# ECONOMETRICS

# The Addison-Wesley Series in Economics

**Abel/Bernanke**
*Macroeconomics*

**Bade/Parkin**
*Foundations of Economics*

**Bierman/Fernandez**
*Game Theory with Economic Applications*

**Binger/Hoffman**
*Microeconomics with Calculus*

**Boyer**
*Principles of Transportation Economics*

**Branson**
*Macroeconomic Theory and Policy*

**Bruce**
*Public Finance and the American Economy*

**Byrns/Stone**
*Economics*

**Carlton/Perloff**
*Modern Industrial Organization*

**Caves/Frankel/Jones**
*World Trade and Payments: An Introduction*

**Chapman**
*Environmental Economics: Theory, Application, and Policy*

**Cooter/Ulen**
*Law and Economics*

**Downs**
*An Economic Theory of Democracy*

**Ehrenberg/Smith**
*Modern Labor Economics*

**Ekelund/Tollison**
*Economics*

**Fusfeld**
*The Age of the Economist*

**Gerber**
*International Economics*

**Ghiara**
*Learning Economics*

**Gordon**
*Macroeconomics*

**Gregory**
*Essentials of Economics*

**Gregory/Stuart**
*Russian and Soviet Economic Performance and Structure*

**Hartwick/Olewiler**
*The Economics of Natural Resource Use*

**Hubbard**
*Money, the Financial System, and the Economy*

**Hughes/Cain**
*American Economic History*

**Husted/Melvin**
*International Economics*

**Jehle/Reny**
*Advanced Microeconomic Theory*

**Johnson-Lans**
*A Health Economics Primer*

**Klein**
*Mathematical Methods for Economics*

**Krugman/Obstfeld**
*International Economics*

**Laidler**
*The Demand for Money*

**Leeds/von Allmen/Schiming**
*Economics*

**Leeds/von Allmen**
*The Economics of Sports*

**Lipsey/Courant/Ragan**
*Economics*

**Melvin**
*International Money and Finance*

**Miller**
*Economics Today*

**Miller**
*Understanding Modern Economics*

**Miller/Benjamin**
*The Economics of Macro Issues*

**Miller/Benjamin/North**
*The Economics of Public Issues*

**Mills/Hamilton**
*Urban Economics*

**Mishkin**
*The Economics of Money, Banking, and Financial Markets*

**Murray**
*Econometrics: A Modern Introduction*

**Parkin**
*Economics*

**Perloff**
*Microeconomics*

**Phelps**
*Health Economics*

**Riddell/Shackelford/Stamos/Schneider**
*Economics: A Tool for Critically Understanding Society*

**Ritter/Silber/Udell**
*Principles of Money, Banking, and Financial Markets*

**Rohlf**
*Introduction to Economic Reasoning*

**Ruffin/Gregory**
*Principles of Economics*

**Sargent**
*Rational Expectations and Inflation*

**Scherer**
*Industry Structure, Strategy, and Public Policy*

**Stock/Watson**
*Introduction to Econometrics*

**Studenmund**
*Using Econometrics*

**Tietenberg**
*Environmental and Natural Resource Economics*

**Tietenberg**
*Environmental Economics and Policy*

**Todaro/Smith**
*Economic Development*

**Waldman**
*Microeconomics*

**Waldman/Jensen**
*Industrial Organization: Theory and Practice*

**Weil**
*Economic Growth*

**Williamson**
*Macroeconomics*

# ECONOMETRICS
## A MODERN INTRODUCTION

## MICHAEL P. MURRAY
*Bates College*

PEARSON
Addison
Wesley

Boston   San Francisco   New York
London   Toronto   Sydney   Tokyo   Singapore   Madrid
Mexico City   Munich   Paris   Cape Town   Hong Kong   Montreal

*For Rosanne, with all my love.*

Publisher: Daryl Fox
Editor-in-Chief: Denise Clinton
Acquisitions Editor: Adrienne D'Ambrosio
Assistant Editor: Amy Fleischer
Editorial Assistant: Ashley Booth
Managing Editor: Nancy Fenton
Senior Production Supervisor: Katherine Watson
Designer: Leslie Haimes, Nesbitt Graphics, Inc.
Cover Designer: Leslie Haimes
Supplements Supervisor: Kirsten Dickerson
Executive Media Producer: Michelle Neil
Media Producer: Bridget Page
Executive Marketing Manager: Stephen Frail
Marketing Coordinator: Kate MacLean
Rights and Permissions Advisor: Shannon Barbe
Manufacturing Buyer: Carol Melville
Production Coordination: Marilyn Dwyer, Nesbitt Graphics, Inc.
Project Manager: Bonnie Boehme, Nesbitt Graphics, Inc.
Composition: Nesbitt Graphics, Inc.
Illustrations: Nesbitt Graphics, Inc.
Cover photo: © Photonica

Library of Congress Cataloging-in-Publication Data
Murray, Michael P., 1946–
  Econometrics : a modern introduction / Michael Murray.
    p. cm.
  Includes bibliographical references and index.
  ISBN 0-321-11361-6 (alk. paper)
  1. Econometrics.  I. Title.
  HB139.M877 2006
  330'.01'5195--dc22                    2005018586

1 2 3 4 5 6 7 8 9 10-CRW-09 08 07 06 05

# Brief Contents

# Contents

# Contents on the Web   www.aw-bc.com/murray

# Preface for Students

This textbook introduces you to the theory and uses of econometrics. Without econometrics, economics would be a rather vague science. For example, economic theory will tell us that a 10% tuition subsidy plan will increase college enrollments, but it won't tell us by how much. Econometrics gives us more specific information. Econometrics tells us that college enrollments will rise, say, 15%, plus or minus 3%, if students get a 10% tuition subsidy.

Econometrics combines data, economic theory, and statistical theory to quantify economic relationships. What is the price elasticity of the demand for cocaine? How much does college financial aid reduce families' saving? How steep is the Phillips curve that relates unemployment rates to changes in the rate of inflation? These are questions that can be answered by using econometrics.

Econometrics also provides tools for testing economic theories. Is the Phillips curve stable, or does it shift when economic policy changes? Is the Cobb–Douglas production function a reasonable representation of the U.S. economy? Does a college education increase lifetime earnings? These are questions for econometricians.

Econometrics also provides tools for forecasting future economic events. What will the GDP be in 2010? What will the unemployment rate be next year? How many cigarettes will R. J. Reynolds sell next year? These, too, are questions for econometricians.

Your background in economic theory and in statistics has prepared you to use econometrics. As you might expect, because economic theory and statistics are both abstract studies, econometrics also requires abstract thinking. But, in the end, econometrics, like economic theory, is not about abstractions; it is about economic behavior.

To keep economic behavior in the foreground as we march through the abstract terrain of econometrics, this text includes Regression's Greatest Hits, an econometric Top 40 that recounts the details of profound, practical, and sometimes amusing real-world econometric studies. You will find the Belgian household expenditure data that Ernst Engel relied on, in 1857, to formulate Engel's Law, which states that food expenditure absorbs a smaller share of consumers' incomes as income rises. You will see the econometric results that supported the Rational Expectations Revolution in macroeconomics. You will see studies of the demands for rye, wheat, cocaine, and watermelons. You will learn how economists measure labor-market discrimination against minorities and women. Economic growth, violence by college students, capital punishment, infant mortality, and health care policy are all subject to econometric study, and all appear in the Greatest Hits feature.

The Greatest Hits also demonstrate the critical thinking skills employed in econometrics studies. You will come to understand the limits of what economists learn. Because all empirical knowledge is conditional, what we think is true today may be contradicted by new data tomorrow. Econometrics will provide you with the ability to assess how much credence to give to economists' latest findings. Sometimes the findings are robust, and worthy of considerable confidence. Sometimes the findings are fragile, and deserve considerable skepticism. Understanding both economic theory and econometrics allows you to make such judgments for yourself, and thereby better understand the economic world in which we live.

# Preface for Teachers

Why this textbook, when there are so many others available? Three features set this text apart from other recent econometrics texts: (i) starting out with the Monte Carlo approach to estimators; (ii) the applied perspective offered by the Greatest Hits feature; and (iii) the multitude of real-world data employed throughout the text. These features are discussed briefly here, and in depth in the following sections.

The book begins with a Monte Carlo exercise that shows students how to compare their own estimators of the slope of a line through the origin. The teacher's manual shows how you can, on the first day of class, get students to devise for themselves several estimators for this slope. By focusing students' attention on how estimators perform across repeated samples, the exercise conditions students to think like econometricians right from the start. The exercise also sets the stage for a very accessible development of the Gauss–Markov Theorem.

The Greatest Hits feature contains exemplary econometric analyses from historical and modern examples. The Greatest Hits feature explores these studies to a depth greater than that usually afforded by a typical textbook example. The additional insight allows students to more fully understand the connection between econometrics and the economic phenomena that they learn about in other economics courses. Many of the Greatest Hits are accompanied by the original data used in the chosen study. For example, Ernst Engel's 1857 study linking food expenditure and income appears among the Greatest Hits, and the Belgian budget data Engel used are available on this textbook's companion Web site (**www.aw-bc.com/murray**).

The book relies heavily on real-world data. The Greatest Hits, the in-text examples, and the 292 end-of-chapter problems span a wide range of economic analyses, and almost all are accompanied by data sets that the students can use to investigate further. In all, the book's companion Web site, **www.aw-bc.com/murray**, contains 105 data sets associated with Greatest Hits, in-chapter examples, and end-of-chapter problems.

My goal in writing this textbook is to engage students in econometrics by showing them how the skills they learn in this course have been applied in the real world, and to encourage them to use their knowledge similarly.

## Why Begin with Monte Carlo?

What are the advantages of beginning with a Monte Carlo approach? Ordinary least squares (OLS) is the usual starting point for econometrics textbooks. Finding a "best fitting" line is an intuitively plausible goal, and the OLS estimator does serve admirably in many analyses. However, starting with OLS has two pedagogical disadvantages. First, the "sum of squared residuals" is a within-sample property of estimators, rather than a sampling property. In 1998, in the *American Economic Review*, Peter Kennedy wrote:

> Contrary to the belief of most econometrics instructors, upon completion of introductory statistics courses, the vast majority of students do not understand the basic logic of classical statistics as captured in the sampling distribution concept.*

Students who do not understand the sampling distribution notion are not yet ready to study econometrics. The study of OLS is at odds with gaining such an understanding. Students are better served by starting with an exercise that highlights sampling distributions rather than with OLS, which ignores them.

Kennedy prefers to begin his classes with a series of problems that ask the students to "explain how to do a Monte Carlo study." I share a similar viewpoint, and thus ask students to begin thinking about Monte Carlo results in Chapter 2. Moreover, this book uses a Monte Carlo exercise that fascinates students because it compares the students' own estimators. (A horse race is always more interesting when your horse is running.) Wondering how his or her own favorite estimator is faring focuses each student's attention on which estimator is performing best when the estimators are used over and over again in repeated samples.

The second pedagogical disadvantage of the OLS strategy is that students are unlikely to uncover it on their own. The OLS estimator is typically given to students by their teachers. Wouldn't students be more invested in the outcomes if they could begin their class by designing their own estimators? Wouldn't the students be more interested if their first analysis in econometrics compared their own estimators? That is the approach this book takes. While devising estimators for the slope and intercept of a straight line is too daunting for most students, a simpler, related problem that students *can* solve asks students to devise an estimator for the slope of a straight line through the origin, beginning by grappling with the cases that have first one, and then two, data points.

For ten years, my students, working with their classmates, have collectively come up with four intuitively plausible estimators for the slope of a line through the origin (all of which are linear, and each of which is BLUE for a suitable data-generating process). I work through this exercise with them on the first day of class, and students feel energized and excited about econometrics at the end of the lecture. With four intuitively plausible estimators in hand, our discussion naturally turns to how we can choose among them. With minimal direction, we find ourselves reviewing the intuitions of mean absolute error, mean square error, unbiasedness, and efficiency.

I initially invite the students to vote for their favorite estimator, but most students quickly realize that this is not an ideal way to find a best estimator. Because

---

*Peter Kennedy, "Teaching Undergraduates Econometrics: A Suggestion for Fundamental Change," *American Economic Review*, 88, no. 2 (May 1998): 487–492.

mean absolute error, mean square error, unbiasedness, and efficiency are all across-sample properties of estimators, a Monte Carlo examination of the students' estimators, in which each estimator is used in many samples, is a well-received strategy for choosing among the estimators. This strategy highlights the sampling distribution concept. The students can see whether their estimator or someone else's performs better when used repeatedly.

The Monte Carlo exercise has another important benefit. In order to conduct a Monte Carlo exercise, students have to make assumptions about the data-generating process. Curiously, students usually make the Gauss–Markov Assumptions when confronted with a series of choices about their DGP. A computer program, available on this book's companion Web site (**www.aw-bc.com/murray**), leads students through the choices they must make to build their Monte Carlo models, and then presents them with the Monte Carlo results. At the end of this exercise, students are keenly aware that they have been looking across samples to assess their estimators, and they are aware that their results might well depend critically on their assumptions—that is, on the Gauss–Markov Assumptions.

Chapter 2 describes this computer program, but in practice, these lessons are most effectively conveyed by working through the computer exercise in class or lab. This Monte Carlo exercise almost always results in a clear winner among the estimators on the basis of mean square error or mean absolute error. What is not clear at the end of the Monte Carlo exercise is whether any of the estimators are unbiased—sampling error muddies the water.

The question of unbiasedness provides the springboard to a more formal statistical analysis of the students' estimators in Chapter 3. Students' estimators are almost always linear estimators; only occasionally do students suggest an estimator that uses medians, which are not linear. Chapter 3 notes the linearity of the students' estimators and asks when, under the Gauss–Markov Assumptions, a linear estimator of the slope of a line through the origin is unbiased. Chapter 3 also derives the variance of a linear estimator. One semester, a student of mine raised his hand at this juncture and asked, "If I minimize that variance, subject to the unbiasedness requirement, can I get an even better estimator?" Not every student leaps unaided to the Gauss–Markov Theorem, but the theorem is easy to motivate once the unbiasedness and variance results are in hand. Moreover, students grasp without great difficulty that the strategy used to get a BLUE estimator under the Gauss–Markov Assumptions could be as easily applied under alternative assumptions; from here, the path to generalized least squares is clear.

The book's Monte Carlo beginning yields three pedagogically valuable fruits: an early experience with competing estimators for a given problem, a clear understanding that econometricians choose estimators for their across-sample properties, and a confident intuition for the strategy of BLUE estimation. Typically, I cover these first three chapters of the text and a lecture-long review of statistics (the material in the book's Statistical Appendix), in four 80-minute lectures and two lab periods. Later on, the text returns to Monte Carlo analyses to facilitate learning about heteroskedasticity, errors in variables, and consistency. Computer programs for these exercises are also on the textbook's companion Web site (**www.aw-bc.com/murray**). Another computer program that visually illustrates the power of hypothesis tests about the OLS estimator is on the Web site as well.

# Regression's Greatest Hits

The Greatest Hits feature serves several purposes in the text. The abstractions needed to do economics are aesthetically appealing for some students, but most students are more interested in econometrics as a toolkit. The first Greatest Hits show students that knowledge obtained with econometrics can be both practical and profound. Early Greatest Hits include Feldstein's investigation of the effect of college financial aid on family saving and Engel's 19th century work on food expenditures and income. A later, more light-hearted Greatest Hit studies the relationship between a wine label's contents and the wine's price.

In the early chapters, the Greatest Hits help students make the leap from the theoretical economics they have studied to the econometrically convenient linear forms in which econometricians usually cast economic theories. The economic theory that students encounter before taking econometrics relies heavily on one economic variable being a function of another, $y = f(x)$, as in a demand equation or in a supply equation, with equilibrium conditions linking the functions. The linear-in-parameters function used in introductory econometrics is a special case of the functions usually found in economic theory, but one that is often unfamiliar to students when they begin their econometrics course. "Why do I care about straight lines?" is a sensible question that is best answered by examples in which straight lines are economically interesting. The Capital Asset Pricing Model and Friedman's permanent income consumption function make straight lines through the origin surprisingly interesting.

Later in the book, the Greatest Hits illustrate how new techniques have been used to obtain practical, profound, or intriguing results. Some Greatest Hits—those categorized as "Classical Favorites"—have each been cited more than 300 times since 1968. Examples include Mincer on wages; Mankiw, Romer, and Weil on growth; Phillips, and later Lucas, on the Phillips curve; and McFadden on transportation. These Greatest Hits show students how much important economic knowledge is grounded in econometric research.

A second subset of Hits—"Golden Oldies"—are equally venerable, but pre-date the Social Science Citation Index. Examples include Engel on the demand for rye (1861); Lehfeldt on the demand for wheat (1914); and Cobb and Douglas on the production function (1928). These Greatest Hits remind students that economics has been an empirical science for a very long time.

A third category—"Pop Tunes"—provides students with practically important or amusing results that illustrate the usefulness of the tools they are learning.

Examples include beer prices and student misbehavior, and capital punishment and murder rates.

The Greatest Hits are written for accessibility. Casual reading should enable students to glean the primary lesson of any Hit. But careful reading should yield richer understandings of both the economics and the econometrics of the Hit. Instructors can use the Greatest Hits as sidebars that illustrate why we study econometrics or as a rich addition to the students' learning.

## Applying Econometrics to Real-World Data

Much of econometrics must be learned by doing econometrics. Though it is true that students cannot understand econometric applications without studying econometric theory, they cannot internalize and fully appreciate the concepts of econometric theory until they have grappled with applications. This book's Greatest Hits and its in-chapter examples show students how econometrics can be richly applied; the end-of-chapter problems charge students with applying econometrics themselves.

In all, 292 end-of-chapter problems ask students to apply their newly learned skills. The problems rely on 105 real-world data sets that are available on the book's companion Web site, **www.aw-bc.com/murray**. (Each data set is available in four formats: EViews, Stata, Excel, and comma-separated ASCII. To allow students to easily apply the methods learned in a given chapter, the data are cleaner than what researchers must usually work with.) Where possible, the data are drawn from published economics articles, so that students can see first-hand the intimate link between econometrics and new economic knowledge.

## Using the Book

I expect that almost all one-term introductory courses will use Chapters 1 through 11. In this case, you would begin with students' own estimators of the slope of a line through the origin and end with generalized least squares applied to models with heteroskedastic or first-order autocorrelated disturbances. However, instructors who do not want to use Monte Carlo methods can skip Chapters 2 and 3 with little disruption. Teachers who assign a term paper in which students do original empirical work can also point students to the Chapter 12 Greatest Hit "Making Music." This hit introduces the microeconomic and macroeconomic data sets that economists work with most often.

Chapters 12 through 19 are written to be taught in almost any order, so that teachers of a semester-long introductory course can select a specialized topic to add to the foundations taught in Chapters 1 through 11. Chapter 12, which introduces consistency and asymptotic distributions, is an especially good prelude to Chapter 13 on IV estimation; otherwise, Chapters 12 through 19 are freestanding. Especially novel is Chapter 15, which introduces students to randomized and natural experiments.

Instructors who prefer to teach matrix algebra with their students will find the chapter appendices that re-present chapter material in matrix form helpful. Early appendices also develop the mechanics of matrix algebra. There is no matrix algebra in the book outside of these appendices. For additional material, teachers can turn to the Web Extensions available on this book's companion Web site. For example, chapters on maximum likelihood estimation and on the generalized method of moments are available online.

Chapters 12 through 19, coupled with the online Web Extensions, are the basis for a second semester of a course in econometrics. Instructors of advanced courses, who need to spend considerable time reviewing introductory econometrics, can select material from Chapters 12 through 19 and the Web Extensions. Advanced courses that follow immediately upon an introductory course can cover most, if not all, of Chapters 12 through 19 and the Web Extensions in a full semester.

# Supplements

For the instructor an Instructor's Manual and PowerPoint presentation slides are available for download at the Instructor's Resource Center on the catalog page for *Econometrics: A Modern Introduction*.

The Instructor's Manual has been designed to provide you with support and suggestions for using this book effectively in your econometrics course. For each chapter in the text, the Instructor's Manual contains:

- Chapter overviews

- Teaching tips, which detail my strategies for helping students achieve success in each topic area

- Answers to the end-of-chapter questions and problems

The Instructor's Manual also contains several suggested pathways for organizing your course.

The Power Point presentation contains a version of my lecture notes, refined and prepared by Stephen Weinberg, who used the book as a Teaching Fellow at Harvard University. The slides also contain the figures and tables from the text.

The Companion Web site for this book can be accessed at **www.aw-bc.com/murray**. This Web site contains a wealth of supplementary material, including

- Eleven Web Extensions—fully developed discussions of the following special topics: A Medley of Regression's Greatest Hits; Using Calculus and Algebra for the Simplest Case: $n = 3$; A Matrix Approach to Consistency; $X$'s Fixed Across Samples; and A Matrix Approach to Consistency with Stochastic Regressors; Local Average Treatment Effects; More Estimators for Systems of Equations; A

Matrix Representation of Panel Data; Multiple Cointegrating Relationships; Log-Odds and Logit Models: Using Grouped Data; Multinomial Models; Generalized Method of Moments Estimators and Identification; and Maximum Likelihood Estimation.

- 105 Data Sets—the data sets that students will use to solve the end-of-chapter problems. The data sets are available in four formats: EViews, Stata, Excel, and comma-separated ASCII.

- Selected Solutions to the end-of-chapter problems

- Six Monte Carlo Simulation Builders—Web-accessible Monte Carlo programs for assessing the small- and large-sample properties of several estimators for various DGPs, including the Gauss–Markov and heteroskedastic cases and the omitted variables case.

- The PowerPoint presentations

- Glossary Flashcards

# Acknowledgments

Few people learn econometrics without help. John Hooper and Dennis Smallwood, my first econometrics teachers, blended technique with intuition to offer a clear introduction to econometrics. Later, Andrew Harvey and Rob Engle helped this microeconomist understand the modern time series methods more common among macroeconomists. More recently, Jack Porter patiently led me through the thickets of nonparametric and semiparametric methods, and discussed meta-issues of econometrics with me at length. I hope this book reveals that I was a good student—I certainly had good teachers.

Many people teach econometrics without the benefit of a colleague equally interested in econometric pedagogy. However, I have been blessed for many years to have Carl Schwinn as my colleague at Bates College. His ideas about teaching econometrics and his critiques of my ideas have enhanced my understanding of how best to teach this difficult subject.

My students have also contributed greatly to this book. They patiently suffered the early drafts, made helpful comments about how the book could better serve them, and diligently reported the typos that, in consequence, dwindled in number over time. Particularly helpful were Michael Coscetta, Matt Ebbel, Eric Fleissig-Greene, Tanner Fahl, Leah Fleck, Karen Guo, John Indellicate, Karl Malloy, Kalina Manova, Ghaffar Mughal, Emily Oster, and Kia Song. Those early drafts also benefited greatly from the keen eyes and minds of my teaching fellows at Harvard, who read the early drafts and made many suggestions for improvements. Especially helpful were Silvia Ardagna, Tuan Le Minh, Christian Pop-

Eleches, Albert Saiz, Seamus Smyth, Marco Stampini, Christel Vermeersch, and Stephen Weinberg. My Bates student assistants, Victoria Finkle, Yang Jerng Hwa, and Carly Rockstroh, helpfully contributed carefully assembled materials for the glossary; Julian Felch, Ben Hagberg, and Andrius Staisiunas commented on end-of-chapter problems.

The Greatest Hits featured in the book span many fields besides microeconomics. I am grateful to David Aschauer, Francesco Caselli, James Hughes, Margaret Maurer-Fazio, Joseph Newhouse, Ron Oaxaca, and Carl Schwinn for technical comments on several Hits.

Many of the data sets in the book have been drawn from published government sources. Many others have been kindly provided by colleagues. I am grateful to Orley Ashenfelter, Robert Barro, Carol Bertaut, Ken Chay, Phillip Cook, Julie Curry, Martin Feldstein, Peter Fishman, Kathryn Graddy, William Hiss, Carolyn Hoxby, James Hughes, Krista Jacobs, Steven Levitt, Katherine Lykens, Aldrin Magne, Greg Mankiw, Jacques Marresse, David Mustard, Thomas Mroz, John Mullahy, Casey Mulligan, John Quigley, Carl Schwinn, Gary Smith, Seamus Smyth, Lawrence Summers, Sam Thompson, and Michael Visser for the data they have shared with me. Co-authors of these contributors and complete citations to their papers are given where the data are used in the book.

Bradley Ewing at Texas Tech University provided some problems for the second half of the book. The book is better for his contributions. Guillermo Covarrubias created the answer keys for the book's end-of-chapter problems. Seamus Smyth provided several data sets and checked nearly all of them for completeness. Stephen Weinberg took my PowerPoint slides for this course and adapted them to better match this version of the book. I am grateful for Stephen's many suggestions for improving both the book and the slides. Victoria Finkle and Oi Yen Lam carefully checked the variable descriptions across the several versions of the data sets.

Later drafts of the book were read (sometimes several times) by a small army of generous colleagues whose comments served to make the book much better than it would have been without them. The reviewers include the following:
Richard Agnello, University of Delaware
Julius Alade, University of Maryland Eastern Shore
Seyhan Arkonac, New York University
Djeto Assane, University of Nevada, Las Vegas
Necati Aydin, Florida A&M University
Christopher R. Bolliger, University of Kentucky
Audie R. Brewton, Northeastern Illinois University
Donald Bruce, University of Tennessee
Robert Burrus, University of North Carolina–Wilmington
Jose Canals-Cerda, University of Colorado, Boulder
Katherine Carson, U.S. Air Force Academy

Chanjin Chung, Oklahoma State University
Victor Claar, Hope College
Sean P. Corcoran, California State University
David Edgerton, Lund University
Eric Eide, Brigham Young University
Can Erbil, Brandeis University
Bradley T. Ewing, Texas Tech University
Barry Falk, Iowa State University
Indranil Ghosh, Penn State Erie
Richard Green, University of California, Davis
Edward Greenberg, Washington University
Li Haizheng, Georgia Institute of Technology
Denise Hare, Reed College
Steve Henson, Western Washington University
Tia Hilmer, Virginia Polytechnic Institute and State University
William Horrace, Syracuse University
Ted Juhle, University of Kansas
Elia Kacapyr, Ithaca College
Chihwa Kao, Syracuse University
Manfred Keil, Claremont McKenna College
Govinda Koirala, University of Rio Grande
Subal Kumbhakar, SUNY–Binghamton
Carlos Martins, Oregon State University
Mary G. McGarvey, University of Nebraska–Lincoln
Robert McNown, University of Colorado
Michael McPherson, University of North Texas
Dmitri M. Medvedovski, Bethel College
Judith Mills, Southern Connecticut State University
Kristen Monaco, California State University Long Beach
Carlisle Moody, College of William and Mary
Adam Murray, Howrey, Simon, and White LLP
Peter Murray, Center for Progressive Leadership
Seth Murray, StreamSage
Yoko Nakajima, Brown University
Nader Nazmi, Lake Forest College
Nick Noble, Miami University, Ohio
Roberto Pedace, University of Redlands
Gabriel Picone, University of South Florida
Jack Porter, University of Wisconsin
Susan Porter-Hudak, Northern Illinois University
Giuseppe Ragusa, University of California, San Diego

Michael Robinson, Mt. Holyoke College
Stephen Rubb, Bentley College
Eric J. Solberg, California State University, Fullerton
John Spencer, Queens University of Belfast
Richard Startz, University of Washington
Diane Stehman, Northeastern Illinois University
Jane Sung, Truman State University
Mark Thoma, University of Oregon
Wim Vijverberg, University of Texas–Dallas
Mary Beth Walker, Georgia State University
Ronald Ward, University of Florida
Mark Wohar, University of Nebraska, Omaha
Zhenhui Xu, Georgia College and State University

I would like to single out several reviewers whose comments were especially detailed and insightful: Catherine Carson, Rosanne Ducey, Denise Hare, Jack Porter, Mark Thoma, Mark Wohar, and one early anonymous reviewer. Mark Thoma was especially generous in checking both the equations and the end-of-chapter problems for errors.

My editors at Addison-Wesley were unfailingly patient and helpful. Jenny Jefferson and Amy Fleischer provided innumerable improvements in concision, flow, and language. Denise Clinton, Adrienne D'Ambrosio, and Sylvia Mallory provided good counsel at critical junctures. Bonnie Boehme (Nesbitt Graphics, Inc.) and Katherine Watson made the tedious copy-editing and production processes bearable. Bridget Page shepherded the creation of both the Monte Carlo computer programs and the book's Web site. Together, the Addison-Wesley team transformed my bland manuscript into a visually exciting and accessible book.

At Harvard, Ann Flack patiently retyped early versions of the text, created the first index for the book, and whipped many of the tables into shape. At Bates, Lorelei Purrington incorporated many of the final editorial corrections into the final draft and carefully compiled the tables of contents, figures, tables, and hits. She cheerfully and carefully made necessary adaptations as the book evolved.

Perhaps the most onerous task fell to my son Ben Murray, who spent a week patiently reading the book to me aloud from the page proofs while I followed along in the original copy; his efforts contributed remarkably to the accuracy of the text in its myriad details.

I have been blessed with the unflagging support of my family throughout the writing of this book. Folksinger Glenn Yarborough once intoned, "'That's OK,' Rose would say. 'Don't you worry none. We'll have good times, by-and-by, next Fall, when the work's all done.'" Hours upon hours that might have been spent with my spouse, Rosanne Ducey, have been spent with my laptop. Now, Fall is a-comin'. I dedicate this book to Rosanne, with all my love.

# PART ONE

# The Linear Regression Model

 *Chapter 1*

# What Is Econometrics?

*The plural of anecdote is data.*

—Variously Attributed

"As the number of college graduates increases, starting wages decrease." "As welfare benefits rise, welfare recipients have more children." Such qualitative statements about economic relationships are the fruit that economic theory offers. But *how much* lower would wages be? *How many* more children would be born? Economic theory is silent about these magnitudes, yet the magnitudes matter greatly. In order to gain a deep understanding and to evaluate policy options judiciously, we must know the magnitudes, and not just the direction, of economic effects. Where economics is silent, econometrics speaks.

**Econometrics** *is the branch of economics that provides the tools to estimate the magnitude of economic relationships.* For example, an econometric analysis might conclude that "a 10% surge in the number of college graduates brings a 6.5% drop in the wage rates employers offer." Econometrics also provides the tools to assess competing claims about the magnitude of an economic relationship. For example, proponents of higher welfare benefits might say, "If the additional welfare benefit from having another child were to rise by 10%, only one welfare recipient in 1,000 would have an additional child," whereas opponents might counter, "such a 10% benefit increase would spur 250 births among 1,000 welfare recipients." Who is right? Can existing data help us to choose sensibly between such claims? Yes, it can, and it is econometrics that informs us how.

How do we define econometrics? The first editor of the Econometric Society's journal, Nobel laureate in economics Ragnar Frisch of Oslo University, wrote in 1936 that econometrics is "the unification of economic theory, statistics, and mathematics."[1] In 1954, three other Nobel laureates in economics, Paul Samuelson of MIT, Tjalling Koopmans of Yale University, and Richard Stone of Cambridge University, offered a definition that emphasizes econometrics' grounding in the everyday economic world in which we live. They said econometrics is "the quantitative analysis of *actual economic phenomena* based on the concurrent development of theory and observation, related by appropriate methods of inference."[2] The italics are added, but the emphasis was evident in the Laureates' discussion of the definition—the deepest understandings of econometrics do not lose sight of the "econ" in econometrics!

Drawing from statisticians, econometricians use probabilistic language to emphasize the uncertainty of their empirical work. For example, they might say, "A 95% confidence interval for employers' price elasticity of demand for recent college graduates is $-.65 \pm .03$," or "A slight majority of studies find a statistically significant positive effect of welfare benefits on fertility, rather than a statistically insignificant effect." Students of econometrics, therefore, need to be familiar with the common language of statistics.

Econometrics also provides tools for making forecasts about the future value of economic variables, for example, "GNP will rise 3.7% in 2010"; "97,000 high school graduates with high test scores will join the army in 2009," and "The real wage rates of black Americans will rise 6.8% between now and 2010." Here, too, econometricians would use cautious technical language to reflect the degree of error that is likely to accompany the forecasts.

Theoretical econometrics relies on models drawn from economic theory and also on tools drawn from mathematical statistics. For applied econometric work, early econometricians relied on hand calculations and mechanical calculators; today, applied econometrics is done almost exclusively on computers. The availability of cheap computing power has led to a growing importance of computers even in the theoretical aspects of econometrics. Some theoretical problems that have been too difficult to solve with formal mathematical tools have proven manageable when tackled with computer exercises called Monte Carlo analyses.

Chapter 1 focuses on two extended examples that illustrate the real-world questions econometricians address and the analytical problems econometricians encounter in the real world. The examples are not meant to be mastered at one sitting. They are simply a roadmap, similar to one that a traveler to China might use on his or her first trip to that country. Looking at such a map would help orient you at the outset of your trip. Some names, perhaps Beijing and Hong Kong, would be familiar to you, but much on the map would seem mysterious and understandable in only the broadest terms—that the Yangtze is a river might be clear, but the Yangtze's economic, cultural, and environmental importance to China would not be evident. Some of the features noted on the map, perhaps the Gobi Desert or the great Three Gorges Dam, might escape your notice altogether. Later, after you visited these places, you would look at the map quite differently. You would see the environmental and economic connections among the Yangtze, the Three Gorges Dam, and the surrounding agricultural lands, as you had seen them firsthand during your travels. So, too, is it with these first examples from econometrics. You will grasp at the outset the broad outline of the questions and problems these examples pose for econometricians. But some, or even many, of the details will seem mysterious—and that's okay, for it is the broad picture that matters now. Later, when you have read more, you can return to these first examples and see in them both the breadth and the depth of econometric analysis.

What you should take away from your study of this map of econometrics is the vocabulary presented in bold letters. Adding these words and phrases to your working vocabulary is the first step in learning to speak the language of econometricians. Some of the words may be familiar to you from studying statistics—statisticians and econometricians speak strikingly similar languages. But don't worry about mastering this vocabulary on your first reading; instead, first enjoy looking over the map and seeing some hints about the journey to come.

## 1.1 A First Example of Econometric Modeling: Financial Aid and Income

Econometrics grew out of economists' efforts to use data to learn about economic phenomena. How much does food consumption change when income changes? What happens to the price of rye when the quantity supplied suddenly surges? These were the specific questions that gave rise to the earliest econometric studies. A question such as how a school changes its financial aid offering as a student's family income rises might be a little closer to home for economics students today. This section relates financial aid to family income to introduce some of the typical concepts and issues that arise in econometric analyses. The next section introduces additional concepts and issues in the context of the relationship between food consumption and income.

### Example 1: Income and Financial Aid

Colleges award most financial aid according to need. To determine need, a financial aid officer looks predominantly, but not exclusively, at a family's income. Qualitatively, we can say that aid varies inversely with a student's family income. We might then ask a more specific, quantitative question: "How much does a student's expected aid change when the student's family income rises by one dollar?"

*We call the relationship between the expected value, or mean, of one variable and the value of one or more other variables a **regression**.* In the case of college financial aid, we could assume that the expected aid for a given level of income is, approximately,

$$expected\ aid\,|\,income = \beta_0 + \beta_1\ income,$$

or, if $A$ represents aid and $I$ represents income,

$$E(A\,|\,I) = \beta_0 + \beta_1 I \qquad\qquad\qquad 1.1$$

where "$E(A\,|\,I)$" reads as "the expected value (or mean) of $A$ given $I$." Here, we are assuming that mean aid is $\beta_0$ when income is zero, and that mean aid changes by $\beta_1$ when income rises by \$1. We call the variable on the left in a regression (here, financial aid) the **dependent variable**, commonly called the **regressand**. (Many basic concepts in econometrics have several names.) We call variables on the right in a regression (here, only income) **independent variables, regressors,** or **explanators,** the last because they "explain," or account for, the expected value of the dependent variable. In turn, we call picking a specific mathematical form for a regression **specifying the functional form** of the regression. The **functional form** is the specific mathematical relationship among the variables, for example a linear, quadratic, or cubic relationship. Equation 1.1 specifies a linear relationship between expected aid and family income.

In the real world of one college's financial aid policies, $\beta_0$ and $\beta_1$ in Equation 1.1 are actual numbers, for example,

$$E(A\,|\,I) = 21,000 - 0.2I,$$

which states that the average student with no income receives \$21,000 in financial aid and that the average aid award is reduced twenty cents for each dollar of income, $I$, that the family earns. But the actual values of $\beta_0$ and $\beta_1$ are usually unknown to the econometrician. To assess how much a student's expected aid changes when the student's family income rises by one dollar, we need to estimate the value of $\beta_1$, the slope of the line relating expected aid to family income. To assess the expected level of aid for a given level of income, we need to estimate both $\beta_0$ and $\beta_1$. *The estimation of unknown values of slopes of lines, such as $\beta_0$ and $\beta_1$, is a central task of econometrics.* We call $\beta_0$ and $\beta_1$ **parameters** of this model. In statistical language, parameters (or **population parameters**) are numerical traits of the population under study. More plainly, parameters are unknown fixed numbers that econometricians estimate. The population mean and population variance are examples of parameters commonly encountered in statistics.

Finding the value of $\beta_1$ would be easy if all students with a given income level received the same aid. A scatterplot of aid and income would be like that in Figure 1.1—a scatterplot without scatter. The slope of the line would be easy to

**Figure 1.1**

Financial Aid and Income Exactly Related

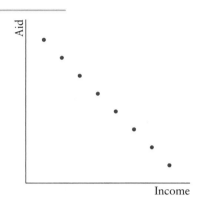

measure. Indeed, if this were the problem, it would hardly qualify as econometrics—we wouldn't estimate $\beta_1$; we'd calculate it exactly. However, individual students with the same income do not each receive the same aid. The relationship between aid and income is inexact.

Students with the same income don't receive the same aid because colleges consider other factors, such as wealth, the number of siblings in college, and numerous special circumstances. Perhaps it would help to pin down the effect of income on aid to add the systematic effects of wealth and siblings to the model, as in

*expected aid|income, wealth, sibs* $= \alpha_0 + \alpha_1 income + \alpha_2 wealth + \alpha_3 sibs$

or

$$E(A|I,W,S) = \alpha_0 + \alpha_1 I + \alpha_2 W + \alpha_3 S, \qquad \textbf{1.2}$$

if we represent wealth by $W$ and the number of siblings by $S$. When the expected value of a variable is related to several other variables, as in Equation 1.2, we sometimes refer to the relationship as a **multiple regression**. We call a regression with an intercept and a single slope a **bivariate regression**.

Even with its richer specification of the determinants of college financial aid, a multiple regression model of expected financial aid is unlikely to yield an exact model of aid levels. Individual students with the same income, wealth, and number of siblings in college do not each receive the same aid because of the myriad special circumstances that influence aid decisions. Casting this situation in statistical terms, we say that individual students receive aid different from the expected value of aid for their income, wealth, and number of siblings in college.

As long as some determinants of aid are not systematic in their effect on aid or are unmeasured (and therefore not available for inclusion in our model), or as long as aid is measured with error, an econometrician cannot calculate aid exactly using observed variables; that is, she does not have access to a deterministic model of financial aid. An econometrician has to settle instead for a deterministic model of individuals' expected, or average, aid levels. How, then, are we to link a model of expected aid with the aid individuals receive?

To capture the cumulative effect of aid determinants not explicitly appearing in a model, we turn to a **stochastic specification** of the financial aid model—one that includes a probabilistic, or random, component. (*Stochastic* is rooted in the Greek verb *stochos*, which means "to guess.") The aid for a student with a specific family income differs by some amount from the average aid for students with that same family income. *In a stochastic specification, the individual discrepancies between actual and expected aid are treated as random, with each value of the discrepancies occurring with some probability.* The discrepancies for a particular sample of students are thought of as a draw from a probabilistic population of discrepancies. For example, if we use the simpler model of Equation 1.1, a stochastic specification of an individual's aid is

$$A = \beta_0 + \beta_1 I + \varepsilon, \qquad\qquad 1.3$$

where $\varepsilon$ is a *random variable* that has a mean equal to zero. A **random variable** is a variable that takes on several possible values, each occurring with some probability. The mean of $\varepsilon$ is zero because the mean of aid, $A$, is $\beta_0 + \beta_1 I$, in accord with Equation 1.1.

$$E(A|I) = \beta_0 + \beta_1 I + E(\varepsilon) = \beta_0 + \beta_1 I$$

only if $E(\varepsilon) = 0$.

If we use the richer model of Equation 1.2, the stochastic specification of a student's financial aid becomes

$$A = \alpha_0 + \alpha_1 I + \alpha_2 W + \alpha_3 S + \nu, \qquad\qquad 1.4$$

where $\nu$ is a random variable with mean zero. In the economics and econometrics literatures, the random variables $\varepsilon$ and $\nu$ are sometimes called **stochastic terms, error terms,** or **stochastic disturbances,** and, most often, just **disturbances** or **errors.** Because one component of financial aid, the disturbance, is a random variable, financial aid is also a random variable. In general, a stochastic specification describes the variable of interest (in this example, financial aid) as a random variable. The error term in equations like Equations 1.3 and 1.4 can arise from numerous sources. Four sources are most common:

1. Variables that affect the dependent variable but are not included among the explanators (for example, determinants of aid *other than* income, wealth, and the number of siblings in college).
2. Mistakes in recording the true value of the dependent variable (for example, mistakes in the recorded aid data).

3. Unaccounted for nonlinearities in the relationship between the dependent variable and the included explanators (for example, aid might depend on the square of income in Equations 1.1 and 1.4).
4. The dependent variable is partially determined by chance (for example, identical students assessed on different days might, by mere chance, get different awards).

Although we refer to the variables $\varepsilon$ and $\nu$ as random variables, both $\varepsilon$ and $\nu$ are actual values in the real world. In our present case, if aid is measured correctly and the relationship between aid and the included explanators is linear, the realized values of $\varepsilon$ and $\nu$ indicate how much individual aid awards differ from the average aid awards for similarly situated students, that is, students with the same income (according to Equation 1.1) or with the same income, wealth, and number of siblings in college (according to Equation 1.2). The discrepancies are then due to chance or to differences among students in variables not included among the explanators. The proportions of students with each discrepancy dictate the probabilities. For example, consider a population of 100 students. If at each level of $I$ or at each combination of $I$, $W$, and $S$, 40 students receive aid \$4 above average, 40 students get aid \$3 below average, and 20 students get aid \$2 below average, then the probability of $+4$ is 0.4, of $-3$ is 0.4, and of $-2$ is 0.2. Notice that these probabilities imply that the mean of the disturbances is, indeed, zero, as required if $\beta_0 + \beta_1 \cdot I$ is to be the average aid level for a given $I$ ($4 \cdot 0.4 - 3 \cdot 0.4 - 2 \cdot 0.2 = 0$). We usually have for study only a sample of students, a sample drawn in some still unspecified way from the total population of students. Notice that we arbitrarily assume in this example that the distribution of the disturbances is the same for every combination of $I$, $W$, and $S$. This is a strong assumption that would warrant testing in an actual study.

If we drew from our population of 100 students a random sample of students at each of several levels of $I$, we might get a scatterplot like that in Figure 1.2. Data drawn from a population observed at a moment in time is called **cross-sectional data**. The data in Figure 1.2 certainly do not trace out a perfectly straight line. Nonetheless, if each of us "fit" a line to these data, we would probably all draw lines with similar slopes (our guesses of $\beta_1$) and intercepts (our guesses of $\beta_0$). When formally describing a sample of observations, such as that underlying Figure 1.2, each observation's distribution needs to be described. For example, if we have $n$ observations in a sample, we describe the expected value of the $i$th observation as

$$\mathrm{E}(A_i \,|\, I_i) = \alpha_0 + \alpha_1 I_i + \alpha_2 W_i + \alpha_3 S_i.$$

How good would your guess of $\beta_1$ be if you fit a line to the data in Figure 1.2? We don't know. To know how good your guess is, we'd need to know $\beta_1$— and there would then be little point in making an estimate, because we'd already

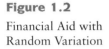

**Figure 1.2**

Financial Aid with
Random Variation

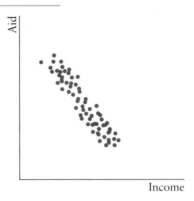

know the answer! In general, even though an econometrician does not know how good a particular *guess* is, she may know how good a particular *guessing procedure* is. For example, she may be able to say, "If I were to use my procedure many times, it would be right on average." And she may be able to say, "No other guessing mechanism that is right on average has squared errors that are smaller on average than my squared errors when used many times." These claims are about the properties of her estimator. Supporting and refuting such claims is one task of econometrics. *However, knowing the properties of estimators does not immediately reveal which estimators are better and which are worse. Econometricians must decide what properties they think desirable for their estimators.*

Econometricians, like statisticians, always distinguish between the procedure they would use to make a guess with any data set and the guess they actually make using that procedure with a specific data set. An **estimator** is a procedure or rule for making guesses about some trait of a population based on samples of data drawn from that population. An **estimate** is a specific guess made by applying an estimator to a specific sample of data. When econometricians estimate the expected value of a variable, $Y$, as a function of one or more explanators, they often say that they **regress $Y$ on its explanators** or **perform the regression of $Y$ on its explanators.**

An econometrician can't assess the precise statistical properties of guessing mechanisms that rely on "eyeballing" a scatterplot. To make precise statements about guessing mechanisms, the econometrician must examine guessing mechanisms, or estimators, that are themselves precise. She needs a mathematical formula to calculate her guesses so she can transform the observed data into a guess of a slope or intercept.

Finally, notice that Equation 1.3 and Equation 1.4 provide *two* models of financial aid, one that uses only income as an explanator and one that uses income, wealth, and siblings in college as explanators. Neither model is "true" insofar as neither provides an exact formula for financial aid. Nor is one model always "better" than the other; either model may be useful. The latter model is richer in detail, and may be preferred for that reason. If we have no data on wealth, though, then the more complex model is useless. Just as a topographical map is sometimes more useful than a plain road map, and sometimes not, purpose and available data determine which econometric model is better.

## What Example 1 Illustrates About Econometrics

Example 1 illustrates five aspects of econometric modeling and practice. First, the example shows how econometricians use a specific functional form to approximate the underlying functional relationship between economic variables. They choose among alternative forms, some more simple, some more elaborate.

Second, the example illustrates how econometricians bridge the gap between the deterministic, or exact, economic relationships usually found in economic

REGRESSION'S
GREATEST HITS

# An Econometric Top 40

## Golden Oldies, Classical Favorites, Pop Tunes

Regression's Greatest Hits selects from famous, influential, and fun regressions that have contributed much to our knowledge of economics. The "Top 40" (or so) countdown unfolds across the chapters of this book. These analyses highlight econometrics' wide applicability to real-world questions. We see in the hits how practical economic questions motivate econometric analysis and how economic theory can profoundly influence the statistical analysis that underpins econometrics. Treat the Econometric Top 40 as you would a friend's CD collection. "Listen" to each, and spend extra time with those you most enjoy.

The Top 40 consists of the following:

**Golden Oldies.** Regression results so well known or so long known that the original papers are seldom cited when the results are used.

**Classical Favorites.** Regression results among the most influential in all of economics—these are "papers that launched a thousand papers."

**Pop Tunes.** Regression results that people are glad to know and glad to repeat. In time, you will settle on your own pop favorites and hum them at unexpected times and places. In addition to the hits in this book, you can find a medley of hits at **www.aw-bc.com/murray**.

The Hit Parade begins in this chapter with a Pop Tune, a regression study of financial aid and family savings. Later comes a Golden Oldie, an early study of consumption and income. Subsequent chapters use the greatest hits to illustrate specific features of econometric analysis. Together, the hits cover a wide range of topics that illustrate the breadth of econometric analyses and accustom you to the kinds of models that econometricians study. ∎

# An Econometric Top 40—A Pop Tune

## Paying for College

College financial aid rules dictate that students receive smaller college aid packages when their parents have accumulated larger financial assets. In the early 1990s, some economists speculated that this "wealth tax" implicit in college aid rules would affect savings little; other economists hypothesized large effects. In 1995, Martin Feldstein of Harvard University asked whether college financial aid rules reduce the accumulation of wealth by parents of prospective students.[3] Using the 1986 Survey of Consumer Finances, Feldstein confronted the question with data.

Feldstein specified a relationship between a family's expected net financial assets (*wealth*), its income (*Y*), the age of the household head (*age*), and the implicit tax rate on assets (how much aid is reduced for each additional dollar in assets) that college aid rules impose (*tax rate*). He examined the financial assets of married couples with at least one child and incomes below $100,000, in households in which the head was between 40 and 50 years of age and no children were yet in college. Feldstein estimated that

$$E(wealth|Y, age, taxrate) = -9934 -$$
$$2.04Y - 1.41(taxrate)(Y) + 0.076(age)(Y).$$

Notice that in this specification, the effects of higher tax rates or greater age on expected wealth depend on the level of the household's income. Feldstein reasonably assumed that an older person with a given level of income tends to have a higher level of wealth than a younger person with the same income—largely because the older person has been accumulating wealth longer. That is, the derivative of expected wealth with respect to age depends on income:

$$\partial wealth / \partial age = 0.076Y.$$

Feldstein also reasonably assumed that a given tax rate tends to reduce the expected wealth of a person with a higher income more than the expected wealth of a person with a lower income because the person with the higher income is apt to have more potential wealth vulnerable to the tax. That is, the derivative of expected wealth with respect to the tax rate depends on income:

$$\partial wealth / \partial taxrate = -1.41Y.$$

According to Feldstein's estimates, an additional year of age would raise expected assets by $0.076Y$—or by $3,040 for a household with an income of $40,000 (about the mean for the sample). The estimated effect of an additional year of age is $4,560 for a household with an income of $60,000. Because the tax rate applied to a family's wealth depends on the number of children a family has in college, both the number of children who attend college and income affect wealth. Feldstein reports that households with one child faced a tax rate on assets of 30% (0.30), and that households with two children faced a tax rate on assets that averaged 41% (0.41).

Without an implicit asset tax, a 45-year-old head of household with a 1986 family income of $40,000 would have expected assets of $45,266 ($-9,934 - 2.04 \cdot 40,000 + 0.076 \cdot 45 \cdot 40,000 - 1.41 \cdot 0.0 \cdot 40,000$). With the implicit tax rates in place, the same head would have expected assets of $28,346 ($45,266 - 1.41 \cdot 0.30 \cdot 40,000$) with one child, or 48% less than $45,266, and only $22,142 ($45,266 - 1.41 \cdot 0.41 \cdot 40,000$) with two children, or 52% less than 45,266. Feldstein's estimates imply that households save dramatically less because of the college aid rules!

**Final Notes**

Economic theory tells us that a tax on wealth reduces saving, thereby reducing wealth, but economic theory alone doesn't tell policy makers enough to fully assess the effects of college aid rules. If college aid rules cause households to cut their savings by 0.05%, policy makers would be unconcerned; if college aid rules cause households to cut their savings by 50.0%, policy makers would be troubled. Theory alone doesn't tell us *how much* any particular tax re-

duces saving—that's an empirical matter, requiring econometric resolution. Feldstein's estimates indicate that college financial tax rules *halve* saving. If his estimates are correct, policy makers should be quite worried about the effect of aid rules on saving. Is Feldstein right or is Feldstein wrong? His striking result raises a question that accompanies every econometric analysis: "How can we assess the reliability of these estimates?" Answering this question is one fundamental task of econometrics.

∎

theory and the random variations from such models actually observed in the world. Econometricians usually introduce randomness by tacking an error term onto their deterministic models; less often, they develop inherently stochastic (that is, probabilistic) economic theories.

Third, the example notes that although we can seldom assess the quality of a specific guess, or *estimate* (for example, "I estimate the mean of $X$ to be 6"), we can often assess the quality of a guessing mechanism, or *estimator* (for example, "I will estimate the mean of $X$ using the sample mean from a simple random sample because the sample mean is right on average").

Fourth, the example illustrates that informal estimation techniques, such as "eyeballing" the data, do not allow formal assessments of the estimator's properties. To judge the value of an estimator, we need to express it in mathematical form. Once we know the properties of an estimator, we need to decide what properties we value.

Finally, the example shows that "models are to be used but not to be believed"[4]; no model is "true," and which of many alternative models we choose depends both on our purposes and on the data at hand.

## 1.2  A Second Example of Econometric Modeling: Consumption and Income

In the previous section, the example of income's relationship to financial aid highlighted five aspects of regression analysis and introduced vocabulary common to econometric studies. Here, the use of regression to estimate the relationship between food consumption and income highlights an additional five aspects of regression analysis, but adds only a few new vocabulary terms.

## Example 2: Income and Food Expenditure

Casual observation reveals that people's food expenditures rise as their incomes rise; people with higher incomes spend more money on food. The 19th century German statistician Ernst Engel, who long headed the Prussian government's statistical department, found that in a sample of Belgian workers, workers with higher incomes devoted a smaller fraction, or share, of their income to food expenditures (see Regression's Greatest Hits: How Income Influences Demand—Engel's Law). The generalization of Engel's finding, that food's income share always falls with increasing income, is known as Engel's Law. Here, we explore Engel's Law by asking whether rising income leads households to spend less on food from each additional dollar of income they earn.

A linear relationship between food expenditure and income, like the linear relationships we used to analyze financial aid in Equations 1.1 and 1.2, could not display declining increments to food expenditure with each additional dollar of income. A linear specification assumes a constant rate of change. How, then, should we specify the relationship between food expenditure and income? We can address this question by expressing the relationship between expected food expenditure and income with a quadratic relationship that involves income and its square:

$$expected\ food\ expenditure = \beta_0 + \beta_1(income) + \beta_2(income^2)$$

or

$$E(F|I) = \beta_0 + \beta_1 I + \beta_2 I^2. \qquad \textbf{1.5}$$

Our interest is in $\beta_1$ and $\beta_2$ because the rate of change of expected food expenditure with respect to income, that is, the derivative of expected food expenditure with respect to income, is $(\beta_1 + 2\beta_2 I)$.

If $\beta_1 > 0$ and $\beta_2 < 0$ in Equation 1.5, expected food expenditure rises at low incomes, and rises less and less as income rises, because the derivative of food expenditure with respect to income starts out as $\beta_1$, when income is zero, and grows smaller, becoming $(\beta_1 + 2\beta_2 I)$, in which $\beta_2$ is negative. In the context of Equation 1.5, to determine whether consumers eventually spend less of additional income on food we would need to test whether $\beta_1 > 0$ and $\beta_2 < 0$. One goal of econometrics is to design such tests.

A drawback of the specification in Equation 1.5 is that when $\beta_1 > 0$ and $\beta_2 < 0$, $(\beta_1 + 2\beta_2 I)$ turns negative when income grows large enough; expected food expenditure is assumed to eventually begin falling with income. Such a downturn in food expenditures when income rises defies common sense. Observed data would be unlikely to display a downturn in expenditures, so few estimates of Equation 1.5 would yield one within the range of observed incomes. Consequently, if our interest lies in incomes that are within the range of the actual data at hand, the quadratic functional form of Equation 1.5 might, in practice, serve well as an approximation. If we wish to extrapolate from the data at hand to incomes well above those observed in the actual data, however, the quadratic function is a poor choice because it gives nonsensical results for sufficiently high incomes. This example illustrates a pitfall common in economic forecasting: Forecasts made outside the range of the observed data may prove quite unreliable.

As in the case of financial aid, we can link expected food expenditure, for which we now have Equation 1.5, to observed food expenditure by adding a stochastic (that is, random or probabilistic) disturbance, $\varepsilon$, to the model:

$$F = \beta_0 + \beta_1 I + \beta_2 I^2 + \varepsilon \qquad\qquad \textbf{1.6}$$

where $\varepsilon$ is a random variable with mean equal to zero. If our data are from households, then $\varepsilon$ is the difference between actual expenditure for a household with income $I$ and the expected food expenditures for a particular household with income $I$.

Notice that in the scatterplot in Figure 1.2, the scatter points are about equally dispersed all along the line. Actual food expenditures are unlikely to be scattered in this same way when graphed against income. People with very low incomes have little discretion over how much food they buy—limited funds but basic needs for nutrition and shelter determine how much low-income households spend on food. In contrast, people with high incomes have much more discretion in choosing how much they spend on food. Some diet-conscious wealthy people spend relatively little on food; others spend lavishly on food. In sum, food expenditures tend to vary less at low incomes than at high incomes; in terms of Equation 1.6, the variance of the disturbance term $w$ depends on the level of income. This fact leads to a scatterplot like that in Figure 1.3, with which we examine the food expenditures of a random sample of households.

Suppose you knew that you could not use the entire sample illustrated in Figure 1.3 for making your estimate of Equation 1.6. You could use either the half of

**Figure 1.3**

Food Expenditures
and Income

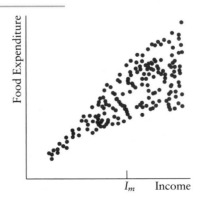

the observations that had income less than $I_m$ or the half of the observations with income more than $I_m$. Given our prior knowledge that households with higher income have more varied consumption levels, given income, which half of the data would you rather use to estimate $\beta_1$ and $\beta_2$? Notice that if the scatterplot in Figure 1.3 is representative, the observations with lower incomes are less plagued by "noise," the distortions arising from the stochastic disturbances to households' food expenditures. These observations fall more closely along the line that defines the expected level of food expenditures than do the observations with higher incomes. Choosing observations with lower incomes would seem advantageous in this case. Notice that there is no such advantage to picking lower or higher income students in Figure 1.2.

By comparing Figures 1.2 and 1.3, we can see that the assumptions we make about the stochastic structure of the model influence which observations we find most informative about the underlying relationship of interest, and therefore influence how we would use the data to estimate the underlying relationship. If some observations are less plagued by noise, we would want to rely more heavily on those observations when estimating $\beta_1$ and $\beta_2$. Furthermore, we would like procedures for differentiating among stochastic structures, so that we know which observations to rely on most heavily. Making assumptions about the distributions of the random components of a model, as when assuming that the disturbances' variance depends on income, is called **specifying the stochastic structure** of the model.

The variance of the disturbances is only one feature of the stochastic structure of a model. There are other features. For example, statisticians give much attention to simple random samples in which all the observations are drawn independently of one another from the same population. In econometrics, the observations in an econometrician's sample are sometimes independent of one another, as in simple random samples, but at other times, econometricians' observations are not statistically independent of one another.

An example of observations that are not statistically independent from one another would be food expenditure data that were quarterly observations of one household's food expenditures and income, instead of observations on a cross section of individuals. Because they are collected over time, we call such data **time series data**. It is highly unlikely that the disturbance to a household's food expenditures in the first quarter of 2003, say, is totally unrelated to the disturbance in the second quarter of that year. If food expenditures are unusually high in the first quarter, it is quite possible that some of the unobserved influences that caused that positive disturbance will persist into the following quarter. Rather than being independent, adjacent disturbances in this example might be positively correlated. Which estimator is best for a given model depends in part on any interdependencies among the model's disturbances.

# An Econometric Top 40—A Golden Oldie

## How Income Influences Demand—Engel's Law

In 1857, German statistician Ernst Engel[5] of Dresden, Germany, formulated his famous law: Households with higher incomes spend a smaller fraction of their income on food. The household budget data for 198 Belgian households, collected by Edouard Ducpetiaux,[6] that Engel used in his study are in the data set Ducfood.*** on this book's companion Web site (**www.aw-bc.com/murray**). (Data sets on the Web site are in four formats: Eviews, for which *** is wf1; STATA, for which *** is dta; Excel, for which *** is xls; and comma delimited text, for which *** is csv. Most data sets appear in three or four of these formats.) Hit Figure 1.1 displays these food expenditure and income data, with total expenditure on all goods and services serving as a measure of income.

These data do not indicate a larger variance for food expenditures at higher incomes as obviously as did the hypothetical observations in Figure 1.3, but the expenditures at higher incomes do appear somewhat more spread out than those at lower incomes. How can we decide whether the variance truly changes with income? One objective of econometrics is to devise formal procedures for answering such questions.

How can we assess Engel's Law with these data? One way to examine whether the fraction of income spent on food falls with income is to estimate the relationship

$$food\ expenditure = \beta_0 + \beta_1(income) + \varepsilon,$$

where $\varepsilon$ is a random variable with mean zero, and ascertain whether $\beta_0$ is positive. In this formulation, the average food consumption for a given income level is $\beta_0 + \beta_1(income)$, so

the fraction of income spent on food, (*food expenditure*)/*income*, is

$$(\beta_0/income) + \beta_1,$$

which falls as income rises if $\beta_0$ is positive, and rises as income rises if $\beta_0$ is negative. If we apply a modern estimator to Ducpetiaux's data, we obtain

$$E(food\ expenditure | income)$$
$$= 84.1 + 0.53 \cdot income. \qquad \text{H1.1}$$

These estimates indicate that in 1855, a Belgian household with no income spent, on average, 84.1 Belgian francs on food (presumably paid for from savings) and that expected food expenditure rose 0.53 francs for each additional

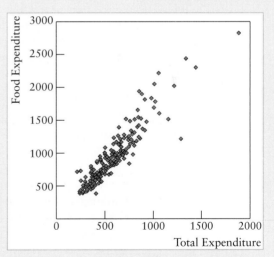

**Hit Figure 1.1**

Food Expenditure and Total Expenditures for 198 Belgian Households in 1855

*Source:* Edouard Ducpetiaux, *Budgets Economiques de Classes de Ouvrieres en Belgique* (Brussels: Hayaz, 1855).

one franc in income. Additional calculations, not shown, indicate that it is highly unlikely that we would obtain an estimate for $\beta_0$ as large as 84.1 if $\beta_0$ were not positive. Thus, we conclude that Engel's Law is, indeed, supported by the data he used.

The second example in this chapter examines an extension of Engel's Law that asserts that as income rises, increases in food expenditures grow at a smaller rate. A quadratic specification in which both income and the square of income affect expected food expenditures allowed a test of that hypothesis. Using Ducpetiaux's data and a quadratic specification, the modern estimator that produced Equation H1.1 yields

$$E(food\ expenditure \mid income) = 86.0 + 0.5 \cdot income + 0.000001 \cdot income^2.$$

The estimated coefficient on income squared is positive, not negative, which, according to the second example, conflicts with shrinking additional food expenditures from additional francs of income. The data do not support the claim that additional food expenditures from additional francs of income are smaller at higher incomes.

Yet another way to examine Engel's Law would be to specify that the relationship between food expenditures and income is a double logarithmic relationship,

$$log(food\ expenditure) = \beta_2 + \beta_3 log(income) + w,$$

where $w$ is a random disturbance of mean zero. It so happens that in such a relationship, $\beta_3$ is the elasticity of food expenditures with respect to income. If $\beta_3$ is less than one, then average food expenditures grow more slowly than does income, because food demand is income inelastic, and the fraction of income spent on food declines as income rises, as Engel's Law posits. When we apply the modern estimator to the double logarithmic specification, we obtain

$$E(log(food\ expenditure) \mid log(income)) = 0.43 + 0.87 \cdot log(income).$$

Further calculations, not shown, indicate that we would be highly unlikely to obtain an estimate as small as 0.87 for $\beta_3$, if $\beta_3$ were not less than one. Again, the data support Engel's Law.

  **Final Notes**

Our discussion of these results from the Ducpetiaux data raises several questions. Would estimators besides the one modern estimator used here suggest different conclusions from the same data? How are we to choose among linear, quadratic, and double logarithmic specifications? And how would we estimate the probability of getting estimates such as those we see, were Engel's Law false? Econometrics addresses all of these questions.

Engel studied food expenditures. Would he have obtained similar conclusions about housing expenditures? About entertainment expenditures? Engel's work inspired generations of studies about the relationship between consumer spending patterns and income. ∎

## What Example 2 Illustrates About Econometrics

This example of income and food expenditure illustrates five new aspects of econometric modeling and practice. First, the example shows how econometricians might specify a model when the relationship between the two variables is not linear. In the example, the proposed model is quadratic.

Second, the example illustrates how an econometrician can test specific economic hypotheses, such as the hypothesis that additional food expenditures decline with income.

Third, the example illustrates that the disturbances in a model need not have the same distribution for every value of the variables on the right-hand side, as was the case with food expenditures' disturbances. An econometrician must understand where his or her data come from so that he or she can properly specify the stochastic structure of the model.

Fourth, the example illustrates that the "best" estimator is determined by the traits of the disturbances, suggesting that econometricians need procedures for determining the traits of disturbances if they are to make "best" estimates.

Last, the example illustrates that the statistical relationship among the observations in a sample depends on how the sample is created. For example, if the data are taken from a simple random sample, the disturbances are independent of one another. If the data are drawn sequentially over time, the observations may well be correlated with one another. How we best form estimates from a sample of data depends on how the observations are related to one another statistically.

## 1.3     Organizing Econometrics

Introductory econometrics is conveniently broken into six categories: (i) What do we assume about where the data come from?; (ii) What makes a good estimator?; (iii) How do we create an estimator?; (iv) What are an estimator's properties?; (v) How do we test hypotheses?; and (vi) How do we forecast? Each category receives considerable attention in this book. Almost every main section of this book is assigned to one of these six categories, listed in the table on page 19. Similar tables appear at the end of each chapter to place the chapters' lessons within this organizational structure.

### What Do We Assume About Where the Data Come From?

In practice, econometricians use data about many different economic phenomena and data gathered in many different ways. One task before us is to devise precise characterizations of where econometric data come from so that we can ask how to make good estimates with such data. What variables belong in our model? Should we include wealth or the number of siblings in our model of financial aid? What is the functional relationship among the variables? Is the relationship linear, quadratic, or something else altogether? What is the stochastic structure of the data? Does the variance of food expenditures rise with income? Are quarterly observations on food expenditures correlated with one another? We needn't provide complete details about where the data come from, but we do need to report the assumptions we rely on about where the data come from.

## What Makes a Good Estimator?

There are many ways to estimate the magnitude of economic relationships. Each estimator has properties, some good, some bad. What are the properties of a good estimator? Why is a sample mean such a popular estimator of a population mean? Why are we likely to guess differently when our disturbances are correlated or when they have variances that change? Once we know where our data come from, what criteria do we use to choose among alternative estimators? Answering these questions is an early task for econometrics because those answers provide criteria for choosing among the many available estimation methods.

## How Do We Create an Estimator?

Early econometricians dwelt almost exclusively on devising estimation procedures. Assessing those estimators came later. Today, we often rely on the estimation procedures devised by the early econometricians, but we also find that we need newer procedures to better use available data. How do econometricians create estimators? For example, if our interest is in the slope and intercept of a linear relationship, what estimators might we consider as candidates for use? How can we create estimators that have the properties we deem good? How do we build an estimator for the slope underlying the financial aid data in Figure 1.2? How do we build an estimator for the curve underlying the food expenditure data in Figure 1.3? Understanding how an estimator is built often gives insight into when it works well and when it does not. Understanding the derivations of older estimators builds a foundation for learning how to construct more modern ones.

## What Are an Estimator's Properties?

We may know what properties would make an estimator attractive to us, but how are we to figure out whether a specific estimator has particular good traits or particular bad traits? For example, if being right on average is a desirable property for an estimator, how do we determine whether a particular estimator has this property? Knowing how an estimator's properties change as the kind of data we are dealing with changes is essential to making sound choices among estimators.

## How Do We Test Hypotheses?

There are two classes of tests that interest us. The first is tests of hypotheses about economic behavior. These tests constitute a fundamental purpose of econometrics. Is Engel's Law true? Does financial aid fall with income? These and other such questions motivate much of econometrics. The second is tests about where our data come from. Do food consumption disturbances have a variance that grows with income? Are our observations statistically independent from one another? Such tests guide us in choosing an estimator appropriate to the data at hand.

## How Do We Forecast?

Estimation provides guesses about the relationships among variables in a population. We might estimate the effect of an additional dollar of income on food expenditure. Forecasting makes predictions about what outcomes will be observed in the future. We might ask what food expenditure is going to be five years from now. These two activities are closely related, but there are subtle distinctions between them.

# Summary

Econometrics is the discipline that seeks quantitative estimates and forecasts of economic relationships; it estimates population parameters and forecasts the future values of random variables. The econometrician specifies both the functional form of a model that relates the expected value of one economic variable to the values of other economic variables and the stochastic structure of the model that states the probabilistic characteristics of the disturbances in the models.

Economic theory often influences the choice of functional form, but usually several alternative functional forms can be differentiated only empirically. Economic theory seldom informs the stochastic specification of a model, but experience has shown that different variances for the disturbances of different observations often plague cross-sectional data, and that correlations among the disturbances across observations often plague time series data. Empirical techniques for these traits of disturbances are necessary if we are to build models that mimic reality well. However, no matter how much care we put into specifying the functional form and stochastic structure of a model, the model is not "true" any more than a good map ever perfectly replicates the terrain it represents. Further-

 *An Organizational Structure for the Study of Econometrics*

1. What do we assume about where the data come from?

2. What makes a good estimator?

3. How do we create an estimator?

4. What are an estimator's properties?

5. How do we test hypotheses?

6. How do we forecast?

more, what constitutes a good model varies from study to study, depending on the real-world process that gave rise to the data, the available data itself, and the questions we wish to ask.

A major task for the econometrician is settling on the best estimator to use in a given situation. Informal procedures, such as "eyeballing" scatterplots, are simple to apply, but it is next to impossible to assess their adequacy. Instead, we need formal mathematical estimators to investigate the estimators' good and bad traits. Unfortunately, no one estimator is going to be best in every circumstance. The stochastic structure of the disturbances greatly influences which estimation procedures are best.

This book will help us answer six key econometric questions: (i) What do we assume about where the data come from?; (ii) What makes a good estimator?; (iii) How do we create an estimator?; (iv) What are an estimator's properties?; (v) How do we test hypotheses?; and (vi) How do we forecast? Ultimately, the econometrician wants to answer practical questions such as "How much does an undernourished factory worker's income in Bangladesh rise if the worker consumes an extra bowl of rice each week?" or "How much do corporate profits change if the corporate income tax rate is lowered by 5%?" Answering our six key questions enables us to address these more pressing issues. The power in answering such practical economic questions makes econometrics useful to all economists. As you progress through your first exposure to econometrics, continually re-ask the question, "How do the concepts and methods I am learning relate to the economic issues that matter most to me?"

## Concepts for Review

# Questions for Discussion

1. Economic theories limit attention to a small number of variables to explain economic phenomena. Econometric models do the same. Are you less comfortable limiting attention to a small number of variables when conducting an empirical analysis than when conducting a theoretical analysis? Discuss.

2. When econometricians use time series data from the past to make inferences about the future, they assume the future and the past are in some sense the same. When econometricians use cross-sectional data from a subset of firms in an industry, they assume that the firms in this industry are in some sense the same. How skeptical are you of this approach? In the case of time series data, how much difference does it make if the data are recent? In the case of cross sections, how much difference does it make if the data are randomly selected? Discuss.

3. We often formulate our economic theories in very general forms, as in

$$investment \ = \ \mathrm{f}(income, \ interest \ rates, \ prices).$$

In econometrics, we usually commit ourselves to a specific functional specification of the data. Does the added specificity of econometric formulae trouble you? Discuss.

# Problems for Analysis

> For the data sets that you will need to solve the problems in this section, go to **www.aw-bc.com/murray.**

1. Invent an example, drawn from the real world, that illustrates the five aspects of econometric modeling and practice highlighted in the income and financial aid examples. Explain, in detail similar to that in the textbook example, how your example illustrates each of those five features of econometric modeling. Provide graphs and equations where appropriate.

2. Invent an example, drawn from the real world, that illustrates the same five aspects of econometric modeling and practice highlighted in the food expenditure and income example. Explain, in detail similar to that in the textbook example, how your example illustrates each of those five features of econometric modeling. Provide graphs and equations where appropriate.

3. For the example you devise in Problem 1, indicate how many observations you would plan on using to conduct such an analysis. Explain how you would measure each variable you discuss and where you think you might find such data.

4. For the example you devise in Problem 2, indicate how many observations you would plan on using to conduct such an analysis. Explain how you would measure each variable you discuss and where you think you might find such data.

5. a. Suppose an econometric analysis finds that the relationship between home runs hit and average annual salary for major league baseball players is

$$expected \ salary \ = \ \$230,\!000 \ + \ \$50,\!000(home \ runs).$$

How much do expected salaries rise for each home run hit?

b. Suppose, instead, that expected salaries prove to be quadratic in home runs:

$$E(salary \mid home\ runs) = \$230,000 + [\$65,000(home\ runs)] - [\$600(home\ runs)^2]$$

(i) What is the derivative of expected salary with respect to home runs for a player who hits 10 home runs? 100 home runs?

(ii) Compute the expected salary of a player who hits 10 home runs.

(iii) Compute the expected salary of a player who hits 11 home runs.

(iv) Compute the expected salary of a player who hits 20 home runs.

c. Why might a player with 10 home runs have a different salary from the expected salary you compute in (bii)?

6. In 2004, David Grabowski and Michael Morrisey of the University of Alabama studied the relationship between gasoline prices and motor vehicle fatalities.[7] Their hypothesis was that higher gasoline prices would bring fewer miles driven, and hence fewer fatalities. In linear regression form, their estimate of the relationship between motor vehicle fatalities per 100,000 individuals is

$$E(fatalities\ per\ 100,000 \mid price) = 20.175 - 3.45(price\ of\ gas\ in\ dollars)$$

in the general population. This estimate implies an elasticity of fatalities with respect to the price of gas of $-0.345$ at the average price of $1.50 per gallon and the average fatalities per 100,000 of 15. For the more accident-prone young drivers, those 17 to 24, Grabowski and Morrisey found that

$$E(fatalities\ per\ 100,000 \mid price) = 42.25 - 11.5(price\ of\ gas\ in\ dollars),$$

which implies an elasticity of fatalities with respect to the price of gas of $-0.69$ at the average price of $1.50 per gallon and the average fatalities per 100,000 of 25.

a. According to Grabowski and Morrisey, how many fewer fatalities per 100,000 individuals occur in the general population when the price of gasoline rises by 10 cents?

b. What do you think explains Grabowski and Morrisey's finding that the elasticity of motor vehicle fatalities with respect to the price of gas is higher for young people than for people in general?

c. What are some of the determinants of motor vehicle fatalities that are not included in the regressions above? (Grabowski and Morrisey actually included several additional explanatory variables in their model.)

## Endnotes

1. Ragnar Frisch, "A Note on the Term 'Econometrics,'" *Econometrica* 4, no. 1 (January 1936): 95.

2. P. A. Samuelson, T. C. Koopmans, and J.R.N. Stone, "Report of the Evaluative Committee for Econometrica," *Econometrica* 22, no. 2 (1954): 141–146.

3. Martin Feldstein, "College Scholarship Rules and Private Saving," *American Economic Review* 85, no. 3 (June 1995): 552–566.
4. Henri Theil, *Principles of Econometrics* (New York: John Wiley, 1971): vi.
5. Ernst Engel, "Die Productions und Consumptionsverhaeltnisse des Koenigsreichs Sachsen," reprinted in *Die Lebenskosten Belgischer Arbeiter-Familien International Statistical Bulletin* 9, no. 1 (Dresden, 1895): 1–124.
6. Edouard Ducpetiaux, *Budgets Economiques de Classes de Ouvrieres en Belgique* (Brussels: Hayaz, 1855).
7. David Grabowski and Michael A. Morrisey, "Gasoline Prices and Motor Vehicle Fatalities," *Journal of Policy Analysis and Management* 23, no. 3 (2004): 575–593.

# Chapter 2

# Choosing Estimators: Intuition and Monte Carlo Methods

*It's a damn poor mind that can only think of one way to spell a word.*
— ATTRIBUTED TO ANDREW JOHNSON (1808–1875)

hen Joseph Jaggers, a British cotton mill engineer, died in 1892, Fred Gilbert penned this popular song in his honor:

*As I walk along the Bois Boulong with an independent air,*
*You can hear the girls declare: "He must be a millionaire."*
*You can hear them sigh and wish to die,*
*You can see them wink the other eye,*
*At the man who broke the Bank at Monte Carlo.[1]*

In 1873, Joseph Jaggers won the equivalent of 4.7 million dollars in today's prices playing roulette in a Monte Carlo casino. That's not the way it's supposed to work.

Casinos count on the promise of statistics' Law of Large Numbers that a properly balanced roulette wheel will almost surely, when spun a very large number of times, land in each of the 37 slots on the machine very close to 1/37th of the time. With that assurance, casinos are almost certain to win when customers play roulette a large number of times. Unfortunately for one casino, and fortunately for Mr. Jaggers, one of the roulette wheels in the casino where he played was not properly balanced, and Jaggers knew which one. The Law of Large Numbers worked as advertised when Jaggers played, but it was he, not the casino, who could count on winning with near certainty. By the time the casino figured out what was going on and fixed their problem, Jaggers had won 6.5 million dollars. He lost 1.8 million of it before deciding that his advantage was gone.

Long after Jaggers was laid to rest, statisticians and econometricians determined how to make computers mimic the random outcomes of roulette wheels and other chance mechanisms. Today, we use computers' random results to assess the performance of estimators that we intend to use many times. We call these assessments **Monte Carlo exercises**. Whether estimating how financial aid or food expenditures change with income, or the price elasticity of the demand for wheat, econometricians can always choose from different methods of estimation. Even for a simple econometric problem, an economist might pursue numerous plausible strategies. In this chapter, we learn how Monte Carlo exercises can help us choose among candidate estimators.

How should econometricians reduce many observations on behavior to provide a single guess? Which estimation strategy is best? Indeed, what do we mean by "best"? The richest responses to these questions are framed in formal statistical terms. This chapter blends statistical notions with some common-sense arguments about what makes good estimation procedures and turns to Monte Carlo methods to find a best estimator among several candidates.

The chapter first discusses some good traits for estimation procedures. It next reviews the estimation of a population mean. It then turns our attention to estimating the slope of a line through the origin. After identifying three intuitively attractive estimators that students often devise themselves, the chapter presents Monte Carlo exercises that ask whether these estimators perform well when used many times. We learn to examine the applications' estimation errors to determine the estimators' properties. The computer program Monte Carlo Builder I on this book's companion Web site (**www.aw-bc.com/murray**) allows you to perform your own Monte Carlo exercises with which to estimate the candidate estimators. This chapter doesn't settle whether the three intuitively appealing estimators are right on average, but we do learn that one estimator among the three is superior. The success of Monte Carlo methods in choosing among these three estimators inspires subsequent applications of Monte Carlo methods to assess the properties of other estimators later in this book and exemplifies the advantages econometricians gain from applying Monte Carlo methods more generally.

## 2.1 How to Sell Econometrics

**WHAT MAKES A GOOD ESTIMATOR?**

Common-sense arguments are especially helpful when economists must convince noneconomists to trust econometric analyses. Although statistical sophistication allows better understandings of the power and limits of econometric methods, many deep statistical insights can be expressed in terms accessible to nonstatisticians. Economists who sell econometric services to businesses and government must often rely on common-sense arguments.

An econometrician who markets her wares by claiming, "I use estimation methods that are guaranteed to be wrong on average," will not find many customers. A much preferable pitch would be, "I use estimation methods that are guaranteed to be right, on average." In technical terms, this latter claim asserts that the econometrician uses an estimator that is *unbiased*. An estimator is **unbiased** if its guesses are right, on average, across all samples, that is, if the expected value of the estimator equals the parameter (for example, the population

**Figure 2.1**

Estimators' Distributions

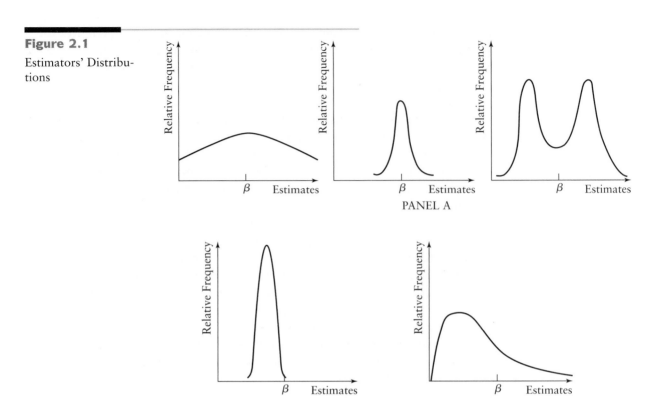

PANEL A

PANEL B

mean) being estimated. Figure 2.1 shows the distributions of several estimators, each an estimator of the population parameter $\beta$. The estimators take on different values with different probabilities across all samples because each sample gives different observations and each estimator uses the observations in its own way. Panel A of the figure shows the distributions of three unbiased estimators—all three estimators are, on average, equal to $\beta$. Panel B shows the distributions of two biased estimators—neither estimator is, on average, equal to $\beta$.

It is better to market estimation procedures that are right, on average, than those that are wrong, on average, but a wary customer might still question an unbiased estimator, saying: "I've heard about the economist with his head in a furnace and his torso in a block of ice who said, 'On average I'm comfortable.' What sorts of mistakes are you likely to make? I'm particularly leery of large errors." A clever econometrician might reply to this sophisticated customer, "If you especially dislike large errors, you are probably more interested in the square of errors than in just the magnitude of the errors. Squaring emphasizes large errors by increasing them relative to the small errors. No one can make unbiased estimates that have smaller average squared errors than mine." In technical terms, this last claim asserts that the econometrician's estimators are *efficient*. An unbiased estimator is **efficient** if across all samples it has a smaller variance than any other unbiased estimator. Econometricians sometimes refer to an unbiased estimator's variance as the estimator's **efficiency**. In Figure 2.1, Panel A, the estimator with its distribution most concentrated around $\beta$ is the most efficient.

An eager competing econometrician might counter, "Mistakes are mistakes. Who cares whether errors result from being wrong on average or from being wrong because of an estimator's variance? My estimators have the smallest squared errors on average, so you should prefer my estimates to hers even though my estimates are biased and hers unbiased." In technical terms, this econometrician is claiming that his estimators have the smallest *mean square error*. The **mean square error** of an estimator is the mean (across all samples) squared deviation of the estimator from the parameter of interest. Numerical calculations would indicate that in Figure 2.1, the estimator in Panel B that has the smaller bias and a distribution very concentrated about its mean has a smaller mean square error than the unbiased estimator in Panel A with the most spread-out distribution—the markedly smaller variance of the estimator in Panel B more than compensates for its unwelcome bias.

Which econometrician's estimates a customer buys depends in part on the customer's purposes. Economic forecasters often don't care about the source of a forecasting error; they care only about the size of their errors. Consequently, economic forecasters will often bypass unbiased estimators in favor of minimum mean square error estimators. In contrast, scientists who ask, "What is the nature of our world?" are more likely to choose unbiased estimators. Such scientists hope that repeated experimentation and analysis will lead to increasingly accurate cumulative assessments. Accepting biased estimators would thwart the scientists' hope from the outset—repeated application of a biased estimator would ultimately converge on a wrong outcome.

Notice that each of our econometricians implicitly suggests a criterion for choosing a "best" estimator: unbiasedness, efficiency, or minimum mean square error. What do these three criteria have in common? Each describes how an estimator performs across samples when we use the estimator over and over again. Why is the focus not on the specific results from a particular sample? Why do the econometricians not tell us whether they will be right, and if they are to be wrong, how much they will err by? They don't tell us because they, like their clients, don't know the right answer; if they knew the right answer, there would be no need for estimation! *We need estimation when we have incomplete information, when we observe only a sample from the population, not the entire population.* What samples we actually obtain in the world is a matter of chance. In formal statistical terms, we can describe our sample observations as random variables, because each value an observation in a sample can take on has some probability of occurring.

Because estimators are a function of the random observations in a sample, estimators are also random variables: Estimators take on different values in different samples, and each estimate has some probability of occurring. The distribution of estimates across all samples is called the estimator's **sampling distribution**. Econometricians often choose estimators based on the properties of the estimator's sampling distribution, called the estimator's **sampling properties**.

Unable to say whether a particular estimate is right or wrong, econometricians peddle their wares with appeals to some property of their estimator's sampling distribution—its mean, or its variance, or its mean square error. In Chapters 1 through 10, we will rely heavily on this sampling perspective for judging estimators.

## 2.2        Estimating a Population's Mean

**WHAT ARE AN ESTIMATOR'S PROPERTIES?**

Estimating the mean of a population is the classic statistics problem. What is the mean family income of California college students? What is the mean weight of breast-fed infants in Calcutta? What is the mean weight of Keebler Crackers in boxes marked 16 ounces? A statistician would say that each of these questions asks about the mean of a population. The populations here are "all California college students," "all breast-fed babies in Calcutta," and "all boxes of Keebler Crackers marked 16 ounces." If we could examine all members of each population, we could calculate the population mean. But if we have only a sample drawn from the population, then we must resort to estimating the population mean. In this section, we review the estimation of a population mean.

Consider a population with a finite mean and a finite variance. Denote the population mean[2] by $\beta$ and the population variance by $\sigma^2$. Statistics teaches that if we draw data from such a sample in a simple random manner (that is, giving each item in the population the same chance of being drawn on every draw and making the draws statistically independent), then the sample mean

$$\overline{Y} = \frac{1}{n}\sum_{i=1}^{n} Y_i,$$

where $n$ is the number of observations and $Y_1, \ldots, Y_n$ are the observations in the sample, is an unbiased estimator of the population mean; that is, the expected value, or mean value, of $\overline{Y}$ across all samples is equal to $\beta$:

$$E(\overline{Y}) = \beta.$$

Also, the variance of $\overline{Y}$ is $\sigma^2$ divided by the number of observations in the sample:

$$\text{var}(\overline{Y}) = \sigma^2/n.$$

The variance of $\overline{Y}$ arises because different samples yield different means. If the underlying population is normally distributed, statistics teaches that the sample mean is also normally distributed and is an efficient estimator of the population mean. And finally, the **Central** (or key) **Limit Theorem** of statistics tells us that in large samples, the sample mean is almost always approximately normally distributed, no matter how the population is distributed.

Just as estimating the mean of a population is the classic statistical problem, estimating the slope of a line is the classic econometric problem. These two seemingly different problems are intimately related. For this reason, we next revisit the estimation of the mean of a population, recasting the problem in a way that facilitates the transition from estimating the mean of a population to estimating the slope of a line.

## The Need for a Precise Statement of Assumptions

A precise, formal statement of the classic statistical estimation problem, estimating the mean of a population, introduces the style of presentation used for stating estimation problems throughout this text. This formal statement adds no new content; it is simply a precise statement of the classic problem of estimating a population's mean when we have a simple random sample. A precise statement of assumptions ensures that we know exactly what we are assuming in an analysis. It allows us to alter assumptions one at a time and to keep track of what changes and what remains the same. Because much of econometrics involves asking how changing assumptions changes the properties of estimators, having a clear format for stating assumptions is very helpful. The next section discusses the random elements of the classic type of data with which we estimate a population mean and thereby establishes this clear format.

## Sampling and Randomness

Suppose we will draw $n$ observations in simple random fashion from a population with mean $\beta$. Call these observations $Y_1, \ldots, Y_n$. Each observation is likely to differ from $\beta$ by some amount. Let us call these differences from the population mean $\varepsilon_1, \ldots, \varepsilon_n$, so that $Y_i = \beta + \varepsilon_i$. Our task is to estimate $\beta$ when $\varepsilon_1, \ldots, \varepsilon_n$ are unknown. If we observed $\varepsilon_1, \ldots, \varepsilon_n$, as well as $Y_i$, we could calculate $\beta$ exactly by subtracting each $\varepsilon_i$ from $Y_i$,—there would be no estimation problem. For example, if we knew how much people slept *and* how much their sleep deviated from average, we could simply calculate, not estimate, the average sleep time. Estimation becomes necessary when we observe only how much some people sleep, not how much their sleep deviates from the unknown average time slept.

Accidents of chance lead us to one sample and not another. If we describe such happenstance in probabilistic terms, as we do when we say that we gather a simple random sample, the observations $Y_1, \ldots, Y_n$, are random variables. In some scientific and social experiments, sample observations are chosen by the actual application of some chance process, such as flipping a coin to select some members of the population for inclusion in the sample and to exclude others. In other applications, a probabilistic description is a convenient fiction that allows us to apply formal statistical notions to real-world processes. For example, each year the economy experiences new shocks, new surprises. GDP, consumption, investment, and so on, *all could have been otherwise*. Econometricians capture this aspect of economic outcomes by describing each year's shocks and surprises as realizations of specific values drawn from some population of what could have been. Unlike samples of individuals drawn from a real human population, there is no real population of alternative economic outcomes from which the observed year is drawn. Here, the population is a convenient fiction. Probabilistic characterizations of real-world events need not assume simple random samples, but simple random samples are the least complicated statistical framework, and are, therefore, a good starting place for introductory analyses.

In any random sample, every member of the population has the same chance of being selected on the $i$th draw. Consequently, in our simple random sample, the distribution of $Y_i$ is exactly the same as the distribution of the population. In particular, the mean of each $Y_i$ is $\beta$ and the variance of each $Y_i$ is the population's variance, $\sigma^2$. In a simple random sample, the observations are all drawn independently, so the $Y_i$'s are mutually statistically independent; similarly, the $\varepsilon_1, \ldots, \varepsilon_n$'s are also statistically independent random variables because they differ from the $Y_i$'s by just the constant $\beta$. Because each $\varepsilon_i$ is the deviation of a random variable ($Y_i$) from its mean ($\beta$), each $\varepsilon_i$ has a mean of zero. Because $\varepsilon_i$ differs from $Y_i$ only by a constant ($\beta$), the variance of $\varepsilon_i$ is also $\sigma^2$. By writing $Y_i = \beta + \varepsilon_i$, we see that $\varepsilon_i$ wholly captures $Y_i$'s randomness.

## Precise Assumptions—the Data-Generating Process

A succinct, formal restatement of our simple random sample assumptions, in a format used repeatedly throughout this text, is

$$Y_i = \beta + \varepsilon_i \qquad i = 1, \ldots, n$$

$$E(\varepsilon_i) = 0 \qquad i = 1, \ldots, n$$

$$\text{var}(\varepsilon_i) = \sigma^2 \qquad i = 1, \ldots, n$$

and $\varepsilon_1, \ldots, \varepsilon_n$ are mutually statistically independent.

These statements exemplify what we call a *data-generating process*. A **data-generating process (DGP)** contains our assumptions about where our data come from. *"What Is the DGP?" rather than "What Do We Assume About Where the Data Come From?" is from now on our name for the first category for organizing in-*

*troductory econometrics*. "What Is the DGP?" is the first category that appears in the end-of-chapter tables organizing the chapters' lessons. The DGP combines what we assume about the underlying population of interest with what we assume about how data are chosen from that population. In the present case, we assume that the population has a finite mean and variance and that the sampling procedure is simple random sampling.

A DGP need not fully specify where our data come from. For example, this first DGP does not state whether the observations are drawn from a normally distributed population or from a population following some other distribution. Conclusions drawn from less restrictive DGPs are more broadly applicable, which is appealing. However, because econometricians can sometimes draw more detailed conclusions from more detailed DGPs, we do sometimes choose to specify more detailed DGPs.

## Interpreting the DGP

The notation in this first DGP is very compact. Some elaboration may help you sharpen your intuition. In econometrics, the $\varepsilon_i$ are variously called "disturbances" or "errors" or "stochastic terms." Saying that $E(\varepsilon_1) = 0$ asserts that across all the samples we might observe, and accounting for those samples' various chances of occurring, the first observations' disturbances (the $\varepsilon_1$ across samples) will average 0. Saying that $E(\varepsilon_2) = 0$ makes a similar claim about the second observations' disturbances across all samples. Saying that $\text{var}(\varepsilon_1) = \sigma^2$ tells us how spread out the disturbances of the first observations are when we look at the first observations of all possible samples and account for the likelihood of each of those samples occurring. Saying that $\text{var}(\varepsilon_2) = \sigma^2$ makes the same claim about how spread out the second observation's disturbances are across samples. Because in this DGP all observations' disturbances have the same variance ($\sigma^2$), we say the disturbances are **homoskedastic**.

Notice that in the formal statement of the DGP, we describe the distribution of the $\varepsilon_1, \ldots, \varepsilon_n$ rather than the distribution of the $Y_1, \ldots, Y_n$. Nonetheless the assumptions made are equivalent. In this DGP, the dependent variables, the $Y_i$, and the disturbances, the $\varepsilon_i$, differ only by $\beta$, so except for their means, their distributions are the same. It is therefore redundant, though instructive, to say that the DGP assumes

$$E(Y_i) = \beta \qquad i = 1, \ldots, n,$$
$$\text{var}(Y_i) = \sigma^2 \qquad i = 1, \ldots, n,$$

and

the $Y_i$ are mutually statistically independent.

As noted earlier, in statistics we learn that for the sample mean from a simple random sampling procedure,

$$\overline{Y} = \frac{(\sum Y_i)}{n}$$

is an unbiased estimator of the population mean, $\beta$. Two rules for manipulating expectations bring us to this unbiasedness conclusion: (i) The expected value of a constant times a random variable equals the constant times the expected value of the random variable, and (ii) the expected value of a sum is the sum of the expected values. Hence:

$$E(\overline{Y}) = E\left(\frac{1}{n}\sum Y_i\right) = \frac{1}{n}E\left(\sum Y_i\right) = \frac{1}{n}\sum E(Y_i) = \frac{1}{n}\sum \beta = \frac{1}{n}n\beta = \beta.$$

The variance of the sample mean is $(\sigma^2/n)$. Two rules for manipulating variances bring us to this variance: (i) The variance of a constant times a random variable equals the constant squared times the variance of the random variable, and (ii) the variance of a sum of independent random variables equals the sum of the variances of the random variables. Therefore,

$$\text{var}(\overline{Y}) = \text{var}\left(\frac{1}{n}\sum Y_i\right) = \left(\frac{1}{n}\right)^2 \text{var}\left(\sum Y_i\right) = \left(\frac{1}{n}\right)^2 \sum \text{var}(Y_i)$$
$$= \left(\frac{1}{n}\right)^2 \sum \sigma^2 = \left(\frac{1}{n}\right)^2 n\sigma^2 = \sigma^2/n.$$

If the disturbances are normally distributed, the sample mean is also the most efficient estimator of $\beta$. In large simple random samples (100 observations and more), the Central Limit Theorem ensures that the sample mean is almost always approximately normally distributed, even when the disturbances are not normally distributed.

## Estimating Means as Estimating Intercepts

The transition from statistics to econometrics is easier when we can see the connection between estimating the mean of a population and estimating the parameters of a straight line (the slope and intercept). The formal statement in Section 2.2 of the classic estimation of a population mean problem invites us to reinterpret that DGP by saying that the estimation of the mean of a population is equivalent to the estimation of a straight line with a slope of zero—that is, with no slope. In this interpretation, $\beta$ is the intercept term of a straight line that has no slope. In the notation of the previous chapter, we might say that

$$E(Y_i|X_i) = \beta + 0X_i \qquad i = 1,\ldots,n,$$

for some $X$ (which $X$ is of little interest, because it has no effect on $Y$), in which case it follows that

$$E(Y_i) = \beta \qquad i = 1, \ldots, n.$$

(If the mean of $Y$ is $\beta$ for each value of $X$, then the mean of $Y$ will be $\beta$ no matter the value of $X$.) This link between the estimation of a population mean and the intercept of a line alerts us to the possibility that a relationship also exists between estimating the mean of a population and estimating the slope of a line. We explore this link in the next section.

## 2.3    Estimating the Slope of a Line with No Intercept: Families of Means

WHAT IS THE DGP?

Estimating a population mean is closely related to the classic econometric problem, estimating the slope of a line. The nature of that relationship is evident in estimating even the simplest straight line, a line that has no intercept term, a line that passes through the origin. Straight lines through the origin do not arise often in economics, but there are several classic cases in which a straight line through the origin does arise from economic theorizing. Two of these examples illustrate the economic relevance of lines through the origin. However, the great advantage of such lines is not their practical applicability, but their relative transparency in exposing the essential nature of estimating slopes of lines. When we understand the estimation of straight lines through the origin, we are far along the path to understanding the estimation of more complex relationships. In addition, we come to that understanding free of superfluous distracting complexity.

### Economic Theory and Lines Through the Origin

Straight lines through the origin do sometimes arise from economic theorizing. Thus, although restrictive, these lines are sometimes of genuine interest to economists.

The first example in which economic theory leads to a straight line through the origin concerns the relationship between an asset's return and its risk. The risk premium of a risky asset is the excess return that the asset gets over what risk-free assets earn in the marketplace. One early finance model assumed that the average risk premium earned by an asset is directly proportional to the riskiness of the asset:

$$E(\textit{risk premium} \mid \textit{risk}) = \beta(\textit{risk}). \qquad \textbf{2.1}$$

The model measures risk by the standard deviation of the asset's returns. Assets with more varied returns are deemed riskier. Figure 2.2, Panel (a), shows a graph of the expected risk premium plotted against risk. The graph is a straight line through the origin. Estimating $\beta$ in this model is estimating the slope of that line with no intercept.

A second example arises when a consumer has a utility function defined for housing and all other goods that has the form

$$U = \alpha[housing]^{\beta}[all\ else]^{(1-\beta)}$$

that economists call the Cobb–Douglas utility function. To maximize utility, this consumer spends a constant fraction of income on housing:

$$E = (housing\ expenditure\,|\,income) = \beta(income) \qquad 2.2$$

Figure 2.2, Panel (b), shows a graph of expected housing expenditures plotted against income. Again, the graph is a straight line through the origin. Estimating $\beta$ in this model is estimating the slope of that line with no intercept.

## Families of Means

Estimating the slope, $\beta$, in these two models is closely related to estimating the mean of a population. How? Notice that the expected return on an asset differs across levels of risk and the expected expenditure on housing differs across levels of income. But in each case, these expected values belong to a well-defined family of means whose members are related in a specific way, by either $\beta(risk)$ or $\beta(income)$. *Thus we see that the classic econometric problem of estimating a line is the estimation of a family of means.* Mean housing expenditure when income is $100,000 ($\beta(\$100,000)$) differs from the mean of housing expenditure when income is $35,000 ($\beta(\$35,000)$), but the two means are related through the linear formula E(*housing expenditure*) = $\beta(income)$.

Recognizing that the econometric problem is about estimating means helps us see the connection between what we learn in statistics and what we learn in econometrics. If the econometric problem is about estimating means, however, why don't we just stick with the methods of statistics? Why don't we just estimate each mean, as described in Section 2.3? We don't because estimating the whole family of means together is more efficient than estimating them one by one. *Recognizing that some means, such as those for housing expenditures at different levels of income, are related allows us to more powerfully use the data we gather.* For example, if we had 50 households with incomes of $100,000 and another 50 households with incomes of $35,000, we could analyze the two samples separately to estimate the mean housing expenditure for each subpopulation. But if

**Figure 2.2**

Risk Premium vs.
Risk and Housing
Expenditure vs. In-
come

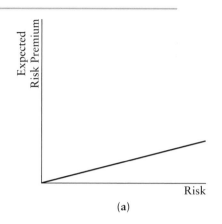

(a)

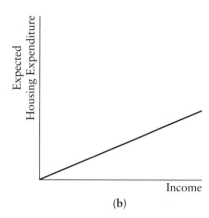

(b)

we exploit the relationship between the two means, and estimate $\beta$ to use in $\beta(income)$, we can use these 100 households to draw inferences about other members of the family—for example, what the expected housing expenditure would be for households with incomes of $60,000 (which is $\beta(\$60,000)$). For another example, if we observed only two assets, each with a risk of 20, we could probably not estimate their expected return very precisely with so few observations. If we also observed 100 assets with a risk of 10 and another 100 assets with a risk of 30, though, an estimate of $\beta$ using all 210 observations might provide a precise estimate of the expected return on assets with a risk of 20 ($\beta(20)$).

## 2.4    Natural Estimators for the Slope of a Line Through the Origin

How Do We Create
an Estimator?

We know that to estimate the mean of a single population, as in the classic statistical problem, we would use the sample mean from a simple random sample. We would calculate

$$\overline{Y} = \sum Y_i/n.$$

But how can we exploit the information that some means belong to a common family, lying along a line through the origin, as with the mean housing expenditures or the mean asset risk premia in our examples? What formula should we use to estimate $\beta$? How should we estimate the family of housing expenditure means or the family of risk premium means? More generally, how should we estimate the slope of a line through the origin?

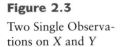

**Figure 2.3**

Two Single Observations on $X$ and $Y$

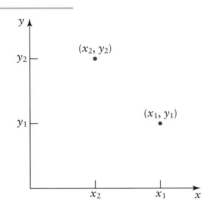

## A First Natural Estimator

To simplify the problem, suppose we have only one observation in our simple random sample $(X_1, Y_1)$. Note that because we are interested in the relationship between $Y$ and $X$, each observation must contain information on both $Y$ and $X$. In the asset return and housing examples, $(X_1, Y_1)$ would be a single asset's observed return and risk, or one person's observed housing expenditure and income. Figure 2.3 plots an illustrative $(X_1, Y_1)$. What is your guess of $\beta$ if you observe $(X_1, Y_1)$? A natural guess would be the slope of the line passing through both $(X_1, Y_1)$ and the origin. This slope is $(Y_1/X_1)$. What if you had a different single data point, $(X_2, Y_2)$? Presumably, with this sample, you would estimate $\beta$ to be $(Y_2/X_2)$, the slope of the line through $(X_2, Y_2)$ and the origin.

What then would you do if you had *both* data points, $(X_1, Y_1)$ and $(X_2, Y_2)$? Many students, when asked this question, suggest as a reasonable estimate

$$\frac{1}{2}\left(\frac{Y_1}{X_1} + \frac{Y_2}{X_2}\right),$$

the mean of the estimates we would make if we had each observation singly. More generally, with $n$ observations, we might propose as a natural estimator

$$\beta_{g1} = \frac{1}{n}\sum\left(\frac{Y_i}{X_i}\right),$$

the mean of the estimates we would make if we had each observation singly. *For our initial estimators, the subscript* g *emphasizes that the formal concept of estimator grows out of the intuitive notion of a guessing mechanism. Here, the numerical subscript "1" distinguishes this initial estimator of the slope of a line through the origin from those that follow.* Notice that no observed $X$ can equal zero if $\beta_{g1}$ is to be well defined; we can't divide by zero. Such restrictions on estimators are common. The concept of estimator grows out of the notion of a guessing mechanism, but not all guessing mechanisms are equal. One fundamental task of econometric theory is to provide us with systematic, well-informed guessing mechanisms worthy of the fancy term "estimator."

The asset risk model of Equation 2.1 slid from favor many years ago, but the Cobb–Douglas utility function continues to be used in many empirical and theoretical studies. Here, we estimate the Cobb–Douglas $\beta$ from Equation 2.2 using data in the file rents.*** on **www.aw-bc.com/murray**. The file contains annual rents and incomes for a sample of 108 New York renters in 1990. Their mean annual income was $35,593 and their mean annual rent $7,718.11. In this sample of New York renters, $\beta_{g1} = 0.29$. If $\beta$ actually equals 0.29—that is, if this estimate is correct—then, on average, New Yorkers spend 29 cents of each dollar on rent.

## A Second Natural Estimator

Not all students asked to estimate the slope of a line through the origin using two data points suggest the mean of the ratios $Y_i/X_i$. Instead, some students look at a graph showing both the $X_i$'s and both the $Y_i$'s and conclude that the most natural estimator would be to use the slope of a line through the origin that splits in half a line connecting the two points. Figure 2.4 illustrates this construction. The point of intersection between the two lines in Figure 2.4 is $([.5(X_1 + X_2)],$ $[.5(Y_1 + Y_2)])$, so this estimator would estimate $\beta$ by the ratio of the average $X$ to the average $Y$, that is,

$$\frac{.5(Y_1 + Y_2)}{.5(X_1 + X_2)} = \frac{(Y_1 + Y_2)}{(X_1 + X_2)}.$$

**Figure 2.4**

Estimating the Slope of a Line with Two Data Points

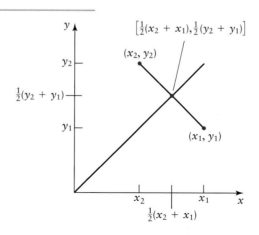

Figure 2.5 shows that an equivalent geometric interpretation of this estimator is to estimate $\beta$ by the slope of the line that passes through the point $[(X_1 + X_2), (Y_1 + Y_2)]$. This latter geometric interpretation has the attractive feature of generalizing to more than two observations (which Figure 2.4 does not). Figure 2.5 suggests we estimate $\beta$ by the ratio of the sum of the $X$'s to the sum of the $Y$'s:

$$\beta_{g2} = \frac{\sum Y_i}{\sum X_i}.$$

Notice the $X_i$ cannot sum to zero if this estimator is to be well defined because we can't divide by zero. Using this method for our sample of New York renters, we find $\beta_{g2} = 0.22$.

Both $\beta_{g1}$ and $\beta_{g2}$ are naturally appealing estimators of $\beta$. Neither $\beta_{g1}$ nor $\beta_{g2}$ is as obvious an estimator as the sample mean was in the classic statistical estimation problem, but both arise from an intuitive examination of the problem.

## A Third Natural Estimator

Although many students suggest $\beta_{g1}$ or $\beta_{g2}$ for estimating the slope of a line through the origin, other students base an estimator on a mathematical insight drawn from calculus. The slope of a line is the rate of change of the left-hand-side variable, $Y$, with respect to the right-hand-side variable, $X$; that is, it is the rise over the run, or the change in $Y$ divided by the change in $X$. With this interpretation of the slope in mind, these students think it most natural to estimate the slope of a line through the origin using two data points by

$$\frac{(Y_1 - Y_2)}{(X_1 - X_2)},$$

the ratio of the change in $Y$ from one observation to the next to the change in $X$ from one observation to the next.

What if we did not have $(X_1, Y_1)$ and $(X_2, Y_2)$ but, instead, had $(X_2, Y_2)$ and a different observation, $(X_3, Y_3)$? Again, we might naturally compute the changes in $Y$ and $X$ from one observation to the next and calculate their ratio to obtain the estimate $(Y_2 - Y_3)/(X_2 - X_3)$. And if we had all three observations? Why not average the two ratios:

$$\frac{1}{2}\frac{(Y_1 - Y_2)}{(X_1 - X_2)} + \frac{1}{2}\frac{(Y_2 - Y_3)}{(X_2 - X_3)}?$$

This latter strategy amounts to first computing the changes in $Y$ and $X$ for successive observations, then averaging the ratios of those successive changes.

**Figure 2.5**

Estimating the Slope
of a Line: $\beta_{g2}$

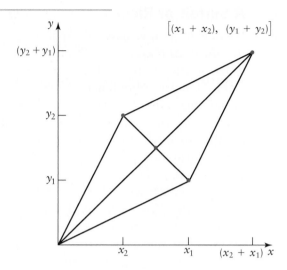

We could reasonably propose some other pairing of these three observations when forming ratios, instead of relying on successive changes. For example, we could pair the first and third observations to replace one of the earlier pairs. Alternatively, we might form all the possible combinations of observations, calculate the associated changes in $Y$ and $X$, and take the mean of the ratios of these changes. In this instance, there would be three possible pairings. With $n$ observations, there would be $n(n-1)/2$ possible pairings. Each of these alternatives would result in yet another estimator to consider. We forgo these alternatives and average the ratios of changes in successive observations' $Y$ and $X$ values.

We choose to analyze the estimator that looks at changes in $Y$ and $X$ in successive observations because this form of the estimator closely approximates an estimator used by some early practitioners of econometrics. Generalizing this estimator to an instance with $n$ observations, we obtain

$$\beta_{g3} = \frac{1}{(n-1)}\sum_{i=2}^{n}\frac{(Y_i - Y_{i-1})}{(X_i - X_{i-1})},$$

that is, the mean ratio of changes in the $Y$'s and $X$'s from observation to observation. Why divide the sum of the ratios of changes in $Y$ to changes in $X$ by $(n-1)$? We do so because there will be one less change than observations; the changes will start at observations 1 and 2 and end at observations $(n-1)$ and $n$, making $(n-1)$ changes in all. If we are to use $\beta_{g3}$ as our estimator, successive $X$'s cannot be equal, because we can't divide by zero. Using this method for our sample of New York renters, we find $\beta_{g3} = 0.28$.

## A Surfeit of Riches

We now have three naturally appealing estimators for the slope of a line through the origin. Applied to our sample of New York renters, these estimators give three different guesses (0.29, 0.22, and 0.28) about the exponent on housing in a Cobb–Douglas utility function, which is the fraction of income households spend on housing. How can we determine which natural estimator is best? We might ask: "Is one of these estimators unbiased? If they are all unbiased, are they all equally efficient?" In subsequent chapters, we examine alternatives to the sampling distribution perspective on what constitutes a best estimator, but in this chapter, and for much of Chapters 1 through 10, we follow a long-standing practice in econometrics and choose a best estimator based on estimators' sampling distributions. Therefore, to choose among $\beta_{g1}$, $\beta_{g2}$, and $\beta_{g3}$ we look at their means, variances, and mean square errors. But can we determine the means, variances, and mean square errors of $\beta_{g1}$, $\beta_{g2}$, and $\beta_{g3}$?

The sampling distributions of our estimators depend on the source of our data, that is, on the DGP that gives us our observations. To compare $\beta_{g1}$, $\beta_{g2}$, and $\beta_{g3}$, or any other natural estimators we might construct, we must first state our assumptions about the population and about the process that generates our sample.

## 2.5    The Data-Generating Process

WHAT IS THE DGP?

In the classic statistical problem of estimating a population mean, we assume the population has a finite mean and variance and that we draw a simple random sample from that population. Now, in the classic econometric problem, we face a family of means that all lie along a line through the origin. An adaptation of our earlier DGP allows for this change from the classic statistical problem to the classic econometric problem. Succinctly stated, the DGP we assume as we compare $\beta_{g1}$, $\beta_{g2}$, and $\beta_{g3}$ is

$$Y_i = \beta X_i + \varepsilon_i \qquad i = 1, \ldots, n$$

$$\mathrm{E}(\varepsilon_i) = 0 \qquad i = 1, \ldots, n$$

$$\mathrm{var}(\varepsilon_i) = \sigma^2 \qquad i = 1, \ldots, n.$$

$\varepsilon_1, \ldots, \varepsilon_n$ are mutually statistically independent.

*Each $X_i$ is fixed across samples.*

As in the classic statistical DGP, all the variation across samples in this classic econometric DGP arises from new disturbances being drawn in each sample; nothing else changes from sample to sample.

## The New Assumptions

This new DGP brings only two changes from the DGP we used earlier when describing the problem of estimating a population mean with a simple random sample.

First, the mean of $Y_i$ is no longer a constant. Instead, $E(Y_i) = \beta X_i$. The underlying population has a family of means, one for each level of $X$, and we wish to estimate the slope, $\beta$, that links those means to $X$. Before, we looked to estimate an intercept term with zero slope. Now we look to estimate a slope with zero intercept. (Later chapters examine lines with both a slope and an intercept.)

Second, we assume that each time we draw a new sample, we use the same $X$'s, so that each $X_i$ is **fixed across samples.** If $X_1$ is 7 in the first sample we draw, then $X_1$ will equal 7 in every sample we draw. This is *not* to say that $X_1 = X_2$. The individual $X_i$, $X_1, \ldots, X_n$, can differ from one another. If $X_1$ is 7, $X_2$ need not be 7; $X_2$ may be 12 or 1004 or any other number. Indeed, if we are to consider $\beta_{g3}$ as a candidate estimator, we must restrict ourselves to cases in which no two successive $X$'s, say $X_1$ and $X_2$, or $X_{13}$ and $X_{14}$ are the same. If $X_1 = 7$, then $X_2$ may not equal 7. The assumption of fixed $X$'s implies that the $X$ value for an observation is chosen before the observation is made. For example, an econometrician settles on an $X$-value for the third observation, say 6, then in every sample she draws, she draws a third observation on $Y$ from the subpopulation in which $X = 6$.

Why do we assume the $X_i$'s are fixed across samples? Some assumption about the $X_i$ is necessary. We need to know where these data come from, just as we need to know where the $Y_i$'s come from. The assumption that $X_i$'s are fixed across samples is the simplest assumption to make. This assumption frees us from having to worry about the distributions of the $X_i$'s because they are fixed, rather than random, variables.

## Are Fixed *X*'s Realistic?

In many practical instances, $X_i$ fixed across samples is not just the simplest assumption; it is also the most realistic assumption. In controlled experiments, econometricians can decide which values of the $X_i$ they will study. An econometrician making a controlled experiment might say, "For my first observation, I will select a household with an income of $25,000; for my second, $30,000," and so on. This researcher will then choose a first observation at random from among all households with an income of $25,000. Then she will choose a second observation, this one from among all households with an income of $30,000, and so on, until the needed number of observations are drawn. If this same researcher were to conduct this study a second time, she would use the same $X_i$'s. Her first observation in the new sample would again be drawn from among all households with

# An Econometric Top 40—A Golden Oldie

## Engel on Price Elasticity

German statistician Ernst Engel is best known for his law about food expenditure and income. In 1861, however, Engel published the earliest known estimate of a price elasticity of demand.[3] He analyzed the demand for rye, a staple grain in 19th-century Europe, and noted that

(*% change in the quantity of rye demanded*)
$$= \beta(\text{\% change in the price of rye})$$

if $\beta$ were the price elasticity of the demand for rye. The data set engelrye.*** on this book's companion Web site (**www.aw-bc.com/murray**) contains Engel's data on these percentage changes for 1847 to 1861. Hit Figure 2.1 contains a scatterplot of Engel's data; the downward slope of the demand curve is apparent in the scatterplot.

If we set $X$ = (% change in quantity) and $Y$ = (% change in price), Engel's specification becomes that of a straight line through the origin. In his paper, Engel implicitly used $\beta_{g2}$ to estimate the price elasticity of demand, reporting an estimated elasticity of $-0.41$. One implication of Engel's finding is that increases in the price of rye resulted in higher expenditures for rye by consumers, because the increase in price was only partially offset by an accompanying decrease in quantity consumed. Higher rye prices would induce consumers to buy less of both rye and other goods.

Had Engel used $\beta_{g3}$, instead of $\beta_{g2}$, he would have estimated the elasticity to be $+1.0$—a positive number at odds with economic theory, which says demand curves slope downward. On the other hand, Engel could not forgo $\beta_{g2}$ and use $\beta_{g1}$ exactly as we have formulated it, because in 1848 there was no change in price (so $X = 0$ that year), and the

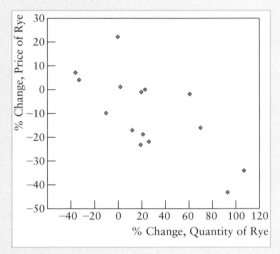

**Hit Figure 2.1**

Percent Changes in the Price and Quantity of Rye (1847–1861)

*Source:* Edouard Ducpetiaux, *Budgets Economiques de Classes de Ouvrieres en Belgique* (Brussels: Hayaz, 1855).

ratio of $Y$ to $X$ was undefined. If we argue that observations at $X = 0$ tell us nothing about the slope of the line, because they don't inform us about where the curve moves from the origin, however, we could adapt $\beta_{g1}$ by ignoring the data for 1848. This procedure yields an elasticity estimate of $-0.31$ from Engel's data.

## Final Notes

Engel and other empirical analysts into the early 20th century had no econometric theory to guide their empirical studies. Authors such as Engel computed estimates according to intuition and plausibility—much as we have done in this chapter. A formal framework for drawing—and assessing—inferences from data collected in the everyday world did not take clear shape until the mid 1940s. That 60-year-old formal framework is the foundation of modern econometric theory, and it forms the basis for this book.

How do we best estimate $\beta$, the slope of the line in the population, from data such as En-

gel's? How do we select among his guess of $-0.41$ and the alternatives of 1.0 and $-0.31$— or should we choose some other estimate altogether? A fundamental task of econometrics is to answer these questions.

■

an income of $25,000, and so on. This is the sense in which we are assuming the $X_i$'s are fixed across samples.

In many other practical instances, it is unrealistic to treat the $X_i$'s as fixed across samples. Consequently, we will eventually want to understand how the assumption of $X$'s being fixed across samples affects which estimator is the best for guessing the slope of a line. The assumption of fixed $X$'s is not the only assumption we will eventually relax. We will know the consequences of relaxing each of the assumptions in the DGP. We will ask what happens when we add an intercept to the DGP and what happens if there are explanatory variables in addition to $X$. We will also ask how the assumptions about homoskedastic and uncorrelated $\varepsilon_i$ affect an estimator. *Much of a first course in econometrics is learning which estimators become the best estimator of a slope as we successively relax the assumptions of this first DGP.*

This new DGP, with its fixed $X$'s, is of inherent interest because it accurately describes the traits of real-world sampling situations. The DGP also serves as a base case from which we can vary our assumptions to analyze alternative sampling situations. If we did not use this DGP, we would still need *some* DGP—we cannot analyze estimation methods without making assumptions about where the sample data come from. In the following sections we'll see that clearly stating the assumptions in the form of a DGP yields benefits. With this particular DGP, we can build Monte Carlo models to mimic and compare the sampling distributions of $\beta_{g1}$, $\beta_{g2}$, and $\beta_{g3}$. In the following sections, we manufacture data for a large number of simple random samples and use those data to assess the performances of $\beta_{g1}$, $\beta_{g2}$, and $\beta_{g3}$, and to determine which, if any, of these three estimators is superior.

## 2.6    Monte Carlo Comparisons

**WHAT ARE AN ESTI-MATOR'S PROPERTIES?**

In Monte Carlo's famous casinos, thousands of tourists try each day to match Joseph Jaggers's ability to grow rich at slot machines and gaming tables. Almost every day, "the house" (the casino) makes money. Let's revisit the European roulette wheels that made Jaggers rich to illustrate how the house makes its money. Eighteen odd numbers on the wheel are colored black, eighteen even numbers red. Zero has no color. For each euro a bettor places on a winning color, red or black, the house pays the bettor one euro in winnings. Because zero causes both red and black to lose, however, the chances of winning on either color are slightly less than 50 percent—18/37, to be exact; on average, betting either red or black will lose money. The Law of Large Numbers, discussed further in the Statistical Appendix, says that with many players, the chance that bettors will, in aggregate, lose money is very close to 100 percent when there are many bettors. All the other games in a casino offer the house a similar small advantage, and we can be sure that while some gamblers may win and some may lose, the bank at Monte Carlo will remain secure.

Statisticians and econometricians rely on the Law of Large Numbers when they use computers to assess the properties of estimators. The analysts' "roulette wheel" is a computer program that generates numbers randomly. Their game is drawing samples of data, over and over again, and using those samples to implement one estimator or another many, many times. If an estimator is unbiased, the Law of Large Numbers ensures that the average error observed across many, many random samples will almost certainly be close to zero. Moreover, the same law ensures that the observed variance of the estimator across those samples will almost certainly be very close to the estimator's true variance. We call a comparison of estimators that uses computers in this way a **Monte Carlo comparison**. As microcomputers have made computing cheap, Monte Carlo comparisons have become an increasingly popular way to explore the properties of statistical methods. In the sections that follow, we conduct a Monte Carlo comparison of $\beta_{g1}$, $\beta_{g2}$, and $\beta_{g3}$ to determine which is best.

## Building a Roulette Wheel

Our motivation for undertaking a Monte Carlo analysis is our desire to know which of our three natural estimators of the slope of a line through the origin, $\beta_{g1}$, $\beta_{g2}$, or $\beta_{g3}$, is superior to the others in terms of bias, variance, or mean square error. Are any of these estimators unbiased? Is one more efficient than the others? Which of the three has the smallest mean square error? These are the questions we want a Monte Carlo analysis to answer.

Unbiasedness, efficiency, and mean squared error are traits of an estimator viewed across all the samples that might possibly arise. When examining these traits of estimators, we cannot rely on calculating them across all samples because the number of possible samples is frequently infinite. Instead, we choose to examine a very large number of samples. The **Law of Large Numbers** assures us that under frequently met conditions, with a very large number of randomly drawn samples, means calculated across observed samples are very likely to be very close to the corresponding means in the population. Because bias, variance, and mean square error are all population means, the Law of Large Numbers applies to them. Just as the casino at Monte Carlo relies on the Law of Large Numbers to guarantee profits from the casino's roulette wheels, we rely on it to ensure that the biases, variances, and mean squared errors obtained from Monte Carlo exercises that draw *many* samples are close to their corresponding values in the population of *all* samples.

This section spells out what we need a roulette wheel to do and how we can go about building a roulette wheel suitable to these needs.

## What Must the Roulette Wheel Do?

Our roulette wheel must give us data with which to compare $\beta_{g1}$, $\beta_{g2}$, and $\beta_{g3}$. In practical applications, econometricians use estimators to make estimates of real economic relationships, using real economic data. Housing expenditure, income, risk premia, and measures of risk are the sorts of data applied econometricians use. When exploring which estimators are best for a given kind of problem, though, econometric theorists often use the manufactured data of Monte Carlo analyses.

Like other economists, econometricians tend to specialize in either theory or application. Econometric theorists design and assess new techniques. Applied econometricians apply existing econometric techniques to real-world data to answer economic questions. Some econometricians move back and forth nimbly between the two roles, but most focus chiefly on one role or the other. Applied econometricians must know enough theory to understand which techniques to use in a given application. Theorists must know applications well enough to know what new techniques would be useful. Students of econometrics need to understand the basics of both theory and application.

Monte Carlo exercises offer two particular advantages over real-world data: First, in a Monte Carlo analysis, the theoretical econometrician knows the traits of the population to be estimated, which the applied econometrician never knows in practice; second, modern computers manufacture Monte Carlo data quickly and cheaply, saving the expense that repeated collection of real-world data would incur. What connects the results of a Monte Carlo analysis to the analysis of real-world data, though? The key is the DGP.

Applied econometricians use a DGP to describe their assumptions about the source of a particular sample. If econometricians gather a simple random sample of breast-fed children's weights or a simple random sample of households' food expenditures and incomes, then the DGPs described in Sections 2.2 and 2.5 would reflect the econometrician's assumptions about the origin of such data. To the extent that a Monte Carlo exercise relies on the same DGP used by the applied econometrician, the lessons from the Monte Carlo analysis advise the applied econometrician about which estimators to use and which to avoid.

# An Econometric Top 40—A Classical Favorite

## Friedman's Permanent Income Hypothesis

John Maynard Keynes's *General Theory*[4] introduced the consumption function, the relationship between consumption spending and income, and gave the function a central place in his macroeconomic theory. Keynes named the rate of change of consumption with respect to income "the marginal propensity to consume." The consumption function is such an important theme in economics that other writers have remade the tune into celebrated analyses of their own. One such analysis is the "Permanent Income Hypothesis" of Nobel laureate Milton Friedman.

In 1957 Friedman[5], of the University of Chicago, objected to the simple Keynesian formulation of the consumption function, in which

$$consumption = \beta_0 + \beta_1 income,$$

where $\beta_1$, the change in consumption with respect to income, is Keynes's marginal propensity to consume. Friedman contended that if income and consumption were properly measured, consumption should be zero when income is zero, or, more strongly, consumption should be strictly proportional to income. Friedman named income properly measured "permanent income" and consumption properly measured "permanent consumption." Thus he specified the consumption function to be

$$permanent\ consumption$$
$$= \beta_1(permanent\ income)$$

with no intercept term.

Friedman linked permanent income very closely to a consumer's wealth. He argued that consumers pay attention to their expected long-term financial circumstances when choosing how much to consume. For example, Friedman would argue that a recent college graduate with no plans for graduate school and earning $35,000 per year is likely to consume less than a young medical student with the same income. The medical student, Friedman would argue, can expect much higher incomes in the future with which to pay for higher spending today. More formally, Friedman described permanent income as "the maximum that one could spend on consumption without lowering one's expected wealth."

Friedman hypothesized that permanent consumption is the average level of consumption for a household with a given permanent income. In formal terms, he said:

$$permanent\ consumption =$$
$$E(consumption \mid permanent\ income).$$

Friedman presumed that households would deviate from their mean consumption levels. To accommodate these deviations, he wrote:

$$consumption = \beta_1(permanent\ income) + v_c,$$

where $v_c$ is a random variable with mean of zero, that is, $E(v_c) = 0$.

Friedman observed that permanent income and income as usually measured would differ from one another in any given year. He hypothesized that, on average, permanent income and income as usually measured would be equal. Thus, he expressed the relationship between income as usually measured and permanent income as

$$income = (permanent\ income) + v_y,$$

where $v_y$ is a random variable with mean zero, $E(v_y) = 0$.

Because permanent income is unobserved, empirical analysis of the marginal propensity to consume must use data on consumption and income as usually measured. Thus, we must estimate $\beta_1$ not from

$$consumption = \beta_1(permanent\ income) + \nu_c,$$

because observations on permanent income aren't available, but instead from

$$consumption = \beta_1(income - \nu_y) + \nu_c$$
$$= \beta_1(income) - \beta_1\nu_y + \nu_c,$$

which is to say, from

$$consumption = \beta_1(income) + u,$$

where $u = -\beta_1\nu_y + \nu_c$.

For reasons that we explore in Chapter 13, Friedman argued that the best way to estimate $\beta_1$ when using consumption and income as usually measured is to use our guessing mechanism $\beta_{g2}$. Friedman compared his estimates of the marginal propensity consumed using $\beta_{g2}$ with those obtained using the estimator that had been commonly employed in studies prior to his.[6] Across 31 household budget studies and 14 time series studies, Friedman's estimates averaged 0.92, whereas previous estimates averaged 0.75; sharply differing conclusions, indeed, about the marginal propensity to consume.

 **Final Notes**

Friedman's great theoretical contribution as described in this Hit was to focus economists' attention on how people incorporated their expectations about the future (in this case about their future incomes) into economic decision making. We will encounter this theme again in other Hits. A striking aspect of Friedman's work is how his economic theory informs us about the econometric relationship at hand. Friedman appeals to theory to explain why the relationship ought to have no intercept term. He also uses economic theory to richly describe the structure of the disturbance term, $u$, in its relationship to random deviations in permanent income and permanent consumption. The "econ" in "econometrics" appears starkly in this great Hit. In 1976, Friedman received the Nobel prize in economics "for his achievements in the fields of consumption analysis, monetary history and theory and for his demonstration of the complexity of stabilization policy."

One econometric question that arises when we contrast Friedman's finding with those of earlier writers is, "Why should we prefer Friedman's estimates to those of previous writers who used the same data but drew different conclusions?" Answering such questions is a central task of econometrics.

Let's look once more at the DGP we'll use to compare the biases, variances, and mean square errors of $\beta_{g1}$, $\beta_{g2}$, and $\beta_{g3}$. Our roulette wheel must produce data with these characteristics:

$$Y_i = \beta X_i + \varepsilon_i \qquad i = 1, \ldots, n$$
$$E(\varepsilon_i) = 0 \qquad i = 1, \ldots, n$$
$$var(\varepsilon_i) = \sigma^2 \qquad i = 1, \ldots, n$$

and $\varepsilon_1, \ldots, \varepsilon_n$ are mutually statistically independent.

Each $X_i$ is fixed across samples.

What must we do to build a roulette wheel with these characteristics? To generate specific numerical data for the $Y_i$, we need (i) the number of observations in each sample, $n$; (ii) the slope of the line, $\beta$; (iii) an explanator value for each observation, that is, the $X_i$; (iv) the common variance shared by the distributions of the disturbances, $\sigma^2$; (v) a specific probability distribution for each disturbance, distributions that all have a zero mean and a variance of $\sigma^2$; and (vi) the $\varepsilon_i$'s themselves, the disturbances for each observation. With $\beta$, the $X_i$, and the $\varepsilon_i$ in hand, we can construct the $Y_i$ from $Y_i = \beta X_i + \varepsilon_i$. Requirements (i) through (iv) and (vi) appear in the DGP. Requirement (v) is necessary so we know to draw the actual observations from a particular probability distribution.

Requirement (v) implies that the specification of our Monte Carlo model is less general than the DGP of interest to us. The DGP does not specify a particular distribution for the disturbances, but requirement (v) does. Monte Carlo models are inherently less general than the usual DGP. To create the Monte Carlo's data, we must specify exactly where the data are to come from. For example, our Monte Carlo results are not for *any* slope $\beta$, but for a *specific* slope $\beta$. Similarly, our Monte Carlo results are not for *any* X-values, but for *the specific* X-values we select. Few DGPs are specified in such complete detail—one attractive trait of DGPs is a generality that makes them broadly applicable. Econometricians cope with the specificity of Monte Carlo models by examining a broad range of Monte Carlo models to check that the results do not vary essentially from one particular embodiment of the DGP's assumptions to another.

When do we make specific choices about our Monte Carlo model? Some choices we make once, at the beginning of the Monte Carlo exercise. These choices include values for $n$, $\beta$, $X_i$, and $\sigma^2$. The values of these items remain the same for all samples we examine. The number of observations, $n$, is the same from one sample to the next. The slope we estimate, $\beta$, and the variance of the disturbances, $\sigma^2$, are traits of the population under study, so they do not change from sample to sample. Also, by assumption, the $X_i$'s do not change from sample to sample. As noted earlier, to pick an $\varepsilon_i$ we need more information than is given by the DGP; we need a specific probability distribution from which to draw it. We need not pick the same distribution for every observation's disturbance, but we can do so. For example, we might assume the disturbances follow the normal distribution with mean zero and variance $\sigma^2$. We choose the distributions for the disturbances only once, also at the beginning of the Monte Carlo exercise. In contrast to our other choices, we pick the $\varepsilon_i$'s themselves repeatedly, freshly with each new manufactured sample. The $\varepsilon_i$'s are random variables whose values differ across samples; they account for the randomness in the $Y_i$'s.

Notice that in our Monte Carlo exercise, we know both $\beta$ and the $\varepsilon_i$, which applied econometricians would not know in practice. We also know the values of $n$, $X_i$, and $Y_i$ in any one particular sample, just as the applied econometrician would. We know everything because we are the builders of the roulette wheel. *The Monte Carlo analysis exploits its complete knowledge about many samples to assess the performance of estimators.* It is this special knowledge, coupled with the power of the Law of Large Numbers, that makes Monte Carlo analyses so informative.

## Building a Roulette Wheel of Your Own: MC Builder I

The book's companion Web site (**www.aw-bc.com/murray**) provides a Monte Carlo builder named "MC Builder I," with which you can conduct your own Monte Carlo analyses of the biases, variances, and mean square errors of $\beta_{g1}$, $\beta_{g2}$, and $\beta_{g3}$. (MC Builder I also analyzes a "mystery guest" called $\beta_{g4}$, which we encounter in Chapter 3.) The site leads you through the choices you have to make to build your own roulette wheel with MC Builder I. You choose (i) the number of observations in each sample, $n$; (ii) the slope of the line in question, $\beta$; (iii) an explanator value for each observation, that is, the $X_i$; (iv) the common variance shared by the distributions of the disturbances, $\sigma^2$; and (v) a specific probability distribution for each disturbance—distributions that all have a zero mean and a variance of $\sigma^2$.

There are several Monte Carlo Builders on this book's companion Web site (**www.aw-bc.com/murray**), each designed for its own special purpose. This book reports many of the lessons we can learn from the Monte Carlo Builders, but the lessons are far more vivid when experienced online, rather than read. Play with the programs and they will reward you many times over.

The most subtle aspect of a roulette wheel is its spinning mechanism. The wheels must be carefully designed to give each slot on the wheel an exactly equal chance of catching the ball when the wheel stops spinning. In econometric roulette wheels, the part of the spinning mechanism is played by a **random number generator**, a computer program that creates series of numbers drawn from a probability distribution with prespecified characteristics. In our Monte Carlo analyses, we need a random number generator to create the disturbances, the $\varepsilon_i$, for each sample. MC Builder I offers the choice of five random number generators from which you can select the values of the $\varepsilon_i$. Using random number generators to produce $\varepsilon_i$ mimics the probabilistic features of the world that lead us to sometimes observe one sample of data and sometimes another. The next section further discusses the connection between randomly generated $\varepsilon_i$ and the real world.

Almost all commercial statistical computer programs, and many other data-handling programs, contain several random number generators, including generators that produce draws from the familiar bell-shaped normal distribution and generators that produce draws from a uniform distribution in which all numbers between some lower and upper bound have an equal chance of being drawn. MC

Builder I offers five random number generators with which to select values of the $\varepsilon_i$: a normal distribution, a uniform distribution, a bimodal distribution, an asymmetric distribution, and a discrete distribution. Each of the random number generators offers flexibility in deciding what variances the observation's distributions will have.

MC Builder I leaves you free to pick the $X_i$'s however you wish, as long as your $X_i$'s never lead an estimator to divide by zero. You can, for example, write down $n$ numbers chosen arbitrarily, as they come to mind. Or you can pick a specific sequence of $n$ numbers.

To ensure that $\beta_{g1}$, $\beta_{g2}$, and $\beta_{g3}$, are always well defined in your Monte Carlo analyses, MC Builder I requires that (i) no $X_i$ is zero (so $\beta_{g1}$ is always defined); (ii) the $X_i$ are all of the same sign (so their sum is never zero, and hence $\beta_{g2}$ is always well defined); and (iii) successive $X$'s are never equal to one another (so the change in $X$ is never zero, and hence $\beta_{g3}$ is always well defined). If you choose $X$-values that violate these rules, the builder asks you to change your $X$-values.

In accord with the DGP's assumption that the $X_i$'s are fixed across samples, MC Builder I uses the same $X_i$-values in every sample. Notice that fixing the $X$'s across samples means the $X_i$'s are not random variables in these Monte Carlo analyses. The only sources of random variation are the disturbances terms, the $\varepsilon_i$.

## Spinning the Roulette Wheel

Once you have picked $\beta$, $\sigma^2$, $n$, the $X_i$, and the probability distribution for your disturbances, the MC Builder I uses the specified random number generator to create a first sample of $\varepsilon_i$'s and computes the corresponding $Y_i$'s by adding the $\varepsilon_i$'s to the $\beta X_i$'s. MC Builder I then uses this first sample of $X_i$'s and $Y_i$'s to estimate $\beta$ using $\beta_{g1}$, $\beta_{g2}$, and $\beta_{g3}$. With the estimates of $\beta$ from $\beta_{g1}$, $\beta_{g2}$, and $\beta_{g3}$, MC Builder I next computes the errors made by each estimator in this first sample. The Monte Carlo builder is able to calculate these errors because we, unlike the practicing econometrician, know the value of $\beta$ in our Monte Carlo world. Together, these steps constitute building the roulette wheel and spinning it once. MC Builder I spins the wheel 10,000 times. With each repetition, MC Builder I (i) creates a new set of $\varepsilon_i$'s and $Y_i$'s based on the specified $\beta$, $n$, $\sigma^2$, $X_i$'s, and probability distribution for the disturbances; (ii) estimates $\beta$ with each estimator using the new sample data; and (iii) computes the estimation errors made by the three estimators in the new sample. Finally, MC Builder I uses the estimates and estimation errors from its 10,000 samples to compute biases, variances, and mean square errors across the 10,000 samples.

The power of the Monte Carlo approach comes from the Law of Large Numbers and from knowing the true value of $\beta$. The Law of Large Numbers assures us that the mean and variance of each estimator's errors across many, many samples (across many, many spins of the wheel) are, with high probability, close to the true mean and variance of that estimator's errors. MC Builder I spins its wheel 10,000 times, giving us 10,000 samples. Choosing too small a number of spins loses the power of the Law of Large Numbers; choosing too large a number of spins results in the analysis taking a very long time on the computer.

## 2.7 Picking $\varepsilon_i$'s and the Real World

WHAT IS THE DGP?

Before you went to bed last night, did you think about how many hours of sleep you would get? Quite possibly you did. Did you think, "The average college student gets 6 hours of sleep. I'm going to get 1 hour more of sleep than average, so I will get 7 hours of sleep."? Probably you didn't. Our Monte Carlo approach operates in this seemingly odd fashion.

Our Monte Carlo technique would arrive at your hours of sleep by first picking a disturbance from some distribution—in your case it would pick $+1$. The Monte Carlo approach would add that hour to the mean sleeping time of 6 hours to arrive at 7 hours of sleep. This mechanical depiction of choosing a disturbance to tag onto a mean is a misrepresentation of how hours of sleep are actually determined. It is a useful misrepresentation, though, because it allows us to create artificial data that conform to a reasonable real-world DGP in which students are sampled in a simple random fashion.

Randomly sampled students deviate from average student behavior. In our artificial Monte Carlo environment, we specify the average behavior of interest and then use a random number generator to make observations deviate from that average behavior. The artificial deviations in our Monte Carlo environment mimic the real-world deviations that would be observed in randomly sampled students.

In the sleep example, arriving at $Y_i$ by a process of addition seems farfetched. But in some real-world settings, arriving at the $Y_i$ by some process of addition is not so farfetched. Households with incomes of \$1,500 per month are aware of their income when they decide how much food to buy. Households with incomes of \$10,000 per month are similarly aware when they buy their food. This awareness of income gives rise to differences in the levels of food expenditure households choose. Characterizing the choice as a precise two-step process, a process in which first an average food expenditure given a household's income is determined and then a disturbance is drawn and added in, strains credibility. It does not strain credibility to think that households have a "target" food expenditure in their minds, however—a target that varies with income—and that they fall short of or exceed their periodic spending target by some accidental amount. The two-step procedure, therefore, contains a grain of real-world truth, while simultaneously allowing us to create artificial data easily.

# 2.8

WHAT ARE AN ESTI-
MATOR'S PROPERTIES?

# Comparing $\beta_{g1}$, $\beta_{g2}$, and $\beta_{g3}$

Our motivation for undertaking a Monte Carlo analysis is our desire to know which of our three natural estimators of the slope of a line through the origin, $\beta_{g1}$, $\beta_{g2}$, or $\beta_{g3}$, is superior to the others in terms of bias, variance, or mean square error. MC Builder I allows you to conduct your own Monte Carlo analysis of these questions. This section reports the results of several Monte Carlo analyses of $\beta_{g1}$, $\beta_{g2}$, and $\beta_{g3}$ that you can conduct using MC Builder I. (Here, the number of spins of the wheel is sometimes smaller than in MC Builder I.)

## A Monte Carlo Exercise

Table 2.1 presents $\beta$, $\sigma^2$, $n$, and the $X_i$'s for one specific roulette wheel with which we can compare $\beta_{g1}$, $\beta_{g2}$, and $\beta_{g3}$. The assumed value of $\beta$ is 271; the assumed value of $\sigma^2$ is 53,970; $n$ is set at 6. The $X$-values range from a low of 0.06 to a high of 3.56. Finally, the assumed distribution for the disturbances is the normal distribution. Table 2.1 also contains the $\varepsilon_i$'s drawn on the first "spin" of this roulette wheel and the implied $Y_i$'s. Each new sample drawn in the Monte Carlo experiment will result in new values for the $\varepsilon_i$'s and hence new values for the $Y_i's$, but $\beta$, $\sigma^2$, $n$, and the $X_i$'s will remain fixed throughout the experiment.

Table 2.2 presents the estimates of $\beta$ from the first five samples, using each of the three estimators. Under each estimate is the error made in that particular sample by that particular estimator. Notice that $\beta_{g1}$ is closest to the true $\beta$ in samples 1 and 4; $\beta_{g2}$ is closest to the true $\beta$ in samples 2, 3, and 5; $\beta_{g3}$ is closest to the true $\beta$ in none of these samples. Unfortunately, in a real-world application, we would not know the true $\beta$, so we could not simply hop among $\beta_{g1}$, $\beta_{g2}$, $\beta_{g3}$, picking the

**TABLE 2.1  Assumed Traits of the Data-Generating Process and One Sample of $Y_i$'s**

$Y = 271X_i + \varepsilon_i \ (i = 1, \ldots, 6)$, $\beta = 271, n = 6$

$\varepsilon_1, \ldots, \varepsilon_n$ distributed independently and $N(0, 53970)$

| $X_1$ | $X_2$ | $X_3$ | $X_4$ | $X_5$ | $X_6$ |
|---|---|---|---|---|---|
| 3.56 | 2.77 | 1.30 | 0.60 | 0.06 | 0.42 |
| $\varepsilon_1$ | $\varepsilon_2$ | $\varepsilon_3$ | $\varepsilon_4$ | $\varepsilon_5$ | $\varepsilon_6$ |
| 62.4 | 425.38 | −236.68 | 215.26 | 67.21 | −153.88 |
| $Y_1$ | $Y_2$ | $Y_3$ | $Y_4$ | $Y_5$ | $Y_6$ |
| 1027.16 | 1176.05 | 115.62 | 377.86 | 83.47 | −40.06 |

**TABLE 2.2** The Estimators and Their Errors in Five Samples

| Sample | | $\beta_{g1}$ | $\beta_{g2}$ | $\beta_{g3}$ |
|---|---|---|---|---|
| 1 | Coef./(error) | 259.7/(−11.3) | 289.4/(18.4) | 1288.6/(1017.6) |
| 2 | Coef./(error) | 334.5/(63.5) | 267.7/ (−3.3) | −4058.1/(−4329.1) |
| 3 | Coef./(error) | 138.8/(−132.2) | 226.6/(−44.4) | −921.1/(1192.1) |
| 4 | Coef./(error) | 266.2/(−4.8) | 296.0/(25.0) | −1505.6/(1776.6) |
| 5 | Coef./(error) | 197.2/(−73.8) | 250.2/(−20.8) | 3172.5/(2901.5) |

best estimate in any particular sample. Indeed, if we did know $\beta$, we would have no need for any estimate. To decide which estimator is best to use in practice, we rely instead on the average characteristics of the estimators. Are the estimators' mean errors zero—that is, are the estimators unbiased? If two or three estimators are unbiased, is one unbiased estimator more efficient than the others? If an estimator is biased, does it have a smaller mean square error than other estimators?

In addition to examining the bias, variance, and mean square error of each of our three estimators, we also examine their *mean absolute errors*. The **mean absolute error** is the mean of the absolute values of the errors made by an estimator. The rationale offered earlier for comparing estimators' mean square errors was that larger errors might be disproportionately costly; squaring errors increases large errors relative to small errors. What if the cost of estimation errors is proportional to the size of the errors? In that case, the magnitudes of errors matter, not their squares. We look at mean absolute errors as well as mean square errors to determine whether our decision to square the mistakes we make much influences which estimator we deem best.

Table 2.3 presents the mean error, the mean square error, and the mean absolute error for each of the three estimators across the first 5 samples drawn and across the first 1,000 samples drawn. Five samples are too few to appeal to the Law of Large Numbers. The errors we observe in five samples might well be idiosyncratic and misleading about the population of all samples. One thousand samples, however, is large enough to expect the Law of Large Numbers to apply, at least in simple problems. What we see in these 1,000 samples is likely to reflect what we would learn from observing all possible samples. Using more samples, for example 10,000 samples, would provide even more reliable results.

The estimator with the smallest observed mean error (−1.2), observed mean square error (1460.9), observed variance (1459.5), and observed mean absolute error (30.5) across the 1000 samples is $\beta_{g2}$. The second-best performer is $\beta_{g1}$, for which the corresponding numbers are 3.8, 30825.2, 30810.8, and 140.9. By far,

**TABLE 2.3** The Performance of $\beta_{g1}$, $\beta_{g2}$, and $\beta_{g3}$ Across Numerous Samples

*Across the First 5 Samples*

|  | $\beta_{g1}$ | $\beta_{g2}$ | $\beta_{g3}$ |
|---|---|---|---|
| Mean error | −31.7 | −5.0 | −675.7 |
| Mean square error | 5422.0 | 675.7 | 6600000.0 |
| Mean absolute error | 57.1 | 22.4 | 2243.4 |

*Across 1,000 Samples*

|  | $\beta_{g1}$ | $\beta_{g2}$ | $\beta_{g3}$ |
|---|---|---|---|
| Mean error | 3.8 | −1.2 | 100.5 |
| (Standard deviation) | (5.5) | (1.2) | (97.9) |
| Mean square error | 30825.2 | 1460.9 | 9600000.0 |
| Variance | 30810.8 | 1459.5 | 9589899.8 |
| Mean absolute error | 140.9 | 30.5 | 2477.2 |

the worst performer is $\beta_{g3}$, for which the corresponding values are 100.5, 9600000, 9589899.8, and 2477.2. It is not necessary that one estimator prove best on all four of these criteria. One estimator might have a smaller bias and another have a smaller variance, for example. However, there is a close relationship among the bias, variance, and mean square error derived in the Statistical Appendix. It is always the case that

$$(bias)^2 + variance = mean\ square\ error.$$

Thus, the fact that $\beta_{g2}$ has both a smaller observed bias and smaller observed variance than the other two estimators ensures that $\beta_{g2}$ also has the smallest mean square error.

The mean error, mean square error, and mean absolute error of $\beta_{g2}$ reported in Table 2.3 are all notably smaller than those for $\beta_{g1}$ and $\beta_{g3}$, which strongly supports a claim that $\beta_{g2}$ is superior to $\beta_{g1}$ and $\beta_{g3}$ for estimating $\beta$ in our Monte Carlo world. Returning to our sample of New York renters, it is now plausible to argue that if we accept this present DGP as applying to our rent and income data, guessing the exponent in the Cobb–Douglas utility function is 0.22 (the value of $\beta_{g2}$ in that sample) is more reasonable than guessing 0.29 or 0.28 (the values of $\beta_{g1}$ and $\beta_{g3}$ in that sample).

## What a Monte Carlo Analysis Can Say About Unbiasedness

What about unbiasedness? Are any of our estimators unbiased? Table 2.3 reveals that none of the three estimators is exactly right on average across the 1,000 samples. The mean errors of 3.8, −1.2, and 100.5 for $\beta_{g1}$, $\beta_{g2}$, and $\beta_{g3}$, respectively, imply that the average estimates from $\beta_{g1}$, $\beta_{g2}$, and $\beta_{g3}$ are 274.8, 269.8, and 371.5, respectively, none of which is equal to the true $\beta$, which is 271. Does this imply that all three estimators are biased? Not necessarily. The Law of Large Numbers ensures that the mean across many samples is likely to be close to the corresponding population mean. The law does not assert that the mean across many samples is exactly equal to the population mean. The observed mean errors might differ from zero by chance, rather than because the estimators are, in fact, biased.

If the observed mean errors are large enough, we might be willing to reject the claim that the estimators are unbiased. But how large is large enough for us to conclude that the estimators are biased? How large an observed error would lead us to reject the claim that the observed mean error differs from zero only by chance?

Statisticians suggest that if so large an observed error as we see would occur very infrequently (say, less than once in 20 draws of 1,000 samples), we should reject the claim that the error differs from zero only by chance. Can we assess the probability of observing mean errors as large as we do if the mean error of the errors in the population were, in fact, zero, that is, if the estimators were unbiased? Yes, we can. Let's see how.

Because our samples are independently drawn, any one estimator's errors are statistically independent across samples. If the number of samples is large, this independence implies that the mean error across samples is approximately normally distributed with a variance equal to the variance of the errors divided by the number of samples. The Monte Carlo exercise provides us with an estimate of the variance of each estimator's errors—the observed errors' variance in the sample. For example, the variance of $\beta_{g1}$'s errors across samples is 30810.8. Thus, if $\beta_{g1}$ is an unbiased estimator, its mean error across 1,000 samples is distributed approximately normally, with a mean of zero (reflecting the assumed unbiasedness of $\beta_{g1}$) and a variance of 30810.8/1000 (if our Monte Carlo estimate of the variance of the errors is correct).

If the mean error of $\beta_{g1}$ across 1,000 samples is distributed $N(0, 30.8108)$, then mean errors larger in magnitude than

$$1.96\sqrt{30.8108} = 1.96 \cdot 5.5 = 10.78$$

would arise less than 5% of the time. (A normally distributed random variable with a mean of zero and a variance of one takes on values greater than 1.96 or less than $-1.96$ 5% of the time. We obtain the corresponding magnitude for a normally distributed random variable with a mean of zero and a variance of $\sigma_{RV}^2$ by multiplying 1.96 by $\sigma_{RV}$.) The observed mean error for $\beta_{g1}$ is 3.8, which is much less than 10.78. Using the statisticians' criterion, we would not reject the claim that $\beta_{g1}$ is unbiased. Nor do similar calculations for $\beta_{g2}$ and $\beta_{g3}$ reject the claims that those estimators are unbiased: $|-1.2| < 1.96\,(1.2)$ and $|100.5| < 1.96\,(97.9)$.

Unfortunately, failing to reject the unbiasedness of our three estimators is not the same as proving they are unbiased. Although the observed mean errors might have arisen unsurprisingly by chance if the estimators are unbiased, the observed mean errors might also have arisen because the estimators are, in fact, biased.

Nor does our inability to reject the claim of unbiasedness indicate that any bias that does exist is inconsequential. For example, the population bias that would most likely give rise to the observed mean error for $\beta_{g2}$ $(-1.2)$ is a bias equal to $-1.2$. Suppose that $X$ were the number of days a division of marines spent in combat under very cold conditions, and $Y$ were the number of frostbitten soldiers, measured in thousands. A bias of $-1,200$ frostbitten soldiers per day is substantial if your job is to provide medical supplies for treating frostbite.

On the other hand, the observed mean errors could be small in practical terms. If $X$ were the number of years a student spent in school and $Y$ were the lifetime earnings of the student in dollars, a bias of \$1,200 in lifetime earnings per year of school might seem inconsequentially small.

In sum, our Monte Carlo experiment leaves us with substantive uncertainty both about whether our estimators are unbiased and, if they are biased, about how practically important those biases are. Nonetheless, despite the uncertainty about unbiasedness, the Monte Carlo model makes clear the superiority of $\beta_{g2}$ over $\beta_{g1}$ and $\beta_{g3}$ in the Monte Carlo model. The next section offers further Monte Carlo evidence about the superiority of $\beta_{g2}$ over $\beta_{g1}$ and $\beta_{g3}$.

## 2.9    Alternative Comparisons of $\beta_{g1}$, $\beta_{g2}$, and $\beta_{g3}$

**WHAT ARE AN ESTI-MATOR'S PROPERTIES?**

For the particular roulette wheel described in Table 2.1, there is almost no doubt that $\beta_{g2}$, with the smallest mean errors, the smallest mean square errors, and the smallest mean absolute errors, is the best of our three intuitively appealing estimators—even if we must remain unsure about whether any of the estimators is indeed unbiased. But what if we had built our roulette wheel differently? Would $\beta_{g2}$ still dominate $\beta_{g1}$? Might $\beta_{g3}$ prove best in some other case? Seeing that $\beta_{g2}$ performs best in one Monte Carlo exercise leaves much room for wondering whether it would perform best under other circumstances. Rather than wonder, statisticians and econometricians who use Monte Carlo methods usually examine several Monte Carlo models to check the *robustness* of their conclusions across different specifications.

## Additional Monte Carlo Exercises

MC Builder I allows you to build numerous Monte Carlo models that satisfy the assumptions of our basic DGP. You can build several different models and learn for yourself whether $\beta_{g2}$ dominates $\beta_{g1}$ and $\beta_{g3}$ in varied circumstances. To explore this **robustness** of $\beta_{g2}$—its capacity to preserve its properties from one roulette wheel to another—we here examine six alternative roulette wheels, all of which conform to the DGP described in Section 2.6, but that use $\beta$, $n$, $\sigma^2$ and $X_i$'s different from those reported in Table 2.1 and different from one another. The question we address is whether $\beta_{g2}$ continues to outperform $\beta_{g1}$ and $\beta_{g3}$. Our study of unbiasedness in the first Monte Carlo exercise revealed that the Monte Carlo exercises are apt to give inconclusive information about the unbiasedness of these three estimators. For this reason, these next Monte Carlo analyses emphasize mean square errors and mean absolute errors rather than unbiasedness.

Table 2.4 summarizes the six alternative roulette wheels we use here; the table reports the sample size $(n)$ and slope $(\beta)$ chosen, the means and variances of the $X$'s picked, and the values selected for the variances of the disturbances $(\sigma^2)$. Tables 2.5 and 2.6 report the mean errors, mean square errors, and mean absolute errors, from 10,000 applications of each alternative roulette wheel.

Table 2.4 shows that the alternative models include a variety of different specifications for study. There are no very large samples (the largest is 36 observations), but there are several very small samples, with 3 observations the smallest.

**TABLE 2.4** Summary Statistics for Six Alternative Monte Carlo Models

| Model | $n$ | $\beta$ | Mean($X$) | Variance($X$) | $\sigma^2$ |
|-------|-----|---------|-----------|---------------|------------|
| 1 | 3 | 0.10 | 2.8 | 1.1 | 25 |
| 2 | 5 | 4 | 5.8 | 19.8 | 160000 |
| 3 | 36 | 2 | −18.5 | 107.9 | 1300000000 |
| 4 | 8 | −12 | 54.0 | 756.0 | 13000000 |
| 5 | 5 | −100 | −87.2 | 5047.6 | 3200000 |
| 6 | 15 | 237 | 66668.8 | 62000000000 | 12000000 |

The slopes range from $-100$ to $237$, the mean $X$'s vary from a $-87.2$ to $66668.8$ (a sample that contains one observation with $X$ equal to a million), and the variance of the $X$'s varies from $1.1$ to $6.2 \times 10^9$. The variance of the disturbances also varies widely, from $25$ to $1.3 \times 10^9$.

Table 2.5 reports the observed mean errors of $\beta_{g1}$, $\beta_{g2}$, and $\beta_{g3}$ for each of the six alternative models. In some of these alternative models, $\beta_{g3}$ has the smallest observed mean error. In Table 2.5, the magnitudes of mean error seem unrelated to the true slopes' sizes, so if there is a bias in an estimator, it is *relatively* larger when the true slope is small.

Table 2.6 reveals that, based on the magnitude of errors made, $\beta_{g2}$ is the best of our three estimators. It has the smallest mean square error and the smallest mean absolute error in each of the six alternative specifications. We also see that $\beta_{g1}$ usually outperforms $\beta_{g3}$, but in two specifications, Models 2 and 6, $\beta_{g3}$ outperforms $\beta_{g1}$. In Chapter 3, we explore why $\beta_{g2}$ performs better than the other estimators and ask if we might find a yet better estimator for the slope of a line through the origin.

The finding that $\beta_{g1}$ usually outperforms $\beta_{g3}$, but that $\beta_{g3}$ sometimes outperforms $\beta_{g1}$, raises a red flag about Monte Carlo investigations. What if we had not examined Model 2 or Model 6? Would we have concluded that $\beta_{g1}$ is generally a better estimator than $\beta_{g3}$? Should we therefore be cautious in claiming that $\beta_{g2}$ is the best of these three estimators? Indeed, we should.

The Law of Large Numbers, from which the Monte Carlo technique derives its power, assures us only that, *for the specifications under study*, the observed

**TABLE 2.5 How $\beta_{g1}$, $\beta_{g2}$, and $\beta_{g3}$ Perform on Average Across Alternative Values for $\beta$, $\sigma^2\ n$, and the $X_i$'s**

*Across 10,000 Samples*

| Model Number | True Slope | | Mean Error | |
|:---:|:---:|:---:|:---:|:---:|
| | $\beta$ | $\beta_{g1}$ | $\beta_{g2}$ | $\beta_{g3}$ |
| 1 | 0.10 | 0.04 | 0.02 | $-0.02$ |
| 2 | 4 | 2.94 | 1.2 | 0.05 |
| 3 | 2 | 66.0 | 33.4 | 21.4 |
| 4 | $-12$ | 2.0 | 1.4 | 0.03 |
| 5 | $-100$ | $-1.3$ | $-0.4$ | 0.23 |
| 6 | 237 | 3.8 | $-0.08$ | $-1.0$ |

**TABLE 2.6** Mean Square and Mean Absolute Errors for $\beta_{g1}$, $\beta_{g2}$, and $\beta_{g3}$ Using Alternative Values of $\beta$, $\sigma^2$ $n$, and the $X_i$'s

*Across 10,000 Samples*

| Model Number | Mean Square Error | | |
| | $\beta_{g1}$ | $\beta_{g2}$ | $\beta_{g3}$ |
|---|---|---|---|
| 1 | 1.5 | 0.6 | 7.6 |
| 2 | 7496 | 930 | 4078 |
| 3 | 1600000 | 107876 | 2400000 |
| 4 | 2116 | 552 | 3731 |
| 5 | 859 | 90 | 2145 |
| 6 | 62644 | 204 | 2105 |

| Model Number | True Slope | | Mean Absolute Error | |
| | $\beta$ | $\beta_{g1}$ | $\beta_{g2}$ | $\beta_{g3}$ |
|---|---|---|---|---|
| 1 | 0.1 | 0.97 | 0.63 | 2.19 |
| 2 | 4.0 | 69.2 | 24.5 | 50.9 |
| 3 | 2.0 | 1021.7 | 262.9 | 1213.5 |
| 4 | −12.0 | 36.6 | 18.8 | 49.0 |
| 5 | −100.0 | 23.4 | 7.4 | 36.6 |
| 6 | 237.0 | 200.3 | 1.5 | 36.6 |

mean biases, the observed mean square errors, and the observed mean absolute errors are unlikely to be far from the true biases, mean square errors, and mean absolute errors. We have no ready assurance that what we observe for one set of specifications will hold true for another. *Consequently, to trust in Monte Carlo techniques, we must examine specifications very much like those we will use in practice.* This fragility of Monte Carlo results, as well as our continuing doubts about the unbiasedness of our estimators, presses us to look for more certain techniques for assessing the properties of estimators. In Chapter 3, we develop such procedures.

## 2.10    Graphical Lessons from the Monte Carlo Exercises

This section graphically analyzes the Monte Carlo performance of our three estimators for several different sample sizes and with disturbances that follow several different distributions. When we estimate a sample mean, rather than the slope of a line through the origin, the Law of Large Numbers assures us that in large samples, the sample mean from a simple random sample will almost surely not lie far from the population mean—the distribution of estimates will collapse around the true mean as the sample size grows. Analytically, this convergence of the sample mean to the population mean stems from the unbiasedness of the sample mean as an estimator of the population mean and the variance of the sample mean being $(\sigma^2/n)$. Notice that as $n$ grows, the variance of the sample mean, $(\sigma^2/n)$, tends toward zero. Hence, as $n$ grows, the distribution of the sample mean collapses around its mean, as the Law of Large Numbers requires. Do our three estimators of the slope of a line through the origin have this same property? Do we get more precise guesses as our sample size grows?

Graphs from our Monte Carlo exercises show that the sampling distributions of our three estimators of the slope of a line through the origin each tend to collapse around a single value as the sample size grows; that is, in large samples, almost all samples yield similar estimates of the slope of a line. Because we have not yet decided whether our estimators are unbiased, however, we cannot conclude from these graphs that the estimators' distributions are collapsing around the slope of the line that we are seeking to estimate; they may each collapse around different numbers.

The Central Limit Theorem assures us that when estimating the mean of a population, in large samples the distribution of estimates will tend toward the normal distribution as the sample size grows. Does the Central Limit Theorem also apply to our three estimators of the slope of a line through the origin? Do we find a similar tendency toward normality when estimating the slope of a line with large samples? We do. Graphs from our Monte Carlo exercises show that the sampling distributions of all three estimators begin looking much like the normal distribution when the number of observations in each sample grows large.

MC Builder II on this book's companion Web site (**www.aw-bc.com/murray**) allows you to study these questions for yourself. Because MC Builder I restricts sample sizes to 100 or less, it is not well suited to studying how our estimators behave when sample sizes grow large. MC Builder II allows you to specify samples with up to 1,000 observations. To make working with so many observations manageable, MC Builder II gives you less free rein over the $X$-values you use than does MC Builder I. In MC Builder II, though, by choosing smaller and larger sample sizes with otherwise similar specifications, you can see how our three estimators behave as the sample size grows large.

## What DGPs Do We Study?

We graphically examine Monte Carlo comparisons of $\beta_{g1}$, $\beta_{g2}$, and $\beta_{g3}$ for two sets of closely related DGPs. In each DGP, the true value of $\beta$ is 4, the standard deviation of the disturbances is 500, and the explanatory variable, X, takes on only two values, 10 and 20. What will vary from model to model are the distributions of the disturbances and the number of observations in each sample.

For the first set of DGPs, we draw the disturbances with a normal random number generator. For the second set of DGPs, we draw the disturbances from a highly skewed distribution in which one third of all values are $-750$ and the remaining two thirds are all 375. (Notice that the expected value of this distribution is zero: $\frac{1}{3}(-750) + \frac{2}{3}(375) = 0$.) Within each of these two sets of DGPs, we design four distinct DGPs, one with 2 observations, one with 20 observations, one with 50 observations, and one with 500 observations. In each of these DGPs, half the X-values are 10, and half are 20.

## What Do We Find?

Panel (a) of Figure 2.6 displays the distributions of $\beta_{g1}$, $\beta_{g2}$, and $\beta_{g3}$ for 10,000 replications from the DGP with normally distributed disturbances and $n = 2$. Panels (b), (c), and (d) of Figure 2.6 do the same for $n = 20$, 50, and 500, respectively. The most striking feature of Figure 2.6 is that $\beta_{g1}$ through $\beta_{g3}$ all share the bell-shaped distribution that we associate with the normal distribution. Even when $n = 2$, the bell-shaped pattern is evident. This pervasive presence of normally distributed estimators stems from using normally distributed disturbances. A second striking feature of Figure 2.6 is that larger sample sizes lead to more precise estimators. As we move from Panel (a) to Panel (d) of Figure 2.6, the distributions of $\beta_{g1}$ through $\beta_{g3}$ all become less spread out. Finally, Figure 2.6 confirms our earlier findings that $\beta_{g2}$ provides guesses that are less spread out than guesses from $\beta_{g1}$ or $\beta_{g3}$.

Figure 2.7 reports the same information as Figure 2.6, but for the DGPs with the highly skewed disturbances. For the DGP with $n = 2$ and skewed disturbances, there are only four possible combinations of Y and X (both disturbances can equal $-750$; both can equal 375; the first can be 375 and the second $-750$, or the first can be $-750$ and the second 375). Consequently, it is not surprising that the distributions of $\beta_{g1}$ through $\beta_{g3}$ are highly non-normal for this DGP, with $n = 2$. What is surprising, though, is that this same highly skewed and discontinuous distribution of disturbances still yields quite normally distributed guesses for $\beta_{g1}$ through $\beta_{g3}$, even when the sample size is only 20. This approximate normality of $\beta_{g1}$ through $\beta_{g3}$ despite non-normal disturbances arises from the same Central Limit Theorem, which

**Figure 2.6**

The Distributions of $\beta_{g1}$, $\beta_{g2}$ and $\beta_{g3}$ for Several Sample Sizes with Normal Disturbances

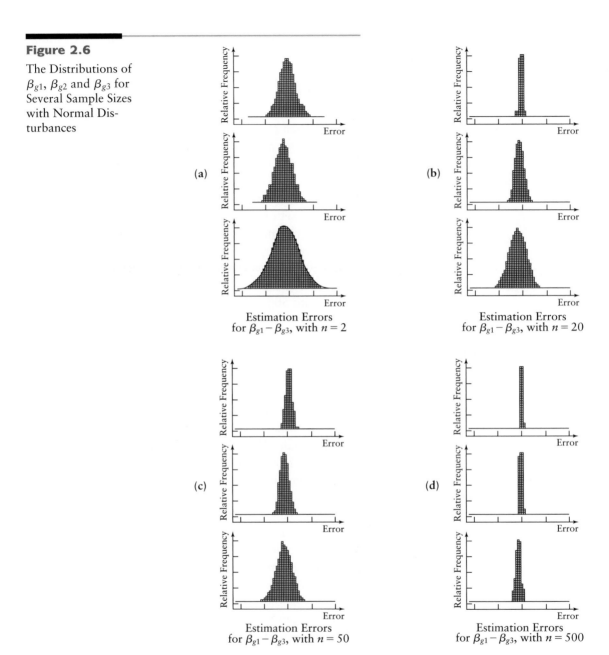

(a) Estimation Errors for $\beta_{g1} - \beta_{g3}$, with $n = 2$

(b) Estimation Errors for $\beta_{g1} - \beta_{g3}$, with $n = 20$

(c) Estimation Errors for $\beta_{g1} - \beta_{g3}$, with $n = 50$

(d) Estimation Errors for $\beta_{g1} - \beta_{g3}$, with $n = 500$

applies to the sample mean from a simple random sample. As with Figure 2.6, Figure 2.7 reveals clearly that larger samples lead to more precise guesses. Also, we find again that $\beta_{g2}$ provides less spread-out guesses than $\beta_{g1}$ or $\beta_{g3}$.

**Figure 2.7**

The Distributions of $\beta_{g1}$, $\beta_{g2}$ and $\beta_{g3}$ for Several Sample Sizes with Skewed Disturbances

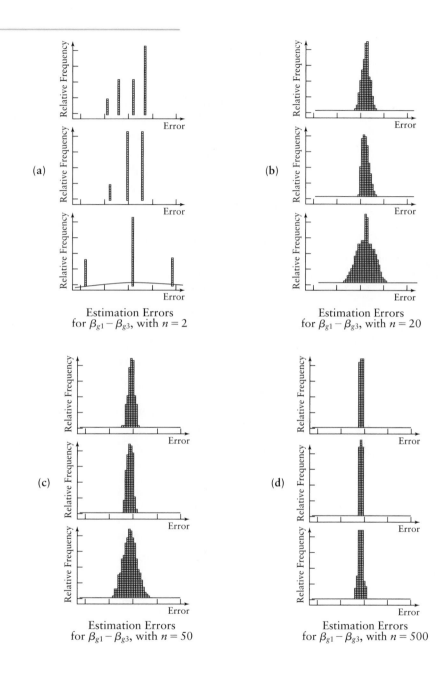

(a)

Estimation Errors for $\beta_{g1} - \beta_{g3}$, with $n = 2$

(b)

Estimation Errors for $\beta_{g1} - \beta_{g3}$, with $n = 20$

(c)

Estimation Errors for $\beta_{g1} - \beta_{g3}$, with $n = 50$

(d)

Estimation Errors for $\beta_{g1} - \beta_{g3}$, with $n = 500$

It is striking that the distributions of all of our estimators collapse and tend toward normality in large samples. Many estimators in econometrics exhibit these traits. The traits arise because the Law of Large Numbers and the Central

Limit Theorem have very broad applicability in statistical matters. In fact, these statistical regularities are so widespread that they inspire an alternative perspective on what makes good estimators. Rather than focusing on the sampling distributions of estimators for a given, finite sample size, we can discuss what happens to the distributions of the estimators as sample sizes grow large. ("If I had all the data in the world, I still couldn't guess the slope correctly," would seem a sorry advertisement for one's estimation methods.) However, keep in mind that in the present context, because we have not yet decided whether our estimators are unbiased, we don't yet know if the estimators' distributions are collapsing around the slope of the line that we are seeking to estimate—maybe our three estimators are collapsing on an incorrect value for the slope of a line through the origin.

We spend more time on the study of large sample properties of estimators in later chapters. When it becomes too difficult to determine the sampling properties of estimators for samples of the size econometricians actually handle, the econometricians often rely instead on the estimators' large sample properties for deciding which estimator is best.

### An Organizational Structure for the Study of Econometrics

#### 1. What Is the DGP?

We specified the data-generating process (DGP):

$$Y_i = \beta X_i + \varepsilon_i \qquad i = 1, \ldots, n$$
$$E(\varepsilon_i) = 0 \qquad i = 1, \ldots, n$$
$$\mathrm{var}(\varepsilon_i) = \sigma^2 \qquad i = 1, \ldots, n$$

and $\varepsilon_1, \ldots, \varepsilon_n$ are mutually statistically independent. Each $X_i$ is fixed across samples.

#### 2. What Makes a Good Estimator?

We focused on the cross-sample properties: small mean square error, unbiasedness, efficiency.

#### 3. How Do We Create an Estimator?

Intuition suggested three estimators: $\beta_{g1}$, $\beta_{g2}$, and $\beta_{g3}$.

#### 4. What Are an Estimator's Properties?

We used Monte Carlo analysis to learn that in the specifications we examined: (i) $\beta_{g2}$ has a smaller MSE than $\beta_{g1}$ or $\beta_{g3}$; (ii) All three estimators' variances shrink as sample size grows.

# Summary

The preceding table places the highlights of this chapter within the organizational structure we established in Chapter 1; every chapter concludes with such a table. This chapter began by describing properties of estimators that consumers of econometric research would find attractive: unbiasedness, minimum mean square error, minimum mean absolute error, and efficiency. All these properties of estimators look at the performance of estimators *across* samples, in effect asking how the estimators perform when used many times. Choosing estimators based on sampling properties is common in econometrics.

Because econometricians often estimate slopes of lines, this chapter introduced a simple prototype of this task: estimating the slope of a line through the origin. Grappling with this special case provides us with techniques and intuitions that generalize broadly. Estimating the slope of a line proved closely related to the classic statistical problem of estimating the mean of a population; the lines econometricians estimate are different in that they define families of means, families whose relationships are determined by the slopes and intercepts of those lines. In addition, just as in statistics we settled on the sample mean as an intuitively appealing estimator for the population mean, we discovered here three intuitively appealing estimators of the slope of a line through the origin.

To choose a best estimator from among the three intuitively appealing candidates, we used each one many times and compared their performances across many samples. We used the computer to generate the many samples, applying a technique known as Monte Carlo experimentation to imitate the repeated use of the estimators across real-world samples. Building the Monte Carlo experiment made clear that assessing the properties of estimators requires careful attention to the source of the data. We called the detailed specification of the source of one's data a data-generating process (DGP). In our Monte Carlo experiments, we assumed that the independent variable's values in our model (the $X_i$'s) reappeared in each new sample, whereas the dependent variable's values (the $Y_i$'s) changed from sample to sample in a simple random fashion. We conceptualized the deviation of each $Y_i$ from its expected value as being "disturbances" drawn independently from a single statistical distribution. To actually draw values for the disturbances in each sample, we relied on computer-generated random numbers. Finally, to complete the Monte Carlo arrangement, we set values for the slope of the line, the $X_i$, the number of observations in a sample, and the variance of the disturbances.

To assess the robustness of our results to alternative choices in building our Monte Carlo models, we conducted seven Monte Carlo experiments, each with different choices for the slope of the line, the $X_i$, and so on. All seven Monte Carlo models found that one estimator among the three makes errors decidedly smaller in magnitude than those made by the other two estimators. None of the seven models indicated that any of the three estimators are decidedly biased, but the models also do not allow us to declare any of the estimators unbiased.

Our graphical examination of Monte Carlo results revealed that normally distributed disturbances appear to result in all the estimators being themselves normally distributed, even in small samples. Moreover, even when the disturbances were highly non-normal, all the estimators appeared approximately normally distributed once sample sizes grew moderately large. The graphical analysis also highlighted the fact that larger samples tend to yield more precise estimators.

The graphical analysis of Monte Carlo results revealed that the Law of Large Numbers and the Central Limit Theorem have broad applicability in statistical matters and that they also influence econometric practice. When determining the sampling properties of estimators for specific sample sizes becomes too difficult, econometricians often choose estimators based on what happens to the estimators' sampling distributions as sample size grows large. Such large sample properties offer an alternative to the (finite) sampling properties criteria for choosing among estimators.

One inherent limitation of Monte Carlo evaluations is that their results are always uncertain. This uncertainty stems from the finite repetitions possible in any Monte Carlo experiment. For some questions, the uncertainty in Monte Carlo analyses is not a burden—we are clear that $\beta_{g2}$ is superior to $\beta_{g1}$ and $\beta_{g3}$ for the DGPs we've studied. For other questions, the uncertainty limits us—we still do not know whether any of our three estimators is unbiased. Could we determine the statistical properties of our three estimators more surely? In the next chapter, we find that we can. Another limitation of Monte Carlo methods is that the number of candidate estimators we can consider is generally rather small. In this chapter we studied three; studying many more with Monte Carlo techniques would be quite tedious. Is there some way we can examine a larger number of candidate estimators to find the best among them? Again, in the next chapter, we find that we can.

## Concepts for Review

## Questions for Discussion

1. Why might a manager of a firm prefer lower mean square errors over lower mean absolute errors when making an estimate in a business setting? Why might another manager prefer the reverse? What might be the costs of various sorts of errors?

2. Why should anyone prefer unbiased estimators with a larger mean square error over biased estimators with a smaller mean square error? Aren't mistakes mistakes, whatever their source? Why might anyone care whether their errors stem from bias or from variance?

3. The data-generating-process (DGP) this chapter uses for comparing $\beta_{g1}$, $\beta_{g2}$ and $\beta_{g3}$ assumes that all the disturbances are statistically independent and that each disturbance has the same variance, $\text{var}(\varepsilon_i) = \sigma^2$. Suppose we were going to estimate individuals' expected incomes, given their levels of education, with

$$income_i = \beta_0 + \beta_1(education_i) + \varepsilon_i.$$

   a. If we gather data by selecting households at random and then interviewing all adults in the chosen households, using each adult in the sample as an observation, do you think the observations will be statistically independent? Discuss.

   b. If we choose half our observations by interviewing a simple random sample of middle-aged adults and choose the other half of our observations by interviewing a simple random sample of young adults, do you think all the disturbances will have the same variance? Discuss.

   c. What are some determinants of individuals' incomes that are captured by the disturbance term, $\varepsilon_i$?

4. Each time we conduct a Monte Carlo experiment, we get different numerical results, even when we keep the DGP fixed. Why does this happen? Should it worry us? Discuss.

5. The results of a Monte Carlo experiment are only informative about the specific DGP we use to generate the results. Can we learn anything general from such specific findings? Discuss.

## Problems for Analyis

For the data sets that you will need to solve the problems in this section, go to **www.aw-bc.com/murray.**

1. Use the MC Builder I on **www.aw-bc.com/murray** to construct your own DGP with which to compare the performances of $\beta_{g1}$, $\beta_{g2}$, and $\beta_{g3}$. Which estimator has the lowest bias? The smallest mean square error? The smallest mean absolute error? Based on the evidence you obtain, do you think any of the estimators is unbiased?

 2. Use the data from 1847 to 1861 in engelrye.*** to confirm the estimates of the price elasticity of the demand for rye reported in this chapter's Greatest Hit about Ernst

Engel and the demand for rye. The percentage changes in price and quantity are in variables named either *perchngpricerye* and *perchngquanrye*, or *chngprice* and *chngquan*, depending on the file used. The differences in the percent changes in the prices and quantities from one observation to the next are in the variables *dchp* and *dchq*, respectively.

3. Trygve Haavelmo used the data from 1922 to 1941 that is in haavelmo.*** to estimate the marginal propensity to consume.[7] Haavelmo reported a marginal propensity to consume of 0.73 when he estimated a consumption function. The measure of consumption in this data set is *real_cons*; the measure of income is *real_gdp*. Milton Friedman later argued[8] that the consumption function passes through the origin, as in

$$consumption = \beta(income) + u,$$

where $\beta$ is the marginal propensity to consume.
   a. Compute the means of consumption and income in this sample.
   b. Estimate the marginal propensity to consume using $\beta_{g2}$, which is the estimator Milton Friedman recommended.
   c. Estimate the marginal propensity to consume using $\beta_{g1}$ and $\beta_{g3}$. (The differences in consumption from one observation to the next are in the variable *dcons*; the differences in income are in the variable *dgdp*.)
   d. In Keynesian macroeconomic theory, an independent change in government spending, $\Delta G$ increases income by $\Delta G/(1 - \beta)$. This is called "the multiplier effect," and "the multiplier" is $1/(1 - \beta)$. What is the range of estimated multipliers across your three estimates of the marginal propensity to consume?

4. For many years, housing economists believed that households spent a constant fraction of income on housing, as in

$$housing\ expenditure = \beta(income) + u.$$

The file housing.*** contains housing expenditures (*housing*) and total expenditures (*total*) for a sample of 19th century Belgian workers collected by Edouard Ducpetiaux.[9] The differences in housing expenditure from one observation to the next are in the variable *dhousing*; the differences in total expenditure are in the variable *dtotal*.
   a. Compute the means of total expenditure and housing expenditure in this sample.
   b. Estimate $\beta$ using $\beta_{g1}$, $\beta_{g2}$, and $\beta_{g3}$, using total expenditure for total income.
   c. If income rises by 100 (it averages around 900 in this sample), what increase in estimated expected housing expenditure results according to each of these estimates?
   d. What economic argument would you make against housing absorbing a constant share of income?
   e. What are some determinants of housing that are captured by $u$?

5. The data set production.*** contains data on U.S. labor costs (*labor*), capital expenditures (*capital*), and the value of output (*output*), for a sample of years.
   a. Use $\beta_{g1}$, $\beta_{g2}$, and $\beta_{g3}$ to estimate labor's share in output, using the model

$$labor\ cost = \beta_1(output) + u.$$

The differences in labor costs from observation to observation are in the variable *dlabor*; the differences in capital are in *dcapital*; and the differences in output's value are in *doutput*.

b. Use $\beta_{g1}$, $\beta_{g2}$, and $\beta_{g3}$ to estimate capital's share in output, using the model

$$capital\ expenditures = \beta_2(output) + \varepsilon$$

6. Use MC Builder II on this book's companion Web site (**www.aw-bc.com/murray**) to determine whether the variances of $\beta_{g1}$, $\beta_{g2}$, and $\beta_{g3}$ shrink as the sample size grows and whether their distributions approach the normal distribution as the sample size grows.

## Endnotes

1. "The Man Who Broke the Bank at Monte Carlo," written and composed by Fred Gilbert, 1892.
2. In introductory statistics courses, the population mean is commonly named $\mu$. The population mean is named $\beta$ here because that name fits more neatly with the symbols commonly used both in econometrics and throughout this text.
3. Ernst Engel, "Die Getreidepreise, die Ernteertraege und die Getreidehandel in preussischen Staate," *Zeitschroft des Koeniglich Preussischen Statistichen Bureaus* I (1861): 249–289.
4. John Maynard Keynes, *The General Theory of Employment, Interest, and Money* (London: Macmillan, 1936).
5. Milton Friedman, *A Theory of the Consumption Function* (Princeton, NJ: Princeton University Press, 1957).
6. Economists prior to Friedman had estimated $\beta_1$ by a formula that we will encounter in Chapter 4.
7. Trygve Haavelmo, "Methods of Measuring the Marginal Propensity to Consume," *Journal of the American Statistical Association* 42 (March 1947): 105–122.
8. Friedman, *A Theory of the Consumption Function.*
9. Edouard Ducpetiaux, *Budgets Economiques de Classes de Ouvrieres en Belgique* (Brussels: Hayaz, 1855).

# Chapter 3

# Linear Estimators and the Gauss–Markov Theorem

*Where all the women are strong, all the men are good looking, and all the children are above average.*

—GARRISON KEILLOR[1]

hree econometricians were hunting deer in the woods. They spied a large buck just 50 yards away, standing broadside to them. The first econometrician raised his gun and fired, hitting a tree two feet behind the deer. The second econometrician fired almost simultaneously, hitting a tree two feet in front of the deer. The third econometrician began jumping up and down, yelling "We got him on average; we got him on average!"

Clearly, there are limitations to the property of unbiasedness. Other things equal, however, being right on average is better than being wrong on average. And had the econometricians' shots landed just two inches from the deer's heart, instead of several feet away, they would have been eating as well as celebrating. Coupled with a small variance, unbiasedness becomes a very attractive property indeed. This chapter explores the unbiasedness and variance of estimators.

In Chapter 2, we used intuition to develop three estimators for the slope of a line that passes through the origin. We then used Monte Carlo techniques to examine the statistical properties of those estimators across samples and to decide which estimator was the best of the three. We concluded that in the models we considered, the ratio of the average $Y$ to the average $X$, which we called $\beta_{g2}$, is superior to the average ratio of the $Y$'s and $X$'s and to the average ratio of the change in $Y$ to the change in $X$, which we called $\beta_{g1}$ and $\beta_{g3}$, respectively. In particular, we decided that with a sample of renters from New York, our favored guess of the share of income they devoted to rent is 0.22, the estimate obtained with $\beta_{g2}$, rather than 0.29 or 0.28, the estimates from $\beta_{g1}$ and $\beta_{g3}$, respectively.

We arrived at $\beta_{g1}$, $\beta_{g2}$, and $\beta_{g3}$ intuitively—but is intuition the best source for good estimators? Might a more systematic approach to devising estimators lead us to an even better estimator for the slope of a line through the origin? Might there be a better estimator than $\beta_{g2}$ for the share of income devoted to rent by New Yorkers?

This chapter introduces formal techniques for developing a "best" estimator for the slope of a line that passes through the origin. These techniques focus on a broad set of estimators, called linear estimators, that includes the three we arrived at intuitively. The techniques let us determine mathematically both the mean and the variance of estimators. Consequently, the techniques can determine which estimators are unbiased and which unbiased estimator has the smallest variance. We settle on efficiency as our criterion for which estimator is best, so we dub the unbiased linear estimator with the smallest variance the *best linear unbiased estimator*, or the *BLUE* estimator. Applying the BLUE estimator to our sample of New York renters, we find our best guess for the share of income that New Yorkers devote to rent is 0.17, which is quite different from the earlier estimates.

<table>
<tr><td>

**3.1**

</td><td>

# Linear Estimators

</td></tr>
<tr><td>

HOW DO WE CREATE AN ESTIMATOR?

</td><td>

Looking across all possible estimators to find the best one is a daunting and generally unmanageable task. Instead, we narrow the range of possibilities by focusing on a broad class of estimators called **linear estimators**. The intuitive estimators of Chapter 2, $\beta_{g1}$, $\beta_{g2}$, and $\beta_{g3}$, all prove to be linear estimators, which illustrates that the class of linear estimators contains very plausible estimators for the slope of a line through the origin.

</td></tr>
</table>

## Linear Estimators and Their Weights

Linear estimators can be computed as a weighted sum of the observations on the dependent variable of a model. An estimator, $g$, is linear if it can be written

$$g = \sum_{i=1}^{n} w_i Y_i,$$

where $Y_i$ is the $i$-th observation on the dependent variable, and $w_i$ is a number. We refer to the $w_i$ as "weights." Notice that if there were no weights (or if all the weights were all equal to one), the estimator would just be the sum of the observations on the dependent variable. As a general notational practice, we can omit the range of a sum, such as "$i = 1$ to $n$" when the range is clear. Thus, we can also say that an estimator, $g$, is linear if

$$g = \sum w_i Y_i.$$

The weights allow us to count some observations more heavily than others in the sum. For example,

$$\left(\frac{1}{3}\right) Y_1 + \left(\frac{1}{6}\right) Y_2 + \left(\frac{1}{10}\right) Y_3$$

is a linear estimator in which the first observation is weighted most heavily and the third observation is weighted least heavily. The weights need not differ from one another. The sample mean is a linear estimator with all the $w_i$ set equal to

$1/n$, where $n$ is the number of observations:

$$\overline{Y} = sample\ mean = \left(\frac{1}{n}\right)\sum Y_i = \sum\left(\frac{1}{n}\right)Y_i.$$

The sample mean weights all observations equally.

The weights in a linear estimator must be numbers, not random variables.[2] If the explanators (the $X_i$) in a model are fixed across samples, then the weights can depend on the $X_i$. If the $X_i$'s are fixed across samples, another example of a linear estimator is

$$\left(\frac{1}{X_1}\right)Y_1 + \left(\frac{1}{X_2}\right)Y_2 + \left(\frac{1}{X_3}\right)Y_3.$$

In this example, the linear estimator weights more heavily observations with small $X$ values (for which $1/X_i$ is large).

Sometimes, an estimator is not linear in $Y_i$ itself but is linear in some transformation of $Y_i$. For example,

$$\sum\left(\frac{1}{n}\right)Y_i^2$$

and

$$\sum\left(\frac{1}{n}\right)\ln(Y_i)$$

are not linear in the $Y$, and therefore are not linear estimators in $Y$, even though they would be linear in $Y_i^2$ and $\ln(Y_i)$, respectively. The following would not be a linear estimator:

$$\sum\left(\frac{1}{n}\right)\ln(Y_i) + \sum\left(\frac{1}{n^3}\right)Y_i^4,$$

because it can't be simplified to

$$\sum w_i f(Y_i)$$

for some $f(Y_i)$.

As already noted, the intuitively appealing estimators of Chapter 2, $\beta_{g1}$, $\beta_{g2}$, and $\beta_{g3}$, are all linear estimators. Consider $\beta_{g1}$. This estimator, which we have written as

$$\left(\frac{1}{n}\right)\sum\left(\frac{Y_i}{X_i}\right),$$

can instead be rewritten as

$$\sum \left( \frac{1}{n\,X_i} \right) Y_i.$$

Here, the weights applied to the $Y_i$ are

$$w_{1i} = \frac{1}{nX_i} \qquad i = 1, \ldots, n.$$

Similarly, the estimator $\beta_{g2}$,

$$\frac{\sum Y_i}{\sum X_i},$$

can be rewritten as

$$\sum \left[ \left( \frac{1}{\sum X_j} \right) Y_i \right],$$

in which every $Y_i$ has the same weight,

$$w_{2i} = \left[ \frac{1}{\sum (X_j)} \right].$$

Finally, the estimator $\beta_{g3}$,

$$\beta_{g3} = \frac{1}{(n-1)} \sum_{i=2}^{n} \frac{(Y_i - Y_{i-1})}{(X_i - X_{i-1})},$$

can be written (after more extensive manipulation) as

$$\frac{1}{(n-1)} \left( \frac{1}{[X_1 - X_2]} \right) Y_1 + \frac{1}{(n-1)} \left( \frac{1}{[X_n - X_{n-1}]} \right) Y_n$$

$$+ \frac{1}{(n-1)} \sum_{(i=2)}^{(n-1)} \left\{ \left( \frac{1}{[X_i - X_{i+1}]} \right) - \left( \frac{1}{[X_{i-1} - X_i]} \right) \right\} Y_i,$$

in which the weights applied to the $Y_i$ are

$$w_{31} = \frac{1}{[X_1 - X_2]} \times \left[ \frac{1}{(n-1)} \right],$$

$$w_{3n} = \frac{1}{[X_n - X_{n-1}]} \times \left[ \frac{1}{(n-1)} \right],$$

# An Econometric Top 40—A Golden Oldie

## The Capital Asset Pricing Model

Most people dislike risk in financial matters. Financial markets recognize this fact and offer people a higher expected rate of return on risky assets. For this reason, the excess of a risky asset's expected return over the return on a riskless asset, such as the return on essentially riskless U.S. government short-term securities, $R_g$, is called the risk premium. Chapter 2 describes one naive model that captures this truism. That model assumes that the expected risk premium on an asset is proportional to the standard deviation of the asset's rate of return. The model's intuition is that the more an asset's return varies, the more investors must be compensated for risk; the higher the standard deviation of the return, the more uncertain investors are about what the return will actually be.

Professional financial analysts used this naive model as recently as the 1950s, but between 1950 and 1970 several Nobel laureates in economics (Harry Markowitz, Merton Miller, William Sharpe, Myron Scholes, and James Tobin) transformed our understanding of risk and return.[3] These writers formalized the folk wisdom "Don't put all your eggs into one basket" as "diversifying your portfolio," and discovered through a formal mathematical analysis what that wisdom means for the risk premia assets receive in financial markets.

The Nobel laureates argued that because investors can diversify their portfolios, the naive model of risk premia in Chapter 2 does not reflect how the market determines risk premia. For example, suppose there are just two assets, swimsuits and umbrellas, that you can invest in next summer. Swimsuits do well if the sun shines, and badly otherwise. Umbrellas do well if it rains, and badly otherwise. If half of summers are sunny and half rainy, both swimsuits

and umbrellas have highly variable returns. The naive model that identifies an asset's risk with its variance that would predict these assets would therefore command considerable risk premia. Not so. Diversification allows you to hold these assets with little risk—simply invest in both umbrellas and swimsuits, and thereby earn an unvarying return.[4] Unfortunately, we cannot diversify away all risk so easily. Suppose some summers are cloudy, without sunshine or rain. Both swimsuits and umbrellas do badly. This risk is unavoidable if there are only these two risky assets, and so the investments in umbrellas and swimsuits would command some risk premium if they were to be held by investors.

The Capital Asset Pricing Model (CAPM) that sprang from the work of the Nobel laureates implies that it is the additional undiversifiable risk that an asset brings to an optimal portfolio that determines the risk premium the asset will receive. The Nobel economists determined that we could measure this riskiness of an asset. When markets are in equilibrium, says the CAPM, the riskiness of an asset relative to the riskiness of the entire asset market would be equal to the slope, $\beta$, in the relationship

*(asset's excess expected return above the riskless rate) = $\beta$(excess return of a "market portfolio" above the riskless rate),*

where a "market portfolio" is a portfolio containing every asset in the marketplace in proportion to its total value. Analysts call the slope of this line the asset's "beta." If an asset's return bounces about its equilibrium value in practice, we can estimate the riskiness of the asset (its beta) by collecting time series observations on the asset's return, $R_A$, the return of a market portfolio, $R_{Mt}$, and the risk-free rate of return, measured by the return on government bonds, $R_g$. We use these data to estimate the model

$$(R_{At} - R_g) = \beta(R_{Mt} - R_g) + e_t$$
$$t = 1, \ldots, T,$$

where the subscript $t$ indicates which time period an observation is drawn from and $T$ is the total number of time series observations on the asset. The slope in an asset's equation is the asset's beta, a measure of the asset's contribution to an optimal portfolio's undiversifiable risk. For many years, stock analysts devoted much attention to discussing the betas of stocks as a guide to assets' pricing. Estimating $\beta$ is estimating the slope of a line with no intercept term.

### Final Notes

The CAPM revolutionized the quantitative analysis of stocks and bonds. Economists quickly exploited the model to assess the performance of mutual funds and other investment institutions. In 1981, Tobin received the Nobel prize in economics "for his analysis of financial markets and their relations to expenditure decisions, employment, production and prices." In 1990, Markowitz, Miller, and Sharpe received the Nobel prize in economics "for their pioneering work in the theory of financial economics." In 1997, Scholes joined the others as a Nobel laureate, receiving his prize "for a new method

to determine the value of derivatives." We'll encounter one such analysis in another Classical Favorite in Chapter 7.

The CAPM epitomizes the importance of the "econ" in "econometrics." In the CAPM, economic theory tells us what variables to study; economic theory guides us to investigate the role of risk in an asset's pricing by examining the asset's excess return relative to the excess return on a market portfolio—and informs us that no other considerations will matter. Economic theory also tells us that the relationship between an asset's excess returns and the market's excess returns is a straight line, with no intercept. And finally, economic theory reveals that the slope of such a line (an asset's beta) depends on the asset's undiversifiable risk. Econometrics goes beyond the "econ." Economic theory tells us only the qualitative relationship between an asset's excess return and the market's excess return. In contrast, econometrics draws on the insights from economic theory and takes the further step of blending the theoretical observations with empirical observation, allowing us to quantify precisely the relationship between an asset's excess return and the market's excess return and to assess whether the received theory fits or is at odds with the observed facts. ∎

and

$$w_{3i} = \left[\frac{1}{[X_i - X_{i+1}]} - \frac{1}{[X_{i-1} - X_i]}\right] \times \left[\frac{1}{(n-1)}\right] i = 2, \ldots, n - 1.$$

The $(n - 1)$ terms in $\beta_{g3}$ arise because there are only $(n - 1)$ changes in the $Y$'s and $X$'s as we go through successive observations from 1 through $n$.

## 3.2     Unbiased Linear Estimators

WHAT ARE AN ESTI-
MATOR'S PROPERTIES?

Being right on average is a desirable trait for estimators. The Monte Carlo analysis of Chapter 2 did not determine whether the intuitively plausible estimators, $\beta_{g1}$, $\beta_{g2}$, and $\beta_{g3}$, are unbiased. Fortunately, their linearity simplifies investigating mathematically whether they are unbiased and, if so, which of them is most efficient. This section introduces the statistical tools needed to investigate unbiasedness and applies those tools to linear estimators of the slope of a line through the origin.

### The DGP

*Always*, an investigation of unbiasedness or efficiency must begin with a statement of the data-generating process (DGP) with which the estimators in question will be used. In our present case, this DGP is

$$Y_i = \beta X_i + \varepsilon_i \qquad i = 1, \ldots, n$$

$$\mathrm{E}(\varepsilon_i) = 0 \qquad i = 1, \ldots, n$$

$$\mathrm{var}(\varepsilon_i) = \sigma^2 \qquad i = 1, \ldots, n$$

$$\mathrm{cov}(\varepsilon_i, \varepsilon_j) = 0 \qquad i \neq j$$

Each $X_i$ is fixed across samples.

This is the DGP that motivated our Monte Carlo studies in Chapter 2, except that the assumption of mutually independent disturbances has been replaced by the weaker assumption of uncorrelated disturbances. (If the disturbances are mutually independent, then they are uncorrelated. Being uncorrelated, they need not be independent.) Our analyses do not require independence of the disturbances.

The primary unknown parameter in this DGP is $\beta$. Like the previous chapter, this chapter focuses on the estimation of $\beta$. However, because $\sigma^2$ is also unknown and proves relevant to the precision of our estimators of $\beta$, in subsequent chapters we also investigate how we might estimate $\sigma^2$. Models in which the expected value of $Y$ depends on one or more explanators, such as $X$, are called regression models. *A common way of saying "estimate the slope coefficient of X in a regression model" is "regress Y on X."*

### Unbiasedness and the Algebra of Expectations

For *any* DGP, a linear estimator, $g$, is an unbiased estimator of $\beta$ if and only if

$$\mathrm{E}(g) = \mathrm{E}\left(\sum_{i=1}^{n} w_i Y_i\right) = \beta.$$

Here we ask which linear estimators unbiasedly estimate $\beta$ in our DGP. The tool we use to answer this question is the *algebra of expectations*, whose key rules are contained in Table 3.1. The **algebra of expectations** tells us how we may manipulate mathematical expectation expressions. The assumption that the explanators (the $X_i$) are fixed across samples makes many of the rules applicable to the linear estimators we study. We maintain this assumption until Chapter 12.

We begin by noting that

$$\mathrm{E}\left(\sum_{i=1}^{n} w_i Y_i\right) = \sum_{i=1}^{n} \mathrm{E}(w_i Y_i),$$

because, according to Table 3.1, the expected value of a sum is the sum of the expected values. Table 3.1 also reports that the expected value of a constant times a random variable is the constant times the expected value of the random variables. We require that the weights of a linear estimator, the $w_i$, be constants (that is, numbers that are fixed across samples), so we can rewrite $\sum \mathrm{E}(w_i Y_i)$ as

$$\sum_{i=1}^{n} w_i \mathrm{E}(Y_i).$$

---

**TABLE 3.1  The Algebra of Expectations**[*]

1. The expected value of a constant times a random variable is the constant times the expected value of the random variable:

$$\mathrm{E}(cY) = c\mathrm{E}(Y),$$

where $c$ is a constant and $Y$ is a random variable.

2. The expected value of a constant is a constant:

$$\mathrm{E}(c) = c.$$

3. The expected value of a constant plus a random variable is the constant plus the expected value of the random variable:

$$\mathrm{E}(c + Y) = c + \mathrm{E}(Y),$$

where $c$ is a constant and $Y$ is a random variable.

4. The expected value of a sum is the sum of the expected values:

$$\mathrm{E}\left(\sum_{i=1}^{n} Y_i\right) = \sum_{i=1}^{n} \mathrm{E}(Y_i),$$

where each $Y_i$ is a random variable.

[*]$\mathrm{E}(Y)$, the expected value of a discrete random variable $Y$, is $\sum_Y Y_i \mathrm{p}(Y_i)$, in which $\mathrm{p}(Y_i)$ is the probability of $Y_i$ and the sum is over all the different values that $Y$ takes on in the population. $\mathrm{E}(Y)$, the expected value of a continuous random variable, is $\int_Y y\mathrm{f}(y)$, in which $\mathrm{f}(y)$ is the probability density function of $Y$ and the integration is over the range of $Y$ in the population.

The $w_i$ for $\beta_{g1}$, $\beta_{g2}$, and $\beta_{g3}$ are constants in the present DGP, because the DGP assumes that $n$ and the $X_i$ are fixed across samples.

The DGP assumes that $Y_i$ equals $\beta X_i + \varepsilon_i$, so we can replace $Y_i$ with $\beta X_i + \varepsilon_i$ in the preceding expression, yielding

$$\sum_{i=1}^{n} w_i \mathrm{E}(\beta X_i + \varepsilon_i),$$

which equals

$$\sum_{i=1}^{n} w_i [\mathrm{E}(\beta X_i) + \mathrm{E}(\varepsilon_i)],$$

which, in turn, simplifies to

$$\sum_{i=1}^{n} w_i \beta X_i,$$

because $\beta$ and $X_i$ are constants and $\mathrm{E}(\varepsilon_i) = 0$ in our DGP. Hence, for linear estimators in our DGP,

$$\mathrm{E}(g) = \sum_{i=1}^{n} w_i \beta X_i = \beta \sum_{i=1}^{n} w_i X_i.$$

Which linear estimators unbiasedly estimate $\beta$ in our DGP? Those for which

$$\sum_{i=1}^{n} w_i X_i = 1.$$

For them,

$$\mathrm{E}(g) = \beta \sum_{i=1}^{n} w_i X_i = \beta(1) = \beta.$$

Notice that if all the observations on $X$ equal zero, no set of weights can satisfy the unbiasedness requirement. In that special case, there exists no linear unbiased estimator of the slope of a line through the origin. Intuitively, if every $X$ is zero, we cannot ascertain how $Y$ changes when $X$ changes. However, if all observations on $X$ are equal to some single nonzero value, we can unbiasedly estimate the slope because we know from the DGP that $\mathrm{E}(Y|X = 0) = 0$. We can compare the observed mean of $Y$ at the nonzero value of $X$ with known zero mean of $Y$ when $X$ is zero, to see how $\mathrm{E}(Y)$ changes when $X$ changes.

## Are Our Intuitive Estimators Unbiased?

Now that we know which linear estimators are unbiased estimators of $\beta$ in our DGP, we could ask if $\beta_{g1}$, $\beta_{g2}$, and $\beta_{g3}$ are among the unbiased estimators of $\beta$, a question left unanswered by our Monte Carlo analyses in Chapter 2.

For example, is $\beta_{g1}$ unbiased? The weights for $\beta_{g1}$ are

$$w_{1i} = \frac{1}{nX_i} \qquad i = 1, \ldots, n.$$

In this case,

$$\sum_{i=1}^{n} w_{1i}X_i = \sum_{i=1}^{n}\left(\left[\frac{1}{(nX_i)}\right]X_i\right) = \sum_{i=1}^{n}\left(\frac{1}{n}\right) = \left(\frac{1}{n}\right)\sum_{i=1}^{n}1 = \left(\frac{1}{n}\right)n = 1,$$

so $\beta_{g1}$ is, indeed, unbiased! (Recall that $\sum_{i=1}^{n}1$ is a sum of $n$ ones and therefore equals $n$.)

Is $\beta_{g2}$ unbiased? The weights for $\beta_{g2}$ are

$$w_{2i} = \frac{1}{\displaystyle\sum_{j=1}^{n}X_j} \qquad i = 1, \ldots, n.$$

In this case,

$$\sum_{i=1}^{n} w_{2i}X_i = \sum_{i=1}^{n}\left(\left[\frac{1}{\displaystyle\sum_{j=1}^{n}X_j}\right]X_i\right) = \frac{\displaystyle\sum_{i=1}^{n}X_i}{\displaystyle\sum_{j=1}^{n}X_j} = 1$$

so $\beta_{g2}$ is, indeed, unbiased!

Similar computations for $\beta_{g3}$ would reveal that it, too, is an unbiased estimator of $\beta$ in our DGP.

All three of our intuitive estimators, $\beta_{g1}$, $\beta_{g2}$, and $\beta_{g3}$, are unbiased estimators of $\beta$. The unbiasedness of all three estimators speaks well of our intuitions about how to estimate the slope of a line through the origin. Determination of the three estimators' unbiasedness using the algebra of expectations also speaks to the power of this formal, mathematical approach to studying estimators. As here, the algebra of expectations can often answer questions that the Monte Carlo exercise cannot—and so the algebra of expectations is a frequently used tool in econometric analysis.

If $\beta_{g1}$, $\beta_{g2}$, and $\beta_{g3}$ are all unbiased estimators of $\beta$, the choice among them turns on which one is the most efficient, that is, on which has the smallest variance. The next section shows how we can determine the variances of these and other linear estimators.

## 3.3    The Variance of a Linear Estimator

WHAT ARE AN ESTI-
MATOR'S PROPERTIES?

The example of econometricians hunting deer highlights the fact that an unbiased estimator is unhelpful if its variance is too large. How are we to assess when an estimator's variance is large? Fortunately, just as linearity simplifies investigating estimators' expected values, linearity simplifies investigating their variances. This section introduces the statistical tools needed to determine the variance of linear estimators and applies those tools to find the variance of linear estimators of $\beta$ in the DGP used in the preceding section.

## Linear Estimators and the Algebra of Variances

What is the variance of a linear estimator? The tool we use to answer this question is the *algebra of variances*, whose key rules are contained in Table 3.2. The **algebra of variances** tells us how we may manipulate variance expressions. As we found for the algebra of expectations, the assumption that the explanators (the $X_i$) are fixed across samples makes the rules of the algebra of variances applicable to linear estimators.

We begin with an expression for the variance of a linear estimator:

$$\text{var}(g) = \text{var}\left(\sum_{i=1}^{n} w_i Y_i\right),$$

which, using the algebra of variances described in Table 3.2, we can rewrite as

$$\sum_{i=1}^{n} \text{var}(w_i Y_i) + 2(\textit{sum of all the covariances among the } w_i Y_i)$$

$$= \sum_{i=1}^{n} \text{var}(w_i Y_i) + \sum_{i=1}^{n} \sum_{\substack{j=1 \\ j \neq i}}^{n} \text{cov}(w_i Y_i, w_j Y_j)$$

$$= \sum_{i=1}^{n} w_i^2 \text{var}(Y_i) + \sum_{i=1}^{n} \sum_{\substack{j=1 \\ j \neq i}}^{n} w_i w_j \text{cov}(Y_i, Y_j).$$

But the DGP tells us that the $\varepsilon_i$, and hence the $Y_i$ (which, in this DGP, differ from the $\varepsilon_i$ by only $\beta X_i$, which is constant across samples), are uncorrelated, so all the covariance terms are zero. Hence, for linear estimators in our DGP,

$$\text{var}(g) = \text{var}\left(\sum_{i=1}^{n} w_i Y_i\right) = \sum_{i=1}^{n} w_i^2 \text{var}(Y_i).$$

However, $Y_i = \beta X_i + \varepsilon_i$, in which $\beta X_i$ is a constant across samples, so

$$\text{var}(Y_i) = \text{var}(\beta X_i + \varepsilon_i) = \text{var}(\varepsilon_i) = \sigma^2.$$

Therefore, the variance of a linear estimator in our DGP can be rewritten as

$$\sum_{i=1}^{n} w_i^2 \sigma^2$$

**TABLE 3.2 The Algebra of Variances**[*]

1. The variance of a constant times a random variable is the constant squared times the variance of the random variable:

$$\text{var}(cY) = c^2\text{var}(Y),$$

where $c$ is a constant and $Y$ is a random variable.

2. The variance of a constant plus a random variable is the variance of the random variable

$$\text{var}(c + Y) = \text{var}(Y),$$

where $c$ is a constant and $Y$ is a random variable.

3. The variance of a sum is the sum of the variances, plus two times the sum of all the covariances among the variables in the original sum:

$$\text{var}\left(\sum Y_i\right) = \sum\text{var}(Y_i) + 2(\textit{sum of all the covariances among the } Y_i)$$

$$= \sum\text{var}(Y_i) + \sum_{i=1}^{n}\sum_{\substack{j=1 \\ j\neq i}}^{n}\text{cov}(Y_i,Y_j),$$

where $Y_i$ and $Y_j$ are random variables. (Because $\text{cov}(Y_i,Y_j) = \text{cov}(Y_j,Y_i)$, each covariance appears twice in the sum.)

4. The covariance of $(Y_i + a)$ and $(Y_j + b)$ is $\text{cov}(Y_i,Y_j)$, where $a$ and $b$ are constants.

5. The covariance of $aY_i$ and $bY_j$ is $ab$ times the $\text{cov}(Y_i,Y_j)$:

$$\text{cov}(aY_i,bY_j) = a\,b\,\text{cov}(Y_i,Y_j).$$

[*]$\text{Var}(Y)$, the variance of a random variable $Y$, is $E[Y - E(Y)]^2$, that is, the mean squared deviation of $Y$ from its own mean. $\text{Cov}(Y_i,Y_j) = E([Y_i - E(Y_i)][Y_j - E(Y_j)])$, that is, the mean of the products of the deviations of $Y_i$ and $Y_j$ from their respective means.

or as

$$\sigma^2\sum_{i=1}^{n}w_i^2. \qquad\qquad 3.1$$

For example, the variance of $\beta_{g1}$ follows from the weights for $\beta_{g1}$, which are

$$w_{1i} = \frac{1}{nX_i} \qquad i = 1,\ldots,n.$$

Inserting these weights into the formula for the variance of a linear estimator in our DGP, we obtain

$$\text{var}(\beta_{g1}) = \sigma^2 \sum \frac{1}{(nX_i)^2} \qquad \text{3.2}$$

Similarly, the weights for $\beta_{g2}$ are

$$w_{2i} = \frac{1}{\sum\limits_{j=1}^{n} X_j} \qquad i = 1, \ldots, n.$$

Inserting these weights into the formula for a linear estimator's variance in our DGP leads to

$$\text{var}(\beta_{g2}) = \frac{n\sigma^2}{\left[ \sum (X_i) \right]^2}. \qquad \text{3.3}$$

The variance formula for $\beta_{g3}$ is very messy and not reported.

## Relative Variances of Linear Estimators

Notice that the variances of linear estimators in this DGP are all proportional to $\sigma^2$. We cannot compute the variances without knowing $\sigma^2$, but we can compare the *relative* variances of linear estimators without knowing $\sigma^2$, as long as we know their weights, which for $\beta_{g1}$, $\beta_{g2}$, and $\beta_{g3}$ depend only on $n$ and the $X_i$. For two linear estimators, $g_A$ and $g_B$, with weights $w_{Ai}$ and $w_{Bi}$, respectively,

$$\frac{\text{var}(g_A)}{\text{var}(g_B)} = \frac{\sum (w_{Ai})^2}{\sum (w_{Bi})^2}.$$

In our sample of New York renters discussed in Chapter 2, and for which the data appear on this book's companion Web site (**www.aw-bc.com/murray**) in the file rents.***, the variances of $\beta_{g1}$, and $\beta_{g3}$ are both about four times that of $\beta_{g2}$ in the present DGP. If all the $X$'s are of the same sign, the variance of $\beta_{g2}$ in the present DGP is always less than that of $\beta_{g1}$; when the $X$'s are not all of the same sign, $\beta_{g1}$ or $\beta_{g3}$ may be more efficient than $\beta_{g2}$ in the present DGP.

## Revisiting Monte Carlo Exercises

In our Monte Carlo exercises in Chapter 2, we knew $n$, $\sigma^2$, and the $X_i$. Knowing these suffices to compute the population variances of $\beta_{g1}$, $\beta_{g2}$, and $\beta_{g3}$, based on the formulae in Equations 3.1 to 3.3. Table 3.3 reports these population variances

**TABLE 3.3** Calculated and Observed Variances for $\beta_{g1}$, $\beta_{g2}$, and $\beta_{g3}$

| | Var($\beta_{g1}$) | | Var($\beta_{g2}$) | | Var($\beta_{g3}$) | |
|---|---|---|---|---|---|---|
| Model | Population | Samples | Population | Samples | Population | Samples |
| 1 | 4.1 | 1.5 | 0.4 | 0.6 | 20 | 7.6 |
| 2 | 7577 | 7496 | 951 | 930 | 4137 | 4078 |
| 3 | 1604379 | 1612675 | 105186 | 107876 | 2112537 | 2438215 |
| 4 | 2148 | 2116 | 556 | 552 | 3673 | 3731 |
| 5 | 341 | 859 | 85 | 90 | 2128 | 2145 |
| 6 | 64145 | 62644 | 0.00012 | 2.04 | 2143 | 2105 |

for $\beta_{g1}$, $\beta_{g2}$, and $\beta_{g3}$ for the six students' models in Chapter 2. The calculated population variance of $\beta_{g2}$ is less than that of either $\beta_{g1}$ or $\beta_{g3}$ in every case, in close accord with our Monte Carlo conclusion, based on observed variances across the 10,000 samples.

Table 3.3 also restates the observed variances of $\beta_{g1}$, $\beta_{g2}$, and $\beta_{g3}$ about their common mean ($\beta$) obtained in a Monte Carlo exercise. The observed variance of $\beta_{g2}$ is smallest in every case. Notice that as with the mean error, the Monte Carlo results are relatively precise for the large variances of $\beta_{g1}$, $\beta_{g2}$, and $\beta_{g3}$, but are *relatively* imprecise for small variances. Indeed, the Monte Carlo observed variances are precise enough that in every case we correctly rank the estimators in order of efficiency. This supports the claim made at the end of Chapter 2 that the Law of Large Numbers ensures that Monte Carlo comparisons of estimators for particular specifications will generally reveal the better estimator. The problem remains, however, that conclusions from one specification do not necessarily generalize to others; for example, $\beta_{g1}$, sometimes, as in Models 2 and 6 in Table 3.3, but not always, dominates $\beta_{g3}$.

To confirm that Monte Carlo analyses can yield conflicting results when we examine additional specifications, consider two others in which we relax the requirement that all the $X$'s be of the same sign, replacing it with the requirement that the sum of the $X$'s cannot be zero (which continues to ensure that $\beta_{g2}$ is well defined). Table 3.4 presents two models in which some of the $X$'s are positive and some negative. In each instance, the mean $X$ is small, and therefore $\beta_{g2}$ is rather imprecise. In both models, $\beta_{g1}$ and $\beta_{g3}$ are more efficient than $\beta_{g2}$! Model 7 is the same as Model 1 except that the signs of some $X$'s have been changed. Even this minor adjustment can alter the relative efficiency of the estimators. The sensitivity of the Monte Carlo results to model specification suggests that a general formula

**TABLE 3.4** Two Additional Monte Carlo Models

| Model | $n$ | $\beta$ | Mean($X$) | Variance($X$) | $\sigma^2$ |
|-------|-----|---------|-----------|---------------|------------|
| 7 | 5 | −1 | 0.8 | 6.6 | 1225 |
| 8 | 3 | 0.10 | 0.4 | 7.5 | 25 |

| | Var($\beta_{g1}$) | | Var($\beta_{g2}$) | | Var($\beta_{g3}$) | |
|-------|------------|----------|------------|----------|------------|----------|
| Model | Population | Observed | Population | Observed | Population | Observed |
| 7 | 112.0 | 109.0 | 383 | 374 | 99.0 | 97.0 |
| 8 | 4.1 | 1.4 | 19 | 30 | 3.2 | 1.1 |

for the variance of an estimator, like that in Equation 3.1, has an advantage over Monte Carlo exercises. With a formula in hand, it is easier to see when one estimator's variance is smaller than that of another and whether it is always so. Monte Carlo models are almost always restricted to a limited set of possible models for comparison.

Tables 3.3 and 3.4 report the variances of the several estimators. This is not the usual practice among econometricians. Instead, econometricians usually report the standard deviations of estimators, that is, the square roots of the variances, to indicate the precision of the estimators. Econometricians typically call the standard deviation of an estimator its **standard error**, because for unbiased estimators, all the variation in an estimator stems from estimation errors (that is, all the variation about the mean of the estimator is variation about the true value). Econometric software packages typically report an estimate of an estimator's standard error right along with any report of the estimator's value in a particular sample.

## 3.4    A More Efficient Linear Estimator

WHAT ARE AN ESTI-
MATOR'S PROPERTIES?

Monte Carlo techniques revealed that for the models in Chapter 2, $\beta_{g2}$ is more efficient than $\beta_{g1}$ or $\beta_{g3}$, but we have now seen that for some other $X$-values, $\beta_{g2}$ is not the most efficient of these estimators in the present DGP. We have also seen that exploiting the power of mathematical statistics yields formulae for the variances of $\beta_{g1}$, $\beta_{g2}$, and $\beta_{g3}$ that would allow us to choose the most efficient of these estimators for any specific set of $X$-values embedded in the present DGP. But should we limit ourselves to $\beta_{g1}$, $\beta_{g2}$, and $\beta_{g3}$? Is some other linear estimator, perhaps, more efficient than any of these? If so, what does such an estimator look like? And is there one that is *always* the most efficient? This section finds a path to a superior estimator by asking why $\beta_{g2}$ is more efficient than $\beta_{g1}$ when the $X$'s are all of the same sign.

## Why Is $\beta_{g2}$ More Efficient Than $\beta_{g1}$?

To discover what a more efficient estimator might look like, let's consider why $\beta_{g2}$ was more efficient than $\beta_{g1}$ in Chapter 2's models. In calculating an estimate, $\beta_{g2}$ weights every $Y_i$ the same. Each $Y_i$ receives the weight $(1/[\sum X_i])$. In contrast, $\beta_{g1}$ (for which the weights are $[1/(nX_i)]$) weights $Y_i$ associated with smaller $X_i$ more than observations associated with larger $X_i$. This difference between $\beta_{g1}$ and $\beta_{g2}$, coupled with the DGP that we assume, implies that $\beta_{g2}$ will be more efficient.

To see why $\beta_{g2}$'s constant weights are preferable to $\beta_{g1}$'s, which weight observations with small $X$-values more heavily, look at Figure 3.1, in which identical $\varepsilon_i$ are assumed at three different $X_i$. (The DGP assumes that the distributions of the $\varepsilon_i$ are identical across the $X_i$'s. Consequently, disturbances of the size shown are equally likely at $X_1$, $X_2$, and $X_3$.) The line $Y = \beta X_i$, which represents $E(Y/X_i)$ in the population, is the solid line in Figure 3.1. Suppose we could choose a single observation, at $X_1$, $X_2$, or $X_3$. At which $X_i$ does this particular disturbance lead us to the largest error in estimating $\beta$?

Notice that with any single observation, $\beta_{g1}$ and $\beta_{g2}$ yield identical estimates. The estimates we would make with either estimator using just one single observation are the dotted lines in Figure 3.1. The largest error in estimating $\beta$ is with $X_1$, and the smallest is with $X_3$. *A given disturbance is more misleading about the slope of the line when the observation has a smaller X than when it has a larger X.* Figure 3.1 makes clear that for our DGP, $Y_i$ associated with smaller $X_i$ are less informative about $\beta$ than $Y_i$ associated with larger $X_i$. Precisely because it gives greater weight to $Y_i$ associated with smaller $X_i$, $\beta_{g1}$ is less efficient than $\beta_{g2}$ when all the $X$'s are of the same sign.

**Figure 3.1**

Effects of a Disturbance for Small and Large $X$

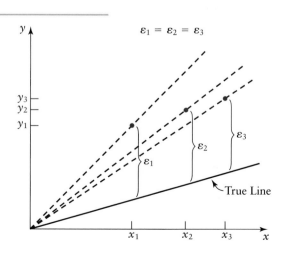

Figure 3.1 shows that more heavily weighting observations with smaller $X$-values is inefficient. The figure further shows that observations with *larger* $X$-values are more informative about $\beta$ than those with smaller $X$-values. Observations with larger $X$-values should therefore receive more weight than those with smaller $X$-values. Weighting all observations equally, as $\beta_{g2}$ does, is not most efficient. How might we more heavily weight $Y_i$ associated with larger $X_i$ to more efficiently estimate $\beta$? By more heavily weighting observations with large $X$'s. But how can we do that?

## What Estimator Might Be More Efficient Than $\beta_{g2}$?

Examining how we mechanically calculate $\beta_{g1}$ points us in the right direction for finding an estimator more efficient than $\beta_{g2}$. The underlying relationship is

$$Y_i = X_i\beta + \varepsilon_i \qquad i = 1, \ldots, n.$$

For $\beta_{g1}$, we first divide both sides of this relationship by $X_i$ for every observation:

$$\frac{Y_i}{X_i} = \frac{\beta X_i + \varepsilon_i}{X_i} \quad i = 1, \ldots, n,$$

and then divide both sides by $n$. We thereby weight each $Y_i$ by $1/(nX_i)$. We then sum these relationships across all the observations:

$$\sum \left(\frac{Y_i}{nX_i}\right) = \beta + \sum \left(\frac{\varepsilon_i}{nX_i}\right).$$

The last term on the right of this expression is the error in our estimate. Because $\beta_{g1}$ is unbiased, the mean of these errors is zero. Because these errors differ from $\beta_{g1}$ only by the constant, $\beta$, their variance is the same as that of $\beta_{g1}$, which, according to Equation 3.2, is $[\sigma^2/n^2]\sum(1/X_i^2)$.

What if, instead of weighting each observation by $(1/X_i)$, we were to weight each observation by $X_i$, so that observations with larger $X$'s are weighted more heavily? Doing so gives us

$$X_iY_i = X_i^2\beta + X_i\varepsilon_i.$$

If we sum both sides across all observations, we obtain

$$\sum(X_iY_i) = \beta\sum(X_i^2) + \sum(X_i\varepsilon_i).$$

To reduce the right-hand side to $\beta$ plus something, we need to divide through by $\sum X_i^2$, which yields a new estimator we call $\beta_{g4}$:

$$\beta_{g4} = \frac{\sum X_iY_i}{\sum X_i^2} = \beta + \frac{\sum X_i\varepsilon_i}{\sum X_i^2}.$$

Notice that

$$\beta_{g4} = \frac{\sum\limits_{i=1}^{n} X_i Y_i}{\sum\limits_{j=1}^{n} X_j^2} = \sum\limits_{i=1}^{n} \left( \frac{X_i}{\sum\limits_{j=1}^{n} X_j^2} \right) Y_i.$$

(Both the $j$'s and the $i$'s take on values $1, \ldots, n$, as needed. The switch from subscript $i$ to subscript $j$ involves no change of meaning but makes it easier to keep track of changes as we execute one summation sign or the other.) Consequently, $\beta_{g4}$ is a linear estimator in which the weights are

$$w_{4i} = \frac{X_i}{\sum X_j^2} \qquad i = 1, \ldots, n.$$

This new linear estimator, $\beta_{g4}$, more heavily weights $Y_i$ associated with larger $X_i$, per Figure 3.1.

If we apply $\beta_{g4}$ to the sample of New York renters examined in Chapter 2, we find $\beta_{g4} = 0.17$ (compared to the estimates 0.29, 0.22, and 0.28 for $\beta_{g1}$, $\beta_{g2}$, and $\beta_{g3}$).

(The New York renter data is in the file rents.*** on this book's companion Web site, **www.aw-bc.com/murray**.) Notice that $\beta_{g4}$ yields a markedly different estimate of the share of income devoted to housing than we obtain from our other linear estimators. Is $\beta_{g4}$ also an unbiased estimator? If so, its difference from the other estimators in this sample gives us good reason to determine which of the estimators is the most reliable (the least likely to be far wrong), that is, the most efficient.

## Is $\beta_{g4}$ Unbiased?

Is $\beta_{g4}$ unbiased? Yes. For our DGP, a linear estimator of the slope of a line that passes through the origin is unbiased if

$$\sum_{i=1}^{n} w_i X_i = 1.$$

To see that the weights for $\beta_{g4}$ satisfy this condition, recall that the weights for $\beta_{g4}$ are

$$w_{4i} = \frac{X_i}{\sum\limits_{j=1}^{n} X_j^2}.$$

In this case,

$$\sum_{i=1}^{n}(w_{4i}X_i) = \sum_{i=1}^{n}\left(\left[X_i/\sum_{j=1}^{n}X_j^2\right]X_i\right) = \sum_{i=1}^{n}\left[X_i^2/\sum_{j=1}^{n}X_j^2\right]$$

$$= \left[\sum_{i=1}^{n}X_i^2\right]/\left[\sum_{j=1}^{n}X_j^2\right] = 1.$$

The last step follows from what precedes because $\sum_{i=1}^{n}X_i^2 = X_1^2 + \cdots + X_n^2 = \sum_{j=1}^{n}X_j^2$—the subscripts $i$ and $j$ are substitutable because they perform the same notational duty. Thus, $\beta_{g4}$ is an unbiased estimator of $\beta$ for our DGP.

We have proved the unbiasedness of $\beta_{g1}$, $\beta_{g2}$, and $\beta_{g4}$ by appealing to the requirement that $\sum w_i X_i = 1$ for a linear estimator to unbiasedly estimate $\beta$ in our DGP. Sometimes unbiasedness is more insightfully proved by examining an estimator directly than by examining the estimator's weights. It is, therefore, helpful to study a second proof that $\beta_{g4}$ is an unbiased estimator of $\beta$.

The expression

$$\frac{\sum X_i Y_i}{\sum X_i^2} = \beta + \frac{\sum X_i \varepsilon_i}{\sum X_i^2}$$

suggests an alternative route to proving that $\beta_{g4}$ is an unbiased estimator of the slope in our DGP. Showing that $E\left(\sum(X_i\varepsilon_i)/\sum(X_i^2)\right)$ equals zero proves the unbiasedness of $\beta_{g4}$. The first step in this proof is to note that

$$E\left(\sum(X_i\varepsilon_i)/\sum(X_i^2)\right) = E\left[\sum X_i\varepsilon_i\right]/\sum(X_i^2)$$

because the sum of the squared $X$'s is a constant across samples. Next note that

$$E\left[\sum X_i\varepsilon_i\right]/\sum(X_i^2) = \left[\sum E(X_i\varepsilon_i)\right]/\sum(X_i^2)$$

and

$$\left[\sum E(X_i\varepsilon_i)\right]/\sum(X_i^2) = \left[\sum(X_i E(\varepsilon_i))\right]/\sum(X_i^2) = 0.$$

Thus, once again, we conclude that, like $\beta_{g1}$ and $\beta_{g2}$, $\beta_{g4}$ is unbiased.

## The Variance of $\beta_{g4}$

Figure 3.1 suggests that more heavily weighting observations with large $X$-values leads to a more efficient estimator of $\beta$ than $\beta_{g2}$ or $\beta_{g1}$. What, then, is the variance of $\beta_{g4}$? The formula for the variance of a linear estimator is

$$var\left(\sum w_i Y_i\right) = \sigma^2 \sum w_i^2.$$

The weights for $\beta_{g4}$ are

$$w_{4i} = \frac{X_i}{\sum\limits_{j=1}^{n} X_j^2} \qquad i = 1, \ldots, n.$$

Consequently, the variance of $\beta_{g4}$ is

$$\sigma^2 \sum_{i=1}^{n} \left( \frac{X_i}{\sum\limits_{j=1}^{n} X_j^2} \right)^2 = \sigma^2 \frac{\sum\limits_{i=1}^{n} X_i^2}{\left( \sum\limits_{j=1}^{n} X_j^2 \right)^2} = \frac{\sigma^2}{\sum\limits_{j=1}^{n} X_j^2}. \qquad 3.4$$

Once again, the last step follows from what precedes because

$$\sum_{i=1}^{n} X_i^2 = X_1^2 + \cdots + X_n^2 = \sum_{j=1}^{n} X_j^2;$$

the subscripts $i$ and $j$ are substitutable because they perform the same notational duty.

Looking at an alternative route to this variance expression for $\beta_{g4}$ prepares us for later derivations of the variances of other estimators. Because

$$\beta_{g4} = \beta + \frac{\sum X_i \varepsilon_i}{\sum X_i^2},$$

in which $\beta$ is a constant, the variance of $\beta_{g4}$ equals that of $\left( \sum (X_i \varepsilon_i) / \sum (X_i^2) \right)$. Thus the variance of $\beta_{g4}$ is

$$\text{var}\left( \sum (X_i \varepsilon_i) / \sum (X_i^2) \right) = \text{var}\left[ \sum X_i \varepsilon_i \right] / \left( \sum X_i^2 \right)^2$$

$$= \frac{\left[ \sum\limits_{i=1}^{n} \text{var}(X_i \varepsilon_i) + \sum\limits_{i=1}^{n} \sum\limits_{\substack{j=1 \\ j \neq i}}^{n} \text{cov}(X_i \varepsilon_i, X_j \varepsilon_j) \right]}{\left( \sum X_i^2 \right)^2}$$

$$= \frac{\left[ \sum\limits_{i=1}^{n} \text{var}(X_i \varepsilon_i) + \sum\limits_{i=1}^{n} \sum\limits_{\substack{j=1 \\ j \neq i}}^{n} X_i X_j \text{cov}(\varepsilon_i, \varepsilon_j) \right]}{\left( \sum X_i^2 \right)^2}$$

$$= \left[ \sum \text{var}(X_i \varepsilon_i) \right] / \left( \sum X_i^2 \right)^2.$$

All the covariance terms disappear because the $\varepsilon_i$ are uncorrelated. Continuing,

$$
\begin{aligned}
\left[ \sum \text{var}(X_i \varepsilon_i) \right] / \left( \sum X_i^2 \right)^2 &= \left[ \sum X_i^2 \, \text{var}(\varepsilon_i) \right] / \left( \sum X_i^2 \right)^2 \\
&= \left[ \sum X_i^2 \sigma^2 \right] / \left( \sum X_i^2 \right)^2 \\
&= \sigma^2 \left[ \sum X_i^2 \right] / \left( \sum X_i^2 \right)^2 \\
&= \sigma^2 / \sum X_i^2.
\end{aligned}
$$

The variance of $\beta_{g4}$ is less than the variance of $\beta_{g2}$. (For our New York renters, $\beta_{g4}$'s variance is about 20% less than that of $\beta_{g2}$.)

### Is There a Linear Estimator More Efficient Than $\beta_{g4}$?

Does $\beta_{g4}$ weight $Y_i$ associated with larger $X_i$ heavily enough or too heavily? Is there a linear estimator more efficient than $\beta_{g4}$? Consider another linear estimator, $\beta_{g5}$, that more heavily weights $Y_i$'s associated with larger $X_i$'s, and does so even more dramatically than $\beta_{g4}$.

$$
\beta_{g5} = \frac{\sum X_i^2 Y_i}{\sum X_i^3}.
$$

For the sample of New York renters we have been examining, $\beta_{g5} = 0.15$. Is $\beta_{g5}$ more or less efficient than $\beta_{g4}$? Rather than comparing the variances of the linear estimators $\beta_{g4}$ and $\beta_{g5}$, viewed in isolation from other estimators, the next section asks and answers a more general question: "What is the most efficient linear unbiased estimator of the slope in our DGP?" With guesses for the exponent of housing in a Cobb–Douglas utility function ranging from 0.15 to 0.29 for the five unbiased linear estimators we have uncovered, we might well want to know which of the guesses is best—claiming households spend 15 cents of each additional dollar of income on housing is quite different than saying those households spend 29 cents of each additional dollar on housing.

## 3.5    A First Gauss–Markov Theorem

How Do We Create an Estimator?

The class of linear estimators contains many intuitively plausible estimators. In Chapter 2, we examined three such estimators using Monte Carlo techniques and found that $\beta_{g2}$ is more efficient than $\beta_{g1}$ or $\beta_{g3}$ for the specifications we looked at. This chapter has introduced a fourth estimator, $\beta_{g4}$, designed to be more efficient than $\beta_{g2}$. But might there be an unbiased linear estimator with even smaller variance than $\beta_{g4}$?

The **best linear unbiased estimator** (BLUE) of $\beta$ is the unbiased linear estimator of $\beta$ that has the smallest variance. Is $\beta_{g4}$ the best linear unbiased estimator

(BLUE) of the slope of a line in our DGP? It is, indeed. This is the simplest version of a deep result that econometricians call the Gauss–Markov Theorem.

## The Gauss–Markov Assumptions

The **Gauss–Markov Theorem** states that $\beta_{g4}$ is the BLUE estimator of a straight line through the origin when the stochastic structure of the DGP satisfies the **Gauss–Markov Assumptions**, namely:

$$E(\varepsilon_i) = 0 \qquad i = 1, \ldots, n$$

$$\text{var}(\varepsilon_i) = \sigma^2 \qquad i = 1, \ldots, n$$

$$\text{cov}(\varepsilon_i, \varepsilon_j) = 0 \qquad i \neq j$$

Each $X_i$ is fixed across samples.

Notice that because the $Y$'s differ from the $\varepsilon$'s by only a constant, these assumptions imply that $\text{var}(Y_i) = \sigma^2$ and $\text{cov}(Y_i, Y_j) = 0$, for $i \neq j$. Finding a BLUE estimator amounts to finding a best set of weights for an unbiased linear estimator.

## Finding the Best Weights

Two traits characterize the "best" weights. First, such weights make the estimator unbiased. For the estimator to be unbiased, it must be true that

$$\sum_{i=1}^{n} w_i X_i = 1.$$

Second, the weights must make the estimator efficient among linear estimators; that is, the weights must yield the estimator with the smallest variance among unbiased linear estimators. Recall, for our DGP, that the variance of any linear estimator is $\sigma^2 \sum w_i^2$. Thus, if the weights of $\beta_{g4}$ solve the following constrained minimization problem[5], then $\beta_{g4}$ is the BLUE estimator of $\beta$ for our DGP:

$$\text{minimize} \qquad \nu = \sigma^2 \sum w_i^2$$

with respect to $w_1, \ldots, w_n$, subject to the restriction that

$$\sum_{i=1}^{n} w_i X_i = 1.$$

Appendix 3.A solves this constrained minimization problem twice. First it solves the problem when there are just two observations. This solution requires only maximizing a function of one variable, which involves standard calculus. The appendix shows that when $n = 2$, the variance of a linear unbiased estimator is minimized by the weights

$$w_1 = \frac{X_1}{\left(X_1^2 + X_2^2\right)}$$

and

$$w_2 = \frac{X_2}{\left(X_1^2 + X_2^2\right)}.$$

Thus, $\beta_{g4}$ is the BLUE estimator of $\beta$ for our DGP when $n = 2$.

When there are $n$ observations, the solution of the constrained minimization problem requires a more sophisticated calculus procedure. Appendix 3.A applies the method of Lagrange multipliers to show that when $n > 2$, the optimal weights are still those of $\beta_{g4}$. The appendix shows that the BLUE estimator under the Gauss–Markov Assumptions has weights

$$w_i = \frac{X_i}{\sum\left(X_i^2\right)},$$

for $i = 1, \ldots, n$. $\beta_{g4}$ *is the BLUE estimator, given the Gauss–Markov Assumptions.*

One special case of the present DGP is that in which $X$ can take on only a single value, 1. This is the case of a simple random sample drawn from a population with a mean equal to $\beta$. If $X_1 = X_2 = \cdots = X_n = 1$, every observation has the same mean, $\beta$. In this case, the weights for $\beta_{g4}$ reduce to

$$X_i/\sum\left(X_i^2\right) = 1/\sum\left(1^2\right) = 1/\sum(1) = \left(1/n\right).$$

Thus, in this special case, $\beta_{g4}$ is the sample mean! Consequently, our derivation of the BLUE estimator for the slope of a line through the origin leads us to a striking conclusion. *The sample mean is the BLUE estimator of the population mean in a simple random sample.*

Returning briefly to our New York renters, if we believe that the Cobb–Douglas utility function reflects consumers' preferences (so expected rent is related to income by a straight line through the origin) and believe that the Gauss–Markov Assumptions accurately reflect where our New York data come from, then our best linear unbiased estimate of the exponent of housing in the Cobb–Douglas production function is 0.17, the estimate based on $\beta_{g4}$. We would guess consumers tend to spend 17 cents of each additional dollar of income on housing.

The Gauss–Markov Theorem tells us that $\beta_{g4}$ is the BLUE estimator of the slope of a line through the origin. Are the intuitive estimators of Chapter 2 useless, then? No. In fact, if we were to replace the Gauss–Markov Assumption that the disturbances all have the same variance with an assumption that the variances were proportional to the $X_i^2$ or to the $X_i$, we would discover that $\beta_{g1}$ and $\beta_{g2}$, respectively, would be the BLUE estimators of $\beta$. Our intuitive estimators reappear in Chapter 10, where we deal with disturbances that have unequal variances.

## 3.6 Replacing Fixed $X$'s with Stochastic $X$'s

**WHAT IS THE DGP?**

The assumption that the explanator values are the same from one sample to the next is unrealistic. Let's consider the empirical studies we've seen thus far in various Greatest Hits boxes. If Martin Feldstein had drawn a new sample of households with which to study financial aid, the new households would have had different incomes and different numbers of children than the households in the original sample. If Ernst Engel had studied the food expenditures of a different sample of Belgian households, the incomes of the new households would have been different from the incomes of the households in the original sample. Economists can almost never ensure that all samples would have the same $X$-values. Is $\beta_{g4}$ still the BLUE estimator of $\beta$ if we replace the Gauss–Markov Assumption that the $X$'s are fixed with an assumption that the $X$'s are random variables? This section shows that $\beta_{g4}$ remains the BLUE estimator of $\beta$ if the $X$'s are a particular, often-encountered sort of random variable.

### Extending the Reach of the Gauss–Markov Assumptions

The Gauss–Markov Assumptions say that the disturbances are homoskedastic and serially uncorrelated, and have a mean of zero, and that the observed $X$-values are the same in every sample. If the $X$-values, instead, change randomly from sample to sample, the Gauss–Markov depiction of the disturbances is incomplete because it does not tell us about the joint distribution of the $X$'s and the disturbances together. To overcome this limitation, let's replace the assumption that the $X$'s are fixed with an assumption that the $X$'s are random, but that for each and every combination of the $X$-values the disturbances remain mean zero, heteroskedastic, serially uncorrelated random variables. This new assumption says that the Gauss–Markov Assumptions hold *conditionally* for any values of $X_1, \ldots, X_n$. We can rewrite this new DGP as

$$
\begin{array}{ll}
Y_i = \beta X_i + \varepsilon_i & i = 1, \ldots, n \\
\mathrm{E}(\varepsilon_i | X_1, \ldots, X_n) = 0 & i = 1, \ldots, n \\
\mathrm{var}(\varepsilon_i | X_1, \ldots, X_n) = \sigma^2 & i = 1, \ldots, n \\
\mathrm{cov}(\varepsilon_i, \varepsilon_j | X_1, \ldots, X_n) = 0 & i \neq j
\end{array}
$$

**3.5**

In this DGP, the $X$'s change from sample to sample, but our expectation for each $\varepsilon_i$ remains the same, no matter what $X$-values appear in a given sample. We continue to expect each disturbance to be zero, to have a mean of zero, a variance of $\sigma^2$, and a zero covariance with each other disturbance.

One implication of this DGP is that each disturbance has a zero covariance with any observation on the explanator—each disturbance is uncorrelated with every observation on $X$; $\text{cov}(\varepsilon_i, X_j) = 0$ for every $i$ and $j$. Many real-world DGPs are accurately depicted by Equations 3.5. In particular, if the disturbances are mean zero, homoskedastic, and serially uncorrelated *in the population* (that is, *across* all possible combinations of the $X$'s), then the new DGP would apply if each $\varepsilon_i$ were statistically independent of $X_1$ through $X_n$, that is, if *each* disturbance were statistically independent of *all* of the observations on $X$.

Conditioning on a specific set of $X$-values, as in Equations 3.5, treats those $X$-values as if they were fixed across samples—it looks only at samples in which the observations on $X$ take on those specific values. Mathematically, this returns us to the case we have been examining thus far, but now all the mathematical results must be interpreted as *conditional on the values of X*.

## The Conditional and Population Properties of $\beta_{g4}$

This chapter has found that when the $X$'s are fixed across samples,

$$E(\beta_{g4}) = \beta$$

and

$$\text{var}(\beta_{g4}) = \sigma^2 / \sum X_i^2.$$

When the $X$'s are random variables across samples and the new extended DGP given by Equations 3.5 applies, these findings become *conditional* findings:

$$E(\beta_{g4} | X) = \beta$$

and

$$\text{var}(\beta_{g4} | X) = \sigma^2 / \sum X_i^2.$$

Thus, the estimator $\beta_{g4}$ is unbiased, given the observed $X$-values, and the variance of $\beta_{g4}$ is $\sigma^2 / \sum X_i^2$, given the observed $X$-values. Furthermore, $\beta_{g4}$ also remains the BLUE estimator for the new DGP, conditional on the $X$-values.

We can infer from these conditional findings what is true about $\beta_{g4}$ in the population as a whole. The **Law of Iterated Expectations** states that for any $Z$ and $X$,

$$E[E(Z | X)] = E(Z).$$

(For example, suppose we observe the mean incomes for Asians, blacks, and whites in a population made up only of those three groups. The Law of Iterated Expectations says that taking the weighted mean of those three group mean incomes, where the weights are the relative frequencies of the races in the population, yields the mean income we would obtain had we averaged across all the individuals in the population.)

Consequently,

$$E(\beta_{g4}) = E[E(\beta_{g4}|X)] = E(\beta) = \beta$$

and

$$var(\beta_{g4}) = \sigma^2 E\left(\frac{1}{\sum X_i^2}\right). \qquad \textbf{3.6}$$

The population variance result in Equation 3.6 follows because $E(\beta_{g4}) = E(\beta_{g4}|X) = \beta$, so that

$$var(\beta_{g4}) = E([\beta_{g4} - \beta)]^2) = E[E([\beta_{g4} - \beta)]^2|X)]$$

$$= E(var(\beta_{g4}|X)) = E(\sigma^2/\sum X_i^2) = \sigma^2 E\left(\frac{1}{\sum X_i^2}\right).$$

Because $\beta_{g4}$ remains the BLUE estimator for the new DGP, conditional on the *X*-values, $\beta_{g4}$ is BLUE in the population of all samples, as well, because no linear estimator has a smaller variance than $\beta_{g4}$ for any set of *X*-values.

Although we can infer the population traits of $\beta_{g4}$ in this new extended version of the Gauss–Markov DGP, the conditional traits matter most to econometricians. If our sample has a small sum of squared *X*'s, it is no comfort to us that across all sets of *X*-values, the variance of $\beta_{g4}$ is small. We are stuck with an observation from a subset of samples in which $\beta_{g4}$ estimates $\beta$ imprecisely, so we must be skeptical of our estimate. Similarly, if we obtain a sample with a fortunately large sum of squared *X*'s, there is only a small probability that our guess is far from the true $\beta$; it doesn't much matter whether across all samples $\beta_{g4}$ imprecisely estimates $\beta$.

The population traits do matter, however, when we are planning to draw a sample for study. The conditional variance of $\beta_{g4}$ tells us that our prospects for precise estimation depend on how likely we are to draw a sample with a large sum of squared *X*'s. If the mean and variance of the *X*'s across all possible samples are both small, we are unlikely to draw an informative sample.

Why assume fixed *X*'s? We do so to make the mathematical analysis less cluttered. Treating the *X*-values as fixed across samples avoids the conditioning notation found in Equations 3.5. However, here we have seen that the results we obtain in the fixed $X$ DGP can be validly and more realistically interpreted as applying conditionally on the observed $X$'s in a DGP like that given by Equations 3.5.

## 3.7    Application: A U.S. Production Function

An analysis of American technology in the 20th century illustrates the advantages of using $\beta_{g4}$ rather than $\beta_{g1}$, $\beta_{g2}$, or $\beta_{g3}$. In 1928, Charles Cobb of Amherst College and Paul Douglas of the University of Chicago (and later a U.S. Senator) published their classic article, "A Theory of Production,"[6] in which they estimated a production function for American manufacturing. They specified the production function to be of the form

$$Q = \alpha L^{\beta} K^{(1-\beta)},$$

where $\alpha$ and $\beta$ are parameters, $Q$ is output, $L$ is labor input, and $K$ is the capital stock used. This specification is called a **Cobb–Douglas production function**.

If firms pay workers and capital their marginal products in an economy with a Cobb–Douglas production function, compensation to workers will be a constant fraction of the value of output, and that fraction will equal $\beta$; that is,

$$W = \beta V,$$

where $W$ is compensation (wages, salaries, and supplements to wages and salaries) and $V$ is the value of output, or total income. What fraction of the value of a firm's output is spent on labor? This section applies the Cobb–Douglas model to a simple random sample of eight years of 20th century U.S. workers' compensation and U.S. national income. The data are in Table 3.5. (A random number generator produced eight numbers between 00 and 95 to obtain the years for this random sample. The data on compensation and income are from those eight years. The sample size of eight is merely illustrative.)

### Estimating the Cobb–Douglas Production Function with $\beta_{g1}$, $\beta_{g2}$, $\beta_{g3}$, and $\beta_{g4}$

Table 3.6 presents estimates of $\beta$ using this data and each of our four estimators, $\beta_{g1}$, $\beta_{g2}$, $\beta_{g3}$, and $\beta_{g4}$. Table 3.6 also reports estimated standard errors for each of the four estimators. (Although econometricians develop their theory in terms of estimators' variances, as noted earlier, they more usually report estimators' standard deviations, calling them the estimators' "standard errors.") Unlike the example of New York renters, for whom $\beta_{g1}$, $\beta_{g2}$, $\beta_{g3}$, and $\beta_{g4}$ provided sharply different estimates of the share of income spent on housing by New York renters, the specific estimates of the share of workers in the Cobb–Douglas production model, $\beta$, reported in Table 3.6, do not differ much from each other. The lowest estimate

**TABLE 3.5** A Random Sample of Compensation and National Income (Measured in Billions of Dollars)

| Year | National Income | Compensation |
|------|-----------------|--------------|
| 1959 | 400.00 | 279.10 |
| 1932 | 42.80 | 31.10 |
| 1975 | 1215.00 | 931.10 |
| 1929 | 86.80 | 51.10 |
| 1933 | 40.30 | 29.50 |
| 1970 | 800.50 | 603.90 |
| 1993 | 5140.30 | 3772.20 |
| 1980 | 2121.40 | 1596.50 |

for $\beta$, 0.702, comes from $\beta_{g3}$; the highest estimate, 0.741, comes from $\beta_{g2}$. All the estimates agree that labor receives a little under three quarters of the value of firms' output in compensation.

In contrast to the similarity of the estimates of labor's share obtained from $\beta_{g1}$, $\beta_{g2}$, $\beta_{g3}$ and $\beta_{g4}$, the estimated standard errors for the three estimators vary dramatically. Recall that the standard error measures how spread out the estimator's guesses are across samples. The estimated standard error of $\beta_{g3}$ is 0.364; if $\beta_{g3}$ were normally distributed (as it probably is, at least approximately), then the central two thirds of $\beta_{g3}$'s distribution would span a range 0.72 wide! If the true value of $\beta$ were 0.50, then in one third of samples, $\beta_{g3}$ would yield guesses bigger than 0.86 or smaller than 0.14.[7] The estimator $\beta_{g3}$ is very imprecise and tells us little about $\beta$. Nearly as uninformative is $\beta_{g1}$, with an estimated standard error of 0.21. In marked contrast, both $\beta_{g2}$ and $\beta_{g4}$ find quite precise information about $\beta$ in these data; their estimated standard errors are 0.006 and 0.004, respectively. In

**TABLE 3.6** Estimates of the Cobb–Douglas Parameter $\beta$, with Standard Errors

| Estimator: | $\beta_{g1}$ | $\beta_{g2}$ | $\beta_{g3}$ | $\beta_{g4}$ |
|------------|--------------|--------------|--------------|--------------|
| Estimate: | 0.719 | 0.741 | 0.702 | 0.738 |
| Estimated Standard Error: | 0.210 | 0.006 | 0.364 | 0.004 |

95% of samples, $\beta_{g2}$ and $\beta_{g4}$ yield estimates within 0.012 and 0.008 of $\beta$, respectively. Keep in mind that these probability assessments depend on ours being the right DGP for these data. If we specify the DGP incorrectly, our claims about the estimators are unwarranted.

By choosing $\beta_{g2}$ or $\beta_{g4}$, instead of $\beta_{g3}$ or $\beta_{g1}$, we find in even this small random sample of eight observations precise information about $\beta$. But if we choose $\beta_{g1}$ or $\beta_{g3}$, instead of $\beta_{g2}$ and $\beta_{g4}$, the estimators are imprecise. Although in this particular sample the four estimators give similar estimates, across other samples, $\beta_{g1}$ or $\beta_{g3}$ would yield far more varied estimates than would $\beta_{g2}$ or $\beta_{g4}$. This example shows that a sample of data that looks uninformative using an inefficient estimator may prove surprisingly rich when we use an efficient estimator.

## Is Ours the Correct DGP for These U.S. Data?

Our assessments of $\beta_{g1}$, $\beta_{g2}$, $\beta_{g3}$, and $\beta_{g4}$ rely on the assumption that ours is the right DGP for these data. Five questions are pertinent to the match between our choice of DGP and the actual origins of our data: (i) From what population are the data drawn? (ii) Are the disturbances likely to be mutually independent? (iii) Are all the disturbances likely to have the same variance? (iv) Are the $X$'s truly fixed in repeated samples? (v) Is the production function really of the Cobb–Douglas form?

*From what population are the data drawn?* The population contains all the years in the 20th century; the variables studied are compensation and national income in each year.

*Are the disturbances likely to be mutually independent?* Data drawn from different time periods, called time series data, often have correlated disturbances because econometricians usually draw observations adjacent in time. In the present study, however, the years are randomly drawn; the year chosen for one observation does not affect which year is chosen next. Time series are not usually drawn in this random fashion, but when they are, the observations are independent of one another and are therefore uncorrelated, as in any simple random sample.

*Are all the disturbances likely to have the same variance?* No. Compensation is likely to vary more in eras when national income is large than when national income is small. Consequently, observations with large national income are likely to have disturbances with larger variance.

*Are the $X$'s truly fixed in repeated samples?* No. Because the years are chosen in a simple random fashion, we would get different values for national income in our first observation as our first observation changes from one sample to the next, and similarly for all the subsequent observations. Thus, the $X$'s vary across samples in this DGP.

*Is the production function really of the Cobb–Douglas form?* Almost surely not. The Cobb–Douglas form is very restrictive and is always viewed as, at best, an approximation to the true underlying production relationship. The Cobb–

Douglas is often a very useful approximation and many econometric analyses rely on it.

The fact that our actual DGP does not match up with the Gauss–Markov Assumptions casts some doubt on the validity of the estimates reported in Tables 3.5 and 3.6, though the substantive point—that plausible estimators can vary widely in their efficiency—is nonetheless correct. In later chapters, we study how best to estimate the slopes of lines when the Gauss–Markov Assumptions do not apply. As we learn more about a variety of DGPs, we return to this Cobb–Douglas problem for a more sophisticated appraisal of this analysis.

The fact that our actual DGP does not match up with the Gauss–Markov Assumptions should not lead us to dismiss the results of our analysis out of hand. No model of complex real-world phenomena perfectly matches the real world. Indeed, one goal of model building is to abstract from many details of a real-world phenomenon so we can think carefully about essential aspects of that world. All our models will be flawed, which is all right. Models are to be used, not believed.

Students of econometrics need to learn to distinguish blemishes in econometric models from crippling inadequacies. Auto-club maps are gross simplifications of the actual countryside, but they get us from home to never-before-visited places quite effectively. On the other hand, those same maps are of much less use in planning a bicycle trip—they lack any indication of topography and could lead us merrily, but needlessly, up and down hills. During one term of study, students of econometrics learn how to read a wide variety of maps so they can use a suitable map when they conduct econometric analyses and can make reasonable judgments about when a particular map is "good enough."

## 3.8  Econometric Software Output

Because $\beta_{g4}$ is the BLUE estimator of the slope of a line through the origin under the Gauss–Markov Assumptions, econometric software packages calculate $\beta_{g4}$ as their standard response when asked to regress a dependent variable on a single explanator and no intercept term. Table 3.7 displays the output from the econometric software package EViews 4.1™ when we ask that package to regress compensation on national income, with no intercept term. Table 3.7 also displays the corresponding output from another econometric software package, Stata 8.2™. The two outputs are similar; most of the information provided in them is commonly found in output from other econometric software packages as well.

Both EViews and Stata report the estimated slope coefficient, 0.738, for national income (named NI in both computer applications) from a regression of compensation on national income, based on $\beta_{g4}$, the same value reported in Table 3.6. Both also report the estimated standard error of $\beta_{g4}$ in this application: 0.0037077, which corresponds to the rounded-up 0.004 reported in Table 3.6.

**TABLE 3.7 Outputs from a Regression* of Compensation on National Income**

EViews 4.1™
Dependent Variable: Comp
Method: Least Squares
Sample: 1 8
Included observations: 8

| Variable | Coefficient | Std. Error | t-Statistic | Prob. |
|---|---|---|---|---|
| NI | 0.738018 | 0.003708 | 199.0479 | 0.0000 |
| R-squared | 0.999721 | Mean dependent var | | 911.8125 |
| Adjusted R-squared | 0.999721 | S.D. dependent var | | 1278.452 |
| S.E. of regression | 21.36736 | Akaike info criterion | | 9.078074 |
| Sum squared resid | 3195.947 | Schwarz criterion | | 9.088004 |
| Log likelihood | -35.31230 | Durbin–Watson stat | | 2.495375 |

* The data are from Table 3.5.

**Stata 8.2**

| Source | SS | df | MS | | |
|---|---|---|---|---|---|
| Model | 18089096.7 | 1 | 18089096.7 | Number of obs = | 8 |
| Residual | 3195.9466 | 7 | 456.5638 | F(1, 7)    = | 39620.09 |
| | | | | Prob > F    = | 0.0000 |
| Total | 18092292.6 | 8 | 2261536.58 | R-squared    = | 0.9998 |
| | | | | Adj R-squared = | 0.9998 |
| | | | | Root MSE    = | 21.367 |

| comp | Coef. | Std. Err. | t | P > \|t\| | [95% Conf. Interval] | |
|---|---|---|---|---|---|---|
| NI | .7380185 | .0037077 | 199.048 | 0.000 | .7292511 | .7467859 |

* The data are from Table 3.5.

(As is common in econometric packages, the output does not explicitly state that the reported standard errors are estimates, but they are.) Both outputs also note that the number of observations is eight. EViews is explicit that the dependent variable is *"comp,"* which is the name given compensation in both computer applications; Stata indicates that *comp* is the dependent variable by listing it in the same row as "Coef.," etc. EViews names the estimation method "Least Squares,"

### An Organizational Structure for the Study of Econometrics

**1. What Is the DGP?**

We specified the data-generating process (DGP):

$$Y_i = \beta X_i + \varepsilon_i \qquad i = 1, \ldots, n$$
$$E(\varepsilon_i) = 0 \qquad i = 1, \ldots, n$$
$$\text{var}(\varepsilon_i) = \sigma^2 \qquad i = 1, \ldots, n$$
$$\text{cov}(\varepsilon_i, \varepsilon_j) = 0 \qquad i \neq j$$

Each $X_i$ is fixed across samples.

**2. What Makes a Good Estimator?**

We focused on unbiasedness and efficiency.

**3. How Do We Create an Estimator?**

BLUE estimation led to $\beta_{g4}$ for the DGP in Question 1.

**4. What Are an Estimator's Properties?**

The algebra of expectations revealed that $\beta_{g1}$, $\beta_{g2}$, $\beta_{g3}$, and $\beta_{g4}$ are all unbiased in the DGP in Question 1 because $\sum_{i=1}^{n} w_i X_i = 1$ for each.

The algebra of variances revealed that the variance of any linear estimator is $\sigma^2 \sum w_i^2$ in the DGP in Question 1.

which is a common name for $\beta_{g4}$. As we expand our knowledge of econometrics, we will understand other items in these outputs.

## Summary

The chapter began by using a typical strategy of econometricians for finding good estimators. Though we restricted attention to the simple case of estimating the slope of a line through the origin, we encountered all the ingredients of more general estimation problems. We began with a set of appealing alternative estimators, settled on what we thought to be an appropriate DGP, and asked which candidate estimator had the best statistical properties.

At the outset of the chapter, we discovered that our three natural estimators for the slope of a line through the origin could all be written in the linear form $g = \sum w_i Y_i$. Estimators of this form we call linear estimators. Econometricians almost always first consider linear estimators for study, which is not surprising, given their simplicity and the number of naturally appealing estimators that fall into this class.

We then saw that for the chapter's DGP, with its Gauss–Markov Assumptions, linear estimators estimate $\beta$ unbiasedly if, and only if, their weights have the property $\sum w_i X_i = 1$. Strikingly, all of our initial intuitive estimators, $\beta_{g1}$, $\beta_{g2}$, and $\beta_{g3}$, proved unbiased. Any linear estimator's variance is $\sigma^2 \sum w_i^2$ under the Gauss–Markov Assumptions. The resultant formulae for the variances of $\beta_{g1}$ and $\beta_{g2}$ revealed that if all the $X$'s are of the same sign, $\beta_{g2}$ is more efficient than $\beta_{g1}$.

Next, the chapter shifted to a second common strategy econometricians use to find attractive estimators, namely, solving mathematically for estimators with appealing properties in a given DGP. Being right on average and making small errors are such appealing properties that we naturally asked which unbiased linear estimator has the smallest variance, that is, which is the "best" linear unbiased, or BLUE, estimator of the slope of the line through the origin. Which linear estimator is BLUE depends critically on the chapter's DGP, with its Gauss–Markov Assumptions, but the basic strategy of the chapter works equally effectively for many other DGPs.

A final example highlighted the importance of choosing efficient estimators. For a sample of U.S. data, $\beta_{g3}$ provided virtually no useful information about the slope of a line, $\beta$, if the data spring from our assumed DGP. In dramatic contrast, applying $\beta_{g2}$ or $\beta_{g4}$ revealed that the sample contained precise information about $\beta$.

## Concepts for Review

Algebra of expectations    77

Algebra of variances    80

Best linear unbiased estimator (BLUE)    90

Cobb–Douglas production function    96

Gauss–Markov Assumptions    91

Gauss–Markov Theorem    91

Law of Iterated Expectations    94

Linear estimator    71

Standard error    84

## Questions for Discussion

1. The reliance on a DGP to decide which estimator to use leads us to make different estimates from the same data if those identical data sets happen to arise from different DGPs. If the data are $(X_1 = 4, Y_1 = 6)$ and $(X_2 = 7, Y_2 = 12)$, for example, why should the DGP matter when we use these data to guess $\beta$?

2. Suppose you and a classmate disagree about the mean income of students' parents at your school. Your best guess is that the mean income is $64,000. Your classmate's best guess is $85,000. In an effort to resolve your difference, you gather a simple random sample of incomes of 25 students at your school. The sample mean from this sample is $70,000. We've learned in this chapter that the sample mean is BLUE if one has a simple random sample. Should you and your classmate ignore your previous

difference of opinion and now agree that the best guess for you to make about the mean income of students at your school is $70,000? Do your prior views have any role in deciding on a new best guess?

3. Your professor asks each student in your class to draw a simple random sample of 15 years from the population of years spanning 1900–2004, and to estimate the relationship between consumption and GDP, using a regression model with no intercept term. The professor tells you the variance of the disturbances over this 105-year period. Suppose that your 15 observations are, by chance, concentrated in the period 1980–2004, and your roommates' observations are, by chance, largely from the early 20th century. When you apply Equation 3.4 to your data, you get a much smaller value for the variance of $\beta_{g4}$ than when your roommate applies that formula. Does the smaller variance you get indicate that your estimate is a better estimate than your roommate's?

# Problems for Analysis

> For the data sets that you will need to solve the problems in this section, go to **www.aw-bc.com/murray.**

1. Suppose you have three observations on X ($X_1 = 10$, $X_2 = 7$, $X_3 = 12$).
   a. What weights does $\beta_{g1}$ use to estimate the slope coefficient?
   b. What weights does $\beta_{g2}$ use to estimate the slope coefficient?
   c. Express $\beta_{g1}$ and $\beta_{g2}$ in terms of these weights and the three observations on Y ($Y_1$, $Y_2$, $Y_3$).

2. Which of the following are linear estimators?
   a. $(1/2)Y_1 + (1/3)Y_2 + Y_3$
   b. $(1/4)Y_1 Y_2 + (1/2)Y_3$
   c. $(X_1/X_2)Y_1 + Y_2 + (1/8)Y_3$

3. a. Demonstrate that $\sum_{i=1}^{n} w_i X_i = 1$ for $\beta_{g3}$.
   b. What does $\sum_{i=1}^{n} w_i X_i = 1$ imply about this linear estimator, given the DGP we use in this chapter?

4. Given the DGP we use in this chapter, demonstrate that the variance of $\beta_{g2}$ is

$$\mathrm{var}(\beta_{g2}) = \frac{\sigma^2 n}{\left[\sum X_i\right]^2}.$$

5. Suppose you have three observations on X ($X_1 = 10$, $X_2 = 7$, $X_3 = 12$). Calculate the ratio of the variance of $\beta_{g1}$ to the variance of $\beta_{g2}$, given the DGP we use in this chapter.

6. Examine Table 3.3.
   a. Why does $\beta_{g2}$ have such a small variance in Model 6?
   b. Why do all three estimators have small variances in Model 1?

7. Suppose your DGP satisfies our Gauss–Markov Assumptions.
   a. Show that the estimator $\beta_{g6} = \sum X_i^2 Y_i / \sum X_i^3$ is a linear estimator.
   b. Determine whether $\beta_{g6}$ is an unbiased estimator of $\beta$.
   c. Express the variance of $\beta_{g6}$ in terms of the weights that $\beta_{g6}$ applies to the $Y_i$'s. Call the variance of the disturbances $\sigma^2$.

8. For the DGP

$$Y_i = \beta X_i + u_i \qquad\qquad i = 1, 2$$
$$u_i \text{ distributed } N(0, \sigma^2) \qquad i = 1, 2$$
$$\text{cov}(u_1, u_2) = \psi,$$
$$X_1 \text{ and } X_2 \text{ fixed across samples.}$$

(Notice that this DGP applies to a sample with just two observations. Notice, too, that the covariance between disturbances is not 0, but $\psi$.)
   a. Derive the variance of a linear estimator, $g$, of $\beta$ in terms of its weights.
   b. What do we require of a linear estimator's weights if the linear estimator is to be an unbiased estimator of $\beta$?
   c. State the mathematical problem whose solution will yield weights' BLUE for this DGP.

9. Suppose that we encounter $n$ observations from a process that differs from our Gauss–Markov Assumptions in only one regard: $\text{var}(u_i) = \sigma^2 X_i^2$, instead of $\text{var}(u_i) = \sigma^2$.
   a. Determine what must be true of a linear estimator's weights if the estimator is to be an unbiased estimator of $\beta$ in this new DGP.
   b. Determine the variance of a linear estimator in this new DGP.
   c. For the case $n = 2$, use substitution and calculus to show that
      $\beta_{g1} = (1/n) \sum (Y_i / X_i)$ is the BLUE estimator of $\beta$ for this alternative DGP.

 10. The data set production.*** contains data on U.S. labor costs (*labor*), capital expenditures (*capital*), and the value of output *(output)* for a sample of years.
   a. Use $\beta_{g1}$, $\beta_{g2}$, $\beta_{g3}$, and $\beta_{g4}$ to estimate labor's share in output, using the model

$$labor\ cost = \beta_1(output) + u.$$

(The differences in labor costs from observation to observation are in the variable *dlabor*; the differences in capital are in *dcapital*; and the differences in output's value are in *doutput*.)
   b. If the Gauss–Markov Assumptions apply to these data, what is the ratio of the variance of $\beta_{g1}$ to the variance of $\beta_{g2}$?
   c. If the Gauss–Markov Assumptions apply to these data, what is the ratio of the variance of $\beta_{g2}$ to the variance of $\beta_{g4}$?
   d. If the Gauss–Markov Assumptions apply to these data, which of $\beta_{g1}$, $\beta_{g2}$, and $\beta_{g4}$ is most efficient? Least efficient?
   e. Use $\beta_{g1}$, $\beta_{g2}$, $\beta_{g3}$, and $\beta_{g4}$ to estimate capital's share in output, using the model

$$capital\ expenditures = \beta_2(output) + \varepsilon.$$

11. For many years, financial analysts measured a stock's riskiness by looking at the slope coefficient in

$$(\text{stock's rate of return} - \text{rate of return on a risk-free asset})$$
$$= \beta \ (\text{market rate of return} - \text{rate of return on a risk-free asset}) + v$$

or, equivalently, in

$$(\text{stock's excess return}) = \beta(\text{market's excess return}) + v.$$

This model is known as the Capital Asset Pricing Model (CAPM). According to this model, investors require a stock with greater non-diversifiable risk to offer a higher return to compensate for that risk. The stock's "beta," the slope $\beta$ in the regression of the firm's excess return on the market's excess return, measures the asset's contribution to an optimal portfolio's undiversifiable risk. In this sense, assets with smaller betas are less risky. The file CAPM1.*** contains excess returns for the market (*mreturn*) and excess returns for two firms in the computer chip business (*freturn*) for each of 192 months. The first 192 observations pertain to firm 1; the next 192 pertain to firm 2. The variable *firm* identifies firms 1 and 2.

a. Compute the means of firms' returns and of the markets' return for firms 1 and 2.

b. Use $\beta_{g1}$, $\beta_{g2}$, $\beta_{g3}$, and $\beta_{g4}$ to estimate a beta for each firm. (The differences in *freturn* from one observation to the next are contained in *dfreturn*; the differences in *mreturn* are contained in *dmreturn*.)

c. What is the ratio of the variance of $\beta_{g1}$ to the variance of $\beta_{g2}$?

d. What is the ratio of the variance of $\beta_{g2}$ to the variance of $\beta_{g4}$?

e. Do the estimators agree about which firm adds more risk to a diversified portfolio?

12. The relationship between votes cast on election day and votes cast by absentee ballot has recently been a celebrated topic. The file election1.*** contains the differences in votes between Democratic and Republican candidates in Pennsylvania State Senate races for election-day vote counts (*electionday* or *eday*) and for absentee vote counts (*absentee*) from 1982 to 1993.[8]

$$electionday = (\text{election-day votes for the Democratic candidates}$$
$$- \text{election day votes for the Republican candidates})$$

$$absentee = (\text{absentee votes for the Democratic candidates}$$
$$- \text{absentee votes for the Republican candidates})$$

On average, among election-day voters, Democratic Senate candidates received 39,007 more votes than their Republican opponents; absentee voters cast, on average 256 more votes for Democrats than for Republicans. One could argue that in any one election year, the Democratic edge in absentee votes should be proportional to its edge in election-day votes:

$$absentee = \beta(\text{electionday}) + v.$$

a. Estimate $\beta$ using $\beta_{g1}$, $\beta_{g2}$, $\beta_{g3}$, and $\beta_{g4}$. (The differences in *electionday* from observation to observation are contained in *delect*; the differences in *absentee* are contained in *dabsent*.)

b. If in a specific year, the Democratic candidates receive 10,000 more election-day votes than the Republican candidates, estimate how many more absentee voters will vote for Democrats than Republicans. Is the answer markedly different, depending upon which estimator we use?

c. What is the ratio of the variance of $\beta_{g1}$ to the variance of $\beta_{g2}$?

d. What is the ratio of the variance of $\beta_{g2}$ to the variance of $\beta_{g4}$?

e. What are some of the determinants of absentee ballot outcomes that are captured by the disturbance term?

 13. The file engelrye.\*\*\* contains data on the percentage change in the price of rye and the percentage change in the quantity of rye demanded for the years 1847–1861. These are the data Ernst Engel used in his 1861 Greatest Hit about the demand for rye.[9] The percentage changes in price and quantity are in variables named either *perchngpricerye* and *perchngquanrye*, or *chngprice* and *chngquan*, depending on the file used. The differences in the percent changes in the prices and quantities from one observation to the next are in the variables *dchp* and *dchq*, respectively. Engel's model was, implicitly,

$$percentage\ change\ in\ quantity\ demanded = \beta(percentage\ change\ in\ price)$$

a. Compute the mean percentage changes in prices and quantities in this sample.

b. Estimate $\beta$ using $\beta_{g1}$, $\beta_{g2}$, $\beta_{g3}$, and $\beta_{g4}$.

c. If the Gauss–Markov Assumptions apply to these data, what is the ratio of the variance of $\beta_{g1}$ to the variance of $\beta_{g2}$?

d. If the Gauss–Markov Assumptions apply to these data, what is the ratio of the variance of $\beta_{g2}$ to the variance of $\beta_{g4}$?

e. If the Gauss–Markov Assumptions apply to these data, which of $\beta_{g1}$, $\beta_{g2}$, and $\beta_{g4}$ is most efficient? Which least efficient?

f. Make up an example, grounded in the real world, that relies on the fact that these data are from 15 successive years to cast doubt on the assumption that the disturbances are statistically independent. Does this cast doubt upon the claim that our estimators, $\beta_{g1}$, $\beta_{g2}$, $\beta_{g3}$, and $\beta_{g4}$, are unbiased? Does it cast doubt on the claim that $\beta_{g4}$ is more efficient than the other three estimators?

g. Is it reasonable to think that the explanatory variable has values that are fixed in repeated samples in this instance? What implication does this have for the claim that $\beta_{g1}$, $\beta_{g2}$, $\beta_{g3}$, and $\beta_{g4}$ are unbiased and that $\beta_{g4}$ is BLUE?

 14. Trygve Haavelmo used the data from 1922 to 1941 in haavelmo.\*\*\* to estimate the marginal propensity to consume.[10] Haavelmo reported a marginal propensity to consume of 0.73 when he estimated a consumption function. The measure of consumption in this data set is *real_cons*; the measure of income is *real_gdp*. Milton Friedman later argued[11] that the consumption function passes through the origin, as in

$$consumption = \beta(income) + u,$$

where $\beta$ is the marginal propensity to consume.

a. Estimate the marginal propensity to consume using $\beta_{g2}$, which is the estimator Milton Friedman recommended.

b. Estimate the marginal propensity to consume using $\beta_{g1}$, $\beta_{g3}$, and $\beta_{g4}$. (The differences in consumption from one observation to the next are in the variable *dcons*; the differences in income are in the variable *dgdp*.)

c. In Keynesian macroeconomic theory, an independent change in government spending, $\Delta G$, increases income by $\Delta G/(1 - \beta)$. This is called "the multiplier effect," and "the multiplier" is $1/(1 - \beta)$. What is the range of estimated multipliers across your four estimates of the marginal propensity to consume?

d. If the Gauss–Markov Assumptions apply to these data, what is the ratio of the variance of $\beta_{g1}$ to the variance of $\beta_{g2}$?

e. If the Gauss–Markov Assumptions apply to these data, what is the ratio of the variance of $\beta_{g2}$ to the variance of $\beta_{g4}$?

f. If the Gauss–Markov Assumptions apply to these data, which of $\beta_{g1}$, $\beta_{g2}$, and $\beta_{g4}$ is most efficient? Least efficient?

g. Make up an example, grounded in the real world, that relies on the fact that these data are from 15 successive years to cast doubt on the assumption that the disturbances are statistically independent. Does this cast doubt on the claim that our estimators $\beta_{g1}$, $\beta_{g2}$, $\beta_{g3}$, and $\beta_{g4}$ are unbiased? Does it cast doubt on the claim that $\beta_{g4}$ is more efficient than the other three estimators?

h. Is it reasonable to think that the explanatory variable has values that are fixed in repeated samples in this instance? What implication does this have for the claim that $\beta_{g1}$, $\beta_{g2}$, $\beta_{g3}$, and $\beta_{g4}$ are unbiased and that $\beta_{g4}$ is BLUE?

 15. For many years, housing economists believed that households spent a constant fraction of income on housing, as in

$$housing\ expenditure = \beta(income) + u.$$

The file housing.*** contains housing expenditures (*housing*) and total expenditures (*total*) for a sample of 19th century Belgian workers collected by Edouard Ducpetiaux.[12] The differences in housing expenditure from one observation to the next are in the variable *dhousing*; the differences in total expenditure are in the variable *dtotal*.

a. Compute the means of total expenditure and housing expenditure in this sample.

b. Estimate $\beta$ using $\beta_{g1}$, $\beta_{g2}$, $\beta_{g3}$ and $\beta_{g4}$, using total expenditure for total income.

c. If income rises by 100 (it averages around 900 in this sample), what increase in estimated expected housing expenditure results according to each of these estimates?

d. What economic argument would you make against housing absorbing a constant share of income?

e. If the Gauss–Markov Assumptions apply to these data, what is the ratio of the variance of $\beta_{g1}$ to the variance of $\beta_{g2}$?

f. If the Gauss–Markov Assumptions apply to these data, what is the ratio of the variance of $\beta_{g2}$ to the variance of $\beta_{g4}$?

g. If the Gauss–Markov Assumptions apply to these data, which of $\beta_{g1}$, $\beta_{g2}$, and $\beta_{g4}$ is most efficient? Least efficient?

h. Make an economic argument against the assumption that each observation's disturbance has the same variance, $\sigma^2$. Does this cast doubt on the claim that our estimators, $\beta_{g1}$, $\beta_{g2}$, $\beta_{g3}$, and $\beta_{g4}$, are unbiased? Does it cast doubt on the claim that $\beta_{g4}$ is more efficient than the other three estimators?

i. Would it have been possible for Ducpetiaux to gather further samples of workers with the same total expenditures as those in this study? Does that warrant his using the assumption of explanators being fixed across samples? If not, what implication does this have for the claims that $\beta_{g1}$, $\beta_{g2}$, $\beta_{g3}$, and $\beta_{g4}$ are unbiased and that $\beta_{g4}$ is BLUE?

j. What are some determinants of housing expenditure that are captured by $u$?

# Endnotes

1. Garrison Keillor, *Lake Wobegon Days* (New York: Penguin Books, 1985).

2. Chapter 11 extends the notion of linear estimators to include some cases in which the weights are themselves random variables.

3. The authors' seminal works include Harry Markowitz, "Portfolio Selection," *Journal of Finance* 7, no. 1 (March 1952): 77–91; Merton Miller and Myron Scholes, "Rates of Return in Relation to Risk: A Re-examination of Some Recent Findings," in Michael C. Jensen, ed., *Studies in the Theory of Capital Markets* (New York: Praeger, 1972): 79–121; William F. Sharpe, "Capital Asset Prices: A Theory of Market Equilibrium Under Conditions of Risk," *Journal of Finance* 19 (September 1964): 425–442; and James Tobin, "Liquidity Preference as Behavior Towards Risk, *Review of Economic Studies*, no. 67 (February 1958): 65–86.

4. In this case, the returns from umbrellas and the returns from swimsuits are perfectly negatively correlated.

5. A constrained minimization problem is one in which we minimize a function subject to some restriction. For example, firms seek to minimize costs subject to a given level of output. We also encounter constrained maximization problems in other parts of economics—individuals maximize utility subject to a budget constraint.

6. Charles Cobb and Paul Douglas, "A Theory of Production," *American Economic Review* 18 (Suppl.) (1928): 139–165.

7. A trait of the normal distribution is that one third of a normally distributed random variable's values lie within one standard deviation of that variable's mean; 95% of values lie within two standard deviations of the mean.

8. Gary Smith of Pomona College generously provided these data.

9. Ernst Engel, "Die Getreidepreise, die Ernteertraege und die Getreidehandel in Preussischen Staate," *Zeitschroft des Koeniglich Preussischen Statistichen Bureaus* I (1861): 249–289.

10. Trygve Haavelmo, "Methods of Measuring the Marginal Propensity to Consume," *Journal of the American Statistical Association* 42 (March 1947): 105–122.

11. Milton Friedman, *A Theory of the Consumption Function* (Princeton, NJ: Princeton University Press, 1957).

12. Edouard Ducpetiaux, *Budgets Economiques de Classes de Ouvrieres en Belgique* (Brussels: Hayaz, 1855).

## Appendix 3.A

# Finding the BLUE Estimator of a Straight Line Through the Origin

This appendix finds the BLUE estimator for $\beta$ in the special case of two observations ($n = 2$) and in the general case in which $n > 2$. The first derivation requires only ordinary calculus. The more general derivation uses the method of Lagrange multipliers, perhaps familiar from microeconomics.

## 3.A.1  The Gauss–Markov Theorem

**WHAT IS THE DGP?**

The Gauss–Markov Theorem states that $\beta_{g4}$ is the best linear unbiased estimator of a straight line through the origin when the stochastic structure of the DGP satisfies the Gauss–Markov Assumptions, namely:

$$E(\varepsilon_i) = 0 \qquad i = 1,\ldots,n$$
$$\mathrm{var}(\varepsilon_i) = \sigma^2 \qquad i = 1,\ldots,n$$
$$\mathrm{cov}(\varepsilon_i, \varepsilon_j) = 0 \qquad i \neq j$$

Each $X_i$ is fixed across samples.

### The Mathematical Problem

For a linear estimator to be unbiased, it must be true that

$$\sum_{i=1}^{n} w_i X_i = 1. \qquad\qquad \textbf{3.A.1}$$

The Gauss–Markov Theorem requires that the weights make the estimator efficient among linear estimators; that is, the weights must yield the estimator with the smallest variance among unbiased linear estimators. Equation 3.A.1 tells us that under the Gauss–Markov Assumptions, the variance of any linear estimator is

$$\mathrm{var}\left(\sum_{i=1}^{n} w_i Y_i\right) = \sigma^2 \sum w_i^2. \qquad\qquad \textbf{3.A.2}$$

Thus, if the weights of $\beta_{g4}$ solve the following constrained minimization problem, then $\beta_{g4}$ is the BLUE estimator of $\beta$ for our DGP:

$$\text{minimize} \quad v = \sigma^2 \sum w_i^2$$

with respect to $w_1, \ldots, w_n$, subject to the restriction that

$$\sum_{i=1}^{n} w_i X_i = 1.$$

## 3.A.2 BLUE Estimation of $\beta$ When $n = 2$

The simplest example of this constrained minimization in Section 3.A.1 is that in which we have just two observations, that is, when $n = 2$. In this case, we can express the problem as the minimization of a function with one argument, for which standard calculus provides a solution.

### Finding the BLUE Estimator

The problem is when $n = 2$ is

$$\text{minimize} \qquad v = \sigma^2 w_1^2 + \sigma^2 w_2^2$$

with respect to $w_1$ and $w_2$, subject to

$$w_1 X_1 + w_2 X_2 = 1.$$

To solve the problem, substitute the constraint (rearranged to be $w_2 = (1 - w_1 X_1)/X_2$, into $v = \sigma^2 w_1^2 + \sigma^2 w_2^2$, and minimize the resulting function with respect to $w_1$. Thus we have

$$\text{minimize} \qquad v = \sigma^2 w_1^2 + \frac{\sigma^2 (1 - w_1 X_1)^2}{X_2^2}$$

$$= \sigma^2 w_1^2 + \frac{\sigma^2}{X_2^2} - 2\sigma^2 w_1 \frac{X_1}{X_2^2} + \sigma^2 w_1^2 \frac{X_1^2}{X_2^2}$$

with respect to $w_1$. Minimizing the function $v$ requires taking the derivative of $v$ with respect $w_1$, setting the resulting derivative equal to zero, and solving for $w_1$. We obtain

$$\frac{dv}{dw_1} = 2\sigma^2 w_1 - 2\sigma^2 \frac{X_1}{X_2^2} + 2\sigma^2 w_1 \frac{X_1^2}{X_2^2} = 0$$

or

$$w_1 - \frac{X_1}{X_2^2} + w_1 \frac{X_1^2}{X_2^2} = 0,$$

so that

$$w_1 + \frac{w_1 X_1^2}{X_2^2} = \frac{X_1}{X_2^2},$$

which, when solved for $w_1$, yields

$$w_1 = \frac{X_1}{(X_1^2 + X_2^2)}.$$

Substituting this expression back into the constraint and solving for $w_2$ yields

$$w_2 = \frac{X_2}{(X_1^2 + X_2^2)},$$

so we find that $\beta_{g4}$ is the BLUE estimator of $\beta$ for our DGP.

## 3.A.3   BLUE Estimation of $\beta$ When $n > 2$

**How Do We Create an Estimator?**

Finding the BLUE estimator when $n > 2$ still requires minimizing the variance of a linear estimator, given by Equation 3.A.2, subject to the unbiasedness constraint given by Equation 3.A.1. For this general case, the method of Lagrange multipliers is the suitable mathematical tool.

### Solving the Constrained Minimization Problem

In the method of Lagrange multipliers, first we form the Lagrangian function corresponding to our constrained minimization problem:

$$L = \sigma^2 \sum w_i^2 - \lambda \left( \sum w_i X_i - 1 \right).$$

Then, we take the derivatives of this function with respect to the $w_i$ and $\lambda$:

$$\frac{\partial L}{\partial w_i} = 2\sigma^2 w_i - \lambda \quad X_i = 0 \qquad \textbf{3.A.3}$$

and

$$\frac{\partial L}{\partial \lambda} = \sum w_i X_i - 1 = 0. \qquad \textbf{3.A.4}$$

From Equation 3.A.3 we can conclude that

$$w_i = \frac{\frac{1}{2}(\lambda X_i)}{\sigma^2},$$

and therefore that $\sum w_i X_i = 1$, which equals 1 by Equation 3.A.4, can be written as

$$\sum w_i X_i = \sum \frac{\left( \frac{1}{2}[\lambda X_i] X_i \right)}{\sigma^2}$$

$$= \frac{\frac{1}{2} \sum (\lambda X_i^2)}{\sigma^2} = \frac{\frac{1}{2} \lambda \sum X_i^2}{\sigma^2} = 1.$$

This implies that

$$\lambda = \frac{2\sigma^2}{\sum(X_i^3)}.$$

Substituting for $\lambda$ in Equation 3.A.3, we then obtain

$$2w_i = \left[\frac{2}{\sum(X_i^2)}\right]X_i,$$

or

$$w_i = \frac{X_i}{\sum(X_i^2)},$$

which are indeed the weights of $\beta_{g4}$. Consequently, $\beta_{g4}$ is the BLUE estimator of $\beta$ for our DGP.

 *Appendix 3.B*

# A Matrix Algebra Representation of Regressions, Linear Estimators, and Linear Unbiased Estimators

Because our DGPs often involve linear relationships, and our estimators are often linear, many of the mathematical relationships we use involve sums of products. This section introduces a new mathematical notation that allows much leaner expression of sums of products. Subsequent chapters will further develop this notation. In this notation, data are presented in rectangular arrays. This new notation for manipulating arrays of numbers and its mathematical use mathematicians call **matrix algebra**.

## 3.B.1        An Alternative to Summation Notation

The first rectangular arrangements of data that matrix algebra treats are individual columns or rows of numbers. The first manipulation of these arrays is a multiplication process that forms a sum of products. Matrix algebra does not have a formal division procedure; it accomplishes division by multiplying by inverses. This appendix introduces row and column matrices, their multiplication, and the notion of an inverse matrix, to derive $\beta_{g4}$ and to reformulate the BLUE estimation problem.

## Column Vectors and Row Vectors

Linear estimators have the form $\sum_{i=1}^{n} w_i Y_i$. The unbiasedness condition for linear estimators of the slope of a line through the origin under the Gauss–Markov conditions is $\sum_{i=1}^{n} w_i X_i = 1$. The BLUE estimator of the slope of a line through the origin is

$$\beta_{g4} = \frac{\sum_{i=1}^{n} X_i Y_i}{\sum_{i=1}^{n} X_i^2}$$

under the Gauss–Markov Assumptions. All of these expressions involve sums of products and the summation sign, $\Sigma$. This section introduces an alternative way of expressing sums of products that relies on a more compact notation than $(Y_1, Y_2, \ldots, Y_n)$ or $(Y_i, i = 1, \ldots, n)$ for representing $n$ observations.

Consider the $n$ observations on $Y$, $(Y_1, Y_2, Y_3, \ldots, Y_n)$. Arrange these $n$ numbers into a single column and call that array $\mathbf{Y}$:

$$\mathbf{Y} = \begin{bmatrix} Y_1 \\ Y_2 \\ Y_3 \\ \cdot \\ \cdot \\ Y_n \end{bmatrix}.$$

$Y$ is called a **column vector** because it consists of a single column of numbers. The number of items in the column is sometimes called the length of the column.

We similarly define a column vector $\mathbf{w}$:

$$\mathbf{w} = \begin{bmatrix} w_1 \\ w_2 \\ w_3 \\ \cdot \\ \cdot \\ w_n \end{bmatrix}$$

that contains the weights we might use in a linear estimator. Had we arranged the data in $\mathbf{w}$ in a row instead of a column, we would call the resulting array a **row**

**vector.** The mathematical operation that turns a column vector into a row vector, or *vice versa*, is indicated by a prime symbol, as in $w'$; $w'$ is called the **transpose** of $w$:

$$w' = [w_1 \; w_2 \; w_3 \ldots w_n].$$

The number of items in a row or column vector we sometimes call the length of the vector.

## Matrix Multiplication

In addition to the transpose operation, mathematicians have defined an operation whereby row vectors and column vectors of equal length can be "multiplied" together. Because mathematicians call an array of numbers a matrix (plural "matrices"), such multiplication is called **matrix multiplication**. (From this point on, matrices are always in bold italics, as in $Y$ and $w$; when matrices are displayed with their elements, the elements appear within brackets.) Matrix multiplication proves quite convenient when talking about linear estimators. The matrix multiplication rule for multiplying a row vector $w'$ times a column vector $Y$ is

$$w'Y = [w_1 \; w_2 \; \ldots \; w_n] \begin{bmatrix} Y_1 \\ Y_2 \\ \cdot \\ \cdot \\ \cdot \\ Y_n \end{bmatrix} = \left[ \sum_{i=1}^{n} w_i Y_i \right]. \qquad \text{3.B.1}$$

A convenient intuitive way to see what this matrix multiplication does is called the **right-hand rule**. Extend your right hand toward the page of the book, pointing at the two matrices above, palm down. Adjust your fingers so that your right thumb points at $w_1$ and your right index finger points at $Y_1$. Now rotate your wrist so that your thumb moves *across* the $w$ row matrix and your index finger moves *down* the column matrix. The matrix multiplication multiplies each pair of numbers, one from the row matrix, the other from the column matrix, and tallies all those products in a sum. When we encounter more complicated matrices later on, we learn this same right-hand rule is at the root of the mechanics of all matrix multiplication. Mathematicians do not think of matrix multiplication in only this mechanical way, but for our purposes, the mechanical interpretation suffices.

Notice that the matrix multiplication in Equation 3.B.1 applies only to the case when the first vector is a row vector and the second vector is a column vector, *with both vectors having the same length, n.* If the first vector does not have the same length as the second, matrix multiplication is not possible.

Applying this rule above to other relationships we have seen, we obtain

$$w'w = \left[\sum(w_i w_i)\right] = \left[\sum(w_i^2)\right],$$

$$w'X = \left[\sum(w_i X_i)\right],$$

$$X'Y = \left[\sum(X_i Y_i)\right],$$

and

$$X'X = \left[\sum(X_i X_i)\right] = \left[\sum(X_i^2)\right].$$

Thus, several results of this chapter can be very succinctly expressed in terms of matrix multiplication.

The first such restatement is that an estimator is a linear estimator if and only if it can be expressed in the form $w'Y$, where $w$ is a vector of weights and $Y$ a vector of observations on our dependent variable.

The unbiasedness requirement for linear estimators can also be expressed in matrix terms. Mathematicians say a matrix containing a single 1 is an example of what they call an **identity matrix**. Identity matrices are symbolized by $I$. Thus, under the Gauss–Markov Assumptions, a linear estimator of the slope of a line through the origin is unbiased if $w'X = I$, where $X$ is a column vector of observations on our independent variable and $I = [1]$.

Intuitively, the BLUE estimator for the slope of a line through the origin under the Gauss–Markov Assumptions, $\beta_{g4}$, might be written $(X'Y)/(X'X)$. However, mathematicians don't actually define a division operation for matrices. Instead, they rely on multiplying by inverses. Recall that in ordinary algebra,

$$\left(\sum X_i^2\right)^{-1} = \frac{1}{\sum X_i^2}$$

and that $\left(\sum X_i^2\right)^{-1} \left(\sum X_i^2\right) = 1$. Mathematicians call $\left(\sum X_i^2\right)^{-1}$ the inverse of $\sum X_i^2$. Mathematicians similarly define the **inverse of a matrix** $M$ to be the matrix $M^{-1}$ such that $M^{-1}M = I$. Thus, the matrix algebra representation of $\beta_{g4}$ is

$$\beta_{g4} = [\beta_{g4}] = (X'X)^{-1}(X'Y). \qquad \text{3.B.2}$$

The matrix notation also allows a succinct description of the regression relationship that relates the $Y_i$ to the $X_i$ and the $\varepsilon_i$. However, this description requires two additional matrix manipulations. First, a matrix, for example $X$ in the present example, multiplied by a single number, like $\beta$ in our DGP, equals a new matrix with the same number of rows and columns—together called the "dimensions" of the matrix—in which every element is equal to its corresponding element in the original matrix times the constant. Thus,

$$X\beta = \begin{bmatrix} \beta X_1 \\ \beta X_2 \\ \cdot \\ \cdot \\ \cdot \\ \beta X_n \end{bmatrix}.$$

A single number, like $\beta$, not set within an array, is called a **scalar**, to contrast it with matrices. Second, column vectors of equal length can be added together by adding together their corresponding elements. (The same holds true for row vectors of equal length.)

Using these two results, arrange the $n$ disturbances in our DGP into a column vector, $\varepsilon$:

$$\varepsilon = \begin{bmatrix} \varepsilon_1 \\ \varepsilon_2 \\ \cdot \\ \cdot \\ \varepsilon_n \end{bmatrix}$$

and write $Y = X\beta + \varepsilon$, which is

$$\begin{bmatrix} Y_1 \\ Y_2 \\ Y_3 \\ \cdot \\ \cdot \\ Y_n \end{bmatrix} = \begin{bmatrix} \beta X_1 \\ \beta X_2 \\ \beta X_3 \\ \cdot \\ \cdot \\ \beta X_n \end{bmatrix} + \begin{bmatrix} \varepsilon_1 \\ \varepsilon_2 \\ \varepsilon_3 \\ \cdot \\ \cdot \\ \varepsilon_n \end{bmatrix} = \begin{bmatrix} \beta X_1 + \varepsilon_1 \\ \beta X_2 + \varepsilon_2 \\ \beta X_3 + \varepsilon_3 \\ \cdot \\ \cdot \\ \beta X_n + \varepsilon_n \end{bmatrix}$$

$$Y_i = X_i\beta + \varepsilon_i \qquad i = 1, \ldots, n.$$

This elegant representation of our model permits an equally elegant presentation of the computational approach to building $\beta_{g4}$ developed in the main text of this chapter. Equation 3.B.2 notes that

$$\boldsymbol{\beta_{g4}} = [\beta_{g4}] = (X'X)^{-1}(X'Y).$$

An intuitive matrix algebra construction of $\boldsymbol{\beta_{g4}}$ starts with

$$Y = X\beta + \varepsilon.$$

The main text of this chapter demonstrates that an efficient estimator of the slope of a line through the origin more heavily weights observations with large X-values. There, the weighting was accomplished by multiplying observations by their

X-values. Where does multiplying $Y$ by $X$ lead us? Matrices follow the distributive rule of ordinary algebra, so multiplying both sides of the preceding equation by $X'$ leads to

$$X'Y = X'X\beta + X'\varepsilon.$$

Multiplying both sides by $(X'X)^{-1}$ to isolate the $\beta$ leads to

$$(X'X)^{-1}X'Y = (X'X)^{-1}X'X\,\beta + (X'X)^{-1}X'\varepsilon$$
$$= I\beta + (X'X)^{-1}X'\varepsilon$$
$$= [\boldsymbol{\beta}] + (X'X)^{-1}X'\varepsilon, \qquad \text{3.B.3}$$

which matches the earlier finding that

$$\beta_{g4} = \frac{\sum X_i Y_i}{\sum X_i^2} = \beta + \frac{\sum X_i \varepsilon_i}{\sum X_i^2}.$$

The unbiasedness of $\beta_{g4}$ follows from the assumption that $E(\varepsilon_i) = 0$ for all $i$. When the expectations operator is applied to a matrix, it means that the operator is to be applied to every element of the matrix. In matrix form, the assumption that the disturbances all have a zero mean is

$$E(\boldsymbol{\varepsilon}) = \begin{bmatrix} E(\varepsilon_1) \\ E(\varepsilon_2) \\ \cdot \\ \cdot \\ E(\varepsilon_n) \end{bmatrix} = \begin{bmatrix} 0 \\ 0 \\ \cdot \\ \cdot \\ 0 \end{bmatrix} = 0.$$

With this assumption in hand, matrix algebra provides another proof that $\beta_{g4}$ is unbiased. Equation 3.B.3 reports that

$$(X'X)^{-1}X'Y = [\beta] + (X'X)^{-1}X'\varepsilon.$$

(Notice that both $(X'X)^{-1}$ and $X'Y$ contain a single number, as do $[\beta]$ and $X'\varepsilon$. Because $E(\boldsymbol{\varepsilon}) = 0$,

$$E(X'\varepsilon) = E\left[\sum(X_i\varepsilon_i)\right]$$
$$= \left[\sum E(X_i\varepsilon_i)\right] = [0].$$

(Notice that $E(\boldsymbol{\varepsilon})$ is a column vector of length $n$, but $E(X'\varepsilon)$ is a matrix with just one element, a single zero.) Consequently,

$$E(\boldsymbol{\beta}_{g4}) = E((X'X)^{-1}X'Y)$$
$$= [\beta] + E((X'X)X'\varepsilon)$$
$$= E((X'X)[0]) = [\beta] + [0] = [\beta].$$

In matrix algebra form, the constrained minimization that leads to the BLUE estimator of the slope of a line through the origin under the Gauss–Markov Assumptions is

$$\text{minimize} \quad \nu = \sigma^2 \, w'w$$
$$\text{with respect to } w,$$
$$\text{subject to } w'X = I.$$

The matrix representation of regression models becomes very powerful when the models include more than one explanator—in those cases, the summation notation proves of only limited usefulness, whereas the matrix notation continues to serve effectively. The matrix algebra proof of the Gauss–Markov Theorem appears in an appendix to Chapter 6, the chapter on multiple regression models.

## Appendix 3.B  Concepts for Review

# *Chapter 4*

# BLUE Estimators for the Slope and Intercept of a Straight Line

*A straight line may be the shortest distance between two points, but it is by no means the most interesting.*

—Dr. Who, BBC

o wage, no work." An unprovocative slogan. I wouldn't work without pay. Would you? The widespread truth of this slogan might tempt us to think that because labor supplied would be zero at a wage of zero, a linear labor supply function would generally pass through the origin, much as in the Capital Asset Pricing Model (CAPM) and Cobb–Douglas examples of Chapter 2. This would be a mistake. Most workers would refuse to work well before the wage rate fell to zero. Consequently, expected hours worked are more likely to depend on the wage rate as pictured in Figure 4.1, with

$$\text{E}(hours\ worked\,|\,wage\ rate) = \beta_0 + \beta_1(wage\ rate)$$

as long as hours worked are not negative. Labor supply functions are unlikely to be straight lines through the origin.

The CAPM and the Cobb–Douglas production and consumption functions do provide theoretical frameworks in which straight lines through the origin are economically interesting, but common sense suggests that many empirical relationships will not pass through the origin. Expected college financial aid is unlikely to be zero for students with no family income; the quantity of cars demanded at a price of zero is unlikely to be zero. Lines through the origin are the exception, not the rule. This chapter explores how we might best estimate the relationship between two variables when both the intercept and the slope are unknown.

**Figure 4.1**

A Labor Supply
Function

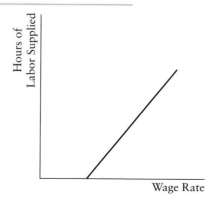

Conceptually, estimating the slope of a straight line with unknown intercept is much like estimating the slope of a line through the origin. Bias, efficiency, and mean square error all matter, just as they did in estimating the slope of a line through the origin. Because linear estimators embraced a wide variety of intuitively appealing estimators in the case of a line through the origin, we focus again on the class of linear estimators. What is the best linear unbiased estimator (the BLUE) estimator of the slope of a line with unknown intercept? What is the BLUE estimator of the intercept of a straight line? These are the core questions that this chapter addresses. Because the properties of an estimator depend on the data-generating process (DGP) from which the data arise, we begin with a new DGP, one that includes a straight line with an unknown intercept. With the new DGP, we can investigate the bias, variance, and covariance of linear estimators when we apply such estimators to data arising from this DGP.

## 4.1     The DGP for a Straight Line with Unknown Intercept

WHAT IS THE DGP?

The first step in deriving estimators with attractive properties is specifying the DGP that describes where the sample data come from. Here, we adapt the DGP of Chapter 3 to include an intercept term:

$$Y_i = \beta_0 + \beta_1 X_i + \varepsilon_i \qquad i = 1, \ldots, n$$
$$E(\varepsilon_i) = 0 \qquad i = 1, \ldots, n$$
$$\text{var}(\varepsilon_i) = \sigma^2 \qquad i = 1, \ldots, n$$
$$\text{cov}(\varepsilon_i, \varepsilon_j) = 0 \qquad i \neq j$$

$X_i$'s fixed across samples.

Notice that we again make the Gauss–Markov Assumptions about the disturbances and the explanator. The only change from the basic DGP of Chapter 3 is the inclusion of an intercept in the regression equation. This change allows us to consider many relationships for which a straight line through the origin would be inappropriate. As noted in the introduction to this chapter, students with no income are likely to receive more, not less, financial aid than others—the relationship between financial aid and income,

$$E(\textit{financial aid}|\textit{family income}) = \beta_0 + \beta_1(\textit{family income}),$$

requires a positive intercept, $\beta_0 > 0$. Similarly, a demand function that describes the number of cars as a function of the price of cars also requires a positive intercept, as in

$$E(\textit{quantity demanded}|\textit{price}) = \beta_0 + \beta_1(\textit{price}),$$

# An Econometric Top 40—A Classical Favorite

## The Phillips Curve

Nations sometimes suffer from high unemployment or high inflation. In 1958, A. W. Phillips of the London School of Economics argued that historical experience in the United Kingdom indicated that a trade-off might exist between these two ills[1]; governments might be able to reduce one malady, but only at the cost of increasing the other.

Phillips distinguished between "demand pull" influences on the general price level—high levels of aggregate demand that put pressure on wage rates—and "cost push" influences—adverse shocks to aggregate supply that put pressure on goods prices.

Phillips emphasized the "demand push" aspect of inflation. Theoretically, he argued that when aggregate demand was high, and labor was therefore relatively scarce, money wage rates would be bid up, contributing to inflation. Empirically, Phillips used a simple curve-fitting technique to estimate the coefficients linking unemployment and changes in money wage rates.[2] Phillips's analysis exposed a long-term negative correlation between the rate of change in money wages and the level of unemployment in the economy. His fitted equation for changes in the money wage rate as a function of the level of unemployment in the United Kingdom from 1861 to 1913 provided a remarkably good fit to data on those variables taken from 1914 to 1957. Phillips presented most of his results graphically, but he did offer the explicit formula for the curve that he fit for 1861–1913:

$$inflation = -0.9 + 9.638$$
$$(unemployment)^{-1.394}.$$

Phillips's analysis led economists to wonder if there is a structural link between unemployment and inflation. Macroeconomists leapt on Phillips's results, arguing that the "Phillips curve" revealed an unfortunate dilemma facing policy makers: One must choose between less unemployment and less inflation—one cannot reduce both simultaneously.

The Phillips curve was soon subjected to further empirical tests. Economists recognized that searching for correlations among numerous unrelated variables will eventually reveal some correlations that arise merely by chance. To test whether the correlations found in such searches are real or mere chance, we must see if the correlation persists in independent data sets. U.S. economists checking Phillips's conjecture with data for the following decade found striking confirmation of Phillips's results. The U.S. economists argued that wage changes would be mirrored in inflation, so they studied

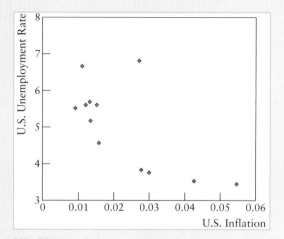

**Hit Figure 4.1**

U.S. Unemployment Vs. Inflation, 1958–1969
*Source:* U.S. Department of Commerce.

the relationship between inflation and unemployment, rather than between wage changes and unemployment. Hit Figure 4.1 shows a scatterplot of the unemployment inflation for the United States for the years 1958–1969. The negative correlation between unemployment and inflation in these data is clear.

 **Final Notes**

The Phillips curve strikingly illustrates the power of econometric analyses to influence economic thought. The Phillips curve had two dramatic effects on macroeconomics. First, it led a generation of macro-policy advisors to talk about a trade-off between unemployment and inflation when discussing government policy alternatives. Second, the Phillips results sparked a theoretical debate about whether the Phillips curve revealed a stable structural relationship between inflation and unemployment or merely a volatile and temporary relationship that could not serve as a guide to government policy. This debate grew into the "rational expectations revolution," which we'll explore in a later Classical Favorite.

Phillips's reliance on curves that fit his data well was acceptable practice in 1958. Few economists then could do more than just hope that curve-fitting exercises would prove statistically sound. Today, economists' insistence on more than just hope for justifying estimation procedures is almost universal. We see later in this chapter that some curve-fitting techniques do prove sound statistically, but it is the estimators' traits, such as unbiasedness, that buy them credence, not simply the fact that the fitted curve reasonably matches the observed data. ∎

to reflect the fact that when the price of a good is zero, the number of cars demanded is greater than zero. Again as noted in the introduction, labor supply equations require an intercept less than zero because workers will stop supplying labor before the wage rate falls to zero. This new DGP with an unknown intercept term is considerably more widely applicable than that used in Chapter 3—it even includes the former DGP as a special case in which $\beta_0 = 0$.

The assumption that $X$ takes on the same values in every sample is unrealistic. When economists draw new samples, the $X$-values are likely to vary. However, we saw in Chapter 3 that if the Gauss–Markov Assumptions about the disturbances hold for all possible combinations of $X$-values, then we can interpret all results based on the assumption of fixed $X$'s as conditional results for random $X$'s, conditional on the observed $X$-values. The arguments in Chapter 3 for a line through the origin apply equally to the case in which the intercept is unknown. *All findings we obtain in this chapter for the fixed $X$'s DGP with unknown slope and intercept apply if the DGP has random $X$-values, as long as the Gauss–Markov Assumptions about the disturbances hold for every pattern of $X$-value. The only change we must make for such random $X$ cases is to make all the expectation and variance statements conditional on the observed values of the $X$'s.* This conditional interpretation of findings is more realistic than assuming fixed $X$'s.

Nonetheless, we continue to use the fixed $X$'s assumption in our analysis to avoid the notational complexity of conditioning all claims on the observed values of $X$.

## 4.2    The Expected Value and Variance of Linear Estimators

**WHAT ARE AN ESTI-MATOR'S PROPERTIES?**

Where are we to look for good estimators of the slope and intercept of a line? Examining *all* possible estimators is too large a task to be feasible. Instead, we continue the strategy that proved fruitful in Chapter 3 and examine the class of linear estimators, seeking best estimators for the slope and intercept from among all linear estimators. Our strategy in Chapter 3 to find a BLUE estimator had three steps: (i) determine when a linear estimator is unbiased for the DGP in hand; (ii) determine the variance of a linear estimator for that DGP; and (iii) find the weights for a linear estimator that minimize that variance, subject to the unbiasedness requirement. This section follows steps (i) and (ii), paving the way for step (iii) in the next section.

### Conditions for Unbiasedness

When is a linear estimator unbiased in this DGP? That is, when does the expected value of a linear estimator equal the parameter, here $\beta_0$ or $\beta_1$, that we are estimating? Recall that a linear estimator is one that can be written in the form

$$g = \sum w_i Y_i.$$

What is $g$'s expected value in this DGP? The key assumptions of the DGP that determine $g$'s expected value are that the mean disturbance is zero and the $X_i$'s are fixed across samples.

$$\begin{aligned} \mathrm{E}(g) &= \mathrm{E}\Big[\sum w_i Y_i\Big] = \mathrm{E}\Big[\sum w_i(\beta_0 + \beta_1 X_i + \varepsilon_i)\Big] \\ &= \sum \mathrm{E}[w_i(\beta_0 + \beta_1 X_i + \varepsilon_i)] \\ &= \sum \mathrm{E}(w_i\beta_0 + w_i\beta_1 X_i + w_i\varepsilon_i) \\ &= \sum [\mathrm{E}(w_i\beta_0) + \mathrm{E}(w_i\beta_1 X_i) + \mathrm{E}(w_i\varepsilon_i)] \\ &= \sum [w_i\beta_0 + w_i\beta_1 X_i + w_i\mathrm{E}(\varepsilon_i)] \\ &= \sum w_i\beta_0 + \sum w_i\beta_1 X_i + \sum w_i 0 \\ &= \beta_0\sum w_i + \beta_1\sum w_i X_i. \end{aligned}$$

The linear estimators that unbiasedly estimate $\beta_1$ use different weights than the linear estimators that unbiasedly estimate $\beta_0$. This section indicates weights used to estimate $\beta_1$, with a superscript 1, and to estimate $\beta_0$, with a superscript 0. Elsewhere in this book, these superscripts appear only if they are necessary for clarity.

If $g$ is to be an unbiased estimator of $\beta_1$, $E(g)$ must equal $\beta_1$. For $E(g)$ to equal $\beta_1$, the weights, $w_1^1, w_2^1, \ldots, w_n^1$ chosen for estimating $\beta_1$ must satisfy two conditions:

$$\sum w_i^1 = 0 \quad and \quad \sum w_i^1 X_i = 1.$$

The second condition is the same as when there is no intercept in the model, as in Chapters 2 and 3. The first condition is new, suggesting that the BLUE estimator of the slope when the intercept is unknown differs from that when the origin is known to be zero, $\beta_{g4}$. Note that when $\beta_0$ equals zero, the sum of the weights need not be zero for a linear estimator to be unbiased. This is precisely the case discussed in Chapters 2 and 3. But when the intercept is unknown, we cannot presume it is zero, so we must choose weights that sum to zero to claim our estimator of the slope is surely unbiased.

Similarly, if $g$ is to be an unbiased estimator of $\beta_0$, $E(g)$ must equal $\beta_0$. For $E(g)$ to equal $\beta_0$, the weights, $w_1^0, w_2^0, \ldots, w_n^0$, chosen for estimating $\beta_0$ must satisfy two conditions:

$$\sum w_i^0 = 1 \quad and \quad \sum w_i^0 X_i = 0.$$

Note that when $\beta_1$ equals zero, the sum of the $w_i^0$ times the $X$'s need not equal zero. This is precisely the classic statistical problem of estimating the mean of a population, in which $E(Y_i) = \beta_0$. We know from Chapter 3 that the BLUE estimator of the population mean, using a simple random sample, is the sample mean, which gives all observations the same weight, $1/n$; in that case, the sum of the weights equals $\sum 1/n$, which equals $n(1/n)$, which does indeed equal one, as required for unbiasedness.

Notice that if all the $X$-values are the same, that is, if $X_1 = X_2 = \cdots = X_n = c$, where $c$ is some constant, the conditions for $g$ to unbiasedly estimate $\beta_1$ cannot be satisfied. In this special case, if the first requirement is met, so $\sum w_i^1 = 0$, then

$$\sum w_i^1 X_i = \sum w_i^1 c = c \sum w_i^1 = 0,$$

which violates the second requirement for $g$ to unbiasedly estimate $\beta_1$. Similarly, if all the $X$-values are the same and, additionally, not equal to zero, $g$ cannot unbiasedly estimate $\beta_0$. In this case, if the second requirement is met, $\sum w_i^0 X_i = 0$ and

$$\sum w_i^0 c = c \sum w_i^0 = 0.$$

If $c$ is not zero, and $c \sum w_i^0 = 0$, then $\sum w_i^0$ cannot equal one, as would be required for $g$ to unbiasedly estimate $\beta_0$. *Sometimes no linear unbiased estimator of a slope or of an intercept exists.*

## The Variance of a Linear Estimator

Next, we determine the variance of a linear estimator when the Gauss–Markov Assumptions apply. We can write the variance of a linear estimator as

$$\text{var}(g) = \text{var}\left(\sum_{i=1}^{n} w_i Y_i\right),$$

which we can rewrite as

$$\sum_{i=1}^{n} \text{var}(w_i Y_i) + 2 \text{ sum of all the covariances among the } w_i Y_i$$

$$= \sum_{i=1}^{n} \text{var}(w_i Y_i) + \sum_{i=1}^{n} \sum_{\substack{j=1 \\ j \neq i}}^{n} \text{cov}(w_i Y_i, w_j Y_j)$$

$$= \sum_{i=1}^{n} w_i^2 \text{var}(Y_i) + \sum_{i=1}^{n} \sum_{\substack{j=1 \\ j \neq i}}^{n} w_i w_j \text{cov}(Y_i, Y_j).$$

But the Gauss–Markov Assumptions tell us that the $\varepsilon_i$, and thus the $Y_i$ (which, in this DGP, differ from the $\varepsilon_i$ by only $[\beta_0 + \beta_1 X_i]$, which is constant across samples), are uncorrelated, so all the covariance terms are zero. Therefore, for linear estimators,

$$\text{var}(g) = \sum_{i=1}^{n} \text{var}(w_i Y_i),$$

which can be rewritten

$$\text{var}(g) = \sum_{i=1}^{n} (w_i^2 \text{var}(Y_i)).$$

In this DGP, the $Y_i$ differ from the $\varepsilon_i$ by $(\beta_0 + \beta_1 X_i)$, which is a constant across samples. Consequently, in this DGP, the variance of $Y_i$ is the same as the variance of the disturbances, $\sigma^2$. Thus,

$$\sum_{i=1}^{n} w_i^2 \text{var}(Y_i) = \sum_{i=1}^{n} w_i^2 \sigma^2,$$

or

$$\text{var}(g) = \sigma^2 \sum_{i=1}^{n} w_i^2.$$

Notice that this expression is the same one we obtained for the variance of a linear estimator in Chapter 3, when we were estimating the slope of a line through the origin under the Gauss–Markov Assumptions. This formula for the variance of a linear estimator also applies to models with multiple explanators, as long as the Gauss–Markov Assumptions are satisfied. Chapter 6 discusses the multiple explanator case.

## 4.3     BLUE Estimation of the Slope and Intercept of a Straight Line

**How Do We Create an Estimator?**

As our hunter-econometricians reminded us in Chapter 3, unbiasedness is a weak property for an estimator if the variance of the estimator is very large. Consequently, in addition to unbiasedness, a best linear estimator should have a smaller variance than any other unbiased linear estimator. We can find such BLUE estimators for the slope, $\beta_1$, and intercept, $\beta_0$, given our DGP, by twice minimizing the variance of linear estimators, $\sigma^2 \sum w_i^2$, with respect to the weights $w_1, \ldots, w_n$. First minimize $\sigma^2 \sum w_i^2$ subject to the two unbiasedness conditions for estimators of $\beta_1$. Then minimize $\sigma^2 \sum w_i^2$ again, this time subject to the two unbiasedness conditions for estimators of $\beta_0$. The resultant calculus and algebra are messier than in the simpler case of a line with no intercept. This section lays out the calculus problems whose solutions are the weights for the BLUE estimators of the slope and intercept of a straight line under the Gauss–Markov Assumptions.

### A BLUE Estimator for the Slope, $\beta_1$

Consider the BLUE estimator for $\beta_1$ when $n = 3$, the simplest case.[3] The variance of a linear estimator, $\nu$, is then

$$\nu = \sigma^2 w_1^2 + \sigma^2 w_2^2 + \sigma^2 w_3^2.$$

To obtain the BLUE estimator in this case,

$$\text{minimize } \nu = \sigma^2 w_1^2 + \sigma^2 w_2^2 + \sigma^2 w_3^2$$

with respect to $w_1$, $w_2$, and $w_3$, subject to

$$w_1 X_1 + w_2 X_2 + w_3 X_3 = 1$$

and

$$w_1 + w_2 + w_3 = 0,$$

which is a calculus problem.

More generally, for any $n$, we can write the constrained minimization problem as

$$\text{minimize } \nu = \sigma^2 \sum_{i=1}^{n} w_i^2$$

with respect to $w_1, w_2, \ldots, w_n$, subject to

$$\sum_{i=1}^{n} w_i = 0$$

and

$$\sum_{i=1}^{n} w_i X_i = 1.$$

Appendix 4.A solves this more general problem and shows that the weights for the BLUE estimator for $\beta_1$ when the Gauss–Markov Assumptions apply are

$$w_i^{1^*} = \frac{(X_i - \overline{X})}{\sum_{j=1}^{n}(X_j - \overline{X})^2}, \qquad \textbf{4.1}$$

where the asterisk in the superscript indicates that these are BLUE weights. In the case when $n = 3$, these weights are

$$w_1^{1^*} = (X_1 - \overline{X})/[(X_1 - \overline{X})^2 + (X_2 - \overline{X})^2 + (X_3 - \overline{X})^2],$$
$$w_2^{1^*} = (X_2 - \overline{X})/[(X_1 - \overline{X})^2 + (X_2 - \overline{X})^2 + (X_3 - \overline{X})^2],$$

and

$$w_3^{1^*} = (X_3 - \overline{X})/[(X_1 - \overline{X})^2 + (X_2 - \overline{X})^2 + (X_3 - \overline{X})^2].$$

Solving the constrained minimization problem for $n = 3$ requires only algebra and minimization of a function in a single variable. The auxiliary Appendix 4.D on this book's companion Web site (**www.aw-bc.com/murray**) contains the derivation for the case $n = 3$.

The BLUE estimator of the slope, which we call $\hat{\beta}_1$, is

$$\hat{\beta}_1 = \sum_{i=1}^{n} \left[ \frac{(X_i - \overline{X})}{\sum_{i=1}^{n}(X_i - \overline{X})^2} Y_i \right] = \frac{\sum_{i=1}^{n}[(X_i - \overline{X})Y_i]}{\sum_{i=1}^{n}(X_i - \overline{X})^2}.$$

We can apply $\hat{\beta}_1$ to estimating the marginal effect of income on housing expenditure for the sample of New York renters examined in Chapters 2 and 3. In Chapters 2 and 3, we assumed rent is strictly proportional to income. Here we allow for an unknown intercept term:

$$rent_i = \beta_0 + \beta_1 income + \varepsilon_i.$$

This specification does not preclude $\beta_0 = 0$, but it does not require it, either.

In the renter data, $\Sigma(X_i - \overline{X})Y_i = 3348436763.78$ and $\Sigma(X_i - \overline{X})^2 = 52674672255.3$. Based on these data, $\hat{\beta}_1 = 0.064$.

The new estimator, $\hat{\beta}_1$, differs dramatically from the estimates of the change in rent with respect to income found in Chapters 2 and 3, using $\beta_{g1}, \beta_{g2}, \beta_{g3}$, and $\beta_{g4}$ (from which we obtained estimates of 0.29, 0.22, 0.28, and 0.17, respectively). What have we done differently? In deriving $\hat{\beta}_1$ we have imposed two unbiasedness constraints, $\Sigma w_i = 0$ and $\Sigma w_i X_i = 1$. In Chapter 3, when we derived the BLUE estimator for a DGP with no intercept term, we imposed only one unbiasedness constraint, $\Sigma w_i X_i = 1$.

The estimators $\beta_{g1}, \beta_{g2}, \beta_{g3}$, and $\beta_{g4}$ are all biased estimators of the slope of the line if the intercept is not zero (unless by happy accident $\Sigma w_i = 0$ for one or more of those estimators—which it does not in the New York renter data). Moreover, given the large difference between $\hat{\beta}_1$ and $\beta_{g1}, \beta_{g2}, \beta_{g3}$, or $\beta_{g4}$, the biases appear substantial. We examine such biases in more detail in Chapter 8.

## An Estimator for $\beta_0$

The strategy we just used to obtain the BLUE estimator for the slope applies equally well to obtain the BLUE estimator for the intercept. We

$$\text{minimize } \nu = \sigma^2 \sum_{i=1}^{n} w_i^2$$

with respect to $w_1, w_2, \ldots, w_n$, subject to

$$\sum_{i=1}^{n} w_i = 1$$

and

$$\sum_{i=1}^{n} w_i X_i = 0.$$

The weights for the BLUE estimator of $\beta_0$ are

$$w_i^{0*} = \left[ \frac{1}{n} - \frac{\overline{X}(X_i - \overline{X})}{\sum(X_i - \overline{X})^2} \right], \qquad 4.2$$

where the asterisk in the superscript again indicates that these are the BLUE weights. These weights imply that when the Gauss–Markov Assumptions apply, the BLUE estimator of $\beta_0$, which we call $\hat{\beta}_0$, is

$$\hat{\beta}_0 = \overline{Y} - \overline{X}\hat{\beta}_1.$$

In our sample of New York renters, $\overline{X} = 35,553$, $\overline{Y} = 7,718.11$, and $\hat{\beta}_1 = 0.064$. Thus, $\hat{\beta}_0 = 5442.18$, which is substantially larger than zero when rents are measured in dollars per year. Perhaps the DGP underlying our rent and income data has a nonzero intercept, contrary to the assumptions of Chapters 2 and 3; perhaps $\beta_{g1}$, $\beta_{g2}$, $\beta_{g3}$, and $\beta_{g4}$ are biased estimators of the rate of change of rent with respect to income. The estimator $\beta_{g4}$ is not BLUE if the intercept term is not zero. *In general, the estimator optimal for one DGP is not optimal for another one. We will need procedures for discerning among various DGPs if we are to be confident about choosing the right estimators for a given problem.*

## An Often Used Property of Certain Sums

Econometric analyses frequently involve the difference between a variable and its mean, for example, $(X_i - \overline{X})$ or $(Y_i - \overline{Y})$. These deviations of variables from their own means often arise in sums of products, as in $\sum(X_i - \overline{X})(Y_i - \overline{Y})$. These expressions have a trait, derived in Appendix 4.C, that is frequently exploited in algebraic manipulations of econometric formulae:

$$\sum[(X_i - \overline{X})Y_i] = \sum[(X_i - \overline{X})(Y_i - \overline{Y})].$$

Thus, we can rewrite the BLUE estimator of $\beta_1$,

$$\hat{\beta}_1 = \frac{\sum(X_i - \overline{X})Y_i}{\sum(X_i - \overline{X})^2},$$

as

$$\hat{\beta}_1 = \frac{\sum[(X_i - \overline{X})(Y_i - \overline{Y})]}{\sum(X_i - \overline{X})^2} = \frac{\sum x_i y_i}{\sum x_i^2}, \qquad \textbf{4.3}$$

where $x_i = (X_i - \overline{X})$ and $y_i = (Y_i - \overline{Y})$.

Expressing $\hat{\beta}_1$ in terms of deviations of $X$ and $Y$ from their own means, as here, is commonplace. This practice is so common that, from this point forward, in estimator formulae, capital letters generally denote the value of variables and the corresponding lowercase letters denote deviations of variables from their own means, as with $X_i$ and $x_i$, or $Y_i$ and $y_i$, discussed earlier.

## A Relationship Between $\hat{\beta}_1$ and $\beta_{g4}$

Viewing the BLUE estimator of the slope in the form given by Equation 4.3,

$$\hat{\beta}_1 = \frac{\sum x_i y_i}{\sum x_i^2},$$

exposes a close similarity between $\hat{\beta}_1$ and $\beta_{g4}$:

$$\beta_{g4} = \frac{\sum X_i Y_i}{\sum X_i^2}.$$

The similarity becomes more pronounced when we consider that the BLUE estimator for $\beta_0$,

$$\hat{\beta}_0 = \overline{Y} - \hat{\beta}_1 \overline{X},$$

implies that

$$\overline{Y} = \hat{\beta}_0 + \hat{\beta}_1 \overline{X}.$$

Just as the estimated line

$$Y_i = \beta_{g4} X_i$$

necessarily passes through the origin, the line estimated with $\hat{\beta}_0$ and $\hat{\beta}_1$ forces the estimated line to pass through $\overline{X}, \overline{Y}$. The transformed variables, $x$ and $y$, have their own origin at $\overline{X}, \overline{Y}$ (because $x_i = 0$ when $X_i = \overline{X}$ and $y_i = 0$ when $Y_i = \overline{Y}$). Thus, we estimate the slope of a line forced through the $x, y$ origin by

$$\hat{\beta}_1 = \frac{\sum x_i y_i}{\sum x_i^2},$$

and we estimate the slope of a line forced through the $X, Y$ origin by

$$\beta_{g4} = \frac{\sum X_i Y_i}{\sum X_i^2}.$$

The two instances differ in that the DGP that led us to $\beta_{g4}$ *assumed* that the line in the population passes through the $X, Y$ origin, whereas when studying a straight line with unknown intercept, we only *estimate* that the line passes through $\overline{X}, \overline{Y}$.

## An Example: The Phillips Curve

Economist A. W. Phillips's 1958 Golden Oldie that introduced this chapter suggested that there is a trade-off between unemployment and inflation. His analysis used a century of British data. Subsequent analysis using a decade of U.S. data supported Phillips's claim. The U.S. data are contained in the data set phillipsearly.*** on this book's companion Web site (**www.aw-bc.com/murray**). Figure 4.2 replicates the U.S. data on unemployment and inflation displayed in Hit Figure 4.1. The line in the figure is the fitted line obtained using the BLUE estimators for the slope and intercept. Table 4.1 reports the BLUE estimators of the

**Figure 4.2**

U.S. Unemployment
and Inflation,
1958–1969

*Source:* U.S. Depart-
ment of Commerce.

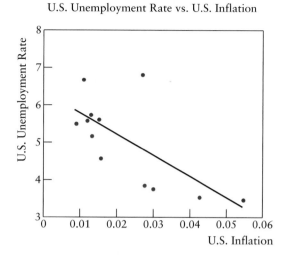

U.S. Unemployment Rate vs. U.S. Inflation

slope and intercept. According to the table, a 0.55 percentage point decrease in unemployment accompanies each one percentage point increase in inflation.

**TABLE 4.1  The Phillips Curve**

Dependent Variable: UNEMPLOY
Method: Least Squares
Sample: 1958 1969
Included observations: 12

| Variable | Coefficient | Std. Error | t-Statistic | Prob. |
|----------|-------------|------------|-------------|-------|
| C | 0.062498 | 0.005003 | 12.49199 | 0.0000 |
| INFL | −0.55256 | 0.190166 | −2.905683 | 0.0157 |
| R-squared | 0.457789 | Mean dependent var | | 0.050069 |
| Adjusted R-squared | 0.403568 | S.D. dependent var | | 0.011640 |
| S.E. of regression | 0.008989 | Akaike info criterion | | −6.43452 |
| Sum squared resid | 0.000808 | Schwarz criterion | | −6.35370 |
| Log likelihood | 40.60715 | F-statistic | | 8.442994 |
| Durbin–Watson stat | 1.112023 | Prob(F-statistic) | | 0.015680 |

## 4.4    $\hat{\beta}_0$ and $\hat{\beta}_1$ Are Intuitively Appealing Estimators

**HOW DO WE CREATE AN ESTIMATOR?**

Chapter 3 restricted attention to linear estimators after showing that several intuitively appealing estimators are linear ones. This chapter begins immediately with linear estimators and sets out to find the BLUE estimators for the slope and intercept of a line. Does the BLUE strategy for constructing an estimator lead us to intuitively appealing estimators? It does, though the intuitions brought to bear are considerably more subtle than the intuitions that led us to several estimators for the slope of a line through the origin. Three intuitions, each more sophisticated than the one before it, lead us to the estimators of the slope and intercept that are BLUE under the Gauss–Markov Assumptions.

### The First Intuition

A first intuition for determining intuitively appealing estimators of $\beta_0$ and $\beta_1$ arises naturally if we consider graphically what the first relationship, $\overline{Y} = \tilde{\beta}_0 + \tilde{\beta}_1 \overline{X}$, requires. Figure 4.3 contains several illustrative scatterplots and "eyeballed" lines fitting those data. You might make different estimates than those shown, but it is likely that your estimates would share one trait with them: Almost surely your estimates would also lie "in the middle of the data" in each case. What constitutes "in the middle" is ambiguous; Panel (c) clarifies the concept somewhat. The fitted line is far from all sample points in that scatter, but it treads a path between the points, nonetheless—and is therefore "in the middle of the data."

The requirement that

$$\overline{Y} = \tilde{\beta}_0 + \tilde{\beta}_1 \overline{X} \qquad \textbf{4.4}$$

**Figure 4.3**

Some Scatterplots and Estimated Lines

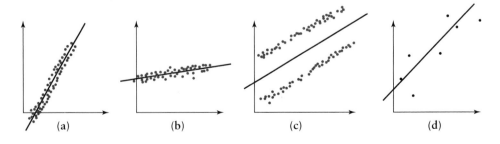

(a)          (b)          (c)          (d)

provides a specific solution to what constitutes "the middle of the data." The middle of the data, by this criterion, is the point $(\overline{X}, \overline{Y})$, and the criterion insists that our estimated line must pass through this point.

## The Second Intuition

Is the point $(\overline{X}, \overline{Y})$ an intuitively appealing specification of "the middle of the data"? It is. Equation 4.4 arises from the insight that the sample mean is an appealing estimator of the population mean. To see this, consider the mean of the sample observations, that is, the mean of the $Y_i = \beta_0 + \beta_1 X_i + \varepsilon_i$,

$$\overline{Y} = \frac{1}{n}\sum Y_i = \frac{1}{n}\sum(\beta_0 + \beta_1 X_i + \varepsilon_i) = \beta_0 + \beta_1\overline{X} + \overline{\varepsilon}.$$

In the population of all possible samples,

$$\mathrm{E}(\overline{Y}) = \mathrm{E}(\beta_0 + \beta_1\overline{X} + \overline{\varepsilon}) = \beta_0 + \beta_1\mathrm{E}(\overline{X}),$$

because $\mathrm{E}(\overline{\varepsilon}) = 0$. If we knew both $\mathrm{E}(\overline{Y})$ and $\mathrm{E}(\overline{X})$ in the population of samples,

$$\mathrm{E}(\overline{Y}) = \beta_0 + \beta_1\mathrm{E}(\overline{X})$$

would give us one equation to use in determining $\beta_0$ and $\beta_1$. Our current DGP asserts that we do know $\mathrm{E}(\overline{X})$, because the $X$'s are the same in every sample, so their mean in the population of samples is the same as the mean in any one sample, $\overline{X}$. But we do not know $\mathrm{E}(\overline{Y})$ in the population of samples. However, an estimator of $\mathrm{E}(\overline{Y})$ is readily available, namely, $\overline{Y}$, the mean $Y$ in a sample. These arguments lead us to require that any guesses of the intercept and slope, $\tilde{\beta}_0$ and $\tilde{\beta}_1$, satisfy

$$\overline{Y} = \tilde{\beta}_0 + \tilde{\beta}_1\overline{X}.$$

## The Third Intuition

Because a plausible estimator will pass through the middle of the data and because $(\overline{X}, \overline{Y})$ is an intuitive location for the middle of the data, we do want the estimators of the intercept and slope to satisfy

$$\tilde{\beta}_0 = \overline{Y} - \tilde{\beta}_1\overline{X}. \tag{4.5}$$

But Equation 4.5 alone is not enough to estimate both $\beta_0$ and $\beta_1$. Equation 4.5 is a single equation with two unknowns. We need a second relationship to uniquely determine estimates of $\beta_0$ and $\beta_1$.

Coupling our insistence that our intuitively plausible estimated line passes through $(\overline{X}, \overline{Y})$ with a minor shift in perspective leads us to a natural second

**Figure 4.4**

Transforming Variables from $X$ and $Y$ to $x$ and $y$

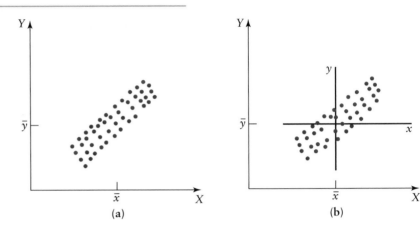

(a)                    (b)

relationship involving our estimators. Figure 4.4, Panel (a), shows a scatter of observations on $X$ and $Y$. To shift our perspective, once again define $x_i$ to be $(X_i - \overline{X})$ and $y_i$ to be $(Y_i - \overline{Y})$. The "origin" for these transformed variables, $x$ and $y$, is simply the point $(\overline{X}, \overline{Y})$, calculated from the untransformed $X$ and $Y$ variables. Panel (b) shows the same scatter, but includes the axes for $x$ and $y$, in addition to the original axes for $X$ and $Y$. Requiring that our estimated line pass through $(\overline{X}, \overline{Y})$ when written in terms of $X$ and $Y$ is the same as requiring the line to pass through the origin when expressed in terms of $x$ and $y$!

We know a fine candidate for estimating the slope of a line through the origin $(x_i = 0, y_i = 0)$: $\Sigma x_i y_i / \Sigma x_i^2$, which is $\hat{\beta}_1$ the BLUE estimator! With this estimator of $\beta_1$ in hand, we now also have an estimator for $\beta_0$. Combining our requirement that any estimator pass through the point $(\overline{X}, \overline{Y})$ with our new estimator of the slope, we arrive at the BLUE estimator for the intercept, $\hat{\beta}_0$:

$$\hat{\beta}_0 = \overline{Y} - \hat{\beta}_1 \overline{X}.$$

In sum, we arrive at $\hat{\beta}_0$ and $\hat{\beta}_1$ by three steps: (i) A good estimated line will pass through the middle of the data; (ii) $(\overline{X}, \overline{Y})$ is a good candidate for middle of the data for the same reasons that the sample mean is a good estimator for the population mean; and (iii) a line that passes through $(\overline{X}, \overline{Y})$ in $X$, $Y$ coordinates passes through the origin in $x$, $y$ coordinates, so $\beta_{g4}$ applied to $x$ and $y$ is an appealing estimator for the slope.

## A Further Insight About BLUE Estimators

In Chapter 3 we learned that when estimating a line through the origin in a DGP with homoskedastic disturbances, $\beta_{g1}$'s more heavily weighting observations associated with smaller $X$'s makes $\beta_{g1}$ inferior to $\beta_{g2}$. Observations associated with smaller $X$'s tend to be more misleading about the true slope than do observations associated with larger $X$'s. Here, with an unknown intercept in the DGP, a similar intuition explains why the BLUE weights for estimating the slope of a line give greater weight to $Y_i$'s associated with $X_i$'s further from the mean of the $X_i$'s. *Disturbances of a given size are less misleading about the slope of a line with unknown intercept when associated with an observation that has an X-value far from the mean X than when associated with an observation that has an X-value closer to the mean X.*

Look at the two scatterplots in Figure 4.5. In both, the means of $X$, $\overline{X}$ and $Y$, $\overline{Y}$ are the same; the disturbances are also the same. Only the $X$-values differ. Which scatterplot do you think provides more accurate guesses about $\beta_1$, that in Panel (a) or Panel (b)? Clearly, the scatterplot in Panel (b) does, even though the disturbances in the two scatters are the same. When the observed $X_i$'s are close together, small changes in the disturbances lead to larger changes in the estimated slope coefficients than when the observed $X_i$'s are far apart. Thus, it is not surprising that the BLUE estimator for $\beta_1$ gives greater weight to $Y_i$'s associated with $X_i$ further from the mean of the $X_i$'s.

It is certainly not the case, however, that we wish to dismiss altogether $Y_i$'s associated with $X_i$'s that lie near the mean of the $X_i$'s, $\overline{X}$. Surely, we would rather have all the data contained in Figure 4.4, not just the data in scatterplot (b). Thus, the optimal weights will give *some* weight to $Y_i$'s associated with $X_i$'s that lie near the mean of the $X_i$'s. It is a mathematical fact that $x_i/\sum x_i^2$, rather than some other formula that would also more heavily weight $Y_i$'s associated with $X_i$'s far from $\overline{X}$, gives the optimal weights.

**Figure 4.5**

Dispersed $X$-values
Yield a More Precise
Estimator

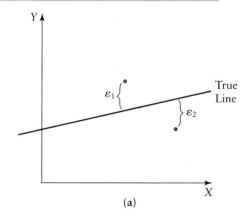

(a)

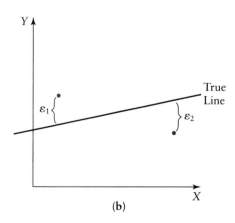

(b)

## 4.5　Logarithms in Econometrics

WHAT IS THE DGP?

In some regressions we have seen, the dependent and independent variables are measured without transformation, as in the consumption function that used consumption and income as its variables. In other regressions, the variables of interest have been transformed. For example, the Cobb–Douglas production function leads naturally to a regression in which the dependent and independent variables are measured in logarithms:

$$\ln(Q) = \beta_0 + \beta_1 \ln(L) + (1 - \beta_1) \ln(K).$$

Econometricians frequently use logarithms to specify econometric relationships. The following subsections discuss the role of logarithmic transformations in econometric analyses.

### The Attraction of Logarithms

Econometricians use logarithms because a close relationship exists between changes in a variable's logarithms and percentage changes in the variable itself. Percentages appear frequently in economic analyses, for example, in interest rates, unemployment rates, and birth rates. Percentages also appear in economic theory in the form of elasticities; for example, the income elasticity of demand for housing is the percentage change in housing consumption that accompanies a 1% change in income. Price elasticities of demand, the percentage change in the quantity demanded in response to a 1% change in price, are especially important in economics. Would a tax on cigarettes increase or decrease consumer spending on cigarettes? It depends on the elasticity. Does the minimum wage increase or decrease the total earnings of low-skill workers? It depends on the price elasticity of the demand for low-skill workers.

Because elasticities are important in so many economic analyses, econometricians are eager to find convenient ways to measure them. Logarithms provide the shortest road.

### Double Logarithmic Specifications and Elasticities

We call the specification in which both the dependent variable and the independent variable are measured in logarithms either the **double logarithmic specification** or the **logarithmic specification**. In a double logarithmic specification, such as

$$\ln(food\ bought) = \beta_0 + \beta_1 \ln(income),$$

$\beta_1$ has a specific interpretation—it is the income elasticity of food. How is this so?

By the chain rule, the derivative of the $\ln(food\ bought)$ with respect to *income* is the same as the derivative of the $\ln(food\ bought)$ with respect to *food bought* times the derivative of *food bought* with respect to *income*. Also, recall that the derivative of the $\ln(x)$ with respect to $x$ is $1/x$. Consequently, taking the derivative of $\ln(\textit{food bought})$, abbreviated as $\ln(F)$, with respect to *income*, abbreviated as $I$, we can write:

$$\frac{d \ln (F)}{dI} = \frac{d \ln (F)}{dF} \frac{d(F)}{dI} = \frac{1}{F} \frac{dF}{dI}.$$

Taking the derivative of $[\beta_0 + \beta_1 \ln (I)]$ with respect to $I$, we can then write:

$$\frac{I}{F} \frac{dF}{dI} = \frac{\beta_1}{I},$$

which implies that the income elasticity of food expenditure with respect to income is equal to $\beta_1$, that is,

$$\frac{I}{F} \frac{dF}{dI} = \beta_1.$$

To see that this is an elasticity, consider the intuitive rearrangement

$$\frac{dF}{F} \frac{I}{dI} = \frac{dF/F}{dI/I} = \frac{\%\ change\ in\ F}{\%\ change\ in\ I}.$$

Thus, $\beta_1$ is the income elasticity of food demand, as claimed. Similar examination of

$$\ln(\textit{cigarettes bought}) = \alpha_0 + \alpha_1 \ln(\textit{price of cigarettes})$$

would reveal that $\alpha_1$ is the price elasticity of cigarette demand. In the Cobb–Douglas production function, $\beta_1$ is the elasticity of output with respect to labor.

## An Example: The Phillips Curve Revisited

When Phillips estimated the relationship between unemployment and inflation, he did not rely on a linear specification of the model. A glance at Figure 4.2 reveals that the observed U.S. data are not scattered at all evenly along the fitted line. The observations at middling inflation levels all bow underneath the fitted line. A nonlinear relationship seems more in accord with the data. Figure 4.6 shows a double logarithmic relationship fit to these same data using the BLUE estimators. The logarithmic specification fits the data better than does the linear relationship in Figure 4.2. On this informal basis, most econometricians study the Phillips curve as a logarithmic relationship rather than a linear one. Table 4.2 reports the logarithmic regression results. The estimated elasticity of the unemployment rate

**Figure 4.6**

A Logarithmic
Phillips Curve

*Source*: U.S. Depart-
ment of Commerce

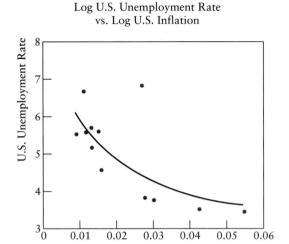

Log U.S. Unemployment Rate
vs. Log U.S. Inflation

with respect to the inflation rate is $-0.30$—a 0.3% (not percentage point) decrease in unemployment accompanies a 1% (not percentage point) increase in inflation. Unfortunately, the double logarithmic specification would not work if inflation were to become zero or negative, because logs are defined only for numbers greater than zero.

**TABLE 4.2**  A Logarithmic Phillips Curve

Dependent Variable: LOG(UNEMPLOY)
Method: Least Squares
Sample: 1958 1969
Included observations: 12

| Variable | Coefficient | Std. Error | t-Statistic | Prob. |
|---|---|---|---|---|
| C | −4.20014 | 0.354422 | −11.85070 | 0.0000 |
| LOG(INFL) | −0.29822 | 0.088681 | −3.362927 | 0.0072 |
| R-squared | 0.530721 | Mean dependent var | | −3.01986 |
| Adjusted R-squared | 0.483793 | S.D. dependent var | | 0.237922 |
| S.E. of regression | 0.170941 | Akaike info criterion | | 0.54398 |
| Sum squared resid | 0.292209 | Schwarz criterion | | 0.46316 |
| Log likelihood | 5.263894 | F-statistic | | 11.30928 |
| Durbin–Watson stat | 1.313309 | Prob(F-statistic) | | 0.007207 |

## Semilog Specifications and Percentage Changes

Elasticities are not the only useful application of logarithms in economic relation-ships. Growth rates also bear a close relationship to logarithms. In econometricians' frequent studies of how variables change over time, a convenient measure of how quickly a variable is growing is its growth rate; for example, "Computer use is growing at 5% per year." A regression with the dependent variable, say computer use, measured in logs, and the dependent variable, say year, measured in levels (for example, 2001, 2002, and so on) exposes such a growth rate. In the relationship

$$\ln(computer\ use) = \beta_0 + \beta_1 year,$$

$\beta_1$ is the annual rate of change of computer use. We call a regression model in which the dependent variable is measured in logs, but the explanators are not, a **semilogarithmic, or semilog, specification**. To see why $\beta_1$ is the annual rate of change of computer use, examine the derivative of *computer use (Y)* with respect to *year (X)* in the semilogarithmic specification:

$$\beta_1 = \frac{d\ln(Y)}{dX} = \frac{d\ln(Y)}{dY}\frac{dY}{dX} = \frac{1}{Y}\frac{dY}{dX} = \frac{dY/Y}{dX}.$$

Thus, because $d\ln(Y)/dX = \beta_1$, we can interpret $\beta_1$ as the percentage change in $Y$ for a one-unit change in $X$, that is, the percentage change in computer use per year.

Another important application of the semilog specification arises when $X$ is a variable that indicates membership or nonmembership in a group. Suppose $X$ equals 1 if an individual is male and 0 if an individual is female. A one-unit change in $X$ corresponds to shifting from observing a man to observing a woman. The coefficient $\beta_1$ is then the percentage difference in $Y$ between a man and a woman.

The derivative of a logarithm is only approximately a percentage change. The approximation invites us to infer from

$$\ln(Y) = \beta_0 + \beta_1 X$$

that

$$(\%\ change\ in\ Y) \approx \beta_1(change\ in\ X).$$

The larger the percentage change in $Y$, the less accurate this approximation is. A similar caveat applies to percentage changes in $Y$ and percentage changes in $X$ when using estimated elasticities; the percentage change interpretations of changes in $\ln(Y)$ and $\ln(X)$ are accurate for relatively small changes in $Y$ and $X$.

## An Example: The Phillips Curve Yet Again

We can re-specify the relationship between unemployment and inflation described in Tables 4.1 and 4.2 as a semilogarithmic relationship. Figure 4.7 shows the fit-ted semilog relationship and Table 4.3 reports the semilog regression results.

**Figure 4.7**

A Semilog Phillips Curve

*Source*: U.S. Department of Commerce

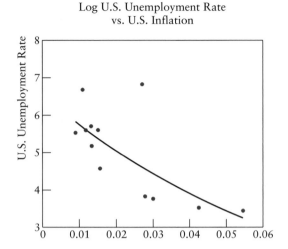

The estimated coefficient 12.27 on inflation implies that a 1% (not percentage point) decrease in unemployment accompanies each one percentage point increase in inflation. The fit of the semilogarithmic specification shown in Figure 4.7 is similar to that of the linear specification. The double log specification ap-

**TABLE 4.3  A Semilog Phillips Curve**

Dependent Variable: LOG(UNEMPLOY)
Method: Least Squares
Sample: 1958 1969
Included observations: 12

| Variable | Coefficient | Std. Error | t-Statistic | Prob. |
|---|---|---|---|---|
| C | −2.74382 | 0.094147 | −29.14405 | 0.0000 |
| INFL | −12.2717 | 3.578510 | −3.429289 | 0.0064 |
| R-squared | 0.540442 | Mean dependent var | | −3.01986 |
| Adjusted R-squared | 0.494486 | S.D. dependent var | | 0.237922 |
| S.E. of regression | 0.169161 | Akaike info criterion | | −0.56491 |
| Sum squared resid | 0.286156 | Schwarz criterion | | −0.4840 |
| Log likelihood | 5.389485 | F-statistic | | 11.76002 |
| Durbin–Watson stat | 1.059311 | Prob(F-statistic) | | 0.006446 |

# An Econometric Top 40—A Golden Oldie

## How Price Influences Demand

In 1914, Robert Lehfeldt[4] of Johannesburg, South Africa, published what has become a well-known estimate of a price elasticity of demand that relied on a double logarithmic specification. Lehfeldt reasoned that variations in weather drive fluctuations in wheat production from one year to the next and that the price of wheat adjusts, so that buyers are willing to buy all the wheat produced. Hence, he argued, the price of wheat observed in any year reflects the demand for wheat.

Lehfeldt was especially clever in his thinking. Because demand curves require *ceteris paribus*—that is, all other things to remain the same—he adjusted the annual data on wheat production to account for population growth and the attendant growth in demand. He also adjusted his price series to account for inflation, thereby effectively holding other prices constant. (The data set lehfwheat.*** on this book's Web site (**www.aw-bc.com/murray**) contains Lehfeldt's adjusted data on the worldwide quantity of wheat and on the world price of wheat as measured by the import price of wheat in Britain.[5]) Hit Figure 4.2 displays Lehfeldt's data, which spanned 1888–1911.

To facilitate estimation of the demand elasticity for wheat, Lehfeldt relied on a double logarithmic specification:

*(natural log of the price of wheat)* $= \beta_0 +$ $\beta_1^*$ *(natural logarithm of quantity of wheat)*.

Lehfeldt explained that $\beta_1$ would be the inverse of the price elasticity, e, of the demand for wheat, where

$$e = \frac{d(quantity)}{d(price)} \cdot \frac{(price)}{(quantity)}.$$

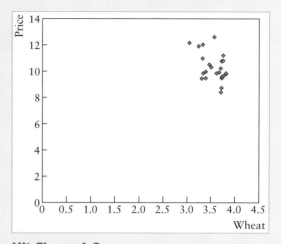

**Hit Figure 4.2**

The Demand for Wheat 1888–1911

*Source*: R. A. Lehfeldt, "The Elasticity of the Demand for Wheat," *Economic Journal* 24(1914): 212–217.

because

$$\beta = \frac{d[\log(price)]}{d[\log(quantity)]}$$

$$= \frac{d(price)}{d(quantity)} \cdot \frac{quantity}{price}$$

From the data in the scatter, Lehfeldt inferred that the price elasticity of the demand for wheat was −0.6 (that is, his estimate of $\beta_1$ was −1.67). Increases in the price of wheat would increase consumers' expenditure on this staple, because the reduction in quantity consumed would not fully offset the increase in price. Increases in wheat prices would reduce consumers' consumption of both wheat and other goods. A modern econometrician would arrive at a different estimate. Using the BLUE estimator, $\hat{\beta}_1$, yields the estimate 0.73 for $\beta_1$, implying a price elasticity of demand of $-1.37$, a markedly different estimate than Lehfeldt's.

 **Final Notes**

As we reflect on Lehfeldt's analysis, a natural question is, "How did Lehfeldt decide on $-0.6$ as his guess of the elasticity, based on his data?" George Stigler, who reports Lehfeldt's data, calls Lehfeldt's method "peculiar."[6] But Lehfeldt's efforts seem peculiar only in the light of modern econometric thought. Lehfeldt's pioneering efforts preceded the systematic thinking that guides modern practitioners of econometrics. As early 20th century economists grew weary of relying on estimators drawn from intuition, a central methodological task of econometrics became to provide criteria with which to separate estimation procedures into the peculiar and the sensible.

∎

pears to fit these data better than do the linear or the semilog specifications. Notice, however, that we could continue to apply the semilog and linear specifications if inflation turned negative (the unemployment rate cannot turn negative).[7]

## Summary

This chapter began by determining the conditions under which a linear estimator is an unbiased estimator of the slope or of the intercept of a straight line when the

 *An Organizational Structure for the Study of Econometrics*

### 1. What Is the DGP?

We specified the data-generating process:

$$Y_i = \beta_0 + \beta_1 X_i + \varepsilon_i \qquad i = 1, \ldots, n$$

plus the Gauss–Markov Assumptions, logarithms, elasticities, and rates of change.

### 2. What Makes a Good Estimator?

Without variation in X, unbiased estimation is impossible.

### 3. How Do We Create an Estimator?

BLUE estimation for the DGP above led to

$\hat{\beta}_1 = \sum x_i y_i / \sum x_i^2$ for the slope, and

$\hat{\beta}_0 = \overline{Y} - \hat{\beta}_1 \overline{X}$ for the intercept.

### 4. What Are an Estimator's Properties?

Best linear unbiased

Gauss–Markov Assumptions apply. We found that estimating the slope unbiasedly requires

$$\sum w_i^1 = 0 \qquad \text{and} \qquad \sum w_i^1 X_i = 1,$$

whereas estimating the intercept unbiasedly requires a different set of weights, satisfying the different restrictions

$$\sum w_i^0 = 1 \qquad \text{and} \qquad \sum w_i^0 X_i = 0.$$

When the $X_i$'s do not vary, these unbiasedness conditions cannot be met, and unbiased estimation is not possible. We then determined that the variance of a linear estimator in this DGP in which the Gauss–Markov Assumptions apply is

$$\sigma^2 \sum w_i^2.$$

The BLUE estimator of the slope for this DGP proved to be

$$\hat{\beta}_1 = \frac{\sum x_i y_i}{\sum x_i^2}.$$

The BLUE estimator of the intercept proved to be

$$\hat{\beta}_0 = \overline{Y} - \hat{\beta}_1 \overline{X}.$$

Finally, the chapter noted the special interpretations that apply to models in which the dependent variable, and perhaps also the independent variable, are measured in logarithms.

## Concepts for Review

| | |
|---|---|
| Double logarithmic, or logarithmic, specification   136 | Semilogarithmic, or semilog, specification   139 |

## Questions for Discussion

1. The Gauss–Markov Theorem narrows attention to bias and efficiency. Are there important features of the estimators or of the world that you think are neglected by this focus on the expected values and variances of estimators? Discuss.

2. Why do you think econometricians dwell so much on unbiased estimators? Suppose that we average estimates from a large number of econometricians who have used separate samples to estimate the price elasticity of demand for housing. How do the implications of bias differ from the implications of variance for the statistical properties of our average?

3. How much do regressions tell us about causality? Discuss this in the context of two regression equations:
   a. *poverty rate* = $\beta_0 + \beta_1(unemployment\ rate) + v$,
      with observations on a sequence of years in the United States, and

b. (*votes for Democratic senate candidate among absentee voters*) $= \alpha_0 + \alpha_1$
   (*votes for Democratic senate candidate cast on election day*),
   with observations from a sequence of Senate elections in New York State.

# Problems for Analysis

> For the data sets that you will need to solve the problems in this section,
> go to **www.aw-bc.com/murray**.

1. Estimate a model with unknown slope and intercept of a line, assuming the Gauss–Markov Assumptions hold. Suppose the mean of the $X_i$'s is 70, the mean of the $Y_i$'s is 100, the $\sum x_i y_i = -3,550$, the $\sum x_i^2 = 2,250$, $\sum y_i^2 = 4,872,040$, $n = 12$, and $\sum e_i^2 = 487,204$. Compute $\hat{\beta}_0$ and $\hat{\beta}_1$.

2. Under the Gauss–Markov Assumptions in a model with unknown slope and intercept, is $\tilde{\beta}_1 = (\sum x_i^2 y_i / \sum x_i^3)$ an unbiased estimator of the slope of the line?

3. Suppose that the DGP (that is, the data-generating process) satisfies all the Gauss–Markov Assumptions except the assumption that $E(\varepsilon_i) = 0$, which is replaced by $E(\varepsilon_i) = \alpha_0$, where $\alpha_0$ is an unknown constant.
   a. What are the expected values of $\hat{\beta}_0$ and $\hat{\beta}_1$?
   b. When the other Gauss–Markov Assumptions hold, are the variances of $\hat{\beta}_0$ and $\hat{\beta}_1$ altered if, instead of $E(\varepsilon_i) = 0$, $E(\varepsilon_i) = \alpha_0$?
   c. How would you describe the consequences of assuming $E(\varepsilon_i)$ equals 0 when $E(\varepsilon_i)$ actually equals $\alpha_0$?

4. For many years, financial analysts measured a stock's riskiness by looking at the slope coefficient in the following equation:

$$(\text{stock's rate of return} \;-\; \text{rate of return on a risk-free asset})$$
$$= \beta \,(\text{market rate of return} \;-\; \text{rate of return on a risk-free asset}) + v,$$

or, equivalently, in

$$(\text{stock's excess return}) = \beta \,(\text{market's excess return}) + v.$$

This model is known as the Capital Asset Pricing Model (CAPM). According to this model, investors require a stock with greater nondiversifiable risk to offer a higher return to compensate for that risk. The stock's "beta," the slope $\beta$ in the regression of the firm's excess return on the market's excess return, measures the asset's contribution to an optimal portfolio's undiversifiable risk. Assets with smaller betas are less risky in this sense. The file CAPM1.*** contains excess returns for the market (*mreturn*) and excess returns for two firms in the computer chip business (*freturn*) for each of 192 months. The first 192 observations pertain to firm 1; the next 192 to firm 2. The variable *firm* identifies firms 1 and 2.

The CAPM model tells us that the relationship between firms' expected excess return and the markets' excess return is a straight line through the origin. If the model is right, then $\beta_{g4}$ is the BLUE estimator of the slope. However, we could still estimate the CAPM model with an intercept included, using $\hat{\beta}_1$ to estimate the slope.

a. If the CAPM is right, is $\hat{\beta}_1$ an unbiased estimator of the slope?

b. For firms 1 and 2, what are the variances of $\hat{\beta}_1$ relative to the variances of $\beta_{g4}$? How would you describe the efficiency gain provided by the theoretical knowledge that $\beta_0 = 0$?

5. Does market power inhibit innovation? Or do noncompetitive economic profits fund advances in technology that more competitive firms can't afford? The file TFP.\*\*\* contains data pertinent to these questions. The two variables in the file are the percentage changes in industries' total factor productivity (TFP) over a 5-year period (*tfp_ch*) and the concentrations of market share (measured in percent) among industries' four largest firms (*conc*).

a. Compute the mean rate of change in TFP for the industries in the sample and the mean four-firm concentration.

b. Create a scatterplot with four-firm concentrations on the horizontal axis and TFP changes on the vertical axis. Is there a strong relationship between TFP growth and four-firm concentration across firms?

c. Regress TFP changes on four-firm concentrations. If the concentration rises one percentage point, by how much do you estimate TFP changes?

6. The file poverty1.\*\*\* contains U.S. poverty rates (*poverty*) and unemployment rates (*unemploy*), both measured in percent, from 1980 to 2003.

a. Compute the mean poverty rate and the mean unemployment rate in this sample.

b. Create a scatterplot with unemployment rates on the horizontal axis and poverty rates on the vertical axis. Is there a strong relationship between poverty rates and unemployment rates?

c. Assume the Gauss–Markov DGP and use the BLUE estimators to estimate the slope and intercept of

$$poverty\ rate = \beta_0 + \beta_1(unemployment\ rate) + v.$$

d. If the unemployment rate rises by one percentage point, by how much does the estimated expected poverty rate rise?

e. These data are from a sequence of years. Does this give you any reason to question the Gauss–Markov Assumption that the disturbances are statistically independent of one another? Did we rely on that assumption of independence when we proved $\hat{\beta}_0$ and $\hat{\beta}_1$ are unbiased in this DGP? Did we rely on that assumption when we proved that those same estimators are BLUE?

7. The file horioka.\*\*\* contains data used in 1980 by Martin Feldstein and Charles Horioka to study the relationship between countries' saving rates (*spergdp*) and investment rate (*ipergdp*).[8] Their model is

$$investment\ rate_i = \beta_0 + \beta_1(saving\ rate_i) + \varepsilon_i,$$

where *investment rate_i* is the 1960–1974 average investment rate for country $i$ and *saving rate_i* is the 1960–1974 average saving rate for country $i$.

a. Compute the mean saving and investment rates in this sample.

b. Create a scatterplot with saving rates on the horizontal axis and investment rates on the vertical axis. These rates are dollars of saving or investment per dollar of gdp. Is there an obvious relationship between investment rates and saving rates?

c. Regress *ipergdp* on *spergdp* and an intercept term. If savings were to fall by 10 cents per dollar of GDP, how much would estimated expected investment per dollar of GDP fall?

d. Is it surprising that countries' savings rates and investment rates are so closely connected? Shouldn't international capital flows allow individual countries' investment rates and savings rates to differ markedly from one another? Or might international capital be less fluid than that?

e. Make up an example, grounded in the real world, that relies on the fact that these data are from 15 successive years to cast doubt on the assumption that the disturbances are statistically independent. Does this cast doubt on the claim that the estimator $\hat{\beta}_1$ is unbiased? Does it cast doubt on the claim that the estimator $\hat{\beta}_1$ is more efficient than other unbiased linear estimators?

f. Is it reasonable in this instance to think that the explanatory variable has values that are fixed in repeated samples? What implication does this have for the claims that the estimator $\hat{\beta}_1$ is (i) unbiased and (ii) BLUE?

8. Are presidential elections affected by the economy? Do voters consider how much unemployment has changed during the election year when casting their votes for or against the party sitting in the White House? The file political.*** contains the change in unemployment in the 12 months immediately preceding the election (*unemploy*) and the percentage of the popular vote obtained by the incumbent presidential party (*incumbent* or *incumb*) in each presidential election (*year*) since 1900.[9] Both *unemploy* and *incumbent* are measured in percent.

a. Compute the means and standard deviations of changes in unemployment and of the incumbent party's proportion of the vote in this sample.

b. Create a scatterplot with the change in unemployment on the horizontal axis and the incumbent party's percent of the popular vote on the vertical axis. Is there a strong relationship between jobs and votes for the incumbent party?

c. Use the BLUE estimators to estimate the slope and intercept of

$$incumbent = \beta_0 + \beta_1(unemploy) + \varepsilon.$$

d. What is the estimated effect of a one percentage point increase in unemployment on the expected percentage of the popular vote that the incumbent party will obtain? Do the estimated sign and magnitude of this effect seem reasonable? Briefly explain.

e. The variables *incumbent* and *unemploy* are both measured in percent. Divide *unemploy* by 100, creating a new variable, *une*, that is the change in unemployment expressed as a fraction. What are the mean and standard deviation of *une*?

f. Regress *incumbent* against *une* and an intercept term. Explain the differences between these results and those in (c).

g. Divide *incumbent* by 100, creating a new variable, *inc*, that is the incumbent party's share of the vote expressed as a fraction. What are the mean and standard deviation of *inc*?

h. Regress *inc* against *unemploy* and an intercept term. Regress *inc* against *une* and an intercept term. Explain the differences between these results and those in (c) and (f).

i. How does the BLUE estimate of $\beta_1$ in this DGP compare with $\beta_{g4}$? Does $\beta_{g4}$ appear to be seriously biased in this application?

9. The relationship between votes cast on election day and votes cast absentee has recently gained increased coverage by the media. The file election.*** contains the differences in votes between Democratic and Republican candidates in Pennsylvania State Senate races for election-day vote counts (*electionday* or *eday*) and for absentee vote counts (*absentee*) from 1982 to 1993.[10]

$$electionday = (election\ day\ votes\ for\ Democratic\ candidates$$
$$- election\ day\ votes\ for\ Republican\ candidates)$$

$$absentee = (absentee\ votes\ for\ Democratic\ candidates$$
$$- absentee\ votes\ for\ Republican\ candidates)$$

On average, among election-day voters, Democratic Senate candidates received 39,007 more votes than their Republican opponents; absentee voters cast, on average 256 more votes for Democrats than for Republicans.

a. Create a scatterplot with *electionday*, the difference between Democratic and Republican candidates' votes in election-day vote counts, on the horizontal axis, and *absentee*, the difference between Democratic and Republican candidates' votes in absentee ballots, on the vertical axis. Is there a strong relationship between the difference in absentee votes and the difference in election-day votes?

b. Use the BLUE estimator to estimate the slope and intercept in

$$absentee = \beta_0 + \beta_1(election\ day) + v.$$

c. If the Democratic candidate receives 10,000 more votes than the Republican candidate from election-day voters, can we estimate how many more absentee votes the Democratic candidate will receive than the Republican candidate?

d. How does the BLUE estimate of $\beta_1$ in this DGP compare with $\beta_{g4}$? Does $\beta_{g4}$ appear to be seriously biased in this application?

10. The American welfare program that serves poor single parents and their children is called Temporary Assistance for Needy Families (TANF). TANF varies widely from state to state, both in its generosity and in its eligibility requirements. The file tanf.*** contains the basic real TANF benefit level for a family of four in each of the 50 states (*tanfreal*). Economists who study welfare across countries have found that countries that are more racially homogeneous have higher welfare benefits. Here, we explore whether this is also true across American states. In all U.S. states, African Americans are a minority. The data in tanf.*** will allow you to determine whether TANF benefits are higher in more racially homogeneous states, that is, in states with a smaller proportion of African Americans in the population. The TANF data set includes among its variables the variable *black*, which reports the fraction of a state's population that is African American.

a. Compute the means of real TANF benefits and of the proportion of states' populations that are African American.

b. Create a scatterplot with the percentage of the state's population that is African American on the horizontal axis and real TANF benefits on the vertical axis. Is there a strong relationship between *tanfreal* and *black*? Does the relationship look more logarithmic than linear?

c. Regress *tanfreal* on *black* and an intercept term. What is the estimated difference in expected real TANF benefits between a state with a population of 5% African Americans and one with 10%? How large is that difference relative to the average real TANF benefit level across all states?

d. Regress ln(*tanfreal*) on *black*. What is the estimated percentage change in real TANF benefits from a 10 percentage point increase in the proportion of African Americans in the population?

e. Regress ln(*tanfreal*) on ln(*black*). What is the estimated elasticity of real TANF benefits with respect to the proportion of the population that is African American? What is the difference between the predicted real TANF benefits in a state whose population is 5% African Americans and one with 15% African Americans?

f. Do the different specifications used in (b), (c), and (d) matter much for the estimated difference in expected real TANF benefits between a state whose population is 5% African Americans and one whose population is 15% African Americans?

11. The file food.\*\*\* contains food expenditures (*food*) and total expenditures (*total*) for a sample of 19th century Belgian workers collected by Edouard Ducpetiaux[11] and studied by Ernst Engel.[12] Chapter 1 used these data to examine Engel's Law about food expenditures and income. Engel's Law posits that a household's food expenditure grows more slowly than its income. Examine Engel's data to confirm the results of Chapter 1. Use total expenditure as your measure of income. Assume the Gauss–Markov Assumptions apply to the DGP for Ducpetiaux's data.

a. Compute the means of total expenditure and food expenditure.

b. Create a scatterplot with total expenditures on the horizontal axis and food expenditures on the vertical axis. Is there a strong relationship between food expenditure and total expenditure?

c. Use the BLUE estimator to estimate the slope and intercept in

$$food\ expenditure = \beta_0 + \beta_1(income) + v.$$

d. How does the BLUE estimate of $\beta_1$ in this DGP compare with $\beta_{g4}$? Does $\beta_{g4}$ appear to be seriously biased in this application?

e. Does your estimate of $\beta_0$ imply that food's share in expenditures falls as income rises?

f. Use the BLUE estimator to estimate the slope and intercept in

$$\ln(food\ expenditure) = \beta_0 + \beta_1 \ln(income) + v.$$

g. How does the BLUE estimate of $\beta_1$ in this DGP compare with $\beta_{g4}$? Does $\beta_{g4}$ appear to be seriously biased in this application?

h. Does your estimate of the income elasticity of food demand support Engel's Law?

i. Make an economic argument against the assumption that the disturbances for housing expenditures all have the same variance. Does this cast doubt on the claim that the estimator $\hat{\beta}_1$ is unbiased? Or that the estimator $\hat{\beta}_1$ is more efficient than other unbiased linear estimators?

j. Would it have been possible for Ducpetiaux to gather further samples of workers with the same total expenditures as those in this study? Does that warrant his using the assumption of explanators being fixed across samples? If not, what implication does this have for the claims that the estimator $\hat{\beta}_1$ is (a) unbiased and (b) BLUE?

k. What are some determinants of food expenditure that are captured by the disturbance terms in the regression equations?

12. The file housing2.*** contains housing expenditures (*housing*) and total expenditures (*total*) for a sample of 19th century Belgian workers collected by Edouard Ducpetiaux[13] and studied by Ernst Engel. Chapter 1 examined Engel's Law about food expenditures and income. Engel's Law posits that a household's food expenditure grows more slowly than its income. Here we examine Engel's data to see if he could have also concluded that housing expenditure grows more slowly than income. Use total expenditure as your measure of income. Assume the Gauss–Markov Assumptions apply to the DGP for Ducpetiaux's data.

a. Create a scatterplot with total expenditures on the horizontal axis and housing expenditure on the vertical axis. Is there a strong relationship between housing expenditure and total expenditure?

b. Two observations in the scatterplot seem mildly anomalous in that two individuals have total expenditures that are almost entirely housing expenditures. Do you believe these two observations are correct? How could you account for this for individuals observed in the middle of the 19th century? Do you think these individuals were starving?

c. Does the scatterplot give a visual impression at odds with the assumption that the disturbance for each observation in a regression of housing expenditures on income has the same variance, $\sigma^2$?

d. Use the BLUE estimator to estimate the slope and intercept in

$$housing\ expenditure = \beta_0 + \beta_1(income) + v.$$

e. How does the BLUE estimate of $\beta_1$ in this DGP compare with $\beta_{g4}$? Does $\beta_{g4}$ appear to be seriously biased in this application?

f. Does your estimate of $\beta_0$ imply that housing's share in expenditures falls as income rises?

g. Use the BLUE estimator to estimate the slope and intercept in

$$\ln(housing\ expenditure) = \beta_0 + \beta_1 \ln(income) + v.$$

h. How does the BLUE estimate of $\beta_1$ in this DGP compare with $\beta_{g4}$? Does $\beta_{g4}$ appear to be seriously biased in this application?

i. Does your estimate of the income elasticity of housing demand support the existence of an Engel's Law for housing?

j. Are your regression results altered much if you delete the two anomalous observations?

k. Make an economic argument against the assumption that the disturbances for housing expenditures all have the same variance? Does this cast doubt on the claim that the estimator $\hat{\beta}_1$ is unbiased? That the estimator $\hat{\beta}_1$ is more efficient than other unbiased linear estimators?

l. Had he wanted to, could Ducpetiaux have gathered further samples of workers with the same total expenditures as those in this study? Does that warrant his using the assumption of explanators being fixed across samples? If not, what implication does this have for the claims that the estimator $\hat{\beta}_1$ is (i) unbiased and (ii) BLUE?

m. What are some determinants of housing expenditure that are captured by the disturbance terms in the regression equations?

13. Suppose you have a sample of observations on firms' investment expenditures (*invest*) and on the real interest rate that firms expect (*realrate*). What equation would you use to estimate the elasticity of investment demand with respect to the expected real interest rate, if you were willing to assume that elasticity is a constant?

 14. The file wineweather.*** contains the natural log of the average 1989 prices (*logprice*) for Bordeaux wines for the vintages from 1952 to 1989 (*vintage* or *vint*). The age of each vintage in 1989 is given by the variable *age*. These data were part of an analysis of Bordeaux wine as an investment by economists Orley Ashenfelter and David Ashmore of Princeton University and Robert LaLonde of the University of Chicago.[14]

a. Compute the mean of the log of the price in this sample. What price of wine has that natural logarithm?

b. Compute the price of wine for each observation. Then compute the mean price of wine in this sample. Why does the mean price of wine in the sample not equal the wine whose price has a logarithm equal to the mean of the logs of the prices of wine in the sample?

c. Create a scatterplot with age on the horizontal axis and the log of price on the vertical axis. Do older wines tend to sell for more than younger wines? Does an older wine always sell for more than a younger wine?

d. Estimate the semilog relationship

$$\ln(price) = \beta_0 + \beta_1(age) + v.$$

How much does the expected price of a bottle of wine grow per year?

e. Estimate the semilog relationship

$$\ln(price) = \alpha_0 + \alpha_1(vintage) + v.$$

How does the estimated coefficient on *vintage* compare with the estimated coefficient on *age*? Briefly explain why this is so. Why do the estimated intercepts in the two equations differ as they do?

 15. The file sat1.*** contains the Scholastic Achievement Test score (*SAT*) measured in total points on a 1600-point scale and four-year grade point average (*totgpa*) on a four-point scale for a sample of Bates College students.

a. Compute the mean SAT score and mean GPA for this sample of Bates students.

b. Create a scatterplot with SAT score on the horizontal axis and GPA on the vertical axis. Is there a strong relationship between SAT score and GPA?

c. Regress *totgpa* on *SAT* and an intercept term. If two students differ by 100 points in their SAT scores, what is the estimated difference in their expected grade point averages?

 16. Trygve Haavelmo used the data from 1922 to 1941 in haavelmo2.*** to estimate the marginal propensity to consume.[15] Haavelmo reported a value of 0.73 when he used these data to estimate a consumption function of the form

$$consumption = \beta_0 + \beta_1(income) + u.$$

The measure of consumption in this data set is *real_cons*; the measure of income is *real_gdp*. Milton Friedman later argued[16] that the consumption function passes through the origin, as in

$$consumption = \beta(income) + u,$$

where $\beta$ is the marginal propensity to consume. Friedman recommended estimating the marginal propensity to consume using $\beta_{g2}$. Across 45 studies, Friedman's estimates average 0.92. We will learn more about Friedman's arguments for omitting the intercept term in a later chapter.

a. Create a scatterplot with gross domestic product (GDP) on the horizontal axis and consumption on the vertical axis. Is there an obvious relationship between consumption and income?

b. Estimate the marginal propensity to consume in Haavelmo's model, $\beta_1$, using $\hat{\beta}_1$, and estimate the marginal propensity to consume in Friedman's specification, $\beta$, using both $\beta_{g2}$ and $\beta_{g4}$.

c. In Keynesian macroeconomic theory, an independent change in government spending, $\Delta G$, increases income by $\Delta G/(1 - \beta)$. This is called "the multiplier effect," and "the multiplier" is $1/(1 - \beta)$. What is the range of estimated multipliers across your three estimates of the marginal propensity to consume? Does omitting the intercept term result in a markedly different estimated multiplier with the Haavelmo data?

d. Make up an example, grounded in the real world, that relies on the fact that these data are from 21 successive years to cast doubt on the assumption that the disturbances are statistically independent? Does this cast doubt upon the claim that the estimator $\hat{\beta}_1$ is unbiased? That the estimator $\hat{\beta}_1$ is more efficient than other unbiased linear estimators?

e. Is it reasonable in this instance to think that the explanatory variable has values that are fixed in repeated samples? What implication does this have for the claims that the estimator $\hat{\beta}_1$ is (i) unbiased and (ii) BLUE?

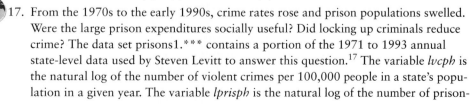 17. From the 1970s to the early 1990s, crime rates rose and prison populations swelled. Were the large prison expenditures socially useful? Did locking up criminals reduce crime? The data set prisons1.*** contains a portion of the 1971 to 1993 annual state-level data used by Steven Levitt to answer this question.[17] The variable *lvcph* is the natural log of the number of violent crimes per 100,000 people in a state's population in a given year. The variable *lprisph* is the natural log of the number of prison-

ers in the state during a given year. The data set also contains *chlvcph* and *chlprisph*, the changes in *lvcph* and *lprisph* from one year to the next in a given state, and the variables *state* and *year* to identify the states and years.

a. Regress the log of the violent crimes per 100,000 people (the log of the violent crime rate) against an intercept term and the log of the number of prisoners per 100,000 people (the log of the incarceration rate). Interpret the estimated coefficients.

b. These data are a combination of time series and cross section, with 23 years of data for each of 50 states and the District of Columbia. California is state number 5; Illinois is number 14; New York is number 34. Restrict the data to each of these states in turn. Create scatterplots for each, first with year on the horizontal axis and violent crime rate on the vertical axis, then with year on the horizontal axis and incarceration rate on the vertical axis. Do the same for one or two other states. What appears to be the consistent pattern of both crime rates and incarceration rates over time?

c. In time series data, there are sometimes third variables that influence both the dependent variable and the explanator, driving both steadily in one direction or another over time and biasing the OLS estimator. Econometricians sometimes sidestep this problem by analyzing *the changes* in the variables, rather than *the levels*. Regress the change in the log of the violent crime rate against the change in the log of the incarceration rate. Interpret the estimated coefficients.

18. Use calculus to derive the BLUE estimator for the intercept of a line in the special case in which $n = 3$. Assume the Gauss–Markov Assumptions hold and that the relationship has a single unknown slope coefficient, as well as the unknown intercept. Alternatively, use the Lagrangian method to derive the estimator for the slope of a line in the general case of $n$ observations.

## Endnotes

1. A.W. Phillips, "The Relation Between Unemployment and the Rate of Change of Money Wages in the United Kingdom, 1861–1957," *Economica* 25 (November 1958): 283–299.

2. Phillips's technique was simple, but his curve was not. He reported his fitted line for 1861–1913 as ln(unemployment) = 0.71 − 0.53ln(inflation − 0.90). Phillips arrived at these numbers by trial and error, picking the combination he thought best fit the data.

3. In Chapter 3, the simplest case of interest was for $n = 2$ because for $n = 1$, the choice of estimator was obvious—connect the one data point to the origin. Similarly, when both the slope and intercept are unknown, if $n$ were 2, a straight line could fit the data perfectly, and the choice among estimators is not difficult—we would fit the line to the data. The simplest case in which the choice of slope and intercept estimators is not obvious is, therefore, that in which $n = 3$.

4. R. A. Lehfeldt, "The Elasticity of the Demand for Wheat," *Economic Journal* 24(1914): 212–217.

5. These data are taken from George Stigler, "The Early History of Empirical Studies of Consumer Behavior," *Journal of Political Economy* 62, no. 2 (April 1954): 95–113.

6. Ibid. 110.

7. The linear, logarithmic, and double logarithmic specifications are all special cases of a more general specification that econometricians call the Box–Cox transformation. The Box–Cox transformation allows us to test formally each of these specifications. For more about the Box–Cox transformation, see William Greene, *Econometric Analysis*, 5th ed. (Englewood Cliffs, NJ: Prentice-Hall, 2002): 173–175.

8. Martin Feldstein and Charles Horioka, "Domestic Savings and International Capital Flows," *Economic Journal* 90 (June 1980): 314–329.

9. Gary Smith of Pomona College generously provided these data.

10. Gary Smith of Pomona College generously provided these data.

11. Edouard Ducpetiaux, *Budgets Economiques de Classes de Ouvrieres en Belgique* (Brussels: Hayaz, 1855).

12. Ernst Engel, "Die Productions und Consumptionsverhaeltnisse des Koenigsreichs Sachsen," reprinted in *Die Lebenskosten Belgischer Arbeiter-Familien*, *International Statistical Bulletin* 9, no. 1 (Dresden, 1895): 1–124.

13. Edouard Ducpetiaux, *Budgets Economiques*.

14. Orley Ashenfelter, David Ashmore, and Robert LaLonde, "Bordeaux Wine Vintage Quality and the Weather," http://www.liquidasset.com/orley.htm (accessed December 1999).

15. Trygve Haavelmo, "Methods of Measuring the Marginal Propensity to Consume," *Journal of the American Statistical Association* 42 (March 1947): 105–122.

16. Milton Friedman, *A Theory of the Consumption Function* (Princeton, NJ: Princeton University Press, 1957).

17. Steven D. Levitt, "The Effect of Prison Population Size on Crime Rates: Evidence from Prison Overcrowding Litigation," *Quarterly Journal of Economics* 111, no. 2 (May 1996): 319–351.

 *Appendix 4.A*

# Finding the BLUE Estimator for the Slope of a Straight Line with an Unknown Intercept

Section 4.3 asserts without proof that the BLUE estimator of the slope of a line with unknown intercept is

$$\hat{\beta}_1 = \frac{\sum (X_i - \overline{X}) Y_i}{\sum (X_i - \overline{X})^2}$$

under the Gauss–Markov Assumptions.

This appendix uses the method of Lagrangian multipliers to derive the BLUE estimator under the Gauss–Markov Assumptions for samples with any number of observations. Available on this book's companion Web site (**www.aw-bc.com/murray**) is an auxiliary appendix that uses more elementary calculus to derive the BLUE estimator for the slope of a straight line with an unknown intercept when samples contain three observations and the Gauss–Markov Assumptions apply.

## 4.A.1    The Lagrangian Approach for the Case of $n$ Observations

This section finds the BLUE estimator for $\beta_1$, the slope coefficient for any number of observations, $n$. Begin by forming the Lagrangian function

$$L = \sigma^2 \sum w_i^2 - \lambda_1\left(\sum w_i\right) - \lambda_2\left(\sum w_i X_i - 1\right).$$

Taking the derivatives of this function with respect to the $w_i$, $\lambda_1$ and $\lambda_2$, we obtain:

$$\partial L/\partial w_i = 2\sigma^2 w_i - \lambda_1 - \lambda_2 X_i = 0, \tag{4.A.1}$$

$$\partial L/\partial \lambda_1 = \sum w_i = 0, \tag{4.A.2}$$

and

$$\partial L/\partial \lambda_2 = \sum w_i X_i - 1 = 0. \tag{4.A.3}$$

From Equation 4.A.1 we can conclude that

$$w_i = \tfrac{1}{2}\sigma^2(\lambda_1 + \lambda_2 X_1), \tag{4.A.4}$$

and therefore that $\sum w_i$ (which equals 0, according to Equation 4.A.2) can be written as

$$\sum w_i = 0 = \sum(\tfrac{1}{2}\sigma^2[\lambda_1 + \lambda_2 X_i]) = \tfrac{1}{2}\sigma^2 \sum \lambda_1 + \tfrac{1}{2}\sigma^2 \sum(\lambda_2 X_i)$$
$$= \tfrac{1}{2}\sigma^2 n\lambda_1 + \tfrac{1}{2}\sigma^2 \lambda_2 \sum X_i.$$

This implies that

$$n\lambda_1 = -\lambda_2 \sum X_i = -\lambda_2 n\overline{X},$$

where $\overline{X}$ is the mean of the $X_i$'s. Thus

$$\lambda_1 = -\lambda_2 \overline{X}.$$

Substituting $-\lambda_2\overline{X}$ for $\lambda_1$ in Equation 4.A.4, we then obtain

$$w_i = \tfrac{1}{2}(-\lambda_2\overline{X} + \lambda_2 X_i) = \tfrac{1}{2}(\lambda_2[X_i - \overline{X}]) = \tfrac{1}{2}\lambda_2 x_i. \qquad \textbf{4.A.5}$$

Substituting this last expression for the $w_i$ in Equation 4.A.3, we obtain

$$\sum(\tfrac{1}{2}\lambda_2 x_i X_i) - 1 = 0,$$

so that

$$\tfrac{1}{2}\lambda_2 \sum(x_i X_i) = 1$$

or

$$\lambda_2 = 2/\sum(x_i X_i) = 2/\sum(x_i^2) \qquad \textbf{4.A.6}$$

because $\sum x_i X_i = \sum x_i^2$. To see that $\sum x_i X_i = \sum x_i^2$, note that $\sum x_i = 0$, which implies that

$$\sum(x_i X_i) = \sum(x_i X_i) - \overline{X}\sum x_i = \sum[x_i(X_i - \overline{X})] = \sum(x_i^2).$$

Combining Equations 4.A.6 and 4.A.5, we arrive at

$$w_i = \tfrac{1}{2}\left[2/\sum(x_i^2)\right](x_i) = x_i/\sum(x_i^2),$$

which are the weights for the BLUE estimator of the slope of a line with an unknown intercept.

## *Appendix 4.B*

# Matrix Algebra and Estimating the Slope of a Straight Line with an Unknown Intercept

The matrix approach developed in Appendix 3.A can be extended to the case of a straight line with an intercept. We can then express the results of the main text of this chapter in matrix algebra notation.

## 4.B.1   Constructing Appealing Linear Estimators of $\hat{\beta}_1$ and $\hat{\beta}_0$

This section presents a matrix formulation of the estimation of both $\hat{\beta}_1$ and $\hat{\beta}_0$. Along the way, the section generalizes the matrix notation and matrix manipulations of Appendix 3.A.

### A Matrix Representation of a Regression Model Including an Intercept

To express the model

$$Y_i = \beta_0 + \beta_1 X_{1i} + \varepsilon_i \qquad i = 1, \ldots, n$$

in matrix form, first consider that $\beta_0$ could be equally well stated as $\beta_0 \cdot 1$. Our rules for adding matrices and for multiplying matrices by scalars suffice for us to write

$$\begin{bmatrix} Y_1 \\ Y_2 \\ Y_3 \\ \cdot \\ \cdot \\ \cdot \\ Y_n \end{bmatrix} = \begin{bmatrix} 1 \\ 1 \\ 1 \\ \cdot \\ \cdot \\ \cdot \\ 1 \end{bmatrix} \beta_0 + \begin{bmatrix} X_{11} \\ X_{12} \\ X_{13} \\ \cdot \\ \cdot \\ \cdot \\ X_{1n} \end{bmatrix} \beta_1 + \begin{bmatrix} \varepsilon_1 \\ \varepsilon_2 \\ \varepsilon_3 \\ \cdot \\ \cdot \\ \cdot \\ \varepsilon_n \end{bmatrix}.$$

Define:

$$\mathbf{Y} = \begin{bmatrix} Y_1 \\ Y_2 \\ Y_3 \\ \cdot \\ \cdot \\ \cdot \\ Y_n \end{bmatrix} \qquad \mathbf{I}_0 = \begin{bmatrix} 1 \\ 1 \\ 1 \\ \cdot \\ \cdot \\ \cdot \\ 1 \end{bmatrix} \qquad \mathbf{X}_1 = \begin{bmatrix} X_{11} \\ X_{12} \\ X_{13} \\ \cdot \\ \cdot \\ \cdot \\ X_{1n} \end{bmatrix}.$$

Then, write:

$$\mathbf{Y} = \mathbf{I}_0 \beta_0 + \mathbf{X}_1 \beta_1 + \boldsymbol{\varepsilon}. \qquad\qquad \text{4.B.1}$$

The matrix $\mathbf{I}_0$, a column of $n$ 1's, is useful in matrix algebra manipulations in its own right, but in the present context, it is illuminating to define

$$\mathbf{X}_0 = \mathbf{I}_0.$$

This notation highlights the fact that the intercept term is quite like other explanators.

Next, define:

$$X = [X_0 X_1] \qquad \text{4.B.2}$$

and

$$\boldsymbol{\beta}' = [\beta_0 \beta_1], \qquad \text{4.B.3}$$

so that the right-hand rule for multiplying matrices allows us to write:

$$Y = X\boldsymbol{\beta} + \boldsymbol{\varepsilon},$$

because $X\boldsymbol{\beta} = X_0\beta_0 + X_1\beta_1$. This very compact notation generalizes to models with many explanators by simply adding more columns to $X$ and more rows to $\boldsymbol{\beta}$.

## Multiplying Matrices Revisited

Appendix 3.A used the multiplication of matrices to represent $\beta_{g4}$ as $(X'X)^{-1}X'Y$. This appendix represents both $\hat{\beta}_1$ and $\hat{\beta}_0$ with matrix multiplication but first generalizes the definition of matrix multiplication beyond the definition given in Appendix 3.A, which sufficed for multiplying vectors. Recall that Appendix 3.A suggested the right-hand rule for multiplying a row vector and a column vector: To multiply a row vector $A$ by a column vector $C$, we (i) point a thumb at the first item on the left of the row vector $A$ and an index finger at the top element in the column vector $C$; (ii) multiply the two elements together; (iii) roll our thumb and index finger to point at the next two elements, multiplying them and adding that product to the preceding; and (iv) continue until we form $[\Sigma A_i C_i]$.

Equation 4.B.2 defines $X$ to be a row vector made up of two matrices, $X_0$ and $X_1$. This depiction allowed us to multiply $X$ and the column vector $\boldsymbol{\beta}$ using our right-hand rule for multiplying a row vector by a column vector: $X\boldsymbol{\beta} = X_0\beta_0 + X_1\beta_1$. An alternative way to picture this same $X$ matrix is to see it as a matrix with 2 columns and $n$ rows:

$$
\begin{bmatrix} Y_1 \\ Y_2 \\ Y_3 \\ \cdot \\ \cdot \\ \cdot \\ Y_n \end{bmatrix}
=
\begin{bmatrix} 1 & X_{11} \\ 1 & X_{12} \\ 1 & X_{13} \\ & \cdot \\ & \cdot \\ & \cdot \\ 1 & X_{1n} \end{bmatrix}
\begin{bmatrix} \beta_0 \\ \beta_1 \end{bmatrix}
+
\begin{bmatrix} \varepsilon_1 \\ \varepsilon_2 \\ \varepsilon_3 \\ \cdot \\ \cdot \\ \cdot \\ \varepsilon_n \end{bmatrix}
$$

$X$ has $n$ rows and 2 columns; such a matrix is said to have **dimensions** $n$ by 2 (often written $n \times 2$), or to be an $n$ by 2 matrix. The matrix containing the intercept and slope coefficients, $\boldsymbol{\beta}$, has 2 rows and 1 column; it is said to be a 2 by 1 matrix. How, then, do we multiply an $n \times 2$ matrix by a $2 \times 1$ matrix? The right-hand rule of Appendix 3.A, applied to each row of the $n \times 2$ matrix in turn, does the trick; each application of the right-hand rule creates a new row for the product matrix. Consequently, the result from multiplying an $n \times 2$ matrix by a $2 \times 1$ matrix will be an $n \times 1$ matrix. The product $X\beta$, therefore, has $n$ rows, just as needed for

$$
\begin{bmatrix} Y_1 \\ Y_2 \\ Y_3 \\ \cdot \\ \cdot \\ Y_n \end{bmatrix} = \begin{bmatrix} \beta_0 + X_{11}\ \beta_1 \\ \beta_0 + X_{12}\ \beta_1 \\ \beta_0 + X_{13}\ \beta_1 \\ \cdot \\ \cdot \\ \beta_0 + X_{1n}\ \beta_1 \end{bmatrix} + \begin{bmatrix} \varepsilon_1 \\ \varepsilon_2 \\ \varepsilon_3 \\ \cdot \\ \cdot \\ \varepsilon_n \end{bmatrix},
$$

which is our model. Notice that applying the right-hand rule repeatedly requires that the first matrix in a multiplication must have the same number of columns as the second matrix has rows, so, in the present case, $X$ has 2 columns and $\beta$ has 2 rows, whereas their product has $n$ rows and one column. Note that these requirements and results generalize. The product of an $n \times m$ matrix and an $m \times p$ matrix will always be an $n \times p$ matrix, and matrix multiplication is possible only if the number of columns in the first matrix matches the number of rows in the second, as in an $n \times m$ matrix times an $m \times p$ matrix.

## A Computational Path to Building $\hat{\beta}_1$ and $\hat{\beta}_0$

Appendix 3.A represented $\beta_{g4}$ as more heavily weighting observations with large $X$-values by initially premultiplying both sides of the regression model by $X'$. In the present instance, $X'$ is defined by

$$
X' = \begin{bmatrix} 1 & 1 & 1 & \cdot & \cdot & 1 \\ X_{11} & X_{12} & X_{13} & \cdot & \cdot & X_{1n} \end{bmatrix}
$$

In that same spirit, write

$$
X'Y = X'X\beta + X'\varepsilon.
$$

Because $X'$ is a $2 \times n$ matrix and $Y$ is an $n \times 1$ matrix, they can be multiplied together using the extended right-hand rule. When matrices have dimensions that permit multiplication, mathematicians say the matrices **conform** to one another.

What is $X'Y$?

$$
X'Y = \begin{bmatrix} 1 & 1 & 1 & \cdot & \cdot & 1 \\ X_{11} & X_{12} & X_{13} & \cdot & \cdot & X_{1n} \end{bmatrix} \begin{bmatrix} Y_1 \\ Y_2 \\ Y_3 \\ \cdot \\ \cdot \\ Y_n \end{bmatrix} = \begin{bmatrix} \sum_{i=1}^{n} Y_i \\ \sum_{i=1}^{n} X_{1i}Y_i \end{bmatrix}.
$$

## Multiplying Matrices When Neither Is a Vector

We now know what $X'Y$ is, but what is $X'X$? Because $X'$ is $2 \times n$ and $X$ is $n \times 2$, they do conform to one another, so multiplication is possible, but *how* do we multiply them together? By repeated applications of the right-hand rule. When we multiply an $n \times m$ matrix by an $m \times p$ matrix, we form the item in the $i$-th row and $j$-th column of the $n \times p$ product matrix by applying the right-hand rule to the $i$-th row of the first matrix and the $j$-th column of the second matrix. Thus $X'X$ is

$$X'X = \begin{bmatrix} 1 & 1 & 1 & \cdot & \cdot & 1 \\ X_{11} & X_{12} & X_{13} & \cdot & \cdot & X_{1n} \end{bmatrix} \begin{bmatrix} 1 & X_{11} \\ 1 & X_{12} \\ 1 & X_{13} \\ \cdot & \cdot \\ \cdot & \cdot \\ 1 & X_{1n} \end{bmatrix} = \begin{bmatrix} n & \sum_{i=1}^{n} X_{1i} \\ \sum_{i=1}^{n} X_{1i} & \sum_{i=1}^{n} X_{1i}^2 \end{bmatrix}.$$

Notice that $X'X$ has dimensions $2 \times 2$. Any matrix with the same number of rows as columns is called a **square matrix**. Notice, too, that the off-diagonal elements of $X'X$ are equal; a square matrix in which the off-diagonal $jk$-th element always equals the off-diagonal $kj$-th element is called a **symmetric matrix**.

## Extending the Notion of an Inverse Matrix

Appendix 3.A isolated $\beta$ in $X'Y = X'X\beta + X'\varepsilon$ by multiplying both sides by $(X'X)^{-1}$. To do this, Appendix 3.A defined the **inverse of a matrix** $M$ to be the matrix $M^{-1}$ such that

$$M^{-1}M = I,$$

where $I$ is an identity matrix. There, $I = [1]$. More generally, the **identity matrix** is

$$I_m = \begin{bmatrix} 1 & 0 & 0 & \cdot & 0 \\ 0 & 1 & 0 & \cdot & 0 \\ \cdot & \cdot & \cdot & & \cdot \\ \cdot & \cdot & \cdot & & \cdot \\ 0 & 0 & 0 & \cdot & 1 \end{bmatrix},$$

with $m$ 1's along the diagonal and 0's elsewhere. $I_m$ is always a square matrix; $m$ can be any strictly positive integer. When the dimensions of an identity matrix are clear from the context, the subscript $m$ is usually omitted. The identity matrix has the property that multiplying it by any matrix with which it is conformable, say $A$, or $B$ results in a product equal to that other matrix, $A$; that is,

$$IA = A$$

or

$$BI = B.$$

## The Estimators $\hat{\beta}_0$ and $\hat{\beta}_1$

Multiplying both sides of

$$X'Y = X'X\beta + X'\varepsilon$$

by $(X'X)^{-1}$ yields

$$\hat{\beta} = \begin{bmatrix} \hat{\beta}_0 \\ \hat{\beta}_1 \end{bmatrix}$$

$$\hat{\beta} = (X'X)^{-1}X'Y = (X'X)^{-1}(X'X)\beta + (X'X)^{-1}X'\varepsilon = \beta + (X'X)^{-1}X'\varepsilon.$$

Determining the inverse for any particular matrix can be complicated. Fortunately, computer algorithms allow us to easily calculate the inverses we need to compute our BLUE estimators. Conveniently, in the special case of a $2 \times 2$ matrix, there is a formula for the inverse. For our $X'X$ matrix, the inverse is

$$[X'X]^{-1} = \begin{bmatrix} \sum_{i=1}^{n} X_i^2 / n \sum_{i=1}^{n} x_i^2 & -\sum_{i=1}^{n}(X_i/n) / \sum_{i=1}^{n} x_i^2 \\ -\sum_{i=1}^{n}(X_i/n) / \sum_{i=1}^{n} x_i^2 & 1/\sum_{i=1}^{n} x_{1i}^2 \end{bmatrix}$$

where $x_i = (X_i - \overline{X})$ as above. Notice that the elements of $(X'X)^{-1}$, were they multiplied by $\sigma^2$, would equal the variances and covariance of $\hat{\beta}_0$ and $\hat{\beta}_1$; thus the matrix notation provides a highly compact rendering of these variances and covariance: $\sigma^2(X'X)^{-1}$. Notice, too, that $(X'X)^{-1}$ is symmetric. The inverse of a symmetric matrix, if it exists, is always symmetric.

Multiplying $(X'X)^{-1}$ by $(X'Y)$, using the extended right-hand rule, reveals that $\hat{\beta}$ is indeed

$$\begin{bmatrix} \hat{\beta}_0 \\ \hat{\beta}_1 \end{bmatrix}$$

because

$$\sum(X_i - \overline{X})^2 = \sum(X_i^2 - 2X_i\overline{X} + \overline{X}^2) = \sum(X_i^2) - n\overline{X}^2$$

implies that

$$\sum(X_i^2) = \sum(x_i^2) + n\overline{X}^2:$$

$$\hat{\boldsymbol{\beta}} = [X'X]^{-1}X'Y = \begin{bmatrix} \sum_{i=1}^{n} X_i^2/n\sum_{i=1}^{n} x_i^2 & -\sum_{i=1}^{n}(X_i/n)/\sum_{i=1}^{n} x_i^2 \\ -\sum_{i=1}^{n}(X_i/n)/\sum_{i=1}^{n} x_i^2 & 1/\sum_{i=1}^{n} x_i^2 \end{bmatrix} \begin{bmatrix} \sum_{i=1}^{n} Y_i \\ \sum_{i=1}^{n} X_i Y_i \end{bmatrix}$$

$$= \begin{bmatrix} \left(\sum_{i=1}^{n} X_i^2/n\sum_{i=1}^{n} x_i^2\right)\left(\sum_{i=1}^{n} Y_i\right) + \left(-\sum_{i=1}^{n}(X_i/n)/\sum_{i=1}^{n} x_i^2\right)\left(\sum_{i=1}^{n} X_i Y_i\right) \\ \left(-\sum_{i=1}^{n}(X_i/n)/\sum_{i=1}^{n} x_i^2\right)\left(\sum_{i=1}^{n} Y_i\right) + \left(1/\sum_{i=1}^{n} x_{1i}^2\right)\left(\sum_{i=1}^{n} X_i Y_i\right) \end{bmatrix}$$

$$= \begin{bmatrix} \left(\left(\sum_{i=1}^{n} X_i^2 + n(\overline{X})^2\right)/n\sum_{i=1}^{n} x_i^2\right)\left(\sum_{i=1}^{n} Y_i\right) + \left((-\overline{X})/\sum_{i=1}^{n} x_i^2\right)\left(\sum_{i=1}^{n} X_i Y_i\right) \\ \left((-\overline{X})/\sum_{i=1}^{n} x_i^2\right)\left(\sum_{i=1}^{n} Y_i\right) + \left(1/\sum_{i=1}^{n} x_{1i}^2\right)\left(\sum_{i=1}^{n} X_i Y_i\right) \end{bmatrix}$$

$$= \begin{bmatrix} \left((1/n) + (\overline{X})^2/\sum_{i=1}^{n} x_i^2\right)\left(\sum_{i=1}^{n} Y_i\right) + \left((-\overline{X})/\sum_{i=1}^{n} x_i^2\right)\left(\sum_{i=1}^{n} X_i Y_i\right) \\ \left((-1/\sum_{i=1}^{n} x_i^2\right)\left(\sum_{i=1}^{n} \overline{X} Y_i\right) + \left(1/\sum_{i=1}^{n} x_{1i}^2\right)\left(\sum_{i=1}^{n} X_i Y_i\right) \end{bmatrix}$$

$$= \begin{bmatrix} (1/n)\sum_{i=1}^{n} Y_i + \left(\overline{X}/\sum_{i=1}^{n} x_i^2\right)\left(\sum_{i=1}^{n} \overline{X} Y_i\right) + \left((-\overline{X})/\sum_{i=1}^{n} x_i^2\right)\left(\sum_{i=1}^{n} X_i Y_i\right) \\ \left((-1/\sum_{i=1}^{n} x_i^2\right)\left(\sum_{i=1}^{n} \overline{X} Y_i\right) + \left(1/\sum_{i=1}^{n} x_{1i}^2\right)\left(\sum_{i=1}^{n} X_i Y_i\right) \end{bmatrix}$$

$$= \begin{bmatrix} \overline{Y} - \overline{X}\left(\sum_{i=1}^{n}(X_i - \overline{X})Y_i\right)/\left(\sum_{i=1}^{n} x_i^2\right) \\ \left(\sum_{i=1}^{n}(X_i - \overline{X})Y_i\right)/\left(\sum_{i=1}^{n} x_i^2\right) \end{bmatrix}$$

$$= \begin{bmatrix} \hat{\beta}_0 \\ \hat{\beta}_1 \end{bmatrix},$$

as stated. Because

$$(X'X)^{-1}X'Y = \boldsymbol{\beta} + (X'X)^{-1}X'\boldsymbol{\varepsilon},$$
$$\mathrm{E}((X'X)^{-1}X'Y) = \boldsymbol{\beta} + \mathrm{E}((X'X)^{-1}X'\boldsymbol{\varepsilon})$$
$$= \boldsymbol{\beta} + 0 = \boldsymbol{\beta},$$

reaffirming that our estimators $\hat{\beta}_0$ and $\hat{\beta}_1$ are unbiased.

Our matrix notation provides a compact representation of the general conditions for unbiased linear estimation of $\beta_0$ and $\beta_1$. Earlier in this chapter, we denoted the weights for unbiased linear estimation of $\beta_0$ by $w_i^0$, and the weights for unbiased linear estimation of $\beta_1$ by $w_i^1$. Define

$$\mathbf{W}' = \begin{bmatrix} w_1^0 & w_2^0 & w_3^0 & \cdots & w_n^0 \\ w_1^1 & w_2^1 & w_3^1 & \cdots & w_n^1 \end{bmatrix}.$$

The conditions for unbiased linear estimation of $\beta$ are then $\mathbf{W}'\mathbf{X} = \mathbf{I}_2$; that is,

$$\begin{bmatrix} \sum w_i^0 & \sum w_i^0 X_i \\ \sum w_i^1 & \sum w_i^1 X_i \end{bmatrix} = \begin{bmatrix} 1 & 0 \\ 0 & 1 \end{bmatrix}.$$

The compact notation developed in this section adds nothing conceptually to our understanding of the estimation of the slope and intercept of a line. The power of this approach will shine through, however, when we turn to models with more than one explanator. The matrix results obtained in this section will generalize directly to models with multiple explanators; we will simply add more columns to the $X$ matrix and more rows to the $\beta$ matrix!

## Appendix 4.B Concepts for Review

 *Appendix 4.C*

# A Commonly Used Property of Certain Sums

Econometricians use the property

$$\sum[(X_i - \overline{X})Y_i] = \sum[(X_i - \overline{X})(Y_i - \overline{Y})]. \qquad \text{4.C.1}$$

so often that a proof of it is in order. Begin by rewriting the right-hand side of

Equation 4.C.1 as

$$\sum[(X_i - \overline{X})(Y_i - \overline{Y})] = \sum[(X_i - \overline{X})Y_i - (X_i - \overline{X})\overline{Y}].$$    **4.C.2**

Breaking up the two pieces of the sum on the right-hand side of Equation 4.C.2 into two distinct sums yields

$$\sum[(X_i - \overline{X})Y_i] - \sum[X_i - \overline{X}]\overline{Y}.$$    **4.C.3**

Factoring out from the second sum in Equation 4.C.3 leads to

$$\sum[(X_i - \overline{X})Y_i] - \overline{Y}\sum[X_i - \overline{X}] = \sum[(X_i - \overline{X})Y_i],$$

with the final step holding because the sum of the deviations of a variable from its own mean is always zero, that is, $\sum(X_i - \overline{X}) = 0$. This establishes that

$$\sum[(X_i - \overline{X})Y_i] = \sum[(X_i - \overline{X})(Y_i - \overline{Y})],$$

or

$$\sum x_i Y_i = \sum x_i y_i$$

where $x_i = (X_i - \overline{X})$ and $y_i = (Y_i - \overline{Y})$.

# Chapter 5

# Residuals

*Yesterday upon the stair*
*I met a man who wasn't there.*
*He wasn't there again today.*
*Gee, I wish he'd go away![1]*

—HUGHES MEARNS

isturbances are much like the man upon the stair. On average, they aren't there (their mean is zero) and economists wish they would go away. It is disturbances that add scatter to a scatterplot and that make econometrics a statistical science, rather than a deterministic one. Econometricians often cope with disturbances by pretending that they can see them—they mimic the disturbances by asking how far the observed $Y$'s lie from the estimated line, though the disturbance is really the distance of $Y$ from the true line. It is a surprisingly effective fiction.

This chapter introduces three ways that econometricians use these imitation disturbances: (i) to estimate the variance of the unseen disturbances, (ii) to measure how well a line fits a given body of data, and (iii) to devise popular and useful estimators of the slope and intercept of a line.

We know from Chapter 3 that the variance of $\beta_{g4}$ depends on the variance of the disturbances, $\sigma^2$; the more variable the disturbances, the less precise our estimates of the slope. In a data-generating process (DGP) with both unknown slope and unknown intercept, the variance of the best linear unbiased estimators (BLUE) of the slope and intercept similarly depend on the variance of the disturbances. Unfortunately, $\sigma^2$ is usually not known. This chapter shows how econometricians estimate $\sigma^2$ and how they use that estimate of $\sigma^2$ to estimate the variances of the estimators of a slope and intercept.

Estimating population parameters, such as a population mean or the slope of a line, is one important task for statistics. Such estimation is a major part of econometrics. Another use of statistics, though, is to provide a summary description of a given set of data, without reference to an underlying population. The sample mean, for example, is often used as a descriptive statistic that summarizes in a single number the central tendency of many observations on a variable. An estimated line can similarly describe the broad pattern displayed in a scatterplot of many observations on two variables. This chapter defines a measure of how well a straight line describes a given set of data. The chapter concludes with the famous estimators of the slope and intercept of a line that best describe a given set of observations. This estimator is the ordinary least squares (OLS) estimator often discussed in statistics courses. The OLS estimator coincides with the BLUE estimator when the Gauss–Markov Assumptions are satisfied.

## 5.1    Estimating $\sigma^2$

**HOW DO WE CREATE AN ESTIMATOR?**

The variances and covariance of $\hat{\beta}_0$ and $\hat{\beta}_1$ depend on $\sigma^2$. Unfortunately, in the real world we seldom know $\sigma^2$, the variance of the disturbances in our DGP. Consequently, we also seldom know the variances of $\hat{\beta}_0$ and $\hat{\beta}_1$. Without knowledge of $\sigma^2$, econometricians estimate it. This section develops the estimator they commonly use.

### An Intuitive Estimator of $\sigma^2$

What intuitions do we have that would help us design an attractive estimator for $\sigma^2$, the variance of the disturbances, the $\varepsilon_i$? The intuition that population means are well estimated by sample means provides us with a key to estimating $\sigma^2$.

First, review the definition of variance. The variance of any random variable, $\nu$, is the expected value of squared deviations of that variable from its own mean:

$$\text{var}(\nu) = E([\nu - E(\nu)]^2).$$

Because under the Gauss–Markov Assumptions the $\varepsilon_i$ have a mean of zero,

$$\text{var}(\varepsilon_i) = E(\varepsilon_i^2) = \sigma^2.$$

Also, note that

$$Y_i = \beta_0 + \beta_1 X_i + \varepsilon_i$$

implies

$$\varepsilon_i = Y_i - \beta_0 - \beta_1 X_i.$$

The mean of the squared sample disturbances,

$$\frac{1}{n}\sum \varepsilon_i^2 = \frac{1}{n}\sum (Y_i - \beta_0 - \beta_1 X_i)^2,$$

has expected value

$$E\left(\frac{1}{n}\sum \varepsilon_i^2\right) = \frac{1}{n}\sum E(\varepsilon_i^2) = \frac{1}{n}\sum \sigma^2 = \sigma^2.$$

This would be an unbiased estimator of $\sigma^2$.

Unfortunately, we do not know $\beta_0$ and $\beta_1$ in real-world applications, so, observing only the $X_i$ and $Y_i$, we can compute neither the disturbances, the

$(Y_i - \beta_0 - \beta_1 X_i)$, nor the mean of their squares. The intuitive estimator is infeasible. But this infeasible intuitive estimator points the way to another appealing estimator that *is* feasible.

## An Unbiased Estimator of $\sigma^2$

If we did know $\beta_0$ and $\beta_1$, the mean of the squared observed disturbances would be an unbiased estimator of $\sigma^2$. Can we adapt this infeasible estimator to make it feasible? Yes. In real-world applications, we replace $\beta_0$ and $\beta_1$ with $\hat{\beta}_0$ and $\hat{\beta}_1$, forming

$$e_i = Y_i - \hat{\beta}_0 - \hat{\beta}_1 X_i$$

to mimic the unobserved $\varepsilon_i$. The $e_i$ are called the **residuals of the regression,** or **residuals.** Figure 5.1 shows the residuals graphically for a sample of three observations. In the figure, the residual is the vertical distance from an observed $Y_i$ to the fitted value of that $Y_i$, $\hat{\beta}_0 + \hat{\beta}_1 X_i$. Notice that this strategy uses $(\hat{\beta}_0 + \hat{\beta}_1 X_i)$ to estimate the expected value of $Y_i$. Econometricians call $(\hat{\beta}_0 + \hat{\beta}_1 X_i)$ the **fitted value of $Y_i$.** The squared residuals from a regression serve in place of the squared disturbances when we estimate $\sigma^2$.

A similar situation arises when estimating the variance of a population with mean $\mu$ using data drawn from a simple random sample. In that case, the population mean, $\mu$, is generally unknown, so instead of examining the mean of the $(Y - \mu)^2$, statisticians examine the $(Y_i - \overline{Y})^2$. However,

$$\frac{1}{n}\sum_{i=1}^{n}(Y_i - \overline{Y})^2$$

proves to be a biased estimator of $\sigma^2$, whereas

$$\frac{1}{n-1}\sum_{i=1}^{n}(Y_i - \overline{Y})^2$$

proves to be unbiased. (See the Statistical Appendix for a demonstration of these claims.) For similar reasons, in a DGP satisfying the Gauss–Markov Assumptions, the mean squared residual from a regression would be a biased estimator of $\sigma^2$, but

$$s^2 = \frac{\sum_{i=1}^{n}(residuals^2)}{(n-2)} = \frac{\sum_{i=1}^{n}\left((Y_i - \hat{\beta}_0 - \hat{\beta}_1 X_i)^2\right)}{n-2}$$

is an unbiased estimator of $\sigma^2$. (Appendix 5.A proves the unbiasedness of $s^2$.) The need in the regression model to divide by $(n-2)$ rather than $(n-1)$ stems from

**Figure 5.1**

A Fitted Line and Its Residuals

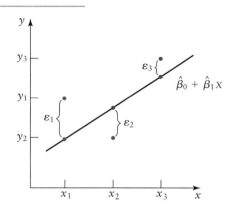

there being two parameters estimated in the residual, $\beta_0$ and $\beta_1$, as opposed to only one, $\overline{Y}$ when estimating $\mu$, in the case of estimating a population variance with data from a simple random sample. In general, when a regression model contains multiple explanators, the denominator of the unbiased estimator of $\sigma^2$ is ($n$ − the number of estimated coefficients). In the present case, that denominator is ($n - 2$) because both the intercept and the slope are estimated.

Econometricians frequently report standard deviations rather than variances. The square root of $s^2$, $s$, estimates the standard deviation of the disturbances. Because the disturbances in regression models are often called "error terms," $s$ is called the **estimated standard error of the regression**.

## 5.2    The Variances and Covariance of $\hat{\beta}_1$ and $\hat{\beta}_0$

The BLUE estimator has a smaller variance than any other linear estimator, but how small is that? If the smallest achievable variance is large, our BLUE estimator isn't very attractive, after all—even if it is better than alternative estimators. This section applies Chapter 4's formulae for the variances of linear estimators to obtain the variances of the BLUE estimators of an unknown slope and an unknown intercept, $\hat{\beta}_1$ and $\hat{\beta}_0$. It then presents the formula for the covariance of two linear estimators and uses that formula to determine the covariance between $\hat{\beta}_1$ and $\hat{\beta}_0$.

### The Variances of $\hat{\beta}_1$ and $\hat{\beta}_0$

Chapter 4 established that under the Gauss–Markov Assumptions, the variance of any linear estimator is $\sigma^2 \sum w_i^2$. The current section uses this formula to obtain the variance of $\hat{\beta}_1$, $\sigma^2_{\hat{\beta}_1}$, and then presents two formulae for the variance of, $\hat{\beta}_0$, $\sigma^2_{\hat{\beta}_0}$.

Equation 4.1 states that the weights for $\hat{\beta}_1$ are

$$w_i^{1*} = \frac{x_i}{\sum\limits_{j=1}^{n} x_j^2} \qquad i = 1, \ldots, n.$$

Therefore,

$$\sigma_{\hat{\beta}_1}^2 = \sigma^2 \sum_{i=1}^{n} (w_i^{1*})^2 = \sigma^2 = \sum_{i=1}^{n} \left( \frac{x_i}{\sum\limits_{j=1}^{n} x_j^2} \right)^2$$

$$= \sigma^2 \sum \left( \frac{x_i^2}{\left[ \sum x_j^2 \right]^2} \right)$$

$$= \sigma^2 \frac{\sum x_i^2}{(\sum x_j^2)^2} = \frac{\sigma^2}{\sum x_i^2}. \tag{5.1}$$

The last step follows from what precedes because $\sum_{i=1}^{n} x_i^2 = x_1^2 + \cdots + x_n^2 = \sum_{j=1}^{n} x_j^2$; the subscripts $i$ and $j$ are substitutable because they perform the same notational duty.

The square root of an unbiased estimator's variance is often called the estimator's **standard error**, rather than its *standard deviation*. Thus, the standard error of $\hat{\beta}_1$ is $\sqrt{\frac{\sigma^2}{\sum x_i^2}}$. The change from *deviation* to *error* reflects the fact that for an unbiased estimator, deviations of the variable from its own mean are also the errors made with the estimator—the deviations of the estimator from the true value of the parameter.

Obtaining $\sigma_{\hat{\beta}_0}^2$ is more complicated than obtaining $\sigma_{\hat{\beta}_1}^2$ because the weights for $\hat{\beta}_0$ are more complicated. Appendix 5.B contains the derivation. The formula for $\sigma_{\hat{\beta}_0}^2$ can be expressed either as

$$\sigma_{\hat{\beta}_0}^2 = \frac{\sigma^2 \sum X_i^2}{n \sum x_j^2}, \tag{5.2}$$

or, equivalently, as

$$\sigma_{\hat{\beta}_0}^2 = \sigma^2 \left( \frac{1}{n} + \frac{\overline{X}^2}{\sum x_j^2} \right). \tag{5.3}$$

Notice that neither $\sigma^2_{\hat{\beta}_0}$ nor $\sigma^2_{\hat{\beta}_1}$ would exist if all the $X_i$ equaled a nonzero constant, say $k$, because in that case $\sum x_i^2$ would equal zero. When the $X_i$ are not all exactly equal to $k$, but are nearly so, so that $1/\sum x_i^2$ is very small, the BLUE estimators of $\beta_0$ and $\beta_1$ are very imprecise. *When there is very little variation in the explanator about its mean, the BLUE estimators of the slope and intercept will tend to be very imprecise.* In such cases it would be cold comfort to learn that $\hat{\beta}_0$ and $\hat{\beta}_1$ are BLUE estimators—what good is having the smallest variances among linear estimators if those variances are very large? The "solutions" to such imprecise estimators are (i) additional observations in which the $x_i$ terms are not very small, or (ii) many more observations of any sort—$\sum x_i^2$ will eventually grow large if there are enough nonzero elements in the sum.

In the special case in which all $X$-values are zero,

$$x_i = (X_i - \overline{X}) = (X_i - 0) = X_i,$$

so $\hat{\beta}_0$ and its variance both exist because the $\sum x_i^2$ in the denominator of the variance formula for $\hat{\beta}_0$ cancels with the $\sum X_i^2$ in the numerator. The variance of $\hat{\beta}_0$ is $\sigma^2/n$—and $\hat{\beta}_0$ reduces to the sample mean. In this special case, though, neither $\hat{\beta}_1$ nor its variance exists.

## The Covariance Between $\hat{\beta}_0$ and $\hat{\beta}_1$

The derivations of Equations 5.2 and 5.3, the variances of $\hat{\beta}_1$ and $\hat{\beta}_0$, rely on Chapter 4's derivation of the variance of a linear estimator. Because $\hat{\beta}_0$ and $\hat{\beta}_1$ are different linear combinations of the same $Y$-values, it is possible that the two estimators are correlated. To study the covariance between $\hat{\beta}_0$ and $\hat{\beta}_1$, we first examine the covariance between two different linear estimators.

The Gauss–Markov Assumptions state that the disturbances, and hence the $Y_i$, are uncorrelated with one another. However, this lack of correlation among the $Y_i$ does not ensure that two linear estimators built using the $Y_i$ are uncorrelated; after all, both estimators depend on the same $Y_i$. Often, but not invariably, linear estimators based on the same $Y_i$ will be correlated with one another. The formula for the covariance between two linear estimators depends on the estimators' weights.

Consider one linear estimator, $R = \sum w_j^R Y_j$, and a second linear estimator, $S = \sum w_i^S Y_i$. The covariance between the two estimators, $R$ and $S$, is defined as

$$\text{cov}(R, S) = E([R - E(R)][S - E(S)]).$$

Appendix 5.B derives the formula for the covariance of two linear estimators, $R$ and $S$, under the Gauss–Markov Assumptions. The formula is

$$\text{cov}(R, S) = \sigma^2 \sum w_i^R w_i^S. \hspace{2cm} \textbf{5.4}$$

This formula for the covariance between linear estimators also applies to models with multiple explanators if the Gauss–Markov Assumptions are satisfied. This formula enables us to derive the covariance of $\hat{\beta}_0$ and $\hat{\beta}_1$.

The weights for $\hat{\beta}_1$, $w_i^{1*}$, are given in Equation 4.1:

$$w_i^{1*} = x_i / \sum x_i^2. \qquad\qquad 5.5$$

The weights for $\hat{\beta}_0$, $w_i^{0*}$, are given in Equation 4.2:

$$w_i^{0*} = \left[ \frac{1}{n} - \overline{X} \frac{x_i}{\sum x_j^2} \right].$$

Substituting from Equation 5.5, we obtain

$$w_i^{0*} = \left[ \frac{1}{n} - \overline{X} \frac{x_i}{\sum x_j^2} \right] = \left[ \frac{1}{n} - \overline{X} w_i^{1*} \right]. \qquad\qquad 5.6$$

From Equations 5.5 and 5.6, it follows that the covariance of $\hat{\beta}_0$ and $\hat{\beta}_1$ is

$$\sigma^2 \sum w_i^{0*} w_i^{1*} = \sigma^2 \sum ([(1/n) - \overline{X} w_i^{1*}] w_i^{1*})$$
$$= \sigma^2 \left( \sum w_i^{1*}/n \right) + \sigma^2 \sum \left( -\overline{X}[w_i^{1*}]^2 \right)$$
$$= (\sigma^2/n)\left( \sum w_i^{1*} \right) - \sigma^2 \overline{X} \sum \left[ (w_i^{1*})^2 \right].$$

But, because $\hat{\beta}_1$ is an unbiased linear estimator of $\beta_1$,

$$\sum w_i^{1*} = 0,$$

so the covariance of $\hat{\beta}_0$ and $\hat{\beta}_1$ is

$$\text{cov}(\hat{\beta}_0, \hat{\beta}_1) = -\sigma^2 \overline{X} \sum (w_i^{1*})^2 = -\overline{X}\text{var}(\hat{\beta}_1) = -\sigma^2 \overline{X}/\sum x_i^2. \qquad 5.7$$

*It follows that (i) $\hat{\beta}_0$ and $\hat{\beta}_1$ are uncorrelated if and only if $\overline{X} = 0$, (ii) $\hat{\beta}_0$ and $\hat{\beta}_1$ are negatively correlated if $\overline{X}$ is positive, and (iii) $\hat{\beta}_0$ and $\hat{\beta}_1$ are positively correlated if $\overline{X}$ is negative.*

## Estimators of Var($\hat{\beta}_0$), Var($\hat{\beta}_1$), and Cov($\hat{\beta}_0$, $\hat{\beta}_1$)

The variances of $\hat{\beta}_0$ and $\hat{\beta}_1$ and their covariance are as follows:

$$\text{var}(\hat{\beta}_1) = \frac{\sigma^2}{\sum x_i^2},$$

$$\text{var}(\hat{\beta}_0) = \frac{\sigma^2 \sum X_i^2}{n \sum x_j^2},$$

and

$$\text{cov}(\hat{\beta}_0, \hat{\beta}_1) = -\frac{\sigma^2 \overline{X}}{\sum x_j^2}.$$

All depend on the unknown variance $\sigma^2$. To assess the precision of our BLUE estimators in a given situation, we need to estimate these statistics.

We can estimate $\sigma^2$ in each of these expressions by using $s^2$ in its place. Thus, we can estimate the variances of $\hat{\beta}_0$ and $\hat{\beta}_1$ and their covariance:

$$\text{estimated var}(\hat{\beta}_1) = s_{\beta_1}^2 = \frac{s^2}{\sum x_i^2}$$

and

$$\text{estimated var}(\hat{\beta}_0) = s_{\beta_0}^2 = \frac{s^2 \sum X_i^2}{n \sum x_j^2}.$$

The estimated standard errors of $\hat{\beta}_0$ and $\hat{\beta}_1$ are $s_{\beta_0}$ and $s_{\beta_1}$, respectively. The estimated covariance of $\hat{\beta}_0$ and $\hat{\beta}_1$ is

$$\text{estimated cov}(\hat{\beta}_0, \hat{\beta}_1) = -\frac{s^2 \overline{X}}{\sum x_i^2}.$$

To illustrate the use of these estimators, return to our sample of New York renters, for whom $Y$ is rent and $X$ is income. We have for these renters the following information:

$$n = 108 \qquad \overline{X} = 35{,}553 \qquad \overline{Y} = 7{,}718.11 \qquad \sum X_i^2 = 189{,}500{,}998{,}162$$

$$\sum x_i^2 = 52{,}674{,}672{,}255.3 \qquad s^2 = (3302.7)^2$$

$$\sum y^2 = 1{,}369{,}057{,}486.67 \qquad \sum e_i^2 = 1{,}156{,}203{,}244.68.$$

Thus, $s_{\beta_1} = 0.0044$; $s_{\beta_0} = 602.78$ (notice these are the square roots of the estimated variances, so they are estimated standard deviations); and $\text{cov}(\hat{\beta}_0, \hat{\beta}_1) = -7.37$. The fact that the estimated intercept 5455.49 is nine times its estimated standard deviation suggests strongly that the intercept is not zero. Were the intercept truly zero, the probability that we would see an estimate nine standard deviations above zero is minuscule. Because the Cobb–Douglas specification of preferences implies no intercept in the rent–income relationship, these results are persuasive that New York renters' housing preferences are not Cobb–Douglas. The simplifying assumption of Chapters 2 and 3, that the expected rent line passes through the origin, is rejected by this more general analysis of the rent and income data.

## 5.3     The Gauss–Markov Theorem and the Expected Value of $Y$, Given $X$

**WHAT ARE AN ESTIMATOR'S PROPERTIES?**

An econometrician's interest often extends beyond $\beta_0$ and $\beta_1$ individually to the value of $\beta_0 + \beta_1 X$ for some specific value of $X$, $X^*$; that is, she may wish to estimate $E(Y|X^*)$. For example, an econometrician might want to estimate the expected level of college financial aid for families with incomes of \$1,500 per month.

A natural way to estimate $E(Y|X^*)$ would be to combine the individual estimates of $\beta_0$ and $\beta_1$:

$$\hat{Y}^* = \hat{\beta}_0 + \hat{\beta}_1 X^*.$$

A remarkable generalization of the BLUE results for estimating $\beta_0$ and $\beta_1$ states that for the Gauss–Markov DGP, the BLUE estimator of *any* linear combination of $\beta_0$ and $\beta_1$ (and, in particular, of $\beta_0 + \beta_1 X^*$) is that same linear combination of $\hat{\beta}_0$ and $\hat{\beta}_1$. Therefore, the "natural" estimator of $E(Y|X^*)$, $\hat{Y}^*$, is indeed the BLUE estimator of $E(Y|X^*)$.[2]

Because $\hat{Y}^*$ is a linear combination of $\hat{\beta}_0$ and $\hat{\beta}_1$, its variance depends on their variances and covariance. Equations 5.2 and 5.3 report that

$$\sigma_{\hat{\beta}_0}^2 = \text{var}(\hat{\beta}_0) = \frac{\sigma^2 \sum X_i^2}{n \sum x_i^2}$$

and that

$$\sigma_{\hat{\beta}_0}^2 = \sigma^2 \left( \frac{1}{n} + \frac{\overline{X}^2}{\sum x_j^2} \right).$$

Equation 5.7 reports that the covariance of $\hat{\beta}_0$ and $\hat{\beta}_1$ is

$$\text{cov}(\hat{\beta}_0, \hat{\beta}_1) = -\overline{X}\text{var}(\hat{\beta}_1).$$

From these variances and covariance, it follows that the variance of $\hat{Y}^*$ is

$$
\begin{aligned}
\hat{\sigma}_{\hat{Y}^*}^2 = \text{var}(\hat{Y}^*) &= \text{var}(\hat{\beta}_0 + \hat{\beta}_1 X^*) \\
&= \text{var}(\hat{\beta}_0) + \text{var}(\hat{\beta}_0 X^*) + 2\text{cov}(\hat{\beta}_0, \hat{\beta}_1 X^*) \\
&= \text{var}(\hat{\beta}_0) + X^{*2}\text{var}(\hat{\beta}_1) + 2 X^*\text{cov}(\hat{\beta}_0, \hat{\beta}_1) \\
&= \sigma^2 \left( \frac{1}{n} + \frac{\overline{X}^2}{\sum x_j^2} + \frac{X^{*2}}{\sum x_j^2} - 2\frac{X^*\overline{X}}{\sum x_j^2} \right) \\
&= \sigma^2 \left[ \frac{1}{n} + \frac{(X^* - \overline{X})^2}{\sum x_i^2} \right]
\end{aligned}
$$

       **5.8**

*The Gauss–Markov Theorem implies that no other unbiased linear estimator of E(Y|X\*) has smaller variance than this variance of $\hat{Y}^*$.* Econometricians call $\sigma_{Y^*}$ the **standard error of the estimator of the expected value of Y given X = X\*.**

The estimated variance of the expected value of Y given $X = X^*$ is

$$s_{Y^*}^2 = s^2\left[\frac{1}{n} + \frac{(X^* - \overline{X})^2}{\sum x_i^2}\right].$$

The estimated standard error of the expected value of Y, given $X = X^*$, is $s_{Y^*}$. In our sample of New York renters, $s_{Y^*} = 317.8$ for $X^* = 35,455$ or, alternatively, $s_{Y^*} = 407.2$ for $X^* = 17,728$.

## 5.4     Confidence Intervals and Prediction Intervals

**HOW DO WE CREATE AN ESTIMATOR?**

The estimators we have examined each provide a single number as the estimated value of a population parameter. Estimators that provide a single number as the estimate are **point estimators.** However, instead of offering a single number as an estimate, econometricians sometimes report a range of values as their estimate. Estimators that provide a range of values are **interval estimators.** The most common interval estimators are *confidence intervals.* Building confidence intervals requires both a point estimate and an estimated standard error for the point estimator. It is the point estimator's estimated standard error that determines the width of the interval.

The most common examples of such interval estimates are the myriad polling results that appear in newspapers: "According to a recent poll, the proportion of Iowans who favor increased farm subsidies is 76%. The result is reliable within ±3%." What newspapers call "an estimate with its margin of error" is usually what statisticians call a *95% confidence interval.*

Confidence intervals have a less-often-encountered relation called a *prediction interval.* Prediction intervals are to forecasts what confidence intervals are to estimates. A typical prediction interval has the form "We predict next year's GDP will be 8.3 trillion dollars, plus or minus 0.3 trillion dollars." This section defines the confidence intervals and prediction intervals commonly used by econometricians.

### Confidence Intervals for the Slope, Intercept, and E(Y|X)

The estimators we have treated so far are all point estimators; that is, they offer a single number as a guess. Point estimators do provide an answer to the question "What is your best guess?" A drawback of these estimators is that they are almost never exactly right. Indeed, if our estimator is imprecise, many of the guesses based on that estimator would be far wrong. How are we to indicate whether we think our best guess is apt to be close to the true value? We build and report a confidence interval.

Confidence intervals offer a range of guesses. A confidence interval is a guessing mechanism that generates a range of values, within which the true parameter value is estimated to lie. We can determine the proportion of successful intervals a particular guessing mechanism will yield. If a particular guessing mechanism produces intervals that cover the true parameter value in $\gamma\%$ of the samples generated by the DGP, we say that the mechanism is a $\gamma\%$ **confidence interval**. Thus, if a guessing mechanism produces correct intervals for 95% of all samples, we call it a 95% confidence interval.

Some caution is needed in interpreting the 95% in "95% confidence interval." The probability 95% is the probability *across all samples* that a randomly drawn sample, and thus a randomly generated 95% confidence interval, will cover the true parameter value. However, 95% does *not* describe the probability that a particular interval generated with a 95% confidence interval covers the true parameter value. For example, a particular 95% confidence interval can be obviously wrong, as in the case of a price elasticity of demand for which the 95% confidence interval contains only positive values. Economic theory indicates that such an interval is plainly wrong and that we have been unlucky in our data.

Computing confidence intervals is straightforward when we begin with a normally distributed and unbiased point estimator. If $\beta_g \sim N(\beta, \sigma_g^2)$, then a $\gamma\%$ confidence interval for $\beta$ when $\sigma_g$ is known is

$$\beta_g \pm [Z_{(1-\gamma)/2}]\sigma_g,$$

where $[Z_{(1-\gamma)/2}]$ is the $(1-\gamma)/2$ cutoff value for the standard normal distribution (1.96 if $\gamma = 0.95$). To generate $\gamma\%$ confidence intervals for $\beta_0, \beta_1$, or $E(Y|X = X^*)$, we need only substitute $\hat{\beta}_0, \hat{\beta}_1$, or $(\hat{\beta}_0 + \hat{\beta}_1 X^*)$ for $\beta_g$ and $\sigma_0^2, \sigma_1^2$, or $\sigma_{Y_0}^2$, for $\sigma_g^2$.

Building a confidence interval using the standard normal probability distribution requires that we know $\sigma_g$. Often we don't know $\sigma_g$. If $\sigma_g$ is unknown, we must replace it with an estimator. As in building test statistics, this substitution shifts us from using the standard normal distribution to using the $t$-distribution. The general $\gamma\%$ confidence interval in such cases is

$$\beta_g \pm \left[t^{n-k-1}_{((1-\gamma)/2)}\right]s_g,$$

where $(t^{n-k-1}_{((1-\gamma)/2)})$ is the $(1-\gamma)/2\%$ cutoff for the $t$-distribution with $(n - k - 1)$ degrees of freedom, and $s_g^2$ is the estimated variance of $\beta_g$. When $n$ is large, the $t$-distribution is approximately the same as the normal distribution.

## Prediction Intervals for Future Values of $Y$

Estimation and forecasting are two different activities. In estimation, we are guessing the value of a population parameter, a fixed number. In forecasting, we are guessing what the realized value of a random variable will be in a particular future period, a transient number that will exist only at one point in time. This subtle distinction matters more to statisticians than to practicing econometricians, but it helps us clarify why interval guesses for forecasts differ from interval guesses for parameters.

Interval guesses for forecasts are called prediction intervals, not confidence intervals. A $\gamma\%$ **prediction interval** is a guessing mechanism that generates intervals that include the actual future value of the forecasted random variable in $\gamma\%$ of all subsequent realizations from the population.

An example clarifies the distinction between estimation and forecasting. When guessing average consumption for people with incomes of \$100,000, we face only one source of error—sampling error—in our guesses of $\beta_0$ and $\beta_1$. When we guess the consumption of a specific individual with an income of \$100,000, however, we face two sources of error—the same sampling error in $\beta_0$ and $\beta_1$ *and* the error due to this particular household's disturbance, $\varepsilon$. Consequently, a $\gamma\%$ prediction interval for $Y$ given $X = X_0$ is wider than the $\gamma\%$ confidence interval for $E(Y|X = X_0)$.

Recall that the variance of $\hat{Y}_0$, our estimator of $E(Y|X_0)$, is

$$\sigma_{\hat{Y}_0}^2 = \sigma^2[(1/n) + (X_0 - \overline{X})^2 / \sum(x_i^2)], \qquad \textbf{5.9}$$

and the estimated value of this variance is

$$s_{\hat{Y}_0}^2 = s^2[(1/n) + (X_0 - \overline{X})^2 / \sum(x_i^2)]. \qquad \textbf{5.10}$$

These variances reflect the sampling errors in $\hat{\beta}_0$ and $\hat{\beta}_1$.

To forecast $Y|X = X_0$, we use the same $\hat{Y}_0 = \hat{\beta}_0 + \hat{\beta}_1 X_0$ that we use to estimate $E(Y|X = X_0)$. Because the forecast is conditioned on a specific value of $X$, we call this a **conditional forecast**. However, the variance of our conditional forecast errors will have a second element beyond the sampling error due to $\hat{\beta}_0$ and $\hat{\beta}_1$—the error due to $\varepsilon$. Because the variance of $\varepsilon$ is $\sigma^2$, we will need to add another $\sigma^2$ to the sampling variance to arrive at the **variance of the conditional forecast error**, $\sigma_{F_0}^2$:

$$\sigma_{F_0}^2 = \sigma^2[1 + (1/n) + (X_0 - \overline{X})^2 / \sum(x_i^2)]. \qquad \textbf{5.11}$$

Similarly, the estimated variance of the conditional forecast error is

$$s_{F_0}^2 = s^2[1 + (1/n) + (X_0 - \overline{X})^2 / \sum(x_i^2)]. \qquad \textbf{5.12}$$

Notice that the 1's in Equations 5.11 and 5.12 differentiate $\sigma_{F_0}^2$ and $s_{F_0}^2$ from their estimation counterparts in Equations 5.9 and 5.10.

# An Econometric Top 40—A Golden Oldie

## The Cobb–Douglas Production Function

In 1928, Charles Cobb of Amherst College and Paul Douglas of the University of Chicago collaborated on a study of production[3] using annual U.S. data for the period 1899–1922. Douglas was later to enter the United States Senate, but his enduring claim to fame is the Cobb–Douglas production function:

$$output = \alpha(labor)^{\beta}(capital)^{1-\beta}.$$

In Chapter 2 we noted that the Cobb–Douglas production function implies that firms will pay labor a fixed proportion of the total value of output. That implication enabled us to estimate $\beta$ using data on labor's compensation and the total value of output (or income). Cobb and Douglas did not rely on this theoretical result. Instead, they estimated both $\alpha$ and $\beta$ using data on *output, labor,* and *capital.* To estimate this relationship, Cobb and Douglas rewrote their production function as

$$\ln(output/capital) = \ln(\alpha)$$
$$+ \beta\ln(labor/capital).$$

Cobb and Douglas reported estimates of 1.01 for $\alpha$ (so the estimate of $\ln(\alpha) = .01$) and .75

for $\beta$. The data they used are contained in cobbdouglas.*** on this book's companion Web site (**www.aw-bc.com/murray**).

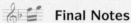 **Final Notes**

Chapter 2 noted that the Cobb–Douglas functional form can represent preferences as well as technology. If consumer's preferences are Cobb–Douglas, then their housing expenditures are a constant fraction of their income. The Cobb–Douglas form's structure permits remarkably easy manipulation of both utility functions and production functions, making it economics' most popular form for theoretical illustrations. Econometric tools to estimate the Cobb–Douglas parameters, $\alpha$ and $\beta$, allow the Cobb–Douglas to be used to draw quantitative, as well as qualitative, conclusions. In another Golden Oldie in this chapter, we encounter a slightly more complex and somewhat less restrictive specification of technology, called the CES production function.

∎

With the variances of the forecast errors in hand, we can then build the $\gamma\%$ prediction interval for $(Y|X = X_0)$. When $\sigma_{F_0}$ is known, the $95\%$ prediction interval is

$$\hat{\beta}_0 + \hat{\beta}_1 X_0 \pm [z_{(1-\gamma)/2}]\sigma_{F_0},$$

where $[Z_{(1-\gamma)/2}]$ is the $(1 - \gamma)/2$ cutoff value for the standard normal distribution, which is 1.96 if $\gamma = 0.95$.

If $\sigma_{F_0}$ is unobserved, it must be replaced with an estimator. As in building confidence intervals, this substitution shifts us from using the standard normal distribution to using the *t*-distribution. The general $\gamma\%$ prediction interval for

$(Y|X = X_0)$ in such cases is

$$\hat{Y}_0 \pm [t^{n-k-1}_{(1-\gamma)/2}]s_{F_0},$$

where $(t)^{n-k-1}_{((1-\gamma)/2)}$ is the $1 - \gamma/2\%$ cutoff for the $t$-distribution with $(n - k - 1)$ degrees of freedom.

## 5.5   Application: A U.S. Production Function

In Chapter 3, we estimated a Cobb–Douglas production function for the United States using labors' compensation and national income data. In that instance, we assumed not only a Cobb–Douglas production function, but also that labor and capital were paid their marginal products. Here we re-estimate the Cobb–Douglas production function for that same random sample of years, this time without assuming factors are paid their marginal products. We do assume constant returns to scale. We compare these new results to those obtained by Cobb and Douglas, who used data from 1899 to 1922.

The Cobb–Douglas production function is

$$Q = \beta_0 L^{\beta_1} K^{\beta_2}.$$

The constant returns to scale Cobb–Douglas production function is

$$Q = \beta_0 L^{\beta_1} K^{(1-\beta_1)},$$

or, in logarithmic form,

$$\ln(Q) = \beta_0 + \beta_1 \ln(L) + (1 - \beta_1)\ln(K)$$

or

$$\ln(Q/K) = \beta_0 + \beta_1 \ln(L/K), \qquad \textbf{5.13}$$

where $Q$ is output, $L$ is labor, and $K$ is capital.

Table 5.1 presents data from the same sample of years as did Table 3.5. Table 5.1 reports for each year a measure of real output, a measure of labor input, a measure of capital stock, the log of the ratio of real output to the capital stock, and the log of the ratio of labor input to the capital stock. Table 5.2 reports regression results for Equation 5.13. The table contains both the BLUE estimates of $\beta_0$ and $\beta_1$ and their estimated standard errors. Neither coefficient is estimated precisely, and .92 seems too high for $\beta_1$. (If labor is paid its marginal product, labor would receive 92% of GDP—an implausibly high fraction.) The high estimated standard errors reflect the difficulty of precisely estimating a model containing two parameters with just eight observations.

**TABLE 5.1** U.S. Data from a Sample of Years

| Year | Real Output (Q) | Labor Input (L) | Capital Input (K) | ln (Q/K) | ln (L/K) |
|------|------|------|------|------|------|
| 1959 | 3.94 | 2.75 | 1.59 | 0.91 | 0.55 |
| 1932 | 1.06 | 0.77 | 1.11 | −0.04 | −0.36 |
| 1975 | 5.96 | 4.57 | 3.08 | 0.66 | 0.39 |
| 1929 | 1.72 | 1.01 | 1.16 | 0.39 | −0.14 |
| 1933 | 1.03 | 0.75 | 1.07 | −0.04 | −0.35 |
| 1970 | 5.92 | 4.47 | 2.54 | 0.84 | 0.56 |
| 1993 | 10.78 | 7.91 | 5.03 | 0.76 | 0.45 |
| 1980 | 7.66 | 5.76 | 3.68 | 0.73 | 0.45 |

Remarkably, Table 3.6, using the data seen here in Table 5.1, reported that $\beta_{g4}$ estimated what is here $\beta_1$ to be 0.738, with an estimated standard error of 0.004, which contrasts sharply with the estimated standard error for $\hat{\beta}_1$ of 0.575 in Table 5.2. The key to the smaller standard errors in Chapter 3 is that the model specification in Chapter 3 exploited information provided by economic theory that is not exploited in specifying Equation 5.13. The theoretical insight that factors of production are paid their marginal products enabled us to estimate the labor elasticity of output ($\beta_1$) with much greater precision in Chapter 3 than we do here. These contrasting estimated standard errors expose an important insight for econometricians. *Economic theory sometimes provides restrictions that greatly increase the information we can glean from a particular DGP.* Whether such increases in efficiency are real or imagined depends on the validity of the economic theory applied. Whether we have estimated the standard errors of our estimators correctly also depends on whether we have properly specified the DGP in ques-

**TABLE 5.2** Estimated Cobb–Douglas Coefficients and Their Estimated Standard Errors

|  | $\beta_0$ | $\beta_1$ |
|------|------|------|
| Estimate: | 0.348 | 0.924 |
| Estimated Standard Error: | 0.245 | 0.575 |

tion. We will return to the example of Chapter 3 in this context when we discuss heteroskedasticity.

Table 5.3 contains output from the estimation of a Cobb–Douglas production function using Cobb and Douglas's original data for 1899–1922. The data are in the file cobbdouglas.*** on this book's companion Web site (**www.aw-bc. com/murray**). The variables in the data set are expenditures on capital (*capital*),

**TABLE 5.3** Cobb and Douglas's Production Function Estimates

EViews 4.1 Output
Dependent Variable: LOGOUTCP
Method: Least Squares
Sample: 1899 1922
Included observations: 24

| Variable | Coefficient | Std. Error | t-Statistic | Prob. |
|---|---|---|---|---|
| C | 0.014545 | 0.019979 | 0.727985 | 0.4743 |
| LOGLABCP | 0.745866 | 0.041224 | 18.09318 | 0.0000 |
| R-squared | 0.937028 | Mean dependent var | | −0.279148 |
| Adjusted R-squared | 0.934166 | S.D. dependent var | | 0.222407 |
| S.E. of regression | 0.057066 | Akaike info criterion | | −2.809574 |
| Sum squared resid | 0.071643 | Schwarz criterion | | −2.711403 |
| Log likelihood | 35.71489 | F-statistic | | 327.3633 |
| Durbin–Watson stat | 1.616390 | Prob(F-statistic) | | 0.000000 |

*Stata 8.0 Output*

| Source | SS | df | MS | |
|---|---|---|---|---|
| Model | 1.06605443 | 1 | 1.06605443 | Number of obs = 24 |
| Residual | .071642712 | 22 | .003256487 | F(1, 22) = 327.36 |
| | | | | Prob > F = 0.0000 |
| Total | 1.13769715 | 23 | .049465093 | R-squared = 0.9370 |
| | | | | Adj R-squared = 0.9342 |
| | | | | Root MSE = .05707 |

| logoutcp | Coef. | Std. Err. | t | P > \|t\| | [95% Conf. Interval] | |
|---|---|---|---|---|---|---|
| loglabcp | .7458658 | .0412236 | 18.093 | 0.000 | .6603734 | .8313583 |
| _cons | .0145446 | .0199793 | 0.728 | 0.474 | −.0268899 | .0559791 |

# An Econometric Top 40—A Golden Oldie

## The CES Production Function

Microeconomists frequently wonder how easily one factor of production can be substituted for another. At one extreme, no substitution is possible at all. For example, each molecule of water requires exactly two hydrogen atoms and one oxygen atom; no substitution of oxygen for hydrogen is possible. Such processes are called "fixed proportions" production processes. At the other extreme, two inputs can be substituted freely for one another. For example, red doors might substitute one for one with blue doors in some construction projects. In another example, quart containers of milk might substitute freely on a four-for-one basis with gallon containers in some recipes. Such inputs are called "perfect substitutes."

Hit Figure 5.1 illustrates these concepts graphically. Panels (a) and (b) show the combinations of two inputs that can produce a given quantity of output, $Q^*$, when other inputs (not shown) are held fixed. (Microeconomists call such curves "isoquants.") In Panel (a), the production process uses the two inputs in fixed proportions. In Panel (b), the inputs are perfect substitutes.

Most production processes lie between these two extremes, with varying degrees of substitutability possible. For example, Panel (c) in Hit Figure 5.1 shows an isoquant for a Cobb–Douglas production function. To measure substitutability, microeconomists have defined an elasticity of substitution, $\kappa$, that reflects the shape of the isoquant. The greater the elasticity of substitution, the more readily the inputs can be substituted, one for the other. The isoquants in Panels (a) and (b) have elasticities of substitution of zero and infinity. Cobb–Douglas production functions always have an elasticity of substitution of one. Microeconomists sometimes shy away from the Cobb–Douglas production

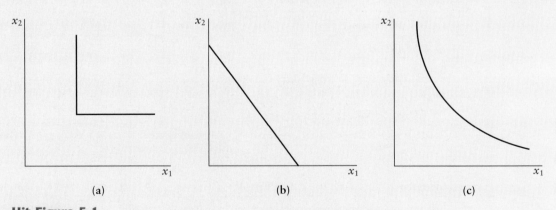

(a)                    (b)                    (c)

**Hit Figure 5.1**

Isoquants for Fixed Proportions, Perfect Substitutes, and Cobb–Douglas Production Processes

function because it imposes a unitary elasticity of substitution. When the degree of substitution between inputs lies at the heart of an economic problem, microeconomists want other production function specifications. The constant elasticity of a substitution production function is one popular choice.

In the early 1960s, Hollis Chenery, B.S. Minhas, and Nobel laureates Kenneth Arrow and Robert Solow noticed that in actual production processes it was often the case that the ratio of inputs' prices moved with the ratio of the inputs' quantities, according to

$$\ln(P_1/P_2) = \beta_0 + \beta_1\ln(X_1/X_2),$$

where $P_1$ and $P_2$ are input prices and $X_1$ and $X_2$ are inputs.

"If inputs are paid their marginal products," these economists asked, "what is the underlying production function that would give rise to this observation?" Their answer, reported in a classic 1961 paper,[4] is the constant elasticity of substitution (CES) production function for which output, $Q$, is related to the inputs, $X_1$ and $X_2$, by

$$Q^\rho = \tau X_1^\rho + X_2^\rho.$$

The function is called the CES because for this production function the elasticity of substitution is constant for all input levels. For the CES production function,

$$\kappa = \frac{1}{\beta_1} = (1 - \rho).$$

That is, the elasticity of substitution for the CES equals the inverse of the coefficient $\beta_1$ in the relationship identified by Arrow, Chenery, Minhas, and Solow,

$$\ln(P_1/P_2) = \beta_0 + \beta_1\ln(X_1/X_2).$$

For appropriate choices of the parameters $\tau$ and $\rho$ of the CES production function, economists can approximate the fixed proportions, perfect substitutes, or Cobb–Douglas production functions; the three are called "limiting cases" of the CES. The CES can also depict technologies for which the elasticity of substitution is not zero, or infinity, or one. The CES can depict any technology for which the elasticity of substitution between inputs is a constant, be it 1, 3, 12, or 0.234.

The CES production function provides a useful alternative to the Cobb–Douglas production function. The CES is more flexible, in that it allows a broader range of technological possibilities, and, mathematically, is almost as easy to manipulate as the Cobb–Douglas.

**HIT TABLE 5.1  The Elasticity of Substitution in Manufacturing**

Dependent Variable: LOG(WAGERATIO)
Method: Least Squares
Sample: 1 15

| Variable | Coefficient | Std. Error |
|---|---|---|
| C | 0.647909 | 0.155259 |
| LOG(KLRATIO) | 0.359554 | 0.121779 |
| R-squared | 0.401402 | |

Hit Table 5.1 contains estimates of the production function for manufacturing. The data, contained in ces.*** on this book's companion Web site (**www.aw-bc.com/murray**), are 15 observations on manufacturing industries; the industries vary in their capital–labor ratios and in the prices they pay capital and labor. According to these data, the estimated elasticity of substitution between capital and labor in manufacturing is 2.78, which is highly elastic.

### Final Notes

The discovery of the CES production function is an exemplar of scientific inquiry. These economists noticed a regularity in the empirical data they had studied in numerous contexts. What were these data telling them about the structure of industrial production? Careful theoretical reasoning led them to the answer. Had these economists settled for the empirical observation, we would have been left with an empirical curiosity, a statistical artifact, without any rationale. Instead, they used microeconomic theory to find the one production function that would account for their empirical finding.

■

payments to labor (*labor*), and the value of output (*output*). The variable *LOGOUTCP* is the log of the output/capital ratio. The variable *LOGLABCP* is the log of the labor/capital ratio. In EViews, the variable C indicates the intercept term, often called "the constant term." In Stata, "_cons" indicates the constant term. With 24 observations, 15 more than in Table 5.1, Cobb and Douglas were able to obtain more precise estimates of the slope and intercept than those reported in Table 5.2; the estimated standard errors for both $\hat{\beta}_0$ and $\hat{\beta}_1$ are much higher in Table 5.2 than in Table 5.3. The 95% confidence interval for the intercept is −0.027 to 0.056. The 95% confidence interval for the slope is 0.660 to 0.831.

## 5.6    The Goodness of Fit of an Estimated Line

WHAT ARE THE PROPERTIES OF AN ESTIMATOR?

Thus far, we have dwelt on the properties of estimators *across* samples, for example, bias and efficiency. Sometimes, however, we wonder how well a given estimated line describes the sample data in hand. Using an estimated line to fit a scatterplot of observed data is much like using a sample mean to describe a sample of observations on a single variable. For example, we often speak of the mean SAT score in a group of students, or of the mean racing time of a particular runner in several races. An estimated line can similarly broadly describe the pattern in a scatterplot of two variables. But how well does a straight line describe a scatterplot? That is the subject of this section.

### Decomposing the Variance of the $Y_i$ Within a Sample

Sometimes, a fitted line closely describes the data in a scatter, as in Panel (a) of Figure 5.2. Other times, observations tend to lie far from the fitted line, as in

Panel (b). In Panel (a), the $Y$-values associated with each $X$-value are almost exactly the values predicted by the fitted line, based on the $X$-values, whereas in Panel (b) the $Y$-values are quite different from those predicted by the fitted line. In both cases, though, we can describe each observed $Y$-value as the sum of the fitted value and the residual for the observation:

$$Y_i = (\hat{\beta}_0 + \hat{\beta}_1 X_i) + e_i.$$

Notice that, given $\hat{\beta}_0$ and $\hat{\beta}_1$, $Y_i$ varies only when $X_i$ or $e_i$ varies. Econometricians often ask how much of the variation in the $Y_i$'s within a sample is attributable to variation in the observed $X_i$'s (how much of the variation in the $Y_i$'s can be "explained" by that in the $X_i$'s), and how much is attributable to the variation in the residuals (how much of the variation in the $Y_i$'s remains unexplained). Notice that the variance we are describing here is the sample variance of the $Y_i$'s across all observations in a given sample, and not a variance across samples.

The variance of the $Y_i$'s within the sample can be expressed as

$$\text{Svar}(Y_i) = \text{Svar}(\hat{\beta}_0 + \hat{\beta}_1 X_i + e_i) = \text{Svar}(\hat{\beta}_0 + \hat{\beta}_1 X_i) + \text{var}(e_i)$$
$$+ 2\,\text{Scov}[(\hat{\beta}_0 + \hat{\beta}_1 X_i), e_i]$$
$$= \hat{\beta}_1^2 \text{Svar}(X_i) + \text{Svar}(e_i) + 2\hat{\beta}_1 \text{Scov}(X_i, e_i).$$

The prefix "$S$" on the variance and covariance terms remind us that (i) these variances are within the sample, so $\hat{\beta}_0$ and $\hat{\beta}_1$ will not vary—only the $X_i$ and $e_i$ will vary; and (ii) the variances are measured about the sample means, $\overline{Y}$ and $\overline{X}$, not about population means. This expression simplifies to

$$= \hat{\beta}_1^2 \text{Svar}(X_i) + \text{Svar}(e_i)$$

**Figure 5.2**

A Good Fit and a Poor Fit

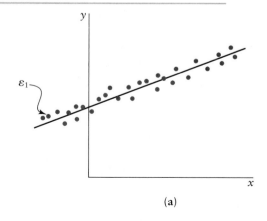

(a)

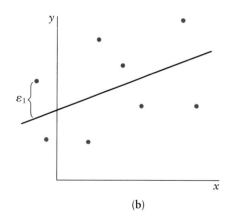

(b)

because $\text{Scov}(X_i, e_i)$ is zero. To prove that the $\text{Scov}(X_i, e_i)$ equals zero, we begin by defining the sample covariance of the $X_i$ and $e_i$:

$$\text{Scov}(X_i, e_i) = \frac{1}{n}\sum(x_i - \overline{X})(e_i - \overline{e}),$$

where overbars denote the mean of the variable in the sample. But from Chapter 4, we know it is always true that

$$\sum(Q_i - \overline{Q})(Z_i - \overline{Z}) = \sum(Q_i - \overline{Q})Z_i, \qquad\qquad 5.14$$

for any $Q$ and $Z$, so we can equally well write this as

$$\text{Scov}(X_i, e_i) = \frac{1}{n}\sum(x_i - \overline{X})e_i = \frac{1}{n}\sum x_i e_i,$$

where $x_i = (X_i - \overline{X})$. Further,

$$\frac{1}{n}\sum x_i e_i = \frac{1}{n}\sum x_i(Y_i - \hat{\beta}_0 - \hat{\beta}_1 X_i)$$

$$= \frac{1}{n}\sum x_i Y_i - \hat{\beta}_0\frac{1}{n}\sum x_i - \hat{\beta}_1\frac{1}{n}\sum x_i X_i,$$

to which we can twice apply the result from Equation 5.14 to continue with

$$= \frac{1}{n}\sum x_i y_i - \hat{\beta}_0\frac{1}{n}\sum x_i - \hat{\beta}_1\frac{1}{n}\sum x_i^2$$

$$= \frac{1}{n}\sum x_i y_i - \hat{\beta}_1\frac{1}{n}\sum x_i^2$$

(which exploits the fact that $\sum x_i = 0$ because the sum of any variable's deviations from its own mean is zero), continuing,

$$= \frac{1}{n}\sum x_i y_i - \left[\sum x_i y_i / \sum x_i^2\right]\frac{1}{n}\sum x_i^2 = 0.$$

Therefore, within any sample of observations, in a model containing both an intercept and a slope,

$$\text{Svar}(Y_i) = \hat{\beta}_1^2\text{Svar}(X_i) + \text{Svar}(e_i) = \hat{\beta}_1^2\frac{1}{n}\sum x_i^2 + \frac{1}{n}\sum(e_i - \overline{e})^2.$$

Because, as we learn in the next section, $\overline{\varepsilon}$ equals zero in OLS regressions that include an intercept term,

$$\text{Svar}(Y_i) = \hat{\beta}_1^2\text{Svar}(X_i) + \text{Svar}(e_i) = \hat{\beta}_1^2\frac{1}{n}\sum x_i^2 + \frac{1}{n}\sum e_i^2,$$

when the model contains an intercept term. When the model does not contain an intercept term (that is, for a line through the origin), $\bar{\varepsilon}$ does not usually equal zero.

Thus, when the model contains an unknown intercept, the variation in the $Y_i$ can be decomposed into (i) variation that OLS attributes to variation in the $X_i$ and (ii) unexplained variation that stems from the variation in the residuals. The smaller the sum of squared residuals (the variation in the residuals), the better the estimated equation fits the data, that is, the more the variation anticipated by the fitted equation (because of variation in the $X_i$) captures the variation observed in the $Y_i$.

Table 5.4 replicates Table 5.3. Stata reports all the elements of the decomposition of the variance of $Y$ by reporting the raw sums: $\sum y_i^2 = 1.13769715$ is commonly referred to as the "total sum of squares" (TSS); it appears in the SS column on the Total row in the Stata output. $\hat{\beta}_1^2 \sum x_i^2 = 1.06605443$ is commonly referred to as the "model sum of squares" (MSS), or "the explained sum of squares"; it appears in the SS column on the Model row in the Stata output. $\sum e_i^2 = .071642712$ is commonly called the "residual sum of squares" (RSS), or the "error sum of squares" (ESS), or the "sum of squared residuals" (SSR), or the "unexplained sum of squares"; it appears in the SS column on the residual row in the Stata output. As shown in the Stata output, TSS = RSS + MSS. EViews reports only the sum of squared residuals.

## The Coefficient of Determination, $R^2$

The decomposition of the variation of the $Y_i$ into two parts,

$$\text{Svar}(Y_i) = \hat{\beta}_1^2 \text{Svar}(X_i) + \text{Svar}(e_i) = \hat{\beta}_1^2 \frac{1}{n} \sum x_i^2 + \frac{1}{n} \sum e_i^2,$$

provides the foundation for a measure of how well an estimated line fits a given sample of data. The fraction of the variation in the $Y_i$ that is accounted for by variation in the $X_i$ is

$$\frac{\hat{\beta}_1^2 \frac{1}{n} \sum x_i^2}{\left[\hat{\beta}_1^2 \sum x_i^2 + \frac{1}{n} \sum e_i^2\right]} = \frac{\hat{\beta}_1^2 \sum x_i^2}{\sum y_i^2}.$$

The fraction of the variation in the $Y_i$ that is unexplained by variation in the $X_i$ is

$$\frac{\frac{1}{n} \sum e_i^2}{\left[\hat{\beta}_1^2 \sum x_i^2 + \frac{1}{n} \sum e_i^2\right]} = \frac{\sum e_i^2}{\sum y_i^2}.$$

**TABLE 5.4** Cobb and Douglas's Production Function Estimates

EViews 4.1 Output
Dependent Variable: LOGOUTCP
Method: Least Squares
Sample: 1899 1922
Included observations: 24

| Variable | Coefficient | Std. Error | t-Statistic | Prob. |
|---|---|---|---|---|
| C | 0.014545 | 0.019979 | 0.727985 | 0.4743 |
| LOGLABCP | 0.745866 | 0.041224 | 18.09318 | 0.0000 |
| R-squared | 0.937028 | Mean dependent var | | −0.27914 |
| Adjusted R-squared | 0.934166 | S.D. dependent var | | 0.222407 |
| S.E. of regression | 0.057066 | Akaike info criterion | | −2.80957 |
| Sum squared resid | 0.071643 | Schwarz criterion | | −2.71140 |
| Log likelihood | 35.71489 | F-statistic | | 327.3633 |
| Durbin–Watson stat | 1.616390 | Prob(F-statistic) | | 0.000000 |

*Stata 8.0 Output*

| Source | SS | df | MS | |
|---|---|---|---|---|
| Model | 1.06605443 | 1 | 1.06605443 | Number of obs = 24 |
| Residual | .071642712 | 22 | .003256487 | F(1, 22) = 327.36 |
| | | | | Prob > F = 0.0000 |
| Total | 1.13769715 | 23 | .049465093 | R − squared = 0.9370 |
| | | | | Adj R − squared = 0.9342 |
| | | | | Root MSE = .05707 |

| logoutcp | Coef. | Std. Err. | t | P > \|t\| | [95% Conf. Interval] | |
|---|---|---|---|---|---|---|
| loglabcp | .7458658 | .0412236 | 18.093 | 0.000 | .6603734 | .8313583 |
| _cons | .0145446 | .0199793 | 0.728 | 0.474 | −.0268899 | .0559791 |

The fraction of the variation in the $Y_i$ attributable to variation in the $X_i$ is the most commonly used measure of the *goodness of fit* of a line, usually denoted by $R^2$:

$$R^2 = \frac{\hat{\beta}_1^2 \sum x_i^2}{\sum y_i^2} = 1 - \frac{\sum e_i^2}{\sum y_i^2}, \qquad 5.15$$

which is called the **coefficient of determination**. As a fraction, $R^2$ will always lie between 0 and 1. When this fraction is high (close to 1), the model "fits" the data well. For example, the $R^2$ would be high in Panel A of Figure 5.5, and low in Panel B. All econometric software programs report the $R^2$ for regression. In Table 5.4, for example, we see Cobb and Douglas obtained an $R^2$ of 0.937 in their study of U.S. production from 1899 to 1922.

The formula for $R^2$ reveals that if we know the $R^2$ and the sum of squared residuals, we can compute the total sum of squares, $\sum y_i^2$. The difference between the total sum of squares and the residual sum of squares is what Stata calls the model sum of squares in Table 5.4. Hence, although EViews does not report the total sum of squares or the model sum of squares, we can compute those two items from the $R^2$ and the sum of squared residuals that EViews does report. Stata, as we noted earlier, reports all the numbers in its output. (Subsequent tables do not contain the output from both EViews and Stata; Tables 3.7 and 5.4 suffice to make the point that having seen the output from one econometric software package, you've seen them all.)

The interpretation of $R^2$ as the fraction of the variation in the sample $Y$'s that can be explained by variation in the $X$'s depends critically on the decomposition of the sample variance of the $Y$'s into those two parts alone—that is, the interpretation depends on the sample covariation between the $X$'s and residuals being zero. If the intercept term is excluded from the model, we have no assurance that the $X$'s and the residuals have no sample covariation. Consequently, if the constant term is excluded from a model, the $R^2$, calculated using Equation 5.15, need not be in the range 0 to 1. In this special case, the interpretation of the $R^2$ as the proportion of the variation in the sample $Y_i$'s is incorrect and the $R^2$ should be ignored.

As a practical matter, econometricians have found that the magnitude of the $R^2$ measure varies across types of data. Models using time series data, such as annual GDP from 1940 through 1995, or total consumption from the first quarter of 1960 through the fourth quarter of 1990, usually yield high $R^2$, on the order of 0.90 or more. (Cobb and Douglas obtained an $R^2$ of 0.93 in their time series study.) Models using time series data on changes in GDP or consumption tend to yield substantially lower $R^2$, on the order of 0.70–0.90. Models using aggregated cross sectional data, for example, GDP and consumption drawn from 50 industrialized countries in 1985, or output and labor inputs across several industries, tend to yield still lower $R^2$, on the order of 0.30–0.70. Finally, models using a cross section of individual household- or firm-level data often find very low $R^2$'s, sometimes as low as 0.05, and seldom above 0.40. For example, based on the data given at the end of Section 5.2 for our New York renters, the OLS estimates of the rent–income relationship slope and intercept result in an $R^2$ of 0.16—variation in income across renters accounts for only 16% of the variation in rents New Yorkers pay.

The high $R^2$ values typically observed in time series data such as consumption and income arise because those data frequently have a common tendency to rise over time. That common upward movement translates into a great deal of common variation. Changes in time series data tend to have smaller $R^2$-values than other time series data because examining changes from period to period washes out the accumulation of shared upward movements. Individual data usually have very low $R^2$-values because the idiosyncratic aspects of behavior are extensive—individuals vary widely in how they respond to changes in income, for example, so much usually remains unexplained when studying individuals. The moderately large $R^2$ seen in changes in time series variables and also in aggregated cross-sectional data, such as labor and output levels across industries, arise chiefly because the aggregation of many industries or of many households (as in changes in national consumption and income) washes away much individual idiosyncracy, leaving broadly shared responses of the (aggregated) independent variable to the (aggregated) explanator.

The $R^2$ measure is seductive. Although the measure is useful, we must keep in mind what it does *not* tell us. A high $R^2$ gives no assurance that our estimators are unbiased. A low $R^2$ does not imply that our estimators are inefficient. If our real interest is in the true value of the slope and intercept, the $R^2$ measure is not the proper guide to success or failure. Students of econometrics and practicing econometricians too often get distracted by their high or low $R^2$'s. *Try not to be overly fond of $R^2$.*

Even though $R^2$ tells us little about how well the fitted line estimates the underlying relationship between $X$ and $Y$, it can still provide useful information. For example, consider an analysis of GDP as a function of government spending. If the econometrician is asking whether stabilizing government spending over the sample period would have stabilized GDP, the $R^2$ measure can be a useful tool. Suppose the DGP that generates GDP and government spending satisfies the assumptions with which we began this chapter, so that $\hat{\beta}_0$ and $\hat{\beta}_1$ are BLUE. Suppose further that we calculate that $R^2$ equals 0.75 for a model that expresses GDP as a linear function of government spending. We therefore estimate that 75% of the variation in GDP is attributable to variation in government spending over the period. We could then argue—as long as we believe that the relationship between government spending and GDP is causal and not merely a statistical happenstance—that had government spending been held at its mean value throughout the sample period, eliminating all the variation in government spending, the variation in GDP would have been reduced by 75%. See the Regression's Greatest Hits—Immobile Capital Markets box on the next page for an $R^2$ finding that spurred more than 200 follow-up studies.

# An Econometric Top 40—A Classical Favorite

## The World's Surprisingly Immobile Capital Markets

A long-cherished maxim of economists of nearly every stripe has been the international mobility of capital. Marxists and other critics of capitalism have objected to the ease with which capital (in the form of financial resources) flees poor countries and lands in rich countries. Neoclassical economists have extolled the efficiency of capital flowing across borders to be put to its most highly valued uses. But is capital really as mobile as economists have made it out to be? Perhaps not, according to a classic regression estimated by Martin Feldstein and Charles Horioka of Harvard University.

The perception that capital is highly mobile rests in part on the observation that liquid financial capital moves rapidly about world financial markets as investors respond to small changes in interest rates in various countries. But most capital is not in this easily transferred form. Much of capital is in the illiquid, long-term form of buildings and equipment. Are investors as willing to sink their funds into these less liquid assets as they are into financial instruments?

Despite the folk wisdom about capital mobility, there are reasons to wonder whether capital is, indeed, so mobile internationally. Investors may perceive investment in foreign economies as particularly risky, and as comprising risks that are difficult to "diversify away" (see the Regression's Greatest Hits—Capital Asset Pricing Model box on p. 74 for a discussion of diversification). Such perceived risks could impede the mobility of international capital. Furthermore, many countries create institutional barriers to capital flows.

Whether capital is mobile has important economic consequences. If capital is immobile,

government policies that increase saving also spur domestic capital formation, as the savings get channeled into domestic uses. In contrast, if capital is internationally mobile, policies to increase savings do not spur domestic investment. The mobility of capital also has serious consequences for who bears taxes. The microeconomic theory of tax incidence shows that taxes are largely borne by immobile factors of production. If capital is immobile, capital will share the burden of taxes in considerable measure with immobile labor, but if capital is internationally mobile, it can escape taxes, and the burden of taxes will be borne more by labor.

In 1980, Feldstein and Horioka subjected the capital mobility folklore to empirical test.[5] They noted that if capital is, in fact, highly mobile, savings and investment would not be bound together from one country to another. Countries with eager savers and few investment opportunities would send their dollars abroad, and countries with little savings and rich investment opportunities would draw cash from elsewhere. Feldstein and Horioka, therefore, proposed examining the relationship between savings and investment in a sample of 21 developed countries belonging to the Organization for Economic Co-operation and Development (OECD). The two economists found capital to be surprisingly immobile.

In the years 1960–1974, saving rates varied widely among these 21 OECD countries, with a high of 37.2% in Japan and a low of 18.4% in the United Kingdom. Across the 15 years, which countries saved a lot and which a little proved very stable; the correlation between countries, savings rates in 1960–1964 and the savings rates in those same countries in 1970–

1974 was 0.86. In the same years, 1960–1974, investment rates also varied comparably widely across these 21 OECD countries, and which countries invested much and which little remained stable across the 15 years.

What Feldstein and Horioka noted was that if capital is truly highly mobile across countries, the investment rates in individual countries should not be accounted for by the saving rates in individual countries. That is, in the regression

*investment rate$_i$ = $\beta_0$ + $\beta_1$(saving rate$_i$) + $\varepsilon_i$*

where *investment rate$_i$* is the 1960–1974 average investment rate for country *i* and *saving rate$_i$* is the 1960–1974 average saving rate for country *i*, most of the variation in the investment rate should be accounted for by variation in $\varepsilon$, not by variation in the saving rate variable; that is, the $R^2$ in this regression should be low. When Feldstein and Horioka conducted this regression, however, the $R^2$ proved to be 0.91. Moreover, they estimated the coefficient $\beta_1$ to be 0.89, indicating that increased savings were

channeled almost dollar for dollar into increased domestic investment. Capital appears to be far less mobile than economists had long thought! The data set horioka.*** on this book's companion Web site (**www.aw-bc.com/murray**) contains the saving and investment rate data that Feldstein and Horioka used.

 **Final Notes**

Feldstein and Horioka's findings were so surprising that they have been repeatedly called "the Feldstein–Horioka Paradox." Their paper epitomizes the insight and inspiration that a carefully conceived simple regression can provide—and the powerful effect a surprisingly high $R^2$ can have. Even now, more than 20 years later, economists are still trying to account for their paradox. Is capital truly so much less mobile than economists had long presumed, or are there economic models with mobile capital that can account for Feldstein and Horioka's results?

■

## 5.7    Two Properties of the BLUE Estimators' Residuals

WHAT ARE THE PROPERTIES OF AN ESTIMATOR?

The residuals that accompany $\hat{\beta}_0$ and $\hat{\beta}_1$ have two properties that prove important in econometric theory:

$$\sum e_i = 0$$

and

$$\sum X_i e_i = 0.$$

Numerous theoretical problems in econometrics stumble on the sum of the residuals or on the sum of the residuals times the corresponding $X$-values. Knowing that these sums equal zero when the residuals are based on $\hat{\beta}_0$ and $\hat{\beta}_1$ simplifies the analysis of such problems. This section derives the properties of these BLUE estimators' residuals. Appendix 5.C expresses the results using matrix algebra.

## The Sum of the Residuals

To prove that the sum of the residuals equals zero when our estimators are $\hat{\beta}_0$ and $\hat{\beta}_1$, recall that in this case,

$$e_i = Y_i - \hat{\beta}_0 - \hat{\beta}_1 X_i$$

so that

$$
\begin{aligned}
\sum e_i &= \sum (Y_i - \hat{\beta}_0 - \hat{\beta}_1 X_i) \\
&= \sum Y_i - \sum \hat{\beta}_0 - \sum \hat{\beta}_1 X_i \\
&= \sum Y_i - n\hat{\beta}_0 - \hat{\beta}_1 \sum X_i \\
&= n\left[\frac{1}{n}\sum Y_i + \frac{1}{n}(n\hat{\beta}_0) + \frac{1}{n}\hat{\beta}_1 \sum X_i\right] \\
&= n[\overline{Y} - \hat{\beta}_0 - \hat{\beta}_1 \overline{X}].
\end{aligned}
$$

It then follows from

$$\sum e_i = n[\overline{Y} - \hat{\beta}_0 - \hat{\beta}_1 \overline{X}]$$

that

$$\sum e_i = 0,$$

as claimed, because the line fitted with $\hat{\beta}_0$ and $\hat{\beta}_1$ passes through $(\overline{X}, \overline{Y})$, that is,

$$\overline{Y} = \hat{\beta}_0 + \hat{\beta}_1 \overline{X}.$$

## The Sum of the *X*'s Times the Residuals

To prove that the sum of the *X*'s times the residuals equals zero, we begin by noting that because the sum of the residuals is zero, the mean residual, $\bar{e}$, is also zero, and we can write

$$\sum X_i e_i = \sum [X_i(e_i - \bar{e})].$$

Recall the rule from Section 5.3 that tells us that for any *Q* and *Z*,

$$\sum (Q_i - \overline{Q})(Z_i - \overline{Z}) = \sum (Q_i - \overline{Q})Z_i.$$

Using this rule, we can write

$$\sum [X_i(e_i - \bar{e})] = \sum [(X_i - \overline{X})(e_i - \bar{e})],$$

which is the covariance of *X* and *e* in the sample, $\text{Scov}(X_i, e_i)$. In Section 5.10, however, we proved that

$$\text{Scov}(X_i, e_i) = 0,$$

so

$$\sum X_i e_i = 0,$$

as claimed.

<table>
<tr><td>**5.8**</td><td># Ordinary Least Squares</td></tr>
</table>

Fitting a scatterplot well provides yet another intuitive approach to estimating a straight line. Historically, and in many econometrics courses, a good-fitting line has been the very first estimator people considered for a straight line with unknown intercept. The $R^2$ measure defined in Section 5.6,

$$R^2 = 1 - \frac{\sum e_i^2}{\sum y_i^2},$$

is largest for the estimates of the slope and intercept that make the sum of squared residuals as small as possible. Note that the term $\sum y_i^2$ is a trait of the sample and is the same for all estimators, and that our choice of estimators can only influence $\sum e_i^2$. One way to define a "best fitting" line, then, is to say that the best fitting line minimizes the sum of squared residuals; that is, the best fitting line minimizes the mean squared distances of observations from the fitted line, with the distance measured as the vertical distance from the observed $(X, Y)$ point to the estimated line. The goal, then, is to minimize

$$\text{sum of squared residuals} = SSR = \sum (Y_i - \tilde{\beta}_0 - \tilde{\beta}_1 X_i)^2$$

with respect to $\tilde{\beta}_0$ and $\tilde{\beta}_1$.

The estimators for $\beta_0$ and $\beta_1$ that minimize the sum of squared residuals are called the **ordinary least squares (OLS) estimators**. The OLS estimators prove to be $\hat{\beta}_0$ and $\hat{\beta}_1$, the BLUE estimators under the Gauss–Markov Assumptions. Historically, $\hat{\beta}_0$ and $\hat{\beta}_1$ first became popular because of their least squares property. The search for BLUE estimators came later.

To conclude that $\hat{\beta}_0$ and $\hat{\beta}_1$ are the OLS estimators, we need to prove that they do minimize the sum of squared residuals. To minimize

$$SSR = \sum (Y_i - \tilde{\beta}_0 - \tilde{\beta}_1 X_i)^2$$
$$= \sum [Y_i^2 + \tilde{\beta}_0^2 + \tilde{\beta}_1^2 X_i^2 + 2(\tilde{\beta}_0 \tilde{\beta}_1 X_i - \tilde{\beta}_0 Y_i - \tilde{\beta}_1 X_i Y_i)]$$

with respect to $\tilde{\beta}_0$ and $\tilde{\beta}_1$, we take the derivative of SSR with respect to $\tilde{\beta}_0$ and with respect to $\tilde{\beta}_1$, and set those derivatives each to zero:

$$\frac{\partial SSR}{\partial \tilde{\beta}_0} = \sum (2\tilde{\beta}_0 + 2\tilde{\beta}_1 X_i - 2Y_i) = 0$$

$$\frac{\partial SSR}{\partial \tilde{\beta}_1} = \sum (2\tilde{\beta}_1 X_i^2 + 2\tilde{\beta}_0 X_i - 2X_i Y_i) = 0.$$

The first of these two equations requires that

$$2\sum (Y_i - \tilde{\beta}_0 - \tilde{\beta}_1 X_i) = 2\sum e_i = 0.$$

The second requires that

$$2\sum (Y_i - \tilde{\beta}_0 - \tilde{\beta}_1 X_i)X_i = 2\sum e_i X_i = 0.$$

Thus, the OLS estimators require that the residuals sum to zero and that the sum of the residuals times the $X_i$'s is also zero. In Section 5.6 we learned that these are properties of $\hat{\beta}_0$ and $\hat{\beta}_1$, so $\hat{\beta}_0$ and $\hat{\beta}_1$ must be the OLS estimators of the intercept and slope.

The OLS estimators are based on a *within-sample property*: They minimize the sum of squared residuals. They have this property without any reference to the underlying DGP. The OLS estimators, $\hat{\beta}_0$ and $\hat{\beta}_1$, happen to have good statistical properties across samples when the Gauss–Markov Assumptions are satisfied. For other DGPs, however, we shall find that $\hat{\beta}_0$ and $\hat{\beta}_1$ are no longer BLUE—even though, as the OLS estimators, these estimators *always* minimize the

## An Organizational Structure for the Study of Econometrics

### 1. What Is the DGP?

We specified the data-generating process:

$$Y_i = \beta_0 + \beta_1 X_i + \varepsilon_i \qquad i = 1, \ldots, n,$$

plus the Gauss–Markov Assumptions.

### 2. What Makes a Good Estimator?

Sometimes a good fit is desirable (OLS).

Too little variation in $X$ yields imprecise estimators.

### 3. How Do We Create an Estimator?

An unbiased estimator of $\sigma^2$ is $\frac{1}{n-2}\sum e_i^2 = \frac{1}{n-2}\sum (Y_i - \hat{\beta}_0 - \hat{\beta}_1 X_i)^2$.

$\hat{\beta}_0$ and $\hat{\beta}_1$ minimize the sum of squared residuals (OLS).

Use confidence intervals.

### 4. What Are an Estimator's Properties?

$$\text{var}(\hat{\beta}_1) = \sigma^2 / \sum x_i^2$$

$$\text{var}(\hat{\beta}_0) = \frac{\sigma^2 \sum X_i^2}{n \sum x_j^2}$$

$$\text{cov}(\hat{\beta}_0, \hat{\beta}_1) = -\sigma^2 \overline{X} / \sum x_i^2$$

### 5. How Do We Make Forecasts?

Use prediction intervals.

sum of squared residuals and therefore *always* maximize $R^2$. In general, there may be a conflict between choosing estimators that are BLUE and choosing those that best fit the observed data. If our goal is to describe well the data in hand, the least squares property becomes paramount. But if our goal is to estimate the values of the population parameters $\beta_0$ and $\beta_1$, our chief concern is the kinds of errors we make in estimating those parameters, and the goodness of fit of our estimated line becomes unimportant. Econometricians are usually more interested in the underlying parameters, $\beta_0$ and $\beta_1$, and less concerned about fit.

From now on, we follow common practice and refer to $\hat{\beta}_0$ and $\hat{\beta}_1$, and their counterparts in models with multiple explanators, as *OLS estimators*, because they do have that within-sample property and because that is their historical root.

## Summary

This chapter began by determining that the variance of a linear estimator in a DGP with unknown slope and intercept, in which the Gauss–Markov Assumptions apply, is

$$\sigma^2 \sum w_i^2,$$

and that the covariance between two estimators in such a DGP is

$$\sigma^2 \sum w_i^R w_i^S.$$

The BLUE estimator of the slope for such a DGP proved to be

$$\hat{\beta}_1 = \frac{\sum x_i y_i}{\sum x_i^2},$$

and the BLUE estimator of the intercept proved to be

$$\hat{\beta}_0 = \overline{Y} - \hat{\beta}_1 \overline{X}.$$

We then determined that in such a DGP, the variances of $\hat{\beta}_0$ and $\hat{\beta}_1$ are

$$\sigma_{\hat{\beta}_0}^2 = \frac{\sigma^2 \sum X_i^2}{n \sum x_j^2}$$

and

$$\sigma_{\hat{\beta}_1}^2 = \sigma^2 / \sum x_i^2,$$

respectively. The square roots of these variances are the estimators' standard errors. When the $X_i$ vary too little about their mean, these variances are very large.

The covariance between $\hat{\beta}_0$ and $\hat{\beta}_1$ is

$$-\sigma^2 \overline{X} / \sum x_i^2.$$

The chapter used the variances and covariance of the BLUE estimators of the slope and intercept of a line to determine the standard error of the estimator of the expected value of $Y$ given $X = X^*$:

$$\sigma_{Y^*} = \sqrt{\sigma^2 \left[ \frac{1}{n} + \frac{(X^* - \overline{X})^2}{\sum x_i^2} \right]}.$$

Because $\sigma^2$ is seldom known, the chapter next developed an estimator of $\sigma^2$ in which we used the residuals from the fitted regression line,

$$e_i = Y_i - \hat{\beta}_0 - \hat{\beta}_1 X_i,$$

to mimic the unobserved disturbances. An unbiased estimator of $\sigma^2$ is

$$s^2 = \frac{1}{n-2} \sum e_i^2.$$

We used estimators' standard errors and estimated standard errors to construct confidence intervals and prediction intervals.

The chapter next noted that the sum of squared residuals is a convenient indicator of how well a regression line fits, or describes, an observed sample of data. The sum of squared residuals underpins a useful measure of goodness of fit, the coefficient of determination, usually denoted by $R^2$:

$$R^2 = \frac{\hat{\beta}_1^2 \sum x_i^2}{\sum y_i^2} = 1 - \frac{\sum e_i^2}{\sum y_i^2}.$$

We concluded by showing that $\hat{\beta}_0$ and $\hat{\beta}_1$ are the estimators of the intercept and slope that minimize the sum of squared residuals (and therefore maximize $R^2$), and are usually called OLS estimators for that reason.

## Concepts for Review

## Questions for Discussion

1. The theoretical concepts of a production function and a utility function are much more general than the Cobb–Douglas specification. How much credence do you think we should give to empirical results based on such specifications? In contrast, do the analyses of Feldstein and Horioka and of Phillips strike you as any more informative than regressions about consumer preferences or the U.S. production function based on the Cobb–Douglas form? Discuss.

2. The OLS estimator *always* provides the best fit to the data in hand, in the sense that it always minimizes the sum of squared residuals. Why *should or shouldn't* we use this as a universal criterion for choosing an estimator?

## Problems for Analysis

> For the data sets that you will need to solve the problems in this section, go to **www.aw-bc.com/murray**.

1. Prove that an unbiased estimator of the variance of the disturbances is

$$s^2 = \frac{1}{n-1}\sum(Y_i - \beta_{g4})^2,$$

when the DGP contains a straight line through the origin and the disturbances satisfy the Gauss–Markov Assumptions.

2. Estimate a model with unknown slope and intercept of a line, assuming the Gauss–Markov Assumptions hold. Suppose the mean of the $X_i$'s is 70, the mean of the $Y_i$'s is 100, $\sum x_i y_i = -3,550$, $\sum x_i^2 = 2,250$, $\sum y_i^2 = 4,872,040$, $n = 12$, $\sum X_i^2 = 61,050$ and $\sum e_i^2 = 487,204$.
   a. Compute, $\hat{\beta}_0$, $\hat{\beta}_1$, $s^2$, and $R^2$.
   b. Construct 95% confidence intervals for $\beta_0$ and $\beta_1$.
   c. Compute the fitted value of $Y$, given $X = 80$.
   d. Compute the estimated standard error of the estimator of the expected value of $Y$, given $X = 80$.
   e. Compute the standard deviation of the conditional forecast error, $\sigma_{F_0}^2$, for the predicted value of $Y$, given $X = 80$.

3. Under the Gauss–Markov Assumptions in a model with unknown slope and intercept, what is the variance of $\tilde{\beta}_1 = (\sum x_i^2 Y_i / \sum x_i^3)$?

4. Does market power inhibit innovation? Or do noncompetitive economic profits fund advances in technology that more competitive firms can't afford? The file tfp.$^{***}$

contains data pertinent to these questions. The two variables in the file are the percentage changes in industries' total factor productivity (TFP) over a five-year period (*tfp_ch*) and the concentrations of market share (measured in percent) among industries' four largest firms (*conc*).

a. Regress TFP changes on four-firm concentrations. If the concentration rises one percentage point, how much do you estimate TFP changes by? Construct a 95% confidence interval for the slope coefficient.

b. How would you describe in words your interval estimate of the amount the expected TFP would change if the four-firm concentration were to rise one percentage point?

c. How much of the variation in TFP changes in this sample can be accounted for by the variation in four-firm concentration?

5. The file poverty1.*** contains U.S. poverty rates (*poverty*) and unemployment rates (*unemploy*), both measured in percent, from 1959 to 2003.

a. Compute the mean poverty rate and mean unemployment rate in this sample. What are their standard deviations?

b. Create a scatterplot with unemployment rates on the horizontal axis and poverty rates on the vertical axis. Is there a strong relationship between poverty rates and unemployment rates?

c. Use the BLUE estimators to estimate the slope and intercept of

$$poverty\ rate = \beta_0 + \beta_1(unemployment\ rate) + v.$$

d. Construct a 95% confidence interval for $\beta_1$. How would you describe in words your interval estimate of the amount the expected poverty rate would change if the unemployment rate were to rise one percentage point?

e. How much of the variation in poverty rates over the period 1959–2003 can be accounted for by variation in the unemployment rate?

f. Divide *unemploy* by 100 to create a new variable *une*, the unemployment rate measured as a fraction. What are the mean and standard deviation of this new variable?

g. Regress *poverty* on *une*. Explain the differences and similarities between the results of this regression and those in (c). Are the estimated coefficients the same? Are their estimated standard errors the same? Is the standard error of the regression the same? Is the $R^2$ the same? Explain each response briefly.

h. Use the regression results from (g) to construct a 95% confidence interval for the slope coefficient. Explain the differences in center and width between this confidence interval and the confidence interval built in (d). Also explain whether the two confidence intervals are reporting the same information.

6. The file wineweather.*** contains the natural log of the average 1989 prices (*logprice*) for Bordeaux wines for the vintages 1952–1989 (*vintage* or *vint*). The age of each vintage in 1989 is given by the variable *age*. These data were part of an analysis of Bordeaux wine as an investment by economists Orley Ashenfelter and David Ashmore of Princeton University and Robert LaLonde of the University of Chicago.[6]

a. Create a scatterplot with age on the horizontal axis and the log of price on the vertical axis. Do older wines tend to sell at a higher price than younger wines? Does an older wine always sell at a higher price than a younger wine?

b. Estimate the semilog relationship

$$\ln(price) = \beta_0 + \beta_1(age) + \nu.$$

c. Construct a 95% confidence interval for the annual growth rate of the expected price of a bottle of wine. Does your interval incline you to reject a claim that the age of wine doesn't matter for its expected price? Briefly explain your response.

d. How much of the variation in the prices of wines across vintages can be accounted for by the age of the wine?

7. The file sat1.*** contains the Scholastic Achievement Test score (*SAT*) measured in total points on a 1600-point scale, and four-year grade point average (*totgpa*) on a four-point scale, for a sample of Bates College students.

a. Create a scatterplot with SAT score on the horizontal axis and grade point average on the vertical axis. Is there a strong relationship between SAT score and grade point average?

b. Regress *totgpa* on *SAT* and an intercept term.

c. Build a 95% confidence interval for the coefficient on *SAT*. Does your interval incline you to reject a claim that grades and SAT scores are unrelated? Does it incline you to reject the claim that SAT scores are an important determinant of grades? Briefly explain your response.

d. How much of the variation in GPAs across Bates students can be accounted for by the variation in their SAT scores?

8. Are presidential elections affected by the economy? Do voters consider how much unemployment has changed during the election year when casting their votes for or against the party sitting in the White House? The file political.*** contains the change in unemployment in the 12 months immediately preceding the election (*unemploy*) and the percentage of the popular vote obtained by the incumbent presidential party (*incumbent* or *incumb*) in each presidential election (*year*) since 1900.[7] Both *unemploy* and *incumbent* are measured in percent.

a. Create a scatterplot with the change in unemployment on the horizontal axis and the incumbent party's percent of the popular vote on the vertical axis. Is there a strong relationship between jobs and votes for the incumbent party?

b. Use the BLUE estimators to estimate the slope and intercept of

$$incumbent = \beta_0 + \beta_1(unemploy) + \varepsilon.$$

c. Construct a 95% confidence interval for the effect of a one percentage point increase in unemployment on the expected percentage of the popular vote that the incumbent party will obtain. Does this interval incline you to reject a claim that the unemployment rate has no effect on the votes obtained by the incumbent party's presidential candidate? Briefly explain your response.

d. How much of the variation in the incumbent party's votes across the past 26 presidential elections can be accounted for by variation in changes in the unemployment rate in the 12 months prior to the election? Do these econometric results lend credence to the popular cry during the 1992 presidential election "It's the economy, stupid"? (How much did the unemployment rate change in the 12 months prior to the 1992 election?)

e. What is the estimated standard error of the regression? How would you explain the practical meaning of this number to your roommate?

 9. The file food.*** contains food expenditures (*food*) and total expenditures (*total*) for a sample of 19th century Belgian workers collected by Edouard Ducpetiaux[8] and studied by Ernst Engel.[9] Chapter 1 used these data to examine Engel's Law about food expenditures and income. Engel's Law posits that a household's food expenditure grows more slowly than its income. Use total expenditure as your measure of income. Assume the Gauss–Markov Assumptions apply to the DGP for Ducpetiaux's DGP.

a. Create a scatterplot with total expenditures on the horizontal axis and food expenditure on the vertical axis. Is there a strong relationship between food expenditure and total expenditure?

b. Estimate the slope and intercept in

$$food\ expenditure = \beta_0 + \beta_1(income) + v.$$

c. Construct a 95% confidence interval for $\beta_0$.

d. Do any of the values in your interval estimate for $\beta_0$ imply that food's share in expenditures rises as income rises?

e. How much of the variation in food expenditures among the sampled workers can be accounted for by variation in incomes?

f. Use the BLUE estimator to estimate the slope and intercept in

$$\ln(food\ expenditure) = \beta_0 + \beta_1\ln(income) + v.$$

g. Construct a 95% confidence interval for $\beta_1$.

h. Do any of the values in your interval estimator for the income elasticity of food demand refute Engel's Law?

10. The file housing2.*** contains housing expenditures (*housing*) and total expenditures (*total*) for a sample of 19th-century Belgian workers collected by Edouard Ducpetiaux[10] and studied by Ernst Engel. Chapter 1 examined Engel's Law about food expenditures and income. Engel's Law posits that a household's food expenditure grows more slowly than its income. Here, you are to examine Engel's data to see if he could have also concluded that housing expenditure grows more slowly than income. You are to use total expenditure as your measure of income. Assume the Gauss–Markov Assumptions apply to the DGP for Ducpetiaux's data.

a. Create a scatterplot with total expenditures on the horizontal axis and housing expenditure on the vertical axis. Is there a strong relationship between housing expenditure and total expenditure?

b. Estimate the slope and intercept in

$$housing\ expenditure = \beta_0 + \beta_1(income) + v.$$

c. Construct a 95% confidence interval for $\beta_0$.

d. Do any of the values in your interval estimate for $\beta_0$ imply that housing's share in expenditures rises as income rises?

e. How much of the variation in housing expenditures among the sampled workers can be accounted for by variation in incomes?

f. Use the BLUE estimator to estimate the slope and intercept in

$$\ln(\textit{housing expenditure}) = \beta_0 + \beta_1 \ln(\textit{income}) + v.$$

g. Construct a 95% confidence interval for $\beta_1$.

h. Do all values in your interval estimator for the income elasticity of housing support an Engel's Law for housing?

 11. The relationship between votes cast on election day and votes cast absentee has recently been covered extensively by the media. The file election.*** contains the differences in votes between Democratic and Republican candidates in Pennsylvania State Senate races for election-day vote counts (*electionday* or *eday*) and for absentee vote counts (*absentee*) from 1982 to 1993.[11]

$$\textit{electionday} = (\textit{election-day votes for the Democratic candidates} \\ - \textit{election-day votes for the Republican candidates})$$

$$\textit{absentee} = (\textit{absentee votes for the Democratic candidates} \\ -\textit{absentee votes for the Republican candidates})$$

On average, among election-day voters, Democratic Senate candidates received 39,007 more votes than their Republican opponents; absentee voters cast, on average, 256 more votes for Democrats than for Republicans.

In the 1993 election in the Second Senatorial District in Philadelphia, which determined which party controlled the Pennsylvania State Senate, the Republican candidate won among the votes cast on election day, 19,691 to 19,127, whereas the Democrat won the absentee ballots, 1,391 to 366. The Democrat won the election by 461 votes. Later, a federal judge ruled that the Democrats had engaged in a "civil conspiracy" to win the election and declared the Republican the winner. The dozen observations in election.*** were part of the evidence given to the judge to support the claim that many absentee ballots in the 1993 Second District election were fraudulent. The election-day ballots were not contested. All agreed that the Democrat received 564 fewer votes than the Republican.

a. Create a scatterplot with *electionday*, the difference between Democratic candidates' votes and Republican candidates' votes in election-day vote counts, on the horizontal axis, and *absentee*, the difference between Democratic candidates' votes and Republican candidates' votes in absentee ballots, on the vertical axis. Is there a strong relationship between the difference in absentee votes and the difference in election-day votes?

b. Estimate the slope and intercept in

$$\textit{absentee} = \beta_0 + \beta_1(\textit{electionday}) + v.$$

c. Build a 95% confidence interval for $\beta_1$. Based on your interval, are you inclined to reject a claim that how much a candidate wins by among election-day voters is irrelevant in assessing whether a candidate is likely to win or lose among absentee voters?

d. Build a 95% prediction interval for the difference in votes between Democrat and Republican conditional on the Democrat's receiving 564 fewer votes from election-day voters. Given this interval, how would you assess the claim that the absentee votes (which favored the Democrat by 1,025 votes) contained many fraudulent votes?

e. Given the interval estimated in (d), what would you say to a claim that perhaps some votes were fraudulent, but that enough were fair votes to overcome the Republican's edge of 564 votes among election-day voters? Briefly explain your reasoning.

f. Parts (d) and (e) direct your attention to the prediction interval for assessing the claims about the absentee ballots. Would 95% confidence intervals be more or less appropriate for guiding these judgments? Briefly explain your reasoning.

12. From the 1970s to the early 1990s, crime rates rose and prison populations swelled. Were the large prison expenditures socially useful? Did locking up criminals reduce crime? The data set prisons1.*** contains a portion of the 1971 to 1993 annual state-level data used by Steven Levitt to answer this question.[12] The variable *lvcph* is the natural log of the number of violent crimes per 100,000 people in a state's population in a given year. The variable *lprisph* is the natural log of the number of prisoners in the state during a given year. The data set also contains *chlvcph* and *chlprisph*, the changes in *lvcph* and *lprisph* from one year to the next in a given state, and the variables *state* and *year* to identify the states and years.

a. In time series data, sometimes third variables influence both the dependent variable and the explanator, driving both steadily in one direction or another over time and biasing the OLS estimator. Econometricians sometimes sidestep this problem by analyzing *the changes* in the variables, rather than *the levels*. Regress the change in the log of the violent crime rate against the change in the log of the incarceration rate. Interpret the estimated coefficients.

b. Build a 95% confidence interval for the slope. Based on this interval, would you be inclined to reject a claim that incarceration rates are unrelated to violent crime rates?

13. The American welfare program that serves poor single parents and their children is called Temporary Assistance for Needy Families (TANF). TANF varies widely from state to state, both in its generosity and in its eligibility requirements. The file tanf.*** contains the basic real TANF benefit level for a family of four in each of the 50 states (*tanfreal*). Economists who study welfare across countries have found that countries that are more racially homogeneous have higher welfare benefits. Here we will explore whether this is also true across American states. In all U.S. states, African Americans are a minority. The data in tanf.*** will allow you to determine whether TANF benefits are higher in more racially homogeneous states, that is, in states with a smaller proportion of African Americans in the population. The TANF data set includes among its variables the variable *black*, which reports the fraction of a state's population that is African American.

a. Create a scatterplot with the percentage of the state's population that is African American on the horizontal axis and real TANF benefits on the vertical axis. Is there a strong relationship between *tanfreal* and *black*?

b. Regress *tanfreal* on *black* and an intercept term. Build a 95% confidence interval for the effect of a one percentage point increase in African Americans' share of a state's population on the expected real TANF payment in the state.

c. Compute the estimated standard error of the estimator of the expected value of real TANF benefits in a state with a population that is 5% African American.

d. How much of the variation in real TANF benefits across states is accounted for by variation in state's African American populations?

14. The Trans-Alaska Pipeline brings to Valdez, on Alaska's south central coast, both crude oil from northern Prudhoe Bay oil fields and "residual refinery oil" from a refinery near Fairbanks, Alaska. (Residual refinery oil is substance left over after crude has been initially refined; residual refinery oil can be refined again, but yields much less product than crude oil itself.) Crude oils of varying quality and the very low quality residual refinery oil are all mixed together in the pipeline, arriving all together at Valdez in one blended quality.

Some oil-field owners provide high-quality crude to the pipeline. Others provide lower quality crudes. The Fairbanks refinery provides very low quality residual oil. Buyers of oil from the pipeline in Valdez pay a single price, appropriate to the quality of the blended crude that flows out of the pipeline. In fairness to high-quality suppliers, the carriers that operate the pipeline pay suppliers higher prices for better quality crude and lower prices for lower quality crude, with the lowest price being for residual refinery oil. The carriers measure quality by "API gravity," with higher gravity indicating higher quality; the unit of measure of API gravity is "API degrees."

The carriers proposed a rule for setting the price paid to suppliers. The implicit premise of the rule was that the market value of a barrel of oil rises $0.15 with each API degree of the oil. Under the rule, each supplier would receive the price per barrel paid in Valdez, plus $0.15 times the difference between the degrees API of the supplier's crude or residual oil and the average quality of the oil delivered in Valdez. (The oil delivered in Valdez was 23 API degree oil.) Suppliers providing oil of above-average quality would get a premium; suppliers of below-average quality oil would incur a penalty. For example, a supplier offering oil of 25 degrees API would receive a premium of $(25 - 23) \cdot (\$0.15$ per barrel). A supplier offering oil of 20 degrees API would incur a penalty of $(20 - 23) \cdot (\$0.15$ per barrel).

The Fairbanks refinery, which stood to incur the largest penalties because of its low-quality residual oil (18 API degrees), challenged the rule before an Administrative Law Judge.[13] The Fairbanks refinery proposed the differential be somewhere between $0.0309 and $0.0535 per degree API per barrel.

The judge found that the basic notion of a price differential was "just and reasonable," as the law requires. The judge then had to settle on an appropriate size for the differential. Unfortunately, there was no observed market price for Alaskan crude oil of various qualities (the only market for Alaskan crude oil was that for blended crude oil in Valdez). Information on the prices of a sample of Persian Gulf crude oils was available, however. The sampled values of crude oils' quality (measured in API degrees) and price per barrel (measured in 1984 dollars) are in the variables *API* and *price* in the file oilprice1.***.

a. Create a scatterplot with quality on the horizontal axis and price on the vertical axis.

b. Use a regression to estimate how much the price per barrel changes when API gravity rises by one degree.

c. Construct a 95% confidence interval for how much the price per barrel changes when API gravity rises by one degree.

d. As an expert witness hired by the judge, what price differential would you propose based on these data? Briefly explain your answer.

e. The judge asks you whether either the price proposed by the carriers or the price proposed by the Fairbanks refinery is a reasonable price to use, given the available data. Answer the judge.

f. Multiply *price* by 100 to create a new variable *p* that measures price in cents. Regress *p* on *API* and an intercept term. Explain the differences between these regression results and those in (b). In particular, why does the standard error of the regression change, but the $R^2$ remain unchanged?

## Endnotes

1. Hughes Mearns, "Antigonish," 1899, reprinted in *Worlds In Small*, John Colombo, ed. (Cacanadadada Press, 1992).

2. Proving this more general Gauss–Markov Theorem requires a messier variant of our derivation of the BLUE estimators for $\beta_0$ and $\beta_1$. A linear estimator of $E(Y|X^*)$ will be of the usual form $\hat{Y}^* = \sum w_i Y_i$. In this instance, we want $E(\hat{Y}^*) = \beta_0 + \beta_1 X^*$, which requires $\sum(w_i) = 1$ and $\sum(w_i X_i) = X^*$. As usual, the variance of the linear estimator is $\sigma^2 \sum(w_i^2)$. The Gauss–Markov Theorem says that the appropriate weights are $w_i^{Y_0} = (w_i^{0^*} + X^* w_i^{1^*})$. Because $\sum(w_i^{0^*}) = 1$ and $\sum(w_i^{1^*}) = 0$, on the one hand, and $\sum(w_i^{0^*} X^*) = 0$ and $\sum(w_i^{0^*} X^*) = 1$, on the other hand, the $w_i^{Y_0}$ satisfy the unbiasedness constraints for estimating $E(Y|X^*)$. The calculus to prove these are the most efficient weights is cumbersome.

3. Charles W. Cobb and Paul Douglas, "A Theory of Production," *American Economic Review* 18, no. 1 (March 1928): 139–165.

4. K. J. Arrow, H. B. Chenery, B. S. Minhas, and R. M. Solow, "Capital-Labor Substitution and Economic Efficiency," *Review of Economics and Statistics* 43, no. 3 (August 1961): 225–250.

5. Martin Feldstein and Charles Horioka, "Domestic Savings and International Capital Flows," *Economic Journal* 90 (June 1980): 314–329.

6. Orley Ashenfelter, David Ashmore, and Robert LaLonde, "Bordeaux Wine Vintage Quality and the Weather," http://www.liquidasset.com/orley.htm (accessed December 1999).

7. Gary Smith of Pomona College generously provided these data.

8. Edouard Ducpetiaux, *Budgets Economiques de Classes de Ouvrieres en Belgique* (Brussels: Hayaz, 1855).

9. Ernst Engel, "Die Productions und Consumptionsverhaeltnisse des Koenigsreichs Sachsen," reprinted in *Die Lebenskosten Belgischer Arbeiter-Familien* (Dresden, 1895).

10. Edouard Ducpetiaux, *Budgets Economiques de Classes de Ouvrieres en Belgique* (Brussels: Hayaz, 1855).

11. Gary Smith of Pomona College generously provided these data.

12. Steven D. Levitt, "The Effect of Prison Population Size on Crime Rates: Evidence from Prison Overcrowding Litigation," *Quarterly Journal of Economics* 111, no. 2 (May 1996): 319–351.

13. Trans-Alaska Pipeline System, FERC ¶ 23, 048 (1983), FERC ¶ 61,123 (1984).

 *Appendix 5.A*

# The Unbiasedness of $s^2$

The variance of the disturbances, $\sigma^2$, is seldom known. Econometricians must estimate it. In the case of a population with a mean $\mu$ and a variance $\sigma^2$, an unbiased estimator of $\sigma^2$ is

$$s^2 = \frac{\sum_{i=1}^{n}(Y_i - \bar{Y})^2}{n - 1}. \qquad \text{5.A.1}$$

The Statistical Appendix proves the unbiasedness of $s^2$.

This appendix proves that for the Gauss–Markov DGP for a line through the origin, an unbiased estimator of $\sigma^2$ is

$$\frac{\sum_{i=1}^{n}(Y_i - \beta_{g4}X_i)^2}{n - 1}, \qquad \text{5.A.2}$$

but that when an unknown intercept is added to that DGP, the unbiased estimator becomes

$$\frac{\sum_{i=1}^{n}(Y_i - \hat{\beta}_0 - \hat{\beta}_1 X_i)^2}{n - 2}. \qquad \text{5.A.3}$$

# 5.A.1     Estimating the Variance of the Disturbances

Although the three estimators given in Equations 5.A.1 to 5.A.3 are different from one another, it is common to name them all $s^2$ and to rely on context to tell which estimator is intended.

The unintuitive aspect of each of these estimators is its denominator. Why do we not divide by $n$, which would be to use the mean squared residual to estimate the mean square disturbance? It is the appearance of the estimators, $\overline{Y}$, $\beta_{g4}$, $\hat{\beta}_0$, and $\hat{\beta}_1$ in the numerators that leads to the need for a denominator less than $n$; if we knew the population mean, $\beta$, $\beta_0$, and $\beta_1$, and used them in our numerators instead of the estimators, dividing by $n$ in each case would unbiasedly estimate $\sigma^2$. This section establishes that knowing $\beta$, $\beta_0$, and $\beta_1$ would lead to estimators of $\sigma^2$ that seem more natural, but that the denominators in Equations 5.A.1 to 5.A.3 needed to unbiasedly estimate $\sigma^2$ if $\beta$, $\beta_0$, and $\beta_1$ are unknown.

## An Infeasible Alternative Estimator

Suppose we do know $\mu$, or $\beta$, or $\beta_0$ and $\beta_1$. We could then subtract the (known) $E(Y_i|X_i)$ from $Y_i$ to obtain the $i$-th disturbance, $\varepsilon_i$. With the sample disturbances in hand, we could estimate $\sigma^2$ by

$$\hat{\sigma}^2 = \frac{1}{n}\sum_{i=1}^{n}\varepsilon_i^2,$$

which would be an unbiased estimator of $\sigma^2$ because

$$E(\hat{\sigma}^2) = E\left(\frac{1}{n}\sum\varepsilon_i^2\right) = \frac{1}{n}\sum E(\varepsilon_i^2) = \sigma^2.$$

Unfortunately, we do not know the $E(Y|X)$, so this estimator is infeasible. In the absence of $E(Y|X)$, we use our estimate of the expected value in its stead and use the $i$-th residual in place of the $i$-th disturbance. However, because our estimates are correlated with the $Y_i$, just replacing the disturbances with the residuals in $\hat{\sigma}^2$ leads to a biased estimator. To preserve unbiasedness, we must also alter the denominator.

## Some Preliminaries

We need several formulae and findings to prove the unbiasedness of $s^2$. First, Appendix 5.B shows that

$$\sum X_i^2 - n\overline{X}^2 = \sum x_i^2.$$

Second, under the Gauss–Markov Assumptions, the variances and covariances of $\beta_{g4}$, $\hat{\beta}_0$, and $\hat{\beta}_1$ are

$$\sigma_{g4}^2 = \frac{\sigma^2}{\sum X_i^2},$$

$$\sigma_{\hat{\beta}_0}^2 = var(\hat{\beta}_0) = \frac{\sigma^2 \sum X_i^2}{n \sum x_i^2},$$

$$\sigma_{\hat{\beta}_1}^2 = var(\hat{\beta}_1) = \frac{\sigma^2}{\sum x_i^2},$$

and

$$cov(\hat{\beta}_0, \hat{\beta}_1) = -\overline{X}\, var(\hat{\beta}_1),$$

respectively. Third, under the Gauss–Markov Assumptions,

$$E\left[\left(\sum \varepsilon_i\right)^2\right] = E\left[\sum_i \sum_j \varepsilon_i \varepsilon_j\right] = \sum \sum E(\varepsilon_i \varepsilon_j) = \sum_i E(\varepsilon_i^2) = n\sigma^2$$

because $E(Y_i Y_j) = 0$, for $i \neq j$, and, similarly,

$$E\left(\varepsilon_i \sum_j Y_j\right) = n\sigma^2.$$

And fourth, because the OLS estimators are unbiased, $\sum w_i X_i = 1$ for the slope estimator's weights, and $\sum w_i = 1$ for the intercept estimator's weights.

## The Unbiasedness of $s^2$

Consider the unbiasedness of

$$\frac{\sum_{i=1}^{n}(Y_i - \hat{\beta}_0 - \hat{\beta}_1 X_i)^2}{n-2}.$$

What is the expected value of the numerator?

Here it is convenient to rewrite the numerator

$$\sum_{i=1}^{n}(Y_i - \hat{\beta}_0 - \hat{\beta}_1 X_i)^2 = \sum (Y_i - \beta_0 - \beta_1 X_i - (\hat{\beta}_0 - \beta_0) - (\hat{\beta}_1 - \beta_1)X_i)^2$$

$$= \sum (\varepsilon_i - (\hat{\beta}_0 - \beta_0) - (\hat{\beta}_1 - \beta_1)X_i)^2.$$

In expectation,

$$E\left[\sum (\varepsilon_i - (\hat{\beta}_0 - \beta_0) - (\hat{\beta}_1 - \beta_1)X_i)^2\right]$$
$$= E\left[\sum \varepsilon_i^2\right] + E\left[\sum(\hat{\beta}_0 - \beta_0)^2\right] + E\left[\sum(\hat{\beta}_1 - \beta_1)^2 X_i^2\right]$$
$$\quad - 2E\left[\sum \varepsilon_i(\hat{\beta}_0 - \beta_0)\right] - 2E\left[\sum \varepsilon_i(\hat{\beta}_1 - \beta_1)X_i\right]$$
$$\quad + 2E\left[\sum(\hat{\beta}_0 - \beta_0)(\hat{\beta}_1 - \beta_1)X_i\right]$$

$$
\begin{aligned}
&= \mathrm{E}\left[\sum \varepsilon_i^2\right] + \mathrm{E}\left[\sum (\hat{\beta}_0 - \beta_0)^2\right] + \mathrm{E}\left[\sum (\hat{\beta}_1 - \beta_1)^2 X_i^2\right] \\
&\quad - 2\sum \mathrm{E}\left[\varepsilon_i \hat{\beta}_0 - \varepsilon_i \beta_0\right] - 2\sum \mathrm{E}\left[\varepsilon_i \hat{\beta}_1 X_i - \varepsilon_i \beta_1 X_i\right] \\
&\quad + 2\sum \mathrm{E}\left[(\hat{\beta}_0 - \beta_0)(\hat{\beta}_1 - \beta_1)X_i\right] \\
&= n\sigma^2 + n\mathrm{var}(\hat{\beta}_0) + \mathrm{var}(\hat{\beta}_1)\sum X_i^2 \\
&\quad - 2\sum \mathrm{E}\left(\varepsilon_i \hat{\beta}_0\right) - 2\sum \mathrm{E}\left(\varepsilon_i \hat{\beta}_1 X_i\right) + 2\mathrm{cov}(\hat{\beta}_0, \beta_1)n\overline{X} \\
&= n\sigma^2 + n\mathrm{var}(\hat{\beta}_0) + \mathrm{var}(\hat{\beta}_1)\sum X_i^2 \\
&\quad - 2\sum_i \mathrm{E}\left[\varepsilon_i \sum_j w_j^0 Y_j\right] - 2\sum_j \mathrm{E}\left[\varepsilon_i X_i \sum_j w_j^1 Y_j\right] \\
&\quad + 2\mathrm{cov}(\hat{\beta}_0, \beta_1)n\overline{X} \\
&= n\sigma^2 + n\mathrm{var}(\hat{\beta}_0) + \mathrm{var}(\hat{\beta}_1)\sum X_i^2 \\
&\quad - 2\sum_i w_i^0 \sigma^2 - 2\sum_i w_i^1 X_i \sigma^2 + 2\mathrm{cov}(\hat{\beta}_0, \hat{\beta}_1)n\overline{X} \\
&= n\sigma^2 + n\mathrm{var}(\hat{\beta}_0) + \mathrm{var}(\hat{\beta}_1)\sum X_i^2 \\
&\quad - 2\sigma^2 - 2\sigma^2 - 2\sum_i w_i^1 X_i \sigma^2 + 2\mathrm{cov}(\hat{\beta}_0, \hat{\beta}_1)n\overline{X} \\
&= n\sigma^2 + \sigma^2 \frac{\sum X_i^2}{\sum x_i^2} + \sigma^2 \frac{\sum X_i^2}{\sum x_i^2} \\
&\quad - 2\sigma^2 - 2\sigma^2 - 2\overline{X}\frac{\sigma^2}{\sum x_i^2}n\overline{X} \\
&= n\sigma^2 + 2\frac{\sigma^2}{\sum x_i^2}\left(\sum X_i^2 - n\overline{X}^2\right) - 4\sigma^2 = (n-2)\sigma^2.
\end{aligned}
$$

from which it follows that

$$
s^2 = \frac{\displaystyle\sum_{i=1}^{n}(Y_i - \hat{\beta}_0 - \hat{\beta}_1 X_i)^2}{n-2}
$$

is an unbiased estimator of $\sigma^2$ in the Gauss–Markov DGP with unknown slope and intercept.

# Appendix 5.B

# The Variance of $\hat{\beta}_0$ and the Covariance Between Linear Estimators

With both the intercept and slope of a line unknown, we need two linear estimators, one for the intercept and one for the slope. This chapter shows that the OLS estimators of the slope and intercept are unbiased estimators and derives the variance of the OLS slope estimator. This appendix derives the variance of the OLS intercept estimator. Because both of these two (different) estimators of the slope and intercept are (different) linear combinations of the same $Y$-values, it is possible that the two estimators are correlated. This appendix also derives the covariance between two linear estimators when the Gauss–Markov Assumptions apply.

## 5.B.1     The Variance of the OLS Intercept Estimator

Obtaining $\sigma^2_{\hat{\beta}_0}$ is more complicated than obtaining $\sigma^2_{\hat{\beta}_1}$ because the weights for $\hat{\beta}_0$ are more complicated. However, it simplifies the derivation of $\hat{\beta}_0$'s variance to first examine $\sum x_i^2$ in some detail.

### A Special Expression for the Sum of the $x_i^2$

The following algebraic relationship allows a simpler expression for $\sigma^2_{\hat{\beta}_0}$:

$$\sum x_i^2 + n\overline{X}^2 = \sum X_i^2. \qquad \text{5.B.1}$$

To see that Equation 5.B.1 is always true, consider

$$\sum x_i^2 = \sum (X_i - \overline{X})^2 = \sum (X_i^2 - 2\overline{X}X_i + \overline{X}^2)$$
$$= \sum X_i^2 - 2\overline{X}\sum X_i + \sum \overline{X}^2,$$

which, because $\sum X_i = n\overline{X}$ and $\sum \overline{X}^2 = n\overline{X}^2$,

$$= \sum X_i^2 - 2n\overline{X}^2 + n\overline{X}^2.$$

Still more simply,

$$\sum x_i^2 = \sum X_i^2 - n\overline{X}^2,$$

which implies that

$$\sum x_i^2 + n\overline{X}^2 = \sum X_i^2.$$

## The Variance of $\hat{\beta}_0$

To obtain the variance of $\hat{\beta}_0$, apply the variance formula for a linear estimator, $\sigma^2 \sum w_i^2$, to the weights for $\hat{\beta}_0$. Equation 4.2 reports that the weights for $\hat{\beta}_0$ are

$$w_i^{0*} = \left[\frac{1}{n} - \frac{\overline{X}x_i}{\sum x_j^2}\right] = \frac{\sum x_j^2 - n\overline{X}x_i}{n\sum x_j^2}.$$

Hence,

$$(w_i^{0*})^2 = \frac{\left(\sum x_j^2 - n\overline{X}x_i\right)^2}{\left(n\sum x_j^2\right)^2} = \frac{\left(\sum x_j^2\right)^2 - 2n\overline{X}x_i\sum x_j^2 + (n\overline{X}x_i)^2}{\left(n\sum x_j^2\right)^2}.$$

Consequently, when we sum the squared weights over all $i$, we obtain

$$\sum(w_i^{0*})^2 = \frac{n\left(\sum x_j^2\right)^2 - 2n\overline{X}\left(\sum x_j^2\right)\sum x_i + n^2\overline{X}^2\sum x_i^2}{\left(n\sum x_j^2\right)^2} \qquad \textbf{5.B.2}$$

$$= \frac{n\left(\sum x_j^2\right)^2 + n^2\overline{X}^2\sum x_i^2}{\left(n\sum x_j^2\right)^2}, \qquad \textbf{5.B.3}$$

with Equation 5.B.3 following from Equation 5.B.2 because $\sum x_i = 0$. Simplifying, we see

$$\sum(w_i^{0*}) = \frac{n\left(\sum x_j^2\right)^2}{n^2\left(\sum x_j^2\right)^2} + \frac{\overline{X}^2}{\sum x_j^2}$$

$$= \frac{1}{n} + \frac{\overline{X}^2}{\sum x_j^2},$$

so that

$$\sigma_{\hat{\beta}_0}^2 = \sigma^2\left(\frac{1}{n} + \frac{\overline{X}^2}{\sum x_j^2}\right). \qquad \textbf{5.B.4}$$

However,

$$\frac{1}{n} + \frac{\overline{X}^2}{\sum x_j^2} = \frac{\sum x_j^2 + n\overline{X}^2}{n\sum x_j^2},$$

and, according to Equation 5.B.1, the numerator in this expression is simply $\sum X_j^2$. Therefore,

$$\sigma_{\hat{\beta}_0}^2 = \frac{\sigma^2\sum X_i^2}{n\sum x_j^2}. \qquad \textbf{5.B.5}$$

## 5.B.2     The Covariance of Linear Estimators

Next, consider the covariance between two linear estimators. In particular, consider one linear estimator, $R = \sum w_j^R Y_j$, and a second linear estimator, $S = \sum w_i^s Y_i$. The covariance between the two estimators, $R$ and $S$, is defined as

$$E([R - E(R)][S - E(S)]).$$

To derive a formula for the covariance between $R$ and $S$ under the Gauss-Markov Assumptions, we will first express $R$, $S$, and their expected values in terms of the $Y_i$. Initially, these substitutions make the covariance expression more complicated, but because the Gauss–Markov Assumptions inform us about the stochastic, that is, probabilistic, nature of the $Y_i$, we can exploit the algebra of expectations to simplify the covariance expression when viewed in terms of the $Y_i$.

We begin with the covariance expression without the expectation operation:

$$[R - E(R)][S - E(S)] = \left[\sum_j (w_j^R Y_j) - E(R)\right]\left[\sum_i (w_i^S Y_i) - E(S)\right],$$

in which

$$E(R) = E\left(\sum_j w_j^R Y_j\right) = \sum [w_j^R E(Y_j)], \qquad\qquad \text{5.B.6}$$

and

$$E(S) = \sum [w_i^S E(Y_i)] \qquad\qquad \text{5.B.7}$$

If we substitute these expressions for $E(R)$ and $E(S)$ in Equations 5.B.6 and 5.B.7, we get

$$
\begin{aligned}
[R - E(R)][S - E(S)] &= \left[\sum_j w_j^R Y_j - E\left(\sum_j w_j^R Y_j\right)\right]\left[\sum_i w_i^S Y_i - E\left(\sum_i w_i^S Y_i\right)\right] \\
&= \left[\sum_j w_j^R Y_j - \sum_j w_j^R E(Y_j)\right]\left[\sum_i w_i^S Y_i - \sum_i w_i^S E(Y_i)\right] \\
&= \left(\sum_j w_j^R [Y_j - E(Y_j)]\right)\left(\sum_i w_i^S [Y_i - E(Y_i)]\right).
\end{aligned}
$$

Multiplying the two terms of the product leads to

$$
\begin{aligned}
&= \sum_i \sum_j w_j^R [Y_j - E(Y_j)] w_i^S [Y_i - E(Y_i)] \\
&= \sum_i \sum_j w_j^R w_i^S [Y_j - E(Y_j)][Y_i - E(Y_i)].
\end{aligned}
$$

Taking the expected value of $[R - E(R)][S - E(S)]$, we find that the covariance of two linear estimators $R$ and $S$ is

$$E([R - E(R)][S - E(S)]) = E(\sum \sum w_j^R w_i^S [Y_j - E(Y_j)][Y_i - E(Y_i)])$$
$$= \sum \sum [w_j^R w_i^S E([Y_j - E(Y_j)][Y_i - E(Y_i)])] \textbf{ 5.B.8}$$

Because the covariances of the $Y$'s are zero according to the Gauss–Markov Assumptions, only the terms where $i = j$ are not zero in the double sum in Equation 5.B.8; thus

$$E([R - E(R)][S - E(S)]) = \sum w_i^R w_i^S E([Y_i - E(Y_i)]^2)$$
$$= \sum w_i^R w_i^S \sigma^2 = \sigma^2 \sum w_i^R w_i^S,$$

an expression for the covariance of any two linear estimators under the Gauss–Markov Assumptions.

This derivation relies only on the Gauss–Markov Assumptions. This formula for the covariance between linear estimators therefore also applies to models with multiple explanators, as long as the Gauss–Markov Assumptions are satisfied.

 *Appendix 5.C*

# Matrix Algebra and the Properties of OLS Residuals

The matrix notation also allows us to describe succinctly both the fitted values and the residuals from an OLS regression. The equation

$$\hat{Y} = X\hat{\beta}$$

expresses the fitted values, and

$$e = Y - X\hat{\beta}$$

expresses the residuals. Three useful relationships stemming from $\hat{\beta}_0$ and $\hat{\beta}_1$ are stated simply as

$$X'_0 e = 0; \; X'_1 e = 0 \text{ (or, more compactly, } X'e = 0); \quad \text{and} \quad \hat{Y}'e = 0.$$

# Chapter 6

# Multiple Regression

*All human actions have one or more of these seven causes: chance, nature, compulsion, habit, reason, passion, and desire.*

—ARISTOTLE

The regression models in Chapters 2 to 5 ignore Aristotle's insight that actions can have multiple causes. Those models allow for only one independent variable to explain any dependent variable. In the real world, however, more complex models are often needed. For example, when families decide where to live, their motivations are multifaceted. Proximity to workplace and amenities, income, the price of housing, and family size all influence families' housing choices. When firms choose locations for their plants, local wages, local taxes, utility availability, and access to markets for materials and machinery all influence the firms' location decisions. Similarly, when economists look at countries' different growth rates, they consider capital stocks, labor force education, political stability, smoothly functioning markets, and well-defined property rights. Multiple influences are the norm, not the exception, when we examine social phenomena. How are we to analyze housing expenditure, firms' locations, or economic growth when there is not one explanator in the relationship, but many?

Regression models with a single explanatory variable are useful pedagogical devices and are frequently useful in practice. However, economic variables such as financial aid, housing expenditure, firms' locations, and economic growth typically depend on multiple factors rather than on a single determinant; most econometric models contain several slope coefficients. Chapter 1 called regression models with multiple explanators *multiple regression models*. This chapter explores multiple regression models in detail.

## 6.1     The DGP for the Regression Model

**WHAT IS THE DGP?**

As before, the first step in deriving estimators with attractive properties is to specify the data-generating process (DGP) that describes the source of the sample data. In this chapter, we adapt the DGP of Chapter 4 to include multiple $X$'s on the right-hand side of the regression equation:

$$Y_i = \beta_0 + \beta_1 X_{1i} + \beta_2 X_{2i} + \cdots + \beta_k X_{ki} + \varepsilon_i \qquad i = 1, \ldots, n$$
$$\mathrm{E}(\varepsilon_i) = 0 \qquad i = 1, \ldots, n$$

$$\text{var}(\varepsilon_i) = \sigma^2 \qquad\qquad\qquad i = 1, \ldots, n$$
$$\text{cov}(\varepsilon_i, \varepsilon_j) = 0 \qquad\qquad\qquad i \neq j$$

Each explanator is fixed across samples.

Notice that the DGP again makes the Gauss–Markov Assumptions about the disturbances and the explanators. The only change from the DGP of Chapter 4 is the inclusion of multiple regressors in the equation. *Each slope coefficient in this multiple regression DGP indicates how much E(Y) changes when the corresponding X changes by one unit, holding all the other explanators fixed.* For example, if $X_{1i}, \ldots, X_{(k-1)i}$ are fixed, and $X_{ki}$ changes by one unit, $E(Y_i)$ rises by $\beta_k$ units. In mathematical language, the slope coefficients are the partial derivatives of E(Y) with respect to the X's.

The assumption that the X's take on the same values in every sample is unrealistic. When economists draw new samples, these values are likely to vary. We saw in Chapter 3, however, that if the Gauss–Markov Assumptions about the disturbances hold for all possible combinations of X-values, then we can interpret all results based on the assumption of fixed X's as conditional results for random X's, conditional on the observed X-values. The arguments in Chapter 3 for a line through the origin apply equally to multiple regressions. All the findings we obtain for the fixed X's DGP apply to a DGP with random X-values, as long as the Gauss–Markov Assumptions about the disturbances hold for every pattern of observations on the several explanators in the model. The only change we must make for such random X cases is to make all the expectation and variance statements conditional on the observed values of the explanators. This conditional interpretation of findings is more realistic than assuming fixed X's. Nonetheless, we continue to use the fixed X's assumption in our analysis to avoid the notational complexity of conditioning all claims on the observed values of X. Appendix 6.A provides the more complex—and more realistic—formulation of the DGP with stochastic X's and offers some additional subtle distinctions that stem from having stochastic regressors.

Like linear regression models with one explanator, multiple regression models can be envisioned geometrically. Figure 6.1 depicts a scatter of data on earnings, education, and experience. The expected value of earnings appears as a plane in the three dimensions of the graph. Our estimates of $\beta_0$, $\beta_1$, and $\beta_2$ determine an estimated plane in the earnings, education, and experience space. When the number of explanators exceeds three, geometric representation begins to fail us.

## Polynomials

The multiple regression model looks at first glance to be a strictly linear relationship. The model is strictly linear when each X represents a new determinant of

**Figure 6.1**

Earnings, Education,
and Experience and
the Expected Value
of Earnings

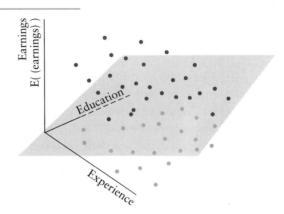

E($Y$). However, the multiple regression form also allows for polynomials, such as

$$Y_i = \beta_0 + \beta_1 Z_i + \beta_2 Z_i^2 + \beta_3 Q_i + \beta_4 Z_i Q_i + \varepsilon_i,$$

which are not linear in the explanators. Defining $X_{1i} = Z_i$; $X_{2i} = Z_{1i}^2$; $X_{3i} = Q_i$; $X_{4i} = Z_i Q_i$ returns us to the multiple regression DGP form. The variable $X_{4i} = Z_i Q_i$ we call an **interaction term**, because with this variable in the model, the change in E($Y_i$) resulting from a change in $Q_i$ depends on $Z_i$, and vice versa. The change in E($Y_i$) resulting from a one-unit change in $Q_i$ in this model is

$$\frac{change\ in\ \mathrm{E}(Y_i)}{change\ in\ Q_i} = \beta_3 + \beta_4 Z_i.$$

The change in E($Y_i$) resulting from a one-unit change in $Z_i$ is complicated by the presence of the quadratic term, $Z_i^2$, as well as by the interaction term:

$$\frac{change\ in\ \mathrm{E}(Y_i)}{change\ in\ Z_i} = \beta_1 + 2\beta_2 Z_i + \beta_4 Q_i.$$

The effect of the quadratic term alone (that is, if $\beta_4 = 0$) is to make the change in E($Y_i$), resulting from a one-unit change in $Z_i$,

$$\frac{change\ in\ \mathrm{E}(Y_i)}{change\ in\ Z_i} = \beta_1 + 2\beta_2 Z_i.$$

(These relationships are the partial derivatives of the E($Y_i$) with respect to $Q_i$ and with respect to $Z_i$). Higher order polynomial terms, such as cubics and quartics, can similarly appear in multiple regressions, as can the logs introduced at the end of Chapter 4 and other functions of the explanators, such as inverses.

# An Econometric Top 40—A Pop Tune

## College Students' Misbehavior and the Price of Beer

Many happy college moments are accompanied by alcohol. Parties, sporting events, and hanging out are often occasions for imbibing. Sadly, alcohol use isn't limited to students who drink responsibly. According to the University of Southern Illinois' Core Alcohol and Drug Surveys of College Students, during the course of a year, while or after drinking or taking drugs, almost a third of college students get into arguments or fights, 1 college student in 8 gets in trouble with authorities, 1 in 14 pulls a fire alarm or damages property, and 1 in 7 has taken sexual advantage of another or has been taken advantage of sexually. These numbers are based on students' reports of their own behavior.

What is the role of alcohol in these behaviors? If everybody drinks (though not everyone does—15% of students say they haven't imbibed in the past year and another 25% report drinking fewer than one drink per week), it would be surprising if misbehaving students weren't also students who drink. Is alcohol a causal contributor to these events or a mere accompaniment? Students themselves seem to think alcohol plays a role—the questions they answered referred to events "caused by" drinking or taking drugs. But is there other evidence that alcohol contributes to these misbehaviors? Yes, there is.

In 1999, Michael Grossman of the City University of New York and Sara Markowitz of Rutgers University combined survey answers from more than 100,000 students at almost 200 colleges and universities with state-level data on beer prices.[1] The price of beer varies widely across states; in the study's sample, a six pack cost between $3.25 and $5.25, depending on the state of purchase. The price differences are largely due to differences in state beer taxes. The authors regressed the yes (= 1) and no (= 0) answers of students to each of the misbehavior questions against the price of beer in the state, and the student's age, gender, race or ethnicity, year in school, work status, and other similar variables. There were separate regressions for each of the four misbehavior categories.

Grossman and Markowitz's regression results indicate that less misbehavior accompanies higher beer prices. A 10% increase in the price of beer is associated with a 4.8% decline in getting in trouble with the authorities because of alcohol and drugs, a 3.3% decrease in the incidence of such arguments and fights, a 5.2% decline in reported property damage, and a 3.6% reduction in reported incidents of sexual exploitation. These findings for college students mirror results in broader populations. Other econometric evidence suggests that rapes and murders would decline 2% to 5% if beer prices rose 10%.[2] Alcohol does not bring out the worst in everyone, but it does in some.

The relationship between beer prices and both minor and major misbehavior supports the claim that alcohol is causally linked to such behavior. If alcohol were merely an accidental companion of misbehavior, observed frequently because students frequently drink, there would be no connection between beer prices and misbehaviors. Instead, we observe connections across a range of misbehaviors—some, such as arguments or pranks, that might be minor, and some, such as property damage and sexual assault, that are serious.

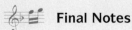 **Final Notes**

Knowing that alcohol consumption leads to appreciable amounts of misbehavior in colleges and elsewhere is not the same as knowing what to do with that information. Ought states raise beer taxes to deter violence? Should colleges and universities hinder drinking to reduce misbehavior? What about the burdens such policies would place on all people who use alcohol responsibly? Shaping sound policies almost always requires more than regression results. But regression analyses can inform policy makers about some likely consequences of alternative policies. Much of the applied work of econometricians is designed to spare policy makers from making uninformed decisions. ∎

## 6.2     BLUE Estimation in a Multiple Regression Model

**How Do We Create an Estimator?**

How are we to estimate the intercept and slopes in a multiple regression? Once again, as in estimating a single slope or an intercept and a single slope, estimators that are unbiased are attractive—we like being right on average. As our hunter econometricians who ate canned corned beef instead of fresh venison demonstrated in Chapter 3, however, unbiased estimators with too large a variance are not very useful. We want efficient estimators, not just unbiased ones. Because the set of linear estimators proved fruitful in earlier chapters, this chapter also looks among linear estimators to find a best estimator. How are we to obtain best linear unbiased estimators (BLUE) for the slopes and intercept in a multiple regression model? The strategy is the same as before. First, we determine the unbiasedness conditions for a linear estimator in this DGP. Second, we determine the variance. And finally, we minimize the variance with respect to the weights of a linear estimator, subject to the unbiasedness constraints.

### What Is Required for Unbiased Linear Estimation?

When is a linear estimator, $g$, an unbiased estimator of the intercept in our multiple regression DGP? To answer this question, examine the $E(g)$ and ask what conditions on the weights of the linear estimator suffice to make $E(g)$ equal $\beta_0$. Linear estimators are those that can be written as

$$E(g) = E\left[\sum w_i Y_i\right] = \sum E(w_i Y_i) = \sum w_i E(Y_i)$$

or

$$E(g) = \sum \left[w_i E(\beta_0 + \beta_1 X_{1i} + \cdots + \beta_k X_{ki} + \varepsilon_i)\right]$$
$$= \sum \left[w_i(\beta_0 + \beta_1 X_{1i} + \cdots + \beta_k X_{ki})\right]$$
$$= \beta_0 \sum w_i + \beta_1 \sum w_i X_{1i} + \cdots + \beta_k \sum w_i X_{ki},$$

which implies that if $g$ is to be an unbiased estimator of $\beta_0$, $(k + 1)$ conditions are needed:

$$\sum w_i = 1, \qquad\qquad\qquad\qquad \text{6.1}$$

and

$$\sum_i w_i X_{ji} = 0, \qquad \text{for each } j = 1, \ldots, k. \qquad \text{6.2}$$

What conditions suffice for a linear estimator, $g$, to be an unbiased estimator of a slope coefficient in our DGP, say $\beta_s$? The required conditions are similar to those needed for unbiased estimation of the intercept. Again, because

$$E(g) = \beta_0 \sum w_i + \beta_1 \sum w_i X_{1i} + \cdots + \beta_k \sum w_i X_{ki},$$

for $g$ to be an unbiased estimator of $\beta_s$, $(k + 1)$ conditions must be met:

$$\sum w_i = 0, \qquad\qquad\qquad\qquad \text{6.3}$$

and

$$\sum w_i X_{ri} = 0 \qquad \text{for } r \neq s \qquad\qquad \text{6.4}$$

and

$$\sum w_i X_{si} = 1. \qquad\qquad\qquad\qquad \text{6.5}$$

The treatment of the intercept is less different than it first appears. If we define a variable $X_{0i} = 1$ for all observations, we can rewrite the multiple regression relationship

$$Y_i = \beta_0 + \beta_1 X_{1i} + \beta_2 X_{2i} + \cdots + \beta_k X_{ki} + \varepsilon_i$$

as

$$Y_i \beta_0 X_{0i} + \beta_1 X_{1i} + \beta_2 X_{2i} + \cdots + \beta_k X_{ki} + \varepsilon_i$$

with no alteration in meaning. Similarly, the requirement that

$$\sum w_i = 0$$

can be rewritten as

$$\sum w_i X_{0i} = 0$$

with no alteration in meaning. In the latter form, the symmetry between the intercept term and the slope coefficients becomes apparent. We will occasionally use this convention of specifying $X_{0i} = 1$ in association with the intercept term in our equations.

Note that if we omit the intercept term from the multiple regression model, there is one less unbiasedness constraint required. As in Chapter 3, we need not impose the restriction that $\sum w_i = 0$ if there is no intercept term in the model.

## What Is the Variance of a Linear Estimator in This DGP?

Section 4.2 noted that the variance of a linear estimator under the Gauss–Markov Assumptions is the same no matter the number of explanators:

$$\text{var}(g) = \sigma^2 \sum w_i^2. \qquad 6.6$$

The covariance between linear estimators is also the same under the Gauss–Markov Assumptions, no matter the number of explanators. For two linear estimators, one with weights $w_i^r$ and the other with weights $w_i^s$, the covariance between the estimators is

$$\sigma^2 \sum w_i^r w_i^s,$$

if the Gauss–Markov Assumptions apply. The derivations of these formulae depend neither on the number of explanators nor on the presence of an intercept in the model, so these variance and covariance formulae apply no matter the number of explanators and with or without an intercept in the model.

## What Are the BLUE Estimators of $\beta_0, \beta_1, \ldots, \beta_k$ in This DGP?

The BLUE estimators $\hat{\beta}_0, \hat{\beta}_1, \ldots, \hat{\beta}_k$, for the coefficients in this DGP follow from minimizing $\sigma^2 \sum w_i^2$ with respect to the weights, subject to the corresponding unbiasedness constraints contained in Equations 6.1 through 6.5. Recall that in the DGP with one explanator and an unknown intercept, there were BLUE weights for estimating the intercept and separate BLUE weights for estimating the slope. In the multiple regression DGP, there are $(k + 1)$ sets of $n$ weights, one set for the intercept and $k$ sets for the $k$ slope coefficients. Appendix 6.B uses matrix algebra to prove that the ordinary least squares (OLS) estimator is BLUE in the multiple regression model when the Gauss–Markov Assumptions hold. Ordinary algebraic formulae for the BLUE estimators are quite complex; their matrix algebra formula is not.[3] The weights become more complicated as the number of explanators grows because the weights depend on the sums of the cross products of all possible combinations of the explanators, that is, on

$$\sum_{i=1}^{n} X_{ji} X_{mi}$$

for both $j$ and $m$ ranging from 0 to $k$.

# An Econometric Top 40—A Pop Tune

## The Demand for Drugs

Medical science tells us that cocaine is addictive. But is there economic evidence of cocaine's addictiveness? If cocaine is addictive, we would expect current consumption to be larger for people whose past consumption is larger. We might also expect consumption to be quite unresponsive to price. Moreover, economists often argue that rational individuals who know a drug is addictive reduce use today if they prefer to consume less in the future (in an effort to reduce their future dependency). Such rational addiction and addiction avoidance would be evidenced by today's consumption being related to tomorrow's, as well as yesterday's.

In 1998, economists Michael Grossman of the City University of New York and Frank Chaloupka of the University of Illinois at Chicago used data on young adults collected by the University of Michigan Institute for Social Research (ISR) and by the U.S. Drug Enforcement Administration (DEA) to study the short-run and long-run elasticities of young adults' cocaine demand.[4] The ISR data contained several years of information on individuals' socioeconomic characteristics, their states of residence, and their consumption of cocaine. The DEA data contained information on the price of cocaine by state and over time.

Grossman and Chaloupka specified the demand for cocaine as

$$C_t = \beta_1 C_{t-1} + \beta_2 C_{t+1} + \beta_3\, price_t$$
$$+ \beta_4\, income + \beta_5\, male$$
$$+ \beta_6\, black + \beta_7[marijuana\ ok]$$
$$+ \beta_8[legal\ drinking\ age] + \varepsilon,$$

where $C_t$, $C_{t-1}$ and $C_{t+1}$ are an individual's cocaine consumption this year, last year, and next year, respectively; $price_t$ is cocaine's price; $income_t$ is the individual's real income; and *legal drinking age* is the legal drinking age in the individual's state. *Male*, *black*, and *marijuana ok* are three variables that equal one when the individual is male, or is black, or lives in a jurisdiction in which marijuana is decriminalized, and that equal zero otherwise.

Grossman and Chaloupka found that present consumption does depend on past consumption, supporting the medical evidence that cocaine is addictive. For example, having consumed more cocaine last year raises the individual's consumption this year. Next year's consumption has a similar estimated effect on this year's consumption, supporting the hypothesis that consumers are rationally addictive.

The price of cocaine has a surprisingly strong estimated effect on cocaine consumption. Despite the addictive character of cocaine, consumers can adjust their consumption levels when prices change. The authors estimate that at the median values of their variables, the long-run price elasticity of demand for cocaine is $-1.35$;[5] the estimated short-run elasticity (the responsiveness in the first year following a permanent change in price) is markedly smaller in magnitude, but still not small: $-0.96$. The responsiveness to a temporary (one-year) change in price is still smaller in magnitude: $-0.50$. Addiction and long-run price responsiveness are not contradictory.

In their analysis, Grossman and Chaloupka separately analyze consumers' average propensity to use cocaine and the extent of cocaine use by those who choose to consume. They concluded that most of the long-run reduction in cocaine use stemming from price increases is due to users going "cold turkey," that is, stopping cocaine use altogether. About a third of the effect stems from users reducing the frequency of their use.

Grossman and Chaloupka's estimates have implications for government drug policies. The demand elasticity in excess of one suggests that policies that raise cocaine providers' costs lower consumers' long-run expenditures on cocaine—higher street prices bring a more than offsetting decrease in quantity demanded. On the basis of this evidence, policies that permanently curb cocaine supply doubly reduce the profits of drug sellers, simultaneously raising their costs and lowering their revenues.

The estimated short-run elasticity of $-0.96$ suggests drug sellers' revenues would not fall immediately after a permanent price increase. The estimated elasticity to a temporary price change, $-0.50$, indicates that transient policies that increase the costs of cocaine suppliers, and hence temporarily raise street prices, increase cocaine suppliers' revenues, as quantities fall only half as much as prices rise in such cases.

The estimated coefficient on *marijuana ok* is positive, indicating that where penalties for marijuana use are lower, the demand for cocaine is higher—marijuana and cocaine appear

to be complements. The estimated coefficient on *minimum drinking age* is also positive, indicating that where access to alcohol is more difficult, cocaine use is higher—alcohol and cocaine appear to be substitutes. If alcohol and cocaine are, indeed, substitutes, policies that curb alcohol use among young people, but that do not address other drugs, spur cocaine use.

 **Final Notes**

Grossman and Chaloupka's results, if correct, have strong implications for policy makers. It is therefore important to know whether their estimates are the best guesses available from these data. If they are, how reliable are these estimates? These are two pressing questions that econometric theory addresses.

Reducing cocaine use in the United States is a challenging, multifaceted problem. Mere econometric analyses cannot solve the problem or answer the related moral and social questions that matter for good policy. However, empirical evidence about the price elasticity of cocaine demand and its relationship to the consumption of other substances can inform policy makers and help them to avoid counterproductive measures as they work to shape effective policies.

∎

Previously, computing BLUE estimates for a multiple regression DGP was an arduous, time-consuming task performed on hand-powered calculating machines; today, computers rapidly do the calculations. The same computers calculate the estimated standard errors and estimated covariances for the BLUE estimators.

As with the BLUE estimators in our earlier DGPs, under the Gauss–Markov Assumptions, the BLUE estimators in the multiple regression model minimize the within-sample sum of squared residuals. That is, they are the OLS estimators.

If we omit the intercept term from the multiple regression model, the formulae for $\hat{\beta}_1, \ldots, \hat{\beta}_k$ change, just as they do whenever the list of regressors is altered. In practice, the computer treats $X_0$ (which always equals one) just like any other explanator when computing the BLUE estimators.

### A More General Gauss–Markov Theorem

The multiple regression model with the Gauss–Markov Assumptions supports the most general form of the Gauss–Markov Theorem, which tells us that

$$\hat{Y}^* = \hat{\beta}_0 X_0^* + \hat{\beta}_1 X_1^* + \hat{\beta}_2 X_2^* + \cdots + \hat{\beta}_k X_k^*$$

is the BLUE estimator of $E(Y \mid X_0^*, X_1^*, X_2^*, \ldots, X_k^*)$. Thus, using the OLS estimators of $\beta_0, \beta_1, \beta_2, \ldots, \beta_k$ is the best linear estimator for the mean of $Y$ for *any* combination of $X$'s. For example, in Grossman and Chaloupka's Greatest Hit, the individual's expected cocaine consumption is expressed as a function of many explanators, the fitted value of $Y_i$ (an individual's cocaine consumption) given that the individual's observed explanator values, $X_{1i}, X_{2i}, \ldots, X_{ki}$,

$$\hat{Y}_i = \hat{\beta}_0 + \sum_{j=1}^{k} \hat{\beta}_j X_{ji},$$

would be the BLUE estimator of $E(Y_i \mid X_{1i}, X_{2i}, \ldots, X_{ki})$, the $i$-th individual's expected cocaine consumption.

## 6.3    An Application: Earnings Equations

This section introduces a specific multiple regression model and estimates it using the BLUE estimator, OLS. The individual's earnings are influenced by numerous factors. Two factors of particular interest to economists are education and experience. Disentangling the contributions of education from those of experience, or from the effects of other factors, requires a multiple regression analysis. When specifying multiple regression models of earnings, economists generally argue that a better dependent variable than earnings itself is the log of earnings, because the log of earnings specification more closely adheres to the Gauss–Markov Assumptions. Such analyses of earnings have also shown that the effects of education and experience on earnings differ among people depending on their race and gender. This section analyzes the earnings equations for black female and black male workers in the United States, but econometricians have estimated the effects of education and experience on earnings for many countries and for many groups.

### BLUE Estimates for Black Women

One multiple regression model for earnings is

$$E(log\ of\ earnings)_i = \beta_0 + \beta_1(years\ of\ education)_i$$
$$+\ \beta_2(years\ work\ experience)_i + \varepsilon_i \qquad \textbf{6.7}$$

For a sample of black female workers drawn from the National Longitudinal Survey of Youth (NLSY), the BLUE estimator yields

Estimated E(*natural log of earnings*) = 6.77 + 0.15(*years of education*)

(estimated standard error)        (0.182) (0.012)

+ 0.05(*years work experience*)

(0.010)

The figures in parentheses are estimated standard errors for the BLUE coefficient estimators. Table 6.1 reports the regression results in more detail. The variable "*lnincome*" is the log of earnings; the variable "*educatn*" is years of education; the variable "*exper*" is years of work experience. These data, for both black men and black women, are contained in the data set earnings1.*** on this book's companion Web site (**www.aw-bc.com/murray**). With multiple explanators, the slopes are the marginal effect on the dependent variable of one explanator, given that the others are fixed. Econometricians say that the presence of multiple explanators **controls** for their individual effects. Thus $\beta_1$ in Equation 6.7 is the marginal effect of education on the expected log of earnings *controlling for work experience*.

Changes in logarithms correspond approximately to percentage changes in the variable whose log we are examining, a fact noted in Section 4.5. In this wage equation, we estimate that the expected log of earnings changes 0.159 when education rises by one year, holding experience fixed. This is to say that expected earnings rise 15.9% with each additional year of education a black woman has, when experience is held constant. Labor economists infer from this regression that the "estimated rate of return on education" is 15.9% for black women. The labor economists say 0.159 estimates the rate of return on education because the regression claims that by forgoing one year's earnings, a black woman can increase her annual earnings by 15.9%. To the extent that tuition and other education-related expenses are small relative to one year's earnings, the return on forgoing a year's earnings in order to get one more year of schooling is thus 15.9%.

## Using Dummy Variables to Capture Categories

Studying the earnings of black women is facilitated by the fact that earnings, years of work experience, and years of education are all numerical variables. What if we were to analyze a sample of black women *and* men, though? How can we model differences in earnings between men and women? Gender is a category that does not have a natural numerical representation. We can envision earnings, or years of work experience, or years of education as a *Y*- or *X*-variable in our models. But what about gender? What numerical values could possibly make sense for male and female? Remarkably, assigning a value of 1 to females and 0 to males (or the other way around) yields an *X*-variable with a coefficient that has a

**TABLE 6.1  OLS Estimation of Black Women's Wage Equation**

Dependent Variable: LNINCOME
Method: Least Squares
Sample: 2 1800 IF FEMALE = 1
Included observations: 655

| Variable | Coefficient | Std. Error | t-Statistic | Prob. |
|---|---|---|---|---|
| C | 6.662385 | 0.208836 | 31.90246 | 0.0000 |
| EDUCATN | 0.159434 | 0.014043 | 11.35301 | 0.0000 |
| EXPER | 0.051263 | 0.011231 | 4.564324 | 0.0000 |
| R-squared | 0.213645 | Mean dependent var | | 9.392007 |
| Adjusted R-squared | 0.211232 | S.D. dependent var | | 0.827973 |
| S.E. of regression | 0.735344 | Akaike info criterion | | 2.227613 |
| Sum squared resid | 352.5565 | Schwarz criterion | | 2.248153 |
| Log likelihood | −726.5433 | F-statistic | | 88.57080 |
| Durbin–Watson stat | 1.995931 | Prob(F-statistic) | | 0.000000 |

very sensible interpretation in the multiple regression DGP above. A variable that takes on the value 1 for observations that fall into a particular category, and a value of 0 for observations that do not, we call a **binary variable** or, more commonly in econometrics, a **dummy variable**.

If we set $X_3 = 1$ for females, and $X_3 = 0$ for males, and allow $Y$ to be an individual's log earnings,

$$Y_i = \beta_0 + \beta_1 X_{1i} + \beta_2 X_{2i} + \beta_3 X_{3i} + \varepsilon_i$$

and the Gauss–Markov Assumptions lead to

$$E(Y_i \mid X_{1i}, X_{2i}, X_{3i}) = E(log\ earnings \mid education_i, experience_i, sex_i)$$

$$= \begin{cases} \beta_0 + \beta_1 X_{1i} + \beta_2 X_{2i} & for\ X_{3i} = 0 \\ \beta_0 + \beta_1 X_{1i} + \beta_2 X_{2i} + \beta_3 & for\ X_{3i} = 1 \end{cases}$$

Thus, $\beta_0$ is the intercept for men and $\beta_0 + \beta_3$ is the intercept for women in this relationship. The variable $X_3$ is a dummy variable equal to 1 for women; its coefficient, $\beta_3$, is the difference between the intercept for women and the intercept for men. On average, earnings by women and men with the same traits differ by $\beta_3$. If $\beta_3 = 0$, on average, men and women with the same education and experience earn the same wage rates.

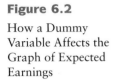

**Figure 6.2**

How a Dummy
Variable Affects the
Graph of Expected
Earnings

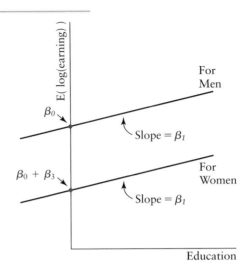

Figure 6.2 illustrates the relationship between log earnings and education for black women and black men, holding experience fixed. In the figure, differing intercepts for men and women reflect the effect of the dummy variable female on earnings. Because we assume the slopes are the same for men and women, the expected log earnings lines are parallel. *A dummy variable explanator equaling 1 shifts the intercept term of a regression model by the amount of the dummy's coefficient, causing a parallel shift in the regression line.*

Table 6.2 reports a regression of log earnings for a sample of black workers, male and female. (The sample women are those studied in Table 6.1.) To the explanators *educatn* and *exper* in Table 6.1, we add the dummy variable *"female"* that equals 1 for women and 0 for men.

The estimated coefficients of *educatn* and *exper* do not change appreciably from the estimates in Table 6.1, though they could. The estimated coefficient for *female*, $-0.21$ indicates that on average, women earn approximately 21% less than men with the same years of education and years of work experience. The estimated intercept term for men in this relationship is 6.986; the estimated intercept for women is $(6.986 - 0.210) = 6.776$. An earnings regression sheds considerable light on the difference between black women's and black men's earnings. Journalists frequently cite large differences between the earnings of men and women. Is the difference simply due to differences in education and work experience between men and women? Not for blacks, according to Table 6.1. Black men and women with the same level of education and work experience have earnings that differ by 21%, on average. *Here we see that one important analytical role for multiple regression is its trait of estimating the effect of one variable while holding others fixed.*

**Table 6.2  OLS Estimation of Black Workers' Wage Equation I**

Dependent Variable: LNINCOME
Method: Least Squares
Sample: 2 1799
Included observations: 1362

| Variable | Coefficient | Std. Error | t-Statistic | Prob. |
|----------|------------|-----------|-------------|-------|
| C | 6.986272 | 0.153630 | 45.47468 | 0.0000 |
| EDUCATN | 0.146139 | 0.009454 | 15.45851 | 0.0000 |
| EXPER | 0.056663 | 0.008505 | 6.662507 | 0.0000 |
| FEMALE | −0.210517 | 0.041334 | −5.093117 | 0.0000 |
| R-squared | 0.188341 | Mean dependent var | | 9.458546 |
| Adjusted R-squared | 0.186548 | S.D. dependent var | | 0.824104 |
| S.E. of regression | 0.743272 | Akaike info criterion | | 2.247424 |
| Sum squared resid | 750.2321 | Schwarz criterion | | 2.262745 |
| Log likelihood | −1526.496 | F-statistic | | 105.0387 |
| Durbin–Watson stat | 2.061926 | Prob(F-statistic) | | 0.000000 |

The regression reported in Table 6.1 specifies that the earnings relationship has both an intercept and a dummy variable for female. We could have specified the same relationship differently, and sometimes it is convenient to do so. A formally equivalent way of specifying this earnings equation would use two dummy variables, one for female and one for male. The variable "*female*" remains 1 for women and 0 for men; the variable "*male*" equals 1 for men and 0 for women. If we estimate the equation

$$Y_i = \beta_1 X_{1i} + \beta_2 X_{2i} + \alpha_3\, Female_i + \alpha_4\, Male_i + \varepsilon_i,$$

then the Gauss–Markov Assumptions lead to

$$E(Y_i \mid X_{1i}, X_{2i}, X_{3i}, X_{4i}) = E(log(earning) \mid education_i, experience_i, female_i, male_i)$$
$$= \begin{cases} \beta_1 X_{1i} + \beta_2 X_{2i} + \alpha_3 & \textit{for women} \\ \beta_1 X_{1i} + \beta_2 X_{2i} + \alpha_4 & \textit{for men.} \end{cases}$$

Here, the coefficient on the dummy variable *male*, $\alpha_4$, is the intercept for men, and the coefficient on the dummy variable *female*, $\alpha_3$, is the intercept for women. No separate constant term is needed in this relationship because the intercepts for men and women are already provided for in $\alpha_3$ and $\alpha_4$. Table 6.3 reports this earnings regression for the same sample of black workers studied in Table 6.2.

The results in Table 6.3 are remarkably similar to those in Table 6.2, but with a few striking differences. The estimated coefficients and standard errors are identical for education and experience. The estimated intercept in Table 6.2 is the same as the estimated coefficient for *male* in Table 6.3—as it should be because both are the estimated intercept for males. The estimated coefficient for *female* has changed, but that is not surprising—so has the interpretation of the coefficient. The new estimated coefficient for *female* in Table 6.3 is 6.77, exactly the same estimated intercept for women as inferred from the estimated coefficients in Table 6.2. Viewed the other way around, the difference between the estimated intercepts for men and women from Table 6.3 yields −0.21, exactly the same difference as estimated in Table 6.2.

Why do the two models yield matching estimates? Recall that the BLUE estimators are the OLS estimators. The estimates in Tables 6.2 and 6.3 both choose slopes for education and experience, and intercepts for men and women that minimize the sum of squared residuals. In both tables, the sum of squared residuals is the same, 750.2321, so both tables obtain the same estimates for the slopes and intercepts. Which specification an econometrician uses is a matter of convenience.

### Table 6.3 OLS Estimation of Black Workers' Wage Equation II

Dependent Variable: LNINCOME
Method: Least Squares
Sample: 2 1799
Included observations: 1362

| Variable | Coefficient | Std. Error | t-Statistic | Prob. |
|---|---|---|---|---|
| EDUCATN | 0.146139 | 0.009454 | 15.45851 | 0.0000 |
| EXPER | 0.056663 | 0.008505 | 6.662507 | 0.0000 |
| FEMALE | 6.775755 | 0.156386 | 43.32708 | 0.0000 |
| MALE | 6.986272 | 0.153630 | 45.47468 | 0.0000 |
| R-squared | 0.188341 | Mean dependent var | | 9.458546 |
| Adjusted R-squared | 0.186548 | S.D. dependent var | | 0.824104 |
| S.E. of regression | 0.743272 | Akaike info criterion | | 2.247424 |
| Sum squared resid | 750.2321 | Schwarz criterion | | 2.262745 |
| Log likelihood | −1526.496 | Durbin–Watson stat | | 2.061926 |

Table 6.2 reports an estimated standard error for the estimated difference in intercepts (the estimated standard error for the coefficient on female), but no estimated standard error for the women's intercept. Table 6.3 does the opposite. Econometricians often choose their specification depending on which estimated standard error they would rather see printed.

Another similarity between Tables 6.2 and 6.3 is that the $R^2$ and model sum of squares (as well as the adjusted $R^2$ and $F$-statistic, two statistics this book has not yet discussed) are identical for these two different models. Eviews computes these statistics using formulae that assume a constant term is included in the model (that is, an explanatory variable, $X_0$, that is equal to 1 for every observation), even when such a variable is excluded. The reason for this reporting convention for models without an intercept term is that $R^2$, the model sum of squares; adjusted $R^2$; and $F$-statistic do not usually have useful interpretations when there is no intercept in the model. When the constant is excluded, as in the estimation for Table 6.3, the formulae that Eviews and most other econometric software packages use are generally misleading—they apply to regressions that have an intercept term—and those statistics should be ignored. Some packages, like Eviews, report the values for these statistics that would sensibly result from including an intercept term, which is misleading when the model without an intercept does not fit the data the same as the model with an intercept term, as is usually the case. Other packages report the values for these statistics that result from the model without an intercept, values that are often uninformative.

## 6.4  Estimating $\sigma^2$

**HOW DO WE CREATE AN ESTIMATOR?**

A major attraction of the BLUE estimator is its efficiency relative to other linear estimators. A BLUE estimator has a smaller variance than other unbiased linear estimators. But just how small is the variance of the BLUE estimator? If the variance is large, then even the BLUE estimator is unattractive. Equation 6.6 reports that the variance of a linear estimator in a multiple regression is

$$\text{var}(g) = \sigma^2 \sum w_i^2, \qquad\qquad \textbf{6.8}$$

when the DGP satisfies the Gauss–Markov Assumptions. This is the same formula that applies to regression models with a single explanator when the Gauss–Markov Assumptions are met. When the regression line is known to pass through the origin, the variance of the BLUE estimator of the slope is

$$\frac{\sigma^2}{\sum X_i^2};$$

when the intercept is unknown, the variance of the BLUE slope estimator is

$$\frac{\sigma^2}{\sum X_i^2}.$$

In the multiple regression model, the weights for the BLUE estimators of the intercept and slopes depend on how many regressors are in the model and on the values of those regressors. We obtain the BLUE weights by solving the constrained minimization problem described in Section 6.2. However, the weights alone do not suffice to compute the BLUE estimators' variances. To calculate the variance of the BLUE estimators, we need both the weights for the estimators and the variance of the disturbances, $\sigma^2$. Unfortunately, $\sigma^2$ is usually unknown. Consequently, to estimate the variances of the BLUE estimators, we must first estimate $\sigma^2$. This section explains how econometricians estimate $\sigma^2$ in the multiple regression DGP.

## Using the Residuals to Mimic the Disturbances

As in Section 5.3, we use the residuals, $e_1, e_2, \ldots, e_n$, from the OLS regression to form an estimator for $\sigma^2$. In the model with a single explanator and an unknown intercept, an unbiased estimator of $\sigma^2$ is

$$s^2 = \frac{\sum e_i^2}{n - 2}.$$

In the multiple regression context, the $i$-th residual is defined as

$$e_i = Y_i - \hat{Y}_i = Y_i - \hat{\beta}_0 - \hat{\beta}_1 X_{1i} - \hat{\beta}_2 X_{2i} - \cdots - \hat{\beta}_k X_{ki},$$

and our unbiased estimator of $\sigma^2$ is

$$s^2 = \frac{\sum e_i^2}{(n - k - 1)},$$

which generalizes our earlier estimator. Appendix 6.B.3 uses matrix algebra to prove the unbiasedness of $s^2$. Notice that $(n - k - 1)$ is the number of observations minus the number of coefficients estimated. In the model with one explanator and an unknown intercept, two coefficients are estimated, so the sum of squared residuals is divided by $(n - 2)$. In the model with only a slope and no intercept, the sum of squared residuals would be divided by $(n - 1)$. Some econometricians begin numbering the $X$'s with $X_1$ as the intercept; for these econometricians $k$ is the number of coefficients to be estimated, so they describe $s^2$ differently, dividing the sum of squared residuals by $(n - k)$. But their concept and ours is the same—divide the sum of squared residuals by the number of observations less the number of estimated coefficients in the regression line.

As in the regression model with a single explanator, we can replace $\sigma^2$ with its estimated value in the expression for a slope estimator's variance to estimate the variance of that estimator. The estimated variance of $\hat{\beta}_s$ is

$$s_{\hat{\beta}_s}^2 = s^2 \sum w_{si}^2,$$

where the weights are the OLS weights for estimating $\beta_s$. The square root of the estimated variance is the estimator's estimated standard error.

## 6.5 Ordinary Least Squares

**How Do We Create an Estimator?**

In Section 5.8, we saw that the BLUE estimator under the Gauss–Markov Assumptions minimizes the sum of squared residuals when there is a single explanator—thus the estimator's name "ordinary least squares" (OLS). The BLUE estimator under the Gauss–Markov Assumptions with multiple explanators also minimizes the sum of squared residuals, which accounts for our calling the estimator the OLS estimator.

### A Visual Approach to OLS

Figure 6.1 shows a 3-D scatter of wages, education, and experience, along with the plane that defines the expected wage, given education and experience. Figure 6.3 shows the same scatter, but with a fitted plane that minimizes the sum of squared residuals, where the residuals are measured by the shortest distance from the sample point to the plane, holding the two explanators fixed—from points A and B, the residuals are measured by the length $e_A$ and $e_B$ in the figure. Ordinary least squares chooses estimates of the slopes and intercept that minimize the sum of squared residuals. Under the Gauss–Markov Assumptions, the OLS estimators happen to be the BLUE estimators. Thus, if the DGP satisfies the Gauss–Markov Assumptions, the fitted plane in Figure 6.3 corresponds to the BLUE estimator of that plane.

### An Implication of OLS

We learned in Chapter 4 that in a regression with an intercept and a single explanatory variable, minimizing the sum of squared residuals requires that

$$\sum e_i = \sum X_{0i} e_i = 0 \qquad \qquad \text{6.9}$$

and

$$\sum X_i e_i = 0. \qquad \qquad \text{6.10}$$

**Figure 6.3**

A Fitted Plane

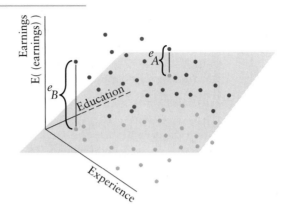

Minimizing the sum of squared residuals in the multiple regression case, in turn, requires that

$$\sum_i X_{ji} e_i = 0 \qquad j = 0, \ldots, k. \qquad\qquad \textbf{6.11}$$

Appendix 6.A proves that the conditions of Equation 6.11 characterize the BLUE estimator for multiple regressions under the Gauss–Markov Assumptions, establishing again that OLS is BLUE under the Gauss–Markov Assumptions. Notice that if there is an intercept term in the model, for which $X_{0i}$ is equal to one for all $i$, the sum of the residuals equals zero. *In regressions with intercepts, the OLS residuals always sum to zero.*

Equation 6.11 follows from minimizing the sum of squared residuals in a multiple regression. The sum of squared residuals is

$$SSR = \sum_{i=1}^{n} (Y_i - \tilde{\beta}_0 X_{0i} - \tilde{\beta}_1 X_{1i} - \cdots - \tilde{\beta}_k X_{ki})^2.$$

To find the estimators that minimize the sum of squared residuals, we set to zero the derivatives of *SSR* with respect to the estimates:

$$\frac{\partial SSR}{\partial \tilde{\beta}_j} = \sum_{i=1}^{n} \left[ 2(Y_i - \tilde{\beta}_0 X_{0i} - \tilde{\beta}_1 X_{1i} - \cdots - \tilde{\beta}_k X_{ki}) X_{ji} \right] = 0$$

$$for\ j = 0, \ldots, k,$$

which we can rewrite as

$$\sum_{i=1}^{n} 2 e_i X_{ji} = \sum_{i=1}^{n} X_{ji} e_i = 0 \qquad for\ j = 0, \ldots, k.$$

## 6.6 $R^2$ in the Multiple Regression Model

WHAT ARE AN ESTI-
MATOR'S PROPERTIES?

How well does an estimated line describe the data at hand? How much of the variation in the dependent variable can be accounted for by the variation in the explanatory variables, once appropriate slope coefficients are chosen for those explanators? Regression lines that account for much of the variation in their dependent variable—that is, regressions with a high $R^2$ (the goodness-of-fit measure introduced in Chapter 5)—can be quite telling. For example, in Chapter 5, Horioka and Feldstein's Regressions Greatest Hits box regression shows that variation in countries' savings can account for almost all the variation in those countries' investment, a result at odds with common notions of international capital mobility. This section explains how $R^2$ is defined in a multiple regression model and introduces a second goodness-of-fit measure.

### $R^2$—the Coefficient of Determination Revisited

Chapter 4 introduced $R^2$, the coefficient of determination, which is the fraction of the variation in the observed $Y$'s in the sample that could be accounted for by variation in the sample $X$'s. Econometricians use the $R^2$ measure as an indicator of goodness of fit in the multiple regression model, too. In the multiple regression model, $R^2$ is defined as

$$R^2 = 1 - \frac{\sum e_i^2}{\sum y_i^2},$$

in which $e_i$ is the $i$-th residual for the fitted line and $y_i$ is the deviation of $Y_i$ from its sample mean, $\overline{Y}$, as usual. In the multiple regression model, $R^2$ measures the fraction of the sample variation of the $Y$'s that can be attributed to the sample variation about their means of all of the $X$'s collectively.

As in the bivariate model, the interpretation of $R^2$ as the fraction of the variation in the sample $Y$'s that can be explained by variation in the $X$'s in the multiple regression model depends critically on the decomposition of the sample variation of the $Y$'s into those two parts alone; that is, the interpretation depends critically on there being no sample covariation between the $X$'s and residuals. If the intercept term is excluded from the model, we have no assurance that the $X$'s and the residuals have no sample covariation. Consequently, if the constant term is excluded from a model, the $R^2$ should be ignored. When the intercept is excluded, the $R^2$ reported by econometric software packages are sometimes not between 0 and 1.

### Adjusted $R^2$

OLS minimizes the sum of squared residuals, thereby maximizing $R^2$. When we add additional explanators to a model, we cannot worsen the fit obtained by

# An Econometric Top 40—A Classical Favorite

## The Solow Model, Old and New

In 1776, Adam Smith created the discipline of economics with his treatise *An Inquiry into the Nature and Causes of the Wealth of Nations*.[6] Why some nations become rich and others don't has remained a core fascination of economists ever since. In 1956 and 1957, future Nobel laureate Robert Solow of the Massachusetts Institute of Technology made theoretical and empirical contributions to the study of economic growth that has shaped much of the subsequent literature on the subject.[7] Solow's theoretical work illuminated technical progress as a likely key to long-run growth in per capita incomes. Solow's empirical work offered a clever approach to disentangling the separate contributions of technical change and capital accumulation to economic growth. Solow studied economic growth in the United States for the first half of the 20th century, a period during which output per worker approximately doubled. How much of that increase in output per worker, he asked, was due to increased capital per worker, and how much to technological change?

In 1992, Gregory Mankiw of Harvard University, David Romer of the University of California at Berkeley, and David Weil of Brown University focused on what Solow's model says about the *level* of per capita GDP in an economy and made a compelling argument that the heart of the Solow model explains a remarkable amount of the variation in per capita GDP across countries.[8] Their data is in the file MRW.*** on this book's companion Web site (**www.aw-bc.com/murray**). Problem 13 at the end of this chapter describes the variables in that file.

The Solow model takes the population growth rate, technological change, and the national saving rate as given from outside the economic model. The model then treats these three elements as the ultimate determinants of per capita GDP in a country. Mankiw, Romer, and Weil argue that technological change is unlikely to account for much of the cross-country differences in per capita GDP because new technologies are observable, and presumably adaptable, by all countries. If Solow's model is on target, say Mankiw, Romer, and Weil, it is differences in saving rates and population growth rates across countries that should account for most of the cross-country differences in GDP.

Mankiw, Romer, and Weil find that the traditional Solow model does not perform well empirically. If the production function is Cobb–Douglas, with the income share of labor equal to $\beta_1$, the Solow model implies that the equilibrium level of GDP per capita is

$$\ln(Q/L) = \beta_0 + \frac{1 - \beta_1}{\beta_1} \ln(s)$$
$$- \frac{1 - \beta_1}{\beta_1} \ln(n + g + d) + \varepsilon.$$

where $s$ is the saving rate in the country, $n$ is the population growth rate in the country, $g$ is a worldwide rate of technological advance, and $d$ is the depreciation rate of capital. We can rewrite this equilibrium level of GDP per capita as

$$\ln(Q/L) = \beta_0 + \frac{1 - \beta_1}{\beta_1} \ln[s/(n + g + d)]$$
$$+ \varepsilon$$
$$= \alpha_0 + \alpha_1 \ln[s/(n + g + d)] + \varepsilon.$$

Mankiw, Romer, and Weil assume the parameters $g$ and $d$ are constant throughout the world and equal to 2% and 3%, respectively. The authors argue that knowledge is available everywhere and that machines and such will depreciate about the same in every country. Reasonable variations in the values of $g$ and $d$ did not alter the authors' results appreciably. The authors used data on $Q$, $L$, $s$, and $n$ from a sample of 98 countries to estimate $\alpha_0$ and $\alpha_1$.

We know from accounting data that the share of labor in GDP ($\beta_1$) is about 2/3; the parameter $\alpha_1$ is therefore about 0.5, if the Solow model is correct. Using GDP per capita, savings rates, and population growth rates from 98 countries, Mankiw, Romer, and Weil estimate that $\alpha_1$ is 1.48, with an estimated standard error of 0.12. This estimate is sharply at odds with the theoretical model and what we know of $\alpha_1$.

Mankiw, Romer, and Weil were not ready to abandon Solow's model altogether, however. They noted that Solow's model makes output dependent only on capital and labor, thereby missing the important effects of human capital on the production of GDP. The authors proposed augmenting the Solow model to include two types of capital, the physical capital traditionally included plus human capital, along with the number of workers. What the authors kept was Solow's treatment of population growth rates and saving rates as given from outside the model. They asked, "How well does the augmented Solow model perform in modeling differences in per capita GDP across countries?" "Remarkably well," was their answer. Differences in population growth rates, saving for physical capital investment, and saving for human capital investment account remarkably well for the cross-country variation in per capita GDP.

The augmented Solow model yields an equilibrium level of per capita GDP:

$$\ln(Q/L) = \beta_0 - \frac{\beta_2 + \beta_3}{1 - \beta_2 - \beta_3}$$
$$\ln(n + g + d)$$
$$+ \frac{\beta_2}{1 - \beta_2 - \beta_3} \ln(S_h)$$
$$+ \frac{\beta_3}{1 - \beta_2 - \beta_3} \ln(s_p) + \varepsilon$$

in which $\beta_2$ is human capital's income share, $\beta_3$ is physical capital's income share, $s_h$ is the saving rate for investment in human capital, and $s_p$ is the saving rate for investment in physical capital. We can rewrite this equilibrium level of per capita GDP as

$$\ln(Q/L) = \beta_0 + \frac{\beta_2}{1 - \beta_2 - \beta_3} \cdot$$
$$\ln[s_h/(n + g + d)]$$
$$+ \frac{\beta_3}{1 - \beta_2 - \beta_3} \cdot$$
$$\ln[s_p/(n + g + d)] + \varepsilon$$
$$= \alpha_0 + \alpha_1 \ln[s_h/(n + g + d)]$$
$$+ \alpha_2 \ln[s_p/(n + g + d)] + \varepsilon.$$

Mankiw, Romer, and Weil note that accounting data reveal that $\beta_3$ is about 1/3. They also argue persuasively that $\beta_2$ is about 1/3. What do the OLS estimates of $\alpha_1$ and $\alpha_2$ imply as estimates of $\beta_2$ and $\beta_3$? Using per capita GDP, population growth rates, saving rates for physical capital, and the fraction of working-age individuals enrolled in secondary schools (which the authors hope is proportional to $s_h$) from 98 countries, the authors' estimate of $\beta_2$ is 0.28 (with an estimated standard error of 0.03), and their estimate of $\beta_3$ is 0.31 (with an estimated standard error of 0.04). These are remarkably close to the values of 1/3 that we expect if the theory is on the mark.

The match of the estimated income shares for human and physical capital to what we expect them to be lends support to the Solow model. But more striking testimony to the power of the Solow model is that the regression with human capital savings as a variable has an $R^2$ of 0.78. Cross-country variations in population growth rates, savings for physical capital investment, and the proportion of working-age individuals enrolled in secondary school account for nearly 80% of the variation in per capita GDP across these 98 countries. Solow's choice to focus on saving and population growth rates does seem to have been inspired. However, if saving rates and population growth rates are so critical to growth, it becomes all the more important to understand what determines those rates—a task the Solow model sets aside from the outset.

Mankiw, Romer, and Weil's results stunned economists studying economic growth. The results seemed almost too good to be true. A host of economists carefully examined the augmented Solow model results. The most telling attention was given to the schooling savings variable that so obviously overlooks primary education and postsecondary education. More recently, growth economists have fruitfully questioned the assumption that technological advance is uniform across countries. And as the $R^2$ of improved specifications goes down, more room is opened for other factors to become important for growth. But even revisionists find that differences across countries in saving rates for physical and human capital and in population growth rates account for perhaps half of

the variation in per capita GDP across countries. Arguably, Solow's intuition about where the most important action lies seems confirmed, even as analysts seek for richer models to offer deeper accounts of why nations differ so much in their per capita incomes.

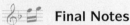 **Final Notes**

Mankiw, Romer, and Weil's paper illustrates how econometrics can be used to test the applicability of economic theories. The paper also highlights how a relatively simple economic theory, here the Solow model that ties cross-country differences in per capita GDP to cross-country differences in population growth rates and savings for human and physical capital, can sometimes succinctly capture very complex real-world phenomena. The fact that these three explanatory variables (as measured by Mankiw, Romer, and Weil) account for almost 80% of the dramatic cross-country variation in per capita GDP challenged all economists who had previously dismissed Solow's model as too simple.

Population growth and saving rates are variables unlikely to be fixed across many samples. Is OLS the appropriate estimator for these data? The saving rate for human capital is only roughly measured by the schooling variable employed by Mankiw, Romer, and Weil. How dependent are their results on this variable? Variants on these two questions must be answered by every economist who undertakes serious econometric work.

■

OLS. Giving the new variable a coefficient of zero and leaving the other estimated coefficients unchanged would keep the fit constant. In most instances, adding another regressor increases $R^2$.

Some researchers like to use goodness of fit to decide whether or not to add an additional explanator to a model. For this purpose $R^2$ is not very attractive, because it is never smaller for more regressors. **Adjusted $R^2$** is a goodness-of-fit measure that grows smaller when an additional regressor is included in the model if the new regressor does not increase $R^2$ by "enough." Adjusted $R^2$, $\overline{R}^2$, is defined by

$$\overline{R}^2 = 1 - \left(\frac{\sum e_i^2/(n-k-1)}{\sum y_i^2/(n-1)}\right),$$

where $k$ is the number of explanators.

The adjusted $R^2$ grows as the sum of squared residuals shrinks, just as with the $R^2$, but the larger $k$ is, the larger the amount we subtract from $n$ to arrive at the adjusted $R^2$. Because adding regressors lowers the sum of squared residuals, but increases $k$, adding regressors may increase or decrease the adjusted $R^2$. The adjusted $R^2$ cannot exceed 1, but it can be less than 0.

Some researchers use the adjusted $R^2$ as a quick indicator of whether or not a regressor should be added to a model. This book does not recommend this practice in anything but descriptive exercises, because the adjusted $R^2$, like the $R^2$ itself, is not grounded in the DGP underlying the data, but simply reflects a trait of the sample in hand.

## 6.7 Four Uses of "Linear" in Econometrics

**WHAT IS THE DGP?**

Chapter 3 defined linear estimators as estimators that can be written in the form

$$g = \sum w_i Y_i,$$

where the $Y_i$ are observations on the dependent variable, and the $w_i$ are weights that do not depend on the $Y_i$. We call a relationship such as $\sum w_i Y_i$ a weighted sum of the $Y_i$. Because many unbiased estimators of the slope of a line are linear and because the Gauss–Markov Theorem provides us with a most efficient linear estimator, linear estimators play an important role in econometrics. Linearity arises in three prominent places in econometrics other than in the definition of linear estimators. *In all, we have four important meanings of* linear *in econometrics: (i) Estimators can be linear in the dependent variable; (ii) regression models can be linear in the dependent and independent variables; (iii) regression models can be linear in their parameters; and (iv) economic theory may impose linear constraints on the parameters of a model.*

A second prominent use of *linear* appears when we say that a regression model is linear in the independent and explanatory variables. A regression model is **linear in the independent and explanatory variables** when the dependent variable can be expressed as a weighted sum of the explanatory variables, plus a random disturbance. Econometricians will frequently specify a linear relationship between the dependent variable and the explanators, as we did in the financial aid example in Chapter 1:

$$aid = \beta_0 + \beta_1 income + \beta_2 wealth + \beta_3 siblings + v.$$

Here, *aid*, the dependent variable, is a weighted sum of the explanatory variables (income, wealth, and siblings). If the relationship between *aid* and its explanators were, instead,

$$aid = \beta_0 + \beta_1 income^2 + \beta_2 \ln(wealth) + \beta_3 siblings + v \qquad \textbf{6.12}$$

or

$$\ln(aid) = \beta_0 + \beta_1 income + \beta_2 wealth + \beta_3 siblings + v \qquad \textbf{6.13}$$

or

$$\ln(aid) = \beta_0 + \beta_1 \ln(income) + \beta_2 \ln(wealth) + \beta_3 \ln(siblings) + v, \quad \textbf{6.14}$$

then the relationship between the dependent variable and the explanators would not be linear, though in the last instance, we could say that the double logarithmic relationship is linear in the logarithms. Nonlinearities among the dependent and explanatory variables pose few difficulties for econometricians.

The third prominent use of *linear* in econometrics is when a model is linear in its parameters and its disturbance. Such models are called **linear regression models**. A linear regression model expresses some observable variable as a weighted sum of the population parameters, plus a random disturbance. The relationships in Equations 6.12 to 6.14 are not linear in the explanators, but are still examples of linear regressions because in all three, the right-hand side is a weighted sum of the parameters of interest to us ($\beta_0$, $\beta_1$, $\beta_2$, and $\beta_3$) and the disturbances. In this "linear regression" perspective on linearity, the weights in the linear relationship are the explanatory variables, be they measured in levels or in logs. With the exception of some models in the last chapters, this book studies linear regression models, or linear regression.

If the relationship between *aid* and its explanators were either

$$aid = \beta_0 + \beta_1 \beta_2 income + \beta_3 wealth + \beta_0 \beta_3 siblings + v$$

or, alternatively (and differently),

$$(aid)^{\beta_0} = \beta_1 income + \beta_2 wealth + \beta_3 siblings + v, \qquad \textbf{6.15}$$

then the model would not be linear in the parameters of interest ($\beta_0$, $\beta_1$, $\beta_2$, and $\beta_3$), nor could we transform it so that it was. Furthermore, if the relationship between *aid* and its explanators were

$$aid = [\beta_0 + \beta_1 \beta_2 income + \beta_2 wealth + \beta_0 \beta_3 siblings] \, v,$$

the relationship would not be a linear regression—because it is multiplicative, not linear, in its disturbance, $v$. We call regressions that are not linear in the parameters of interest to us or in their disturbances **nonlinear regressions**. Prior to the introduction of inexpensive fast computers, nonlinear regressions often posed difficult computational problems for econometricians. Now, the chief difficulties are analytical.

Linear estimators play a dominant role in this book, though we grapple with some of the most important nonlinear regression models in later chapters. Whether models should be specified to be linear or nonlinear in their parameters depends on a balancing of realism and simplicity.

Finally, constraints on the parameters of a model may be "linear." Economic theories often imply that specific relationships hold among the coefficients of a model. For example, because income and wealth are related, we might construct a theory that implies the coefficient on income in Equation 6.15 is equal to the square root of the coefficient on wealth, that is, that $\beta_1 = \sqrt{\beta_2}$. In general, such constraints need not be linear in form. When the hypothesized constraints among the coefficients can be written as a linear combination of the coefficients, for example, if we believed $\beta_1 - 2\beta_0 + 4\beta_3 = 0$ in that same nonlinear aid regression, we would say that there are **linear constraints** on the coefficients.

 ***An Organizational Structure
for the Study of Econometrics***

---

**1. What Is the DGP?**

We specified the data-generating process,

$$Y_i = \beta_0 + \beta_1 X_{ii} + \ldots + \beta_k X_{ki} + \varepsilon_i \qquad i = 1, \ldots, n,$$

with the Gauss–Markov Assumptions.

Dummy variables can quantify categorical variables.

---

**2. What Makes a Good Estimator?**

BLUE

---

**3. How Do We Create an Estimator?**

Maximize $R^2$. That is, minimize the sum of squared residuals (OLS).

An unbiased estimator of $\sigma^2$ is

$$\frac{1}{n-k-1}\Sigma e^2 = \frac{1}{n-k-1}\Sigma(Y_i - \hat{\beta}_0 - \hat{\beta}_1 X_{1i} - \cdots - \hat{\beta}_k X_{ki})^2.$$

---

**4. What Are an Estimator's Properties?**

OLS is BLUE for this DGP.

# Summary

In economic relationships, numerous causal factors are often at work. Economists seek to ascertain the separate effects of each causal factor. For example, how much does education increase wages and how much does work experience increase wages? Multiple regression models allow a dependent variable to be influenced by several explanators. This chapter asked how we should estimate the slopes of each of several explanators in a multiple regression model. These slopes tell us how the dependent variable changes when one factor is changed, holding all the others fixed.

The chapter began by determining the conditions under which a linear estimator is an unbiased estimator of a slope or of the intercept of a straight line with multiple explanators when the Gauss–Markov Assumptions apply. We found that estimating the coefficient $\beta_s$ unbiasedly requires

$$\sum_i w_i^s X_{si} = 1$$

and

$$\sum_i w_i^s X_{ri} = 0 \qquad \textit{for } r \neq s.$$

Minimizing the variance of a linear estimator ($\sigma^2 \sum w_i^2$ when the Gauss–Markov Assumptions apply), subject to the unbiasedness constraints, yields the BLUE estimators of the slopes and intercept (if there is one) in the multiple regression model.

We also introduced binary, or dummy, variables to describe categorical phenomena such as race or sex. Each category is assigned a variable that takes on the value 1 when an observation falls into that category, and the value 0 otherwise. The chapter describes the appropriate interpretation of dummy variable's coefficients.

To know just how efficient the BLUE estimators are, we need to know their variances. The variance of the BLUE estimators in the multiple regression model depends on the variance of the disturbances. Because we don't usually know the variance of the disturbances, $\sigma^2$, we have to estimate it. The chapter shows how to estimate $\sigma^2$ from a regression's residuals so we can infer the precision of our estimators of slopes and the intercept.

The chapter concludes by defining the goodness-of-fit measure, $R^2$, for multiple regression models and by introducing the alternative measure of fit, adjusted $R^2$. Because the BLUE estimator for a multiple regression under the Gauss–Markov Assumptions minimizes the sum of squared residuals, and thereby maximizes $R^2$, the BLUE estimator is called the ordinary least squares (OLS) estimator.

# Concepts for Review

Adjusted $R^2$   234

Binary variable   223

Controls   222

Dummy variable   223

Interaction term   214

Linear constraints   237

Linear in the independent and
explanatory variables   235

Linear regression models   236

Nonlinear regression   237

# Questions for Discussion

1. The multiple regression model allows us to include many influences in studying economic phenomena. What concerns do you have about what can and cannot be included in our regression models? How persuaded are you that Chaloupka and Grossman accurately portray the demand for cocaine or that Mankiw, Romer, and Weil advance our understanding of the determinants of economic growth through their studies described in Greatest Hits boxes in this chapter? Are you troubled that the drug study only accounts for the state a person lives in or that Mankiw, Romer, and Weil do not include any political or institutional variables in their model? Discuss these issues.

2. With the multiple regression model in hand, do we have any use for simpler models, such as a straight line through the origin or a straight line with an intercept and a single slope? What analytical purposes might such simpler models serve?

3. Consider a Gauss–Markov DGP in which $Y_i$ depends on both $X_{1i}$ and $X_{2i}$, as in

$$Y_i = \beta_0 + \beta_1 X_{1i} + \beta_2 X_{2i} + u_i,$$

but for which we also know that $X_2$ depends linearly on $X_1$, too, as in

$$X_{2i} = \alpha_1 X_{1i} + v_i.$$

Suppose the government can manipulate $X_1$. Make up an example, rooted in the real world, in which the government is more interested in knowing the estimated coefficient on $X_1$ from a regression of $Y$ on $X_1$ and an intercept term than in knowing the estimated coefficient on $X_1$ in a regression of $Y$ on $X_1$ and $X_2$. Compare your example with others' examples and identify what makes them similar to one another.

# Problems for Analysis

For the data sets that you will need to solve the problems in this section, go to **www.aw-bc.com/murray**.

1. Does the separation of corporate control from corporate ownership lead to inflated executive salaries and worse firm performance? George Stigler and Claire Friedland

have addressed these questions empirically using a sample of firms.[9] A subset of their data are in the file execcomp.***. The variables in the file are

*ecomp*      Average total annual compensation in thousands of dollars for a firm's top three executives

*assets*      Firm's assets in millions of dollars

*profits*      Firm's annual profits in millions of dollars

*mcontrol*    A dummy variable indicating management control of the firm

a. Regress executives' compensation on the firm's assets and profits, the control dummy, and an intercept term. What proportion of the variation in top executive's compensation in this sample is accounted for by these variables?

b. If the firm's profits rise by one million dollars, by how much do you estimate the top executives' average compensation will change, if assets and the form of control remain fixed?

c. If the firm's assets rise by one million dollars, by how much do you estimate the top executives' average compensation will change, if assets and the form of control remain fixed?

d. What is the estimated difference between the expected average compensations of top executives in management-controlled firms and top executives in ownership-controlled firms, if assets and the form of control remain fixed?

e. Regress firm profits on firm assets and the management-control dummy. How much of the variation in the firm's profits in this sample can be accounted for by variation in assets and the form of control?

f. If the firm's assets rise by one million dollars, by how much do you estimate the profits will change, if assets and the form of control remain fixed?

g. What is the estimated difference between the expected profits in management-controlled firms and in ownership-controlled firms, if assets and the form of control remain fixed?

h. Are the empirical results in (a) and (e) consistent with the claim that management control hurts firm performance and leads to higher pay for executives?

i. Construct 95% confidence intervals for the coefficients on *mcontrol* in the regressions in (a) and (e). Do these intervals make you sympathetic to the claim that managerial control has no discernible effect on either profits or executive compensation?

2. Suppose an econometric analysis finds that in Ghana average annual per capita grain consumption follows the relationship

$$\ln(grain) = 170 + .8\ln(annual\ per\ capita\ income) - .5\ln(price\ of\ grain),$$

where grain is measured in kilograms per person, annual per capita income in Kenyan shillings, and the price of grain in shillings per kilogram.

a. What is per capita grain consumption when per capita income equals 1,000 Kenyan shillings and the price of grain is 10 Kenyan shillings per pound?

b. If income rises from 1,000 to 1,010 Kenyan shillings, compute what happens to grain production. How does this computation compare with the prediction from elasticity that a 1% rise in income will bring an .8% rise in consumption?

c. If income rises from 1,000 to 1,500 Kenyan shillings, compute what happens to grain production. How does this computation compare with the prediction from elasticity that a 50% rise in income will bring a 40% rise in consumption?

d. What do you conclude from (b) and (c) together?

3. Suppose an econometric study finds that in France, average per capita wine consumption has been changing over time, according to the relationship

$$\ln(wine_t) = 47 + 1.6\ln(per\ capita\ income_t) - 0.1\ln(price\ of\ wine_t) - 0.07t,$$

where wine is measured in gallons per person per year, income is annual per capita income in euros, the price of wine is measured in euros per gallon, and $t = 1$ in 1970 and changes by one each year. Further suppose that per capita income and the price of wine were constant from 1970 until 2000, at values of 20,000 euros and 10 euros per gallon, respectively.

a. Compute how much average wine consumption per capita changed from 1970 to 1971. How does this amount compare with the simple interpretation of the estimated coefficient ($-0.07$) on the variable time that claims that consumption declines by 7% per year?

b. Compute how much average wine consumption per capita changed from 1970 to 2000 (30 years)? How does this amount compare with the simple interpretation of the estimated coefficient ($-0.07$) on the variable time that claims that consumption declines by 7% per year?

c. What do you conclude from (a) and (b) together?

4. Earnings data for a sample of Hispanic men and women interviewed in the National Longitudinal Survey of Youth, is contained in the file earnings2.***. The variables are: the natural log of earnings, *lnincome*; education in years, *educatn*; experience in years, *exper*; score on the Armed Forces Qualifications Test, *AFQT*; and whether the individual is female or not, the dummy variable *female*.

a. Estimate an earnings equation for Hispanic women by regressing the natural log of earnings on years of education, years of experience, and an intercept term. (Do not include men in this regression.)

b. What is the estimated rate of return from education for Hispanic women?

c. Construct a 95% confidence interval for the rate of return from education.

d. How much of the variation in Hispanic women's earnings is accounted for by variation in their education and experience? What does this say about the importance of other determinants of earnings in accounting for the variation in Hispanic women's earnings? What are some of these other determinants?

e. The Armed Forces Qualifications Test (AFQT) was administered to all individuals in this sample. This test gives some indication of an individual's intelligence. Add AFQT score to the earnings regression for Hispanic women. How much more of the variation in Hispanic women's earnings does the model now account for?

f. Estimate an earnings equation like that in (e), but for men and women together, including a dummy variable, *male*, that equals 1 for men and 0 for females.

g. According to the estimates in (f), how much less than men do women earn, on average, given the same levels of education, experience, and AFQT score?

h. Re-estimate the earnings equation of (f), but this time without an intercept term and with both *male* and *female* included.

i. Relate the estimated coefficients on *male* and *female* in (h) to the estimated intercept and the estimated coefficient on *male* in (f). Briefly explain.

5. Some colleges and universities no longer require SAT scores as part of their application process. Suppose your school's admissions director wishes to review your school's SAT policy. As part of her analysis, she wants to learn more about the relationship between SAT scores and class performance for students who have already enrolled. You have been selected to design this study. The agreed-upon measure of performance is grade point average.

   a. Would it be better to study the grade point average of students in their first year, or the grade point average of students at graduation? Briefly explain your reasoning.

   b. What other variables would you include in your regression model besides SAT scores? Explain your reasoning for each variable. Note which of the variables you seek are likely to be included in the dossiers of enrolled students.

   c. Do you recommend using the composite SAT score, or the individual components as explanators?

   d. Your analysis applies to enrolled students. Is this the correct population to be studying to analyze admissions policy? What pitfalls do you see with using enrolled students?

   e. Offer suggestions for overcoming the pitfalls you note in (d).

   f. The data in sat2.*** are pertinent to this investigation. The sample contains the entering students from one class at Bates College. The variables include

   | | |
   |---|---|
   | *GPA* | First year grade point average (on a 4.0 scale) |
   | *quant* | Score on the math portion of the Scholastic Aptitude Test (SAT) |
   | *verbal* | Score on the verbal portion of the Scholastic Aptitude Test (SAT) |
   | *SAT* | The sum of *quant* and *verbal* |
   | *female* | = 1 if female, = 0 if male |
   | *prv* | = 1 if student attended a private school; = 0 otherwise |
   | *rank* | Percentage rank in high school class; for example, 0.01 indicates the student finished in the top 1% of his or her graduating class. |

   Regress *GPA* on *SAT*, *rank*, *prv*, and *female*.

   g. If two students are the same except for a 100-point difference in their SAT scores, what is the estimated difference in the students' expected GPAs? Does this strike you as a substantial effect of SAT score on GPA, or as a weak effect?

   h. How much of the variation in *GPA* in this sample is accounted for by the variation in the explanators? What does this indicate about the importance of other determinants of *GPA* for explaining the differences among students' GPAs? Identify some of those other determinants.

   i. Rerun the regression without *SAT*. How much less of the variation in *GPA* can be accounted for when *SAT* is omitted?

6. For many years, Major League Baseball (MLB) had an unusual labor rule that tied each player to a single team—players were not allowed to change to a new team without the old team's permission. In 1976, this rule changed and baseball players

became able to periodically declare themselves "free agents." When they did, they could change teams freely before the following season. Fans and economists have questioned whether free agency increased, decreased, or left unchanged the competitive balance among teams in their league play. Peter Fishman used the data from 1950 to 2004 in the file baseball.*** to settle this debate.[10]

To measure the competitiveness of baseball teams in any given season, the data set provides the standard deviation of winning percentages (the proportion of games played that a team won) across all teams in the league, *stdevwp*. When teams are competitive, they win similar numbers of games, and the standard deviation is low. When some teams dominate and others perform badly, the standard deviation is high. The number of players that declare free agency prior to a given season is *fragents*.

Several other variables can affect the competitiveness of teams. From 1965 on, MLB had a draft of amateur players in which the poorest performing teams of the previous season get first choices in the draft. The purpose of this practice is to improve competitiveness among teams. *Draft* is a dummy variable indicating years from 1965 on. The number of teams in MLB affects the standard deviation of winning percentages. Each dominant team and each poor team has a smaller impact on the mean deviation of winning percentages from their overall mean when there are more teams in the league. *Teams* is the number of teams in MLB during the season. And finally, when a larger proportion of the U.S. population is playing baseball, the variance in ability among players is greater than when a smaller proportion (presumably the very best) plays. The variable *poppct* is the fraction of the U.S. population who are MLB players.

a. Regress *stdevwp* against *fragents*, *draft, teams, poppct*, and an intercept term. What do you conclude about the effect of free agency on the competitiveness of MLB teams?

b. Do the remaining explanators have their expected signs? Briefly explain.

c. How large an effect does the preferential amateur draft have on competitiveness, relative to the mean standard deviation of winning percentages in this sample?

d. Build a 95% confidence interval for the effect of 10 more free agents relative to the mean standard deviation of winning percentages in this sample.

e. How much of the variation in the standard deviation of winning percentages across the years in this sample can be accounted for by the explanators?

 7. When police arrest more people for murder, are there fewer murders? The data set murder1.*** contains a subset of the data that David Mustard used to address this question.[11] Among the variables in the file are

*arrmurd*    County's murder arrests as a percentage of murders in the county
*lratmurd*   Natural log of county's annual murder rate per 100,000 people
*density*    County's population density
*ppb*       The percentage of the county's population who are African American
*incom*    The county's per capita income.

a. Regress the log of the murder rate on the logs of income, the murder arrest rate, population density, and the proportion of the population who are African American. Do the estimated signs of the variables' coefficients conform to your expectations? Briefly explain.

b. What is the estimated elasticity of murder rates with respect to arrest rates?

c. Construct a 95% confidence interval for the elasticity of murder rates with respect to arrest rates.

d. Do you estimate that expected murder rates in a county fall faster than expected incomes rise?

e. Does a 95% confidence interval for the elasticity of murder rates with respect to income include −1.0?

f. How much of the variation in the log of murder rates in this sample is accounted for by variation in the explanatory variables? What other variables do you think might be important for murder rates, besides those in this regression?

 8. French wine bottles' labels contain information about the wine. Is the wine red or white? What is the wine's vintage? Which region is the wine from? And what class does the producer claim for the wine (for example, *gran cru classe* or *clu non classe*)? But what consumers probably want from a wine are superb sensory traits. Is the wine too acidic? Does it have fine tannins? Does it offer complex aromas? These are the sorts of traits that wine drinkers and professional wine tasters look for. Three French economists, Pierre Combris, Sebastien Lecocq, and Michael Visser, used data from wine bottle labels and from professional wine tasters to ask which traits, the traits reported on the label or the sensory traits, better account for the price of French wines.[12] The file wine.*** contains a subsample of the wines these authors used.

The variables in the file, and their meanings, are as follows:

*PRICE*   The wine's price

*GRADE*   Professional tasters' grade for the wine

**Label Traits**

*RANK*   Cru or gran cru (3); cru bourgeois (2); cru non classe (1)

*RED*   Red wine (2); white wine (1)

*WHIT*   White wine (2); red wine (1)

*AN89*   Vintage 1989 (2); otherwise (1)

*AN90*   Vintage 1990 (2); otherwise (1)

*AN91*   Vintage 1991 (2); otherwise (1)

*BORD*   Bordeaux group (2); otherwise (1)

*COTE*   Cote group (2); otherwise (1)

*MEGR*   Medoc and graves group (2); otherwise (1)

*SEPF*   Saint-Emilion Pomerol Frosnac group (2); otherwise (1)

*BLSE*   Blanc Secs group (2); otherwise (1)

*BLDO*   Blanc Doux group (2); otherwise (1)

**Sensory Traits**

*INTE*   Aromatic intensity strong (3); classic (2); discrete (1)

*FINE*   Finesse of aromas yes (2); no (1)

*COMP*   Complexity of aromas yes (2); no (1)

*FIRM*   Firmness of attack yes (2); no (1)

*ACID*   Excessive acidity yes (2); no (1)

*SUPP*    Supple yes (2); no (1)
*FAT*    Plump (3); medium (2); lean (1)
*FLAT*    Flat yes (2); no (1)
*WCON*    Well concentrated yes (2); no (1)
*HARM*    Well-balanced components (3); balanced (2); unbalanced (1)
*TANI*    Fine tannins yes (2); no (1)
*FINI*    Finish long (3); medium (2); short (1)
*ALCO*    Alcohol excess yes (2); no (1)
*STAL*    Trace of staleness yes (2); no (1)
*REDU*    Touch of reduction (2); no (1)
*KEEP*    Needs keeping before drinking yes (2); no (1)

a. Regress the natural log of the price of wine against the wine's sensory traits and an intercept term. How much of the variation in the log of wine's price in this sample is accounted for by the variation in the wines' sensory traits?

b. Regress the natural log of the price of wine against *RANK*, the three vintage variables, and all region variables except *BORD*. Do not include a constant term. Using all three vintage variables is akin to using both *male* and *female* in the earnings equation in the chapter; omitting *BORD* is akin to using only *female* or *male*. How much of the variation in the log of wine's price in this sample is accounted for by the variation in the wines' traits that are reported on the bottles' labels?

c. If wine markets were perfect, so that consumers had perfect information, would we see the results that we do in (a) and (b)? Briefly explain.

9. This exercise examines the returns to education using data on 340 individuals who have twins. The data file for this problem is twin1.***. This data extract is from a survey of twins conducted by Orley Ashenfelter and Cecelia Rouse of Princeton University at the Twins Day Festival in Twinsburg, Ohio.[13] The observational unit of the data is the individual. Here we look at the data for one twin from each pair of twins.

The key variables are
*hrwage*        The self-reported hourly wage of the individual (in dollars)
*lwage*        The natural log of the hourly wage
*age* and *age2*    The age of a person (*age*) and its square (*age2*)
*female*        = 1 if the person is female; = 0 otherwise
*white*        = 1 if the person is white; = 0 otherwise
*educ*        The educational attainment of the individual

a. Regress hourly wage on the indicator for white. Repeat this using the log–wage measure, instead of hourly wage. Are you surprised by what you find?

b. Examine the summary statistics for the variable *white*. What probably accounts for the results in (a)?

c. Regress hourly wage on a constant, education, age, age-squared, and on the gender indicator. What do the coefficients on age and age-squared say about the life profile of earnings?

d. Regress the log of hourly wage on a constant, education, age, age-squared, and on the gender indicator. What do the coefficients on age and age-squared say about the life profile of earnings?

e. How much of the variation in hourly wages is accounted for by variation in the explanatory variables?

f. Which of the Gauss–Markov Assumptions are likely to be violated in the DGP underlying these data? Briefly explain your concerns.

g. Suppose that in addition to the 340 observations in this data set, you also had the corresponding data on these individuals' twin siblings, giving you 680 observations in all. In addition to any concerns noted in (e), which Gauss–Markov Assumptions are likely to be violated by this new larger data set? Briefly explain your concerns.

10. Nitrogen dioxide ($NO_2$) is a pollutant that attacks the human respiratory system; it increases the likelihood of respiratory illness. One common source of nitrogen dioxide is automobile exhaust. The file NO2 pollution.*** contains a subset from 500 hourly observations made from October 2001 to August 2003.[14] The variables in the data set are

| | |
|---|---|
| LNO2 | Natural logarithm of the concentration of $NO_2$ (particles) |
| LCARS | Natural logarithm of the number of cars per hour |
| TEMP | Temperature 2 meters above ground (degree C) |
| WNDSPD | Wind speed (meters/second) |
| TCHNG23 | The temperature difference between 25 meters and 2 meters above ground (degrees C) |
| WNDDIR | Wind direction (degrees between 0 and 360) |
| HOUR | Hour of day |
| DAYS | Day number from October 1, 2001 |

a. Regress $NO_2$ concentration on the log of the number of cars, the two temperature variables, the two wind variables, and the time index (*DAYS*). Build a 95% confidence interval for the elasticity of $NO_2$ pollution with respect to car traffic.

b. What is the estimated rate of change in $NO_2$ pollution per day?

c. Is it correct to estimate the annual growth rate in $NO_2$ pollution by multiplying your estimate in (b) by 365? Briefly explain your response.

d. How much of the variation in the log of hourly levels of $NO_2$ pollution in this sample is accounted for by the variation in the explanators?

e. How much of the variation in the log of hourly levels of $NO_2$ pollution in this sample could be accounted for by the variation in *DAYS* alone?

11. How do growing weather and a wine's age influence a Bordeaux wine's price? The data set wineweather1.*** contains average 1989 prices for Bordeaux wines for the vintages from 1952 to 1989, along with data on weather conditions when each vintage was being grown. These data were part of an analysis of Bordeaux wine as an investment by economists Orley Ashenfelter, David Ashmore, and Robert LaLonde.[15] The variables in the file are

| | |
|---|---|
| logprice | Natural log of the price of Bordeaux wines relative to the price of the 1961 vintage |
| degrees | Average temperature in the growing season |
| hrain | Rainfall in the harvest season |
| wrain | Winter rainfall prior to harvest season |
| Time_sv | Time from 1989 back to the wine's vintage year. |

a. Use multiple regression to explore how growing-season temperatures, harvest-season rainfall, off-season rainfall, and the age of a wine influence the natural log of a vintage's price.
b. Are the signs on the variables what you expect? Briefly explain.
c. How much of the variation in vintages' prices in this sample is accounted for by these explanators?
d. Regress the log of price on vintage and an intercept term. How do you interpret the coefficients on vintage in this regression and in the regression in (a)?
e. Why does the variable *logprice* have the value zero in 1961?

12. Robert Barro studied economic growth in a cross section of countries.[16] The file barrogrowth.\*\*\* contains Barro's variables for a slightly different sample of countries, with an inferior measure of assassinations. The variables in the file are as follows:

| | |
|---|---|
| *ASIAE* | East Asia dummy |
| *ASSAS* | Assassinations per year |
| *COUNTRY* | Name of Country |
| *GCY* | Government Consumption as a % of GDP average 70–85 |
| *GDP60* | GDP 1960 |
| *GDP70* | GDP 1970 |
| *GR6085* | GDP Growth 60–85 (average) |
| *GR7085* | GDP Growth 70–85 (average) |
| *LAAM* | Latin America dummy |
| *PPI60DEV* | Deviations from PPP for Investment 1960 |
| *PRIM60* | Percent Enrolled in Primary School 1960 |
| *PRIM70* | Percent Enrolled in Primary School 1970 |
| *PREVCOUP* | Revolutions and Coups a year |
| *SAFRICA* | Sub-Saharan Africa dummy |
| *SEC60* | Percent Enrolled in Secondary school 1960 |
| *SEC70* | Percent Enrolled in Secondary School 1970 |
| *SHCODE* | Summers–Heston Country code |
| *STTEAPRI* | Student–Teacher Ratio in Primary Schools 1960 |
| *STTEASEC* | Student–Teacher Ratio in Secondary Schools 1970. |

a. Regress GDP growth from 1960 to 1985 on GDP in 1960 and an intercept term. What does the estimated slope's sign suggest about whether poorer countries were catching up to richer ones in the 1960–1985 period?
b. Regress GDP growth from 1960 to 1985 on GDP in 1960, government consumption as a fraction of GDP, the percents enrolled in primary and secondary education, revolutions and coups a year, and the measure of economic distortion, *PPI60DEV*. What does the sign of the estimated coefficient for GDP60 tell you about the propensity of poorer countries to catch up with countries otherwise like themselves? Do the signs of the other estimated coefficients accord with your intuition?

13. Greg Mankiw, David Romer, and David Weil examined the Solow growth model by looking at its implications for both the levels of countries' GDPs and the growth rates

of countries' GDPs.[17] The data they used are in the file MRW.\*\*\*. The variables in that file are

| | |
|---|---|
| COUNTRY | Number representing country |
| GDP60 | GDP per working-age population in 1960 |
| GDP85 | GDP per working-age population in 1985 |
| GDPGR | GDP growth rate '60–'85 |
| INTER | Dummy variable indicating MRW's intermediate group |
| INVEST | Investment as a percentage of GDP |
| NONOIL | Dummy variable for non-oil-producing country |
| OECD | Dummy variable for OECD country |
| POPGR | Population growth rate in percent |
| SCHOOL | Percent of working-age population in secondary school. |

a. The Regression's Greatest Hits box on p. 232 of this chapter that describes Mankiw, Romer, and Weil's work describes the variables they derived from the data in MRW.\*\*\*. Create their variables

$$X_1 = \ln\left(\frac{s}{n + g + d}\right) = \ln\left(\frac{s_p}{n + g + d}\right) = \ln\left(\frac{invest}{popgr + 2 + 3}\right)$$

and

$$X_2 = \ln\left(\frac{s_h}{n + g + d}\right) = \ln\left(\frac{school}{popgr + 2 + 3}\right).$$

b. Restrict the sample to countries that are not oil producers. Regress the log of GDP85 on $X_1$ and an intercept term. Confirm that you get Mankiw, Romer, and Weil's estimate for the slope linking investment rates and population growth to GDP.

c. Restrict the sample to countries that are not oil producers. Regress the log of GDP85 on $X_1$, $X_2$, and an intercept term. Confirm that you get Mankiw, Romer, and Weil's results for the parameters they call $\beta_2$ and $\beta_3$ in their augmented Solow model (as described in this chapter's Greatest Hit about their work).

d. How much of the variation in the log of output per working-age person is attributable to variation in the log of investments in human capital (*school*), physical capital (*invest*), and population growth (*popgr*)? Would you conclude that the augmented Solow model explains a considerable portion of cross-country income differences, and that investment and population growth are important contributors to differences in countries' GDP levels?

e. What are some additional determinants of GDP that are absorbed in the disturbance term of the augmented Solow model?

f. Continue to restrict the sample to countries that are not oil producers. Regress the difference in the logs of GDP in 1985 and GDP in 1960 (which is the log of their ratio) on an intercept and GDP in 1960. Construct a 95% confidence interval for the slope. Does this confidence interval incline you to reject the claim that from 1960 to 1985 poorer countries grew faster than rich ones?

g. How much of the variation in the countries' growth rates in this sample is accounted for by variation in 1960 GDPs in this model?

h. For non-oil-producing countries, regress the log of ($GDP85/GDP60$) on an intercept, the log of GDP in 1960, the log of investment as a percent of GDP, and the log of ($popgr + 5$) (the last is the log of population growth plus the rate of technological advance plus the depreciation rate). Construct a 95% confidence interval for the slope of the log of *invest*. Does this confidence interval incline you to reject the claim that from 1960 to 1985 poorer countries grew faster than rich ones, if their rates of investment and population growth were equal?

i. How much more of the variation of countries' growth rates in this sample is accounted for by adding the investment and population growth variables to the model?

j. Looking back to the augmented Solow growth model in (c), what else might you include in the model of growth rates? Try it. How much does your addition increase the model's explanatory power, as measured by $R^2$?

14. You are interested in examining two questions about juries: (i) Is the composition of juries representative of the adult population? (ii) Is it representative of the pool of available jurors?[18]

You have cross-sectional data on a random sample of 100,000 people from the United States. All of the people in the sample are age 45. The variables are

$J$ = number of times the individual has served on a jury during his or her life (up to his or her current age of 45)

$S$ = individual's years of schooling

$H$ = individual's usual hours of work per week as an adult (this can be equal to zero)

$D_{female}$ = 1 if individual is female; 0 otherwise

$D_{AfricAm}$ = 1 if individual is African American; 0 otherwise

$D_{Hispanic}$ = 1 if individual is Hispanic; 0 otherwise

$D_{Asian}$ = 1 if individual is Asian; 0 otherwise

$R$ = number of months since his or her 18th birthday that the individual has been registered to vote

Suppose that all the individuals in your sample live in states where potential jurors are drawn from the list of registered voters. Therefore, the more months a person has been registered to vote (from the age of 18 to his or her current age of 45), the more chances the individual has had to be drawn for potential jury duty.

If you are unfamiliar with the U.S. jury system, you will need to know that not all potential jurors (i.e., the jury pool) are assigned to jury duty. Lawyers can object to certain people in the pool and prevent them from being on juries. Other potential jurors may be relieved of jury duty if they claim certain hardships.

a. Explain *briefly* why the questions (i) and (ii) are different and why the answer to *each* of the two questions could be useful.

b. Set up the regression equation that you would use to answer the first question. Which parameters would you look at in order to answer it?

c. Set up the regression equation that you would use to answer the second question. Which parameters would you look at in order to answer it?

d. Some states have "motor-voter" laws, whereby voter registration automatically occurs when a person gets a driver's license. As a result, motor-voter states draw their potential jurors from the list of all people who have drivers' licenses. Suppose that some of the 100,000 people in your sample are from states that have motor-voter laws and the rest are from states that use traditional voter registration lists that contain only the people who show up at a government office.

The data set has an additional variable: $D_{MotorVoter} = 1$ if individual is from a motor-voter state; 0 otherwise. Set up the equation that would allow you to examine the question "Do motor-voter laws change the ways in which juries are non-representative of the adult population?" Which parameters would you look at to answer this question?

15. In this question, $Y$, $X$, and $Z$ are the variables; the parameters of interest are $\beta_1$ and $\beta_2$. Which of the following models are linear in the dependent and independent variables? Briefly explain your answers.

a. $Y_i = \beta_1 X_i + \beta_2 Z_i + u_i$
b. $\ln(Y_i) = \beta_1 X_i + \beta_1 \beta_2 Z_i + u_i$
c. $Y_i = \beta_1 X_i^2 + \beta_2 Z_i + u_i$
d. $Y_i = \beta_1 X_i + \beta_1^2 Z_i + u_i$
e. $Y_i^4 = \beta_1 X_i + \beta_1^2 Z_i + u_i$

16. In this question, $Y$, $X$, and $Z$ are the variables; the parameters of interest are $\beta_1$ and $\beta_2$. Which of the following models are linear in the parameters of interest? Briefly explain your answers.

a. $Y_i = \beta_1 X_i + \beta_2 Z_i + u_i$
b. $\ln(Y_i) = \beta_1 X_i + \beta_1 \beta_2 Z_i + u_i$
c. $Y_i = \beta_1 X_i^2 + \beta_2 Z_i + u_i$
d. $Y_i = \beta_1 X_i + \beta_1^2 Z_i + u_i$
e. $Y_i^4 = \beta_1 X_i + \beta_1^2 Z_i + u_i$

## Endnotes

1. Michael Grossman and Sara Markowitz, "Alcohol Regulation and Violence on College Campuses," in *Economics of Substance Abuse*, eds. M. Grossman and C. Hsieh (Northhampton, United Kingdom: Edward Elgar, 2001): 155–177.
2. Frank Chaloupka and Henry Saffer, "Alcohol, Illegal Drugs, Public Policy, and Crime" (paper presented at the annual meeting of the Western Economic Association, San Francisco, July 1992); Phillip J. Cook and Michael J. Moore, "Economic Perspectives on Reducing Alcohol-related Violence," in *Alcohol and Interpersonal Violence: Fostering Interdisciplinary Perspectives*, ed. Susan Martin, NIH Publication No. 93-3496 (Washington, D.C.: Government Printing Office, 1993): 193–211.
3. In matrix form, the BLUE estimator is $(X'X)^{-1} X'Y$, the same formula obtained in the matrix algebra appendix of Chapter 4 for the BLUE estimators of the intercept and slope with a single explanator.

4. M. Grossman and Frank J. Chaloupka, "The Demand for Cocaine by Young Adults: A Rational Addiction Approach," *Journal of Health Economics* 17, no. 4 (August 1998): 427–474. The consumption data are described in L. D. Johnston, P. M. O'-Malley, and J. G. Bachman, "National Survey Results on Drug Use from the Monitoring the Future Study, 1975–1994" (Washington, D.C.: U.S. Government Printing Office, 1995). The price data were from The DEA's System to Retrieve Information from Drug Evidence.

5. Linear demand curves, like the one Grossman and Chaloupka use, do not have constant elasticities, so one must pick a point along the curve at which to calculate the demand elasticity. In the long run, cocaine demand is the same yesterday, today, and tomorrow. To obtain the long-run demand curve, one imposes this requirement on the specified (estimated) demand curve and solves for quantity as a function of price.

6. Adam Smith, *An Inquiry into the Nature and Causes of the Wealth of Nations.* 2 vols. (London: W. Strahan & T. Cadell, 1776).

7. R. M. Solow, "A Contribution to the Theory of Economic Growth," *Quarterly Journal of Economics* 70, no. 1 (1956): 65–94; R. M. Solow, "Technical Change and the Aggregate Production Function," *Review of Economics and Statistics* 39: 312–320.

8. N. Gregory Mankiw, David Romer, and David Weil, "A Contribution to the Empirics of Economic Growth," *Quarterly Journal of Economics* 107, no. 2 (May 1992): 407–437. Mankiw, Romer, and Weil also examine per capita GDP growth rates, with results similar to those they obtain from examining per capita GDP levels.

9. George J. Stigler and Claire Friedland, "The Literature of Economics: The Case of Berle and Means" *Journal of Law and Economics* 26, no. 2 (June 1983): 237–268.

10. Peter Fishman, "Competitive Balance and Free Agency in Major League Baseball," *The American Economist* 47, no. 2 (Fall 2003): 86–91.

11. David Mustard, "Reexamining Criminal Behavior: The Importance of Omitted Variable Bias," *Review of Economics and Statistics* 85, no. 1 (February 2003): 205–211.

12. Pierre Combris, Sebastien Lecocq, and Michael Visser, "Estimation of a Hedonic Price Equation for Bordeaux Wine: Does Quality Matter?" *Economic Journal* (March 1997): 390–402.

13. Orley Ashenfelter and Cecelia Rouse, "Income, Schooling, and Ability: Evidence from a New Sample of Identical Twins," *Quarterly Journal of Economics* 113, no. 1 (February 1998): 253–284.

14. These data come from the Statlib archive of Carnegie Mellon University. They were originally posted there by Aldrin Magne.

15. Orley Ashenfelter, David Ashmore, and Robert LaLonde, "Bordeaux Wine Vintage Quality and the Weather," http://www.liquidasset.com/orley.htm, December 1999.

16. Robert J. Barro, "Economic Growth in a Cross Section of Countries." *Quarterly Journal of Economics* 106, no. 2 (May 1991): 407–443.

17. N. Gregory Mankiw et al., "A Contribution to the Empirics of Economic Growth."

18. Caroline Hoxby kindly provided this question.

*Appendix 6.A*

# Blue Estimation in a DGP with Stochastic Regressors

The assumption of fixed regressors is convenient, but unrealistic. This appendix analyzes a DGP in which all the results from the Gauss–Markov DGP are preserved, except that in this DGP, those results are all conditional on the observed $X$-values. This new, stochastic regressor DGP assumes that the Gauss–Markov Assumptions about the disturbances hold for each and every possible combinations of $X$-values. In this DGP, the usual BLUE estimators continue to be unbiased and efficient among linear estimators. *In essence, if OLS is BLUE for each and every combination of X-values, it is BLUE when those X-values occur probabilistically.*

This appendix first revisits unbiased linear estimation in the context of stochastic regressors. It then determines the BLUE estimator for the DGP with disturbances that satisfy the Gauss–Markov Assumptions for every combination of $X$-values.

## 6.A.1     Unbiasedness Conditions for Linear Estimators

**WHAT ARE AN ESTI-
MATOR'S PROPERTIES?**

A linear estimator is of the form

$$g = \sum w_i Y_i.$$

When we assumed that explanators were fixed across samples, however, we limited linear estimators to weights that were constant across samples. Now, because we still want to allow the weights to depend on the $X$'s, which are allowed to be random variables, we must allow the weights to be random variables, too.

For a linear estimator, such as OLS, to be unbiased, its expectation must equal the parameter of interest. What, then, is the expected value of a linear estimator when the estimator's weights may be random variables? Consider the case of a straight line with unknown intercept and slopes, and with $E(\varepsilon_i) = 0$:

$$E(g) = E\left(\sum w_i Y_i\right) = \sum E(w_i Y_i)$$

$$= \sum_{i=1}^{n} E\left(w_i\left[\left(\sum_{j=0}^{k}\beta_j X_{ji}\right) + \varepsilon_i\right]\right)$$

$$= \sum_{i=1}^{n}\left[E\left(w_i\sum_{j=0}^{k}\beta_j X_{ji}\right) + E(w_i\varepsilon_i)\right].$$

In our earlier analysis of unbiased linear estimators, the weights were constants, allowing us to argue that $E(w_i\varepsilon_i) = w_iE(\varepsilon_i) = 0$. This simplification led to the restrictions for unbiasedly estimating $\beta_s$:

$$\sum_{i=1}^{n} w_iX_{ri} = 0 \qquad \textit{for } r \neq s \qquad\qquad \textbf{6.A.1}$$

and

$$\sum_{i=1}^{n} w_iX_{si} = 1. \qquad\qquad \textbf{6.A.2}$$

Does $E(\varepsilon_i) = 0$ imply that $E(w_i\varepsilon_i) = 0$ when the weights are not constants but are instead random variables? Not necessarily. Let us suppose for the moment, though, that $E(w_i\varepsilon_i)$ does equal zero. Do we then arrive at the same unbiasedness conditions for a linear estimator? Not quite. If $E(w_i\varepsilon_i) = 0$, we can simplify the expression for $E(g)$ and write:

$$
\begin{aligned}
E(g) &= \sum_{i=1}^{n} E\left(w_i\sum_{j=0}^{k}\beta_jX_{ji}\right) = \sum_{i=1}^{n} E\left(\sum_{j=0}^{k}w_i\beta_jX_{ji}\right) \\
&= \sum_{i=1}^{n}\left(\sum_{j=0}^{k}E[w_i\beta_jX_{ji}]\right) = \sum_{i=1}^{n}\sum_{j=0}^{k}E[w_i\beta_jX_{ji}] = \sum_{j=0}^{k}\sum_{i=1}^{n}E[w_i\beta_jX_{ji}] \\
&= \sum_{j=0}^{k}\sum_{i=1}^{n}\beta_jE[w_iX_{ji}] = \sum_{j=0}^{k}\left(\beta_j\sum_{i=1}^{n}E[w_iX_{ji}]\right),
\end{aligned}
$$

which differs from what we obtained when the explanators were nonstochastic only in that $E(w_iX_{ji})$ now appears in the final term, where previously we had $w_iX_{ji}$. A linear estimator will be an unbiased estimator of $\beta_s$ if

$$\sum_{i=1}^{n}E(w_iX_{ri}) = E\left(\sum_{i=1}^{n}w_iX_{ri}\right) = 0 \qquad \textit{for } r \neq s \qquad\qquad \textbf{6.A.3}$$

and

$$\sum_{i=1}^{n}E(w_iX_{si}) = E\left(\sum_{i=1}^{n}w_iX_{si}\right) = 1. \qquad\qquad \textbf{6.A.4}$$

Notice that any estimator satisfying Equations 6.A.1 and 6.A.2 satisfies Equations 6.A.3 and 6.A.4, too. Equations 6.A.3 and 6.A.4 impose weaker requirements than do Equations 6.A.1 and 6.A.2. When the explanators are stochastic, for $E(g) = \beta_s$, the weights times the $X$'s, need not sum to zero (or one, as the case may be) in every sample, only on average across all samples. For example, $\sum w_iX_{si}$ could be more then 1 for some values of the $X$'s and be less than 1 for other values, as long as the sum equaled 1 on average across all samples. Because relying on these quite weak conditions would greatly complicate the analysis of linear estimators, econometricians choose not to exploit this weaker requirement. Instead, they point out that these conditions are met if, in fact, the weights sum to zero (or 1, as the case may be) in *every* sample, as we require when the $X$'s are fixed.

When considering stochastic regressors, econometricians call an estimator an unbiased estimator of $\beta_s$ if

$$E(g|X_{11}, \ldots, X_{1n}, X_{21}, \ldots, X_{2n}, \ldots, X_{k1}, \ldots, X_{kn}) = \beta_s,$$

that is, if the expected value of $g$, *conditional on the $X$'s*, equals $\beta_s$. This is a more stringent requirement than $E(g) = \beta_s$, because $E(g)$ could equal $\beta_s$ on average across all combinations of $X$-values without equaling $\beta_s$ for *each* combination of $X$-values. But, when $g$, on average, equals $\beta_s$ for each combination of $X$-values, as required in this definition, then $g$, on average, also equals $\beta_s$ across all samples of $X$'s. The argument here is a special case of the Law of Iterated Expectations, which states that for any $Z$ and $X$,

$$E[E(Z|X)] = E(Z).$$

In our definition of an unbiased estimator, we require $E(g|X) = \beta_s$, that is, that conditional on the $X$-values in the sample, the expected value of $g$ is $\beta_s$. By the Law of Iterated Expectations, it follows then that $E(g) = E[E(g|X)] = E[\beta_s] = \beta_s$. The stronger unbiasedness requirement implies the weaker one.

Insisting that a linear estimator be unbiased for every combination of $X$-values means that the unbiasedness constraints must hold *conditional on the $X$'s*. Replacing the simple expectations in the derivation of Equations 6.A.3 and 6.A.4 with conditional expectations conditioned on the $X$'s makes the weights and $X$'s fixed, not random, returning us to the unbiasedness conditions in Equations 6.A.1 and 6.A.2, rather than to the new, weaker requirements of Equations 6.A.3 and 6.A.4.

Conditioning on the $X$'s in deriving the unbiasedness conditions would have replaced $E(w_i\varepsilon_i)$ with $E(w_i\varepsilon_i|X_{11}, \ldots, X_{1n}, X_{21}, \ldots, X_{2n}, \ldots, X_{k1}, \ldots, X_{kn})$. Therefore, instead of relying on $E(\varepsilon_i) = 0$ to yield $E(w_i\varepsilon_i) = 0$ and the unbiasedness conditions in Equations 6.A.1 and 6.A.2, as we did with fixed regressors, we now make the stronger assumption that

$$E(\varepsilon_i|X_{11}, \ldots, X_{1n}, X_{21}, \ldots, X_{2n}, \ldots, X_{k1}, \ldots, X_{kn}) = 0 \qquad \textbf{6.A.5}$$

to arrive at that destination with stochastic regressors. Equation 6.A.5 ensures that

$$E(w_i\varepsilon_i|X_{11}, \ldots, X_{1n}, X_{21}, \ldots, X_{2n}, \ldots, X_{k1}, \ldots, X_{kn})$$
$$= w_i E(\varepsilon_i|X_{11}, \ldots, X_{1n}, X_{21}, \ldots, X_{2n}, \ldots, X_{k1}, \ldots, X_{kn}) = 0,$$

with the last step following because, conditional on the $X$'s, $w_i$ is a constant and therefore leads to Equations 6.A.1 and 6.A.2 as the unbiasedness conditions for linear estimators.

## Adapted Gauss–Markov Assumptions

The following DGP adapts the Gauss–Markov Assumptions to the stochastic regressor setting:

$$Y_i = \beta_0 + \beta_1 X_{1i} + \beta_2 X_{2i} + \ldots + \beta_k X_{ki} + \varepsilon_i \qquad i = 1, \ldots, n$$

$$E(\varepsilon_i | X_{11}, \ldots, X_{1n}, \ldots, X_{k1}, \ldots, X_{kn}) = 0 \qquad i = 1, \ldots, n$$

$$\text{var}(\varepsilon_i | X_{11}, \ldots, X_{1n}, \ldots, X_{k1}, \ldots, X_{kn}) = \sigma^2 \qquad i = 1, \ldots, n$$

$$\text{cov}(\varepsilon_i, \varepsilon_j | X_{11}, \ldots, X_{1n}, \ldots, X_{k1}, \ldots, X_{kn}) = 0 \qquad i \neq j.$$

In this DGP, any estimator unbiased for fixed $X$'s, including OLS and its least squares kin, is unbiased for stochastic regressors. This DGP differs from the original Gauss–Markov DGP only in that the $X$'s are stochastic and the expectations are all conditional on the $X$'s. *All of the statistical results of Chapters 3 through 11 apply for stochastic regressors if the distributional and moment assumptions made in those chapters are replaced by assumptions about expectations conditional on the X's. The results are then conditional on the X's as well.* Unfortunately, although Equation 6.A.5 is often true in practice, it is also often untrue. When Equation 6.A.5 is untrue, this DGP is not applicable, and OLS may be biased.

One condition under which Equation 6.A.5 is true is when each $\varepsilon_i$ is statistically independent of all the $X$'s in all $n$ sample observations. Notice that the assumption requires each disturbance to be independent of *all* explanators jointly. The disturbance in one observation must be independent of the $X$'s in all the observations because the $X$-values from all may appear in the weights of a linear estimator; for example, $\sum x_i^2$ appears in the denominator of the OLS estimator. Equation 6.A.5 also arises as a trait of some models in which individuals or firms maximize utility or profit conditional on available information.

## OLS BLUE in This DGP

To see that in this adapted Gauss–Markov DGP, OLS also remains BLUE, begin with a question: "What is the variance of a linear estimator $g$ that unbiasedly estimates $\beta$?"

$$\text{var}(g) = E([g - \beta]^2).$$

By the Law of Iterated Expectations,

$$\text{var}(g) = E([g - \beta]^2) = E(E([g - \beta]^2 | X)) = E(\text{var}(g | X)),$$

that is, the variance of $g$ is the average variance of $g$ across all sampled $X$'s. For example, when the explanators are stochastic and there is an unknown intercept and an unknown slope, the variance of $\hat{\beta}_1$ is no longer

$$\sigma^2 / \sum x_i^2$$

but is

$$E(\sigma^2/\sum x_i^2) = \sigma^2 E(1/\sum x_i^2)$$

6.A.6

instead.

Because OLS makes the variance of $g$ smallest—among linear unbiased estimators—for each combination of $X$-values, OLS must have the smallest average variance among linear estimators across $X$-values as well. Hence, in this DGP, OLS still yields the BLUE estimators for the slopes and intercept.

Notice that in claiming that OLS is still BLUE, the definitions of both linear estimators and unbiasedness are slightly altered. The weights in a linear estimator can be random variables. And to be an unbiased estimator, a linear estimator must be right on average *for each possible combination of X-values.*

 # Appendix 6.B

# Matrix Algebra and Multiple Regression

The weights of BLUE estimators of the slopes and intercept of a straight line are the solutions to the constrained minimization problem in which the variance of a linear estimator is minimized, subject to unbiasedness restrictions. When there is a single explanator, ordinary algebra suffices to obtain the BLUE weights from the first-order conditions of the constrained minimization problem. For more than one explanator, matrix algebra provides the better route to defining the weights for the BLUE estimators.

This appendix presents a matrix algebra representation of the multiple regression model. This representation is used to demonstrate the unbiasedness of the OLS estimator and to compactly represent the variances and covariances of the OLS estimators. The appendix then derives the BLUE estimator for a multiple regression model under the Gauss–Markov Assumptions.

## 6.B.1    A Matrix Representation of the Multiple Regression Model

Matrices allow a highly compact representation of the multiple regression model. Compactness is just one virtue of the matrix representation; in subsequent sections, we will demonstrate that matrix algebra is a powerful tool for analysis.

## The Multiple Regression Model in Matrix Form

Consider first the multiple regression model written as

$$Y_i = \beta_0 + \beta_1 X_{1i} + \beta_2 X_{2i} + \cdots + \beta_k X_{ki} + \varepsilon_i \qquad i = 1, \ldots, n,$$

and as written in matrix form.

$$Y_i = \beta_0 + \beta_1 X_{1i} + \beta_2 X_{2i} + \cdots + \beta_k X_{ki} + \varepsilon_i \qquad i = 1, \ldots, n$$

$$
\begin{bmatrix} Y_1 \\ Y_2 \\ Y_3 \\ \vdots \\ Y_n \end{bmatrix}
=
\begin{bmatrix}
\beta_0 + X_{11}\beta_1 + X_{21}\beta_2 + \cdots + X_{k1}\beta_k \\
\beta_0 + X_{12}\beta_1 + X_{22}\beta_2 + \cdots + X_{k2}\beta_k \\
\beta_0 + X_{13}\beta_1 + X_{23}\beta_2 + \cdots + X_{k3}\beta_k \\
\vdots \\
\beta_0 + X_{1n}\beta_1 + 1X_{2n}\beta_2 + \cdots + X_{kn}\beta_k
\end{bmatrix}
+
\begin{bmatrix} \varepsilon_1 \\ \varepsilon_2 \\ \varepsilon_3 \\ \vdots \\ \varepsilon_n \end{bmatrix}
$$

$$
\begin{bmatrix} Y_1 \\ Y_2 \\ Y_3 \\ \vdots \\ Y_n \end{bmatrix}
=
\begin{bmatrix}
1 & X_{11} & X_{21} & \cdots & X_{k1} \\
1 & X_{12} & X_{22} & \cdots & X_{k2} \\
1 & X_{13} & X_{23} & \cdots & X_{k3} \\
& & \vdots & & \\
1 & X_{1n} & X_{2n} & \cdots & X_{kn}
\end{bmatrix}
\begin{bmatrix} \beta_0 \\ \beta_1 \\ \beta_2 \\ \cdot \\ \beta_k \end{bmatrix}
+
\begin{bmatrix} \varepsilon_1 \\ \varepsilon_2 \\ \varepsilon_3 \\ \vdots \\ \varepsilon_n \end{bmatrix}
$$

$$Y = X\beta + \varepsilon$$

Notice that $Y$, $X$, and $\varepsilon$ each have $n$ rows, one for each observation, while $\beta$ has $(k + 1)$ rows, one for each explanator, including the constant term.

## The Gauss–Markov Assumptions in Matrix Form

The Gauss–Markov Assumptions say that the disturbances are zero, on average, that is, that $E([\varepsilon]) = 0$, that $X$ is fixed in repeated samples, and that the disturbances are homoskedastic and serially uncorrelated.

To represent the Gauss–Markov Assumptions about the variances and covariances of the disturbances, consider the $n \times n$ matrix $\varepsilon\varepsilon'$ for the case in which $n = 4$:

$$
\varepsilon\varepsilon' =
\begin{bmatrix} \varepsilon_1 \\ \varepsilon_2 \\ \varepsilon_3 \\ \varepsilon_4 \end{bmatrix}
[\varepsilon_1 \varepsilon_2 \varepsilon_3 \varepsilon_4]
=
\begin{bmatrix}
\varepsilon_1^2 & \varepsilon_1\varepsilon_2 & \varepsilon_1\varepsilon_3 & \varepsilon_1\varepsilon_4 \\
\varepsilon_2\varepsilon_1 & \varepsilon_2^2 & \varepsilon_2\varepsilon_3 & \varepsilon_2\varepsilon_4 \\
\varepsilon_3\varepsilon_1 & \varepsilon_3\varepsilon_2 & \varepsilon_3^2 & \varepsilon_3\varepsilon_4 \\
\varepsilon_4\varepsilon_1 & \varepsilon_4\varepsilon_2 & \varepsilon_4\varepsilon_3 & \varepsilon_4^2
\end{bmatrix}.
$$

The expected values of the diagonal elements are the variances of the disturbances for the $n$ observations. The expected values of the off-diagonal elements are the covariances among the disturbances of the $n$ observations. Consequently, $E(\varepsilon\varepsilon')$ is the matrix containing the variances and covariances among the disturbances about which we have made assumptions in our models. $E(\boldsymbol{\varepsilon\varepsilon}')$ is called the **variance–covariance matrix of the disturbances.**

We can represent the Gauss–Markov Assumption of homoskedastic disturbances with no serial correlation as follows:

$$E(\boldsymbol{\varepsilon\varepsilon}') = \begin{bmatrix} \sigma^2 & 0 & 0 & 0 \\ 0 & \sigma^2 & 0 & 0 \\ 0 & 0 & \sigma^2 & 0 \\ 0 & 0 & 0 & \sigma^2 \end{bmatrix} = \sigma^2 \begin{bmatrix} 1 & 0 & 0 & 0 \\ 0 & 1 & 0 & 0 \\ 0 & 0 & 1 & 0 \\ 0 & 0 & 0 & 1 \end{bmatrix} = \sigma^2 I$$

We can thus use the matrices to restate the Gauss–Markov Assumptions that make the OLS Estimator, $\hat{\boldsymbol{\beta}}$, BLUE:

$$Y = X\boldsymbol{\beta} + \boldsymbol{\varepsilon}$$
$$E[\boldsymbol{\varepsilon}] = 0$$
$$E[\boldsymbol{\varepsilon\varepsilon}'] = \sigma^2 I$$
$$X \text{ is fixed across samples.}$$

## 6.B.2    Estimating the Multiple Regression Model's Coefficients

The multiple regression model contains $(k + 1)$ coefficients, one intercept, and $k$ slopes, $\beta_0, \beta_1, \beta_2, \ldots, \beta_k$, which are contained in the matrix $\boldsymbol{\beta}$. How should we estimate the elements of $\boldsymbol{\beta}$? This section takes three routes to constructing an estimator for $\boldsymbol{\beta}$. The first approach extends the intuition of more heavily weighting observations with larger $X$-values. The second minimizes the sum of squared residuals to obtain the OLS estimator of $\boldsymbol{\beta}$. The third examines the $(k + 1)$ elements of $\boldsymbol{\beta}$ individually, then minimizes the variance of each element's estimator subject to the unbiasedness requirements, to obtain the BLUE estimator of $\boldsymbol{\beta}$.

### An Intuitive Approach to Estimating $\beta$

In Chapter 3 we learned that more heavily weighting observations with large $X$-values is efficient when estimating a line through the origin. In Chapter 4, we learned that weighting observations that have $X$-values far from the mean of $X$ is efficient when estimating a line with unknown slope. Here, we ask what estimator results if we weight the matrix of observations, $Y$, by the matrix of explanators, $X$. To make these two matrices amenable to multiplication, we must use the transpose of $X$, $X'$:

$$Y = X\boldsymbol{\beta} + \boldsymbol{\varepsilon}$$

$$X'Y = X'X\boldsymbol{\beta} + X'\boldsymbol{\varepsilon} \qquad \text{6.B.1}$$

Because we wish to estimate $\boldsymbol{\beta}$, we move to isolate $\boldsymbol{\beta}$ by multiplying both sides of the preceding equation by $[X'X]^{-1}$. The assumption that $[X'X]^{-1}$ exists is the assumption that the explanators are not perfectly collinear. Multiplying both sides of Equation 6.B.1, we obtain

$$[X'X]^{-1}X'Y = [X'X]^{-1}X'X\boldsymbol{\beta} + [X'X]^{-1}X'\boldsymbol{\varepsilon}$$
$$[X'X]^{-1}X'Y = \boldsymbol{\beta} + [X'X]^{-1}X'\boldsymbol{\varepsilon}.$$

Thus, an intuitive estimator for $\boldsymbol{\beta}$ is

$$\hat{\boldsymbol{\beta}} = [X'X]^{-1}X'Y. \qquad \text{6.B.2}$$

This estimator, $\hat{\boldsymbol{\beta}}$, is an unbiased estimator of $\boldsymbol{\beta}$:

$$E[\hat{\boldsymbol{\beta}}] = E[[X'X]^{-1}X'Y] = E[\boldsymbol{\beta}] + E[[X'X]^{-1}X'\boldsymbol{\varepsilon}]$$
$$= \boldsymbol{\beta} + [X'X]^{-1}X'(E[\boldsymbol{\varepsilon}]) = \boldsymbol{\beta}$$

## Ordinary Least Squares

Ordinary least squares seeks the value of $\tilde{\boldsymbol{\beta}}$ that minimizes the sum of squared residuals, $SSR$, where

$$SSR = \sum(Y_i - \tilde{\beta}_0 X_{0i} - \tilde{\beta}_1 X_{1i} - \cdots - \tilde{\beta}_k X_{ki})^2.$$

In matrix form, the sum of squared residuals is

$$\tilde{e}'\tilde{e} = [Y - \tilde{\boldsymbol{\beta}}X]'[Y - \tilde{\boldsymbol{\beta}}X].$$

Note that $[Y - \tilde{\boldsymbol{\beta}}X]$ is an $(n \times 1)$ matrix, so $[Y - \tilde{\boldsymbol{\beta}}X]'$ is $(1 \times n)$, and $\tilde{e}'\tilde{e}$ is $1 \times 1$. We can rewrite the sum of squared residuals as

$$\tilde{e}'\tilde{e} = [Y - \tilde{\boldsymbol{\beta}}X]'[Y - \tilde{\boldsymbol{\beta}}X] = Y'Y - \boldsymbol{\beta}'X'Y - Y'X\boldsymbol{\beta} + \boldsymbol{\beta}'X'X\boldsymbol{\beta}. \quad \text{6.B.3}$$

Recall from Chapter 4 that $[ZQ]' = Q'Z'$. Because each element of Equation 6.B.3 is $(1 \times 1)$, we can simplify the equation to

$$\tilde{e}'\tilde{e} = Y'Y - 2Y'X\tilde{\boldsymbol{\beta}} + \tilde{\boldsymbol{\beta}}'X'X\tilde{\boldsymbol{\beta}}.$$

Differentiation of matrices has two rules of interest to us here. First,

$$\frac{\partial Z'\boldsymbol{\beta}}{\partial \boldsymbol{\beta}} = Z.$$

Notice that $Z'$ appears in the function being differentiated and $Z$ appears in the derivative. Second,

$$\frac{\partial \boldsymbol{\beta}'Z\boldsymbol{\beta}}{\partial \boldsymbol{\beta}} = 2Z\boldsymbol{\beta},$$

when $Z$ is symmetric. A matrix is symmetric when the off-diagonal element $jh$ always equals the off-diagonal element $hj$. We can apply this second differentiation rule to our problem because $X'X$ is a symmetric matrix.

To see that $X'X$ is symmetric, examine the case in which $k = 3$. First, consider $X$ itself:

$$X = \begin{bmatrix} 1 & X_{11} & X_{21} & \cdots & X_{31} \\ 1 & X_{12} & X_{22} & \cdots & X_{32} \\ 1 & X_{13} & X_{23} & \cdots & X_{33} \\ & & \vdots & & \\ 1 & X_{1n} & X_{2n} & \cdots & X_{3n} \end{bmatrix}.$$

The transpose of $X$ is, therefore,

$$X' = \begin{bmatrix} 1 & 1 & 1 & \cdots & 1 \\ X_{11} & X_{12} & X_{13} & \cdots & X_{1n} \\ X_{21} & X_{22} & X_{23} & \cdots & X_{2n} \\ X_{31} & X_{32} & X_{33} & \cdots & X_{3n} \end{bmatrix},$$

and $X'X$ is the symmetric matrix of cross products of the X-variables. Thus,

$$X'X = \begin{bmatrix} 1 & 1 & 1 & \cdot & 1 \\ X_{11} & X_{12} & X_{13} & \cdot & X_{1n} \\ X_{21} & X_{22} & X_{23} & \cdot & X_{2n} \\ X_{31} & X_{32} & X_{33} & \cdot & X_{3n} \end{bmatrix} \begin{bmatrix} 1 & X_{11} & X_{21} & \cdots & X_{k1} \\ 1 & X_{12} & X_{22} & \cdots & X_{k2} \\ 1 & X_{13} & X_{23} & \cdots & X_{k3} \\ & & \vdots & & \\ 1 & X_{1n} & X_{2n} & \cdots & X_{kn} \end{bmatrix}$$

$$= \begin{bmatrix} n & \sum_{i=1}^{n} X_{1i} & \sum_{i=1}^{n} X_{2i} & \sum_{i=1}^{n} X_{3i} \\ \sum_{i=1}^{n} X_{1i} & \sum_{i=1}^{n} X_{1i}^2 & \sum_{i=1}^{n} X_{1i}X_{2i} & \sum_{i=1}^{n} X_{1i}X_{3i} \\ \sum_{i=1}^{n} X_{2i} & \sum_{i=1}^{n} X_{2i}X_{1i} & \sum_{i=1}^{n} X_{2i}^2 & \sum_{i=1}^{n} X_{2i}X_{3i} \\ \sum_{i=1}^{n} X_{3i} & \sum_{i=1}^{n} X_{3i}X_{1i} & \sum_{i=1}^{n} X_{3i}X_{2i} & \sum_{i=1}^{n} X_{3i}^2 \end{bmatrix}.$$

To find the estimator of $\beta$ that minimizes the sum of squared residuals, we set the derivative of the sum of squared residuals with respect to to $\tilde{\beta}$ zero:

$$\frac{\partial \tilde{e}'\tilde{e}}{\partial \tilde{\beta}} = -2X'Y + 2X'X = 0,$$

which implies that the OLS estimator, $\hat{\boldsymbol{\beta}}$, in the multiple regression model is

$$[X'X]^{-1}X'Y,$$

which is the same formula that applies when there is a single explanator, with or without an intercept term. The assumption that $[X'X]^{-1}$ exists is the assumption that the explanators are not perfectly collinear.

## Linear Estimators in the Multiple Regression Model

Linear estimators have proven a fruitful set to examine. We can describe linear estimators of the matrix $\boldsymbol{\beta}$. Let

$$\mathbf{W}^{r\prime} = \begin{bmatrix} w_1^r w_2^r \cdots w_n^r \end{bmatrix} \qquad \text{6.B.4}$$

be the $n$ weights to be applied to our $n$ observations when estimating the $r$-th coefficient; the corresponding linear estimator would be $\mathbf{W}^{r\prime}Y$. If we collect the weights for estimating all the coefficients in a matrix,

$$\mathbf{W} = (\mathbf{W}^1\mathbf{W}^2\cdots\mathbf{W}^k),$$

we can express the linear estimator of the matrix $\boldsymbol{\beta}$ as $\mathbf{W}'Y$.

For example, for the OLS estimator, $\mathbf{W} = X(X'X)^{-1}$. To see that these are, indeed, the weights for OLS, look to the linear estimator $\mathbf{W}'Y$ using these weights, that is, examine $[X(X'X)^{-1}]'Y$. Because $[Q'Z]'$ always equals $Z'Q$,

$$[X(X'X)^{-1}]' = [(X'X)^{-1}]'X'.$$

Further, because the matrix $[X'X]$ is symmetric, the matrix $[X'X]^{-1}$ is also symmetric, so

$$[[X'X]^{-1}]' = [X'X]^{-1}.$$

Thus, we find that using the assumed weights for OLS we obtain $\mathbf{W}'Y = [X'X]^{-1}X'Y$, just as in Equation 6.B.2.

## Unbiasedness Conditions for Linear Estimators

We can also use the Gauss–Markov Assumptions to determine the conditions under which a linear estimator is unbiased. Unbiasedness requires that $E(\mathbf{W}'Y) = \boldsymbol{\beta}$. Because $Y = X\boldsymbol{\beta} + \boldsymbol{\varepsilon}$,

$$E(\mathbf{W}'Y) = E(\mathbf{W}'[X\boldsymbol{\beta} + \boldsymbol{\varepsilon}]) = \mathbf{W}'X\boldsymbol{\beta},$$

which implies that $\mathbf{W}'X = I_k$ is the unbiasedness condition for linear estimators to unbiasedly estimate $\boldsymbol{\beta}$.

## The Variance of Linear Estimators

The variance–covariance matrix of any set of $k$ linear estimators is

$$
\mathrm{E}([W'Y - \mathrm{E}(W'Y)][W'Y - \mathrm{E}(W'Y)]')
$$
$$
= \mathrm{E}([W'Y - W'\mathrm{E}(Y)][W'Y - W'\mathrm{E}(Y)]')
$$
$$
= \mathrm{E}([W'[Y - \mathrm{E}(Y)][W'[Y - \mathrm{E}(Y)]'
$$
$$
= \mathrm{E}(W'[Y - \mathrm{E}(Y)][Y - \mathrm{E}(Y)]'W)
$$
$$
= W'\mathrm{E}([Y - \mathrm{E}(Y)][Y - \mathrm{E}(Y)]')W
$$

$$
= W'(\sigma^2 I)W = \sigma^2 W'W. \qquad \text{6.B.5}
$$

Notice that because $[W'Y - \mathrm{E}(W'Y)]$ is $(k \times 1)$, multiplying it by its transpose yields a $(k \times k)$ matrix.

## The Variances and Covariances of the OLS Estimator

Matrix algebra provides a succinct expression for the variances and covariances of the coefficient estimators. In general, the variance–covariance matrix for an estimator of $\boldsymbol{\beta}$ is $\mathrm{E}([\tilde{\boldsymbol{\beta}} - \boldsymbol{\beta}][\tilde{\boldsymbol{\beta}} - \boldsymbol{\beta}]')$. In the particular case of the OLS estimator under the Gauss–Markov Assumptions when $k = 2$, the variance–covariance matrix of the estimators is

$$
\mathrm{E}[[\hat{\beta} - \beta][\hat{\beta} - \beta]']
$$
$$
= \begin{bmatrix}
\mathrm{E}[[\hat{\beta}_0 - \beta_0]^2] & \mathrm{E}[[\hat{\beta}_0 - \beta_0][\hat{\beta}_1 - \beta_1]] & \mathrm{E}[[\hat{\beta}_0 - \beta_0][\hat{\beta}_2 - \beta_2]] \\
\mathrm{E}[[\hat{\beta}_1 - \beta_1][\hat{\beta}_0 - \beta_0]] & \mathrm{E}[[\hat{\beta}_1 - \beta_1]^2] & \mathrm{E}[[\hat{\beta}_1 - \beta_1][\hat{\beta}_2 - \beta_2]] \\
\mathrm{E}[[\hat{\beta}_2 - \beta_2][\hat{\beta}_0 - \beta_0]] & \mathrm{E}[[\hat{\beta}_2 - \beta_2][\hat{\beta}_1 - \beta_1]] & \mathrm{E}[[\hat{\beta}_2 - \beta_2]^2]
\end{bmatrix}.
$$

More generally, the variance–covariance matrix of the OLS estimators is

$$
\mathrm{E}[[\hat{\beta} - \beta][\hat{\beta} - \beta]']
$$
$$
= \begin{bmatrix}
\mathrm{E}[[\hat{\beta}_0 - \beta_0]^2] & \mathrm{E}[[\hat{\beta}_0 - \beta_0][\hat{\beta}_1 - \beta_1]] & \mathrm{E}[[\hat{\beta}_0 - \beta_0][\hat{\beta}_2 - \beta_2]] \\
\mathrm{E}[[\hat{\beta}_1 - \beta_1][\hat{\beta}_0 - \beta_0]] & \mathrm{E}[[\hat{\beta}_1 - \beta_1]^2] & \mathrm{E}[[\hat{\beta}_1 - \beta_1][\hat{\beta}_2 - \beta_2]] \\
\mathrm{E}[[\hat{\beta}_2 - \beta_2][\hat{\beta}_0 - \beta_0]] & \mathrm{E}[[\hat{\beta}_2 - \beta_2][\hat{\beta}_1 - \beta_1]] & \mathrm{E}[[\hat{\beta}_2 - \beta_2]^2]
\end{bmatrix}.
$$

$$
= [X'X]^{-1}X'\boldsymbol{uu}'X[X'X]^{-1}
$$
$$
= [X'X]^{-1}X'[\sigma^2 I]X[X'X]^{-1}
$$
$$
= \sigma^2[X'X]^{-1}X'X[X'X]^{-1}
$$
$$
= \sigma^2[X'X]^{-1}. \qquad \text{6.B.6}
$$

The variance obtained in Equation 6.A.4 is confirmed by inserting the OLS weights, $X[X'X]^{-1}$, for $W$ in Equation 6.A.5:

$$\sigma^2 W'W = \sigma^2\left[[X'X]^{-1} X'([X'X]^{-1}X)'\right]$$
$$= \sigma^2[X'X]^{-1}X^1X[X^1X]^{-1} = \sigma^2[X'X]^{-1}.$$

## OLS Is BLUE Under the Gauss–Markov Assumptions

Minimizing the variance of a linear estimator subject to the unbiasedness conditions would determine the BLUE estimators under the Gauss–Markov Assumptions. But that derivation, which would involve both matrix algebra and Lagrange multipliers, is lengthy and unnecessarily complex. In Chapters 3 and 4 we learned that the OLS estimator is BLUE under the Gauss–Markov Assumptions. It is therefore natural to ask whether any other unbiased linear estimator, for example, $C'Y$, has a smaller variance than the OLS estimator in the multiple regression model when the Gauss–Markov Assumptions apply.

Consider a linear estimator $C'Y$, with weights that differ from the OLS weights by some amount. Define the matrix $D'$ by

$$D' = C' - [X'X]^{-1}X'$$

so that

$$C' = [X'X]^{-1}X' + D'.$$

$D'$ contains the differences between the OLS weights and the weights of the linear estimator $C'Y$.

The unbiasedness of $C'Y$ requires that $C'X = I_{k+1}$. Consequently,

$$(D' + [X'X]^{-1}X')X = I_{k+1}.$$

But OLS is also unbiased, so

$$D'X + [X'X]^{-1}X'X = D'X - I_{k+1} = I_{k+1},$$

which implies that

$$D'X = 0.$$

The next step in proving that OLS is BLUE is to show that the variances of the $(k + 1)$ elements of $C'Y$ are all larger than the corresponding $(k + 1)$ variances of the OLS estimators. Because the variance–covariance matrix of a linear estimator $W'Y$ is $\sigma^2[W'W]$, the variances of $C'Y$'s $(k + 1)$ estimators are the diagonal elements of

$$\sigma^2 C'C = \sigma^2(D' + [X'X]^{-1}X')(X[X'X]^{-1} + D)$$
$$= \sigma^2(D'X[X'X]^{-1} + D'D + [X'X]^{-1}X'X[X'X]^{-1} + [X'X]^{-1}X'D)$$

$$= \sigma^2(0 + D'D + [X'X]^{-1} + 0)$$
$$= \sigma^2(D'D + [X'X]^{-1}).$$

Just as the diagonal elements of $X'X$ are the sums of the squared $X$'s, $\sum_{i=1}^{n} X_{ji}^2$ for $j = 0, 1, \ldots, k$, the diagonal elements of $D'D$ are the sums of the squares of the differences between the OLS weights and the weights of $C'Y$. The diagonal elements of $D'D$ are necessarily positive if $C'Y$ differs from the OLS estimator.

Recall that the variance of the OLS estimators are $\sigma^2$ times the diagonal elements of $[X'X]^{-1}$. Therefore, no unbiased estimator $C'Y$ different from the OLS estimator can provide smaller variances than OLS because the diagonal elements of $D'D + [X'X]^{-1}$ are larger than those of $[X'X]^{-1}$.

This proof that no other estimator has a smaller variance than OLS under the Gauss–Markov Assumptions illustrates how proofs by contradiction are sometimes simpler than direct attacks. This "proof by contradiction" is about half as long as the corresponding derivation of the BLUE estimators using matrix algebra and Lagrange multipliers.

## A Relationship Among Explanators and Residuals for the OLS Estimator

Section 6.9 finds that for the multiple regression OLS model, it must be the case that

$$\sum_i X_{ji}e_i = 0 \qquad j = 0, \ldots, k.$$

In matrix form, this condition states that

$$X'e = 0. \qquad\qquad \text{6.B.6}$$

When two matrices, $A$ and $B$ have the property that $A'B = 0$, we say that the columns of $A$ are **orthogonal** to the columns of $B$. To prove that the columns of $X$ are orthogonal to $e$, recall that

$$e = Y - X\hat{\beta} = Y - X(X'X)^{-1}X'Y.$$

It follows that

$$X'e = X'Y - X'X(X'X)^{-1}X'Y$$
$$= X'Y - IX'Y$$
$$= X'Y - X'Y = 0,$$

as we found in Section 6.9.

## 6.B.3    Estimating $\sigma^2$

Econometricians use the sum of squared residuals from the OLS regression to estimate $\sigma^2$. The estimator they use,

$$s^2 = \frac{\sum e_i^2}{(n - k - 1)},$$

is unbiased. To demonstrate the unbiasedness of $s$ requires defining the **trace** of a square matrix, which is the sum of the matrix's diagonal elements. A key characteristic of the trace is that the trace of a product of matrices, tr($ABCD$), is equal to the trace of any conformable permutation of its elements, for example, tr($ABCD$) = tr($BCDA$). Also, tr($A + B$) = tr($A$) + tr($B$).

Recall that

$$e = Y - X\hat{\beta} = Y - X(X'X)^{-1}X'Y$$

or

$$e = (I_n - X(X'X)^{-1}X')Y = MY,$$

where $M = (I_n - X(X'X)^{-1}X')$. $M$ is a matrix such that $M'M = M$. Any matrix $M$ with the property that $M''M = M$ we call **idempotent**. Thus,

$$e = M(X\beta + \varepsilon) = MX\beta + M\varepsilon.$$

However,

$$MX = (I_n - X(X'X)^{-1}X')X = (I_n X - X(X'X)^{-1}X'X) = X - X = 0.$$

Therefore,

$$e = M\varepsilon$$

and

$$e'e = \varepsilon'M'M\varepsilon.$$

But because $M'M = M$,

$$e'e = \varepsilon'M\varepsilon.$$

Because $e'e$ is $1 \times 1$, it equals its trace:

$$e'e = \text{tr}(\varepsilon'M\varepsilon).$$

But

$$\text{tr}(\boldsymbol{\varepsilon}'\boldsymbol{M}\boldsymbol{\varepsilon}) = \text{tr}(\boldsymbol{M}\boldsymbol{\varepsilon}\boldsymbol{\varepsilon}')$$

by the rule for the traces of permutations.

Because the trace is a sum (of diagonal elements of the matrix),

$$\text{E}(\text{tr}(\boldsymbol{A})) = \text{tr}(\text{E}(\boldsymbol{A})).$$

Consequently,

$$\text{E}(e'e) = \text{tr}(\text{E}(\boldsymbol{M}\boldsymbol{\varepsilon}\boldsymbol{\varepsilon}')).$$

Because $X$ is a constant across samples,

$$\text{E}(\boldsymbol{M}\boldsymbol{\varepsilon}\boldsymbol{\varepsilon}') = \boldsymbol{M}(\text{E}(\boldsymbol{\varepsilon}\boldsymbol{\varepsilon}')) = \boldsymbol{M}(\sigma^2 I_n) = \sigma^2 \boldsymbol{M}.$$

Thus,

$$\text{E}(e'e) = \sigma^2 \text{tr}(\boldsymbol{M}).$$

The trace of $\boldsymbol{M}$

$$= \text{tr}((I_n - X(X'X)^{-1}X')) = \text{tr}(I_n) - \text{tr}(X(X'X)^{-1}X').$$

By the rule for the traces of permutations, the trace of $X(X'X)^{-1}X'$ is

$$\text{tr}(X(X'X)^{-1}X') = \text{tr}((X'X)^{-1}X'X) = \text{tr}(I_{k+1}).$$

Thus, we conclude that

$$\text{E}(e'e) = \sigma^2 \text{tr}(\boldsymbol{M}) = \sigma^2(n - k - 1), \qquad \text{6.B.7}$$

because the trace of an $m \times m$ identity matrix is $m$.

Equation 6.6 implies that

$$\text{E}(s^2) = \text{E}(e'e/(n - k - 1)) = \sigma^2.$$

# Appendix 6.B Concepts for Review

# PART TWO

# Specification and Hypothesis Testing

 *Chapter 7*

# Testing Single Hypotheses in Regression Models

*Torture data enough and it will confess to anything.*

—VARIOUSLY ATTRIBUTED

Skepticism about empirical analysis is widespread. Humorist Mark Twain took an extreme stand: "Get your facts first, then you can distort them as you please." But computer guru Charles Babbage counters, "Errors using inadequate data are much less than those using no data at all." Can we overcome skepticism and satisfy our common sense with empirical arguments that use "inadequate" data?

The Regression's Greatest Hits boxes and other applications we have seen in the first six chapters address a broad array of questions. Table 7.1 contains five questions drawn from these Greatest Hits. Why do the authors of these analyses think that the uncertain analysis of econometrics yields insights worthy of attention? When Martin Feldstein claims that his data reveal a negative effect of college financial aid on family saving, or when Grossman and Chaloupka claim that cocaine use is higher where marijuana laws are more lenient, or when Mankiw, Romer, and Weil claim that the simple Solow growth model conflicts with observed cross-country per capita income differences, why do they reject objections that what they observe is just an accident, arising by chance? We know econometric knowledge is uncertain—we have repeatedly examined the probabilistic nature of samples. How, then, are we to make confident claims based on uncertain data? This chapter addresses these questions.

**TABLE 7.1  Five Hypotheses Encountered Thus Far**

1. Does college financial aid reduce family savings? (Feldstein, p. 10)

2. Was the inflation–unemployment relationship observed in the 1960s a statistical accident? (Phillips, p. 121)

3. Is there a strong positive relationship between investment and savings? That is, are international capital markets mobile? (Feldstein and Horioka, p. 189)

4. Are marijuana and cocaine complements? That is, do weaker anti-marijuana laws lead to more cocaine use? (Grossman and Chaloupka, p. 219)

5. Are cross-country differences in per capita income in accord with either a simple or an augmented Solow model of growth? (Mankiw, Romer, and Weil, p. 232)

All the authors cited argue implicitly that if their claims were untrue, their data would be very surprising. If college financial aid does not deter saving, Feldstein's data would be very surprising. If cocaine and marijuana are not complements, Grossman and Chaloupka's substantial negative estimated substitution effect would be very surprising. If Solow's simple model is not at odds with the reality of cross-country per capita income differences, Mankiw, Romer, and Weil's estimates would be very surprising. The measure of surprise in each case is a probability, in particular, the probability of observing data like those in hand were the authors wrong in their claims.

Sherlock Holmes once said that a dog that didn't bark was the key to solving a case.[1] Watson was puzzled, because a dog might fail to bark in myriad circumstances. But in some circumstances, a silent dog was highly unlikely. In Holmes's investigation, ruling out the circumstances in which the dog was unlikely to be quiet left only one solution to the case—and it proved to be the right one. Like Holmes, our econometricians build their cases with one strategic use of hypothesis testing. They note that if we wish to disagree with their claims, we are left making a counterclaim that, if it were true, would make the data like theirs highly unlikely. They argue that we should reject the counterclaim for that reason and agree with them instead. Statisticians call such counterclaims "null hypotheses," and the claims of Holmes and company "alternative hypotheses." Holmes and our econometricians reject the null hypotheses with which they are faced and consequently look instead to their alternative hypotheses. Holmes could have been wrong; so, too, might be our economists. By carefully choosing their methods of analysis, however, Holmes and his modern economic counterparts are right unless they are unlucky.

This chapter begins by reviewing the steps of hypothesis testing. It then develops the methods econometricians use to test some common hypotheses that arise in econometrics. Hypothesis testing is one device econometricians use to grapple with the uncertainty of econometric analyses.

## 7.1 Rejecting and Failing to Reject Hypotheses

In a hypothesis test, we may reject the null hypothesis (as Holmes did) or not. Suppose data like that at hand would be likely to occur were the null hypothesis true. In that case, the data at hand do not urge us away from the null hypothesis, and we should not reject the null hypothesis. *Caution: When we fail to reject the null hypothesis, we ought not be quick to say that we accept the null hypothesis.* Often data are unsurprising both under the null and under the alternative hypothesis, so we can reject neither claim—leaving us unable to accept either claim. However, if we have strong prior reasons for believing the null hypothesis, new data that lead us not to reject that null hypothesis will leave our beliefs largely intact. Thus, a test that fails to reject the null hypothesis that the moon is made of green cheese ought not lead you to embrace that null hypothesis, whereas a test that fails to reject the null hypothesis that the sun will rise in the east tomorrow should leave your prior confidence in that null hypothesis intact.

We can err in either of two ways when we test hypotheses: We can reject a true null hypothesis, or we can fail to reject a false null hypothesis. These two errors are called **Type I errors** and **Type II errors**, respectively. Given the probabilistic nature of econometric evidence, each of these errors occurs with some probability. Econometricians keep track of these errors by assessing the conditional probability of rejecting the null hypothesis if it is true and of failing to reject the null hypothesis if it is false. In U.S. courts, defendants are presumed innocent (the null hypothesis) until proven guilty. Insisting on "proof beyond a reasonable doubt" stems from wanting a low probability of Type I error—innocent individuals are to be convicted infrequently. If the courts were instead loath to let the guilty go free, they would insist on a low probability of Type II error—juries should not acquit guilty people often. In practice, there is a tension between the goal of protecting the innocent, which may lead to acquitting some guilty individuals, and of increasing conviction rates for the guilty, which generally means convicting more innocent people. Statisticians face similar trade-offs between risking Type I errors and risking Type II errors.

Hypothesis testing requires us to make precise statements about the probability with which an estimator will take on one particular value or another. This requires more detailed knowledge about the distribution of disturbances in our data-generating process (DGP) than we have thus far assumed. An often reasonable, and simplifying, distributional assumption is that the disturbances are normally distributed. In many applications in which the disturbances are not normal, the test procedures we develop for the normal case prove to be good approximations. This chapter augments the DGP of Chapter 6 with an assumption of normally distributed disturbances:

$$Y_i = \beta_0 + \beta_1 X_{1i} + \beta_2 X_{2i} + \cdots + \beta_k X_{ki} + \varepsilon_i \qquad i = 1, \ldots, n$$

$$E(\varepsilon_i) = 0 \qquad i = 1, \ldots, n$$

$$\text{var}(\varepsilon_i) = \sigma^2 \qquad i = 1, \ldots, n$$

$$\text{cov}(\varepsilon_i, \varepsilon_j) = 0 \qquad \text{for } i \neq j$$

Each explanator is fixed across samples.
The disturbances are jointly normally distributed.

In this DGP, the disturbances are mutually independent because uncorrelated normally distributed random variables are statistically independent. Furthermore, the $Y_i$'s are also normally distributed and statistically independent because they differ from the disturbances only by constants. Finally, linear estimators are normally distributed with this DGP because linear combinations of normally distributed random variables are themselves normally distributed.

In the next section, we detail six steps in conducting hypothesis tests. These steps establish what risks of Type I and Type II errors we undertake and the specific criteria for rejecting or failing to reject a particular null hypothesis.

## 7.2    Six Steps to Hypothesis Testing

**How Do We Test Hypotheses?**

Sherlock Holmes didn't examine every detail of the dog's behavior in his case. Instead, he summarized the dog's behavior: It didn't bark. Holmes used that summary information to reject some possibilities as he sought a dastardly villain. Econometricians similarly boil down their data to manageable proportions by calculating statistics, such as sample means, sample variances, and estimated slopes, from the data in hand. Econometricians base their hypothesis tests on such statistics, calling them **test statistics**. We call the set of test statistic values that would lead an econometrician to reject a null hypothesis the **critical region** of the test; if the test statistic lies in the critical region, the null hypothesis is rejected. We call the probability of rejecting the null hypothesis when the null hypothesis is true the **significance level** or the **size** of the test, the test's **probability of Type I error**.

Hypothesis tests require six steps: (i) frame the null and alternative hypotheses (for example, make the null hypothesis be that the mean income of Philadelphians is $83,000, and make the alternative be that the mean is not $83,000); (ii) choose a test statistic with which to summarize the sample data (for example, choose the mean income among a sample of 100 randomly selected Philadelphians); (iii) choose a probability of rejecting the null hypothesis when it is true (for example, choose 5%); (iv) determine a set of values for the test statistic that would lead us to reject the null hypothesis (for example, reject the null if the observed mean is further than $9,000 from $83,000); (v) determine the value of the test statistic in the sample at hand (for example, the sample mean income we observe is $72,000); and (vi) reject or fail to reject the null hypothesis, depending on whether or not the observed value of the test statistic falls in the chosen critical region (in the example, we would reject the null hypothesis because $72,000 differs from $83,000 by more than $9,000). This section discusses these six steps.

## Framing the Null and Alternative Hypotheses

The first step in testing hypotheses is to frame the null and alternative hypotheses. The **null hypothesis** is the specific hypothesis under which the data will be deemed unsurprising or surprising enough to warrant rejection. The **alternative hypothesis** is what would be true if the null hypothesis were not. The null hypothesis "the slope is zero" (commonly depicted by $H_0$: $\beta_1 = 0$) and the alternative hypothesis "the slope is not zero" (commonly depicted by $H_1$: $\beta_1 \neq 0$), and the null hypothesis "the intercept is 6" and the alternative hypothesis "the intercept is not 6" are two examples. If we are willing to rule out positive slopes from the outset, "the slope is zero" and "the slope is strictly negative" would also serve as null and alternative hypotheses.

We call the assumptions we rely on and don't question in a hypothesis test the test's **maintained hypothesis**. For example, if we rule out positive slopes from the outset, that assumption is a part of our maintained hypothesis. Similarly, if our test procedure relies on the disturbances in a DGP being normally distributed and uncorrelated, then those assumptions are part of our maintained hypothesis. The formal probability statements of a hypothesis test are grounded in the test's maintained hypothesis. The assumptions of a test's maintained hypothesis are drawn from the assumptions made in the DGP. Just as claims about the statistical properties of estimators depend on the validity of the DGP used to establish those claims, hypothesis tests depend on the validity of the test's maintained hypothesis. If the maintained hypothesis is wrong, the test results may be, too.

The term "null hypothesis" stems from early agricultural applications of hypothesis tests. The null hypothesis was often a claim that some particular agricultural treatment had no effect on crop yields, hence the name "null." However, the key feature of a null hypothesis is not that it pertains to some noneffect, but rather that the hypothesis is precise enough to enable us to make the exact probability statements needed to define the critical region for a test. Some null hypotheses are so narrowly defined that they facilitate probability assessments. For example, a null hypothesis that "mean SAT scores are the same for males and females," (for which the alternative is "mean SAT scores for males and females differ") implies that the difference in mean scores in the population is exactly zero. Other null hypotheses are more complex and complicate assessing probabilities. Particularly troublesome are null hypotheses that embrace a wide variety of circumstances. One such null hypothesis is "smoking either enhances health or has no effect" (for which the alternative is "smoking harms health"). What we would observe if smoking markedly enhances health differs greatly from what we would observe if smoking has no effect on health. With markedly varying patterns of observation associated with a single null hypothesis, it is difficult to determine whether potential critical regions incur the probability of Type I error required by the test's significance level. Later in this chapter, we further discuss such complicated null hypotheses.

When testing hypotheses, either the null hypothesis or the alternative hypothesis can be the focal point of interest. Choosing a focal point is not about asserting our prior beliefs; rather, it is about conveniently structuring the question we are asking in our research. Grossman and Chaloupka, on the one hand, place the focus of their analysis on their alternative hypothesis, that marijuana and cocaine are complements. These authors declare their null hypothesis to be that marijuana and cocaine are neither substitutes nor complements. When they reject this null hypothesis in favor of the alternative that the goods are complements, they consider the case for complementarity strongly made. On the other hand, Mankiw, Romer, and Weil make the null hypothesis their focal point when they test the simple Solow growth model. These authors declare as the null hypothesis an implication of the simple Solow model (that a particular slope is one third); it is the rejection of this null hypothesis (and thus the rejection of the simple Solow model) and not the alternative hypothesis, that absorbs their attention. Mankiw, Romer, and Weil also make the null hypothesis their focal point when they test their augmented Solow growth model. In this case, the authors declare as their null hypothesis an implication of their model—that three slopes in a regression sum to zero. Because they fail to reject this null hypothesis, they are encouraged about their augmented Solow model.

## Choosing a Test Statistic

The second step in testing hypotheses is choosing a test statistic. The intuition of hypothesis testing rests on rejecting null hypotheses that make data like that in hand very surprising. But how do we assess whether the data in hand are very surprising? Can we summarize all the observations in a single number and declare that value "surprising" if the null hypothesis were true? We can and we do. These are the numbers we call test statistics.

There is an infinite number of ways to combine sample data. We call each function whose arguments are the sample observations, $f(Y_1, \ldots, Y_n)$, a **sample statistic**. The design of good hypothesis tests rests on artfully selecting a useful statistic for the test. Linear estimators are sample statistics because they are functions of the observed data. Functions of several linear estimators are also sample statistics. The sum of squared residuals is another sample statistic. When econometricians use a sample statistic as the foundation for a hypothesis test, the statistic is called a test statistic. The most common test statistics in econometrics involve manipulating the estimators of coefficients and the residuals from regressions.

Historically, an important trait of useful test statistics was ease of looking up the probabilities associated with the statistics. Early econometricians avoided intuitively appealing test statistics if calculating the probabilities for those statistics would be too cumbersome. For example, to test the null hypothesis that the slope $\beta_s$ in our DGP is equal to a specific value, $\beta_s^*$, the estimated slope, $\hat{\beta}_s$ is a natural candidate as a test statistic. If $\hat{\beta}_s$ were sufficiently far (in some probabilistic sense) from $\beta_s^*$, we would reject the null hypothesis. Tables for the probability distribution of $\hat{\beta}_s$ are not generally available, though, and before the advent of computers, econometricians needed such tables for their work. The early econometricians did not use $\hat{\beta}_s$ as a test statistic. Instead, they worked with a transformation of $\hat{\beta}_s$ with a probability distribution that was readily accessible. Computers now look up probabilities for us, so convenience is less an issue today, but econometricians continue to rely heavily on the test statistics that were most convenient in the past.

## The *t*-Statistic

What transformation of $\hat{\beta}_s$ yields a convenient test statistic? Clues lie in what we know about the distribution of $\hat{\beta}_s$. The estimator $\hat{\beta}_s$ is normally distributed because it is a linear estimator, and all linear estimators are normally distributed in the DGP we are considering. The mean and variance of $\hat{\beta}_s$ are $\beta_s$ and $\sigma^2_{\hat{\beta}_s}$, respectively. To read probabilities for $\hat{\beta}_s$, given the null hypothesis directly from a table, we would need a probability table for the $N(\beta_s^*, \sigma^2_{\hat{\beta}_s})$ distribution, a daunting prospect because there would need to be a different table for each possible combination of $\beta_s^*$, and $\sigma^2_{\hat{\beta}_s}$. The lack of such tables made the estimated coefficient, $\hat{\beta}_s$, an inconvenient test statistic for early econometricians. But recognizing that $\hat{\beta}_s$ is distributed $N(\beta_s^*, \sigma^2_{\hat{\beta}_s})$, given the null hypothesis, leads to the transformation that the early econometricians used as a test statistic for hypotheses about $\hat{\beta}_s$.

Recall two properties of normally distributed random variables. Adding a constant to a normally distributed random variable results in another normally distributed random variable. So does multiplying a normally distributed random variable by a constant. The early econometricians exploited these rules to transform $\hat{\beta}_s$ into a standard normal distribution, with a mean of zero and a variance of one. The statistic

$$Z = \frac{\hat{\beta}_s - \beta_s^*}{\sigma_{\hat{\beta}_s}^2}$$

is distributed N(0, 1)if $\beta_s^*$, the value asserted under the null hypothesis, is the true value of $\beta_s$. $Z$ is not as obvious a test statistic as $\hat{\beta}_s$, but its probabilities are readily available in a standard normal table.

A practical problem with both $\hat{\beta}_s$ and $Z$ as test statistics is that we do not usually know $\sigma_{\hat{\beta}_s}^2$. Fortunately, we have an estimator for $\sigma_{\hat{\beta}_s}^2$, $s_{\hat{\beta}_s}$ the estimated standard error of $\hat{\beta}_s$ developed in Section 6.4. When we replace $\sigma_{\hat{\beta}_s}^2$ with $s_{\hat{\beta}_s}$ in the $Z$-statistic based on $\hat{\beta}_s$, we obtain a statistic that follows the $t$-distribution with $(n - k - 1)$ degrees of freedom, where $n$ is the number of observations in the sample and $(k + 1)$ is the number of explanators, including the intercept, in the regression model. We call any test statistic that follows the $t$-distribution a **t-statistic**. The statistic

$$t = \frac{\hat{\beta}_s - \beta_s^*}{s_{\hat{\beta}_s}} \sim t_{n-k-1},$$

if $\beta_s^*$, the value asserted under the null hypothesis, is the true value of $\beta_s$, so it is a $t$-statistic. There are tables that report probabilities associated with the $t$-distribution for various degrees of freedom.

The degrees of freedom of the t-statistic's distribution stem from the fact that $s_{\hat{\beta}_s}$ is based on the sum of squared residuals, which are not statistically independent; in essence, each estimated coefficient in the regression model "uses up" one observation, leaving $(n - k - 1)$ independent pieces of information from the sample for estimating $\sigma_{\hat{\beta}_s}^2$. The "$t$-distribution" is actually a family of distributions, with each family member identified by its number of degrees of freedom.

Notice that the $t$-statistic for the null hypothesis that $\beta_s = 0$ is the ratio of the estimated coefficient to its standard error. Econometric software packages always report this particular $t$-statistic for each coefficient. The packages can also compute the $t$-statistics associated with other specific hypotheses about a coefficient; you need only provide the hypothesized value of $\beta_s$, $\beta_s^*$.

Returning to our sample of New York renters, discussed in Chapters 2 through 6, we can now formally test the hypothesis that the rent–income relationship has a nonzero intercept term. This is the hypothesis that $\beta_0 = 0$. In Chapter 5 we found that $\hat{\beta}_0 = 5,455$ and its estimated standard error is 672. The $t$-statistic for the null hypothesis

$$H_0: \beta_0 = 0$$

is thus

$$t = (5{,}455 - 0)/673 = 9.01.$$

We estimate that $\hat{\beta}_0$ lies nine standard deviations from $\beta_0$'s hypothesized value of zero. Does a $t$-statistic this large lead us to reject the null hypothesis of no intercept term in the rent–income relationship? We soon learn that it does. It appears that, as we speculated in Chapter 5, New York renters' preferences for housing are not Cobb–Douglas.

The $t$-distribution applies exactly to the $t$-statistic if the underlying disturbances are normally distributed. If the underlying distribution is not normal, the $t$-statistic's distribution in small samples is not generally known, but in large samples (say, 100 or more observations), if the underlying disturbances are not normal, the $t$-statistic is likely to be approximately normally distributed. This approximation stems from the workings of the Central Limit Theorem.

## Choosing a Significance Level

The third step in testing hypotheses is choosing a significance level. Viewed from a rhetorical rather than a scientific standpoint, hypothesis testing is a clever approach to argument. Suppose my goal is to make you doubt some claim you have made, for example, "Smoking is harmless." I begin by yielding to you, which is surely a pleasant ploy. "Let us suppose you are right in your claim (the null hypothesis)," I say. "Is the observed difference in lung cancer rates between smokers and nonsmokers surprising to you? The difference (our test statistic) is large—surprisingly large. If you are right, we would expect to see so large a difference in lung cancer rates just less than once in 100 samples! We must be very unlucky to get so large a test statistic, if you are correct. But why should I suppose us so unlucky? I fear you are wrong after all. Wouldn't you agree?" If the observed test statistic is sufficiently surprising, then given your claim, I might well persuade you to reject your initial claim. How surprising is surprising enough? We call the level of sufficient surprise the significance level of the test. My ploy is effective only if the significance level is low. The data need to be quite surprising given the null hypothesis, if I am to successfully challenge your view in this way. Traditionally, analysts choose significance levels of 0.01, 0.05, or 0.10, with 0.05 the most common value.

Statisticians call the probability that the test statistic would take on a value even more extreme than what we observe the **P-value** of the test. *If the P-value of our observed test statistic is less than the significance level, we reject the null hypothesis.*

Apart from its rhetorical role in setting a level of sufficient surprise, the selection of a significance level fixes the probability that we will reject the null hypothesis, given it is true; that is, the significance level is the probability of a Type I error. If the significance level in the smoking example were 0.05, there would be a 5% chance that we would reject the null hypothesis that smoking is harmless, were the hypothesis true.

## Choosing a Critical Region

The fourth step in testing hypotheses is choosing the values of the test statistic that would lead us to reject the null hypothesis. With the probability of Type I error predetermined by the chosen significance level, our only remaining control over mistakes in designing a good test is over the probability of Type II error (the probability of failing to reject the null hypothesis when it is false). Our choice of a critical region determines the probability of Type II error. In principle, we choose the values of the critical region to make the probability of Type II error as small as possible. In practice, minimizing the probability of Type II error is usually infeasible because the best critical region for one specific version of the alternative hypothesis is different from that for another specific version, so we use rough rules of thumb to settle on a suitable critical region. Most commonly, we place the critical region either at both extremes of the test statistic's values or at just one extreme. When the critical region is at one extreme, we are conducting a **one-tailed test**; when the critical region is divided between the two extremes of the test statistic, we are conducting a **two-tailed test**.

John Dillinger said he robbed banks because that is where people put their money. Just as Dillinger's goal was to obtain money, our goal is to reject false null hypotheses. Just as he put his efforts into robbing the banks with the most money, we put our critical region where the alternative hypothesis has the most probability mass. We choose a critical region that we are relatively likely to observe if the alternative hypothesis is true, because then the probability of Type II error is relatively small—we're giving ourselves a better chance of the statistic's taking on a value in the critical region when the null hypothesis is false.

For example, consider Martin Feldstein's interest in college financial aid. Economic theory indicates that college financial aid decreases family saving. When Martin Feldstein tested the hypothesis of no effect of financial aid on family savings, he conducted a one-tailed test. He expected, in accord with economic theory, that if the null hypothesis were wrong, the data were much more likely to show a decline than an increase in family savings. The critical region for Feldstein's $t$-test contained only negative values. In contrast, in their classic economic growth paper, Mankiw, Romer, and Weil chose to conduct a two-tailed test of the simple Solow growth model. If the simple Solow model is correct, one slope, $\beta_s$, in Mankiw, Romer, and Weil's regression, is one third. If Solow's model is wrong, we have no idea what that coefficient is—it could be larger than one third or it could be smaller. Mankiw, Romer, and Weil's null hypothesis was $\beta_s = 1/3$. The alternative hypothesis was $\beta_s \neq 1/3$. They conducted a two-tailed test, choosing the critical region of their $t$-test to contain both positive and negative values. The negative values in their critical region were intended to reject the null hypothesis if $\beta_s$ were really less than one third (when the $t$-statistic is likely to be negative across samples) and the positive ones to reject the null hypothesis if $\beta_s$ were really greater than one third (when the $t$-statistic is likely to be positive across samples).

Panel (a) of Figure 7.1 shows the distribution of the $t$-statistic with 10 degrees of freedom and the critical region for a two-tailed test at the 0.05 significance level. The values of the statistic that separate the critical region from the rest of the distribution, $-2.28$ and $2.28$ in Panel (a), we call the **critical values** of the test. The two-tailed test divides the probability of Type I error into errors that could arise either from surprisingly large $t$-statistics or from surprisingly small $t$-statistics. Panel (b) also shows the distribution of the $t$-statistic with 10 degrees of freedom, but with the critical region for a one-tailed test when the alternative hypothesis is that $\beta_s < 0$. The critical value for the one-tailed test is 1.81. As the number of degrees of freedom grows large, the $t$-distribution approaches normal; the corresponding critical values for the two-tailed test approach 1.96 and $-1.96$, and the corresponding critical value for the one-tailed test approaches $-1.64$.

Our goal in choosing the critical region can be expressed in two equivalent ways: Either we are trying to make as large as possible the probability of rejecting the null hypothesis if it is false or we are trying to make the **probability of Type II error** small. We call the probability of rejecting the null hypothesis when it is false the **power of a test**. If a test has a high probability of rejecting the null hypothesis when that hypothesis is false, we say the test is "powerful" or "has high power." If a test has a low probability of rejecting the null hypothesis when that hypothesis is false, we say the test is "weak" or has "low power." Weak tests are not very useful, though they are better than no test. Failure to reject the null hypothesis

**Figure 7.1**

Critical Regions for Two-Tailed and One-Tailed $t$-Statistics with a 0.05 Significance Level and 10 Degrees of Freedom

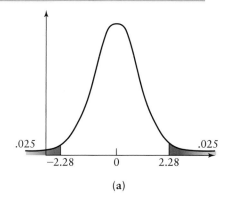

(a)

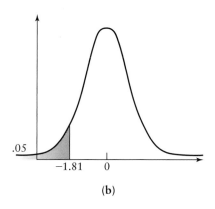

(b)

with a weak test tells us little about the null hypothesis. Unfortunately, we cannot always construct tests with high power.

## The Power of a Test

When the alternative hypothesis is complex, a test's power will vary with the actual alternative value that occurs. For example, in Barro's study of income convergence, the alternative hypothesis is complex: "The coefficient on 1960 income is negative." In this case, the $t$-test's power will vary with the actual negative value the slope takes on. The $t$-test may be quite powerful against alternatives with a very negative slope value—when poor countries catch up rapidly with the rich— but be relatively weak for negative slope values close to zero—when poor countries catch up extremely slowly. For another example, in an estimated wage equation, we might be unlikely to reject a false null hypothesis of no age discrimination in wages if the actual amount of discrimination is small, but be quite likely to reject that same false null hypothesis if the actual amount of discrimination is large. Figure 7.2 illustrates this point.

In Figure 7.2, the null hypothesis is that $\beta_s = 0$; the alternative is that $\beta_s < 0$. The standard error of the estimator is such that if the null hypothesis were true, we would reject the null hypothesis when the estimated $\beta_s$ is less than $-2$; that is, 5% of the estimates across samples will be less than $-2$, if $\beta_s = 0$. The rightmost bell curve in the figure is that for the estimator when $\beta_s = 0$. The leftmost bell curve is that for the estimator when $\beta_s = -2$; 50% of estimates will be less than $-2$, if $\beta_s = -2$. The power of the test against the alternative that $\beta_s = -2$ is 50%. The third bell curve corresponds to the distribution of the estimator when $\beta_s$ is a small negative number, close to zero. Barely more than 5% of the estimates will be less than $-2$ in this case. The power of this $t$-test is little

**Figure 7.2**

Distribution of $\hat{\beta}_s$ for $\beta_s = -2$, 0, and a Little Less Than 0

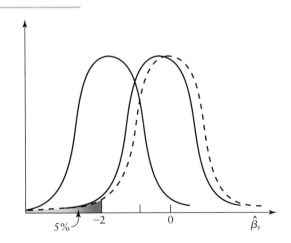

more than 5% against the alternative that $\beta_s$ is a small negative number close to zero. If the true alternative is that $\beta_s$ is very much less than $-2$, the power of the test is much greater than 50%. *It is generally the case that t-tests are relatively weak when the false null hypothesis is close to the true alternative, and that t-tests become relatively powerful when the false null hypothesis is far from the true alternative.*

Another way to envision the power of a test is to plot the probability of rejecting the null hypothesis against the actual value of the parameter. Figure 7.3 pictures twice the power of a two-tailed test of the hypothesis that $\beta_s = 0$ when the test is at the 0.05 significance level. Notice that in Figure 7.3 at $\beta_s = 0$ the probability of rejecting the null hypothesis is 0.05, which equals the significance level of the test. The flatter power curve corresponds to a test based on a less efficient estimator of $\beta_s$, the less flat power curve corresponds to a test based on a more efficient estimator of $\beta_s$. *More efficient estimators allow more powerful tests. The smaller the variance of our estimator, the more powerful our t-tests.*

## Critical Regions and Complex Null Hypotheses

Sometimes we want the null hypothesis to be more complex than "Smoking is harmless"; we want the null hypothesis to be "Smoking is harmless or beneficial," so that the alternative is "Smoking is harmful." The common practice in such cases is to simplify the null hypothesis to the case that makes the null hypothesis hardest to reject, and to ignore the remaining cases in the null hypothesis. The rhetorical interpretation of hypothesis testing rationalizes this practice. Rhetorically, I want rejection of the null to be compelling. Higher lung cancer rates for smokers than for nonsmokers would be even more surprising if smoking

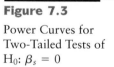

**Figure 7.3**

Power Curves for
Two-Tailed Tests of
$H_0: \beta_s = 0$

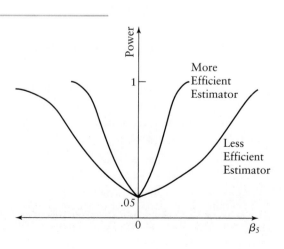

were beneficial to health than if smoking were just harmless. If you will be persuaded by my rejection of the null hypothesis when the null hypothesis is that smoking is harmless, you will also be persuaded if the null hypothesis were instead that smoking confers health benefits. This rhetorical strategy in designing tests leads to one-tailed tests with stated significance levels that are correct for the hardest to reject form of the null hypothesis (smoking is harmless), but too high for the other versions of the null hypothesis (smoking is beneficial).

One-tailed $t$-tests thus arise in two ways. First, they arise when we can preclude some values of $\beta_s$ from the outset (as in Feldstein's study of college financial aid, in which economic theory precluded the possibility that "college financial aid increases family savings"). In assessing several of the hypotheses in Table 7.1, the econometricians could plausibly rule out a subset of outcomes. For example, econometricians might be willing to presume that raising the probability that murderers receive the death penalty does not increase the murder rate, which would imply that the coefficient on the execution probability in Ehrlich's model is not positive. The realistic options are that the coefficient here is zero (the null hypothesis) or negative (the alternative hypothesis). Second, one-tailed $t$-tests arise when the rhetorical interest is in credibly establishing a one-sided alternative (such as "smoking is harmful"). For rejections of the null hypothesis to be convincing, the hardest to reject version of the null hypothesis is tested ("smoking is harmless").

Understanding how complex null hypotheses can lead to one-sided tests completes the conceptual underpinnings of hypothesis testing. We have now learned about (i) the formulation of simple and complex null hypotheses, along with their accompanying alternative hypotheses; (ii) the need for test statistics to summarize the data at hand; (iii) the standard choice of a low probability of Type I error, that is, a low significance level, for tests; and (iv) the relationship between a test's chosen critical region and its power. What remains are the mechanical steps of computing a specific test statistic and drawing a conclusion from that statistic.

## Computing the Test Statistic and Drawing a Conclusion

The fifth step in testing hypotheses is computing the chosen test statistic. The sixth step is to reject or fail to reject the null based on the value of the test statistic. The hypotheses in Table 7.1 require tests about the value of a single coefficient, making the $t$-statistic

$$t = \frac{\hat{\beta}_s - \beta_s^*}{s_{\hat{\beta}_s}} \sim t_{(n-k-1)},$$

where $\beta_s^*$ is the hypothesized value of $\beta_s$, appropriate for testing those hypotheses. The appropriate value for $s_{\hat{\beta}_s}$ varies from application to application. Because we have explicit formulae for $\beta_{g4}$, $\hat{\beta}_1$, and $\hat{\beta}_0$, and for their estimated standard errors, we can devise standard algebraic formulae for their $t$-statistics. In multiple regression models, however, we need to rely on the computer's calculations or on matrix algebra to provide us with estimated standard errors.

The $t$-statistic for $\beta_{g4}$ when the null hypothesis is $H_0$: $\beta = \beta^*$ is

$$t = \frac{\beta_{g4} - \beta^*}{\sqrt{s^2/\left(\sum X_i^2\right)}} \sim t_{n-1},$$

where $s^2$ is the sum of squared residuals from that regression, divided by $(n - 1)$. This $t$-statistic has $(n - 1)$ degrees of freedom.

The $t$-statistic for $\hat{\beta}_1$ when the null hypothesis is $H_0$: $\beta_1 = \beta_1^*$ is

$$t = \frac{\hat{\beta}_1 - B_1^*}{\sqrt{s^2/\left(\sum x_i^2\right)}} \sim t_{n-2},$$

where $s^2$ is the sum of squared residuals from that regression, divided by $(n - 2)$. This $t$-statistic has $(n - 2)$ degrees of freedom. The $t$-statistic for $\hat{\beta}_0$ when the null hypothesis is $H_0$: $\beta_0 = \beta_0^*$ is

$$t = \frac{\hat{\beta}_0 - \beta_0^*}{\sqrt{[(s^2 \sum X_i^2/(n\sum x_i^2)]}} \sim t_{n-2},$$

where $s^2$ is the sum of squared residuals from that regression, divided by $(n - 2)$. This $t$-statistic has $(n - 2)$ degrees of freedom. In general, we rely on econometric software programs to compute the appropriate value for $s_{\hat{\beta}_s}$ in each application.

Table 7.2 presents the hypotheses of Table 7.1 and the pertinent $t$-statistics reported in the original studies. Four of the five reported $t$-statistics are larger in magnitude than the reported critical values for the tests, leading us to reject these eight hypotheses and to fail to reject the remaining two. When we reject a null hypothesis that a regression coefficient, $\beta_s$, is different from some value, $\beta_s^*$, we say that $\beta_s$ is **statistically significantly different from** $\beta_s^*$. If $\beta_s$ is statistically significantly different from zero, we say $\beta_s$ is **statistically significant**.

Let's apply these new expressions to some of the results in Table 7.2. The hypothesis we fail to reject is that the coefficient on savings in Feldstein and Horioka's cross-country investment equation equals one. The savings coefficient is not statistically significantly different from one. In contrast, the relevant coefficient in the simple Solow regression estimated by Mankiw, Romer, and Weil differs significantly from 0.33 because we reject the null hypothesis that the coefficient equals 0.33.

**TABLE 7.2** Six Illustrative *t*-Tests

(All null hypotheses are $\beta = \beta^0$. $\beta^0 = 0$ unless otherwise noted)

| | $n$ | Est. coef. | Est. s.e. | *t*-stat | $\alpha = 0.05$ Crit. *t* |
|---|---|---|---|---|---|
| **One-Tailed Tests in Which Rejection Would Support "Yes" and H$_1$: $\boldsymbol{\beta > \beta^0}$** | | | | | |
| Does college financial aid reduce family savings? (Feldstein, p. 10) | 161 | −1.41* | 0.60 | −2.35 | −1.65 |
| **Two-Tailed Tests in Which Rejection Would Support "No"** | | | | | |
| Is unemployment unrelated to inflation? (Phillips, p. 121) | 12 | −0.55 | 0.19 | −2.91 | 2.23 |
| Are cross-country differences in per capita income consonant with the simple Solow model of growth? (H$_0$: $\beta = 0.5$) (Mankiew, Romer, and Weil, p. 232) | 98 | 1.48 | 0.12 | 8.17 | 1.99 |
| **One-Tailed Tests in Which Rejection Would Support "No" and H$_1$: $\boldsymbol{\beta > \beta^0}$** | | | | | |
| Are international capital markets immobile? (H$_0$: $\beta = 1$) (Feldstein and Horioka, p. 189) | 16 | 0.94 | 0.091 | −0.68 | 1.75 |
| **One-Tailed Tests in Which Rejection Would Support "Yes" and H$_1$: $\boldsymbol{\beta > \beta^0}$** | | | | | |
| Are marijuana and cocaine complements? (Grossman and Chaloupka, p. 219) | 38,855 | .008* | 0.0035 | *2.29 | 1.64 |

*This hit did not use OLS. The estimator was approximately normally distributed.

## A Caveat About Maintained Hypotheses

The probability statements used in hypothesis tests depend critically on the DGP. If we incorrectly specify the DGP, we are likely to compute incorrect probabilities. The assumptions about the DGP that we make and use, but do not test, make up the maintained hypothesis for the test. Many, perhaps most, substantive debates about econometric test results are about what the appropriate DGP really is. It is therefore important to repeat the point made earlier: *If our maintained hypothesis is wrong, our hypothesis tests may well be faulty.*

## Tests Undermined

Under the Gauss–Markov Assumptions, the *t*-tests described in this chapter work as advertised, with significance levels and power that can be determined by applying the *t*-distribution to the proffered *t*-statistics. If the underlying disturbances are normally distributed, the tests hold exactly; otherwise, the tests apply well approximately in large samples. When the Gauss–Markov Assumptions are violated, however, the suggested *t*-tests can go awry in any of four ways.

Recall that the significance level, or the size, of a test is the probability that the test procedure would reject the null hypothesis if the hypothesis were true and that the power of a test is the probability that the test procedure would reject the null hypothesis if the hypothesis were false. Each of the four ways a test procedure can go awry relates to the power or significance level of the test. First, a test may be a *weak test*. A **weak test** is one that is unlikely to reject some or all alternatives of interest; tests based on inefficient estimators tend to be weaker than those based on efficient estimators. Second, a test may be a *biased test*. A **biased test** is one that is more likely to reject the null hypothesis when it is true than when it is false, at least for some alternatives—that is, the significance level of the test is higher than the power of the test for some alternative. Notice this is a different meaning of biased than in "biased estimator," but the two are linked—biased estimators often give rise to biased tests. Third, a test may be an *inconsistent test*. An **inconsistent test** is a test with a power that does not approach 1.0 against every alternative for a given significance level; that is, even with an infinite amount of data we cannot be certain of rejecting the null when it is false. Fourth, a test's distribution may diverge from what we assume, leading to stated significance levels that are false. We call any difference between the actual significance level of a test and the stated significance level a **size distortion**.

In sum, statistical tests can go awry as follows:

1. A test can be weak; that is, a test's power can be small.
2. A test can be biased; that is, a test's power can exceed its significance level for some alternatives.
3. A test can be inconsistent; that is, a test's power can fail to approach 1.0 for a given significance level as the sample size grows without bound.
4. A test's size can be distorted; that is, a test's stated significance level can be incorrect.

## 7.3    Degrees of Freedom Revisited

Econometricians frequently rely on sums of squared residuals when forming test statistics. For example, the $t$-statistic defined in Section 7.2 has $s^2$ in its denominator to estimate $\sigma^2$, where

$$s^2 = \frac{\sum(Y_i - \hat{\beta}_0 - \hat{\beta}_1 X_{1i} - \cdots - \hat{\beta}_k X_{ki})^2}{n - k - 1}.$$

When the residuals are normally distributed, the sum of squared residuals divided by $\sigma^2$,

$$\sum e_i^2 / \sigma^2 = \sum_{i=1}^{n}\left(Y_i - \hat{\beta}_0 - \hat{\beta}_1 X_i\right)^2 / \sigma^2,$$

is a sum of squared standard ($N(0, 1)$) normals. Sums of squared standard normals make up a probability distribution family called chi-square distributions, which are reviewed in the Statistical Appendix at the end of this book. Members of the chi-square family are differentiated from one another by the number of independent squared normals in their sums. Statisticians call the number of independent squared normals in a sum of squared normals the sum's **degrees of freedom**. Test statistics that involve one or more sums of squared standard normals are also differentiated by the numbers of degrees of freedom in those sums.

Recall that we use

$$s^2 = \frac{\sum(Y_i - \hat{\beta}_0 - \hat{\beta}_1 X_{1i} - \cdots - \hat{\beta}_k X_{ki})^2}{n - k - 1}$$

to estimate $\sigma^2$, because the mean squared disturbance in our sample,

$$\hat{\sigma}^2 = \frac{\sum(Y_i - \beta_0 - \beta_1 X_{1i} - \cdots - \beta_k X_{ki})^2}{n},$$

is unavailable (the slopes and intercept are unknown). The numerator of $\hat{\sigma}^2$ is a sum of $n$ squared independent mean zero normals. But because the estimated slopes and intercepts in the numerator of $s^2$ depend on all of the observed $Y$-values, the elements of that sum are not independent. The numerator of $s^2$ contains only $(n - k - 1)$ independent elements. As a consequence, the $t$-statistic defined in Section 7.2 has $(n - k - 1)$ degrees of freedom.

Why are there only $(n - k - 1)$ independent elements? We learned in Chapter 3 that the ordinary least squares (OLS) residuals (the $e_i$) from fitting a line through the origin satisfy

$$\sum X_i e_i = 0.$$

We learned in Chapter 5 that the OLS residuals from fitting a line with an unknown slope and intercept satisfy

$$\sum X_i e_i = 0$$

and

$$\sum e_i = 0.$$

And we learned in Chapter 6 that the OLS residuals from fitting a multiple regression model satisfy

$$\sum_{i=1}^{n} X_{ji} e_i = 0 \qquad for \; j = 0, 1, \ldots, k.$$

Thus, the residuals in the model without an intercept are constructed subject to a single constraint: The sum of the residuals times the $X$'s equals zero. If we know $(n - 1)$ residuals, we can compute the remaining one from the constraint. The residuals in the model with an unknown intercept and slope are constructed subject to two constraints. If we know $(n - 2)$ residuals, we can compute the other two from those constraints. The residuals in the multiple regression model satisfy $(k + 1)$ constraints. If we know $(n - k - 1)$ residuals, we can compute the remaining $(k + 1)$ residuals from those constraints. From this difference in constraints stems the difference in the degrees of freedom of the $t$-statistic for models with differing numbers of observations and explanators.

We build the estimator of $\sigma^2$ from a sum of $n$ squared residuals, residuals that are not independent of one another. In the multiple regression model, there are only $(n - k - 1)$ independent pieces of information contained in the residuals; in the model with an unknown slope and intercept, there are only $(n - 2)$ such pieces; and in the model without an intercept, there are $(n - 1)$. The number of such independent pieces of information in the denominator of a $t$-statistic is the degrees of freedom of the statistic. In more formal language, the sum of squared residuals is a sum of $(n - k - 1)$ independent squared mean zero normal random variables, which implies that the sum of squared residuals divided by $\sigma^2$ is distributed chi-square with $(n - k - 1)$ degrees of freedom.

# An Econometric Top 40—A Classical Favorite

## The Capital Asset Model Revisited

Financial analysis was transformed in the 1960s when John Lintner and William F. Sharpe independently proposed the model we know today as the Capital Asset Pricing Model (CAPM). This model, elegant in its simplicity, gave students of financial markets a convenient tool for assessing the performance of asset prices. In the discussion of the CAPM Classic Hit in Chapter 3, we learned that per the CAPM, when markets are in equilibrium, the riskiness of an asset relative to the riskiness of the entire asset market would be equal to the slope, $\beta$, in the relationship

(asset's excess return above the riskless rate)=
$\quad \beta$(excess return of a "market portfolio"
$\qquad$ above the riskless rate) $+ u$,

where a "market portfolio" is a portfolio containing every asset in the marketplace in proportion to its total value, and $u$ is a mean zero, serially uncorrelated, homoskedastic disturbance term. The coefficient $\beta$ in this model, called by many the asset's "beta," measures the marginal contribution of the asset to a market portfolio's undiversifiable risk. If beta were 0.5, then when the market excess return rises by 10%, this asset's excess return would rise by 5%. Many financial analysts have long paid much attention to assets' betas.

In the years following the CAPM's introduction, several economists questioned whether the relationship between an asset's excess return and the excess return of a market portfolio is a straight line with no intercept. In 1972, economists Fischer Black of the University of Chicago, Michael C. Jensen of the University of Rochester, and Myron Scholes of the Massachusetts Institute of Technology explained why

earlier tests of whether the intercept is truly zero, based on cross-sectional data, were faulty. They proposed an alternative test of the hypothesis based on a regression of the form

$$R_{At} = \beta_0 + \beta_1 R_{Mt} + \varepsilon_t \qquad t = 1, \ldots, T$$

where $R_{At}$ is the asset's excess return over the riskless rate, $R_{Mt}$ is the excess return of a market portfolio over the riskless rate, the subscript $t$ is the time period an observation is drawn from, $T$ is the total number of time series observations on the asset, and $\varepsilon_t$ is a random disturbance. Black, Jensen, and Scholes rejected the null hypothesis that $\beta_0 = 0$ and concluded that the CAPM was a faulty model because it precludes the nonzero intercept that they observed empirically.

Black, Jensen, and Scholes next ask how the CAPM goes astray. One possible difficulty the authors note was that the CAPM assumes investors can always borrow or lend some risk-free asset. Relaxing this assumption, the authors arrive at an alternative model that, like the CAPM model, implies a linear relationship between an asset's excess return and the excess return of a market portfolio. But, unlike the CAPM model, the alternative model also implies a linear relationship with a nonzero intercept term. Black, Jensen, and Scholes name their model "a two-factor model" because the theory looked not to one, but two, excess returns to explain equilibrium asset prices. The work of Black, Jensen, and Scholes spawned a cottage industry of financial models, each with more factors than the one before it.

The CAPM model and the two-factor model describe the asset pricing for a single stock. There are many stocks in the market. Which asset, then, should we use to test the CAPM? Presumably, we should look at many assets and garner information from them all. Black, Jensen, and Scholes address this question and note that combining the information from numerous stocks requires particular care because the disturbances for some stocks are correlated in any one time period (good years for some often mean good years for many; bad years for some often mean bad years for many), contrary to the Gauss–Markov Assumptions. The authors propose a clever estimation procedure that allows them to use information from all the stocks in their sample without being misled by the correlations among observations across stocks.

 **Final Notes**

Like many of the Regression's Greatest Hits, the Black, Jensen, and Scholes paper illustrates the interplay between theory and empirical work in econometrics. The CAPM theory guides the initial specification of the model for testing. When the authors find the CAPM wanting, they seek a theory consonant with the data in hand. Such back and forth shifting between new theories, new empirical analyses, and still newer theories, is how economic understanding advances. The paper also illustrates the care that must be taken in specifying our maintained hypotheses correctly. The DGP that aptly describes each stock individually proved faulty when looking across stocks. Finally, the tale of Black, Jensen, and Scholes should hearten us that reasonable estimation and testing strategies are available when we stray from the Gauss–Markov Assumptions. ∎

## 7.4     An Application: The Capital Asset Pricing Model Revisited

Table 7.2 presents numerous tests about the slopes of lines. Sometimes, though, it is not the slopes in a regression analysis, but rather the intercept term, that is telling about a theory. Here we test the null hypothesis that an intercept term is zero in the classic Capital Asset Pricing Model (CAPM) discussed in Chapter 3 and in the previous section's Regression's Greatest Hits.

The CAPM implies that when markets are in equilibrium, the riskiness of an asset relative to the riskiness of the entire asset market would be equal to the slope, $\beta$, in the relationship

*(asset's excess return above the riskless rate) =*

$\beta$ *(excess return of a "market portfolio" above the riskless rate) + u,*

where a "market portfolio" is a portfolio containing every asset in the marketplace in proportion to its total value, and *u* is a disturbance term that satisfies the

**TABLE 7.3** *t*-Tests of the Capital Asset Pricing Model

| Firm | Estimated Intercept | Std. Error | *t*-Statistic | Prob. |
|------|---------------------|------------|---------------|-------|
| AMD | −0.004337 | 0.011815 | −0.367084 | 0.7140 |
| Intel | 0.010561 | 0.007520 | 1.404376 | 0.1618 |
| Boise-Cascade | −0.006868 | 0.005302 | −1.295336 | 0.1968 |
| Weyerhaeuser | −0.003961 | 0.004534 | −0.873636 | 0.3834 |
| Delta Airlines | −0.004094 | 0.005266 | −0.777420 | 0.4379 |
| US Air | −0.004462 | 0.009553 | −0.467046 | 0.6410 |

Gauss–Markov Assumptions. This relationship is a straight line through the origin. In a previous Classic Hit, on p. 286, Black, Jensen, and Scholes devised an alternative theory, called the two-factor model, that implies there should be an intercept term where the CAPM says there is none.

The data set CAPM.***, which you can access at **www.aw-bc.com/murray**, contains monthly observations for 16 years on the excess returns for eight stocks on the U.S. Stock Exchange (two from each of four industries) and for a market portfolio. (This file is too large for the student version of EViews; it can be used with other versions of EViews.) Table 7.3 contains the estimated intercepts for six of these stocks from regressions of a stock's excess returns on the market excess return. The table also reports the estimated standard errors and *t*-statistics. For example, for AMD, the first firm in the table, the information from the regression output includes the estimated intercept, −0.004337; its estimated standard error, 0.011815; and its *t*-statistic for the null hypothesis that $\beta = 0$, −0.367084, which derives from

$$t = \frac{-0.004377}{0.011815} = -0.367084.$$

Each of the other *t*-statistics is similarly computed.

Table 7.3 also reports, in the column labeled "Prob.", P-values for each estimate. Econometric software packages usually report as the P-value for *t*-statistics the probability that the *t*-statistic is larger *in magnitude* than the observed value, given the null is true. This is the P-value appropriate for a two-tailed test. If the reported P-value is less than the chosen significance level of a two–tailed test, we reject the null hypothesis. For a one-tailed *t*-test, it would be necessary to divide the reported P-value by two. None of the five *t*-statistics in Table 7.3 are statistically significant at any conventional significance level (0.01, 0.05, or 0.10). For these firms, the data do not lead us to reject the CAPM model in favor of the two-factor model of Black, Jensen, and Scholes.

## 7.5 Tests About a Linear Combination of Coefficients

**HOW DO WE TEST HYPOTHESES?**

The $t$-tests we have discussed so far focus on a single coefficient, testing whether that coefficient takes on a specific value. Econometricians are often interested not just in one particular coefficient, but in a relationship among the coefficients. We need procedures to test hypotheses about such relationships. For example, we saw in Chapter 5 that the constant returns to scale Cobb–Douglas production function, in logarithmic form, is

$$\ln(Q) = \beta_0 + \beta_1 \ln(L) + (1 - \beta_1)\ln(K).$$

The requirement that the coefficients on labor and capital sum to one reflects a common assumption that there are constant returns to scale (doubling inputs doubles output). Is this assumption warranted? If we freed up the coefficient on capital and called it $\beta_2$, how do we test the null hypothesis that $\beta_1 + \beta_2 = 1$?

For another example, Mankiw, Romer, and Weil, in their Classic Hit discussed in Chapter 6, develop an augmented Solow growth model that includes human capital. According to that model, the equilibrium level of per capita GDP is

$$\ln(Q/L) = \alpha_0 - \frac{\beta_2 + \beta_3}{1 - \beta_2 - \beta_3}\ln(n + g + d)$$

$$+ \frac{\beta_2}{1 - \beta_2 - \beta_3}\ln(s_h) + \frac{\beta_3}{1 - \beta_2 - \beta_3}\ln(s_p) + \varepsilon,$$

in which $\beta_2$ is human capital's income share, $\beta_3$ is physical capital's income share, $s_h$ is the saving rate for investment in human capital, $s_p$ is the saving rate for investment in physical capital, $n$ is the population growth rate in the country, $g$ is the worldwide rate of technological advance, and $d$ is the depreciation of capital. Note from the equation that the theory implies that the coefficients of the three explanators sum to zero. If we name these three coefficients $\alpha_1$, $\alpha_2$, and $\alpha_3$, so that,

$$\alpha_1 = -\frac{\beta_2 + \beta_3}{1 - \beta_2 - \beta_3},$$

$$\alpha_2 = \frac{\beta_2}{1 - \beta_2 - \beta_3},$$

and

$$\alpha_3 = \frac{\beta_3}{1 - \beta_2 - \beta_3},$$

how do we test the null hypothesis that

$$\alpha_1 + \alpha_2 + \alpha_3 = 0?$$

This section develops tests for such hypothesis about linear combinations of coefficients.

## Another *t*-Statistic

The intuition for selecting a test statistic for a null hypothesis about a linear combination of coefficients ($\sum_{j=0}^{k} c_j \beta_j = \nu^*$) is that if the null were true, it would be surprising to see the same linear combination of the estimated coefficients much different than the hypothesized value. (In the sum, $c_j$ can be zero for some values of $j$—not all coefficients need be included in the linear combination.) That is, $\sum_{j=0}^{k} c_j \hat{\beta}_j$ should not be very far from the hypothesized value, $\nu^*$. As in the case of a single coefficient, it is convenient to transform the weighted sum of coefficients into a *t*-statistic with $(n - k - 1)$ degrees of freedom:

$$t = \frac{\left( \sum_{j=0}^{k} c_j \hat{\beta}_j \right) - \nu^*}{\left( est.\ stnd.\ error\ of\ \sum_{j=0}^{k} c_j \hat{\beta}_j \right)} \sim t_{n-k-1},$$

where the estimated standard error of $\sum_{j=0}^{k} c_j \hat{\beta}_j$ is

$$\sqrt{s^2 \left( \sum_{j=0}^{k} c_j^2 \text{var}(\hat{\beta}_j) + \sum_{j=0}^{k} \sum_{\substack{l=0 \\ l \neq j}}^{k} c_j c_l \text{cov}(\hat{\beta}_j, \hat{\beta}_l) \right)}.$$

The numerator in this expression is normally distributed in our DGP, because a linear combination of normally distributed random variables is normally distributed. The variance of the numerator is the variance of a linear combination of our estimated coefficients, and so depends on the variances and covariances of the estimated coefficients. Because we don't know $\sigma^2$, the variance of the disturbances, we need to use $s^2$ to estimate the standard error of the numerator.

The *t*-distribution applies exactly to the *t*-statistic just discussed if the underlying disturbances are normally distributed. If the underlying distribution is not normal, the *t*-statistic's distribution in small samples is not generally known. In large samples (say 100 or more observations), however, even if the underlying disturbances are not normal, the *t*-statistic is very often approximately normally distributed.

## Two Examples of Testing for a Relationship Among Regression Coefficients

Are the returns to scale in the Cobb–Douglas production function constant, as Cobb and Douglas supposed? Testing Cobb and Douglas's assumption is our first example of testing a hypothesis about a relationship among regression coefficients. The data, which appear in cobbdouglas.***, a data set available at **www.aw-bc.com/murray**, are the original Cobb and Douglas data that we first used in Chapter 5. Table 7.4 reports regression results from regressing the log of output on an intercept term and the logs of labor and capital:

$$\ln(Q) = \beta_0 + \beta_1 \ln(L) + \beta_2 \ln(K) + u.$$

The table also reports the estimated variances and covariances of the estimated coefficients from that regression. Econometric software packages allow users to ask for the estimated variances and covariances of the coefficients.

Returns to scale are constant in the Cobb–Douglas production function if

$$\beta_1 + \beta_2 = 1.$$

**TABLE 7.4**  A Cobb–Douglas Production Function with Possibly Non-Constant Returns to Scale

Dependent Variable: LOG(OUTPUT)
Sample: 1899 1922

| Variable | Coefficient | Std. Error | *t*-Statistic | Prob. |
|---|---|---|---|---|
| C | −0.177310 | 0.434293 | −0.408272 | 0.6872 |
| LOG(LABOR) | 0.807278 | 0.145076 | 5.564513 | 0.0000 |
| LOG(CAPITAL) | 0.233053 | 0.063530 | 3.668415 | 0.0014 |
| R-squared | 0.957425 | Mean dependent var  5.077336 | | |
| S.E. of regression | 0.058138 | | | |

### Estimated Variances and Covariances

| | C | LOG(LABOR) | LOG(CAPITAL) |
|---|---|---|---|
| C | 0.188610 | −0.059547 | 0.019984 |
| LOG(LABOR) | −0.059547 | 0.021047 | −0.008383 |
| LOG(CAPITAL) | 0.019984 | −0.008383 | 0.004036 |

To test this hypothesis, we need the estimated standard error of $\hat{\beta}_1 + \hat{\beta}_2$. Applying the algebra of variances to $\text{var}(\hat{\beta}_1 + \hat{\beta}_2)$ we find

$$\text{var}(\hat{\beta}_1 + \hat{\beta}_2) = \text{var}(\hat{\beta}_1) + \text{var}(\hat{\beta}_2) + 2\text{cov}(\hat{\beta}_1, \hat{\beta}_2),$$

which, using the numbers from Table 7.4, implies that

$$\text{var}(\hat{\beta}_1 + \hat{\beta}_2) = 0.021047 + 0.004036 + 2(-0.008383) = 0.008317.$$

The square root of this variance, 0.091198, is the estimated standard error of $\hat{\beta}_1 + \hat{\beta}_2$. To test the null that $\hat{\beta}_1 + \hat{\beta}_2 = 1$, the test statistic is thus

$$t = \frac{\hat{\beta}_1 + \hat{\beta}_2 - 1}{s_{\hat{\beta}_1 + \hat{\beta}_2}} = \frac{0.807278 + 0.233053 - 1}{0.091198} = 0.4421.$$

A $t$-table indicates that the critical values for a two-tailed $t$-test with 21 degrees of freedom and a significance level of 0.05 are $\pm 2.08$. The P-value of the observed $t$-statistic is 0.6628. We fail to reject the null hypothesis of constant returns to scale. The data Cobb and Douglas used was not at odds with their assumption of constant returns to scale.

Econometricians generally rely on their econometric software programs, rather than on hand calculations, to compute the statistics necessary for such hypothesis tests as these. In Mankiw, Romer, and Weil's study, for example, the authors report a P-value of 0.41 for the test of their hypothesis that $\alpha_1 + \alpha_2 + \alpha_3 = 0$ in their augmented Solow model.[2] That P-value corresponds to a $t$-value of plus or minus 0.84 because 0.84 is the value of a $t$-statistic with 98 degrees of freedom, beyond which lies 20.5 of the $t$-distribution's probability mass. The reported P-value leads us to fail to reject the implications of Mankiw, Romer, and Weil's augmented Solow model. Given that the authors had prior reasons for liking their model, their test left their enthusiasm intact. As noted earlier, other economists jumped on the Mankiw, Romer, and Weil bandwagon largely because of the model's high $R^2$. However, had the model failed this test of the relationship among $\alpha_1$, $\alpha_2$, and $\alpha_3$, and had it indicated instead that $\alpha_1 + \alpha_2 + \alpha_3 \neq 0$, the high $R^2$ would likely not have drawn the adherents it did.

## A Special Case: The Expected Value of Y Given X

Economists sometimes make claims about the expected value of $Y$ given particular values of explanators. For example, in his study of college financial aid, Martin Feldstein estimates an equation whose dependent variable is family assets and whose explanators are the household head's age, $X_1$, family income, $X_2$, and the financial aid tax rate faced by the family. The tax rate depends on income, number of kids, $X_3$, and proximity in age of kids, $X_4$. We might wish to test a claim

# An Econometric Top 40—A Classical Favorite

## A Deeper Look at Discrimination

In his classic book on earnings equations, economist Jacob Mincer argued that much of the variation in earnings could be explained by variation in education. Later economists used his methods to explore the extent to which other factors contribute to income inequality. In 1973, economist Ron Oaxaca of the University of Arizona studied the wage gap between white women and white men, and economist Alan Blinder of Princeton University studied the wage gap between black men and white men.[3]

Average wage rates of men and women, or of blacks and whites, may differ for either of two reasons. First, men and women (or blacks and whites) may differ in the attributes they bring to the labor market. For example, women have traditionally had less work experience than men, and blacks once had substantially less education than whites. Second, men and women (or blacks and whites) may be rewarded differently for the same attributes. Oaxaca and Blinder independently devised a method for measuring these two different contributions to wage gaps. Their methods have subsequently been called "Oaxaca/Blinder decompositions."

If two groups are rewarded differently for the same traits, as Oaxaca and Blinder suspected in their studies, the slope coefficients in a wage equation will be different for the two groups, so we should not estimate a single wage equation for both groups together. Both Blinder and Oaxaca started their studies by testing the hypothesis that the two groups under study had the same slope coefficients, but perhaps different intercepts. Both economists rejected the null of shared slope coefficients. Wage differences could, indeed, stem from either different traits or different rewards for the same traits. How, then, can we estimate both

sources of wage differences? How do we perform the Oaxaca/Blinder decompositions?

The Oaxaca/Blinder decompositions are based on separately estimated wage functions for each group under study. Consider Oaxaca's study of white men's and white women's wages. In addition to the education and experience variables called for by Mincer, Oaxaca allowed wage rates to vary with an individual's occupation, industry, sector, part-time or full-time status, marital status, health status, distance to work, size of urban area, and region. Oaxaca used his regressions to answer two questions.

First, how would women's and men's expected wages differ if they each had the mean traits for their group and were paid according to the men's estimated wage equation? This addresses the first reason for wage differences: Some of the difference in men and women's earnings may be attributable to differences in their traits. This difference, $\Delta_T$, is

$$\Delta_T = \sum_{j=0}^{k} \hat{\beta}_j^M \left( \overline{X}_j^W - \overline{X}_j^M \right).$$

(Alternatively, we could use the estimated women's wage equation coefficients.) Notice that the sum is over the $(k + 1)$ explanators, including the intercept term. If, on balance, women have less marketable traits than men, $\Delta_T$ is negative. Testing the hypothesis that $\Delta_T = 0$ calls for a $t$-test about a linear combination of regression coefficients.

Second, how would a woman's wage differ if she had the traits of an average woman but in one instance was paid according to the men's estimated wage equation, and in another instance was paid according to the women's estimated wage equation? This question addresses the second reason for wage differences: Women may earn less than men, in part, because they get a lower return than men for the same traits. This difference, $\Delta_R$, is

$$\Delta_R = \sum_{j=0}^{k} \left(\hat{\beta}_j^W - \hat{\beta}_j^M\right)\overline{X}_j^W.$$

(We could alternatively do this for men.) If, on balance, women receive less of a return than men for the same marketable traits, $\Delta_R$ is negative. Testing the hypothesis that $\Delta_R = 0$ calls for a *t*-test about a linear combination of regression coefficients.

The sum of these measures of the two sources of wage differences is the average difference between men's and women's wages in the sample at hand. To see this character of the sum, consider that

$$\Delta_T + \Delta_R = \sum_{j=0}^{k} \hat{\beta}_j^M \left(\overline{X}_j^W - \overline{X}_j^M\right)$$

$$+ \sum_{j=0}^{k} \left(\hat{\beta}_j^W - \hat{\beta}_j^M\right)\overline{X}_j^W$$

$$= \sum_{j=0}^{k} \hat{\beta}_j^M \overline{X}_j^W - \sum_{j=0}^{k} \hat{\beta}_j^M \overline{X}_j^M$$

$$+ \sum_{j=0}^{k} \hat{\beta}_j^W \overline{X}_j^W - \sum_{j=0}^{k} \hat{\beta}_j^M \overline{X}_j^W.$$

The first and last terms in the preceding expression cancel one another, leaving

$$\Delta_T + \Delta_R = -\sum_{j=0}^{k} \hat{\beta}_j^M \overline{X}_j^M + \sum_{j=0}^{k} \hat{\beta}_j^W \overline{X}_j^W$$

$$= \sum_{j=0}^{k} \hat{\beta}_j^W \overline{X}_j^W - \sum_{j=0}^{k} \hat{\beta}_j^M \overline{X}_j^M.$$

Because the fitted OLS regression line passes through the point of means, $\sum \hat{\beta} X_j^W$ equals women's mean wage, $\overline{Y}^W$, and $\sum \hat{\beta} X_j^W$ equals men's mean wage, $\overline{Y}^M$. Thus,

$$\Delta_T + \Delta_R = \overline{Y}^W - \overline{Y}^M.$$

This characteristic of the measures $\Delta_T$ and $\Delta_R$ led to their being called "wage gap decomposi-

tions." Oaxaca estimated that between 58% and 75% of the 54 percentage point difference between white men's and white women's wages was due to differences in what the market paid men and women for the same attributes. The lower numbers arose when industry, sector, and occupation are included in the regression. The higher numbers arose when those factors were deleted. To the extent that discrimination operates by channeling men and women into separate industries or jobs, it is the higher numbers that better capture labor market discrimination. In the 30 years since Oaxaca wrote, women have made substantial gains in the labor market. The overall gap between white men's and white women's wages is now about 30%, but it remains the case that more of the discrepancy can be attributed to differences in returns than to differences in men and women's productive traits.

Blinder estimated that differences in what the market paid black men and white men for the same attributes accounted for about 40% of the 50 percentage point difference between white men's wages and black men's wages. Blinder's model included occupation, but not industry. In the 30 years since Blinder wrote, blacks have made substantial gains in the labor market. The overall gap between working black men's wages and working white men's wages is now about 20%; it remains the case that almost half of the discrepancy can be attributed to differences in returns rather than to differences in blacks' and whites' productive traits.

Different returns for the same traits is, on the face of it, discriminatory. Why should men and women, or blacks and whites, be rewarded differently for the same attributes? However, we must be careful that the traits we measure are, indeed, the same. For example, if one group receives lower quality education, then the returns to education might be unequal, without the labor market discriminating unfairly. Oaxaca/Blinder decompositions require careful attention to using comparably measured traits.

Interpreting the wage differences that stem from differences in marketable traits requires particular care. Well-functioning labor markets should pay people for their productive attributes, so workers with better productive qualities should get paid more. But what if the traits that are rewarded are not actually productive, but instead serve to provide higher rewards to one group of workers at the expense of others? For example, if we include dummy variables for where workers live as explanators in our wage equations, higher wages paid to workers who live in mostly white neighborhoods would make $\Delta_T$ negative, even if a worker's residential neighborhood has nothing to do with the worker's productivity. Extra wage payments for such a trait would be discriminatory. We need to be careful about what we include as traits in Oaxaca/Blinder wage equations.

The example of differing returns to education for groups that receive lower quality education raises another important point about Oaxaca/Blinder decompositions. Discrimination outside the labor market can lead to varying outcomes in even nondiscriminating labor markets. For example, for many years, black Americans were offered education of inferior quality in schools that were called "separate but equal." Oaxaca/Blinder decompositions don't look beyond the traits workers bring to the marketplace to ask if it is discrimination in other parts of society that account for one group of workers having fewer marketable skills than others. Oaxaca/Blinder decompositions are a powerful tool for investigating labor market discrimination, but as with most regression tools applied to complex social issues, they tell only one part of the story.

 ## Final Notes

Oaxaca's and Blinder's work highlights how economists can fruitfully extract subtle insights from econometric models. The decomposition of wage gaps into a gap attributable to differences in traits and a gap attributable to differences in returns to traits also highlights the care we must give to interpreting regression results if they are to guide, and not mislead, policy makers and public discourse. The need for hypothesis tests to determine whether the calculated differences attributable to either traits or to returns are genuine, rather than being mere statistical accidents, reminds us of the importance of $t$-tests for sound econometric reasoning. ∎

that a 45-year-old household head with two kids two years apart in age and earning \$40,000 per year has expected assets of \$30,000,

$$H_0: E(Y\,|\,X_1 = 45, X_2 = 40, X_3 = 2, X_4 = 2) = 30,$$

against the alternative that the expected assets for such an individual are less than \$30,000. The null hypothesis can be rewritten as

$$H_0: E(Y) = \beta_0 + \beta_1 45 + \beta_2 40 + \beta_3 2 + \beta_4 2 = 30,$$

which is another null hypothesis about a linear combination of the coefficients.

Feldstein reports that the estimated expected income for such an individual is \$22,142, but he does not report the estimated standard error for this estimate, so we do not know whether his data would lead us to reject the claim of $30,000. However, with 161 observations and four estimated coefficients, the critical value for a $t$-statistic would be $-1.64$ if we conduct a one-sided test at the 0.05 significance level. If the estimated standard error of the estimator of the expected assets were no larger than $4,791, we would reject the null hypothesis:

$$(22{,}142 - 30{,}000)/4{,}791 = -1.64.$$

Feldstein does not use OLS in his analysis, but, because his sample size is large, his estimators are approximately normally distributed, so the test is approximately correct as described. This example illustrates how the $t$-test for $E(Y|X)$ is one more powerful arrow in the econometrician's quiver.

Many hypotheses can be tested using a $t$-test. We can test whether a specific coefficient is zero or some particular nonzero value. We can test whether a specific linear combination of coefficients equals a particular value, which implies that we can test whether the expected value of $Y$ for a specific combination of explanator values equals a particular value. What we cannot use $t$-tests for is testing several different hypotheses about the coefficients in a model. Testing multiple hypotheses all together is the subject of Chapter 9.

 ***An Organizational Structure for the Study of Econometrics***

**1. What Is the DGP?**

The Gauss–Markov Assumptions

Normally distributed disturbances

**2. What Makes a Good Estimator?**

_____

**3. How Do We Create an Estimator?**

_____

**4. What Are the Properties of an Estimator?**

_____

**5. How Do We Test Hypotheses?**

Use $t$-tests for individual coefficients.

Use $t$-tests for single linear combinations of coefficients.

# Summary

The chapter began by reviewing the steps of hypothesis testing. It then developed the methods econometricians use to make the probability assessments required to test two common kinds of hypotheses that arise in econometrics: hypotheses about a single slope or intercept coefficient, and hypotheses about a linear combination of coefficients.

# Concepts for Review

# Questions for Discussion

1. Why do we use the conventional significance levels of .10, .05, and .01? What would it mean to conduct a test at the .50 significance level? Discuss.

2. If we reject the null hypothesis at the .05 significance level, does that mean we are 95% certain the hypothesis is wrong? Discuss.

3. Hypothesis tests in economics are meaningless because the maintained hypotheses upon which the tests are based are always wrong. Discuss.

## Problems for Analysis

For the data sets that you will need to solve the problems in this section, go to **www.aw-bc.com/murray**.

1. Assume our model contains an unknown slope and intercept with a DGP that satisfies the Gauss–Markov Assumptions. Suppose $\overline{X} = 70$, $\overline{Y} = 100$, $\sum x_i y_i = -3,550$, $\sum x_i^2 = 2,250$, $\sum X_i^2 = 58,800$, $n = 12$, and $s^2 = 69.8$.
   a. What is $\hat{\beta}_1$?
   b. What is $\hat{\beta}_0$?
   c. Test the null hypothesis that $\beta_1 = -2$ against the alternative that $\beta_1 > -2$, at the .10 significance level.
   d. Test the null hypothesis that $\beta_0 = 0$ against the alternative that it does not, at the .01 significance level.

2. For many years, housing economists believed that households spent a constant fraction of income on housing, as in

$$housing\ expenditure = \beta(income) + u.$$

The file housing.*** contains housing expenditures (*housing*) and total expenditures (*total*) for a sample of 19th century Belgian workers collected by Edouard Ducpetiaux.[4]
   a. Regress housing expenditure on total expenditure and an intercept term. Test at the 5% significance level the null hypothesis that the intercept term is zero, against the alternative that it is not. What do you conclude about housing economists' long-held belief?
   b. Add the square of total expenditure to the regression. Test at the 5% significance level the null hypothesis that the coefficient on the square of housing expenditure is zero.

3. Are students influenced by their peers? In a study of college students' alcohol drinking and academic performance,[5] Michael Kremer and Dan Levy report the following estimated coefficients from an OLS regression of 456 male students' first- or second-year college GPAs on the students' own high school GPA, SAT score, and high school drinking habits, and the students' randomly assigned roommates' high school drinking habits (estimated standard errors are in parentheses):

| | |
|---|---|
| *Own high school GPA* | 0.112 (0.043) |
| *Own SAT score divided by 100* | 0.442 (0.082) |
| *Student drank frequently in high school.* | −0.109 (0.150) |
| *Student drank occasionally in high school.* | −0.028 (0.119) |
| *Roommate drank frequently in high school.* | −0.282 (0.128) |
| *Roommate drank occasionally in high school.* | −0.263 (0.101) |

Dependent Variable: own college GPA
   a. Which of these coefficients are statistically significant at the 5% level of significance? At the 10% level?

b. The estimated effect of a roommate who drinks moderately on one's expected GPA is equivalent to how much worse of a high school GPA? And this is equivalent to how much worse an SAT score?

c. To assess the practical significance the effect one's roommate has on one's performance, compare the effect of a roommate who drank frequently in high school to the standard deviation of college GPAs among these students, 0.58 points on a four-point scale. Assume GPAs are normally distributed. A student whose GPA is 0.282 points below the mean GPA is in what percentile of the GPA distribution?

d. Speculate why the estimated coefficients on one's roommate's high school drinking habits and one's own high school drinking habits differ in their magnitudes and statistical significance in this regression.

 4. The chapter notes that the validity of the Capital Asset Pricing Model (CAPM) can be tested by asking whether $\beta_0 = 0$ in

*(stock's rate of return − rate of return on a risk-free asset)*

$\quad = \beta_0 + \beta_1 (market\ rate\ of\ return - rate\ of\ return\ on\ a\ risk-free\ asset) + v,$

or, equivalently, in

$\quad\quad (stock's\ excess\ return) = \beta_0 + \beta_1 (market's\ excess\ return) + v.$

The file capm1.*** contains excess returns for the market (*mreturn*) and excess returns for two firms in the computer chip business (*freturn*) for each of 192 months. The first 192 observations pertain to firm 1, the next 192 pertain to firm 2. The variable *firm* identifies firms 1 and 2. For firm 1 and for firm 2, test the null hypothesis that $\beta_0 = 0$. What do you conclude about the CAPM from these data?

 5. Does the separation of corporate control from corporate ownership lead to inflated executive salaries and worse firm performance? George Stigler and Claire Friedland have addressed these questions empirically using a sample of firms.[6] A subset of their data is in the file execcomp.***. The variables in the file are

ecomp    Average total annual compensation in thousands of dollars for a firm's top three executives

assets    Firm's assets in millions of dollars

profits    Firm's annual profits in millions of dollars

mcontrol    A dummy variable indicating management control of the firm

a. Regress executives' compensation on the firm's assets and profits, the control dummy, and an intercept term. Test at the 10% significance level the null hypothesis that managerial control has no discernible effect on executive compensation.

b. Regress firm profits on firm assets and the management control dummy. Test at the 10% significance level the null hypothesis that managerial control has no discernible effect on profits.

c. Test at the 10% significance level the null hypothesis that executives in firms controlled by managers receive $17,300 more in expected compensation than do executives in otherwise similar owner-controlled firms ($17,300 is 20% of the mean executives' salary in this sample), against the alternative that they receive less than that much more often.

d.  Do you fail to reject the null hypothesis that the form of control does not matter for executive compensation? Do these data make you confident that the form of control does not have a substantial effect on executives' compensation? In technical terms, how would you describe the limitations of these data for assessing the effect of managerial control of the firm on executives' compensation?

6.  The file wineweather.*** contains the natural log of the average 1989 prices (*logprice*) for Bordeaux wines for the vintages from 1952 to 1989 (*vintage* or *vint*). The age of each vintage in 1989 is given by the variable *age*. These data were part of an analysis of Bordeaux wine as an investment by economists Orley Ashenfelter and David Ashmore of Princeton University and Robert LaLonde of the University of Chicago.[7]

a.  Create a scatterplot with age on the horizontal axis and the log of price on the vertical axis. Do older wines tend to sell for more than younger wines? Does an older wine always sell for more than a younger wine?

b.  Estimate the semilog relationship

$$\ln(price) = \beta_0 + \beta_1(age) + v.$$

c.  Test at the 5% significance level the null hypothesis that the age of wine doesn't matter for its expected price against the alternative that wines grow more valuable with age.

7.  The American welfare program that serves poor single parents and their children is called Temporary Assistance for Needy Families (TANF). TANF varies widely from state to state, both in its generosity and in its eligibility requirements. The file tanf.*** contains the basic real TANF benefit level for a family of four in each of the 50 states (*tanfreal*). This TANF data set includes among its variables the variable *black*, which reports the fraction of a state's population that is African American.

a.  Regress *tanfreal* on *black* and an intercept term. Test at the 1% significance level the null hypothesis that real TANF benefits do not depend on race, against the alternative that they do.

b.  What would you have done differently in (a) if the test had been at the 5% significance level?

c.  Economists who study welfare across countries have found that countries that are more racially homogeneous have higher welfare benefits. This problem explores whether this is also true across American states. In all U.S. states, African Americans are a minority. Use the data in TANF.*** to test at the 1% significance level the null hypothesis that real TANF benefits are not higher in more racially homogeneous states, that is, in states with a smaller proportion of African Americans in the population, against the alternative that real TANF benefits are higher in more racially homogeneous states. The TANF data set includes among its variables the variable *black*, which reports the fraction of a state's population that is African American.

    d. What is the difference between the test suitable for (a) and the test suitable for (b)?

    e. Hypothesis tests can go awry in four ways. If we use the test procedure suitable for (a), when our interest is in (b), how might the test go awry?

8. Are presidential elections affected by the economy? Do voters consider how much unemployment has changed during the election year when casting their votes for or against the party sitting in the White House? The file political.*** contains the change in unemployment in the 12 months immediately preceding the election (*unemploy*) and the percentage of the popular vote obtained by the incumbent presidential party (*incumbent* or *incumb*) in each presidential election (*year*) since 1900.[8] Both *unemploy* and *incumbent* are measured in percent.

    a. Use OLS to estimate the slope and intercept of

$$incumbent = \beta_0 + \beta_1 (unemploy) + \varepsilon.$$

    Test at the 5% significance level the null hypothesis that changes in the unemployment rate in the 12 months prior to the presidential election have no effect on the incumbent party's popular vote in the presidential election against the alternative that increases in the unemployment rate hurt the incumbent party's prospects.

    b. Is it reasonable to structure the test in (a) as a one-tailed test? Briefly explain.

    c. If the one-tailed test is reasonable in (b), why is it preferable to use a one-tailed test?

    d. A political pundit has argued that if the unemployment rate rises by two percentage points in the 12 months prior to the election, an incumbent party's "goose is cooked," and "they can't expect to get even 47% of the popular vote." Test the claim that the incumbent party's expected vote is 47% or more, against the alternative that the expected vote is less than 47%, given that the unemployment rate rises two percentage points in the 12 months prior to the election.

9. In a dispute about pricing on the Trans-Alaska Pipeline,[9] one side argued that the market price of crude oil rises $0.15 per barrel when the oil's quality improves by "one degree API" ("degrees API" is a standard measure of oil's quality). The opposing side argued that price rises only $0.053 per barrel when the oil's quality improves by one API degree. The administrative court judge in the case had access to a sample of Persian Gulf oils prices and qualities. The sampled values of crude oil's qualities (measured in API degrees) and price per barrel (measured in 1984 dollars) are in the variables *API* and *price* in the file oilprice1.***.

    a. Use the sample data to test at the 10% significance level the null hypothesis that the expected price of crude oil changes $0.15 per barrel when quality improves one degree API.

    b. Use the sample data to test at the 10% significance level the null hypothesis that the expected price of crude oil changes $0.53 per barrel when quality improves one degree API.

    c. Test at the 5% significance level the null hypothesis that the expected price of a barrel of oil is $20 if its API quality is 40.

10. Does year-to-year economic growth alter the poverty rate? Is poverty low where economic growth is high? These two similar questions are slightly different from one another. The first asks whether *changes* in the poverty rate are related to *changes* in GDP. The second asks whether the *level* of the poverty rate depends on *changes* in GDP. The file poverty2.*** contains

*poverty*    U.S. poverty rates
*gdpgrow*    U.S. GDP growth rates
*unemploy*   U.S. unemployment rates

all measured in percents.

a. Regress changes in the poverty rate on GDP growth and an intercept term. Is GDP growth statistically significant at the 5% significance level?

b. Regress the poverty rate on GDP growth and an intercept term. Is GDP growth statistically significant at the 5% significance level?

c. Interpret, and resolve, the seemingly conflicting findings about statistical significance in (a) and (b).

d. Regress changes in the poverty rate on GDP growth, changes in the unemployment rate, and an intercept term. Which variables are statistically significant at the 5% significance level? At the 10% level?

e. Interpret, and resolve, the seemingly conflicting findings about statistical significance in (a) and (d). In particular, assess the unqualified claim that "Year to year, economic growth reduces poverty." Relate your assessment to the concern during the 2000 presidential election that the economic recovery of that period was "a jobless recovery."

11. Nitrogen dioxide ($NO_2$) is a pollutant that attacks humans' respiratory systems; it increases the likelihood of respiratory illness. One common source of nitrogen dioxide is automobile exhaust. The file NO2pollution.*** contains a subset from 500 hourly observations made from October 2001 to August 2003.[10] The variables in the data set are

*lno2*      Natural logarithm of the concentration of $NO_2$ (particles)
*lcars*     Natural logarithm of the number of cars per hour
*temp*      Temperature 2 meters above ground (degrees C)
*wndspd*    Wind speed (meters/second)
*tchng23*   Temperature difference between 25 and 2 meters above ground (degrees C)
*wnddir*    Wind direction (degrees between 0 and 360)
*hour*      Hour of day
*days*      Day number from October 1, 2001.

Regress the log of $NO_2$ concentration on the log of the number of cars, the two temperature variables, the two wind variables, and the time index (*days*). Which variables are statistically significant at the 5% level? At the 10% level?

12. For many years, major league baseball (MLB) had an unusual labor rule that tied each player to a single team—players were not allowed to change to a new team without the old team's permission. In 1976, this rule changed, and baseball players became able to periodically declare themselves "free agents." When they did, they

could change teams freely before the following season. Fans and economists have questioned whether free agency increased, decreased, or left unchanged the competitive balance among teams in the league. Peter Fishman used the data from 1950 to 2004 in the file baseball.*** to settle this debate.[11]

To measure the competitiveness of baseball teams in any given season, the data set provides the standard deviation of winning percentages (the proportion of games played that a team won) across all teams in the league, *stdevwp*. When teams are competitive, they win similar numbers of games, and the standard deviation is low. When some teams dominate and others perform badly, the standard deviation is high. The number of players that declare free agency prior to a given season is *fragents*.

Several other variables can affect the competitiveness of teams. Beginning in 1965, MLB had a draft of amateur players in which the poorest performing teams of the previous season get first choices in the draft. The purpose of this practice is to improve competitiveness among teams. *Draft* is a dummy variable indicating years from 1965 on. The number of teams in MLB affects the standard deviation of winning percentages. Each dominant team and each poor team has a smaller impact on the mean deviation of winning percentages from their overall mean when there are more teams in the league. *Teams* is the number of teams in MLB during the season. And finally, when a larger proportion of the U.S. population is playing baseball, the variance in ability among players is greater than when a smaller proportion (presumably the very best) plays. The variable *poppct* is the fraction of the U.S. population who are MLB players.

a. Regress *stdevwp* against *fragents*, *draft*, *teams*, *poppct*, and an intercept term. Test at the 5% significance level the null hypothesis that free agency has no effect on the competitiveness of MLB, against the alternative that it does. What do you conclude about the effect of free agency on baseball's competitiveness on the playing field?

b. Do the remaining explanators have their expected signs? Briefly explain.

c. Are the remaining variables statistically significant at the 5% level of significance?

 13. Robert Barro studied economic growth in a cross section of countries.[12] The file barrogrowth.*** contains Barro's variables for a slightly different sample of countries, and with an inferior measure of assassinations. Among the variables in the file are

| | |
|---|---|
| *gcy* | Government consumption as a % of GDP 70–85 (average) |
| *gdp60* | GDP 1960 |
| *gdp70* | GDP 1970 |
| *gr6085* | GDP Growth 60–85 (average) |
| *gr7085* | GDP Growth 70–85 (average) |
| *ppi60dev* | Deviations from PPP for investment 1960 |
| *prim60* | Percent enrolled in primary school 1960 |
| *prim70* | Percent enrolled in primary school 1970 |
| *prevcoup* | Revolutions and coups a year |
| *sec60* | Percent enrolled in secondary school 1960 |
| *sec70* | Percent enrolled in secondary school 1970 |

a. Regress GDP growth from 1960 to 1985 on GDP in 1960 and an intercept term.

b. What does the sign of the estimated slope in (a) suggest about whether poorer countries were catching up with the richer countries over the sample period? Is the estimated slope in (a) statistically significant at the 5% level?

c. Regress GDP growth from 1960 to 1985 on GDP in 1960, government consumption as a fraction of GDP, the percents enrolled in primary and secondary education in 1960, revolutions and coups in a year, the measure of economic distortions, *PPI60DEV*, and an intercept term.

d. What does the sign of the estimated coefficient on GDP in 1960 in (c) suggest about whether poorer countries were catching up with otherwise similar richer countries over the sample period? Is the estimated slope in (c) statistically significant at the 5% level?

e. Which other explanators in Barro's model are statistically significant at the 5% significance level? Which are significant at the 1% significance level? Which are not significant at even the 10% significance level? Do the signs on the statistically significant coefficients accord with your intuition?

f. Regress GDP growth from 1970 to 1985 on GDP in 1970, government consumption as a fraction of GDP, the percents enrolled in primary and secondary education in 1970, revolutions and coups in a year, and the measure of economic distortions, *PPI60DEV*. Which variables found significant in (d) remain so in this regression? Which do not?

 14. The sudden growth of homelessness in the 1980s is often attributed to the release of many individuals from mental hospitals during that period. Housing economists, however, have painted a more complex picture, pointing to housing market conditions and economic circumstances as significant contributors to the problem. John Quigley, Steven Raphael, and Eugene Smolensky addressed the roots of homelessness with several data sets.[13] One of their data sets, covering 273 urban areas and based on the 1990 U.S. Census, is contained in homeless1.***. The variables in that file are

| | |
|---|---|
| *hmlss* | Natural log of the homelessness rate 1990 |
| *vac* | Natural log of the rental vacancy rate 1990 |
| *grossr* | Natural log of the median gross rent 1990 |
| *mdhhinc* | Natural log of the median household income 1990 |
| *rntincrt* | Natural log of the rent/income ratio 1990 |
| *unemploy* | Natural log of the unemployment rate 1990 |
| *mhosp* | The change in mental hospital population per 100,000 people 1981–1992 |
| *prison* | The change in prison population per 100,000 people 1981–1992 |
| *jantemp* | Natural log of the average January temperature |
| *ssipop* | Natural log of the city's supplemental security income recipients |
| *pop* | Natural log of the city's total population |

a. Regress the log of the homelessness rate on an intercept term, the logs of gross rent, median household income, January temperature, unemployment, and the changes in mental health and prison populations.

b. Which variables are statistically significant at the 5% level? At the 10% level? Are these results supportive of Quigley and Smolensky's contentions that homelessness is more complex than just an issue of deinstitutionalization and that housing market conditions are also a part of the story?

15. Do good SAT scores indicate a good college GPA? The data in sat2.*** are pertinent to this question. The sample contains the students from an incoming class at Bates College. The variables include

*GPA*   First-year grade point average (on a 4.0 scale)

*quant*   Score on the math portion of the Scholastic Aptitude Test (SAT)

*verbal*   Score on the verbal portion of the Scholastic Aptitude Test (SAT)

*SAT*   Sum of *quant* and *verbal*

*female*   = 1 if female, = 0 if male

*prv*   = 1 if student attended a private school; = 0

*rank*   Percentage rank in high school class; for example, 0.01 indicates the student finished in the top 1% of his or her graduating class.

a. Regress *GPA* on *SAT*, *rank*, *prv*, and *female*. Test at the 5% significance level the null hypothesis that Bates students with higher SAT scores do not have better expected GPAs than students with lower SAT scores, against the alternative that they do.

b. Test at the 5% significance level the null hypothesis that female Bates students have the same expected GPA as otherwise similar male students, against the alternative that they do not.

c. Regress *GPA* on *quant*, *verbal*, *rank*, *prv*, and *female*. Test at the 5% significance level the null hypothesis that math and verbal SAT scores have the same effect on expected GPA as one another, against the alternative that they do not. (Equivalently, test the null hypothesis that the difference between the coefficients of *quant* and *verbal* is zero, against the alternative that it is not.)

16. Table 5.1 (in Chapter 5), p. 178, contains data for a sample of 20th century years on output ($Q$), capital ($K$), and labor ($L$) in the United States. Use these data to test the null hypothesis that the U.S. production function displays constant returns to scale.

17. The file equipmentandgrowth.*** contains data on economic growth between 1960 and 1985 for 106 countries. De Long and Summers[14] used these data to investigate the effect of equipment investment on economic growth. The six variables in the file are

*gdp60vus*   The natural log of a country's income per capita in 1960 relative to that in the United States in 1960

*gdpgr*   The growth rate of income per worker for a country between 1960 and 1985

*noneqinv*   Nonequipment investment for the country between 1960 and 1985

*equipinv*   Equipment investment for the country between 1960 and 1985

*lofgr6085*   The growth rate of the labor force between 1960 and 1985

*continent*   The continent of the country

a. Regress the growth rate on the other four variables, besides *continent*, and a constant term. Test at the 5% significance level the null hypothesis that, with other things equal, countries with lower incomes per capita in 1960 grew no faster than countries with larger incomes against the alternative that they did.

b. In that same regression, test at the 5% significance level the null hypothesis that growth does not depend on equipment investment.

c. A one percentage point increase in equipment investment is estimated to cause how large an increase in GDP growth?

d. Test the null hypothesis that the effects of nonequipment investment and equipment investment on economic growth are the same (that is, that the difference between their coefficients is zero).

e. Continents 3 and 4 are Europe and North America. Re-estimate the model for countries on these continents. Test at the 5% significance level the null hypothesis that equipment investment is unimportant for economic growth in countries on these continents.

f. Re-estimate the model for countries on continents other than Europe and North America. Test at the 5% significance level the null hypothesis that equipment investment is unimportant for economic growth in countries on these continents.

 18. Greg Mankiw, David Romer, and David Weil examined the Solow growth model by looking at its implications for both the levels of countries' GDPs and the growth rates of countries' GDPs.[15] The data they used are in the file mrw.***. The variables in that file are

| | |
|---|---|
| *country* | Number representing country |
| *gdp60* | GDP per working-age population in 1960 |
| *gdp85* | GDP per working-age population in 1985 |
| *gdpgr* | GDP growth rate 1960–1985 |
| *inter* | Dummy variable indicating MRW's intermediate group |
| *invest* | Investment as a percentage of GDP |
| *nonoil* | Dummy variable for non-oil-producing country |
| *oecd* | Dummy variable for OECD country |
| *popgr* | Population growth rate in percent |
| *school* | Percent of working-age population in secondary school |

The chapter notes that a test of the validity of Mankiw, Romer, and Weil's augmented Solow growth model is whether the slope coefficients sum to zero in the regression

$$\ln(GDP85) = \beta_0 + \beta_1\ln(POPGR + 5) + \beta\ln(INVEST) + \beta\ln(SCHOOL) + \nu.$$

a. Test at the 5% significance level the null hypothesis that the three slopes sum to zero.

b. What is the implication of your test result for the validity of the augmented Solow model?

19. Explain what "size distortion" means in the following: "Standard hypothesis testing procedures applied to this estimator results in a size distortion of 25%. Interpret the so-called 5% significance level for this test accordingly."

20. In a Gauss–Markov DGP with an intercept term and one slope coefficient, the BLUE estimator of a straight line through the origin, $\beta_{g4}$, is biased. Suppose that in our particular DGP, $\beta_{g4}$ is biased upward. Assume an econometrician estimates the slope

with $\beta_{g4}$ anyway, forgetting that it is a biased estimator, and uses $\beta_{g4}$ to test the null hypothesis that the slope is equal to zero. Show graphically that the econometrician's test is biased.

## Endnotes

1. The case was "Silver Blaze" in Sir Arthur Conan Doyle's, *Memoirs of Sherlock Holmes*, 1894.
2. N. Gregory Mankiw, David Romer, and David Weil, "A Contribution to the Empirics of Economic Growth," *Quarterly Journal of Economics* 107, no. 2 (May 1992): 407–437.
3. Alan Blinder, "Wage Discrimination: Reduced Form and Structural Estimates," *Journal of Human Resources* 8, no. 4 (Fall 1973): 436–455. Ronald Oaxaca, "Male–Female Wage Differentials in Urban Labor Markets," *International Economic Review* (October 1973): 693–709.
4. Edouard Ducpetiaux, *Budgets Economiques de Classes de Ouvrieres en Belgique*, (Brussels: Hayaz, 1855).
5. Michael Kremer and Dan Levy, "Peer Effects and Alcohol Use Among College Students" (Cambridge, MA: NBER Working Paper 9876, 2003).
6. George J. Stigler and Claire Friedland, "The Literature of Economics: The Case of Berle and Means," *Journal of Law and Economics* 26, no. 2 (June 1983): 237–268.
7. Orley Ashenfelter, David Ashmore, and Robert LaLonde, "Bordeaux Wine Vintage Quality and the Weather," December 1999, http://www.liquidasset.com/orley.htm.
8. Gary Smith of Pomona College generously provided these data.
9. Trans-Alaska Pipeline System, FERC ¶ 23, 048 (1983), FERC ¶ 61,123 (1984).
10. These data come from the Statlib archive of Carnegie Mellon University. They were originally posted there by Aldrin Magne.
11. Peter Fishman, "Competitive Balance and Free Agency in Major League Baseball," *The American Economist* 47, no. 2 (Fall 2003): 86–91.
12. Robert J. Barro, "Economic Growth in a Cross Section of Countries," *Quarterly Journal of Economics* 106, no. 2 (May 1991): 407–443.
13. John M. Quigley, Steven Raphael, and Eugene Smolensky, "Homeless in America, Homeless in California," *Review of Economics and Statistics* 83 (February 2001): 37–51.
14. J. Bradford DeLong and Lawrence H. Summers, "How Strongly Do Developing Countries Benefit from Equipment Investment?" *Journal of Monetary Economics* 32, no. 3 (1994): 395–415.
15. Mankiw, Romer, and Weil, "A Contribution to the Empirics of Economic Growth."

# Chapter 8

# Superfluous and Omitted Variables, Multicollinearity, and Binary Variables

*"When I use a word," Humpty Dumpty said, in a rather scornful tone, "it means just what I choose it to mean—neither more nor less."*
*"The question is," said Alice, "whether you can make words mean so many things."*
*"The question is," said Humpty Dumpty, "who is to be master—that's all."[1]*

—LEWIS CARROLL

The question, say econometricians, is whether regression models are as arbitrary as Humpty Dumpty would have them, or are their structures less flexible than that. The prospect of numerous explanators introduces this question in two guises. First, can we, without adverse consequence, omit explanators that actually influence the expected value of the dependent variable? For example, does neglecting wealth or siblings in studying the effect of income on financial aid lead to bad estimates of the effect of income on financial aid? Second, can we, without adverse consequence, include explanatory variables that do not actually influence the expected value of the dependent variable? For example, would adding the price of shoelaces in Siberia as an explanator in the financial aid equation lead to bad estimates of the effect of income on financial aid? This chapter asks whether we are free to follow Humpty Dumpty in being masterful when we build regression models. It asks, "What variables should we include in our regressions, and why?"

## 8.1 Including Superfluous Variables

WHAT ARE AN ESTIMATOR'S PROPERTIES?

The multiple regression model allows us to include any variables we wish in a regression analysis. How do we choose which variables to include and which to exclude? Are there adverse consequences from adding superfluous variables? From omitting relevant variables? The key to answering these questions is recognizing that we obtain the best linear unbiased estimators (BLUE) by minimizing the variance of a linear estimator subject to unbiasedness restrictions. The smaller we can make that variance, the more efficient our estimator. Efficiency applies only to unbiased estimators, however; without our unbiasedness restrictions, we risk creating biased estimators. This section explains that including superfluous variables harms efficiency. The next section discusses how omitting relevant variables causes bias.

## Superfluous Variables and Lost Efficiency

Multiple regression allows us to include any variables we wish in our data-generating process (DGP). One temptation is to include all the variables at our disposal—"everything but the kitchen sink." Is this an unwise strategy? What are the consequences if we include "explanators" in our DGP that do not matter, that is, for which the true coefficients are zero? Including superfluous variables in our DGP results in less efficient BLUE estimators. We can improve efficiency without cost by excluding such superfluous explanators, resulting in no bias and enhanced efficiency.

Recall that the expected value of a linear estimator for our multiple regression DGP is

$$E(g) = \beta_0 \Sigma w_i + \beta_i \Sigma w_i X_{1i} + \cdots + \beta_k \Sigma w_i X_{ki},$$

or, if we define a variable $X_{0i} = 1$ for every observation,

$$E(g) = \beta_0 \Sigma w_i X_{0i} + \beta_1 \Sigma w_i X_{1i} + \cdots + \beta_k \Sigma w_i X_{ki}. \qquad \textbf{8.1}$$

To unbiasedly estimate $\beta_s$, we choose $w_i^s$ such that

$$\Sigma w_i^s X_{ri} = 0 \qquad \text{for } r \neq s$$

to ensure that

$$\beta_r \Sigma w_i^s X_{ri} = 0 \qquad \text{for each } r \neq s$$

in Equation 8.1. But if we know the variable $X_{qi}$'s coefficient, $\beta_q$, is zero, we don't need such a restriction on $\Sigma(w_i^s X_{qi})$. *Thus, we can omit explanators we know to be superfluous and still obtain unbiased estimates of the other variables' coefficients.*

By excluding superfluous variables, we reduce the number of constraints needed when deriving the BLUE estimator and thereby enhance the efficiency of the estimators. If, for example, we know for certain that $\beta_q = 0$, we can obtain unbiased estimators of the remaining coefficients without requiring that

$$\Sigma w_i X_{qi} = 0.$$

With fewer constraints imposed on our minimization problem, we will generally achieve a lower—and never a larger—minimum variance than we would with additional constraints. *Including superfluous variables in our models risks inefficiency.* Only when the superfluous variable is perfectly uncorrelated with the remaining variables does omitting it not improve efficiency.

# A Monte Carlo Experiment

## Prelude to Omitted Variables

Just as Chapter 2 provided a Monte Carlo prelude to the more formal analysis of Chapter 3, the Monte Carlo exercises here precede this chapter's formal investigation of the consequences of omitting relevant explanators from a regression model. Here a Monte Carlo exercise asks whether omitting variables causes ordinary least squares (OLS) to be biased. The software for this exercise, MC Builder III, is available on this book's companion Web site (**www.aw-bc.com/murray**). The DGP underlying this Monte Carlo exercise is a multiple regression model with an intercept and two explanators:

$$Y_i = \beta_0 + \beta_1 X_{1i} + \beta_2 X_{2i} + \varepsilon_i.$$

The Gauss–Markov Assumptions apply and the disturbances in the model are normally distributed. The question addressed by the Monte Carlo exercise is whether OLS yields an unbiased estimator of $\beta_0$ and $\beta_1$ if the analyst incorrectly overlooks $X_2$ and applies the OLS estimator that is suitable for the model

$$Y_i = \beta_0 + \beta_1 X_{1i} + \eta_i.$$

Any bias caused by omitting a relevant variable is likely to depend in part on how the omitted variable is related to the included variables. The Monte Carlo model allows for such a relationship by letting us specify a relationship among $X_2$, the intercept, and $X_1$:

$$X_{2i} = \gamma_0 + \gamma_1 X_{1i} + \nu_i.$$

If $\gamma_0$ and $\gamma_1$ are both equal to zero, the omitted variable is unrelated to the included variables. In MC Builder III, the user assigns values for $\gamma_0$ and $\gamma_1$. A $N(0, \sigma_\nu^2)$ random number generator provides values for the $\nu_i$. Because MC Builder III assumes the $X$'s are fixed across samples, the user assigns values for the $X$'s just once. The user also assigns a value for the variance of the $\nu_i$, $\sigma_\nu^2$.

Building the model has six steps:

1. Choose a number of observations (less than 100, for speed), $n$, to use in every sample.
2. Choose coefficients for the intercept and for the included and omitted explanators, $\beta_0$, $\beta_1$, and $\beta_2$.
3. Choose coefficients for a regression relationship between the omitted and included variables, $X_1$ and $X_2$.
4. Choose $n$ values for the included variable, $X_1$.
5. Choose a variance for the disturbances, $\sigma^2$.
6. Choose a nonzero variance, $\sigma_\nu^2$, for the $\nu_i$ in the relationship between the included and omitted explanators, $X_1$ and $X_2$.

The first thing MC Builder III does is construct values for $X_2$ from $X_1$ by the following formula:

$$X_{2i} = \gamma_0 + \gamma_1 X_{1i} + \nu_i,$$

where the $\nu_i$ are $n$ draws from a $N(0, \sigma_\nu^2)$ random number generator. (As an alternative to constructing $X_2$ from $X_1$, MC Builder III allows you to enter your own distinct values for $X_2$.) The same $X_2$ values then appear in every sample, so the explanators are fixed across samples, in accord with the Gauss–Markov Assumptions. MC Builder III reports $\hat{\gamma}_1$, the regression coefficient on $X_1$ that results from regressing $X_2$ on $X_1$ and an intercept term. The program also reports $\hat{\gamma}_0$, the estimated slope in that same regression. These regression coefficients, not the Builder inputs $\gamma_0$ and $\gamma_1$, describe how the actual $X_{2i}$ variable is related to the intercept term and $X_{1i}$.

MC Builder III next creates $n$ values for $Y$ to use as a first sample. These are generated according to

$$Y_i = \beta_0 + \beta_1 X_{1i} + \beta_2 X_{2i} + \varepsilon_i$$
$$for\ i = 1, \ldots, n,$$

where the $\varepsilon_i$ are $n$ draws from a N$(0, \sigma^2)$ random number generator. These observations are then used to form OLS estimators of $\beta_0$ and $\beta_1$ as if $X_2$ were not in the relationship.

MC Builder III generates 10,000 such samples and 10,000 such OLS estimates of $\beta_0$ and $\beta_1$. The program then reports the mean estimated values of $\hat{\beta}_0$ and $\hat{\beta}_1$ and their mean estimation errors across the 10,000 samples. In the same table, the program reports $\beta_0$ and $\hat{\gamma}_0$ and $\beta_1$ and $\hat{\gamma}_1$.

Use MC Builder III to examine the performance of OLS when a variable is omitted. Conduct four Monte Carlo experiments, trying several different values for the $\beta$'s, and the $\gamma$'s. Allow the values to vary considerably. Each time, write down the values of the $\beta$'s, the $\gamma$'s, and the $\hat{\gamma}$'s. After the first experiment, ask:

1. Is OLS a biased estimator when a variable is omitted, according to the Monte Carlo exercise?

2. What is the magnitude of any bias in estimating $\beta_0$, according to the Monte Carlo exercise?

3. What is the magnitude of any bias in estimating $\beta_1$, according to the Monte Carlo exercise?

After each succeeding experiment, ask questions 1–3 again. Also ask:

4. Is there an approximate relationship between the biases in estimating $\beta_0$ and $\beta_1$ and the magnitudes of $\beta_3$, $\hat{\gamma}_0$, and $\hat{\gamma}_1$?

Next, conduct Monte Carlo exercises with (i) $\gamma_0 = 0$, but $\gamma_1 \neq 0$; (ii) $\gamma_0 \neq 0$, but $\gamma_1 = 0$; and (iii) $\gamma_0 = 0$, and $\gamma_1 = 0$. Use a large value for $\beta_2$ in each of these experiments. After each of these experiments, ask

5. What happens to the biases in estimating $\beta_0$ and $\beta_1$ in these cases? ∎

---

Efficiency insists that we exclude superfluous variables from our regressions. What about excluding relevant variables? Are there adverse consequences if, in our efforts to exclude superfluous variables, we inadvertently omit relevant variables? Yes, there are. Excluding relevant variables risks biased estimators for the remaining coefficients.

## 8.2    Omitting Relevant Variables

WHAT ARE AN ESTIMATOR'S PROPERTIES?

Including superfluous variables in a regression costs efficiency. Omitting relevant variables can have the frequently more calamitous consequence of biasing the OLS estimates of the remaining coefficients in the model. This section establishes that omitting relevant variables can cause OLS to be biased, presents a formula for that bias, illustrates how omitted variables can poison a regression analysis, and discusses when omitting relevant variables is acceptable.

### Omitted Variable Bias

We have learned that to unbiasedly estimate $\beta_s$, we choose $w_i^s$ such that

$$\sum w_i^s X_{ri} = 0 \qquad \text{for } r \neq s,$$

to ensure that

$$\beta_r \sum w_i^s X_{ri} = 0 \qquad \text{for each } r \neq s$$

in Equation 8.1. Not imposing such a restriction for a variable $X_{qi}$ does not bring any bias if the coefficient of $X_{qi}$, $\beta_q$, is truly zero, that is, if $X_{qi}$ is a superfluous variable. If $\beta_q$ does not equal zero, however, to neglect the restriction by omitting $X_q$ from the model risks using biased estimators for the remaining variables. Note that the risk would not materialize if

$$\sum w_i^s X_{qi} = 0$$

by happenstance; otherwise the risk would materialize. *Omitting relevant variables from our models risks bias.* We call this bias **omitted variable bias**. Only when an excluded relevant variable is perfectly uncorrelated with all of the remaining explanators does omitting the relevant variable not introduce bias.

When we omit a relevant explanator from our analysis, the estimates of the remaining variables' coefficients reflect, to the extent that they can, the effects of the omitted variable. When we omit relevant variables from a model, we muddy the estimates of the remaining variables' effects as they become mixed with the effects of the omitted variables.

## A Formula for Omitted Variable Bias

What, precisely, is the bias in estimating $\beta_s$ if we omit $X_{OMV}$ when $X_{OMV}$'s coefficient is *not* zero? If we do not ensure that

$$\sum w_i^s X_{OMVi} = 0$$

when $\beta_{OMV} \neq 0$, then

$$E(g) = \beta_s + \beta_{OMV} \sum w_i^s X_{OMVi}$$

and the bias in estimating $\beta_s$ is

$$\beta_{OMV} \sum w_i^s X_{OMVi}, \qquad\qquad 8.2$$

which we call **omitted variable bias**. (If several relevant variables were omitted, each would contribute to the bias in $g$ as just as omitting $X_{OMV}$ does; the biases would be added together. Appendix 8.A uses matrix algebra to provide a general analysis of omitted variable bias.) Some economists refer to inadvertently omitted relevant variables as "lurking" variables that bring us unrecognized bias in estimating the coefficients of the included variables.

The appearance of $\beta_{OMV}$ in the bias expression indicates that omitting variables with larger effects (larger coefficients) leads to greater biases in the other coefficients. But what interpretation can we give to the second portion of the bias, the term

$$\sum w_i^s X_{OMVi}?$$

This weighted sum of the $X_{OMVi}$ is itself a linear estimator. The weighted sum equals the linear estimator we would use to obtain a coefficient on $X_s$ if we were to regress the omitted variable, $X_{OMVi}$, on all the variables included in the model. This term reflects the extent to which $X_s$ can predict $X_{OMV}$, given all the other variables included in the model. In essence, the bias in our estimator of $\beta$ stems from $X_s$ trying to reflect, as best it can, the effect of the omitted $X_{OMV}$. *The biases arising from an omitted variable will be small to the extent that the omitted variable's effect is small and to the extent that the included variables do not account for the omitted variables' value.*

Consider a special case. The BLUE estimator of the slope of a line through the origin, $\beta_{g4}$, is a biased estimator of the slope if the intercept term is not actually zero. In this case, $X_{OMVi} = X_{0i} = 1$ for all observations. The bias in estimating the slope of a single explanator if we wrongly omit the intercept (the intercept is nonzero) and use $\beta_{g4}$ is

$$\beta_0 \sum \left[ \left( \frac{X_i}{\sum X_j^2} \right) X_{0i} \right] = \beta_0 \sum \left( \frac{X_i}{\sum X_j^2} \right) = \frac{\beta_0 \sum X_i}{\sum X_j^2},$$

which is zero if

$$\sum X_i = n\overline{X} = 0.$$

Thus, incorrectly omitting the intercept term leads to biased estimation of the slope, unless the mean $X$ is zero.

These biases are evident from the Monte Carlo experiments we can conduct with MC Builder III. Table 8.1 contains the results of four such Monte Carlo exercises conducted with MC Builder III. The Monte Carlo exercises result in observed biases quite close to the theoretical biases in every instance. In each case, the bias in estimating $\beta_0$ is approximately equal to its theoretically correct value, $\beta_2 \hat{\gamma}_0$, and the bias in estimating $\beta_1$ is approximately equal to its theoretically correct value, $\beta_2 \hat{\gamma}_1$.

To further illustrate the bias that arises from erroneously omitting the intercept term, return once more to the sample of New York renters that we examined in earlier chapters. We found in Chapter 4 that the OLS estimate of the slope in the rent–income relationship was dramatically lower when we included an intercept term ($\hat{\beta}_1 = 0.06$) than when we omitted the constant term ($\beta_{g4} = 0.17$). In the New York data, $\overline{X}$, the mean income is $35,553, $n = 108$, and

**TABLE 8.1** Theoretical and Monte Carlo Measures of Omitted Variable Bias

| $n$ | $\beta_0$ | $\beta_1$ | $\beta_2$ | $\hat{\gamma}_0$ | $\hat{\gamma}_1$ | $\sigma^2$ | $\sigma_\nu^2$ | Monte Carlo Est. Bias | $\hat{\gamma}_1$ | $\beta_2 A \hat{\gamma}_1$ Exact Bias in OLS Est. |
|-----|-----------|-----------|-----------|------------------|------------------|------------|----------------|-----------------------|------------------|---------------------------------------------------|
| 20  | 4         | 12        | 20        | $-3$             | 0.2              | 2500       | 100            | 7.47                  | 0.372            | 7.44                                              |
| 15  | $-30$     | 27        | 4         | 10               | 2.0              | 900        | 600            | 8.91                  | 2.245            | 8.98                                              |
| 12  | $-8$      | $-10$     | $-5$      | 20               | 0.5              | 3600       | 2500           | 6.75                  | $-1.36$          | 6.80                                              |
| 20  | 4         | 12        | 20        | $-3$             | $-2.0$           | 2500       | 100            | $-34.4$               | $-1.83$          | $-36.6$                                           |

$\sum X_i^2 = 189,500,998,162$. We do not know the true value of $\beta_0$, so we cannot compute the true bias that stems from omitting the intercept term. We do have an estimate of $\beta_0$, however. We found the estimated value of $\beta_0$ to be $5,442 = \hat{\beta}_0$. If we replace $\beta_0$ in the bias expression with 5,442, we obtain an estimated bias of 0.11, which is exactly the difference between the estimates with and without an intercept.

For yet another illustration of the biases that stem from omitting relevant explanators, turn to the data in sat2.*** on this book's companion Web site (**www.aw-bc.com/murray**). The data report first-year college grade point average, *GPA*, quantitative SAT score, verbal SAT score, rank in high school class, and gender for students in one incoming class at Bates College. If we regress first-year grade point average on both SAT scores, gender, and the log of rank in class, we obtain

$$\text{estimated } E(GPA) = 1.28 + .089\textit{female} + 0.00069\textit{quant}$$
$$+ 0.00146\textit{verbal} - 0.133\ln(\textit{rank}).$$

If we omit the verbal score variable, we obtain instead,

$$\text{estimated } E(GPA) = 1.86 + 0.082\textit{female} + 0.00109\textit{quant} - 0.129\ln(\textit{rank}).$$

The estimated coefficient on *quant* rises more than 40% when *verbal* is omitted. The reason for this increase is the coefficient on *verbal* and the considerable relationship between math and verbal scores in these data:

$$\text{estimated } E(verbal) = 399.45 + 0.28\textit{quant} - 4.66\textit{female} + 2.47\ln(\textit{rank}).$$

The estimated coefficient on *quant* is biased upward by 28% of the coefficient on *verbal* (which we estimate to be 0.00146) when the verbal score is omitted from the regression.

## What to Include, What to Exclude

Deciding which variables to include and which to exclude from a model is a common dilemma for economists. Including superfluous variables leads to inefficiency, but excluding relevant variables incurs bias. Academic economists tend to worry more about bias than inefficiency, so they tend to err on the side of including too many variables. Many more applied economists worry more about mean square error than about bias and are therefore more willing to omit variables in an effort to reduce the variance of their estimators.

To determine whether a variable belongs in a model, economists often turn to economic theory to guide their reasoning. For example, consumer income, a good's own price, and the price of closely related goods belong in a demand equation. Economists also often use their practical intuition as a guide to what variables to include in a model. For examples, weather in a growing region belongs in a supply relationship for an agricultural commodity, and an indicator of an ongoing civil war belongs in the GDP equation for a strife-torn country.

## When Omitted Relevant Variables Are Acceptable

There are two situations in which omitted variable bias does not trouble economists. The first is when our interest is in forecasting $Y$, and some relevant variables are not observed. In this case, omitted variable bias sometimes yields better forecasts of $Y$ than we would otherwise obtain. If the omitted variable is unobserved, we cannot include it in our model, so we cannot explicitly account for that variable in making forecasts. We can, however, hope that the relationship between the omitted and included variables is the same in the periods for which we are making forecasts as it is in our observed sample data. In that case, the biased estimated coefficients from the observed sample will incorporate into our forecasts the effects of the unobserved omitted variable, though only to the extent that the included variables can predict the omitted variables. Thus, forecasters are less troubled by omitted variable bias than are other economists.

For example, a Pop Tune in this chapter (p. 325) specifies that expected GPA for a population of college students depends on the students' math and verbal SAT scores. One purpose of the model is forecasting the performance of prospective students. If math SAT scores are highly correlated with verbal SAT scores, a grade point average regression that omits verbal SAT scores while including math SAT scores might predict grade point average nearly as well as one that includes both scores.

The second situation in which omitted relevant variables are all right arises when analysts are not interested in cases in which one variable is manipulated while all other things remain equal. Sometimes policy makers can affect one explanator, say $X_1$, directly, and $X_1$, in turn, affects another explanator, say $X_2$. For

# An Econometric Top 40—A Classical Favorite

## The Expectations-Augmented Phillips Curve

This Classical Favorite looks at how an omitted variable problem led many economists prematurely to proclaim the demise of the famous "Phillips curve" of the 1950s and 60s. In 1958, A. W. Phillips used a century of United Kingdom data to argue that there is a trade-off between inflation and unemployment. In studying Phillip's classic hit in Chapter 4, we saw that U.S. experience through the 1960s provided empirical support for Phillips's findings from U.K. data. But the 1960s also brought theoretical objections to Phillips's notion that monetary phenomena such as inflation could affect the long-run values of real variables such as the unemployment rate. (The data for this section are contained on this book's companion Web site (**www.aw-bc.com/murray**) in the data set phillipsall.\*\*\*.)

Those who argued against a long-run Phillips curve claimed that government could not systematically sustain higher output with higher inflation. Their argument was straightforward. Consider your hourly wage and the prices of goods, all computed in cents. Perhaps your pay is 1,000 cents per hour and milk costs 90 cents per quart. These prices lead consumers and firms to work and produce at particular levels. The theoretical objection to the Phillips curve was that in the long run, when people have had time to adjust to changes in prices, multiplying every price (including your wage) by 100 (or any other factor) should not change peoples' decisions. It should not matter if pay becomes $1,000 per hour and milk costs $90, instead of 1,000 cents and 90 cents (if all other goods' prices change similarly).

### Evidence for and Against the Bivariate Phillips Curve

The 1958–1969 scatterplot of unemployment versus inflation for the United States accords

well with Phillips's hypothesis, as shown in Hit Figure 8.1:

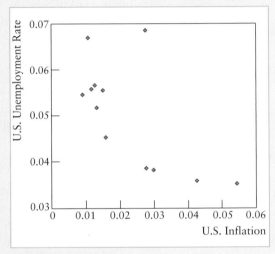

**Hit Figure 8.1**

U.S. Unemployment and Inflation 1958–1969

The same scatterplot, but from 1958 to 2004, shown in Hit Figure 8.2, however, provides no such support.

The negative relationship between unemployment and inflation disappears after 1970, giving empirical support to the theoretical objections to the Phillips curve. Regressions of U.S. inflation on U.S. unemployment using the data from 1958 to 1969 and 1958 to 2004 mirror the graphical depictions. The regression for 1958–1969, reported in Panel A of Hit Table 8.1, estimates that inflation and unemployment move in opposite directions. The regression for 1958–2004, reported in Panel B, estimates that inflation and unemployment move in the same direction.

What had happened to the Phillips curve after 1970? Was Phillips completely wrong in his

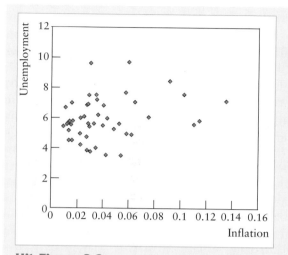

**Hit Figure 8.2**

U.S. Unemployment and Inflation 1958–2004

In brief, Phelps argued from microeconomic principles that anticipated inflation would not change real behavior; only unexpected price increases would spur employment. Expectations-augmented Phillips curves soon became the standard specification among econometricians studying macroeconomics.

### The Expectations-Augmented Phillips Curve

The data from 1958 to 1969 and 1958 to 2004 seem to offer very different pictures of the relationship between unemployment and inflation. But watch what happens when we introduce expected inflation into the story. Suppose, as Phelps argued, that only unexpected inflation can spur employment. In that case, instead of

$$inflation_t = \beta_0 + \beta_1 unemployment_t + u_t,$$

we have

$$inflation_t - (expected\ inflation_t) = \beta_0 + \beta_1 unemployment_t + u_t$$

hypothesis? The answer, said macroeconomists, is rooted in expectations about inflation. In 1967, University of Pennsylvania economist Edmund Phelps laid out a case for including expectations about inflation in the Phillips curve.[2]

**HIT TABLE 8.1** **Regressions of Inflation on Unemployment, 1958–1969 and 1958–2004**

**Panel A (1958–1969)**
Dependent Variable: INFL
Method: Least Squares
Sample: 1958 1969
Included observations: 12

| Variable | Coefficient | Std. Error | t-Statistic | Prob. |
|---|---|---|---|---|
| C | 0.063975 | 0.014625 | 4.374235 | 0.0014 |
| UNEMPLOY | −0.828485 | 0.285126 | −0.2905683 | 0.0157 |

**Panel B (1958–2004)**
Dependent Variable: INFL
Method: Least Squares
Sample: 1958 2004
Included observations: 41

| Variable | Coefficient | Std. Error | t-Statistic | Prob. |
|---|---|---|---|---|
| C | 0.008736 | 0.018306 | 0.477214 | 0.6355 |
| UNEMPLOY | 0.542127 | 0.330264 | 1.805503 | 0.0777 |

or

$$inflation_t = (expected\ inflation_t) + \beta_0$$
$$+ \beta_1 unemployment_t + u_t.$$

If it is unexpected inflation that spurs employment, our earlier Phillips curve regressions omit a relevant variable—expected inflation. The estimated coefficients in Hit Table 8.1 suffer from omitted variable bias if the omitted variable, expected inflation, is correlated with the included variable, unemployment, a bias that could be different in the 1958–1969 sample than in the longer 1958–2004 sample. Does the anomalous instability in the relationship between inflation and unemployment disappear if we incorporate the missing variable in our model? Let's see.

Adding expectations to our econometric analysis requires that we measure expectations. How can we measure expectations of inflation? One simple (and perhaps naive) approach to expectations says that people expect this period's inflation to equal last period's inflation; that is,

$$(expected\ inflation_t) = inflation_{t-1}.$$

If we adopt this convenient measure of expectations, we can specify that

$$inflation_t = inflation_{t-1} + \beta_0$$
$$+ \beta_1 unemployment_t + u_t.$$

The Phillips curve modified to include expectations of inflation is called the "expectations-augmented Phillips curve." Because we need the inflation from the preceding time period as a variable in this regression, the number of observations shrinks by one: The 1958–2004 sample does not contain the 1957 inflation rate for use as a variable in 1958. The expectations-augmented Phillips curve proves quite stable over the two sample periods, 1959–1969 and 1959–2004.

Hit Table 8.2 presents augmented Phillips curves estimated for 1959–1969 and 1959–

2004. The inflation variable is $infl(-1)$. Adding lagged inflation reduces the sample size by one from that in Hit Table 8.1 because the data do not contain inflation in 1957, which is needed to compute $infl(-1)$ for 1958. The estimated unemployment coefficient for 1959–1969 is again negative, as in Hit Table 8.1, but now the unemployment coefficient for 1959–2004 is also negative and is of the same magnitude as found in the early period.

## Rational Expectations and the Augmented Phillips Curve

At first, the augmented Phillips curve

$$(inflation_t - inflation_{t-1}) =$$
$$\beta_0 + \beta_1(unemployment_t) + u_t$$

just moves the policy trade-off from unemployment and inflation to unemployment and changes in inflation—a government willing to accept ever increasing inflation would seem able to support a lower unemployment rate. We must keep in mind, however, that the lagged value of inflation is only serving as a proxy for expected inflation. The augmented curve is, in truth,

$$(inflation_t) - (expected\ inflation_t) =$$
$$\beta_0 + \beta_1(unemployment_t) + u_t.$$

In our regressions, we assumed that lagged inflation accurately measures expected inflation. What if that assumption is wrong? The process by which economic agents form their expectations proves critical to the policy consequences of the augmented Phillips curve. If agents optimally use all the historical information available to them in forming their expectations, that is, if they form their expectations "rationally," then only unpredictable changes in inflation are accompanied by declines in unemployment. Systematic government inflation policies that follow rules based on past economic outcomes

**HIT TABLE 8.2  An Expectations-Augmented Phillips Curve, 1959–1969 and 1959–2004**

**Panel A (1959–1969)**
Dependent Variable: INFL
Method: Least Squares
Sample(adjusted): 1959 1969
Included observations: 11 after adjusting endpoints

| Variable | Coefficient | Std. Error | t-Statistic | Prob. |
|---|---|---|---|---|
| C | 0.051149 | 0.017577 | 2.910065 | 0.0196 |
| UNEMPLOY | −0.828586 | 0.278415 | −2.976079 | 0.0177 |
| INFL(−1) | 0.561564 | 0.277551 | 2.023281 | 0.0777 |

**Panel B (1959–2004)**
Dependent Variable: INFL
Method: Least Squares
Sample(adjusted): 1959 2004
Included observations: 46 after adjusting endpoints

| Variable | Coefficient | Std. Error | t-Statistic | Prob. |
|---|---|---|---|---|
| C | 0.038913 | 0.010023 | 3.882169 | 0.0004 |
| UNEMPLOY | −0.677368 | 0.194650 | −3.479923 | 0.0012 |
| INFL(−1) | 1.021775 | 0.093617 | 10.91446 | 0.0000 |

can be predicted by economic agents and hence cannot influence unemployment. Herein lies the "rational expectations revolution" that argued monetary policy is ineffective.

 **Final Notes**

The failure of the simple Phillips curve after 1970 reflects the perils of omitting relevant variables from econometric models. Omitted variables bias can lead us far astray in our guesses—witness the positive effect of unemployment on inflation when we estimate in the bivariate model with the 1958–2004 data. We have also uncovered one signal of omitted variable bias, however: instability of parameter estimates across samples.

If including relevant variables is so important to reliable estimates, how are we to decide which variables belong in a model, and which do not? Economic theory often provides us our best guide, but the economic reasoning sometimes needs to be deep. Incorporating expectations into an augmented Phillips curve requires one level of sophisticated economic reasoning. Indeed, the augmented Phillips curve is an example that dramatically underscores the "econ" in "econometrics." In another Classical Hit in this chapter, by Robert Lucas (p. 333), you can see how the rational expectations revolution took thinking about the Phillips curve to an even deeper level.

■

example, an increase in the marginal income tax rate, $X_1$, that a worker faces directly reduces work effort, $Y$, by increasing the marginal opportunity cost of working, but also changes work effort through an income effect of lowering the worker's take-home pay, $X_2$. The true effect of the policy is the combined direct effect of $X_1$ on $Y$, *plus* the indirect effect of $X_1$ on $Y$ operating through the effect of $X_1$ on $X_2$. The coefficient of $X_1$ in a regression that also includes $X_2$ as an explanator only captures the direct effect of $X_1$ on $Y$. Omitting $X_2$ from the regression leads to an estimated coefficient for $X_1$ that includes the indirect effect operating through $X_2$ if the only reason for the correlation of $X_1$ with $X_2$ is the causal effect of $X_1$ on $X_2$. Thus, to estimate the full effect of a change in the marginal tax rate on work effort, we would omit take-home pay as an explanator, including only the marginal tax rate.

For a different example, consider admissions officers at Bates College who recently assessed Bates's policy of not requiring that applicants submit SAT scores. The admissions officers wanted to know whether enrolled nonsubmitters perform as well as enrolled submitters. The admissions officers regressed students' GPAs on an intercept term and a dummy variable, *submit*, indicating whether the student had submitted an SAT score. This regression omits all other determinants of students' GPAs from the model because the admissions officers weren't interested in whether nonsubmitters perform like other students who share similar characteristics, such as class rank and other factors that might affect GPA. They were only interested in finding out if students who submit SAT scores perform better than students who don't. The estimated coefficient on *submit* in the Bates admission officer's analysis was 0.04; submitters had an average GPA 0.04 above that of nonsubmitters, an inconsequential difference. In this case, omitting traits besides submitting SAT scores allowed the admissions officers to argue that the enrolled submitters do not perform appreciably better than enrolled nonsubmitters, without regard to other ways in which the two groups might differ.

In brief, omitting relevant explanators causes bias if the omitted variable is correlated with the included variables. Such biases undermine our interpreting an explanator's estimated slope coefficients as indicating the marginal effect of that explanator on the dependent variable, holding other things equal. When forecasting, or when uninterested in the case of "other things being equal," such omitted variable biases need not worry us.

## 8.3    Multicollinearity

WHAT ARE AN ESTI-
MATOR'S PROPERTIES?

Cities with high unemployment rates, low education levels, and high population density have high crime rates. Individuals whose mother and father have high education levels tend to get lots of education. But how do unemployment, education, and population density each contribute to crime rates? Whose education contributes more to the education prospects of a child, the mother's or the father's? These are precisely the sorts of questions we hope multiple regression can answer. The regression framework isolates the separate effect of each influence on the dependent variable. Can we always disentangle the various effects in practice, though? Unfortunately not. This section shows that when explanators move too closely together, estimating their separate effects efficiently becomes difficult—and, in the extreme, impossible.

## Correlated Explanators

When unemployment rates, education levels, and high population density move closely with one another as we look from city to city, it is difficult to tease out the separate influence of each explanator. When the educations of children's fathers and mothers are very similar within families, it is difficult to isolate the influence of each parent's education. *When explanators vary closely together, we say they are **multicollinear** or, equivalently, **collinear**.*

In the extreme, when two explanators move in perfect lock step with one another, so that one is a multiple of another, we say the explanators are **perfectly collinear**. Perfect collinearity can also arise among three or more explanators; when three or more variables are perfectly collinear, one of the variables can be expressed as an exact linear combination of the others. For example, the three explanators $X_{0i}$, $X_{1i}$, and $X_{2i}$ are perfectly collinear if

$$X_{2i} = \gamma_0 X_{0i} + \gamma_0 X_{1i} = \gamma_0 + \gamma_1 X_{1i} \qquad i = 1, \ldots, n,$$

with the last equality holding because $X_{0i} = 1$ for all $i$; similarly, the four explanators $X_1$, $X_2$, $X_3$, and $X_4$ are perfectly collinear if

$$X_{4i} = \gamma_1 X_{1i} + \gamma_2 X_{2i} + \gamma_3 X_{3i} \qquad i = 1, \ldots, n$$

and $\gamma_1$, $\gamma_2$, and $\gamma_3$ are nonzero. Note that if $\gamma_1$ and $\gamma_2$ were nonzero and $\gamma_3$ were zero, $X_1$, $X_2$, and $X_4$ would be perfectly collinear.

If the relationship among multiple explanators is not exact, but nearly so, we describe them, too, as collinear or multicollinear; if we regress one explanator on the others, say $X_{1i}$ on $X_{0i}$, $X_{2i}, \ldots, X_{ki}$, and obtain a small sum of squared residuals from that regression, $\sum e_{1i}^2$, where

$$e_{1i} = X_{1i} - \hat{\alpha}_0 - \hat{\alpha}_2 X_{2i} - \cdots - \hat{\alpha}_k X_{ki}, \qquad \textbf{8.3}$$

then $X_1$ is collinear with the one or more of the other explanators. If $\sum e_{1i}^2$ is *not* small, $X_1$ is not collinear with the other explanators. Notice that if $n$ is large enough, $\sum e_{1i}^2$ is unlikely to be small. Increasing $n$ is likely to eventually overcome collinearity problems.

## The Consequences of Multicollinearity

When variables move closely together, it is difficult to differentiate their individual effects. *Consequently, estimators of the coefficients of collinear explanators tend to have large variances.* In a multiple regression such as

$$Y_i = \beta_0 + \beta_1 X_{1i} + \beta_2 X_{2i} + \cdots + \beta_k X_{ki} + \varepsilon_i \qquad i = 1, \ldots, n \qquad \textbf{8.4}$$

some, all, or none (but not just one) of the explanators may suffer from multicollinearity. Multicollinearity affects the variances of only the collinear explanators, and not the variances of other explanators in the model. *In the extreme, when some explanators are perfectly collinear, there exists no unbiased linear estimator for their coefficients.*

To obtain some algebraic intuition for the imprecision caused by multicollinearity, consider the special case in which the collinearity arises because $X_1$ is almost exactly a multiple of $X_0$ (that is, when $X_1$ is almost constant) and in which $X_0$ and $X_1$ are the only two explanators. In this special case in which we regress $Y_i$ on $X_{0i}$ and $X_{1i}$,

$$Y_i = \beta_0 + \beta_1 X_{1i} + \varepsilon_i,$$

the BLUE estimator of the slope is

$$\hat{\beta}_1 = \frac{\sum x_{1i} y_i}{\sum x_{1i}^2}$$

and the variance of that estimator is

$$\text{var}(\hat{\beta}_1) = \frac{\sigma^2}{\sum x_{1i}^2}. \qquad \textbf{8.5}$$

In this case, the check for whether $X_1$ is collinear with $X_0$ calls for regressing $X_1$ on $X_0$ (that is, on just an intercept term),

$$X_{1i} = \alpha X_{0i} + v_i = \alpha + v_i,$$

which, we learned in Chapter 3, yields $\overline{X}_1$. Consequently, in this special case the residual in Equation 8.3 is

$$e_{1i} = X_{1i} - \overline{X}_1 = x_{1i}. \qquad \textbf{8.6}$$

When the sum of squared $e_{1i}$ from Equation 8.6 is small, the variance of the BLUE estimator of $X_1$'s coefficient, $\beta_1$, (given by Equation 8.5) is large (unless the variance of the disturbances, $\sigma^2$, is small). Furthermore, because the variance of the BLUE estimator of the intercept is

$$\text{var}(\hat{\beta}_0) = \frac{\sigma^2 \sum X_{1i}^2}{n \sum x_{1i}^2},$$

collinearity between $X_1$ and $X_0$ generally means $\text{var}(\hat{\beta}_0)$ is large, too. If the collinearity were perfect, $X_1$ would be a constant and the BLUE estimator of $\beta_1$ would not exist. The OLS estimator of the slopes of collinear variables are generally imprecise for much the same reason as seen in this example.

## Perfect Multicollinearity

When some explanators are collinear, there is too little separate variation in those explanators to allow precise estimation of their individual effects on $Y$. In the extreme, when some explanators move in lock-step with one another, there exists no unbiased linear estimator for their coefficients. For example, suppose we are studying the effect of temperature and humidity on the sale of sunglasses, and that in each observation in our data, humidity is equal to the temperature divided by 2; every time temperature rises by two, humidity rises by one. With such data we cannot distinguish the effect of changes in temperature from the effect of changes in humidity. Did sales rise because humidity rose or because temperature rose? There is no way to tell with our data, because the two always happen together in our data.

More generally, explanators suffer from perfect multicollinearity whenever one explanator, say $X_s$, equals a weighted sum of the other variables, that is:

$$X_{si} = \sum_{\substack{j=0 \\ j \neq s}}^{k} \alpha_j X_{ji}$$

for all $i$. We say $X_s$ is perfectly collinear with the set of explanators that have nonzero coefficients in this equation. When explanators are perfectly collinear, no weights exist that satisfy the unbiasedness conditions for unbiased estimation of their coefficients. The reasoning goes as follows. Unbiased estimation of $\beta_s$ requires

$$\sum_i w_i^s X_{ri} = 0 \qquad \text{for } r \neq s$$

and

$$\sum_i w_i^s X_{si} = 1.$$

However, if

$$X_{si} = \sum_{\substack{j=0 \\ j \neq s}}^{k} a_j X_{ji}$$

then, substituting,

$$\sum_i w_i^s X_{si} = \sum_i \left[ w_i^s \left( \sum_{\substack{j=0 \\ j \neq s}}^{k} a_j X_{ji} \right) \right]$$

$$= \sum_i \left[ \left( \sum_{\substack{j=0 \\ j \neq s}}^{k} w_i^s a_j X_{ji} \right) \right],$$

because multiplying the second sum by $w_i^s$ is the same as multiplying each term in that sum by $w_i^s$,

$$= \sum_{\substack{j=0 \\ j \neq s}}^{k} \left[ \sum_i w_i^s a_j X_{ji} \right],$$

because the order of a sum does not matter,

$$= \sum_{\substack{j=0 \\ j \neq s}}^{k} a_j \left[ \sum_i w_i^s X_{ji} \right],$$

because $a_j$ doesn't vary with $i$ and thus can be factored out, and,

$$= \sum_{\substack{j=0 \\ j \neq s}}^{k} a_j \left[ \sum_i w_i^s X_{ji} \right] = 0,$$

because each term in brackets is zero if we are to unbiasedly estimate $\beta_s$. Hence, if $X_s$ is perfectly collinear with other explanators, $\beta_s$ cannot be unbiasedly linearly estimated because $\sum_i w_i^s X_{si}$ cannot equal both 0 and 1.

## Coping with Multicollinearity

The least controversial way of overcoming multicollinearity in data is to add more observations—preferably observations for which the explanators are *not* collinear, and certainly observations in which the explanators are not perfectly collinear.

A frequent, but often problematic, strategy to avoid multicollinearity is to omit one or another variable from a model. For example, education, experience, and age are often collinear in moderately sized samples of workers. Labor econo-

**REGRESSION'S GREATEST HITS**

# An Econometric Top 40—A Pop Tune

## Who Needs SAT Scores?

The Scholastic Aptitude Test (SAT) has been a rite of passage for generations of prospective college students. Most colleges require the SAT or its cousin, the ACT, for admission. The tests have sparked considerable controversy over the years, because critics worry that the tests are not accurate predictors of college performance and that the tests might be biased against some groups of students. In 1984, Bates College broke ranks with its sisters and announced that it would no longer require SAT scores of applicants. Bates based its decision, in part, on a regression analysis of test scores and subsequent academic performance of students who attended Bates.[3] Bates was able to study the academic performance and SAT scores of nonsubmitters because the scores were submitted after admission.

Did Bates find that SAT scores do not predict GPA? Did they find that those who submit SAT scores do no better than those who do not? No. Bates's initial analysis revealed that students with higher SAT scores have higher GPAs on average. The subsequent analyses found that submitters have higher average GPAs than nonsubmitters. But the Bates analyses reveal that these differences are small.

The early Bates data indicate that students whose SAT scores differ by 100 points, a substantial difference, on average differ in their GPAs by only 0.12 points on a 4.00 scale when other variables are kept fixed. The file sat2.\*\*\* on this book's companion Web site (**www.aw-bc .com/murray**) contains SAT scores and first-year GPAs for a class of Bates students that entered the college when SAT scores were required.

Hit Table 8.3 contains a regression of Bates students' first-year GPAs, *GPA*, (measured on a 4.0 scale) on four variables: (i) *SAT*, which is SAT score (which ranges from 400 to 1600 nationally); (ii) *RANK*, which is the student's high school percentile rank in class; (iii) *FEMALE*, which is equal to one for females and zero for males; and (iv) *PRIV*, which is equal to one for those who attended private high schools and zero for others. The data are from sat2.\*\*\*. The estimated coefficient on SAT is 0.0012. The estimated standard deviation of the SAT coefficient estimator is 0.0002, indicating quite precise estimation of the SAT coefficient. The variable SAT score could be replaced by the scores on the individual component tests that make up the SAT test, math and verbal. However, if we were to include the separate math and verbal scores, we could not also include the SAT variable, as it would be perfectly collinear with the math and verbal scores, being the sum of those two scores.

How much predictive power is lost when SAT scores are not included in a GPA regression? The $R^2$ in the GPA equation falls from 0.14 to 0.06 when SAT score is excluded. This is not a trivial decline. However, a more informative way to see the relative unimportance of SAT scores for predicting first-year GPA is to consider the following mental experiment. Suppose Bates' first-year class had to be half its actual size, say, 158 students instead of the 317 first-year students in the prepolicy sample of sat2.\*\*\*. We could assess the relative unimportance of SAT scores by asking how well GPA regressions, with and without SAT scores, would predict which of the 317 sample's enrolled students would have the top 158 first-year GPAs? Would Bates pick a better entering class of 158 students if it knew the students'

**HIT TABLE 8.3  SAT and GPA**

Dependent Variable: GPA
Method: Least Squares
Sample: 1 317
Included observations: 317

| Variable | Coefficient | Std. Error | t-Statistic | Prob. |
|---|---|---|---|---|
| C | 1.532618 | 0.264339 | 5.797922 | 0.0000 |
| PRV | 0.122989 | 0.102278 | 1.202496 | 0.2301 |
| RANK | 0.701015 | 0.176137 | 3.979946 | 0.0001 |
| FEMALE | 0.130242 | 0.053678 | 2.426384 | 0.0158 |
| SAT | 0.001178 | 0.000218 | 5.400013 | 0.0000 |
| R-squared | 0.143634 | Mean dependent var | 2.860637 | |
| Adjusted R-squared | 0.132655 | S.D. dependent var | 0.494186 | |
| S.E. of regression | 0.460242 | Akaike info criterion | 1.301518 | |
| Sum squared resid | 66.08862 | Schwarz criterion | 1.360806 | |
| Log likelihood | −201.2905 | F-statistic | 13.08255 | |
| Durbin–Watson stat | 1.942173 | Prob(F-statistic) | 0.000000 | |

SAT scores? Do the regressions with and without SAT score identify equally well the high-achieving first-year students?

Not quite. In the prepolicy sample of first-year students, the list of the top 158 predicted GPA students contains 101 of the 158 actual above-median achievers if SAT score is included in the prediction regression and 97 of the actual above-median achievers if SAT score is omitted from the prediction regression. Losing the SAT information and relying only on rank in class, gender, and whether one attended a private high school causes Bates to misclassify 2.5% more high achievers than does having the SAT scores. The benefits from having SAT score are smaller still when nonquantifiable information, such as letters of recommendation and interviews, are considered.

But why would Bates stop asking for SAT scores if those scores have any predictive value whatsoever? There are three plausible explanations. First, if the SAT is indeed biased against

some groups, forgoing reliance on the tests avoids that bias. Because the relationship between SAT score and GPA is weak, Bates incurs little cost by not requiring SAT scores, so even a small risk of bias might justify Bates's decision. Second, Bates anticipated that by becoming the first highly ranked liberal arts college to not require SAT scores, it would quickly become a favored back-up school for potential applicants worried about their SAT scores. The altered SAT requirement might enrich Bates's applicant pool and bring to Bates some strong students who would otherwise not apply. And third, Bates's policy change brought the college favorable nationwide publicity. Subsequently, several other colleges followed Bates's lead, reducing somewhat the gains from enriched applicant pools and free publicity. The controversy about potential biases in the SAT, however, has grown more heated over time. Optional SAT submission remains Bates's policy.

**Final Notes**

Bates's use of SAT scores highlights a difference between forecasting and other uses of regression models. Admissions officers worry more about predicting the future performance of applicants and less about whether estimates of particular coefficients are unbiased. Social scientists, on the other hand, seek to understand the causal links among variables, and for such work, they want unbiased estimators that isolate the actual effect of one variable on another.

The Bates analysis illustrates how regression analysis can contribute to complex policy analyses. As when deciding whether SAT scores should be optional, regression results are seldom more than one part in many when arriving at policy decisions. For Bates, regression analysis showed that making SAT scores optional would not much impair the college's ability to predict student performance. But whether the small loss in information from forgoing SAT scores was worth the benefits of the policy was a question that went well beyond the reach of the regressions. ∎

mists estimating wage equations frequently include only education and experience variables in their wage models, and omit age.

The labor economists' strategy of omitting one explanator is sound if there is a good reason to think that the omitted explanator has no influence on the dependent variable, because omitting an irrelevant variable from the DGP causes no bias in the estimators of the remaining variables and improves the efficiency of the BLUE estimators. Indeed, even if the excluded explanator is not entirely irrelevant, omitting a variable whose true coefficient is very small introduces little bias, and may well improve the mean square error of the estimators of the remaining coefficients.

Thus, when estimating wage equations, if economists think age has no effect on wage for the population under study, omitting age from a wage equation is a justifiable approach to overcoming multicollinearity in the data. If age *does* matter for wages (for example, when age discrimination is a salient feature of the labor market under study), however, then omitting age to overcome multicollinearity is unwarranted because it may introduce appreciable omitted variables bias in the remaining variables in the wage equation.

In short, there are two helpful ways of coping with the imprecise estimates that can result from multicollinearity. First, we can add observations to our sample. Unfortunately, economists seldom have the luxury of adding observations—they usually use all the available observations to start with. Second, we can drop superfluous variables from the regression model. Unfortunately, multicollinearity among several relevant variables can't be coped with this way, because dropping relevant variables introduces biases into the estimates of the remaining variables' coefficients. Often, when our standard errors are large because of multicollinearity, we must simply acknowledge that the data in hand do not offer much information about the coefficients we estimate imprecisely. The most frequent way of coping with multicollinearity is to live with it.

## 8.4    The Earnings Example Extended—More About Dummy Variables

WHAT IS THE DGP?

Section 6.3 estimated earnings equations for black men and black women. In that section we use a dummy variable that distinguishes women from men to show that earnings differ between black men and black women and that this remains true when differences in workers' educations and work experiences are accounted for, or are "controlled for." This section elaborates on the uses—and pitfalls—of dummy variables in regression analyses.

### Using Multiple Dummy Variables to Estimate Means

Earnings differ between black men and black women. Earnings also differ among racial and ethnic groups. Our particular National Longitudinal Survey of Youth (NLSY) sample of workers contains only three groups—Hispanics, non-Hispanic blacks, and non-Hispanic whites—each of which might have different earnings experiences. To analyze such differences, we construct three dummy variables: H (= 1 if the individual is Hispanic, and = 0 otherwise), B (= 1 if the individual is a non-Hispanic black, and = 0 otherwise), and $W$ (= 1 if the individual is a non-Hispanic white, and = 0 otherwise).

Were we to ignore other explanators, we could analyze the average earnings of these three groups in any of several ways. For one, specifying

$$E(\ln(earnings)) = \beta_H H + \beta_B B + \beta_W W$$

would yield coefficients $\beta_H$, $\beta_B$, and $\beta_W$ equal to the average log of earnings for the respective groups. In this specification,

$$E(\ln(earnings)|H = 1, B = 0, W = 0) = \beta_H + \beta_B 0 + \beta_W 0 = \beta_H$$

$$E(\ln(earnings)|H = 0, B = 1, W = 0) = \beta_H 0 + \beta_B + \beta_W 0 = \beta_B$$

and

$$E(\ln(earnings)|H = 0, B = 0, W = 1) = \beta_H 0 + \beta_B 0 + \beta_W 1 = \beta_W.$$

The sample of workers in the file earnings.*** on this book's companion Web site (www.aw-bc.com/murray) yields the following regression result:

$$\text{estimated } E(\ln(earnings)) = 9.73W + 9.54H + 9.46B. \qquad \textbf{8.7}$$

$$\text{(e.s.e.)} \qquad (0.01) \quad (0.05) \quad (0.02)$$

(This data file is too large for the student version of EViews, but not for other versions.) Alternatively, we could specify the relationship with an intercept term corresponding to the mean of one group and dummy variables that allow the other groups' means to differ from that first group's mean. For example:

$$E(\ln(earnings)) = \beta_0 + \beta_1 H + \beta_2 W$$

specifies $\beta_0$ as the mean log of earnings for blacks ($E(\ln(earnings)|H = 0, B = 1, W = 0) = \beta_0$), while $\beta_1$ and $\beta_2$ indicate how Hispanics' and non-Hispanic whites' mean log earnings differ from non-Hispanic blacks':

$$E(\ln(earnings)|H = 1, B = 0, W = 0) = \beta_0 + \beta_1,$$
$$E(\ln(earnings)|H = 0, B = 0, W = 1) = \beta_0 + \beta_2.$$

The group we choose to represent with a constant term is a matter of convenience. For example, we might wish to know how much less Hispanics and non-Hispanic blacks earn when compared to non-Hispanic whites. Using the sample of workers in earnings.***, we find this specification estimates expected log earnings to be

$$\text{estimated } E(\ln(earnings)) = 9.73 - 0.19H - 0.27B, \qquad \textbf{8.8}$$

$$\text{(e.s.e.)} \qquad\qquad (0.01) \quad (0.05) \quad (0.02)$$

indicate that both Hispanics and non-Hispanic blacks earn appreciably less than non-Hispanic whites. Because $e^{-0.19} = 0.83$ and $e^{-0.27} = 0.76$, we would compute that Hispanics earn 83% of what non-Hispanic whites do, and non-Hispanic blacks earn 76% of what non-Hispanic whites do.[4]

Note that in each of the specifications above we omit either the constant term or the dummy variable for one of the categories. Not to do so would introduce multicollinearity into the model because the sum of all the dummy variables is always one (in our subpopulation, an individual always belongs to just one of the categories). That is,

$$H + B + W = 1,$$

so that the $X_0$ (equal to one for every observation) always equals the sum of all the dummies. This fact implies perfect multicollinearity among the dummies and the constant term. Causing multicollinearity by including in a regression's explanators *all* the categorical dummies *and* an intercept term we call the **dummy variable trap**.

The choice to omit the constant or one dummy variable will not alter the estimates of mean effects. The estimates from Equation 8.8, which provide one group's means and the other group's divergences from the mean, match up with the estimates from Equation 8.7, which provide the mean effects for each group by omitting a constant. The choice depends only on ease of interpreting one's output.

If we are interested in the differences between non-Hispanic white and non-Hispanic blacks and between Hispanics and whites, the reported estimated coefficients of Equation 8.8—and their reported standard errors—are precisely what we are interested in. To use the estimates from Equation 8.7, we would have to subtract the estimated coefficient for non-Hispanic white from those for non-Hispanic black and Hispanic in order to compute the figures of interest to us, and the standard errors would have to be obtained separately. On the other hand, if the intercepts for the various groups are what interest us, Equation 8.7 tells us precisely what we are interested in—the intercepts and their estimated standard errors. We should run the regressions in a form that spares us extra calculations.

When including an intercept and omitting one dummy variable, keep in mind that the coefficients on the included variables measure how those groups differ from the omitted group. If the omitted group's intercept is imprecisely measured, we are likely to imprecisely measure how the other groups differ from the omitted group as well. *Consequently, when choosing a dummy variable to omit from our model, we should usually not omit the dummy variable of a group for which we have only a small number of observations, because that group's intercept is likely to be imprecisely measured.*

## Using Multiple Dummies to Estimate Intercepts

When additional explanators are included in the model, the coefficients on the dummy variables no longer correspond to the means for the categories, but instead correspond to the intercepts. Thus, if we specify

$$E(\ln(earnings)) = \beta_H Hispanic + \beta_B black + \beta_W(non\text{-}Hispanic\ white)$$
$$+ \beta_1 education + \beta_2 experience + \beta_3(experience\ squared),$$

$\beta_H$ is the intercept for Hispanics, $\beta_B$ the intercept for non-Hispanic blacks, and $\beta_W$ the intercept for non-Hispanic whites. Similarly, if we specify

$$E(\ln(earnings)) = \alpha_0 + \alpha_1 H + \alpha_2 B + \beta_1 education$$
$$+ \beta_2 experience + \beta_3(experience\ squared),$$

then $\alpha_0$ will be the intercept term for the omitted category (in this case, non-Hispanic whites) and $\alpha_0 + \alpha_1$ will be the effective intercept term when $H = 1$ and $B = 0$, so $\alpha_0 + \alpha_1$ is the intercept term for Hispanics, and $\alpha_0 + \alpha_2$ will be the intercept term for non-Hispanic blacks. Figure 8.1 illustrates the exact correspondence of these two specifications by graphing each for a fixed level of experience. The figure depicts the expected value of log earnings for Hispanics, non-Hispanic blacks, and non-Hispanic whites. Notice that the intercept for Hispanics is $\beta_H = \alpha_0 + \alpha_1$, for non-Hispanic blacks is $\beta_B = \alpha_0 + \alpha_2$, and for non-Hispanic

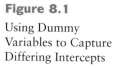

**Figure 8.1**

Using Dummy
Variables to Capture
Differing Intercepts

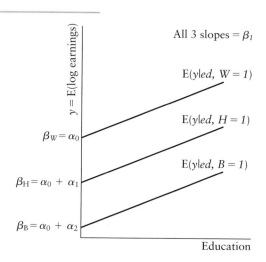

whites is $\beta_W = \alpha_0$. In the figure, $\alpha_0$ and $\alpha_2$ are both negative, so expected log earnings are less for Hispanics and non-Hispanic blacks than for non-Hispanic whites.

## Using Multiple Dummies to Categorize Along Several Dimensions

We can place individuals into multiple categories. For example, individuals can be Hispanic and female. In such cases, two sets of dummies are needed, one for race/ethnicity and one for sex. If we include an intercept in such a model, one dummy from each categorization needs to be omitted from the model—the intercept then represents the intercept for individuals with the omitted traits. For example, if Hispanic males are the omitted category, the dummies for Hispanic and male need to be omitted from the model, and the intercept is the intercept for Hispanic males. When an intercept is included in the model, the coefficients on the remaining dummies are how the intercept for that coefficient's group (say Hispanics, if the dummy is 1 for Hispanics and 0 otherwise) differs from the intercept of otherwise similar non-Hispanics. Alternatively, we can omit the intercept from the model and include in the model all the dummy variables for some one categorization. The coefficients on the dummy variables for that categorization then indicate the contribution to the intercept term of being in that dummies' group. For example, if one categorization is male/female, and another is black/white, then omitting the intercept allows us to include either both the male and female dummies, or both the black and white dummies. If we include both the male and female dummies, their estimated coefficients are the intercepts for males and females, respectively.

Distinguishing among the workers in the file earnings.*** on this book's companion Web site (**www.aw-bc.com/murray**) by ethnicity and sex, yields:

$$\text{estimated } E(\ln(earnings)) = 7.45 - 0.04H - 0.20B - 0.39female$$
$$\text{(e.s.e.)} \qquad (0.13) \quad (0.04) \quad (0.02) \quad (0.018)$$

$$+ \ 0.12education + 0.11experience$$
$$(0.004) \qquad\qquad (0.024)$$

$$- \ 0.003 \ (experience \ squared)$$
$$(0.001)$$

Notice that adding controls for education, experience, and sex markedly reduces the coefficient on $H$, but only modestly reduces the coefficient on $B$. This suggests that much of the difference in earnings between Hispanics and non-Hispanic whites is due to differences in education, experience, and sex. In contrast, the differences between non-Hispanic blacks and non-Hispanic whites persist for individuals with otherwise similar traits.

## Using Dummy Variables to Allow Different Slopes for Different Groups

Dummy variables can also be used to investigate whether slopes differ between groups. Suppose we wish to ask what the effect of education is for females. If the dummy for female is $F$ and that for male $M$, we can form the interaction terms for sex and education, that is, the one variable multiplied by the other: $(F \cdot education)$ and $(M \cdot education)$. Notice $(F \cdot education)$ equals education when $F$ equals 1 and equals 0 otherwise. Similarly, $(M \cdot education)$ equals education when $M = 1$ and equals 0 otherwise.

Thus, we can specify

$$E(\ln(earnings)) \ = \ \alpha_0 + \alpha_1 H + \alpha_2 B + \alpha_3 F$$
$$+ \ \beta_1(F \cdot education) + \beta_2(M \cdot education)$$
$$+ \ \beta_3 experience + \beta_4(experience \ squared).$$

The coefficient $\beta_1$ is the effect of education for women, and $\beta_2$ is the effect of education for men. Notice that we omit education itself to avoid multicollinearity. Alternatively, we could include education itself, and omit one interaction term:

$$E(\ln(earnings)) = \alpha_0 + \alpha_1 H + \alpha_2 B + \alpha_3 F$$
$$\beta_1 education + \beta_2(M \cdot education) +$$
$$\beta_3 experience + \beta_4(experience \ squared),$$

## An Econometric Top 40—A Classical Favorite

### The Rational Expectations Revolution

In 1973, Nobel laureate Robert Lucas of the University of Chicago wrote a profoundly influential paper that provided microeconomic foundations for the new Keynesian-augmented Phillips curve and empirical support for what became the rational expectations revolution.[5] The augmented Phillips curve posits that unemployment fluctuates with unexpected changes in inflation. Lucas argued that such a relationship could stem from producers' uncertainty about the general price level. He reasoned that when a firm is faced with an increased willingness by consumers to spend money on its product, the firm would not know for sure if (i) a beneficial relative price increase had befallen their good or if (ii) a general price increase (that is, inflation) was under way. To the extent that the relative price of the firm's good had risen, the firm would want to expand output; to the extent that the price increase reflected general inflation, no change in the firm's output would be warranted.

Lucas suggested that the firm would resolve its uncertainty about why consumers are spending more by making a probabilistic assessment. The "rational" approach, said Lucas, would be to look at past experience, asking the historical extent of the two kinds of price changes, and to form a judgment about the current price change based on the laws of probability and past experience. In environments in which inflation had seldom occurred in the past, a rational firm would expect much of any current price increase to be a relative price increase. In environments in which inflationary episodes had occurred frequently in the past, much of any price increase would be attributed to inflation. Firms acting as Lucas expected would give rise to an augmented Phillips

curve—inflation would spur firms to increase output (and decrease inflation) to the extent that they estimated the rising prices reflected relative price changes.

A striking conclusion from Lucas's reasoning is that firms' output, and hence unemployment, will be more responsive to changes in the nominal demand for goods in those countries where general price changes have been less frequent. Thus, Lucas could test his theory by looking at how real output, which determines unemployment, varies with changes in nominal output, which reflects changes in households' willingness to spend money on goods. In conformity with the usual augmented Phillips story, Lucas predicts that the change in nominal income will be positively related to the level of real output. Lucas's theory further predicts, in particular, that the coefficient on nominal income will be smaller in those countries with more volatile price levels.

Lucas tested his theory by examining 16 countries. For each country, he regressed current real output on both the most recent change in nominal income and the lagged (one-year) level of real output. Lucas included a lagged value of real output to capture cyclical components of real output. In equation form, Lucas estimated a "supply curve" of the following form:

$$(real\ output_t) = \beta_0$$
$$+ \beta_1(unpredicted\ change\ in\ nominal\ income_t)$$
$$+ \beta_2(unpredicted\ real\ output_{t-1}) + u_t.$$

Lucas measured unpredicted real output and unpredicted changes in nominal output by the deviations of real output and nominal output from their time trends. He assumed people would predict that real and nominal outputs would follow their historical trends. The augmented Phillips curve says $\beta_1$ will be positive—unexpected monetary stimuli spur output (and hence reduce unemployment). In 13 of the 16 countries he examined, Lucas found $\beta_1$ to be significantly positive.

Lucas's theory further states that from one country to the next, $\beta_1$ will be lower in countries in which unpredicted price changes (and thus nominal income changes) are more variable. It is in those countries that firms will attribute less of unexpected increases in consumer spending to relative price changes. Lucas pointed with satisfaction to the fact that in the two countries in his sample in which prices are highly unstable, $\beta_1$ was estimated to be one-tenth the magnitude of even the smallest estimate of $\beta_1$ among the other, relatively price-stable, countries.

Subsequent researchers formalized tests of Lucas's theory about the behavior of $\beta_1$ across countries. For example, Ball, Mankiw, and Romer used a sample of 43 countries to estimate a relationship between country-specific estimates of $\beta_1$ and the variance of each country's change in nominal income variable.[6] They estimated that

$$E[\hat{\beta}_{1i}] = 0.388 - 1.639 variance_i,$$
$$(e.s.e.)\quad (0.057)\quad (0.482)$$

where $\hat{\beta}_{1i}$ is the estimate of $\beta_1$ in the $i$-th country, and ($variance_i$) is the variance over time in the $i$-th country's changes in nominal income about their trend. Notice the novelty of this analysis. There are two steps. First, the authors estimate the "Lucas supply curve" for numerous countries. Then, the authors focus on how the supply curve coefficient estimates vary across countries.

Ball and colleagues, like others conducting similar analyses, found the coefficient on *variance* statistically significant and negative; that is, $\beta_1$ is smaller in those countries in which firms have less reason to attribute unexpected

increases in consumer spending to relative price changes. This finding supports Lucas's theory and lends credibility to the rational expectations claim that monetary policies can only affect output to the extent that the monetary authorities can surprise economic agents. In Lucas's words, "Thus the apparent short-term trade-off (between inflation and unemployment) is favorable as long as it remains unused. . . . These results are, of course, inconsistent with the existence of even moderately stable Phillips curves. On the other hand, they follow directly from the view that inflation stimulates real output if, and only if, it succeeds in 'fooling' suppliers of labor and goods into thinking *relative* prices are moving in their favor."[7]

 **Final Notes**

Lucas's paper is an example of the blending of theory and statistics that marks the best econometric work. The original Phillips paper was largely a provocative statistical exercise in which the economic theory was not compelling. The initial efforts to question the Phillips curve were purely theoretical exercises that challenged the plausibility of the statistical results but did not offer an alternative empirical analysis. Lucas married theory and statistics in his paper, accounting for Phillips's results both empirically and theoretically, while simultaneously offering a fresh and critical understanding of the available data. Not all economists have accepted Lucas's conclusions about monetary policy, but Lucas's work placed a heavy burden on proponents of alternative views to substantiate their claims with equally strong theory and statistics. In 1995, Lucas received the Nobel prize in economics "for having developed and applied the hypothesis of rational expectations, and thereby having transformed macroeconomic analysis and deepened our understanding of economic policy."

in which $\beta_1$ is the effect of education for females (that is, the effect of education when $M = 0$), and $\beta_2$ is how education's effect differs for males from what it is for females.

When estimating such interactions between categorical variables and other variables, it is wise to allow the intercept to vary with the categorical variables, lest the interaction estimate suffer omitted variable bias. Using dummy variables to capture group characteristics such as sex, race, and ethnicity is commonplace. Dummy variables can also be used to differentiate between historical epochs, such as pre–World War II and post–World War II.

Interacting categorical variables with all of the other variables in a model and simultaneously allowing the intercept to vary across the categories, yields the same coefficient estimates as estimating separate equations for each category. Although the coefficient estimates are the same with these two approaches, the $t$-statistics are likely to differ. A single regression estimates one variance for the disturbances and applies that estimate to estimating all standard errors. Separate regressions estimate separate variances for the distinct groups and apply those distinct variance estimates when estimating standard errors.

## Summary

Including superfluous regressors in the model brings unnecessary constraints to the derivation of the BLUE estimator, reducing efficiency. Omitting relevant regressors causes us to overlook needed unbiasedness constraints. We see that when

 ***An Organizational Structure for the Study of Econometrics***

### 1. What Is the DGP?
Dummy variables can quantify categorical variables.

### 2. What Makes a Good Estimator?
——

### 3. How Do We Create an Estimator?
Multicollinearity precludes unbiased estimation.

### 4. What Are an Estimator's Properties?
Omitting relevant variables causes bias.

Including superfluous variables loses efficiency.

Beware the dummy variable trap.

the omitted variable is $X_q$, the resulting omitted variable bias in estimating $\beta_s$ is $\beta_q \sum w_i^s X_{qi}$.

When explanators move too closely together, differentiating their separate effects is difficult. Such closely co-varying explanators are said to be multicollinear or collinear. The variances of collinear variables' estimated coefficients are large. The usual cure for multicollinearity is more observations. In the extreme, when explanators move in lock-step, so that one explanator can be expressed as an exact linear combination of others, the unbiasedness conditions for estimating all those variables' coefficients cannot be met. In such cases, we say the data suffer from perfect multicollinearity.

The chapter describes the appropriate interpretation of dummy variable's coefficients when there are multiple categories and when slopes differ among groups. It also warns us to avoid the dummy variable trap—that is, do not include both an intercept and all the categorical dummies in a regression model, because doing so will result in perfect multicollinearity.

## Concepts for Review

Collinear   321

Dummy variable trap   329

Multicollinear   321

Omitted variables bias   312

Perfectly collinear   321

## Questions for Discussion

1. Regression models, even multiple regression models, contain a limited number of variables. With the vast number of influences that impinge on any economic phenomenon, regression models invariably suffer from omitted variables. Doesn't this fatally wound regression analysis as a tool for learning about the world?

2. When a data set contains a very large number of possible explanatory variables, analysts sometimes try many combinations, ultimately excluding those variables that have poor $t$-statistics and keeping those with good $t$-statistics. In what way is it wrong to claim that the variables in the final model are statistically significant at some conventional significance level, based upon their $t$-statistics?

## Problems for Analysis

> For the data sets that you will need to solve the problems in this section, go to **www.aw-bc.com/murray**.

 1. Does year-to-year economic growth alter the poverty rate? The file poverty2.\*\*\* contains, for 1980–2003 (all measured in percents):

> *poverty*    U.S. poverty rates
> *gdpgrow*    U.S. GDP growth rates
> *unemploy*   U.S. unemployment rates

a. Regress changes in the poverty rate on the GDP growth rate, changes in the unemployment rate, and an intercept term. Does economic growth seem to be a superfluous variable in this regression?

b. Repeat the regression, omitting GDP growth. What is the percentage change in the estimated standard error on unemployment's coefficient that results from dropping GDP growth from the model?

c. Regress changes in the poverty rate on the GDP growth rate. Why might a policy maker be as interested in this regression as in the regression in (a)?

d. Interpret, and resolve, the seemingly conflicting findings about the statistical significance of GDP growth in (a) and (c).

 2. Can omitting an intercept term lead to serious bias? Consider the data in haavelmo2.***. Regress real consumption (*real_cons*) on real GDP (*real_GDP*). Add an intercept term to the regression. Is the estimated marginal propensity to consume substantially different in the two regressions?

 3. When police arrest more people for murder, are there fewer murders? Many econometricians have addressed this question. However, only one economist, David Mustard, has had data on conviction rates and sentence lengths, as well as on arrest rates. Mustard used his data to ask whether earlier analyses lack of conviction and sentence data seriously biased their estimates of the effects of arrests on crime.[8] The data set murder1.*** contains a subset of Mustard's data. Among the variables in the file are:

*arrmurd*    County's murder arrests as a percentage of murders in the county

*convmurd*   County's convictions for murder as a percentage of arrests for murder in the county

*lratmurd*   Natural log of county's annual murder rate per 100,000 people

*density*    County's population density

*ppb*        Percentage of the county's population who are African American

*incom*      County's per capita income

a. Regress the log of the murder rate on the logs of income, the murder arrest rate, population density, and the proportion of the population that is black. Then add the log of the conviction rate to the regression. Compare the estimated elasticities of murder rates with respect to arrest rates. Was the effect of omitting conviction rates from the regression substantial?

b. Briefly explain what must be true about the relationship between arrest rates and conviction rates to account for the results in (a)? Check the correlation between arrest rates and conviction rates in this sample. Does this conform with what you obtained in (a)?

c. Speculate about why conviction rates for murder and arrest rates for murder might be correlated.

 4. How do growing weather and a wine's age influence a Bordeaux wine's price? The data set wineweather1.*** contains average 1989 prices for Bordeaux wines for the

vintages from 1952 to 1989, together with data on weather conditions when each vintage was being grown. These data were part of an analysis of Bordeaux wine as an investment by economists Orley Ashenfelter, David Ashmore, and Robert LaLonde.[9] The variables in the file are

*logprice*    Natural log of the price of Bordeaux wines relative to the price of the 1961 vintage

*degrees*    Average temperature in the growing season

*hrain*    Rainfall in the harvest season

*wrain*    Winter rainfall during the growing season

*time_sv*    Time from 1989 back to the wine's vintage year

a. Regress *logprice* on rainfall during the harvest and the vintage of the wine.

b. Add winter rainfall to the regression in (a). Does winter rainfall seem to be a superfluous variable?

c. Add average temperature during the growing season to the regression in (b). Explain what happens to the estimated coefficient on winter rain when you add *degrees* to the regression by referencing a regression of *degrees* on *wrain*, *hrain*, and an intercept term. Also give an intuitive explanation without explicit reference to the *degrees* regression.

5. U.S. states differ in the generosity of their welfare programs. The file TANF2.*** reports the maximum real benefits each state offers poor single parents with three children. The variables in the file are

*tanfreal*    State's real maximum benefit for single parent with three kids

*black*    Percent of state's population who are African American

*blue*    State voted Democratic in 2004 presidential election

*mdinc*    Median income in state

*west*    = 1 if state is in west; = 0 otherwise

*south*    = 1 if state is in south; = 0 otherwise

*midwest*    = 1 if state is in midwest; = 0 otherwise

*northeast*    = 1 if state is in northeast; = 0 otherwise

a. Regress real benefits on the percent of the population who are African American and an intercept term. Repeat the regression, adding the dummy for whether the state voted Democratic in the 2004 election. Does omitting the political party variable appreciably bias the estimate of race on benefits?

b. Add *west*, *northeast*, and *midwest* to the regression that includes *black*, *blue*, and an intercept term. What do the coefficients on these three additional dummy variables tell us?

c. Did the omission of the regional dummy variables appreciably bias the estimated coefficient on *black*?

d. Modify the regression in (c) to allow the slope for *black* to be different for the Midwest than for the other regions. Is the effect of *black* on real welfare benefits different in the Midwest than elsewhere? Briefly explain your response.

e. Add *south* to the model. Explain what happens.

f. Use regression and the regional dummies to compute the mean welfare benefits in each region over the sample period.

6. Greg Mankiw, David Romer, and David Weil examined the Solow growth model by looking at its implications for both the levels of countries' GDPs and the their growth rates. The data they used are in the file MRW.\*\*\*. The variables in that file are

COUNTRY   Number representing country
GDP60     GDP per working-age population in 1960
GDP85     GDP per working-age population in 1985
GDPGR     GDP growth rate 1960–1985
INTER     Dummy variable indicating MRW's intermediate group
INVEST    Investment as a percentage of GDP
NONOIL    Dummy variable for non-oil-producing country
OECD      Dummy variable for OECD country
POPGR     Population growth rate in percent
SCHOOL    Percent of working-age population in secondary school

   a. Mankiw, Romer, and Weil's Greatest Hit described in Chapter 7 (p. 232) analyzes two growth model specifications—one that ignores human capital and one that does not. Their data is in MRW.\*\*\*. Create their variable that captures physical capital, $X_1$,

$$X_1 = \ln\left(\frac{s}{n+g+d}\right) = \ln\left(\frac{s_p}{n+g+d}\right) = \ln\left(\frac{invest}{popgr+2+3}\right)$$

(*popgrow* is the population growth rate), and their variable that captures human capital, $X_2$,

$$X_2 = \ln\left(\frac{s_h}{n+g+d}\right) = \ln\left(\frac{school}{popgr+2+3}\right).$$

   b. Restrict the sample to countries that are not oil producers. Regress the log of GDP85 on $X_1$ and an intercept term and regress the log of GDP85 on $X_1$, $X_2$, and an intercept term.

   c. Build a 95% confidence interval for the coefficient on X using the results of the second regression. Is there evidence that the corresponding coefficient estimate in the first regression is biased?

7. Nitrogen dioxide ($NO_2$) is a pollutant that attacks the human respiratory systems; it increases the likelihood of respiratory illness. One common source of nitrogen dioxide is automobile exhaust. The file NO2pollution.\*\*\* contains a subset from 500 hourly observations made from October 2001 to August 2003.[10] The variables in the data set are

LNO2      Natural logarithm of the concentration of $NO_2$ (particles)
LCARS     Natural logarithm of the number of cars per hour
TEMP      Temperature two meters above ground (degrees C)
WNDSPD    Wind speed (meters/second)
TCHNG23   Temperature difference between 25 and 2 meters above ground (degrees C)
WNDDIR    Wind direction (degrees between 0 and 360)

*HOUR*      Hour of day
*DAYS*      Day number from October 1, 2001

a. Regress the log of $NO_2$ concentrations on the log of cars per hour. What is the estimated elasticity of $NO_2$ concentrations with respect to cars? Build a 95% confidence interval for the elasticity.

b. Regress the log of $NO_2$ concentration on the log of the number of cars, the two temperature variables, the two wind variables, and the time index (*DAYS*). Does this regression estimate a different elasticity of $NO_2$ concentrations with respect to cars? Are you inclined to say that the first estimate suffered from bias? (Does the new estimated elasticity fall within the old 95% confidence interval?)

c. These data are hourly observations, and the number of cars probably varies widely across the hours of the day—as might other contributors to $NO_2$ levels. Add one dummy variable for each hour of the day (24 in all). Does including the hourly dummies reveal a serious bias in the elasticity estimate in (b)? (This part of the problem cannot be done with the student version of EViews.)

8. Labor economists have learned from extensive work that the log of earnings (*lnincome*) is usually a better measure than earnings (*income*) for use in econometric analyses that examine the determinants of earnings. These economists have also found that explanators such as age (*age*) and education (*educatn*) appear in earnings linearly, with no taking of logs. They have also learned that experience and sometimes its square contribute to explaining the log of earnings. Furthermore, these economists frequently capture "ability" in earnings equations by including an individual's score on the Armed Forces Qualifying Test (*afqt*). The file earnings3.*** contains these variables for a sample of Hispanic workers.

a. Use the regress command to estimate a log–linear earnings equation in which the explanators are education, experience, AFQT score, sex, and an intercept term. In a log–linear specification, the dependent variable—here earnings—is measured in logs, and the explanatory variables are measured linearly—this contrasts with log–log specifications, in which all variables are in logs, and the usual plain linear specification. Briefly state whether the explanators' estimated coefficients in your regression conform to your expectations.

b. Re-run the regression, omitting AFQT score. What happens to the estimated coefficient on education? Would you describe this difference between the two estimates as attributable to a bias? Briefly explain.

c. Regress AFQT score on the remaining explanators. What in these results would allow you to predict the results of the regression in (b), given the results in (a)?

d. To what group of people does the intercept term in your estimated equation directly apply?

e. How would you modify the regression in (a) to allow Hispanic males and Hispanic females each to have their own distinct return to education (that is, their own distinct coefficient on *educatn*)? Explain precisely the variables you would form for inclusion in your regression model to achieve this end. Then run the regression and report the results.

f. Use the regression in (e) to test at the 5% significance level the null hypothesis that Hispanic males and Hispanic females have the same return to education, against the alternative that they do not.

9. The file equipmentandgrowth.*** contains data on economic growth between 1960 and 1985 for 106 countries. De Long and Summers[11] used these data to investigate the effect of equipment investment on economic growth. The six variables in the file are

| | |
|---|---|
| *GDP60vUS* | Natural log of country's per capita income in 1960, relative to that in the United States in 1960 |
| *GDPGR* | Growth rate of income per worker for country between 1960 and 1985 |
| *NONEQINV* | Nonequipment investment for country between 1960 and 1985 |
| *EQUIPINV* | Equipment investment for country between 1960 and 1985 |
| *LFGR6085* | Growth rate of labor force between 1960 and 1985 |
| *CONTINENT* | Continent of the country: 1 = Africa; 2 = Asia; 3 = Europe; 4 = North America; 5 = Oceana; and 6 = South America |

a. Regress the growth rate of income per worker on six dummy variables, one dummy for each continent. Interpret the estimated coefficients. Oceana has the fewest observations in this data set. Does this fact account for any feature of the regression results?

b. Add the other four variables to the regression. Then create a dummy variable for a country being in either Europe or North America. Use this dummy variable to augment this regression to allow countries in Europe and North America to have a different coefficient than other countries for equipment investment. Does this analysis make us more or less confident that equipment investment is important in less developed countries? How would you describe the findings about equipment investment in European and North American countries?

c. Add an intercept term to the regression in (b). Explain what happens.

10. Superfluous explanators, omitted variables bias, and multicollinearity can all arise when studying the relationship between students' SAT scores and their GPAs. The data in sat3.*** are pertinent to this question. The sample contains a random sample of 745 Bates College students. The variables include

| | |
|---|---|
| *HS_GPA* | Adjusted high school G.P.A. |
| *ADRANK* | Admissions rank category |
| *FEMALE* | = 1 if female; = 0 if male |
| *HS_TYPE* | Public high school = 0; independent = 1; religious = 2 |
| *HSPCNTL* | Percentile rank in high school |
| *MATH* | Math SAT score |
| *SAT* | Total sat score—math + verbal |
| *SUBMIT* | Asked that SAT score be considered in admissions |
| *GPA* | Cumulative G.P.A. |
| *VERBAL* | Verbal SAT score |

a. Regress *GPA* on an intercept term, *math*, *verbal*, *hs_gpa*, and *female* and on an intercept term, *verbal*, *hs_gpa*, and *female*. What is the percentage change in the estimated coefficient on *verbal* when *math* is omitted from the regression?

b. Regress *GPA* on an intercept term, *math*, *verbal*, *hs_gpa*, *female*, and *hspcntl*. Does *hspcntl* appear to be a superfluous variable? How do you reach your conclusion?

c. Which variable's estimated standard error is most affected by including *haspcntl* in the regression. Does this make intuitive sense?

d. Test at the 5% significance level the null hypothesis that the coefficients on *math* and *verbal* are equal, against the alternative that they are not.

e. What specific numerical coefficients would you obtain if you regressed individual total (math plus verbal) SAT scores for a sample of students on two variables in a multiple regression, the individual math scores and the individual verbal scores?

f. Add SAT score to the regression in (a). What happens? Why?

g. Applicants who ask that their SAT scores not be considered in the Bates admissions process often say that they are "better students than their SAT scores show." Replace *math* and *verbal* with *SAT* and add *submit* in the regression in (a). What does the coefficient on *submit* tell us about nonsubmitters?

h. Use the variables *GPA* and *submit* in a regression analysis to estimate the difference in the expected GPAs of submitters and nonsubmitters, without regard for how else the two groups might differ.

i. Explain the difference between the results in (g) and (h).

# Endnotes

1. Lewis Carroll, *Through the Looking Glass* (New York: Mansfield and Wessels, 1899).

2. Edmund S. Phelps, "Phillips Curves, Expectations, and Optimal Unemployment over Time," *Economica* (August 1967).

3. William C. Hiss, "Optional SATs at Bates: 17 Years and Not Counting," *The Chronicle of Higher Education* (October 26, 2001): B10–B12.

4. This interpretation is only approximate, but it usually serves as a reasonable approximation in earnings functions. OLS unbiasedly estimates the slope, intercept, and dummy variable coefficients in the double log relationship. Thus, it unbiasedly estimates $E(\ln(Y))$. But $e^{E(\ln(Y))}$ does not equal $E(Y)$ because the transformation is nonlinear. $E(\ln(Y))$ is, in general, less than $\ln(E(Y))$. For a more exact treatment, see Arthur Goldberger, *Topics in Regression Analysis* (New York: Macmillan, 1978): 120.

5. Robert E. Lucas, Jr., "Some International Evidence on Output-Inflation Tradeoffs," *American Economic Review* 63, no. 3 (June 1973): 326–334.

6. Laurence N. Ball, Gregory Mankiw, and David Romer, "The New Keynesian Economics and the Output-Inflation Tradeoff," *Brookings Papers on Economic Activity* no. 1 (1988).

7. Lucas, "Some International Evidence . . . ," 333.

8. David Mustard, "Reexamining Criminal Behavior: the Importance of Omitted Variable Bias," *Review of Economics and Statistics* 85, no. 1 (February 2003): 205–211.

9. Orley Ashenfelter, David Ashmore, and Robert LaLonde, "Bordeaux Wine Vintage Quality and the Weather," http://www.liquidasset.com/orley.htm (December 1999).

10. These data come from the Statlib archive of Carnegie Mellon University. They were originally posted there by Aldrin Magne.
11. J. Bradford DeLong, Lawrence H. Summers, "How Strongly Do Developing Countries Benefit from Equipment Investment?" *Journal of Monetary Economics* 32, no. 3 (1994): 395–415.

 *Appendix 8.A*

# Matrix Algebra, Omitted Variables, and Perfect Collinearity

## 8.A.1    A Matrix Representation of Omitted Variable Bias

Suppose the true DGP is that $Y = X\beta + Q\tau + \epsilon$, but we wrongly ignore $Q$. The expected value of the wrongly applied OLS estimator is

$$E[[X'X]^{-1}X'Y] = E[[X'X]^{-1}X'X\beta + [X'X]^{-1}X'Q\tau + [X'X]^{-1}X'\epsilon]$$
$$= \beta + (X'X)^{-1}X'Q\tau,$$

and we see once again that the bias from omitting relevant variables consists of two parts, one the coefficient of the omitted variable(s), here $\tau$, the other the coefficients one would get by regressing the omitted variable(s) against the included variables, here $(X'X)^{-1}X'Q$.

## 8.A.2    Matrix Representation of Perfect Collinearity

The inverse of a square matrix does not exist if some one or more of the columns can be expressed as a linear combination of other columns. Thus, perfect multicollinearity among the explanators in a regression model reveals itself in matrix algebra by $[X'X]^{-1}$ not existing. An noninvertible square matrix is called **singular**.

### Appendix 8.A Concept for Review

**Singular**   343

# Chapter 9

## Testing Multiple Hypotheses

*It's simple: Truth is complex.*

The hypothesis tests presented in Chapter 7 each dealt with a single claim about the coefficients in a regression model. This chapter describes how to test multiple claims about the coefficients. For example, in a wine tasting study by French economists Combris, Lecocq, and Visser (a Greatest Hit that appears in this chapter on p. 345), the authors wondered which factors explained wine prices; the wine's sensory characteristics that are not included on the wine's label, such as flavor and consistency or other traits of the wine that are included on the label, such as appellation and vintage, and so on. The authors concluded that 14 of 15 sensory traits of the wine that were not reported on the wine's label had no effect on the wine's price—leaving most of the explanation of price to nonsensory traits noted on the wine's label. How were the authors able to do this? They found themselves unable to reject the null hypothesis that 14 sensory variable coefficients in their model were zero—notice that is 14 distinct assertions, one about each of 14 coefficients, made all at once. Testing such multiple claims is the subject of this chapter.

The chapter begins by laying aside *t*-statistics when assessing multiple claims. It then develops an intuitively plausible test statistic for assessing multiple claims. Because the intuition has several elements, the development proceeds with successive notions about what might be a good statistic, each new statistic building on the one before it. The statistic we end up with proves to be the classic test statistic for assessing multiple claims about regression coefficients. The chapter then looks at three commonly encountered special cases: (i) assertions that a subset of variables in the model has coefficients of zero (as in the wine example); (ii) assertions that two groups have the same expected value relationship (for example, that black men and black women have the same earnings function); and (iii) assertions that a regression relationship changed at some particular moment in time (for example, that the Phillips curve underwent a shift in 1970).

## 9.1 The Error in Combining *t*-Statistics

**HOW DO WE TEST HYPOTHESES?**

Can we assess multiple claims about a model's coefficients by using the *t*-statistics we have already developed to assess single claims? Consider the wine example that began this chapter. If we include all 14 sensory variables that Combris, Visser, and Lecocq call insignificant as explanators in a wine price regression

# An Econometric Top 40—A Pop Tune

## Life Is Too Short to Drink Bad Wine!

When you buy expensive wine, do you get good wine or just an impressive-looking label? If consumers value wines for the sensory characteristics, such as aromatic intensity, suppleness, flatness, harmony between components, and finish, and have complete information about wines, one would expect that two wines with the same qualities would sell for the same price, no matter what their labels say about the wine's objective characteristics, such as color, appellation, chateau, vintage, and class. But consumers probably don't have complete information about the sensory traits of the wines they buy—labels do not (reliably) inform consumers about sensory traits—so the objective traits found on labels are most likely to matter. How much do labels matter, though, and how much do a wine's qualities matter? Three French analysts say that a wine's sensory traits don't affect price at all beyond what we learn from the objective traits given on the label.

In 1997,[1] economists Pierre Combris and Michael Visser of the French Institute for Agricultural Research, and economist Sebastien Lecocq of the University of Paris, asked whether the price of a Bordeaux wine depends on the wine's sensory characteristics, as assessed by a panel of experts, or on the wine's objective characteristics that are noted on the label. The authors specified a regression model in which both sensory and objective characteristics could influence the price of a wine. A simplified version of their model that conveys the model's spirit is

$$price = \beta_0 + \beta_1(aromatic\ intensity)$$
$$+ \beta_2(finish) + \beta_3(flatness)$$
$$+ \beta_4(class) + \beta_5(1989\ vintage)$$
$$+ \beta_6(Cotes\ group) + \varepsilon \qquad \text{H9.1}$$

The actual list of characteristics the authors use was longer—allowing, in all, for a dozen color, vintage, and appellation characteristics and 16 sensory characteristics. (The data from the original study are contained in the file wineprice1.***. That file is too large for the student version of Eviews. The files' variables are defined in problem 9 of Chapter 6, where a smaller version of the file is also referenced.)

The authors quantified the sensory characteristic data for use in the regression. For example, consider the variables in Equation H9.1. Aromatic intensity took on values of 1 to 3, depending on the judges' assessment of the wine as "strong," "classic," or "discreet." Finish also took on values of 1 to 3, depending on the judges' assessments of "long," "medium," or "short." Flatness was a binary (two-valued) variable, depending on whether the judges deemed the wine "flat" or "not flat." As for the objective characteristics in Equation H9.1, rank took on the value 3 for wines labeled "cru or grand cru classe," value 2 if the wine was labeled "cru bourgeois," and value 1 otherwise. The vintage 1989 was a variable with just two values, one value for 1989, and another value for any other year. Cote group was yet another variable with just two values, one value indicating a wine labeled as officially a Burgundy of the Cote type, and the other value indicating all other wines.

The authors explain almost two thirds of the variation in Bordeaux wine prices with a set of seven objective characteristics and just one sensory characteristic (whether the wine was judged to need further keeping, a trait associated with higher predicted price for the wine). The remaining 5 objective characteristics and 15 of the 16 sensory characteristics added essentially nothing to the analysts' ability to predict the price of Bordeaux wines. The authors concluded that it is the label that matters for wine prices.

But do a wine's sensory characteristics matter for *something*, if not for price? The French analysts concluded that sensory characteristics do matter for a wine's gastronomic value. The analysts took wine judges' ratings (on a scale of 1 to 20, with 20 being best) of the wines under study and asked whether sensory characteristics or objective characteristics could explain the judges' ratings. The basic model was the same as for explaining price, but now the dependent variable was "judges' rating." Here, 12 sensory characteristics and just 3 objective characteristics (being from the St. Emilion-Pomerol-Fronsac appellations, being a 1990 vintage, and being red were all associated with higher judges' ratings, *ceteris paribus*) enabled the analysts to account for half the variation in judges' ratings. The remaining objective and sensory characteristics added essentially nothing to the analysts' ability to account for the judges' ratings of the wine. Perhaps unsurprisingly, the judges liked fat, firm, supple, well-concentrated wines with a complex nose, strong aromatic intensity, fine tannins, a longer finish, and in which the harmony of components is well balanced. What regression adds to these commonplace insights is the quantitative importance of each of these traits—and evidence of the unimportance of other traits, such as the class of the wine reported on the bottle or the flatness of the wine. On the basis of these results, the authors concluded that the gastronomic quality of the wine is explained most heavily by its sensory traits and hardly at all by the objective characteristics found on the bottle.

 **Final Notes**

Uncovering the determinants of price is one important application of regression analysis. Regression relationships, like that in Equation Hit 9.1 that explain a good's price in terms of its attributes are called "hedonic price regressions" or "hedonic regressions." Harvard University econometrician Zvi Griliches popularized hedonic regressions with his 1961 analysis of automobile prices,[2] but the name traces back to a 1939 analysis by A. T. Court, in which he, too, studied automobiles.[3] More recently, economists have used hedonic price regressions to study the effect of technological change on the price of computers. Disentangling the numerous influences that determine a complicated commodity's price is an ideal use of multiple regression.

■

model, the econometric software reports of the OLS regression would include a *t*-statistic for each of these variables. Would these *t*-statistics offer grounds for rejecting or failing to reject the null that all 14 coefficients are zero? Unfortunately, no. The *t*-statistics are good only for assessing individual claims separately from one another. Why? If our claim that all 14 sensory coefficients are zero is true, we would expect a separate *t*-test about any one of the coefficients to lead to a failure to reject that hypothesis (rejections would occur at the small rate of the significance level of the test, say, 5%). Doesn't this offer a path toward a suitable test? Couldn't we do many *t*-tests to test the multiple claims, rejecting the null hypothesis if any one coefficient proves significant? Unfortunately, no. If each *t*-test is conducted at the 5% level, the combined significance level could be 5%. It would be 5% if the test results across the 14 coefficients always agreed about rejecting or failing to reject. But the true significance level could also be 70%. It would be 70% (14 times 5%) if each coefficient's rejections occurred separately from the rejections of the others. And the true significance level could be anything between 5% and 70%. *The t-statistics in the t-tests are not usually independent from one another, so we have no easy way of traversing from a significance level for a collection of claims to significance levels for the corresponding individual t-tests, or the other way around.*

Difficulty in assigning a significance level is only one problem posed by relying on multiple *t*-statistics, however. Multiple *t*-tests are apt to provide a weak test of hypotheses involving multiple claims about coefficients. Considering the case of two relevant, but highly collinear, variables highlights this power issue. In such a case, each coefficient is likely to have a low *t*-statistic, because it will have a high standard error, attributable to the collinearity. Suppose the null hypothesis is that both coefficients are zero. Further suppose that one coefficient is, in fact, not zero. The low *t*-statistics for each coefficient separately, which is the usual consequence of collinear variables, make it very likely that we will fail to reject the null hypothesis for either variable assessed separately—and therefore make it very likely that we will wrongly fail to reject the null hypothesis. We are often able to construct a more powerful test of the null hypothesis.

The weakness of the *t*-statistic–based test lies in the *t*-test looking at each coefficient separately. When one of these two variables is omitted from the model, we'll barely miss it, as the other will absorb its effect on the dependent variable, in the fashion described in the analysis of omitted variable bias. But if these two variables are not correlated with other explanators, and we were to omit them both from the model, our model might fit the data noticeably less well than when the two were included. Herein lies a clue to how we can test multiple claims at once. We can look at what happens to the fit of the model when all the restrictions of the null hypothesis are imposed. If the fit deteriorates badly, we are apt to think the null hypothesis is wrong.

## 9.2    *F*-Tests: The Intuition

HOW DO WE TEST HYPOTHESES?

If we compare the fit of a regression that includes 15 sensory explanators with the fit of a regression that excludes 14 of those explanators, we would expect the two fits to be similar only if the excluded sensory variables' coefficients were truly zero. If the null hypothesis that the 14 excluded explanators all have zero coefficients is true, then the sensory variables' coefficients would probably get estimates close to zero when included, much like the zeros we impose when we exclude the variables, so the two regressions would tend to fit the data similarly. But if the sensory coefficients were not zero, if the null hypothesis were false, the model that includes the sensory explanators might well fit the data appreciably better than the model that excludes them.

To formalize this intuition about the deterioration of fit into a test statistic, follow these steps:

1. Estimate the model by ordinary least squares (OLS), ignoring the constraints of the null hypothesis.
2. Compute the sum of squared residuals, $SSR^u$, from this unconstrained regression (unconstrained, that is, by the requirements of the null hypothesis).
3. Estimate the model by OLS, imposing the constraints of the null hypothesis (in the wine example, in which the hypothesized values are zeros, this requires estimating the model with the 14 sensory variables omitted).
4. Compute the sum of squared residuals, $SSR^c$, from this constrained regression.
5. Compute the difference between the two sums of squared residuals $(SSR^c - SSR^u)$.

The difference between the sums of squared residuals, $(SSR^c - SSR^u)$, measures the deterioration in fit stemming from imposing the constraints of the null hypothesis. In the wine case, there are 14 such constraints. The difference $(SSR^c - SSR^u)$ will always be non-negative because adding explanators cannot reduce fit, and usually improves it. Is $(SSR^c - SSR^u)$, the difference between the unconstrained and constrained sums of squared residuals, a good test statistic for multiple assertions?

The fact that $(SSR^c - SSR^u)$ is never negative alerts us to a potential problem that would make this sample statistic a poor test statistic. Every time we introduce another constraint in our null hypothesis, we expect the $SSR^c$ to rise; with fewer coefficients to estimate, we will generally fit the data less well. The more constraints we impose, then, the larger the deterioration we expect in fit, even when the null hypothesis is true. To accommodate this expectation, we consider not the simple change in fit, but rather the change in fit per constraint imposed—14 constraints in the current example and, say, $r$ constraints more generally. Thus, we should look at

$$(SSR^c - SSR^u)/r,$$

not just

$$(SSR^c - SSR^u),$$

when judging the deterioration in fit.

There is a second consideration in assessing the deterioration in fit: How large is the deterioration relative to the unconstrained fit itself? That the fit deteriorates by 100 per constraint imposed is far more worrisome if the unconstrained sum of squared residuals were 200 than if it were 20,000. In the former case, the sum of squared residuals increases by 50%; in the latter case, it increases by only 0.5%. Surely, it is the relative increase in the sum of squared residuals that should concern us. We should look at

$$[(SSR^c - SSR^u)/r]/SSR^u,$$

rather than just

$$(SSR^c - SSR^u)/r.$$

Finally, there is a third consideration that should condition our assessment of the deterioration of fit. If we have a vast amount of data, we would think it likely that the unconstrained estimation procedure obtains coefficient estimates close to the true coefficients. Therefore, even a modest deterioration of fit from imposing the null hypothesis' constraints might well persuade us that the null is false. But if we have very little data, we must be open to the possibility that our unconstrained estimates are simply wrong, and that a modest deterioration in fit is attributable not to a false null hypothesis, but to imprecise estimates in the unconstrained estimation. Thus, a given deterioration in fit worries us more about the null hypothesis, the more data we have in hand.

To capture this effect of more data, we weight the relative deterioration per constraint by the number of independent residuals in our unconstrained sum of squared residuals. With $(k + 1)$ coefficients in the model ($k$ slopes and an intercept term), this is $(n - k - 1)$. Thus we propose looking at

$$(n - k - 1)[(SSR^c - SSR^u)/r]/SSR^u$$

or

$$F = \frac{\dfrac{SSR^c - SSR^u}{r}}{\dfrac{SSR^u}{(n - k - 1)}}, \qquad \text{9.1}$$

to test the null hypothesis. We called the statistic $F$ defined in Equation 9.1 the **F-statistic** for testing linear constraints on the coefficients of a regression equation. When the underlying disturbances in the data-generating process (DGP) are normally distributed, this statistic will follow the $F$-distribution with $r$ degrees of freedom in the numerator and $(n - k - 1)$ in the denominator, so we can conduct formal statistical tests of our null hypothesis using this statistic.

Figure 9.1 illustrates the $F$-test when the null hypothesis is

$$H_0: \beta_1 = \beta_1^0 \quad \text{and} \quad \beta_2 = \beta_2^0.$$

**Figure 9.1**

Values of $\hat{\beta}_1$ and $\hat{\beta}_2$ for Which the F-Statistic Does Not Exceed Its Critical Value

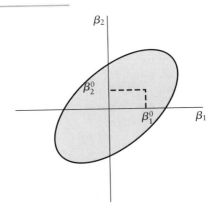

The F-statistic exceeds its critical value whenever $(\hat{\beta}_1, \hat{\beta}_2)$ lies outside the ellipsoid shown in the figure. If the estimators were statistically independent, then the axes of the ellipsoid would be horizontal and vertical, instead of tilted.

## 9.3    *F*-Tests for Multiple Linear Restrictions on Regression Coefficients

**HOW DO WE TEST HYPOTHESES?**

The F-test applies to a broad range of hypotheses about a regression model's coefficients, but not to all hypotheses. Computing the F-statistic requires OLS residuals from the constrained model. Consequently, the constraints imposed by the null hypothesis must result in a regression model that is still linear in its parameters to which OLS would apply. Constraints that do this are called linear constraints. Thus, the F-test applies to null hypotheses that impose linear constraints on the coefficients of the regression model. Examples of linear constraints are

1. $\beta_3 = 1$                                             $r = 1$
2. $\beta_1 = \beta_2 = \beta_3 = 0$                          $r = 3$
3. $\beta_1 = 4\,\beta_2$ and $\beta_3 - 3\,\beta_4 = \beta_5$  $r = 2$
4. $\beta_1 = 7$ and $\beta_4 = 12$                           $r = 2$
5. $\beta_1 + 2\beta_2 = 12$                                  $r = 1$

Notice that the number of constraints is the number of linear relationships imposed on the coefficients. It does not depend on the number of parameters involved in those relationships. Why does (2) impose three constraints? Because (2) could be re-written as

$$(2')\ \beta_1 = 0;\ \beta_2 = 0;\ \text{and}\ \beta_3 = 0 \qquad r = 3.$$

In the special case of $r = 1$, the F-statistic proves to be the square of the t-statistic. Because of this, some econometric software packages use the F-test with $r = 1$ instead of the *t*-statistic for hypothesis tests about single restrictions on the parameters besides $\beta_s = 0$.

Examples of nonlinear constraints, for which the *F*-test is not applicable, are

1. $\beta_1\beta_2 = \beta_3$,
2. $\beta_1 = \beta_2^3$, and
3. $\beta_2 = 1/(1 - \beta_1)$.

## The Distribution of the *F*-Statistic

Proving that the *F*-statistic indeed follows the *F*-distribution with $r$ and $(n - k - 1)$ degrees of freedom when the disturbances are normal is complicated. This section sketches the proof so that we understand how *F*-tests rely on the normality of a model's disturbances and are ready to consider what we might do when normality fails. The key point is that under suitable conditions, the *F*-statistic is the ratio of two independent chi-square distributions, which implies that the statistic follows the *F*-distribution.

Recall that when the disturbances are normally distributed, the OLS residuals are linear combinations of normally distributed random variables. Why? The observed $Y_i$ are normally distributed and, because the estimators of the slope and intercept are normally distributed, so are the fitted values; hence the residuals, obtained by subtracting the normally distributed fitted values from the normally distributed $Y$'s, are also normally distributed. The residuals also have an expected value of zero, because the OLS estimators of the regression coefficients are unbiased. Consequently, the sum of squared residuals is a sum of squared homoskedastic mean zero normals. A sum of squared homoskedastic mean zero normals divided by their variance is distributed chi-square. Earlier we noted that the sum of squared residuals is the sum of $(n - k - 1)$ independent squared mean zero normals. Consequently, the sum of squared residuals divided by $\sigma^2$ is distributed chi-square with $(n - k - 1)$ degrees of freedom.

The further mathematical steps in showing that the *F*-statistic follows the *F*-distribution are two: first, to show that $(SSR^c - SSR^u)$ is equivalent to a sum of $r$ independent squared homoskedastic mean zero normals; and second, to show that $(SSR^c - SSR^u)$, which appears in the numerator of *F*, is statistically independent from $SSR^u$, which appears in the denominator. In fact, we can show that $(SSR^c - SSR^u)/\sigma^2$ and $(SSR^u)/\sigma^2$ are independently distributed chi-square variables. Therefore, dividing each by its number of statistically independent components—this is where the $r$ and $(n - k - 1)$ come from statistically—and taking their ratio,

$$\frac{(SSR^c - SSR^u)/[r\sigma^2]}{SSR^u/[(n - k - 1)\sigma^2]} = \frac{(SSR^c - SSR^u)/r}{SSR^u/(n - k - 1)} = F,$$

yields a variable, the *F*-statistic, that follows the *F*-distribution.

Note that the denominator of the $F$-statistic $[SSR^u/(n - k - 1)]$ is $s^2$, our unbiased estimator for the variance of the disturbances. The statistical role of this denominator in the $F$-statistic is to estimate $\sigma^2$. If we knew $\sigma^2$, we could use it in our test statistic instead of $[SSR^u/(n - k - 1)]$. The statistic $(SSR^c - SSR^u)/\sigma^2$ is then a sum of $r$ squared independent standard normals, and we could use this chi-square distributed variate with $r$ degrees of freedom as our test statistic, instead of relying on the $F$-distribution. As the number of degrees of freedom in the numerator, $(n - k - 1)$, grows large, $s^2$ becomes an increasingly good estimator of $\sigma^2$ and the statistic $rF$ approaches the chi-square distribution with $r$ degrees of freedom.

## A Special Case Commonly Encountered

The $F$-statistic can provide a check on whether a model is useless. When is a model useless? When none of its supposed explanators explain anything; that is, when all the slope coefficients in the model are zero. Testing the null hypothesis that all the explanators have zero coefficients is a basic diagnostic for regressions. The $F$-test for this hypothesis is always reported in econometric software package outputs for regressions.

We can calculate the $F$-statistic for testing the hypothesis that a model is useless using the model's $R^2$. If all the slope coefficients are zero, the constrained sum of squares, $SSR^c$, is the variation of $Y$ about its own mean, $\sum y_i^2$. In this special case, we can write the $F$-statistic as

$$F = \frac{\dfrac{SSR^c - SSR^u}{k}}{\dfrac{SSR^u}{(n - k - 1)}} = \frac{\dfrac{\sum y_i^2 - \sum e_i^2}{k}}{\dfrac{\sum e_i^2}{(n - k - 1)}}.$$

If we divide the numerator and denominator of this expression by $\sum y_i^2$, we obtain

$$F = \frac{\dfrac{\sum y_i^2 - \sum e_i^2}{k}}{\dfrac{\sum e_i^2}{(n - k - 1)}} = \frac{\dfrac{\sum y_i^2 - \sum e_i^2}{k \sum y_i^2}}{\dfrac{\sum e_i^2}{(n - k - 1) \sum y_i^2}} = \frac{\dfrac{1 - \dfrac{\sum e_i^2}{\sum y_i^2}}{k}}{\dfrac{\dfrac{\sum e_i^2}{\sum y_i^2}}{(n - k - 1)}}$$

$$= \frac{R^2/k}{(1 - R^2)/(n - k - 1)},$$

or

$$F = \frac{(n - k - 1) R^2}{k(1 - R^2)},$$

which should offer solace to lovers of the $R^2$ measure because this $F$-statistic says that a high enough $R^2$ implies we would reject the null that none of the explanators in the model explain $Y$.

# Relaxing Assumptions

The above theoretical development of $F$-tests rests on normally distributed disturbances and fixed regressors. This section discusses the consequences of relaxing those assumptions.

## Letting Go of Normality

Our need to use the $F$-distribution instead of the chi-square distribution for testing linear restriction on a model's coefficients is directly analogous to our earlier need to use the $t$-distribution instead of the normal distribution. In the case of the $t$-statistic, we used $s^2$ instead of $\sigma^2$ to normalize coefficient estimates when testing a single restriction on the coefficients; using the random variable $s^2$ in lieu of the constant $\sigma^2$ changed the distribution of the test statistic from the standard normal distribution to the $t$-distribution. In the case of the $F$-statistic, using $s^2$ instead of $\sigma^2$ in the statistics denominator required using the $F$-distribution rather than the chi-square distribution. The analogy to the earlier case goes still further.

The $F$-distribution applies exactly to the $F$-statistic if the underlying disturbances are normally distributed. If the underlying distribution is not normal, the $F$-statistic's distribution in small samples is not generally known. In large samples, say of 100 or more observations, the $F$-statistic multiplied by $r$ ($rF$) has approximately the same distribution as the chi-square distribution with $r$ degrees of freedom. Consequently, we can use $rF$ to test hypotheses in large samples even if the underlying disturbances are not normally distributed.

In the case of $t$-tests, the loss of normality does not require us to look at a new test statistic. The $t$-statistic still works; it is approximately normally distributed in large samples. Nor does it matter whether we look in the normal table or the $t$-table to obtain our critical values, because in the large samples where the approximations hold, the $t$- and normal distributions are approximately the same. In the case of $F$-tests, does the loss of normality require us to look at a new test statistic, $rF$? Must we, instead of looking at the $F$-statistic and the $F$-table, look at $rF$ and the chi-square distribution when the underlying disturbances are not normal? No. We can, but we don't have to. The $F$-statistic will still work for us in large samples. The critical values for the $F$-distribution approach those for the chi-square distribution divided by $r$, as $(n - k - 1)$ grows large. In large samples, the two approaches yield the same results, so we can use either. Econometric software packages sometimes report an $F$-statistic, sometimes a chi-square statistic, and sometimes both.

## Letting Go of Fixed Regressors

Assuming fixed $X$'s is a convenient fiction that simplifies our notation. Chapters 3, 4, and 6 note that econometricians more realistically interpret the many results we have obtained for the fixed regressor case as applying conditional on the $X$-values that we observe in a stochastic regressor DGP for which the Gauss–Markov Assumptions about the disturbances apply for every combination of $X$-values. In this view, OLS is unbiased conditional on any specific set of $X$-values, and its variance is $\sigma^2 / \sum x_i^2$, conditional on the observed $X$-values.

An advantage of using an unbiased estimator for any combination of $X$-values is that the estimator is then necessarily unbiased for the particular $X$-values in hand. Frequently, econometricians only know the particular $X$-values they are dealing with. They do not know the other values the explanators take on or the frequency with which various values occur. *Econometricians' standard practice is to conduct all hypothesis tests and to construct any confidence intervals, conditional on the particular set of $X$'s in a given sample.* The computations for estimators, tests, and confidence intervals are the same whether we assume fixed $X$'s or assume that the $X$'s are stochastic and the Gauss–Markov Assumptions about the disturbances apply for all combinations of $X$-values. If we assume the latter, however, then all the probability statements associated with estimators, hypothesis tests, or confidence intervals are only true *given the X-values we observe*. Furthermore, to test hypotheses when the explanators are stochastic, we also need to make the normality assumption about the disturbances conditional on the $X$'s.

## A Caveat About Multiple Tests

Economists do not test all possible hypotheses about the coefficients in their models. They choose their hypotheses selectively. When the choices about hypothesis tests are settled on *before* examining the data, such selectivity poses little worry. Often, though, economists choose which tests to run *after* examining their data. This common, and needed, practice has consequences for how we interpret test results. To illustrate these consequences, we return to the study of wine prices by Combris, Lecocq, and Visser. They note that 14 of 15 sensory characteristics are statistically insignificant explanators of the prices of wines at the 5% significance level. Presumably, they arrived at this conclusion by the following route: (i) The $t$-statistics for 14 sensory explanators in their initial regression were less than the critical value for a 5% significance level, and one (that for "the wine needs aging") was greater than the critical value; and (ii) an $F$-test with a 5% significance level for the 14 coefficients failed to reject the null that those 14 sensory variables had zero coefficients. This is a common and informative strategy for assessing regression results. However, a caveat is in order. The significance level of their $F$-test is not 5%, as the formal analysis suggests, nor is the significance level for the "significant" sensory trait, "need for aging," 5%.

Why is the "need for aging" variable not genuinely statistically significant at the 5% level? The conclusion would be correct had the authors begun by wondering if the need for aging mattered and had therefore looked at that $t$-statistic; they would then have been testing the coefficient on the need for aging in isolation from other considerations. Instead, the authors examined 15 test statistics and claimed the need for aging significant. If all 15 coefficients were zero, and if the $t$-statistics had been statistically independent—which they can be—then, for a 5% percent significance level, in 54% of samples, the authors would have found one or more statistically significant coefficients among the 15. If all the sensory variables have coefficients of zero, the author's strategy would find at least one significant variable in 54% of samples, not in 5% of samples.

The true significance is also misstated for the $F$-test about the remaining 14 variables. Combris, Visser, and Lecocq focused attention on these fourteen precisely because their $t$-stats are low, a circumstance that arises more often when the estimated coefficients are, indeed, close to zero. The authors' test procedure shies away from examining a coefficient's contribution to explanatory power in precisely those cases when the coefficient has the greatest impact—when its estimated coefficient is large. The true significance level of the authors' strategy is less than 5%.

In many econometric analyses, we are genuinely interested in numerous coefficients and in numerous hypotheses about those coefficients. We cannot avoid the problem faced by Combris, Lecocq, and Visser, and their solution is a reasonable one. The caveat of this section is to be cautious in interpreting significance levels literally. *In particular, econometricians should avoid drawing firm conclusions from studies that examine a wide array of variables and serve up a few "statistically significant" coefficients as discovery.* Such "fishing expeditions" (also called **data mining**) can mislead us greatly if we rely on the stated significance levels in them. However, if we use such investigations wisely, they can inform us about what empirical regularities appear in available data—they just can't offer reliable probability statements to tell us which fish are edible and which are not.[4]

## 9.5 An Application: Linear Coefficient Constraints and the Earnings of Blacks

HOW DO WE TEST HYPOTHESES?

In Chapter 6, we estimated an earnings equation for blacks that included a dummy variable "female" to allow black women and black men to have different intercept terms. Table 9.1 reports that earnings equation based on data from the National Longitudinal Survey of Youth (NLSY). These data are in the file earnings.*** on this book's companion Web site (**www.aw-bc.com/murray**). We now know that the $t$-statistic on *female*'s coefficient, $-5.57$, rejects the null hypothesis of no difference in expected wages between black women and black men.

**TABLE 9.1  Earnings Equation for Black Men and Women (NLSY Data)**

*Earnings Equation for Blacks with Different Intercepts for Men and Women*
Dependent Variable: LNINCOME
Method: Least Squares
Sample: 1 6540 IF BLACK = 1
Included observations: 1801

| Variable | Coefficient | Std. Error | t-Statistic | Prob. |
|---|---|---|---|---|
| C | 7.059470 | 0.134586 | 52.45328 | 0.0000 |
| EDUCATN | 0.147228 | 0.008277 | 17.78738 | 0.0000 |
| EXPER | 0.048906 | 0.007442 | 6.571437 | 0.0000 |
| FEMALE | −0.201094 | 0.036129 | −5.566018 | 0.0000 |
| R-squared | 0.179315 | Mean dependent var | | 9.456713 |
| Adjusted R-squared | 0.177945 | S.D. dependent var | | 0.824032 |
| S.E. of regression | 0.747127 | Akaike info criterion | | 2.257057 |
| Sum squared resid | 1003.084 | Schwarz criterion | | 2.269263 |
| Log likelihood | −2028.479 | F-statistic | | 130.8780 |
| Durbin–Watson stat | 2.004969 | Prob(F-statistic) | | 0.000000 |

But is the difference between black women's wages and black men's wages only a difference in their intercept terms, or do black women and men also obtain different returns for their productive traits; that is, are the coefficients on education and experience different for black women than for black men? Here we return to those NLSY data and test whether black women and black men obtain the same returns for their productive traits. The alternative hypothesis is that they do not receive the same returns; that is, the alternative is that black women and black men have distinctly different earnings functions.[5]

There are three ways to envision distinct earnings functions for black women and black men. One way is to write down two separate functions, one for men, one for women:

$$\text{For women:} \quad \ln(earnings) = \alpha_0 + \alpha_1 education + \alpha_2 experience + \varepsilon \qquad 9.2$$

$$\text{For men:} \quad \ln(earnings) = \beta_0 + \beta_1 education + \beta_2 experience + \varepsilon \qquad 9.3$$

Equivalently, we can use dummy variables for male and female to combine Equations 9.2 and 9.3 into one equation:

$$\ln(earnings) = \alpha_0 female + \alpha_1 (education)(female)$$
$$+ \alpha_2 (experience)(female)$$
$$+ \beta_0 male + \beta_1 (education)(male)$$
$$+ \beta_2 (experience)(male) + \varepsilon,$$

which, when applied to a woman or a man reduces to the same expressions as Equations 9.2 and 9.3. In both of these formulations, our first null hypothesis is

$$H_0: \alpha_0 = \beta_0; \alpha_1 = \beta_1; \alpha_2 = \beta_2,$$

and the alternative hypothesis is

$$H_1: \text{otherwise.}$$

The third formulation uses only the dummy variable female (a corresponding specification using only male is also possible):

$$\ln(earnings) = \beta_0 + \beta_1 education + \beta_2 experience$$
$$+ \beta_3 female + \beta_4 (education)(female)$$
$$+ \beta_5 (experience)(female) + \varepsilon,$$

where the coefficients in the three formulations are connected by

$$\beta_0 + \beta_3 = \alpha_0, \beta_1 + \beta_4 = \alpha_1 \qquad \textbf{9.4}$$

and

$$\beta_2 + \beta_5 = \alpha_2. \qquad \textbf{9.5}$$

In this third rendering, our first null hypothesis is

$$H_0: \beta_3 = 0; \beta_4 = 0; \beta_5 = 0.$$

All three of these formulations are equivalent in the sense that OLS will yield the same sum of squared residuals for each formulation, the same estimated coefficients for the first two formulations, and estimated coefficients for the third formulation that match the first two through the equalities given in Equations 9.4 and 9.5.

Consider first the null hypothesis that the intercept, slope on education, and slope on experience are the same for black women as for black men, against the alternative that the intercept and slopes differ between the two groups. The unconstrained sum of squared residuals, $SSR^u$, is the sum of the sums of squared residuals from an earnings regression for women and an earnings regression for men. Table 9.2 reports these regressions in Panels A and B. From the regression sum of squares reported there, we conclude

$$SSR^u = (455.41 + 547.34) = 1,002.75.$$

The constrained sum of squared residuals, $SSR^c$, is that from a regression including both black women and black men. Table 9.2 also includes the output from this regression. We see there that $SSR^c = 1,020.378$.

The number of constraints, $r$, in the null hypothesis is 3, because we are constraining an intercept and two slopes to be the same for each group. There are 1,801 observations in the sample, so in the unconstrained model, in which there are 6 coefficients (2 intercepts and 4 slopes), $(n - k - 1) = (1,801 - 6) = 1,795$. The critical value for an $F$-test at the 5% significance level when the numerator has $r = 3$ degrees of freedom and the denominator has $(n - k - 1) = 1,795$ degrees of freedom is 2.60.

We calculate $F$ as follows:

$$F = \frac{\dfrac{SSR^c - SSR^u}{r}}{\dfrac{SSR^u}{(n - k - 1)}} = \frac{\dfrac{1020.37 - 1002.75}{3}}{\dfrac{1002.75}{1795}} = 10.51,$$

so we reject the null that the earnings equations are the same for black women and black men.

Having rejected the null hypothesis of identical earnings functions, we might choose to proceed on the supposition that black women and black men have fundamentally different earnings functions. However, many economists like parsimonious models, that is, models with as few coefficients as can be justified. Consequently, it is a common practice in a model such as this to ask whether the differences in earnings functions between black women and black men can be captured more simply than by letting all the coefficients in the earnings functions differ. In particular, is the simpler earnings model reported in Table 9.1, with the dummy variable female included, appropriate for describing the earnings of black women and black men? That is, is

$$\ln(earnings) = \beta_0 + \beta_1 education + \beta_2 experience + \beta_3 female + \varepsilon$$

an appropriate model? Economists would examine these data to determine whether to reject a null hypothesis that black women and black men have the same earnings functions except for differing intercept terms. The alternative is, as above, that all the coefficients differ between the two groups.

**TABLE 9.2** Unconstrained and Constrained Earnings Equations for Black Men and Women (NLSY Data)

*Panel A*
*Earnings Equation for Black Women*
Dependent Variable: LNINCOME
Method: Least Squares
Sample: 1 6540 IF BLACK = 1 and FEMALE = 1
Included observations: 855

| Variable | Coefficient | Std. Error | t-Statistic | Prob. |
|---|---|---|---|---|
| C | 6.770812 | 0.182408 | 37.11912 | 0.0000 |
| EDUCATN | 0.150336 | 0.012089 | 12.43582 | 0.0000 |
| EXPER | 0.052809 | 0.009757 | 5.412683 | 0.0000 |
| R-squared | 0.201342 | Mean dependent var | | 9.399373 |
| Adjusted R-squared | 0.199467 | S.D. dependent var | | 0.817127 |
| S.E. of regression | 0.731104 | Akaike info criterion | | 2.214981 |
| Sum squared resid | 455.4054 | Schwarz criterion | | 2.231652 |
| Log likelihood | −943.9045 | F-statistic | | 107.3948 |
| Durbin–Watson stat | 1.910221 | Prob(F-statistic) | | 0.000000 |

*Panel B*
*Earnings Equation for Black Men*
Dependent Variable: LNINCOME
Method: Least Squares
Sample: 1 6540 IF BLACK = 1 and FEMALE = 0
Included observations: 946

| Variable | Coefficient | Std. Error | t-Statistic | Prob. |
|---|---|---|---|---|
| C | 7.174183 | 0.204386 | 35.10119 | 0.0000 |
| EDUCATN | 0.143802 | 0.011443 | 12.56726 | 0.0000 |
| EXPER | 0.043089 | 0.011543 | 3.733066 | 0.0002 |
| R-squared | 0.153632 | Mean dependent var | | 9.508536 |
| Adjusted R-squared | 0.151837 | S.D. dependent var | | 0.827240 |
| S.E. of regression | 0.761853 | Akaike info criterion | | 2.297039 |
| Sum squared resid | 547.3357 | Schwarz criterion | | 2.312427 |
| Log likelihood | −1083.500 | F-statistic | | 85.58611 |
| Durbin–Watson stat | 2.084601 | Prob(F-statistic) | | 0.000000 |

*continues*

**TABLE 9.2** *(continued)*
*Panel C*
*Earnings Equation for Black Women and Men*
Dependent Variable: LNINCOME
Method: Least Squares
Sample: 1 6540 IF BLACK = 1
Included observations: 1801

| Variable | Coefficient | Std. Error | *t*-Statistic | Prob. |
|---|---|---|---|---|
| C | 7.016878 | 0.135484 | 51.79128 | 0.0000 |
| EDUCATN | 0.138407 | 0.008191 | 16.89658 | 0.0000 |
| EXPER | 0.053955 | 0.007448 | 7.244126 | 0.0000 |
| R-squared | 0.165166 | Mean dependent var | | 9.456713 |
| Adjusted R-squared | 0.164238 | S.D. dependent var | | 0.824032 |
| S.E. of regression | 0.753331 | Akaike info criterion | | 2.273039 |
| Sum squared resid | 1020.378 | Schwarz criterion | | 2.282194 |
| Log likelihood | −2043.872 | F-statistic | | 177.8611 |
| Durbin–Watson stat | 1.970390 | Prob(F-statistic) | | 0.000000 |

The constrained sum of squared residuals for this second null hypothesis is the residual sum of squares reported in Table 9.1 from a regression using both black women and black men, and including a dummy variable for female: 1,003.08. Under this null hypothesis, the slope coefficients for both education and experience are constrained to be the same for women as for men, so $r$ is 2. The unconstrained sum of squared residuals is again 1,002.75. The critical value for an $F$-test at the 5% significance level when the numerator has $r = 2$ degrees of freedom and the denominator has $(n - k - 1) = 1,795$ degrees of freedom, is 3.00. We calculate $F$ to be

$$F = \frac{\dfrac{SSR^c - SSR^u}{r}}{\dfrac{SSR^u}{(n - k - 1)}} = \frac{\dfrac{1003.08 - 1002.75}{2}}{\dfrac{1002.75}{1795}} = 0.30,$$

so we fail to reject the null that the earnings equations are the same, but for different intercept terms.

In our NLSY sample, black women earn 11% less than men, on average. The regression estimates in Table 9.1 indicate that women earn 20% less than men with the same education and experience. The difference between these figures, 9%, reflects the rewards for black women's more marketable traits; black women in our NLSY sample have 8/10 a year more education than the black men in our sample, and 5/10 a year less work experience. According to the coefficients on education and experience in Table 9.1, the 8/10 of a year education garners 12% greater earnings (0.8 · .15); the half year of work experience brings $2\frac{1}{2}$% in earnings (0.5 · .05).

## 9.6 An Application: Linear Coefficient Constraints in a Model of Deficits

HOW DO WE TEST HYPOTHESES?

We have seen that econometric relationships can vary across groups. Do econometric relationships also change over time? Often they do. How are we to test whether a relationship changes in a particular instance? The F-tests of the previous subsection offer a formal way to test whether two time periods have different intercepts and slopes. When the coefficients of a regression relationship change over time, we say a **regime shift** occurs. If we can say in advance when the structure of a relationship might have changed, we can treat the period up until the possible change and the period afterward just as we treated the two groups, black women and black men.

For example, consider the relationship between long-term interest rates and the Federal budget deficit, which we assume depends on four explanators, plus an intercept term:

$$(Long\text{-}term\ interest\ rate) = \beta_0 + \beta_1(expected\ inflation)$$
$$+ \beta_2(real\ short\text{-}term\ interest\ rate)$$
$$+ \beta_3(change\ in\ real\ per\ capita\ income)$$
$$+ \beta_4\ (real\ per\ capita\ deficit) + \varepsilon.$$

Did the extensive deregulation of financial markets that began in 1982 cause the relationship determining long-term interest rates to change? Was there a regime shift after 1981? The data in deficit1.*** on this book's companion Web site (**www.aw-bc.com/murray**) contain data from 1960 to 2004. Here we analyze the first 35 years of data, saving the additional data for your experimentation. The null hypothesis that we will test is that the same coefficients persisted across the entire period from 1960 to 1994. The U.S. deficit and the change in GDP are measured in 1996 dollars per capita. Interest rates and expected inflation are in percent. The expected inflation measure is the mean of the expectations of economists questioned in the Livingston surveys that are now conducted by the Federal Reserve Bank of Philadelphia.

To test the hypothesis of no regime shift, we first estimate the model for the entire period, 1960–1994. We then estimate the model for each of the two time

**TABLE 9.3  A Model of Long-Term Interest Rates (Sample: 1960–1994)**

*Dependent Variable: Interest Rate on 10-Year U.S. Bonds*

| Variable | Coefficient | Std. Error | *t*-Statistic |
|---|---|---|---|
| Constant | 1.314283 | 0.210446 | 6.245213 |
| Real short rate (*realsr*) | 0.788127 | 0.049647 | 15.87457 |
| Expected inflation (*expinfl*) | 0.778786 | 0.029093 | 26.76919 |
| Income growth (*incchng*) | −2.04E-05 | 0.000156 | −0.13098 |
| U.S. deficit (*usdef*) | 0.001926 | 0.000166 | 11.61971 |
| *R*-squared | 0.979308 | | |

*F-Test for a Change in Regime in 1982*

| **F-statistic** | **Probability** |
|---|---|
| 1.313506 | 0.290334 |

*Dummy Variable for Post-1981 (nwfinsys)*

| | Coefficient | Std. Error | *t*-Statistic |
|---|---|---|---|
| Post-1982 Dummy | −0.382897 | 0.33136 | −1.156315 |

*Dummy Variable for Oil Crises (shock1 and shock2)*

| | Coefficient | Std. Error | *t*-Statistic |
|---|---|---|---|
| 1973–1974 Oil Dummy | −0.619800 | 0.285131 | −2.173739 |
| 1977–1978 Oil Dummy | 0.255626 | 0.312746 | 0.817361 |

*F-Test That Both Oil Dummies Are Zero*

| **F-statistic** | **Probability** |
|---|---|
| 2.8074 | 0.078 |

periods, 1960–1981 and 1982–1994, separately. We construct the *F*-statistic for this null hypothesis from the constrained sum of squared residuals, $SSR^c$, (the sum of squared residuals obtained from a single regression for the entire period, 1960–1994) and the unconstrained sum of squared residuals, $SSR^u$, (the sum of the sums of squared residuals obtained for the two time periods analyzed separately from one another). There are five constraints ($r = 5$) in the null hypothesis (one intercept and four slopes are equal to one another), and there are 35 observations and 10 coefficients in the unconstrained model ($(n - k - 1) = 25$). Table 9.3 reports the *F*-statistic for this test using our data: 1.31. The critical value for an $F$-test with 5 and 25 degrees of freedom is 2.60 for a significance level of .05. Because the observed $F$-statistic is less than the critical value, we fail to reject the hypothesis that the two periods all have the same coefficients for these variables.

## 9.7      Two Additional Tests for Regime Shifts

This section introduces two additional tests for whether a regression's coefficients differ between two time periods.

### Chow Tests

We have seen that an $F$-statistic can sometimes determine whether the coefficients in a model differ between two time periods. A problem arises for such tests when there are too few observations in one subperiod to estimate the model separately for both subperiods. The **Chow prediction test** allows us to test for model stability when one subperiod is too short to allow separate estimation of the model in that subperiod. Like the $F$-statistic, the Chow prediction test results in a test statistic that follows the $F$-distribution, but the construction of the statistic and the degrees of freedom are different than in the classic $F$-test that we have already seen.

The Chow strategy is to estimate the model for only the longer subperiod, which we suppose has $n_1$ observations, which is greater than the number of parameters to be estimated. Because the number of parameters in the model exceeds the number of observations in the shorter time period, $n_2$, the parameters of the model cannot be estimated using just the shorter time period's data, as we would in a classic $F$-test. The Chow strategy instead assumes a perfect fit for the shorter subperiod in the unconstrained model of a classic $F$-test. Thus, the unconstrained sum of squared residuals is that for the longer subperiod. In the numerator of the test statistic, we do not put a change in the sum of squared residuals; rather, we include the sum of squared *forecast* errors for the shorter period, based on the longer period's coefficient estimates.

In Chow's procedure, we don't view the size of the distortion in fit in the light of some number of restrictions, but rather in the number of periods for which forecasts are made. The question is, "What is the average squared forecast error in the shorter period when we use the longer period's coefficients to make forecasts?" We view this averaged squared forecast error relative to the unconstrained sum of squared residuals and the amount of data in hand:

$$Chow = \frac{\frac{1}{n_2}\sum_{j=1}^{n_2}(forecast\ error_j)^2}{\frac{1}{n_1-k-1}\sum_{i=1}^{n_1}e_i^2} \sim F(n_2,[n_1-k-1]).$$

The Chow prediction tests made such an impression on econometricians that they refer to all tests for regime shift that rely on the $F$-distribution as **Chow tests**.

## Using Dummy Variables to Test for Regime Shifts

When the number of coefficients in the model is large, Chow-style $F$-tests sometimes lack power—it need not be the case that *all* the coefficients change in a regime shift, and power is lost by looking for changes in every coefficient. For this reason, a common complement to Chow tests is to test the hypothesis that time periods differ in a single coefficient, the intercept term. We test this hypothesis by using dummy variables, just as in the earlier earnings example. Let us consider a regime shift that we believe would happen only once during our sample data. If $D_i$ is a dummy variable, and $X_i$ an ordinary explanator, we have

$$E(Y_i) = \beta_0 + \beta_1 D_i + \beta_2 X_i.$$

When $D_i = 0$ (say in 1982 or earlier, before the possible regime shift), we have

$$E(Y_i) = \beta_0 + \beta_2 X_i,$$

and when $D_i = 1$ (say after 1982, after the possible regime shift), we have

$$E(Y_i) = (\beta_0 + \beta_1) + \beta_2 X_i.$$

Thus, the intercept term in the relationship is $\beta_0$ when $D_i = 0$, and $(\beta_0 + \beta_1)$, when $D_i = 1$. To test the hypothesis that the intercepts are different in two time periods, we need only look at the $t$-statistic for $\hat{\beta}_1$ and ask whether it differs significantly from zero. The dummy variable allows for a parallel shift to occur in the relationship between $Y$ and the explanators when we move from one time period to the other. Table 9.3 contains the $t$-statistic for a deregulation dummy, *nwfinsys*, that equals 0 prior to 1983 and 1 thereafter. We find no evidence of a shift in the intercept term in our model following financial market deregulation.

Such temporal dummy variables can also be useful when the regime shift lasts quite briefly, making it unlikely that we could precisely estimate an effect on each variable in the model. For example, in 1973–1974 and again in 1977–1978, the world was buffeted by oil crises. Did these crises temporarily alter the relationship between long-term interest rates and other variables? Introducing two dummy variables, one for each episode, allows us to test this hypothesis. Table 9.3 contains the $t$-statistics for the coefficients on each of these oil crisis dummy variables, *oil1* and *oil2*, and the $F$-statistic for the joint hypothesis that both coefficients are zero. The coefficient on the first crisis dummy is statistically significant when assessed alone; the coefficient on the second crisis dummy is not. However, when viewed jointly, as we ought to view them, because we introduced the variables together and are apt to interpret them together (we are tempted by the

**REGRESSION'S GREATEST HITS**

# An Econometric Top 40—A Classical Favorite

## Unanticipated Money

We have seen how Robert Lucas pointed to the instability of the Phillips curve as evidence that anticipation of inflation by consumers prevents governments from systematically lowering unemployment by exploiting the Phillips trade-off between inflation and unemployment. In 1977 and 1978, economist Robert Barro, then of the University of Rochester, produced two classical favorites that addressed the efficacy of monetary policy more directly. In his papers, Barro provides evidence that unanticipated changes in the money supply bring changes in output and unemployment, but that anticipated changes bring no changes in these areas. Barro also presents evidence that anticipated changes in the money supply are absorbed completely by inflation, whereas unanticipated changes are partially absorbed by inflation but also bring about changes in output and unemployment.

Barro's first task is to divide observed changes in the money supply into anticipated and unanticipated components. His strategy is to estimate current rates of change in the money supply (changes that consumers do not observe until they have occurred) as a function of past variables that consumers would have already observed. Barro assumes that the fitted value of money's growth rate is the anticipated change in the money supply, and that the residual is the unanticipated change. In essence, Barro assumes his regression model mirrors consumers' expectations. He then asks whether either anticipated or unanticipated changes in the money supply are relevant explanators in equations for output, unemployment, and inflation.

Barro measures the rate of change in the money supply by the change in the logarithm of the money supply from year to year ($DM_t = \ln(money\ supply_t) - \ln(money\ supply_{t-1})$). His

data span 1941–1976. Barro speculates that when government spending is unusually high, the government may expand the money supply to facilitate fund raising. He also argues that when unemployment is unusually high, the government will attempt to spur the economy by increasing the money supply. Barro therefore includes in his model of the money supply both a measure of the previous year's unemployment rate ($UN_{t-1}$) and a measure of government spending ($G_{t-1}$) committed last year for expenditure this year. Barro reasonably anticipates that people will look to recent rates of growth in the money supply as an indicator of how much the money supply will grow in the future. For this reason, he includes in his money supply model the rates of change in the money supply in the two preceding years ($DM_{t-1}$ and $DM_{t-2}$).

Barro's money supply equation is thus

$$E(DM_t) = \beta_0 + \beta_1 DM_{t-1} + \beta_2 DM_{t-2} + \beta_3 G_{t-1} + \beta_4 UN_{t-1},$$

with the following estimated coefficients:

$$DM_t = 0.082 + 0.41 DM_{t-1} + 0.21 DM_{t-2} + 0.072 G_{t-1} + 0.026 UN_{t-1} + e_t,$$
$$(0.027)\quad(0.14)\quad(0.12)\quad(0.016)\quad(0.009)$$

where $e_t$ is the residual from period $t$, and estimated standard errors of the coefficients are in parentheses. Barro uses the residuals from this regression to measure unanticipated changes in the money supply, $UDM_t$, and these fitted values that Barro uses to measure the anticipated changes in the money supply, $ADM_t$. The $t$-statistics for these five coefficients are 3.0, 2.9, 1.8, 4.5, and 2.9; the first two and last two are significant at the 0.05 level of significance, and the middle one is significant at the 0.10 level of significance. The $R^2$ for the estimated equation is 0.90, indicating that consumers can anticipate much of the variation over time in the growth in the money supply.

Barro's core concern is whether unanticipated and anticipated changes in the money supply differ in their effects on unemployment, output, and prices. Let's examine Barro's models and findings for each of these relationships.

To examine the relationship between the money supply growth and unemployment, Barros specifies an unemployment equation. Barro argues that unemployment was affected by the military conscription that took place in many years 1941–1976. He defines a variable ($MIL_t$), that equals zero in years when there was no draft and equals the size of the military relative to the male population aged 15 to 44. Barro includes $MIL$ in his model of unemployment. Barro also argues that changes in the minimum wage over time affect unemployment, so he includes a measure of the magnitude and coverage of the minimum wage ($MWAGE_t$) in his model. Finally, Barro allows current and past values of anticipated and unanticipated money growth to influence unemployment. The model used to test hypotheses is thus

$$UN_t = \beta_0 + \beta_1 ADM_t + \beta_2 ADM_{t-1}$$
$$+ \beta_3 ADM_{t-2} + \beta_4 UDM_t$$
$$+ \beta_5 UDM_{t-1} + \beta_6 UDM_{t-2}$$
$$+ \beta_7 MIL_t + \beta_8 MWAGE_t + \nu_t.$$

Barro's key hypotheses about the relationship between money supply growth and unemployment are that the coefficients on the anticipated money growth variables are zero and that the coefficients on the unanticipated money growth variables are not zero. Barro reports an $F$-statistic of 1.4 for the former null hypothesis and an $F$-statistic of 15.7 for the latter. The critical value for an $F$-test with 3 and 19 degrees of freedom (3 constraints and a regression with 10 co-efficients estimated for the 29 years 1946–1973) at a 0.05 significance level is 3.1. Barro fails to reject the null hypothesis that anticipated money growth does not influence unemployment. In contrast, he rejects the null hypothesis that unanticipated money growth does not influence unemployment. Systematic, that is, predictable, monetary policy does not appear to affect unemployment. Barro's findings offer discouraging counsel to officials hoping to influence the economy through monetary policy. The findings are consistent with rational expectations models of the economy, but also with some other models. Having found money growth's effects on unemployment to depend on expectations about that growth, Barro next asks about the effect of money growth on output.

Barro's model for output is very similar to that for unemployment, and the implications are the same. $F$-tests fail to reject the hypothesis that anticipated changes in the money stock influence output, but they do reject the hypothesis that unanticipated changes in the money stock have no influence on output. Together, the unemployment and output results support the claim that predictable changes in the stock of money do not affect real dimensions of the economy. What, then, of the effect of money supply growth on prices? Barro turns next to this question.

Barro built his model for prices on the demand for money. Transactions, that is, sales and purchases of goods, require dollars. Given constant prices, more transactions require consumers and firms to have more dollars. Viewed the other way around, given a constant quantity of money, more transactions suggest lower prices. Similarly, more dollars, given constant transactions, suggest higher prices, as more dollars chase the same number of goods; indeed, given constant transactions, we expect dollars and prices to change by the same percentage.

Barro's model of the level of prices includes both output (which, when bought and sold entails transactions) and the quantity of money. The actual price level, $P_t$, Barro notes, depends on how determinedly people hold their money for anticipated transactions. People expecting many transactions will be slow to part with dollars on any one transaction, whereas people expecting only a few transactions will be more willing to commit dollars on any one transaction. Further, the more willing people are to commit dollars to any one transaction, the higher they bid up prices. Thus, for a given money supply, $M_t$, prices are higher the more transactions people expect. How many transactions do people expect? Barro returns to his output equation to argue that people's expected output, and hence expected transactions, depend on the unanticipated changes in the money supply. These considerations lead Barro to include unanticipated money growth in his price model. He also recognizes that higher interest rates, $r_t$, will make people less willing to hold dollars and will therefore influence the price level. The basic version of Barro's model of prices is

$$\ln(P_t) = \alpha_0 + \alpha_1 \ln(M_t) + \alpha_2 UMD_t \\ + \alpha_3 UMD_{t-1} + \alpha_4 UMD_{t-2} \\ + \alpha_5 r_t + \alpha_6 t + u_t.$$

where $t$ is an index of time that grows year by year. The actual money supply appears in log form. The $UMD$ terms capture expected output. Barro found that the non-$UMD$ variables from his output equation are statistically insignificant in the price equation, so he omitted them.

How do changes in the money supply affect prices in this model? Anticipated changes appear only through their effect on $\log(M_t)$. An antici-

pated rate of change in the supply of money of 1% will increase $P_t$ by $\alpha_1$ %. An unanticipated rate of change in the money supply this period of 1% ($UMD_t = 1$) will change prices by $(\alpha_1 + \alpha_2)$, as the change affects $M_t$ by 1% and has its own independent effect. Barro's theory claims $\alpha_1 = 1$. What does he find in the data? The estimated coefficient on $\ln(M_t) = 1.02$, with an estimated standard error of 0.07. The $t$-statistic for the null hypothesis that $\alpha_1 = 1$ is $(1.02 - 1.0)/0.07 = 0.29$, well below any classic critical value. We fail to reject the null hypothesis that $\alpha_1 = 1$, a conclusion that offers some corroboration of Barro's model.

 **Final Notes**

Barro's empirical results in these two papers profoundly influenced economists' thinking about the efficacy of monetary policy to influence output or unemployment systematically. Hypothesis tests, in particular $F$-tests, performed a critical role in making Barro's empirical analysis compelling. Had Barro only presented the estimated coefficients of his model, naysayers could have easily dismissed his results as "statistical accidents" that tell us little about the workings of the economy. Barro's $F$-tests about the coefficients on unanticipated money growth and on anticipated money growth refuted such critics forcefully. The $F$-tests Barro performed offered strong evidence in favor of his contention that monetary policy cannot be systematically exploited by policy makers who wish to increase output or lower unemployment. $F$-tests serve other economists equally well in a vast array of econometric studies.

∎

$t$-statistics to say "the first dummy's coefficient is significant, but the second is not"), the $F$-statistic's value does not lead us to reject at the 5% level of significance the joint hypothesis that both dummies have coefficients of zero.

### An Organizational Structure for the Study of Econometrics

**1. What Is the DGP?**

The data-generating process includes Gauss–Markov Assumptions and normally distributed disturbances.

**2. What Makes a Good Estimator?**

_____

**3. How Do We Create an Estimator?**

_____

**4. What Are the Properties of an Estimator?**

_____

**5. How Do We Test Hypotheses?**

Use $F$-tests for multiple linear combinations of coefficients.

Use $F$-tests for regime shifts.

Use Chow tests for regime shifts.

**6. How Do We Make Forecasts?**

_____

## Summary

Hypothesis tests are the tools econometricians most often use to draw confident conclusions from uncertain data. This chapter developed tests for multiple hypotheses about a regression model's parameters. The unifying notion of the chapter is the $F$-test. All of the tests in this chapter are variations on the $F$- test. Indeed, the $F$-test even embraces the $t$-tests of Chapter 7 as special cases because the $t$-statistic with $(n - k - 1)$ degrees of freedom is simply the square root of an $F$-statistic with one and $(n - k - 1)$ degrees of freedom.

## Concepts for Review

## Questions for Discussion

1. We know that omitted variables and superfluous variables are undesirable in regression analysis. Consequently, we should try all combinations of available regressors and choose the regression with largest list of all significant coefficients. Discuss.

2. The regime change tests offered in the chapter require that we know when the regime shift might occur. Discuss intuitive adaptations of this approach for use when you are uncertain about when the break occurs.

## Problems for Analysis

For the data sets that you will need to solve the problems in this section, go to **www.aw-bc.com/murray**.

1. Do changes in unemployment rates or GDP growth rates matter for changes in the poverty rate? The file poverty2.\*\*\* contains, for 1980–2003:

   *poverty*    U.S. poverty rates
   *gdpgrpw*   U.S. GDP growth rates
   *unemploy*  U.S. unemployment rates

   These values are measured in percents.

   a. Regress changes in the poverty rate on changes in the unemployment rate, the GDP growth rate, and an intercept term. Use the $R^2$ statistic to compute the $F$-statistic for the null hypothesis that changes in neither the unemployment rate nor the GDP growth rate matter for changes in the poverty rate.

   b. This sample has 24 observations. Does the validity of the $F$-test described in (a) rest heavily on having normally, or almost normally, distributed disturbances?

2. Nitrogen dioxide ($NO_2$) is a pollutant that attacks the human respiratory system; it increases the likelihood of respiratory illness. One common source of nitrogen dioxide is automobile exhaust. The file NO2pollution.\*\*\* contains a subset from 500 hourly observations made from October 2001 to August 2003.[6] The variables in the data set are

   *LNO2*        Natural logarithm of the concentration of $NO_2$ (particles)
   *LCARS*       Natural logarithm of the number of cars per hour
   *TEMP*        Temperature 2 meters above ground (degrees C)
   *WNDSPD*    Wind speed (meters/second)
   *TCHNG23*   The temperature difference between 25 and 2 meters above ground (degrees C)
   *WNDDIR*    Wind direction (degrees between 0 and 360)
   *HOUR*        Hour of day
   *DAYS*        Day number from October 1, 2001

   a. Regress the log of $NO_2$ concentration on the log of the number of cars, the two temperature variables, the two wind variables, and the time index (*DAYS*). Use the

$R^2$ statistic to compute the $F$-statistic for the null hypothesis that none of the variables in the regression matter for $NO_2$ pollution.

b. This sample has 500 observations. Does the validity of the $F$-test described in (a) rest heavily on having normally, or almost normally, distributed disturbances?

3. Does the separation of corporate control from corporate ownership lead to inflated executive salaries and worse firm performance? George Stigler and Claire Friedland addressed these questions empirically using a sample of firms.[7] A subset of their data are in the file execcomp.***. The variables in the file are

ecomp     Average total annual compensation in thousands of dollars for a firm's top three executives

assets     Firm's assets in millions of dollars

profits     Firm's annual profits in millions of dollars

mcontrol Dummy variable indicating management control of the firm

a. Regress executives' compensation on the firm's assets, the managerial control dummy, a variable that is the product of profits and the managerial control dummy, and an intercept term. Test at the 10% significance level the null hypothesis that managerial control has no discernible effect on executive compensation.

b. Regress firm profits on firm assets, the management control dummy, a variable that is the product of assets and the managerial control dummy, and an intercept term. Test at the 10% significance level the null hypothesis that managerial control has no discernible effect on profits.

c. Interpret the coefficients on the variables in (a) and (b) that involve multiplying the control dummy by assets or profits.

d. Explain why (a) and (b) require $F$-tests and why using two $t$-tests in each case would not be appropriate.

4. The sudden growth of homelessness in the 1980s is often attributed to the release of many individuals from mental hospitals during that period. Housing economists, however, have painted a more complex picture, pointing to housing market conditions and economic circumstances as significant contributors to the problem. John Quigley, Steven Raphael, and Eugene Smolensky addressed the roots of homelessness with several data sets.[8] One of their data sets, covering 273 urban areas and based on the 1990 U.S. Census, is contained in homeless1.***. The variables in that file are

HMLSS          Natural log of the homelessness rate 1990
VAC            Natural log of the rental vacancy rate 1990
GROSSR         Natural log of the median gross rent 1990
MDHHINC        Natural log of the median household income 1990
RNTINCRT       Natural log of the rent/income ratio 1990
UNEMPLOY       Natural log of the unemployment rate 1990
MHOSP          The change in mental hospital population per 100,000 people 1981–1992
PRISON         The change in prison population per 100,000 people 1981–1992
JANTEMP        Natural log of the average January temperature
SSIPOP         Natural log of the city's supplemental security income recipients
POP            Natural log of the city's total population

Regress the log of the homelessness rate on an intercept term, the logs of gross rent, median household income, January temperature, unemployment, and the changes in mental health and prison populations. Use the $R^2$ statistic to compute the $F$-statistic for the null hypothesis that none of the variables in the regression matter for homelessness.

5. The labels on French wine bottles contain information about the wine. Is the wine red or white? What is the wine's vintage? Which region is the wine from? And what class does the producer claim for the wine (for example *gran cru classe* or *clu non classe*)? But what consumers probably want from a wine are superb sensory traits. Is the wine too acidic? Does it have fine tannins? Does it offer complex aromas? These are traits that wine drinkers and professional wine tasters look for. Three French economists, Pierre Combris, Sebastien Lecocq, and Michael Visser, used data from wine bottle labels and from professional wine tasters to ask which traits—the traits reported on the label or the sensory traits—better account for the price of French wines.[9] The file wine.*** contains a subsample of wines these authors used.

The variables in the file and their meaning are

| | |
|---|---|
| PRICE | The wine's price |
| GRADE | Professional tasters grade for the wine |

**Label Traits**

| | |
|---|---|
| RANK | Cru or gran cru (3); cru bourgeois (2); cru non classe (1) |
| RED | Red wine (2); white wine (1) |
| WHIT | White wine (2); red wine (1) |
| AN89 | Vintage 1989 (2); otherwise (1) |
| AN90 | Vintage 1990 (2); otherwise (1) |
| AN91 | Vintage 1991 (2); otherwise (1) |
| BORD | Bordeaux group (2); otherwise (1) |
| COTE | Cote group (2); otherwise (1) |
| MEGR | Medoc and graves group (2); otherwise (1) |
| SEPF | Saint-Emilion Pomerol Frosnac group (2); otherwise (1) |
| BLSE | Blanc Secs group (2); otherwise (1) |
| BLDO | Blanc Doux group (2); otherwise (1) |

**Sensory Traits**

| | |
|---|---|
| INTE | Aromatic intensity strong (3); classic (2); discrete (3) |
| FINE | Finesse of aromas yes (2); no (1) |
| COMP | Complexity of aromas yes (2); no (1) |
| FIRM | Firmness of attack yes (2); no (1) |
| ACID | Excessive acidity yes (2); no (1) |
| SUPP | Supple yes (2); no (1) |
| FAT | Plump (3); medium (2); lean (1) |
| FLAT | Flat yes (2); no (1) |
| WCON | Well concentrated yes (2); no (1) |
| HARM | Well balanced components (3); balanced (2); unbalanced (1) |
| TANI | Fine tannins yes (2); no (1) |
| FINI | Finish long (3); medium (2); short (1) |
| ALCO | Alcohol excess yes (2); no (1) |

*STAL*      Trace of staleness yes (2); no (1)

*REDU*      Touch of reduction (2); no (1)

*KEEP*      Needs keeping before drinking yes (2); no (1)

a. Regress the natural log of the price of wine against the wine's sensory traits, *RANK*, *AN90*, *AN89*, five of the six group variables (omit *BORD*), and an intercept term. Use the $R^2$ statistic to compute the $F$-statistic for the null hypothesis that neither the label traits nor the sensory traits matter for the price of wine. Show all work.

b. Re-run the regression omitting all the sensory traits except *KEEP*. Compute the $F$-statistic for the null hypothesis that none of the omitted sensory variables matter for the price of wine. At the 5% significance level, what do you conclude about these omitted sensory variables? Show all work.

6. The file somedata.\*\*\* contains a dependent variable $Y$ and 30 explanatory variables, $X1$–$X30$. Regress $Y$ on all 30 explanators and an intercept term.

a. Which variables are statistically significant at the 10% level?

b. Use the $R^2$ statistic to compute the $F$-statistic for the null hypothesis that none of the variables $X1$–$X30$ matter for $Y$. Do you reject the null hypothesis at the 10% significance level?

c. Assess the assertion "I interpret the results from (a) and (b) taken together to indicate that at the 10% significance level I should argue that first two variables $X1$ and $X2$ matter for $Y$, but $X3$ through $X30$ do not."

d. Is your finding in (a) at odds with, or consistent with, the claim that all the variables in somedata.\*\*\* are independently drawn random samples from a standard normal distribution and are entirely unrelated to one another.

7. The file deficit1.\*\*\* contains data from 1960 to 2004 for studying the relationship between deficits and long-term interest rates in the United States. Do the data for the full period support the analysis in the chapter that relied on only the years from 1960 to 1994?

8. Robert Barro studied economic growth in a cross section of countries.[10] The file barrogrowth.\*\*\* contains Barro's variables for a slightly different sample of countries, and an inferior measure of assassinations. The variables in the file are

*ASIAE*         East Asia dummy

*ASSAS*         Assassinations per year

*COUNTRY*       Name of country

*GCY*           Government consumption as a % of GDP average 70–85

*GDP60*         GDP 1960

*GDP70*         GDP 1970

*GR6085*        GDP growth 60–85 (average)

*GR7085*        GDP growth 70–85 (average)

*LAAM*          Latin America dummy

*PPI60DEV*      Deviations from PPP for Investment 1960

*PRIM60*        Percent enrolled in primary school 1960

*PRIM70*        Percent enrolled in primary school 1970

*PREVCOUP*      Revolutions and coups a year

| | |
|---|---|
| *SAFRICA* | Sub-Saharan Africa dummy |
| *SEC60* | Percent enrolled in secondary school 1960 |
| *SEC70* | Percent enrolled in secondary school 1970 |
| *SHCODE* | Summers–Heston country code |
| *STTEAPRI* | Student teacher ratio in primary schools 1960 |
| *STTEASEC* | Student teacher ratio in secondary schools 1970. |

a. Regress GDP growth from 1960 to 1985 on GDP in 1960, government consumption as a fraction of GDP, the percents enrolled in primary and secondary education, revolutions and coups in a year, the measure of economic distortions, *PPI60DEV*, and the dummy variables for East Asia, Latin America, and sub-Saharan Africa. Test at the 5% significance level the null hypothesis that none of the three geographic dummies matter for GDP growth, against the alternative hypothesis that they do. Show all work.

b. Test at the 10% significance level the null hypothesis that the coefficient on 1960 GDP is the same in East Asia, Latin America, and sub-Saharan Africa as elsewhere, against the alternative that at least one of these three regions has its own distinct coefficient on 1960 GDP. (This requires another regression besides that in [a].) Show all work.

c. Test at the 10% significance level the null hypothesis that the coefficient on 1960 GDP is the same in East Asia, Latin America, and sub-Saharan Africa as elsewhere, against the alternative that these three regions have a common coefficient on 1960 GDP that is distinct from the coefficient on GDP elsewhere.

9. This exercise examines the returns to education using data on individuals who have twins. The data file for this problem is twin1.***. This data extract is from a survey of twins conducted by Orley Ashenfelter and Cecelia Rouse of Princeton University at the Twins Day Festival in Twinsburg, Ohio.[11] The observational unit of the data is the individual. For sets of twins, information was collected on the earnings, education, age, race, gender, and so on, of individuals. Here we look at the data for one twin from each pair of twins.

The key variables are

| | |
|---|---|
| *hrwage* | Self-reported hourly wage of the individual (in dollars) |
| *lwage* | Natural log of the hourly wage |
| *age* and *age2* | Age of a person (*age*) and its square (*age2*) |
| *female* | = 1 if the person is female; = 0 otherwise |
| *white* | = 1 if the person is white; = 0 otherwise |
| *educ* | Educational attainment of the individual |

a. Test the hypothesis that men and women have the same wage equation against the alternative that they have completely different wage equations.

b. Test the hypothesis that men and women have the same wage equation, but for different intercept terms.

c. Test the hypothesis that age, race, and gender all have zero effect on expected wages.

10. The data set CAPM2.*** contains monthly returns data for six firms, two from each of three industries, for a 16-year period. The variables provided are an indicator of

the firm (*firm*, equal to 1 through 6), an indicator of industry (*ind*, equal to 1 through 3), an indicator of the time period (*month*, equal to 1 through 360), the excess return of the firm's stock over the riskless rate of return in the given month (*freturn*), and the excess return from a market portfolio in the given month (*mreturn*).

a. For Firm 5 and Firm 6, test the capital asset pricing model (CAPM) by testing the hypothesis that the intercept in a regression of *freturns* on *mreturns* is zero.

b. Some economists would argue that betas should be stable over time. For Firm 3 and then for Firm 4, test the hypothesis that the firm's beta was the same in the first eight years of the sample as in the last eight years. Include an intercept term in the equations.

c. Some economists would argue that firms in the same industry should have comparable betas. For each industry, test the hypothesis that the two firms in the industry have the same betas. Include an intercept term in the equations.

d. If the CAPM is true, what are the consequences of including the intercepts in (b) and (c)? If the CAPM were false, what would be the consequences of excluding the intercept term?

e. Does Firm 5 have the same risk characteristics as the market? (Is its beta one?)

 11. How do growing weather and a wine's age influence a Bordeaux wine's price? The data set wineweather1.*** contains average 1989 prices for Bordeaux wines for the vintages from 1952 to 1989, together with data on weather conditions when each vintage was being grown. These data were part of an analysis of Bordeaux wine as an investment by economists Orley Ashenfelter, David Ashmore, and Robert LaLonde.[12] The variables in the file are

*logprice*  Natural log of the price of Bordeaux wines relative to the price of the 1961 vintage

*degrees*  Average temperature in the growing season
*hrain*  Rainfall in the harvest season
*wrain*  Winter rainfall is in *wRn*
*Time_sv*  Time from 1989 back to the wine's vintage year

a. Regress the natural log of a vintage's price on growing-season temperatures, harvest-season rainfall, off-season rainfall, and the age of a wine. Use the $R^2$ statistic to compute the F-statistic for the null hypothesis that none of the variables in the regression matter for the price of wine.

b. Test at the 5% significance level the null hypothesis that the effect of average temperature in the growing season is the same for all wines against the alternative that one or more of the four decades 1951–1960, 1961–1970, 1971–1980, and 1981–1990 had its own distinct coefficient for average temperature.

c. The regression used for (b) should include a dummy variable for each decade, and no constant, or a dummy for each of three decades and a constant. Briefly explain why.

 12. U.S. states differ in the generosity of their welfare programs. The file TANF2.*** reports the maximum real benefits each state offers poor single parents with three children. The variables in the file are

| *tanfreal* | State's real maximum benefit for single parent with three kids |
| *black* | Percent of state's population who are African American |
| *blue* | State voted Democratic in 2004 presidential election |
| *mdinc* | Median income in state |
| *west* | = 1 if state is in west; = 0 otherwise |
| *south* | = 1 if state is in south; = 0 otherwise |
| *midwest* | = 1 if state is in midwest; = 0 otherwise |
| *northeast* | = 1 if state is in northeast; = 0 otherwise |

The basic model in this question specifies that expected real maximum welfare benefits depend on the percent of the population who are African American, whether the state voted for Kerry over Bush in the 2004 U.S. presidential election, and an intercept term.

a. Test at the 5% significance level the null hypothesis that the coefficients for states in the Midwest are the same as for other states.

b. Test at the 5% significance level the null hypothesis that the coefficients for states in the Midwest are the same as for other states, except, perhaps, for the intercept in the Midwest.

c. Test the null hypothesis that states outside the Midwest have the same coefficients as one another, except, perhaps for their intercept terms, against the alternative hypotheses that the three regions (North, South, and West) all have different coefficients.

d. Summarize in nontechnical terms what you conclude from (a), (b), and (c) taken together.

13. Do students with better SAT scores achieve higher grade point averages (GPAs)? The data in sat3.*** are pertinent to this question. The sample contains a random sample of 745 Bates College students. The variables include

| *HS_GPA* | Adjusted high school GPA |
| *ADRANK* | Admissions rank category |
| *FEMALE* | = 1 if female; = 0 if male |
| *HS_TYPE* | Public high school = 0; independent = 1; religious = 2 |
| *HSPCNTL* | Percentile rank in high |
| *MATH* | Math SAT score |
| *SAT* | Total SAT score − math + verbal |
| *SUBMIT* | Asked that SAT score be considered in admissions |
| *GPA* | Cumulative GPA |
| *VERBAL* | Verbal SAT score |

a. Restrict the sample to students who submit their SAT scores for consideration in admission (*submit* = 1). Regress *GPA* on an intercept term, *sat*, *hs_gpa*, and *female*. Test at the 5% significance level the null hypothesis that Bates students with higher SAT scores do not have better than expected GPAs than students with lower SAT scores, against the alternative that they do.

b. Re-run the regression and hypothesis test in (a) for male and female students separately. Is the test result the same for males as for females?

    c. Test at the 5% significance level the null hypothesis that female Bates students and male students have the same coefficients in the regressions in (b).

    d. Test at the 5% significance level the null hypothesis that female Bates students and male students have the same coefficients in the regression in (b), except, perhaps, for the intercept term.

 14. The file equipmentandgrowth.\*\*\* contains data on economic growth between 1960 and 1985 for 106 countries. De Long and Summers[13] used these data to investigate the effect of equipment investment on economic growth. The six variables in the file are

| | |
|---|---|
| *GDP60vUS* | Natural log of a country's per capita income in 1960 relative to that in the United States |
| *GDPGR* | Growth rate of income per worker for a country between 1960 and 1985 |
| *NONEQINV* | Nonequipment investment for the country between 1960 and 1985 |
| *EQUIPINV* | Equipment investment for the country between 1960 and 1985 |
| *LFGR6085* | Growth rate of the labor force between 1960 and 1985 |
| *CONTINENT* | Continent of the country |

The basic model for this problem specifies that a country's expected GDP growth rate depends on the country's investments in both nonequipment and equipment capital, the growth of the country's labor force since 1960, and the country's GDP in 1960.

    a. Test at the 10% significance level the null hypothesis that countries in North America and in Europe have the same coefficients in this model, except, perhaps, for the intercept term.

    b. Test at the 10% significance level the null hypothesis that European and North American countries have the same coefficients in this model as do other countries, except for, perhaps, their intercept terms, against the alternative that the North American and European countries have the same coefficients as one another, except, perhaps for the intercept term, but have different coefficients than the Europeans. (Under the null hypothesis, the North Americans and Europeans may have different intercept terms from one another and from all other countries lumped together.)

    c. Test at the 10% significance level the null hypothesis that the North Americans and Europeans do not differ from the rest of the world except for their intercept terms and their coefficients on equipment investment, against the alternative that American and European countries have the same coefficients as one another, except, perhaps, for the intercept term, but have different coefficients than the Europeans. (Under the null hypothesis, the North Americans and Europeans may have different intercept terms and equipment investment coefficients from one another and from all other countries lumped together.)

 15. For many years, Major League Baseball (MLB) had an unusual labor rule that tied each player to a single team—players were not allowed to change to a new team without the old team's permission. In 1976, this rule changed and baseball players became able to periodically declare themselves "free agents." When they did, they could change teams freely before the following season. Fans and economists have

questioned whether free agency increased, decreased, or left unchanged the competitive balance among teams in their league play. Peter Fishman used the data from 1950 to 2004 in the file baseball.*** to settle this debate.[14]

To measure the competitiveness of baseball teams in any given season, the data set provides the standard deviation of winning percentages (the proportion of games played that a team won) across all teams in the league, *stdevwp*. When teams are competitive, they win similar numbers of games, and the standard deviation is low. When some teams dominate and others perform badly, the standard deviation is high. The number of players that declare free agency prior to a given season is *fragents*.

Several other variables can affect the competitiveness of teams. From 1965 on, MLB had a draft of amateur players in which the poorest performing teams of the previous season get first choices in the draft. The purpose of this practice is to improve competitiveness among teams. *Draft* is a dummy variable indicating years from 1965 on. The number of teams in MLB affects the standard deviation of winning percentages. Each dominant team and each poor team has a smaller impact on the mean deviation of winning percentages from their overall mean when there are more teams in the league. *Teams* is the number of teams in MLB during the season. And finally, when a larger proportion of the U.S. population is playing baseball, the variance in ability among players is greater than when a smaller proportion (presumably the very best) plays. The variable *poppct* is the fraction of the U.S. population who are MLB players.

a. Regress *stdevwp* against *fragents*, *draft*, *teams*, *poppct*, and an intercept term. Test at the 5% significance level the null hypothesis that free agency has no effect on the competitiveness of MLB, against the alternative that it does. What do you conclude about the effect of free agency on baseball's competitiveness on the playing field?

b. The data in baseball.*** cover 55 years. Test at the 5% and 10% significance levels the hypothesis that the intercept and the coefficients on *teams*, *draft,* and *popct* in (a) were the same prior to 1975 as in 1975 onward.

c. Can you test the hypothesis that the coefficient on *fragents* was the same in the earlier period as in the later period?

d. Are the results in (a) sensitive to deleting the years 1950–1975 from the analysis?

## Endnotes

1. Pierre Combris, Sebastien Lecocq, and Michael Visser, "Estimation of a Hedonic Price Equation for Bordeaux Wine: Does Quality Matter?" *Economic Journal* (March 1997): 390–402.

2. Zvi Griliches, "Hedonic Prices for Automobiles: An Econometric Analysis of Quality Change," in *The Price Statistics of the Federal Government*, General Series No. 73 (New York: Columbia University Press, for the National Bureau of Economic Research): 137–196.

3. A. T. Court, "Hedonic Price Indexes with Automotive Examples," in *The Dynamics of Automobile Demand* (New York: The General Motors Corporation, 1939).

4. An informative array of multiple tests appears in Sala-i-Martin's article "I Just Ran Two Million Regressions," *American Economic Review* 87, no. 2 (May 1997):

178–183, which examined which potential determinants of economic growth appear persistently in a humongous variety of specifications. For its title alone, the paper deserves an econometric Oscar!

5. This chapter considers differences in the slopes and intercepts of women's and men's earnings equations when the variances of the disturbances are the same for men and women. Chapter 10 considers DGPs in which the variances of the disturbances are different for women and men. When the disturbances do not have a common variance, a test of the hypothesis of equal slopes and intercepts proceeds differently than here.

6. These data come from the Statlib archive of Carnegie Mellon University. They were originally posted there by Aldrin Magne.

7. George J. Stigler and Claire Friedland, "The Literature of Economics: The Case of Berle and Means," *Journal of Law and Economics* 26, no. 2 (June 1983): 237–268.

8. John M. Quigley, Steven Raphael, and Eugene Smolensky, "Homeless in America, Homeless in California," *Review of Economics and Statistics* 83 (February 2001): 37–51.

9. Pierre Combris, Sebastien Lecocq, and Michael Visser, "Estimation of a Hedonic Price Equation for Bordeaux Wine: Does Quality Matter?" *Economic Journal* (March 1997): 390–402.

10. Robert J. Barro, "Economic Growth in a Cross Section of Countries," *Quarterly Journal of Economics* 106, no. 2 (May 1991): 407–443.

11. Orley Ashenfelter and Cecilia Rouse, "Income, Schooling, and Ability: Evidence from a New Sample of Identical Twins," *Quarterly Journal of Economics* 113, no. 1 (February 1998): 253–284. Professor Ashenfelter kindly provided these data for use in this book.

12. Orley Ashenfelter, David Ashmore, and Robert LaLonde, "Bordeaux Wine Vintage Quality and the Weather," http://www.liquidasset.com/orley.htm (December 1999).

13. J. Bradford DeLong and Lawrence H. Summers, "How Strongly Do Developing Countries Benefit from Equipment Investment?" *Journal of Monetary Economics* 32, no. 3 (1994): 395–415.

14. Peter Fishman, "Competitive Balance and Free Agency in Major League Baseball," *The American Economist* 47, no. 2 (Fall 2003): 86–91.

# Appendix 9.A

# Matrix Algebra and Hypothesis Testing

Matrix algebra provides a compact notation for hypothesis testing in the multiple regression model. This appendix assumes a DGP in which the Gauss–Markov Assumptions apply and in which the disturbances are normally distributed. Thus, $\varepsilon \sim N(0, \sigma^2 I_n)$. The $t$-statistic in the special case in which there is a single explanator and a known intercept equal to zero provides a useful starting point in which to ground our intuition.

## 9.A.1    The Case of a Straight Line Through the Origin Revisited

A $t$-test is appropriate to test the hypothesis that the slope, $\beta$, of a line through the origin is equal to the constant $c$; that is $H_0$: $\beta = c$. The corresponding $t$-statistic is

$$t = \frac{\beta_{g4} - c}{\sqrt{s^2/\sum X_i^2}} = \frac{\beta_{g4} - c}{\sqrt{\sum e_i^2/(n-1)/\sum X_i^2}}.$$

This $t$-statistic has $(n - 1)$ degrees of freedom. The $t$-test is grounded in the intuition that if our estimated value of the slope is sufficiently far from the hypothesized value, the estimate is sufficiently surprising (given the null hypothesis) to make us skeptical of the null hypothesis. The greater the variance in our estimator of the slope, the larger the discrepancy between estimated and hypothesized values must be to waken our skepticism.

This same intuition generalizes to testing more complex linear hypotheses in multiple regression models: If the estimated coefficients violate the hypothesized restrictions too severely, we reject the null hypothesis. How large the discrepancies must be depends on how precise the coefficient estimators are. To adapt the $t$-statistic to more general hypotheses, we first examine its square:

$$t^2 = \frac{(\beta_{g4} - c)^2}{\sum e_i^2/(n-1)/\sum X_i^2}.$$

This squared $t$-statistic follows the $F$-distribution with 1 and $(n - 1)$ degrees of freedom. To see this, consider that

$$t^2 = \frac{\left(\dfrac{\beta_{g4} - c}{\sqrt{\sigma^2 / \sum X_i^2}}\right)^2 / 1}{\sum \left(e_i^2 / \sigma^2\right) / (n - 1)}.$$

The numerator on this expression is a single squared standard normal divided by 1. Thus the numerator is a chi-square variable (with one degree of freedom) divided by its degrees of freedom. The denominator contains a sum of squared mean zero normals, $\sum e_i^2 / \sigma^2$, divided by $(n - 1)$. We could prove with advanced methods that $\sum e_i^2 / \sigma^2$ is distributed chi-square with $(n - 1)$ degrees of freedom (and is distributed chi-square with $[n - k - 1]$ degrees of freedom in the multiple explanator case). Thus, the denominator is a chi-square variable divided by its degrees of freedom. Because the numerator and denominator prove to be statistically independent of one another, it follows that $t^2$ follows the $F$-distribution with 1 and $(n - 1)$ degrees of freedom.[1]

The road to a matrix algebra $F$-statistic for multiple hypotheses in a multiple regression model begins with the matrix representation of the squared $t$-statistic and passes through an extension of this analysis to a model with one explanator and an unknown slope. The first step in the journey is to rewrite $t^2$ with matrix notation for the numerator:

$$t^2 = (\beta_{g4} - c)' \, \sigma^2 \, (\mathbf{X}'\mathbf{X})^{-1} (\beta_{g4} - c) / (s^2 / \sigma^2).$$

This matrix expression is a special case of the more general form of the $F$-statistic for testing multiple linear constraints on the coefficients of a multiple regression model. The next step in the journey is to complicate the analysis by adding an unknown intercept and testing a null hypothesis that constrains both the slope and the intercept.

## 9.A.2    Testing Linear Constraints on Both the Slope and Intercept

Now consider a hypothesis that constrains both the intercept (now assumed to be unknown) and the slope. For example,

$$\text{H}_0: 3\beta_0 = c_0 \text{ and } 4\beta_1 = c_1,$$

where the numbers 3 and 4 are arbitrarily chosen, and could be replaced by any other constants, and $c_0$ and $c_1$ are specific hypothesized values for $3\beta_0$ and $4\beta_1$. The intuition of the $t$-test would have us look at the magnitudes of $3\hat{\beta}_0 - c_0$ and

$4\beta_1 = c_1$ and reject the null hypothesis if the magnitudes were sufficiently large. As with the $t$-test, "sufficiently large" would be relative to the precision with which the coefficients are estimated. Suppose the estimators of the slope and intercept were statistically independent. A natural extension of the $t^2$ statistic would then be

$$W = \frac{(3\hat{\beta}_0 - c_0)^2}{\text{var}(3\hat{\beta}_0)} + \frac{(4\hat{\beta}_1 - c_1)^2}{\text{var}(4\hat{\beta}_1)}. \qquad \text{9.A.1}$$

This statistic weights discrepancies of the estimates from their hypothesized values in accord with the precisions of the estimators. Test statistics that follow this strategy are called **Wald statistics**. Wald statistics count discrepancies from each constraint of the null hypothesis. The squaring of the discrepancies avoids discrepancies in one direction from canceling with discrepancies in the other direction, which seems a reasonable trait for the test statistic.

Can we express $W$ in matrix notation? Yes, we can.

Consider the matrix

$$R = \begin{bmatrix} 3 & 0 \\ 0 & 4 \end{bmatrix}$$

and the matrix

$$\beta = \begin{bmatrix} \beta_0 \\ \beta_1 \end{bmatrix}.$$

The matrix

$$R\beta = c = \begin{bmatrix} c_0 \\ c_1 \end{bmatrix}$$

states the two claims of the null hypothesis. Because the slope and intercept estimators are independent by assumption,

$$\sigma^2(X'X)^{-1} = \begin{bmatrix} \text{var}(\hat{\beta}_0) & 0 \\ 0 & \text{var}(\hat{\beta}_1) \end{bmatrix},$$

and

$$\sigma^2 R (X'X)^{-1} R' = \begin{bmatrix} 9\text{var}(\hat{\beta}_0) & 0 \\ 0 & 16\,\text{var}(\hat{\beta}_1) \end{bmatrix},$$

and

$$(\sigma^2 R (X'X)^{-1} R')^{-1} = \begin{bmatrix} \dfrac{1}{\text{var}(3\hat{\beta}_0)} & 0 \\ 0 & \dfrac{1}{\text{var}(4\hat{\beta}_1)} \end{bmatrix}.$$

A matrix representation of $W$ is, therefore,

$$(R\hat{\beta} - c)' \, (\sigma^2 \, R(X'X)^{-1} \, R')^{-1} \, (R\hat{\beta} - c).$$

Examining Equation 9.A.1 reveals that the numerator has in it the sum of two squared mean zero normals (under the null hypothesis). If we know $\sigma^2$, $W$ follows the chi-square distribution. If we do not know $\sigma^2$, we must estimate it with $s^2$, and we will again be dealing with the ratio of two chi-square variables. To transform $W$ into a statistic that follows the $F$-distribution requires dividing $W$ by 2, because it is the sum of two independent mean zero squared normals. More generally, the analog of $W$ for a null hypothesis with $r$ constraints would require dividing by $r$, as the numerator would contain $r$-squared discrepancies:

$$F = (R\hat{\beta} - c)'(s^2 R(X'X)^{-1}R')^{-1} (R\hat{\beta} - c)/r. \qquad \text{9.A.2}$$

This $F$-statistic follows the $F$-distribution with $r = 2$ and $(n - 2)$ degrees of freedom in the present case and with $r$ and $(n - k - 1)$ degrees of freedom in the more general case.

We arrived at this $F$-statistic by assuming that the coefficient estimators are statistically independent of one another. However, it applies equally well to cases in which the estimators are not statistically independent of one another. The variance–covariance matrix of the disturbances, $\sigma^2(X'X)^{-1}$, takes appropriate account of interdependencies to maintain the $F$-distribution of the statistic. The statistic also applies equally well when there are $k$ explanatory variables in the DGP.

## 9.A.3     Any Linear Constraint Can Be Expressed with $R\beta = c$

The constraint matrix $R$ can be written to express any number of linear constraints on the coefficients. Consider, for example, three linear constraints on the coefficients of a model with four slopes and an intercept term:

$$\alpha_{01}\beta_0 + \alpha_{11}\beta_1 + \alpha_{21}\beta_2 + \alpha_{31}\beta_3 + \alpha_{41}\beta_4 + \alpha_{51}\beta_5 = c_1$$
$$\alpha_{02}\beta_0 + \alpha_{12}\beta_1 + \alpha_{22}\beta_2 + \alpha_{32}\beta_3 + \alpha_{42}\beta_4 + \alpha_{52}\beta_5 = c_2$$

and

$$\alpha_{03}\beta_0 + \alpha_{13}\beta_1 + \alpha_{23}\beta_2 + \alpha_{33}\beta_3 + \alpha_{43}\beta_4 + \alpha_{53}\beta_5 = c_3.$$

Any of the $\alpha$'s could be zero. Note that there cannot be more constraints than there are coefficients to be estimated; any additional constraints would be either redundant or inconsistent with the others. In this case, the matrix $R$ is

$$R = \begin{bmatrix} \alpha_{01} & \alpha_{11} & \alpha_{21} & \alpha_{31} & \alpha_{41} \\ \alpha_{02} & \alpha_{12} & \alpha_{22} & \alpha_{32} & \alpha_{42} \\ \alpha_{03} & \alpha_{13} & \alpha_{23} & \alpha_{33} & \alpha_{43} \end{bmatrix}.$$

One special case of interest is when there is a single linear constraint on the coefficients, so that the constraint matrix has a single row. The variance of $R\hat{\beta}$ in this special case is

$$R(\sigma^2(X'X)^{-1})R' = \sigma^2 \sum_{i=0}^{k} \sum_{j=0}^{k} \alpha_{i1} \, \alpha_{j1} \, \nu_{ij}, \qquad \text{9.A.3}$$

where $\nu_{ij}$ is the $ij$-th element of $(X'X)^{-1}$. We know that this variance, being a variance, cannot be negative. If no subset of the explanators is perfectly collinear, this variance also cannot be zero, so it must be positive. In the more abstract representations of matrix algebra, strictly positive forms like those in Equation 9.A.3 are given a name. A symmetric matrix $Q$, such as that for any row matrix $A$ that is not all zeros, $AQA' > 0$ is called **positive definite**. If $Q$ is positive definite, $Q^{-1}$ exists and is also positive definite.

## 9.A.4 Goodness of Fit and Deviations from the Null Hypothesis

Building the $F$-statistic based on discrepancies between the estimated and hypothesized coefficients, as this appendix does, differs intuitively from the development of $F$-tests in Section 9.2. There, the $F$-statistic followed from examining the deterioration of fit caused by imposing the null hypothesis when estimating the model. However, the $F$-statistics we arrive at by these two routes are computationally equivalent when (i) the model is linear in its parameters; (ii) the hypothesized constraints are linear in the parameters; and (iii) the DGP satisfies the Gauss–Markov Assumptions. A corollary of this observation is that the standard $t$-test is equivalent to a standard $F$-test conducted for a single constraint.

## 9.A.5 A General Gauss–Markov Theorem

Appendix 5.A.2 proved that under the Gauss–Markov Assumptions, OLS is the best linear unbiased estimator (BLUE) of the slopes and intercept of a straight line. Sometimes, however, econometricians' interest is not in the coefficients themselves, but in linear combinations of the coefficients. For example, an econometrician might wish to estimate the expected value of the money supply given that the interest rate is 7% and GDP is 8 trillion dollars:

$$\text{E}(\textit{money supply}) = \beta_0 + \beta_1(7 \textit{ percent}) + \beta_2(8 \textit{ trillion dollars}).$$

What is the BLUE estimator of this linear combination of the coefficients? The Gauss–Markov Theorem states that under the Gauss–Markov Assumptions, the

BLUE estimator of such a linear combination of the coefficients is that same linear combination of the OLS estimators of the coefficients. More generally, if our interest is in estimating a linear combination $X^*\boldsymbol{\beta}$, the BLUE estimator is $X^*\hat{\boldsymbol{\beta}}$. The variance of $X^*\hat{\boldsymbol{\beta}}$ is similar in form to the variance of $R\hat{\boldsymbol{\beta}}$ when $R$ contains a single row, as given by Equation 9.A.3. The variance of $X^*\hat{\boldsymbol{\beta}}$ is

$$\sigma^2 X^*(X'X)^{-1}X^{*\prime}.$$

The variance of any other unbiased linear estimator of $X^*\hat{\boldsymbol{\beta}}$ is larger than that of the OLS-based estimator. Appendix 6.B.2 determined that the variance–covariance matrix of an unbiased estimator different from OLS, $C'Y = (D' + [X'X]^{-1}X')Y$ differs from the OLS variance–covariance matrix, $\sigma^2[X'X]^{-1}$. The variance–covariance matrix of $C'Y$, we learned, is $([X'X]^{-1} + D'D)$. The variance of a linear unbiased estimator of $X^*\boldsymbol{\beta}$, $X^*C'Y$, is

$$\sigma^2 X^*([X'X]^{-1} + D'D)X^{*\prime}$$
$$= \sigma^2 X^*[X'X]^{-1}X^{*\prime} + \sigma^2 X^*D'DX^{*\prime}.$$

If the coefficient estimators given by $C'Y$ differ from the OLS estimators, then $D'D$ is positive definite and $X^*\hat{\boldsymbol{\beta}}$ must have a smaller variance than $X^*C'Y$ because $\sigma^2 X^*D'DX^{*\prime}$ is positive.

## Appendix 9.A Concepts for Review

### Endnote

1. For proofs that the denominator times $(n - k - 1)$ is distributed chi-square with $(n - k - 1)$ degrees of freedom, and that the numerator and denominator are independent, see W. H. Greene, *Econometric Analysis,* 5th ed. (Englewood Cliffs, NJ: Prentice Hall, 2003).

# PART THREE

# Further Topics in Regression

## *Chapter 10*

# Heteroskedastic Disturbances

*Hal White, he found it fantastic—*
*errors were heteroskedastic!*
*OLS is not BLUE. No, it just is not true*
*that the world is homoskedastic.*

Homoskedasticity fails frequently in the real world. Spending on food provides a good example. Some wealthy people are fond of fine foods and spend large sums on food, either at home or in restaurants. Some other wealthy people are very diet-conscious, eating simply and spending little on food. Consequently, food expenditures vary widely among individuals with high incomes. In contrast, poor households have little flexibility in how much they spend on food. Those poor people who like fine food can afford only a little more spending on food than poor people who consume a minimally adequate diet. Put briefly, the variances of food expenditure are much less for poor people than for wealthy people. These different variances in expenditure imply that the Gauss–Markov Assumptions do not apply when studying households' food expenditures as a function of income—when analyzing food expenditures across income levels, we cannot claim that $\text{var}(\varepsilon_i) = \sigma^2$ $(i = 1, \ldots, n)$.

Chapters 3 through 9 relied on the Gauss–Markov Assumptions to establish the unbiasedness and efficiency of the ordinary least squares (OLS) estimator. When the Gauss–Markov Assumption of homoskedasticity fails, as it does for the realistic model of food expenditure, does OLS remain unbiased? Does OLS remain efficient? More generally, what are the consequences of relaxing any of the Gauss–Markov Assumptions, not just homoskedasticity? The next several chapters examine the consequences of relaxing the Gauss–Markov Assumptions, one by one. When the chapters demonstrate that relaxing the assumptions makes OLS biased or inefficient, as it sometimes does, the chapters further ask which alternative estimators are unbiased and which are efficient.

This chapter examines the consequences of relaxing the Gauss–Markov Assumption that all the disturbances have the same variance. We find that the OLS estimators are no longer best linear unbiased estimators (BLUE) and that the usual estimators of the OLS estimators' standard errors are biased when disturbances are not homoskedastic, which undermines the usual $t$- and $F$-tests from Chapters 7 and 9. In practice, we need to check for homoskedasticity before we rely on it. This chapter introduces three formal tests of homoskedasticity, including one devised by econometrician Hal White of the University of California at San Diego, and then derives the BLUE estimators for the slope and intercept of a line when disturbances are not homoskedastic. The chapter concludes by introducing a new, consistent estimator, also attributable to White, for the OLS estimators' standard errors, to be used when BLUE estimation of the model is not feasible.

## 10.1    Visualizing Heteroskedasticity

WHAT IS THE DGP?

Sometimes a visual inspection of the data is the simplest way to find that the disturbances in a model are not homoskedastic. For example, this is the case with our sample of 108 New York renters that we have examined repeatedly. A visual inspection reveals that the disturbances in the rent–income model violate the Gauss–Markov Assumption that $var(\varepsilon_i) = \sigma^2$; the disturbances are not homoskedastic, but *heteroskedastic*. **Heteroskedastic disturbances** differ from one another in their variances, with $var(\varepsilon_i) = \sigma_i^2$ $(i = 1, \ldots, n)$ and $\sigma_i^2 \neq \sigma_j^2$ for two or more observations.

Figure 10.1, the scatterplot of rents and incomes for the sample of New Yorker renters contained in the file rents.*** on this book's companion Web site (**www.aw-bc.com/murray**) is striking. You might think, "Why didn't we look at this before?" Casual inspection of the figure insists on a nonzero intercept term, denies homoskedasticity, and makes no objection to linearly relating the expected rent to income. A visual fitting of a regression line would happily draw a rising straight line that would not pass through the origin but that would, instead, have a positive intercept. Furthermore, the observations seem more spread out at higher levels of income than at low levels of income (with the exception of the highest levels of income, where there are not very many observations with which to establish a pattern), indicating heteroskedastic, not homoskedastic, disturbances. Such visual examination of a model's variables can be quite revealing, es-

**Figure 10.1**

Rents and Incomes
for a Sample of New
Yorkers

*Source:* U.S. Annual
Housing Survey

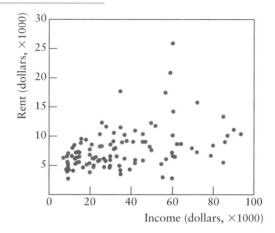

pecially when examining bivariate relationships such as that between the two variables, rent and income.

What are the implications of heteroskedastic disturbances like those found in Figure 10.1? Would the Monte Carlo results of Chapters 2 and 3 have been different had the Monte Carlo experiments contained heteroskedastic disturbances? Would $\beta_{g1}$, $\beta_{g2}$, or $\beta_{g3}$ outperform $\beta_{g4}$ if the disturbances were heteroskedastic? More generally, would the unbiasedness restrictions for linear estimators change? Would the variance of a linear estimator be different than $\sigma^2 \sum w_i^2$? Would OLS still be BLUE? Would the $t$-tests and $F$-tests described in Chapters 7 and 9 still be valid? This chapter addresses these questions in detail, but a graph of heteroskedastic disturbances suffices to expose one consequence of heteroskedasticity: OLS may no longer be BLUE.

A return to Figure 3.1, replicated here as Figure 10.2, reveals why OLS may no longer be BLUE if the disturbances are heteroskedastic. The figure shows the true line (solid) and the lines that would fit (dotted) if we had just one data point (a small $X$, a middle-sized $X$, or a large $X$) with which to estimate the true line. When the disturbances are homoskedastic, we anticipate the same size disturbances at both small $X$'s and large $X$'s. In Figure 10.2, for the case of a straight line through the origin, we see that with equal-sized disturbances at $X_1$, $X_2$, and $X_3$, the observations with larger $X$'s are less misleading about the true slope of the line for any given disturbance. Because with homoskedastic disturbances, the sizes of disturbances are the same at $X_1$, $X_2$, and $X_3$, we concluded in Chapter 3 that when estimating the slope of a line through the origin, we want to more heavily weight observations with larger $X$'s. In Chapter 4, we found that this translated into OLS more heavily weighting observations further from the mean $X$ when estimating a line with an unknown intercept.

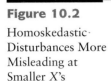

**Figure 10.2**

Homoskedastic·
Disturbances More
Misleading at
Smaller $X$'s

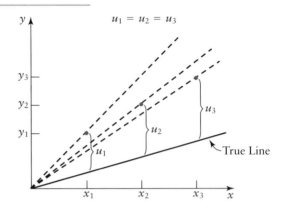

Deciding how to weight observations is more complex when the disturbances are heteroskedastic. Figure 10.3 supposes that the typical disturbance at $X_3$ is larger in magnitude than the typical disturbance at $X_1$—the disturbances are heteroskedastic, and observations with larger $X$'s have more variable disturbances. If the disturbances at $X_3$ are sufficiently larger, as depicted in Figure 10.3, observations with smaller $X$'s are less misleading about the true slope of the line. *In general, other things being the same, when disturbances are heteroskedastic, we wish to less heavily weight those observations with the larger variances.* OLS does not do this, so OLS may not be BLUE when the disturbances are heteroskedastic.

Just how much less a BLUE estimator weights observations with larger variances depends on the specific form of heteroskedasticity in a given data-generating process (DGP). To isolate the consequences of heteroskedasticity for BLUE estimation, consider a DGP that maintains the other Gauss–Markov Assumptions. To allow for the most general form of heteroskedasticity, each observation's disturbance

**Figure 10.3**

Heteroskedasticity
with Smaller Distur-
bances at Smaller $X$'s

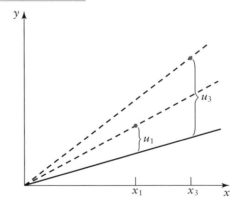

# A Monte Carlo Experiment

## Prelude to Heteroskedasticity

Just as Chapter 2 was a Monte Carlo prelude to the more formal analysis of Chapter 3, the Monte Carlo exercises here precede this chapter's formal investigation of heteroskedasticity's consequences for linear estimators. Recall the initial Monte Carlo investigations of Chapters 2 and 3. There we found that $\beta_{g4}$ outperforms $\beta_{g1}$, $\beta_{g2}$, and $\beta_{g3}$ in estimating the slope of a line through the origin. But those Monte Carlo exercises assumed homoskedastic disturbances. Might $\beta_{g1}$, $\beta_{g2}$, or $\beta_{g3}$ outperform $\beta_{g4}$ when the disturbances are heteroskedastic? MC Builder IV and MC Builder V, which are on this book's companion Web site (**www.aw-bc.com/murray**), support Monte Carlo studies of $\beta_{g1}$, $\beta_{g2}$, $\beta_{g3}$, and $\beta_{g4}$, in which the disturbances are heteroskedastic.

Heteroskedasticity can come in many forms. Harvard economist Robert Barro, in his classic study of a growing money supply, found that disturbances in his money supply equation were much more variable during World War II than in the postwar period, though within each period the disturbances were homoskedastic. The single change in variance was abrupt, occurring just after the war ended in 1945. In contrast, the rent–income scatterplot in Figure 10.1 is consistent with disturbances with variances that grow smoothly with income. In addition to abrupt changes in variances and smoothly increasing variances, myriad other patterns are also possible. MC Builder IV and MC Builder V support Monte Carlo comparisons of $\beta_{g1}$, $\beta_{g2}$, $\beta_{g3}$, and $\beta_{g4}$ as estimators of the slope of a line through the origin for two specific kinds of smoothly shifting heteroskedasticity.

MC Builder IV assumes the disturbances have variances proportional to the magnitude of $X$, $\text{var}(\varepsilon_i) = \sigma^2|X_i|$. MC Builder V assumes the disturbances have variances proportional to the square of $X$, $\text{var}(\varepsilon_i) = \sigma^2 X_i^2$. Notice that both of these specifications accompany larger $X$-values with larger variances for the disturbances, as in the rent–income example. What differs between the two specifications is how rapidly the variance grows. MC Builder IV and MC Builder V ask users to make the same kinds of choices as those made in MC Builder I. Both programs use a random number generator to create values for the disturbances. MC Builder IV and V draw numbers, $\nu_i$, from a homoskedastic random number generator with variance $\sigma^2$. MC Builder IV then multiplies each drawn $\nu_i$ by $\sqrt{|X_i|}$ to create the sample disturbances, the $\varepsilon_i$, which are then suitably heteroskedastic:

$$\text{var}(\varepsilon_i) = \text{var}(\nu_i\sqrt{|X_i|}) = \sigma^2|X_i|.$$

MC Builder V multiplies each drawn $\nu_i$ by $X_i$ to create the sample disturbances, the $\varepsilon_i$. The $\varepsilon_i$ are then suitably heteroskedastic:

$$\text{var}(\varepsilon_i) = \text{var}(\nu_i X_i) = \sigma^2 X_i^2.$$

Conduct several Monte Carlo experiments with each program. Ask:

1. Which estimator performs best when the disturbances' variances are proportional to $|X_i|$?
2. Which estimator performs best when the disturbances' variances are proportional to $X_i^2$?
3. How do you explain the differences between the findings in MC Builder IV and MC Builder V and those obtained in Chapters 2 and 3, where $\beta_{g4}$ outperformed the other estimators, and $\beta_{g3}$ performed second best?

The results from these Monte Carlo experiments highlight the sensible nature of the guessing mechanisms you and other students chose when first examining the estimation of a straight line through the origin. Each intuitively plausible estimator in Chapter 2 proves best for some relatively common DGP, two of them for coping with the common forms of heteroskedasticity found in MC Builder IV and MC Builder V. However, just as knowing that $\beta_{g4}$ outperformed three other estimators when the disturbances were homoskedastic invites wondering if there were a yet better estimator, the Monte Carlo comparisons of $\beta_{g1}$, $\beta_{g2}$, $\beta_{g3}$, and $\beta_{g4}$ with heteroskedastic disturbances invites wondering whether some estimator besides $\beta_{g1}$, $\beta_{g2}$, $\beta_{g3}$, and $\beta_{g4}$ is best in the face of heteroskedasticity. Answering that question requires a formal examination of regression models with heteroskedastic disturbances.

should have its own distinct variance. Consequently, to formalize the discussion of heteroskedasticity, consider the DGP

$$Y_i = \beta_0 + \beta_1 X_{1i} + \cdots + \beta_k X_{ki} + \varepsilon_i \qquad i = 1, \ldots, n$$
$$\mathrm{E}(\varepsilon_i) = 0 \qquad i = 1, \ldots, n$$
$$\mathrm{var}(\varepsilon_i) = \sigma_i^2 \qquad i = 1, \ldots, n$$
$$\mathrm{cov}(\varepsilon_i, \varepsilon_j) = 0 \qquad i \neq j$$

Each explanator is fixed across samples.

In this process, all the Gauss–Markov Assumptions are satisfied, with the exception that the disturbances are no longer homoskedastic, but instead, each observation's disturbance can have its own specific variance.

## 10.2 The Consequences of Heteroskedasticity for the OLS Estimators

**WHAT ARE AN ESTIMATOR'S PROPERTIES?**

OLS is BLUE under the Gauss–Markov Assumptions. But some notable economic phenomena, such as consumers' expenditures, do not follow the Gauss–Markov Assumptions. Monte Carlo experiments with MC Builder IV and MC Builder V make it clear that OLS is not necessarily BLUE when the disturbances are heteroskedastic. Other plausible estimators can have smaller variances. Does OLS at least remain unbiased in the face of heteroskedasticity? What about our other plausible estimators of the slope of a line through the origin, $\beta_{g1}$, $\beta_{g2}$, and $\beta_{g3}$? Are they still unbiased when disturbances are heteroskedastic? More generally, what happens to the unbiasedness conditions for linear estimators derived in Chapter 3? And, beyond estimation, are the test procedures developed in Chapters 7 and 9 still appropriate if the disturbances are heteroskedastic?

This section discusses how heteroskedasticity adversely affects OLS and other linear estimators—and the $t$-tests and $F$-tests based on them. We first learn that slope and intercept estimators that are unbiased with homoskedastic disturbances are unbiased with heteroskedastic disturbances. We then find confirmation of the Monte Carlo result that OLS is inefficient in the face of heteroskedasticity. Finally, we learn that the usual estimators of the variances of OLS estimators are biased when the disturbances are heteroskedastic, which undermines the hypothesis-testing procedures based on OLS that were developed in Chapters 7 and 9.

## Unchanged Unbiasedness Conditions

The good news for OLS when there is heteroskedasticity is that OLS remains unbiased when we preserve all the Gauss–Markov Assumptions except homoskedasticity. *OLS and all other linear estimators unbiased under the Gauss–Markov Assumptions remain unbiased when disturbances are heteroskedastic.* Heteroskedasticity does not change the unbiasedness conditions for linear estimators. Recall the analysis of Chapter 6 that asked when a linear estimator, $g = \sum w_i Y_i$, is an unbiased estimator of the intercept in our multiple regression DGP. That analysis looked at the expected value of $g$:

$$E(g) = E[\sum w_i Y_i] = \sum E(w_i Y_i) = \sum w_i E(Y_i)$$

or

$$
\begin{aligned}
E(g) &= \sum [w_i E(\beta_0 X_0 + \beta_1 X_{1i} + \cdots + \beta_k X_{ki} + \varepsilon_i)] \\
&= \sum [w_i(\beta_0 X_0 + \beta_1 X_{1i} + \cdots + \beta_k X_{ki})] \\
&= \beta_0 \sum w_i X_0 + \beta_1 \sum w_i X_{1i} + \cdots + \beta_k \sum w_i X_{ki},
\end{aligned}
$$

and found that if $g$ is to be an unbiased estimator of some one coefficient in our DGP, say $\beta_s$,

$$\sum w_i X_{ri} = 0 \quad \text{for} \quad r \neq s,$$

and

$$\sum w_i X_{si} = 1,$$

so that $E(g)$ would equal $\beta_s$. These unbiasedness conditions rely only on $E(\varepsilon_i) = 0$, the $X$'s being fixed across samples, and the linearity of the regression equation in its parameters. The variances of the disturbances play no role in determining the unbiasedness of a linear estimator, so the unbiasedness conditions do not depend on whether the disturbances are homoskedastic or heteroskedastic.

## The Changed Variance of a Linear Estimator

The bad news for OLS when there is heteroskedasticity begins with the fact that OLS is not BLUE when the disturbances are heteroskedastic. Although heteroskedasticity does not change the unbiasedness conditions for linear estimators, heteroskedasticity does change the variance of a linear estimator, leading to a BLUE estimator different from the OLS estimator. *In the face of heteroskedasticity, OLS, though unbiased, is inefficient.* To verify the inefficiency of OLS when disturbances are heteroskedastic, we return to Chapter 4's derivation of the variance of a linear estimator:

$$\text{var}(g) = \text{var}\left(\sum_{i=1}^{n} w_i Y_i\right),$$

which we can rewrite as

$$\sum_{i=1}^{n} \text{var}(w_i Y_i) + (\text{sum of all the covariances among the } w_i Y_i)$$

$$= \sum_{i=1}^{n} \text{var}(w_i Y_i) + \sum_{i=1}^{n} \sum_{\substack{j=1 \\ j \neq i}}^{n} \text{cov}(w_i Y_i, w_j Y_j)$$

$$= \sum_{i=1}^{n} w_i^2 \text{var}(Y_i) + \sum_{i=1}^{n} \sum_{\substack{j=1 \\ j \neq i}}^{n} w_i w_j \text{cov}(Y_i, Y_j)$$

Under the Gauss–Markov Assumptions, the $\varepsilon_i$ are uncorrelated and the $Y_i$ differ from the $\varepsilon_i$ by only $[\beta_0 + \beta_1 X_{1i} + \cdots + \beta_k X_{ki}]$, which is constant across samples. Consequently, the $Y_i$ are also uncorrelated. Because $Y_i$ is uncorrelated with $Y_j (i \neq j)$, $\text{cov}(Y_i, Y_j) = 0$ for all $i$ not equal to $j$, so the covariance terms in the previous expression are all zero. With uncorrelated disturbances, then,

$$\text{var}(g) = \sum_{i=1}^{n} w_i^2 \text{var}(Y_i).$$

In this DGP, the variance of $Y_i$ is the same as the variance of the $\varepsilon_i$ $(\sigma_i^2)$ because the $Y_i$ differ from the $\varepsilon_i$ by only $[\beta_0 + \beta_1 X_{1i} + \cdots + \beta_k X_{ki}]$, which is a constant across samples. Consequently, in this DGP with heteroskedastic disturbances,

$$\text{var}(g) = \sum_{i=1}^{n} w_i^2 \sigma_i^2.$$

This last expression does not simplify to $\sigma^2 \sum w_i^2$ because the disturbance's variances are not all the same.

The altered expression for the variance of a linear estimator ($\sum_{i=1}^{n} w_i^2 \sigma_i^2$, instead of $\sigma^2 \sum w_i^2$) alters the BLUE estimators for the slopes and intercept of a regression line. Minimizing $\sum_{i=1}^{n} w_i^2 \sigma_i^2$ with respect to $w_1, \ldots, w_n$, subject to the (unchanged) unbiasedness constraints, does not lead to OLS. (OLS followed from minimizing $\sigma^2 \sum w_i^2$.) OLS is no longer efficient. One task for this chapter is to add to our arsenal of econometric tools estimators for the slopes and intercept of regression lines that are BLUE when the disturbances are heteroskedastic, so that we can efficiently estimate regression relationships when faced with heteroskedastic disturbances.

To see how we can derive a BLUE estimator when disturbances are heteroskedastic, consider heteroskedastic disturbances in a DGP with a single explanator and an unknown intercept. The lessons from this case generalize to the multiple regression case.

With heteroskedastic disturbances in a DGP with unknown slope and intercept, $\hat{\beta}_1$ is no longer the BLUE estimator of $\beta_1$. Moreover, the variance of $\hat{\beta}_1$ is no longer $\sigma^2/\sum x_i^2$. Recall that the OLS weights for the slope when the intercept is unknown are $x_i/\sum x_i^2$ $i = 1, \ldots, n$, a result derived in Chapter 4. Consequently, when the disturbances are heteroskedastic, the variance of the OLS slope estimator is

$$\text{var}(\hat{\beta}_1) = \sum w_i^2 \sigma_i^2 = \sum \left(\frac{x_i}{\sum x_j^2}\right)^2 \sigma_i^2 = \frac{\sum x_i^2 \sigma_i^2}{(\sum x_j^2)^2},$$

which would simplify to our previous result if $\sigma_i^2 = \sigma^2$. If all disturbances' variances are less than some finite number, the denominator $\sum (x_i^2 \sigma_i^2)/(\sum x_i^2)^2$ grows faster with $n$ than does the numerator, so the $\text{var}(\hat{\beta}_1)$ converges to zero in large samples when the disturbances are heteroskedastic, just as they do when the *disturbances* are homoskedastic. For both heteroskedastic and homoskedastic disturbances, the distribution of $\hat{\beta}_1$ collapses around the true slope value as $n$ grows large.

There is, then, further bad news for OLS when the disturbances are heteroskedastic. *Heteroskedasticity undermines the validity of the t-tests and F-tests devised in Chapters 7 and 9.* Those tests are valid in large samples if the Gauss–Markov Assumptions are met, and they are valid in small samples if we add to the Gauss–Markov Assumptions a further assumption of normally distributed disturbances. But in the face of heteroskedasticity, because $\text{var}(\hat{\beta}_1)$ is no longer $\sigma^2/\sum x_i^2$, we would be mistaken to estimate the variance of $\hat{\beta}_1$ by $s^2/\sum x_i^2$, as advocated in Chapter 5, and as is appropriate under the Gauss–Markov Assumptions. (Recall, $s^2 = \frac{1}{n-k-1} \sum e_i^2$, where the $e_i$ are the OLS residuals.) Chapter 7's standard $t$-test for hypotheses about $\hat{\beta}_1$ uses

$$t = \frac{\hat{\beta}_1 - \beta_1^0}{\sqrt{s^2/\sum x_i^2}};$$

this $t$-statistic relies on $s^2$, a mistaken estimator of the variance of $\hat{\beta}_1$ if the disturbances are heteroskedastic. Chapter 9 introduced an $F$-test to assess multiple claims about the slopes and intercept of a regression model. That $F$-test also relies on $s^2$. Consequently, that $F$-test is not the appropriate procedure for testing hypotheses about linear combinations of slopes and intercepts if the disturbances are heteroskedastic.

How does heteroskedasticity undermine the *t*-tests and *F*-tests of Chapters 7 and 9? Heteroskedasticity tends to reduce the power of the tests and distort their size; that is, it tends to make the tests less likely to reject a false null hypothesis and to make the critical values based on the *t*-distribution or *F*-distribution misleading. The stated significance levels of Chapters 7 and 9's tests are wrong when the disturbances are heteroskedastic. For the most commonly encountered forms of heteroskedasticity, the standard *t*-test rejects the null when it is true more often than the stated significance level indicates.

## 10.3        Tests for Heteroskedasticity

Because the efficiency of OLS and the validity of the usual OLS test statistics depend on homoskedasticity, we should test the hypothesis of homoskedasticity before relying on OLS and the standard tests based on it. Sometimes, a visual check suffices to reveal heteroskedasticity, as in Figure 10.1. At other times, though, heteroskedasticity is present but is not obvious to the eye, as in cases where there are several explanatory variables in the model. To allow us to expose heteroskedasticity when visual inspection is insufficient, this section develops three formal statistical tests of the null hypothesis of homoskedasticity.

The first two formal statistical tests both use regressions to ask whether the squared OLS residuals vary systematically with other variables. If the squared residuals do vary with other variables, we reject homoskedasticity. *The White test for heteroskedasticity is the most general heteroskedasticity test.* The White test has some power (sometimes a lot, sometimes a little) against all the forms of heteroskedasticity that undermine the good properties of OLS. *The Breusch–Pagan test for heteroskedasticity is particularly powerful when the econometrician knows something about the forms of heteroskedasticity that might be present.* The Breusch–Pagan test is particularly weak when the econometrician is wrong about the structure of the heteroskedasticity present.

The third formal test for heteroskedasticity, the *Goldfeld–Quandt test*, examines two subsets of the observations in a sample, asking whether the expected squared disturbance in one group differs from that in the other. This is the procedure Robert Barro used in deciding that disturbances to the supply of money during World War II had a larger variance than disturbances after the war. The test is best suited to models in which it is natural to divide the data into distinct groups.

### The White Test

Economist Hal White, of the University of California at San Diego, developed the most general test of heteroskedasticity in 1980.[1] White's approach applies to all multiple regression models, but describing his strategy is simplest in the model with unknown slope and intercept. White's test relies on two expressions for the variance of $\hat{\beta}_1$. As noted earlier, if the disturbances are heteroskedastic,

$$\text{var}(\hat{\beta}_1) = \frac{\sum x_i^2 \sigma_i^2}{(\sum x_i^2)^2}. \qquad \textbf{10.1}$$

If the disturbances are homoskedastic, Equation 10.1 reduces to

$$\text{var}(\hat{\beta}_1) = \frac{\sum x_i^2 \sigma^2}{(\sum x_i^2)^2} = \frac{\sigma^2 \sum x_i^2}{(\sum x_i^2)^2}. \qquad \textbf{10.2}$$

Generally, we don't know either $\sigma^2$ or the $\sigma_i^2$, so we can't compute either of these two variance expressions. However, recall that the $\sigma_i^2 = E(\varepsilon_i^2)$. When we constructed our estimator of $\sigma^2$ in Chapter 5, we found it sensible to replace $E(\varepsilon_i^2)$ with its sample analog, $e_i^2$; we do that again here. Econometricians frequently use observed residuals instead of unobserved disturbances when the residuals are constructed with unbiased estimators. We estimate $\sum x_i^2 \sigma_i^2$ with $\sum x_i^2 e_i^2$, and therefore estimate the variance expression in Equation 10.1 by

$$\widetilde{\text{var}}(\hat{\beta}_1) = \frac{\sigma^2 \sum x_i^2}{(\sum x_i^2)^2}. \qquad \textbf{10.3}$$

We call this estimator of the variance of $\hat{\beta}_1$ **White's heteroskedasticity-consistent variance estimator.** The estimator is called "consistent" because in large samples, its distribution collapses around the true value. The estimator is consistent whether or not the disturbances are heteroskedastic.

When the disturbances are homoskedastic, we can unbiasedly estimate $\sigma^2$ by $s^2 = \frac{1}{n-k-1} \sum e_i^2$. Replacing $\sigma^2$ with this estimator in the variance expression in Equation 10.2, we obtain

$$\frac{\left(\frac{1}{n-k-1}\sum e_i^2\right)\sum x_i^2}{(\sum x_i^2)^2} = \frac{s^2}{\sum x_i^2} = s_{\hat{\beta}_1}^2, \qquad \textbf{10.4}$$

our standard estimator of the variance of $\hat{\beta}_1$ under the Gauss–Markov Assumptions. When the disturbances are homoskedastic, $E(\varepsilon_i^2) = \sigma^2$. When the disturbances are homoskedastic, $\sum(x_i^2 s^2)$ is also a more precise estimator of $\sum(x_i^2 \sigma^2)$ than is $\sum(x_i^2 e_i^2)$. Consequently $s_{\hat{\beta}_1}^2$ is the more efficient estimator of the variance of $\hat{\beta}_1$ when the disturbances are homoskedastic. When the disturbances are heteroskedastic, however, $s_{\hat{\beta}_1}^2$ is an inconsistent estimator of $\text{var}(\hat{\beta}_1)$.

White's insight was that if the disturbances are homoskedastic, these two estimators will tend to be approximately equal in large samples, but if the disturbances are heteroskedastic, the two estimators will tend to differ. In other words, if the disturbances are homoskedastic, both estimators have distributions collapsing around the true variance; if the disturbances are heteroskedastic, the two estimators' distributions collapse around different numbers. Formally, White based his test statistic on the difference between the estimators given by Equations 10.3 and 10.4.

In practice, the **White test** is a test for heteroskedasticity that looks at the relationship between the squared OLS residuals and the levels and squares of explanators. The five steps for conducting the White test are as follows:

1. Estimate the underlying bivariate or multiple regression relationship of interest by OLS.
2. Compute the OLS residuals, $e_1, \ldots, e_n$, from step 1.
3. Regress the $e_i^2$ against all of the explanators in the original model, their squares, the cross products of all the original explanators, and an intercept term. Call the number of slopes in this regression $p$.
4. Compute the $R^2$ from the equation in step 3.
5. $nR^2$ is distributed approximately chi-square with $p$ degrees of freedom in large samples. Reject homoskedasticity if the test statistic $nR^2$ exceeds the critical value for the chi-square distribution with $p$ degrees of freedom at your chosen significance level.

A secondary equation, like that in step 3, estimated as part of a test, or as a step in a multistep estimation procedure, is called an **auxiliary equation**. The regression in step 3 contains squared terms and interaction terms, in addition to the original explanators. Intuitively, the squared terms allow the test to capture heteroskedasticity in which the disturbances' variances are proportional to the square of an explanator (as in MC Builder V), and the interaction terms allow the disturbances' variances to move in still more complex ways as the explanators vary. Occasionally, when the number of observations is small, White's test is conducted without using the interaction terms.

In essence, White's test checks to see if the expected squared residuals are constant (the intercept in the auxiliary regression) or vary with one or more of the explanators in the auxiliary equation. If the $R^2$ in the auxiliary equation is high enough, we reject the null of homoskedasticity because the expected squared disturbance appears to vary across observations, whereas homoskedasticity says it is constant.

To illustrate White's test, suppose we are asking whether the disturbances in a wage equation are homoskedastic. If the equation has three explanators, education, experience, and IQ, then the White test would proceed in the following steps:

1. *estimate* $wage_i = \beta_0 + \beta_1 education_i + \beta_2 experience_i + \beta_3 IQ_i + \varepsilon_i$.

2. Form the residuals, $e_1, \ldots, e_n$, from the OLS estimated wage equation.
3. Regress the $e_i^2$ against *education, experience, IQ, education,*[2] *experience,*[2] *IQ,*[2] *education* · *experience, education* · *IQ, experience* · *IQ*, and an intercept term.
4. Compute the $R^2$ from the auxiliary regression in step 3. $nR^2$ is asymptotically distributed chi-square with $p = 9$ degrees of freedom. (There are nine slopes in the auxiliary regression.)
5. Reject homoskedasticity if $nR^2$ from the auxiliary equation in step 3 exceeds the critical value for the chi-square distribution with 9 degrees of freedom (16.92, if the significance level is .05). If $n = 100$ and the $R^2$ in step 3 were .25, $nR^2 = 25$; we would reject the null hypothesis of homoskedasticity.

The number of explanators in White's auxiliary equation grows quickly as the number of explanators in the underlying model grows. For example, when there are 6 explanators in the underlying model, the auxiliary equation contains 26 explanators.

White's test tends to perform poorly in small samples. Consequently, econometricians are divided between White's test, which has some power against all forms of heteroskedasticity that undermine the good properties of OLS, and an alternative test proposed earlier by econometricians Trevor Breusch and Adrian Pagan of the Australian National University that works better in small samples, but that requires more prior information about the form of heteroskedasticity.[2]

## The Breusch–Pagan Test

Breusch and Pagan of the Australian National University offer a test that is simpler than White's test. They assume the econometrician can specify a series of variables that account for the variation in the disturbances across observations. For example, in our rent–income study, we might argue that the variance of the disturbances is some function of income. The list of specified variables can include some, all, or none of the explanators in the underlying model, and it may contain other variables. Only the specified variables appear in Breusch and Pagan's alternative auxiliary regression. As in the White test, the dependent variable in the Breusch–Pagan test depends on the residuals from the OLS estimation of the equation of interest.

The **Breusch–Pagan test** is a test for heteroskedasticity that looks at the relationship between the squared OLS residuals and the levels of a prespecified subset of explanators. It requires six steps:

1. Estimate the underlying relationship of interest by OLS.
2. Compute the OLS residuals, $e_1, \ldots, e_n$, from step 1.
3. Choose the set of $m$ variables with which we assume the $\sigma_i^2$ vary.
4. Regress the $e_i^2$ against all chosen variables.

5. Compute the $R^2$ from the equation in step 4.
6. $nR^2$ is asymptotically distributed chi-square with $m$ degrees of freedom. Reject the null hypothesis of homoskedasticity if $nR^2$ exceeds the critical value for a chi-square statistic with $m$ degrees of freedom at your chosen significance level.

The chi-square distribution of the $nR^2$ statistic applies strictly only in large samples. In small samples, relying on $nR^2$ following the chi-square distribution is often unwarranted—both the White and Breusch–Pagan tests often suffer distorted sizes in small samples; that is, their stated significance levels are often incorrect. *For analyses using small samples, it is in practice preferable to modify the White and Breusch–Pagan procedures by replacing the chi-square tests in those procedures with an F-test of the hypothesis that the auxiliary regression explanators all have zero coefficients.*

Breusch and Pagan's procedure has more power than White's test if the chosen explanators in the Breusch–Pagan auxiliary regression are correct. If the chosen explanators in the Breusch–Pagan auxiliary regression omit variables with which the variances of the underlying disturbances are actually correlated, the stated significance level of the Breusch–Pagan test becomes misleading, the test loses much or all of its power, and the test becomes both biased and inconsistent. It is somewhat arbitrary to assume that the variance of the disturbances is captured by a linear regression with $m$ predetermined explanators, but to do so often proves a useful approximation in practice.

Alternative specifications of the structure of the heteroskedasticity are also possible. Some econometricians replace the $e_i^2$ with the $|e_i|$ as the dependent variable in step 4 of the Breusch–Pagan procedure. Still others use the natural logarithm of the $e_i^2$, $\ln(e_i^2)$. Each of these choices implies a different structure for the heteroskedasticity. If an econometrician guesses the correct form, the corresponding Breusch–Pagan style test is more powerful for detecting the presence of heteroskedasticity than if the econometrician had guessed incorrectly. Some econometricians conduct several tests for heteroskedasticity, taking comfort when they get the same test result from each and urging caution when some tests indicate rejecting homoskedastic disturbances and some tests do not.

## An Example Comparing the White Test and the Breusch–Pagan Test

In Figure 10.1, rents of higher income renters appear decidedly more spread out than those of lower income renters. Do the White and Breusch–Pagan tests confirm this? Table 10.1 contains the OLS rent–income results for our sample of New York renters. White's procedure calls for both income and income squared in the auxiliary regression. Table 10.2 contains the White test auxiliary regression.

**TABLE 10.1  Rent and Income in New York**

Dependent Variable: RENT
Method: Least Squares
Sample: 1 108
Included Observations: 108

| Variable | Coefficient | Std. Error | t-Statistic | Prob. |
|---|---|---|---|---|
| C | 5455.483 | 602.7776 | 9.050573 | 0.0000 |
| INCOME | 0.063568 | 0.014390 | 4.417505 | 0.0000 |
| R-squared | 0.155475 | Mean dependent var | | 7718.111 |
| Adjusted R-squared | 0.147508 | S.D. dependent var | | 3577.000 |
| S.E. of regression | 3302.662 | Akaike info criterion | | 19.06119 |
| Sum squared resid | $1.16E + 09$ | Schwarz criterion | | 19.11086 |
| Log likelihood | −1027.304 | F-statistic | | 19.51435 |
| Durbin–Watson stat | 2.012384 | Prob(F-statistic) | | 0.000024 |

**TABLE 10.2  White's Auxiliary Regression**

Dependent Variable: $R^2$
Method: Least Squares
Sample: 1 108
Included Observations: 108

| Variable | Coefficient | Std. Error | t-Statistic | Prob. |
|---|---|---|---|---|
| C | −14657900 | 9288994 | −1.577986 | 0.1176 |
| INCOME | 1200.579 | 495.1663 | 2.424598 | 0.0170 |
| $INCOME^2$ | −0.010007 | 0.005355 | −1.868714 | 0.0644 |
| R-squared | 0.082134 | Mean dependent var | | 10515952 |
| Adjusted R-squared | 0.064651 | S.D. dependent var | | 29847739 |
| S.E. of regression | 28866783 | Akaike info criterion | | 37.22167 |
| Sum squared resid | $8.75E + 16$ | Schwarz criterion | | 37.29617 |
| Log likelihood | −2006.970 | F-statistic | | 4.697874 |
| Durbin–Watson stat | 1.864571 | Prob(F-statistic) | | 0.011115 |

**TABLE 10.3** Breusch–Pagan Auxiliary Regression

Dependent Variable: $R^2$
Method: Least Squares
Sample: 1 108
Included Observations: 108

| Variable | Coefficient | Std. Error | t-Statistic | Prob. |
|---|---|---|---|---|
| C | −361594.3 | 5330126. | −0.067840 | 0.9460 |
| INCOME | 305.6033 | 127.2458 | 2.401676 | 0.0181 |
| R-squared | 0.051607 | Mean dependent var | | 10515952 |
| Adjusted R-squared | 0.042660 | S.D. dependent var | | 29847739 |
| S.E. of regression | 29204145 | Akaike info criterion | | 37.23586 |
| Sum squared resid | 9.04E + 16 | Schwarz criterion | | 37.28553 |
| Log likelihood | −2008.737 | F-statistic | | 5.768048 |
| Durbin–Watson stat | 1.908828 | Prob(F-statistic) | | 0.018061 |

Breusch and Pagan do not dictate what variables appear in their auxiliary regression. We shall assume that only income, the variable that appears in the regression model, appears in the Breusch–Pagan auxiliary equation. Table 10.3 contains the Breusch–Pagan auxiliary regression.

The $R^2$ from White's auxiliary equation is 0.082. The test statistic, $nR^2$, is 8.87, well in excess of the critical value of 5.99 for the chi-square statistic, with 2 degrees of freedom at the .05 significance level. The $R^2$ from the Breusch–Pagan auxiliary regression is 0.0516. The test statistic, $nR^2$, is 5.57, which is greater than the critical value of 3.84 for the chi-square statistic with 1 degree of freedom at the .05 significance level. Both tests roundly reject the null hypothesis of homoskedasticity. Had the tests arrived at differing conclusions about heteroskedasticity among New York renters, which test should we rely on? With 108 observations and a single explanator, the tests are conducted with a relatively large sample—the number of degrees of freedom is considerable. In such a case, the power of White's test makes it the preferred test. Had the number of degrees of freedom been markedly smaller, the Breusch–Pagan test would be preferable—and the preferred test statistics would be the $F$-statistics reported in each auxiliary regression (4.69 in White's auxiliary regression and 5.77 in the Breusch–Pagan auxiliary regression).

## The Goldfeld–Quandt Test

White's test and the Breusch–Pagan test both focus on smoothly changing variances for the disturbances. But what if the variance changes abruptly, as Barro found for disturbances during and after World War II in his Regression's Greatest Hits Classical Favorite study of the money supply described in Chapter 9 (see p. 365)? What if our interest is in whether men and women's wages vary differently around their respective means? How do we test for abruptly changing variances? The **Goldfeld–Quandt test** for heteroskedasticity divides the $n$ observations into groups and tests whether two specific groups have disturbances with the same variance. Because disturbances are unobserved, the test compares mean squared residuals for the groups instead. The test has six distinct steps:

1. Divide the $n$ observations into $h$ groups. Let $n_1, \ldots, n_h$ denote the number of observations in groups $1, \ldots, h$.
2. Choose two groups, say Groups 1 and 2, for which to test the null hypothesis that the disturbances for observations in Group 1 have the same variance as the disturbances for observations in Group 2:

$$H_0\!: \sigma_1^2 = \sigma_2^2 \quad H_1\!: \sigma_1^2 \neq \sigma_2^2.$$

3. Estimate the $k$-explanator model of interest by OLS using the $n_1$ observations in Group 1. Form the sum of squared residuals from this regression, $SSR_1$, and divide it by $(n_1 - k)$.
4. Estimate the $k$-explanator model of interest by OLS using the $n_2$ observations in Group 2. Form the sum of squared residuals from this regression, $SSR_2$, and divide it by $(n_2 - k)$.
5. Name the larger of $(SSR_1/(n_1 - k))$ and $(SSR_2/(n_2 - k))$ "$(SSR_L/(n_L - k))$," and name the smaller "$(SSR_S/(n_S - k))$." Form the statistic

$$G = \frac{SSR_L/(n_L - k)}{SSR_S/(n_S - k)}.$$

6. If $G$ exceeds the critical value for an $F$-statistic with $(n_L - k)$ and $(n_S - k)$ degrees of freedom at the chosen significance level, reject the null hypothesis of equal variances.

The Goldfeld–Quandt test is valid if the underlying disturbances are normally distributed. It is approximately valid if both $(n_1 - k)$ and $(n_2 - k)$ are large and the disturbances are not normally distributed.

The most frequent applications of the Goldfeld–Quandt test involve dividing the sample into two groups, as in Barro's study. However, Goldfeld and Quandt originally proposed this test not for abruptly changing variances, but for smoothly changing variances. If the variance is thought to increase with, say, $X_k$,

Goldfeld and Quandt proposed dividing the sample into three groups, those with low values of $X_k$, those with high values of $X_k$, and those with middle values of $X_k$, and testing whether the high $X_k$ observations' disturbances have a different variance than the low $X_k$ observations' disturbances. White's test and the Breusch–Pagan test have supplanted this original use of the Goldfeld–Quandt test, but the Goldfeld–Quandt test remains useful for dealing with abrupt changes in variances.

## An Example of the Goldfeld–Quandt Test

Do men and women's incomes vary similarly about their respective means, given individuals' education and experience? Answering this question is a classic application of the Goldfeld–Quandt procedure. This example uses the income data in the file earnings.*** on this book's companion Web site (**www.aw-bc.com/murray**); the file is too large for the student version of EViews, but it works with other versions. Regressing the log of income against education, experience, experience-squared, and an intercept for the 3,146 women in the sample results in a sum of squared residuals equal to 1,851.52. Thus,

$$s_w^2 = \frac{1,851.52}{3,146 - 4} = 0.5893.$$

The same regression for the 3,394 men in the sample results in a sum of squared residuals equal to 1736.64. Thus,

$$s_M^2 = \frac{1,736.64}{3,394 - 4} = 0.5123.$$

The ratio of the larger to the smaller estimated variance is

$$\frac{0.5893}{0.5123} = 1.15.$$

The P-value for this $F$-statistic with 3,142 and 3,390 degrees of freedom is 0.99997, so we reject the null hypothesis of equal variances at any conventional significance level.

## Omitted Variables and Heteroskedasticity Tests

Incorrect functional form or omitted variables can confuse any test of heteroskedasticity. Showing how omitted variables can lead the White test and the Breusch–Pagan test to reject the null hypothesis of homoskedasticity when the real problem is omitted variables illustrates this confusion.

Labor economists have learned through long experience that wage equations should contain both age and age squared as explanators when no data on experience are available. To illustrate the potential misleading effect of an omitted variable on heteroskedasticity tests, we estimate a wage equation with only education (*educ*) and age (*age*) as explanators for a sample of men who are not self-employed; the dependent variable is the log of the wage (*lwage*). The data are in the file twin1.*** on this book's companion Web site (**www.aw-bc.com/murray**). The self-employed are excluded from the regression because the connections among wages, education, and age are different for them than for other workers; the sample is individuals for whom *female* = 0 and *selfemp* = 0. The data are from a study of twins by economists Orley Ashenfelter and Cecelia Rouse of Princeton University.[3]

Table 10.4, Panel A, reports tests of the null hypothesis of homoskedastic disturbances in this misspecified wage equation that omits age squared. We use the residuals from the wage equation to estimate the White and Breusch–Pagan auxiliary equations. White's procedure dictates which explanators enter the auxiliary

**TABLE 10.4** **Heteroskedasticity Tests for a Wage Equation with an Omitted Age-squared Variable**

*Panel A*

$$\ln(wage) = \beta_0 + \beta_1 education + \beta_2 age + \varepsilon$$

| Test | Statistic | Distribution | Critical Value |
|------|-----------|--------------|----------------|
| White | 18.72 | $\chi^2(5)$ | 11.07 |
| Breusch-Pagan* | 4.59 | $\chi^2(2)$ | 5.99 |
| Breusch-Pagan† | 18.34 | $\chi^2(4)$ | 9.49 |

*Panel B*

$$\ln(wage) = \beta_0 + \beta_1 education + \beta_2 age + \beta_3 age^2 + \varepsilon$$

| Test | Statistic | Distribution | Critical Value |
|------|-----------|--------------|----------------|
| White | 12.82 | $\chi^2(8)$ | 15.51 |
| Breusch-Pagan‡ | 6.61 | $\chi^2(3)$ | 7.82 |
| Breusch-Pagan§ | 8.83 | $\chi^2(5)$ | 11.07 |

*Education and age in auxiliary equation
†Education, age, education squared, and age squared in auxiliary equation
‡Education, age, age squared in auxiliary equation
§Education, age, age squared, education squared, age to the fourth power in auxiliary equation.

regression. The Breusch–Pagan test incorporates any special knowledge about the form of the heteroskedasticity when it is available. Absent other information, the usual Breusch–Pagan procedure is to include all the explanators and maybe their squares. We try two versions of the Breusch–Pagan statistic, one that includes just education and age as the auxiliary equation regressors and another that includes education, age, education squared, and age squared. Table 10.4, Panel A, contains the test results.

White's auxiliary regression has education, age, education squared, age squared, and education times age as its explanators, along with an intercept term. Table 10.4, Panel A, reports that the $nR^2$ statistic from this auxiliary regression is $(112 \cdot .167169) = 18.72$, which exceeds 11.07, the .05 significance level critical value for a chi-square statistic with five degrees of freedom. The White test strongly rejects the null hypothesis of homoskedastic disturbances.

Table 10.4, Panel A, also reports our two Breusch–Pagan test statistics. The Breusch–Pagan statistic from our first Breusch–Pagan test, using only education and age in the auxiliary regression, is 4.59, which is less than 5.99, the .05 significance level critical value for a chi-square statistic with two degrees of freedom. The Breusch–Pagan statistic from our second Breusch–Pagan test, using education, age, and age squared in the auxiliary regression, is 18.34, which exceeds 9.49, the .05 significance level critical value for a chi-square statistic with four degrees of freedom. The Breusch–Pagan test either fails to reject or rejects the null hypothesis of homoskedasticity, depending on which variables are included in the auxiliary regression. The contrasting results illustrate an important point. *We may miss heteroskedasticity with the Breusch–Pagan test if we choose the wrong set of explanators for the auxiliary regression.*

But the problem detected by the heteroskedasticity tests may not be heteroskedastic disturbances at all. The problem may be an omitted variable, age squared. We re-estimate the wage equation regressing the log of the wage against education, age, and age squared. The heteroskedasticity test results for this better specification are in Table 10.4, Panel B. The White $nR^2$ statistic for this regression equals $112 \cdot (.114477) = 12.82$, which is less than 16.92, the .05 significance level critical value for a chi-square statistic with nine degrees of freedom. White's auxiliary regression now includes eight explanators: education, age, education squared, age squared, age to the fourth power, education times age, education times age squared, and age cubed.

Table 10.4 also shows the results for two Breusch–Pagan tests for the better specification. The Breusch–Pagan statistic with education, age, and age squared in the auxiliary regression is 6.61, which is less than 7.82, the .05 significance level critical value for a chi-square statistic with three degrees of freedom. The Breusch–Pagan statistic with the explanators and their squares (education, age, age squared, education squared, and age to the fourth power) in the auxiliary equation is 8.83, which is less than 11.07, the .05 significance level critical value for a chi-square statistic with five degrees of freedom.

Neither the White test nor the Breusch–Pagan tests indicate heteroskedasticity in the disturbances once age squared is included in the wage equation. The heteroskedasticity results in Panel A of Table 10.4 reflect an omitted variable problem, not heteroskedasticity.

Why does it matter whether a test indicates heteroskedasticity or an omitted variable? Because the remedies for the two differ greatly. Taking steps to appropriately accommodate heteroskedastic disturbances does not cure omitted variables bias. The lesson? *Heteroskedasticity tests can be relied on to detect heteroskedasticity only if the model is otherwise properly specified.*

## The RESET Specification Test

The accumulated wisdom of labor economists forewarns that age squared should be included in a wage equation. That knowledge made it easy to distinguish true heteroskedastic disturbances from a heteroskedasticity stemming from an omitted squared age variable in constructing Table 10.4. But how are we to guard against missing variables more generally, so that we do not confuse heteroskedasticity with omitted variables? New York University econometrician James B. Ramsey has proposed one approach, the **RESET (regression specification error test) test** for omitted variables,[4] which has three steps:

1. Conduct OLS, using the explanators we think appropriate.
2. Calculate the fitted values, $\hat{Y}_1, \ldots, \hat{Y}_n$, for the regression in step 1.
3. Conduct an $F$-test of the null hypothesis that $\hat{Y}_i^2$ and $\hat{Y}_i^3$ have coefficients of zero when added to the regression in step 1.

Failure to reject the null hypothesis is evidence that relevant explanators are omitted from the original specification—explanators correlated with the powers of the fitted values.

The RESET test can be used to check that what appears to be heteroskedasticity is not attributable to omitted variables. When the RESET test indicates that there are omitted variables, though, the real work has only just begun. The RESET test does not tell what variables are omitted. Economic theory and common sense need to be applied to uncover these variables. In practice, the RESET test should be conducted prior to testing for heteroskedasticity—we don't know how to interpret the heteroskedasticity tests unless there are no omitted variables.

A drawback of the RESET test is that it frequently lacks power. For example, a RESET test does not expose the omission of squared age from the wage equation studied in Table 10.4.

## 10.4

How Do We Create
an Estimator?

# BLUE Estimation When Disturbances Are Heteroskedastic

If homoskedasticity is the only Gauss–Markov Assumption violated in our DGP, how should we estimate the slopes and intercept of regression models? The most straightforward approach is to assume the new heteroskedastic DGP presented in Section 10.1 and derive the BLUE estimators for that DGP. Following the strategy developed in Chapters 3, 4, and 6, we could minimize the variance of a linear estimator with respect to its weights, subject to the unbiasedness conditions for the new DGP.

Section 10.2 derived the variance expression and the unbiasedness conditions for a linear estimator when the only deviation from the Gauss–Markov Assumptions is that $\text{var}(\varepsilon_i) = \sigma_i^2$. To obtain the BLUE estimator of $\beta_s$ in the face of heteroskedasticity, we minimize that variance:

$$\sum_{i=1}^{n} w_i^2\, \sigma_i^2,$$

with respect to $w_1, \ldots, w_n$, subject to the those unbiasedness constraints:

$$\sum w_i\, X_{ri} = 0 \qquad \text{for } r \neq s,$$

and

$$\sum w_i X_{si} = 1.$$

The weights that solve this problem, $w_1^s, \ldots, w_n^s$ define the BLUE estimator for $\beta_s$ when the disturbances are heteroskedastic.

Obtaining the BLUE estimator for the heteroskedastic DGP by solving a constrained minimization problem highlights the generality of the estimation strategy developed in Chapters 3, 4, and 6. Econometricians have not traditionally taken this approach to determining the BLUE estimator for DGPs with heteroskedastic disturbances, however. Rather than taking the given data with its new DGP and deriving a corresponding new BLUE estimator, econometricians choose to transform the data in a way that makes OLS, when applied to the transformed data, still the BLUE estimator. Transforming the data provides an alternative intuitively appealing and powerful strategy for finding BLUE estimators when the Gauss–Markov Assumptions fail. The two approaches always lead to the same estimators, but by different routes.

## Transforming the Data to Account for Heteroskedasticity

As recently as the late 1950s and early 1960s, calculating estimates was an onerous chore that required careful detailing of the necessary steps for assistants to follow on mechanical calculators. To have a single estimation procedure that applied to many problems was very attractive. Even later, when computers were first becoming widespread, programming estimators was sufficiently burdensome to make it very appealing to have one estimator that fit many circumstances. Early econometricians found it quite convenient computationally to separate data preparation from estimation, and any simple manipulation of the data that allowed continued use of OLS as one's estimator was welcome. Today, exploring the reasoning of these early econometricians offers us rich insight into estimating models with heteroskedastic disturbances.

Because heteroskedasticity can be easily "corrected for" as part of preparing data for analysis, early econometricians avoided devising specific estimators for heteroskedastic DGPs and instead chose to transform their data to account for heteroskedasticity. Can we, too, transform data to overcome heteroskedasticity? For example, how might we transform the rent and income data about New York City renters to allow use of OLS for BLUE estimation? Exploring this example exposes the reasoning of the early econometricians.

The key to appropriately transforming the data to overcome heteroskedasticity lies in examining the specific form heteroskedasticity takes on in our DGP:

$$\text{var}(\varepsilon_i) = \sigma_i^2.$$

If the disturbances were homoskedastic, all the variances would take on a single value, $\sigma^2$. This connection between the homoskedastic and heteroskedastic cases is more apparent if we rewrite the general form for the $\text{var}(\varepsilon_i)$ in our DGP as

$$\text{var}(\varepsilon_i) = \sigma_i^2 = \sigma^2 d_i^2.$$

If all the $d_i^2$ terms are the same (for example, all equal to one), then the disturbances are homoskedastic (with variance $\sigma^2$ if all the $d_i^2$ equal one), in which case, OLS would be the BLUE estimator. Differences among the $d_i^2$ terms in the variances keep OLS from being BLUE. Can we transform the data so as to neutralize the effects of differing $d_i^2$ terms? We can.

Recall that the variance of a constant times a random variable is the constant squared times the variance of the random variable. Thus, if we divide $\varepsilon_i$ by $d_i$, as in $\eta_i = \varepsilon_i/d_i$, we obtain $\text{var}(\eta_i) = \sigma^2$. The $\eta_i$ are homoskedastic. Let us transform the data by dividing every element by $d_i$, creating a new DGP that is, in statistical content, equivalent to the original:

$$Y_i/d_i = \beta_0(1/d_i) + \beta_1 X_i/d_i + \varepsilon_i/d_i \qquad i = 1,\ldots,n$$

$$E(\varepsilon_i/d_i) = 0 \qquad I = 1,\ldots,n$$

$$\text{var}(\varepsilon_i/d_i) = \sigma^2 \qquad i = 1,\ldots,n$$

$$\text{cov}(\varepsilon_i/d_i,\, \varepsilon_j/d_j) = 0 \qquad i \neq j$$

Each $X_i/d_i$ is fixed across samples.

Notice that the coefficients in this transformed relationship, $\beta_0$ and $\beta_1$, are the slope and intercept of the original regression relationship. However, also notice that in the transformed relationship, $\beta_0$ is no longer an intercept, but the slope on $(1/d_i)$, and $\beta_1$ is the slope on $(X_i/d_i)$.

Now, we can define $Q_i = Y_i/d_i$, $Z_{1i} = 1/d_i$, $Z_{2i} = X_i/d_i$, and $\eta_i = \varepsilon_i/d_i$, and rewrite the transformed DGP as

$$Q_i = \beta_0 Z_{1i} + \beta_1 Z_{2i} + \eta_i \qquad i = 1, \ldots, n$$

$$E(\eta_i) = 0 \qquad i = 1, \ldots, n$$

$$\mathrm{var}(\eta_i) = \sigma^2 \qquad i = 1, \ldots, n$$

$$\mathrm{cov}(\eta_1, \ldots, \eta_n) = 0 \qquad i \neq j$$

Each $Z_{ji}$ is fixed across samples.

This is a DGP that satisfies the Gauss–Markov Assumptions! Thus OLS applied to $Q_i$, $Z_{1i}$, and $Z_{2i}$, with no intercept term in the model, provides BLUE estimators of $\beta_0$ and $\beta_1$. These estimators are the same ones we would have arrived at by solving for the linear estimators that minimize $\sum w_i^2 \sigma_i^2 = \sigma^2 \sum w_i^2 d_i^2$ subject to the unbiasedness constraints for $\beta_0$ and $\beta_1$.

Because the BLUE estimators for DGPs with heteroskedastic disturbances can be formulated as OLS estimators for appropriately transformed variables, the early econometricians named these BLUE estimators **generalized least squares** estimators, or **GLS** estimators. *When all the Gauss–Markov Assumptions but homoskedasticity apply, t-tests and F-tests based on GLS estimators have the same attractive properties that OLS provides under the Gauss–Markov Assumptions.* The tests apply exactly if the disturbances are normally distributed and apply approximately in large samples otherwise.

## Weighting Observations with Larger $\sigma_i^2$

To better understand GLS estimators, consider the case of heteroskedastic disturbances in a DGP with one explanator and an intercept known to be zero. A look at the weights used by GLS when estimating the slope of a line through the origin illuminates the efficient use of information when disturbances are heteroskedastic.

GLS applies OLS to the data transformed to account for heteroskedasticity. The usual OLS estimator for the slope of a line through the origin is

$$\beta_{g4} = \sum \left( \frac{X_i}{\sum X_j^2} \right) Y_i = \sum w_i^{OLS} Y_i,$$

where $w_i^{OLS} = [X_i / \sum X_j^2]$. If we apply that formula to the transformed data,

$Y_i/d_i$, $X_i/d_i$, we obtain the GLS estimator

$$\beta_{GLS} = \Sigma \left( \frac{\dfrac{X_i}{d_i}}{\Sigma \left( \dfrac{X_j}{d_j} \right)^2} \right) \frac{Y_i}{d_i} = \Sigma \left( \frac{\dfrac{X_i}{d_i^2}}{\Sigma \left( \dfrac{X_j}{d_j} \right)^2} \right) Y_i = \Sigma\, w_i^{GLS}\, Y_i,$$

where

$$w_i^{GLS} = \left[ \frac{(X_i/d_i^2)}{\Sigma (X_j/d_j)^2} \right].$$

The denominator in $w_i^{GLS}$ is the same for every observation. It is the numerator, therefore, that determines which observations receive more weight. As in the homoskedastic case, other things being the same, GLS more heavily weights observations with larger $X$'s. But also note that $(1/d_i^2)$ appears in the numerator. *Other things being the same, GLS less heavily weights observations with disturbances that have bigger variances.* This result matches the conclusion drawn from Figures 10.2 and 10.3.

Chapter 8 noted that omitting relevant explanators from a regression model risks biasing the OLS estimator. Omitted variables are also likely to bias GLS estimators. The GLS estimator merely alters the weighting of observations from OLS. Dividing variables by $d_i$ is highly unlikely to undo correlation between included and omitted variables. Thus, if heteroskedasticity tests reflect omitted variables rather than heteroskedasticity, the estimators that would be BLUE if there is heteroskedasticity are likely to be biased if there are omitted variables.

## Two Special Cases of Heteroskedastic Disturbances

The GLS estimators require that we know $d_i$. Often we do not. Without knowledge of the $d_i$, we cannot use the GLS estimator. Fortunately, two specific forms of heteroskedasticity do arise with some frequency, and the GLS estimator we use often relies on their weights. In the first frequently encountered form of heteroskedasticity, $d_i = X_i$, a specification that says the variance of the disturbances is proportional to the square of the explanator $(\sigma_i^2 = \sigma^2 X_i^2)$. In the second, $d_i = \sqrt{X_i}$, a specification that says the variance of the disturbances is proportional to the magnitude of the explanator $(\sigma_i^2 = \sigma^2 X_i)$. These are the forms of heteroskedasticity examined in MC Builder IV and MC Builder V.

In the first case, $Q_i = Y_i/X_i$, $Z_{1i} = 1/X_i$ and $Z_{2i} = 1$. Thus, in the first special case,

$$Q_i = \beta_0 Z_{1i} + \beta_1 Z_{2i} + \eta_i = \beta_0 \left( \frac{1}{X_i} \right) + \beta_1 + \eta_i,$$

which is a straight line through the origin with a single explanator, $1/X_i$.

# An Econometric Top 40—A Golden Oldie

## Complete Systems of Demand Equations

The modern formulation of consumer demand theory, in place since early in the 20th century, lies at the heart of economic analysis. According to this theory, the demand functions for every commodity—food, housing, transportation, clothing, and so on—flow from consumers' buying the most favored bundle of goods they can afford. This theory shows how all of a consumer's demands are interrelated; for example, it demonstrates how the responsiveness of the demand for sugar to the price of tea relates to the responsiveness of the demand for tea to the price of sugar.

Empirical demand studies, such as the early econometric work of economists Ernst Engel and Robert Lehfeldt, are even older than modern consumer theory, some dating back more than 150 years. But the early demand studies examined the demand for one good or another in isolation from any others. It wasn't until the mid-20th century that empirical demand studies fully incorporated the interdependencies identified by economic theory.

In 1954, economist Richard Stone of Cambridge University published a pathbreaking work in which he presented Great Britain with a system of demand equations that satisfied the requirements of economists' consumer theory while also allowing estimation by linear regression.[5] Stone's system of demand equations is called the Linear Expenditure System (LES) because it expresses the expenditure on each good ($Y_i = P_iQ_i$) as a linear function of all goods' prices (the $P_i$) and income ($I$). In 1984, Richard Stone received the Nobel prize in economics for his contributions to National Income Accounting.

In the linear expenditure system, expenditures on each of $k$ goods can be expressed as

$$Y_j = P_jQ_j = P_j\gamma_j + \beta_jI - \sum_{g=1}^{k} P_g\beta_j\gamma_g \qquad \textbf{H10.1}$$

where $j$ denotes the $j$-th good. Stone estimated the expenditure equations using several years of aggregate data drawn from Great Britain. Expressing the linear expenditure system in a form slightly modified from Equation H10.1 exposes one fruitful way of thinking about the behavior of people who spend in accord with the LES:

$$Y_j = P_jQ_j = P_j\gamma_j + \beta_j\left(I - \sum_{g=1}^{k} P_g\gamma_g\right).$$

This form suggests a consumer who first buys base amounts of each good, $\gamma_j$, (spending $P_j\gamma_j$ on the j-th good, initially) and then spends additionally on each good $j$ a fixed fraction, $\beta_j$, of any additional income left over, that is, spends on the $j$-th good an additional $\beta_j$ of ($I - \sum_{g=1}^{k} P_g\gamma_g$).

We can rewrite Equation Hit 10.1 in a form suitable for linear regression:

$$Y_{jt} = \beta_jI_t + \alpha_{j1}P_{1t} + \alpha_{j2}P_{2t} + \cdots$$
$$+ \alpha_{jk}P_{kt} + \varepsilon_{jt} \qquad j = 1,\ldots,k,$$

in which

$$\alpha_{jg} = \beta_j\gamma_g \qquad g = 1, \ldots, k$$
$$\text{but} \quad g \neq j$$

and

$$\alpha_{jj} = (1 - \beta_j)\gamma_j.$$

The subscript $t$ reflects the fact that Stone used data drawn over time. For the linear expenditure system to conform to economic theory, each $\beta_j$ must be less than 1, the $\beta_j$ must sum to 1, and each $Q_j$ must exceed $\gamma_j$. If we estimate the $k$ expenditure equations separately from one another, we obtain $k(k + 1)$ estimated parameters. But in truth, there are only $2k$ distinct parameters in the system, $\beta_1, \ldots, \beta_K$ and $\gamma_1, \ldots, \gamma_k$. A central insight of modern economic theory is how the $k$ separate demand functions are linked through such shared parameters.

Every $\gamma_g (g = 1, \ldots, k)$ in the linear expenditure system can be estimated from each expenditure equation:

$$\gamma_g = \alpha_{jg}/\beta_j \qquad \text{for } g \text{ not equal to } j.$$

The estimates of $\gamma_g$ we obtain from one expenditure equation need not be the same as the estimate of $\gamma_g$ from another expenditure equation if we estimate each equation separately. Estimating the separate equations yields $k(k + 1)$ estimated parameters, whereas the LES contains only $2k$ distinct parameters. To obtain a unique set of estimates for the $2k$ parameters of the linear expenditure system, we must impose on our estimators the constraint that $\alpha_{jg}/\beta_j = \alpha_{ig}/\beta_i$ for all $i$ and $j$ not equal to $g$. Testing whether these constraints are true amounts to a test of consumer demand theory!

Stone applied the linear expenditure function to aggregate time series data. Such data need not conform to the consumer theory that applies to individual households. One year after Stone published his work, economists Hendrik Houthakker of Harvard University and S. J. Prais, then of Cambridge University, published a classic book that examines individual household demands.[6] Prais and Houthakker do not employ a system of demand functions that satisfy all the requirements of consumer demand theory, but they do give considerable attention to specifying functional forms that conform to the observed data and to using efficient estimation procedures.

Prais and Houthakker find that the semilog specification fits food item demands best, whereas other commodities' demands are best fit by double log specifications. Prais and Houthakker also observe that household demand disturbances are heteroskedastic—demands, even when measured in logs, are more spread out at higher levels of income than at lower levels of income. Consequently, these authors argue that demand relationships are most efficiently estimated by an estimation procedure called feasible generalized least squares (FGLS). This procedure to efficiently estimate regression models with heteroskedastic disturbances will be developed later in this chapter.

## Final Notes

A valid test of consumer demand theory requires a well-specified DGP. Tests valid when disturbances are homoskedastic are not valid when disturbances are heteroskedastic. Estimators that are efficient when disturbances are homoskedastic are not efficient when disturbances are heteroskedastic. The FGLS estimator used by Prais and Houthakker to examine consumer demands is an efficient estimator that can support valid $t$-tests and $F$-tests when disturbances are heteroskedastic.

Finally, notice that economic theory reduces the number of parameters to be estimated in a linear expenditure system from $k(k + 1)$ to just $2k$. In a system of six expenditure equations, economic theory reduces the number of parameters we need to estimate from 42 to 12. Economic theory confers a marked increase in degrees of freedom and, with that, a potentially substantial increase in efficiency.

■

In the second case, $Q_i = Y_i/\sqrt{X_i}$, $Z_{1i} = 1/\sqrt{X_i}$ and $Z_{2i} = \sqrt{X_i}$. Thus, in this second special case,

$$Q_i = \beta_0 Z_{1i} + \beta_1 Z_{2i} + \eta_i = \beta_0 \frac{1}{\sqrt{X_i}} + \beta_1 \sqrt{X_i} + \eta_i.$$

One or the other of these two forms often approximates the structure of heteroskedasticity found in bivariate models. Let us now see if either of these transformations absorbs the heteroskedasticity we have observed in the rent–income relationship—that is, whether the transformation leads to a dependent variable with disturbances that are homoskedastic.

## 10.5    An Application: GLS Estimation of the Rent–Income Relationship

Econometricians frequently assume disturbances' variance are proportional to the square of an explanator or to the absolute value of an explanator, and they apply GLS accordingly. This section examines the rent–income relationship for our sample of New Yorkers using these strategies. The analysis twice transforms the rent–income data for New York renters in an effort to find a transformation in which the disturbances are homoskedastic. If one of the transformations reflects the actual form of the heteroskedasticity of the disturbances in the rent–income relationship, the resulting estimates of the transformed variables would be the GLS (and therefore BLUE) estimates of $\beta_0$ and $\beta_1$, the slope and intercept of the untransformed rent–income relationship:

$$rent_i = \beta_0 + \beta_1 income_i + \varepsilon_i.$$

### Disturbances with Variances Proportional to Income Squared

We first assume that the disturbances in the rent–income relationship have variances proportional to income squared: $var(\varepsilon_i) = (\sigma^2 income_i^2)$. If the disturbances in the rent–income relationship are heteroskedastic in exactly this way, the BLUE estimators for the slope and intercept of the underlying rent–income ratio can be obtained by applying OLS to

$$(rent/income)_i = \beta_0(1/income) + \beta_1 + \eta_i.$$

The OLS estimated coefficient on (*rent/income*) is the BLUE estimator of the intercept in the untransformed rent–income relationship. The estimated intercept is the BLUE estimator of the slope of the untransformed rent–income relationship.

Table 10.5 reports the results of this regression. If we have correctly specified the form of heteroskedasticity in the untransformed DGP, the estimates in Table 10.5 are BLUE estimators and have been obtained by GLS.

The estimated intercept in Table 10.5, 0.08567, which estimates $\beta_1$, turns out to be about a third larger than the OLS estimate of $\beta_1$, 0.063, reported in Table 10.1. The estimated standard error for this new estimator is larger than the estimate for the OLS estimator used in Table 10.1, but the fact that the original OLS standard error estimator is surely biased in this heteroskedastic case makes this comparison largely uninformative. The estimated slope, 4,811, in the transformed equation is about 10% smaller than the OLS estimate of 5,455 reported in Table 10.1.

Are the estimates in Table 10.5 BLUE? Not according to either the White test or the Breusch–Pagan test. The White $nR^2$ statistic for the null hypothesis that the disturbances in the transformed equation underlying Table 10.5 are homoskedastic is 7.17, well above 5.99, the .05 significance level critical value for a chi–square statistic with two degrees of freedom. If the disturbances in the rent–income relationship have variances proportional to income squared, the disturbances in the transformed relationship would be homoskedastic. (The table does not show the auxiliary regressions underlying these White and Breusch–Pagan tests. Most econometric software programs report only the test statistics.)

**TABLE 10.5 Estimating a Transformed Rent–Income Relationship, $\mathrm{var}(\varepsilon_i) = \sigma^2\, X_i^2$**

Dependent Variable: RENT/INCOME
Method: Least Squares
Sample: 1 108
Included observations: 108

| Variable | Coefficient | Std. Error | t-Statistic | Prob. |
|---|---|---|---|---|
| C | 0.085679 | 0.016701 | 5.130303 | 0.0000 |
| 1/INCOME | 4811.862 | 322.2745 | 14.93094 | 0.0000 |
| R-squared | 0.677746 | Mean dependent var | | 0.291701 |
| Adjusted R-squared | 0.674706 | S.D. dependent var | | 0.171429 |
| S.E. of regression | 0.097774 | Akaike info criterion | | −1.793980 |
| Sum squared resid | 1.013325 | Schwarz criterion | | −1.744311 |
| Log likelihood | 98.87494 | F-statistic | | 222.9331 |
| Durbin-Watson stat | 1.900821 | Prob(F-statistic) | | 0.000000 |

The corresponding Breusch–Pagan statistic is 9.52, well above 3.84, the .05 significance level critical value for a chi–square statistic with one degree of freedom. Rejecting the homoskedasticity of the disturbances in the transformed relationship rejects the variances of the disturbances being proportional to income squared in the rent–income relationship.

Figure 10.4 plots the rent–income ratio (the dependent variable in the transformed regression of Table 10.5) against the inverse of income (the explanator in Table 10.5). The observations at higher values of the inverse of income, measured along the horizontal axis, appear more spread out than at lower values of inverse income. The transformed disturbances on observations with lower income now have the larger variance. We seem to have overcorrected for heteroskedasticity.

## Disturbances with Variances Proportional to Income

We now examine a second assumption about the variance of the disturbances in the untransformed rent–income DGP. Instead of assuming the variances of the disturbances are proportional to income squared, we assume the variances are proportional to income: $\text{var}(\varepsilon_i) = (\sigma^2 income_i)$. If this alternative specification is correct, BLUE estimates of $\beta_0$ and $\beta_1$ will result from OLS applied to the original variables divided by $\sqrt{income_i}$. The resulting transformed equation for which OLS would be BLUE if this assumption about the heteroskedasticity is correct is

$$rent_i/\sqrt{income_i} = \beta_0 \frac{1}{\sqrt{income_i}} + \beta_1\sqrt{income_i} + \eta_i,$$

which is an equation with no intercept and two explanators. Table 10.6 contains the OLS estimates for this second transformed relationship.

**Figure 10.4**

The Rent–Income Ratio Plotted Against the Inverse of Income

*Source:* U.S. Annual Housing Survey

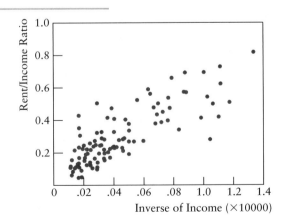

**TABLE 10.6** **Estimating a Second Transformed Rent–Income Relationship,** $\text{var}(\varepsilon_i) = \sigma^2 X_i$

Dependent Variable: RENT/(INCOME$^{0.5}$)
Method: Least Squares
Sample: 1 108
Included observations: 108

| Variable | Coefficient | Std. Error | t-Statistic | Prob. |
|---|---|---|---|---|
| 1/(INCOME$^{0.5}$) | 5085.513 | 411.4241 | 12.36076 | 0.0000 |
| INCOME$^{0.5}$ | 0.073963 | 0.014269 | 5.183325 | 0.0000 |
| R-squared | 0.121359 | Mean dependent var | | 44.92013 |
| Adjusted R-squared | 0.113070 | S.D. dependent var | | 17.41882 |
| S.E. of regression | 16.40451 | Akaike info criterion | | 8.451335 |
| Sum squared resid | 28525.45 | Schwarz criterion | | 8.501004 |
| Log likelihood | −454.3721 | Durbin–Watson stat | | 1.964951 |

The tests for whether the new transformed disturbances are homoskedastic pose two important questions. First, what are the appropriate variables to include in White's auxiliary equation? The White procedure gives us a rule to apply: Include the explanators, their squares, their cross products, and an intercept term. The explanators in this example are the square root of income and its inverse. Their squares are income and its inverse. Because the cross product of the square root of income and its inverse is always equal to one, that cross product cannot account for any variability in the squared residuals. We therefore exclude that cross product from the auxiliary regression (which is essential because it would be perfectly collinear with the intercept term if we did not exclude it). The White test therefore has four degrees of freedom. White's $nR^2$ statistic is 6.19 (we do not show the associated auxiliary regression results), which is markedly less than 9.49, the critical value at the .05 significance level for a chi-square statistic with four degrees of freedom. We fail to reject the null hypothesis of homoskedasticity in the transformed equation.

The second important question posed by our tests is, "What are the appropriate explanators in the Breusch–Pagan auxiliary equation?" The choice of which variables to include seems quite arbitrary. Absent other information, most econometricians would opt for the square root of income and its inverse because they are the explanators in the model. But including the squares of those two explanators instead is also reasonable. With the square root of income and its inverse, the Breusch–Pagan test statistic is 3.63; with income and its inverse, the Breusch–Pagan statistic is 3.23. Both are less than 5.99, the .05 significance level critical value for a chi-square statistic with two degrees of freedom. We fail to reject the null hypothesis of homoskedasticity. Consequently, we fail to reject the null hypothesis that the disturbances in the rent–income relationship have variances proportional to income.

Notice that with two explanators, as in the second transformed model just discussed, there is no simple graph we can examine to confidently expose heteroskedasticity. The formal tests of homoskedasticity are, therefore, essential in multiple regression models.

## A Need for Caution

In our first attempt to correct for heteroskedasticity, we divided both sides of the original equation by income. That strategy over-corrected for the original heteroskedasticity. We then experimented with dividing both sides of the original equation by the square root of income. This seems to have compensated for the original heteroskedasticity; we cannot reject the hypothesis that this second transformed model has homoskedastic disturbances. Thus, the estimates in Table 10.6 would seem to be quite close to what we would obtain if we knew the true degree of heteroskedasticity and had performed GLS. Nonetheless, we need to be cautious. Failing to reject the null hypothesis does not ensure that we can embrace it. It is quite possible that the true degree of heteroskedasticity differs from that assumed in our second transformation. If we have not correctly assigned the degree of heteroskedasticity in the untransformed disturbances, the standard errors and F-tests that we might perform using the supposed GLS estimators do not have the attractive properties that we presume. Fortunately, when the degree of heteroskedasticity is small, the inefficiency of OLS is also small, as are the biases in the usual OLS standard error estimators. Consequently, if our second transformation reduces heteroskedasticity to a low level, this not-quite-GLS estimator will perform almost as well as the true GLS estimator.

## 10.6    Feasible Generalized Least Squares

How Do We Create an Estimator?

In most applied problems, the true form of heteroskedasticity is no more apparent than in the rent–income example. GLS estimation is usually unavailable to us because the $d_i$ are unknown. However, econometricians are frequently willing to estimate the unknown $d_i$ and then use those estimates in GLS as if they were the true values. We call GLS conducted with estimated $d_i$ in place of the true $d_i$ **feasible generalized least squares** (FGLS). For example, Robert Barro, in the second of his classic unanticipated money supply papers discussed in Chapter 9, used

FGLS to estimate his money supply equations after estimating the $d_i$. FGLS is generally efficient in large samples.

Estimating the structure of heteroskedasticity in a DGP requires making assumptions about the nature of the heteroskedasticity. Barro assumed that the values of the $d_i$ took on one single value for all observations prior to World War II and another single value for all observations after World War II. Other analysts assume the variance of the disturbances varies systematically with one or more explanators. Such assumptions are necessary because a sample with $n$ observations is not sufficient for estimating $n$ distinct and unrelated values for the $d_i$. Let us now look at making such assumptions in the context of the rent–income model for New Yorkers that we have repeatedly examined.

## FGLS and the Rent–Income Relationship

How might we apply FGLS to the rent–income data? Let us assume that var$(\varepsilon_i) = \sigma^2 X_i^h$, where $h$ is an unknown constant, which we can rewrite as

$$\ln(\mathrm{E}(\varepsilon_i^2)) = \ln(\sigma^2) + h \ln(X_i).$$

When $h = 2$, we have the first frequently encountered form of heteroskedasticity noted earlier; when $h = 1$, we have the second. Next, we follow the strategy we have often previously pursued, replacing $\mathrm{E}(\varepsilon_i^2)$ by its sample analog, the squared OLS residual from the untransformed regression equation:

$$\ln(e_i^2) = \ln(\sigma^2) + h \ln(X_i) + \zeta_i.$$

We then use the OLS estimate of $h$, $\hat{h}$, as if it were the true value. Doing so allows us to transform the data in the fashion of GLS, dividing each observation by $\sqrt{X_i^{\hat{h}}} = X_i^{\hat{h}/2}$.

Thus, FGLS proceeds in four steps:

1. Estimate the underlying untransformed relationship by OLS.
2. Estimate $h$ by regressing the logs of squared residuals against the log of the $X_i$ and a constant.
3. Use the estimated $h$ from (2) to divide every variable by $\sqrt{X_i^{\hat{h}}} = X_i^{\hat{h}/2}$.
4. Apply OLS to the transformed data.

Other strategies for estimating $h$ are possible. A common one in multiple regression models is to replace the $X_i$ in step 2 with the absolute values of the fitted values from the regression in step 1. Using the fitted values in this way allows all of the explanators to have some effect on the variance of the disturbances.

Table 10.7 contains the regression results from step 2. The estimated coefficient on the $\ln(X)$ is 1.21, which indicates we should divide every observation by $X$ to the 0.605 power. This is so close to 0.5 that the resulting GLS estimates are

**TABLE 10.7** ln(*Squared Residual*) vs ln(*Income*) Following *RENT* vs. *INCOME* by OLS

Dependent Variable: LOG ($e^2$)
Method: Least Squares
Sample: 1 108
Included observations: 108

| Variable | Coefficient | Std. Error | t-Statistic | Prob. |
|----------|-------------|------------|-------------|-------|
| C | 2.083771 | 2.994793 | 0.695798 | 0.4881 |
| LOG(INCOME) | 1.216408 | 0.290830 | 4.182539 | 0.0001 |
| R-squared | 0.141656 | Mean dependent var | | 14.58387 |
| Adjusted R-squared | 0.133559 | S.D. dependent var | | 2.142308 |
| S.E. of regression | 1.994121 | Akaike info criterion | | 4.236629 |
| Sum squared resid | 421.5110 | Schwarz criterion | | 4.286298 |
| Log likelihood | −226.7780 | F-statistic | | 17.49363 |
| Durbin–Watson stat | 1.843326 | Prob(F-statistic) | | 0.000060 |

very close to those reported in Table 10.6, where we had divided all the variables by $\sqrt{X_i}$. Moreover, the standard error of the estimate of $h$ suggests $h$ does not differ statistically from 1, further supporting use of that earlier transformation.

FGLS provides a viable alternative to OLS. To the extent that an econometrician approximates well the true form of the heteroskedasticity, FGLS estimators are optimal, and they provide a good foundation for $t$-tests and $F$-tests of the sort described in Chapters 7 and 9. Such tests, however, generally apply correctly only in large samples, and then only approximately. To the extent that an econometrician misspecifies the form of heteroskedasticity, the FGLS estimators still suffer the same kinds of problems as OLS applied to heteroskedastic data: The estimators are inefficient and the $t$-tests and $F$-tests based on the FGLS estimators are invalid.

## 10.7   White's Heteroskedasticity-Consistent Standard Errors

**How Do We Test Hypotheses?**

When we are confident about the form of heteroskedasticity in our DGP, FGLS provides an efficient estimator that supports valid test procedures. But what if we do not know it? In recent years, more and more econometric software packages have included White's heteroskedasticity-consistent standard errors for OLS as a convenient option. Consequently, when the form of heteroskedasticity is unknown, econometricians have increasingly relied on OLS estimators of the slopes and intercept, coupled with White's heteroskedasticity-consistent estimators of the OLS variances and covariances. (Remember that the standard error is the square root of an estimator's variance.) Some econometricians go so far as to say that OLS coupled with White's heteroskedasticity-consistent standard errors is superior to FGLS when any uncertainty exists about the form of the heteroskedasticity in the DGP. These econometricians argue that FGLS's gains in efficiency over OLS are generally modest and that its risks of invalid statistical inference are too great.

In Section 10.2, we derived White's heteroskedasticity-consistent estimator for the variance of $\hat{\beta}_1$ in a regression model with unknown slope and intercept:

$$\tilde{\text{var}}(\hat{\beta}_1) = \frac{\sum x_i^2 \, e_i^2}{\left( \sum x_i^2 \right)^2}.$$

The strategy White used to obtain this estimator generalizes to yield not just $t$-tests robust to heteroskedasticity, but also $F$-tests. To illustrate the application of White's heteroskedasticity-consistent standard errors, Table 10.8 contains the original OLS estimates of the rent–income model, but this time with heteroskedasticity-consistent estimated standard errors reported.

**TABLE 10.8** OLS Estimates of the Rent–Income Relationship with Robust Standard Errors

Dependent Variable: RENT
Method: Least Squares
Sample: 1 108
Included observations: 108
White Heteroskedasticity-consistent Standard Errors and Covariance

| Variable | Coefficient | Std. Error | t-Statistic | Prob. |
|----------|-------------|------------|-------------|-------|
| C | 5455.483 | 403.2469 | 13.52889 | 0.0000 |
| INCOME | 0.063568 | 0.014759 | 4.307218 | 0.0000 |

| | | | | |
|----------|-------------|------------|-------------|-------|
| R-squared | 0.155475 | Mean dependent var | | 7718.111 |
| Adjusted R-squared | 0.147508 | S.D. dependent var | | 3577.000 |
| S.E. of regression | 3302.662 | Akaike info criterion | | 19.06119 |
| Sum squared resid | 1.16E + 09 | Schwarz criterion | | 19.11086 |
| Log likelihood | −1027.304 | F-statistic | | 19.51435 |
| Durbin-Watson stat | 2.012384 | Prob(F-statistic) | | 0.000024 |

The estimated coefficients in Table 10.8 are the same as in Table 10.1—the estimator is still OLS. However, the estimated standard errors are different—that on the slope estimator is larger, whereas that on the intercept estimator is smaller. The square roots of White's heteroskedasticity-consistent variance estimators, called **White's heteroskedasticity-consistent standard errors** or **White's robust standard errors**, have become a standard tool of econometricians. *When an otherwise properly specified regression displays evidence of heteroskedastic disturbances of uncertain form, econometricians apply OLS with robust standard errors, and they conduct the corresponding robust tests of any hypotheses about the model's intercept and slopes.*

Because more efficient estimators yield more powerful tests of hypotheses, when the form of heteroskedasticity is known, FGLS is superior to OLS used with White's robust standard errors. In practice, the choice between the two strategies is a matter of individual judgment. But because we often do not know the form of heteroskedasticity, our debt to White is great.

## 10.8    Logarithms and Heteroskedasticity

WHAT IS THE DGP?

FGLS and OLS with robust standard errors are two strategies econometricians use to cope with heteroskedastic disturbances. There is another, older strategy that is still in common use. Analyzing the logarithm of a variable sometimes gets rid of heteroskedastic disturbances. Figure 10.5 illustrates the point. Panel (a) in the figure plots wages against education for the sample of twins studied earlier. Panel (b) plots the log of wages against education. Heteroskedasticity is mildly more apparent in Panel (a). A regression analysis of these same data makes the point more definitively. If we had studied not the log of wages as a function of education, age, and age squared in Section 10.5, but just wages as a function of those same variables, we would have found evidence of persisting heteroskedasticity, despite the inclusion of age squared in the regression.

Table 10.9 contains the heteroskedasticity tests results for both the log-wage equation (from Table 10.4) and the wage (*hrwage*) equation, with education, age, and age squared the explanators in both cases. White's test statistic is 17.78, which is greater than 16.92, the .05 significance level critical value for a chi-square statistic with nine degrees of freedom, and also more than the 12.82 test statistic for the log-wage equation. The Breusch–Pagan test yields similar results. The Breusch–Pagan statistics rise from 6.61 and 8.83 in the log-wage equation to 10.84 and 16.87 in the wage equation. Heteroskedasticity that appears in the wage equation is absent from the log-wage equation. This finding in this small data set confirms what labor economists have often found in other wage studies—that taking the log of wages markedly reduces heteroskedasticity in wage-equation disturbances.

**Figure 10.5**

Wages and Log
Wages vs. Education

*Source*: Professor Orley
Ashenfelter, Princeton
University

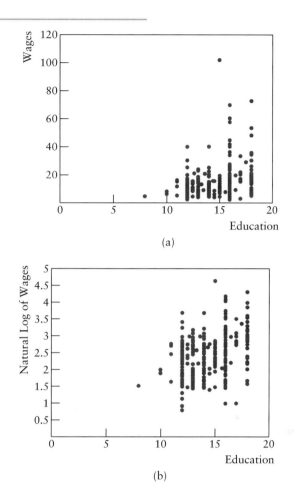

(a)

(b)

Taking the log of wages is not without side effects, however. A semilog speci-fication such as that used in most wage studies imposes a particular shape on the relationship between wages and education and age. A specification linear in wages would impose a different particular shape on that relationship. In the ranges of data observed in most wage studies, the difference between the linear and semilog specifications has not usually made substantive differences in the economic inter-pretations of the data, but we should always check to see whether the choice of form alters the economic interpretations of the data in hand when choosing be-tween linear and semilog (or log) specifications in contexts besides wages.

Furthermore, taking logs does not always dissolve heteroskedasticity. Return-ing to the New York renters data and testing whether the disturbances are het-eroskedastic in a regression of the log of rent on the log of income, we find that the Breusch–Pagan test statistic is 8.65, with just the log of income in the

**TABLE 10.9** Heteroskedasticity Tests and Omitted Variables

| Test | Statistic | Distribution | Critical Value |
|---|---|---|---|
| $\log(wage) = \beta_0 + \beta_1 education + \beta_2 age + \beta_3 age^2 + \varepsilon$ | | | |
| White | 12.82 | $\chi^2(8)$ | 15.51 |
| Breusch–Pagan* | 6.61 | $\chi^2(3)$ | 7.82 |
| Breusch–Pagan† | 8.83 | $\chi^2(5)$ | 11.07 |
| $wage = \beta_0 + \beta_1 education + \beta_2 age + \beta_3 age^2 + \varepsilon$ | | | |
| White | 17.78 | $\chi^2(8)$ | 16.92 |
| Breusch–Pagan* | 10.84 | $\chi^2(3)$ | 7.82 |
| Breusch–Pagan† | 16.87 | $\chi^2(5)$ | 11.07 |

* Education, age, age squared in auxiliary equation.
†Education, age, age squared, education squared, education to the fourth power in auxiliary equation.

Breusch–Pagan auxiliary equation, which greatly exceeds 3.84, the .05 critical value for a chi-square test statistic with one degree of freedom. Thus, functional form can influence heteroskedasticity, but it need not do so. *Heteroskedasticity should be dealt with directly, by FGLS or by heteroskedasticity-consistent standard errors and test procedures. Functional form should be chosen to reflect the observed (or theoretically determined) shape of the relationship between the expected value of the dependent variable and its explanators.* When neither theory nor data distinguish between the linear and logarithmic specifications, we are free to choose the more convenient specification.

## Summary

This chapter relaxes the Gauss–Markov Assumption of heteroskedasticity. We find that when disturbances are heteroskedastic, OLS remains unbiased but is no longer BLUE. We also find that the OLS-based $t$-statistics and $F$-statistics we developed in Chapters 7 and 9 are no longer valid—the tests become inefficient and their stated significance levels are wrong.

The chapter presents three formal tests for heteroskedasticity, the White test, the Breusch–Pagan test, and the Goldfeld–Quandt test. White's test is the most general heteroskedasticity test; it has some power against all the forms of heteroskedasticity that undermine the good properties of OLS. The Breusch–Pagan test is particularly powerful when we know something about the forms of het-

**An Organizational Structure for the Study of Econometrics**

**1. What Is the DGP?**

The Gauss–Markov Assumptions, except $\text{var}(\varepsilon_i) = \sigma_i^2 \neq \sigma^2$

The Gauss–Markov Assumptions, except $\text{var}(\varepsilon_i) = \sigma^2 X_i^2$

The Gauss–Markov Assumptions, except $\text{var}(\varepsilon_i) = \sigma^2 X_i$

**2. What Makes a Good Estimator?**

**3. How Do We Create an Estimator?**

Minimize the variance subject to unbiasedness constraints.

Transform the model to satisfy the Gauss–Markov Assumptions.

White's heteroskedasticity-consistent standard errors

**4. What Are an Estimator's Properties?**

OLS is unbiased and consistent, but inefficient.

GLS is BLUE.

FGLS is consistent and asymptotically efficient.

**5. How Do We Test Hypotheses?**

White's test

Breusch–Pagan test

Goldfeld–Quandt test

Heteroskedasticity vs. omitted variables (RESET test)

eroskedasticity that might be present; the test is particularly weak when we are wrong about the structure of the heteroskedasticity that is present. The Goldfeld–Quandt test is especially useful when distinct groups of observations have different variances for their disturbances.

We next learned two approaches to finding the BLUE estimators for a linear relationship's slopes and intercept when the disturbances are heteroskedastic. The first approach is the standard constrained minimization approach of Chapters 3, 4, and 6. The second approach finds a suitable transformation of the data such that the transformed data satisfy the Gauss–Markov Assumptions. OLS applied to the transformed data is then BLUE. The BLUE estimators with heteroskedastic disturbances are called generalized least squares (GLS) estimators. GLS weights less heavily observations with disturbances that have larger variances.

GLS requires that we know the mathematical form of the heteroskedasticity. Sometimes we know less than required for GLS, but enough to estimate the structure of heteroskedasticity. If we conduct GLS using an estimated structure for the heteroskedasticity, the estimators are called feasible generalized least squares (FGLS) estimators. If the heteroskedasticity is sufficiently well estimated, FGLS is asymptotically efficient.

Unfortunately, we frequently lack even the information required for FGLS. Consequently, we often rely on the unbiased, but inefficient, OLS estimators, even when the disturbances are heteroskedastic. The chapter concludes with a strategy for consistently estimating the variances and covariances of the OLS estimators when the disturbances are heteroskedastic, so that we can use OLS to conduct valid hypothesis tests, despite heteroskedastic disturbances. These estimators are called White's heteroskedasticity-consistent standard errors.

## Concepts for Review

## Questions for Discussion

1. FGLS and OLS with White's heteroskedasticity-consistent standard errors yield different estimates of the marginal propensity to spend on rent for our New York renters. Do these estimates suggest that the model is misspecified? How would the results have to change for you to change your answer to this question? Discuss.

2. Charlie says, "Heteroskedasticity has important policy implications. For example, I regressed rates of operating table deaths (% of operations in which the patient dies on the operating table) during a rare medical procedure on the size of hospitals. I estimated zero effect of the size of hospital on the death rate. Based on just this finding, you might think it doesn't matter where you get this operation. But the disturbances in my equation are heteroskedastic. For example, a hospital that performs five of these operations has twice the variance in its disturbance term as a hospital that does ten of these operations. Obviously, the quality of care is more varied in the hospitals that do few of these operations—it's riskier to get operated on in those hospitals!" Discuss.

# Problems for Analysis

For the data sets that you will need to solve the problems in this section, go to **www.aw-bc.com/murray.**

1. On this book's companion Web site (**www.aw-bc.com/murray**) you will find the Monte Carlo Makers called MC Builder IV and MC Builder V. These Monte Carlo programs allow you to re-examine our original four linear estimators to see which is best if the disturbances are heteroskedastic.
   a. Conduct a Monte Carlo exercise to determine which estimator performs best when the variance of the disturbances is equal to $\sigma^2 X_i$.
   b. Conduct a Monte Carlo exercise to determine which estimator performs best when the variance of the disturbances is equal to $\sigma^2 X_i^2$.

2. If the variance of the disturbances is $\sigma_i^2 = \sigma^2 X_i^{-2}$, how do you transform the data such that OLS is BLUE in the transformed DGP?

3. If the variance of the disturbances is $\sigma_i^2 = \sigma^2 X_i^b$, how do you transform the data such that OLS is BLUE in the transformed DGP? What is the BLUE estimator of the slope of a line through the origin in this case?

4. You have run a multiple regression with data from a DGP that you think satisfies all the Gauss–Markov Assumptions except, perhaps, that of homoskedastic disturbances. You conclude, based on White's test of heteroskedasticity, that the disturbances are heteroskedastic, but you do not know the form of the heteroskedasticity. If you decide to rely on your OLS regression coefficient estimates for drawing inferences, what precautionary measure should you take in light of the likely heteroskedasticity of the disturbances?

 5. The file equipmentandgrowth.*** contains data on economic growth between 1960 and 1985 for 106 countries. De Long and Summers[7] used these data to investigate the effect of equipment investment on economic growth. The six variables in the file are as follows:

   | | |
   |---|---|
   | GDP60vUS | Natural log of a country's per capita income in 1960 relative to that in the United States in 1960 |
   | GDPGR | Growth rate of income per worker for a country, 1960–1985 |
   | NONEQINV | Nonequipment investment for the country, 1960–1985 |
   | EQUIPINV | Equipment investment for the country, 1960–1985 |
   | LFGR6085 | Growth rate of the labor force, 1960–1985 |
   | CONTINENT | Continent of the country. |

   a. Regress the growth rate of income on the other four variables and a dummy variable for each continent. Test at the 5% significance level the null hypothesis that, other things being equal, countries with higher nonequipment investment have faster growth than other countries.
   b. Conduct, at the 5% significance level, White's test for heteroskedastic disturbances. What do you conclude?

c. Conduct the test described in (a), but now use White's heteroskedastic-consistent standard errors. What do you conclude?

6. The budget data Ernst Engel used when he established his famous law about food expenditure is in the file ducfood1.***. The data include both food expenditure (*food*) and housing expenditure (*housing*) data. This problem examines the bivariate relationship between expenditure on food and total expenditure (*total*, a proxy for income).

a. Does a scatterplot with total expenditures on the horizontal axis and food expenditures on the vertical axis visually indicate heteroskedastic disturbances in the food expenditure DGP?

b. Test for heteroskedastic disturbances in the food expenditure data using White's test. What do you conclude at the 5% significance level?

c. Test for heteroskedastic disturbances in the food expenditure data using the Breusch–Pagan test. Assume the heteroskedasticty can depend only on total income. What do you conclude at the 5% significance level?

d. Test for heteroskedastic disturbances in the food expenditure data using the Breusch–Pagan test. Assume the heteroskedasticty can depend on total income and total income squared. What do you conclude at the 5% significance level?

e. Determine whether the observed heteroskedasticity is not heteroskedasticity at all, but a consequence of inadvertently omitting the square of total expenditure from the regression.

f. What are the pros and cons of using the Breusch–Pagan test rather than White's test?

g. What are the pros and cons of conducting the test as in (c), rather than (d)?

h. In these data, which do you prefer to use, the $F$-statistics or the $nR^2$ statistics in (ii), (iii), and (iv)? Briefly explain.

i. Construct a valid 95% confidence interval for the marginal propensity to consume food as total expenditures rise. Base your interval on the OLS coefficient estimates.

j. Construct an arguably more efficient 95% confidence interval for the marginal propensity to consume food as total expenditures rise. Briefly argue for the superiority of the confidence interval you design.

7. The budget data Ernst Engel used when he established his famous law about food expenditure is in the file ducfood1.***. The data include both food expenditure (*food*) and housing expenditure (*housing*) data. This problem examines the bivariate relationship between expenditure on housing and total expenditure (*total*, a proxy for income).

a. Regress housing expenditures on total expenditures. Use White's test to check for heteroskedastic disturbances. What do you conclude at the 5% significance level?

b. Does a scatterplot with total expenditures on the horizontal axis and housing expenditures on the vertical axis visually suggest homoskedastic disturbances in the housing expenditure DGP?

c. Are there two particularly odd points in the scatterplot?

d. Restrict the sample to observations for which total expenditure is greater than or equal to the sum of food expenditure and housing expenditure. Re-examine the scatterplot of housing expenditures on total expenditures. Does the scatterplot visually suggest homoskedastic disturbances in the housing expenditure DGP?

e. Repeat (a), this time restricting the sample to observations in which *total* ≥ *housing* + *food*).

f. Did the "bad" observations in the data markedly alter the estimated marginal propensity to spend on housing? (Examine the percentage change in the estimated coefficient, as well as the magnitude of the change.)

g. Did the bad observations markedly affect the estimated standard error of the estimated marginal propensity to consume housing? Is the appropriate comparison between the estimated standard errors in (a) and (e) or between the estimated standard error in (a) and White's heteroskedastic-consistent standard errors for (e)? Briefly explain.

h. Estimate the marginal propensity to spend on food with and without the bad observations. Do the results support the suspicion that housing expenditures, rather than total expenditures, are misreported in the bad observations?

i. Determine whether the observed heteroskedasticity in the restricted sample is not heteroskedasticity at all but a consequence of inadvertently omitting the square of total expenditures from the regression.

8. Return to the data set twin1.***. Perform a Goldfeld–Quandt test at the 5% significance level of the null hypothesis that the logs of wages for men and for women vary the same about their expected values. Exclude the self-employed from the sample. The variables in the file are as follows:

| | |
|---|---|
| *hrwage* | Self-reported hourly wage of the individual (in dollars) |
| *lwage* | Natural log of the hourly wage |
| *age* and *age2* | Age of a person (*age*) and its square (*age2*) |
| *female* | = 1 if the person is female; = 0 otherwise |
| *white* | = 1 if the person is white; = 0 otherwise |
| *educ* | Educational attainment of the individual |
| *selfemp* | = 1 if self-employed; = 0 otherwise. |

9. Nitrogen dioxide ($NO_2$) is a pollutant that attacks the human respiratory system; it increases the likelihood of respiratory illness. One common source of nitrogen dioxide is automobile exhaust. The file NO2 pollution.*** contains a subset from 500 hourly observations made from October 2001 to August 2003.[8] The variables in the data set are

| | |
|---|---|
| *LNO2* | Natural logarithm of the concentration of $NO_2$ (particles) |
| *LCARS* | Natural logarithm of the number of cars per hour |
| *TEMP* | Temperature 2 meters above ground (degrees C) |
| *WNDSPD* | Wind speed (meters/second) |
| *TCHNG23* | Temperature difference between 25 meters and 2 meters above ground (degrees C), |
| *WNDDIR* | Wind direction (degrees between 0 and 360) |
| *HOUR* | Hour of day |
| *DAYS* | Day number from October 1, 2001. |
| *one* and *twentythree* | Dummy variables for two-hour intervals, starting at 0000. |

   a. Regress the log of $NO_2$ concentration on the log of the number of cars, the two temperature variables, the two wind variables, and the time index (*DAYS*). Use White's test for heteroskedastic disturbances. What do you conclude at the 5% significance level?
   b. Add to the regression the two-hour interval dummies, *one* through *twentythree*. Conduct White's test for heteroskedastic disturbances. What do you conclude about the heteroskedasticity finding in (a)?

10. From the 1970s to the early 1990s, crime rates rose and prison populations swelled. Were the large prison expenditures socially useful? Did locking up criminals reduce crime? The data set prisons4.*** contains a portion of the 1971–1993 annual state-level data used by Steven Levitt to answer these questions.[9] The variable chl*vcph* is the annual change in the natural log of the number of violent crimes per 100,000 people in a state's population in a given year. The variable *chlprisph* is the annual change in the natural log of the number of prisoners in the state during a given year.
   a. Regress the change in the log of the violent crimes per 100,000 people (the log of the violent crime rate) against an intercept term and the change in the log of the number of prisoners per 100,000 people (the log of the incarceration rate). Interpret the estimated coefficients.
   b. Conduct White's test for heteroskedastic disturbances. What do you conclude at the 5% significance level?
   c. Use White's heteroskedasticity-consistent estimator for the estimated standard errors of the OLS estimators in (a). Are White's estimated standard errors much different than the ordinary ones in this instance?

11. Does market power inhibit innovation? Or do noncompetitive economic profits fund advances in technology that more competitive firms can't afford? The file TFP.*** contains data pertinent to these questions. The two variables in the file are the percentage changes in industries' total factor productivity (TFP) over a five-year period (*tfp_ch*) and the concentrations of market share (measured in percent) among industries' four largest firms (*conc*).
   a. Regress TFP changes on four-firm concentrations. If the concentration rises one percentage point, how much do you estimate TFP changes by?
   b. Conduct White's test for heteroskedasticity in this DGP's disturbances. What do you conclude at the 5% significance level?
   c. Build a 95% confidence interval for the effect of market share on changes in TFP. Should you use White's heteroskedastic standard errors in this case?

12. Does the separation of corporate control from corporate ownership lead to worse firm performance? George Stigler and Claire Friedland have addressed this question empirically using a sample of firms.[10] A subset of their data are in the file execcomp.***. The variables in the file are as follows:

*ecomp*      Average total annual compensation in thousands of dollars for a firm's top three executives
*assets*     Firm's assets in millions of dollars
*profits*    Firm's annual profits in millions of dollars
*mcontrol*   Dummy variable indicating management control of the firm

a. Regress firm profits on firm assets and the management control dummy. Use White's test to determine whether the disturbances are heteroskedastic. What do you conclude at the 5% significance level?

b. Divide all of the variables (including the intercept term) in (a) by the square root of assets. Re-estimate the parameters of (a) using these data. These new estimates are BLUE if what is true about the disturbances in the DGP in (a)?

c. Conduct White's test for the disturbances in (b) being heteroskedastic. What do you conclude at the 5% significance level?

d. Divide all the variables (including the intercept term) in (a) by the firm's assets. Re-estimate the parameters of (a) using these data. These new estimates are BLUE if what is true about the disturbances in the DGP in (a)?

e. Conduct White's test for the disturbances in (b) being heteroskedastic. What do you conclude at the 5% significance level?

f. Construct 95% confidence intervals for the coefficients on *mcontrol* using the estimates from the regressions in (a) and (d). (Which estimated standard errors should you use in each case?) Which confidence interval is more efficient, in principle?

g. Conduct at the 5% significance level a Goldfeldt–Quandt test of the null hypothesis that in the transformed specification of the model in (d), management-controlled firms' disturbances have the same variance as do the disturbances of owner-controlled firms. In principle, White's test could detect heteroskedasticity stemming from different variances in the disturbances for owner-controlled firms than for management-controlled firms. Briefly explain why the Goldfeldt–Quandt test might have more power against that alternative than would White's test.

h. Do the intervals in (f) make you sympathetic to the claim that managerial control has no large effect on corporate profits?

 13. When police arrest more people for murder, are there fewer murders? The data set murder1.*** contains a subset of the data that David Mustard used to address this question.[11] Among the variables in the file are

*arrmurd*    County's murder arrests as a percentage of murders in the county

*lratmurd*   Natural log of county's annual murder rate per 100,000 people

*density*    County's population density

*ppb*       Percentage of the county's population who are African American

*incom*     County's per capita income.

a. Regress the log of the murder rate on the logs of income, the murder arrest rate, population density, and the proportion of the population who are African American. Do the estimated signs of the variables' coefficients conform to your expectations? Briefly explain.

b. Conduct White's test for the heteroskedasticity of the disturbances in (a). What do you conclude at the 5% significance level?

c. With other things being the same, how will the variance in murder rates in communities with a very low murder rate compare to that in otherwise similar places with moderate murder rates? Offer an intuitive response. (To get an intuition, recall what happens to the variance of a sample proportion as the probability of success gets lower.)

d. With other things being the same, how will the variance in murder rates in communities with a smaller population compare with that in larger, but otherwise similar, places. Offer an intuitive response. (To get an intuition, recall what happens to the variance of the sample proportion as the probability of success gets lower, or think about the Law of Large Numbers.)

e. If small communities tend to have low murder rates, on average, and if murder rates in moderate-sized places are about the same as those in larger places, what do (c) and (d) imply about the variance of the disturbances in (a) as population size grows?

f. Conduct a Breusch–Pagan test with population and its square as the chosen variables to test the hypothesis about heteroskedasticity described in (e). Is your intuition confirmed?

g. Given the finding in (f), is it likely that dividing both sides of the regression equation used in (a) by either population or its square root will overcome the heteroskedasticity of the disturbances?

h. Construct a 95% confidence interval for the effect of arrests on the log of the murder rate. Briefly explain why you chose the estimation procedure and estimated standard errors that you do.

 14. The labels on French wine bottles contain information about the wine. Is the wine red or white? What is the wine's vintage? Which region is the wine from? And what class does the producer claim for the wine (for example, *gran cru classe* or *clu non classe*)? Three French economists, Pierre Combris, Sebastien Lecocq, and Michael Visser, used data from wine bottle labels to account for the price of French wines.[12] The file wine.*** contains a subsample of wines these authors used.

The relevant variables in the file, and their meanings, are

*PRICE*     Wine's price

*GRADE*   Professional tasters grade for the wine

**Label Traits**

*RANK*     Cru or gran cru (3); cru bourgeois (2); cru non classe (1)

*RED*        Red wine (2); white wine (1)

*WHIT*      White wine (2); red wine (1)

*AN89*      Vintage 1989 (2); otherwise (1)

*AN90*      Vintage 1990 (2); otherwise (1)

*AN91*      Vintage 1991 (2); otherwise (1)

*BORD*     Bordeaux group (2); otherwise (1)

*COTE*      Cote group (2); otherwise (1)

*MEGR*    Medoc and graves group (2); otherwise (1)

*SEPF*       Saint-Emilion Pomerol Frosnac group (2); otherwise (1)

*BLSE*       Blanc Secs group (2); otherwise (1)

*BLDO*      Blanc Doux group (2); otherwise (1)

a. Regress the natural log of the price of wine against *RANK*, the three vintage variables, and all of the region variables except *BORD*. Do not include a constant term; the region variables are mutually exclusive and exhaustive. How much of the variation in the log of wine's price in this sample is accounted for by the variation in the wines' traits that are reported on the bottles' labels?

b. Conduct White's test for heteroskedastic disturbances. At the 5% significance level, what do you conclude?

c. Do you think the variance of older wines' prices will be greater than that of younger wines? Do you think the wines of some regions will be more variable than the wines from other areas?

d. Conduct a Breusch–Pagan analysis that would allow you to address the hypotheses you formulate in (c). Begin by regressing the squared residuals from (a) on the variables in (a). What do you conclude about your hypotheses in (c)?

e. Compare the estimated standard errors for the OLS coefficients in (a) with their White's heteroskedasticity-consistent standard error estimator counterparts.

## Endnotes

1. Halbert White, "A Heteroskedasticity-Consistent Covariance Matrix Estimator and a Direct Test for Heteroskedasticity," *Econometrica* 48, no. 4 (May 1980): 817–838.

2. T. S. Breusch and A. R. Pagan, "A Simple Test for Heteroskedasticity and Random Coefficient Variation," *Econometrica* 47, no. 5 (September 1979): 1287–1294.

3. Orley Ashenfelter and Cecelia Rouse, "Income, Schooling, and Ability: Evidence from a New Sample of Identical Twins," *Quarterly Journal of Economics* 113, no. 1 (February 1998): 253–284. Professor Ashenfelter kindly provided these data for use in this book.

4. James B. Ramsey, "Tests for Specification Error in Classical Linear Least Squares Regression Analysis," *Journal of the Royal Statistical Society* B 31 (1969): 350–371.

5. J.R.N. Stone, "Linear Expenditure Systems and Demand Analysis: An Application to the Patterns of British Demand," *Economic Journal* 64 (1954): 511–527.

6. S. J. Prais and Hendrik Houthakker, *The Analysis of Household Budgets* (Cambridge, UK: Cambridge University Press, 1955).

7. J. Bradford DeLong and Lawrence H. Summers, "How Strongly Do Developing Countries Benefit from Equipment Investment?" *Journal of Monetary Economics* 32, no. 3 (1994): 395–415.

8. These data come from the Statlib archive of Carnegie Mellon University. They were originally posted there by Aldrin Magne.

9. Steven D. Levitt, "The Effect of Prison Population Size on Crime Rates: Evidence from Prison Overcrowding Litigation," *Quarterly Journal of Economics* 111, no. 2 (May 1996): 319–351.

10. George J. Stigler and Claire Friedland, "The Literature of Economics: The Case of Berle and Means," *Journal of Law and Economics* 26, no. 2 (June 1983): 237–268.

11. David Mustard, "Reexamining Criminal Behavior: The Importance of Omitted Variable Bias," *Review of Economics and Statistics* 85, no. 1 (February 2003): 205–211.

12. Pierre Combris, Sebastien Lecocq, and Michael Visser, "Estimation of a Hedonic Price Equation for Bordeaux Wine: Does Quality Matter?" *Economic Journal* (March 1997): 390–402.

# *Appendix 10.A*

# Matrix Algebra and Generalized Least Squares I

This appendix uses matrix algebra to examine the consequences of heteroskedasticity for the OLS and GLS estimators in the multiple regression model.

## 10.A.1    The Heteroskedastic Variance–Covariance Matrix

The Gauss–Markov Assumptions state that disturbances are homoskedastic and uncorrelated. Homoskedasticity is a claim about the variances of the disturbances. A lack of correlation is a claim about the covariances among the disturbances. A **variance–covariance matrix** represents the disturbances' variances and their covariances together in matrix form.

### The Disturbances' Variance–Covariance Matrix

The disturbances' variances and covariances are the expected value of the $n \times n$ matrix $V = \boldsymbol{\varepsilon}\boldsymbol{\varepsilon}'$. For the case in which $n = 4r$,

$$V = \boldsymbol{\varepsilon}\boldsymbol{\varepsilon}' = \begin{bmatrix} \varepsilon_1 \\ \varepsilon_2 \\ \varepsilon_3 \\ \varepsilon_4 \end{bmatrix} [\varepsilon_1\ \varepsilon_2\ \varepsilon_3\ \varepsilon_4] = \begin{bmatrix} \varepsilon_1^2 & \varepsilon_1\varepsilon_2 & \varepsilon_1\varepsilon_3 & \varepsilon_1\varepsilon_4 \\ \varepsilon_2\varepsilon_1 & \varepsilon_2^2 & \varepsilon_2\varepsilon_3 & \varepsilon_2\varepsilon_4 \\ \varepsilon_3\varepsilon_1 & \varepsilon_3\varepsilon_2 & \varepsilon_3^2 & \varepsilon_3\varepsilon_4 \\ \varepsilon_4\varepsilon_1 & \varepsilon_4\varepsilon_2 & \varepsilon_4\varepsilon_3 & \varepsilon_4^2 \end{bmatrix}.$$

The expected values of the diagonal elements are the variances of the $n$ disturbances. The expected values of the off-diagonal elements are the covariances among the $n$ disturbances. $E(\boldsymbol{\varepsilon}\boldsymbol{\varepsilon}')$ is called the variance–covariance matrix of the disturbances. Because $E(\varepsilon_i\varepsilon_j) = E(\varepsilon_j\varepsilon_i)$, $V$ is symmetric. The variance–covariance matrix of $Y$ is also $V$, because $Y$ differs from $\boldsymbol{\varepsilon}$ by just the constant $X\boldsymbol{\beta}$.

The Gauss–Markov Assumptions claim that the disturbances are homoskedastic, that is, that the diagonal elements of $V$ are equal to one another, and that the disturbances are uncorrelated, that is, that the off-diagonal elements of $V$ are all zero. For the case in which $n = 4$, the Gauss–Markov Assumptions claim that

$$V = E(\boldsymbol{\varepsilon}\boldsymbol{\varepsilon}') = \begin{bmatrix} \sigma^2 & 0 & 0 & 0 \\ 0 & \sigma^2 & 0 & 0 \\ 0 & 0 & \sigma^2 & 0 \\ 0 & 0 & 0 & \sigma^2 \end{bmatrix} = \sigma^2 \begin{bmatrix} 1 & 0 & 0 & 0 \\ 0 & 1 & 0 & 0 \\ 0 & 0 & 1 & 0 \\ 0 & 0 & 0 & 1 \end{bmatrix} = \sigma^2 I_4.$$

## The Heteroskedastic Variance–Covariance Matrix

In this chapter, we keep the assumption of uncorrelated disturbances, so the off-diagonal elements of $V$ are still zero, but we do not require homoskedastic disturbances. For the most general heteroskedastic case with uncorrelated disturbances, we can write the variance–covariance matrix as

$$V_0 = E[\boldsymbol{\varepsilon}\boldsymbol{\varepsilon}']) = \begin{bmatrix} \sigma^2 d_1^2 & 0 & .. & 0 \\ 0 & \sigma^2 d_2^2 & .. & 0 \\ : & : & : & : \\ 0 & 0 & .. & \sigma^2 d_n^2 \end{bmatrix}.$$

Two special cases of heteroskedasticity that frequently arise are disturbances with variances proportional to the square of one variable, for example, $X_2$, and disturbances with variance proportional to the absolute value of one variable, for example, $X_2$. In the former case, if $n = 4$, the variance–covariance matrix is

$$V_1 = E([\boldsymbol{\varepsilon}\boldsymbol{\varepsilon}']) = \begin{bmatrix} \sigma^2 X_{21}^2 & 0 & 0 & 0 \\ 0 & \sigma^2 X_{22}^2 & 0 & 0 \\ 0 & 0 & \sigma^2 X_{23}^2 & 0 \\ 0 & 0 & 0 & \sigma^2 X_{24}^2 \end{bmatrix}$$

$$= \sigma^2 \begin{bmatrix} X_{21}^2 & 0 & 0 & 0 \\ 0 & X_{22}^2 & 0 & 0 \\ 0 & 0 & X_{23}^2 & 0 \\ 0 & 0 & 0 & X_{24}^2 \end{bmatrix}. \qquad \text{10.A.1}$$

In the latter case, if $n = 4$, the variance–covariance matrix is

$$V_2 = \begin{bmatrix} \sigma^2 |X_{21}| & 0 & 0 & 0 \\ 0 & \sigma^2 |X_{22}| & 0 & 0 \\ 0 & 0 & \sigma^2 |X_{23}| & 0 \\ 0 & 0 & 0 & \sigma^2 |X_{24}| \end{bmatrix}$$

$$= \sigma^2 \begin{bmatrix} |X_{21}| & 0 & 0 & 0 \\ 0 & |X_{22}| & 0 & 0 \\ 0 & 0 & |X_{23}| & 0 \\ 0 & 0 & 0 & |X_{24}| \end{bmatrix}. \qquad \text{10.A.2}$$

## 10.A.2    OLS, GLS, and Heteroskedasticity

Heteroskedasticity undermines the BLUE property of OLS. However, OLS applied to appropriately transformed data yields the BLUE estimates when all the Gauss–Markov Assumptions except homoskedasticity are met. The BLUE estimation procedure for heteroskedastic disturbances is an example of GLS.

### Heteroskedasticity and OLS

The unbiasedness conditions for linear estimators do not depend on the variances or covariances of the disturbances, so OLS remains unbiased when the disturbances are heteroskedastic. However, heteroskedasticity changes the variance of the OLS estimator. When the variance–covariance matrix for $Y$ is $V_0$,

$$\text{var}(\hat{\beta}) = \text{var}((X'X)^{-1}X'Y) = (X'X)^{-1}X'(\text{var}(Y))X(X'X)^{-1}$$
$$= (X'X)^{-1}X'V_0X(X'X)^{-1}, \tag{10.A.3}$$

which would simplify to the standard variance expression for OLS, $\sigma^2(X'X)^{-1}$, if $V_0 = \sigma^2 I_n$, but not generally. Estimating the variance of the OLS estimator by $s^2(X'X)^{-1}$ results in biased estimates if the disturbances are heteroskedastic. Because the standard OLS-based $t$-tests and $F$-tests rely on this biased estimator, they are invalid when the disturbances are heteroskedastic.

### Heteroskedasticity and GLS

The BLUE estimator when disturbances are heteroskedastic results from minimizing the diagonal elements of the variance expression in Equation 10.A.3, with respect to the linear estimator's weights, $W'$, subject to the unbiasedness conditions, $W'X = I_n$.

Alternatively, the BLUE estimates result from appropriately transforming the regression model and applying OLS to the transformed variables. If the regression model is

$$Y = X\beta + \varepsilon,$$

what is the appropriate transformed model,

$$TY = TX\beta + T\varepsilon,$$

such that OLS applied to it is BLUE? That is, what $n \times n$ matrix $T$ yields an $n \times 1$ matrix $Q = TY$, an $n \times k$ matrix $Z = TX$, and an $n \times 1$ matrix $v = T\varepsilon$, such that OLS applied to

$$Q = Z\beta + v \tag{10.A.4}$$

is BLUE? To answer these questions, first note that $E(\nu) = 0$. Next, consider the variance of OLS applied to 10.A.4, in which $\nu = T\varepsilon$. The variance–covariance matrix for $\nu$ is

$$E(\nu\nu') = E(T\varepsilon\varepsilon'T) = T(E(\varepsilon\varepsilon'))T' = TV_0T'.$$

Consequently, OLS applied to 10.A.4 is BLUE if $TV_0T' = \sigma^2 I_n$, because then the model in Equation 10.A.4 satisfies the Gauss–Markov Assumptions. Computation reveals that $TV_0T' = \sigma^2 I_n$, if

$$T = \begin{bmatrix} \dfrac{1}{d_1} & 0 & .. & 0 \\ 0 & \dfrac{1}{d_2} & .. & 0 \\ \vdots & \vdots & \vdots & \vdots \\ 0 & 0 & .. & \dfrac{1}{d_n} \end{bmatrix}. \qquad \text{10.A.5}$$

In the special cases represented by $V_1$ and $V_2$, we know the values of the $d$; they are $X$ and $\sqrt{|X_i|}$, respectively. In such cases, GLS is a feasible estimator. Notice that, in general, $T$ is symmetric, so $TT' = T'T$ and that $TT' = \sigma^2 V_0^{-1}$. (The inverse of a diagonal matrix is one with diagonal elements that are the inverses of the original matrix's diagonal elements.) Thus, the GLS estimator for the DGP in which all the Gauss–Markov Assumptions but homoskedasticity are met is

$$\begin{aligned} \boldsymbol{\beta}_{GLS} &= (Z'Z)^{-1}Z'Y = (X'T'TX)^{-1}X'TT'Y \\ &= (X'(\sigma^2 V_0^{-1})X)^{-1} X'(\sigma^2 V_0^{-1})Y \\ &= (X'V_0^{-1}X)^{-1}X'V_0^{-1}Y. \end{aligned}$$

The variance of this GLS estimator is

$$\begin{aligned} \sigma^2(Z'Z)^{-1} &= \sigma^2(X'T'TX)^{-1} \\ &= \sigma^2(X'\sigma^2 V_0^{-1} X)^{-1} = (X'V_0^{-1}X)^{-1}. \end{aligned}$$

The standard $t$-tests and $F$-tests developed in Chapters 7 and 9 are valid for OLS applied to the transformed model if the disturbances in the underlying model are normally distributed, and they apply approximately in large samples, even if the underlying disturbances are not normally distributed.

# Appendix 10.A Concept for Review

Variance–covariance matrix   432

# Chapter 11

# Autoregressive Disturbances

*Those who cannot remember the past are condemned to repeat it.*[1]
—GEORGE SANTAYANA

The ancient philosopher Heraclitus, who said, "You cannot step into the same river twice,"[2] might have approved of our Gauss–Markov data-generating process, (DGP) in which each observation offers wholly new information independently of the observations that come before or after it. The modern philosopher George Santayana reminds us that the world is not so simple, however. Because the past often reappears in the future, data gathered over time frequently do not contain independent pieces of information. This chapter grapples with regression models in which the disturbances are correlated over time, rather than being independent of one another.

Economists gather many data series periodically, on an annual, quarterly, monthly, or even more frequent basis. These are the data that Chapter 1 named *time series data*. Such data, drawn from successive periods, are unlikely to satisfy the Gauss–Markov Assumption that the disturbances are uncorrelated. Correlations across such disturbances are apt to arise because random disturbances that affect the economy in one period often affect the future, as well. For example, an earthquake that destroys several factories may have its greatest immediate impact on local employment but in some number of subsequent periods, perhaps for several years after the event, employment would tend to be different than we would otherwise expect, because not all the factories have yet been replaced. Weather, war, sicknesses, and other influences can all press an economic outcome to be above average, or below average, for several periods in a row. When these influences are not measured, they are part of the disturbance terms in regression models, and they contribute to correlations across disturbances.

Because many phenomena observed over time conflict with the Gauss–Markov Assumption that disturbances are uncorrelated, we must often forgo that assumption. This chapter investigates the consequences of correlated disturbances for estimation and inference in regression models. Do correlated disturbances make ordinary least squares (OLS) an inappropriate estimation procedure? As in the case of heteroskedasticity, the answer is both "Yes and no."

The impacts of earthquakes, weather, sicknesses, and other shocks on an economy spill over from one period to the next, but, frequently, they also diminish over time. This chapter replaces the Gauss–Markov Assumption that disturbances are uncorrelated with an assumption that all disturbances are correlated, but with disturbances further apart in time more weakly correlated than ones close together in time. For this new DGP, OLS is unbiased, but it is not BLUE (the best linear unbiased estimator), and the OLS-based $t$-statistics and $F$-statistics developed in Chapters 7 and 9 are no longer valid.

Because correlated disturbances undermine the desirable properties of our original OLS-based testing procedures, in practice we need to ask whether disturbances are uncorrelated before applying those standard procedures. This chapter presents two formal statistical tests of the null hypothesis of uncorrelated disturbances. It also derives the BLUE estimators of the slope and intercept of a line if the disturbances are correlated. The BLUE estimators require more information than we usually have, but they point the way to feasible generalized least squares (FGLS) estimators that become unbiased and efficient in large samples.

Unfortunately, we sometimes know too little about the structure of correlations among the disturbances to support FGLS estimation. Consequently, econometricians often rely on the unbiased, but inefficient, OLS estimator, even when the disturbances are serially correlated. This chapter concludes with a strategy for estimating the variances and covariances of the OLS estimators when the disturbances are correlated over time, but in an unknown fashion. These variance and covariance estimators support valid hypothesis tests based on OLS, despite correlated disturbances.

# 11.1    The Serially Correlated DGP

**WHAT IS THE DGP?**

Persistence in economic influences can lead to correlations among the disturbances in time series data. This section graphically illustrates the correlations that can characterize economic variables in such data and provides a vocabulary for describing these correlations. If the covariances among the disturbances in time-series data are not all zero, we say the disturbances are **serially correlated**; otherwise, we say the disturbances are **serially uncorrelated**. If the correlations between time periods are positive, we say there is **positive serial correlation**. If the correlations between time periods are negative, an infrequently encountered case in econometrics, we say there is **negative serial correlation**.

## Visualizing Serial Correlation

Serial correlation most often appears in the form of observations close in time being positively correlated with one another. For example, inflation in the United States has been positively serially correlated for at least 100 years. We expect above-average inflation in a given period if there was above-average inflation in the previous period, and we expect below-average inflation in a given period if there was below-average inflation in the preceding period.

Figure 11.1, Panel A, shows deviations of inflation in the United States from its mean in the 30 years, 1973–2002, following the first oil price surge caused by

**Figure 11.1  U.S. Inflation's Deviations from Its Mean**

*Source:* U.S. Bureau of Labor Statistics Wholesale Price Index

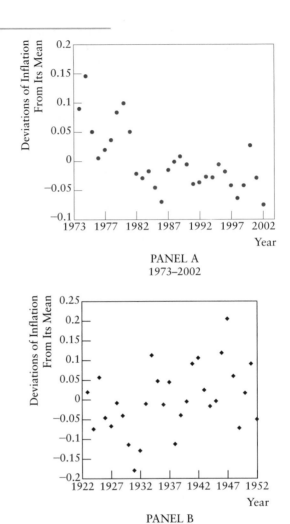

the Organization of the Petroleum Exporting Countries (OPEC). Inflation is positively serially correlated in this period. Years with above-average inflation in Panel A are almost always followed by other years with above-average inflation; years with below-average inflation are almost always followed by other years with below-average inflation. Indeed, price changes moved from above-average one period to below-average the next, or vice versa, only five times in 30 years. We can count these switches by counting the number of times (five) that the line in Panel A crosses a horizontal line along the mean deviation value of zero.

Inflation has not always shown such strong serial correlation. Panel B of Figure 11.1 shows inflation in the United States for the 30 years 1923–1952. In those 30 years, inflation goes from above average to below average, or vice versa, 13 times. This larger number of crossings suggests that deviations of inflation from its mean were less persistent between 1923 and 1952 than between 1973 and 2002, but in both periods, inflation displays positive serial correlation of one degree or another.

## The DGP

A formal analysis of serial correlation requires an explicit DGP. The core DGP for this chapter maintains all the Gauss–Markov Assumptions but one. Instead of uncorrelated disturbances, the DGP assumes that

$$\text{cov}(\varepsilon_t, \varepsilon_{t'}) = \text{E}(\varepsilon_t\, \varepsilon_{t'}) = \sigma_{tt'} \neq 0,$$

for some or all differing values of $t$ and $t'$. When discussing DGPs that apply chiefly to time series data, econometricians usually use $t$, instead of $i$, as the subscript to denote specific observations; they also use $T$, instead of $n$, to denote the sample size. The DGPs in this chapter assume

$$Y_t = \beta_0 + \beta_1 X_{1t} + \cdots + \beta_k X_{kt} + \varepsilon_t,$$
$$\text{E}(\varepsilon_t) = 0 \qquad t = 1, \ldots, T,$$
$$\text{var}(\varepsilon_t) = \sigma^2 \qquad t = 1, \ldots, T,$$

$$\text{E}(\varepsilon_t\, \varepsilon_{t'}) = \sigma_{tt'}\, \sigma_{tt'} \neq 0 \text{ for some or all unequal } t \text{ and } t'.$$
Each explanator is fixed across samples.

The DGPs also assume that the covariance between observations $t$ and $t'$ depends only on the distance between them in time, $|t - t'|$. Thus, we can write

$$\text{E}(\varepsilon_t\, \varepsilon_{t'}) = \sigma_{tt'} = \sigma_{|t-t'|} \text{ for all } t \text{ and } t'.$$

Because the disturbances are homoskedastic, with the common variance $\sigma^2$,

$$\text{E}(\varepsilon_t\, \varepsilon_t) = \text{var}(\varepsilon_t) = \sigma_{|t-t|} = \sigma_0 = \sigma^2.$$

These assumptions are common to all the DGPs in this chapter. Some DGPs in the chapter add further assumptions that ensure that the correlations between disturbances more distant in time from one another shrink toward zero. Valid $t$-tests and $F$-tests in small samples require the additional assumption that the disturbances are normally distributed.

## Stationarity

The assumption that $\sigma_{tt'}$ depends only on $|t - t'|$ requires that economic shocks persist similarly in different parts of the time period under study—shocks happening in 1988 influenced 1990 in the same way that shocks in 2001 influenced 2003. If (i) $\sigma_{tt'}$ depends only on $|t - t'|$, the distance between the observations in

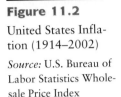

**Figure 11.2**

United States Inflation (1914–2002)

*Source:* U.S. Bureau of Labor Statistics Wholesale Price Index

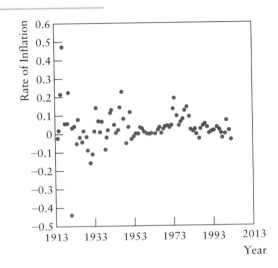

time and (ii) the disturbances are homoskedastic, then we say that the disturbances are **covariance stationary.** If any aspect of the joint distribution of observations (not just the variances or covariances) depends not only on how far apart the observations are from one another but also on when in time the observations take place, we say the time series is **nonstationary.** In essence, nonstationarity says that the DGP that applies to one span of years is different from the DGP that applies to another span of years.

Figure 11.1 suggests that inflation might not be covariance stationary. Figure 11.2 pictures inflation in the United States all the way from 1913 to 2002. We have already observed that the covariance between adjacent disturbances seems greater recently than in the past. With the entire history before us, it seems that the variance changed over time, too. The variance appears quite large early in the century and quite small from 1953 to 1972. Apparently, inflation doubly violates the requirements of covariance stationarity; both the variance of inflation and its covariances changed across the 90 years.

Notice that here we are examining inflation in isolation from other variables. Figure 11.2 suggests that a univariate model of inflation is nonstationary. It is possible that adding explanators of inflation to the model would explain this apparent nonstationarity, with variation in the explanatory variables accounting for the changing variance and covariances of inflation over time.

If no aspect of the joint distribution of observations depends on when in time the observation takes place, we say the DGP is **stationary.** This chapter assumes disturbances are stationary. With the new DGP in hand, we can ask how OLS performs in the face of serially correlated disturbances.

**11.2**

# The Consequences of Serial Correlation for the OLS Estimators

How do serially correlated disturbances adversely affect OLS estimators and the $t$-tests and $F$-tests based on them? We learn first that linear estimators that are unbiased with serially uncorrelated disturbances are also unbiased with serially correlated ones. Next, we learn that when the disturbances are serially correlated, OLS, though still unbiased, is inefficient and that our usual estimators of the variances of OLS estimators are biased. The biases in the standard variance estimators for OLS undermine the OLS-based hypothesis testing procedures developed in Chapters 7 and 9.

## The Unchanged Unbiasedness Conditions

Like heteroskedasticity, serial correlation does not change the unbiasedness conditions for linear estimators. *Slope and intercept estimators that are unbiased with serially uncorrelated disturbances are unbiased with serially correlated disturbances.* To verify this statement, we return to Chapter 6's analysis that asked, When is a linear estimator, $g = \sum w_t Y_t$, an unbiased estimator of the intercept in our multiple regression DGP? Recall that $t$ is now the subscript for individual observations and $T$ is the sample size. In Chapter 6, we looked at the expected value of $g$:

$$E(g) = E[\sum w_t Y_t] = \sum E(w_t Y_t) = \sum w_t E(Y_t)$$

or

$$
\begin{aligned}
E(g) &= \sum[w_t E(\beta_0 X_{0t} + \beta_1 X_{1t} + \cdots + \beta_k X_{kt} + \varepsilon_t)] \\
&= \sum[w_t(\beta_0 X_{0t} + \beta_1 X_{1t} + \cdots + \beta_k X_{kt})] \\
&= \beta_0 \sum w_t X_{0t} + \beta_1 \sum w_t X_{1t} + \cdots + \beta_k \sum w_t X_{kt},
\end{aligned}
$$

and found that if $g$ is to be an unbiased estimator of some one coefficient in our DGP, say $\beta_s$,

$$\sum w_t X_{rt} = 0 \text{ for } r \neq s,$$

and

$$\sum w_t X_{st} = 1,$$

so that $E(g)$ would equal $\beta_s$. These unbiasedness conditions rely only on $E(\varepsilon_t) = 0$, the $X$'s being fixed across samples, and the linearity of the regression equation in its parameters. The covariances among the disturbances play no role. Any linear estimator unbiased when disturbances are uncorrelated is also unbiased when they are correlated.

## The Changed Variance of a Linear Estimator

Serially correlated disturbances change the variance of a linear estimator, leading to a BLUE estimator different from the OLS estimator. *OLS, though unbiased, is inefficient when the disturbances are serially correlated.* To verify the inefficiency of OLS when disturbances are serially correlated, return to Chapter 4's analysis that derived the variance of a linear estimator:

$$\text{var}(g) = \text{var}\left(\sum_{t=1}^{T} w_t Y_t\right),$$

which we can rewrite as

$$\sum_{t=1}^{T} \text{var}(w_t Y_t) + \text{sum of all the covariances among the } w_t Y_t$$

$$= \sum_{t=1}^{T} \text{var}(w_t Y_t) + \sum_{t=1}^{T} \sum_{\substack{t'=1 \\ t' \neq t}}^{T} \text{cov}(w_t Y_t, w_{t'} Y_{t'}). \tag{11.1}$$

$$= \sum_{t=1}^{T} w_t^2 \text{var}(Y_t) + \sum_{t=1}^{T} \sum_{\substack{t'=1 \\ t' \neq t}}^{T} w_t w_{t'} \text{cov}(Y_t, Y_{t'}). \tag{11.2}$$

In our new DGP, the $\varepsilon_t$ are no longer mutually independent. We now assume, instead, that

$$\text{E}(\varepsilon_t \varepsilon_{t'}) = \sigma_{tt'} = \sigma_{|t-t'|}.$$

The $Y_t$ differ from the $\varepsilon_t$ by only $[\beta_0 + \beta_1 X_{1t} + \cdots + \beta_k X_{kt}]$, which is constant across samples under the Gauss–Markov Assumptions. Consequently, the $Y_t$ are also no longer uncorrelated; instead $\text{cov}(Y_t, Y_{t'}) = \text{E}(\varepsilon_t \varepsilon_{t'}) = \sigma_{|t-t'|}$. The covariance terms in Equations 11.1 and 11.2 are not all zero, as they have been in our earlier analyses. With serially correlated disturbances, then, the variance of linear estimators no longer reduces to

$$\sum_{t=1}^{T} w_t^2 \text{var}(Y_t),$$

but instead remains equal to

$$\sum_{t=1}^{T} w_t^2 \text{var}(Y_t) + \sum_{t=1}^{T} \sum_{\substack{t'=1 \\ t' \neq t}}^{T} w_t w_{t'} \text{cov}(Y_t, Y_{t'}).$$

In this DGP, the variance of $Y_t$ is the same as that of the $\varepsilon_t$, $\sigma^2$, because the $Y_t$ differ from the $\varepsilon_t$ by only $[\beta_0 + \beta_1 X_{1t} + \cdots + \beta_k X_{kt}]$, which is a constant across samples. Similarly, the covariance of the $Y$'s equals $\text{E}(\varepsilon_t \varepsilon_{t'})$, which we denote by $\sigma_{|t-t'|}$. Thus, when disturbances are serially correlated, we can write the variance of $g$ as

$$\text{var}(g) = \sigma^2 \sum_{t=1}^{T} w_t^2 + \sum_{t=1}^{T} \sum_{\substack{t'=1 \\ t' \neq t}}^{T} w_t w_{t'} \sigma_{tt'}$$

$$= \sigma^2 \sum_{t=1}^{T} w_t^2 + \sum_{t=1}^{T} \sum_{\substack{t'=1 \\ t' \neq t}}^{T} w_t w_{t'} \sigma_{|t-t'|}.$$

This last expression does not simplify to $\sigma^2 \Sigma w_t^2$, because the $\sigma_{|t-t'|}$ are not all equal to zero for differing $t$ and $t'$. Notice that if any of the $\sigma_{|t-t'|}$ are nonzero, we have a new expression for the variance of linear estimators. We can write the variance of $g$ more compactly as

$$\text{var}(g) = \sum_{t=1}^{T} \sum_{t'=1}^{T} w_t w_{t'} \sigma_{tt'} \qquad \text{11.3}$$

or as

$$\text{var}(g) = \sum_{t=1}^{T} \sum_{t'=1}^{T} w_t w_{t'} \sigma_{|t-t'|},$$

because we have adopted the convention that $\sigma_0 = \sigma^2$.

The altered expression for the variance of a linear estimator alters the BLUE estimator for the slopes and intercept of a regression line. Minimizing

$$\text{var}(g) = \sum_{t=1}^{T} \sum_{t'=1}^{T} w_t w_{t'} \sigma_{|t-t'|}$$

with respect to $w_1, \ldots, w_T$, subject to the (unchanged) unbiasedness constraints does not lead to OLS. (OLS followed from minimizing $\sigma^2 \Sigma w_t^2$.) Because OLS is no longer BLUE, OLS is no longer efficient. One task for this chapter is to find what estimators are BLUE, and therefore efficient, in the face of serial correlation.

## The Biased Standard Estimator of $\text{Var}(\hat{\beta}_1)$

To understand how serial correlation alters the variance of the OLS estimator, consider serially correlated disturbances in a DGP that has a single explanator and an unknown intercept. In this case, $\hat{\beta}_1$ is no longer the BLUE estimator of $\beta_1$, and the variance of $\hat{\beta}_1$ is no longer $\sigma^2 / \sum x_t^2$. Instead,

$$\text{var}(\hat{\beta}_1) = \sum_t \sum_{t'} w_t w_{t'} \sigma_{|t-t'|} = \sum_t \sum_{t'} \frac{x_t x_{t'}}{\left( \sum_k x_k^2 \right)^2} \sigma_{|t-t'|},$$

because the weights for OLS are $w_i = x_i / \Sigma x_k^2$, $i = 1, \ldots, T$.

The $\text{var}(\hat{\beta}_1)$ converges to zero as the sample size grows, as long as $\sigma_{|t-t'|}$ shrinks quickly enough as $|t - t'|$ grows large. We often rely on $\sigma_{|t-t'|}$ shrinking fast enough that $\hat{\beta}_1$ collapses around the true value of $\beta_1$; in effect, we assume that shocks to the economy that occurred in the distant past tend to have little effect in the present, so that the correlation between $\varepsilon_t$ and $\varepsilon_{t'}$ grows small as $|t - t'|$ grows large.

*Because $\text{var}(\hat{\beta}_1)$ is no longer $\sigma^2/\sum x_t^2$, serial correlation undermines the validity of the t-tests and F-tests devised in Chapters 7 and 9.* As is the case with heteroskedasticity, we would be mistaken to estimate the variance of $\hat{\beta}_1$ by $s^2/\sum x_t^2$, as is appropriate under the Gauss–Markov Assumptions. Recall, $s^2 = \frac{1}{T-k-1}\sum e_t^2$, where the $e_t$ are the OLS residuals. The standard $t$-test for $\hat{\beta}_1$, which relies on

$$t = \frac{\hat{\beta}_1 - \beta_1^0}{\sqrt{s^2/\sum x_t^2}},$$

is also incorrect because it depends on this mistaken estimator of the variance of $\hat{\beta}_1$. *If X is growing over time and there is positive serial correlation among the disturbances, $s^2/\sum x_t^2$ underestimates the variance of $\hat{\beta}_1$, misleading us about the precision of the OLS estimator and too often rejecting true null hypotheses about $\beta_1$.* The F-test developed in Chapter 9 relies on $\sigma^2$, estimated by $s^2$, in a similar fashion, and is consequently not the appropriate procedure for testing hypotheses about linear combinations of the slope and intercept if the disturbances are serially correlated.

Test statistics developed for OLS in the multiple regression case are similarly flawed when the disturbances are serially correlated. In both the bivariate and the multiple regression models, when disturbances are positively serially correlated, OLS-based $t$-tests and $F$-tests reject a true null hypothesis more often than the stated significance level of the test claims; that is, the size of these tests is distorted by serially correlated disturbances. Furthermore, when the disturbances are positively serially correlated, the calculated power of OLS-based tests tends to overstate the actual power of such tests. Understated significance levels and overstated power are serious deficiencies, but despite these deficiencies, serial correlation in the disturbances does not make the standard OLS-based tests biased or inconsistent; that is, the significance level of the tests is not higher than the power for any alternative, and as the sample size grows, the power of the tests approaches one for any true alternative hypothesis as the sample.

## The Newey–West Serial Correlation Consistent Standard Error Estimator

If $s^2/\sum x_t^2$ is no longer an unbiased estimator of the variance of $\hat{\beta}_1$, we need an alternative estimator that performs better. White's heteroskedasticity-consistent variance estimator for $\hat{\beta}_1$, developed in Chapter 10, suggests a strategy for estimating the variance of $\hat{\beta}_1$ when the disturbances are serially correlated. For simplicity, let's continue to consider the special case of serially correlated disturbances in a DGP with a single explanator and an unknown intercept. Substituting the OLS weights into Equation 11.3, the variance of $\hat{\beta}_1$ when the disturbances are serially correlated is

$$\text{var}(\hat{\beta}_1) = \sum_t \sum_{t'} w_t w_{t'} \sigma_{tt'} = \sum_t \sum_{t'} \frac{x_t x_{t'}}{\left(\sum_m x_m^2\right)^2} \sigma_{tt'}. \qquad \textbf{11.4}$$

Can we estimate well the variance of $\hat{\beta}_1$ given by Equation 11.4 by following the spirit of White's approach to heteroskedasticity? That is, can we estimate $\text{var}(\hat{\beta}_1)$ well by replacing each $\sigma_{tt'} = \text{E}(\varepsilon_t \varepsilon_{t'})$ in Equation 11.4 by its sample analog, $(e_t e_{t'})$, the product of the OLS residuals for observations $t$ and $t'$,

$$\tilde{\text{var}}(\hat{\beta}_1) = \sum_t \sum_{t'} \frac{x_t x_{t'}}{\left(\sum_m x_m^2\right)^2} e_t e_{t'}? \qquad \textbf{11.5}$$

Unfortunately, there is an important difference between White's heteroskedasticity problem and the serial correlation problem here that undermines the application of White's strategy to the serial correlation problem. White's expression for the variance of $\hat{\beta}_1$ in the face of heteroskedasticity involved one unknown variance for each observation. Here, there are $1/2\, T(T-1)$ distinct correlations among the disturbances (if $\text{cov}(\varepsilon_{t-j}, \varepsilon_t)$ were not equal to $\text{cov}(\varepsilon_t, \varepsilon_{t-j})$, there would be $T(T-1)$ correlations). This large and rapidly growing number of covariances makes the estimator of $\tilde{\text{var}}(\hat{\beta}_1)$ suggested in Equation 11.5 unsuitable for use. Even as $T$ grows very large, $\tilde{\text{var}}(\hat{\beta}_1)$ remains a biased estimator.

Fortunately, econometricians Whitney Newey of MIT and Ken West of the University of Wisconsin, have proposed a modified version of $\tilde{\text{var}}(\hat{\beta}_1)$ that is an unbiased estimator of $\text{var}(\hat{\beta}_1)$ in large samples. The **Newey–West heteroskedasticity and serial correlation consistent variance estimator** is an attractive estimator of the variances of the OLS coefficient estimators when disturbances are heteroskedastic or serially correlated, or both. The estimator is called "consistent" because in large samples, its distribution collapses around the true value. The Newey–West estimator requires the user to choose a lag, $L$, for example, four periods, beyond which serial correlation is small enough to ignore, that is $\sigma_{|t-t'|} \approx 0$ for all $|t-t'| > L$. In most applications, the covariance of $\varepsilon_t$ and $\varepsilon_{t-j}$ do shrink markedly as $j$ grows, so choosing an appropriate $L$ is feasible—values from 2 to 4 in annual or quarterly data and up to 12 in monthly data usually suffice. The Newey–West procedure extends to support consistent $t$- and $F$-tests in multiple regression models with serially correlated disturbances.[3]

Both White's heteroskedasticity consistent variance estimator and the Newey–West variance estimator are unbiased in large samples in the face of heteroskedasticity. White's estimator is more efficient if there is heteroskedasticity and no serial correlation. When the disturbances satisfy the Gauss–Markov Assumptions, the standard OLS variance estimator is more efficient than either the White or Newey–West estimators. Most econometric software packages report the standard variance estimates as a matter of course and either the White or Newey–West estimator upon request.

## 11.3    Tests for Serial Correlation

HOW DO WE TEST HYPOTHESES?

Because OLS is inefficient and standard OLS-based test procedures are invalid when the disturbances are correlated, we should test the hypothesis of serially uncorrelated disturbances before relying on OLS and its standard test procedures. This section introduces two formal statistical tests of the null hypothesis of serially uncorrelated disturbances. Both tests ask whether the OLS residuals are correlated with one another. If the residuals prove correlated, we reject the hypothesis that the disturbances are serially uncorrelated.

### The Durbin–Watson Test

James Durbin of the London School of Economics and G. S. Watson of Princeton University offered economists their first test statistic for serially correlated disturbances.[4] The Durbin–Watson statistic focuses on the correlation between adjacent disturbances, $\varepsilon_t$ and $\varepsilon_{t-1}$. Correlation between adjacent disturbances is called **first-order serial correlation**. Because the disturbances are unobserved, Durbin and Watson suggest we examine the correlation between adjacent OLS residuals instead. The strategy of using observed residuals in place of unobserved disturbances appears frequently in econometrics.

The **Durbin–Watson statistic** is defined as

$$d = \sum_{t=2}^{T} (e_t - e_{t-1})^2 / \sum_{t=1}^{T} e_t^2.$$

It is not transparent that $d$ can reveal the presence of serial correlation. To see how this statistic can, indeed, reveal the presence of serial correlation, we rewrite the Durbin–Watson statistic as

$$d = \left[ \sum_{t=2}^{T} \left( e_t^2 + e_{t-1}^2 - 2e_t e_{t-1} \right) \right] / \sum_{t=1}^{T} e_t^2$$

or

$$d = \left( \sum_{t=2}^{T} e_t^2 + \sum_{t=2}^{T} e_{t-1}^2 - 2 \sum_{t=2}^{T} e_t e_{t-1} \right) / \sum_{t=1}^{T} e_t^2.$$

In large samples, we can divide the numerator by $(T - k - 2)$ and the denominator by $(T - k - 1)$ without much altering the value of the statistic:

$$d \approx \left[ \frac{1}{T-k-2} \left( \sum_{t=2}^{T} e_t^2 + \sum_{t=2}^{T} e_{t-1}^2 - 2 \sum_{t=2}^{T} e_t e_{t-1} \right) \right] \Bigg/ \left[ \frac{1}{T-k-1} \sum_{t=1}^{T} e_t^2 \right]$$

$$= \left[ \frac{1}{T-k-2} \left( \sum_{t=2}^{T} e_t^2 + \frac{1}{T-k-2} \sum_{t=2}^{T} e_{t-1}^2 - \frac{2}{T-k-2} \sum_{t=2}^{T} e_t e_{t-1} \right) \right] \Bigg/$$

$$\left[ \frac{1}{T-k-1} \sum_{t=1}^{T} e_t^2 \right].$$

**11.6**

In the denominator in Equation 11.6, and in the first two terms of the numerator, we have estimators of the variance of the disturbances. In large samples, these estimators collapse around the true variance of the disturbances. Similarly, the third term in the numerator in Equation 11.6 collapses around the covariance between adjacent disturbances. Consequently, in large samples, $d$ will collapse around

$$\frac{[2\sigma_u^2 - 2\text{cov}(u_t, u_{t-1})]}{\sigma_u^2} = 2 - \frac{2\text{cov}(u_t, u_{t-1})}{\sigma_u^2}.$$

**11.7**

Values of $d$ far from two are indicative of serial correlation between adjacent disturbances. The correlation coefficient, $\rho$, between adjacent disturbances is the ratio of the covariance of $\varepsilon_t$ and $\varepsilon_{t-1}$ to their common variance, $\sigma^2$. This correlation coefficient is the rightmost term of Equation 11.7. The correlation coefficient is at its largest when adjacent disturbances are perfectly positively correlated—the covariance equals $\sigma^2$ in that case, and $\rho = 1$. The ratio is at its smallest when adjacent disturbances are perfectly negatively correlated—the covariance equals $-\sigma^2$ in that case, and $\rho = -1$. These bounds on the correlation between $\varepsilon_t$ and $\varepsilon_{t-1}$ imply that the Durbin–Watson statistic is bounded between zero (when adjacent disturbances are perfectly positively correlated) and four (when adjacent disturbances are perfectly negatively correlated). If there is no correlation between adjacent disturbances, we can expect a Durbin–Watson statistic close to two. *Note that the Durbin–Watson statistic only exposes first-order serial correlation; it is insensitive to correlations between disturbances that are not adjacent.*

## Critical Values for the Durbin–Watson Statistic

Unfortunately, the distribution of the $d$ statistic depends on both the number of regressors in the model *and* on the correlation structure of those explanators. Durbin and Watson performed a great service for econometricians by computing critical values for the $d$-statistic under various scenarios, including two extreme versions of the correlation structure among the explanators.

For a given significance level and a given number of slope coefficients, a table for the Durbin–Watson statistic contains two critical values, one effectively an upper bound for the critical value, the other effectively a lower bound. The "true" critical value, which will lie between these two extremes, depends on the actual correlation structure of the explanators in a given data set. Table 11.1 contains the upper and lower critical values for a 5% significance level.

Figure 11.3, Panel A, illustrates the possibilities for a model with 20 observations and a significance level of .05, with the null hypothesis of no correlation between adjacent disturbances (that is, that $\rho = 0$) against the one-sided alternative that adjacent disturbances are positively correlated (that is, that $\rho > 0$). Whether to do a one-sided or two-sided test depends on whether we admit both positive and negative serial correlations as possible alternatives if there is serial correlation, or admit only positive correlations. Few economic applications would exclude positive serial correlation from the outset. In the figure, the lower and upper bounds on the critical value are $d_L$ and $d_U$.

In a one-sided test with an alternative hypothesis of positive serial correlation (that is, $\rho > 0$), if the Durbin–Watson statistic, $d$, is *less* than $d_L$, we confidently *reject* at the .05 significance level the null hypothesis of no first-order correlation among the disturbances. If $d$ is *greater* than $d_U$, we confidently fail to reject the null at the .05 significance level. If $d$ lies *between* $d_L$ and $d_U$, we are *uncertain* whether to reject or fail to reject the null hypothesis.

Because the Durbin–Watson statistic is symmetric around two, the critical regions above two lie exactly as far above two as their counterparts fall below two. Figure 11.3, Panel B, illustrates the possibilities for a model with 20 observations and a significance level of .05, with the null hypothesis of no serial correlation (that is, that $\rho = 0$) against the two-sided alternative of some sort of serial correlation (that is, that $\rho \neq 0$). In this case, there are two uncertain regions, as well as two regions of rejection and failure to reject. Table 11.2 summarizes the possible test outcomes for the Durbin–Watson test.

When using the Durbin–Watson statistic, we must keep three warnings in mind:

1. The Durbin–Watson statistic may be low or be high for reasons other than $E(\varepsilon_t \varepsilon_{t-1})$ being nonzero; for example, wrongly omitted explanators, especially a wrongly omitted explanator that is the lagged value of the dependent variable, can cause the Durbin–Watson statistic to be low.

2. $E(\varepsilon_t \varepsilon_{t-1})$ being zero does not prevent disturbances from being correlated at *other* lags—the Durbin–Watson statistic has low power against correlations in the disturbances that begin at a lag of more than one period.

3. For reasons too advanced for discussion here, the Durbin–Watson statistic should not be used when there are lagged values of the dependent variable included among the explanators.[5]

**TABLE 11.1** Upper and Lower Critical Values for the Durbin–Watson Statistic (5% significance level)

| $j$ $n$ | $k = 1$ $d_L$ | $d_U$ | $k = 2$ $d_L$ | $d_U$ | $k = 3$ $d_L$ | $d_U$ | $k = 4$ $d_L$ | $d_U$ | $k = 5$ $d_L$ | $d_U$ |
|----|-------|-------|-------|-------|-------|-------|-------|-------|-------|-------|
| 6  | 0.610 | 1.400 | —     | —     | —     | —     | —     | —     | —     | —     |
| 7  | 0.700 | 1.356 | 0.467 | 1.896 | —     | —     | —     | —     | —     | —     |
| 8  | 0.763 | 1.332 | 0.559 | 1.777 | 0.368 | 2.287 | —     | —     | —     | —     |
| 9  | 0.824 | 1.320 | 0.629 | 1.699 | 0.455 | 2.128 | 0.296 | 2.588 | —     | —     |
| 10 | 0.879 | 1.320 | 0.697 | 1.641 | 0.525 | 2.016 | 0.376 | 2.414 | 0.243 | 2.822 |
| 11 | 0.927 | 1.324 | 0.658 | 1.604 | 0.595 | 1.928 | 0.444 | 2.283 | 0.316 | 2.645 |
| 12 | 0.971 | 1.331 | 0.812 | 1.579 | 0.658 | 1.864 | 0.512 | 2.177 | 0.379 | 2.506 |
| 13 | 1.010 | 1.340 | 0.861 | 1.562 | 0.715 | 1.816 | 0.574 | 2.094 | 0.445 | 2.390 |
| 14 | 1.045 | 1.350 | 0.905 | 1.551 | 0.767 | 1.779 | 0.632 | 2.030 | 0.505 | 2.296 |
| 15 | 1.077 | 1.361 | 0.946 | 1.543 | 0.814 | 1.750 | 0.685 | 1.977 | 0.562 | 2.220 |
| 16 | 1.106 | 1.371 | 0.982 | 1.539 | 0.857 | 1.728 | 0.734 | 1.935 | 0.615 | 2.157 |
| 17 | 1.133 | 1.381 | 1.015 | 1.536 | 0.897 | 1.710 | 0.779 | 1.900 | 0.664 | 2.104 |
| 18 | 1.158 | 1.391 | 1.046 | 1.535 | 0.933 | 1.696 | 0.820 | 1.872 | 0.710 | 2.060 |
| 19 | 1.180 | 1.401 | 1.074 | 1.536 | 0.967 | 1.685 | 0.859 | 1.848 | 0.752 | 2.023 |
| 20 | 1.201 | 1.411 | 1.100 | 1.537 | 0.998 | 1.676 | 0.894 | 1.828 | 0.792 | 1.991 |
| 21 | 1.221 | 1.420 | 1.125 | 1.538 | 1.026 | 1.669 | 0.927 | 1.812 | 0.829 | 1.964 |
| 22 | 1.239 | 1.429 | 1.147 | 1.541 | 1.053 | 1.664 | 0.958 | 1.797 | 0.863 | 1.940 |
| 23 | 1.257 | 1.437 | 1.168 | 1.543 | 1.078 | 1.660 | 0.986 | 1.785 | 0.895 | 1.920 |
| 24 | 1.273 | 1.446 | 1.188 | 1.546 | 1.101 | 1.656 | 1.013 | 1.775 | 0.925 | 1.902 |
| 25 | 1.288 | 1.454 | 1.206 | 1.550 | 1.123 | 1.654 | 1.038 | 1.767 | 0.953 | 1.886 |
| 26 | 1.302 | 1.461 | 1.224 | 1.553 | 1.143 | 1.652 | 1.062 | 1.759 | 0.979 | 1.873 |
| 27 | 1.316 | 1.469 | 1.240 | 1.556 | 1.162 | 1.651 | 1.084 | 1.753 | 1.004 | 1.861 |
| 28 | 1.328 | 1.476 | 1.255 | 1.560 | 1.181 | 1.650 | 1.104 | 1.747 | 1.028 | 1.850 |
| 29 | 1.341 | 1.483 | 1.270 | 1.563 | 1.198 | 1.650 | 1.124 | 1.743 | 1.050 | 1.841 |
| 30 | 1.352 | 1.489 | 1.284 | 1.567 | 1.214 | 1.650 | 1.143 | 1.739 | 1.071 | 1.833 |

*continues*

**TABLE 11.1** (*continued*)

| $j$ | $k = 1$ | | $k = 2$ | | $k = 3$ | | $k = 4$ | | $k = 5$ | |
|---|---|---|---|---|---|---|---|---|---|---|
| $n$ | $d_L$ | $d_U$ | $d_L$ | $d_U$ | $d_L$ | $d_U$ | $d_L$ | $d_U$ | $d_L$ | $d_U$ |
| 31 | 1.363 | 1.496 | 1.297 | 1.570 | 1.229 | 1.650 | 1.160 | 1.735 | 1.090 | 1.825 |
| 32 | 1.373 | 1.502 | 1.309 | 1.574 | 1.244 | 1.650 | 1.177 | 1.732 | 1.109 | 1.819 |
| 33 | 1.383 | 1.508 | 1.321 | 1.577 | 1.258 | 1.651 | 1.193 | 1.730 | 1.127 | 1.813 |
| 34 | 1.393 | 1.514 | 1.333 | 1.580 | 1.271 | 1.652 | 1.208 | 1.728 | 1.144 | 1.808 |
| 35 | 1.402 | 1.519 | 1.343 | 1.584 | 1.283 | 1.653 | 1.222 | 1.726 | 1.160 | 1.803 |
| 36 | 1.411 | 1.525 | 1.354 | 1.587 | 1.295 | 1.654 | 1.236 | 1.724 | 1.175 | 1.799 |
| 37 | 1.419 | 1.530 | 1.364 | 1.590 | 1.307 | 1.655 | 1.249 | 1.723 | 1.190 | 1.795 |
| 38 | 1.427 | 1.535 | 1.373 | 1.594 | 1.318 | 1.656 | 1.261 | 1.722 | 1.204 | 1.792 |
| 39 | 1.435 | 1.540 | 1.382 | 1.597 | 1.328 | 1.658 | 1.273 | 1.722 | 1.218 | 1.789 |
| 40 | 1.442 | 1.544 | 1.391 | 1.600 | 1.338 | 1.659 | 1.285 | 1.721 | 1.230 | 1.786 |
| 45 | 1.475 | 1.566 | 1.430 | 1.615 | 1.383 | 1.666 | 1.336 | 1.720 | 1.287 | 1.776 |
| 50 | 1.503 | 1.585 | 1.462 | 1.628 | 1.421 | 1.674 | 1.378 | 1.721 | 1.335 | 1.771 |
| 55 | 1.528 | 1.601 | 1.490 | 1.641 | 1.452 | 1.681 | 1.414 | 1.724 | 1.374 | 1.768 |
| 60 | 1.549 | 1.616 | 1.514 | 1.652 | 1.480 | 1.689 | 1.444 | 1.727 | 1.408 | 1.767 |
| 65 | 1.567 | 1.629 | 1.536 | 1.662 | 1.503 | 1.696 | 1.471 | 1.731 | 1.438 | 1.767 |
| 70 | 1.583 | 1.641 | 1.554 | 1.672 | 1.525 | 1.703 | 1.494 | 1.735 | 1.464 | 1.768 |
| 75 | 1.598 | 1.652 | 1.571 | 1.680 | 1.543 | 1.709 | 1.515 | 1.739 | 1.487 | 1.770 |
| 80 | 1.611 | 1.662 | 1.586 | 1.688 | 1.560 | 1.715 | 1.534 | 1.743 | 1.507 | 1.772 |
| 85 | 1.624 | 1.671 | 1.600 | 1.696 | 1.575 | 1.721 | 1.550 | 1.747 | 1.525 | 1.774 |
| 90 | 1.635 | 1.679 | 1.612 | 1.703 | 1.589 | 1.726 | 1.566 | 1.751 | 1.542 | 1.776 |
| 95 | 1.645 | 1.687 | 1.623 | 1.709 | 1.602 | 1.732 | 1.579 | 1.755 | 1.557 | 1.778 |
| 100 | 1.654 | 1.694 | 1.634 | 1.715 | 1.613 | 1.736 | 1.592 | 1.758 | 1.571 | 1.780 |
| 150 | 1.720 | 1.746 | 1.706 | 1.760 | 1.693 | 1.774 | 1.679 | 1.788 | 1.665 | 1.802 |
| 200 | 1.758 | 1.778 | 1.748 | 1.789 | 1.738 | 1.799 | 1.728 | 1.810 | 1.718 | 1.820 |

*Note:* $n$ = number of observations; $k$ = number of explanatory variables excluding the constant term.

Adapted from N. E. Savin and K. J. White, "The Durbin–Watson Test for Serial Correlation, with Extreme Small Samples or Many Regressors," *Econometrica*, 45, (Nov 1997): 1989–1996.

**Figure 11.3**

Durbin–Watson
Lower and Upper
Critical Values for
$n = 20$ and a Single
Explanator, $\alpha = 0.5$

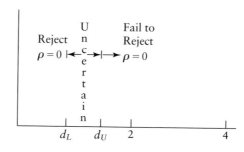

Panel A
One Tail

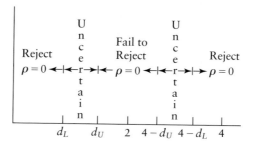

Panel B
Two Tail

**TABLE 11.2 The Durbin–Watson Test**

| *One-sided Test Against $\rho > 0$* | | |
|---|---|---|
| $d < d_L$ | $d_L < d < d_U$ | $d > d_U$ |
| Reject $H_0$ | Inconclusive | Fail to Reject $H_0$ |
| *One-sided Test Against $\rho < 0$* | | |
| $d > (4 - d_L)$ | $(4 - d_U) < d < (4 - d_L)$ | $d < (4 - d_U)$ |
| Reject $H_0$ | Inconclusive | Fail to Reject $H_0$ |
| *Two-sided Test Against $\rho \neq 0$* | | |
| $d < d_L$ | $d_L < d < d_U$ | $d > d_U$ |
| **or** | **or** | **or** |
| $d > (4 - d_L)$ | $(4 - d_U) < d < (4 - d_L)$ | $d < (4 - d_U)$ |
| Reject $H_0$ | Inconclusive | Fail to Reject $H_0$ |

## The Breusch–Godfrey Test

Econometricians Trevor Breusch of the Australian National University and Leslie Godfrey of York University have proposed an alternative to the Durbin–Watson test. Like the Breusch–Pagan test for heteroskedasticity, the **Breusch–Godfrey test** for serial correlation is based on a regression in which residuals appear. The dependent variable in this auxiliary regression is the OLS residual from the equation of basic interest. The explanators in the auxiliary equation include the $X$'s from the equation of interest and some number of lagged residuals. If the lagged residuals explain enough of the variation of the current residual, we reject the null hypothesis of serially uncorrelated disturbances. Breusch and Godfrey tell us how to determine how much explanation is enough.

The Breusch–Godfrey test has three steps:

1. Estimate the equation of interest by OLS.
2. Regress the residuals from step 1 against the explanators in that equation of interest (the $X$'s) and some chosen number, $L$, of the residuals' lagged values:

$$e_t = a_0 + a_1 X_{1t} + \cdots + a_k X_{kt} + a_{k+1} e_{t-1} + \cdots + a_{k+L} e_{t-L} + v_t.$$

3. If $TR^2$ from the auxiliary regression in step 2 exceeds the critical value at the chosen level of significance for a chi-square statistic with $L$ degrees of freedom, reject the null of serially uncorrelated disturbances.

With annual data, choices of $L$ between 2 and 4 are common. With quarterly data, choices of 4 or 8 are common. With monthly data, choices of 12 or 24 are common. Unlike the Durbin–Watson test, the Breusch–Godfrey test is sensitive to correlations between disturbances that are not adjacent to one another, as well as to correlations between adjacent disturbances. The choice of $L$ determines the degree of this sensitivity.

The chi-square distribution of the $TR^2$ statistic in step 3 applies strictly only in large samples. In small samples, relying on $TR^2$ following the chi-square distribution is often unwarranted—the Breusch–Godfrey test often suffers distorted sizes in small samples; that is, its stated significance levels are often incorrect. For analyses using small samples, it is preferable to modify the Breusch–Godfrey procedure by replacing the chi-square test in step 3 with an $F$-test of the hypothesis that the lagged residuals in the auxiliary regression in step 2 all have zero coefficients.

The Durbin–Watson statistic focuses on $E(\varepsilon_t \varepsilon_{t-1})$ alone. In addition, the Breusch–Godfrey test takes into account correlations among disturbances lagged more than once. This difference makes the two tests powerful in different circumstances. The Durbin–Watson test is more powerful than the Breusch–Godfrey test when $E(\varepsilon_t \varepsilon_{t-j})$ is markedly greater for $j = 1$ than for $j > 1$. For example, the Durbin–Watson test is more powerful than the Breusch–Godfrey test when the disturbances follow the particular form of serial correlation studied at length later in this chapter. The Breusch–Godfrey test is more powerful than the Durbin–Watson statistic when $E(\varepsilon_t\varepsilon_{t-1})$ is small but $E(\varepsilon_t\varepsilon_{t-j})$ is not small for some $j$ other than 1. For example, in quarterly data, there might be seasonal effects that would make observations correlated at intervals of one year (that is, at a lag of four quarters), even if the observations were uncorrelated at a lag of one quarter.

## An Example of Checking for Serial Correlation

Serial correlation in the disturbances is a technical statistical consideration that often arises as we grapple with substantive economic questions. Usually the economic question comes first, followed by an econometric analysis that may be influenced by serial correlation. For example, economists wonder how much unemployment affects poverty—one consequence of increased unemployment is increased poverty. When more people are out of work, more people live below the level of income that the Federal government calls "the poverty line." In 2003, the poverty line for a family of four was an income slightly above $18,400 per year. How much, economists ask, does the poverty rate rise when the unemployment rate rises? The econometric analysis of this question encounters serially correlated disturbances.

Table 11.3 reports the EViews output for an OLS regression of the U.S. poverty rate against the U.S. unemployment rate with data from 1980 to 2003.

**TABLE 11.3 Poverty and Unemployment 1980–2003 (OLS)**

Dependent Variable: POVERTY RATE
Method: Least Squares
Sample: 1980 2003
Included observations: 24

| Variable | Coefficient | Std. Error | t-Statistic | Prob. |
|---|---|---|---|---|
| C | 9.792052 | 0.611186 | 16.02138 | 0.0000 |
| UNEMPLOY. RATE | 0.586614 | 0.094726 | 6.192734 | 0.0000 |
| R-squared | 0.635460 | Mean dependent var | | 13.47917 |
| Adjusted R-squared | 0.618890 | S.D. dependent var | | 1.095437 |
| S.E. of regression | 0.676259 | Akaike info criterion | | 2.135173 |
| Sum squared resid | 10.06116 | Schwarz criterion | | 2.233344 |
| Log likelihood | −23.62207 | F-statistic | | 38.34995 |
| Durbin–Watson stat | 0.323725 | Prob(F-statistic) | | 0.000003 |

The data are contained in the file poverty1.*** on this book's companion Web site (**www.aw-bc.com/murray**).

The OLS estimates in Table 11.3 indicate that for each one percentage point rise in the unemployment rate, the poverty rate rises by almost six tenths of a percentage point. Because the U.S. population is about twice the size of the labor force, these rate numbers translate into each additional unemployed person bringing 1.17 more people into poverty. Are the $t$-statistics in Table 11.3 credible? Look at the Durbin–Watson statistic, 0.32. The lower bound of the critical value for the $d$ statistic with $T = 24$ and one slope coefficient is 1.27, so we reject the null hypothesis of serially uncorrelated disturbances.

Table 11.4 contains the auxiliary regression for the Breusch–Godfrey test. The test statistic is $0.76 \cdot 22 = 16.72$. The 5% critical value for a chi-square statistic with two degrees of freedom is 5.99. The Breusch–Godfrey test also rejects the null hypothesis of serially uncorrelated disturbances.

The estimated standard errors in Table 11.3 are biased; the positive serial correlation in the disturbances is probably imparting a downward bias in those estimated standard errors. Thus, we cannot assess the statistical properties of the estimates in the table with the information in hand. The remaining sections of this

**TABLE 11.4** The Breusch–Godfrey Auxiliary Regression for Poverty and Unemployment

Dependent Variable: RESID
Method; Least Squares
Sample (adjusted): 1982 2003
Included observations: 22 after adjustments

| Variable | Coefficient | Std. Error | t-Statistic | Prob. |
|---|---|---|---|---|
| C | −0.77352 | 0.386543 | −2.001119 | 0.0607 |
| UNEMPLOY | 0.121246 | 0.060607 | 2.000527 | 0.0608 |
| RESID(−1) | 0.70975 | 0.219957 | 3.226764 | 0.0047 |
| RESID(−2) | 0.264418 | 0.246816 | 1.071313 | 0.2982 |
| R-squared | 0.764423 | Mean dependent var | | 0.057323 |
| Adjusted R-squared | 0.72516 | S.D. dependent var | | 0.651709 |
| S.E. of regression | 0.341659 | Akaike info criterion | | 0.852961 |
| Sum squared resid | 2.101161 | Schwarz criterion | | 1.051333 |
| Log likelihood | −5.38257 | F-statistic | | 19.46936 |
| Durbin–Watson stat | 1.869066 | Prob(F-statistic) | | 0.000007 |

chapter discuss how we might efficiently estimate the relationship between poverty and unemployment and how we might test hypotheses about that relationship. First, however, we see that omitted variables can confuse serial correlation tests, just as they can confuse heteroskedasticity tests.

## Omitted Variables and Serial Correlation Tests

Serial correlation tests are valuable because they can alert us when serially correlated disturbances make OLS inefficient and make its estimated standard error misleading. However, serial correlation tests can also lead us to reject the null hypothesis of no serial correlation when the real problem is omitted variables or an inappropriate functional form. To better understand this potential problem with serial correlation tests, suppose the true model is

$$Y_t = \beta_0 + \beta_1 X_{1t} + \beta_2 X_{2t} + \varepsilon_t, \qquad\qquad \textbf{11.8}$$

but we estimate

$$Y_t = \beta_0 + \beta_1 X_{1t} + \nu_t, \qquad\qquad \textbf{11.9}$$

in which

$$\nu_t = \beta_2 X_{2t} + \varepsilon_t.$$

We learned in Chapter 8 that mistakenly omitting $X_2$ may bias the estimated coefficient for $X_1$. The new insight here is that if $X_2$ is serially correlated, the $\nu_t$ will also be serially correlated, even if the $\varepsilon_t$ are not. Omitted variables can be mistaken for serial correlation in the disturbances.

To illustrate how omitted variables can be mistaken for serial correlation, let us return to the augmented Phillips curve example from Chapter 8. The augmented Phillips curve involves two suppositions:

1. Employment is linked to unexpected surges in prices.
2. Last year's inflation is a good proxy for what price increases people expect this year.

In this model, the relationship between inflation and unemployment includes a third variable, last year's inflation. Table 11.5 contains the OLS regression results for the augmented Phillips curve estimated with data from 1958 to 2004. The data are contained in phillipsall.*** on this book's companion Web site (**www. aw-bc.com/murray**).

Because the augmented Phillips curve relationship includes a lagged dependent variable, the Durbin–Watson test is not valid. The Breusch–Godfrey statistic with residuals lagged once included in the auxiliary regression (the auxiliary regression is not shown) is 3.01, which is below 3.84, the .05 significance level for a

**TABLE 11.5  The Augmented Phillips Curve (OLS)**

Dependent Variable: INFL
Method: Least Squares
Sample: 1959 2004
Included observations: 46 after adjustments

| Variable | Coefficient | Std. Error | t-Statistic | Prob. |
|---|---|---|---|---|
| C | 0.038913 | 0.010023 | 3.882169 | 0.0004 |
| UNEMPLOY | −0.677368 | 0.194650 | −3.479923 | 0.0012 |
| INFL(−1) | 1.021775 | 0.093617 | 10.91446 | 0.0000 |
| R-squared | 0.753836 | Mean dependent var | | 0.041197 |
| Adjusted R-squared | 0.742415 | S.D. dependent var | | 0.029805 |
| S.E. of regression | 0.015127 | Akaike info criterion | | −5.481707 |
| Sum squared resid | 2.924930 | Schwarz criterion | | −5.362448 |
| Log likelihood | 129.0793 | F-statistic | | 65.84976 |
| Durbin–Watson stat | 1.533848 | Prob(F-statistic) | | 0.000000 |

chi-square statistic with one degree of freedom. Thus, we fail to reject the null hypothesis of no serial correlation in the disturbances. The augmented Phillips curve is an example of Equation 11.8, in which there are two explanators and serially uncorrelated disturbances.

The large $t$-statistic on expected inflation in Table 11.5 indicates that expected inflation does, indeed, belong in the model. The original Phillips curve model mistakenly specified a bivariate relationship between inflation and unemployment, with expected inflation omitted. The original Phillips curve relationship is an example of Equation 11.9, in which an explanator is omitted. Table 11.6 reports OLS estimates of the original Phillips curve model. The very low Durbin–Watson statistic there, 0.448, illustrates how omitting the explanator "expected inflation," which corresponds to $X_2$ in Equation 11.8, can result in disturbances, the $\nu_t$ in Equation 11.9, that indicate serial correlation. Because we know from the analysis of the augmented Phillips curve that the serial correlation is not attributable to serial correlation in the underlying disturbances, the $\varepsilon_t$ in Equation 11.8, it must be attributable to the omission of expected inflation from the model. The lesson? *Serial correlation tests may mistakenly indicate serial correlation if the model is not otherwise properly specified.*

**TABLE 11.6** The Original Phillips Curve (OLS)

Dependent Variable: INFL
Method: Least Squares
Sample: 1958 2004
Included observations: 47

| Variable | Coefficient | Std. Error | t-Statistic | Prob. |
|---|---|---|---|---|
| C | 0.008736 | 0.018306 | 0.477214 | 0.6355 |
| UNEMPLOY | 0.542127 | 0.300264 | 1.805503 | 0.0777 |
| R-squared | 0.067548 | Mean dependent var | | 0.040902 |
| Adjusted R-squared | 0.046827 | S.D. dependent var | | 0.029548 |
| S.E. of regression | 0.028848 | Akaike info criterion | | −4.21930 |
| Sum squared resid | 0.037449 | Schwarz criterion | | −4.133291 |
| Log likelihood | 100.9804 | F-statistic | | 3.259841 |
| Durbin–Watson stat | 0.448168 | Prob(F-statistic) | | 0.077688 |

Why does it matter whether a test indicates serial correlation or an omitted variable? Because the remedies for the two differ greatly. Notice that the estimated coefficient on unemployment in the misspecified model of Table 11.6 is misleadingly different from the corresponding estimate in the well-specified model of Table 11.5—the omitted variable bias in Table 11.6 is considerable. Estimating the original Phillips curve relationship using an estimator that would appropriately accommodate serially correlated disturbances would not overcome this omitted variables bias.

## 11.4    A DGP with First-Order Autoregressive Disturbances

**What Is the DGP?**

Section 11.2 noted that serial correlation, in its most general form, brings $(1/2)T(T-1)$ unknown covariance parameters, a number that quickly becomes much larger than $T$ as $T$ grows. So many unknown parameters can greatly complicate efficient estimation. To devise efficient estimators, we must forgo the general case and instead deal with special cases of serial correlation. In this and the next section, we focus on one special case that arises frequently in practice, called *first-order autoregressive disturbances*.

# An Econometric Top 40—A Classical Favorite

## Is Public Expenditure Productive?

From the 1930s to the late 1980s, macroeconomists viewed government spending as rather homogeneous. They asked whether government spending crowded out private investment, drove up interest rates, or spurred consumer spending. They argued whether funding government expenditures by taxation had different effects than funding by issuing new government debt. They gave relatively little attention, however, to the different ways the government spends its money—on defense, on roads, on food stamps, and so on. Economist David Aschauer of Bates College dramatically altered macroeconomists' view of government spending with a paper he wrote in 1989, however.[6] Aschauer's analysis places a particular kind of government spending—nonmilitary public investments, such as roads—at center stage. Aschauer finds government investment is so important for private sector productivity that a decline in public sector investment might account for much of the productivity slowdown observed in the 1970s and 1980s.

Aschauer asks whether private sector productivity is improved by public sector investments, and whether public sector investments have a different effect on private sector productivity than does other government spending. He assumes a Cobb–Douglas style of production function and uses two dependent variables—output and a measure of productivity called "total factor productivity—to study the effects of government spending on productivity." Aschauer assumes that both output and productivity depend on labor, the private capital stock, the public nonmilitary capital stock (for example, roads), and, perhaps, on other government spending. He also allows output to

depend on the intensity with which the capital stock is being used, as measured by the capacity utilization rate of the private sector.

When Aschauer estimates an output equation that accounts for labor, capital, capacity utilization, and a time trend, his Durbin–Watson statistic is 0.63. Either there is serial correlation in the model's underlying disturbances, or an important variable has been omitted. When Aschauer adds the public stock of nonmilitary capital to the output equation, the Durbin–Watson statistic no longer evidences serial correlation, and public capital becomes statistically significant. The public, nonmilitary capital stock is also significant in Aschauer's productivity equation. Public investment expenditures translate into higher private sector productivity and higher private sector output.

Aschauer finds no evidence of public military capital raising output or productivity, nor does he find the flow of spending on noncapital goods to have any effect on output or productivity. Public spending raises private sector productivity to the extent that public sector spending is on nonmilitary capital goods. How government spends its money matters! It is not government spending, as such, that spurs private productivity, but rather specific government investments in capital goods that makes the private sector more productive.

We could reasonably worry that the direction of causation runs not from government spending to output, but the other way around, from output (which translates into income) to government spending. But if this were the reason for Aschauer's findings, we would expect both military and nonmilitary capital to reflect such an effect of output on expenditure. The fact that only public-sector spending on nonmilitary capital goods shows a link with output suggests that the effect we see reflects a causal effect running from nonmilitary capital to output, and not the other way around. Note that asking which way causality runs is asking which variable is really the dependent variable in our analyses. Chapter 14 examines the particularly complex cases in which causality runs both ways, as would be the case if government spending affected output and output affected GDP.

 **Final Notes**

Aschauer's work has spurred an intensive research effort, undertaken by many economists, to identify the specific investments by government that are most productive and the channels through which those investments enhance private sector productivity. Where Aschauer focused on national productivity and the national public capital stock, others have focused on particular regions, on particular public investments, and on productivity gains in particular private sector activities. This evolution of the analysis from a broad aggregated perspective to an increasingly detailed and microeconomic perspective is instructive. Econometricians often first look for broad, easier to observe patterns in data and then follow up with more detailed studies in those areas where the broader studies suggest there is rich insight to be gained from the more difficult, intensive scrutiny.  ∎

To narrow our focus to a manageable (and empirically important) case, we assume that each period's disturbance includes two parts: first, an **innovation**, or fresh shock that hits the economy in the present period, with no link to the past (so this shock component is uncorrelated with past shocks); and second, an "inheritance" passed on from the previous period's disturbance, on the supposition that whatever made yesterday different from average will persist in its influence, at least partially, into today. (The unit of time need not be a day. It could be a month, a quarter, or a year.) Econometricians call such disturbances **autoregressive** and most commonly account for serial correlation by specifying autoregressive disturbances.

### Visualizing First-Order Autoregressive Disturbances

Figure 11.4 presents two illustrative samples of 75 autoregressive disturbances. Panel A shows innovations (the lines with open circles) and disturbances (the lines with solid circles) when 80% of the previous period's disturbance is inherited. Panel B shows a similar case, but with 98% of the previous period carrying forward. The innovations follow the Gauss–Markov Assumptions—they are mean zero, homoskedastic, and serially uncorrelated random variables. The disturbances themselves are the sum of a fresh innovation and a fraction (here 80% or 98%) of the previous period's disturbance. Autoregressive disturbances are correlated with one another. In particular, they are most highly correlated with their neighbors nearest in time. When the correlation is positive, as here, autoregressive disturbances tend

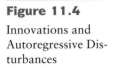

**Figure 11.4**

Innovations and
Autoregressive Dis-
turbances

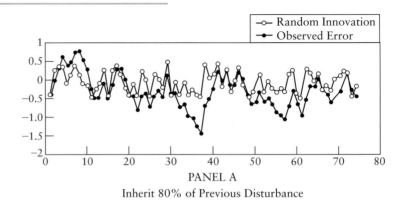

PANEL A
Inherit 80% of Previous Disturbance

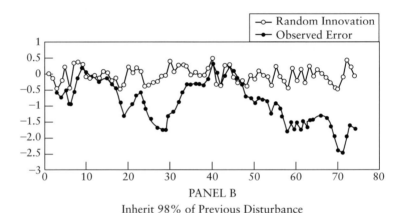

PANEL B
Inherit 98% of Previous Disturbance

to lie on the same side of average (zero) as their near-in-time neighbors. To see how inheriting a fraction of previous disturbances induces correlation in the disturbances, try the following exercise: Count the number of times the innovations switch from below average to above or vice versa. This is the number of times the lines with open circles cross the horizontal zero axis. The lines with open circles have about 30 crossings in Panel A and about 33 in Panel B. Next, count the number of crossings for the lines with solid circles. The lines with solid circles cross the horizontal zero axis about 15 times in Panel A and only 5 times in Panel B. Positively correlated autoregressive disturbances tend to lie on the same side of average (zero) as their near-in-time neighbors.

The Excel program that generated these samples, Autoregressor.xls, is available for download from this book's companion Web site (**www.aw-bc.com/murray**). The program allows the user to look at successive samples for a given degree of inheritance by pressing the F9 key on a PC. The program also allows the user to enter a new inheritance value to view successive samples with that degree of inheritance.

## The DGP

Mathematically, we express the two-part nature of the *first-order autoregressive disturbances* by

$$\varepsilon_t = \rho\varepsilon_{t-1} + \nu_t,$$

where $\varepsilon_t$ is the disturbance in period $t$, $\nu_t$ is the new shock (or innovation) in period $t$, $\rho$ is the fraction of one day's disturbance that carries over into the next, and $\rho\varepsilon_{t-1}$ is the inheritance today from yesterday's disturbance—that part of yesterday's disturbance that reappears in today's disturbance. Econometricians call $\rho$ the **autocorrelation coefficient**. Notice that the equation for $\varepsilon_t$ has the form of a regression relationship that connects $\varepsilon_t$ to its own lagged value, $\varepsilon_{t-1}$. Because "auto" means "self" in Greek, econometricians call these disturbances the $\varepsilon_t$, autoregressive. Furthermore, because $\varepsilon_t$ appears lagged only once on the right-hand side (there are no terms such as $\varepsilon_{t-2}$ or $\varepsilon_{t-3}$ appearing on the right-hand side of the equation), econometricians say that these disturbances follow a **first-order autoregressive process**, or that they are **first-order autoregressive disturbances.**

Our first special case of a DGP with serially correlated disturbances includes all of the Gauss–Markov Assumptions but one. Instead of assuming disturbances are uncorrelated, this new DGP assumes the disturbances follow a first-order autoregressive process. The DGP is

$$Y_t = \beta_0 + \beta_1 X_{1t} + \cdots + \beta_k X_{kt} + \varepsilon_t$$
$$\varepsilon_t = \rho\varepsilon_{t-1} + \nu_t \qquad |\rho| < 1$$
$$\mathrm{E}(\nu_t) = 0$$
$$\mathrm{var}(\nu_t) = \sigma_\nu^2$$
$$\mathrm{cov}(\nu_t, \nu_{t'}) = 0 \qquad t \neq t'$$

$X_t$'s are fixed across samples.

The assumption that $|\rho| < 1$ ensures that the correlations among the disturbances shrink toward zero as the observations become further apart in time. Notice that in this DGP, the innovations, the $\nu_t$, satisfy the Gauss–Markov Assumptions.

## How the Disturbances Are Correlated

The autoregressive structure of the disturbances in this DGP implies that the disturbances, the $\varepsilon_t$, are correlated, even though the innovations, the $\nu_t$, are uncorrelated. In particular, $\mathrm{cov}(\varepsilon_t, \varepsilon_{t-1}) \neq 0$. The proof of this claim begins by noting that because we will learn that $\mathrm{E}(\varepsilon_t) = 0$ for all $t$, $\mathrm{cov}(\varepsilon_t, \varepsilon_{t-1}) = \mathrm{E}(\varepsilon_t, \varepsilon_{t-1})$. Thus,

$$\mathrm{cov}(\varepsilon_t\varepsilon_{t-1}) = \mathrm{E}(\varepsilon_t\varepsilon_{t-1}) = \mathrm{E}([\rho\varepsilon_{t-1} + \nu_t]\varepsilon_{t-1})$$
$$= \mathrm{E}(\rho\varepsilon_{t-1}\varepsilon_{t-1} + \nu_t\varepsilon_{t-1}) = \mathrm{E}(\rho\varepsilon_{t-1}\varepsilon_{t-1}) + \mathrm{E}(\nu_t\varepsilon_{t-1}),$$

which, because $v_t$ is uncorrelated with anything from the past,

$$= \rho E(\varepsilon_{t-1} \varepsilon_{t-1}) = \rho \text{var}(\varepsilon_{t-1}),$$

which is not zero.

## The Mean and Variance of the Disturbances

What, then, are the mean and variance of $\varepsilon_{t-1}$? Because the DGP gives us the mean and variance of the innovations, the $v_t$, we can determine the mean and variance of the disturbances by first expressing the disturbances solely in terms of the innovations. To do this, note first that just as

$$\varepsilon_t = \rho \varepsilon_{t-1} + v_t, \tag{11.10}$$

$$\varepsilon_{t-1} = \rho \varepsilon_{t-2} + v_{t-1}. \tag{11.11}$$

We can therefore substitute the right-hand side of Equation 11.11 for $\varepsilon_{t-1}$ in Equation 11.10. This substitution yields

$$\varepsilon_t = \rho \varepsilon_{t-1} + v_t = \rho(\rho \varepsilon_{t-2} + v_{t-1}) + v_t$$

$$= \rho^2 \varepsilon_{t-2} + \rho v_{t-1} + v_t. \tag{11.12}$$

We can substitute for $\varepsilon_{t-2}$ in Equation 11.12 in the same way that we did for $\varepsilon_{t-1}$ in Equation 11.10, because

$$\varepsilon_{t-2} = \rho \varepsilon_{t-3} + v_{t-2}. \tag{11.13}$$

Substituting the right-hand side of Equation 11.13 for $\varepsilon_{t-2}$ in Equation 11.12 yields

$$\varepsilon_t = \rho^2[\rho \varepsilon_{t-3} + v_{t-2}] + \rho v_{t-1} + v_t$$

$$= \rho^3 \varepsilon_{t-3} + \rho^2 v_{t-2} + \rho v_{t-1} + v_t. \tag{11.14}$$

We could continue substituting in this way indefinitely, which would lead us in the end to

$$\varepsilon_t = v_t + \rho_{t-1} v + \rho^2 v_{t-2} + \rho^3 v_{t-3} + \rho^4 v_{t-4} + \ldots = \sum_{j=0}^{\infty} \rho^j v_{t-j}. \tag{11.15}$$

Thus, we discover that the first-order autoregressive scheme assumes shocks to the economic systems that never wither away entirely. Shocks from the past continue to have an effect forever, albeit a diminishing one. Notice that if $\rho$ were greater than one, shocks that occurred in the past would have an ever-increasing impact on the economic system and that if $\rho$ were one, each innovation would have the same effect in every subsequent period, with no shrinking. This chapter assumes $\rho$ is less than one in magnitude.

Equation 11.15 facilitates determining the mean and variance of $\varepsilon_t$. The expected value of $\sum_{j=0}^{\infty}\rho^j v_{t-j}$ in Equation 11.15 is zero, because each $v$ has a zero mean:

$$\mathrm{E}\left(\sum_{j=0}^{\infty}\rho^j v_{t-j}\right) = \sum_{j=0}^{\infty}\mathrm{E}(\rho^j v_{t-j}) = \sum_{j=0}^{\infty}\rho^j \mathrm{E}(v_{t-j}) = 0.$$

The variance of this same infinite sum is

$$\mathrm{var}(\varepsilon_t) = \mathrm{var}\left(\sum_{j=0}^{\infty}\rho^j v_{t-j}\right) = \sum_{j=0}^{\infty}\mathrm{var}(\rho^j v_{t-j}),$$

in which there are no covariance terms because the innovations are uncorrelated. Thus,

$$\mathrm{var}\,(\varepsilon_t) = \sum_{j=0}^{\infty}\rho^{2j}\mathrm{var}(v_{t-j})$$

$$= \sum_{j=0}^{\infty}\rho^{2j}\sigma_v^2 = \sigma_v^2\sum_{j=0}^{\infty}\rho^{2j} = \frac{\sigma_v^2}{1-\rho^2}.$$

Because this variance, which is denoted by $\sigma_\varepsilon^2$, is the same for every $t$, our disturbances in this first-order autoregressive model are homoskedastic. Also, because $\mathrm{cov}(\varepsilon_t, \varepsilon_{t-1}) = \rho\mathrm{var}(\varepsilon_{t-1})$, $\mathrm{cov}(\varepsilon_t, \varepsilon_{t-1}) = \rho\sigma_\varepsilon^2 = \frac{\rho}{1-\rho^2}\sigma_v^2$.

## More Covariances Among Disturbances

We have now learned that first-order autoregressive disturbances display a particular first-order serial correlation—the covariance of adjacent disturbances is $\rho\sigma_\varepsilon^2$. Do first-order autoregressive disturbances cause disturbances that are not immediately adjacent in time to be correlated as well? They do. To see this, notice that the earlier finding in Equation 11.12 that

$$\varepsilon_t = \rho^2\varepsilon_{t-2} + \rho v_{t-1} + v_t$$

implies that

$$\mathrm{E}(\varepsilon_t\varepsilon_{t-2}) = \mathrm{E}(\rho^2\varepsilon_{t-2}^2 + \rho\varepsilon_{t-2}v_{t-1} + \varepsilon_{t-2}v_t)$$

$$= \rho^2\,\mathrm{var}(\varepsilon_{t-2}) = \frac{\rho^2\sigma_v^2}{1-\rho^2},$$

because disturbances are uncorrelated with future innovations (so $\varepsilon_{t-2}$ is uncorrelated with $v_{t-1}$ and $v_t$). Similarly, the earlier finding in Equation 11.14 that

$$\varepsilon_t = \rho^3 \varepsilon_{t-3} + \rho^2 v_{t-2} + \rho v_{t-1} + v_t,$$

implies that

$$E(\varepsilon_t \varepsilon_{t-3}) = E(\rho^3 \varepsilon_{t-3}^2 + \rho^2 \varepsilon_{t-3} v_{t-2} + \rho \varepsilon_{t-3} v_{t-1} + \varepsilon_{t-3} v_t)$$

$$= \rho^3 \, var(\varepsilon_{t-3}) = \frac{\rho^3 \sigma_v^2}{1 - \rho^2}.$$

More generally, in our DGP with first-order autoregressive disturbances,

$$cov(\varepsilon_t, \varepsilon_{t-q}) = \frac{\rho^q \sigma_v^2}{1 - \rho^2}.$$

### An Alternative Expression of the New DGP

Taken together, the mean, variance, and covariances of the first-order autoregressive disturbances allow an alternative form for the DGP:

$$Y_t = \beta_0 + \beta_1 X_{1t} + \cdots + \beta_k X_{kt} + \varepsilon_t \qquad t = 1, \ldots, T$$

$$E(\varepsilon_t) = 0 \qquad t = 1, \ldots, T$$

$$var(\varepsilon_t) = \sigma_\varepsilon^2 = \frac{\sigma_v^2}{1 - \rho^2} \qquad t = 1, \ldots, T \, |\rho| < 1$$

$$cov(\varepsilon_t, \varepsilon_{t-q}) = \rho^q \sigma_\varepsilon^2 = \frac{\rho^q \sigma_v^2}{1 - \rho^2}$$

$X_t$'s are fixed across samples.

This form of the DGP highlights that the only change from the Gauss–Markov Assumptions is replacing the assumption of uncorrelated disturbances with a particular form of serial correlations among the disturbances. We can now ask our familiar questions: "When is a linear estimator unbiased in this new DGP? What is the variance of a linear estimator in this new DGP? What is the BLUE estimator for this new DGP?" The next section addresses these questions.

## 11.5     BLUE Estimation if Disturbances Are First-Order Autoregressive

HOW DO WE CREATE
AN ESTIMATOR?

As with estimation in heteroskedastic models, there are two possible approaches to BLUE estimation in models with serially correlated disturbances. The first approach is the direct one: We leave the data alone and look for the BLUE estimator by minimizing the variance of a linear estimator, subject to the unbiasedness conditions. The second approach leaves the estimator alone (continuing to rely on OLS), but transforms the data to meet the Gauss–Markov Assumptions, so that OLS applied to the transformed data yields the BLUE estimators of the intercept and slopes.

## Constrained Minimization to Obtain BLUE Estimators

The first approach to obtaining BLUE estimators of the intercept and slopes of a regression model is the constrained minimization approach. Section 11.1 derived the unbiasedness conditions for linear estimators when disturbances are serially correlated. If $g$ is to be an unbiased linear estimator of some one coefficient in our DGP, say $\beta_s$,

$$\sum w_t X_{rt} = 0 \qquad \text{for } r \neq s,$$

and

$$\sum w_t X_{st} = 1,$$

so that E$(g)$ would equal $\beta_s$. Section 11.1 also derived an expression for the variance of a linear estimator when the disturbances are serially correlated:

$$\text{var}(g) = \sigma^2 \sum_{t=1}^{n} w_t^2 + \sum_{t=1}^{n} \sum_{\substack{t'=1 \\ t' \neq t}}^{n} w_t w_{t'} \sigma_{tt'}.$$

In the notation of our first-order autoregressive DGP,

$$\sigma^2 = \sigma_\varepsilon^2$$

and

$$\text{cov}(\varepsilon_t, \varepsilon_s) = \sigma_{|t-s|} = \rho^q \sigma_\varepsilon^2 = \frac{\rho^q \sigma_\nu^2}{1 - \rho^2},$$

where $q = |t - s|$. Thus, we obtain the BLUE estimator of $\beta_s$ for a DGP in which the disturbances follow a first-order autoregression by minimizing

$$\text{var}(g) = \sigma_\varepsilon^2 \sum_{t=1}^{T} w_t^2 + \sum_{t=1}^{T} \sum_{\substack{t'=1 \\ t' \neq t}}^{T} w_t w_{t'} \sigma_\varepsilon^2 \rho^{|t-t'|}$$

with respect to $w_1, \ldots, w_n$, subject to the preceding unbiasedness constraints. The weights that solve this problem, $w_1^s, \ldots, w_n^s$, define the BLUE estimator of $\beta_s$ when the disturbances follow a first-order autoregressive process. The constrained minimization problem for the BLUE estimators is complex enough that we welcome the approach to BLUE estimation that transforms the data appropriately, such that OLS applied to the transformed data is BLUE.

Notice that the constrained minimizations to find BLUE estimators require that we know $\rho$. We will, however, seldom know $\rho$. Consequently, we will rarely be able to implement the BLUE estimator. FGLS is usually the best we can hope for in estimating models with serially correlated disturbances. Nonetheless, deriving the BLUE estimators provides crucial insight into how to construct the FGLS estimator.

## Transforming the Data to Obtain BLUE Estimators

The second approach to obtaining BLUE estimators of the intercept and slopes of a regression model requires transforming the data so that OLS is again BLUE. How can we transform the $X$ and $Y$ data in our sample if we want OLS to yield BLUE estimates when applied to the transformed data? To simplify the exposition, consider a DGP with an unknown intercept and only one unknown slope. Rewriting the first element of our DGP, in this case

$$Y_t = \beta_0 + \beta_1 X_t + \varepsilon_t \qquad t = 1, \ldots, T$$

in the equivalent form

$$Y_t = \beta_0 + \beta_1 X_t + \rho \varepsilon_{t-1} + \nu_t \qquad t = 1, \ldots, T \qquad \text{11.16}$$

simultaneously reveals the correlation problem and suggests a possible way around it. The term $(+\rho \varepsilon_{t-1})$ in $Y_t$ means $Y_t$ will be correlated with $Y_{t-1}$. The consequence of the correlation among observations is that the variance of a linear estimator that uses the $Y$'s will have nonzero covariance terms involving all the $Y$'s, markedly complicating the variance formula. If we could subtract out this element of $Y_t$, though, the correlation problem would disappear. How can we do this?
   Notice that

$$Y_{t-1} = \beta_0 + \beta_1 X_{t-1} + \varepsilon_{t-1},$$

and

$$\rho Y_{t-1} = \rho(\beta_0 + \beta_1 X_{t-1} + \varepsilon_{t-1}) = \rho \beta_0 + \rho \beta_1 X_{t-1} + \rho \varepsilon_{t-1}$$

so that subtracting $\rho Y_{t-1}$ from $Y_t$ would cancel out the $\rho \varepsilon_{t-1}$ that appears on the right-hand side of Equation 11.16:

$$
\begin{aligned}
Y_t - \rho Y_{t-1} &= (\beta_0 + \beta_1 X_t + \rho \varepsilon_{t-1} + \nu_t) - (\rho \beta_0 + \rho \beta_1 X_{t-1} + \rho \varepsilon_{t-1}) \\
&= (1 - \rho)\beta_0 + \beta_1(X_t - \rho X_{t-1}) + \rho \varepsilon_{t-1} - \rho \varepsilon_{t-1} + \nu_t \\
&= (1 - \rho)\beta_0 + \beta_1(X_t - \rho X_{t-1}) + \nu_t. \qquad \text{11.17}
\end{aligned}
$$

Therefore, if we define $Z_t$ by $(Y_t - \rho Y_{t-1})$ and $Q_t$ by $(X_t - \rho X_{t-1})$, we can express our DGP in terms of the transformed variables:

$$Z_t = \beta_0(1 - \rho) + \beta_1 Q_t + \nu_t \qquad t = 2,\ldots,T$$

$$\mathrm{E}(\nu_t) = 0 \qquad\qquad t = 2,\ldots,T$$

$$\mathrm{Var}(\nu_t) = \sigma_\nu^2 \qquad\qquad t = 2,\ldots,T$$

$$\mathrm{Cov}(\nu_t, \nu_s) = 0 \qquad\qquad \text{for } t \neq s$$

$X_t$'s are fixed across samples.

This form of the DGP satisfies the Gauss–Markov Assumptions. Consequently, OLS applied to the $Z$'s and $Q$'s would be the BLUE estimator of $\beta_0$ (the BLUE estimator of $\beta_0$ times a known constant, such as $(1 - \rho)$, is also the BLUE estimator of $\beta_0$) and $\beta_1$, but for one complication: This DGP has only $(T - 1)$ observations, running from $t = 2$ through $t = T$. There is no way to construct $(Y_1 - \rho Y_0)$ or $(X_1 - \rho X_0)$, because we don't observe the earlier $Y$- and $X$-values, so we can't transform $Y_1$ and $X_1$, as we can the other observations. How can we add the information contained in the first observation into our data set without upsetting the Gauss–Markov Assumptions?

Two observations suggest how to alter the transformed DGP to include the first observation. First, $Y_1 = \beta_0 + \beta_1 X_1 + \varepsilon_1$ has a disturbance, $\varepsilon_1$, that is uncorrelated with all future innovations ($\nu_t, t > 1$); hence $Y_1$ and $X_1$ do not require any transforming to make the first disturbance uncorrelated with the other disturbances in the transformed DGP. Second, the variance of $\varepsilon_1$, $\sigma_\nu^2/(1 - \rho^2)$, does differ from that of the $\nu_t$, which have variance $\sigma_\nu^2$; therefore, the first observation does need transformation to avoid heteroskedasticity. If we define

$$Z_1 = Y_1(1 - \rho^2)^{1/2} \text{ and } Q_1 = X_1(1 - \rho^2)^{1/2},$$

then the variance of the first observation in the transformed DGP will, indeed, be $\sigma_\nu^2$, just as it is for all other observations. Transforming the first observation in this way requires that we multiply the *entire* right-hand side by $(1 - \rho^2)^{1/2}$, however, which leads to

$$Y_1(1 - \rho^2)^{1/2} = \beta_0(1 - \rho^2)^{1/2} + \beta_1 X_1(1 - \rho^2)^{1/2} + \varepsilon_1(1 - \rho^2)^{1/2}.$$

With this first observation added to the transformed DGP, the first term on the right-hand side of the model in the DGP is no longer a constant term: For every observation but the first, we have $\beta_0$ times $(1 - \rho)$, whereas for the first observation we have $\beta_0$ times $(1 - \rho^2)^{1/2}$. The BLUE estimation of the model with autoregressive disturbances, therefore, requires applying OLS to a model with two slope coefficients ($\beta_0$ and $\beta_1$) and *no intercept term*.

When $T$ is large, the consequences of ignoring the first observation are small, so the addition of the first observation to the transformed DGP is unnecessary.

We can apply simple OLS with an intercept to transformed observations 2 through $T$. In small samples, though, ignoring the first observation can bring considerable inefficiency. When the first observation is included in the estimation, the estimator is the Generalized Least Squares (GLS) estimator for the coefficients of our model with first-order autoregressive disturbances.

When the model has additional explanators, transforming each as we have $X_t$ makes OLS BLUE. The $m$-th explanator, $X_{mt}$, is transformed to be the $m$-th transformed explanator, $Q_{mt}$:

$$Q_{mt} = X_{mt}(1 - \rho^2)^{1/2} \qquad \text{for } t = 1$$

and

$$Q_{mt} = (X_{mt} - \rho X_{mt-1}) \qquad \text{for } t = 2, \ldots, T.$$

OLS applied to

$$Z_t = \beta_0 Q_{0t} + \beta_1 Q_{1t} + \cdots + \beta_k Q_{kt} + \eta_t$$

is BLUE.

## Estimation When $\rho$ Is Unknown

Unfortunately, the transformation of $X$ and $Y$ into $Q$ and $Z$ requires knowing $\rho$. Seldom, if ever, do we know $\rho$; economic theory sheds little light on how much shocks to the economy carry over from one period to the next. In practice, we have to estimate $\rho$. Fortunately, the autoregressive form that describes $\varepsilon_t$ as $\rho\varepsilon_{t-1} + \nu_t$ points toward a natural way to estimate $\rho$: If we knew the $\varepsilon_t$, we could regress $\varepsilon_t$ on $\varepsilon_{t-1}$ to obtain an estimate of $\rho$. We don't, however, know the $\varepsilon_t$, the disturbances. Instead, we once again use the OLS residuals in place of the unobserved disturbances.

Econometricians Donald Cochrane and Guy Orcutt of Cambridge University[7] were the first to suggest that we use the OLS residuals to estimate models with first-order autoregressive disturbances. The **Cochrane–Orcutt estimator** is the most commonly encountered estimator of regression models with serially correlated disturbances. The estimator has four steps:

1. Conduct OLS using the $X$ and $Y$ data.
2. Regress the OLS residuals against their own lagged values to obtain an estimate of $\rho$, $\hat{\rho}$:

$$e_t = \rho e_{t-1} + \eta_t$$

3. Transform the data as you did earlier, but replace $\rho$ with $\hat{\rho}$.
4. Estimate the transformed model with OLS.

In large samples, the distribution of $\hat{\rho}$ collapses around the true $\rho$ and the transformations in step 3 converge to the GLS transformations, making this estimator efficient in large samples.

Cochrane and Orcutt suggested we ignore the first observation in conducting steps 3 and 4. Economists S. J. Prais of Great Britain's National Institute of Economics and Social Research and Christopher Winsten of the Cowles Commission later suggested adding the first observation in steps 3 and 4 after transforming it to avoid heteroskedasticity; econometricians call this the **Prais–Winsten estimator**.[8] Cochrane and Orcutt made their proposal to simplify computing. With today's computers, there is no reason to exclude the first observation when performing step 3.

The Prais–Winsten estimator is a FGLS estimator, in which we approximate generalized least squares by substituting an estimator of the correlation structure of the disturbances into the GLS estimator of the coefficients. Several econometricians have suggested alternative ways to estimate $\rho$, so we can use a variety of FGLS estimators. All the common FGLS estimators for DGPs with first-order autoregressive disturbances are unbiased and efficient in large samples. We know little about how the various estimators perform in small samples, so choosing among the FGLS estimators is rather arbitrary.

## Iterating the Estimators

The Prais–Winsten estimator is more efficient than OLS. Thus, residuals based on those estimates mimic the true disturbances better than do the OLS residuals. For this reason, after using the Prais–Winsten estimator, it might be preferable to re-estimate $\rho$ using the new, better, residuals, to obtain an improved estimate of $\rho$, with which we could presumably better transform the data for FGLS.

If we do repeat steps 2–4 in the Prais–Winsten procedure, we can claim that the new slope and intercept estimates are better than the preceding ones. The argument that invites us to perform steps 2–4 a second time, though, invites us to perform them yet again—and again and again. Fortunately, this iterative procedure converges quickly; further iterations soon bring almost no change in the estimates.

In large samples, the Prais–Winsten procedure is efficient, so iterating actually gains nothing in large samples. However, many econometricians think iteration is superior in smaller samples, so they conduct Prais–Winsten in this iterative fashion.

## Nonlinear Estimation of Models with Autoregressive Disturbances

The advent of cheap, high-speed computing has popularized another approach to efficiently estimating models with autoregressive disturbances. Adapting Equation 11.17, we can write

$$Y_t = \rho Y_{t-1} + (1 - \rho)\beta_0 + \beta_1(X_t - \rho X_{t-1}) + \nu_t.$$

This relationship is nonlinear in the parameters to be estimated. Econometricians have developed least squares procedures for estimating models of this sort. Many modern econometric packages actually estimate models with autoregressive disturbances in just this way. These nonlinear least squares strategies grapple with the use of a first observation much as we did above. The estimators obtained this way are efficient in large samples.

Some econometric software packages do not offer Prais–Winsten estimation as a standard procedure, but instead estimate autoregressive models using this nonlinear specification. The nonlinear specification is superior to Prais–Winsten if the model contains lagged dependent variables or if there are higher order auto-correlations in the disturbances. In other cases, the nonlinear and Prais–Winsten approaches have the same asymptotic properties.

## Serial Correlation Corrections and Omitted Variables

The GLS, FGLS, and nonlinear estimators that account for serially correlated disturbances do not overcome omitted variable biases. Thus, if serial correlation tests reflect not serially correlated disturbances, but omitted variables, transformation of the data still results in biased estimators. For example, we could use any of the standard estimation procedures that account for autoregressive errors to estimate the original, misspecified version of the Phillips curve that excludes expected inflation. In that application, all the procedures yield negative, but statistically insignificant, coefficients on unemployment, with estimates much smaller than those obtained in Table 11.5, in which the model is correctly specified. Before conducting tests for serial correlation, we should, therefore, test for omitted variable bias, using the RESET test described in Chapter 10.

## Testing Hypotheses

The standard OLS-based tests of hypotheses are invalid when the disturbances are serially correlated. Do our new estimators support valid test procedures when disturbances are first-order autoregressive? If the Gauss–Markov Assumptions are met except for disturbances that follow a first-order autoregressive process, the test procedures we developed in Chapters 7 and 9 for use with OLS are valid with GLS if the disturbances are normally distributed. GLS, FGLS, and the non-linear least squares estimator all validly support those same tests in large samples, even if the disturbances are not normally distributed. If the serial correlation of the disturbances differs from first-order autoregressive specification, however, those standard testing procedures are invalid with any of these estimators, unless the correlation pattern of first-order autoregressive disturbances approximates the true correlation pattern well. When the disturbances follow the first-order autoregressive pattern only approximately, the test procedures are only approximately valid.

## An Example of Estimation with Autoregressive Disturbances

The various estimators that account for first-order autoregressive disturbances yield different estimates in particular samples. It is generally the case, however, that the several estimators provide estimates more in agreement with one another than with the OLS estimates. This example illustrates this point. Table 11.7 reports four estimations of the relationship between poverty and unemployment. The table repeats the OLS estimates from Table 11.3 and adds estimates based on the Prais–Winsten estimator, the iterated Prais–Winsten estimator, and the nonlinear estimator. The estimates of $\rho$ are denoted by rho.

All three estimators that account for serial correlation estimate an effect of unemployment on poverty rates comparable to that estimated with OLS. Because the U.S. population is about twice the size of the labor force, the unemployment coefficients for the non-OLS estimators indicate that from 1.12 to 1.20 individuals enter poverty for each person entering unemployment—quite close to the OLS estimate of 1.17.

**TABLE 11.7** Four Estimations of the Poverty–Unemployment Relationship

*OLS*

|  | coef. | Stnd Er. | t-stat. | p-value |
|---|---|---|---|---|
| C | 9.792052 | 0.611186 | 16.02138 | 0.0000 |
| UNEMPLOY. RATE | 0.586614 | 0.094726 | 6.192734 | 0.0000 |

*Cochrane-Orcutt AR(1) regression—no iteration rho = .8074629*

|  | coef. | Stnd Er. | t-stat. | p-value |
|---|---|---|---|---|
| unemployl | .5834373 | .0976036 | 5.98 | 0.000 |
| _consl | 9.890137 | .7132942 | 13.87 | 0.000 |

*Prais–Winsten AR(1) regression—iterated estimates rho = .855351*

|  | coef. | Stnd Er. | t-stat. | p-value |
|---|---|---|---|---|
| unemployl | .5631339 | .0981236 | 5.74 | 0.000 |
| _consl | 9.643552 | .7628442 | 12.64 | 0.000 |

*Nonlinear Estimator*

|  | coef. | Stnd Er. | t-stat. | p-value |
|---|---|---|---|---|
| C | 9.819377 | 0.715818 | 13.71770 | 0.0000 |
| UNEMPLOY RATE | 0.599118 | 0.104034 | 5.758883 | 0.0000 |
| RHO | 0.780437 | 0.122409 | 6.375643 | 0.0000 |

## Newey–West Serial Correlation Consistent Variances

If the disturbances do not follow a first-order autoregressive process, the FGLS estimator that assumes the disturbances are autoregressive yields hypothesis tests that are invalid. However, tests based on FGLS are still usually more powerful than the standard OLS-based tests in such cases. Nonetheless, in recent years, many econometricians have shied away from FGLS, finding its gains in efficiency over OLS generally modest and its risks of invalid statistical inference too great. Chapter 10 noted that when disturbances are heteroskedastic, econometricians frequently use the OLS estimators of the slopes and intercept, but couple them with White's heteroskedasticity-consistent estimators of the OLS variances and covariances. When the disturbances are serially correlated, heteroskedastic or not, econometricians often use the OLS estimators of the slopes and intercept, but couple them with Newey and West's heteroskedasticity and serial correlation consistent variance estimator. As with the White estimators, we can extend the Newey–West procedures to provide valid tests of multiple claims about linear combinations of regression model coefficients.

Table 11.8 contains the OLS coefficient estimates of the poverty–unemployment relationship with Newey–West heteroskedasticity and serial correlation consistent standard errors. (Remember, standard errors are the square root of an estimator's variance.) The Newey–West standard errors are slightly larger than the standard OLS estimates reported in Table 11.7 on p. 471.

Disagreements among the various estimators do occur. The differences seen in the poverty rate example are all within two estimated standard deviations of the coefficients, so they might well be due to chance. If the disturbances in the poverty–unemployment relationship are first-order autoregressive, the FGLS estimator is preferable to OLS in large samples. If the disturbances are not approximately first-order autoregressive and the sample size is large or the degree of serial correlation is large, then OLS with Newey and West's robust standard errors are preferable. In small samples (say, $T < 25$) with relatively weak autocorrelation (say, $\rho < 0.30$), standard OLS is preferable.

**TABLE 11.8** Poverty and Unemployment (OLS)

*Newey–West Standard Errors*

| Variable | Coefficient | Std. Error | t-Statistic | Prob. |
|----------|-------------|------------|-------------|-------|
| C | 9.792052 | 0.744832 | 13.14665 | 0.0000 |
| UNEMPLOY | 0.586614 | 0.105420 | 5.564560 | 0.0000 |

The assumption that serially correlated disturbances are the root cause of observed serial correlation in the residuals is particularly suspect in a bivariate relationship, like that between poverty and unemployment. A bivariate analysis of poverty and unemployment surely omits other factors that influence the poverty rate. A worry whenever we find serial correlation in the disturbances is whether the problem is truly serial correlation in the random component of the model, or is instead an omitted variables problem. RESET, a test described in Chapter 10, is one way to cope with this worry.

## 11.6 Serial Correlation and Heteroskedasticity Together

**WHAT IS THE DGP?**

Chapter 10 dealt with heteroskedasticity. This chapter has dealt with serial correlation. Unfortunately, serial correlation and heteroskedasticity can occur together, which further complicates the econometrician's work. There are two models in which both serial correlation and heteroskedasticity occur. The first has disturbances that are both heteroskedastic and serially correlated. The second is a model in which the variance of the disturbances is autoregressive in its structure. This section introduces the standard treatment of these two cases.

### Generalized Least Squares

When the DGP satisfies all the Gauss–Markov Assumptions but two—uncorrelated disturbances and heteroskedastic disturbances—the BLUE estimator is GLS. Conceptually, this DGP adds nothing new to what we have already learned about heteroskedasticity and serial correlation. OLS is unbiased, but inefficient, when the DGP has disturbances that are both serially correlated and heteroskedastic. The Newey–West standard errors support valid inference with OLS in this DGP. BLUE estimators result from appropriately transforming the data and applying OLS to the transformed data, in essence combining the transformations used for heteroskedastic and first-order autoregressive disturbances. Appendix 11.A uses matrix algebra to obtain the GLS estimator for the general linear model. In practice, the structure of variances and covariances is often not known, so FGLS methods are frequently needed, rather than GLS. FGLS supports valid $t$-tests and $F$-tests in large samples for this DGP.

### Autoregressive Conditional Heteroskedasticity

Stock prices are sometimes volatile, sometimes not. Inflation is sometimes erratic, sometimes not. Variance is one way of measuring how volatile stock prices are or how erratic inflation is. A glance at Figure 11.2 suggests that inflation, at least, has a variance that shifts over time. Stock price data suggest the same thing. Periods in which stock prices are highly volatile persist, as do periods in which stock price movements are small. The second model to combine serial correlation and heteroskedasticity assumes that heteroskedasticity itself follows a first-order autoregressive pattern. This structure allows above-average variances and below-average variances to persist over time, in accord with the observed patterns of some variables, such as stock prices and inflation. The practical importance of stock pricing models makes models with time-varying heteroskedasticity very popular among financial economists. In 2003, economist Robert Engle, New York University, received the Nobel prize in economics for devising methods of analyzing economic time series with time-varying volatility. Engle called his model for analyzing time-varying volatility the **autoregressive conditional heteroskedasticity (ARCH) model.**[9]

The autoregressive conditional heteroskedasticity (ARCH) model begins with the Gauss–Markov Assumptions but then imposes a special structure on the homoskedastic disturbances. In particular, the disturbances are assumed to satisfy

$$E(\varepsilon_t) = 0 \qquad\qquad t = 1,\ldots,T$$

$$\text{var}(\varepsilon_t) = E(\varepsilon_t^2) = \sigma^2 \qquad t = 1,\ldots,T \qquad\qquad \textbf{11.18}$$

and

$$E(\varepsilon_t \varepsilon_{t'}) = 0 \quad t \neq t'.$$

Because these assumptions suffice to make OLS BLUE, OLS is BLUE in the ARCH model. But the ARCH model adds a further assumption about the variance of the disturbances: Conditional on $\varepsilon_{t-1}$, the variance of $\varepsilon_t$ is

$$E(\varepsilon_t^2 | \varepsilon_{t-1}) = \alpha_0 + \alpha_1 \varepsilon_{t-1}^2. \qquad\qquad \textbf{11.19}$$

If $\alpha_1 > 0$, then when the disturbance in one period is far from zero, the disturbance in the next period will also tend to be far from zero—though not necessarily on the same side of zero. In other words, the larger $\alpha_1$, the more persistent episodes of volatility or quiet will tend to be. As with the autocorrelation coefficient for first-order autoregressive disturbances, $|\alpha_1| < 1$.

## Conditional and Unconditional Variances

What is the connection between Equations 11.18 and 11.19? The ARCH specification assumes a world that is, ultimately, homoskedastic. That is the import of Equation 11.18. That overall homoskedasticity unfolds with episodes of highly variable observations and other episodes of mildly variable observations, however. That is the import of Equation 11.19. Because the overall homoskedasticity results from a collection of specific heteroskedastic realizations, Equations 11.18 and 11.19 are linked quite closely.

Equation 11.18 gives the mean of the variance of $\varepsilon_t$ across the entire distribution of $\varepsilon_{t-1}$. That is,

$$E(E(\varepsilon_t^2 | \varepsilon_{t-1})) = E(\varepsilon_t^2)$$
$$= E(\alpha_0 + \alpha_1 \varepsilon_{t-1}^2)$$
$$= \alpha_0 + \alpha_1 E(\varepsilon_{t-1}^2).$$

Because the Gauss–Markov Assumption states that $E(\varepsilon_t^2) = E(\varepsilon_{t-1}^2) = \sigma^2$,

$$E(\varepsilon_t^2) = \sigma^2 = \alpha_0 + \alpha_1 \sigma^2,$$

so

$$\sigma^2 = \frac{\alpha_0}{1 - \alpha_1}.$$

On average, across all realizations of the ARCH process, the variance of any observation's disturbances is $\sigma^2$. When a specific value of $\varepsilon_{t-1}$ has occurred, though, the next period's disturbance will be drawn from a distribution in which the variance of $\varepsilon_t$ is given by Equation 11.19.

## Testing for ARCH

Equation 11.19 suggests a test for ARCH in the disturbances. If we observed the disturbances, we could regress $\varepsilon_t^2$ on $\varepsilon_{t-1}^2$ and a constant and conduct a $t$-test of the null hypothesis that $\alpha_1$ is zero. Because we don't observe the disturbances, we instead replace them with the OLS residuals in this procedure. The test is valid in large samples.

Table 11.9 reports a test for ARCH disturbances in a model of inflation using the 90 years of data seen in Figure 11.2. The data are in the file inflation.*** on this book's companion Web site (**www.aw-bc.com/murray**). The model regresses inflation on a constant. The squared residuals from that OLS regression are used in the test in Table 11.9. The $t$-statistic on the lagged squared residual is 1.11, so we fail to reject the null hypothesis of no autoregressive structure to inflation's variance.

Does the absence of ARCH contradict our visual assessment of Figure 11.2 that inflation was more variable from 1923 to 1952 than from 1973 to 2002? No, it does not. A Goldfeld–Quandt test of equal variances for the disturbances in the two periods rejects the null of homoskedastic disturbances. The $F$-statistic is 2.53 and the degrees of freedom are 29 and 29 (because there are 30 years in each time period). The .05 significance level critical value for the $F$-statistic is 1.86. The

**TABLE 11.9  Is Inflation ARCH?**

*ARCH Test:*

| | | | | |
|---|---|---|---|---|
| F-statistic | 1.229395 | Probability | | 0.270616 |
| Obs*R-squared | 1.240256 | Probability | | 0.265422 |

Test Equation:
Dependent Variable: RESID$^{\wedge}2$
Method: Least Squares
Sample(adjusted): 1915 2002
Included observations: 88 after adjusting endpoints

| Variable | Coefficient | Std. Error | t-Statistic | Prob. |
|---|---|---|---|---|
| C | 0.007913 | 0.003484 | 2.271359 | 0.0256 |
| RESID$^{\wedge}2(-1)$ | 0.118710 | 0.107063 | 1.108781 | 0.2706 |
| R-squared | 0.014094 | Mean dependent var | | 0.008977 |
| Adjusted R-squared | 0.002630 | S.D. dependent var | | 0.031458 |
| S.E. of regression | 0.031417 | Akaike info criterion | | −4.060467 |
| Sum squared resid | 0.084885 | Schwarz criterion | | −4.004164 |
| Log likelihood | 180.6606 | F-statistic | | 1.229395 |
| Durbin–Watson stat | 1.981283 | Prob(F-statistic) | | 0.270616 |

observed pattern of inflation is inconsistent with ordinary homoskedasticity. This example highlights the very special nature of the ARCH specification, which places conditional heteroskedasticity in a fundamentally homoskedastic environment. Not every pattern of variable volatility can be well represented by an ARCH model. Some additional generality is possible within the ARCH framework, however. Equation 11.19 is sometimes replaced by

$$E(\varepsilon_t^2 \mid \varepsilon_{t-1}, \ldots, \varepsilon_{t-p}) = \alpha_0 + \alpha_1 \varepsilon_{t-1}^2 + \cdots + \alpha_p \varepsilon_{t-p}^2, \qquad \textbf{11.20}$$

which allows for a more complex pattern of correlations among the squared disturbances. Equation 11.20 is called a $p$-th order ARCH model.

Because the ARCH DGP satisfies the Gauss–Markov Assumptions, OLS is BLUE. However, the information contained in the conditional variance makes possible nonlinear estimators that are more efficient than OLS in large samples. The development of those estimators lies beyond the scope of this book.[10]

*An Organizational Structure for the Study of Econometrics*

### 1. What Is the DGP?

Serially correlated disturbances: $E(\varepsilon_t, \varepsilon_{t-j}) \neq 0$ for some or all $j$

First-order autoregressive disturbances: $\varepsilon_t = \rho\varepsilon_{t-1} + \mu_t$

ARCH

### 2. What Makes a Good Estimator?

———

### 3. How Do We Create an Estimator?

Minimizing variance subject to unbiasedness conditions

Transforming variables to satisfy the Gauss–Markov Assumptions

### 4. What Are an Estimator's Properties?

OLS is unbiased and consistent, but inefficient if disturbances are serially correlated.

GLS is BLUE if disturbances are serially correlated.

Prais–Winsten is consistent and asymptotically efficient if disturbances are first-order autoregressive.

### 5. How Do We Test Hypotheses?

The Durbin–Watson test

The Breusch–Godfrey test

Is it serial correlation or is it omitted variables?

## Summary

This chapter relaxes the Gauss–Markov Assumption of independent errors, replacing it with an assumption of serially correlated errors. The chapter examines the consequences of serially correlated disturbances for the estimation and testing procedures developed in Chapters 3 through 9. We find that OLS remains unbiased, but is no longer BLUE. We also find that the OLS-based $t$-statistics and $F$-statistics we developed in earlier chapters are no longer valid.

The chapter presents two formal statistical tests of the null hypothesis of serially uncorrelated disturbances. The Durbin–Watson test for serial correlation focuses attention on $E(\varepsilon_t \varepsilon_{t-1})$; it is particularly powerful against the first-order autoregressive alternative hypothesis. The Durbin–Watson test is not suitable when the equation contains lagged dependent variables. The Durbin–Watson statistic is also sometimes unable to either reject or not reject a hypothesis. The second test for serial correlation is the Breusch–Godfrey test. The Breusch–Godfrey test is less powerful than the Durbin–Watson statistic against first-order autoregressive disturbances, but it is generally a more powerful test. The Breusch–Godfrey test is valid with lagged dependent variables.

Because so many variations of serial correlation are possible, BLUE estimation must focus on a specific sort. A frequently encountered form of serial correlation has first-order autoregressive disturbances. Autoregressive disturbances are made up of two parts: (i) a serially uncorrelated innovation, and (ii) an inheritance of some fraction of the previous period's disturbance. The chapter derives the BLUE estimator for the first-order autoregressive case.

Because the autocorrelation coefficient—the inherited fraction of the previous period's disturbance—is not generally known, GLS is not usually feasible. The chapter therefore describes several estimation procedures that use an estimate of the autocorrelation coefficient:

1. The Cochrane-Orcutt estimator
2. The Prais–Winsten FGLS estimator in two forms, a two-step procedure and an iterative procedure
3. A nonlinear least squares estimator.

All of these estimation procedures are efficient in large samples. Hypothesis tests of the sort developed in Chapters 7 and 9 are valid in large samples with these three estimation procedures.

If the true structure of serial correlation differs from the first-order autoregressive pattern, Prais–Winsten and the nonlinear estimator posed for the autoregressive case are consistent, but tests based on them are invalid. Consequently, econometricians often rely on the unbiased, but inefficient, OLS estimators even when the disturbances are serially correlated. The chapter provides a strategy for consistently estimating the variances and covariances of the OLS estimators when the disturbances are serially correlated, so that we can use OLS to conduct valid hypothesis tests, despite serially correlated disturbances. These estimators are called Newey–West heteroskedasticity and serial correlation consistent standard errors.

Finally, the chapter briefly discusses two ways in which serial correlation and heteroskedasticity may be combined in a model: disturbances that are both heteroskedastic and serially correlated, and the ARCH model.

## Concepts for Review

## Questions for Discussion

1. We could reasonably argue that all disturbance terms are made up of unobserved variables that influence the dependent variable. If this is so, is serial correlation always an omitted variables problem? Should we never settle for Prais–Winsten or some other procedure for efficiently estimating regressions when the disturbances are serially correlated? If we should sometimes settle, what needs to be true for us to do so?

## Problems for Analysis

> For the data that you will need to solve the problems in this section, go to **www.aw-bc.com/murray**.

1. The chapter reports that deviations of inflation from its mean crossed zero 5 times in the 30 years between 1973 and 2002, but 13 times during the 30 years between 1923 and 1952. If inflation were not serially correlated, we would expect it to cross zero every other time. Use the binomial distribution to determine how likely it is that independent observations' deviations from their means would cross zero in a sample of 30 observations (the probability of a crossing is one half). Would this finding lead you to reject the null hypothesis that inflation was serially uncorrelated between 1973 and 2002? Between 1923 and 1952? Across all 60 years?

2. Suppose $E(\varepsilon_t \varepsilon_{t-1})$ is not zero, but that disturbances are uncorrelated at all other lags. Further suppose you have done OLS and found that the Durbin–Watson statistic is below the lower bound critical value, so you correctly reject the null of no serial correlation. You have 200 observations.
   a. Suppose you randomly reorder your observations and rerun OLS. What is likely to happen to your Durbin–Watson statistic? Briefly explain.
   b. Suppose you find that the Durbin–Watson statistic is close to 2 after you have conducted OLS with the shuffled data. Does this suggest that data shuffling is a good way to correct for serial correlation? Briefly explain.
   c. How will the estimated coefficients, estimated standard errors, and $R^2$ from these two OLS estimations compare? Briefly explain.

3. Plot the time series paths of the various processes from a single shock ($\varepsilon_0 > 0$). Ignore $\varepsilon_t, t = 1, 2, \ldots T$ and assume that $y_{t-j} = E(y_t)$.

   a. $y_t = \phi y_{t-1} + \varepsilon_t$ where $\phi = 0.5$
   b. $y_t = \phi y_{t-1} + \varepsilon_t$ where $\phi = -0.5$
   c. $y_t = \phi y_{t-1} + \varepsilon_t$ where $\phi = 1.5$
   d. $y_t = \phi y_{t-1} + \varepsilon_t$ where $\phi = 0.9$
   e. Compare your results in parts (a)–(d) and describe how the responses of the dependent variable differ depending on the value of $\phi$.

4. The serial correlation that troubles us in this chapter is serial correlation in the disturbances. There need not even be any explanatory variables for this problem of serial correlation to exist. The data set cement.*** contains the rate of return (*rate*) on investors' capital for a cement company for each of 14 years, measured in percents.

   a. Regress the rate of return on an intercept term. Interpret the estimated coefficient.
   b. Does the Breusch–Godfrey test statistic indicate serially correlated disturbances at the 10% significance level if a single lagged value of the residuals is included in the auxiliary regression?
   c. Re-estimate the intercept term, using a FGLS-style estimator. Does the estimated standard error change much?

5. One of the fastest growing forms of renewable energy is produced from the wind. Typically, large turbines transform wind into electricity that is then delivered to a utility company. The production process for wind energy depends on a number of technological factors (including turbine design, transformer capacity, management information systems, etc.), physical capital (turbines and generators), and labor (mainly in the form of maintenance and repair). Perhaps the most important element in the production of wind energy is the modeling of wind speed because the operation of the turbines is constrained by minimum and maximum wind speeds. In particular, given the high cost of "turning on" a line of turbines (typically installed in groups of six to eight), a minimum amount of wind speed is required (about 10 mph) and is called the "cut in" speed. In addition, too much wind can damage the turbines, and the corresponding "cut out" speed is in the range of 56 mph. Accurate econometric models of wind speed can assist wind plant managers to operate profitably. The data in wind.*** were collected by engineers in the Wind Science and Engineering Research Center at Texas Tech University at a Mesonet in West Texas, where wind plants are a common sight. Wind turbines are often 70 meters high, but wind speed may be faster or slower depending on distance from the ground. The extent to which wind speed measured at one height is related to wind speed at another height is important information to the wind plant manager. These relationships are referred to as wind profiles. Perform a regression where *X160* (wind speed measured at 160 feet above the ground) is the dependent variable and *X33* (wind speed measured at 33 feet) is the explanatory variable; include an intercept term.

   a. Interpret the estimated coefficient on *X33*. Plot the residuals. Describe the information contained in the residuals.
   b. Test for serial correlation in the disturbances using the Durbin–Watson test and the Breusch–Godfrey test. Do you get similar results from these two tests?

c. Estimate the model by OLS using the Newey–West standard errors and interpret the point estimate of the coefficient on *X33*. Plot the residuals and describe the information contained therein. Are your estimated slope coefficient and its estimated standard error any different than in part (a)? Explain why or why not.

d. Re-estimate the model in (a) using FGLS. Interpret the estimated coefficient on *X33*. Compare your FGLS slope estimate and its estimated standard error to those in parts (a) and (c).

e. Which estimates do you prefer, those from (a), those from (c), or those from (d).

6. This problem uses the poverty rate and unemployment data in poverty1.***.

a. Estimate the poverty rate model separately for 1981–1992 and for 1993–2000. Include a time trend. Separately test the hypothesis of no serial correlation for each specification.

b. Conduct an *F*-test of the hypothesis that the poverty rate model's slope and intercept are the same before and after 1993.

c. What do you conclude about the suitability of applying the Prais–Winsten estimator to these data, as is done in this chapter?

7. Suppose the disturbances in our bivariate DGP have the character $\varepsilon_t = \rho\varepsilon_{t-2} + v_t$, a form of second-order autoregression. Suppose the $v_t$ are mean zero, serially uncorrelated, homoskedastic random variables.

a. What transformation of the model will result in an equivalent DGP for which OLS is BLUE?

b. If $\rho$ is unknown, how would you propose we estimate it, and how would you use that estimate to perform FGLS?

8. You are interested in the relationship $Y_t = \beta_0 + \beta_1 X_t + \varepsilon_t$ with a large sample from a DGP that you think satisfies all the Gauss–Markov Assumptions except that the disturbances, $\varepsilon_t$, have the structure

$$\varepsilon_t = \gamma v_{t-2} + v_t \qquad 0 < \gamma < 1,$$

where the $v_t$ follow the Gauss–Markov Assumptions. If you conduct OLS, which is more likely to reject the null hypothesis of no serial correlation, the Durbin–Watson test or a Breusch–Godfrey test using residuals lagged 1–4 periods? (In both cases, suppose the significance level for the test is .05.) Briefly explain your response. (If one test or the other is likely to have particularly low power, be sure to explain why that is so.)

9. College administrators make staffing decisions based in part on the number of students they expect to enroll. In addition, the school's long-term planning strategy, which includes how many dormitories and dining halls to build and how many parking spaces are needed (yes, schools do care about student parking!), depends on accurately assessing what factors affect enrollment. Economic theory suggests that as the economy improves and job prospects get better, the opportunity cost of attending school for some individuals will rise. Thus, real economic growth may correspond to lower enrollment. On the other hand, it is also possible that this same growth may lead some students to stay in school; perhaps it is now more affordable if their parents' income rises. In any event, the answer to the question of whether or not eco-

nomic growth is good or bad for enrollment can be decided empirically. The National Center for Education Statistics, U.S. Department of Education, tracks the number of students enrolled in U.S. colleges and universities. These and related data are in educ172.***. Estimate a regression using OLS of *logtem* (log of the total number of males enrolled in colleges and universities) on a constant term.

a. Use the Durbin–Watson statistic to confirm the presence of serial correlation.

b. Re-estimate the model including the lagged value of *logtem* as an explanatory term. Now test for the presence of serial correlation, using the Breusch–Godfrey statistic. Describe the information obtained from inclusion of the lagged dependent variable in the model.

c. Now test to see if real economic growth, measured by the growth rate in industrial production, is associated with more or less enrollment.

d. Use White's test to determine if heteroskedasticity exists in the model from part (c).

e. If the economy is currently booming, but inflation is relatively stable and low by historical standards, what would you tell university administrators regarding expected enrollments?

 10. Open haavelmo1.***. The Norwegian economist Trygve Haavelmo assumed that real government spending and real investment did not depend on current income, but was instead autonomously determined by other factors. An early Keynesian, Haavlmo argued that a regression of real income on real autonomous expenditures would measure the multiplier effect described by Keynesian macroeconomics. Regress real income (*realinc*) on real autonomous expenditures (*realauto*); the coefficient on *realauto* is the multiplier effect of autonomous investment.

a. Test for serial correlation in the disturbances. Do you obtain the same conclusion from both the Durbin–Watson test and the Breusch–Godfrey test?

b. Estimate the model by OLS using Newey–West standard errors. Do any of your conclusions about the coefficients change substantially?

c. Estimate the model by some method that takes explicit account of serial correlation in the estimation procedure. Do any of your conclusions about the coefficients change substantially?

d. Which estimates do you think are superior? Briefly explain.

11. This problem considers the effects of rain at different stages of the wine-growing process. The data are in wineweather.***. The data were part of an analysis of Bordeaux wine as an investment by economists Orley Ashenfelter, David Ashmore, and Robert LaLonde.[11] The variables in the data set are as follows:

*logprice*   Natural log of the 1983 average price for wines of the vintage
*hrain*      Rainfall during the harvest season
*wrain*      Rainfall during the winter preceding the harvest
*degrees*    Average temperature April–September in harvest year
*time_sv*    Wine's vintage

a. Regress the log of price on *wrain*, *hrain*, *degrees*, *time_sv*, and a constant. Test for serial correlation in the disturbances. Do you obtain the same conclusion from both the Durbin–Watson test and the Breusch–Godfrey test?

b. Estimate the model by OLS using Newey–West standard errors. Do any of your conclusions about the coefficients change substantially?

c. Estimate the model by some method that takes explicit account of serial correlation in the estimation procedure. Do any of your conclusions about the coefficients change substantially?

d. Which estimates do you think are superior? Briefly explain.

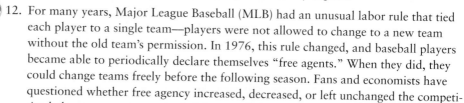

12. For many years, Major League Baseball (MLB) had an unusual labor rule that tied each player to a single team—players were not allowed to change to a new team without the old team's permission. In 1976, this rule changed, and baseball players became able to periodically declare themselves "free agents." When they did, they could change teams freely before the following season. Fans and economists have questioned whether free agency increased, decreased, or left unchanged the competitive balance among teams in their league play. Peter Fishman used the data from 1950 to 2004 in the file baseball.*** to settle this debate.[12]

To measure the competitiveness of baseball teams in any given season, the data set provides the standard deviation of winning percentages (the proportion of games played that a team won) across all teams in the league, *stdevwp*. When teams are competitive, they win similar numbers of games, and the standard deviation is low. When some teams dominate and others perform badly, the standard deviation is high. The number of players that declare free agency prior to a given season is *fragents*.

Several other variables can affect the competitiveness of teams. From 1965 on, MLB had a draft of amateur players in which the poorest performing teams of the previous season get first choices in the draft. The purpose of this practice is to improve competitiveness among teams. *Draft* is a dummy variable indicating years from 1965 on. The number of teams in MLB affects the standard deviation of winning percentages. Each dominant team and each poor team has a smaller impact on the mean deviation of winning percentages from their overall mean when there are more teams in the league. *Teams* is the number of teams in MLB during the season. And finally, when a larger proportion of the U.S. population is playing baseball, the variance in ability among players is greater than when a smaller proportion (presumably the very best) plays. The variable *poppct* is the fraction of the U.S. population who are MLB players.

a. Regress *stdevwp* against *fragents*, *draft*, *teams*, *poppct*, and an intercept term. What do you conclude about the effect of free agency on the competitiveness of MLB teams? Which variables are statistically significant at the 5% significance level?

b. Conduct the Durbin–Watson test for serial correlation and the Breusch–Godfrey test with two lagged values of the residuals in the auxiliary regression. At the 5% significance level, what do you conclude?

c. Compute the Newey–West consistent standard errors for the OLS estimator used in (a). Which variables are statistically significant at the 5% significance level?

d. Re-estimate the relationship in (a) using a FGLS-style estimator. Which variables are statistically significant at the 5% significance level?

e. How many observations are in this data set? How many degrees of freedom? What are the competing concerns in deciding whether the results in (d) are superior in quality to those in (c) and those in (a)?

13. Nitrogen dioxide ($NO_2$) is a pollutant that attacks the human respiratory system; it increases the likelihood of respiratory illness. One common source of nitrous oxides is automobile exhaust. The file NO2pollution3.*** contains successive 500 hourly observations made from October 2001 to August 2003.[13] The variables in the data set are as follows:

LNO2          Natural logarithm of the concentration of $NO_2$ (particles)
LCARS         Natural logarithm of the number of cars per hour
TEMP          Temperature 2 meters above ground (degrees C)
WNDSPD        Wind speed (meters/second)
TCHNG23       Temperature difference between 25 meters and 2 meters above ground (degrees C),
WNDDIR        Wind direction (degrees between 0 and 360)
HOUR          Hour of day
DAYS          Number of the day in the sequence of 500 days
one–twentythree   Dummy variables for two hour intervals, starting at 0000.

a. Regress the log of $NO_2$ concentration on the log of the number of cars, the two temperature variables, the two wind variables, and the time index (DAYS). Does the Durbin–Watson statistic indicate serial correlation at the 5% significance level?

b. Conduct a Breusch–Godfrey test for serial correlation in (a), with two lagged values of the residuals in the auxiliary regression. What do you conclude at the 5% significance level?

c. Use White's test for heteroskedastic disturbances. What do you conclude at the 5% significance level?

d. Add to the regression the two-hour-interval dummies, one through twentythree. Conduct White's test for heteroskesdastic disturbances. What do you conclude about the heteroskedasticity finding in (c)?

e. What does the Durbin–Watson statistic for the regression in (d) indicate about the serial correlation of the disturbances, at the 5% significance level?

f. Conduct a Breusch–Godfrey test for serial correlation in (d), with two lagged values of the residuals in the auxiliary regression. What do you conclude at the 5% significance level?

g. Re-estimate the regression in (d), using an estimation procedure that accounts for first-order autoregressive disturbances.

h. Conduct a Breusch–Godfrey test for serial correlation in (d), with two lagged values of the residuals in the auxiliary regression. What do you conclude at the 5% significance level? Does the first-order autoregressive specification seem to account for the serial correlation in the disturbances?

14. The Chicago Mercantile Exchange (CME) trades options on weather derivatives for a select group of cities (e.g., Minneapolis, Los Angeles, Las Vegas, and about a dozen others). These financial instruments are referred to as derivatives, and, to date, the largest participants in this market are utility companies. In fact, many electric utility

companies use weather derivatives to protect themselves from unusually large swings in demand that arise when weather is unseasonably cold or hot. A key element in structuring a weather contract is knowledge about how weather in one area is correlated with weather in another location. Econometric analysis is one way in which to measure correlations among several locations. For example, suppose you operate a utility in Albuquerque, New Mexico, and have an interest in reducing your weather-related risk, specifically that which is caused by unusual temperatures. It is possible to construct a CME-based portfolio using weather derivatives traded for Las Vegas and Minneapolis, but in order to reduce your risk, you will need to know how temperatures in Albuquerque compare (i.e., correlate) with those in these other cities. The file temper1.*** contains temperature data for Albuquerque, Las Vegas, and Minneapolis.

a. Regress the temperature in Albuquerque (*albtemp*) on the temperatures in Las Vegas (*lvtemp*) and Minneapolis (*mntemp*). Check for serial correlation using the Durbin–Watson statistic.

b. Use White's test for heteroskedastic disturbances. What do you find?

c. Based on your results in (a) and (b), re-estimate the model using a FGLS to account for serial correlation and heteroskedasticity.

15. Environmental economists are often involved in ecological management, and many wildlife areas are governed by federal regulations that mandate the survival of endangered species. The maintenance of population densities in an ecological system requires information on how organisms relate to each other. A popular way of characterizing some of these relationships is with the "predator–prey model."[14] B. G. Villeaux collected time series data on two freshwater organisms, one of which is a predator and the other the prey. These data are in water.***.

a. Estimate a regression using OLS where *preyg* (prey density growth rate) is the dependent variable and *predg* (predator density growth rate) is the explanatory variable; include an intercept term. What does the model tell you about the relationship between predator and prey?

b. Test the residuals for serial correlation. Does your answer to part (a) change?

c. Test the residuals for the presence of ARCH effects. Interpret your results.

d. Estimate a model that takes into account any violations of the OLS model detected in parts (b) and (c). Interpret your results and explain your findings.

16. Financial analysts often use Engle's ARCH model for assessing the returns of many assets. One of the reasons is that while returns have been difficult to model, the volatility can be characterized quite well using Engle's method. The model provides useful information to investors, as the price of assets may depend on the inherent risk. The file dj1.*** contains daily observation of the Dow Jones spot and futures prices. Estimate a regression using OLS that includes only a constant term and in which *ds* (the first-difference of the log of the spot price) is the dependent variable. Note that the estimated coefficient from this regression is really an estimated average return measure for an asset made up of a portfolio of the Dow Jones stocks; the spot price is the spot price of such an asset.

a. Use the Durbin–Watson statistic to confirm the presence of serial correlation. What information about the spot market can you infer from the results?

b. Re-estimate a model including the past change in log spot price and re-test for serial correlation using the Breusch–Pagan statistic. Does your answer to part (a) change?

c. Test for the presence of ARCH (of order 1) in the disturbances of the model in (b). Explain what it means to have this property present in your residuals.

d. Now estimate the ARCH model and describe the results you get for the variance equation. Is the variance process "well behaved"? Derive an estimate of $\sigma^2$ based on your results.

e. What might an informed Wall Street advisor tell clients about the behavior of the spot price of this asset, and specifically about the returns on this asset?

f. Interpret the coefficient on Las Vegas and Minneapolis temperatures and test for joint significance of the temperature variables. Does it appear that the temperatures in Las Vegas and Minneapolis are at all related to the temperature in Albuquerque? Explain why or why not?

## Endnotes

1. George Santayana, *Life of Reason*, vol. 1 ch. 12 (New York: Scribner, 1905).

2. Heraclitus, as quoted by Plato in 360 B.C. in Plato's "Cratylus," trans., Benjamin Jowett, in *The Collected Dialogues of Plato*, eds., E. Hamilton and H. Cairns (New York: Pantheon Books, 1963.)

3. Newey and West did not only drop terms in Equation 11.5 that involved lags longer than *L*. Equation 11.5, truncated or not, can yield (nonsensically) negative variance estimates in some samples. Newey and West adapted Equation 11.5 to avoid that possibility. W. K. Newey and K. D. West, "A Simple, Positive Semi-definite Heteroskedasticity and Autocorrelation Consistent Covariance Matrix," *Econometrica* 55: 703–708.

4. J. Durbin and G. S. Watson, "Testing for Serial Correlation in Least Squares Regressions," *Biometrika* 37 (1950): 409–428.

5. Durbin offered an alternative to the Durbin–Watson statistic, called Durbin's *h*, to be used when lagged dependent variables appear among the explanators. Durbin's *h* statistic is sometimes reported by econometric computer programs. It has been replaced in practice by the more general Breusch–Godfrey test.

6. David Alan Aschauer, "Is Public Expenditure Productive?" *Journal of Monetary Economics* 23 (1989): 177–200.

7. D. Cochrane and G. H. Orcutt, "Applications of Least Squares Regressions to Relationships Containing Autocorrelated Terms," *Journal of the American Statistical Association* 44 (1949): 32–61.

8. S. J. Prais and C. B. Winsten, *Trend Estimators and Serial Correlation*. Cowles Commission Discussion Paper No. 33 (New Haven, CT: Yale University Press, 1954).

9. R. Engle, "Autoregressive Conditional Heteroskedasticity with Estimates of the Variance of United Kingdom Inflations," *Econometrica* 50 (1982): 987–1008.

10. For more on ARCH models, see R. F. Engle, "GARCH101: The Use of ARCH/GARCH Models in Applied Econometrics," *Journal of Economic Perspectives* 15, no. 4 (Fall 2001): 157–168; or T. Bollerslev, R. F. Engle, and D. B. Nelson, "ARCH Models," in *Handbook of Econometrics*, Vol. 4, eds. R. F. Engle and D. L. McFadden (Amsterdam: North Holland, 1994), 2959–3038.

11. Orley Ashenfelter, David Ashmore, and Robert LaLonde, "Bordeaux Wine Vintage Quality and the Weather," http://www.liquidasset.com/orley.htm (December 1999).
12. Peter Fishman, "Competitive Balance and Free Agency in Major League Baseball," *The American Economist* 47, no. 2 (Fall 2003): 86–91.
13. These data come from the Statlib archive of Carnegie Mellon University. They were originally posted there by Aldrin Magne.
14. B. G. Villeux, "An Analysis of the Predatory Interaction Between Didinium and Paramecium," *Journal of Animal Ecology* 48 (1979): 787–803.

 *Appendix 11.A*

# Matrix Algebra and Generalized Least Squares II

This appendix uses matrix algebra to examine the consequences of serial correlation for the OLS and GLS estimators in the multiple regression model.

## 11.A.1  The Serial Correlation Variance–Covariance Matrix

The Gauss–Markov Assumptions state that disturbances are homoskedastic and uncorrelated. Homoskedasticity is a claim about the variances of the disturbances. A lack of correlation is a claim about the covariances among the disturbances. The disturbances' variances and their covariances are represented together in matrix form by a variance–covariance matrix.

### The Disturbances' Variance–Covariance Matrix

As noted in earlier chapters, the disturbances' variances and covariances are the expected value of the $n \times n$ matrix $\boldsymbol{v} = \boldsymbol{\varepsilon}\boldsymbol{\varepsilon}'$. For the case in which $n = 4$:

$$\boldsymbol{v} = \boldsymbol{\varepsilon}\boldsymbol{\varepsilon}' = \begin{bmatrix} \varepsilon_1 \\ \varepsilon_2 \\ \varepsilon_3 \\ \varepsilon_4 \end{bmatrix} \begin{bmatrix} \varepsilon_1 & \varepsilon_2 & \varepsilon_3 & \varepsilon_4 \end{bmatrix} = \begin{bmatrix} \varepsilon_1^2 & \varepsilon_1\varepsilon_2 & \varepsilon_1\varepsilon_3 & \varepsilon_1\varepsilon_4 \\ \varepsilon_2\varepsilon_1 & \varepsilon_2^2 & \varepsilon_2\varepsilon_3 & \varepsilon_2\varepsilon_4 \\ \varepsilon_3\varepsilon_1 & \varepsilon_3\varepsilon_2 & \varepsilon_3^2 & \varepsilon_3\varepsilon_4 \\ \varepsilon_4\varepsilon_1 & \varepsilon_4\varepsilon_2 & \varepsilon_4\varepsilon_3 & \varepsilon_4^2 \end{bmatrix}.$$

The expected values of the diagonal elements are the variances of the $n$ disturbances. The expected values of the off-diagonal elements are the covariances among the $n$ disturbances. $\Omega = E(\nu) = E(\varepsilon\varepsilon')$ is called the variance–covariance matrix of the disturbances. Because $E(\varepsilon_i\varepsilon_j) = E(\varepsilon_j\varepsilon_i)$, $\Omega$ is symmetric. The variance–covariance matrix of $Y$ is also $\Omega$, because $Y$ differs from $\varepsilon$ only by the constant $X\beta$.

The Gauss–Markov Assumptions claim that the disturbances are homoskedastic, that is, that the diagonal elements of $\Omega$ are equal to one another, and the disturbances are uncorrelated, that is, that the off-diagonal elements of $\Omega$ are all zero. For the case in which $n = 4$, the Gauss–Markov Assumptions claim that

$$\Omega = E(\nu) = E(\varepsilon\varepsilon') = \begin{bmatrix} \sigma^2 & 0 & 0 & 0 \\ 0 & \sigma^2 & 0 & 0 \\ 0 & 0 & \sigma^2 & 0 \\ 0 & 0 & 0 & \sigma^2 \end{bmatrix} = \sigma^2 \begin{bmatrix} 1 & 0 & 0 & 0 \\ 0 & 1 & 0 & 0 \\ 0 & 0 & 1 & 0 \\ 0 & 0 & 0 & 1 \end{bmatrix} = \sigma^2 I_4.$$

## The Serial Correlation Variance–Covariance Matrix

Here, we keep the assumption of homoskedastic disturbances, so the diagonal elements of $\Omega$ are still equal to one another, but we do not require uncorrelated disturbances. Allowing serial correlation lets the off-diagonal elements of $\Omega$ take on almost any values, but some restrictions do apply.

Because $\Omega$ is a variance–covariance matrix, it is symmetrical. Further, consider the variance of a linear combination of disturbances $A\varepsilon$, where $A$ is a $1 \times n$ row matrix with at least one nonzero element. The variance of $A\varepsilon$, which equals $A(E(\varepsilon\varepsilon'))A'$, or $AVA'$, cannot be negative, because variances are never negative.

The discussion of Equation A6.1.2 noted that a symmetric matrix $Q$, such that, for any row in matrix $A$ that is not all zeros, $AQA' > 0$ is called positive definite. If $Q$ is positive definite, $Q^1$ exists and is also positive definite. In this appendix, we replace the Gauss–Markov Assumption that the disturbances are uncorrelated with the assumption that $V$ is positive definite; this assumption ensures that $\Omega^{-1}$ exists. This assumption excludes the possibility that var($A\varepsilon$) could be zero for some nonzero $A$.

This chapter treats in detail the special case of first-order autoregressive disturbances. The variance–covariance matrix for first-order autoregressive disturbances is

$$\Omega_{ar1} = E([\varepsilon\varepsilon']) = \sigma_\varepsilon^2 \begin{bmatrix} 1 & \rho & \rho^2 & \cdot\cdot & \rho^{n-2} & \rho^{n-1} \\ \rho & 1 & \rho & \cdot\cdot & \rho^{n-3} & \rho^{n-2} \\ \rho^2 & \rho & 1 & \cdot\cdot & \rho^{n-4} & \rho^{n-3} \\ \vdots & \vdots & \vdots & \vdots & \vdots & \vdots \\ \rho^{n-2} & \rho^{n-3} & \rho^{n-4} & \cdot\cdot & 1 & \rho \\ \rho^{n-1} & \rho^{n-2} & \rho^{n-3} & \cdot\cdot & \rho & 1 \end{bmatrix}, \qquad \text{11.A.1}$$

where

$$\sigma_\varepsilon^2 = \frac{\sigma_\nu^2}{1 - \rho^2},$$

and $\sigma_\nu^2$ is the variance of the underlying innovations.

We noted earlier that if the disturbances are first-order autoregressive, disturbances from the distant past contribute some amount, albeit an increasingly small amount, to today's disturbances. According to the first-order autoregressive disturbances specification, shocks to the economy never cease altogether to have effects on the economy. This assumption does not accurately portray some economic phenomena. For example, a contract could dictate that a late delivery entails a large penalty payment one month, a smaller penalty payment the next month, and no penalties thereafter. Suppose late deliveries are uncorrelated across time. If, in a model of this contract's costs, the disturbances are these penalties, then an innovation (the shock to costs from new late deliveries) affects costs for only two months. This month's disturbance includes any penalties incurred by new late payments, plus any penalties spilling over from last month's late deliveries. The disturbance one month is correlated with the disturbances in immediately adjacent months, but with no others. Processes in which serial correlation becomes zero after some number of periods are called "moving average" processes. The disturbances described for the model of contract costs are called "first-order moving average disturbances," because the correlation ends after one period.

The variance–covariance matrix for a first-order moving average process is

$$\mathbf{\Omega}_{ma1} = \mathrm{E}([\boldsymbol{\varepsilon}\boldsymbol{\varepsilon}']) = \sigma^2 \begin{bmatrix} 1 & \tau & 0 & 0 & \cdot\cdot & 0 & 0 & 0 \\ \tau & 1 & \tau & 0 & \cdot\cdot & 0 & 0 & 0 \\ 0 & \tau & 1 & \tau & \cdot\cdot & 0 & 0 & 0 \\ : & : & : & : & : & : & : & : \\ 0 & 0 & 0 & 0 & \cdot\cdot & 1 & \tau & 0 \\ 0 & 0 & 0 & 0 & \cdot\cdot & \tau & 1 & \tau \\ 0 & 0 & 0 & 0 & \cdot\cdot & 0 & \tau & 1 \end{bmatrix}, \qquad \text{11.A.2}$$

where $\tau$ is the correlation between adjacent months' disturbances.

## 11.A.2  OLS, GLS, and Serial Correlation

Serial correlation undermines the BLUE property of OLS. However, OLS applied to appropriately transformed data yields the BLUE estimates when all the Gauss–Markov Assumptions except uncorrelated disturbances are met. The BLUE estimation procedure for serially correlated disturbances is an example of GLS.

## Serial Correlation and OLS

The unbiasedness conditions for linear estimators do not depend on the variances or covariances of the disturbances, so OLS remains unbiased when the disturbances are serially correlated. Serial correlation changes the variance of the OLS estimator, however. When the variance–covariance matrix for $Y$ is $\Omega$,

$$\text{var}(\hat{\boldsymbol{\beta}}) = \text{var}\,((X'X)^{-1}X'Y) = (X'X)^{-1}X'(\text{var}(Y))X(X'X)^{-1}$$

$$= (X'X)^{-1}X'\,\Omega X(X'X)^{-1}, \qquad \text{11.A.3}$$

which would simplify to the standard variance expression for OLS, $\sigma^2(X'X)^{-1}$, if $\Omega = \sigma^2 I_n$, but not generally. Estimating the variance of the OLS estimator by $s^2(X'X)^{-1}$ results in biased estimates if the disturbances are correlated. Because the standard OLS-based $t$-tests and $F$-tests rely on this biased estimator, they are invalid when the disturbances are correlated.

## Serial Correlation and GLS

The BLUE estimator for serially correlated disturbances results from minimizing the diagonal elements of the variance expression in Equation 11.A.3, with respect to the linear estimator's weights, $W'$, subject to the unbiasedness conditions, $W'X = I_n$.

Alternatively, the BLUE estimates result from appropriately transforming the regression model and applying OLS to the transformed variables. If the regression model is

$$Y = X\boldsymbol{\beta} + \boldsymbol{\varepsilon},$$

what is the appropriate transformed model,

$$TY = TX\boldsymbol{\beta} + T\boldsymbol{\varepsilon},$$

such that OLS applied to it is BLUE? That is, what $n \times n$ matrix $T$ yields an $n \times 1$ matrix $Q = TY$, an $n \times k$ *matrix* $Z = TX$, and an $n \times 1$ matrix $\boldsymbol{v} = T\boldsymbol{\varepsilon}$, such that OLS applied to

$$Q = Z\boldsymbol{\beta} + \boldsymbol{v} \qquad \text{11.A.4}$$

is BLUE? To answer these questions, first note that $E(\boldsymbol{v}) = 0$. Next, consider the variance of OLS applied to 11.A.4, in which $\boldsymbol{v} = T\boldsymbol{\varepsilon}$. The variance–covariance matrix for $\boldsymbol{v}$ is

$$E(\boldsymbol{v}\boldsymbol{v}') = E(T\boldsymbol{\varepsilon}\boldsymbol{\varepsilon}'T) = T(E(\boldsymbol{\varepsilon}\boldsymbol{\varepsilon}'))T' = T\Omega T'.$$

Consequently, OLS applied to 11.A.4 is BLUE if $T\Omega T' = \sigma^2 I_n$, because then the model in Equation 11.A.4 satisfies the Gauss–Markov Assumptions.

Every positive definite matrix can be conveniently decomposed. For example, $\Omega^{-1}$ can be rewritten as the product of some invertible matrix $P'$ and its transpose, $P$; that is,

$$\Omega^{-1} = P'P.$$

A further property of matrices is that $(AB)^{-1} = B^{-1}A^{-1}$, if both $A$ and $B$ are invertible.

Consequently,

$$\Omega = P^{-1}P'^{-1},$$

so that

$$P\Omega P' = PP^{-1}P'^{-1}P' = I_n.$$

Thus, if we set $T = P$, OLS is BLUE when applied to the regression model in Equation 11.A.4. The GLS estimator for the DGP in which all the Gauss–Markov Assumptions but uncorrelated disturbances are met is

$$\beta_{GLS} = (Z'Z)^{-1}Z'Y = (X'P'PX)^{-1}X'PP'Y$$
$$= (X'\Omega^{-1}X)^{-1}X'\Omega^{-1}Y.$$

The variance of this GLS estimator is

$$\sigma^2(Z'Z)^{-1} = \sigma^2(X'P'PX)^{-1}$$
$$= (X'\Omega^{-1}X)^{-1}.$$

The standard $t$-tests and $F$-tests developed in Chapters 7 and 9 are valid for OLS applied to the transformed model if the disturbances in the underlying model are normally distributed, and they apply approximately in large samples, even if the underlying disturbances are not normally distributed.

Even for the simplest serial correlation patterns, such as first-order autoregressive disturbances or first-order moving average disturbances, economic theory seldom tells us the specific values of $\Omega$. GLS is, therefore, seldom a feasible estimator in the face of serial correlation. The real value of GLS for DGPs with serial correlation is that it points us to the FGLS estimators that rely on estimates of the correlation coefficients, $\rho$ and $\tau$, seen in Equations 11.A.1 and 11.A.2. The standard $t$-tests and $F$-tests apply approximately to FGLS estimators in large samples.

## Chapter 12

# Large-Sample Properties of Estimators: Consistency and Asymptotic Efficiency

*As far as the laws of mathematics refer to reality,*
*they are not certain,*
*and as far as they are certain,*
*they do not refer to reality.[1]*

—ALBERT EINSTEIN, (1879–1955)

ne Saturday night, a drunk was crawling on his hands and knees, underneath a lamppost. Officer Friendly happened by. "Watchya doin'?" inquired the officer.

"I'm lookin' fer my car keys," slurred the drunk.

"Oh, dropped 'em here, did ya?" asked the policeman.

"No, I dropped 'em over there," answered the drunk, pointing to a dark alley, "but the light's better over here."

The drunk's strategy warns us about one peril in econometric modeling. Simplifying assumptions and analytical concessions to convenience can undermine empirical work, dooming you to frustration from the outset. Nonetheless, well-chosen simplifying assumptions and analytical conveniences are essential aids in advancing understanding.

Unbiasedness and consistency are intuitively appealing criteria for choosing among estimators. In the data-generating processes (DGPs) we will encounter in coming chapters, though, the search for unbiased estimators is often thwarted. Either finding an unbiased estimator is mathematically beyond us or unbiased estimators require information we don't have. To overcome these difficulties, econometricians look in new places for best estimators. They design convenient analytical alternatives to unbiasedness and efficiency as criteria for selecting estimators. In these new analyses, econometricians ask how estimators perform as the sample size grows infinitely large.

This chapter first explores a large sample property called *consistency* that is of fundamental interest to econometricians and asks whether the unbiased estimators we have studied in earlier chapters are also consistent estimators. A central finding of the chapter is that the least squares estimators may be either consistent or inconsistent for the realistic case in which the explanators are not fixed across samples. Because many estimators can be consistent in a given DGP and just as many can be unbiased, the chapter next introduces the notion of *asymptotic efficiency*, with which we can choose among alternative consistent estimators. Determining the asymptotic efficiency of an estimator requires determining what happens to the estimator's distribution as the sample size grows toward infinity.

When applied haphazardly, the concepts of consistency and asymptotic distributions can be as misguided as the drunk's search under the street light. But when applied judiciously, these notions can lead us to good estimators and valid inferences when unbiased estimators are not available.

## 12.1    The Large-Sample, or Asymptotic, Perspective

WHAT ARE AN ESTI-MATOR'S PROPERTIES?

We have focused thus far on the traits of the estimates from many samples of a given size: "Is an estimator unbiased? What is its variance?" We wanted to know which estimators have the "best sampling properties" in a sample of size *n*. This chapter's new perspective offers an alternative focus. It looks to the **large-sample properties** or **asymptotic properties** of estimators, which are the traits of the estimators as the sample size grows toward infinity.

When we relax the Gauss–Markov Assumptions, or trade in our linear-in-the-parameters models for nonlinear models, unbiasedness and efficiency often become unachievable goals. *When stumped in the search for estimators with good across-sample properties, econometric theorists usually turn to deriving estimators with good large-sample properties, with the often fulfilled hope that estimators, which perform well in very large samples, will work well in moderately sized samples, too.*

Why do we settle for properties that apply to nearly infinite samples, when our samples are always much less than infinite? We do this because determining an estimator's sampling properties, such as unbiasedness and efficiency, is sometimes too difficult. *We turn to the large-sample perspective because large-sample properties are often easier to analyze mathematically than are finite sample properties.*

The new perspective does not abandon the old one altogether, however. The context for asking about large-sample properties is still what happens across many samples, but instead of asking about expectations across samples of given size, the new perspective focuses on the probabilities of favorable and unfavorable outcomes across samples as the size of the samples grows infinitely large.

The large-sample approach doesn't only yield estimators that perform well; it also can inform us about the distribution of estimators, and thereby facilitate hypothesis testing. *When the distribution of an estimator is too difficult to ascertain for finite samples, econometricians hope the large-sample distribution of the estimator provides a good approximation to the finite sample distribution.* If this hope is fulfilled, as it often is, inferences based on the large-sample distribution are a good guide to the inferences econometricians would draw if they knew the estimator's finite sample distribution.

Large-sample properties are cold comfort when one's own data series is short. One extensive industry within econometrics is devoted to Monte Carlo studies of the small-sample properties of estimators made popular by their large-sample properties. Econometricians frequently find that estimators that perform well in large samples perform poorly in small ones.

## Picturing Consistency and Asymptotic Distributions

Pictures can expose to plain view the core large-sample concepts of *consistency* and *asymptotic distributions*. Figures 12.1 and 12.2 replicate Figures 2.6 and 2.7, which show the Monte Carlo experiment distributions of our earliest intuitive estimators, $\beta_{g1}$, $\beta_{g2}$, and $\beta_{g3}$, as the sample sizes in the DGPs grow from 200 to 500. (The experiments reported in Figures 12.1 and 12.2 were conducted using MC Builder II.) As the sample sizes grow, the distributions of $\beta_{g1}$, $\beta_{g2}$, and $\beta_{g3}$ all collapsed around a single value. In Chapter 3, we learned that the distributions of $\beta_{g1}$, $\beta_{g2}$, and $\beta_{g3}$ all have an expected value of $\beta$ under the Gauss–Markov Assumptions. Consequently, the single value the three estimators collapse around is $\beta$, the true value. If such a collapse upon the true value of $\beta$ continues unchecked as the sample size tends toward infinity—that is, if the variance of an unbiased estimator shrinks to zero in the limit—we would say the estimator is a *consistent estimator* of $\beta$.

The Monte Carlo experiment behind Figure 12.1 assumes the disturbances are normally distributed; that behind Figure 12.2 assumes they arise from a highly skewed and discrete distribution that takes on the value $-750$ with probability one third and the value $375$ with probability two thirds. The fact that our estimators appear consistent for such disparate disturbances suggests that the consistency of these estimators is quite robust. What gives rise to this robust consistency? *Mathematically, the consistency of $\beta_{g1}$, $\beta_{g2}$, and $\beta_{g3}$ rests on the Law of Large Numbers.* The **Law of Large Numbers** says that, under suitable conditions, the distribution of a sample mean tends to collapse around the corresponding population mean in large samples.

Figure 12.1 reveals that for all sample sizes, the distributions of $\beta_{g1}$, $\beta_{g2}$, and $\beta_{g3}$ look very much like the normal distribution when the underlying disturbances are normally distributed—which they should, because linear combinations of normally distributed variables are themselves normally distributed. Figure 12.2 offers the more surprising revelation that even for a sample size as small as 20, the distributions of $\beta_{g1}$, $\beta_{g2}$, and $\beta_{g3}$ look much like the normal distribution when the disturbances themselves are quite non-normal. *The approximate normality of*

**Figure 12.1**

The Distributions of $\beta_{g1}$, $\beta_{g2}$, and $\beta_{g3}$ for Several Sample Sizes with Normally Distributed Disturbances

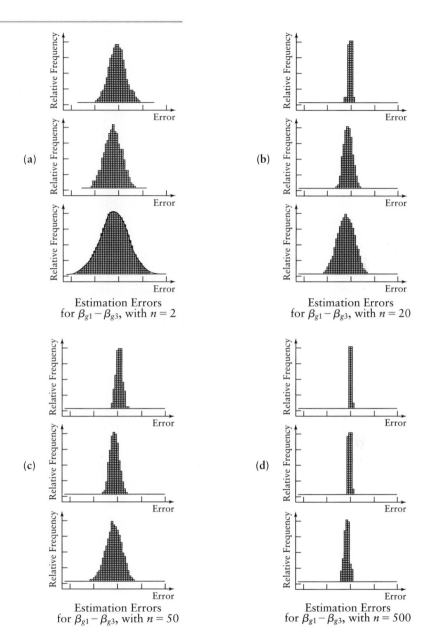

(a) Estimation Errors for $\beta_{g1} - \beta_{g3}$, with $n = 2$

(b) Estimation Errors for $\beta_{g1} - \beta_{g3}$, with $n = 20$

(c) Estimation Errors for $\beta_{g1} - \beta_{g3}$, with $n = 50$

(d) Estimation Errors for $\beta_{g1} - \beta_{g3}$, with $n = 500$

**Figure 12.2**

The Distributions of $\beta_{g1}$, $\beta_{g2}$, and $\beta_{g3}$ for Several Sample Sizes with Skewed, Discrete Disturbances

(a)

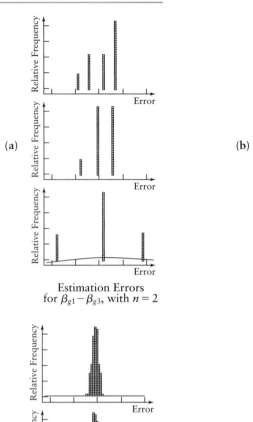

Estimation Errors
for $\beta_{g1} - \beta_{g3}$, with $n = 2$

(b)

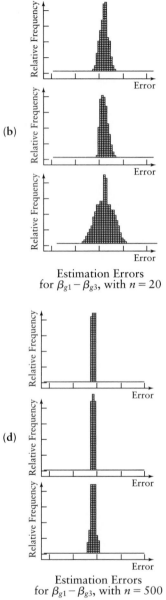

Estimation Errors
for $\beta_{g1} - \beta_{g3}$, with $n = 20$

(c)

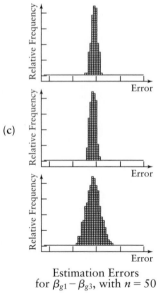

Estimation Errors
for $\beta_{g1} - \beta_{g3}$, with $n = 50$

(d)

Estimation Errors
for $\beta_{g1} - \beta_{g3}$, with $n = 500$

$\beta_{g1}$, $\beta_{g2}$, *and* $\beta_{g3}$ *in large samples, despite non-normal disturbances, stems from statistics' famous Central (or "key") Limit Theorem.* The **Central Limit Theorem** says that under suitable conditions, the distribution of a sample mean tends to be approximately normally distributed in large samples.

When the Central Limit Theorem applies to an estimator, we say that the estimator's *asymptotic distribution* is the normal distribution. The Central Limit Theorem justifies econometricians' reliance on the normal distribution and its relatives for conducting statistical inference in large samples even when disturbances are not normally distributed. Chapter 9 noted the applicability of *t*-tests and *F*-tests in large samples despite non-normal disturbances; it is the Central Limit Theorem that ensures the *t*- and *F*-statistics are approximately *t*- and *F*-distributed in large samples. It is heartening that standard hypothesis testing is valid in large samples for the commonly encountered distributions of disturbances, and not just for normally distributed disturbances, because we often do not know the actual distribution of the disturbances in our models.

## 12.2 Asymptotic Unbiasedness, Consistency, and Probability Limits

WHAT MAKES A
GOOD ESTIMATOR?

Intuitive descriptions of statistical properties like unbiasedness and consistency help econometricians explain their work to nonspecialists. But determining which estimators do and do not have a particular statistical property requires a formal definition that can be applied to specific estimators. This section defines two large-sample properties of estimators, asymptotic unbiasedness and consistency. Determining the consistency of estimators often requires a new analytical tool that we call a *probability limit*—also introduced in this section.

### Asymptotic Unbiasedness

One natural large-sample property is **asymptotic unbiasedness**. If the bias of an estimator has a limit of zero as the number of observations grows without bound, the estimator is asymptotically unbiased. *An estimator that is unbiased for every n is also asymptotically unbiased, but many estimators that are biased for every sample size n are nonetheless asymptotically unbiased.* For example, consider the sample variance from a simple random sample of $n$ observations as an estimator of the population variance. The sample variance,

$$\hat{\sigma}^2 = \frac{1}{n}\sum_{i=1}^{n}(Y_i - \overline{Y})^2,$$

is a biased estimator of the population variance, $\sigma^2$, because

$$E(\hat{\sigma}^2) = \frac{n-1}{n}\sigma^2.$$

Notice that as $n$ grows large, $(n-1)/n$ converges to one and the bias of the sample variance disappears. The sample variance is a biased estimator of the population variance, but an asymptotically unbiased estimator.

## Consistency

An ideal estimation procedure would be exactly right all the time. This lofty ideal is beyond our reach. Nonetheless, some estimators are almost always almost right if their sample size is large enough. The distribution of such an estimator collapses around the true value of the parameter being estimated. We call such an estimator a **consistent estimator**. More precisely, an estimator is **consistent** if beyond some sample size the probability converges to one that its estimate will be as close as we like to the true parameter's value. Unfortunately, but unavoidably, consistent estimators usually still run some small risk of being further from right than we would like, even with a large sample.

A consequence of consistency is that as the sample size grows, the estimator's distribution collapses around the true value of the parameter being estimated. Figure 12.3 illustrates the collapse of the distribution of a consistent estimator $\tilde{\beta}$ about the true value $\beta$. The figure shows the distribution of $\tilde{\beta}$ for samples of 5, 20, 50, and 500, all in one figure. Because $\tilde{\beta}$ is a consistent estimator of $\beta$, the distribution of estimates becomes more concentrated at larger sample sizes, and the concentration accrues increasingly closer to $\beta$.

*One often encountered example of a consistent estimator is an asymptotically unbiased estimator whose variance converges to zero as the sample size grows.* The distribution of such an estimator collapses around the true value as the sample size grows large. However, there are seldom encountered pathological cases in which a consistent estimator is not asymptotically unbiased. One such pathological example helps clarify just what consistency means.

Suppose we wish to estimate $\beta$ with an estimator, $\tilde{\tilde{\beta}}$, that takes on one of just two values, $(\beta + 2n)$ or $(\beta + 1/n)$, the former with probability $1/n$, and the latter with probability $(1 - 1/n)$. This estimator is pathological in that as we get more observations, we risk an ever larger estimation error equal to $2n$. The expected value of this estimator is

$$E(\tilde{\tilde{\beta}}) = 2n\left(\frac{1}{n}\right) + \left(\beta + \frac{1}{n}\right)\left(1 - \frac{1}{n}\right) = 2 + \beta\left(1 - \frac{1}{n}\right) + \frac{1}{n} - \frac{1}{n^2},$$

**Figure 12.3**

The Collapse of a
Consistent Estima-
tor's Distribution as
*n* Grows

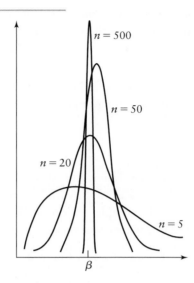

which will, in general, differ from $\beta$, so the estimator $\tilde{\tilde{\beta}}$ is a biased estimator of $\beta$. As $n$ goes to infinity, the expected value of $\tilde{\tilde{\beta}}$ approaches $\beta + 2$, so $\tilde{\tilde{\beta}}$ is also an asymptotically biased estimator.

Nonetheless, $\tilde{\tilde{\beta}}$ is a consistent estimator of $\beta$ because as $n$ grows large, the probability approaches one that $\tilde{\tilde{\beta}}$ is within an ever shrinking $(1/n)$ of $\beta$. The large error associated with $\tilde{\tilde{\beta}}$'s value $(\beta + 2n)$ becomes increasingly unlikely to occur, and the ever more likely to occur $(\beta + 1/n)$ value grows ever closer to $\beta$.

Estimators that are both inconsistent and asymptotically biased are encountered more frequently than consistent estimators that are asymptotically biased. Econometricians avoid such estimators whenever possible, but to avoid them requires methods to identify them. *Probability limits* are the statistical tool econometricians use to distinguish consistent estimators from inconsistent ones.

## Probability Limits

Econometricians say that a consistent estimator *converges in probability* to the true parameter value that we seek. A random variable $\beta^*$ **converges in probability** to a constant value $c$ if, as the sample size grows large, the probability approaches one that $\beta^*$ takes on a value as close to $c$ as we could wish.[2] In such cases, we call $c$ the **probability limit**, or **plim**, of $\beta^*$. Not every estimator's distribution collapses as the sample size grows large, so not every estimator converges in probability to a constant. Among estimators that do converge in probability to a constant, only some converge to the true value we are seeking, so only some estimators are consistent. We read the notation

$$\text{plim}(\beta^*) = d$$

as "$\beta^*$ converges in probability to $d$," or, equivalently, as "the probability limit of $\beta^*$ is $d$," or "the plim of $\beta^*$ is $d$." The estimator $\beta^*$ is a consistent estimator of $\beta$ if, and only if,

$$\text{plim}(\beta^*) = \beta.$$

One frequently encountered example of a random variable that converges to a constant is a random variable with a mean of $d$ and a variance that converges to zero as the sample size grows. This corresponds to the consistency of an unbiased estimator whose variance converges to zero as the sample size grows.

Econometricians are often interested in the large-sample properties of random variables that are sample means of some variable or function of variables, such as the sample variance of the disturbances or the sample covariance between a disturbance and an explanator. The statistical Law of Large Numbers states that, under suitable conditions, a sample mean converges in probability to its expected value in the population. Econometricians often appeal to the Law of Large Numbers to link the probability limit of a random variable to its expected value. We have already seen one pair of conditions under which the Law of Large Numbers holds: (i) The random variable in question is a sample mean whose expected value is always equal to a finite number, $d$, coupled with (ii) the variance of the sample mean converges to zero as the sample size grows. The law holds in many other, but not all, circumstances. *Unbounded variances often upset the Law of Large Numbers.* Appendix 12.A contains a more formal discussion of probability limits and consistency.

## 12.3    The Consistency of $\beta_{g4}$ and $\hat{\beta}_1$

WHAT ARE AN ESTI-
MATOR'S PROPERTIES?

We learned in Chapters 3 and 4 that $\beta_{g4}$ and $\hat{\beta}_1$ are the best linear unbiased estimators (BLUE) under the Gauss–Markov Assumptions. These properties are appealing enough that there would be little reason to develop the probability limit tool just to find one more appealing trait of the least squares estimators. The real worth of consistency and of probability limits is in the analysis of more complicated DGPs than the Gauss–Markov framework. Given our familiarity with the least squares estimators and the Gauss–Markov Assumptions, however, they provide a fertile first place to look at consistency and probability limits. Therefore, this section examines the consistency of $\beta_{g4}$ and $\hat{\beta}_1$ under the Gauss–Markov Assumptions.

The ordinary least squares (OLS) estimators $\beta_{g4}$ and $\hat{\beta}_1$ are consistent under the Gauss–Markov Assumptions, but only if we add further assumptions about what additional $X$-values we observe as the sample size grows. This section's proof of $\beta_{g4}$'s consistency under the Gauss–Markov Assumptions rests on an elementary application of the Law of Large Numbers. The section's proof of $\hat{\beta}_1$'s consistency is more elaborate; it serves as a template for examining the consistency of other estimators in subsequent chapters.

## The Consistency of $\beta_{g4}$ Under the Gauss–Markov Assumptions

We learned in Chapter 3 that under the Gauss–Markov Assumptions the BLUE estimator of the slope of a line through the origin,

$$\beta_{g4} = \frac{\sum X_i Y_i}{\sum X_i^2},$$

has expected value equal to $\beta$ and variance equal to $\sigma^2 / \sum X_i^2$. Because $\beta_{g4}$ is an unbiased estimator ($E(\beta_{g4}) = \beta$), $\beta_{g4}$ is consistent if its variance converges to zero as the sample size grows. Thus, $\beta_{g4}$ is consistent if $\sum X_i^2$ grows without bound as the sample size increases.

Nothing in the Gauss–Markov Assumptions, however, tells us what $X$-values we would add to our analysis if the sample size were to grow. We know only that observation $i$ gets $X$-value $X_i$ in every sample with an $i$-th observation. If we are to ensure that the variance of $\beta_{g4}$ converges to zero in large samples, we need to assume that $\sum X_i^2$ grows without bound as $n$ grows. This is a modest requirement, but it does exclude some DGPs. For example, a time series study that uses the number of Dodo birds (now extinct) as an explanator would not satisfy the requirement that $\sum X_i^2$ grows without bound as $n$ grows—the sum stops growing after the period in which the Dodo bird becomes extinct; $X_i$ then equals zero ever after. Similarly, often satisfied assumptions, coupled with the Gauss–Markov Assumptions, suffice to make our other unbiased estimators consistent.

Notice that the consistency of $\beta_{g4}$ depends $\sigma^2$ on being finite. If the disturbances in our DGP had an infinite variance, the term $\sigma^2$ in the numerator of the estimators' variances might counter the effect of a growing denominator, and the variance might not converge to zero. In economic applications, we need to check whether the assumption of finite variances is warranted. In cross sectional data, variances are almost always finite. In time series data, however, variances sometimes grow without bound. Unbounded variances can make the Law of Large Numbers fail to apply and OLS inconsistent.

## Manipulating Probability Limits

The following are common rules for manipulating probability limits:

1. plim(constant) = constant.
2. plim(sequence of constants) = lim(sequence of constants).

When $\alpha$ and $\beta$ are random variables for which plim($\alpha$) and plim($\beta$) are finite:

3. plim($\alpha + \beta$) = plim($\alpha$) + plim($\beta$).
4. plim($\alpha\beta$) = plim($\alpha$)plim($\beta$).
5. plim($\beta/\alpha$) = plim($\beta$)/plim($\alpha$) if plim($\alpha$) $\neq$ 0.
6. plim($g(\beta)$) = $g$(plim($\beta$)) for continuous $g$.

(The Law of Large Numbers states that under suitable conditions, the difference between a sample mean and its expected value converges in probability to zero. The law applies routinely when a sample mean's expected value is finite and its variance has a limit of 0 as $n$ grows without bound.) The striking feature of these relationships is that they require neither the independence of $\beta$ and $\alpha$, nor the linearity of $g$, making probability limits easier to manipulate than are expected values of products or ratios.

These rules are similar to those for manipulating expectations, but with some important differences. First, expectations apply to random variables with realizations that we see across samples, whereas probability limits apply to the random variables that arise when we draw successively larger samples. Second, rules 4, 5, and 6 are generally untrue of expectations unless the random variables in question are statistically independent, but they apply to probability limits, no matter what the correlations are among the random variables. It is the applicability of rules 4, 5, and 6 to both statistically independent and statistically nonindependent random variables that makes analysis of consistency easier than analysis of bias.

## The Consistency of $\hat{\beta}_1$

We already learned that OLS consistently estimates the slope of a line through the origin under the Gauss–Markov Assumptions as long as, additionally, $\sum X_i^2$ grows without bound as the sample size grows. Here, we use the rules for manipulating probability limits from the previous section to prove the consistency of $\hat{\beta}_1$ when the Gauss–Markov Assumptions apply. Once again, we need an additional assumption about the new values of $X$ that occur as $n$ grows. The assumption is that $\lim(1/n\sum x_i^2)$ equals $Q$, a nonzero, finite constant. One way to prove the consistency of $\hat{\beta}_1$ would be to look at the mean and variance of $\hat{\beta}_1$, as in the proof of the consistency of $\beta_{g4}$. A somewhat more elaborate proof of the consistency of $\hat{\beta}_1$ provides a template for examining the consistency of estimators besides OLS, however, so this section follows the more elaborate path.

Recall that

$$\hat{\beta}_1 = \frac{\sum x_i Y_i}{\sum x_i^2} = \beta_1 + \frac{\sum x_i \varepsilon_i}{\sum x_i^2},$$

which we can rewrite as

$$\hat{\beta}_1 = \beta_1 + \frac{\frac{1}{n}\sum x_i \varepsilon_i}{\frac{1}{n}\sum x_i^2}.$$

The OLS estimator is consistent if it converges in probability to $\beta_1$, that is, if

$$\text{plim}(\hat{\beta}_1) = \text{plim}\left(\beta_1 + \frac{\frac{1}{n}\sum x_i \varepsilon_i}{\frac{1}{n}\sum x_i^2}\right) = \beta_1.$$

Rule 3 in our rules for manipulating probability limits is that the plim of a sum is the sum of the plims. Thus,

$$\text{plim}\left(\beta_1 + \frac{\frac{1}{n}\sum x_i \varepsilon_i}{\frac{1}{n}\sum x_i^2}\right) = \text{plim}(\beta_1) + \text{plim}\left(\frac{\frac{1}{n}\sum x_i \varepsilon_i}{\frac{1}{n}\sum x_i^2}\right).$$

Rule 1 says that the plim of a constant is a constant. Thus,

$$\text{plim}(\beta_1) + \text{plim}\left(\frac{\frac{1}{n}\sum x_i \varepsilon_i}{\frac{1}{n}\sum x_i^2}\right) = \beta_1 + \text{plim}\left(\frac{\frac{1}{n}\sum x_i \varepsilon_i}{\frac{1}{n}\sum x_i^2}\right).$$

Rule 5 says that the plim of a ratio is the ratio of the plims, if the plim in the denominator is not zero. Thus, if $\text{plim}\left(\frac{1}{n}\sum x_i^2\right)$ is not zero,

$$\beta_1 + \text{plim}\left(\frac{\frac{1}{n}\sum x_i \varepsilon_i}{\frac{1}{n}\sum x_i^2}\right) = \beta_1 + \frac{\text{plim}\left(\frac{1}{n}\sum x_i \varepsilon_i\right)}{\text{plim}\left(\frac{1}{n}\sum x_i^2\right)}. \qquad \textbf{12.1}$$

Increasing the sample size requires adding new $X$-values. These new $X$-values may change the mean squared $X$. Consequently, the mean of squared $X$'s is best viewed as a sequence of numbers that may change when the sample size changes. Our new assumptions say that the limit of this sequence is $Q$. Rule 2 says that the plim of a sequence of constants is the limit of that sequence, so $\text{plim}\left(\frac{1}{n}\Sigma x_i^2\right)$ equals $\lim\left(\frac{1}{n}\Sigma x_i^2\right)$, which equals $Q$, by assumption. We can rewrite Equation 12.1:

$$\beta_1 + \frac{\text{plim}\left(\frac{1}{n}\Sigma x_i\varepsilon_i\right)}{\text{plim}\left(\frac{1}{n}\Sigma x_i^2\right)} = \beta_1 + \frac{\text{plim}\left(\frac{1}{n}\Sigma x_i\varepsilon_i\right)}{Q}.$$

Thus, the consistency of $\hat{\beta}_1$ rests on whether $\text{plim}\left(\frac{1}{n}\Sigma x_i\varepsilon_i\right)$ equals zero.

The Gauss–Markov Assumptions imply that $\text{E}\left(\frac{1}{n}\Sigma x_i\varepsilon_i\right)$ equals zero. Therefore, if the variance of $\left(\frac{1}{n}\Sigma x_i\varepsilon_i\right)$ converges to zero as $n$ grows, $\text{plim}\left(\frac{1}{n}\Sigma x_i\varepsilon_i\right)$ will, indeed, equal zero because its distribution will collapse on its mean as the sample size grows. What is the variance of $\left(\frac{1}{n}\Sigma x_i\varepsilon_i\right)$? It is

$$\text{var}\left(\frac{1}{n}\Sigma x_i\varepsilon_i\right) = \frac{1}{n^2}\Sigma x_i^2\text{var}(\varepsilon_i)$$

because $n$ and the $x$ are constants and the covariances among the disturbances are zero under the Gauss–Markov Assumptions. Thus, we find that

$$\frac{1}{n^2}\Sigma x_i^2\text{var}(\varepsilon_i) = \frac{1}{n^2}\Sigma x_i^2\sigma^2 = \frac{\sigma^2}{n}\frac{1}{n}\Sigma x_i^2,$$

the limit of which as $n$ grows, is

$$\lim\left(\frac{\sigma^2}{n}\frac{1}{n}\Sigma x_i^2\right) = \lim\left(\frac{\sigma^2}{n}\right)\lim\left(\frac{1}{n}\Sigma x_i^2\right) = 0Q = 0.$$

The OLS estimator, $\hat{\beta}_1$, is a consistent estimator of $\beta_1$. Appendix 12.C in Extension 3 on this book's Web site (**www.aw-bc.com Murray**) contains a matrix algebra proof for the consistency of OLS in the multiple regression case; there, too, mild assumptions about the character of additional $X$-values are required. These mild assumptions ensure that the explanators do not become perfectly collinear in large samples and that the $X$-values don't suffer Dodo bird–like problems.

## Consistent Estimators and Specifying DGPs

A feature of this analysis of $\hat{\beta}_1$'s consistency is frequently found in econometric work. Econometricians don't always assume only what they minimally need to assume. They often make stronger assumptions than are strictly necessary. At one level, Equation 12.1 tells us what needs to be true for $\hat{\beta}_1$ to be a consistent estimator of $\beta_1$. We need

$$\text{plim}\left(\frac{1}{n}\Sigma x_i\varepsilon_i\right) = 0 \tag{12.2}$$

and

$$\text{plim}\left(\frac{1}{n}\Sigma x_i^2\right) = Q, \text{ a nonzero constant.} \tag{12.3}$$

When 12.2 fails, but 12.3 holds, the OLS estimator is both asymptotically biased and inconsistent; the estimator's distribution collapses around the wrong value.

Instead of assuming Equations 12.2 and 12.3 directly, though, the proof of the consistency of $\hat{\beta}_1$ derives Equations 12.2 and 12.3, using the Law of Large Numbers, from the extended Gauss–Markov Assumptions:

1. The explanators are fixed across samples.
2. $E(x_i\varepsilon_i) = 0.$      **12.4**
3. $\lim\limits_{n\to\infty}\left(\frac{1}{n}\Sigma x_i^2\right) = Q$, a nonzero constant.      **12.5**

Equations 12.4 and 12.5 are stronger assumptions than are absolutely necessary for Equations 12.1 and 12.2 to be true when the explanators are fixed across samples. Why do econometricians make stronger assumptions than necessary? Why don't they simply assume Equations 12.1 and 12.2 are true?

One major advantage of assuming Equations 12.4 and 12.5 instead of Equations 12.1 and 12.2 is that there are straightforward tests of the hypothesis that $E(x_i\varepsilon_i) = 0$, but no direct way of empirically examining the $\text{plim}(\frac{1}{n}\Sigma x_i\varepsilon_i)$, because it involves the limit of an infinite sequence. One goal of econometricians in specifying their models is to make their assumptions testable. A second reason that econometricians often rely on assumptions about expectations, coupled with the Law of Large Numbers, to establish asymptotic convergence results is that economic theory more often yields constraints on expected values than on probability limits. Econometricians grounding their DGPs in economic theory are, therefore, likely to rely on expected value assumptions drawn from economic theory, coupled with the Law of Large numbers, to assess the consistency of their estimators.

## An Example: Haavelmo and the Consumption Function

In this section, we learn that when our interest is in a nonlinear transformation of an unbiased estimator, the transformation may lose us unbiasedness. Consistency, on the other hand, is preserved by all continuous transformations. The following example makes this point.

In a Golden Oldie later in this chapter (see p. 508), Trygve Haavelmo shows that we can estimate the marginal propensity to consume, *mpc*, by examining the Keynesian multiplier expression that links changes in GDP, $\Delta GDP$, to changes in autonomous investment expenditure (which is what macroeconomists call investment that is unaffected by income changes), $\Delta Inv$:

$$\Delta GDP_i = \frac{1}{1 - mpc}\Delta Inv_i + \varepsilon_i = \beta \Delta Inv_i + \varepsilon.$$

We know that $\beta_{g4}$ estimates $\beta$ unbiasedly and consistently, if the Gauss–Markov Assumptions are satisfied. Our interest here is not in $\beta$, though but rather in the marginal propensity to consume,

$$mpc = 1 - \frac{1}{\beta}.$$

Is the estimator of the marginal propensity to consume based on $\beta_{g4}$,

$$\widehat{mpc} = 1 - \frac{1}{\beta_{g4}},$$

an unbiased estimator of *mpc*? Is $\widehat{mpc}$ a consistent estimator of *mpc*?

The estimator $\widehat{mpc}$ is an unbiased estimator of *mpc* if $E(\widehat{mpc}) = mpc$; that is, if

$$E\left(1 - \frac{1}{\beta_{g4}}\right) = E\left(1 - \frac{\sum \Delta inv_i^2}{\sum \Delta inv_i \Delta GDP_i}\right) = 1 - E\left(\frac{\sum \Delta inv_i^2}{\sum \Delta inv_i \Delta GDP_i}\right) = mpc.$$

Unfortunately, our algebra of expectations does not tell us how to go from

$$E(\Delta GDP_i) = \beta \Delta Inv_i$$

to a simple expression for

$$E\left(\frac{\sum \Delta Inv_i^2}{\sum \Delta Inv_i \Delta GDP_i}\right); \qquad\qquad\qquad 12.6$$

our algebra of expectations applies to linear transformations of a random variable, but not to nonlinear transformations. (The appearance of the dependent variable, $\Delta GDP$, in the denominator of Equation 12.6 makes the expression nonlinear.) However, more advanced methods would reveal that $E(\widehat{mpc})$ does not generally equal *mpc*, so $\widehat{mpc}$ is not an unbiased estimator of *mpc*. Nonlinear transformations of unbiased estimators usually lose the unbiasedness property.

Is $\widehat{mpc}$ a consistent estimator of *mpc*? Yes, it is. Rule 6 of our rules for manipulating probability limits tells us that for continuous functions, the plim of a function is the function of the plims. Thus, if $\text{plim}(\beta_{g4})$, which equals $mpc$, is not zero,

$$\text{plim}\left(1 - \frac{1}{\beta_{g4}}\right) = 1 - \frac{1}{\text{plim}(\beta_{g4})} = 1 - \frac{1}{\beta} = mpc,$$

and $\widehat{mpc}$ is a consistent estimator of $mpc$. Consistency is maintained when an estimator is continuously transformed.

This example highlights the simplicity of manipulating probability limits relative to manipulating expectations. The large-sample analysis assures us that although $\widehat{mpc}$ is a biased estimator of $mpc$, in sufficiently large samples, that bias will become inconsequential. Haavelmo's estimation strategy has considerable appeal when our samples are large, and it highlights why consistency is a convenient property for estimators to have.

## 12.4   Replacing Fixed $X$'s with Stochastic $X$'s

**What Is the DGP?**   The assumption that the $X$'s take on the same values in every sample is unrealistic. When economists draw new samples, the values that the explanators take on are likely to vary. Does OLS remain a consistent estimator under the extended Gauss–Markov Assumptions if the $X$'s are not fixed, but instead vary randomly across samples? This is the question that this section addresses. The good news is that OLS may be consistent when the explanators are not fixed across samples. The bad news is that OLS may instead be inconsistent when the explanators are not fixed.

### Assumptions About the Disturbances and Stochastic $X$'s

Chapter 3 argued that its findings about the means and variances of linear estimators for the fixed $X$-case could be extended to the random $X$-case, but only if the DGP included a suitable assumption about the joint distribution of the disturbances and the $X$'s. That chapter showed that if we replace the assumption of fixed $X$'s with the assumption that the Gauss–Markov Assumptions about the disturbances hold conditional on every particular set of values for random $X$'s, then we preserve the findings about the expected values and variances of linear estimators, except that all such statements became true only conditional on the observed $X$-values.

Chapters 4 and 6 noted that these same conclusions apply to OLS in the bivariate and multiple regression models. Does some similar assumption suffice for OLS to be a consistent estimator when the $X$'s vary from sample to sample? Yes, there is an assumption about the joint distribution of the disturbances and the $X$'s for which OLS is consistent. However, just as in the case of fixed $X$'s, a proof of

# An Econometric Top 40—A Golden Oldie

## The Marginal Propensity to Consume

In his classic 1936 book[3] that reshaped the field of macroeconomics, John Maynard Keynes, a Cambridge University economist, placed much emphasis on what he termed the "marginal propensity to consume." In simple form, he claimed that

$$consumption = \beta_0 + \beta_1 income, \qquad \text{H12.1}$$

where $\beta_1$, the change in consumption with respect to income, is the marginal propensity to consume. Keynes argued that the marginal propensity to consume is between zero and one. He also explained that increases in government spending or in investment could spur total output by more than the amount of that increase. The magnitude of this "multiplier effect" depends on the marginal propensity to consume. For example,

$$(change\ in\ income) =$$
$$(change\ in\ government\ expenditure)/(1 - \beta_1).$$
$$\text{H12.2}$$

Keynes's multiplier is thus

$$1/(1 - \beta_1). \qquad \text{H12.3}$$

Because Keynes assumed $0 \le \beta_1 \le 1$, his theory implies a multiplier greater than or equal to one, but on the question of how large the multiplier actually is, Keynes's theory is silent. Enter the econometricians. In 1947, Nobel laureate in economics Trygve Haavelmo of Oslo University, estimated the marginal propensity to consume,[4] and, by implication, the multiplier effect.

Haavelmo used data on consumption and income to estimate the $\beta_1$ shown in Equation H12.1. Using the U.S. data on real per capita consumption and real per capita income for 1922–1941 shown in Hit Figure 12.1, Haavelmo estimated the marginal propensity to consume to be 0.732, which, according to Equation H12.3, implies a multiplier of 3.73. Next, Haavelmo used the multiplier relationship shown in Equation H12.2 (with autonomous expenditure replacing government spending) to estimate $1/(1 - \beta_1)$ directly. Haavelmo's direct estimate of the multiplier, 3.048, implied an estimated marginal propensity to consume of 0.672. Haavelmo's data on income, consumption, and what he termed "autonomous expenditure," essentially, government spending plus investment, are contained in haavelmo.***.

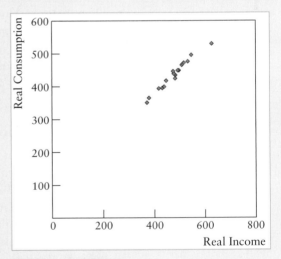

**Hit Figure 12.1**

Real Consumption and Real GDP, 1922–1941

*Source*: Trygve Haavelmo, "Methods of Measuring the Marginal Propensity to Consume," *Journal of the American Statistical Association* 42 (March 1947): 105–122.

**Final Notes**

From a macroeconomic perspective, Haavelmo's two estimates, 3.73 and 3.048, are substantially different. Haavelmo argued forcefully that the estimator using Equation H12.2 was superior to the estimate based on Equation H12.1, reminding us to keep in mind the question: "Why should an economist prefer one guess about the marginal propensity to consume to another guess based upon the same data?" In 1989, Haavelmo received the Nobel prize in economics "for his clarification of the probability theory foundations of econometrics and his analyses of simultaneous economic structures."

∎

the consistency of OLS also requires a new assumption about the behavior of the $X$'s in large samples to avoid Dodo-bird outcomes.

Equation 12.1 reports that

$$\text{plim}(\hat{\beta}_1) = \beta_1 + \text{plim}\left(\frac{\frac{1}{n}\Sigma x_i \varepsilon_i}{\frac{1}{n}\Sigma x_i^2}\right) = \beta_1 + \frac{\text{plim}\left(\frac{1}{n}\Sigma x_i \varepsilon_i\right)}{\text{plim}\left(\frac{1}{n}\Sigma x_i^2\right)}.$$

The assumptions needed for OLS to be consistent are those given in Equations 12.2 and 12.3:

$$\text{plim}\left(\frac{1}{n}\Sigma x_i \varepsilon_i\right) = 0 \qquad\qquad \textbf{12.7}$$

and

$$\text{plim}\left(\frac{1}{n}\Sigma x_i^2\right) = Q, \text{ a nonzero constant.} \qquad\qquad \textbf{12.8}$$

Equation 12.7 requires that the sample covariance between $X_i$ and $\varepsilon_i$ converges in probability to zero. Notice that this lack of correlation in large samples applies only to each disturbance and the corresponding observation on $X$; it imposes no restriction on the correlation between a disturbance, $\varepsilon_i$, and the values $X$ takes on in other observations. Equation 12.7 refers only to each disturbance and its corresponding observation on $X$. In words we express this condition by saying that the disturbances are **contemporaneously uncorrelated asymptotically**. Equation 12.8 is the stochastic counterpart to Equation 12.3; it excludes random Dodo-like explanators.

For the practical and theoretical reasons discussed in the preceding section, econometricians often don't assume Equation 12.7, but instead make assumptions about the covariance of the $\varepsilon_i$ and the $X_i$ in the population that ensure, by the Law of Large Numbers, that Equation 12.7 holds. In particular, they usually rest the consistency of OLS on whether

$$E(x_i\varepsilon_i) = 0 \qquad\qquad \textbf{12.7}'$$

and some variant of

$$\lim_{n\to\infty}\left[\operatorname{var}\!\left(\tfrac{1}{n}\Sigma x_i\varepsilon_i\right)\right] = 0.^5 \qquad\qquad \textbf{12.7}''$$

When the disturbances and $X$'s satisfy 12.7′, we say that the disturbances and explanators are **contemporaneously uncorrelated**. When Equations 12.7′ and 12.7″ hold, OLS is a consistent estimator even if the $X$'s are not fixed across samples.

What might make a real-world DGP violate Equation 12.7′ and, thereby Equation 12.7? How could the disturbances and explanators be contemporaneously correlated? One example, the demand function for wheat, sheds much light on these questions. Let the demand for wheat be

$$Q_i^d = \beta_0 + \beta_1 P_i + \varepsilon_i^d,$$

where $Q^d$ is the quantity of wheat demanded and $P$ is the price of wheat. The interactions of supply and demand in the market for wheat make the explanator $P$, the price of wheat, contemporaneously correlated with the disturbances in the demand relationship. A surge in wheat demand above its expected value will be accompanied by a surge in the price of wheat, as long as supply is not perfectly elastic. Similarly, an unexpectedly low demand for wheat will be accompanied by an unexpectedly low price. These deviations of the quantity of wheat demanded and of the price of wheat from their expected values make the explanator, price, contemporaneously correlated with the disturbances in the demand equation—the $E(X_i\varepsilon_i)$ would not be zero in such a case. Chapter 13 introduces several other commonly encountered situations in which the disturbances and explanators will be contemporaneously correlated. Nonetheless, explanators and disturbances are very often contemporaneously uncorrelated in real-world DGPs, making OLS a frequently consistent estimator.

Why do we need an assumption like Equation 12.7″ in addition to Equation 12.7′? Why does it not suffice to assume Equation 12.7′? We need Equation 12.7″, or something like it, because if the $\operatorname{var}(x_i\varepsilon_i)$ grows infinite as the sample size grows, the Law of Large Numbers might not apply, and, therefore, $(1/n)\Sigma x_i\varepsilon_i$ might not converge in probability at all. Consequently, the consistency of OLS would be threatened, despite the fact that $E(x_i\varepsilon)_i = 0$. In many economic applications, Equation 12.7″ is a reasonable assumption; in others, it is not. Chapter 18 treats cases in which Equation 12.7″ fails. All other chapters assume Equation 12.7″ holds.

## OLS: Sometimes Consistent, Sometimes Not

OLS is consistent when Equations 12.7 and 12.8 hold. When Equation 12.7 fails and Equation 12.8 holds, OLS is inconsistent. Thus when explanators are stochastic, OLS may be either consistent or inconsistent. *When the disturbances and explanators are contemporaneously uncorrelated and the Law of Large Numbers applies, OLS is a consistent estimator. When the disturbances and explanators are contemporaneously correlated and the Law of Large Numbers applies, OLS is not consistent.* In such cases, the asymptotic bias of OLS equals its inconsistency, namely

$$\frac{\text{plim}(\Sigma x_i \varepsilon_i)}{Q},$$    12.9

which is zero when the explanators are contemporaneously uncorrelated asymptotically.

Why is it that contemporaneous correlation between disturbances and explanators makes OLS inconsistent? The example of the demand for wheat sheds considerable light on the reason OLS is inconsistent in such cases. The inconsistency of OLS arises because OLS attributes all of the co-movement between price and quantity, the numerator in

$$\hat{\beta}_1 = \frac{\Sigma x_i y_i}{\Sigma x_i^2},$$

to the effect of $X$ on the expected value of $Y$. When $X_i$ is uncorrelated with $\varepsilon_i$, this is a good strategy. When $X_i$ is correlated with $\varepsilon_i$, it is not.

## The Finite Sample Bias in OLS When $E(x_i \varepsilon_i) = 0$

OLS is consistent when the $X$'s and disturbances are contemporaneously uncorrelated. Is OLS unbiased in such DGPs, too? Often, it is not. The OLS estimator is

$$\hat{\beta}_1 = \frac{\Sigma x_i Y_i}{\Sigma x_i^2} = \beta_1 + \frac{\Sigma x_i \varepsilon_i}{\Sigma x_i^2}.$$

Thus,

$$E(\hat{\beta}_1) = E\left(\frac{\Sigma x_i Y_i}{\Sigma x_i^2}\right) = \beta_1 + E\left(\frac{\Sigma x_i \varepsilon_i}{\Sigma x_i^2}\right).$$

When the $X$'s are fixed, the last term on the right becomes

$$\frac{\Sigma x_i E(\varepsilon_i)}{\Sigma x_i^2},$$

and OLS is unbiased. But when the $X$'s are stochastic,

$$\sum \mathrm{E}\left[\left(\frac{x_i}{\sum x_i^2}\right)\varepsilon_i\right]$$

does not generally equal

$$\sum\left(\mathrm{E}\left[\frac{x_i}{\sum x_i^2}\right]\mathrm{E}(\varepsilon_i)\right)$$

unless *each* disturbance is statistically independent of *all* observations on $X$, which is a much stronger condition than $\mathrm{E}(X_i\varepsilon_i) = 0$. It is the appearance of all observations on $X$ in the denominator of each term in the sum that makes the needed independence assumption so strong.

Similarly, we learned in earlier chapters that OLS is BLUE if regressors are stochastic if the Gauss–Markov Assumptions hold for *every* combination of observations on the explanators. This assumption condition would imply that *each* disturbance is uncorrelated with *every* observation on the explanators. This, too, is a stronger condition than the disturbances and explanators being contemporaneously uncorrelated. Thus, for OLS to be unbiased requires more than that the disturbances and explanators be contemporaneously uncorrelated.

## Multiple Regression Models, GLS, and FGLS

In a multiple regression, OLS is consistent if (i) Equation 12.7 applies to each explanator in the model and (ii) an assumption corresponding to Equation 12.8 excludes both Dodo-bird explanators and multicollinearity among the explanators in the probability limit. Unfortunately, in the multiple regression model, some explanators may be uncorrelated with the disturbance term, whereas others are correlated with it. One explanator contemporaneously correlated with the disturbances can spoil the whole barrel—one such variable can make the OLS estimates of all coefficients of a model inconsistent. Appendix 12.D in Extension 3 on this book's Web site (**www.aw-bc.com/murray**) uses matrix algebra to discuss in more detail the consistency of OLS in multiple regressions with stochastic regressors.

What we have learned about the consistency of OLS applies as well to generalized least squares (GLS). GLS is generally a consistent estimator under the same conditions as OLS. For feasible generalized least squares (FGLS) to be consistent, some additional assumptions are needed about how the structures of heteroskedasticity and serial correlation are estimated.[6] When the disturbances and explanators are contemporaneously correlated, OLS, GLS, and FGLS are usually inconsistent; that is, they usually converge on the wrong answer.

## A Monte Carlo Experiment

### Prelude to Asymptotic Efficiency

Figures 12.1 and 12.2 illustrate that consistent estimators tend to collapse around the true value. In all but exceptional (and only occasionally interesting) cases, the variances of these consistent estimators are collapsing toward zero. How are we to compare the variances of consistent estimators as the sample size grows large if almost all of them have zero variance in the limit? How are we to describe the shape of such distributions if they are collapsing onto a single point? The key is to look at the distribution of an estimator's errors under a magnifying glass. Then we can see which estimators are collapsing more rapidly and what shape the distribution of the estimator takes on as the sample size grows toward infinity.

The magnification that we use multiplies all the errors an estimator makes by some power of $n$, the sample size. MC Builder VI is like MC Builder II from its beginning almost to its end. The key difference between MC Builder II and MC Builder VI is that MC Builder VI adds one new graph for each estimator to those provided by MC Builder II. MC Builder VI asks the user for a degree of magnification for the errors made by each estimator. The default magnification value is 0.5. The graphs of the errors for each estimator at each of several sample sizes are then displayed, as in Figures 12.1 and 12.2, together with the distributions of the magnified errors, that is, the errors multiplied by $n^c$, where $c$ is the chosen magnification. Thus, MC Builder VI graphs the distribution of

$$(\beta_{gj} - \beta)n^c$$

for each of the three estimators, $\beta_{g1}$, $\beta_{g2}$, and $\beta_{g3}$, as calculated in 10,000 samples of varying sizes.

Conduct three Monte Carlo experiments with MC Builder VI choosing normally distributed disturbances. In the first, use the default magnification. In the second, magnify the errors by $n$ to a power less than 0.5; in the third, magnify the errors by $n$ to a power greater than 0.5. Which magnification will allow you to figure out which estimator's variance collapses to zero fastest? Repeat the exercise, using nonnormal disturbances. Do these Monte Carlo results depend on choosing normally distributed disturbances?

In real-world applications, regressors are stochastic, not fixed. Consequently, we cannot blindly trust OLS to be unbiased, even in large samples. We must learn to identify situations in which OLS performs badly. Chapter 13 describes several other commonly encountered situations in which the disturbances and explanators are contemporaneously correlated and OLS is both biased and inconsistent.

Because stochastic regressors can make least squares both biased and inconsistent, we need alternatives to the least squares estimators. Chapter 13 builds on the notion of linear estimators to uncover an alternative to least squares that is consistent when least squares is not.

## 12.5     Asymptotic Efficiency and Asymptotic Distributions

Consistency is a desirable trait for an estimator. However, just as there are many unbiased estimators of the slope of a line through the origin, there are also many consistent estimators. How are we to choose among them? We chose among unbiased estimators by looking for the unbiased estimator with the smallest variance. We called that estimator efficient. Similarly, we choose among consistent estimators based on an efficiency criterion that we call *asymptotic efficiency*. An **asymptotically efficient** estimator is one with a variance that is the smallest among all consistent estimators for all sample sizes greater than $N$, where $N$ is some finite number.

In studying the sampling properties of estimators, we devised hypothesis testing techniques based on the distributions of the estimators. Similarly, we can construct hypothesis testing procedures based on what we call the *asymptotic distribution* of an estimator. Loosely speaking, the asymptotic distribution of an estimator is the shape its distribution takes on as $n$ grows large. This section examines both asymptotic efficiency and asymptotic distributions in some detail.

### Asymptotic Efficiency

Asymptotic efficiency is a subtle concept. Although it is straightforward to ask which of several unbiased estimators has the smallest variances, and to thereby determine which of those estimators is most efficient, we cannot do the same when comparing consistent estimators. In the limit, all consistent estimators collapse around the true parameter value, and, therefore, nearly all consistent estimators have zero variance in the limit. We cannot fruitfully define asymptotic efficiency in terms of the limits of the estimators' variances. We must define it in some other way.

The key step in defining an estimator's asymptotic distribution is ascertaining how quickly the estimator is converging toward the true parameter value. For a consistent estimator, the estimation errors made in successively larger samples tend to grow smaller. To counter this shrinkage, we "magnify" these errors by even larger amounts as the sample size grows. Just as a magnifying glass makes objects look twice or thrice—or whatever number of times—larger than they really are, magnifying errors multiply each error by some number to make it appear larger—and easier to view. If the magnifying effect is too small, with larger samples, even the magnified errors shrink toward zero. If the magnifying effect is too large, the magnified errors tend to explode as the magnification grows even greater with sample size. An aptly chosen magnification of errors might just balance out the effect of increasing sample size, however, and the distribution of the magnified errors might conveniently converge to some recognizable form, such as the normal distribution. Econometricians call this apt magnification the **convergence rate** of an estimator, and they call the distribution that the errors converge to an **asymptotic distribution**.

## The Rate of Convergence of $\beta_{g4}$

To magnify the distribution of $\beta_{g4}$ by just the right amount, so that the magnified distribution neither shrinks nor explodes as the sample size grows, we need to know how fast $\beta_{g4}$ collapses toward $\beta$. Because the variance of $\beta_{g4}$ is $\sigma^2/\sum X_i^2$, one reasonable answer is to say that $\beta_{g4}$ collapses toward $\beta$ as fast as the sum of squared $X$'s grows. But there is another answer that interests econometricians more: How fast does the collapse occur in terms of the sample size?

Econometricians think about the collapse of $\beta_{g4}$ toward $\beta$ in terms of how fast $\beta_{g4}$'s errors in guessing $\beta$ converge toward zero. These errors have the same variance as $\beta_{g4}$, so the errors collapse toward zero just as fast as $\beta_{g4}$ collapses toward $\beta$. Thus, the focus of our attention still needs to be $\sum X_i^2$, which tells us how fast the squared errors converge toward zero. Each additional observation brings the prospect of increasing $\sum X_i^2$, so the growth of $\sum X_i^2$ seems linked to the growth of $n$. Consequently, next, we examine the convergence of $\sum X_i^2$ in terms of $n$.

We can rewrite $\sum X_i^2$ as $[n(1/n)\sum X_i^2]$. In many applications, it makes sense to assume that the mean squared $X$ approaches a finite, nonzero constant, $Q$, as $n$ grows. For example, suppose our explanator is income and we draw a simple random sample of observations from the U.S. population. In very large samples, the mean squared income in the sample, $1/n\sum X_i^2$, will almost certainly mirror that in the population. (This follows from the Law of Large Numbers.) As a consequence, the mean squared income will not grow infinitely large; instead, it will converge to some number, a number we call $Q$. Under the Gauss–Markov Assumptions, the $X_i$ are fixed across samples rather than drawn at random from some population. In the Monte Carlo experiments underlying Figures 12.1 and 12.2, we used the same two $X$-values, 10 and 20, over and over, ensuring that the mean squared $X$ in our samples was always 250, because we drew two observations at a time. $Q$ equals 250 in our Monte Carlo experiments (first $[10^2 + 20^2]/2$, then $[10^2 + 20^2 + 10^2 + 20^2]/4$, and so on.).

When the mean squared $X$ approaches a nonzero, finite number $Q$ as $n$ grows, we can say

$$\lim[\text{var}(\beta_{g4})] = \frac{\sigma^2}{nQ},$$

which shows that the variance of the guessing errors (and of $\beta_{g4}$) converges to zero with the same speed that $n$ approaches infinity, which econometricians call "rate $n$." Because the squared errors shrink as fast as $n$ grows, the (unsquared) errors shrink as fast as the square root of $n$ grows. Thus, econometricians say that $\beta_{g4}$ and its errors **converge at the rate root $n$**: If we magnify the errors $\beta_{g4}$ makes in guessing $\beta$ by $\sqrt{n}$, the variance of these magnified errors will neither shrink nor explode:

$$\text{var}_m(\sqrt{n}\,(\beta_{g4} - \beta)) = n\left(\frac{\sigma^2}{nQ}\right) = \frac{\sigma^2}{Q}.$$

We have thus determined that $\beta_{g4}$ is **root $n$ consistent**, that is, that $\beta_{g4}$ converges at the rate root $n$. When the magnification is at the estimator's convergence rate, the variance of an estimator's magnified errors is called the estimator's **asymptotic variance**; $\beta_{g4}$'s asymptotic variance is thus $\sigma^2/Q$. The larger an estimator's convergence rate (the faster the estimator's variance collapses toward zero), the more efficient the estimator. We sometimes call an estimator's asymptotic variance its **asymptotic efficiency**. Among estimators with the same convergence rate, the consistent estimator with the smallest asymptotic variance is called asymptotically efficient among estimators with that convergence rate.

When the sum of squared $X$'s converges to $Q$ as $n$ grows, $\beta_{g4}$ is root $n$ consistent. When might the mean-squared $X$ not converge to a nonzero finite constant, but instead grow without bound? It will grow without bound if the explanator is time. If the explanator in our model is time, then each additional observation has a larger value for $X$ as time progresses. When there is such a time trend in the model, the variance of $\beta_{g4}$ shrinks toward zero because $n$ is growing without bound *and* because the average squared $X$ is growing without bound. The convergence of $\beta_{g4}$ and its errors is therefore *faster* than root $n$ when the explanator is time.

## The Root $n$ Consistency and Asymptotic Normality of $\beta_{g1}$, $\beta_{g2}$, $\beta_{g3}$, and $\beta_{g4}$

Figure 12.4 illustrates the root $n$ consistency of $\beta_{g1}$, $\beta_{g2}$, $\beta_{g3}$, and $\beta_{g4}$ using experiments conducted with MC Builder IV, which is like MC Builder II, except that MC Builder IV includes $\beta_{g4}$ among the estimators examined. Columns 1 and 3 of these figures mirror Figures 12.1 and 12.2, except that $\beta_{g4}$ is included in the new figures, and the distributions are centered around zero instead of around $\beta$, because the graphs are of the estimation errors, rather than of the estimates. (The errors and the estimators have the same variance, so we can examine either to study the variances of the estimators.) We magnify the errors, rather than magnifying the estimates themselves, because multiplying a mean zero distribution by any number leaves its mean at zero. Had we multiplied the estimates themselves by

$\sqrt{n}$, the distribution's mean would explode with $n$. The asymptotic distribution of a consistent estimator's errors, in contrast, has both a mean of zero and a finite, nonzero variance. Columns 1 and 2 are based on normally distributed disturbances; columns 3 and 4 are based on highly skewed disturbances. Panels A through D rely on sample sizes of 2, 20, 50, and 500, respectively.

Columns 2 and 4 of Figure 12.4 graph the estimation errors of $\beta_{g1}$, $\beta_{g2}$, $\beta_{g3}$, and $\beta_{g4}$, magnified by, as $n$ grows large $\sqrt{n}$. These distributions are called the asymptotic distributions of the estimators' errors. For large enough $n$, the asymptotic distribution of the errors provides probability statements about the errors that are as close to correct as we wish. The asymptotic distributions of $\beta_{g1}$, $\beta_{g2}$, $\beta_{g3}$, and $\beta_{g4}$ are normal, as suggested by Figure 12.4. Their normality rests on the Central Limit Theorem, which says that under suitable conditions, the distribution of the deviations of a large number of random variables from their asymptotic mean is asymptotically normally distributed. Like the Law of Large Numbers, the Central Limit Theorem usually requires bounded variances. Indeed, the Central Limit Theorem is generally more demanding in this regard than the Law of Large Numbers. Consequently, sometimes estimators are consistent, but do not follow the normal distribution asymptotically.[7] Appendix 12.B discusses in more detail the kinds of assumptions needed for the Central Limit Theorem to apply and for OLS to be approximately normally distributed in large samples. Chapter 18 treats cases in which the OLS estimators are not normally distributed asymptotically; in other chapters, we assume OLS estimators are normally distributed asymptotically.

## Hypothesis Testing

The chief use of asymptotic distributions is for statistical inference when the finite sample distribution of an estimator is unknown. In moderately large samples, say 100 or more, asymptotic distributions often serve as fair approximations to finite sample distributions.

When OLS is consistent and asymptotically normally distributed, it supports all the asymptotic hypothesis tests described in Chapters 7 and 9. When the disturbances are heteroskedastic or serially correlated and FGLS is consistent, economic DGPs frequently support the Central Limit Theorem. In such cases, the FGLS estimator is asymptotically normally distributed and the standard tests using FGLS are appropriate in large samples.

Because least squares estimators are usually inconsistent when the disturbances and explanators are contemporaneously correlated, hypothesis tests based on those estimators are usually invalid for such DGPs. *When least squares estimators are inconsistent, the standard hypothesis tests based on them are biased and inconsistent, and their stated significance levels are misleading.*

**Figure 12.4**

The Distributions of Errors for $\beta_{g1}$, $\beta_{g2}$, $\beta_{g3}$, and $\beta_{g4}$ for Various $n$ and Normal and Skewed, Discrete Disturbances

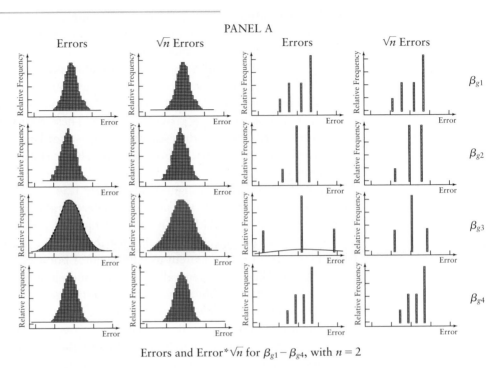

PANEL A

Errors and Error*$\sqrt{n}$ for $\beta_{g1} - \beta_{g4}$, with $n = 2$

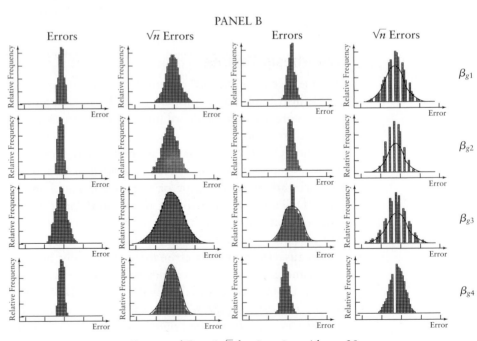

PANEL B

Errors and Error*$\sqrt{n}$ for $\beta_{g1} - \beta_{g4}$, with $n = 20$

**Figure 12.4**

*(continued)*

PANEL C

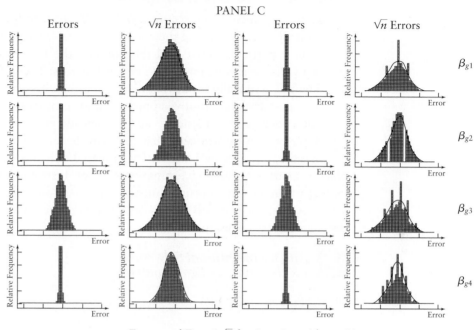

Errors and Error*$\sqrt{n}$ for $\beta_{g1} - \beta_{g4}$, with $n = 50$

PANEL D

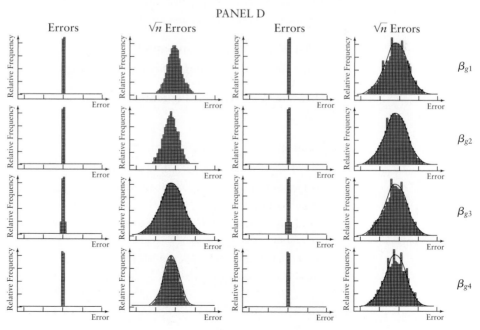

Errors and Error*$\sqrt{n}$ for $\beta_{g1} - \beta_{g4}$, with $n = 500$

## Alternatives to BLUE Estimation

Chapters 3 through 11 emphasized the BLUE strategy for designing estimators. The strategy requires finding the conditions under which a linear estimator is unbiased in a particular DGP and then finding the linear estimator that has the smallest variance among unbiased linear estimators. The BLUE strategy was motivated by the desirability of having unbiased estimators with a small variance and by the tractability and intuitive appeal of linear estimators.

The concepts of consistency and asymptotic efficiency similarly motivate a search for estimation strategies that can provide consistent and asymptotically efficient estimators when OLS is neither unbiased nor consistent. *Instrumental variables* estimation is one such estimation strategy. Instrumental variables estimators belong to the class of linear estimators. The next chapter, Chapter 13, exposes several situations in which OLS is both biased and inconsistent and describes the instrumental variables approach.

### *An Organizational Structure for the Study of Econometrics*

1. **What Is the DGP?**

   Asymptotic analysis requires adding assumptions about additional $X$'s; for example, $\lim(\sum X_i^2)$ is finite and nonzero. Variances are bounded, so the Law of Large Numbers and the Central Limit Theorem will apply.

2. **What Makes a Good Estimator?**

   Consistency and asymptotic efficiency

3. **How Do We Create an Estimator?**

   ———

4. **What Are an Estimator's Properties?**

   OLS is consistent under the Gauss–Markov Assumptions if the mean sum of squared $X$'s doesn't converge to zero.

   OLS is inconsistent under the Gauss–Markov Assumptions if explanators are stochastic and contemporaneously correlated with the disturbances asymptotically.

5. **How Do We Test Hypotheses?**

   ———

REGRESSION'S
GREATEST HITS

# An Econometric Top 40—A Classical Favorite

## Making Music

Econometricians need data just as musicians need tunes. Econometricians often improvise, finding data that no one else has used. At other times, econometricians play variations on well-known themes, using data that have been examined frequently by others. This Hit describes nine well-known data sources that econometricians have turned to over and over.

None of these heavily used data sources provides data that would satisfy the assumption of explanators fixed across samples. For example, each new Current Population Survey studies new households, with new traits. The Survey of Income and Program Participation sometimes reinterviews households, but even then, the household's traits change from survey year to survey year. And if researchers were to rebuild any of these surveys anew, the new observations drawn would have different values for most variables than do the original observations. These data sources remind us emphatically that we must relax the simplifying assumption of explanators fixed across samples and understand well the implications of stochastic regressors.

### The Current Population Survey (CPS)

The CPS provides views of the U.S. labor force and population between census years. Each month, the U.S. Census Bureau interviews about 50,000 households, asking labor market questions regarding employment, unemployment, earnings, and hours of work, and demographic questions regarding age, sex, race, marital status, and educational attainment. The employment questions are asked for all household members 15 years of age and older. Each sampled household is interviewed in 8 months over a 16-month period and is then replaced with a newly sampled household.

The CPS is the broadest frequently snapped picture of U.S. households. In addition to its basic data, the CPS has frequently added supplemental questions on special topics, such as education, fertility, and immigration.

The U.S. Census Bureau (www.census.gov) maintains a CPS home page with a great deal of information about the CPS and information on how to download recent CPS surveys. The National Bureau of Economic Research (www.nber.org) sells a CD file that contains the fourth and final month (the months in which earnings and wage data are gathered) interview data for all surveyed households from 1976 to 2000.

### The Survey of Income and Program Participation (SIPP)

SIPP is a series of relatively specialized surveys; its purpose is to document who is eligible for and who participates in U.S. social welfare programs. Some other surveys do ask questions about participation in social welfare programs, but those surveys pose questions that invite respondents to mix together many different programs. For example, the CPS asks about "subsidized housing," which some respondents do interpret as government's public housing, but which other respondents interpret as employer-subsidized housing or housing provided by relatives. SIPP is designed to ascertain the specific program in which respondents participate. No data set is better suited to investigating households' eligibility for and participation in U.S. social welfare programs.

The first SIPP panel of households was initially interviewed in 1983. The most recent panel of households was first interviewed in 1996. The SIPP surveys are longitudinal in nature; that is, they follow the same households for an extended period of time—two to four years. SIPP is not purely longitudinal, as one group of interviewed households replaces another after some years.

The U.S. Census Bureau (www.census.gov) maintains a Web site with information about how to obtain the SIPP data.

## The Panel Survey of Income Dynamics (PSID)

The PSID is a longitudinal survey of a representative sample of American families. The sample was drawn in 1968, and the families have been followed with annual interviews. As younger family members formed their own households, they—and their own families—were still followed in the PSID. The original 4,800 families has grown to more than 7,000. The focus of the survey is income, its sources and amounts, and family composition changes, including births, adoptions, deaths, and changes in marital status and living arrangements. With up to 34 years of data on some individuals, and with data that span parents and children across a generation, the PSID is the best data set for investigating the dynamics of income change in the United States.

In 1997, the PSID's interviewing switched from annual interviews to every other year. In 1997, the PSID dropped some families from the sample and added a new group of immigrant families to improve the contemporary representativeness of the sample. The PSID has a particularly low drop-out rate, so the sample has long been a particularly representative look at the U.S. population.

The University of Michigan (www.umich .edu) maintains a Web site with information

about the PSID, including information about its public use files.

## The National Longitudinal Surveys (NLS)

The NLS is made up of seven surveys, each of which follows a sample of individuals over many years. Some surveys initially interview teens, others initially interview the children of people interviewed in another of the samples, and still others begin with middle-aged individuals. The first NLS was begun in 1966. The most recent NLS was begun in 1997. The samples are representative of the American population in the age cohorts studied.

The NLS allows studies of the varied experiences of groups of Americans born in specific years. The data collected include income, employment, education, training investments, assets, welfare receipt, childcare costs, insurance coverage, health conditions, alcohol and substance abuse, sexual activity, marriage, fertility, and demographic characteristics.

The Bureau of Labor Statistics of the U.S. Department of Labor (www.bls.gov) maintains a Web site with information about ordering NLS data.

## The National Income and Product Accounts

The Federal Reserve Bank of St. Louis (www.stls.frb.org) provides online access to over 800 variables drawn from the U.S. National Income and Product Accounts, including GDP, investment, and consumption, with some series dating back to 1946. These are aggregate data, usually for the entire United States, but sometimes for specific regions. Some of the data are gathered monthly, some are gathered quarterly, and still other data are gathered annually. The St. Louis Fed supplements these macroeconomic data with many monetary series that they gather, including interest rates, the Consumer Price Index, and the money supply. These data, obtained from the St. Louis Fed or from any of several commercial sources, are the stuff from which most U.S. macroeconomic econometric studies are built.

### The Penn World Tables (PWT)

Economists Alan Heston and Robert Summers have compiled an international macroeconomic database called the Penn World Tables (pwt.econ.upenn.edu). The PWT contains macroeconomic data for some 150 countries. To allow meaningful cross-country comparisons of data that were originally compiled in national currencies, Heston and Summers use purchasing power parity deflators to make all variables comparable across countries. To allow meaningful comparisons over time, Heston and Summers also express all variables in constant dollar terms. Many studies of comparative economic growth have used the Penn World Tables.

### The NBER Historical Data

The National Bureau of Economic Research (NBER) has compiled an extensive set of macroeconomic variables for the period 1900–1939. The series include data on production, employment, money, and prices. The data are chiefly for the United States, but there is some coverage of the United Kingdom, France, and Germany. Better historical data on the U.S. economy are difficult to come by. These data are available online at the NBER Web site (www.nber.org).

### The Living Standards Measurement Surveys (LSMS)

In 1980, the World Bank began a program of gathering data on household behavior and households' circumstances around the world. It has conducted Living Standards Measurement Surveys in about two dozen countries, spanning Africa, Asia, South America, and Eastern Europe. The surveys are frequently longitudinal in character, with households tracked for two or three years. The surveys obtain extensive information on income and its sources, the health status of household members, nutritional data, and demographic characteristics. Given the varied forms in which income is generated across developing economies, each LSMS is designed to account for the particular conditions of the country in which the survey is taken. There are no better data on representative samples of households in developing countries. These data are available for purchase from the World Bank (www.worldbank.org/lsms).

### The City–County Data Books

The library of the University of Virginia (fisher.lib.virginia.edu) makes available online the 1988 and 1994 County and City Data Books, which contain extensive data on counties and cities in the United States. The U.S. Census Bureau makes available online the year 2000 County and City Data book in pdf format.

 **Final Notes**

The data sets described in this Hit are among the most widely used sources for econometric analysis. However, literally thousands of other data sets are available around the world, each dealing with its own specialized topic. The Internet is an excellent source of these data sets, as are college and university research libraries. Government agencies frequently make data available over the Internet or in published documents.

■

# Summary

The chapter began by introducing visually the large sample concepts of consistency, asymptotic efficiency, and asymptotic distribution. It then formally defined two large sample properties: asymptotic unbiasedness and consistency. We learned that $\beta_{g4}$ is a consistent estimator of $\beta$ under the Gauss–Markov Assumptions, as long as we add a mild assumption about what additional $X$-values we use as the sample size grows large. The proof of the consistency of $\beta_{g4}$ points toward similar proofs that would show the consistency of our earlier unbiased estimators if we add similar mild assumptions about the $X$-values to the usual Gauss–Markov Assumptions. When the $X$'s are not fixed across samples, however, the least squares estimators are biased and inconsistent unless the $X$'s are contemporaneously uncorrelated with the disturbances.

Just as there are many unbiased estimators for the slope of a line, there are also often many consistent estimators. We adapted the across-sample property of efficiency to the large sample framework, calling the notion asymptotic efficiency. Asymptotic efficiency proves a more complex notion than efficiency because all consistent estimators have variances that collapse to zero as sample size grows. To compare estimators with errors that are shrinking toward zero, we magnify all the errors, so that they do not shrink. We defined an asymptotic variance that looks at the variance of magnified estimation errors. Among estimators with variances that shrink toward zero at the same rate, we prefer those with the smallest asymptotic variance; we call these preferred estimators asymptotically efficient.

Least squares estimators are often normally distributed asymptotically. When these estimators are both consistent and asymptotically normally distributed, they support the standard hypothesis testing procedures in large samples. When least squares estimators are inconsistent, tests based on them are biased and inconsistent.

# Concepts for Review

## Questions for Discussion

1. "Asymptotic properties are inherently irrelevant. We will never have an infinite sample, or anything close to it, so what happens when a sample becomes infinite is uninformative." Do you agree or disagree? Discuss.

2. Across-sample properties are inherently irrelevant. We have only the sample we gather. What would happen in other samples is irrelevant. Discuss.

## Problems for Analysis

> For the data that you will need to solve the problems in this section,
> go to **www.aw-bc.com/murray.**

1. Show that the sample mean from a simple random sample is a consistent estimator of the population mean, as long as the variance of the population is finite.

2. Show that $\beta_{g1}, 1/n \sum (Y_i/X_i)$, is a consistent estimator of the slope of a line through the origin if the Gauss–Markov Assumptions are met and no $X$-value at any sample size is smaller than a finite, nonzero number $M$. (The variance of $\beta_{g1}$ is $\frac{\sigma^2}{n^2} \sum \frac{1}{X_i^2}$.) Explain in words what the assumption about the $X$-values prevents.

3. Provide a mild assumption about the $X$-values that, when coupled with the assumption that $E(\varepsilon_i) = 0$, implies that $\beta_{g2}$, $\sum Y_i / \sum X_i$ is a consistent estimator of the slope of a line through the origin. Demonstrate the consistency of $\beta_{g2}$ under these assumptions.

4. In 1914, Robert Lehfeldt[8] of Johannesburg, South Africa, published what has become a well-known estimate of a price elasticity of demand that relied on a double logarithmic specification. Lehfeldt reasoned that variations in weather drive fluctuations in wheat production from one year to the next, and that the price of wheat adjusts so that buyers are willing to buy all the wheat produced. Hence, he argued, the price of wheat observed in any year reflects the demand for wheat. The file lehfwheat.*** contains Lehfeldt's data.
   a. Regress the natural log of the price of wheat (*logprice*) on the log of the quantity of wheat (*logwheat*) and an intercept term. The inverse of the slope in this relationship is the price elasticity of the demand for wheat.
   b. Demonstrate that if the Gauss–Markov Assumptions apply, the inverse of the OLS estimator of the slope in (a) is a consistent estimator of the price elasticity of the demand for wheat.

5. An OLS regression of infant mortality rates ($M$) on physicians per capita ($P$) and an intercept term yields

$$E(M) = 0.0012 - 0.0250P,$$
$$(0.0003) \quad (0.010)$$

where the figures in parentheses are estimated standard errors. Assume the disturbances, the $\varepsilon_i$, are serially uncorrelated and distributed normally with mean zero and variance $\sigma^2$.

a. Suppose each disturbance is statistically independent of all observations on $M$. If $n = 12$, how would you test the hypothesis that the coefficient on $P$ is zero?

b. Suppose each disturbance is *not* statistically independent of all observations on $M$, but that $E(P_i\varepsilon_i) = 0$ for all $i$. How would the fact that $n = 12$ influence your interpretation of a standard $t$-test that the coefficient on $P$ is zero?

c. Suppose each disturbance is *not* statistically independent of all observations on $M$, but that $E(P_i\varepsilon_i) = 0$ for all $i$. If $n$ were 3,500, instead of 12, how would your interpretation of a standard $t$-test that the coefficient on $P$ is zero change from the case in which $n = 12$?

d. Suppose that $E(P_i\varepsilon_i) \neq 0$ for all $i$. If $n$ were 3,500, how would your interpretation of a standard $t$-test that the coefficient on $P$ is zero change from the case in which $n = 3,500$ and $E(P_i\varepsilon_i) = 0$ for all $i$?

e. Suppose each disturbance is *not* statistically independent of all observations on $M$, but that $E(P_i\varepsilon_i) = 0$ for all $i$, and $n = 3,500$. If the variance of $\varepsilon_i$ were $\sigma^2 X_i^2$, instead of $\sigma^2$, how would you recommend the relationship between infant mortality and physicians per capita be estimated?

 6. Are presidential elections affected by the economy? Do voters consider how much unemployment has changed during the election year when casting their votes for or against the party sitting in the White House? The file political.\*\*\* contains the change in unemployment in the 12 months immediately preceding the election (*unemploy*) and the percentage of the popular vote obtained by the incumbent presidential party (*incumbent* or *incumb*) in each presidential election (*year*) since 1900.[9] Both *unemploy* and *incumbent* are measured in percent. Use OLS to estimate the slope and intercept of

$$incumbent = \beta_0 + \beta_1(unemploy) + \varepsilon.$$

Test at the 5% significance level the null hypothesis that changes in the unemployment rate in the 12 months prior to the presidential election have no effect on the incumbent party's popular vote in the presidential election against the alternative that increases in the unemployment rate hurt the incumbent party's prospects. How is your interpretation of the test result altered by the fact that the unemployment rate is not fixed in repeated samples and our sample size is small? What difference would it make in that discussion if unemployment were still not fixed in repeated samples, but the size of the sample were large?

 7. The file equipmentandgrowth.\*\*\* contains data on economic growth 1960–1985 for 106 countries. De Long and Summers[10] used these data to investigate the effect of equipment investment on economic growth. The six variables in the file are as follows:

GDP60vUS    Natural log of a country's per capita income in 1960 relative to that in the United States in 1960

GDPGR    The growth rate of income per worker for a country, 1960–1985

*NONEQINV*     Nonequipment investment for the country, between 1960–1985
*EQUIPINV*      Equipment investment for the country, 1960–1985
*LFGR6085*      Growth rate of the labor force, 1960–1985
*CONTINENT*    Continent of the country

Regress the growth rate on the other four variables, besides *continent*, and a constant term. Test at the 5% significance level the null hypothesis that, other things being equal, countries with lower per capita incomes in 1960 grew no faster than countries with larger per capita incomes in 1960 against the alternative that they did. How is your interpretation of the test result altered by the fact that the unemployment rate is not fixed in repeated samples and our sample size is small? What difference would it make in that discussion if the unemployment rate were still not fixed in repeated samples, but the size of the sample were large?

8. This exercise examines the returns to education using data on individuals who have twins. The data file for this problem is twin1.***. This data extract is from a survey of twins conducted by Orley Ashenfelter and Cecelia Rouse of Princeton University at the Twin's Day Festival in Twinsburg, Ohio.[11] The observational unit of the data is the individual. For sets of twins, information was collected on the earnings, education, age, race, gender, and so on, of individuals. Here we look at the data for one twin from each pair of twins.

The key variables are as follows:

*hrwage*       Self-reported hourly wage of the individual (in dollars)
*lwage*        Natural log of the hourly wage
*age* and *age2*   Age of a person (*age*) and its square (*age2*)
*female*         = 1 if the person is female; = 0 otherwise
*white*          = 1 if the person is white; = 0 otherwise
*educ*         Educational attainment of the individual

Test the hypothesis that men and women have the same wage equation against the alternative that they have different wage equations. How is your interpretation of this test result altered if we acknowledge that the explanators are not fixed in repeated samples? How would this interpretation change if the number of observations were small?

9. The file wineweather.*** contains the natural log of the average 1989 prices (*logprice*) for Bordeaux wines for the vintages 1952–1989 (*vintage* or *vint*). The age of each vintage in 1989 is given by the variable *age*. These data were part of an analysis of Bordeaux wine as an investment by economists Orley Ashenfelter and David Ashmore of Princeton University and Robert LaLonde of the University of Chicago.[12]

a. Estimate the semilog relationship

$$\ln(price) = \beta_0 + \beta_1(age) + v.$$

Test at the 5% significance level the null hypothesis that the age of wine doesn't matter for its expected price against the alternative that wines grow more valuable with age.

b. A friend is going to gather another sample of Bordeaux wines from this same period. If your sample and hers are both simple random samples of all Bordeaux wines from these several years, assess the accuracy of the following claim: "Your statistical results will differ from mine only because of the sampling variation in the disturbances." If you think the claim inaccurate, what qualifications would you add to make the claim true?

c. Is the estimator in (a) an unbiased estimator?

d. Regress the natural log of a vintage's price on growing-season temperatures, harvest-season rainfall, off-season rainfall, and the age of a wine. Use the $R^2$ statistic to compute the $F$-statistic for the null hypothesis that none of the variables in the regression matter for the price of wine. How is your interpretation of this test result altered if we acknowledge that the explanators are not fixed in repeated samples? How would this interpretation change if the number of observations were large?

 10. Cindy's Coffee Shop operates 30 stores and competes fiercely with StarStrucks Coffee, a national coffee store chain. Cindy's has determined that their competitive advantage is in providing high-quality service at low prices. However, competing on price means that they must be thoroughly knowledgeable about how responsive the demand for their product is to changes in price as well as to other determinants of demand. One way they have managed to remain competitive is by establishing good supply chain relationships that enable them to buy in bulk for all 30 stores at a substantial discount. The coffee is shipped directly from a wholesaler to each of the stores using a just-in-time (JIT) inventory system. Although JIT keeps stock levels and thus production costs low, there is a risk that a store may not be able to satisfy a higher than expected demand on a given day. Consequently, this strategy depends critically on determining unit sales revenue at the store level. The data for the last full year of operation for each of the stores are in cindyscoffee.*** .

a. Estimate a demand function (*qty*) for Cindy's coffee using the average price charged for a sale (*cprice*) and a constant term in the regression. Enter the variables in natural logs. Plot the residuals from this regression. Explain why the disturbances and *cprice* may be contemporaneously correlated.

b. What does your answer to (a) imply for interpreting the statistical significance of the estimated coefficients? What assumptions are necessary for you to interpret the estimated coefficient on *cprice* as a consistent estimator of the price elasticity of demand?

c. Suppose OLS consistently estimates this demand function. Interpret the meaning of the coefficient on *cprice*. How sensitive are Cindy's customers to changes in price? Would raising the price increase or decrease total revenue?

d. Re-estimate the demand function in (a), adding as explanators the natural log of the average price charged by StarStrucks (*sprice*), and the natural log of the average household income (*income*) for the market in which a store operates as the determinants of demand. Include a constant term in the regression. Now interpret the estimated coefficients in terms of price elasticity of demand, cross-price elasticity of demand, and income elasticity.

e. Cindy's also has information on whether the store is located in a suburb or in the city. The dummy variable *suburb* takes on the value one if the store is in a suburb and zero if it is in the city. Using the explanatory variables seen in part (a), test the hypothesis that suburban stores and city stores have the same demand equations against the alternative that they have completely different demand equations.

f. Interpret the results in (e) in light of the sample size. Explain whether or not you think the explanators are fixed in repeated samples and how, if at all, this affects your conclusions.

11. Cindy's coffee shop operates 22 company-owned stores and has 8 franchise stores. The owners of the franchises believe that they have been treated unfairly by Cindy's top managers. They contend that they were given the least desirable locations where traffic is less, household incomes are lower, and StarStrucks stores charge lower prices, all of which lead to lower sales. You are hired to look into this matter by an arbitrator. Open cindyscoffee.*** data on the Modern Introduction Web site.

a. Estimate a model in which log(*qty*) is regressed on log(*income*), log(*sprice*), log(*cprice*), and a constant term (variables are as defined in Problem 10). Test the hypothesis that franchise stores and company-owned stores have the same demand equations against the alternative that they have completely different demand equations. What would you tell the franchise owners?

b. Suppose the franchise owners argued that your results are meaningless because there are only 30 stores all together and, further, there are only 8 franchise owners. How would you respond?

c. The arbitrator wants you to test whether location matters. Augment the above model with the *suburb* variable. Do your results change? Would your results change if the number of franchise stores were 22 and the number of company stores were 8? Why or why not?

12. The Edwards Aquifer Authority in San Antonio, Texas, is in charge of monitoring and maintaining the groundwater in the region surrounding the city. San Antonio is a large and growing city that gets its water from the aquifer. The city's growing demand for water is a major concern for the Authority. Econometric techniques can be used to model the spring flow rates, a critical element in the assessing the availability of fresh water. The data for this problem are in water1.***.

a. Estimate by OLS a model in which the spring flow rate (*flow*) is the dependent variable and surface air temperature (*temp*) and a measure of the well water level (*well*) are explanatory variables, and include a constant term. Be sure that your final specification accounts for serial correlations and, if necessary, utilizes White's correction for heteroskedastic disturbances.

b. The Authority reports aquifer level (water) in feet above sea level, and the spring flow rate is measured in cubic feet per second. Interpret your results in part (a) in terms of how each variable helps to explain the variation in flow rate. Plot the residuals. Do you think that the assumption of normality holds in this case? How does your conclusion regarding normality affect your interpretation of the model?

c. If aquifer level and temperature are negatively correlated, what is the inconsistency in the slope coefficient of a regression of water on temperature?

# Endnotes

1. Albert Einstein, *Sidelights on Relativity* (New York: Dover, 1983).

2. Strictly speaking, just as ordinary mathematical limits apply to *sequences* of numbers, rather than to a single number, probability limits apply to *sequences* of random variables. This distinction reflects the fact that, for example, the sample mean becomes a different random variable each time the sample size changes—it depends on a different number of random observations than before the change. For notational simplicity, this book overlooks that distinction here and in subsequent chapters. Appendix 12.A provides a more precise discussion of probability limits.

3. John Maynard Keynes, *The General Theory of Employment, Interest, and Money* (New York: Harcourt, Brace, 1936).

4. Trygve Haavelmo, "Methods of Measuring the Marginal Propensity to Consume," *Journal of the American Statistical Association* 42 (March 1947): 105–122.

5. A deeper examination of the consistency of $\hat{\beta}_1$ would investigate the conditions under which the $\text{var}\left(\frac{1}{n}\sum x_i \varepsilon_i\right)$ converges to zero as $n$ grows, if the $E(x_i \varepsilon_i) = 0$. For such advanced treatments, see William H. Greene, *Econometric Analysis*, 5th ed. (Englewood Cliffs, NJ: Prentice-Hall, 2003): 66–68, or Fumio Hayashi, *Econometrics* (Princeton, NJ: Princeton University Press, 2000): 109–113.

6. For a more advanced discussion of the consistency of FGLS, see William Greene, *Econometric Analysis*, 5th ed. (Englewood Cliffs, NJ: Prentice-Hall, 2003): 209–210.

7. The Law of Large Numbers has been proven to hold under a variety of differing circumstances. So has the Central Limit Theorem. Thus, there are numerous Laws of Large Numbers and numerous Central Limit Theorems. Which law implies consistency and which theorem implies asymptotic normality varies from one setting to another. We do not dwell on the details of these various laws in this book. In a similar vein, econometric theorists define several kinds of convergence, not just convergence in probability. See William H. Greene, *Econometric Analysis*, 5th ed. (Englewood Cliffs, NJ: Prentice-Hall, 2003) for treatment of these advanced topics.

8. R.A. Lehfeldt, "The Elasticity of the Demand for Wheat," *Economic Journal* 24 (1914): 212–217.

9. Gary Smith of Pomona College generously provided these data.

10. J. Bradford DeLong and Lawrence H. Summers, "How Strongly Do Developing Countries Benefit from Equipment Investment?" *Journal of Monetary Economics*, 32, no. 3 (1993): 345–415.

11. Orley Ashenfelter and Cecelia Rouse, "Income, Schooling, and Ability: Evidence from a New Sample of Identical Twins," *Quarterly Journal of Economics* (February 1998): 253–284.

12. Orley Ashenfelter, David Ashmore, and Robert LaLonde, "Bordeaux Wine Vintage Quality and the Weather," *Chance* 8, no. 4 (1995): 7–14.

# *Appendix 12.A*

# Probability Limits and Consistency

Consistency is an intuitively appealing trait for an estimator. We would like to be increasingly sure that our guesses aren't far wrong as we gather more data. Formalizing this intuition requires some care. This appendix provides a formal definition of probability limits and consistency.

## 12.A.1 Defining Probability Limits and Consistency

**WHAT MAKES A GOOD ESTIMATOR?**

When we define a consistent estimator, we first must note that, strictly speaking, there isn't usually one single estimator for all sample sizes, because estimators ordinarily use all the observations in the sample. Adding more observations changes most estimators. For example, the sample mean is $(Y_1 + Y_2)/2$ when $n = 2$, but it becomes $(Y_1 + Y_2 + Y_3/3$ when $n = 3$. When looking across sample sizes, we are actually examining *a sequence* of estimators, with a new (though closely related) estimator for each sample size. A subscript $n$ added to an estimator can highlight when we are actually discussing a sequence of estimators. For example, $\overline{Y}$ denotes the sample mean, which we often use to estimate the population mean. A sequence of means is denoted by $\overline{Y}_n$:

$$\overline{Y}_n = \left\{ Y_1, \frac{1}{2}(Y_1 + Y_2), \frac{1}{3}(Y_1 + Y_2 + Y_3), \ldots, \frac{1}{n}(Y_1 + \cdots + Y_n) \right\}.$$

When attention is obviously on a sequence of estimators, and the argument isn't too formal, econometric studies often omit the subscript $n$. In this formal introduction to large sample properties, sequences of estimators are indicated with a subscript. Elsewhere in this book, and often in the economics literature, the subscripts are omitted.

In more formal terms, an estimator $\tilde{\beta}_n$ of some population parameter $\beta$ is a consistent estimator of $\beta$ if and only if the probability limit of $\tilde{\beta}_n$ (denoted plim($\tilde{\beta}_n$)) is $\beta$, or, in mathematical notation, if and only if

$$\text{plim}(\tilde{\beta}_n) = \beta,$$

where

$$\text{plim}(\tilde{\beta}_n) = \beta \quad \textit{if and only if} \quad \lim_{n \Rightarrow \infty} (\text{Pr}[|\tilde{\beta}_n - \beta| < c]) = 1$$

for any $c > 0$. The expression " $\lim_{n \Rightarrow \infty} [\text{Pr}(A_n \textit{ is an event } A^*)] = 1$" says that as $n$ grows large, the probability that event $A^*$ is the realized value of the $n^{\text{th}}$ random variable in a sequence of random variables, $A_n$, eventually grows as close to one as you wish it to, or, alternatively, for any proximity to certainty that you wish to choose, say, $1 - v$, for any $v > 0$, there is an $n$, for example, N, large enough that

*probability(event $A^*$ is the realized value of $A_n$) $> 1 - v$*

for all $n > N$. When the probability limit of $\tilde{\beta}_n$ is $\beta$, econometricians say that $\tilde{\beta}_n$ converges in probability to $\beta$. More informally, they say that converges in probability to $\beta$, or that $\tilde{\beta}$ consistently estimates $\beta$. *The distribution of an asymptotically unbiased estimator of $\beta$ whose variance converges to zero as n grows large collapses around $\beta$ as n grows large; consequently, such an unbiased estimator is a consistent estimator of $\beta$.*

Earlier in the chapter (p. 502), we learned rules for manipulating probability limits of random variables. Those rules are not explicit about probability limits referring to *sequences* of random variables. A more precise rendering of the rules would refer not to random variables, but to sequences of random variables and would place a subscript $n$ on each random variable in the list to indicate that the reference is actually to a sequence of random variables with elements that differ in their value of $n$. For example, rule (3) would become "When $\alpha_n$ and $\beta_n$ are sequences of random variables for which $\text{plim}(\alpha_n)$ and $\text{plim}(\beta_n)$ are finite:

$$(3) \ \text{plim}(\alpha_n + \beta_n) = \text{plim}(\alpha_n) + \text{plim}(\beta_n)."$$

This list of rules also gives a somewhat imprecise description of the Law of Large Numbers. The statistical subtleties that the rules skirt lie beyond the scope of this book. The subtleties arise because not only is the sample mean a sequence, when viewed asymptotically, that is $\left\{ \varepsilon_1, \dfrac{\varepsilon_1 + \varepsilon_2}{2}, \ldots, \dfrac{1}{n} \sum_{i=1}^{n} \varepsilon_i, \ldots \right\}$, but the expected value of that sample mean is also a sequence, $\left\{ \text{E}(\varepsilon_1), \text{E}\left(\dfrac{\varepsilon_1 + \varepsilon_2}{2}\right), \ldots, \right.$ $\left. \text{E}\left(\dfrac{1}{n}\sum_{i=1}^{n} \varepsilon_i\right), \ldots \right\}$. Implicitly, referring to a single expected value for the sequence of random variables, as in the statement of the law in our list of rules, assumes that all the elements of the sequence of expected values take on the same one value. We frequently do assume a single expected value for a sequence of expectations, for example, $\text{E}(\varepsilon_i) = 0$ or $\text{E}(\hat{\beta}_1) = \beta_1$; however, there are more general statements of the Law of Large Numbers that allow for the sequence of expectations to have multiple values that converge to some limit.[1]

### Endnote

1. For a more intense discussion of the Law of Large Numbers, see Fumio Hiyashi, *Econometrics* (Princeton, NJ: Princeton University Press, 2000).

 *Appendix 12.B*

# Asymptotic Normality and OLS

**WHAT ARE AN ESTI-
MATOR'S PROPERTIES?**

This appendix discusses the asymptotic normality of OLS. Consider the case of a DGP for a straight line with unknown slope and intercept, in which Equations 12.7 and 12.8,

$$\text{plim}\left(\frac{1}{n}\Sigma\, x_i\varepsilon_i\right) = 0$$

and

$$\text{plim}\left(\frac{1}{n}\Sigma\, x_i^2\right) = Q,\ \text{a nonzero constant,}$$

are true. In such a DGP, the OLS estimator,

$$\hat{\beta}_1 = \beta + \frac{\left(\frac{1}{n}\Sigma\, x_i\varepsilon_i\right)}{\left(\frac{1}{n}\Sigma\, x_i^2\right)},$$

is consistent.

We generally examine asymptotic distributions by putting random variables under a microscope, that is, by multiplying them by a number such as the square root of the sample size. If we were to multiply a random variable with a nonzero mean this way, the magnified mean would explode toward infinity. Consequently, to find a random variable's asymptotic distribution, we examine the deviations of the random variable from its own mean. Here, we look at

$$(\hat{\beta} - \beta) = \frac{\left(\frac{1}{n}\Sigma\, x_i\varepsilon_i\right)}{\left(\frac{1}{n}\Sigma\, x_i^2\right)}.$$

A rule of mathematical statistics says that because the denominator on the right-hand side converges in probability to $Q$, the asymptotic distribution of $(\hat{\beta} - \beta)$ is the same as the asymptotic distribution of

$$\frac{\frac{1}{n}\sum x_i \varepsilon_i}{Q}.$$

Thus, if $(1/n \sum x_i \varepsilon_i)$ is normally distributed asymptotically in this DGP, so is $\beta$. The assumptions of the present DGP are not enough to ensure that $\hat{\beta}$ is normally distributed asymptotically, because the Central Limit Theorem requires more conditions than this DGP provides to ensure that $(1/n \sum x_i \varepsilon_i)$ is normally distributed asymptotically.

Like the Law of Large Numbers, the Central Limit Theorem may not apply if some moments of, and among, the explanators and disturbances are unbounded. The Central Limit Theorem may also not apply if correlations among the observations are too strong, or if some observations weigh so heavily in the estimator that they swamp the rest asymptotically. Thus, for $\hat{\beta}$ to be normally distributed asymptotically when regressors are stochastic, assumptions similar to the following need to be added to the DGP:

1. The first through fourth moments of and among the disturbances and explanators in each observation are less than some finite number.
2. The observations are statistically independent.
3. $\lim_{n->\infty}(x_i^2/\sum_{j=1}^{n} x_j^2) = 0$, which ensures that the weight of each observation shrinks fast enough that no observation's distribution overwhelms the tendency toward normality.

Replacing the independence assumption (2) with other assumptions that allow for serially correlated explanators and serially correlated disturbances without losing the Central Limit Theorem is also possible. For many economic DGPs, the Central Limit Theorem applies and OLS is asymptotically normally distributed. The most frequently encountered violations of the Central Limit Theorem's requirements are observations too strongly correlated and unbounded moments. Such violations make OLS non-normal even in large samples. Central Limit Theorems are more sensitive to unbounded moments than are Laws of Large numbers.[1] For example, sometimes, when $var(1/n \sum x_i \varepsilon_i)$ does not converge to zero, consistency is maintained, but asymptotic normality is lost.

## Endnote

1. To learn more about Central Limit Theorems and the Laws of Large Numbers, see William H. Greene, *Econometric Analysis*, 5th ed. (Englewood Cliffs, NJ: Prentice-Hall, 2003): 896–918.

# Chapter 13

# Instrumental Variables Estimation

*Give me a lever long enough and a place to stand and I will move the world.*
—ARCHIMEDES, 280 B.C.

Econometricians frequently find themselves wishing for levers of their own with which to consistently estimate traits of the world. An econometrician peddling his wares finds customers unhappy when he says, "My estimators are wrong on average" or, worse yet, "Even with all the data in the world, my estimators are almost surely wrong by more than a little."

Unfortunately, these sad assessments usually apply to ordinary least squares (OLS) and its generalized least squares (GLS) and feasible generalized least squares (FGLS) kin ("the least squares estimators") if any explanators in the model are contemporaneously correlated with the disturbances. For such cases, econometricians need an estimator other than the least squares estimators—they need a lever. This chapter explains how mismeasured explanators, omitted variables, jointly determined variables, and lagged dependent variables with serially correlated disturbances all give rise to the contemporaneous correlations between disturbances and explanators that can make least squares biased and inconsistent. It also presents an alternative linear estimation procedure, called *instrumental variables* estimation, that is consistent when least squares is not and that provides a sound asymptotic base for hypothesis testing when least squares does not. When the least squares estimators are consistent, we prefer them to instrumental variables estimators, because the least squares estimators are more efficient, but when the disturbances and explanators are correlated, we need an alternative estimation strategy, a lever, that avoids the biases of least squares. Instrumental variables estimation often provides such a lever.

## 13.1 Friedman and the Consumption Function Revisited

Chapter 3 showed that OLS can be best linear unbiased estimators (BLUE) when the explanators in a regression model are stochastic, as long as the Gauss–Markov Assumptions about the disturbances apply for each and every possible combination of $X$-values. Sometimes this needed assumption holds, and OLS remains the estimator of choice. We saw in Chapter 12 that the disturbances may, in fact, be contemporaneously correlated with the explanators, though, in which case OLS is not only no longer BLUE, it is not even consistent.

# An Econometric Top 40—A Classical Favorite

## Heart Attacks and Heart Treatments

Does more intensive treatment following heart attacks increase the longevity of elderly heart attack patients? Do cardiac catheterization, revascularization, and other intensive medical procedures reduce mortality among these elderly? Mark McClellan, Barbara McNeil, and Joseph Newhouse, all of Harvard University, asked these questions in 1994.[1] Such medical questions may seem odd in an econometrics textbook, but intensive treatments of heart attack patients are very costly procedures. There is an important economic dimension to the choice of heart procedures. Longevity and costs are not the only considerations in undertaking medical procedures, but increased longevity is the primary justification offered by physicians for intensive medical procedures for heart patients. If these intensive procedures do not reduce mortality, their costs become much harder to defend. Moreover, this particular study is of econometric interest because the authors rely on instrumental variables estimation to determine the effectiveness of intensive treatment for elderly heart attack patients.

Can a simple comparison of means determine whether intensive treatment following heart attacks reduces mortality among elderly heart attack patients? Does it suffice to compare mortality rates of elderly heart attack patients who do and don't receive intensive treatment and ask who lives longer? Those who receive the more intensive care do have lower mortality rates, right away and subsequently. But no, this is not enough to answer the question. The recipients and nonrecipients differ in many other ways besides receiving different treatments. Those who receive the more intensive treatment are on average younger, more likely to live in urban areas, more likely to be

white, and more likely to be male. These observable differences between the intensively treated and others are correlated with mortality rates in the general population. Such traits, rather than the intensive treatment such people receive, may account for the lower mortality rates of the treated.

To control for these observed traits and ask if intensive treatment still lowers mortality rates, we can perform OLS regressions that estimate the effect of intensive treatment given other observed traits:

$$Mortality = \beta_0 +$$
$$\beta_1(dummy\ for\ intensively\ treated)$$
$$+ \beta_2\ race + \cdots + \beta_k\ urban + \varepsilon.$$

OLS estimates indicate that more intensive treatment reduces mortality immediately and subsequently. This analysis is not conclusive, however. Patients chosen for intensive treatment are a select group—they differ in many observable ways. Are they not also likely to differ in many unobserved ways? Can we be confident that our regression does not suffer from an omitted variables bias that would cloud our results? We cannot.

Many medical professionals are accustomed to the usual way in which experiments are conducted, with random assignment of individuals to treatments. When we randomize who gets a treatment and who does not, we reduce to a low probability the prospect that the treated and untreated differ systematically in ways that account for observed outcomes. Looking for differences between groups in randomized trials is a convincing way to assess the effectiveness of treatments. Medical professionals, accustomed to the randomized trials that mark much scientific investigation, often view OLS regressions that may suffer omitted variable bias with skepticism and even outright scorn. But randomized trials are not a feasible way to learn about the effects of intensive heart treatment. Who among us is willing to deny some elderly heart attack patients, in the name of scientific inquiry, the intensive treatment that their physicians deem suitable?

The explanator in the mortality equation that may bias OLS estimation is the dummy variable that indicates a person has been intensively treated. Some are concerned that this variable is correlated with unobserved traits that directly influence mortality. McClellan, McNeil, and Newhouse propose an instrument for this variable: the shortest geographic distance from the home of the individual to a hospital that has the facilities for intensive treatment. The authors observe that distance to a hospital that can give intensive treatment is correlated with receipt of such treatment. They argue that this geographic accident is likely to be uncorrelated with unobserved traits that influence mortality. These two traits, being correlated with the explanator that may bias OLS and being uncorrelated with the disturbances, are the key features of valid instruments.

When the authors estimate the mortality relationship using instrumental variables (IV) estimation, they find very small positive effects on mortality from the intensive treatment. Moreover, most of the improved mortality rate occurs because patients assigned to intense treatment die less often in the first days of hos-

pitalization—which is before the intensive treatment is actually given! Thus, it would seem that the gains are not from the intensive treatment itself, but from other features of those hospitals that are most likely to give intensive treatment. McClellan, McNeil, and Newhouse point out that some patients are in genuine and obvious need of more intensive treatment. The IV results suggest that it is only these patients who are likely to be living longer because of the treatments. The authors recommend that government and hospitals reduce the healthcare system's provision of such intensive treatments.

 **Final Notes**

Assessing the effects of public programs is a frequent task for economists. The McClellan, McNeil, and Newhouse paper illustrates how useful IV estimation can be in determining which programs have positive effects, which negative effects, and which no effect. IV estimation is an increasingly popular tool among econometricians who assess the effects of public programs. Valid instruments can be hard to come by, but when they are available, they frequently provide more credible estimates of a program's effects than the estimates obtained from OLS. The principal challenge in conducting IV estimation is finding valid instruments. If a candidate variable is either correlated with the disturbances or uncorrelated with the explanator that biases OLS, it is not a valid instrument.

■

We call explanators that are contemporaneously correlated with the disturbances **troublesome variables**. In Chapter 12, for example, the price of wheat was a troublesome explanator in the demand equation for wheat, unless the supply curve for wheat was perfectly elastic. That troublesome variable made OLS inconsistently estimate the demand for wheat. In this section, we find that mismeasured explanators are also troublesome and make OLS inconsistent. Nobel laureate

Milton Friedman of the University of Chicago puts a mismeasured explanator at the center of his classic study of the consumption function study that appears as a Golden Oldie in Chapter 2 (see p. 46). Friedman's clever strategy for consistent estimation in his study points the way to a general strategy for consistent estimation when OLS is inconsistent.

## Consumption and Permanent Income

Friedman hypothesizes that consumption depends not on current income, but on a longer term notion of income that he names "permanent income." A key point in Friedman's analysis is that the common practice of estimating consumption functions using current income makes OLS biased in estimating the marginal propensity to consume. Friedman's observation that mismeasured explanators makes OLS biased generalizes to models other than the consumption function, and his novel alternative estimator is a precursor to a more general strategy for coping with mismeasured $X$'s and other sources of contemporaneous correlation between $X$'s and disturbances.

Friedman specifies that

$$consumption_t = \beta(permanent\ income)_t + \varepsilon_t.$$

Friedman's theory implies that the consumption function passes through the origin. Friedman further argues that current income differs from permanent income by a random amount $v_t$ that is independent of both $\varepsilon_t$ and permanent income. That is,

$$(current\ income)_t = (permanent\ income)_t + v_t,$$

which implies that

$$(permanent\ income)_t = (current\ income)_t - v_t.$$

Because we do not observe permanent income, Friedman, like many economists before and after him, relies on current income as an imperfect measure of permanent income:

$$
\begin{aligned}
consumption_t &= \beta(current\ income_t - v_t) + \varepsilon_t \\
&= \beta(current\ income)_t - \beta v_t + \varepsilon_t \\
&= \beta(current\ income)_t + \eta_t, \qquad \textbf{13.1}
\end{aligned}
$$

in which $\eta_t = \varepsilon_t - \beta v_t$. Friedman recognizes that because current income at time $t$ depends on $v_t$, it follows that the regressor in Equation 13.1 is contemporaneously correlated with the equation's disturbance, $\eta_t$ (which equals $\varepsilon_t - \beta v_t$), that is,

$$E[(current\ income)_t \varepsilon_t] \neq 0.$$

Consequently, OLS is biased and inconsistent.

## OLS's Measurement Error Bias

We call bias that stems from mismeasured explanators **measurement error bias.** How Friedman overcomes this bias is best seen by looking at what makes OLS a biased and inconsistent estimator. Call current income $M_i$, permanent income $X_i$, and consumption $Y_i$. Friedman would like to estimate

$$Y_i = \beta X_i + \varepsilon_i,$$

but is limited to examining

$$Y_i = \beta M_i - \beta v_i + \varepsilon_i = \beta M_i + \eta_i. \qquad \textbf{13.2}$$

If in a regression we use mismeasured $X_i$, that is if we use $M_i$, then an analysis of $\beta_{g4}$ will be the same as previously, except that $M_i$ and its properties will replace $X_i$ and its properties. OLS applied to Equation 13.2 is biased and inconsistent. The bias in OLS is apparent when we examine the formula for the expected value of $\beta_{g4}$ when the explanatory variable is $M_i$. The estimator is

$$\beta_{g4} = \frac{\sum M_i Y_i}{\sum M_i^2} = \frac{\sum M_i(\beta M_i + \eta_i)}{\sum M_i^2} = \frac{\beta \sum M_i M_i}{\sum M_i^2} + \frac{\sum M_i \eta_i}{\sum M_i^2} \qquad \textbf{13.3}$$

and its expectation is

$$E(\beta_{g4}) = E\left(\beta + \frac{\sum M_i \eta_i}{\sum M_i^2}\right) = \beta + E\left(\frac{\sum M_i \eta_i}{\sum M_i^2}\right). \qquad \textbf{13.4}$$

The expectation on the right-hand side of Equation 13.4 is not easy to evaluate because it has random variables in both its numerator and its denominators, but the fact that $E(M_i\eta_i)$ in its numerator is not equal to zero does, in fact, make the expectation nonzero. OLS is biased when there is measurement error in the explanator. Is OLS at least consistent when the regressor is measured with error? No, it is not.

To see the inconsistency of OLS explicitly, let's again consider the OLS estimator, $\beta_{g4}$, when the explanatory variable is $M_i$ but now rewrite Equation 13.3 as

$$\beta_{g4} = \beta + \frac{\sum M_i \eta_i}{\sum M_i^2} = \beta + \frac{\frac{1}{n}\sum M_i \eta_i}{\frac{1}{n}\sum M_i^2}.$$

It is convenient to multiply both the numerator and the denominator of

$$\frac{\sum M_i \eta_i}{\sum M_i^2}$$

by $\left(\frac{1}{n}\right)$ because otherwise neither the numerator nor the denominator would converge as the sample size grows because the variance of a sum grows large as the number of uncorrelated elements in the sum grows large. The plim of $\beta_{g4}$ is

$$\text{plim}(\beta_{g4}) = \text{plim}\left(\beta + \frac{\frac{1}{n}\sum M_i \eta_i}{\frac{1}{n}\sum M_i^2}\right).$$

In Chapter 12, we learned that the plim of a sum is the sum of the plims, and the plim of a constant is the constant, so we can write

$$\text{plim}(\beta_{g4}) = \text{plim}(\beta) + \text{plim}\left(\frac{\frac{1}{n}\sum M_i \eta_i}{\frac{1}{n}\sum M_i^2}\right) = \beta + \text{plim}\left(\frac{\frac{1}{n}\sum M_i \eta_i}{\frac{1}{n}\sum M_i^2}\right).$$

In Chapter 12 we also learned that the plim of a ratio is the ratio of the plims, as long as the plim of the denominator is not zero. Thus, if we assume that $\text{plim}(\frac{1}{n}\sum M_i^2)$ does not equal zero, we can write

$$\text{plim}(\beta_{g4}) = \beta + \frac{\text{plim}\left(\frac{1}{n}\sum M_i \eta_i\right)}{\text{plim}\left(\frac{1}{n}\sum M_i^2\right)}.$$

If we assume that the Law of Large Numbers applies to this DGP, then means converge to their corresponding expected values. In this case,

$$\text{plim}(\beta_{g4}) = \beta + \frac{E(M_i \eta_i)}{E(M_i^2)}. \tag{13.5}$$

The numerator of Equation 13.5 is not zero, so $\beta_{g4}$ is inconsistent. The inconsistency of OLS stems from the correlation of the explanator $M_i$ with the disturbance, $\eta_i$. Notice that the larger the covariation between $M_i$ and $\eta_i$ is, the larger the inconsistency of OLS is; as that covariance goes to zero, so, too, does the inconsistency of OLS. Appendix 13.A shows that if the explanator is mismeasured in a model with an unknown intercept and one unknown slope,

$$\frac{\text{plim}\left(\frac{1}{n}\sum M_i \eta_i\right)}{\text{plim}\left(\frac{1}{n}\sum M_i^2\right)} = \frac{-\beta \sigma_\nu^2}{[Q + \sigma_\nu^2]}, \tag{13.6}$$

where $Q$ is the variance of the underlying true (and unobserved) explanator values, permanent income, and $\sigma_\nu^2$ is the variance in the measurement errors. Notice that this inconsistency (which economists commonly refer to as a bias) is opposite in sign and proportional to $\beta$; the OLS estimator tends to understate the magnitude of $\beta$. For this reason, measurement error bias is sometimes called **attenuation bias** when there is a single explanator. The larger the variance of the measurement errors relative to the variance of the underlying $X_i$, the larger the inconsistency of OLS. If the variance of the measurement errors is much smaller than the variance of the underlying $X_i$, the inconsistency of OLS is negligible. With a single explanator, measurement error in the explanator always biases OLS toward zero; however, when there are multiple explanators in the model, measurement error in the explanators can bias OLS toward or away from zero.

The seed of OLS's bias is planted in the first step toward constructing the OLS estimator, $\beta_{g4}$. The first step in constructing $\beta_{g4}$ is to weight each observation by $M_i$:

$$M_i Y_i = \beta M_i^2 + M_i \eta_i.$$

The disturbances get multiplied by the explanator in this step. It is the fact that $E(M_i \eta_i)$ does not equal zero (because $M_i$ and $\eta_i$ are correlated) that makes OLS biased. Friedman suggests avoiding this bias by using a different estimator. His approach avoids multiplying by $M_i$. Instead of applying OLS ($\beta_{g4}$), Friedman uses another of our early linear estimators, $\beta_{g2}$:

$$\beta_{g2} = \frac{\Sigma \; dependent \; variable_i}{\Sigma \; (explanator)_i}.$$

## The Consistency of $\beta_{g2}$

To prove that $\beta_{g2}$ is a consistent estimator of $\beta$, despite relying on $M$, the mismeasured $X$-value, as our explanatory variable, start with $\beta_{g2}$'s construction from

$$Y_i = \beta M_i + \eta_i.$$

We do not weight each observation by $M_i$, as we do for $\beta_{g4}$, but instead immediately sum both sides and divide through by $\Sigma M_i$:

$$\frac{\Sigma Y_i}{\Sigma M_i} = \frac{\Sigma(\beta M_i + \eta_i)}{(\Sigma M_i)} = \beta + \frac{(\Sigma \eta_i)}{(\Sigma M_i)} = \beta_{g2},$$

or

$$\beta_{g2} = \beta + \frac{\left(\frac{1}{n}\Sigma \eta_i\right)}{\left(\frac{1}{n}\Sigma M_i\right)}.$$

The probability limit of $\beta_{g2}$ is

$$\text{plim}(\beta_{g2}) = \text{plim}\left(\beta + \frac{\left(\frac{1}{n}\Sigma\eta_i\right)}{\left(\frac{1}{n}\Sigma M_i\right)}\right).$$

The plim of a sum is the sum of the plims, and the plim of a constant is the constant, so

$$\text{plim}(\beta_{g2}) = \beta + \text{plim}\left(\frac{\left(\frac{1}{n}\Sigma\eta_i\right)}{\left(\frac{1}{n}\Sigma M_i\right)}\right).$$

The inconsistency of $\beta_{g2}$ is, therefore,

$$\text{plim}\left[\frac{\left(\frac{1}{n}\Sigma\eta_i\right)}{\left(\frac{1}{n}\Sigma M_i\right)}\right].$$

Because the plim of a ratio is the ratio of the plims, as long as the plim of the denominator is not zero, we can write

$$\text{plim}\left[\frac{\left(\frac{1}{n}\Sigma\eta_i\right)}{\left(\frac{1}{n}\Sigma M_i\right)}\right] = \frac{\text{plim}\left(\frac{1}{n}\Sigma\eta_i\right)}{\text{plim}\left(\frac{1}{n}\Sigma M_i\right)},$$

if we assume that $\text{plim}(\frac{1}{n}\Sigma M_i)$ is not zero (that is, if we assume current income does not converge to an average value of zero over time). If we further assume that the data-generating process (DGP) here is such that the Law of Large Numbers applies, so that means converge in probability to their corresponding expected values, then we can claim that

$$\frac{\text{plim}\left[\frac{1}{n}\Sigma\eta_i\right]}{\text{plim}\left[\frac{1}{n}\Sigma M_i\right]} = \frac{E(\eta_i)}{E(M_i)} = \frac{0}{E(M_i)} = 0,$$

which implies that $\beta_{g2}$ is a consistent estimator when applied to mismeasured explanators in a DGP with no intercept and a single explanator.

Milton Friedman was the first to suggest using $\beta_{g2}$ to consistently estimate the marginal propensity to consume in his consumption function model. Unfortunately, the consistency of $\beta_{g2}$ rests on the model having no intercept term. We saw in Chapter 4 that except in the special case in which the average explanator value is zero, $\beta_{g2}$ is biased for every sample size if there is an intercept term in the model. Friedman's estimator does not provide a general solution to estimating models in which OLS is inconsistent. Moreover, Friedman's strategy may not be the most efficient approach to estimation even when there is no intercept term. The next section builds on Friedman's insight to develop an even better estimation strategy for models in which OLS is inconsistent.

## 13.2    Instrumental Variables Estimation

**How Do We Create an Estimator?**

The estimator $\beta_{g2}$ provides a consistent estimator for Friedman's problem and others in which the slope of a line through the origin cannot be consistently estimated by OLS. But can we do better than $\beta_{g2}$? Remember why OLS ($\beta_{g4}$) outperformed $\beta_{g2}$ when we had no measurement error: For a DGP with a straight line through the origin and homoskedastic disturbances, observations with larger explanatory values mislead us less about the true slope than do those with smaller explanatory values. Can we weight our observations on $Y$ in a more efficient fashion than $\beta_{g2}$ does? Sometimes we can.

### Improving on $\beta_{g2}$

Suppose we could find a new variable, $Z_i$, that has two characteristics:

1. It is correlated with the underlying $X_i$'s, that is, with permanent income (so it is an indicator of the value of the underlying explanator for each observation).

2. It is uncorrelated with the disturbances in the equation to be estimated—in this case the $\eta_i$.

In Friedman's consumption function example, if the $Z_i$ are uncorrelated with both the measurement errors in the $M_i$ (the $\nu_i$) and the disturbances of the underlying model (the $\varepsilon_i$), then they will be uncorrelated with the $\eta_i$.

The variable $Z$ we seek here is an example of an *instrumental variable*. An **instrumental variable**, or more simply, an **instrument**, is (i) contemporaneously correlated with a troublesome variable and (ii) contemporaneously uncorrelated with the disturbance. To be useful in overcoming the biases caused by a troublesome variable, an instrument cannot itself be an explanator in the model.

### Illustrative Instruments

What are typical instrumental variables? Four examples offer an informative portrait of instrumental variables. First, in the Classical Favorite earlier in this chapter, which studies the efficacy of intensive procedures for treating elderly severe heart attack patients, Mark McClellan and his coauthors consider the dummy variable *intensively treated* a troublesome variable. They fear that people selected for intensive heart treatment differ from other heart patients in unobserved ways relevant to mortality, making the dummy correlated with the omitted variables in the disturbance term. These authors use the distance of the patient's residence from a hospital able to perform intensive procedures as their instrument for the troublesome variable.[2] They argue that (i) the kind of treatment elderly patients receive is correlated with the patients' proximity to hospitals that provide the most intensive treatment and that (ii) where the elderly patient lives is not correlated with unobserved determinants of the patients' survival prospects that make up the disturbance term.

Second, in his widely cited study of how military service affects individuals' lifetime earnings, economist Joshua Angrist of MIT finds military service to be a troublesome variable because serving in the military might be correlated with unobserved traits that appear in the disturbance term. Angrist turns to a draft lottery conducted for all 18-year-olds during the Vietnam War for an instrument. He uses whether one's birthday was a draft lottery "winner" as an instrument for military service.[3] Angrist argues that (i) lottery winners were more likely than other people to serve in the military and that (ii) one's birth date is not correlated with unobserved determinants of earnings.

Third, in a paper examining consumption and the permanent income hypothesis, econometrician Fumio Hiyashi of the University of Tokyo uses lagged variables, including lagged per capita exports and lagged per capita government spending as instruments for his troublesome variable, permanent income.[4] Hiyashi implicitly argues that (i) past exports and government spending are correlated with consumers' permanent incomes, and that (ii) although deviations of current income from permanent income might be correlated with current exports and current government spending, those deviations are not correlated with past exports or past government spending.

Fourth, in a study of the determinants of wages, economists Orley Ashenfelter and Cecelia Rouse of Princeton University considered individual's self-reported education levels a troublesome variable because individuals may misreport their own education.[5] They use siblings' reports of the individuals' years of education as an instrument for the individuals' self-reported years of education. Ashenfelter and Rouse argue that siblings' reports of individuals' education are likely to be (i) highly correlated with the individuals' actual education, and (ii) have reporting errors uncorrelated both with the errors in the self-reports and with the underlying disturbances in the wage equation for individuals.

## The Instrumental Variables Estimator

Now, having seen what instrumental variables look like, suppose that in Friedman's consumption function example we find a suitable instrumental variable, $Z$, for $M$, the mismeasured regressor. Further suppose that $Z_i$ and $M_i$ are *positively* correlated. When faced with a mismeasured independent variable, such as permanent income, so that instead of estimating the true relationship,

$$Y_i = X_i\beta + \varepsilon_i,$$

we estimate

$$Y_i = M_i\beta + \eta_i = (X_i + v_i) + (-\beta v_i + \varepsilon_i),$$

we can use $Z$ to construct a better estimator of $\beta$ than $\beta_{g2}$.

Recall that $\beta_{g2}$ weights every observation equally, with a weight equal to $\sum X_i$. However, because higher $Z_i$ tend to correspond to higher $X_i$, we have reason to more heavily weight observations associated with larger $Z_i$, just as in OLS we weight observations with larger $X$-values more heavily. Therefore, let us construct a new estimator by first weighting each observation by $Z_i$:

$$Z_i Y_i = \beta Z_i M_i + Z_i \eta_i. \qquad \textbf{13.7}$$

Notice that $M_i$ appears in Equation 13.7 where we might ordinarily expect $X_i$. This is because we are assuming that we are limited to using $M_i$, the mismeasured $X_i$, in our regression, instead of $X_i$ itself.

Next we sum both sides:

$$\sum Z_i Y_i = \sum \beta Z_i M_i + \sum Z_i \eta_i,$$

and then divide by $\sum Z_i M_i$ (rather than by $\sum M_i^2$, as OLS would):

$$\frac{(\sum Z_i Y_i)}{(\sum Z_i M_i)} = \beta + \frac{(\sum Z_i \eta_i)}{(\sum Z_i M_i)} = \beta_{IV}. \qquad \textbf{13.8}$$

We call $\beta_{IV}$ an **instrumental variables (IV) estimator**.[6]

The intuition underlying the IV estimator has three parts. Recall that $Z$ (our instrument) is correlated with $M$ (our troublesome variable), but not with the disturbances—and in particular, not with the measurement errors that appear in both $M$ and the disturbances. The first element of the intuition is that $Z$ and $M$ move together only through the workings of $X$ because $Z$ is not correlated with the measurement error in $M$. The second element of the intuition is that $Z$ and $Y$ move together only through the workings of $X$, because $Z$ is uncorrelated with the disturbances. These first two elements combine to yield the third element of the intuition: The co-movement of $Z$ and $Y$ relative to the co-movement of $Z$ and $M$ reflects the movement of $Y$ brought about by $X$, and nothing else.

Does this strategy require that $Z$ and $M$ be *positively* correlated? No! Even if $Z$ and $M$ were *negatively* correlated, the estimator would still work. Why?

Consider the denominator and numerator of the left-hand side of Equation 13.8. If $Z$ and $M$ were *negatively* correlated, $\sum Z_i M_i$ would tend to be negative—unlike $\sum X_i^2$, which appears in the denominator of the OLS estimator. But $\sum Z_i Y_i$ would also tend to have the opposite sign from $\sum X_i Y_i$, which appears in the numerator of the OLS estimator. Consequently, the IV estimator would tend to end up with the same sign as OLS. *The lesson is that a variable can be either positively or negatively correlated with the troublesome variables and serve equally well as an instrument.*

How well does the IV estimator perform, though? Is it biased? Is it consistent? Let's find out.

## The Bias of an IV Estimator

For the IV estimator, $\beta_{IV}$, to be unbiased, its expected value must equal $\beta$. The expected value of $\beta_{IV}$, is

$$E(\beta_{IV}) = \beta + E\left(\frac{\sum Z_i \eta_i}{\sum Z_i M_i}\right).$$

We *cannot* rewrite this expression as

$$E(\beta_{IV}) = \beta + \sum\left(E\left(\frac{Z_i}{\sum Z_i M_i}\right)E(\eta_i)\right),$$

which would equal $\beta$, because the $\eta_i$ are correlated with the $M_i$. *The IV estimator is biased.* Indeed, it turns out that the finite sample bias of instrumental variables is in the same direction as the bias of OLS.

## The Consistency of an IV Estimator

If the IV estimator is biased, is it at least consistent? For the IV estimator, $\beta_{IV}$, to be consistent, its probability limit must equal $\beta$. The probability limit of $\beta_{IV}$ is

$$\text{plim}(\beta_{IV}) = \text{plim}\left(\beta + \frac{(\sum Z_i \eta_i)}{(\sum Z_i M_i)}\right) = \beta + \text{plim}\left(\frac{(\sum Z_i \eta_i)}{(\sum Z_i M_i)}\right).$$

To see that $\beta_{IV}$ is consistent, note that

$$\text{plim}\left[\frac{\sum(Z_i \eta_i)}{\sum(Z_i M_i)}\right] = \frac{\text{plim}\left[\left(\frac{1}{n}\sum Z_i \eta_i\right)\right]}{\text{plim}\left[\left(\frac{1}{n}\sum Z_i M_i\right)\right]},$$

as long as $\text{plim}(\frac{1}{n}\sum Z_i M_i)$ does not equal zero. If we further assume that the Law of Large Numbers applies in this DGP, so that sample means converge in probability to the corresponding expected values, then

$$\frac{\text{plim}\left[\left(\frac{1}{n}\right)\sum Z_i \eta_i\right]}{\text{plim}\left[\left(\frac{1}{n}\right)\sum Z_i M_i\right]} = \frac{0}{\text{plim}\left[\left(\frac{1}{n}\right)\sum Z_i(X_i + v_i)\right]}$$

$$= \frac{0}{\left(\text{plim}\left[\left(\frac{1}{n}\right)\sum Z_i X_i\right] + \text{plim}\left[\left(\frac{1}{n}\right)\sum Z_i v_i\right]\right)}$$

$$= \frac{0}{\left[\text{plim}\left[\left(\frac{1}{n}\right)\sum Z_i X_i\right] + 0\right]} = \frac{0}{[E(Z_i X_i) + 0]} = 0,$$

because by assumption $Z_i$ is uncorrelated with $v_i$ and $\varepsilon_i$, and is correlated with $X_i$. Thus,

$$\text{plim}(\beta_{IV}) = \beta + 0 = \beta.$$

*The IV estimator is a consistent estimator with mismeasured explanators.* This result does not only apply to a regression line with one slope and no intercept term. Appendix 13.B shows that IV estimation is also consistent in a multiple regression model with mismeasured explanators.

A review of this proof that IV is a consistent estimator underscores the idea that the IV estimator would be consistent even if the correlation between the instrument and the troublesome explanator were negative, not positive. As we have learned already, instruments negatively correlated with a troublesome explanator can be just as effective antidotes for bias as instruments positively correlated with that explanator.

## The Variance of an IV Estimator

Any valid instrument yields a consistent IV estimator. Just as some unbiased estimators are more efficient than others, though, some instruments yield more efficient IV estimators than others.

The asymptotic variance of the instrumental variables estimator $\beta_{IV}$ given by Equation 13.8 is as follows:

$$\frac{1}{n}\sigma_\eta^2 \frac{\text{plim}\left(\frac{1}{n}\sum Z_i^2\right)}{\text{plim}\left(\frac{1}{n}\sum Z_i M_i\right)^2},$$

**13.9**

where $\sigma_\eta^2 = \text{var}(\eta_i)$. When there is an intercept term in the underlying model, $\beta_{IV}$ becomes $\Sigma z_i y_i / \Sigma z_i x_i$ and the asymptotic variance of $\beta_{IV}$ becomes

$$\frac{1}{n}\sigma^2 \frac{\text{plim}\left(\frac{1}{n}\Sigma z_i^2\right)}{\text{plim}\left(\frac{1}{n}\Sigma z_i m_i\right)^2},$$

13.10

where, as usual, $z$ and $m$ are the deviations of $Z$ and $M$ from their respective means. Appendix 13.B derives this variance in the context of multiple regression.

Notice that the asymptotic covariance of $Z$ with $M$ appears in the denominator of $\beta_{IV}$'s variance, and the asymptotic variance of $Z$ appears in the numerator. *An instrument that has a high covariance with the troublesome explanator and a small variance yields a more efficient instrumental variance estimator.*

## The Multiple Regression Case

IV estimation generalizes to models with multiple explanators. *In the multiple regression case, IV estimation remains consistent when contemporaneous correlation between the disturbances and one or more explanators makes OLS biased and inconsistent.* Instruments for a specific troublesome variable have two traits:

1. Contemporaneous correlation with that troublesome variable
2. No contemporaneous correlation with the disturbances

Troublesome variables are explanators whose correlation with the disturbances biases OLS. Perfect multicollinearity among the set of instruments and nontroublesome variables undermines IV estimation, just as perfect multicollinearity undermines OLS estimation. *Successful IV estimation in multiple regression models requires at least one instrument for each troublesome variable in the model, not counting the nontroublesome explanators in the model.* If the only valid instruments are themselves explanators in the model, the instruments are perfectly correlated with the nontroublesome explanators, and IV estimation fails. There is always a perfect instrument for each nontroublesome variable—itself; each nontroublesome variable is contemporaneously uncorrelated with the disturbances and perfectly correlated with itself. Because nontroublesome explanators serve as instruments for themselves, they are not available to serve as effective instruments for troublesome variables. The instruments for troublesome variables must be variables that are not themselves explanators in the model.

## Identification

We can use IV estimation to consistently estimate models with troublesome explanators as long as there is at least one instrument available for each troublesome variable. When we have just enough instruments for consistent estimation, we say that the regression equation is **exactly identified**. When we have more than enough instruments, we say that the equation is **overidentified**. If the model cannot be consistently estimated because we have too few instruments, we say that the equation is **underidentified**. Because the instruments for troublesome variables cannot themselves be explanators in the model, identification requires that our model must exclude from the regression equation at least as many potential instrumental variables as there are troublesome explanators. We call this requirement the **order condition for identification**.

*The order condition is a necessary condition for the identification of an equation.*

## 13.3   Sources of Contemporaneous Correlation

WHAT IS THE DGP?

We have just seen that mismeasured explanators make OLS biased and inconsistent and that IV estimation consistently estimates the parameters of the model in this case. This section explains how IV estimation can provide consistent estimates in three other often encountered settings in which contemporaneously correlated explanators and disturbances make OLS biased and inconsistent. The three settings are (i) omitted relevant explanators, (ii) lagged dependent variables coupled with serially correlated disturbances, and (iii) jointly determined dependent and independent variables.

### Instrumental Variables and Omitted Variables Bias

When relevant explanatory variables are excluded from the model, they become a part of the disturbance term. If

$$Y_i = \beta_0 + \beta_1 X_{1i} + \beta_2 X_{2i} + \varepsilon_i,$$

but we mistakenly specify

$$Y_i = \beta_0 + \beta_1 X_{1i} + \eta_i,$$

then $\eta_i = \beta_2 X_{2i} + \varepsilon_i$. We learned in Chapter 8 that omitted variables bias arises when the included variables are correlated with the omitted relevant variables, that is, when $E(x_{1i}x_{2i}) \neq 0$. In such cases, the included explanators are not contemporaneously uncorrelated with the disturbances, $E(x_{1i}\eta_i) = E(x_{1i}(\beta_2 X_{2i} + \varepsilon_i)) \neq 0$, so OLS suffers from the bias and inconsistency that we call omitted variables bias.

Notice that in the omitted variable case, our goal is to estimate the coefficient on the regressor included in our model, $X_{1i}$ itself. This is in contrast to the mismeasured explanator case, when our interest is in the effect of the actual variable, not the effect of the regressor, $M_i$. In the present case, then, the IV estimator is

$$\beta_{IV} = \frac{(\sum Z_i Y_i)}{(\sum Z_i X_{1i})},$$

because $X_1$ is itself the troublesome variable.

IV estimation can overcome omitted variables bias if the instruments are valid ones, that is, if they satisfy our two conditions: (i) they are correlated with the troublesome variable; and (ii) they are uncorrelated with the disturbance. For example, Josh Angrist in his study of the effect of military service on earnings, and Mark McClellan and his coauthors in their study of the efficacy of heart disease treatments, use IV estimation to overcome omitted variables bias.

Satisfying requirement (ii) is often particularly difficult when seeking instruments to overcome omitted variables bias. Omitted variable bias arises because the included $X$'s are correlated with the omitted variables. Valid instruments in this case must be variables that are correlated with the included $X$'s and uncorrelated with the omitted $X$'s. A difficult problem in choosing instruments to overcome omitted variable bias is establishing that the instruments are uncorrelated with the omitted variables. McClellan and his coauthors confronted this issue directly. In their heart treatment paper, they conduct formal tests of their success in choosing a suitable instrumental variable. In contrast, Angrist offered only intuitive support for his choice of a lottery "winning" birthday dummy variable as an instrument. How, he asked, could the randomized lottery outcome be correlated with traits of the individuals? Angrist's persuasive rationale is the rhetorical and substantive foundation of the randomized experiments that are often conducted in both the natural and the social sciences.

## Instrumental Variables Estimation and Lagged Dependent Variables

Lagged dependent variables are another potential destroyer of the consistency of OLS. Robert Barro's classic money growth equations, discussed in Chapter 6, contained money growth lagged once and lagged twice. We learn here that if the disturbances are serially correlated, OLS may be inconsistent in models with lagged dependent variables.

To see that when lagged dependent variables are coupled with serially correlated disturbances, OLS may become inconsistent, suppose the dependent variable lagged once appears as an explanator in a DGP with first-order autoregressive disturbances:

$$Y_t = \beta_0 + \beta_1 Y_{t-1} + \varepsilon_t$$

$$\varepsilon_t = \rho \varepsilon_{t-1} + \nu_t. \qquad \qquad \text{13.11}$$

We can rewrite $Y_t$, substituting for $Y_{t-1}$. This exposes the appearance of $\varepsilon_{t-1}$ within the explanators:

$$Y_t = \beta_0 + \beta_1 Y_{t-1} + \varepsilon_t$$
$$= \beta_0 + \beta_1(\beta_0 + \beta_1 Y_{t-2} + \varepsilon_{t-1}) + \varepsilon_t. \qquad \textbf{13.12}$$

The appearance of $\varepsilon_{t-1}$ in Equation 13.12 makes it clear that OLS is inconsistent in this DGP because Equation 13.11 ensures that $E(\varepsilon_t\varepsilon_{t-1})$ is not zero; the explanator $Y_{t-1}$ is contemporaneously correlated with the disturbance, $\varepsilon_t$. *A lagged dependent variable among the explanators and serially correlated disturbances often combine together to make OLS inconsistent.* Serial correlation and lagged dependent variables *may* not make OLS inconsistent, however. For example, suppose that instead of first-order serial correlation, the DGP has a serial correlation in which $E(\varepsilon_t\varepsilon_{t-1}) = 0$, but $E(\varepsilon_t\varepsilon_{t-2}) \neq 0$. In such a case, OLS would be consistent. (Barro found no serial correlation in his disturbances, so he was spared these concerns about the consistency of OLS.)

Notice that in the present case, our goal is to estimate the coefficient on the regressor in our model, $Y_{t-1}$. This differs from the mismeasured explanator case, in which our interest is in the effect of the true independent variable, not the effect of the regressor, $M_i$. In the present case, then, the IV estimator is

$$\beta_{IV} = \frac{(\sum Z_t Y_t)}{(\sum Z_t Y_{t-1})},$$

because $Y_{t-1}$ is the troublesome variable.

IV estimation can consistently estimate the parameters of a model with lagged dependent variables when the disturbances are serially correlated. Finding suitable instruments for the lagged dependent variables is frequently difficult, however. If an explanator besides the lagged dependent variable is present in the model, econometricians sometimes use lagged values of that explanator as an instrument for the lagged dependent variable. Unfortunately, lagged explanators are frequently highly collinear with their current values. In such cases, IV estimators have a high variance for the same reason that OLS estimators have a high variance when explanators are highly collinear.

## Instrumental Variables and Jointly Determined Variables

Many economic variables are interdependent. For example, the price of an audio CD influences the quantity of CDs bought and sold, but the quantity produced for sale also influences the CD's price. Similarly, the number of people in jail influences crime rates, but crime rates also influence the number of people in jail. OLS is often biased when used to estimate regression models involving such interdependent variables.

To understand why OLS is biased in such regressions, return to the demand curve for a staple agricultural commodity, wheat, that we examined in Chapter 12. Rather than making the expected quantity demanded strictly proportional to the price of wheat, as we did in Chapter 12, consider a richer specification of the demand for wheat,

$$Q_i = \beta_0 + \beta_1 P_i + \beta_2 I_i + \varepsilon_i^d,$$

in which $Q$ is the quantity of wheat demanded, $P$ is the price of wheat, and $I$ is income, and consider the supply curve for wheat:

$$P_i = \alpha_0 + \alpha_1 Q_i + \alpha_2 W_i + \varepsilon_i^s,$$

where $W$ is an indicator of weather conditions. When there is an above-average quantity of wheat demanded because the demand disturbance, $\varepsilon_i^d$, is greater than zero, price will tend to be higher than if the shock to demand were zero—the higher quantity tends to move farmers up their supply curves. As a consequence, price is contemporaneously correlated with the disturbances in the demand curve, and OLS is biased if it is used to estimate the demand curve. This bias is called **simultaneity bias** because it stems from price and quantity being simultaneously determined.

Fortunately, there is a natural instrumental variable for the troublesome price variable in the demand equation. Weather meets the two requirements for a valid instrument. It is correlated with price because it appears in the supply curve and is also unlikely to be correlated with the shocks in the demand for wheat. IV estimation can sometimes consistently estimate the parameters of a model that contains explanators that are jointly determined with the dependent variables, even though OLS cannot. We call explanators that are jointly determined with the dependent variables **endogenous variables** because they are determined within the system of equations. In this example, price is an endogenous variable that appears as an explanator in the demand equation. Weather, on the other hand, is an example of what we call **exogenous variables** because it is determined outside this system of equations. Exogenous variables are uncorrelated with the disturbances of the system, so they are good candidates for use as instruments. Weather is a good instrument for the demand equation because it does not appear as an explanator in that equation.

OLS applied to the supply equation also suffers from simultaneity bias. In the supply equation, it is quantity that is the troublesome endogenous explanator. Weather is not a useful instrument for quantity in the supply equation because weather already appears in that equation as an explanator. Fortunately, there is a natural instrument for quantity in the supply equation—the income variable that appears in the demand equation, but not in the supply equation. Income is plausibly determined outside the supply-and-demand system for wheat and is therefore plausibly an exogenous variable.

Suitable instruments are not always available when variables are jointly determined. When fewer exogenous variables are excluded from an equation than there are endogenous explanators in the equation, the order condition for identification fails and the equation's coefficients cannot be consistently estimated. Even when enough exogenous variables are excluded from an equation to satisfy the order condition, sometimes no consistent estimator of an equation is possible. Each equation in a system of equations needs its own independent exclusion restrictions. When an equation satisfies the order condition, and the equations' exclusion restrictions are not redundant with the restrictions of other equations in the model, we say that the equation satisfies the **rank condition for identification**. *The rank condition is a sufficient condition for the identification of an equation.*

### Lagged Dependent Variables and Identification

We have seen that explanators that are lagged dependent variables make OLS biased and inconsistent if the disturbances are serially correlated. When the disturbances are not serially correlated, however, lagged dependent variables can facilitate consistent estimation of an equation. When there is no serial correlation in the disturbances, lagged dependent variables are uncorrelated with the disturbances. Consequently, if a lagged dependent variable is correlated with a troublesome variable, it can serve as an instrumental variable. Econometricians call a model's exogenous and lagged dependent variables the model's **predetermined variables**.

## 13.4    An Application: Wage Equations and IV Estimation

We have looked at wage equations several times. One striking feature of wage equations is the many variables they do *not* contain. We explain wages with years of education, age and age squared (or better, experience), sex, race, and occasionally a measure of intelligence. Many other traits do not get measured and therefore do not get included. Did a person's parents read to them, restrict television viewing, send them to good schools, or make them do their homework? All these variables might influence one's future wages, but we do not usually include them in wage equations, because we usually don't measure them. Do these omitted traits bias the OLS estimates we obtain from our wage equations?

Instrumental variables is one strategy for overcoming the omitted variables problem in wage equations. Another strategy is to look at the differences in earnings between identical twins, for whom many of the unobserved traits that might influence wages are very similar, if not exactly equal. Orley Ashenfelter and Cecelia Rouse of Princeton University have implemented this approach.[7] Their data are in the file bothtwins.*** on this book's companion Web site (**www.aw-bc.com/murray**); the variables in that file are described in this chapter's problem 5.

This section first uses the Ashenfelter–Rouse data to estimate the return to education by OLS using differences between identical twins. (The differences data are in the file twindiff.*** on this book's companion Web site, **www.aw-bc.com/murray**; the variables in that file are described in this chapter's Problem 1.) A second estimation problem in wage equations, besides omitted variables, is that individuals may misreport their level of education, inducing measurement error bias in OLS estimates of the wage equation. Differences between twins' self-reported education levels is similarly tainted by such measurement error. To ascertain the extent of measurement error bias in the OLS estimates based on differences between twins, the section compares IV estimates of the returns to education with the OLS estimates. In the context of this chapter, it is the IV application that is most pertinent; however, the use of differences between twins to overcome omitted variable bias proves to be a powerful tool in its own right.

## Using Twins to Overcome Omitted Variable Bias

Wage equations apply to twins as much as to anyone. If we examine one such equation applied to two siblings who are identical twins, we would write

$$
\begin{aligned}
\text{Twin 1:} \quad wage_1 = {} & \beta_0 + \beta_1 education_1 + \beta_2 age_1 + \beta_3 age_1^2 \\
& + \beta_4 white_1^2 + \beta_5 female_1 + \beta_6 (mother's\ education)_1 \\
& + \beta_7 (parents'\ income)_1 + \beta_8 IQ_1 \\
& + \beta_9 (number\ of\ siblings)_1 + \varepsilon_1,
\end{aligned} \tag{13.13}
$$

and

$$
\begin{aligned}
\text{Twin 2:} \quad wage_2 = {} & \beta_0 + \beta_1 education_2 + \beta_2 age_2 + \beta_3 age_2^2 + \beta_4 white_2 \\
& + \beta_5 female_2 + \beta_6 (mother's\ education)_2 \\
& + \beta_7 (parents'\ income)_2 + \beta_8 IQ_2 \\
& + \beta_9 (number\ of\ siblings)_2 + \varepsilon_2.
\end{aligned} \tag{13.14}
$$

Suppose mother's education, parents' income, and how many siblings the individual has are all unmeasured variables, along with the disturbance terms. A wage equation estimated using these observations on twins risks omitted variable bias—the included variables, education, age, and age squared, might be correlated with the omitted variables.

What happens if we examine the *difference* between these twins' wages?

$$wage_1 - wage_2 = \beta_1(education_1 - education_2) + \beta_2(0) + \beta_3(0) + \beta_4(0)$$
$$+ \beta_5(0) + \beta_6(0) + \beta_7(0) + \beta_8(IQ_1 - IQ_2) + \beta_7(0) + \varepsilon_1 - \varepsilon_2 \qquad \textbf{13.15}$$

Three potential sources of omitted variable bias disappear altogether from the regression (parents' income, age, and number of siblings), and another grows small (IQ). Notice that parents' income and IQ are particularly worrisome potential sources of bias in earnings equations. Taking differences of twins' wages effectively eliminates these, and perhaps other, unnoted, sources of omitted variables bias. OLS estimates of the differences equation will therefore be free of some biases that might plague ordinary wage equations. One important benefit of examining differences between twins is that by comparing regressions based on the twins' individual wages with regressions based on the differences between twins' wages, we can investigate whether standard wage regressions suffer serious omitted variable bias.

## The Extent of Omitted Variables Bias in Wage Equations

To measure the extent of omitted variable bias in wage equations, we compare estimates of the returns to education based on the differences in twins' wages with estimates of the return to education based just on the individual wages for every twin. If the estimated rate of return differs sharply between the two approaches, it could be that standard OLS wage equation estimates for non-twins are seriously biased by omitted variables bias.

Table 13.1 reports estimates of the return to education based on OLS applied to the difference in twins' wages and educations, using Ashenfelter and Rouse's twins data.

The dependent variable, *dlwage*, is the difference in log wage between the twins, with each twin reporting his or her own hourly wage. (Problem 1 in this chapter defines all of the variable names for twindiff.***.) The independent variable, *deduc*, is the difference in reported years of education, with each twin reporting his or her own education. The differences in education are small, with a mean slightly different from zero and a standard deviation of about 1.5 years. The estimated return to education in Table 13.1 is 0.061.

Table 13. 2 reports a log wage regression using all the individual twins as observations. The data are in the file bothtwins.*** on this book's companion Web site (**www.aw-bc.com/murray**). Problem 2 in this chapter describes all the variables in that file. The estimated return to education of 0.061 based on the differences in twins' wages and reported in Table 13.1 contrasts sharply with the estimate, 0.11, reported in Table 13.2. If the results in Tables 13.1 and 13.2 are reliable, they are strong evidence that usual wage equation estimates, like those in

**TABLE 13.1** The Return to Education for Twins (OLS): Differences in Log Wages and Years of School

Dependent Variable: DLWAGE
Method: Least Squares
Sample: 1 340
Included observations: 340

| Variable | Coefficient | Std. Error | t-Statistic | Prob. |
|---|---|---|---|---|
| DEDUC | 0.061044 | 0.018712 | 3.262354 | 0.0012 |
| C | −0.029562 | 0.027530 | −1.073822 | 0.2837 |
| R-squared | 0.030527 | Mean dependent var | | −0.032494 |
| Adjusted R-squared | 0.027659 | S.D. dependent var | | 0.514514 |
| S.E. of regression | 0.507348 | Akaike info criterion | | 1.486627 |
| Sum squared resid | 87.00197 | Schwarz criterion | | 1.509150 |
| Log likelihood | −250.7266 | F-statistic | | 10.64296 |
| Durbin–Watson stat | 2.269220 | Prob(F-statistic) | | 0.001218 |

Table 13.2, suffer from omitted variable bias. (Recall that the regression in Table 13.1 is freed from some potential omitted variable biases that could plague the regression in Table 13.2.)

However, before we can confidently conclude that omitted variables bias is a serious problem in ordinary wage equations, we need to rule out the alternative explanation for the differences between Tables 13.1 and 13.2—that the different estimates might stem not from omitted variable bias, but from measurement error bias caused by mistaken self-reports of education levels. Instrumental variables estimation can shield the regression results from such measurement error biases.

Ashenfelter and Rouse gathered their twins data very cleverly. Because the self-reports of education are at risk of appreciable measurement error, Ashenfelter and Rouse collected an excellent instrumental variable for individuals' educations. The education variables in Tables 13.1 and 13.2 are based on individuals' self-reports of their education. But each twin also reported their twin's education level. These sibling reports of an individual's education are a very plausible instrument for the individual education variable of Equations 13.13 and 13.14. The difference between these sibling reports for a given pair of twins is a plausible instrument for the difference in education variable of Equation 13.15. The sibling reports are likely to be correlated with the individuals' actual education levels—siblings should know quite a lot about one another—and there is no particular

**TABLE 13.2** The Return to Education for Twins (OLS): One Twin's Log Wage, Education, and so on

Dependent Variable: LWAGE
Method: Least Squares
Sample: 1 680
Included observations: 680

| Variable | Coefficient | Std. Error | t-Statistic | Prob. |
|---|---|---|---|---|
| C | −1.094912 | 0.261239 | −4.191227 | 0.0000 |
| AGE | 0.103942 | 0.010499 | 9.900300 | 0.0000 |
| AGE2 | −0.001063 | 0.000126 | −8.432745 | 0.0000 |
| EDUC | 0.109992 | 0.009558 | 11.50808 | 0.0000 |
| FEMALE | −0.317994 | 0.040031 | −7.943619 | 0.0000 |
| WHITE | −0.100095 | 0.072211 | −1.386160 | 0.1662 |

| | | | | |
|---|---|---|---|---|
| R-squared | 0.338756 | Mean dependent var | | 2.440960 |
| Adjusted R-squared | 0.333850 | S.D. dependent var | | 0.620855 |
| S.E. of regression | 0.506729 | Akaike info criterion | | 1.487104 |
| Sum squared resid | 173.0660 | Schwarz criterion | | 1.527005 |
| Log likelihood | −499.6154 | F-statistic | | 69.05803 |
| Durbin–Watson stat | 1.559457 | Prob(F-statistic) | | 0.000000 |

reason to think that the mistakes made by individuals in reporting their years of education would be correlated with the mistakes made in their sibling's report.

Tables 13.3 and 13.4 estimate the same wage equations as Tables 13.1 and 13.2, this time using an IV estimator, instead of OLS, to guard against measurement error biases. The instrument for self-reported education is siblings' reports of the individuals' education; the instrument for the difference in self-reported education is the difference in siblings' reports for one another. The IV estimated rate of return to education in Table 13.4 (0.116) differs little from the corresponding OLS estimate in Table 13.2 (0.110)—measurement error bias seems inconsequential in this regression. But the IV estimate of that same return in Table 13.3 (0.107) is markedly higher than the corresponding estimate in Table 13.1 (0.061)—measurement error bias seems considerable in this regression.

From an economic standpoint, the important result is that the IV estimate of the return to education based on the differenced data is almost the same as the OLS and IV estimates based on the individual's logged wages. Wiping out some potential omitted variable biases has little effect. Omitted variables common to

**TABLE 13.3** The Return to Education for Twins (IV): Differences in Log Wages and Years of School

Dependent Variable: DLWAGE
Method: Two-Stage Least Squares
Sample: 1 340
Included observations: 340
Instrument list: DEDUCT C

| Variable | Coefficient | Std. Error | t-Statistic | Prob. |
|---|---|---|---|---|
| DEDUC | 0.107010 | 0.029562 | 3.619892 | 0.0003 |
| C | −0.027354 | 0.027796 | −0.984097 | 0.3258 |
| R-squared | 0.013218 | Mean dependent var | | −0.032494 |
| Adjusted R-squared | 0.010299 | S.D. dependent var | | 0.514514 |
| S.E. of regression | 0.511857 | Sum squared resid | | 88.55525 |
| F-statistic | 13.10362 | Durbin-Watson statistic | | 2.254436 |
| Prob(F-statistic) | 0.000340 | | | |

the twins do not appear to have biased OLS in the standard wage equations. This is comforting news for economists who have long relied on standard wage equations.

The formula for the bias caused by mismeasured explanators demonstrates why IV matters for the regressions in Table 13.1 and 13.3, but not for the regressions in Table 13.2 and 13.4. Equation 13.5 reports that the inconsistency created by measurement error in a bivariate model is

$$\frac{-\beta \sigma_\nu^2}{[Q + \sigma_\nu^2]},$$

where $Q$ is the variance of the underlying true (and unobserved) explanator values and $\sigma_\nu^2$ is the variance in the measurement errors. *When the variance of the underlying explanator is much greater than that of the measurement errors, measurement error bias is inconsequential. When the variance of the underlying explanator is small relative to the measurement errors, measurement error bias is large.* Because twins' education varies more across twins than does the difference in twins' educations ($Q$ is larger for the raw twins data than for the differenced data), measurement error is a more serious problem in the differenced equation.

**TABLE 13.4** The Return to Education for Twins (IV): Each Twin's Log Wage, Education, and so on

Dependent Variable: LWAGE
Method: Two-Stage Least Squares
Sample: 1 680
Included observations: 680
Instrument list: EDUCT_T C AGE AGE2 FEMALE WHITE

| Variable | Coefficient | Std. Error | t-Statistic | Prob. |
|---|---|---|---|---|
| C | −1.187928 | 0.268570 | −4.423169 | 0.0000 |
| AGE | 0.104032 | 0.010502 | 9.905765 | 0.0000 |
| AGE2 | −0.001062 | 0.000126 | −8.421153 | 0.0000 |
| EDUC | 0.116017 | 0.010370 | 11.18817 | 0.0000 |
| FEMALE | −0.315643 | 0.040074 | −7.876545 | 0.0000 |
| WHITE | −0.098029 | 0.072245 | −1.356905 | 0.1753 |
| R-squared | 0.338366 | Mean dependent var | | 2.440960 |
| Adjusted R-squared | 0.333457 | S.D. dependent var | | 0.620855 |
| S.E. of regression | 0.506878 | Sum squared resid | | 173.1680 |
| F-statistic | 67.58081 | Durbin–Watson stat | | 1.563301 |
| Prob(F-statistic) | 0.000000 | | | |

## 13.5  Instrumental Variables and Two-Stage Least Squares

HOW DO WE CREATE AN ESTIMATOR?

Although economists are sometimes hard pressed to find even one valid instrument for each troublesome variable in a model, frequently the problem is an overabundance of candidate instruments. If several variables satisfy the requirements for valid instruments, how are we to choose which candidate instrument to use in our IV estimator? This section outlines a strategy for applying IV estimation when we have extra candidate instruments. It then introduces a computational procedure that econometricians frequently use to implement IV estimation.

### Combining Multiple Candidate Instruments

One guiding principle for choosing among candidate instruments stems from our early insight that we weight observations with larger X-values (or larger x-values if there is an intercept) because such observations are less misleading about the true slope of the line. This insight makes it natural to argue that we'd like an instrument that is most correlated with the troublesome explanator. Do we, then, choose the candidate instrument that has the highest correlation with the troublesome variable? No. We can, in fact, do better still. There is probably a linear combination of the candidate instruments that is even more highly correlated with the troublesome explanator than is any one candidate alone. Regressing the troublesome explanator on the candidate instruments using OLS yields the highest possible correlation between the troublesome variable and any linear combination of candidate instruments.

We would like to use the instrument that has the highest correlation with the troublesome explanator *in the population*. Unfortunately, the best we are likely to do is to find the instrument with the highest correlation *in the sample*. In practice, to form one instrument from $m$ candidates, we find the linear combination of $m$ candidate instruments, $Z_1, Z_2, \ldots, Z_m$, that is most highly correlated with the troublesome explanator in our sample. To find that linear combination, we use OLS to regress the troublesome explanator against the $Z$'s. OLS maximizes $R^2$, providing the maximum correlation in this sample between the troublesome explanator and a linear combination of the $Z$'s. The fitted values from this auxiliary regression is our instrument for the troublesome variable. If $Z_1, Z_2, \ldots, Z_m$ are uncorrelated with the disturbances—as they must be, to be candidate instruments—any linear combination of $Z_1, Z_2, \ldots, Z_m$, will also be uncorrelated with the disturbances. Our instrument, therefore, satisfies both requirements for a valid instrument.

This strategy for constructing one instrument from a number of candidates has two steps:

1. Divide the $X$'s into two sets, $s$ troublesome $X$'s $(X_1, \ldots, X_s)$ and $(k + 1 - s)$ nontroublesome $X$'s $(X_0, X_{s+1}, \ldots, X_k)$. Regress *each* troublesome $X$ $(X_1, \ldots, X_s)$ on all the additional candidate instruments $(Z_1, \ldots, Z_g)$, *and* all the nontroublesome $X$'s $(X_0, X_{s+1}, \ldots, X_k)$. That is, estimate by OLS the auxiliary equations

$$X_{ji} = \alpha_1 Z_{1i} + \cdots + \alpha_g Z_{gi} + \gamma_0 + \gamma_1 X_{(s+1)i} + \cdots + \gamma_{k-s} X_{ki} + \eta_i.$$

   for each $j = 1, \ldots, s$. (If there is no intercept term, the number of nontroublesome variables would be $(k + 1 - s)$.)

2. Use the fitted values from the auxiliary regressions in step 1 as the instrumental variables for the troublesome variables and perform IV estimation.

In the case of a straight line with an unknown slope, the two-step IV estimator is

$$\frac{\sum \hat{x}_i y_i}{\sum \hat{x}_i x_i}.$$

13.16

In computing Equation 13.16, $\hat{X}_i$ is the fitted value of $X$ from the first-step auxiliary regression, and $\hat{x}_i$ is the deviation of that fitted value from its own mean. In the first step, $X$ is regressed against $Z$ and an intercept term. Notice that if $X$ were regressed against itself in the first stage, the fit would be perfect, so $\hat{x}$ would equal $x_i$, and the IV estimator would be the same as OLS.

Including the nontroublesome $X$'s (if any) as explanators in the auxiliary regressions is not essential to this procedure. Because the nontroublesome $X$'s are uncorrelated with the disturbances, including any nontroublesome $X$'s in the auxiliary regressions does not cause the fitted values to violate step 2. If a particular nontroublesome explanator doesn't satisfy step 1, it will tend to get a zero coefficient in the auxiliary regression, so all that is lost by including it among the candidate instruments is efficiency. Including the nontroublesome $X$'s in the auxiliary regressions *is* essential in the next estimation procedure we study, which, we will learn, is the procedure almost universally used to conduct IV estimation.

## Two-Stage Least Squares

In practice, econometricians do not usually calculate the instrumental variable estimator for simultaneous equations models in the way just described. They use an alternative computational procedure that happens to yield the same answer—**two-stage least squares (2SLS)**. *The first stage of 2SLS coincides with the first step of IV estimation: Regress each troublesome variable individually against all the predetermined variables and compute the fitted values from these auxiliary regressions.* The second stage of 2SLS differs from the second step of IV estimation. *In the second stage of 2SLS, estimate the equation of interest by Ordinary Least Squares, but with the fitted values of troublesome variables replacing the troublesome variables themselves.* That is, to perform 2SLS estimation,

1. Divide the $X$'s into two sets, $s$ troublesome $X$'s $(X_1, \ldots, X_s)$ and $(k + 1 - s)$ nontroublesome $X$'s $(X_0, X_{s+1}, \ldots, X_k)$. Regress *each* troublesome $X$ $(X_1, \ldots, X_s)$ on all the additional candidate instruments $(Z_1, \ldots, Z_g)$ *and* all the nontroublesome $X$'s $(X_0, X_{s+1}, \ldots, X_k)$. That is, estimate by OLS the auxiliary equation

$$X_{ji} = \alpha_1 Z_{1i} + \cdots + \alpha_g Z_{gi} + \gamma_0 + \gamma_1 X_{(s+1)i} + \cdots + \gamma_{k-s} X_{ki} + \eta_i. \quad \textbf{13.17}$$

for each $j = 1, \ldots, s$. (If there is no intercept term, the number of nontroublesome variables would be $(k + 1 - s)$.)

2. Replace the troublesome variables with their fitted values, $\hat{X}_{ji}$, from the auxiliary regressions in (1) and perform OLS. That is, perform OLS on the equation

$$Y_i = \beta_0 + \beta_1 \hat{X}_{1i} + \cdots + \beta_s \hat{X}_{si} + \beta_{s+1} X_{(s+1)i} + \cdots + \beta_k X_{ki} + \mu_i. \quad \textbf{13.18}$$

2SLS yields exactly the same estimates as the two-step IV estimator; therefore, 2SLS is a consistent estimation procedure. *However, if we were to omit the non-troublesome X's from the auxiliary regressions, the IV and 2SLS procedures would differ in their results and 2SLS would not be a consistent estimator, even though the IV estimator would be consistent.* Appendix 13.B proves the equivalence of the two-step IV procedure and 2SLS. Econometricians originally used 2SLS to perform IV estimation because 2SLS could be performed with the already existing OLS software; they continue to rely on it out of habit.

In the case of a straight line with unknown slope, the 2SLS estimator is

$$\frac{\sum \hat{x}_i y_i}{\sum \hat{x}_i^2},$$                                           13.19

where $\hat{X}_i$ is the fitted value of $X$ from the first-stage auxiliary regression, and $\hat{x}_i$ is the deviation of that fitted value from its own mean.

## Testing Hypotheses Using 2SLS

The estimated standard errors that an econometric software package would report if it were only given the regression in Equation 13.18 to perform by OLS would not be the correct standard errors for the 2SLS estimator. The OLS standard error estimates would not take into account the fact that some of the explanators are fitted values from a previous regression. An OLS package used to estimate Equation 13.18 would assume the asymptotic variance of the estimator is

$$\frac{\sigma^2}{\text{plim}\left(\frac{1}{n}\sum \hat{x}_i^2\right)},$$                                           13.20

but we know from Equation 13.10 that the variance of the IV estimator is

$$\frac{1}{n}\sigma^2 \frac{\text{plim}\left(\frac{1}{n}\sum \hat{x}_i^2\right)}{\text{plim}\left(\frac{1}{n}\sum \hat{x}_i x_i\right)^2},$$                                           13.21

which does not generally equal the expression in Equation 13.20. When the user indicates 2SLS as the estimation procedure, econometric software packages report the appropriate estimated standard errors, based on Equation 13.21 or its multiple regression generalization. These packages do, however, use the OLS estimator of Equation 13.19, or its multiple regression generalization, to compute IV coefficient estimates. In fact, the IV estimates reported in Tables 13.3 and 13.4 were produced using 2SLS.

If the disturbances and explanators are contemporaneously correlated, the test procedures developed in Chapters 7 through 11 are valid asymptotically when the estimator is 2SLS, as long as the other Gauss–Markov Assumptions are met. The appropriate $F$-statistic is slightly altered from the OLS case, however. Recall that Chapter 9 developed the $F$-statistic for a null hypothesis that imposes $r$ constraints:

$$F = \frac{(change\ in\ sum\ of\ squared\ residuals)/r}{(unconstrained\ sum\ of\ squared\ residuals)/(n - k - 1)}.$$

The change in the sum of squared residuals in the numerator of this $F$-statistic captures the deterioration of fit that results from imposing the constraints of the null hypothesis. The sum of squared residuals in the denominator appears as an estimate of the variance of the disturbances. The same intuitive roles lead to slightly altered calculations when the regression is conducted by 2SLS.

The sum of squared residuals in the second stage of 2SLS is smaller when the hypothesized constraints are not imposed than when the constraints are imposed. This deterioration of fit appears in the numerator of the $F$-statistic. These sums of squared residuals rely on the fitted values of the explanators that are used in the second stage of 2SLS—they are the sums of squared residuals that an OLS package would report if the fitted values were inserted as the explanators, $SSR^2_{u2SLS}$ and $SSR^2_{c2SLS}$. How this sum of squared residuals changes when the hypothesized constraints are imposed, $SSR^2_{c2SLS} - SSR^2_{u2SLS}$, is the change in sum of squared residuals that goes in the $F$-statistic.

The sum of squared residuals used to estimate the disturbances in the denominator is the sum of squared residuals in the unconstrained regression based on the actual explanator values, $SSR^2_u$. These residuals are

$$\tilde{e}^u_i = Y_i - \sum_{j=0}^{k} \tilde{\beta}^u_j X_i,$$

where the $\tilde{\beta}^u_j$ are the unconstrained 2SLS coefficient estimates. The residuals for $SSR^2_{u2SLS}$ differ from those $SSR^2_u$ for in that they use $\hat{X}_i$, instead of $X_i$.

The $F$-statistic for $F$-tests that rely on 2SLS is

$$F = \frac{(SSR^2_{c2SLS} - SSR^2_{u2SLS})/r}{SSR^2_u/(n - k - 1)},$$

where $r$ is the number of constraints imposed by the null hypothesis. The degrees of freedom are, as with OLS-based $F$-tests, $r$ and $(n - k - 1)$.

## Weak Instruments

Often, IV estimation is unavailable to economists because no valid instruments are available, that is, variables correlated with the troublesome variable, but uncorrelated with the disturbances. But it is also possible to find a valid instrument and still not be able to exploit the virtues of IV estimation. *If instruments are too weakly correlated with the troublesome X's, IV estimation will do little to overcome OLS' bias in even quite large samples.* We call such instruments **weak instruments**.[8] Because OLS has a smaller variance than the IV estimator, weak instruments yield IV estimators that can have a larger mean square error than OLS. Weak instruments also distort the size of standard hypothesis tests that are based on the asymptotically normal distribution of the IV estimator. In even quite large samples, the exact distribution of the IV estimator can differ greatly from the normal when the instruments are weak. Consequently, we should not use IV estimation when instruments are weak. But how can we detect weak instruments?

Econometricians James Stock and Motohiro Yogo of Harvard University offer statistics and critical values for detecting weak instruments.[9] In the case of a single troublesome regressor (that is, for $s = k = 1$ in Equation 13.17), the statistic is an $F$-statistic. The null hypothesis tested is that all the candidate instruments that do not themselves appear in the equation of interest have coefficients equal to zero in the first-stage auxiliary regression of 2SLS. The choice of critical values depends on our purpose. Table 13.5, Column A, contains the critical values if the

**TABLE 13.5** Critical Values for Testing the Null Hypothesis that Instruments are Weak

| Number of Instruments | A<br>Reduce Bias<br>90% | B<br>Hold Size Below 15%<br>for Nominal 5% |
|---|---|---|
| 1 | ——— | 8.96 |
| 2 | ——— | 11.59 |
| 3 | 9.08 | 12.83 |
| 5 | 10.83 | 15.09 |
| 10 | 11.49 | 20.88 |
| 15 | 11.51 | 26.80 |

# An Econometric Top 40—A Pop Tune

## Are Public Housing Projects Bad for Kids?

Public housing projects, subsidized by the Federal Government since 1937, have long had a bad reputation. But do public housing projects compromise the well-being of their residents and their children? Economists Janet Currie of UCLA and Aaron Yelowitz of the University of Kentucky addressed this question econometrically in a paper published in 2000.[10] They asked whether public housing tenants were more crowded than if they had been residents of private dwellings and whether living in a project damages children's life chances.

Currie and Yelowitz used crowding, density, and being held back in school as their indicators of poor outcomes for families and their children. They performed three OLS regressions in which their three outcome variables were the dependent variable, and the explanators were a dummy variable indicating the household lives in a public housing project (named *PROJECT*) and a series of household traits: the number of boys in the family, the number of children in the family, and the household head's age, gender, race, education, and marital status (named $X_2, \ldots, X_8$). Currie and Yelowitz drew these data from the Survey of Income and Program Participation (SIPP), described in a Greatest Hit in Chapter 12 (see p. 521).

In these regressions,

$$outcome = \beta_0 + \beta_1 PROJECT_1$$
$$+ \sum_{j=2}^{8} \beta_j X_{ji} + \varepsilon_i,$$

$\hat{\beta}_1$ was positive and statistically significant in each, indicating that project residents live in more crowded and denser situations than otherwise similar people who do not live in the projects and that children living in projects are more likely to be left behind one or more grades than are children from otherwise similar households who do not live in the projects. At first look, then, public housing projects inflict on resident households and their children the poor outcomes that journalists lead us to expect. But is public housing really bad for kids—or are the OLS results misleading?

Currie and Yelowitz worried that the OLS estimates suffered from serious omitted variable bias. They wrote, "Whether or not a family lives in a project reflects choices made by both households and program administrators. Many unobserved factors, such as whether the family can double up with family or friends or has recently been homeless, are likely to affect both participation and outcomes."[11] Where would public housing residents be living if they weren't in public housing? Perhaps in even worse circumstances.

Currie and Yelowitz argued for IV estimation of the outcome equations to lay to rest any concerns about omitted variable bias. The instrument they posed stems from a government rule that uses the gender mix of children in a household to determine what size apartment a family should receive.

A public housing rule precludes boys and girls from having to share a room. A consequence of the rule is that families with one boy and one girl receive a three bedroom apartment, whereas families with two children of the same sex receive a two-bedroom apartment. Public housing rents depend only on family income, so families receiving a three-bedroom apartment also receive a bigger subsidy. Currie and Yelowitz found that two-children families entitled to a larger apartment because of their childrens' sexes were 24% more likely to enter public housing than were similar two-child families entitled to a smaller apartment.

The public housing rule most impacts two-children households, so Currie and Yelowitz limited their attention to families with two children when they turned to IV estimation. The correlation between PROGRAM and the sex mix of the family's children was by far strongest among two-children households, making IV estimation more efficient among that group. The IV results for all families were similar to those for families with just two children, but the standard errors were larger.

Currie and Yelowitz emphasized a potential error that researchers risk when choosing instruments. We must avoid choosing as candidate instruments variables that themselves belong in the model. A relevant variable omitted from the model cannot be uncorrelated with the disturbances, so relevant omitted variables cannot be valid instruments. Currie and Yelowitz went to special lengths to dispel concerns that their instrument was itself an omitted relevant variable and therefore correlated with the disturbance term.

The instrumental variable Currie and Yelowitz actually used, ESTPROBPROJ, was the estimated probability that a household participates in public housing, based on the nontroublesome explanators in the outcome equation and a dummy variable, BOYANDGIRL. BOYANDGIRL was equal to one if the family had one boy and one girl and was equal to zero otherwise. ESTPROBPROJ was the fitted value from the auxiliary regression

$$PROJECT_i = \alpha_0 + \alpha_1 BOYANDGIRL_i + \sum \alpha_j X_{ji} + \eta_i.$$

Initially, Currie and Yelowitz estimated the PROJECT auxiliary equation using the SIPP data, intending to conduct IV estimation by the two-stage least squares (2SLS) procedure described in this chapter. Currie and Yelowitz found that the SIPP sample was too small to support this use of instrumental variables, however. The fitted values from the PROJECT auxiliary equation based on the SIPP data proved to be what this chapter calls a "weak instrument." The 2SLS procedure was unsuited to analyzing the SIPP data. To cope with this problem, Currie and Yelowitz turned to another strategy to construct their instrument.

Unlike SIPP, the Current Population Survey (CPS), also described in Chapter 12 (see p. 521), contains no information on the outcome variables of interest to Currie and Yelowitz, so, the CPS is not suited to asking whether public housing is bad for children. The very large CPS data set does contain information on whether households are in public housing, though, and it also contains information on the nontroublesome explanators in Currie and Yelowitz's model, as well as on the gender composition of a family's children. Consequently, the CPS data provided precise estimates of the auxiliary regression that has PROJECT as its dependent variable.

Currie and Yelowitz used estimated coefficients from the CPS-based PROJECT auxiliary regression to form new estimates of the probability that a family was in public housing, ESTPROBPROJ. BOYANDGIRL was highly significant in this CPS-based regression; fitted values from this new PROJECT regression were not weak instruments. The authors then used the new ESTPROBPROJ as their instrumental variable with which to re-estimate the outcome equations. The strategy of estimating the PROJECT equation with one sample and performing instrumental variables with another sample is called "two-sample instrumental variables (2SIV)." 2SIV was first proposed by economists Joshua Angrist of MIT and Alan Krueger of Princeton University.[12]

What did Currie and Yelowitz find when they estimated the outcome equations by instrumental variables? Households in public housing were less likely to live in crowded or dense circumstances and their children were 11 percentage points less likely to be held back a grade than were children from otherwise similar households that do not live in public housing. The 11% figure was only significant at the 10% level, however, so its standard error was relatively large.

These Currie–Yelowitz findings contrast sharply with the public perception of public housing. How can they be right? There are two likely explanations. First, public housing is more diverse than the common image suggests. Currie and Yelowitz pointed out that there are 3,300 public housing agencies spread across the United States, with a total of about 13,200 projects. Of these agencies, 2,300 operate fewer than 300 units. Public housing is not as dense, on average, as people usually think. Second, many households who come to public housing have housing alternatives that are quite bleak. Public housing may seem unattractive, but it is frequently an improvement for its tenants.

 **Final Notes**

Currie and Yelowitz's work highlights how econometric analysis can expose misinformation that might otherwise lead policy makers to bad decisions. It underscores that economists need to be alert to circumstances that bias the OLS estimator. If Currie and Yelowitz had not turned to IV estimation, they would have been misled by OLS.

Currie and Yelowitz's findings also highlight two technical lessons about IV estimation. First, we need instruments that are not weak if we are to benefit from IV estimation. Careful attention to available information can sometimes provide such instruments even when a first inspection indicates that only weak instruments are available. Second, a model is not identified unless we have at least one candidate that does not itself belong in the model of interest. To trust our IV estimates, we must trust that we have such a variable. Currie and Yelowitz markedly improved the credibility of their IV estimates by using evidence from the literature and their own samples to support their claim that the gender composition of the household was not an omitted relevant explanator.

■

goal is to reduce the bias obtained with OLS by at least 90%.[13] Column B contains the appropriate critical values if the goal is to keep the true significance level of hypothesis tests about the troublesome variable's coefficient in the second stage of 2SLS at less than 15% when the nominal level of the test is 5%. Although the critical value depends in both cases on the number of candidate instruments in the first-stage regression, notice that limiting size distortion places the more stringent requirement on the observed strength of the instruments.

In the analysis of wage differences between twins, the $F$-statistic from regressing the difference between twins' reports of their own education on the difference between their reports of one another's education and an intercept is 232.8. The difference between twins' reports of one another's educations is not a weak instrument.

Earlier, we learned that to overcome the bias stemming from a lagged dependent variable coupled with serially correlated disturbances, economists sometimes use the lagged values of other explanators to conduct IV estimation. We also learned that if the other lagged explanator values are highly correlated with their current values, the IV estimator has a large variance. Such a high degree of correlation between lagged and current explanator values is also likely to lead to weak instruments—even in moderately large samples, IV estimates will be biased about as much as OLS.[14]

## 13.6    Testing Whether $E(X_i\varepsilon_i)$ Equals Zero

HOW DO WE TEST HYPOTHESES?

When disturbances and explanators are contemporaneously uncorrelated, least squares estimation provides a sound basis for hypotheses tests. How are we to determine whether or not $E(X_i\varepsilon_i) = 0$? This section presents a procedure that tests the null hypothesis that there are no troublesome explanators in an equation.

### A Test for Troublesome Explanators

OLS is often markedly more efficient than IV estimation if there is no measurement error in the explanators, no omitted variables, and no endogenous explanators. In such cases, IV estimation needlessly sacrifices a great deal of efficiency. When can we exploit OLS and its better efficiency, and when should we use IV estimation despite its higher variance? To answer this question, econometrician De-Min Wu of the University of Kansas has proposed a test for the null hypothesis that no explanators are contemporaneously correlated with the disturbances.[15] Because Wu's test belongs to a more general class of tests later proposed by Jerry Hausman of MIT, this test is called the **Hausman–Wu specification test**.[16]

We can see Wu's strategy by considering a model with a single, potentially troublesome explanator. Assume that

$$Y_i = \beta_0 + \beta_1 X_i + \varepsilon_i. \qquad \textbf{13.22}$$

OLS is an inconsistent estimator of the parameters of Equation 13.22 if the disturbances are contemporaneously correlated with the disturbances. If $X$ is, in fact, a troublesome variable, OLS is inconsistent. To test hypotheses about Equation 13.22, we need to be able to consistently estimate it—we need at least one valid instrument for $X$. With such an instrument, we can consistently estimate Equation 13.22 by 2SLS. Wu assumes we have at least one such instrument.

Wu's strategy augments Equation 13.22 by adding to it the residuals from the first stage of 2SLS, $\nu$, as an explanator:

$$Y_i = \beta_0 + \beta_1 X_i + \tau_1 \nu_i + \varepsilon_i, \qquad \textbf{13.23}$$

where $\nu_i = (X_i - \hat{X}_i)$ and the $\hat{X}_i$ are the fitted values that are used as explanators in the second stage of 2SLS. Because $\nu$ does not appear in the true model, given by Equation 13.21, our maintained hypothesis assumes that $\tau_1 = 0$.

If neither the $X_i$ nor the $\nu_i$ are correlated with the $\varepsilon_i$, OLS consistently estimates both Equation 13.21 and Equation 13.22, and

$$\text{plim}(\hat{\tau}_1) = 0,$$

because the OLS estimator of $\tau_1$ is consistent. However, if $X_i$ is contemporaneously correlated with $\varepsilon_i$, then $\nu_i$ is also contemporaneously correlated with $\varepsilon_i$ and

$$\text{plim}(\hat{\tau}_1) \neq 0.$$

These two claims about $\text{plim}(\hat{\tau}_1)$ provide the foundation for Wu's test. The proof of the latter claim, that $\text{plim}(\hat{\tau}_1) \neq 0$, follows.

Wu's procedure constructs the residuals from the first stage of 2SLS, that is, the $\nu_i$, are taken from

$$X_i = \hat{X}_i + \nu_i.$$

The $\hat{X}_i$ are defined as linear combinations of nontroublesome variables, so whether $X_i$ is correlated with $\varepsilon_i$, or not, the $\hat{X}_i$ are uncorrelated with the disturbances. Consequently, for $X_i$ to be correlated with $\varepsilon_i$, $\nu_i$ must be correlated with $\varepsilon_i$. It follows that when $X$ is contemporaneously correlated with the disturbances, so is $\nu$, and OLS applied to Equation 13.23 is an inconsistent estimator of $\tau_1$. In such cases, $\text{plim}(\hat{\tau}_1) \neq 0$, as claimed.

Finding that $\text{plim}(\hat{\tau}_1) \neq 0$ is at odds with the null hypothesis that the explanator is not a troublesome variable. Wu's strategy estimates Equation 13.23 by OLS and rejects the null hypothesis that $X$ and $\varepsilon_i$ are contemporaneously uncorrelated if a $t$-test or $F$-test rejects the null that $\tau_1 = 0$.

The Hausman–Wu test generalizes to a DGP in which there are $s$ potentially troublesome variables, $X_1, \ldots, X_s$, and $(k + 1 - s)$ surely untroublesome explanators, $X_0, X_{s+1}, X_{s+2}, \ldots, X_k$, as well as $(r > k)$ valid instruments for the potentially troublesome variables. The dependent variable is $Y$ and

$$Y_i = \beta_0 + \sum_{j=1}^{k} \beta_j X_{ji} + \varepsilon_i.$$

The Hausman–Wu specification test has two steps:

1. Use OLS to regress each potentially troublesome explanator, $X_{1i}$ through $X_{si}$, on the candidate instrumental variables, $Z_{1i}$ through $Z_{ri}$, including among the candidate instruments the $(k + 1 - s)$ surely nontroublesome explanators, and compute the residuals, $\nu_{1i}$ through $\nu_{si}$, from these regressions:

$$\nu_{ji} = X_{ji} - (\hat{\alpha}_0 + \hat{\alpha}_{1j} Z_{1i} + \cdots + \hat{\alpha}_{rj} Z_{ri}) = X_{ji} - \hat{X}_{ji} \ (j = 1, \ldots, s).$$

2. Use OLS to regress the model's dependent variable, $Y_i$, on both the $(k + 1)$ potentially troublesome and surely nontroublesome explanators, and the $s$ residuals computed in the first stage, the $\nu_i$:

$$Y_i = \beta_0 + \sum_{j=1}^{k} \beta_j X_{ji} + \sum_{j=1}^{s} \tau_j \nu_{ji} + \varepsilon_i,$$

and conduct at some chosen level of significance an $F$-test of the hypothesis that

$$\tau_1 = \tau_2 = \cdots = \tau_s = 0.$$

The $F$-statistic has $s$ and $(n - k - s - 1)$ degrees of freedom.

## Testing Whether the Difference in Twins' Educations Is Troublesome

For an application of the Hausman–Wu test, let's return to the OLS and 2SLS analyses of twins' wages studied in Tables 13.1 and 13.3. There we found that the OLS and 2SLS estimators of the rate of return to education differed appreciably. Did that difference in estimates arise because the difference in siblings' educations variable suffered from attenuation bias? Yes, it seems so. Table 13.6 reports the Hausman–Wu regression, including as an explanator the residuals from having

**TABLE 13.6  Hausman–Wu Test Of $E(X_i \varepsilon_i)$ Equaling Zero**

Dependent Variable: DLWAGE
Method: Least Squares
Sample: 1 340
Included observations: 340

| Variable | Coefficient | Std. Error | t-Statistic | Prob. |
|----------|-------------|------------|-------------|-------|
| C | −0.027354 | 0.027422 | −0.997524 | 0.3192 |
| DEDUC | 0.107010 | 0.029164 | 3.669282 | 0.0003 |
| REZ | −0.077620 | 0.037898 | −2.048137 | 0.0413 |
| R-squared | 0.042446 | Mean dependent var | | −0.032494 |
| Adjusted R-squared | 0.036763 | S.D. dependent var | | 0.514514 |
| S.E. of regression | 0.504967 | Akaike info criterion | | 1.480138 |
| Sum squared resid | 85.93232 | Schwarz criterion | | 1.513923 |
| Log likelihood | −248.6235 | F-statistic | | 7.469211 |
| Durbin–Watson stat | 2.261881 | Prob(F-statistic) | | 0.000670 |

regressed *deduc* on deduct and a constant term. (The IV estimator in Table 13.3 used *deduct* and an intercept term to construct its instrument.) Because the alternative hypothesis is that there is measurement error bias, in which case the coefficient on the residual is negative, the appropriate test is a one-tailed test. The *t*-statistic on the residual variable, *rez*, is 2.05, which is larger than 1.64, the .05 significance level one-sided critical value for a *t*-test with hundreds of degrees of freedom. We therefore reject the null hypothesis of no measurement error.

The Hausman–Wu procedure requires valid instruments that are not weak. In the twins example, we are confident that our instrument is both valid and strong. We can have confidence in the Hausman–Wu test result that the OLS estimates of the equation explaining the difference between twins' wages are inconsistent.

### An Organizational Structure for the Study of Econometrics

**1. What Is the DGP?**

Stochastic regressors

Disturbances and $X$'s contemporaneously correlated

Omitted variables

Mismeasured explanators

Lagged dependent variables

Random coefficients

**2. What Makes a Good Estimator?**

Consistency

**3. How Do We Create an Estimator?**

Instrumental variables (IV)

Two-stage least squares (it's IV)

**4. What Are an Estimator's Properties?**

OLS is BLUE if disturbances independent of all explanators.

OLS is consistent if disturbances and $X$'s contemporaneously uncorrelated.

Lagged dependent variables make OLS biased.

Jointly determined variables make OLS biased and inconsistent (simultaneity bias).

Lagged dependent variable and serial correlation make OLS inconsistent.

Mismeasured $X$'s make OLS biased and inconsistent.

**5. How Do We Test Hypotheses?**

Hausman–Wu test that E($X_i\varepsilon_i$) = 0

# Summary

OLS and its GLS and FGLS kin are not always consistent estimators. When they are not, hypothesis tests based on them are not valid. Least squares estimators lose their consistency when $E(X_i\varepsilon_i) \neq 0$, that is, when the disturbances and explanators are contemporaneously correlated. We call explanators that are contemporaneously correlated with the disturbances "troublesome."

This chapter reviewed four circumstances in which disturbances and explanators are contemporaneously correlated: omitted variables, mismeasured explanators, jointly determined variables, and lagged dependent variables coupled with serially correlated disturbances. The chapter introduced an alternative to OLS, the instrumental variables (IV) estimator, which provides consistent estimates when the explanators are contemporaneously correlated with the disturbances.

Valid instrumental variables are correlated with the troublesome explanators but uncorrelated with the disturbances. The chapter described a computational procedure for obtaining IV estimates, called two-stage least squares (2SLS). IV estimation is less efficient than OLS, or its GLS and FGLS kin, when the disturbances are contemporaneously uncorrelated with the explanators. If the disturbances and explanators are contemporaneously correlated, the test procedures developed in Chapters 7 through 11 are generally valid asymptotically when based on IV estimates. The chapter also added a new test procedure, the Hausman–Wu test that no explanators are troublesome.

The chapter noted that instrumental variables may be weak, in which case they reduce the bias found in OLS by little and lead to tests biased in size in even quite large samples. Finally, the chapter introduced random coefficients models in which the slope coefficients in a model vary across observations. In such models, IV estimates may tell us about the average effect of an explanator on $Y$ for a non-representative subset of the population.

## Concepts for Review

# Questions for Discussion

1. McClellan, McNeil, and Newhouse use the distance of the patient's residence from a hospital able to perform intensive procedures as their instrument for the intensive procedure dummy variable. Ashenfelter and Rouse used the difference between twin's reports of one another's educations as an instrument for the difference between the twins' reports of their own educations. Currie and Yelowitz use a dummy variable indicating the mix of boys and girls in a family as an instrument for participation in public housing. Are you skeptical of the instruments used by McClellan, McNeil, and Newhouse? By Ashenfelter and Rouse? By Currie and Yelowitz? Discuss.

2. Are lagged values of the explanators likely to serve as legitimate instrumental variables in time series data? Offer several examples and discuss.

# Problems for Analysis

> For the data sets that you will need to solve the problems in this section, go to **www.aw-bc.com/murray**.

1. Return to Ashenfelter and Rouse's identical twins data in twindiff.***. The variables in the file are

   *deduc*      Own report of difference in twins' educations (this twin's minus the other's)

   *deduct*     Twin's report first difference in twin's educations (this twin's minus the other's)

   *dlwage*     Difference in logs of twins' wages (this twin's minus the other's)

   *dmarried*   Difference in twins' ever married status (this twin's minus the other's)

   We have two imperfect measures of the difference in education between twins: *deduc* and *deduct*.

   a. In the chapter, we made *deduct* an instrument for *deduc* and compared OLS and IV results for regressions of *dlwage* on *deduc*. However, both *deduc* and *deduct* are measures of the same thing—the difference in the twins' educations. Reverse the roles of the two variables in OLS and IV regression with *dlwage* as the dependent variable. Compare the results to those in the chapter.

   b. Determine whether *deduc* is a weak instrument for *deduct*.

   c. Use the Hausman–Wu test to determine whether *deduct* is measured with error.

2. Return to Ashenfelter and Rouse's identical twins data in bothtwins.***. The variables in the file are

   | | |
   |---|---|
   | *AGE* | Age |
   | *AGE2* | Age squared |
   | *DADED* | Father's education |
   | *EDUC* | This twin's report of own education |
   | *EDUC_T* | Other twin's report of other twin's education |
   | *EDUCT* | This twin's report of other twin's education |

$EDUCT\_T$    Other twin's report of this twin's education
$FEMALE$     Female
$HRWAGE$     Hrwage
$LWAGE$      Lwage
$LWAGE\_T$    Sibling's wage
$MARRIED$    Married
$MOMED$      Mother's education
$SELFEMP$    Self-employed
$WHITE$      White

a. In the chapter, we made $EDUCT\_T$ an instrument for $EDUC$ and compared OLS and IV results for regressions of $LWAGE$ on $EDUC$, $AGE$, $AGE$ $SQUARED$, $FEMALE$, and $WHITE$. However, both $EDUC$ and $EDUCT\_T$ are measures of the same thing, the education of the twin in this observation. Reverse the roles of $EDUC$ and $EDUCT\_T$ in the OLS and IV regressions of the chapter. Compare the results to those in the chapter.

b. Is $EDUC$ a weak instrument for $EDUCT\_T$?

3. In Ashenfelter and Rouse's study of wages using twins, a sibling's reports of the other individuals' education is used as an instrument to overcome measurement error in the self-reported education variable. If the actual problem is not measurement error in self-reported education, but omitted variables, such as parents' income and mother's education, is the siblings' report of individuals' education a valid instrument? Briefly explain why or why not.

4. For much of the past half-century, there has been a flow of central city residents to the suburbs. One oft cited cause of this exodus is central city crime rates. Julie Cullen and Stephen Levitt investigated empirically the connection between a city's population changes and its crime rate. To capture the adjustments made by city residents when crime rates change, Cullen and Levitt focused on changes in population and changes in crime rates. The file flight2.*** contains a subset of Cullen and Levitt's data. (Their full set of annual data are in the file flight1.***, which is too large for the student version of Eviews to read.) The sample has annual data from 1985 to 1993 for 127 cities. The model for this problem specifies that

*(annual change in the natural log of city's population)*$_i$ =

$\beta_0 + \beta_1$*(annual change in city's crime rate)*$_i$

$+ \beta_2$*(annual change in the crime rate in the rest of the urban area)*$_i$

$+ \beta_3$*(annual change in local area unemployment)*$_i + v_i$.

Cullen and Levitt were concerned that there might be feedback effects from changes in population to changes in the crime rate, so they estimated their model with IV methods, as well as OLS. The instruments they chose were the changes in the rates at which the city's state imprisoned felons and released felons from prison in each of the three years preceding the observed change in population and crime rates.

   The choice of the change in logs for the population variable and changes in rates for the crime variable results in a specification in which $-\beta_1$ is the number of city residents who *leave* the city when one additional crime is committed. The one-year change in the natural log of population is

$$\ln(population_t) - \ln(population_{t-1}) = \ln(population_t / population_{t-1})$$

$$= \ln\left(\frac{population_{t-1} + \Delta population_t}{population_{t-1}}\right)$$

$$= \ln\left(1 + \frac{\Delta population_t}{population_{t-1}}\right) \approx \frac{\Delta population_t}{population_{t-1}}.$$

(The approximation holds well when the percent change in population from one year to the next is small.) With the percent change in population on the left-hand side of the regression equation, and "additional crimes per person" as the variable attached to $\beta_1$, the interpretation of $\beta_1$ is "number of additional people per additional crime."

The variables in flight2.*** are

| | |
|---|---|
| *c1_crim* | 1-year change in the city's crime rate |
| *c1_scr* | 1-year change in the rest of SMSA's crime/population |
| *d1_pop* | 1-year change in the log of the city's population |
| *dz1_ccom* | Prior-year change in log of rate at which state sends people to prison |
| *dz2_ccom* | 2-year-prior change in log of rate at which state sends people to prison |
| *dz3_ccom* | 3-year-prior change in log of rate at which state sends people to prison |
| *dz1_rele* | Prior year change in log of rate at which the state releases people from prison |
| *dz2_rele* | 2-year-prior change in log of rate at which the state releases people from prison |
| *dz3_rele* | 3-year-prior change in log of rate at which the state releases people from prison |
| *c1_unem* | 1-year change in the % unemployed |

a. Regress the change in the log of population on the changes in the crime rates of the city and of the surrounding urban area, including the change in the local unemployment rate and an intercept term. Interpret the estimated coefficient on the change in the city's crime rate.

b. There are about twice as many people in a city's surrounding urban area as in the city itself. With this in mind, interpret the estimated coefficient on the crime rate in the surrounding urban area.

c. Re-estimate the relationship in (a) using IV estimation. Use the three lagged values of the change in imprisonment and release rates as the instruments. What do you conclude from the IV estimation?

d. Test whether the instruments in (c) are weak.

e. Use the Hausman–Wu test to determine whether IV estimation was needed.

5. Does a mother's smoking during pregnancy adversely affect her baby's birth weight? John Mullahy addressed this question using IV estimation.[17] The file whitebweight.*** contains a subset of Mullahy's data that includes all of the white mothers in his sample. The variables in the file are as follows:

| | |
|---|---|
| *lnbwt* | Natural log of birth weight |
| *male* | = 1 if the baby is male; = 0 otherwise |
| *parity* | Number of children the woman has borne |

*cigspreg*   Number of cigarettes the mother smoked daily during pregnancy
*famincom*  Family income
*edfather*   Father's education
*edmother*  Mother's education

With so few explanatory variables in hand, Mullahy worried that his estimate of smoking's effect on birth weight might suffer omitted variables bias. To counter this, Mullahy turned to IV estimation. He noted that previous research indicated that birth weight was not related to parents' educations or to family income. Since education and income are correlates of smoking, Mullahy used these variables as instruments. (He also used some other variables not included here, and he did not limit his analysis to white mothers.)

a. Regress the log of birth weight on the baby's sex, the mother's parity, and the number of cigarettes the mother smokes per day. Use both OLS and IV estimation. Use father's and mother's educations and family income as instruments.

b. What is the percentage difference in the estimated effect of a cigarette per day on birth weight between the OLS and IV estimators?

c. Are the instruments in (a) weak?

d. Explain the likely consequence for the IV estimator if Mullahy were wrong about parental education or income not belonging in the model for birthweight.

e. Use the Hausman–Wu test to check Mullahy's concern that the OLS regression in (a) yields biased estimates.

f. Does your intuition support Mullahy's choice of instruments? Briefly explain your reasoning. (Your answer should address what constitutes a valid instrument.)

6. In 1971, only 85 Americans of every 100,000 were in prison. By 1993, the imprisonment rate had risen to 325 per 100,000. Surprisingly, crime rates did not fall during this period, leading some people to wonder if imprisonment had no effect on crime rates. Steven Levitt addressed this question using IV estimation.[18] The file prisons6.\*\*\* contains a 1981–1993 subset of Levitt's data. This file requires EViews 5. or STATA. The variables in that file are as follows:

*pcvcrimr*   Annual percent change in the violent crime rate in a state
*pcpcrimr*   Annual percent change in the property crimes rate in a state
*pcmprsnr*  Annual percent change in the imprisonment rate in a state
*final*      = 1 if within 3 years of an overcrowding judgment against the state
*year*       Year of the observation
*state*      Numerical index indicating the state of the observation

Levitt examined changes in states' crime rates and imprisonment rates. His intuition was that increases in the prison population would decrease crime rates, so it was natural to look at the changes in crime and imprisonment rates. However, Levitt was concerned that in addition to any effect of imprisonment rates on crime, there might be a feedback effect of crime rates on imprisonment rates. He was also concerned that in his relatively simple model, OLS might suffer from omitted variables bias (although his full data set had some explanators not included here). Consequently, Levitt turned to IV estimation.

   The instrument available in prisons6.\*\*\* is a dummy variable that indicates whether a state has been successfully sued recently for prison overcrowding. If a final judgment of overcrowding occurred in year $y$ in a state, then the dummy variable *final* takes on the value 1 in years $y + 1$, $y + 2$, and $y + 3$.

a. Regress the percent change in the violent crime rate on the percent change in the previous year's imprisonment rate and a dummy variable for each year from 1981 to 1993, using both OLS and IV estimation. (In EViews, the command @expand facilitates entering such dummy variables.) What is the difference in the estimated effect of a 1% change in imprisonment rates on expected violent crime rates?

b. Is *final* (lagged one year) a weak instrument for the percentage change in the imprisonment rate (lagged one year)?

c. Repeat (a), but with the percentage change in property crimes as the dependent variable.

d. Does using an instrument for *pcmprsnr* that is not weak ensure that hypothesis tests about *pcmprsnr's* coefficient are powerful? (*Hint:* Examine the regression in (c).)

e. Does your intuition support Levitt's choice of *final* as an instrument? Briefly explain your reasoning. (Your answer should address what constitutes a valid instrument.)

7. This problem examines several estimates of the marginal propensity to consume. It relies on the data set haavelmo1.\*\*\* .

a. Estimate the marginal propensity to consume:
   (i) by OLS, including an intercept term;
   (ii) by OLS, excluding the intercept term; and
   (iii) using $\beta_{g2}$, excluding the intercept term.

b. Use the Hausman–Wu test to assess whether current income suffers measurement error bias if the model contains no intercept term. Use the intercept term as the available valid instrument.

c. What relationship is there between the second step regression in the Hausman–Wu procedure and regression a(i)? Briefly explain.

8. Does alcohol dependency interfere with people's ability to find work? John Mullahy and Jody Sindelar addressed this question using data from the 1988 National Health Interview Survey.[19] Their study examined the unemployment and employment of U.S. men and women between the ages of 25 and 59, and used several measures of problem drinking. The file alchunemp.\*\*\* contains a subsample of Mullahy and Sindelar's data: African American males 30 to 59 years of age. The variables in the file are as follows:

| | |
|---|---|
| *stalccon* | Per capita alcohol consumption in the person's state |
| *stunempl* | Unemployment rate in the individual's state |
| *momalc* | = 1 if individual's birth mother was an alcoholic; = 0 otherwise |
| *dadalc* | = 1 if individual's birth father was an alcoholic; = 0 otherwise |
| *educ* | Individual's years of education |
| *beertax* | Tax rate on beer in the individual's state |
| *married* | = 1 if the individual is married; = 0 otherwise |
| *poorhlth* | = 1 if the individual is in poor health; = 0 otherwise |
| *unemploy* | = 1 if the individual is unemployed; = 0 otherwise |
| *alcdep* | A measure of alcohol dependency/abuse; = 1 if dependent; = 0 otherwise. |

Mullahy and Sindelar note that although problem drinking may interfere with an individual's ability to find work, other explanators not in their data set might be correlated with alcohol abuse, and unemployment itself might cause some alcohol problems. They are concerned that OLS estimates of the relationship between unemployment and problem drinking might be biased because of omitted variables or because of simultaneity.

a. Regress the unemployment indicator on the state's unemployment rate and on the individual's education, marital status, health status, and the dependency measure. What is the estimated effect of problem drinking (as measured by *alcdep*) on the employment rate?

b. Re-estimate the relationship in (a) using 2SLS, with *momalc*, *dadalc*, *stalccon*, and *beertax* as instruments for *alcdep*. How does the estimated coefficient on *alcdep* change from the OLS estimate? What happens to the estimated standard error of that coefficient?

c. Regress *alcdep* on the other explanators in (a), the instruments in (b), and an intercept term. Test the hypothesis that the coefficients on the instruments are all zero. Do the instruments appear weak?

d. Interpret the results from (a) and (b) taken together. Does the magnitude of the IV coefficient on *alcdep* make you think the analysis is flawed?

e. Do you think the instruments in (b) are valid instruments? Briefly explain.

9. Does alcohol dependency interfere with people's ability to work? John Mullahy and Jody Sindelar addressed this question using data from the 1988 National Health Interview Survey.[20] Their study examined the employment and unemployment of U.S. men and women between the ages of 25–59, and used several measures of alcohol dependency. Problem 8 examines individuals' unemployment status. This problem examines their employment status (the remaining category is out-of-the-labor-force.) The file alchemploy.*** contains a subsample of Mullahy and Sindelar's data: African American males 30–59 years of age. The variables in the file are the same as in problem 9, except that *unemploy* is replaced by *employed*, a dummy variable equal to one if the individual is employed.

Mullahy and Sindelar note that although problem drinking may interfere with an individual's ability to work, other explanators not in their data set might be correlated with alcohol abuse, and work itself might cause some alcohol problems. They are concerned that OLS estimates of the relationship between employment and problem drinking might be biased because of omitted variables or because of simultaneity.

a. Regress the employment indicator on the state's unemployment rate and on the individual's education, marital status, health status, and the dependency measure. What do you find is the effect of problem drinking (as measured by *alcdep*) on the employment rate?

b. Re-estimate the relationship in (a) using 2SLS, with *momalc*, *dadalc*, *stalccon*, and *beertax* as instruments for *alcdep*. How does the estimated coefficient on *alcdep* change from the OLS estimate? What happens to the estimated standard error of that coefficient?

c. Interpret the results from (a) and (b) taken together.

d. Regress *alcdep* on the other explanators in (a), the instruments in (b), and an intercept term. Test the hypothesis that the coefficients on the instruments are all zero. Do the instruments appear weak?

e. Does using instruments that are definitely not weak ensure that hypothesis tests based on them will be powerful?

10. In what sense is $\beta_{g2}$ an instrumental variable estimator in Friedman's permanent income consumption function specification? Think about $X_0$, the explanator that always equals 1.

11. Joshua Angrist's draft lottery study uses having a lottery "winning" birthday as an instrument for having military service. "Winners" were more apt to serve in the military than losers.

a. The correlation between winning the lottery and military service stems from some winners being drafted and others joining the military voluntarily to avoid being drafted. The dependent variable is lifetime earnings. Policy makers might want to know whether joining the service increases the lifetime earnings of young men who choose the service as their first employment. If this is our interest, what hesitations should we have about the interpretation of Angrist's estimate of the effect of military service on lifetime earnings?

b. Suppose that in a regression of "having military service" on "having a winning birthday" and the nontroublesome explanators in Angrist's study, the $t$-statistic on "having a winning birthday" is 2.10. Would this make you worry about the suitability of Angrist's instrument? Briefly explain your answer.

12. Some economists argue that a tight labor market leads to higher wages for workers and, in turn, this leads to upward pressure on output prices as firms attempt to maintain their profit margins. In light of this, inflation forecasters will often include measures of wage growth in their models. Open serv1.*** data on the Modern Introduction Web site. This data set includes the rate of inflation in consumer prices (*inf*), the growth rate in manufacturing wages (*mg*), the growth rate in wages for workers in services-producing industries (*sg*), and the growth rate in wages for workers in goods-producing industries (*gg*).

a. Use OLS to estimate an inflation equation that includes a constant term and *mg*. Now estimate an IV model in which *gg* is the instrument. Compare the two models. Do you think *gg* is a good instrument for *mg* (i.e., is it a valid instrument)? Explain.

b. Now use OLS to estimate an inflation equation that includes a constant term and *mg*. Estimate an IV model in which *sg* is the instrument. Compare the two models. Do you think *sg* is a good instrument for *mg*? Briefly explain.

c. Is *gg* a weak instrument for *mg*?

## Endnotes

1. Mark McClellan, Barbara McNeil, and Joseph Newhouse, "Does More Intensive Treatment of Acute Myocardial Infarction in the Elderly Reduce Mortality?" *Journal of the American Medical Association* 272, no. 11 (September 1994): 859–893.
2. Ibid.

3. Joshua Angrist, "Lifetime Earnings and the Vietnam Era Draft Lottery: Evidence from Social Security Administrative Records," *American Economic Review* 30, no. 3 (June 1990): 313–336.

4. Fumio Hiyashi, "The Permanent Income Hypothesis: Estimation and Testing by Instrumental Variables," *Journal of Political Economy* 90, no. 5 (October 1982): 895–916.

5. Orley Ashenfelter and Cecelia Rouse, "Income, Schooling, and Ability: Evidence from a New Sample of Identical Twins," *Quarterly Journal of Economics* 113, no. 1 (February 1998): 253–284.

6. The first development and use of instrumental variables estimation appeared in Philip Wright, *The Tariff on Animal and Vegetable Oils*, New York; Macmillan, 1928. The contribution was overlooked for many years. The paper that brought IV estimation to wide attention among economists was R. C. Geary, "Determination of Linear Relations Between Systematic Parts of Variables with Errors of Observation the Variances of Which Are Unknown," *Econometrica* 17, no. 1 (January 1949): 30–58.

7. Ashenfelter and Rouse, "Income, Schooling, and Ability: Evidence from a New Sample of Identical Twins."

8. Charles R. Nelson and Richard Startz, "The Distribution of the Instrumental Variables Estimator and Its *t* Ratio When the Instrument Is a Poor One," *Journal of Business* 63 (1990): S125–S140, first drew sharp attention to the weak instruments problem.

9. James H. Stock and Motohiro Yogo, "Testing for Weak Instruments in Linear IV Regression," in *Identification and Inference for Econometric Models: Essays in Honor of Thomas Rothenberg*, D. W. K. Andrews and J. H. Stock, eds. (London: Cambridge University Press, 2005). Stock and Yogo also present test statistics and critical values for detecting weak instruments in models with more than one troublesome variable.

10. Janet Currie and Aaron Yelowitz, "Are Public Housing Projects Good for Kids?" *Journal of Public Economics* 75 (January 2000): 99–124.

11. Ibid, 104.

12. Joshua Angrist and Alan Krueger, "The Effect of Age at School Entry on Educational Attainment: An Application of Instrumental Variables with Moments from Two Samples," *Journal of the American Statistical Association* 87, no. 418 (June 1992): 328–337.

13. The numbers in the table are taken from James H. Stock, Jonathan H. Wright, and Motohiro Yogo, "A Survey of Weak Instruments and Weak Identification in Generalized Method of Moments," *Journal of Business and Economic Statistics* 20, no. 4 (October 2002): 518–529. Stock, Wright, and Yogo also review alternative valid confidence interval estimators based on weak instruments.

14. For methods for constructing valid confidence intervals using weak instruments, see Eric Zivot, Richard Startz, and Charles R. Nelson, "Valid Confidence Intervals and Inference in the Presence of Weak Instruments," *International Economic Review* 39, no. 4 (1998): 1119–1144.

15. De-Min Wu, "Alternative Tests of Independence Between Stochastic Regressors and Disturbances," *Econometrica* 41 (1973): 733–750.

16. Jerry A. Hausman, "Specification Tests in Econometrics," *Econometrica* 46, no. 6 (1978): 1251–1272.

17. John Mullahy, "Instrumental-Variable Estimation of Count Data Models: Applications to Models of Cigarette Smoking Behavior," *Review of Economics and Statistics* (1997): 586-593.
18. Steven Levitt, "The Effect of Prison Population Size on Crime Rates: Evidence From Prison Overcrowding Litigation," *Quarterly Journal of Economics* 111, no. 2 (May 1996): 319–351.
19. John Mullahy and Jody Sindelar, "Employment, Unemployment, and Problem Drinking," *Journal of Health Economics*, 15, 1996, 409–434.
20. Ibid.

# *Appendix 13.A*

# The Magnitude of Measurement Error Bias

Milton Friedman's model of permanent income highlights the difference between current income and permanent income. Formally, Friedman defined permanent income as the maximum amount the consumer could spend and still leave his or her wealth unchanged. Because current income mismeasures permanent income, OLS yields biased estimates of the consumer's marginal propensity to consume, $\beta$, in the consumption function

$$Y_i = \beta X_i + \varepsilon_i,$$

in which $Y$ is consumption and $X$ is permanent income. This appendix derives the magnitude of the bias incurred using OLS.

## 13.A.1   The Measurement Error DGP

**WHAT IS THE DGP?**

The DGP we study varies from the Gauss–Markov Assumptions as little as possible, but adds mismeasurement of the explanator. The DGP is

$$Y_i = \beta X_i + \varepsilon_i \qquad i = 1, \ldots, n.$$
$$E(\varepsilon_i) = 0 \qquad i = 1, \ldots, n.$$
$$\mathrm{var}(\varepsilon_i) = \sigma_\varepsilon^2 \qquad i = 1, \ldots, n.$$
$$\mathrm{cov}(X_i, \varepsilon_i) = 0.$$
$$M_i = X_i + \nu_i.$$

$$E(\nu_i) = 0 \qquad i = 1, \ldots, n.$$

$$\text{var}(\nu_i) = \sigma_\nu^2 \qquad i = 1, \ldots, n.$$

$$\text{cov}(X_i, \nu_i) = 0.$$

$\varepsilon_1, \ldots, \varepsilon_n, \nu_1, \ldots, \nu_n$ are mutually statistically independent.

Not all $X_i$ are zero.

The $X_i$ are unobserved, but the $M_i$ are observed.

The measurement errors and underlying disturbances are mutually statistically independent, which implies that they are uncorrelated with one another both contemporaneously and across observations.

## 13.A.2   The Magnitude of Measurement Error Bias

Recall the construction of the BLUE estimator, $\beta_{g4}$. We first weighted each observation by its explanator:

$$M_i Y_i = \beta M_i^2 + M_i \eta_i.$$

We then summed both sides:

$$\sum M_i Y_i = \sum \beta M_i^2 + \sum M_i \eta_i.$$

and then divided both sides by $\sum M_i^2$:

$$\frac{\left(\sum M_i Y_i\right)}{\left(\sum M_i^2\right)} = \beta + \frac{\left(\sum M_i \eta_i\right)}{\left(\sum M_i^2\right)}.$$

The last term on the right determines the bias of the OLS formula applied to $M$ and $Y$. The bias in OLS is

$$E\left[\frac{\sum M_i \eta_i}{\left(\sum M_i^2\right)}\right].$$

The bias, $\dfrac{\sum M_i \eta_i}{\sum M_i^2}$, is more easily assessed if we reintroduce $X_i$, $\varepsilon_i$, and $\nu_i$.

First, we replace $M_i$ with $(X_i + \nu_i)$:

$$\frac{\left(\sum M_i \eta_i\right)}{\left(\sum M_i^2\right)} = \frac{\left(\sum (X_i + \nu_i)\eta_i\right)}{\left(\sum (X_i + \nu_i)^2\right)}.$$

Then, we replace $\eta_i$ with $(-\beta v_i + \varepsilon_i)$:

$$\frac{[\sum(X_i + v_i)\eta_i]}{[\sum(X_i + v_i)^2]} = \frac{[\sum(X_i + v_i)(-\beta v_i + \varepsilon_i)]}{[\sum(X_i + v_i)^2]}$$

We can then expand the numerator:

$$\sum(X_i + v_i)(-\beta v_i + \varepsilon_i) = -\beta\sum(X_i v_i) + \sum(X_i \varepsilon_i) - \beta\sum v_i^2 + \sum v_i \varepsilon_i,$$

and we can expand the denominator:

$$\sum(X_i + v_i)^2 = \sum X_i^2 + \sum v_i^2 + 2\sum X_i v_i.$$

Thus, the bias in applying OLS to the mismeasured explanator is

$$\mathrm{E}\left[\frac{[-\beta\sum(x_i v_i) + \sum(X_i \varepsilon_i) - \beta\sum v_i^2 + \sum v_i \varepsilon_i]}{[\sum X_i^2 + \sum v_i^2 + 2\sum X_i v_i]}\right].$$

Unfortunately, with random variables appearing in both the numerator and the denominator, there is no simple way to evaluate this expectation, though advanced methods do show that the expectation is not equal to zero; OLS is, in fact, biased. What is easier to show is that OLS is inconsistent when the explanators are mismeasured.

The analysis of measurement error bias provides an instructive example of the power of asymptotic analysis when an analysis of sampling properties is difficult. In the following analysis, we examine consistency. The analysis of consistency establishes that measurement errors in explanators cause OLS to be biased and yields a simple expression for the magnitude of the inconsistency.

The plim of a ratio is the ratio of the plims, as long as the plim in the denominator is not zero. Consequently,

$$\mathrm{plim}\left[\frac{[-\beta\sum(X_i v_i) + \sum(X_i \varepsilon_i) - \beta\sum v_i^2 + \sum v_i \varepsilon_i]}{[\sum X_i^2 + \sum v_i^2 + 2\sum X_i v_i]}\right]$$

$$= \frac{\mathrm{plim}[[-\beta\sum(X_i v_i) + \sum(X_i \varepsilon_i) - \beta\sum v_i^2 + \sum v_i \varepsilon_i]]}{\mathrm{plim}[\sum X_i^2 + \sum v_i^2 + 2\sum X_i v_i]}$$

$$= \frac{\mathrm{plim}\left[\frac{1}{n}[-\beta\sum(X_i v_i) + \sum(X_i \varepsilon_i) - \beta\sum v_i^2 + \sum v_i \varepsilon_i]\right]}{\mathrm{plim}\left[\frac{1}{n}[\sum X_i^2 + \sum v_i^2 + 2\sum X_i v_i]\right]}.$$

We can break up and simplify the denominator:

$$\text{plim}\left[\frac{1}{n}[\Sigma X_i^2 + \Sigma v_i^2 + 2\Sigma X_i v_i]\right]$$

$$= \text{plim}\left(\frac{1}{n}\Sigma X_i^2\right) + \text{plim}\left(\Sigma v_i^2\right) + 2\text{plim}\left(\frac{1}{n}\Sigma X_i v_i\right),$$

which, if we include sufficient additional assumptions in the DGP to ensure that the Law of Large Numbers applies so that these plims equal the corresponding expected values,

$$= Q + \sigma_v^2 + 0.$$

It would suffice to add the assumption that $E(X_i^4)$, $E(v_i^4)$, and $E(X_i^2 v_i^2)$ are bounded by some finite value because then the variances of the means would converge to zero as the sample size grows.

Similarly, the numerator can be broken up and simplified:

$$\text{plim}\left[\frac{1}{n}\left[-\beta\Sigma(X_i v_i) + \Sigma(X_i \varepsilon_i) - \beta\Sigma v_i^2 + \Sigma(v_i \varepsilon_i)\right]\right]$$

$$= -\beta\text{plim}\left(\frac{1}{n}\Sigma X_i v_i\right) + \text{plim}\left(\frac{1}{n}\Sigma X_i \varepsilon_i\right) - \beta\text{plim}\left(\frac{1}{n}\Sigma v_i^2\right) + \text{plim}\left(\frac{1}{n}\Sigma v_i \varepsilon_i\right),$$

which, again assuming the Law of Large Numbers applies,

$$= -0 + 0 - \beta\sigma_v^2 + 0.$$

It would suffice to invoke the Law of Large Numbers to add the assumptions that $E(X_i^2 \varepsilon_i^2)$, $E(v_i^4)$, and $E(v_i^2 \varepsilon_i^2)$ are bounded by some finite value, which would ensure that the variances of all the sums converge to zero as the sample size grows.

Thus, we have found that OLS applied to mismeasured explanators yields inconsistent estimates of the slope, with the inconsistency

$$\frac{-\beta\sigma_v^2}{[Q + \sigma_v^2]}.$$

Except in pathological cases, this inconsistency equals the asymptotic bias of the OLS estimators. Advanced methods can show that expression for the asymptotic bias approximates the small sample bias of OLS, being off by a factor of less than $(1/n)$.

Econometricians often call this bias in OLS that arises from mismeasured explanators in a bivariate regression attenuation bias because its effect is to systematically underestimate the magnitude of the slope. When the slope is positive, this bias is negative ($-\beta$ will be negative, whereas $[\sigma_v^2/(Q + \sigma_v^2)]$ is always positive), but smaller than $\beta([\sigma_v^2/(Q + \sigma_v^2)]$ will always be a fraction if there is measurement error, leading to coefficient estimates that tend to be closer to zero than is $\beta$. When the slope is negative, this bias is positive, but smaller than $\beta$ in magnitude, leading again to coefficient estimates that are closer to zero than is $\beta$. The size of the asymptotic bias is proportional to the magnitude of $\beta$.

When there is a constant term in the regression, the bias expression is the same, except that $Q$, in that case, is the probability limit of $\frac{1}{n}\sum x_i^2$, not of $\frac{1}{n}\sum X_i^2$. In multiple regression models, the bias expression is more complex, and the multiple regression biases are not always toward zero.

The expression for this measurement error bias also sheds light on when we can expect the bias due to measurement error to be small. *If the variance of the measurement errors is small relative to the variation in the underlying true explanators, measurement error bias will be small.* This result generalizes to models with multiple explanators. In many practical applications, it is reasonable to assert that the measurement errors in the data are quite small relative to the underlying variation in the true explanators. In such applications, it is reasonable to ignore attenuation bias and use OLS confidently.

## 13.A.3   Mismeasured Explanators in Multiple Regression

WHAT ARE THE
PROPERTIES OF AN
ESTIMATOR?

Mismeasured explanators can plague OLS in multiple regression, too. Consider the $n$ observation, $k + 1$ explanator DGP in which the explanators are not directly observed, but are, instead, measured with error. In matrix form, this DGP is

$$Y = X\beta + \varepsilon$$
$$M = X + \nu$$
$$\mathrm{E}(\varepsilon) = 0$$
$$\mathrm{E}(\nu) = 0$$
$$\mathrm{E}(\varepsilon\varepsilon') = \sigma_\varepsilon^2 I_n$$
$$\mathrm{E}(\nu\nu') = \sigma_\nu^2 I_n$$

$X, \varepsilon,$ and $\nu$ are mutually statistically independent.

$\frac{1}{n}X'X = Q_n$ and $\frac{1}{n}M'M = \Omega_{MM}$ are always positive definite.

$$\mathrm{E}\left(\frac{1}{n}X'X\right) = Q$$
$$\mathrm{E}\left(\frac{1}{n}M'M\right) = \Omega_{MM}.$$

OLS is biased in this DGP if $M$ is our measure of $X$. If $M$ is our measure of $X$, the relationship we can estimate is

$$Y = M\beta + \eta = (X + \nu)\beta + \eta,$$

where $\eta = \varepsilon - \nu\beta$. The expected value of $\hat{\beta}$ is

$$E(\hat{\beta}) = E[(M'M)^{-1}M'Y] = \beta + E[(M'M)^{-1}M'\eta].$$

The bias in OLS when there are mismeasured explanators is

$$\begin{aligned}
E[(M'M)^{-1}M'\eta] &= E[(M'M)^{-1}M'(\varepsilon - \nu\beta)] \\
&= E[(M'M)^{-1}M'\varepsilon] - E[(M'M)^{-1}M'\nu\beta] \\
&= E[(M'M)^{-1}M']\,E[\varepsilon] - E[(M'M)^{-1}M'\nu]\beta \\
&= 0 - E[(M'M)^{-1}M'\nu]\beta = -E[(M'M)^{-1}M'\nu]\beta.
\end{aligned}$$

Advanced methods can show that this last expression is not, in general, zero. We can see the nature of the bias by considering the expression's probability limit instead of its expectation.

$$\begin{aligned}
\text{plim}(-(M'M)^{-1}M'\nu\beta) &= \text{plim}\left[-\left(\tfrac{1}{n}M'M\right)^{-1}\right]\text{plim}\left[\left(\tfrac{1}{n}\right)M'\nu\right]\beta \\
&= -\left[\text{plim}\left(\tfrac{1}{n}X'X\right) - \text{plim}\left(\tfrac{1}{n}\nu'\nu\right)\right]^{-1}\text{plim}\left[\left(\tfrac{1}{n}\right)(X+\nu)'\nu\right]\beta \\
&\quad -\left[\text{plim}\left(\tfrac{1}{n}X'X\right) - \text{plim}\left(\tfrac{1}{n}\nu'\nu\right)\right]^{-1}\text{plim}\left[\left(\tfrac{1}{n}\right)\nu'\nu\right]\beta.
\end{aligned}$$

If the Law of Large numbers applies, so that these plims equal their expectations, we arrive at the inconsistency being

$$(Q + \sigma_\nu^2 I_n)^{-1}\sigma_\nu^2 I_n\beta = (Q + \sigma_\nu^2 I_n)^{-1}\sigma_\nu^2\beta.$$

# Appendix 13.B

# Matrix Representations of Instrumental Variables and 2SLS Estimators

When OLS is inconsistent because the explanators and disturbances are correlated, instrumental variables estimation can provide a consistent alternative to OLS. The most common way econometricians implement IV estimation is by conducting 2SLS. This appendix demonstrates the consistency of the IV estimator and the equivalence of IV estimator and 2SLS to a particular IV estimator. The consistency of 2SLS depends on its equivalence to an IV estimator.

## 13.B.1    The DGP

WHAT IS THE DGP?

The DGP here assumes that

$$Y = X\beta + \varepsilon$$

and

$$\text{plim}\left(\frac{1}{n}(X'X)\right) = Q, \ Q \text{ positive definite.} \qquad \text{13.B.1}$$

Equation 13.B.1 rules out (i) data sources in which the $X$ values are unbounded and (ii) an approach to perfect multicollinearity as $n$ approaches infinity.

The DGP here also assumes that

$$\text{plim}\left(\frac{1}{n}X'\varepsilon\right) = C, \text{ in which some elements are nonzero.} \qquad \text{13.B.2}$$

What restrictions on expectations ensure that 13.B.2 holds if the $X$-values are stochastic? Three assumptions taken together suffice: (i) the explanators are not perfectly collinear, so $(X'X) = Q_n$, and $Q_n^{-1}$ exists; (ii) $\text{E}(\frac{1}{n}X'\varepsilon\varepsilon'X\frac{1}{n})$ goes to zero in the limit; and (iii) $\text{E}(X'\varepsilon) = C$. The last of these three conditions states that the explanators and disturbances are contemporaneously correlated.

To examine the consistency of an instrumental variables estimator, we need some assumptions about the instruments. We assume that

$$\text{plim}\left(\frac{1}{n}Z'\boldsymbol{\varepsilon}\right) = 0 \qquad \text{13.B.3}$$

and

$$\text{plim}\left(\frac{1}{n}Z'X\right) = \boldsymbol{\Omega}_{ZX}, \text{ a positive definite matrix.} \qquad \text{13.B.4}$$

Assumptions about expectations that suffice to ensure 13.B.3 and 13.B.4 are that $E(Z'\boldsymbol{\varepsilon}) = 0$, $E(Z'X) = \boldsymbol{\Omega}_{ZX}$, a positive definite matrix, and both $E(\frac{1}{n}Z'\boldsymbol{\varepsilon}\boldsymbol{\varepsilon}'Z\frac{1}{n})$ and $E(\frac{1}{n}Z'XX'Z\frac{1}{n})$ converge to zero as the sample size grows. To facilitate analyzing the variance of the IV estimator, we also assume that

$$\text{plim}\left(\frac{1}{n}Z'\boldsymbol{\varepsilon}\boldsymbol{\varepsilon}'Z\right) = \sigma^2\boldsymbol{\Omega}_{ZZ}, \text{ a positive definite matrix.}$$

## 13.B.2     The OLS and IV Estimators

This section asks whether OLS or IV estimation is consistent in the preceding DGP. It also examines the behavior of the variation in the IV estimator about $\boldsymbol{\beta}$.

### Consistency

In this DGP, $\hat{\boldsymbol{\beta}}$ is not a consistent estimator of $\boldsymbol{\beta}$. Consider

$$\hat{\boldsymbol{\beta}} = (X'X)^{-1}X'Y = \boldsymbol{\beta} + (X'X)^{-1}X'\boldsymbol{\varepsilon},$$

so that

$$\text{plim}(\hat{\boldsymbol{\beta}}) = \text{plim}(\boldsymbol{\beta} + (X'X)^{-1}X'\boldsymbol{\varepsilon})$$
$$= \boldsymbol{\beta} + \text{plim}\left(\left(\frac{1}{n}X'X\right)^{-1}\right)\text{plim}\left(\frac{1}{n}X'\boldsymbol{\varepsilon}\right) = \boldsymbol{\beta} + Q^{-1}C \neq \boldsymbol{\beta}.$$

However, the IV estimator is consistent in this DGP. Consider

$$\tilde{\boldsymbol{\beta}}_{IV} = (Z'X)^{-1}Z'Y = \boldsymbol{\beta} + (Z'X)^{-1}Z'\boldsymbol{\varepsilon},$$

so that

$$\text{plim}(\tilde{\boldsymbol{\beta}}_{IV}) = \text{plim}(\boldsymbol{\beta} + (Z'X)^{-1}Z'\boldsymbol{\varepsilon})$$
$$= \boldsymbol{\beta} + \text{plim}\left(\left(\frac{1}{n}Z'X\right)^{-1}\right)\text{plim}\left(\frac{1}{n}Z'\boldsymbol{\varepsilon}\right) = \boldsymbol{\beta} + Q^{-1}0 = \boldsymbol{\beta}.$$

## The Variation of $\tilde{\beta}_{IV}$ About $\beta$

How do the squared errors of the instrumental variables estimator behave as sample size grows? Consider

$$\begin{aligned}
\text{plim}[(\tilde{\beta}_{IV} - \beta)(\tilde{\beta}_{IV} - \beta)'] &= \text{plim}[(Z'X)^{-1}Z'\varepsilon\varepsilon'Z(X'Z)^{-1}] \\
&= \text{plim}\left[\frac{1}{n}(Z'X)^{-1}\right]\text{plim}\left[\frac{1}{n}Z'\varepsilon\varepsilon'Z\frac{1}{n}\right]\text{plim}\left[\frac{1}{n}(X'Z)^{-1}\right] \\
&= \frac{1}{n}\text{plim}\left[\frac{1}{n}(Z'X)^{-1}\right]\text{plim}\left[\frac{1}{n}Z'\varepsilon\varepsilon'Z\right]\text{plim}\left[\frac{1}{n}(X'Z)^{-1}\right] \\
&= \frac{1}{n}\Omega_{zx}^{-1}(\sigma^2\Omega_{zz})(\Omega'_{ZX})^{-1} = \frac{\sigma^2}{n}\Omega_{zx}^{-1}(\Omega_{zz})(\Omega'_{ZX})^{-1}.
\end{aligned}$$

A consistent estimator of $\sigma^2$ relies on the sum of squared residuals from the IV regression, adjusted for the number of degrees of freedom:

$$\tilde{s}^2 = (Y - X\tilde{\beta}_{IV})'(Y - X\tilde{\beta}_{IV})/(n - k - 1).$$

The estimated asymptotic variance of $\tilde{\beta}_{IV}$ is

$$\tilde{s}^2(Z'X)^{-1}Z'Z(X'Z)^{-1}.$$

# 13.B.3  2SLS and IV

How Do We Make
an Estimator?

When an equation contains several troublesome variables, that is, explanators correlated with the disturbances, we can divide the explanators into troublesome and nontroublesome explanators, and write the equation as

$$Y = W^*\alpha + X\beta + \varepsilon, \qquad \text{13.B.5}$$

in which $W^*$ contains the troublesome variables and $X$ contains the nontroublesome explanators. Additionally, consider a set of potential instruments, $Z^*$. Because $E(W^{*\prime}\varepsilon)$ does not equal zero, OLS is inconsistent, but both IV estimators and 2SLS consistently estimate the coefficients of Equation 13.B.5. This section presents the 2SLS estimator in matrix form and shows it is equivalent to a particular IV estimator.

## 2SLS in Matrix Form

To perform 2SLS,

1. Use OLS to regress of each element of $W^*$ on $Z^*$ and $X$ (as nontroublesome variables, the elements of $X$ will serve as fine instruments for themselves). Form the fitted values from these OLS regressions.

2. Conduct OLS on 13.B.5, but replace the elements of $W^*$ with their fitted values from stage 1.

Notice that if we modify step 1 and regress both the elements of $W^*$ and the elements of $X$ on $Z^*$ and $X$, the fitted values for each element of $X$ will equal that element of $X$, because a perfect fit results when we regress a variable on itself. We could then similarly modify step 2 to replace the elements of both $W^*$ and $X$ with their fitted values without at all altering the final estimates obtained. This modified, but equivalent, version of 2SLS makes it easier to determine the matrix algebra formula for 2SLS.

To exploit this modified 2SLS procedure's computational advantages, define $W = [W^*X]$, $Z = [Z^*X]$, and $\gamma' = [\alpha\ \beta]$, so that we can rewrite Equation 13.B.5 as

$$Y = W\gamma + \varepsilon.$$

Conducting the modified 2SLS procedure requires that we do two things:

1′. Conduct OLS for each element of $W$ and assemble these OLS coefficient estimates in a $(k + 1) \times (k + 1)$ matrix, $\hat{\beta}$, in which each column consists of the OLS estimates for one equation:

$$\hat{\beta} = (Z'Z)^{-1}Z'W.$$

The fitted values, $\hat{W}$, of the elements of $W$ are

$$\hat{W} = Z\hat{\beta} = Z(Z'Z)^{-1}Z'W. \qquad \text{13.B.6}$$

2′. Perform OLS, replacing the elements of $W$ with their fitted values. The 2SLS estimator for $\gamma$ is therefore

$$\begin{aligned}
\tilde{\gamma}_{2SLS} &= (\hat{W}'\hat{W})^{-1}\hat{W}'Y \\
&= (W'Z(Z'Z)^{-1}Z'Z(Z'Z)^{-1}Z'W)^{-1}W'Z(Z'Z)^{-1}Z'Y \\
&= (W'Z(Z'Z)^{-1}Z'W)^{-1}W'Z(Z'Z)^{-1}Z'Y. \qquad \text{13.B.7}
\end{aligned}$$

## 2SLS and IV Estimation

The 2SLS estimator is equivalent to a particular IV estimator. Equation 13.B.6 defines, $\hat{W}$, a particular set of linear combinations of the valid potential instruments in this model. Linear combinations of valid instruments are also valid instruments because they, too, are uncorrelated with the disturbances and correlated with the troublesome variables. Consequently, the elements of $\hat{W}$ are valid instruments for the elements of $\mathbf{W}$. The IV estimator for $\boldsymbol{\gamma}$ that uses $\hat{\mathbf{W}}$ as the instruments is

$$\tilde{\boldsymbol{\gamma}}_{\text{IV}} = (\hat{\mathbf{W}}'\mathbf{W})\hat{\mathbf{W}}'\mathbf{Y} = (\mathbf{W}'\mathbf{Z}(\mathbf{Z}'\mathbf{Z})^{-1}\mathbf{Z}'\mathbf{W})^{-1}\mathbf{W}'\mathbf{Z}(\mathbf{Z}'\mathbf{Z})^{-1}\mathbf{Z}'\mathbf{Y},$$

which is the same expression as in 13.B.7. The 2SLS estimator is equivalent to an IV estimator that uses the fitted values from (1′) as instruments in estimating 13.B.5. Because we know IV is a consistent estimation procedure, we also know 2SLS is a consistent estimation procedure.

## The Special Nature of 2SLS

2SLS poses a puzzle when juxtaposed against the mismeasured explanators bias of OLS: It is consistent even if we deliberately replace explanators in OLS with mismeasured versions of themselves. 2SLS doesn't suffer from measurement error bias because of the very special way it mismeasures variables. The mismeasured variables used in 2SLS have two features that combine to avoid measurement error bias:

1. Fitted values from OLS regressions are always uncorrelated with the corresponding residuals. Consequently, unlike the classic mismeasured explanators in DGP, the mismeasured variables in 2SLS are not correlated with the corresponding mismeasurement term introduced into the disturbance term.
2. Each fitted value in 2SLS is a linear combination of explanators from the first-stage regression. OLS always produces residuals uncorrelated with each explanator. As linear combinations of those same explanators, each fitted value in the second stage is uncorrelated with all of the mismeasurement terms introduced by using fitted values in place of actual values in the second stage of 2SLS.

These two features of 2SLS cause the explanators in the second stage of 2SLS to not be correlated with the disturbances in that regression. Consequently, the 2SLS estimator does not suffer measurement error bias.

Features 1 and 2 of 2SLS are essential to its consistency. If the fitted values in the second stage were not all linear combinations of *the same* variables, or if any of the nontroublesome explanators were omitted from the first-stage regression, 2SLS would be vulnerable to mismeasurement bias and its consistency would be lost.

IV estimation is more general than 2SLS. For example, IV estimation can construct instruments for different troublesome variables from different lists of candidate instruments without losing its consistency. Suppose that we know that $\mathbf{Z}_1$ contains valid candidate instruments for $\mathbf{W}_1^*$ and that $\mathbf{Z}_2$ contains valid candidate instruments for $W_2^*$, and, further, that the candidate instruments for one variable are not correlated with the other troublesome variable. In this case, it would be more efficient to construct instruments by regressing $W_1^*$ on $Z_1$ and $W_2^*$ on $Z_2$ than by regressing $W_1^*$ and $W_2^*$ on both $Z_1$ and $Z_2$. If the instruments are constructed in this more efficient manner, though, it is not a consistent estimator to perform OLS using those fitted values in place of the troublesome variables. Using those fitted values as instruments in a true IV formula, however, is consistent. Most software packages conduct IV estimation by performing 2SLS because the computations are easier to do that way. In most applications, this approach is fine. In the special cases in which we know that instruments should be built using separate candidate lists, we need to avoid 2SLS and use the true IV formulae.

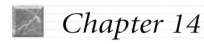

## *Chapter 14*

# Systems of Equations

*Teach a parrot to say Supply and Demand and you've got an economist.*
— THOMAS CARLYLE (1795–1881)

W hy has college grown so expensive? Supply and demand. Why have computers grown so cheap? Supply and demand. In the 19th century, Cambridge University economist Alfred Marshall taught us that supply and demand work together to determine prices and quantities; he wrote, "We might as reasonably dispute whether it is the upper or the under blade of a pair of scissors that cuts a piece of paper, as whether value is governed by utility or cost of production."[1] If econometrics is to be relevant to economics, it needs to grapple with the two blades of supply and demand by working with models that include not just one equation, but two or more. And it is not just microeconomics' supply and demand that force economists to consider systems of equations. GDP, investment, consumption, savings, and many other variables of macroeconomics are jointly determined in a complex system of relationships.

In our regression models thus far, we have assumed that one variable under scrutiny, the dependent variable, is determined by the variables that we call the independent variables. We have generally overlooked the interdependencies that characterize supply and demand and other economic equilibrium mechanisms. Economics requires an econometrics that can account for interdependencies, that is, for systems of equations. This chapter examines the consequences of multiple equations for the methods developed in earlier chapters.

The chapter begins with the example of supply and demand as a prototype for systems of equations. This example offers three lessons that generalize to other systems of equations: (i) ordinary least squares (OLS) is generally inconsistent when applied to simultaneous equations; (ii) when simultaneity makes OLS perform badly, instrumental variables estimation often serves us well; and (iii) sometimes we can't consistently estimate some individual equations in a system of equations; that is, some equations in a system of equations may not be *identified*. Most of this chapter concentrates on introducing consistent estimation procedures for equations that *are* identified. Some of these procedures estimate the equations one by one; others estimate them jointly. These methods enable us to grapple with the complex interdependencies that characterize real-world economic relationships. With them in hand, we will not be daunted when some parrot looks at our estimated demand curve for college or computers, and says, "What about supply?"

## 14.1    Endogenous and Exogenous Variables in Simultaneous Equations

The data-generating process (DGPs) we have considered so far have had only one equation. This chapter considers the estimation of systems of equations that simultaneously determine several variables. To understand how to construct a DGP with more than one equation, consider a simplified supply and demand specification for personal computers. The data might be gathered from several European countries that each produces its own personal computers, in which case the unit of observation is a country. Or the data might be gathered in the United States over time, in which case the unit of observation is a time period.

On the demand side, we assume that the quantity of personal computers demanded, $Q_i^d$, depends only on the price of personal computers, $P_i$, and a stochastic disturbance, $\varepsilon_i^d$. On the supply side, we assume that competitive conditions rule in the market for personal computers, so the marginal cost conditions faced by firms determine the supply curve, with higher marginal costs incurred at higher output levels. We use $Q_i^s$ to denote the quantity of personal computers produced by firms. The price of personal computers asked for by competitive, profit-maximizing suppliers, $P_i$, equals the marginal cost of personal computers.

Because the supply curve is a portion of the marginal cost curve, and marginal cost equals price in competitive markets, we can express the supply function as price (marginal cost) varying with the quantity produced. We assume that the price of plastic materials, $M_i$, also affects the marginal cost of producing personal computers, as does a stochastic disturbance, $\varepsilon_i^s$.

We assume that markets clear, that is, that $Q_i^d = Q_i^s$, and we simplify quantity to just $Q_i$. Using a linear form for both the supply and demand relationships, we have the demand curve

$$Q_i = \beta_0 + \beta_1 P_i + \varepsilon_i^d, \tag{14.1}$$

and the supply curve

$$P_i = \alpha_0 + \alpha_1 Q_i + \alpha_2 M_i + \varepsilon_i^s. \tag{14.2}$$

We assume that $\varepsilon_i^s$ and $\varepsilon_i^d$ individually satisfy the Gauss–Markov conditions, have variances $\sigma_s^2$ and $\sigma_d^2$, and are uncorrelated with one another, except for a possible contemporaneous correlation reflected in $\text{cov}(\varepsilon_i^s, \varepsilon_i^d) = \sigma_{sd}$. We further assume that the personal computer industry's use of plastic is too small to affect the price of plastic materials, $M_i$, and so the price of plastic materials is determined outside our supply and demand model. Econometricians call systems of interdependent equations that jointly determine variables, as supply and demand jointly determine price and quantity, systems of **simultaneous equations**.

Because the price and quantity of personal computers are jointly determined within the supply and demand model, there is not a "natural" choice of a dependent variable, as we have assumed previously. We could represent demand as the price consumers are willing to pay for a given quantity of the good. In such an alternative representation of demand, price would be the dependent variable in the demand relationship, and quantity could appear as an explanator. Similarly, instead of specifying supply as the marginal cost of the producer for a given quantity, we could represent supply by the quantity a producer would be willing to sell at a given price. In such an alternative specification of supply, quantity would appear as the dependent variable and price as an explanator.

Which of these representations we choose is arbitrary. Here, to emphasize that both quantity and price are variables determined within the system, Equations 14.1 and 14.2 specify one equation with quantity as the dependent variable and one equation with price as the dependent variable. What we should not do is specify the price of plastic materials as the dependent variable in the supply relationship, nor should we specify it as depending on the stochastic disturbances of our system of simultaneous equations, because we have assumed that the price of plastic materials is not determined within the supply and demand relationship, but is, instead, given from outside the system.

## Endogenous and Exogenous Variables

Equations 14.1 and 14.2 contain two dependent variables, $P$ and $Q$. Intuitively, we can describe $P$ and $Q$ as the variables that are determined *inside* our system; econometricians call such variables **endogenous**. In contrast, $M$, the price of plastic materials, is determined *outside* our system; econometricians call these variables **exogenous**. The constant term in a model is another example of an exogenous variable, albeit a variable whose value does not vary at all.

We assume the price of plastic materials is exogenous on the presumption that the computer industry's use of plastic is too small a part of the entire demand for plastic to influence the price of plastic. In formal terms, we are assuming that

$$E(\varepsilon_i^s | M_1, \ldots, M_n) = 0$$

and

$$E(\varepsilon_i^d | M_1, \ldots, M_n) = 0.$$

These two conditions are the formal way of saying that the price of plastic materials is exogenous to supply and demand. These conditions imply that exogenous variables are uncorrelated with the disturbances in our DGP. These assumptions about the price of plastic materials could be wrong; we will need formal statistical tests to check them.

Endogenous variables appear as dependent variables in a simultaneous system and may also appear as explanators. Exogenous variables appear only as explanators. In many econometric models, lagged values of endogenous variables also appear as explanators. We call exogenous variables and lagged endogenous variables **predetermined variables**. Exogenous variables are predetermined because they are determined outside the system of equations; exogenous variables are always contemporaneously uncorrelated with the disturbance. Lagged dependent variables are predetermined in the sense that when the endogenous values in time $t$ are determined, their earlier values have already been determined; however, lagged endogenous variables that serve as explanators may or may not be contemporaneously correlated with the disturbances. Chapter 13 introduced the convention of calling variables that are contemporaneously correlated with the disturbances "troublesome." Exogenous explanatory variables are never troublesome. Lagged endogenous explanators can be either troublesome or nontroublesome; when the disturbances are serially uncorrelated, lagged dependent variables are not troublesome.

## 14.2     The Simultaneity Bias of OLS

WHAT ARE AN ESTI-
MATOR'S PROPERTIES?

How are we to estimate the intercepts and slopes of the supply and demand equations in our new simultaneous equations DGP? Because both supply and demand contain explanators that are correlated with the disturbances, OLS is neither unbiased nor consistent. This section explores in more detail the properties of OLS when estimating simultaneous equations.

### Estimating the Demand for Personal Computers

Consider first estimating the demand equation for personal computers. OLS applied to the demand equation yields biased estimates. Intuitively, feedback from demand shocks to price causes the bias. For example, if the demand for personal computers were surprisingly high ($\varepsilon_i^d > 0$), the supply equation indicates that the price for personal computers would also be higher than it would otherwise be (assuming, as we do, that $\alpha_1 > 0$). Therefore, the price variable, $P_i$, would be correlated with the disturbance term, $\varepsilon_i^d$, in the demand equation. *Endogenous explanators are often contemporaneously correlated with the disturbances of the equations in which they appear.* In short, endogenous explanators are often troublesome explanators. This lesson is not new; we saw it in Chapter 13. But it is important enough to merit repetition.

### Structural Equations and Reduced Form Equations

We can express the correlation between $P_i$ and $\varepsilon_i^d$ formally. Such a formal expression is a first step toward quantifying the bias of OLS, which will reveal whether the bias is large or small. We arrive at the supply and demand equations in Equations 14.1 and 14.2 by considering the institutional and behavioral relationships that hold among economic variables. Econometricians call such a representation of a system of equations the **structural form** of the model and call these equations the **structural equations** of the model. In a structural equation, exogenous and endogenous variables may both serve as explanators. Because economists are deeply interested in the behavioral relationships that determine economic outcomes, the parameters of the structural form are frequently of central interest to them. An alternative representation of a system is possible, however; we can express the endogenous variables in a system as functions of the predetermined variables and the disturbances alone. The representation of a simultaneous system of equations that expresses the endogenous variables as functions of the predetermined variables and the disturbances alone we call the **reduced form** of the model.

In the personal computers example, we can solve for price and quantity as functions of the price of plastic materials and the two disturbances alone. The reduced form equation for price is

$$P_i = \frac{(\alpha_0 + \beta_0\alpha_1)}{(1 - \alpha_1\beta_1)} + \frac{(\alpha_2 M_i)}{(1 - \alpha_1\beta_1)} + \frac{(\alpha_1\varepsilon_i^d + \varepsilon_i^s)}{(1 - \alpha_1\beta_1)}, \qquad \textbf{14.3}$$

which we rewrite as

$$P_i = \pi_{p0} + \pi_{p1}M_i + \mu_i^p. \qquad \textbf{14.4}$$

The reduced form equation for quantity is

$$Q_i = \frac{(\beta_0 + \alpha_0\beta_1)}{(1 - \alpha_1\beta_1)} + \frac{\alpha_2\beta_1 M_i}{(1 - \alpha_1\beta_1)} + \frac{(\varepsilon_i^d + \beta_1\varepsilon_i^s)}{(1 - \alpha_1\beta_1)}, \qquad \textbf{14.5}$$

which we rewrite as

$$Q_i = \pi_{q0} + \pi_{q1}M_i + \mu_i^q. \qquad \textbf{14.6}$$

The coefficients $\pi_{p0}$, $\pi_{p1}$, $\pi_{q0}$, and $\pi_{q1}$ in Equations 14.4 and 14.6 are the parameters of the **reduced form equations.**

*Reduced form equations are sometimes all we need to know, depending on our purposes.* For example, suppose the government required that both buyers and sellers of computers pay a tax of $T$ dollars at the purchase of a computer. Further suppose that this tax is exogenous to the supply and demand for computers. The variable, $T$, would appear as an explanator in both the supply and the demand equations. In the reduced form equation for the quantity of personal computers, $Q$, the coefficient on $T$ would tell us how the expected equilibrium quantity of personal computers would change if $T$ changed. Without the structural equations' parameters, we would be unable to describe the mechanism by which the tax alters $Q$—does the tax work chiefly through its discouraging influence on supply, or through its discouraging influence on demand, or evenhandedly through both? We can't tell from the reduced form equation. If our primary concern is with how much a change in $T$ effects $E(Q)$, and not on the mechanism by which $T$ has its effects, though, then the reduced form equation tells us what we need to know—what $T$ does to the quantity of computers we expect to see exchanged in the marketplace.

## Simultaneity Bias

The reduced form representation of the supply and demand model given in Equations 14.3 and 14.5 reveals that both $P_i$ and $Q_i$ vary as either $\varepsilon_i^s$ or $\varepsilon_i^d$ varies. Thus, $P_i$ and $\varepsilon_i^d$ are correlated, implying that OLS estimation of the demand parameters is biased and inconsistent. Similarly, $Q_i$ and $\varepsilon_i^s$ are correlated, so OLS applied to the supply equation is also biased and inconsistent. Such a bias we call **simultaneous equations bias**.

A more formal analysis uncovers the magnitude of these simultaneous equations biases. Let's consider the inconsistency of OLS applied to the demand curve. The appearance of $\varepsilon_i^d$ in Equation 14.3 reveals that $P_i$ is correlated with the disturbance of the demand equation, as long as $\alpha_1 \neq 0$, that is, as long as marginal cost depends on quantity. If we treat $M_i$ as fixed across samples, we find from Equation 14.3 that the covariance between $P_i$ and $\varepsilon_i^d$ is

$$E(p_i\varepsilon_i^d) = E(\mu_i^P\varepsilon_i^d) = E\left(\frac{\alpha_1\varepsilon_i^d + \varepsilon_i^s}{1 - \alpha_1\beta_1}\varepsilon_i^d\right) = \frac{\alpha_1\sigma_d^2 + \sigma_{sd}}{1 - \alpha_1\beta_1}. \qquad \textbf{14.7}$$

Equation 12.9 reported that when the explanator in a bivariate regression is correlated with the disturbance, as price is here, the inconsistency of OLS is

$$\frac{\mathrm{plim}\left(\frac{1}{n}\Sigma p_i\varepsilon_i^d\right)}{Q},$$

where $Q = \mathrm{plim}\left(\frac{1}{n}\Sigma p_i^2\right)$, which we assume is not zero. If the Law of Large Numbers also applies, then $\mathrm{plim}\left(\frac{1}{n}\Sigma p_i\varepsilon_i^d\right) = E(p_i\varepsilon_i^d)$, and the larger the right-hand side of Equation 14.7 relative to $Q$, the larger the inconsistency of OLS in estimating the slope of the demand curve.

OLS isn't always biased when applied to structural equations in a simultaneous system. For example, suppose that the price of plastic materials in Equation 14.2, $M_i$, is not an exogenous variable, but is an endogenous variable instead, and that the structural equation determining the price of plastic materials depends on just exogenous variables and a disturbance term, $\varepsilon_i^M$. Further assume that the exogenous variables in the price of plastic equation are transport costs for plastic and the crude oil's price, and that $\varepsilon_i^M$ is uncorrelated with $\varepsilon_i^s$ and $\varepsilon_i^d$. Thus,

$$M_i = \gamma_0 + \gamma_1 transport\ costs_i + \gamma_2 crude\ oil\ price_i + \varepsilon_i^M.$$

In such a case, the reduced form equation for the price of plastic materials would be the same as the structural equation, and the price of plastic materials would still not be correlated with the disturbances in the supply or demand equations. OLS would provide unbiased and consistent estimates of the parameters of the price of plastic materials equation in such an expanded simultaneous system.

Although OLS estimates of structural equations are, in general, vulnerable to simultaneous equations bias, OLS consistently estimates reduced form equations if the predetermined variables in the model are not troublesome. The exogenous variables are uncorrelated with all the disturbances in the model, so the exogenous explanators in the reduced form equation do not upset the consistency of OLS estimates of the reduced form equations. If there are lagged endogenous variables in the reduced form equation, but serially uncorrelated disturbances in the structural model, then those lagged endogenous variables are not troublesome, so they, too, do not upset the consistency of OLS. *Serially correlated disturbances in the structural equations, when coupled with lagged endogenous variables in the reduced form, can undermine the consistency of OLS estimates of the reduced form parameters.* We return to the case of serially correlated reduced form disturbances at the end of the chapter.

## Recursive Systems

Sometimes OLS estimates structural equations without incurring simultaneous equations bias. It is feedback between price and quantity that can give rise to simultaneity bias in Equations 14.1 and 14.2. When feedback is absent and the disturbances in the structural equations are not correlated, simultaneous equations bias disappears. For example, in Equation 14.3, if $\alpha_1 = 0$ and $\sigma_{sd} = 0$, then the price of personal computers is uncorrelated with the disturbance in the demand equation; there would be no simultaneous equations bias in applying OLS to the demand equation under these conditions. Notice that in such a case, the endogenous variable quantity demanded would depend on the endogenous variable price, but price would not, in turn, depend on quantity (because $\alpha_1 = 0$). There would be no feedback from quantity to price.

When a system has endogenous variables appearing as explanators without feedback, the relationship between those dependent endogenous variables and their endogenous explanators is said to be **recursive**. Recursive relationships do not suffer from simultaneous equations bias if the disturbances are not correlated across equations.

## 14.3        The Identification Problem

Sometimes a DGP contains too little information to permit us to consistently estimate a population parameter of interest. When the DGP is such that no amount of data would allow us to differentiate between several (maybe infinitely many) values of an unknown population parameter, we say that the embarrassment of riches—too many values of the parameters that are equally consistent with any data—stems from DGPs that are **observationally equivalent**. We also say that those unknown parameters are *underidentified*. The structural equations of simultaneous equations models are particularly vulnerable to underidentification.

Reduced form equations are usually **identified**; that is, they can be consistently estimated. For example, if a reduced form contains no lagged dependent variables, and its explanators, the exogenous variables, are not perfectly collinear, then the reduced form equations are identified. A sufficient condition for the reduced form equations to be identified is that no predetermined variables in the structural equations are troublesome. In this case, OLS consistently estimates the reduced form's parameters. Perfect multicollinearity precludes consistent estimation of some parameters in a model, so perfect multicollinearity among the predetermined variables makes some reduced form parameters underidentified.

### Indirect Least Squares

Less clear in simultaneous systems is whether the parameters of each structural equation are identified. At first look, identification of the reduced form equations offers a straightforward path to identifying the structural equations. The parameters of the reduced form depend on those of the structural model, as is evident from a comparison of Equations 14.3 and 14.5 with Equations 14.1 and 14.2. Is it possible to infer the structural parameters from the parameters of the reduced form? If so, we need only transform the consistent OLS estimates of the reduced form to obtain consistent estimates of the structural parameters. This result follows from the rule given in Chapter 12 that $g(\text{plim}[x_n]) = \text{plim}[g(x_n)]$, transforming a consistent estimator yields a consistent estimator of the transformation!

Estimating the structural parameters by transforming the reduced form parameters is called **indirect least squares** (ILS). When we can successfully implement ILS to estimate structural parameters, those parameters are identified, because we can consistently estimate them. However, we cannot always extract the structural parameters by a transformation of the reduced form parameters—sometimes, structural parameters are underidentified. Inferring the structural parameters from the reduced form parameters requires prior knowledge about how some variables affect others. The most common prior restriction on effects of variables is to assume that some predetermined variables do not appear in some structural equations.

## Underidentified, Exactly Identified, and Overidentified Parameters

The strategy of moving from the reduced form parameters to the structural parameters succeeds for the demand relationship in Equation 14.2. Reduced forms may, indeed, support the identification of structural equations. But the strategy fails for identifying the supply relationship in Equation 14.1. Reduced forms may not support the identification of structural equations.

The reduced form equations in Equation 14.3 and 14.5 contain just enough information to uniquely determine the structural parameters of the demand equation; econometricians say the demand function is **exactly identified** in such a case. That same reduced form contains too little information to ascertain the structural parameters of the supply function; econometricians call the supply function **underidentified**. A third logical possibility is that the reduced form equations contain so much information that several different solutions exist for the structural parameters; econometricians label a structural equation whose parameters suffer this fate **overidentified**. These are the same identification concepts that we saw in Chapter 13.

## Identification in the Supply and Demand Example

In our supply and demand example, the structural equations give $P$ and $Q$ in terms of the structural parameters. The reduced form equations give $P$ and $Q$ in terms of the reduced form parameters. The representations of the reduced form in Equations 14.3 through 14.6 imply that

$$\pi_{p0} = \frac{(\alpha_0 + \beta_0\alpha_1)}{(1 - \alpha_1\beta_1)}$$

$$\pi_{p1} = \frac{\alpha_2}{(1 - \alpha_1\beta_1)}$$

$$\pi_{q0} = \frac{(\beta_0 + \alpha_0\beta_1)}{(1 - \alpha_1\beta_1)}$$

and

$$\pi_{q1} = \frac{\alpha_2\beta_1}{(1 - \alpha_1\beta_1)}.$$

14.8

These relationships among the reduced form and structural parameters imply that

$$\alpha_1\pi_{q0} = (-\alpha_0 + \pi_{p0})$$

14.9

and

$$\alpha_1\pi_{q1} = (\pi_{p1} - \alpha_2)$$

for the structural supply parameters, and for the structural demand parameters
they imply that

$$\beta_0 = \pi_{q0} - \left(\frac{\pi_{q1}\pi_{p0}}{\pi_{p1}}\right) \qquad \text{14.10}$$

and

$$\beta_1 = \frac{\pi_{q1}}{\pi_{p1}}. \qquad \text{14.11}$$

Because we have *two* relationships between the *two* structural demand parameters and the reduced form parameters, we can just determine the structural
demand parameters from the reduced form parameters; the demand equation is
exactly identified. Because we have *two* relationships among the *three* supply parameters and the reduced form parameters, however, we cannot solve for the
structural supply parameters from the reduced form equations; the supply equation is underidentified. Equations 14.10 and 14.11 support ILS estimation for the
demand equation, which is exactly identified:

$$\beta_0^{ILS} = \hat{\pi}_{q0} - \left(\frac{\hat{\pi}_{q1}\hat{\pi}_{p0}}{\hat{\pi}_{p1}}\right) \qquad \text{14.12}$$

and

$$\beta_1^{ILS} = \frac{\hat{\pi}_{q1}}{\hat{\pi}_{p1}}. \qquad \text{14.13}$$

There are no corresponding equations for the supply equation's parameters; they
are underidentified.

## A Graphical Depiction of the Identification Problem

The identification problem has a graphical representation, too. Figure 14.1, Panel
(a), shows the supply, $S^0$, and demand, $D^0$, for personal computers, with quantity
on the horizontal axis and price on the vertical axis. Panel (b) shows supply shifting with the price of plastic materials. In Panel (b), the original supply curve is to
the left of the new curves, $S^1$, $S^2$, and $S^3$, each of which corresponds to an increasingly favorable (low) price of plastic materials. Because changing the price of plastic materials affects supply, but not demand, the changing price of plastic materials
traces out the demand curve. The demand curve is identified, as we have already
determined. The supply curve is not identified because there is no variable in the
model that shifts demand without influencing supply. If there were such a variable,
supply would also be identified. For example, suppose we had a variable $I$, in-

come, that appears in the demand equation, but not in the supply equation. Figure 14.1, Panel (c), shows demand shifting with income. In Panel (c), the original demand curve is to the left of the new curves, $D^1$, $D^2$, and $D^3$, each of which corresponds to a higher income and greater demand for personal computers, which is a normal good. Because changing income affects demand, but not supply, changing income traces out the supply curve. Income identifies the supply curve.

A changing exogenous variable need not identify either supply or demand. Figure 14.2 shows supply and demand, with both affected by such an exogenous variable, $Z$. Because $Z$ shifts both supply and demand, the price quantity combinations we observe trace out neither a supply curve nor a demand curve. Indeed, we cannot distinguish with these data between the demand and supply curves $D^1$, $D^2$, and $D^3$, and $S^1$, $S^2$, and $S^3$, shown by the solid lines, and alternative demand and supply curves such as $d^1$, $d^2$, and $d^3$, and $s^1$, $s^2$, and $s^3$, depicted by the dashed lines. An exogenous variable that appears in both equations does not help

**Figure 14.1**

Identifying Supply and Demand

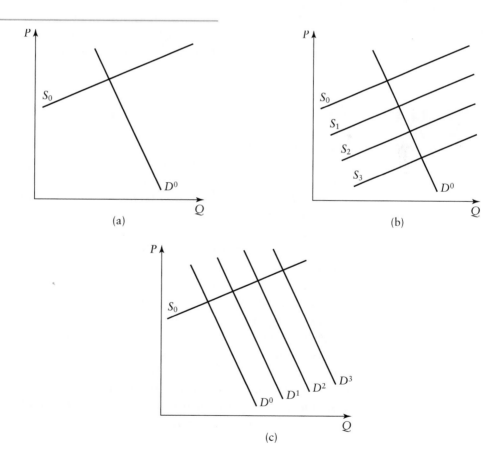

(a)

(b)

(c)

**Figure 14.2**

A Changing Exogenous Variable that Identifies Neither Supply nor Demand

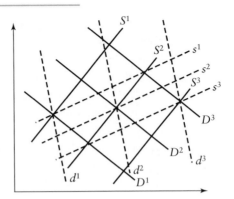

us identify either equation. Notice, too, that variables that appear in neither the demand curve nor the supply curve do not aid in distinguishing the two relationships and hence do not help in identifying either equation.[2]

## 14.4    An Application: The Fulton Fish Market

In this application, we apply the supply and demand framework to the demand and supply for fish in the Fulton Fish Market in New York City, illustrating the conceptual findings of Sections 14.1 through 14.3.

In 1995, economist Kathryn Graddy of Oxford University studied the daily supply and demand for whiting, a particular type of fish, in New York's Fulton Fish Market.[3] Graddy's study has subsequently appeared in the econometrics literature to typify simultaneous supply and demand studies.[4] Here, too, her data illustrate simultaneous equations estimation. First, we analyze the demand and supply for whiting using the same model as in the personal computer example, but with the wind speed in the fishing area off the coast of New York City playing the role of the price of plastic materials as an exogenous variable pertinent to the supply of whiting in New York City. The data are in the file whiting.*** on this book's companion Web site (**www.aw-bc.com/murray**). Ideally, we would like to know the quantity of whiting sold each day across the entire market. Instead, we examine the sales of one dealer, on the assumption that the dealer maintained a constant share of the total market (an assumption Graddy supported both theoretically and with her personal observations of the market).

The biased OLS regression for the supply relationship in Equation 14.1, adapted to the whiting market, is

$$P = -1.25 - 0.095\ Q + 0.65\ windspeed.$$
$$(0.69)\quad (0.046)\qquad (0.16)$$

The biased OLS regression for the demand relationship in Equation 14.2, adapted to the whiting market, is

$$Q = 8.42 - 0.54P.$$
$$(0.76)\quad (0.18)$$

The estimated demand equation conforms to economic theory—the estimated coefficient on price is negative as demand theory requires—but we know the OLS estimator is nonetheless inconsistent, because it suffers from simultaneity bias. In contrast, not only is the supply curve estimate inconsistent, it is at odds with economic theory, which calls for an upward sloping or horizontal supply curve. Noting that the supply curve is underidentified does not prevent us from estimating its parameters by OLS—but the results of OLS, or of any other estimation procedure, applied to the supply equation are necessarily inconsistent because supply is not identified.

The reduced form equation for quantity in this model is

$$Q = 11.21 - 0.94windspeed.$$
$$(0.94)\quad (0.33)$$

We know from the structural equations that wind speed enters into supply and demand only through the supply equation. We can therefore interpret this reduced form result with a supply story: Fewer fish are captured on days when the seas are churned up by strong winds.

The reduced form equation for price in this model is

$$P = -2.32 + 0.74windspeed.$$
$$(0.46)\quad (0.16)$$

As with the reduced form quantity equation, we can interpret this reduced form result with a supply story: Higher wind speeds at sea make catching fish more difficult; the higher prices associated with higher wind speeds in the reduced form equation reflect this difficulty. Notice that if wind speed appeared in both the supply and the demand equations, we would not be able to disentangle the supply-side effects from the demand-side effects using only the reduced form equations; the reduced form coefficients would be an amalgam of supply-side and demand-side influences.

The analysis of identification in Section 14.3 revealed that when the demand curve excludes one variable—there the price of plastic materials, here wind speed—but the supply curve excludes no variable that appears in the demand equation, the demand equation parameters are exactly identified and the supply equation parameters underidentified. We saw, too, that ILS provides consistent estimators of the demand parameters. Equation 14.13 gives the ILS estimator of the slope of the demand curve:

$$\beta_1^{ILS} = \hat{\pi}_{d1}/\hat{\pi}_{s1}.$$

This expression links the reduced form equation parameters to the slope of price in the demand curve. Using $\beta_1^{ILS}$, we obtain $-0.938/0.74 = -1.26$ as the ILS estimator of $\beta_1$. This consistent ILS estimate is 2 1/2 times the OLS estimate $(-0.54)$. Because simultaneous equations often make OLS this strongly biased, econometricians need consistent estimators to use when OLS is inconsistent.

## 14.5    ILS, Overidentification and Underidentification

**What Is the DGP?**

We've seen that ILS provides consistent estimates of exactly identified parameters. We've also seen that ILS cannot consistently estimate underidentified parameters (no estimator can). Can ILS also provide consistent estimates of overidentified parameters? Is there anything that an econometrician can say empirically about underidentified parameters? This section addresses these questions.

### Identification and the DGP

Identification is a property of the DGP. The identification of a structural equation logically precedes estimating the equation's parameters. The relationships among reduced form and structural parameters hold among the true parameters; they are not simply characteristics of estimates.

For example, if we had an infinite number of observations, and therefore knew with certainty the true values of the reduced form coefficients for the supply and demand model of Equations 14.1 and 14.2, we would still be unable to determine the supply equation parameters of Equation 14.1. An infinite set of possible structural parameters would be equally consistent with the reduced form information. As noted earlier, econometricians say that such sets of possible structural parameter values are observationally equivalent. The essence of an underidentified equation is that no amount of data will permit us to consistently estimate its true parameters; we cannot distinguish among all the observationally equivalent alternatives.

## A Surfeit of Riches: Overidentification

Structural equations may be underidentified, exactly identified, or overidentified. Overidentification occurs when there are more relationships among the structural parameters of an equation and the reduced form parameters than there are structural parameters in the equation. When a parameter is overidentified, ILS does not provide a unique estimate of the parameter but, rather, multiple estimates. This richness, however, is not an embarrassment; we will see that overidentification is actually a desirable trait for a DGP's parameters.

In essence, when faced with determining the structural parameters from the reduced form parameters, we have more equations than we have unknowns. Viewed from a population perspective, overidentification poses no logical difficulty. The numerous relationships among the reduced form parameters and the structural parameters are mutually consistent with one another; they all hold true at once. However, when we turn to estimation, overidentification presents us with a practical problem.

In estimation, we do not work with the actual values of the reduced form equations. We work with estimates of those parameters. If we estimate the reduced form equations by OLS, as is reasonable, we do not impose the identifying restrictions on our data. Consequently, our empirical estimates may not satisfy all the theoretical restrictions that do hold among the actual reduced form parameters. However, we can choose one subset or another of the theoretical restrictions, a subset just large enough to exactly determine a set of structural estimates from the reduced form estimates.

In infinite samples, it does not matter which subset of restrictions we choose to rely on; they are all mutually consistent with one another. But in finite samples, when our reduced form estimates differ from the true reduced form parameters, we will get different estimates of the structural parameters, depending on the restriction we choose to impose. Thus, estimating structural parameters of overidentified equations from reduced form parameter estimates has a degree of arbitrariness that makes it an unappealing strategy, even though all the arbitrary choices do yield consistent estimates of the structural parameters if we estimate the reduced form parameters consistently.

Overidentification poses practical problems, but more information is better than less. Overidentification is, on balance, an attractive trait in a DGP. The consistent estimators for simultaneous equations models that we devise in the next sections generally perform better in finite samples when the parameters being estimated are overidentified.

## Overidentification in the Supply and Demand Model

The difficulty that overidentification poses for ILS appears in the supply and demand model of Equations 14.1 and 14.2 if we assume that $\beta_0$ is zero, that is, that the demand curve is a straight line through the origin. What would become of the ILS procedure? When $\beta_0 = 0$, the relationships in Equation 14.8 simplify to

$$\pi_{p0} = \frac{(\alpha_0)}{(1 - \alpha_1\beta_1)}$$

$$\pi_{p1} = \frac{(\alpha_2)}{(1 - \alpha_1\beta_1)}$$

$$\pi_{q0} = \frac{(\alpha_0\beta_1)}{(1 - \alpha_1\beta_1)}$$

$$\pi_{q1} = \frac{(\alpha_2\beta_1)}{(1 - \alpha_1\beta_1)}.$$

Consequently, we can derive *two* expressions for $\beta_1$:

$$\beta_1 = \frac{\pi_{q0}}{\pi_{p0}}$$

and

$$\beta_1 = \frac{\pi_{q1}}{\pi_{p1}}.$$

Thus, when we exclude both the price of plastic materials and the constant term from the demand equation, the slope of the demand equation becomes overidentified. ILS leaves us with several alternative estimators to choose from.

In any given sample, we have no assurances that the estimated reduced form coefficients will coincide with their population values. Thus, estimating $\beta_1$ with the OLS estimates of $\pi_{p0}$, $\pi_{q0}$, $\pi_{p1}$, and $\pi_{q1}$ yields two different estimates of $\beta_1$. Asymptotically, both estimators converge on the true value of $\beta_1$.

## Underidentification in the Supply and Demand Model

We have now seen that overidentification indicates we have more information than we minimally need to consistently estimate a parameter, and that exact identification indicates we have the minimally required information to consistently estimate a parameter. The truly troublesome case arises when we have underidentification, or too little information to consistently estimate a parameter. Note well though, that underidentification does *not* mean we have *no* information about the parameters in the underidentified equation. It only means we cannot, even in principle, sensibly estimate the underidentified structural parameters. We may be able to do some other worthwhile things, however.

In particular, even though we cannot test hypotheses about the value of a particular parameter, we may be able to test hypotheses about joint restrictions on several of the parameters of the structural equation. For example, in the supply and demand model of Equations 14.1 and 14.2, Equations 14.3 through 14.6 led to Equation 14.9

$$\alpha_1 \pi_{q0} = (-\alpha_0 + \pi_{p0}).$$

Therefore, if someone hypothesizes that $\alpha_0 = 4$ and $\alpha_1 = 6$ in the structural supply equation, we could use the reduced form equation to test the hypothesis that $6\pi_{q0} = (-4 + \pi_{p0})$, despite the fact that both $\alpha_0$ and $\alpha_1$ are underidentified.

## 14.6    Instrumental Variables and Simultaneity Bias

**How Do We Make an Estimator?**

How do we estimate overidentified structural equations? OLS suffers from simultaneity bias when estimating structural equations. ILS isn't suitable for estimating overidentified structural equations because there isn't a unique mapping from reduced form parameters to structural parameters when an equation is overidentified. This section argues that the instrumental variables (IV) estimator introduced in Chapter 13 can consistently estimate identified structural equations.

### Instrumental Variables and Simultaneous Equations

We have already learned that the inconsistency of OLS for estimating simultaneous equations arises because endogenous explanatory variables are, in general, contemporaneously correlated with the disturbances. In the demand equation, $E(p_i \varepsilon_i^d) > 0$; in the supply equation, $E(q_i \varepsilon_i^s) < 0$, both of which violate the requirements for OLS to be a consistent estimator. This important result is worth another look. We have also learned in Chapter 13 that IV estimation can consistently estimate equations in which explanators and disturbances are contemporaneously correlated. This important result is also worth revisiting. The IV estimator, which, in the case of a straight line through the origin, is

$$\beta_{IV} = \frac{\sum Z_i Y_i}{\sum Z_i X_i},$$

weights observations by a variable that is both correlated with a troublesome explanator and uncorrelated with the equation's disturbances, asymptotically. This practice, we shall now see once more, yields consistent estimates of the equation's parameters.

For estimating the slope of a straight line through the origin, the OLS estimator, $\beta_{g4}$, is inconsistent if the disturbances and the explanator, $X$, are contemporaneously correlated. But if we find a variable, $Z$, that is both correlated with $X$, and uncorrelated with the disturbances, then

$$\beta_{IV} = \frac{\sum Z_i Y_i}{\sum Z_i X_i} = \frac{\sum Z_i(\beta X_i + \varepsilon_i)}{\sum Z_i X_i} = \beta + \frac{\sum Z_i \varepsilon_i}{\sum Z_i X_i} = \beta + \frac{\frac{1}{n}\sum Z_i \varepsilon_i}{\frac{1}{n}\sum Z_i X_i}$$

is a consistent estimator of $\beta$ because $\text{plim}(\beta_{IV}) = \beta$. To see this, consider

$$\text{plim}(\beta_{IV}) = \text{plim}\left(\beta + \frac{\frac{1}{n}\sum Z_i \varepsilon_i}{\frac{1}{n}\sum Z_i X_i}\right),$$

which we can rewrite as

$$\text{plim}(\beta_{IV}) = \text{plim}\left(\beta + \frac{\frac{1}{n}\sum Z_i \varepsilon_i}{\frac{1}{n}\sum Z_i X_i}\right) = \beta + \text{plim}\left(\frac{\frac{1}{n}\sum Z_i \varepsilon_i}{\frac{1}{n}\sum Z_i X_i}\right),$$

because, according to the rules from Chapter 12, the plim of a sum is the sum of the plims and the plim of a constant is the constant. Also, because the plim of a ratio is the ratio of the plims, as long as the plim in the denominator is not zero, we can write

$$\beta + \text{plim}\left(\frac{\frac{1}{n}\sum Z_i \varepsilon_i}{\frac{1}{n}\sum Z_i X_i}\right)$$

as

$$\beta + \frac{\text{plim}\left(\frac{1}{n}\sum Z_i \varepsilon_i\right)}{\text{plim}\left(\frac{1}{n}\sum Z_i X_i\right)}.$$

We choose the variable $Z$ such that $Z$ and $X$ are correlated asymptotically, so $\text{plim}\left(\frac{1}{n}\sum Z_i X_i \neq 0\right)$. We also choose $Z$ such that $Z$ and $\varepsilon$ are uncorrelated asymptotically, so $\text{plim}\left(\frac{1}{n}\sum Z_i \varepsilon_i\right) = 0$. Thus, $\beta_{IV}$ is, indeed, a consistent estimator of $\beta$:

$$\text{plim}(\beta_{IV}) = \beta + \frac{\text{plim}\left(\frac{1}{n}\sum Z_i \varepsilon_i\right)}{\text{plim}\left(\frac{1}{n}\sum Z_i X_i\right)} = \beta + 0 = \beta.$$

The multiple regression extension of this IV estimator consistently estimates the coefficients of equations in which the explanators are contemporaneously correlated with the disturbances. Thus, the IV estimator promises to consistently estimate identified structural equations. The key to fulfilling this promise is finding suitable instrumental variables.

Valid instruments are as follows:

1. They are contemporaneously correlated with the troublesome explanators, those explanators that are contemporaneously correlated with the disturbances. In the simultaneous equations context, this means that valid instruments must be correlated with an equation's endogenous explanators.
2. They are contemporaneously uncorrelated with the disturbances. In the simultaneous equations context, exogenous variables and untroublesome lagged endogenous variables have this characteristic.

## Instrumental Variables and the Demand for Personal Computers

Which instrumental variables could we use to estimate the demand for personal computers as given by Equation 14.2? $P$ is the troublesome variable in the demand equation. What variable might we use as an instrument for $P$? A quick check of the supply and demand equations suggests $M$ as a natural instrument for $P$. A lower price for plastic materials drives costs down for producers, tending the system toward lower prices. A higher price of plastic materials has the opposite effect. Hence, $M$ is plausibly correlated with $P$. Moreover, as an exogenous variable, $M$ is uncorrelated with the disturbances. Therefore, $M$ meets both requirements for a viable instrumental variable. We can consistently estimate the parameters of the demand equation using an IV estimator.

Now consider the supply equation for personal computers. $Q$ is the troublesome variable in the supply equation. What instrument might we use for $Q$? Unfortunately, all the variables relevant to the problem already appear in the supply equation: The constant term, $Q$, and $M$ are explanators, and $P$ is the dependent variable. If we were to use $M$ as an instrument for $Q$, as we proposed doing for $P$ to estimate the demand equation, the instrument for $P$, which is $M$, would be perfectly correlated with the explanator $M$. The IV estimator would, consequently, suffer from perfect multicollinearity and therefore not exist. Similarly, the constant term appears in the supply equation, so it cannot be used as an instrument for $Q$, although it, like $M$, is an exogenous variable. Consequently, no variable is available for use as an instrumental variable to consistently estimate the supply equation. This lack of the instruments necessary for conducting IV estimation reflects the underidentification of the supply equation.

Our success in finding an appropriate instrument for $P$ in the demand equation highlights the central role of the untroublesome variables in a system in providing instrumental variables. Exogenous variables are always candidate instrumental variables, because exogenous variables are, by definition, uncorrelated with the disturbances. If the disturbances in a model are serially uncorrelated,

**TABLE 14.1  The Demand for Whiting Estimated by Instrumental Variables**

Dependent Variable: QTY
Method: Two-Stage Least Squares
Sample: 1 111
Included observations: 111
Instrument list: C WINDSPD

| Variable | Coefficient | Std. Error | t-Statistic | Prob. |
|----------|-------------|------------|-------------|-------|
| C | 8.278343 | 0.117064 | 70.71667 | 0.0000 |
| PRICE | −1.265414 | 0.473054 | −2.674989 | 0.0086 |
| R-squared | −0.061634 | Mean dependent var | | 8.523430 |
| Adjusted R-squared | −0.071373 | S.D. dependent var | | 0.741672 |
| S.E. of regression | 0.767684 | Sum squared resid | | 64.23788 |
| F-statistic | 7.155565 | Durbin–Watson stat | | 1.270212 |
| Prob(F-statistic) | 0.008625 | | | |

lagged endogenous variables are also candidate instrumental variables. In contrast, the endogenous variables in the system do not help us in building instrumental variables because they themselves are contemporaneously correlated with the disturbances in the system.

## More Fish: IV Estimation and the Fulton Fish Market

To see the IV approach to estimating simultaneous equations at work, let's return to the Fulton Fish Market. Table 14.1 contains the IV regression for the demand for whiting fish in New York's Fulton Fish Market, based on Graddy's data. Wind speed is the instrumental variable for price in the demand equation. (The negative $R^2$ in the table stems from using an estimator other than OLS. Only for OLS is the $R^2$ measure a proportion bounded between zero and one.)

The IV estimator of the slope coefficient on this example is the same as the ILS estimate, −1.26. This result reflects a general characteristic of the IV estimator: When an equation is exactly identified, the IV estimator coincides with the ILS estimator. The output for the IV estimation also provides the estimated standard error for the IV and ILS estimators: 0.47.

# An Econometric Top 40—A Golden Oldie

## The Supply and Demand for Watermelons

Agricultural economists pioneered the use of econometrics because the supply and demand for agricultural products are natural targets for econometric study. Some of the first to estimate supply or demand functions understood that the simultaneous determination of price and quantity could invalidate OLS estimates of demand and supply elasticities, but the formal techniques for estimating simultaneous equation models that make up the heart of this chapter were created by the macroeconomists of the 1930s and 1940s.

When the macroeconomists developed their new tools, the agricultural economists were quick to recognize the applicability of the new estimators to supply and demand. In 1955, Daniel Suits of the University of Michigan published the first study to apply the then new simultaneous equations estimation procedures to supply and demand.[5] He selected the watermelon market for his work, using annual national data from the United States for the years 1930–1951.

Suits's work is novel in recognizing that suppliers make two decisions: planting and harvesting. He specifies a watermelon-planting equation that depends on the previous year's price of watermelon, price of cotton (which Suits treats as the opportunity cost of planting watermelon for southern producers), and the average price of "truck farm produce" (which Suits treats as the opportunity cost of planting watermelon for northern producers). Suits then specifies a harvesting equation that depends on the current price of watermelon, the cost of transporting watermelons to market, and the quantity of watermelons under cultivation. These two equations complete the supply side

of the watermelon market. On the demand side, Suits specifies that the price consumers are willing to pay depends on income and on the quantity of watermelons consumed.

Suits argues that because the explanators in the planting equation are all predetermined, he can validly apply OLS to that equation. He estimates the harvest and demand equations with the simultaneous equations technique called *limited information maximum likelihood* (LIML). LIML first appeared in the literature in 1949[6] and is described in an online extension. Suits estimates that the elasticity of planting with respect to the previous year's watermelon price is 0.6, that the cross-price elasticity of planting with respect to the previous year's cotton price is −0.3, and that the cross-price elasticity of planting with respect to the previous year's truck farm produce is −0.1. He estimates that the elasticity of the harvest with respect to the current price of watermelons is 0.2. (Suits argues, reasonably, that price should influence planting more than harvesting, as he finds.) Finally, Suits estimates an income elasticity of demand equal to 1.4 and a price elasticity of −0.9. All these estimated elasticities, except for the truck farm produce price elasticity, are significantly different from zero.

Because planting depends on past prices, not current prices, Suits's model has a dynamic dimension absent from the other supply and demand models in this chapter. Suits computes the dynamic equilibrium path of prices implied by his model for his sample period, 1930–1951, and compares that estimated equilibrium path with the observed path of crops and prices. He also uses his model to forecast watermelon crops and watermelon prices through

1954. Suits's forecasts performed reasonably well in those years.

### Final Notes

Suits was the first agricultural economist to borrow the macroeconometricians' new estimation procedures, but an even earlier agricultural economist had independently solved the simultaneity problem. In 1928, the Brookings Institution's Phillip G. Wright published a study of the demand and supply of flax seed.[7] Wright avoided the simultaneity bias of OLS by proposing an alternative estimator that we now call the IV estimator. Sadly, Wright's contribution, in the appendix of a book on animal and vegetable oils, went unnoticed by econometricians; it was not until 1949 when R. C. Geary independently published the IV strategy[8] in a widely read journal that econometricians added IV estimation to their toolkit. Wright's unfortunate obscurity reminds us that productive academic advances occur not in isolation, but as part of a broad conversation.

■

## 14.7 Optimal Instruments and Two-Stage Least Squares

**HOW DO WE MAKE AN ESTIMATOR?**

Earlier in this chapter, choosing an instrument for $P$ in the personal computer and whiting fish demand equation examples was simplified because there was only one viable candidate—the price of plastic materials, in the one case, and wind speed, in the other. What would we have done if there had been two untroublesome variables in the supply equation that were excluded from the demand equation? For example, suppose supply depended on both transport costs for plastic ($T$) and the price of crude oil ($C$). Which variable would we choose as an instrument, $T$ or $C$? Or would we use some combination of the two? This section reviews the strategy for choosing among candidate instruments developed in Chapter 13. The section also reviews the steps of the two-stage least squares (2SLS) estimator, also detailed in Chapter 13, that econometricians generally use to conduct IV estimation.

### Choosing Optimal Instruments

The intuition that first led to IV estimation leads us to an appropriate strategy for choosing an instrument for $P$. The role of our instruments is to weight our observations in an efficient fashion. The troublesome variables would be an excellent guide to such efficient weighting, but using them gives rise to the bias problems that we wish to avoid. Our instruments are meant to achieve a similar weighting without bringing the bias that plagues weighting by the troublesome variables. It thus is appealing to choose an instrument that is as highly correlated with the troublesome variable as is possible without choosing an instrument correlated with the disturbances; this comes as close as we dare go to weighting as OLS would. In the personal computers example, the linear combination of $C$ and $T$ that would be most highly correlated with $P$ would be the fitted value from a regression of $P$ on $C$, $T$, and a constant term. These fitted values generate the most (asymptotically) efficient combination of $C$, $T$, and a constant term for use as an instrument in an IV estimator. This is the strategy for performing IV estimation with competing instruments detailed in Chapter 13.

## Two-Stage Least Squares

In practice, econometricians have calculated the IV estimator for simultaneous equations models by employing an alternative but equivalent strategy, called two-stage least squares. The 2SLS estimation procedure has two steps:

1. Construct fitted values for all the troublesome explanators from the reduced form equations of the model. That is, estimate the reduced form by OLS and compute the fitted values for all the troublesome explanators based on their reduced form equations.
2. Estimate each structural equation by OLS but with the fitted values of troublesome variables from step 1's reduced form equations replacing the troublesome variables themselves.

As long as the instruments used in step 2 are the fitted values from the system's reduced form, the 2SLS formulae give the same result as IV estimation, so 2SLS is a consistent estimator. (Appendix 13.B proves this result.)

If we were to use an econometric software package's OLS command to conduct step 2 of 2SLS, the reported standard errors on the coefficients would be incorrect because they would not take into account the fact that the explanators are fitted values from another regression. According to Equation 13.9, the asymptotic variance of the IV estimator, and, therefore, of the equivalent 2SLS estimator, is

$$\frac{1}{n}\sigma^2 \frac{\text{plim}\left(\frac{1}{n}\Sigma\ \hat{p}_i^2\right)}{\text{plim}\left(\frac{1}{n}\Sigma\ \hat{p}_i p_i\right)^2},$$

not

$$\frac{\sigma^2}{\text{plim}\left(\frac{1}{n}\Sigma\ \hat{p}_i^2\right)},$$

as OLS packages assume. The 2SLS commands in econometric software packages report the correct standard errors, accounting for the constructed nature of the second-stage explanators. Notice that the output in Table 14.1 reports the estimation method as 2SLS.

If the disturbances and explanators are contemporaneously correlated, the test procedures developed in Chapters 7 through 13 are valid asymptotically when the estimator is 2SLS if the other Gauss–Markov Assumptions are met. We saw in Chapter 13 that the appropriate $F$-statistic is slightly altered from the OLS case. For $F$-tests based on OLS, the numerator of the test statistic contains the difference between the sums of squared residuals from the constrained and unconstrained regressions, and the denominator contains the sum of squared residuals from the unconstrained regression. For $F$-tests based on 2SLS, the numerator of the test statistic contains the difference between the sums of squared residuals in the second stage of 2SLS, with and without the hypothesized constraints imposed, $SSR^2_{u2SLS}$ and $SSR^2_{c2SLS}$; these residuals are based on the fitted values of the explanators that appear in the second stage of 2SLS. However, the sum of squared residuals used to estimate the disturbances in the denominator is the sum of squared residuals in the unconstrained regression, based on the actual explanator values, $SSR^2_u$. These residuals are

$$\tilde{e}^u_i = Y_i - \sum_{j=0}^{k} \tilde{\beta}^u_j X_i,$$

where the $\tilde{\beta}^u_j$ are the unconstrained 2SLS coefficient estimates. The residuals for $SSR^2_{u2SLS}$ differ from those for $SSR^2_u$ in that they use $\hat{X}_i$, instead of $X_i$. The $F$-statistic for $F$-tests that rely on 2SLS is

$$F = \frac{(SSR^2_{c2SLS} - SSR^2_{u2SLS})/r}{SSR^2_u/(n - k - 1)},$$

where $r$ is the number of constraints imposed by the null hypothesis. The degrees of freedom are, as with OLS-based $F$-tests, $r$ and $(n - k - 1)$.

## 14.8    Order and Rank Conditions for Identification

WHAT IS THE DGP?

This section explores more deeply the connection between the identification of a structural equation and finding suitable instruments for IV estimation of that equation. Econometricians have found two conditions for determining whether a structural equation is identified. One is necessary for identification. If it is not met, the equation is not identified. The other condition is sufficient for identification. If it is met, the equation is identified.

### The Order Condition for Identification

Not just any predetermined variable can serve as an instrument for a troublesome variable. A predetermined variable that already appears in a specific equation cannot serve as an instrument for a troublesome variable in that same equation; instrumental variables cannot be perfectly collinear with other explanators or other instruments. (Recall from Chapter 13 that in IV estimation, nontroublesome variables serve as their own instruments.) Thus, we cannot consistently estimate a structural equation with troublesome explanators unless at least one untroublesome variable is excluded from the equation. For example, the price of plastic materials is excluded from the demand equation for personal computers, so that equation might be identified, but no untroublesome variable is excluded from the supply equation, so that equation is not identified.

Excluding a single untroublesome variable can fall short of identifying an equation. If there are several troublesome variables in a specific structural equation, we need a different instrument for each of those variables—using the same instrument twice would mean we had perfectly collinear instruments. *If we are to consistently estimate a structural equation by instrumental variables, that structural equation must exclude at least one untroublesome variable for each troublesome variable in the equation.* Econometricians call this condition the **order condition for identification**. The order condition is necessary, but not sufficient, for identification.

## Exclusion Restrictions and Covariance Restrictions

We have seen that in the simultaneous supply and demand model, excluding the intercept term makes an exactly identified equation overidentified. We usually employ a similar strategy to identify equations within simultaneous equations models. We assume that some variables, either exogenous variables or lagged dependent variables, are contemporaneously uncorrelated with the disturbances in our equations. We call this assumption a **covariance restriction**. We also assume that some of these untroublesome variables are excluded from certain structural equations. We call this assumption an **exclusion restriction**.

IV estimation exploits the covariance restriction that makes a variable $Z$ exogenous to estimate the effects of an endogenous explanator, $Y^*$. The variable $Z$ works as an instrument for the endogenous explanator only if $Z$ is not itself a variable in the equation, which is an exclusion restriction, and only if $Z$ and $Y^*$ are asymptotically correlated, which is yet another covariance restriction.

## The Rank Condition for Identification

The order condition says that an equation is not identified if there are not enough exclusion and covariance restrictions. But does having the called-for number of exclusion and covariance restrictions guarantee that the equation is identified? Unfortunately, it does not. The order condition is necessary, but not sufficient, to ensure identification through exclusions. We may exclude enough predetermined variables from an equation and still fail to identify the equation. To understand the potential difficulty, consider the slightly altered demand and supply model for personal computers, in which the supply curve is

$$P_i = \alpha_0 + \alpha_1 Q_i + \alpha_2 M_i + \varepsilon_i^s,$$

which, unlike Equation 14.1, contains $M_i$ as an explanator, the demand curve is still

$$Q_i = \beta_0 + \beta_1 P_i + \beta_2 M_i + \varepsilon_i^d,$$

and there is an equation for the price of plastic materials:

$$M_i = \gamma_0 + \gamma_1 transport\ cost_i + \gamma_2 crude\ oil\ price_i + \varepsilon_i^w.$$

This simultaneous system contains three endogenous variables: the price of personal computers, the quantity of personal computers, and the price of plastic materials. The system also contains three exogenous variables: the constant term, transport costs, and the price of crude oil.

The price of plastic materials equation is identified because it only contains exogenous explanators. Neither the supply curve nor the demand curve is identified, though, despite each excluding not just one, but two, exogenous variables. What is the difficulty? The demand and supply curves both exclude *the same* exogenous variables, and shifts in those two variables affect both supply and demand, working through $M_i$. When either transport costs for plastic or the price of crude oil shifts, both supply and demand are affected (through shifts in $M_i$)—we do not trace out either curve by examining how price and quantity vary as transport costs or the price of crude oil varies. Satisfying the order condition is necessary for identification, but not sufficient. *For an equation to be identified by exclusion restrictions, or by other restrictions on the parameters of predetermined variables, each equation needs its own distinct identifying restrictions.* The mathematical representation of an equation having its own distinct identifying restrictions is called the **rank condition for identification**. The rank condition is necessary and sufficient for an equation to be identified.

The requirement that an equation have its own distinct identifying restrictions does not mean that a single exogenous variable can't be excluded from two equations if they are both to be identified. Suppose that in addition to transport costs and the price of crude oil, our model had another exogenous variable that measures software availability. Excluding transport costs and the price of crude oil from the personal computer demand equation would be a set of exclusion restrictions distinct from excluding transport costs and software availability from the personal computer supply equation.

Appendix 14.A, which can be found in Extension 5 on this book's Web site (**www .aw-bc.com/murray**), uses matrix algebra to derive the rank and order conditions for identification, using a matrix representation of simultaneous equations models.

## Some Rules of Thumb for Identification

Several rules of thumb for checking the identification of equations in a simultaneous system can spare us from the often tedious chore of checking the formal rank condition:

1. If each equation contains an untroublesome variable that appears in no other equation, all the equations of the system are identified.
2. An equation with no troublesome explanators is identified.
3. An equation that excludes no variables at all is not identified.
4. An equation that excludes fewer untroublesome variables than it has endogenous explanators is not identified (the order condition).
5. If two equations contain the same set of variables, differing only in which is the dependent variable, neither equation is identified.
6. If a proper subset of the variables in one equation are the only variables in a second equation, the first equation is not identified.
7. If the variables excluded from one equation do not contain at least one variable from each other equation, the one equation is not identified.

## Hausman's Test of Overidentifying Restrictions

2SLS consistently estimates an equation only if the covariance restrictions on which we rely to identify that equations are correct. In practice, econometricians are frequently unsure whether one variable or another is, indeed, uncorrelated with the disturbances. Testing the covariance restrictions is made difficult by the fact that an underidentified equation cannot be consistently estimated. We cannot test restrictions that exactly identify an equation because we cannot consistently estimate the equation without relying on those restrictions. Only when an equation is overidentified can we test some of the identifying restrictions.

Econometrician Jerry Hausman of MIT provides a test for the validity of instruments in excess of those needed to identify an equation exactly.[9] Hausman's test does not require naming the culprits among the proposed instruments, nor does it tell us the culprits. The null hypothesis in Hausman's test is that all the variables that are assumed to be nontroublesome are, in fact, nontroublesome. However, the test is inconsistent unless the equation is overidentified. Consequently, the test does not apply to underidentified or exactly identified equations. Hausman's test has two steps:

1. Estimate the model by 2SLS using all the proposed instruments (including any nontroublesome $X$'s) to create instruments in the first stage of 2SLS.

Form residuals based on the actual $X$- and $Y$-values and the 2SLS parameter estimates. (Notice that these are *not* the residuals from the second-stage regression in 2SLS, which would be based on the fitted $X$-values from the first stage of 2SLS.)

2. Regress the residuals from step 1 against all the proposed instruments used in the first stage of 2SLS. Conduct an $F$-test of the null hypothesis that all the coefficients in this regression are zero. Alternatively, use $n$ times the $R^2$ from this regression as the test statistic; it is distributed chi-square asymptotically, with degrees of freedom equal to the number of instruments in excess of the number of troublesome explanators. The null hypothesis is that the extra instruments are valid.

If 2SLS provided exactly correct parameter estimates, the residuals constructed in step 1 would be the disturbances in the model. Step 2 would then be directly testing the null hypothesis that the disturbances are uncorrelated with each and every proposed instrument. This would be a fine test of the validity of the proposed instruments. Because 2SLS is consistent under that null hypothesis, in large samples, the Hausman test almost certainly closely approximates the test with the true disturbances.

Hausman originally proposed using the chi-square test based on $nR^2$, but the asymptotically equivalent $F$-test seems to perform better in small to moderately sized samples. As in all 2SLS $F$-tests, the $F$-statistic uses in its numerator the change in the sum of squared residuals based on the fitted values of the explanators, and in its denominator the sum of squared residuals based on the true explanator values. Unfortunately, Hausman's test suffers from considerable size distortions in small samples, so it is most useful with large samples and is not at all useful in small samples.

An attractive feature of the Hausman procedure is that it tests for the validity of any subset of extra instruments. When we fail to reject the null hypothesis using the Hausman test, our confidence is shored up in all our instruments (though the result could also stem from the test being weak in our application), as long as we believe *some* set of exactly identifying restrictions does hold true. On the other hand, the same feature is unattractive when the test rejects the null hypothesis; the rejection provides no information about which instruments are invalid.

In large samples, Hausman's test has power against alternatives in which proposed instruments are correlated with the disturbances. Hausman's test does not detect weak instruments, that is, instruments uncorrelated with the disturbances, but only weakly correlated with the explanators.

## 14.9   An Application: 2SLS at the Fulton Fish Market

To see the 2SLS estimation procedure at work, let's return once more to Graddy's Fulton Fish Market data. Graddy's data contain more information than we used earlier. Six weather-related indicators can be reasonably assumed to be exogenous: rainy, stormy, mixed, cold, and two measures of wind speed. Including these additional variables in the supply equation makes demand overidentified. We now write the supply curve for whiting as

$$price_t = \alpha_0 + \alpha_1 QTY_t + \alpha_2 windspd_t + \alpha_3 cold_t + \alpha_4 rainy_t \\ + \alpha_5 stormy_t + \alpha_6 mixed_t + \alpha_7 windspd2_t + \varepsilon_t^s.$$

Table 14.2 reports the 2SLS estimates of the demand equation with all six exogenous weather-related variables included in the first-stage reduced form. The coefficient on price is 25% smaller than in Table 14.1. Furthermore, the standard error of the price coefficient estimate has fallen from 0.47 to 0.38—the additional excluded exogenous variables support a more efficient IV estimator for the demand equation.

### TABLE 14.2  2SLS Estimates of the Overidentified Demand for Whiting

Dependent Variable: QTY
Method: Two-Stage Least Squares
Sample: 1 111
Included observations: 111
Instrument list: C WINDSPD WINDSPD2 COLD RAINY MIXED STORMY

| Variable | Coefficient | Std. Error | t-Statistic | Prob. |
|---|---|---|---|---|
| C | 8.324852 | 0.101988 | 81.62585 | 0.0000 |
| PRICE | −1.025282 | 0.382113 | −2.683191 | 0.0084 |
| R-squared | 0.015352 | Mean dependent var | | 8.523430 |
| Adjusted R-squared | 0.006319 | S.D. dependent var | | 0.741672 |
| S.E. of regression | 0.739325 | Sum squared resid | | 59.57958 |
| F-statistic | 7.199512 | Durbin–Watson stat | | 1.383351 |
| Prob(F-statistic) | 0.008429 | | | |

Graddy's work offers an even richer specification of the supply and demand model for whiting. The demand for whiting varies systematically across the days of the week. Consequently, we can specify the demand curve more elaborately as

$$QTY_t = \beta_0 + \beta_1 price_t + \beta_2 monday_t + \beta_3 tuesday_t$$
$$+ \beta_4 wednesday_t + \beta_5 thursday_t + \varepsilon_t^d,$$

where the days of the week indicate dummy variables for those days. The day-of-the-week dummies offer exogenous variables that are excluded from the supply equation.

With the exogenous day-of-the-week variables excluded from the supply equation, that equation is now identified, even overidentified. With the additional weather-related variables excluded from the demand equation, but included in the supply equation, the demand equation moves from being exactly identified to being overidentified. We can now use 2SLS to estimate both supply and demand by 2SLS.

**TABLE 14.3** 2SLS Estimates of Supply and Demand for Whiting When Both Equations Are Identified

Panel A Demand
Dependent Variable: QTY
Method: Two-Stage Least Squares
Sample: 1 111
Included observations: 111
Instrument list: C WINDSPD WINDSPD2 COLD RAINY MIXED
STORMY DAY1 DAY2 DAY3 DAY4

| Variable | Coefficient | Std. Error | t-Statistic | Prob. |
|---|---|---|---|---|
| C | 8.539577 | 0.156067 | 54.71736 | 0.0000 |
| PRICE | −0.933768 | 0.345268 | −2.704469 | 0.0080 |
| DAY1 | −0.012161 | 0.208390 | −0.058355 | 0.9536 |
| DAY2 | −0.525926 | 0.202373 | −2.598797 | 0.0107 |
| DAY3 | −0.562691 | 0.207042 | −2.717764 | 0.0077 |
| DAY4 | 0.100051 | 0.202898 | 0.493109 | 0.6230 |
| R-squared | 0.184330 | Mean dependent var | | 8.523430 |
| Adjusted R-squared | 0.145489 | S.D. dependent var | | 0.741672 |
| S.E. of regression | 0.685600 | Sum squared resid | | 49.35496 |
| F-statistic | 5.001714 | Durbin–Watson stat | | 1.349732 |
| Prob(F-statistic) | 0.000378 | | | |

Table 14.3 reports the 2SLS estimates for demand and supply based on this expanded list of exogenous variables. The estimated coefficient for *price* is somewhat smaller than in Table 14.2, and its estimated standard error is slightly smaller. The *t*-statistics for the day-of-the-week variables indicate that demand does shift across the days. Based on the *t*-statistic for *quantity*, 0.41, in Panel B, we fail to reject the hypothesis that the supply price is unaffected by quantity, that is, that supply is perfectly elastic.[10] Unfortunately, the estimated standard error on QTY is large; we do not have precise information about the relationship between price and quantity in the supply function. The test of the hypothesis that supply is perfectly elastic is low in power because of the high variance of the estimated effect of quantity on price. We do, however, see that stormy and mixed weather both lead to higher marginal costs for the suppliers of whiting fish.

The Durbin–Watson statistics in these equations, especially in the supply equation, should give us pause about relying on the usual estimated standard errors. However, using Newey–West estimated standard errors instead does not, in

**TABLE 14.3** (*continued*)
Panel B Supply
Dependent Variable: PRICE
Method: Two-Stage Least Squares
Sample: 1 111
Included observations: 111
Instrument list: C WINDSPD WINDSPD2 RAINY COLD MIXED

STORMY DAY1 DAY2 DAY3 DAY4

| Variable | Coefficient | Std. Error | t-Statistic | Prob. |
|---|---|---|---|---|
| C | −3.080187 | 5.872025 | −0.524553 | 0.6010 |
| QTY | 0.050564 | 0.124702 | 0.405474 | 0.6860 |
| WINDSPD | 1.446541 | 4.067415 | 0.355641 | 0.7228 |
| RAINY | −0.003661 | 0.093281 | −0.039249 | 0.9688 |
| COLD | 0.046887 | 0.077916 | 0.601763 | 0.5487 |
| STORMY | 0.388965 | 0.143127 | 2.717621 | 0.0077 |
| MIXED | 0.212301 | 0.096118 | 2.208745 | 0.0294 |
| WINDSPD2 | −0.228898 | 0.705276 | −0.324551 | 0.7462 |
| R-squared | 0.193912 | Mean dependent var | | −0.193681 |
| Adjusted R-squared | 0.139129 | S.D. dependent var | | 0.381935 |
| S.E. of regression | 0.354371 | Sum squared resid | | 12.93460 |
| F-statistic | 4.282148 | Durbin–Watson stat | | 0.733186 |
| Prob(F-statistic) | 0.000343 | | | |

this case, alter any of the inferences we have drawn—the robust standard error estimates do not differ much from the standard estimates of Table 14.3. As always, the low Durbin–Watson statistics should spur us to ask if we have omitted any important variables whose omission might be biasing our estimates.

## Testing the Overidentifying Restrictions in the Whiting Market

Are the overidentifying restrictions in the supply and demand equations for whiting valid? Let's use Hausman's test to answer this question. The residuals from the 2SLS estimation of the demand equation are named *hdresid*. Table 14.4, Panel A,

**TABLE 14.4** Testing the Overidentifying Restrictions on the Supply and Demand for Whiting

Panel A Demand
Dependent Variable: HDRESID
Method: Two-Stage Least Squares
Sample: 1 111
Included observations: 111
Instrument list: C DAY1 DAY2 DAY3 DAY4 RAINY COLD MIXED
STORMY WINDSPD WINDSPD2

| Variable | Coefficient | Std. Error | t-Statistic | Prob. |
|----------|-------------|------------|-------------|-------|
| C | −8.592736 | 11.53642 | −0.744836 | 0.4581 |
| RAINY | 0.068699 | 0.184224 | 0.372912 | 0.7100 |
| COLD | 0.037239 | 0.152936 | 0.243493 | 0.8081 |
| MIXED | 0.132721 | 0.189027 | 0.702129 | 0.4842 |
| STORMY | 0.156766 | 0.282967 | 0.554007 | 0.5808 |
| WINDSPD | 6.350609 | 8.030640 | 0.790797 | 0.4309 |
| WINDSPD2 | −1.177412 | 1.391182 | −0.846339 | 0.3994 |
| DAY1 | 0.040554 | 0.216985 | 0.186895 | 0.8521 |
| DAY2 | 0.012551 | 0.212309 | 0.059116 | 0.9530 |
| DAY3 | −0.045203 | 0.215162 | −0.210088 | 0.8340 |
| DAY4 | −0.023716 | 0.208393 | −0.113805 | 0.9096 |

| | | | | |
|---|---|---|---|---|
| R-squared | 0.021994 | Mean dependent var | | 4.98E-15 |
| Adjusted R-squared | −0.075806 | S.D. dependent var | | 0.669837 |
| S.E. of regression | 0.694762 | Sum squared resid | | 48.26944 |
| F-statistic | 0.224889 | Durbin-Watson stat | | 1.385866 |
| Prob(F-statistic) | 0.993342 | | | |

shows the results from regressing those residuals against all the supposedly exogenous variables.

The Wald statistic for Hausman's test applied to the demand equation, which tests the overidentifying exclusion of the weather-related variables from demand, is $111 \cdot (0.022) = 2.442$, which is much less than the .05 significance level critical value for a chi-square statistic with 5 degrees of freedom, 11.07. The appropriate degrees of freedom number is 5 because there is one troublesome variable in the demand equation (price) and six excluded exogenous variables; one troublesome variable requires only one excluded exogenous variable, so the remaining five exclusions are overidentifying. The *F*-statistic in Panel A, 0.224, leads to the same conclusion. We fail to reject the validity of the overidentifying restrictions in the demand equation.

**TABLE 14.4** (*continued*)

Panel B Supply
Dependent Variable: HSRESID
Method: Two-Stage Least Squares
Sample: 1 111
Included observations: 111
Instrument list: C DAY1 DAY2 DAY3 DAY4 RAINY COLD MIXED
STORMY WINDSPD WINDSPD2

| Variable | Coefficient | Std. Error | t-Statistic | Prob. |
|---|---|---|---|---|
| C | −0.085432 | 5.890721 | −0.014503 | 0.9885 |
| RAINY | −0.010301 | 0.094068 | −0.109505 | 0.9130 |
| COLD | −0.002542 | 0.078092 | −0.032546 | 0.9741 |
| MIXED | −0.022034 | 0.096521 | −0.228280 | 0.8199 |
| STORMY | −0.043000 | 0.144489 | −0.297599 | 0.7666 |
| WINDSPD | −0.030370 | 4.100601 | −0.007406 | 0.9941 |
| WINDSPD2 | 0.028726 | 0.710364 | 0.040438 | 0.9678 |
| DAY1 | −0.141154 | 0.110797 | −1.273987 | 0.2056 |
| DAY2 | −0.060595 | 0.108409 | −0.641966 | 0.5224 |
| DAY3 | −0.038285 | 0.109866 | −0.348469 | 0.7282 |
| DAY4 | 0.029864 | 0.106409 | 0.280652 | 0.7796 |

| | | | | |
|---|---|---|---|---|
| R-squared | 0.026998 | Mean dependent var | | $-3.67E - 16$ |
| Adjusted R-squared | −0.070302 | S.D. dependent var | | 0.342910 |
| S.E. of regression | 0.354759 | Sum squared resid | | 12.58540 |
| F-statistic | 0.277472 | Durbin–Watson stat | | 0.728527 |
| Prob(F-statistic) | 0.984838 | | | |

The residuals from the 2SLS estimation of the supply equation are named *hsresid*. The results from regressing those residuals against all the supposedly exogenous variables are in Table 14.4, Panel B. The Wald statistic for Hausman's test applied to the supply equation, which tests the overidentifying exclusion of the day-of-the-week variables from supply, is $111 \cdot (0.027) = 2.997$, which is much less than the .05 significance level critical value for a chi-square statistic with 3 degrees of freedom, 7.81. The appropriate degrees of freedom number is three because there is one troublesome variable in the demand equation (price) and four excluded exogenous variables; one troublesome variable requires only one excluded exogenous variable, so the remaining three exclusions are overidentifying. The *F*-statistic in Panel A, 0.277, leads to the same conclusion. We fail to reject the validity of the overidentifying restrictions in the supply equation.

## Serially Correlated Disturbances in Simultaneous Equations

If there are serially correlated disturbances in a simultaneous equations model, and there are also lagged endogenous variables, any lagged dependent variables put in the reduced form equations would be contemporaneously correlated with the disturbances, and therefore OLS would not consistently estimate the reduced form. The reduced form equation used for two-stage least squares must be limited to truly predetermined variables. But instruments for the endogenous explanators—for example, the fitted values from a reduced form—are not all we need in this instance. The lagged dependent variables also require instruments.

We can consistently estimate a structural equation with lagged dependent variables and serially correlated disturbances if the structural equation has a large enough number of excluded exogenous variables. If the number of excluded exogenous variables is larger than the number of endogenous and lagged endogenous explanators in the equation, then IV estimation of the equation is consistent (assuming the appropriate rank condition for identification is also met). With consistent IV estimates of the equation's parameters in hand, we can consistently estimate the autocorrelation coefficients for the structural disturbances, much as in the Cochrane–Orcutt procedure. Using these estimates of the correlation coefficients, we can transform the data in the Cochrane–Orcutt fashion to arrive at data purged of serial correlation. These transformed data allow consistent application of two-stage least squares. For example, if the disturbances follow a first-order autoregressive process, the estimation procedure has four steps:

1. Estimate the structural equation with an IV estimator, treating both endogenous and lagged dependent variables as troublesome.
2. Regress the residuals from step 1 on their own lagged values to estimate the autocorrelation coefficient for the disturbances.

**REGRESSION'S GREATEST HITS**

# An Econometric Top 40—A Pop Tune

## Incarceration and Crime

Macroeconometric interest in simultaneous equations models waned in the 1980s because the Lucas critique of structural macroeconometric models dramatically reduced research on such models. In the 1990s, however, microeconometric interest soared. We have already seen that the simultaneous determination of price and quantity requires microeconomists to ponder how they can identify and unbiasedly estimate elasticities when studying markets. But in the 1990s, microeconomists expanded their efforts to investigate the microeconomics of many nonmarket phenomena such as crime, fertility, discrimination, and classroom behavior. Simultaneity also reared its ugly head in many of these efforts. Microeconomists repeatedly asked, "How am I to identify and estimate the behavioral equations of interest?" One lesson came from the macroeconomists: estimate only the relationship of direct interest—don't risk inheriting specification error biases from equations that don't much interest you. But the central puzzle remained: How does one identify the relationship of interest?

Let's consider, for example, the problem facing economists who wish to estimate the effect that jailing criminals has on the crime rate. Jailing criminals reduces crime in two ways. First, the risk of jail time may deter potential criminals. Second, those who are imprisoned are less likely to assault or rob us as long as they are in jail. However, the link between incarceration and crime is not one way. The greater the number of crimes, the higher the expected number of people in jail. Incarceration rates and crime rates are simultaneously determined, each affecting the other. Consequently, an OLS regression of crime on incarceration rates does not unbiasedly estimate the effect of incarceration

rates on crime. In

$$crimes_t = \beta_0 + \beta_1(incarcerated_t) + \varepsilon_t^C,$$  H14.1

the independent variable is correlated with the disturbance term because

$$incarcerated_t = \alpha_0 + \alpha_1(crimes_t) + \varepsilon_t^I$$

as well.

The simultaneity bias of OLS is the least of our problems in this specification. No consistent estimator of the crime equation coefficients exists; the crime equation is underidentified. The incarceration equation is also underidentified.

In 1996, Steven Levitt of the University of Chicago identified Equation Hit 14.1 and estimated the effect of prison population on crime rates. The file prisons.*** on this book's companion Web site (**www.aw-bc.com/murray**) contains Levitt's data. (This file is too large for the student version of EViews.) He used as his instruments dummy variables indicating the status of prison crowding lawsuits brought in a state.[11] Levitt argues that prison crowding suits result in reductions in prison populations and influence crime rates only through these consequent reductions in prison populations. His analysis focuses on changes in prison populations and changes in crime rates. Levitt's model claims that

$$\Delta incarcerated_t = \gamma_0 + \gamma_1(\Delta crimes_t) + \gamma_2(litigation\ status_t) + \varepsilon_t^I,$$

(where $\Delta$ indicates the change in the variable), but that litigation status does not appear in the crimes equation:

$$\Delta crimes_t = \tau_0 + \tau_1(\Delta incarcerated_t) + \varepsilon_t^C.$$

Levitt carefully shows that the crowding litigation dummies are, indeed, correlated with changes in prison populations. In the 12 states with entire prison systems under state control, prison population growth rates were 2.3 percentage points above the national average before the suits were filed and 2.5 percentage points below the national average after the suits were filed. In his analysis, Levitt distinguishes among (i) states with no suits, (ii) states in which suits have been filed without determination of outcome, (iii) states in which courts have made preliminary determinations against the state, (iv) states in which the courts have made final determinations against the state, and (v) states released from court control.

Levitt next shows that past changes in crime rates do not predict crowding litigation. Were he to find otherwise, we would doubt the exogeneity of the crowding legislation. Levitt concludes his analysis with another check for correlation between the litigation dummies and the disturbances in the change in crime rates equation. With numerous litigation dummies, Levitt's change-in-crime-rates equation is overidentified, so he can test the validity of the overidentifying restrictions. He fails to reject their validity.

To guard against the litigation dummies being weak instruments, Levitt shows that in a reduced form model, crowding litigation contributes significantly to explaining changes in crime rates. Thus, prison crowding litigation status holds promise as a valid and strong instrument for changes in prison population in a changes in crime rate equation: The litigation dummies appear (i) correlated with the troublesome variable (changes in prison population), (ii) exogenous to the variable of interest (changes in crime rates), and (iii) to be reasonably important contributors to the reduced form crime equation's explanatory power.

### Final Notes

Levitt's analysis illustrates the traits that a compelling analysis of a structural equation needs to have: (i) instruments that are plausibly exogenous—even better would be overidentifying restrictions whose exogeneity is not rejected, and (ii) instruments strongly correlated with the endogenous explanator.

Levitt's analysis also illustrates that simultaneity bias can be quite substantial. Levitt estimates two to three times the effect of incarceration rates on crime rates as analysts who have relied on OLS. According to Levitt's analysis, each additional prisoner results in 15 fewer crimes per year. Given the cost of incarceration and the damage done by crimes, Levitt's number suggest that at the margin, incarceration pays off financially.

■

3. Transform the structural equation as in the Cochrane–Orcutt procedure for estimating models with first-order autoregressive disturbances.
4. Conduct 2SLS estimation using the transformed data from step 3.

## Summary

This chapter explores the estimation of models involving dependent variables and explanators with values jointly determined within a system of relationships. The simultaneous equations that link the variables of the model are called simultane-

### An Organizational Structure for the Study of Econometrics

**1. What Is the DGP?**

Structural equations

Reduced form equations

The identification problem: the rank and order conditions

**2. What Makes a Good Estimator?**

Consistency

Efficiency

**3. How Do We Create an Estimator?**

Indirect least squares (ILS)

Two-stage least squares (2SLS)

**4. What Are An Estimator's Properties?**

The simultaneity bias of OLS

**5. How Do We Test Hypotheses?**

Hausman's test of overidentifying restrictions

ous equations. Those variables with values determined by the simultaneous equations are called endogenous variables; those variables with values determined outside the system, and which are, therefore, independent of the disturbances in the system, are called exogenous variables. Lagged values of the explanatory variables may also appear as explanators in economic models. Along with exogenous variables, lagged endogenous explanators are called predetermined variables. Both endogenous and predetermined variables can appear as explanators in simultaneous equations. The behavioral and institutional relationships among the variables of a system are called structural equations. An alternative representation of a system expresses each endogenous variable as a function of the system's predetermined variables.

The chapter shows how the appearance of endogenous variables among the explanators can make OLS inconsistent as an estimator of simultaneous equations. The chapter also exposes the more fundamental problem that the appearance of endogenous variables among the explanators of an equation can make that equation's parameters underidentified. A necessary condition for identification of an equation is that it exclude at least as many exogenous variables as it contains endogenous explanators; this is called the order condition for identification. The order condition is only necessary and not sufficient because each equation needs its own distinct identifying restrictions; if an equation satisfies the order condition, but excludes the same variables as another structural equation in the system, identification may be lost.

We next revisit an IV estimator, 2SLS, that can consistently estimate identified equations in a simultaneous system. The 2SLS estimator allows us to test any overidentifying restrictions assumed in the DGP; the test is called a Hausman test. This estimator is one of several consistent estimation strategies that estimate the equations in a system one at a time.

## Concepts for Review

| | |
|---|---|
| Covariance restriction   617 | Predetermined variables   596 |
| Endogenous variables   595 | Rank condition for identification   618 |
| Exactly identified   601 | Recursive   599 |
| Exclusion restriction   617 | Reduced form   597 |
| Exogenous variables   595 | Reduced form equations   597 |
| Identified   600 | Simultaneous equations   594 |
| Indirect least squares   600 | Simultaneous equations bias   598 |
| Observationally equivalent   600 | Structural equations   597 |
| Order condition for identification   617 | Structural form   597 |
| Overidentified   601 | Underidentified   601 |

## Questions for Discussion

1. Is the identification problem the Achilles heel of econometrics? Is econometric knowledge informative if it requires that we begin with identifying assumptions? Does the identification problem plague other kinds of learning and knowing, outside the realm of econometrics?

2. If everything depends on everything else, can we construct meaningful econometric models that have a limited number of variables?

## Problems for Analysis

For the data sets that you will need to solve the problems in this section, go to **www.aw-bc.com/murray**.

1. Determine the magnitude of OLS's simultaneity bias in estimating the supply curve of Equation 14.2. Express the bias in terms of the coefficients of Equations 14.1 and

14.2 and the variances and covariances of the disturbances in those equations. Make explicit any assumptions you rely on.

2. You have a two-equation simultaneous equation model. The structural equations are

$$Y_{1i} = \alpha_0 + \alpha_1 X_i + \alpha_2 Y_{2i} + \varepsilon_{1i}$$

and

$$Y_{2i} = \beta_0 + \beta_1 Y_{1i} + \varepsilon_{2i}.$$

The estimated reduced form equations are

$$Y_{1i} = 2 + 4X_i$$

and

$$Y_{2i} = 1 + 8X_i.$$

a. Which structural parameters are identified?
b. Estimate the identified structural parameters. State what kind of estimator you are using.
c. Assume $\alpha_2 = 0$. Estimate the identified structural parameters.

3. Is either equation identified in the following system of equations in which $X_{1i}$ is exogenous?

$$Y_{1i} = \alpha_0 + \alpha_1 X_{1i} + \alpha_2 Y_{2i} + \varepsilon_{1i}$$
$$Y_{2i} = \beta_0 + \beta_1 X_{1i} + \beta_2 Y_{1i} + \varepsilon_{2i}$$

Briefly explain.

4. "Simultaneity between prisoner populations and crime rates makes it difficult to isolate the causal effect of changes in prison populations on crime."[12] With this observation, Steven Levitt introduced his study of crime rates and prison populations that used instrumental variables to isolate the causal effect of changes in prison populations on crime. The file prisons6.*** contains a 1981–1993 subset of Levitt's data. This file requires EViews 5. or STATA. The variables in the file are

pcvcrimr    Annual percent change in the violent crime rate in a state
pcpcrimr    Annual percent change in the property crime rate in a state
pcmprsnr    Annual percent change in the imprisonment rate in a state
final       = 1 if within 3 years of an overcrowding judgment against the state
year        Year of the observation
state       Numerical index indicating the state of the observation

Levitt examined changes in states' crime rates and imprisonment rates. His intuition was that increases in the prison population would decrease crime rates, so it was natural to look at the changes in crime and imprisonment rates. However, Levitt was concerned that in addition to any effect of imprisonment rates on crime, there might be a feedback effect of crime rates on imprisonment rates. He was also concerned that in his simple model, OLS might suffer from omitted variables bias. Consequently, Levitt turned to IV estimation.

The instrument available in prisons6.*** is a dummy variable that indicates whether a state has been recently successfully sued for prison overcrowding. If a final judgment of overcrowding occurred in year $y$ in a state, then the dummy variable *final* takes on the value 1 in years $y + 1$, $y + 2$, and $y + 3$.

a. Regress the percent change in the violent crime rate on the previous year's percentage change in the imprisonment rate and a dummy variable for each year from 1981 to 1993, using both OLS and IV estimation. (In EViews, the command expand facilitates entering such dummy variables.) What is the difference in the estimated effect of a 1% change in imprisonment rates on expected violent crime rates?

b. Is *final* a weak instrument for the percentage change in the imprisonment rate?

   A larger portion of Levitt's data from 1971 to 1993 are in the file prisons5.***; this file is too large for the student version of Eviews, so the rest of this problem is for students with access to other software. The variables in this file are

| | |
|---|---|
| *state* | Numerical indicator of the state |
| *year* | Year of the observation |
| *popul* | State's population |
| *lprison* | Natural log of the number of imprisoned per 100,000 population in the state in the year |
| *lpcrim* | Natural log of the number of property crimes per 100,000 population in the state in the year |
| *lvcrim* | Natural log of the number of violent crimes per 100,000 population in the state in the year |
| *lincome* | Natural log of annual per capita income in the state |
| *unemp* | State's unemployment rate in the year |
| *black* | Percentage of the state's population who are African American |
| *metrop* | Percentage of the state's population who live in cities |
| *filed* | Overcrowding suit is filed in the year in the state |
| *prel_dec* | Preliminary overcrowding judgment is reached in the year in the state |
| *furt_act* | Further action on an overcrowding suit is taken in the year in the state |
| *fina_dec* | Final judgment of overcrowding is announced in the year in the state |
| *release* | State's prisons are released from outside control in the year. |

c. Regress the change in the log of the violent crimes rate on a dummy variable for each year in the sample, the changes in the logs of the imprisonment rate (lagged one year) and income, and the changes in (i) the unemployment rate, (ii) the proportion of the population who are African American, and (iii) the proportion of the population who live in cities.

d. Re-estimate the regression in (a) using IV estimation. The instruments are the five overcrowding litigation related variables, each lagged 1 year, 2 years, and 3 years. What happens to the magnitude of the estimated coefficient for imprisonment? What happens to its standard error?

e. Use Hausman's test to test the overidentifying restrictions in the IV estimation in (d).

5. Lawrence Klein built one of the earliest models of the macro economy and estimated it for the United States.[13] Klein's Model I contains a consumption function in which consumption $(C)$ depends on wages and salaries in the public and private sectors $(W_g$ and $W_p)$ and on property income $(P)$:

$$C_t = \alpha_0 + \alpha_1(W_{gt} + W_{pt}) + \alpha_2 P_t + \varepsilon_t^C.$$

The exogenous variables in Klein's system were government spending $(G)$, government wages $(W_g)$, indirect business taxes plus net exports $(X)$, and a time trend $(T)$. Additional predetermined variables were the capital stock, which was measured at the beginning of the year $(K)$, lagged property income $(P_{t-1})$, and lagged national product $(Y_{t-1})$. The file klein1.*** contains Klein's original data.
a. Estimate Klein's consumption function by OLS and by 2SLS. Compare the results.
b. Test the overidentifying restrictions for the regression in (a).

6. Again Consider Lawrence Klein's model of the macro economy. Klein's Model I contains an investment equation in which investment $(I)$ depends on current and lagged property income and on the initial stock of capital $(K)$:

$$I_t = \beta_0 + \beta_1 P_t + \beta_2 P_{t-1} + \beta_3 K_t + \varepsilon_t^I.$$

The exogenous variables in Klein's system and additional predetermined variables were the same as in Problem 4. The file klein1.*** contains Klein's original data.
a. Estimate Klein's investment function by OLS and by 2SLS. Compare the results.
b. Test the overidentifying restrictions for the regression in (a).

7. For a third time, consider Lawrence Klein's model of the macro economy. Klein's Model I contains a wage equation in which wages depend on current and lagged national product $(Y)$ and a time trend $(T)$:

$$W_t = \gamma_0 + \gamma_1 Y_t + \gamma_2 Y_{t-1} + \gamma_3 T_t + \varepsilon_t^W.$$

The exogenous variables in Klein's system and additional predetermined variables were the same as in Problems 4 and 5. The file klein1.*** contains Klein's original data.
a. Estimate Klein's wage function by OLS and by 2SLS. Compare the results.
b. Test the overidentifying restrictions for the regression in (a).

8. Does alcohol dependency interfere with people's ability to find work? John Mullahy and Jody Sindelar addressed this question using data from the 1988 National Health Interview Survey.[14] Their study examined the unemployment and employment of U.S. men and women between the ages of 25 and 59, and used several measures of problem drinking. The file alchunemp.*** contains a subsample of Mullahy and Sindelar's data: African American males 30 to 59 years of age. The variables in the file are as follows:

*stalccon*    Per capita alcohol consumption in the person's state.
*stunempl*   Unemployment rate in the person's state
*momalc*   = 1 if individual's birth mother was an alcoholic; = 0 otherwise
*dadalc*    = 1 if individual's birth father was an alcoholic; = 0 otherwise
*educ*      Individual's years of education

| | |
|---|---|
| *beertax* | Tax rate on beer in the person's state |
| *married* | = 1 if the individual is married; = 0 otherwise |
| *poorhlth* | = 1 if the individual is in poor health; = 0 otherwise |
| *unemploy* | = 1 if the individual is unemployed; = 0 otherwise |
| *alcdep* | A measure of alcohol dependency/abuse; = 1 if dependent; = 0 otherwise. |

Mullahy and Sindelar note that although problem drinking may interfere with an individual's ability to find work, unemployment itself might cause some alcohol problems. They are concerned that OLS estimates of the relationship between unemployment and problem drinking might be biased because of simultaneity.

a. Regress the unemployment indicator on the state's unemployment rate, the individual's education, marital status, health status, and the dependency measure. What is the estimated effect of problem drinking (as measured by *alcdep*) on the employment rate?

b. Re-estimate the relationship in (a) using 2SLS, with *momalc*, *dadalc*, *stalccon*, and *beertax* as instruments for *alcdep*. How does the estimated coefficient on *alcdep* change from the OLS estimate? What happens to the estimated standard error of that coefficient?

c. Use Hausman's procedure to test the overidentifying restrictions that Mullahy and Sindelar rely on. This part of the problem cannot be done with the student version of EViews.

 9. A resurgence in trade agreements and cooperation among countries has led to changing market shares in global commodity trade. In fact, as the presence of multinationals operating in a particular country (the host) increases, it becomes increasingly difficult for that country's policymakers to make farm and food policy within the confines of its borders. This difficulty in policy implementation arises because domestic production includes the supply of product from host country companies as well as that produced by multinationals located in the host country, not to mention the influx of imports that comes with opening borders to trade. The data for this problem are in the file integration1.***. This file contains data on the market share of foreign multinationals in the oilseed industry for Argentina (*AOS*) and Brazil (*BOS*) over the 1991–2003 period, as well as other information. Many U.S. multinationals locate in both Argentina and Brazil and produce the same products. This operational strategy helps the multinational hedge itself against a number of risks that may include political changes, demand uncertainties, exchange rate risk, and supply chain disruptions, but it makes it difficult to isolate the causal effect of changes in the market share of foreign multinationals in one country relative to those in another, which might be useful information when constructing domestic farm and food policy as well as designing and enforcing trade agreements.

a. Estimate the market share model for Argentina's oilseed industry by OLS and by 2SLS. The basic market share model is $AOS = \beta_0 + \beta_1 BOS + \varepsilon$ (where the time subscripts have been suppressed). The predetermined variables for use in the 2SLS estimation are the one-period lagged values of *AOS* and *BOS*. Compare the 2SLS and OLS results.

b. Re-estimate the market share model for Argentina's oilseed industry by 2SLS using two additional predetermined variables: the market share measures for a major competing industry in both countries. The competing industry is flour mill production in Argentina and Brazil (*AFM* and *BFM*, respectively) Compare these 2SLS results with the OLS results in (a) and OLS results.

c. Test the overidentifying restrictions for the regressions in (a) and (b).

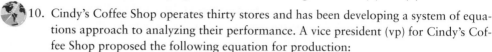 10. Cindy's Coffee Shop operates thirty stores and has been developing a system of equations approach to analyzing their performance. A vice president (vp) for Cindy's Coffee Shop proposed the following equation for production:

$$qty = \beta_0 + \beta_1 franchise + \beta_2 age + \varepsilon$$

where *qty* is the quantity of coffee sold and franchise is a dummy variable that equals one for a franchise store and 0 for a company-owned store. The number of years the store has been in operation is denoted by *age*. The VP recently read that 2SLS estimation can be superior to OLS. Consequently, the VP decides to instrument for *age* and *franchise* when estimating his production model. The VP argues that the average price charged for a sale by the competitor (*sprice*) and the average price charged for a sale by Cindy's (*cprice*) are exogenous because Cindy's has no control over what others charge and because their own prices are set by the company (though the average sale may vary by location). In addition, the average household income for the market area in which the store operates is exogenous. The data for one full year of operation for each of the stores are in cindyscoffee.\*\*\*.

a. Estimate the VP's production model by OLS and by 2SLS. Compare the results.

b. Determine whether or not the model is overidentified.

c. Do you think that the VP is correct to assert that *sprice* and *cprice* are exogenous? Briefly explain.

d. Do you think that *franchise* is a troublesome variable for which we need an instrument? Briefly explain.

e. Do you think that *age* is a troublesome variable for which we need an instrument? Briefly explain.

f. If we are instrumenting for *franchise* or *age* needlessly, what is the consequence for our estimates? Explain.

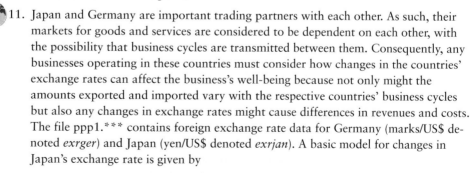 11. Japan and Germany are important trading partners with each other. As such, their markets for goods and services are considered to be dependent on each other, with the possibility that business cycles are transmitted between them. Consequently, any businesses operating in these countries must consider how changes in the countries' exchange rates can affect the business's well-being because not only might the amounts exported and imported vary with the respective countries' business cycles but also any changes in exchange rates might cause differences in revenues and costs. The file ppp1.\*\*\* contains foreign exchange rate data for Germany (marks/US$ denoted *exrger*) and Japan (yen/US$ denoted *exrjan*). A basic model for changes in Japan's exchange rate is given by

$$\Delta \ln(exrjan)_t = c + \beta_1 \Delta \ln(exrger)_t + \beta_2 \Delta \ln(exrjan)_{t-1} + \varepsilon_t$$

where $\Delta$ denotes the first difference. Furthermore, firms in both countries conduct a significant amount of business with U.S. companies. The exogenous variable in this model is the U.S. price level (*pus*). Use the first difference of the log of this variable as a candidate instrument in what follows; use $\Delta\log(exrjan)_{t-2}$ and the lagged change in the U.S. price level as predetermined variables. Instrument for both explanators in the model.

a. Estimate the equation by OLS and by 2SLS. Compare the results.

b. Test the overidentifying restrictions for the regression in (b).

c. What are the possible consequences for our choice of instruments if the disturbances are serially correlated?

 12. Enrollment levels at private colleges and universities may be particularly susceptible to the state of the economy. The National Center for Education Statistics, U.S. Department of Education, tracks the number of students enrolled in private U.S. colleges and universities. A sample of such data are in the file educ172.***. The variable *totenpriv* denotes the number of students enrolled in private colleges and universities. The enrollment model is of the following form:

$$totenpriv_t = \alpha + \beta_1 T_t + \beta_2 ip_t + \beta_3 ip_{t-1} + \beta_4 totenpriv_{t-1} + \varepsilon_t,$$

which specifies that current enrollment at private colleges depends on last period's enrollment, current national output (*ip*), and lagged output, as well as a time trend (*T*). Suppose current output, $ip_t$, is an endogenous variable, and lagged output, $ip_{t-1}$, and $totenpriv_{t-1}$ are predetermined variables. Exogenous variables in the model are the fed funds rate (*ff*) and the consumer price level (*cpi*).

a. Estimate an enrollment function by OLS and by 2SLS. Compare the OLS and 2SLS results.

b. Private college enrollment might depend on the number of students choosing to go to state-supported schools. Add the number of students enrolled in public colleges (*totenpub*) to the model in (a). Estimate the respecified model using 2SLS with an additional predetermined variable, the lagged value of the number of students enrolled in public colleges, added to those used in (a). How have your results changed?

 13. Many economists adhere to the notion that the spread between a long-term interest rate and a short-term interest rate helps to explain future changes in real output. A model of the macroeconomy might include an equation in which the rate of change (or first difference of the log) in industrial production (*ip*) depends on last period's spread between the 30-year bond rate and the one-year bill rate (*tbond30* and *tbill1yr*). The disturbances in this equation are likely to be serially correlated. The exogenous variables in this system include the predetermined value of the money supply (*m1*), the contemporaneous return on stocks (*return*), and the current and lagged difference between the natural rate of unemployment (*natur*) and the unemployment rate (*ur*). U.S. data for estimating this model are in the file month1.***.

a. Estimate the following equation by OLS and by 2SLS, not accounting for the serial correlation. Note that $T$ is an exogenous time trend. Compare the results.

$$\Delta\ln(ip)_t = \beta_0 + \beta_1(tbond30 - tbill1yr)_{t-1} + \beta_2 T_t + \varepsilon_t$$

b. Because the equation in (a) is overidentified, 2SLS consistently estimates the relationship in (a). Adapt 2SLS to account for serial correlation in the disturbances and more efficiently estimate the relationship in (a).

c. It may be that the relationships among interest rates are affected by the monetary policy decisions of the central bank and thus the money supply. Moreover, changes in interest rates affect the balance sheets of firms and households. The result of these relationships may be to introduce a simultaneity bias in the model of changes in real output. Use Hausman's procedure to test the overidentifying restrictions in (a).

14. One standard model of the macroeconomy includes, among other equations, structural equations for the supply of and demand for loanable funds. The supply of loanable funds depends on the actions of the Federal Reserve, whereas the demand function is based on the behavior of individual agents in the economy. In equilibrium, these supply-and-demand relationships jointly determine the equilibrium interest rate. The U.S. data in money1.*** suffice to estimate these supply-and-demand equations. The supply of loanable funds depends on the money supply and the default risk of (potential) borrowers, and the demand for loanable funds depends on income (or aggregate output). In money1.***, real output growth is given by the variable *growth*, the level of the money supply is denoted *fm1*, and the spread between the rates on corporate paper and the risk-free Treasury bill rate is denoted *sprd*. The demand for loans is believed to depend on *growth*, as this provides businesses (i.e., borrowers) with information about future demand for their goods and services. Exogenous variables are the money supply and *sprd*, and $\Delta ir_{t-2}$ is predetermined.

a. Estimate the following interest rate (*ir*) function by OLS and by 2SLS. Compare the results.

$$\Delta(ir)_t = \beta_0 + \beta_1 growth_t + \beta_2 \Delta(ir)_{t-1} + \varepsilon_t$$

b. Because the equation in (a) is overidentified, 2SLS consistently estimates the relationship. Adapt 2SLS to account for serial correlation in the disturbances and more efficiently estimate the relationship.

c. Test the overidentifying restrictions for the regression in (a).

15. Are any equations identified in the following system of equations in which $X_{1i}$ is exogenous?

$$Y_{1i} = \alpha_0 + \alpha_1 X_{1i} + \alpha_2 Y_{2i} + \varepsilon_{1i}$$
$$Y_{2i} = \beta_0 + \beta_1 X_{1i} + \beta_2 Y_{1i} + \varepsilon_{2i}$$
$$Y_{3i} = \gamma_0 + \gamma_1 Y_{1i} + \varepsilon_{3i}.$$

Briefly explain.

16. Are any equations identified in the following system of equations in which $X_{1i}$ is exogenous?

$$Y_{1i} = \alpha_0 + \alpha_1 X_{1i} + \alpha_2 Y_{2i} + \varepsilon_{1i}$$
$$Y_{2i} = \beta_0 + \beta_1 X_{1i} + \beta_2 Y_{1i} + \varepsilon_{2i}$$
$$Y_{3i} = \gamma_0 + \gamma_1 Y_{1i} + \varepsilon_{3i}$$
$$Y_{4i} = \tau_0 + \tau_1 Y_{1i} + \varepsilon_{4i}$$

Briefly explain.

17. Are any equations identified in the following system of equations in which $X_{1i}$ is exogenous?

$$Y_{1i} = \alpha_0 + \alpha_1 X_{1i} + \alpha_2 Y_{2i} + \alpha_3 Y_{3i} + \alpha_4 Y_{4i} + \varepsilon_{1i}$$

$$Y_{2i} = \beta_0 + \beta_1 X_{1i} + \beta_2 Y_{1i} + \beta_3 Y_{3i} + \beta_4 Y_{4i} + \varepsilon_{2i}$$

$$Y_{3i} = \gamma_1 Y_{1i} + \gamma_2 Y_{4i} + \varepsilon_{3i}$$

$$Y_{4i} = \tau_1 Y_{2i} + \tau_2 Y_{3i} + \varepsilon_{4i}$$

Briefly explain.

## Endnotes

1. Alfred Marshall, *Principles of Economics*, 9th (variorum) ed., Vol. 1, part 8, C. W. Guillebaud, ed. (London: Macmillan, 1961): 348.

2. Restrictions on a model's coefficients can identify an equation. Is there other prior information that might identify a structural equation? Yes. For example, prior information about the variances and covariances of the disturbances in a model can suffice to identify an equation. See William H. Green, *Econometric Analysis*, (Englewood Cliffs, NJ: Prentice Hall, 2003): 394–395.

3. Kathryn Graddy, "Testing for Imperfect Competition at the Fulton Fish Market," *RAND Journal of Economics* 26, no. 1 (Spring 1995): 75–92.

4. Joshua Angrist, Kathryn Graddy, and Guido Imbens, "The Interpretation of Instrumental Variables Estimators in Simultaneous Equations Models with an Application to the Demand for Fish," *Review of Economic Studies* 67, no. 3 (July 2000): 499–527.

5. Daniel B. Suits, "An Econometric Model of the Watermelon Market," *Journal of Farm Economics* 24 (1955): 237–251.

6. T. W. Anderson and H. Rubin, "Estimation of the Parameters of a Single Equation in a Complete System of Stochastic Equations," *Annals of Mathematical Statistics* 20 (1949): 46–63.

7. Phillip G. Wright, *The Tariff on Animal and Vegetable Oils* (New York: Macmillan, 1928).

8. R. C. Geary, "Determination of Linear Relations Between Systematic Parts of Variables with Errors of Observation the Variances of Which Are Unknown" *Econometria* 17, no. 1 (January 1949): 30–58. Like Wright's book, Olav Reiersol, "Confluence Analysis by Means of Instrumental Sets of Variables," *Mathematik, Astronomi, och Fysik* 32, no. 4 (1945): 1–119, developed an IV estimator, but was overlooked by economists for some years.

9. Jerry A. Hausman, "Specification and Estimation of Simultaneous Equation Models," Chapter 7 in *Handbook of Econometrics*, Vol. 1, Z. Griliches and M. D. Intrilligator, eds. (Amsterdam: North Holland, 1983).

10. In her original study, Graddy found that price varied with race, suggesting a noncompetitive market in which firms exert market power.

11. Steven D. Levitt, "The Effect of Prison Population Size on Crime Rates: Evidence from Prison Overcrowding Legislation," *Quarterly Journal of Economics* (May 1996): 319–351.

12. Ibid.
13. Lawrence Klein, *Economic Fluctuations in the United States 1921–1941* (New York: John Wiley, 1950).
14. John Mullahy and Jody Sindelar, "Employment, Unemployment, and Problem Drinking," *Journal of Health Economics* 15 (1996): 409–434.

# Chapter 15

# Randomized Experiments and Natural Experiments

*Life is short, the art long, opportunity fleeting,*
*experiment treacherous, judgment difficult.*

—HIPPOCRATES (460–370 B.C.)

Why do soda bottles pop their caps when left in a hot car? Why do tennis balls go flat in winter? It's all about how gases behave in enclosed spaces when temperature changes. The science of heated and cooled gases is well understood because scientists have long conducted careful experiments to study gases in controlled environments. Physical scientists can often design experiments in which two things change (say, the gas's temperature and the pressure the gas places on the container) while everything else that might matter (for example, the amount of a gas in a container and the container's volume) stays fixed. Such *controlled experiments* facilitate determining the effect of one variable on another, as in finding how pressure changes when temperature changes, with other things being the same.

Economists do not study why soda bottles pop and tennis balls plop, or other physical phenomena. Instead they try to explain the workings of the social world. Moreover, unlike physical scientists, economists rarely have the luxury of controlling the values that their variables take on—they can't exert the control on their working environment that physical scientists often do. Nonetheless, like physical scientists, economists ask, "What causes what?" Does the Head Start program improve poor children's subsequent academic performance? Does a new state income tax revision spur economic growth? Is living in the suburbs better for the poor than living in the inner city?

We might hope to answer such questions without controlled experiments by determining whether random samples drawn from those treated, such as poor children who participated in Head Start, and from those untreated, such as poor children who did not participate in Head Start, have statistically different means. Unfortunately, although the difference in such estimated means does consistently estimate whether the two sampled populations differ in their means, we would, in general, be wrong to infer from such a comparison that Head Start gives students an academic head start—maybe it is just that the more able children are sent to Head Start by their parents.

This chapter explores the distinction between estimating and interpreting the difference between two populations' means. It also introduces several experimental designs—*controlled experiments*, *randomized experiments*, and *natural experiments*—that physical and social scientists rely on to uncover the causal effects of programs or treatments. The results from controlled experiments and from randomized experiments are generally compelling. Natural experiments are inherently less compelling. The chapter first discusses the estimation and interpretation of differences in means between two populations.

## 15.1 Estimating Means and Interpreting Differences in Means

**WHAT IS THE DGP?**

Studying specific examples is an instructive way to understand the distinction between estimating and interpreting differences in means. Let's consider two simple random samples, one drawn from fourth graders from poor families who attended Head Start and the other drawn from fourth graders from poor families who did not attend Head Start. Such samples suffice to validly *estimate* the difference between the populations' mean performance on a fourth-grade exam. The difference between the sample means is an unbiased estimator of the difference between the populations' means. But to *interpret* any difference in those sample means is less straightforward than the statistical estimation itself. We cannot confidently claim that such a difference is *caused* by Head Start. More detailed assumptions about the data-generating process (DGP) at hand are necessary before we can confidently interpret the practical import of an observed difference in means.

What complicates interpreting the difference between two populations' means? When can we validly interpret a difference between the means of treated and untreated populations (for example, those who attended Head Start and those who did not) as reflecting a causal effect of the treatment? These questions are the chief concern of this and the following sections. This section first elaborates on the distinction between *estimating* and *interpreting* the difference between two populations' means. It then introduces a real-world example of two populations whose means differ. The example reappears throughout the chapter to illustrate new concepts.

### Estimation vs. Interpretation

A random sample drawn from the population of all poor children who participate in Head Start does yield an unbiased estimate of the population mean for that group. Similarly, a random sample of all poor children who do not participate in Head Start does yield an unbiased estimate of the population mean for that group. Moreover, we can unbiasedly estimate the difference in these two popula-tion means by differencing the sample means. Equivalently, we can define a dummy variable, $D$, that takes on the value one when the observation is on a Head Start participant and that takes on the value zero when the observation is on a poor child who does not participate in Head Start. We can then estimate the difference in means in a regression model; we can ask, "Is $\beta_1$ equal to zero in

$$Y_1 = \beta_0 + \beta_1 D_i + \varepsilon_i?"$$

If the sample means differ significantly, that is, if we reject the null hypothesis that $\beta_1 = 0$, we can validly infer from the estimates that the two populations have dif-ferent means. But can we validly *interpret* such a difference in means as measuring the causal effect, or **treatment effect**, of the Head Start program? No, we cannot.

If poor children's participation in Head Start is not random, then the dummy indicating participation in the program may be correlated with any traits of the children omitted from the regression and relevant to $Y$. Such a correlation biases ordinary least squares (OLS) as an estimator of the treatment effect of Head Start. The two populations may have different means for $Y$, a difference that OLS can capture, but Head Start may not be the cause of any such difference.

Valid interpretation of differences in population means as treatment effects invariably rests on more assumptions about where the data come from than are needed to just test for a difference in populations' means. Subsequent sections in this chapter describe three foundations for interpreting differences in means as treatment effects. Each copes, more and less well, with the biases that can arise if $D$ is correlated with the disturbances. The first foundation is controlled experi-ments. The second is randomized experiments, and the third natural experiments. Because we so often want to know the effects of a treatment or program, we have a profound interest in finding foundations for validly assessing treatment effects.

Before elaborating on these foundations for interpreting differences in popu-lation means as treatment effects, we turn to an example that exposes why it can be wrong to interpret differences in population means as treatment effects.

## The Neighborhood Poverty Example

In some countries, the poor are evenly spread geographically throughout the pop-ulation, but in most American cities the poor tend to live in concentrated areas. For many years, large metropolitan regions in the United States reinforced this pattern by building their public housing units in the poorer parts of their inner cities. More recently, social scientists have wondered whether the dense poverty of inner city neighborhoods is detrimental to the prospects of the poor. Would poor households fare better if they lived in neighborhoods with less poverty?

A simple way to answer this question is to compare a sample of high-poverty neighborhood residents with low levels of education (for whom $D_i = 0$) with a sample of low-poverty neighborhood residents with low levels of education (for whom $D_i = 1$), asking whether those who live in low-poverty neighborhoods fare better than those in high-poverty neighborhoods. We could determine "faring better," $Y_i$, by earnings, the probability of employment, the educational attainment of children, or other measures of well-being. In practice, social scientists have used many measures of well-being. Such tests generally find that poor households whose heads have low education, but who live in low-poverty neighborhoods, fare better than their counterparts in high-poverty neighborhoods ($\beta_1$ is positive and statistically significantly different from zero). But does this finding imply that living in a low-poverty neighborhood *makes* one fare better? Unfortunately, it does not. To understand why, let's consider earnings as a measure of "faring better."

Households choose for themselves where to live, but high-poverty neighborhoods offer lower rents—a major factor for poor households. Low-education household heads with better earnings prospects are more apt to choose to live in low-poverty neighborhoods. The causal link between higher earnings and living in low-poverty neighborhoods may be that higher earnings allow one to live in those neighborhoods, not that living in low-poverty neighborhoods ensures higher earnings. It may well be the case that household heads with low education who locate in low-poverty neighborhoods are the heads who, for some reason other than location, have better earnings prospects.

The phrase "for some reason other than location" invites the question, "What other reasons?" If we could quantify those reasons, and account for them in our analysis, we could discover whether the difference in mean earnings for low-education household heads in the low-poverty neighborhoods and high-poverty neighborhoods persists after we account for those "other reasons." A multiple regression analysis could, in principle, account for those other reasons:

$$earnings\ rate_i = \beta_0 + \beta_1(low\ poverty_i) + \beta_2 X_{2i} + \cdots + \beta_k X_{ki} + u_i, \quad \textbf{15.1}$$

where "*low poverty*" is the dummy variable for living in a low-poverty neighborhood, and the X-variables are other factors that could influence individuals' earnings. Variables that researchers have sometimes included among the X's are time since last move, age of the household head, ages of children, years of welfare receipt, and the household head's years of welfare receipt, education, and job training. The coefficient on *low poverty* indicates how the expected earnings rate varies between low- and high-poverty neighborhoods. In applications, such multiple regression analyses continue to find that household heads with little education who live in low-poverty neighborhoods fare better than their high-poverty neighborhood counterparts.

But does finding that $\beta_1$ is positive imply that living in the low-poverty neighborhoods *leads* to higher average earnings? In practice, the answer is "No." We measure numerous potential determinants of earnings, but there are many other potential determinants that we do not measure. There are inevitably omitted relevant variables that could bias the OLS estimator of the coefficient on *low poverty*. If the omitted, often unmeasured, relevant variables are correlated with *low poverty*, OLS yields biased estimates of the effect of neighborhood poverty on earnings. For example, it might be that workers who are particularly reliable on the job—a trait very hard to measure—are also the sort of reliable tenants that can more easily obtain housing in low-poverty areas. An omitted measure of reliability would influence wages and be correlated with living in a low-poverty area. When there are omitted relevant traits among a study's subjects, econometricians say that there is **unobserved heterogeneity** among the subjects.

If we interpret the coefficient on *low poverty*, $\beta_1$, to be the causal effect of residing in a low-poverty neighborhood, the choices of households may bias the OLS estimate of $\beta_1$ by making *low poverty* correlated with the omitted unobserved traits of the households. The omitted variables bias that can result from using data in which households select themselves into categories is called **self-selection bias**. How might we avoid self-selection bias? More generally, how might we ensure that unobserved heterogeneity does not lead to biases in our estimate of $\beta_1$ and undermine our causal interpretation of $\beta_1$? The next sections address these questions.

## 15.2    Controlled and Randomized Experiments

WHAT IS THE DGP?

Physical scientists have for centuries relied on experiments to make credible inferences about causal relationships. In the past century, social scientists have followed suit. Two strategies for assessing causal relationships are particularly compelling: controlled experiments and randomized experiments. This section describes these strategies in some detail.

### Controlled Experiments

A core difficulty in analyzing causality in samples of self-selected low-poverty neighborhood dwellers and high-poverty neighborhood dwellers is that many unobserved variables may differ in value between the two groups we study. Multiple regression models can control for numerous observed factors by including them as explanators in a model, but it remains the case that when we see differences in, say, location and income, unobserved differences in other variables are also present. A causal interpretation of an observed relationship is not possible unless we have ensured that other things are kept equal. *Ceteris paribus* is Latin for "other things being equal." Thus, one problem analysts can stumble over is that *ceteris* may not be *paribus*.

Physical scientists often cope with the *ceteris paribus* problem by rigidly controlling the environment in which they gather their observations. They use airtight containers from which all air has been evacuated, zero gravity simulators, and other devices to control an experimental environment to ensure that all other things are, indeed, equal when studying some phenomenon. When scientists can make other things equal in this fashion, they say their data come from a **controlled experiment.** *Controlled experiments avoid the dangers of unobserved heterogeneity by banishing it.*

A controlled experiment systematically varies some aspects of the environment across observations. For example, if we wish to confirm the thermodynamic relationship that for an ideal gas enclosed in a confined space,

$$PV = mRT,$$

where $P$ = pressure, $V$ = volume, $m$ = the number of molecules in the gas (measured in moles), $R$ = Avogadro's number (a specific constant), and $T$ = temperature, we want to vary $P$, $V$, $m$, and $T$ across many values so we can estimate the regression:

$$\ln(P_i) = \beta_0 + \beta_1 \ln(m_i) + \beta_2 \ln(T_i) + \beta_3 \ln(V_i) + \varepsilon_i,$$

in which the index $i$ refers to a particular replication of the experiment. This regression allows us to test the null hypothesis that

$$\beta_0 = \ln(R); \beta_1 = 1; \beta_2 = 1; \text{ and } \beta_3 = -1.$$

In well-controlled experiments, scientists often attribute the disturbance term to measurement error. As long as they measure the traits varied in the experiment, multiple regression can statistically control for the varying conditions. If scientists mismeasure only the dependent variable, OLS unbiasedly estimates the treatment effect. If they also mismeasure explanators, repeated, independent measurements of the explanators provide valid instruments for consistent instrumental variables (IV) estimation of the treatment effects.

Unfortunately, many physical scientists and most social scientists are unable to manipulate the environments in which they gather data completely enough to guarantee that they are holding other things equal. For example, horticulturists studying the effects of fertilizer cannot ensure that every plot of soil is the same except for the amount of fertilizer in use. Sunlight, moisture, and the mineral content of the soil itself will vary from site to site. Just as individuals with low education will differ from one another in unmeasured and unmeasurable ways, plots of land will display unobserved heterogeneity, too. Although plots of land won't select themselves into treated and untreated sites, farmers may do the selecting in equally unfortunate ways. For example, some plots in a farmer's care may be harder to get to with fertilizing equipment than are others, and farmers may choose not to treat such plots. If those harder to reach plots differ systematically in their inherent fertility from easier to reach plots, the self-selection bias reappears through farmers' choices.

## Randomized Experiments

When controlled experiments are not feasible, *randomized experiments* offer a powerful alternative strategy for avoiding the perils of selection bias. In a **randomized experiment,** experimenters randomly draw sample participants from a population (for example, all persons eligible for subsidized housing or all corn fields in Iowa) and randomly assign individual participants in the study to be treated or untreated (that is, either given a suburban subsidized dwelling or given an inner-city subsidized dwelling, or either fertilized, or not). The treated individuals, called the **treatment group,** are compared with the untreated. We call the untreated individuals the **control group,** because they are, within the bounds of sampling error, the same as the treated group, except for the treatment itself and its consequences. Thus, the control group reflects the effects of everything but the treatment itself. *In randomized experiments, the control group's statistically reliable similarity to the treatment group in any regard but the treatment itself serves the role that rigid physical control of the environment sometimes achieves for physical scientists.*

For example, classic agricultural experiments randomly assign sample plots of land to either receive fertilizer, or not. Such experiments ask whether the fertilizer causes higher yields; that is, in

$$yield_i = \beta_0 + \beta_1(dummy\ for\ fertilized)_i + u_i,$$

is the coefficient on the fertilizer dummy greater than zero? Random assignment ensures that across samples the treatment dummy will be uncorrelated with omitted relevant variables that are embedded in the disturbance term—the control group differs systematically from the treatment group only in being untreated. The Law of Large Numbers guarantees that as the number of plots in the sample grows large, the average difference between the treated and untreated plots in any specified finite number of traits besides the application of fertilizer almost surely becomes small. Large treatment and control groups ensure a high degree of likely similarity between the two groups in anything but the treatment and its effects. OLS analysis of the data from such randomized experiments yields unbiased and consistent estimates of the treatment effect of fertilizer.

We can unbiasedly estimate the effect of a randomized treatment by regressing the outcome on an intercept and the treatment dummy. Randomization makes sure the treatment dummy is uncorrelated with any other variables that influence the outcome variable—there can be no omitted variable bias. Nonetheless, analysts using experimental data do often include in their regressions relevant variables in addition to the treatment dummy, as in

$$yield_i = \beta_0 + \beta_1(dummy\ for\ fertilized)_i + \beta_2 X_{2i} + \beta_3 X_{3i} + w_i.$$

By including additional relevant explanators, the analysts reduce the variance of the disturbance term by removing from it any variation in the $X$'s across samples. An analyst estimates the treatment effect of a fertilizer more precisely when the additional relevant variables are included.

That randomization is a sound foundation for drawing causal inferences from sample means ranks as one of the great scientific insights of the late 19th and early 20th centuries. Agriculture and pharmacology have blossomed because of the lessons we have learned from randomized experiments. Economists have used large randomized social experiments to learn about health insurance, housing programs, and negative income taxes, and in recent decades, a new subfield of economics, experimental economics, has used small-scale randomized experiments to test many features of economic theory.

## The Neighborhood Poverty Example Revisited

The Department of Housing and Urban Development (HUD) is conducting an on-going randomized experiment, called the Moving to Opportunity Program, to study the effect of a low neighborhood poverty rate on the well-being of disadvantaged residents. In this program, HUD randomly assigned a sample of low-income public housing tenants who offered to participate in the experiment through either (i) receipt of a special housing voucher good only for living in a neighborhood with a poverty rate less than 10% (these people are the treatment group or the "voucher group"); or (ii) participation in a control group that receives no voucher and to which the subsidy recipients can be compared.[1] A comparison of subsequent job and education outcomes for voucher and control households promises rich and reliable information about the benefits to disadvantaged households from living in low-poverty neighborhoods. Early analyses examine the effects of the Moving to Opportunity Program in its first two years of operation; longer term analyses will examine the program's effects after 10 years.

Random assignment of the households between the treatment and control groups guarantees that any unobserved heterogeneity among the households is not correlated across samples with receipt of a voucher. Moreover, if the samples are large enough, the probability that any particular subset of unobserved traits is more than slightly correlated with treatment type in a randomly chosen sample is very small. In this housing location example, randomizing assignment eliminates the self-selection biases that could occur if households or bureaucrats were to systematically assign households to the voucher group or the control group. In the actual randomized experiment, the 961 voucher and control households did not differ in statistically significant fashion across a spectrum of 48 measured traits.

If the Moving to Opportunity experimental design accurately represents the data-generating process that gives rise to the experiment's data, the disturbances in Equation 15.1 are uncorrelated with the treatment dummy, *low poverty*. OLS applied to the Moving to Opportunity data would yield unbiased estimates of the treatment effect of a low-poverty neighborhood.

## Sources of Bias in Randomized Experiments

Random experiments do not cure all statistical ills. Random assignment of households to treatment and control groups avoids self-selection bias, but other sources of bias can still arise. In the Moving to Opportunity experiment, not everyone offered a voucher has succeeded in finding a place to live in a low-poverty neighborhood.[2] The unsuccessful recipients have tended to remain in their housing projects, as have the control households. Furthermore, not everyone who entered the experiment has continued answering subsequent surveys about his or her experiences. Finally, some households who cooperated initially later dropped out of the program. Consequently, the randomized design of the experiment may not fully capture the process that generates the experimental data.

If the unsuccessful voucher recipients or the nonreporting households differ in unobserved ways from the successful voucher recipients or from the survey-responding households, the *low poverty* dummy is once again correlated with omitted variables. The bias that can result from voucher-group households failing to find housing in low-poverty neighborhoods is an instance of self-selection bias. **Nonresponse bias** can stem from participating households not reporting their experiences. **Attrition bias** can stem from households leaving the experiment before it is done.

Another form of bias arises when the sample households are not initially drawn randomly from the population of interest. The Moving to Opportunity experiment is likely to tell us how public housing residents who are willing to relocate to low-poverty neighborhoods benefit from living in such neighborhoods. But what about disadvantaged households that don't live in public housing or that would be unwilling to make such a move? Would such households differ systematically from those that applied to the Moving to Opportunity experiment? Quite possibly. If the population sampled differs from that in which we are truly interested, the bias risked is called **sample selection bias**.

When self-selection, sample selection, nonresponse, and attrition biases are arguably small in a randomized experiment, the experiment offers a foundation

# An Econometric Top 40—A Classical Favorite

## The Social Experiments: Labor Supply, Housing Allowances, and Health Insurance

In the 1970s and 1980s, the U.S. government sponsored three large social science experiments. First were a series of four negative-income tax experiments that sought to understand how American households would alter their work effort if given a guaranteed minimum income. Second were two housing allowance experiments that probed into how low-income American households would respond to housing vouchers that work much like food stamps. Third was a national health insurance experiment that examined how American households would respond to universal health insurance.

These randomized social experiments all randomly sampled U.S. households in the subpopulations of interest. Selected households were then randomly assigned to treatment and control groups. In each instance, the experiments focused on potential public policies of great scope. Many conservative and liberal social analysts hoped that the patchwork quilt of American social welfare programs could be replaced by a single program, a guaranteed minimum income that would be slowly taxed away as one's income rose (the benefit a household received would be based on a formula: benefit = minimum income − [tax rate] · [earned income]). Others, skeptical about the prospects for a guaranteed income and dissatisfied with public housing projects as a solution to the housing needs of the poor, hoped for a system of housing vouchers that would pay part of the rent of low-income families as they found their homes in the private housing market. Still others saw health insurance as a national need that could be provided best by a universal, subsidized insurance program. Before such complex programs could garner the political support they would need, the most serious doubts about the programs had to be addressed, which was the goal of the experiments.

Would a guaranteed minimum income cause millions of people to go on the dole and abandon work? Would housing vouchers increase the demand for housing, only to see rents skyrocket and low-income households made no better off by the allowances? Would a free national health plan bankrupt government? Would national health insurance improve health outcomes in the United States? The available economic and medical evidence on all these questions was too fragile to serve as the basis for vastly expensive public policies. The hope was that randomized experiments, freed of the biases that threaten the validity of most social science empirical work, could provide the informational basis for sound policy making.

The experiments were complex undertakings. In the four negative-income tax (NIT) experiments, more than 8,000 households received guaranteed incomes, some receiving guaranteed incomes for up to 20 years. One housing allowance experiment, called the supply experiment, offered housing allowances to all income-eligible households in two small cities, South Bend, Indiana, and Green Bay, Wisconsin. The other housing allowance experiment offered allowances to a random sample of income-eligible households in two larger cities, Phoenix and Pittsburgh. The health insurance experiment sampled some 5,000 people across six cities. Each experiment lasted a minimum of several years.

The NIT experiments established that a guaranteed minimum income would have non-negligible, but also noncatastrophic, effects on work effort. Male heads of two-parent households would not react much to the minimum income guarantee itself, but would cut their work hours because of the tax rate on earnings that draws down the subsidy as income rises. Men in the program who faced the highest marginal tax rates decreased their hours worked by about 11%. Single female household heads who participated would cut their hours worked by as little as nothing or as much as 15%; these women would react to both the guarantee itself (an income effect that increases the consumption of leisure, which is a normal good) and to the tax rate (a substitution effect that follows on a decrease in the opportunity cost of leisure). Participating women in two-parent households would cut their hours of work most dramatically, by as much as 20% to 30%. (Because married women have become more attached to market work in the past 30 years, this last result might prove different today; married women might behave more like their husbands now.)

Despite these results, the political will for a guaranteed minimum income did not materialize. When Richard Nixon proposed his Family Assistance Plan, a variant on a guaranteed minimum income, it fell to a coalition of conservatives who disliked the idea altogether and liberals who found the plan insufficiently generous.

The experimental data from the NIT experiments did, however, provide labor economists with a rich trove of information to explore with economic models and econometric tools. The division of reductions in work effort into income and substitution effects required econometric estimates of labor supply models that went well beyond comparing the mean hours worked of treatment groups and controls. The sophistication of labor economics grew dramatically during the 1970s and 1980s as a direct result of analyzing the experimental data.

The housing allowance supply experiment established that a city-wide housing allowance program need not drive up rents. Four factors contributed to keeping prices in check in South Bend and Green Bay. First, eligible households only slowly took advantage of their vouchers, giving the market time to adjust to the increased demands. Second, housing vacancies served as a buffer, absorbing new demands for better housing. Third, landlords upgraded units to provide additional housing that met the requirements of the allowance program. Fourth, among those who used their vouchers, the program subsidies spurred housing demand less than anticipated. Much doubt remained, nonetheless, about whether housing market experiences in small places such as South Bend and Green Bay told us enough about large-city markets such as New York or Los Angeles.

The housing allowance demand experiment rigorously established that price and income elasticities of demand for housing are smaller than had been previously believed. Voucher plans that would pay a percentage of households' rents would spur demand less than anticipated. Program requirements that insisted on housing units meeting specific physical standards (such as treads on the building's stairways) did increase the proportion of households meeting those standards, but the correlation among standards met was rather low, so the only way to ensure a standard would be met was to set the standard explicitly. Unfortunately, physical standards discouraged substantial numbers of otherwise eligible households from finding compliant housing. Perhaps the most important finding of the experiment was that housing allowances enabled households to obtain housing as good as that found in public housing at a much lower cost to government.

In the years since the housing allowance experiment, federally subsidized housing programs have increasingly used voucher programs, and less and less used subsidized construction for the poor. Because the voucher programs are cheaper, more households are getting housing subsidies today than in the past, while the quality of the housing that subsidized households receive has not been adversely affected.

The National Health Insurance Experiment (NHIE) established that income has a positive effect on outpatient services and a negative effect on inpatient services for insured households, leading to a shallow U-shaped relationship between income and total expenditures. Furthermore, the experimental results imply that changes in insurance coverage over time accounted for only a small fraction of the rise in health care costs since World War II. But perhaps the most important finding of the NHIE was that modest cost sharing by patients (with a cap on maximum out-of-pocket expenditures) reduces medical expenditures but does not measurably change health outcomes.

The NHIE did not lead to a national health insurance program. The lesson about cost sharing seems to have changed insurance practices in the United States, however. The fraction of major companies with cost-sharing insurance plans rose from 30% to 63% in the years immediately following the publication of the experimental results. Within a decade of the experiment, the resulting cost savings on the consequent avoided medical expenses was about $7 billion.

 **Final Notes**

All of the large social experiments had to grapple with serious logistical and statistical problems. Do short-duration experimental programs tell us much about actual long-term programs? Do attrition bias and nonreporting bias invalidate the inferences from the experiments? Are the locations chosen for the experiments representative of the nation as a whole—can we generalize from South Bend to New York or from Seattle to Atlanta? Researchers overcame enough of these problems by applying well-known statistical methods and by inventing new methods, so that all the experiments added richly to our understanding of the social policies they addressed.

The great social experiments of the 1970s and 1980s did not lead to the vast new programs that their sponsors had hoped for, but each has had a lasting positive impact on social policy. Despite this success, few additional social experiments have followed in the wake of these first efforts. The cost of social experiments is high—the NHIE cost almost $150 million—and government seldom funds such big-ticket items in times of fiscal distress. But if we compare the $150 million cost of the NHIE with the $7 billion cost savings from knowing to use modest cost sharing in health insurance policies, we might conclude that additional social experiments can be worthwhile social investments.

■

for credible inferences about the treatment effects of the experimental program or treatment in the population of interest. The Moving to Opportunity program draws from an important population. Many disadvantaged households live in public housing and would be willing to move to a low-poverty neighborhood. (As evidence, many more households applied to participate in the Moving to Opportunity experiments than could be accommodated.) If self-selection and attrition biases prove minimal and response rates prove high, the Moving to Opportunity program promises considerable insight into the importance of location for many impoverished Americans.

Randomized social experiments are generally costly. Such experiments are seldom undertaken unless there is strong reason to believe they will provide valuable information. What led the U.S. government to think that the Moving to Opportunity experiment is likely to yield valuable information? The impetus for this experiment was an unusual natural experiment in Chicago. *Natural experiments* arise when the workings of ordinary social changes happen to give rise to conditions that seem similar to a randomized experiment. The next section discusses natural experiments in detail.

## 15.3    Natural Experiments

WHAT IS THE DGP?

*Natural experiments are usually less compelling than either controlled or randomized experiments. They are also less expensive.* A **natural experiment** is one that relies on chance circumstances mimicking the conditions of a randomized experiment. Inevitably, the messy unfolding of real-world events falls short of the clean random separation of treatment and control groups obtained in randomized experiments. As a consequence, the results of natural experiments are inherently less compelling than those from comparable randomized or controlled experiments. This section studies one particular natural experiment, called the Gautreaux program, to illustrate the pitfalls of natural experiments. The section following this one redeems natural experiments with a statistical technique that can make the results of natural experiments more reliable.

### The Gautreaux Experiment

The natural experiment that spurred the Moving to Opportunity program grew out of a 1966 civil rights lawsuit brought by Chicago public housing tenants. The lawsuit, called the Gautreaux lawsuit, charged that the Chicago public housing authority had employed racially discriminatory policies. The U.S. Supreme Court agreed with the charge and, in 1976, ruled that black public housing residents in Chicago be given subsidized housing vouchers that would enable them to live in private market apartments. The distribution of vouchers in the Gautreaux experience appeared to be unsystematic in ways akin to the random assignment of voucher and control households in the Moving to Opportunity experiment.

In the 15 years following the Supreme Court's Gautreaux ruling, about 4,000 households received vouchers under the ruling. Almost all of the voucher recipients came from inner city neighborhoods. Many of these households received vouchers for suburban communities, while others received vouchers for inner city communities. In practice, which households got which vouchers seemed to be dictated chiefly by the happenstance of what vouchers were available when a given family applied. Households did not appear to exercise much self-selection about where their vouchers would let them live. If the assignments of households to the suburbs or inner city were, in effect, random, the Gautreaux experience offered a natural experiment about the effects of location on the life outcomes of disadvantaged households.

In the Gautreaux experience, all households moved either within the inner-city or from the inner city to the suburbs. The inner city neighborhoods from which the Gautreaux households came were generally high-poverty ones. The Gautreaux households that stayed in the inner city tended to live in high-poverty neighborhoods, whereas the Gautreaux households that moved to the suburbs generally moved to middle-income suburbs. Thus, the inner-city/suburb contrast in the Gautreaux experience matches closely to the low-poverty neighborhood/high-poverty neighborhood contrast of the Moving to Opportunity experiment.

The Gautreaux experience typifies what economists call natural experiments. Real-world programs and treatments are sometimes applied in ways that seem to mimic a randomized experiment. Such natural experiments are sometimes more convincingly akin to random experiments, sometimes less. For example, in the Vietnam draft lottery discussed in Chapter 13, the lottery assigned numbers by random draw; the real-world policy divided 18-year-olds into two groups, those who had "winning" lottery numbers and those who did not, just as a randomized experiment would. In contrast, no randomization device was used in the Gautreaux experiment; we have only anecdotal information to support the contention that the assignment of households to inner-city or suburban locations was unsystematic.

## Differences in Means in the Gautreaux Experience

A decade after the first households in the Gautreaux program moved to new neighborhoods, economists randomly selected a sample of Gautreaux participants for study.[3] These analysts were convinced that the Gautreaux experience was a fine natural experiment that mimicked well a randomized experiment. Two thirds of the households chosen by the analysts were found and answered the analysts' questions. Here we consider what the analysts learned about employment rates for female household heads who were Gautreaux participants. More important, we use this Gautreaux analysis as the springboard to the next section, in which we develop an important estimation strategy used in analyzing many natural experiments.

The analysts found that the employment rate for female household heads who moved to the suburbs was 64%, while the employment rate for female

**TABLE 15.1** The Difference in Means Between Suburban Movers and Inner-City Movers

Employment Rates of Females Who Move to:

|  | Suburbs | Inner City | Difference |
|---|---|---|---|
| After move | 64% | 51% | 13% |

household heads who remained in the inner city was 51%. These observed employment rates are the sample means of a binary variable that takes on the value one if a woman is employed and the value zero if she is not. The difference between these estimated means was significantly different from zero. Table 15.1 displays this comparison of employment rates. The comparison suggests that a suburban location may confer a considerable employment advantage on poor females who head households.

Why might we be skeptical of this estimate of the treatment effect of a suburban location on employment? If the assignment of households in the Gautreaux experience was essentially random, we ought not be skeptical of the finding. But was the assignment truly random? Even if the individuals exercised no control over their new location, might not program administrators influence the assignments? Perhaps the administrators assigned to the suburbs those women who they thought were best able to handle that environment, so that the women in urban and suburban locations have unobserved special traits that account for their different employment levels. The anecdotal evidence suggests otherwise, but there is still considerable room for skepticism.

Fortunately, the Gautreaux data allow us to check on the cross-sectional estimate of the effect of moving to the suburbs on employment. These data contain information on sample program participants both before and after their receipt of their vouchers. The time series dimension of these data has two observations, one from before and one from after receiving the Gautreaux vouchers. (The cross-sectional dimension has 332 observations, 224 on women who received suburban location vouchers and 108 on women who received inner city location vouchers.) Do the time series data tell the same story as the cross-sectional data?

In the Gautreaux cross section, we find suburban dwellers observed 10 years after moving had employment rates 13 percentage points higher than the inner-city dwellers. Do the time series data reinforce this evidence of a strong effect of location on employment? In the time series, we compare the employment rates of suburban-bound household heads before they moved with employment rates of

**TABLE 15.2 The Difference in Before and After Means for Suburban Movers**

Females Who Move to:

|  | Suburbs | Inner City | Difference |
|---|---|---|---|
| After move | 64% | 51% | 13% |
| Before move | 64% |  |  |
| Difference | 0% |  |  |

suburban-bound household heads after they moved. In the sample, 64% of the suburb-bound female household heads were employed before moving, the same employment rate these women had after moving. The difference in employment rates is zero, suggesting that perhaps the suburban location bestowed no employment advantages on these women. Table 15.2 displays both this time series analysis comparison and the earlier cross-sectional comparison.

Which results are we to believe, the difference in cross-section means or the difference in time series means? Just as there are omitted variable stories that could undermine the cross-sectional results, there are also arguments to counter the suggestion from the time series data that location has no effect on employment. Perhaps economic conditions in Chicago, such as the overall metropolitan unemployment rate, changed in the decade between our two measures of the women's employment status, masking the effect of location.

The potential for selection biases from administrative interventions has meant that the large difference in employment rates between these two groups of women does not persuade skeptical analysts that the suburbs confer employment benefits on low-income female household heads. The prospect that the time series result reflects not the suburban location's effect, but other time-related conditions, has meant that the time series finding of no effect on employment similarly does not persuade skeptical analysts that location is unimportant for the employment of low-income household heads. The Gautreaux natural experiment, like many other natural experiments, is flimsy enough in its guarding against biases arising from omitted variables that simple differences in means, as between the suburban and urban populations studied or between the suburban populations observed at two moments in time, constitute weak evidence of a causal effect of location on employment. Fortunately, the Gautreaux data allow better estimators of treatment effects than simple differences in means. The next section introduces one such estimator.

## 15.4     Difference in Differences Estimation

HOW DO WE CREATE
AN ESTIMATOR?

We mistrust the Gautreaux time series estimates because there might be employment-relevant circumstances other than location that changed in the decade between the two observed time periods. We mistrust the Gautreaux cross-sectional estimates because there might be omitted employment-relevant traits of the suburban and urban groups that are unmeasured and also correlated with the households' assignments to suburban or inner-city locations. In this section, we devise an estimator, the *difference in differences estimator*, that overcomes both these concerns. The difference in differences estimator overcomes the first concern. In essence, the estimator uses the households who stay in the inner city to determine what circumstances relevant to employment, other than location, changed between the two time periods. The same difference in differences estimator overcomes the second concern by using the pre-move data to determine how the two assignment groups differ from one another. The difference in differences estimator is sufficiently complicated that it is best discovered before it is formally defined. This section uncovers the estimator in several steps.

### The Difference in Differences Estimator

To check our concern about the time series comparison, we turn to the Gautreaux participants who did not leave the inner city. The employment rates of these female heads of household was 60% before their moves. The continuing inner-city dwellers (who did have to move within the inner city to use their vouchers) experienced a 9% decline in their employment rates 10 years after moving!

What are we to make of the experience of these women who remained in the inner city before and after receiving vouchers? Perhaps employment rates fell in Chicago between these years, or perhaps moving disrupted the employment prospects of women who moved but stayed in the inner city. In either case, we could expect that suburban dwellers would presumably also suffer city-wide employment changes or would also suffer dislocations from moving, just like the program participants who stayed in the city center. But note again that the employment rates of suburban dwellers did not fall at all after moving. The 9% decline in employment rates for the inner-city stayers and the 0% change in employment rates for suburban-bound women differed significantly; a reasonable conclusion is that the suburban location conferred substantial employment benefits on suburban dwellers. Table 15.3 displays this comparison of changes in employment for inner-city stayers and suburban-bound women; the table also repeats the earlier comparisons.

The experience of the inner-city stayers "controls" for the effects of moving and for Chicago-wide employment changes (because the Gautreaux experience changed nothing else for those women), allowing us to translate the 0% change in

**TABLE 15.3** The Difference in Differences in Before and After Means for Suburban and Inner City Movers

Females Who Move to:

|  | Suburbs | Inner City | Difference |
|---|---|---|---|
| After move | 64% | 51% | 13% |
| Before move | 64% | 60% |  |
| Difference | 0% | −9% | 9% |

employment for movers to the suburbs into an overall positive effect of 9% for a suburban locale (because the women who moved to the suburbs did not suffer the 9% decline that the stayers did, but were, presumably, exposed to the same disruptions and metropolitan economic forces as the stayers). This procedure that leads to the 9% estimate of the effect of locating in the suburbs is free from taint by shifts over time in city-wide employment opportunities.

We can similarly check our concern about the cross-sectional difference in means between urban and suburban dwellers after their moves. The 4% difference in pre-move employment rates between suburb movers and inner-city stayers gives us a "control" for the differences in fundamental employability of these two groups. Netting this 4% from the 13% difference we observe after the moves leads to the same 9% difference in employment rates obtained by comparing the changes in employment for suburban-bound women and women who stayed in the inner city. Viewed this way, we see that the procedure that leads to the 9% estimate of the effect of locating in the suburbs is free from taint by persistent differences in the urban and suburban dwellers. Table 15.4 conveniently displays these comparisons.

The 9% estimate of the favorable effect of a suburban location on employment results from differencing the differences in two means (either the 0% and

**TABLE 15.4** The Difference in Before and After Differences in Means for Suburban and Inner-City Movers

Females Who Move to:

|  | Suburbs | Inner City | Difference |
|---|---|---|---|
| After move | 64% ($\overline{Y}_1$) | 51% ($\overline{Y}_2$) | 13% |
| Before move | 64% ($\overline{Y}_3$) | 60% ($\overline{Y}_4$) | 4% |
| Difference | 0% | −9% | 9% |

−9% or the 13% and 4%). The estimator that results is the **difference in differences estimator**, which econometricians often call "diff-in-diffs" for short. Is it an accident of this example that the two calculations both lead to the same result, 9%? No. The two approaches are just rearrangements of one expression. Table 15.4 uses $\overline{Y}_1$, $\overline{Y}_2$, $\overline{Y}_3$, and $\overline{Y}_4$ instead of the particular numerical results from the Gautreaux program, to indicate arbitrary percentages of employment. Using these arbitrary values, the two strategies for computing the difference in differences estimator are

$$(\overline{Y}_1 - \overline{Y}_3) - (\overline{Y}_2 - \overline{Y}_4) = \overline{Y}_1 + \overline{Y}_4 - \overline{Y}_3 - \overline{Y}_2$$

and

$$(\overline{Y}_1 - \overline{Y}_2) - (\overline{Y}_3 - \overline{Y}_4) = \overline{Y}_1 + \overline{Y}_4 - \overline{Y}_3 - \overline{Y}_2.$$

The two strategies always yield the same result.

Because the diff-in-diffs estimator controls for both shifts over time in city-wide employment opportunities and persistent differences between the urban and suburban dwellers other than location, this estimator is a much more convincing estimator of the effect of suburban living on the earnings of poor women than were the two difference in means estimators reported in Tables 15.1 and 15.2.

## The Variance of the Diff-in-Diffs Estimator

The diff-in-diffs estimator involves adding and subtracting four sample means. If the means are mutually statistically independent, then the variance of the diff-in-diffs estimator is the sum of the variances of the four sample means. If the variances of $\overline{Y}_1$, $\overline{Y}_2$, $\overline{Y}_3$, and $\overline{Y}_4$ are $\frac{\sigma_1^2}{n_1}$, $\frac{\sigma_2^2}{n_2}$, $\frac{\sigma_3^2}{n_3}$, and $\frac{\sigma_4^2}{n_4}$, respectively, then

$$\text{var}[\overline{Y}_1 - \overline{Y}_2] - [\overline{Y}_3 - \overline{Y}_4] = \frac{\sigma_1^2}{n_1} + \frac{\sigma_2^2}{n_2} + \frac{\sigma_3^2}{n_3} + \frac{\sigma_4^2}{n_4}.$$

If $\sigma_1^2 = \sigma_2^2 = \sigma_3^2 = \sigma_4^2 = \sigma^2$, and the sample variances corresponding to the sample means $\overline{Y}_1$, $\overline{Y}_2$, $\overline{Y}_3$, and $\overline{Y}_4$ are $\tilde{\sigma}_1^2$, $\tilde{\sigma}_2^2$, $\tilde{\sigma}_3^2$, and $\tilde{\sigma}_4^2$, respectively, then an unbiased estimator of $\sigma^2$ is

$$\tilde{s}^2 = \frac{n_1\tilde{\sigma}_1^2 + n_2\tilde{\sigma}_2^2 + n_3\tilde{\sigma}_3^2 + n_4\tilde{\sigma}_4^2}{n_1 + n_2 + n_3 + n_4 - 4},$$

and an unbiased estimator of the variance of the diff-in-diffs estimator is

$$s_{DinD}^2 = \tilde{s}^2\left(\frac{1}{n_1} + \frac{1}{n_2} + \frac{1}{n_3} + \frac{1}{n_4}\right).$$

If the observations underlying the sample means are also normally distributed, or if our samples are all large, we can test hypotheses about the treatment effect being estimated with the diff-in-diffs estimator. In those cases, the appropriate $t$-statistic for the hypothesis that the treatment effect equals $\beta^*$ is

$$t = \frac{([\overline{Y}_1 - \overline{Y}_2] - [\overline{Y}_3 - \overline{Y}_4]) - \beta^*}{s_{DinD}},$$

which follows the $t$-distribution with $(n_1 + n_2 + n_3 + n_4 - 4)$ degrees of freedom.

## A Regression Formulation of Diff-in-Diffs

Constructing the difference in differences estimator as we do, moving from Table 15.1 to Table 15.4, exposes the workings of the estimator. We can also shed light on the diff-in-diffs strategy by viewing it as a regression model:

$$employment_{it} = \beta_0 + \beta_1(in\ suburb_{it}) + \beta_2(after_{it})$$
$$+ \beta_3(assigned\ to\ suburb_{it}) + \varepsilon_{it}, \qquad \textbf{15.2}$$

where $in\ suburb = 0$ unless the observation is on a person assigned to the suburbs once the person is in the suburbs, when it equals 1; $after = 1$ in the period after households have moved and zero before; and $assigned\ to\ suburb = 1$ for households who received suburban vouchers and $= 0$ otherwise. The index $i$ takes on the value 1 through $n$, where $n$ is the number of people participating in the program; the index $t$ takes on the value 1 prior to moving and 2 subsequent to moving. In a randomized experiment, there would be no need for the variable - $assigned\ to\ suburb$ because randomization ensures that its coefficient is zero— there is no mean difference across samples between the controls and the treatment group. If we were to examine individuals both before and after a randomized experiment, we would, however, need the dummy $after$ because the randomization is not done with respect to time. $In\ suburb$ is surely correlated with $after$. Notice that Equation 15.2 uses two subscripts to capture the two dimensions of the data. The data have a cross-sectional dimension that reflects the individuals under study and a time series dimension that reflects the time periods before and after moving. We call data that provide a time series of cross sections (which we could equally well call a cross section of time series) **panel data**.

Equation 15.2 allows that individuals assigned to the suburbs differ in traits other than location from individuals assigned to the inner city. People assigned to the suburbs but not yet moved (when they still live in the inner city) have E(employment) $= \beta_0 + \beta_3$, whereas before moving, those assigned to the inner city have E(employment) $= \beta_0$. The specification also allows employment to change from before moving to after moving (because of either moving costs or metropolitan-wide employment changes). Observations from after moving have E(employment) larger by $\beta_2$ compared to observations from before moving. Finally, the specification allows a specific effect for being located in the suburbs, $\beta_1$.

The cross-sectional and time series differences in means that we first examined (in Tables 15.1 and 15.2) are biased estimators of $\beta_1$ when the coefficients on *after* and *assigned to suburb* do not equal zero in this regression model—the differences in means implicitly omit these two variables from the model. On the other hand, the diff-in-diffs estimator is an unbiased estimator of $\beta_1$ in this specification; indeed, diff-in-diffs is the OLS estimator of $\beta_1$ for this model. Based on Table 15.4, the least squares estimates of $\beta_0$, $\beta_1$, $\beta_2$, and $\beta_3$ yield

$$\widehat{emp}_{it} = 0.60 + 0.09(in\ suburb_{it}) - 0.09(after_{it})$$
$$+ 0.04\ (assigned\ to\ suburb_{it}) + \varepsilon_{it}.$$

Among the Gautreaux households, better employment outcomes were not the only better outcomes for suburban dwellers. The study found substantial benefits of suburban location for the children of suburban households. The children of suburban dwellers had better school and job outcomes after moving than did their inner-city-staying counterparts. Half the suburban children went on to college; a fifth of the urban children went on to college. Of the grown children who did not go to college, three quarters of the suburban dwellers were employed, whereas only a fifth of their urban counterparts were working. Collectively, the Gautreaux results were so striking that they spurred HUD to design the Moving to Opportunity experiment in which assignments of households have the true randomization lacking in the Gautreaux voucher assignments.

## The Achilles Heel of Diff-in-Diffs

The difference in differences analysis is vulnerable to a possibly serious source of bias. The difference in differences estimator controls for city-wide shift in employment and for persistent differences in the traits of suburban and urban women, but what if the suburban women underwent some experiences, unrelated to their living in the suburbs, that the inner-city women did not? Such events could account for the results in Table 15.4, instead of some effect of living in the suburbs.

In terms of the regression model of Equation 15.2, if the assignment of women resulted in $E(\varepsilon_{12})$ not equaling $E(\varepsilon_{22})$, the diff-in-diffs estimator is biased. That is, the diff-in-diffs estimator is biased if Equation 15.2 mistakenly omits an interaction term between *after* and *assigned to suburb*. For example, if the women assigned suburban vouchers were also sent to a job placement service, any better employment rate attributable to that service would appear as a treatment effect of the suburbs. Or if pregnant women were always assigned inner-city vouchers, their subsequent lower employment rates would be translated into a positive treatment effect for living in the suburbs.

If Equation 15.2 wrongly omits a relevant interaction term between *after* and *assigned to suburb*, then the differences in means are likely to be biased even if the coefficients of *after* and *assigned to suburb* are both zero. The diff-in-diffs estima-

# An Econometric Top 40—A Pop Tune

## Fast Food and the Minimum Wage

Since the Fair Labor Standards Act was enacted in 1938, setting a minimum wage of 25 cents per hour in industry, the minimum wage has been a contentious political topic in the United States. Hit Figure 15.1 shows the path of both the nominal and the real minimum wages from 1938 to 2000. The lower curve shows the upward march of the nominal minimum wage from $0.25 in 1938 to $5.15 in 2000. The real minimum wage, in contrast, goes up and down as inflation eats away at the purchasing power of the nominal minimum wage unless Congress increases the nominal minimum wage sufficiently to restore purchasing power. The real minimum wage reached a maximum in 1968, but it has tended, on average, to decline since

then. In 2000, the real minimum wage was about the same as in the late 1950s.

As inflation eats away at the purchasing power of the minimum wage, supporters of the law press for increases, arguing that low-skill workers need the protection of a minimum wage sufficient to allow them a minimal level of economic well-being.[4] Opponents reply that the minimum wage is misguided, because it destroys jobs that unskilled workers could otherwise fill. The popular debate, in the press and among politicians, focuses on the poor, their wages and their employment, but always lurking in the background are the interests of employers, whose profits go down when the minimum wage goes up. In 1994, economists David

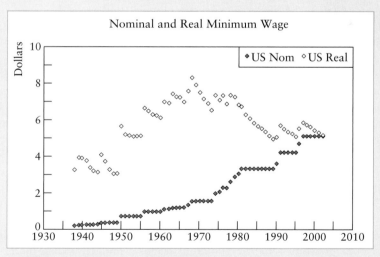

**Hit Figure 15.1**

The Nominal and Real Minimum Wage

*Source:* U.S. Department of Commerce

Card of the University of California at Berkeley and Alan Krueger of Princeton University analyzed a natural experiment that shed new and surprising light on the minimum wage controversy.[5]

Does the minimum wage help or hurt low-skill workers? If the wage rate increase is large enough relative to the employment loss, then raising the minimum wage raises the total wages paid to low-skill workers. If the employment losses are large enough relative to the wage-rate increase, then the total wages paid to low-skill workers decline. Economists have long examined the minimum wage empirically. Virtually all studies find that the declines in employment are not nearly large enough to cause the total wages paid to low-skill workers to fall. However, an increase in the total wages paid to low-skill workers need not mean that all low-skill workers get paid more when the minimum wage is increased.

If unemployment is spread evenly across low-skill workers, then over time all low-skill workers share in the higher payments to low-skill workers caused by the increases in the minimum wage. But if the jobs destroyed by the minimum wage are chiefly jobs held by a particular subset of low-skill workers, those workers end up with lower incomes, not higher incomes, when the minimum wage is increased. Opponents of the minimum wage have often focused on low-skill teenage workers as likely losers from an increase in the minimum wage. Low-skill teens, argue the opponents, are harmed by increases in the minimum wage.

Card and Krueger uncovered a natural experiment with which to determine whether employers of low-skill teens employ fewer such teens in response to a higher minimum wage. On April 1, 1992, New Jersey's state-mandated minimum wage rose from $4.25 to $5.05. Neighboring Pennsylvania's minimum wage did not change. If the opponents of minimum wage increases are correct, teen employment in New Jersey should have fallen relative to that in Pennsylvania following the 1992 increase in New Jersey's minimum wage.

Fast-food establishments are a major employer of unskilled teens. Card and Krueger asked what happened to employment in a sample of fast-food stores in New Jersey and eastern Pennsylvania between early 1992, before the minimum wage rose in New Jersey, and late 1992, six or more months after the minimum wage rose. Card and Krueger identified their fast-food establishments by selecting all Burger King, KFC, Roy Roger's, and Wendy's stores that had listed phone numbers in New Jersey or eastern Pennsylvania, where the Pennsylvania–New Jersey border lies. The response rate to Card and Krueger's inquiries was almost 90%, most of them by telephone. In all, 410 of 473 stores reported their employment numbers in early 1992; 399 of those 410 again reported employment numbers in late 1992. The authors excluded McDonald's from their study at the outset because earlier work had revealed that McDonald's stores respond to such inquiries infrequently.

Card and Krueger conducted numerous sophisticated analyses of their data to ensure the robustness of their results. The core finding of their study, however, comes from a difference in differences estimation of the effect of the minimum wage increase on employment in New Jersey. Hit Table 15.1 reports the diff-in-diffs results. Average employment rose in New Jersey stores over the period, but fell in Pennsylvania, though the difference is not statistically significant. The data are also consistent with a small decline in employment from the minimum wage increase, but not with any large decline. Card and Krueger reinforced their finding from the diff-in-diffs estimator by showing that firms in New Jersey that were already paying above the new minimum wage

**HIT TABLE 15.1 Diff-in-Diffs Estimate of the Employment Effect of New Jersey's Minimum Wage Increase**

Average Employment in a Sample of Fast-food Stores (Number of Employees)

|  | New Jersey | Pennsylvania | Difference |
| --- | --- | --- | --- |
| Early 1992 | 29.8 | 33.1 | −3.3 |
| Late 1992 | 30.0 | 30.9 | −0.9 |
| Difference | −0.2 | 2.2 | −2.4 |

level and firms that had previously been paying less than the new minimum wage had very similar changes in their average employment levels between the two time periods. The New Jersey/Pennsylvania natural experiment indicates that the minimum wage does not much hurt the employment of low-skill teens.

Natural experiments are less compelling than randomized experiments. Even when difference in differences estimation puts to rest concerns that New Jersey fast-food stores are simply different from those in Pennsylvania or that demand conditions for fast food changed between early and late 1992, there remains the worry that changes over time idiosyncratic to New Jersey or to Pennsylvania bias the diff-in-diffs estimates of the effect of the minimum wage change. Some critics also worried that the telephone survey methods that Card and Krueger used measured employment unreliably. In 2000, Card and Krueger responded to their critics.[6]

To address the critics who didn't like the telephone survey, Card and Krueger obtained data from the U.S. Bureau of Labor Statistics (BLS) on the employment numbers for the stores in Card and Krueger's sample. Their results were essentially unchanged by the new data. To address critics who worried that the adjustment to the minimum wage would take more than one year, Card and Krueger used

BLS data for 1993 and 1994 to estimate the changes in employment levels in the two states. Their results were essentially unchanged. To quiet critics who worried that the seven Pennsylvania counties included in the original study were somehow peculiar, Card and Krueger used the BLS data to double the number of Pennsylvania counties included in their analysis. Their results were essentially unchanged.

Perhaps the most telling extension in Card and Krueger's second study was the inclusion of a second natural experiment. In 1996, the national minimum wage in the United States rose from $4.25 to $4.75. This increased the minimum wage in Pennsylvania, but it had no effect on New Jersey's still higher minimum wage of $5.05. Card and Krueger used the BLS data to conduct a second diff-in-diffs analysis, this time using the increase in the minimum wage in Pennsylvania to estimate the effect of an increase in the minimum wage on employment in the fast-food industry.

With the reversal of roles between Pennsylvania and New Jersey in this new natural experiment, any peculiarities between the trends in fast-food employment in New Jersey and those in Pennsylvania that biased the earlier findings against seeing an effect of the minimum wage would bias the results of the new experiment in the opposite direction. The new findings mirrored the original findings, however. The authors found no significant (or appreciable) effect of the minimum wage increase in Pennsylvania on employment levels in Pennsylvania's fast-food industry. Card and Krueger conclude that teen employment is less sensitive to changes in the minimum wage than opponents of minimum wage increases have argued.

 ### Final Notes

Taken together, the Card and Krueger papers are models of fine empirical analysis. In the first paper, the authors take great pains to anticipate challenges to the validity of their re-

sults and to offer what empirical analyses they can to answer those challenges. Then, once done with their study, rather than dropping the matter and getting on to their next research project, Card and Krueger looked for better data to check whether their initial findings were valid, and they looked for a new natural experiment to check their earlier findings. Card and Krueger's tenacity in answering a question thoroughly and their openness to having been wrong initially are virtues every econometrician should develop.

∎

tor, in contrast, is unbiased if the coefficient of either *after* or *assigned to suburb* is nonzero, and is biased only if their interaction has a nonzero effect. Thus, the difference in means estimators are more vulnerable to bias than is the diff-in-diffs estimator. Herein lies the rationale for claiming that natural experiments that allow diff-in-diffs estimation are more credible than natural experiments that must rely on a difference in means.

Diff-in-diffs estimators are moderately compelling when coupled with a plausible natural experiment. In the case of the Gautreaux experiment, the evidence was compelling enough to warrant the further (expensive) Moving to Opportunity experiment—and was also uncompelling enough to require such further experimentation.

## The Strength of Randomized Experiments

Randomized experiments guard against an interaction between *after* and *assigned to suburb* by the very process of randomization. With randomization, the $E(\varepsilon_{12}) = E(\varepsilon_{22})$ and the coefficient on the interaction between *after* and *assigned to suburb* is zero. Randomization similarly ensures that the coefficient *assigned to suburb* is zero. Natural experiments guarantee no similarly effective guard against these potential sources of bias in differences in means estimators or in the diff-in-diffs estimator. If we believe the natural experiment managed a quasi-randomization, we dismiss these vulnerabilities of natural experiments; if we are skeptical of the degree of randomizing achieved in the natural experiment, we worry considerably about relevant events systematically befalling either the treated subjects alone or the untreated subjects alone in the second period of the experiment.

## 15.5    Average and Marginal Treatment Effects

WHAT ARE THE
PROPERTIES OF AN
ESTIMATOR?

If a treatment or a program would affect everyone the same way, the estimated treatment effects from a randomized experiment or from a lucky natural experiment are unbiased estimates of how anyone would be affected by the treatment or program in question. Frequently, though, people are affected by a treatment or program in different ways. This section briefly explores the consequences of heterogeneity in people's responsiveness for interpreting estimated treatment effects.

### Average Treatment Effects on the Treated

To explore the consequences of varied responsiveness to treatments and programs, consider again the Moving to Opportunity program. That program does not sample from the population of all disadvantaged individuals in the inner city, but instead, selects from public housing tenants applying for a housing subsidy that requires moving to a low-poverty neighborhood. If all households assigned to the voucher group use their voucher, the experimental results can estimate unbiasedly the average effect of suburban placement on the population of disadvantaged inner-city dwellers who would apply for and be eligible for a housing subsidy, but not the effects on other disadvantaged households. We say that the experimental results can unbiasedly estimate the **average effect of the treatment on the treated**, that is, the average effect of the treatment across all subjects treated. However, the effects of suburban living for eligible applicants might be greater or less than for all disadvantaged inner-city dwellers. If the program were expanded to cover a broader segment of inner-city inhabitants, the average effect of moving to a suburban dwelling might change. Similarly, if the program were narrowed to focus on a smaller subset of the disadvantaged city dwellers (for instance, only the very poorest households), the average effect of suburban dwelling in such a program might also differ from the average effect observed in the experiment. When the average effect of a treatment changes with the population treated, we say that the marginal treatment effects differ from the average treatment effect. In such cases, we want to use caution when making generalizations from the experimental data.

Incomplete participation by treatment group households also requires caution in interpreting results. If not all households in the voucher group use their vouchers, some members of the treatment group will not undergo the treatment of living in a low-poverty neighborhood. In such cases, we distinguish between the average effect of the treatment on the treated (the effect of living in a low-poverty neighborhood on those who actually use their vouchers) and the **average effect of the treatment on those we intend to treat**. The average effect on those we intend to treat is the total treatment effect (here accrued only by those who use their vouchers) divided by the number of households in the treatment group. Both averages can be of interest. The effect on the treated tells us something about the effect of living in low-poverty neighborhoods. The effect on those whom we intend to treat tells us about the average effect a real-world program would have across all eligible households.

## Early Results from the Moving to Opportunity Experiment

The Gautreaux analysis was conducted more than 15 years after the Supreme Court decision in favor of the Gautreaux tenants by Lawrence Katz, Jeffrey Kling, and Jeffrey Liebman. The Moving to Opportunity experiment is ongoing, and the preliminary analysis treats only the first 2 years of the program.[7] We ought not expect the short-run effects of living in low-poverty neighborhoods to match the long-term effects. Indeed, interviews with the Gautreaux participants indicate that the employment effects for suburban households did not appear until several years after households moved. It is revealing to see what Katz and his colleagues observed in the first 2 years of the Moving to Opportunity experiment, nonetheless.

In contrast to the findings over a longer time period included from the Gautreaux experience, Katz and his colleagues find that after 2 years, employment rates do not differ between voucher and control households. In the experiment, 39% of control participants were employed after 2 years, whereas 40% of voucher participants were employed. There have been some better outcomes for children whose families moved to low-poverty neighborhoods in the first stage of the experiment. Among controls, 32.6% of mothers report behavior problems with their sons, whereas only 23.6% of voucher mothers report such problems. The difference is statistically significant, mirroring the better outcomes for suburban children in the Gautreaux experiment. The authors also find better mental health among the parents who receive vouchers. Control adults report being in "good health" less frequently (57.8%) than do voucher households (69.3%). We must await the later results from the experiment to see if the long-term economic outcomes turn out brighter for the voucher households. Table 15.5 displays these early results of the Moving to Opportunity program.

## Experimental Effects on the Treated and on Those We Intend to Treat

The initial Moving to Opportunity results provide a striking illustration of the need to distinguish between average effects on the treated and average effects on those we intend to treat. Only about half of the Moving to Opportunity voucher group actually found housing (within two years) in low-poverty neighborhoods where they could put their vouchers to use. The gains from the vouchers accrue to these successful voucher households. (The unsuccessful households in the voucher group are in essentially the same circumstances as the control households and are therefore unlikely to experience any treatment effect.) The effects reported in

**TABLE 15.5** Some Initial Outcomes in the Moving to Opportunity Program

| Voucher Recipients | Controls | Effect |
|---|---|---|
| **Employment Rates for Household Heads** | | |
| 40% | 39% | 1.0% |
| **Household Heads' Sons with Behavior Problems** | | |
| 23.6% | 32.6% | −9.0% |
| **Household Heads in Good Mental Health** | | |
| 69.3% | 57.8% | 11.5% |

Table 15.5 for the voucher group are the average treatment effects on those whom the program intends to treat in the Moving to Opportunity program. The average treatment effect on the treated is about double the average treatment effect on those the program intends to treat.

The large split between voucher households that succeeded in finding housing and those that didn't introduces the specter of self-selection bias for the experiment's early results. The self-selection, much of it attributable not so much to a household's choices as to a household's inability to find a place to live in a low-poverty neighborhood, may be considerable. Because the division between successful and unsuccessful is not randomized, the average effect on the treated may not reflect the effect the treatment would have on untreated households; the marginal effects of treatment may not equal the average effects.

To estimate the average treatment on those we intend to treat and the average treatment effect on the treated, Katz and colleagues specify two distinct models. Let $Z$ be a dummy variable indicating that a household is offered a voucher. Let $V$ be a dummy variable indicating that the household actually uses a voucher. Let $Y$ measure an outcome of interest, such as earnings. The first model is

$$Y_i = \alpha_0 + \alpha_1 Z_i + \alpha_2 X_{2i} + \cdots + \alpha_k X_{ki} + \varepsilon_i,$$

where $X_2, \ldots, X_k$ are other explanators of $Y$.

What is $\alpha_1$? It is the difference in the expected value of $Y$ between control group households and voucher group households; that is, $\alpha_1$ is the average treatment effect on those we intend to treat. OLS unbiasedly estimates $\alpha_1$, because randomization ensures that $Z_i$ is uncorrelated with $\varepsilon_i$.

Omitting the $X$-variables would not bias the OLS estimate of $\alpha_1$, because randomization also ensures that the assignment to the voucher group variable, $Z$, is uncorrelated with the individual's traits. However, including these other explanators reduces the variance of the disturbances because the $X$-variable effects would be a part of the disturbance if they were omitted. Consequently, including these other explanators helps to estimate $\alpha_1$ more precisely.

Because not all voucher households actually use vouchers, $\alpha_1$ is not the treatment effect of vouchers on the treated. To estimate the average treatment effect on the treated, the authors turn to a second model:

$$Y_i = \beta_0 + \beta_1 V_i + \beta_2 X_{2i} + \cdots + \beta_k X_{ki} + \nu_i. \qquad \textbf{15.3}$$

In this specification, $\beta_1$ is the average treatment effect on the treated (those for whom $V = 1$). However, we have no assurances that $V$ is uncorrelated with the disturbance term; for example, those who use the voucher may be people who would have unusually good outcomes even without a voucher. OLS would inconsistently estimate $\beta_1$ if there were such a correlation. Fortunately, we have a fine instrument for $V$, namely, $Z$. Being eligible for a voucher ($Z = 1$) is correlated with using a voucher ($V = 1$), and is also uncorrelated with $\nu$ (because voucher eligibility is randomly assigned). Katz and his colleagues use IV to estimate the vouchers' average treatment effects on the treated. As noted earlier, these effects are about double the estimated average treatment effect on those whom we intend to treat.

Does our IV estimator of $\beta_1$ tell us how $E(Y)$ would change for the unsuccessful treatment group members if they were to use a voucher and move to the suburbs? Not necessarily. If the effect of suburban living differs among people in the sampled population, then perhaps those who have succeeded in using their vouchers differ systematically from those who do not. For example, maybe those who would gain most from suburban living manage to find places in the suburbs. Our IV estimator consistently estimates the average effect on the treated; if the treated differ from other treatment group households in the efficacy of suburban living, our estimated $\beta_1$ does not tell us how using vouchers would help the unsuccessful treatment group households. Because the estimated effect of the "treatment," suburban living, applies to only a subset of all households, econometricians say the effect is a "local" effect. Because the effect may not be the same for all the households in the subset, econometricians say the effect is an "average" effect. Consequently, econometricians say that using $Z$ as an instrument to estimate $\beta_1$ in Equation 15.3 estimates the **local average treatment effect** for treated households.

What *can* we infer generally from our IV estimator of $\beta_1$? We can infer that the control group (and population) households that are like the successful treatment group households could expect to benefit from living in the suburbs to an extent similar to that experienced by the successful treatment group households. That is, households similar to the treated households can expect to add our estimate of $\beta_1$ to their $Y$'s, too, if they were to receive vouchers to live in the suburbs.

Moreover, because the experiment assigned subjects randomly, the fraction of such similar households in the control group (and population) is probably about the same as we observe in the treatment group.

## Randomized vs. Natural Experiments

The Moving to Opportunity analysis highlights two important features of randomized experiments compared with natural experiments. First, in the Gautreaux natural experiment, panel data were important to the study's credibility because the ability to control for differences between groups and between time periods was essential. *After* and *assigned to suburb* were quite apt to have nonzero coefficients, which would make simple differences in means biased estimates of a treatment effect. In contrast, because of its randomization, the Moving to Opportunity analysis can rely confidently on differences in means. The randomization ensures that the control group and voucher group are the same (within sampling error) except for the voucher scheme. Second, we see that the randomization provides a useful instrumental variable to overcome the self-selection that can arise even in randomized experiments.

### An Organizational Structure for the Study of Econometrics

**1. What Is the DGP?**

*Controlled, randomized, and natural experiments*

**2. How Do We Create an Estimator?**

*Difference in differences*

**3. What Are an Estimator's Properties?**

*OLS estimation of treatment effects can be biased by*

(a) *Sample selection bias*

(b) *Self-selection bias*

(c) *Nonresponse bias*

(d) *Attrition bias*

**4. How Do We Test Hypotheses?**

———

**5. How Do We Make Forecasts?**

———

Despite their analytical advantages, randomized social experiments are conducted infrequently because they are very expensive. We are often limited to natural experiments with which to infer the effects of social programs. Such natural experiments are more credible when they are viewed through panel data, allowing estimators such as diff-in-diffs with which to overcome omitted variables biases.

## Summary

This chapter discusses controlled, randomized, and natural experiments. The goal of such experiments is to ascertain the causal effect of some intervention, be it a vaccine, a social program, or a new fertilizer. To achieve that goal, an experiment must preclude or overcome omitted variable biases; otherwise, the estimated coefficients would not reflect the effect of the intervention.

Controlled experiments guard against unobserved heterogeneity by banishing it. Randomized experiments rely on random assignment to control and treatment groups to avoid unobserved heterogeneity. Natural experiments are treatment and control groups arising in everyday life that to a greater or lesser degree mimic the random assignment imposed in randomized experiments.

Omitted variables bias can creep into analyses through several routes. Self-selection, nonresponse, and attrition can all undermine even well-intentioned randomized experiments and can even more easily undermine natural experiments. An estimation technique called difference in differences, or diff-in-diffs estimation, proves a guardian against some varieties of bias in natural experiments. The technique is available when the data are drawn both across individuals, some of whom are treated and some of whom are untreated, and across time, with observations before and after treatment.

The difference in differences estimator guards against underlying differences between treatments and controls by exploiting information about those differences before the treatment. The difference in differences estimator guards against temporal changes unrelated to the treatment by exploiting the changes experienced by the controls over time.

The difference-in-differences estimator illustrates how a combination of cross-section data and time series data can guard against omitted variables bias. The next chapter discusses estimators other than OLS and IV that are available for estimating models in DGP that combine cross-section and time series data.

## Concepts for Review

## Questions for Discussion

1.  Compare and contrast Josh Angrist's use of the Vietnam War draft lottery as a natural experiment with the Gautreaux experience as a natural experiment. Angrist used having a low lottery number (a low number made getting drafted more likely) as an instrument for military service in an earnings equation. How does each experiment differ from a random experiment? In what ways do you find the information from these natural experiments compelling, and in what ways are you skeptical of that information?

2.  Describe and discuss how you would construct randomized experiments that would allow you to estimate each of the following effects:
    a.  Whether small financial incentives affect students' willingness to truthfully report their GPAs to another student.
    b.  Whether small financial incentives affect students' willingness to perform a simple repetitive task some large number of times.
    c.  The effect of a training program on the earnings of high-school dropouts.
    d.  Whether increasing the number of police officers who patrol on foot reduces crime rates.

In each case discuss costs, practical barriers, and potential biases.

## Problems for Analysis

For the data sets that you will need to solve these problems,
go to **www.aw-bc.com/murray.**

1.  In March 1995, County A in Kansas implemented a mandatory motivation program for its welfare recipients, requiring them to listen to a monthly afternoon motivational speech (someone talks to the recipients to inspire them to search hard for a job). Neighboring County B did not change anything about its welfare program over the period considered. The average monthly earnings for a welfare recipient in County A were $240 in February 1995 and $220 in June 1995. The average monthly earnings for a welfare recipient in County B were $180 in February 1995 and $150 in June 1995.
    a.  What is the difference in differences estimate of the effect of the motivation program on earnings?

b. Suppose you are given the individual earnings data. Provide the regression equation that gives the same estimate as in (a).

c. Which coefficient in the regression is estimated by the difference in differences estimator in (a)?

d. One critic mentions that seasonal variation in jobs could cause a problem in the difference in differences estimator. How would you respond?

2. In their reanalysis of the minimum wage and fast food employment, Card and Krueger found that employment grew 2% in New Jersey and 10% in Pennsylvania between September 1996, before the increase in Pennsylvania's minimum wage from $4.25 to $4.75, and September 1997, nearly 1 year after the change. What is the difference in differences estimator of the change in the log of Pennsylvania employment due to the increase in the minimum wage?

3. Merit pay for teachers is a hotly contested issue in many communities. Randall Eberts, Kevin Hollenbeck, and Joe Stone analyzed a natural experiment about merit pay for teachers.[8] In 1996, a Michigan high school introduced merit pay for its teachers, with pay linked to the rate at which a teacher's students dropped out of the teacher's courses by the term's end. A nearby, otherwise similar high school in the same school district did not introduce merit pay. Did merit pay increase student retention?

In 1994–1995, the merit pay school's retention rate was 50.92%; the other school's retention rate was 39.02%; in 1998-1999, the merit pay school's retention rate was 71.66%; the other school's retention rate was 54.57%. Eberts and colleagues report that the estimated standard error of the diff-in-diffs estimator of merit pay's effect on retention was 1.60%. In neither school was teachers' pay linked to the grades of students. In 1994–1995, the merit pay school's average GPA was 2.71; in the other school, the average GPA was 2.19. In 1998–1999, the merit pay school's average GPA was 2.19; in the other school it was 1.82. Eberts and colleagues report that the estimated standard error of the diff-in-diffs estimator of merit pay's effect on GPAs was 0.11.

a. The estimated effects of merit pay on student retention and GPAs based on the changes in the observed means at the merit pay school are 20.74% and −0.53, respectively. The reported estimated standard errors for these effects are 0.89% and 0.06. Both effects are statistically significant at even the 1% level. Describe the potential biases in these estimates that could be guarded against by difference in differences estimation.

b. What are the difference in differences estimates of the effect of merit pay on student retention and on GPAs?

c. Which of the estimated effects in (b) are statistically significant at the .05 significance level?

4. Few taxpayers' returns are audited by the government. Would increasing the frequency of audits increase tax collection? Joel Slemrod, Martha Blumenthal, and Charles Christian report a randomized experiment in Minnesota that addressed this question.[9] In early 1995, a random sample of Minnesota taxpayers were sent letters

informing them that their not-yet submitted income tax returns for 1994's income would be closely scrutinized by auditors and if errors were found, the taxpayers would be required to pay any additional taxes required and any corresponding penalties.

The total taxes that letter-recipients reported owing for both 1993 and 1994 were compared in difference in differences fashion to the reported taxes owed in 1993 and 1994 for a random sample of taxpayers who received no letter. Among the 397 households receiving the letter and reporting incomes between $10,000 and $100,000 in 1994, reported tax liability went from $5,082 in 1993 to $6,201 in 1994. Among the 1318 households not receiving the letter and reporting incomes between $10,000 and $100,000 in 1994, reported tax liability went from $5,162 in 1993 to $5,606 in 1994. The data also yield a value of $4,866.34 for $\tilde{s}$.

a. What is the difference in differences estimate of the effect of the audit letter on taxpayers' reported income tax?

b. Is the estimated effect in (a) statistically significant at the .10 significance level?

5. Many health insurance plans require subscribers to make a copayment when receiving covered care. Typically, the copayment is some fraction of the cost of the service. Do higher copayments lead to lower demands for physicians' services? Bart Cockx and Carine Brasseur address this question using data from a natural experiment in Belgium.[10]

In 1994, Belgium raised the copayment for physicians' home visits by a third. However, the increased copayment did not apply to widowed, disabled, retired, or orphaned individuals. The authors used these latter individuals as the control group in a natural experiment. From 1993 to 1994, the average number of physicians' home visits to women in the control group rose from 8.32 to 8.34. The average number of physicians' home visits to women for whom copayments rose (the treatment group) fell from 1.59 to 1.47.

a. What is the difference in differences estimate of the effect of the increased copayment rate on the demand for physicians' home visits?

b. What is the effect of increased copayment rate expressed as a percentage of treatment group women's 1993 visits?

c. What is the estimated price elasticity of demand for physicians' home services among Belgian women based on the result in (b)?

d. What is the percentage change in visits for the treatment group from 1993 to 1994? And for the control group?

e. How would you use the results in (d) in the spirit of diff-in-diffs estimation to estimate the percentage change in physician visits demanded attributable to the increased copayment rate?

f. What is the estimated price elasticity of demand for physicians' home services among Belgian women based on the result in (e)?

g. Given the large discrepancy between the numbers of visits for the treatments and controls, which estimator for the price elasticity of demand do you prefer? Briefly explain.

h. Why might the control and treatment groups in this natural experiment make diff-in-diffs a biased estimator?

6. State workers' compensation plans, which provide income to injured workers, are an important component of the social safety net in the United States. One concern about generous workers' compensation plans is that they give injured workers an incentive to stay off the job longer than necessary. Bruce Meyer, Kip Viscusi, and David Durbin report a natural experiment that sheds light on this concern that the duration of injury times would grow if compensation were made more generous.[11] Workers' compensation plans replace a fraction of injured workers' income, up to some maximum amount per week. States vary in their replacement rates and maximum payments. In 1982, Kentucky increased its maximum payment by 50%. Injured workers receiving less than the maximum payment amount were unaffected by the rule change; these workers are the control group in the natural experiment. The treatment group in the experiment was those injured workers who would receive the maximum payment under either maximum payment plan. A 20% random sample of compensation claim records for workers injured either before or after the change in the maximum payment has a sample mean of the logs of injury time that was 1.13 before and 1.13 after the change in maximum payments for the control group, and 1.38 before and 1.58 after the change for the treatment group. The study reports an estimated standard error for the difference in differences estimator equal to 0.17.

   a. What is the difference in differences estimate of the effect of the 50% change in payments on the mean log of injury time?

   b. Is the effect estimated in (a) statistically significant at the .05 significance level?

   c. Based on the result in (b), what is the estimate of the elasticity of injury time with respect to the compensation payment?

7. The "spatial mismatch hypothesis" contends that the segregation of African Americans and Hispanics into ghettoes and barrios isolates many of the residents from the locations where jobs suitable to their skills can be found. Harry Holzer, John Quigley, and Steven Raphael investigate the spatial mismatch hypothesis by examining a natural experiment in the San Francisco Bay area.[12] They used a regression analysis to arrive at their conclusions. Here, we examine their data in a difference in differences framework.

When people live in one place and jobs are in another, transportation becomes important for employment. If the separation of jobs and employment is especially sharp for minorities, improvements in transportation are apt to benefit them disproportionately. In 1997, the Bay Area Rapid Transit (BART) District opened a long-planned new rapid transit line designed to reduce automobile commuting from the suburbs into the city. The new line also improved transportation from the city to the suburbs by adding new stations in the suburbs. In this problem, we look to see if the line's new stations improved employment opportunities for Hispanics more than for other workers.

If the new BART line affects everyone the same, we would not expect hiring of Hispanics by employers located close to the new stations to change relative to hiring of other groups. Nor would we expect hiring of Hispanics by employers located far from (that is, not near) the new stations to be affected relative to the hiring of other groups. A survey of employers taken both shortly before and shortly after the opening of the new line asked whether an employer's most recent hire for a position not requiring a college degree was Hispanic. The following table reports the percentages for employers located close to the new stations and for employers located far from the new stations, both before and after the stations' opening; the numbers in parentheses are the reported estimated standard errors. For the purposes of this question, assume that the numbers of jobs in the near and far locations are the same.

|  | After | Before | Difference |
|---|---|---|---|
| Employer Near to Station | 0.295 | 0.196 | 0.099 |
|  | (0.043) | (0.038) | (0.058) |
| Employer Far from Station | 0.211 | 0.316 | −0.105 |
|  | (0.047) | (0.054) | (0.066) |
|  |  |  | D-in-D |
| Difference | 0.084 | −0.120 | 0.204 |
|  | (0.058) | · (0.064) | (0.089) |

a. Do the numbers in the table indicate that for Hispanics the new station improved employment opportunities near the new stations?

b. Assume that the means in the table are all normally distributed. What is the $p$-value of the observed change in the percentage of most recent hires that were Hispanic among employers located near the new stations?

c. The year 1997 was one of general employment growth in Oakland. In light of that fact, offer a reasonable explanation for the negative sign on the change in the percentage of most recent hires that were Hispanic among employers located far from the new stations.

d. What is the $p$-value for the change discussed in (c)?

e. If asked whether the new stations increased the number of Hispanics employed, what would you conclude based on these data?

f. If asked whether the new stations improved the welfare of Hispanic workers, what would you conclude based on these data?

g. The estimated standard error on the difference in differences is computed assuming the means are statistically independent of one another. Is that a reasonable assumption in this case?

h. To validly interpret the difference in differences estimate in the table as an indicator of the effect of the new line on Hispanics' overall opportunities, what must we assume about the effect of the new line on employers far from the new stations? Are you comfortable with making that assumption?

 8. Some school systems place students in classes with others of like ability, rather than mixing all students together. This practice is called "tracking." There is much debate about the educational and social consequences of tracking. Eric Hanushek and

Ludger Wössmann have investigated whether tracking students in primary school leads to greater inequality in achievement test outcomes at the secondary school level.[13]

The file tracking.*** contains Hanushek and Wössmann's measure of test outcome inequality (*ineq*) for 17 countries in each of two test administrations. The variable *ineq* is the standard deviation of students' achievement test scores (less the mean standard deviation across countries) in a given country. The first of the two achievement tests was administered to fourth graders, before tracking begins in any of the 17 countries. The second test was administered soon after students began secondary school studies, by which time, students in some sample countries had been tracked and students in other sample countries had not been tracked. The variable *secondary* takes on the value 1 if *ineq* refers to tests taken in secondary school and the value 0 if *ineq* refers to tests taken in primary school. The variable *primtrck* takes on the value 1 if the observation is for a country with tracking at the primary school level (but still after the fourth grade) and the value 0 if the observation is for a country that does not track at the primary school level.

a. For the observations on tests administered during secondary school (after tracking has taken place in countries for which *primtrck* equals 1), regress *ineq* on *primtrck* and an intercept term. Does the estimated difference in mean inequality between tracking and nontracking countries support the claim that tracking leads to increased inequality?

b. Repeat the regression in (a) for the observations on tests taken in primary school, before there is any tracking. What does this regression tell us about which countries tend to introduce tracking prior to secondary school?

c. What doubt does the result in (b) cast upon the test in (a)?

d. To counter the concern in (c), compute the difference in differences estimator of the effect on achievement test outcome inequality of tracking at the primary school level. What does this estimate say about the effect of tracking on inequality?

e. Conduct a regression in which the coefficient on the interaction between *secondary* and *primtrck* is the diff-in-diffs estimator of the effect of tracking on the inequality measure. What does this regression indicate about the statistical significance of the effect estimated in (d)?

## Endnotes

1. The random assignment also offered some applicants a geographically unrestricted housing voucher. For more on the experiment and its early results, see Lawrence F. Katz, Jeffrey Kling, and Jeffrey Liebman, "Moving to Opportunity in Boston: Early Results of a Randomized Mobility Experiment," *Quarterly Journal of Economics* 116, no. 2 (May 2001): 607–654. Because any real program subsidizing moves to the suburbs would be voluntary, limiting the experiment to volunteers focused on households of interest.

2. Voucher recipients were given extensive assistance finding housing in low-poverty neighborhoods. However, within the first 2 years, only about half of the voucher

group had actually found housing in low-poverty neighborhoods; the rest of the voucher group had not yet used the vouchers available to them.

3. James E. Rosenbaum, "Changing the Geography of Opportunity by Expanding Residential Choice: Lessons from the Gautreaux Program," *Housing Policy Debate* 6 (1995): 231–269.

4. Even in 1968, when the real minimum wage was at its highest, a full-time worker earning the minimum wage was below the poverty level for supporting a family of four.

5. David Card and Alan B. Krueger, "Minimum Wages and Unemployment: A Case Study of the Fast-food Industry in New Jersey and Pennsylvania," *American Economic Review* 84 (September 4, 1994): 772–793.

6. David Card and Alan B. Krueger, "Minimum Wages and Employment: A Case Study of the Fast-food Industry in New Jersey and Pennsylvania: A Reply," *American Economic Review* 90, no. 5 (December 2000): 1397–1420.

7. Lawrence F. Katz, "Moving to Opportunity in Boston."

8. Randall Eberts, Kevin Hollenbeck, and Joe Stone, "Teacher Performance Incentives and Student Outcomes," *Journal of Human Resources* 37, no. 4 (2002): 913–927.

9. Joel Slemrod, Martha Blumenthal, and Charles Christian, "Taxpayer Response to an Increased Probability of Audit: Evidence from a Controlled Experiment in Minnesota," *Journal of Public Economics* 79, no. 2 (2001): 455–483.

10. Bart Cockx and Carine Brasseur, "The Demand for Physicians Services: Evidence from a Natural Experiment," *Journal of Health Economics* 22 (2003): 881–913.

11. Bruce D. Meyer, W. Kip Viscusi, and David L. Durbin, "Workers' Compensation and Injury Duration: Evidence from a Natural Experiment, *American Economic Review* 85, no. 3 (June 1995): 322–340.

12. Harry J. Holzer, John M. Quigley, and Steven Raphael, "Public Transit and the Spatial Distribution of Minority Employment: Evidence from a Natural Experiment," *Journal of Policy Analysis and Management* 22, no. 3 (2003): 415–441.

13. Eric Hanushek and Ludger Wössmann, "Does Educational Tracking Affect Performance and Inequality? Difference in Differences Evidence Across Countries," National Bureau of Economic Research, Working Paper 1124, February 2005. The inequality data in this problem are approximated from the paper's Figure 1.

# Chapter 16

# Analyzing Panel Data

*When I'm playful, I use the meridians of longitude and parallels of latitude for a seine, and drag the Atlantic Ocean for whales.[1]*

—Child of Calamity

In many countries, an educated workforce facilitates economic growth from decade to decade. Looking at data across countries and over decades can tell us much about the strength of the effect of education on economic growth. In this instance, economists can fruitfully use data that have both cross-sectional and time series dimensions. How are we to analyze such data? In Chapters 1 through 14 our formal data-generating process (DGP) contained either cross-sectional data or time series data, but not both. In Chapter 15, for the first time we analyzed data that had both temporal and cross-sectional dimensions. There we saw that developing methods specific to these special data, such as the difference in differences estimator, can overcome biases that sometimes plague studies of a single cross section or a single time series. This chapter further examines how to exploit data that have both cross-sectional and time series dimensions.

In recent years, statistical agencies have increasingly assembled data sets containing both time series and cross-sectional information. For example, the Organization for Economic Cooperation and Development (OECD), which comprises most of the highly industrialized nations of the world, publishes time series data for each of its member countries. The University of Michigan publishes its Panel Survey of Income Dynamics (PSID) containing household data for the large number of U.S. households that have contributed information to the PSID annually since 1968. Economists have exploited these data as they have become available. Along the way, econometricians have developed formal methods suitable to studying such data. This chapter introduces those methods.

The chapter begins by introducing the two kinds of DGPs that economists most often use when specifying the statistical traits of data that have both cross-sectional and time series dimensions. These DGPs both allow for unobserved differences among the individuals who appear in the panel. In the first kind of DGP, each individual differs from others in the sample in ways that remain fixed across samples. In the second, each individual differs from others in the sample, but the differences among individuals change randomly across samples. The chapter then presents estimators suitable for each sort of DGP. It also presents testing procedures pertinent to DGPs that contain both cross-sectional and time series data and shows how the estimation procedures developed for data with temporal and cross-sectional dimensions also apply to some other DGPs in which observations have dual dimensions.

# 16.1    Panel Data

Some data sets combine information about one cross section of individuals at one moment in time with information about a different cross section of individuals at a different moment in time. We do not study that sort of data in this chapter. Instead, we focus on data that contain information about the same individuals viewed at several moments in time. We call data that contain such a time series of cross sections (or, equivalently, such a cross section of time series) **panel data**. The difference in differences estimator introduced in Chapter 15 reveals how we can sometimes exploit panel data to overcome the omitted variables problem that we call *unobserved heterogeneity*. **Unobserved heterogeneity** refers to omitted variables with values that are constant for an observed individual over at least the time span of one panel data sample. This section introduces the most common specifications for a panel data DGP in which there is unobserved heterogeneity.

To illustrate unobserved heterogeneity, consider the PSID. Each household in the PSID is apt to differ systematically from all others in unobserved ways. Consequently, all the observations on one household share some commonality not shared with other observations. Also consider the OECD panel data. Each OECD country has its idiosyncrasies. Consequently, all the observations on one country share some commonality not shared with other observations. Commonalities can also be shared by all the observations in a single time period, and by no others. For example, all PSID households observed in a given year, say 2003, will be subject to a common set of U.S. economic conditions, and all OECD countries observed in a given year, say 2002, will be subject to a common set of international economic conditions.

If there were no persistent unobserved commonality for each individual in a panel, the analysis of panel data would not differ much from that of other DGPs we have seen. Indeed, if there is no such commonality and no serial correlation in the disturbances over time, panel data could satisfy the Gauss–Markov Assumptions and ordinary least squares (OLS) would again be the best linear unbiased estimator (BLUE). Absent persistent unobserved individual idiosyncrasies, the chief advantage of panel data is that it increases the number of observations in our sample relative to a single time series or cross section. The extra observations may also bring additional variation in the explanators. But persistent unobserved idiosyncrasies usually do appear in panel data. The central question in analyzing panel data is how to deal with these idiosyncrasies. *Panel data offer three chief advantages over studying a single cross section or time series: (i) a panel increases*

*sample size; (ii) the additional observations of a panel may bring additional varia-*
*tion in the explanators; and (iii) panel data can overcome some omitted variable*
*biases that might plague a single cross section.*

Unobserved heterogeneity in panel data is a special sort of omitted variable. This omitted variable has a specific value for each individual. All the observations on an individual in a given sample contain this common unobserved effect. For example, if the panel consists of time series observations on a set of firms, there is a firm-specific effect common to each temporal observation on a specific firm. The unobserved heterogeneity might combine several traits of the individual, each of which could be an explanator if measured. For example, corporate culture, the CEO's style, and the rules of the company's bylaws might each give rise to a firm-specific effect that is constant over all the time periods in a sample. However, because the effects of all these traits are unobserved (by assumption), we can deal only with their sum in our analysis—we cannot disentangle what may be a complex of unobserved traits.

Panel data with unobserved heterogeneity come in two varieties. The unobserved heterogeneity may be the same from one sample to the next, or it may vary randomly from one sample to the next. **Distinct intercepts DGPs** are those in which the unobserved differences among groups are the same from one sample to the next. **Error components DGPs** are those in which the unobserved differences among groups vary randomly from one sample to the next. Error components DGPs are more common in practice, but distinct intercepts DGPs do sometimes arise. Because the estimation strategy for distinct intercepts DGPs is more transparent, we begin with the distinct intercepts case (Extension 6 on this book's Web site, **www.aw-bc .com/murray**, contains a matrix algebra exposition of panel data DGP's.)

A more general treatment of panel data would explore in some detail temporal effects common to all individuals. We limit our attention to the special case of a distinct intercept term for each time period and treat such temporal dummies as explanators akin to any other.

## Distinct Intercepts DGPs

To understand the distinct intercepts DGP, consider the following example. Individual states in the United States vary in how many of their youths join the military. Some of this variation is attributable to measurable socioeconomic differences among the states, but some of the variation is rooted in long-standing traditions in states' cultures. Economists who study military recruiting repeatedly draw samples over time. Typically, these economists obtain data from all the states in a given time period. Consequently, the same cultural influences reappear in each sample of data. This example typifies what we call a distinct intercepts DGP—the effect of a state's culture on recruiting is the same from one sample to the next.

Let us first consider a distinct intercepts DGP that differs as little as possible from our standard Gauss–Markov DGP. Suppose that in the military recruiting example, we draw samples containing $T$ years, with all $n$ U.S. states included in each sample. A sample thus has $nT$ observations in all. The dependent variable is the number of recruits from a given state in a given year. The explanators might include military pay relative to civilian pay, the size of recruiting bonuses, the number of recent high school graduates in the state, and the state's unemployment rate. We assume the disturbances have a mean of zero and are homoskedastic and serially uncorrelated. We also assume the explanators are contemporaneously uncorrelated with the disturbances. The distinct intercepts DGP is

$$Y_{it} = \beta_{0i} + \beta_1 X_{1it} + \cdots + \beta_K X_{Kit} + \varepsilon_{it} \qquad i = 1, \ldots, n; \qquad \textbf{16.1}$$
$$t = 1, \ldots, T$$
$$\mathrm{E}(\varepsilon_{it}) = 0 \qquad i = 1, \ldots, n; t = 1, \ldots, T$$
$$\mathrm{var}(\varepsilon_{it}) = \sigma^2 \qquad i = 1, \ldots, n; t = 1, \ldots, T$$
$$\mathrm{E}(\varepsilon_{it}\varepsilon_{i't'}) = 0 \qquad \text{if } i \neq i' \text{ or } t \neq t'$$
$$\mathrm{E}(X_{jit}\varepsilon_{it}) = 0 \qquad \text{for all } j, i, t$$

The two new features of this DGP are (i) the data are a cross section of time series so that observations have two subscripts, $i$ and $t$—the index $i$ indicates which individual (state) the observation is from and the index $t$ indicates which time period the observation is from; and (ii) each individual has its own intercept term, $\beta_{0i}$.

In the distinct intercepts DGP, the individual specific intercept terms are parameters, traits of the population that remain the same from one sample to the next. The coefficients $\beta_{0i}$ capture the sum of all unobserved influences on $Y$ that remain constant over the time periods of the sample for individual $i$. In this DGP, $\varepsilon_{it}$ is contemporaneously uncorrelated with the explanators, so OLS is consistent if the explanators are not asymptotically perfectly collinear.

The distinct intercepts model may be appropriate if our observations are always drawn from the same individuals, as in drawing all the states of the United States, but if the individuals observed vary from sample to sample, that model is inappropriate. When we observe different individuals in each sample, we do not have distinct individual intercepts; instead we have an individual effect that is constant for all observations on a specific individual in a given sample, but that is random across samples. Such data require an error components DGP.

## Error Components Models

To understand the error components DGP, let's modify our previous example. Each county in the United States is assigned to a Military Recruiting District.

Each recruiting district contains many counties, sometimes counties from several states. Each recruiting district has a commander in charge of recruiting. Commanders stay in place for several years. Recruiting commanders differ in their ability and their enthusiasm for their jobs. How many recruits sign up in a recruiting district depends greatly on the productive efforts of the local recruiting commander. For simplicity, in this subsection, we assume there are none of the state-specific distinct intercepts discussed earlier.[2]

We assume the commanders change from one panel sample to the next. For further simplicity, we also assume that each recruiting district has only one commander for all the years in any one sample. Because the commanders we observe change from sample to sample, the effect of commanders on recruiting in this scenario is not fixed across samples. Instead of capturing the recruiting district-specific effects of commanders by distinct intercepts for each recruiting district, the effect appears in the DGP as a random disturbance that is the same for every observation on a given district in a given sample, but that is random across samples. The recruiting district specific disturbance is one component of the total disturbance term. We call a DGP with such effects an error components DGP.

The notion of an error component deserves some elaboration. In one sample, the individual effect for the first observation (that for the Military Recruiting District Number One in the first year of the sample) refers to the effect of one recruiting commander, perhaps Captain Ramirez. In the next sample, the individual effect for the first observation (once again for the Military Recruiting District Number One in the first year of the sample) refers to the effect of a different recruiting commander, perhaps Captain Silmer. In error components models, we account for this variation in the individual effect across samples by treating the recruiting commander effect as a random variable that makes up one component of an observation's disturbance term. Captain Ramirez's effect appears in each first-sample observation on Military Recruiting District Number One. Captain Silmer's effect appears in each second-sample observation. The individual error component varies across individuals in a sample but not across the temporal observations in a sample. We denote the individual error component for the $i$-th individual in a sample by $\nu_i$.

The number of recruits in a district in a given time period depends on many unmeasured influences in addition to the traits of the commander. These unmeasured influences also appear in the disturbance term for an observation. We represent the sum of these unmeasured observation-specific effects for the $it$-th observation by the random variable $\mu_{it}$. The total disturbance in the $it$-th observation in an error components model is $(\nu_i + \mu_{it})$.

To formalize the notion of an error components DGP, let's first consider an error components DGP that differs as little as possible from our standard Gauss–Markov DGP. In this first error components DGP, then, following the spirit of the Gauss–Markov Assumptions, (i) the two sorts of disturbances, the $\mu_{it}$ and $\nu_i$, have means of zero and are homoskedastic; (ii) the $\mu_{it}$ are uncorrelated over time and across individuals; (iii) the $\nu_i$ are uncorrelated across individuals; and (iv) the $\mu_{it}$ and $\nu_j$ are uncorrelated. The first error components DGP deviates from the Gauss–Markov Assumptions in one regard, namely, that the disturbances contain a random component for each individual in a given sample, $\nu_i$, that is fixed from one time period to the next. Finally, as noted earlier, the first error components DGP allows the explanators to be random variables but assumes that the explanators are contemporaneously uncorrelated with the disturbances. We assume that our data are a panel of $n$ individuals (for example, military recruiting districts) observed for $T$ time periods, providing $nT$ observations in all. Here is our first error components DGP:

$$Y_{it} = \beta_0 + \beta_1 X_{1it} + \cdots + \beta_K X_{Kit} + \nu_i + \mu_{it} \qquad i = 1,\ldots,n; \qquad \textbf{16.2}$$
$$t = 1,\ldots,T$$

$$\begin{aligned}
\mathrm{E}(\mu_{it}) &= 0 & i &= 1,\ldots,n;\ t = 1,\ldots,T \\
\mathrm{var}(\mu_{it}) &= \sigma_\mu^2 & i &= 1,\ldots,n;\ t = 1,\ldots,T \\
\mathrm{E}(\mu_{it}\mu_{i't'}) &= 0 & &if\ i \neq i'\ or\ t \neq t' \\
\mathrm{E}(\nu_i) &= 0 & i &= 1,\ldots,n \\
\mathrm{var}(\nu_i) &= \sigma_\nu^2 & i &= 1,\ldots,n \\
\mathrm{E}(\nu_i\nu_j) &= 0 & &for\ i \neq j \\
\mathrm{E}(\mu_{it}\nu_j) &= 0 & &for\ all\ i,\ j,\ t \\
\mathrm{E}(X_{jit}\mu_{it}) &= 0 & &for\ all\ i,\ j,\ t \\
\mathrm{E}(X_{jit}\nu_i) &= 0 & &for\ all\ i,\ j,\ t.
\end{aligned}$$

The DGP described in Equation 16.2 is frequently used by economists. A second error components DGP is also frequently used, however. These two error components DGPs differ in only one regard. In the error components model described in Equation 16.2, the explanators are assumed to be uncorrelated with the disturbances. In the second model, the explanators are allowed to be contemporaneously correlated with the individual effects (the $\nu_i$), but are assumed to be contemporaneously uncorrelated with the $\mu_{it}$. We shall see that the best estimator to use differs between the two DGPs.

In the first error components DGP, the error components and the explanators are contemporaneously uncorrelated. OLS is a consistent estimator in this DGP. In the second one, the individual specific error components are correlated with the explanators. OLS is not a consistent estimator in this second DGP.

Formally, the second error components DGP is also given by Equation 16.2, except for the last assumption. In this DGP,

$$\mathrm{E}(X_{jit}\nu_i) \neq 0 \quad for\ at\ least\ some\ j,\ i,\ and\ t.$$

Why might the explanators be correlated with the individual specific error components? Consider the military recruiting example. One observed variable affecting the number of recruits that sign up in a military recruiting district is the district's recruiting budget. Especially able recruiting commanders, one for whom the individual error component $v_i > 0$, may lobby quite effectively for higher budgets. If so, districts with above-average values for $v_i$ are likely to have above-average values for the budget explanator—the explanators and error components would be correlated.

### Choosing a Fixed or Error Components DGP

Notice that in both error components specifications and in the preceding distinct intercepts specification, the "individuals" for whom we specify individual effects are defined by their geography, a state in one instance and a military recruiting district in the other. *What makes a distinct intercepts DGP appropriate for one and an error components DGP appropriate for the other is the persistence or variability of the individual specific effect across samples.*

To determine whether we are dealing with distinct intercepts or an error component, we must ask ourselves about the sampling context of our study. Note, too, that geography is certainly not the only way in which individuals might be identified. Individual firms, each observed over time, would constitute a panel. Households, each observed over time, would similarly constitute a panel. The distinct intercepts and error components distinction would once again turn on whether we expected to repeatedly sample the same firms or households, or to draw new firms or households in subsequent samples.

## 16.2    Estimation with Panel Data

How Do We Make an Estimator?

This section introduces estimators for the previous section's distinct intercepts and error components DGPs. *One estimator, the fixed effects estimator, is appropriate for estimating slopes both in the distinct intercepts DGP and in the second error components DGP (in which the random individual effects are correlated with the disturbances). Another estimator, the random effects estimator, is suitable for estimating slopes in the first error components model (in which the random individual effects are uncorrelated with the disturbances).* Because the appropriate estimator depends on the error components DGP we are using, we also need to discuss a test for distinguishing between the two error components DGPs.

### Estimation in the Distinct Intercepts DGP

In the distinct intercepts DGP, each individual has its own intercept term, $\beta_{0i}$. We have seen distinct intercepts for subsets of observations before—dummy variable explanators give distinct intercepts to distinct groups. If we include a dummy

# An Econometric Top 40—Two Golden Oldies

## The Early Panel Studies

### Management Bias

Many people attend graduate schools of management to make themselves more valuable to firms. Owners of firms know that able managers contribute to the success of firms, and they are willing to pay top salaries to employ good managers. However, despite their importance, managers are invisible in many econometric studies of firms. Production functions traditionally include capital, labor, and sometimes land and materials, as explanators of output, with management nowhere to be seen. In 1962, Yair Mundlak of the Hebrew University argued that using panel data can overcome the omitted variable bias that arises from ignoring management.[3] If capital or labor or materials use are correlated with management, then OLS applied to a production relationship that omits management yields biased estimates of the technological relationship between output and inputs.

Mundlak argues that management poses particularly difficult measurement problems. In what units do we measure management? We might include variables we think are related to management, but the concept itself is sufficiently vague as to make accurate measurement all but impossible. However, we can sidestep the measurement problem, Mundlak claims, if within a given firm management is constant across several years. The key is to use a cross section of time series observations on several firms. Mundlak's analysis of management bias is the first published use of a fixed effects estimator. Because many economic analyses are plagued by similarly difficult-to-measure, but relevant variables, Mundlak's success provides a tool applicable to many econometric studies.

Mundlak's sample consists of 66 family farms in Israel, each observed annually from 1954 to 1958. The data contain information on output of labor, materials, capital (livestock, in the case of the Israeli farms of that time), and land. Mundlak argues that a farm-specific intercept term can capture the effect of farm management if the farm management effect is constant for each farm across the five years in the sample. The time series information for each farm allows Mundlak to estimate the farm-specific intercepts.

What did Mundlak find? Does accounting for management matter? Indeed, it does. The OLS-estimated elasticity of output with respect to all measured inputs is 0.97 when management is ignored. The elasticity drops to 0.80 when management is accounted for. Mundlak is careful to note that if there are unmeasured aspects of the farms other than management, the estimated farm-specific effect combines these effects with the management effect. Mundlak suggests that in a larger sample, we might use a geographic dummy variable for farms in the same village to control separately for local fertility advantages and the like. Mundlak also suggests including a dummy variable for each time period to capture productivity changes that occur from one year to the next and are apt to affect all farms similarly. Such temporal dummies have become a fixture in many subsequent panel data analyses.

Mundlak's 1962 paper was the first to introduce distinct intercepts to control for omitted variables bias in panel data. Subsequently, a host of researchers have adopted Mundlak's DGP. The first application of an error components DGP to panel data came in 1969, when economists Pietro Balestra of Universite de Fribourg and Marc Nerlove of Yale University used such a model to study the demand for natural gas.

## Natural Gas

Balestra and Nerlove linked their study of the demand for natural gas to the well-developed theory of durable consumption goods. Economists distinguish between durable consumption goods (goods enjoyed repeatedly over a length of time) and nondurable consumption goods (goods consumed all at once). Cars, washers, dryers, and stoves are durable consumption goods; bananas, beverages, gasoline, and heating or cooking fuels are nondurable ones. Economists long understood that analyzing the demand for durable consumption goods requires a dynamic analysis—purchases made in the past affect purchases made today because some of the durable goods bought in the past are still available today for consumption. If how much of a durable consumption a consumer would buy today depends on how much the consumer has bought in the past, a demand model for today's demand for a durable consumption good would include a lagged dependent variable as an explanator.

Reasoning similarly, we might be tempted to argue that the demands for nondurable consumption goods do not require a dynamic analysis—each period, we can make new choices about how many bananas to buy, how many movies to see, and how much fuel to consume, without relating them to our past choices. In 1969, Balestra and Nerlove of Yale University pointed out that some nondurable consumption does require a dynamic analysis.[4] Energy consumption depends on the stock of appliances that one holds. Past decisions to purchase appliances influence today's demands for energy. Thus, an explanator in energy demand equations should be lagged appliance ac-

cumulations. Moreover, they note, the current prices of energy sources should appear in demand equations for appliances. Balestra and Nerlove focused their attention on one particular energy source: natural gas.

The demand for natural gas depends on many factors, including weather, population, the relative price of natural gas, income, and the stock of gas-using appliances. In turn, the demand for gas-using appliances depends on those same factors, the prices of alternative fuels, and the prices of appliances that use alternative fuels. Balestra and Nerlove argue that once an appliance stock is in place, households will substitute little, if at all, between energy sources. Thus, it is the appliance demands, not the energy demands, that depend on the prices of alternative fuels.

Balestra and Nerlove gather state-level demand data for the years 1950–1962. Natural gas was available in 36 states during that period. Unfortunately, during the start-up years of natural gas availability, 1950–1956, supply limits constrained consumption in many states. Data from those years are not informative about the responsiveness of demand to economic influences. However, the data from the six years 1957–1962 were informative about demand. By requiring that the industry interrupt supply to businesses if that were necessary to meet consumer demand, state regulations made the supply of natural gas to consumers infinitely elastic. Moreover, state regulations made current prices independent of current demand—the regulatory system put price structures in place that did not change without time-consuming regulatory hearings.

Balestra and Nerlove pooled the data from the 36 states in which natural gas was available across the six years in which quantities observed reflected movements along the demand curve for natural gas. The authors' panel data model is dynamic in that the demand for natural gas depends on accumulated stocks of appliances, and the stocks of appliances are sensitive to the path of energy prices and income.

Balestra and Nerlove were aware of the fixed effects estimator for panel models. However, they were loath to sacrifice the 36 degrees of freedom that state-specific dummy variables would require. They offered, instead, the innovative (in 1969) suggestion that they treat the state-specific effects as random variables, and that the appropriate estimator is a variant of what we now call the random effects estimator. (Their estimator differs from the random effects estimator we examine because they grappled with the appearance of dynamic effects, whereas we do not allow for such temporal concerns in our error components DGPs.)

Balestra and Nerlove's insight that the demand for natural gas depends on accumulated appliance stocks proves crucial to their analysis. OLS estimation of a static model without appliances leads to a statistically insignificant effect of the price of natural gas on the demand for natural gas. When the model is made dynamic, though, by including appliance accumu-lation, the estimated long-run own-price elasticity is −0.63 and statistically significant. Because the estimated depreciation rate on natural gas appliances is 2% per year, Balestra and Nerlove find relatively little estimated short-run responsiveness of natural gas demand to the price of natural gas.

 **Final Notes**

Mundlak and Balestra and Nerlove stand in a long tradition of economists driven to make econometric innovations by the twin pressures of applied interests and available data. When they wrote, panel data was unusual; they needed to innovate to use such data. Today, panel data are increasingly available, and all applied economists should familiarize themselves with the econometric tools for analyzing such data. But just as Balestra and Nerlove looked to the specifics of natural gas demand and their panel data to reach beyond the ready tool of distinct intercept DGPs, the best applied econometricians will always ask if their particular analytical problem invites the development of new econometric tools.

∎

variable for each individual (for each state in the distinct intercepts military recruiting example), the coefficients on those dummies are the $\beta_{0i}$ of the distinct intercepts model. OLS applied to the model with these dummy variables included yields unbiased estimates of all the coefficients in the model. This estimator is commonly called the **least squares dummy variable (LSDV) estimator**. In this DGP, the LSDV estimator efficiently estimates the coefficients of the model. Unfortunately, the number of individuals in a panel may be large. For example, if we were to analyze military recruiting at the county level, we would find that there are about 3,000 counties in the United States. Coping with 3,000 dummy variables can be quite cumbersome—even 50 dummies, one for each state, lead to messy, unmanageable computer reports.

Frequently in distinct intercepts panel data applications, we are interested in the slope coefficients assumed to be common across individuals and over time rather than in the intercept terms varying across individuals. For example, U.S.

Defense Department analysts are more interested in how many more recruits they can entice to join the military by raising recruiting bonuses than in how recruiting differs between Androscoggin County, Maine, and Orange County, California. Consequently, the analysts have little or no need for the intercepts in the recruit model.

If our interest is only in the slope coefficients, and not in the intercepts, there exists a shortcut that avoids LSDV's need for many dummy variables. Recall the change in OLS brought by moving from a straight line through the origin to a straight line with unknown intercept. The OLS formula for the slope of the line changed only in that instead of using $X_i$ and $Y_i$ in the least squares formula, we used the deviation of $X_i$ from its sample mean, $\overline{X}$, that is, $(X_i - \overline{X}) = x_i$, and the deviation of $Y$ from its own sample mean, $\overline{Y}$, that is, $(Y_i - \overline{Y}) = y_i$, so that

$$\frac{\sum X_i Y_i}{\sum X_i^2}$$

became

$$\frac{\sum x_i y_i}{\sum x_i^2}.$$

The transformation of $X$ to $x$ and of $Y$ to $y$ conveniently links the estimation of the slope of a line through the origin to the estimation of a single slope when the intercept is unknown.

Similar transformations of $X$ and $Y$ avoid the need for estimating each intercept term in the distinct intercepts model. The **fixed effects estimator** is OLS applied to the distinct intercepts model, expressed in terms of the deviations of each observation from the sample mean for the individual in that observation. (There are $T$ observations for each individual. The deviations for any one individual used in the fixed effects estimator are the differences of every observation for the individual from the mean for that individual over those $T$ observations.) Thus, we rewrite the model as

$$y_{it} = \beta_1 x_{1it} + \cdots + \beta_k x_{kit} + (\varepsilon_{it} - \overline{\varepsilon}_i), \qquad \text{16.3}$$

in which $y_{it} = (Y_{it} - \overline{Y}_i)$ and $x_{jit} = (X_{jit} - \overline{X}_{ji})$, where

$$\overline{Y}_i = \frac{1}{T}\sum_{t=1}^{T} Y_{it}, \ \overline{X}_{ji} = \frac{1}{T}\sum_{t=1}^{T} X_{jit}, \text{ and } \overline{\varepsilon}_i = \frac{1}{T}\sum_{t=1}^{T} \varepsilon_{it}.$$

The fixed effects estimator yields the same efficient estimates and standard errors for the slope coefficients as does LSDV, but it provides no estimates of the intercepts. The fixed effects estimator is a convenient shortcut to the OLS estimates of the slope coefficients. Notice that any variable, $X_m$, that does not vary over time for any individual has $x_{mi}$ equal to zero for every observation. The coefficient for such an $X_m$ does not appear in Equation 16.3 and cannot be estimated consistently by any estimator because it is perfectly collinear with the set of distinct intercepts.

## Fixed Effects Estimation as Within Estimation

Because the fixed effects estimator relies on each observation expressed as a deviation from the individual's mean, the estimator does not exploit any of the variation of the $X$'s *across* individuals to estimate the slopes. For example, in the case of a single explanator, the fixed effects estimator of $\beta_1$ is

$$\tilde{\beta}_1^{FE} = \hat{\beta}_1^{LSDV} = \frac{\sum_{t=1}^{T}\sum_{i=1}^{n}(X_{it} - \overline{X}_i)(Y_{it} - \overline{Y}_i)}{\sum_{t=1}^{T}\sum_{i=1}^{n}(X_{it} - \overline{X}_i)^2}. \qquad \textbf{16.4}$$

This formula uses the deviations of each observation from its individual-specific mean, rather than deviations of observations about the overall means of $X$ or $Y$. How one observation differs from others on that same individual matters for the fixed effects estimator; how one observation differs from the means for other individuals does not. In this sense, the variation across individuals does not matter for the fixed effects estimator.

The variation not exploited in Equation 16.4 is that of the individual's means about the overall mean. To understand this claim, let's define

$$\overline{X} = \frac{1}{nT}\sum_{t=1}^{T}\sum_{i=1}^{n}X_{it} \quad \text{and} \quad \overline{Y} = \frac{1}{nT}\sum_{t=1}^{T}\sum_{i=1}^{n}Y_{it}.$$

We can then decompose the total variation in the $X$'s about their overall mean, $\overline{X}$, into two parts:

$$\sum_{t=1}^{T}\sum_{i=1}^{n}(X_{it} - \overline{X})^2 = \sum_{t=1}^{T}\sum_{i=1}^{n}(X_{it} - \overline{X}_i)^2 + \sum_{i=1}^{n}(\overline{X}_i - \overline{X})^2. \qquad \textbf{16.5}$$

Similarly,

$$\sum_{t=1}^{T}\sum_{i=1}^{n}(X_{it} - \overline{X})(\overline{Y}_{it} - \overline{Y}) = \sum_{t=1}^{T}\sum_{i=1}^{n}(X_{it} - \overline{X}_i)(\overline{Y}_{it} - \overline{Y}_i)$$
$$+ \sum_{i=1}^{n}(\overline{X}_i - \overline{X})(\overline{Y}_i - \overline{Y}). \qquad \textbf{16.6}$$

If there were a single intercept in the DGP, instead of distinct ones, the OLS estimator of $\beta_1$ would be the ratio of the left-hand side of Equation 16.6 to the left-hand side of Equation 16.5. In contrast, the fixed effects estimator, given by Equation 16.4, is the ratio of the first term on the right-hand side of Equation 16.6 to the first term on the right-hand side of 16.5. The fixed effects estimator does not include

$$\sum_{i=1}^{n}(\overline{X}_i - \overline{X})(\overline{Y}_i - \overline{Y})$$

in the numerator or

$$\sum_{i=1}^{n}(\overline{X}_i - \overline{X})^2$$

in the denominator because the co-movements of $\overline{X}_i$ and the $\overline{Y}_i$ about $\overline{X}$ and $\overline{Y}$ may be attributable to *either* the effects of the $\overline{X}_i$ varying or the effects of differences in the individual's intercept terms, the $\beta_{0i}$.

In the distinct intercepts DGP, an estimator based on the variation between group means

$$\tilde{\beta}_1^G = \frac{\sum_{i=1}^{n}(\overline{X}_i - \overline{X})(\overline{Y}_i - \overline{Y})}{\sum_{i=1}^{n}(\overline{X}_i - \overline{X})^2} \qquad 16.7$$

would be a biased estimator of $\beta_1$ because the effects of differing intercepts would be folded into the effects of $X$. If the individuals shared a common intercept, $\tilde{\beta}_1^G$ would estimate $\beta_1$ consistently, but inefficiently.

*The fixed effects estimator relies entirely on the variation of the X's that happens within the observations for individuals. For this reason, the fixed effects estimator is sometimes called the "within" estimator.* The aptness of the description of the fixed effects estimator as the "within" estimator might become more clear if we consider a case in which each $X$-variable has a constant value over time for each individual, but individuals have different $X$-values from one another; that is, $X_{it} = X_{it'}$ for all $i$, $t$, and $t'$, but $X_{it} \neq X_{i't}$ for $i \neq i'$. For example, if $X$ is years of education and our sample is made up of older men, each individual's education is apt to be constant across all the observations on the individual. In such a special case, there is no variation of any of the $X$'s within individuals, but there is variation across individuals. Because there is no variation of the $X$'s within individuals, the mean value of each $X$ equals that constant value for each individual: $X_{it} = \overline{X}_i$. Consequently, $x_{it} = 0$ for all $i$ and $t$, and the fixed effects estimator does not exist. Thus, without within-individual variation in the $X$'s, the fixed effects estimator does not exist. In contrast, if the $X_{it}$'s are the same for all $i$, instead of for all $t$, there is no variation *across* individuals, and the fixed effects estimator continues to exist.

Because the distinct intercepts DGP differs from the original Gauss–Markov Assumptions only in having one dummy variable for each individual, the LSDV estimator is BLUE for that DGP; OLS is BLUE in the multiple regression model under the Gauss–Markov Assumptions. Because the fixed effects estimator yields the same slope estimates as LSDV, fixed effects is also BLUE for estimating the slopes of a line in a distinct intercepts DGP. Is OLS similarly BLUE for estimating either of the error components DGPs? Let's turn to this question next.

## Estimation in the First Error Components DGP

The explanators in the first error components DGP are contemporaneously uncorrelated with the disturbances, $\nu$ and $\mu$. OLS therefore yields consistent estimates of the parameters of the first error components DGP. The disturbances in the first error components DGP are homoskedastic (with variance equal to $\sigma_\nu^2 + \sigma_\mu^2$), but the disturbances are *not*, in general, uncorrelated with one another because all the observations on a given individual share an identical value for $\nu$.

The covariance between disturbances for a given individual is

$$\text{cov}([\nu_i + \mu_{it}], [\nu_i + \mu_{it'}]) = \text{E}(\nu_i^2 + \nu_i\mu_{it'} + \nu_i\mu_{it} + \nu_{it}\nu_{it'})$$
$$= \text{E}(\nu_i^2) + 0 + 0 + 0 = \sigma_\nu^2.$$

Therefore, the correlation coefficient for the disturbances of any one individual is

$$\frac{\sigma_\nu^2}{\sigma_\nu^2 + \sigma_\mu^2}. \qquad \textbf{16.8}$$

Because some disturbances are correlated, OLS is not the efficient estimator for the first error components DGP. However, because there is a single intercept in this error components DGP, OLS, the fixed effects estimator, and the estimator $\tilde{\beta}_1^G$ defined in Equation 16.7 are all unbiased estimators of $\beta_1$. However, none of these estimators efficiently estimates $\beta_1$; the efficient estimator for this first error components DGP takes into account the correlation among observations on each individual.

If $\sigma_\nu^2$ and $\sigma_\mu^2$ were known, we could use Equation 16.8 and the generalized least squares (GLS) estimator to efficiently estimate $\beta_1$ in the first error components DGP. The GLS estimator is a weighted average of the within-groups fixed effects estimator, $\tilde{\beta}^{FE}$, and the between-group mean estimator, $\tilde{\beta}^G$. But because the two variances are usually unknown, in practice we rely on a feasible generalized least squares (FGLS) estimator for the first error components model. The **random effects estimator** is the FGLS estimator that takes into account the estimated correlations among all observations on each individual. Many econometrics software packages provide such a random effects estimator for the error components model.

## Implementing the FGLS Random Effects Estimator

The random effects estimator requires consistent estimators of $\sigma_\nu^2$ and $\sigma_\mu^2$. We obtain these by using the residuals from two different initial estimates of the model. The first initial estimate is from fixed effects estimation. The fixed effects estimator ignores variation across the individuals, looking only at that within individuals. The residuals from a fixed effects estimation, the $\tilde{u}_{it}$, mimic the $\mu_{it}$ because within an individual's observations, there is no variation in $\nu_i$. We estimate the variance of $\mu$ by

$$s_\mu^2 = \frac{\sum_{t=1}^{T}\sum_{i=1}^{n}\left(\tilde{u}_{it} - \frac{1}{T}\sum_{j=1}^{T}\tilde{u}_{ij}\right)^2}{n(T - k - 1)}. \qquad 16.9$$

The second estimation is OLS. The OLS residuals, the $e_{it}$, mimic the total disturbances in each observation, $(\nu_i + \mu_{it})$, so $s^2$, the usual estimator of the disturbances' variance, consistently estimates $(\sigma_\nu^2 + \sigma_\mu^2)$. We estimate $\sigma_\nu^2$ by

$$s_\nu^2 = s^2 - s_\mu^2.$$

The random effects FGLS estimator uses these estimates of $\sigma_\nu^2$ and $\sigma_\mu^2$ to efficiently weight all the observations in the sample to obtain efficient estimates of the slopes and intercept of the error components model. *The random effects estimator relies on all the variation in the explanators, both the variation within the observations on individuals and the variation across the different means of the explanators for different individuals. OLS also uses both of these sources of variation, but weighs the observations differently than random effects estimation.*

## Estimation in the Second Error Components DGP

The second error components DGP differs from the first in that its explanators may be correlated with the individual error components, as in the case of good recruiting commanders and good recruiting budgets. Because the explanators are contemporaneously correlated with the disturbances, neither OLS nor FGLS is a consistent estimator of the parameters of this second error components DGP. If OLS and FGLS are not consistent, how are we to estimate the slopes in this DGP? We once again use the fixed effects estimator.

Recall that the fixed effects estimator applies OLS to

$$Y_{it} = \beta_1 x_{1it} + \cdots + \beta_k x_{kit} + (\varepsilon_{it} - \overline{\varepsilon}_i),$$

in which $y_{it} = (Y_{it} - \overline{Y}_i)$ and $x_{jit} = (X_{jit} - \overline{X}_{ji})$, where $\overline{Y}_i = \frac{1}{T}\sum_{t=1}^{T} Y_{it}$, $\overline{X}_{ji} = \frac{1}{T}\sum_{t=1}^{T} X_{jit}$, and $\overline{\varepsilon}_i = \frac{1}{T}\sum_{t=1}^{T} \varepsilon_{it}$. In the random effects estimator, the disturbance $\varepsilon_{it} = \nu_i + \mu_{it}$. Consequently, $(\varepsilon_{it} - \overline{\varepsilon}_i) = (\nu_i + \mu_{it} - \overline{\nu}_i - \overline{\mu}_i)$, which equals

$(\mu_{it} - \overline{\mu}_i)$, because the individual random components, the $\nu_i$, are constant over the sample time periods (and are therefore equal to their own temporal averages, the $\overline{\nu}_i$). OLS applied to the deviations of the explanators from their means for each individual is consistent because the $x_{jit}$ are contemporaneously uncorrelated with the $(\mu_{it} - \overline{\mu}_i)$. The fixed effects estimator efficiently estimates the parameters of the second error components DGP.

The disturbances in panel data can be heteroskedastic or serially correlated. Conceptually, these problems have the same consequences as discussed in Chapters 10 and 11. The mathematics becomes more complicated when the serial correlation coefficients differ across individuals in the distinct intercepts DGP and by the presence of two components in the disturbances in the error components DGP. GLS and FGLS apply in these cases.

## An Example of Estimation with Panel Data: Manufacturing Firms

How capital and labor contribute to output is one of the long-standing questions in economics. One measure of the contributions of labor and capital is found in estimates of production functions. Zvi Griliches of Harvard University and Jacques Mairesse of the Institut National de la Statistique in Paris have several times used large panels of firms to estimate Cobb–Douglas production functions.[5] Here we use a recent panel provided by Mairesse. The data cover 625 firms from 16 countries for a period of eight years, with 5,000 observations in all. The data are in cobbdoug2.*** on this book's companion Web site (**www.aw-bc.com/murray**); this file is too large for the student version of Eviews to read.

Table 16.1 contains the random effects estimates of the Cobb–Douglas production function:

$$Q_i = \beta_0 L_i^{\beta_1} K_i^{\beta_2} \varepsilon_i,$$

which we estimate in logarithmic form. The estimated coefficients of 0.30 for capital and 0.69 for labor are similar to those we have obtained using U.S. data. If markets are competitive and firms maximize profits, these estimates are consistent with a constant return to scale technology in which labor receives 70% of output and capital receives 30%. Notice that the table reports estimates of the variance of both the individual error components and the observation-specific component of the disturbance term (in this case, 93% of the total disturbance variance is attributable to the individual error components). Notice, too, that the specification in Table 16.1 includes a "fixed effect" for time; that is, a dummy variable for each year is included in the model. The time dummies capture technological change from year to year.

**TABLE 16.1** Random Effects Estimation of a Cobb–Douglas Production Function for a Sample of Manufacturing Firms

Dependent Variable: LOGOUT
Method: Panel EGLS (Cross-section random effects)
Sample: 1987 1994
Cross-sections included: 625
Total panel (balanced) observations: 5000
Swamy and Arora estimator of component variances

| Variable | Coefficient | Std. Error | t-Statistic | Prob. |
|---|---|---|---|---|
| C | 4.165682 | 0.104866 | 39.72390 | 0.0000 |
| LOGKAP | 0.298934 | 0.011588 | 25.79625 | 0.0000 |
| LOGLABOR | 0.693189 | 0.011761 | 58.93992 | 0.0000 |

| Effects Specification | | |
|---|---|---|
| | S.D. (of disturbances) | Rho (Proportion of total disturbance variance) |
| Cross-section random | 0.557931 | 0.9307 |
| Period fixed (dummy variables) | | |
| Idiosyncratic random | 0.152279 | 0.0693 |

If we use the random effects estimator, the asymptotic version of the $F$-test described in Chapter 12 leads us to fail to reject the hypothesis that French manufacturing operates subject to constant returns to scale, that is, that $\beta_1 + \beta_2 = 1$:

**Wald Test:**

| Test Statistic | Value | df | Probability |
|---|---|---|---|
| F-statistic | 0.674375 | (1, 4990) | 0.4116 |
| Chi-square | 0.674375 | 1 | 0.4115 |
| Null Hypothesis Summary: | | | |
| Normalized Restriction ( = 0) | Value | Std. Err. | |
| $-1 + C(2) + C(3)$ | $-0.007877$ | 0.009592 | |

**TABLE 16.2** Fixed Effects Estimation of a Cobb–Douglas Production Function for a Sample of Manufacturing Firms

Dependent Variable: LOGOUT
Method: Panel Least Squares
Sample: 1987 1994
Cross-sections included: 625
Total panel (balanced) observations: 5000

| Variable | Coefficient | Std. Error | t-Statistic | Prob. |
|----------|-------------|------------|-------------|-------|
| C | 4.305700 | 0.153644 | 28.02385 | 0.0000 |
| LOGKAP | 0.312343 | 0.014494 | 21.54940 | 0.0000 |
| LOGLABOR | 0.658524 | 0.013222 | 49.80464 | 0.0000 |

Effects Specification
Cross-section fixed (dummy variables)
Period fixed (dummy variables)

| | | | |
|----------|-------------|------------|-------------|
| R-squared | 0.993690 | Mean dependent var | 13.78478 |
| Adjusted R-squared | 0.992775 | S.D. dependent var | 1.791519 |
| S.E. of regression | 0.152279 | Akaike info criterion | −0.808193 |
| Sum squared resid | 101.2430 | Schwarz criterion | 0.018187 |
| Log likelihood | 2654.482 | F-statistic | 1086.156 |
| Durbin–Watson stat | 0.780115 | Prob(F-statistic) | 0.000000 |

Table 16.2 shows that we would obtain estimates similar to the random effects estimates from fixed effects estimation. Again, there is a dummy variable for each year, accounted for by including a fixed effect in the time dimension.

Fixed effects estimation ignores all the variation in the explanators across individuals in the sample. Checking whether this is necessary is a sensible precaution; we don't want to discard information unnecessarily. The appropriate test is an $F$-test of the hypothesis that all the individual effects are equal. Because dummy variables are included both for each firm and for each time period, the test checks each set of dummies separately and both sets together. The test rejects the null hypotheses that the dummies are unnecessary.

### Redundant Fixed Effects Tests

Equation: Untitled
Test cross-section and period fixed effects

| Effects Test | Statistic | d.f. | Prob. |
|---|---|---|---|
| Cross-section F | 108.313459 | (624,4366) | 0.0000 |
| Cross-section Chi-square | 14010.870912 | 624 | 0.0000 |
| Period F | 14.680958 | (7,4366) | 0.0000 |
| Period Chi-square | 116.326040 | 7 | 0.0000 |
| Cross-Section/Period F | 107.472148 | (631,4366) | 0.0000 |
| Cross-Section/Period Chi-square | 14026.642787 | 631 | 0.0000 |

This $F$-test is appropriate if we think the DGP is a distinct intercepts one. Because we would likely observe a different sample of French firms were we to draw a new sample, the appropriate DGP here is one of the error components DGPs.

Unlike the random effects estimation, the fixed effects estimator leads us to reject the null hypothesis that French manufacturing firms experience constant returns to scale:

### Wald Test:

| Test Statistic | Value | df | Probability |
|---|---|---|---|
| F-statistic | 4.381288 | (1, 4366) | 0.0364 |
| Chi-square | 4.381288 | 1 | 0.0363 |

Null Hypothesis Summary:

| Normalized Restriction ( = 0) | Value | Std. Err. |
|---|---|---|
| $-1 + C(2) + C(3)$ | $-0.029133$ | 0.013918 |

Restrictions are linear in coefficients.

Although the test results are different, the point estimates of $\beta_1 + \beta_2$ do not differ much between the random effects and fixed effects estimators: 0.99 and 0.97, respectively. Returns to scale seem very nearly constant in manufacturing.

## 16.3    Related DGPs

WHAT IS THE DGP?

Data sets can have multiple dimensions without having both a cross-sectional and a time-series component. For example, we might study each child in a sample of many households. Here, the two dimensions are household and child. Children in a given household share a common household environment, and hence a common household effect. The individual effects we find in panel data can recur in other multiple dimension data. If we do not attend to individual effects in our data, we will needlessly introduce biases or inefficiencies into our studies.

We call observations that share a common effect **clustered**. In specifying clustered models, we must decide whether the individual effect is a distinct intercept or an error component. We then choose our estimator according to the same criteria, as in panel data. Whether to specify error components or distinct intercepts depends on where additional samples would come from. For example, an industry economist who always samples from the same firms should settle on a distinct intercepts DGP. But if the firms observed vary from sample to sample, the appropriate DGP is an error components DGP. In contrast, household surveys are likely to be drawn in an error components setting; new households would be chosen in any resampling.

If individual effects are fixed, the appropriate estimator is the distinct intercepts estimator. If they are random and are uncorrelated with the explanators in the model, the appropriate estimator is the random effects estimator. If they are random and are correlated with the explanators, then the fixed effects estimator is appropriate. As with panel data, the Hausman test may distinguish between the two error components DGPs.

An alternative estimation strategy for clustered data is to use OLS, but with robust standard error estimates that reflect the correlation of disturbances within groups. This is less efficient than error components estimation; we should avoid OLS when panel data software are available. In any case, we should not use OLS without robust standard errors if the data are clustered—the standard OLS variance estimators are biased in this case, and the bias is usually toward zero.

Our discussion of panel data focuses on two dimensions, the cross section and the time series. Some data sets are more complex than this, and they require generalizations of fixed or random effects estimators to account for that complexity. For example, the Russian Living Standards Measurement Survey of the World Bank provides time series observations on each child and household in a sample, allowing three dimensions in the data: time, household, and child. The concepts of distinct intercepts and error components, and their applications, carry over into the estimation of models using these more complex data.

## An Example of a Clustered Data Set: Children in Russian Households in 1995

The World Bank has conducted Living Standards Measurement Surveys (LSMS) in about two dozen countries. The surveys examine multiple dimensions of children's physical well-being, including indications of their health and nutrition. Children who are below expected height at a young age frequently grow up to have health

# An Econometric Top 40—A Classical Favorite

## Specification Tests and an Earnings Function

OLS is wonderful if the Gauss–Markov Assumptions apply. But how are we to know whether the disturbances are homoskedastic, serially uncorrelated with one another, and uncorrelated with the explanators? Tests for heteroskedasticity and serial correlation occupied much of econometricians' energy in the 1950s and 1960s, and continued to attract attention through the 1970s. These tests, described in Chapters 10 and 11, allow us to settle on an efficient estimator, be it OLS or some variety of FGLS.

Surprisingly, econometricians paid less attention to finding specification tests for correlation between the disturbances and explanators. This is surprising because failure of the assumption that the disturbances and explanators are contemporaneously uncorrelated undermines the consistency of all the usual least squares estimators. In 1978, Jerry Hausman of MIT closed the gap with a stunning article that offered a strategy for testing for correlations between disturbances and explanators stemming from mismeasured, omitted, or endogenous explanators; from error components that are correlated with explanators; or from misspecified equations in simultaneous systems. Hausman applied his theoretical approach to panel data on earnings, finding that relying on random effects estimators for earnings equations to increase efficiency probably comes at the cost of incurring omitted variables biases.

Hausman's strategy is brilliantly simple in concept. There are estimators that are consistent, but not necessarily efficient, even when the disturbances are correlated with the explanators. There are estimators that are efficient when the disturbances are uncorrelated with the explanators but inconsistent otherwise. Hausman argues that if the potentially efficient estimators are consistent, they ought not differ much from the always consistent estimators, relative to sampling errors. Thus, we can test the appropriateness of the potentially efficient estimators, say $\beta^*$, by comparing their estimates with those of the surely consistent estimators, say $\tilde{\beta}$.

Implementing Hausman's strategy requires an expression for the variance of $(\tilde{\beta} - \beta^*)$. Hausman exploits the efficiency of $\beta^*$ under the null hypothesis to show that under the null hypothesis, the variance of $(\tilde{\beta} - \beta^*)$ is $[\text{var}(\tilde{\beta}) - \text{var}(\beta^*)]$. With this variance in hand, he is able to determine a test statistic that is distributed asymptotically as chi-square with $k$ degrees of freedom, where $k$ is the number of coefficients in the model under the null hypothesis.

Because Hausman's strategy is so broadly applicable, the roles of $\beta^*$ and $\tilde{\beta}$ vary from one application to the next. When checking for omitted variable bias or mismeasured explanators, $\beta^*$ is OLS and $\tilde{\beta}$ is instrumental variables (IV). When checking for simultaneity bias, $\beta^*$ is OLS and $\tilde{\beta}$ is two-stage least squares (2SLS). When checking for error components correlated with explanators, $\beta^*$ is the random effects estimator and $\tilde{\beta}$ is the fixed effects estimator. When checking for misspecified equations in a simultaneous system, $\beta^*$ is 2SLS and $\tilde{\beta}$ is three-stage least squares (3SLS).

Hausman applies his strategy to an earnings function that he estimates with panel data from the University of Michigan's Panel Study of Income Dynamics. He asks if the error components in his model are uncorrelated with the explanators in the model. He rejects the null hypothesis and concludes that the random effects estimates differ significantly from the fixed effects estimates. Hausman used this example to offer an important caveat to the use of his test in panel data.

Rejecting the null of no difference between the fixed and random effects estimates may indicate that the error components are correlated with the disturbances, or it may reflect that mismeasurement of the explanators is more serious in the fixed effects estimation than in the random effects estimation. In the former case, fixed effects estimation is preferable to random effects estimation. In the latter case, the reverse is preferable (though IV is preferable to both). Hausman argues that we must think carefully about the potential for measurement error problems before leaping to settle on fixed effects estimation.

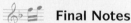 **Final Notes**

The Hausman test is a powerful tool for econometricians. But equally important for us is the final lesson from his empirical work, because it generalizes to many other hypothesis tests. What we infer from a hypothesis test, be it a test for omitted variables bias in random effects estimators or a test for heteroskedasticity in our DGP, depends critically on our maintained hypothesis, the features of the DGP that we are taking for granted. If we assume that the explanators are well measured, Hausman's test can reveal omitted variables bias. Similarly, if we assume no omitted variables, White's heteroskedasticity test can reveal heteroskedasticity. But if variables are mismeasured in the former case, or omitted in the latter, the appropriate interpretation of the test results changes. Hausman's counsel, that we consider long and carefully the assumptions we will subsequently take for granted in our DGP, is wise indeed. Maintained hypotheses should be arrived at with care.

∎

problems. Here we use the LSMS data to examine determinants of height for young children (0 to 4 years of age) in Russia in 1995. Because we have several observations on children in many families, this data set has some of the features of a panel, with any distinct intercept or error component common among all the children in a given household. A subset of the Russian LSMS data are in the file russia2.*** on this book's companion Web site (**www.aw-bc.com/murray**).

For each child in the sample, the survey compared the child's height to that of other Russian children of the same age. The data set contains a "Z-score" for the child's percentile ranking in height among other children his or her age. The Z-score is the value of a standard normal variate that would be in that same percentile in a population that follows the standard normal distribution. Thus, a child at the median height gets a Z-score of 0. A child in the 97.5 percentile gets a Z-score of 1.96. The Z-scores of the children are our dependent variable ($z\_w\_haz\_6$). We ask if the daily caloric intake of the child ($totcal6$), the total household food expenditure ($totexpn6$), the education of the mother ($meduc6$), or the number of siblings ($numsib6$) in the household matter for a given child's Z-score. Table 16.3 contains the results of random effects estimation. The estimation report is in the format used by Stata 8.0; the information is quite similar to

**TABLE 16.3** Determinants of Children's Height Random Effects Estimates

| Random-effects GLS regression | | | | Number of obs = 403 | | |
|---|---|---|---|---|---|---|
| Group variable (i) : t | | | | Number of groups = 363 | | |
| R-sq: within = 0.2339 | | | | Obs per group: min = 1 | | |
| between = 0.0424 | | | | avg = 1.1 | | |
| overall = 0.0483 | | | | max = 3 | | |
| Random effects $u\_i$ ~ Gaussian | | | | Wald chi2(4) = 22.13 | | |
| corr(u_i, X) = 0 (assumed) | | | | Prob > chi2 = 0.0002 | | |
| z_haz_6| | **Coef.** | **Std. Err.** | **z** | **P > |z|** | **[95% Conf. Interval]** | |
| totcal6 | | .0004738 | .0001464 | 3.24 | 0.001 | .000187 | .0007607 |
| totexpn6 | | $1.95e-08$ | $4.57e-08$ | 0.43 | 0.669 | $-7.01e-08$ | $1.09e-07$ |
| numsib6 | | −.165441 | .073901 | −2.24 | 0.025 | −.3102844 | −.0205977 |
| meduc6 | | .0626431 | .0295771 | 2.12 | 0.034 | .0046731 | .1206132 |
| _cons | | −1.528885 | .4214247 | −3.63 | 0.000 | −2.354862 | −.7029076 |
| sigma_u | | .92516599 | | | | | |
| sigma_e | | 1.1303565 | | | | | |
| rho | | .40116092 | (fraction of variance due to u_i) | | | | |

that provided by EViews. Notice that the household-specific effects account for only 40% of the total variance of the disturbances in this example, in contrast to the French manufacturing example in which firm-specific effects accounted for 93% of the variance in the disturbances.

We find that once the individual child's daily caloric intake is accounted for, total food expenditures for the family do not matter. However, having additional siblings does reduce one's height, even given caloric intake. This suggests that additional siblings may lead to a deterioration in the quality of food intake, beyond what it might do to food consumption. More educated mothers have taller children, even when caloric intake is constant, suggesting that more educated mothers provide either better quality food or otherwise healthier living conditions.

## 16.4    Distinguishing Among Panel Data DGPs

**HOW DO WE TEST HYPOTHESES?**

To choose the efficient estimator to use with panel data requires that we know which of our three panel data DGPs applies to the data at hand. A misjudgment about the DGP can lead us to choose an inefficient, or even an inconsistent, estimator. How, then, do we choose among the panel data DGPs? The choice between distinct intercept and error components DGPs depends on the sampling context for a given study. Do we expect to study the same potentially heterogeneous individuals in one sample after another? If so, the distinct intercepts DGP is appropriate. Do we expect to study different potentially heterogeneous individuals in one sample after another? If so, an error components DGP is appropriate. The choice of a distinct intercepts or an error components DGP is not grounded in the data at hand but rather in the context of our study. In cases in which we have settled upon an error components framework, though, there is a formal hypothesis test that allows us to infer from the data which of our two error components DGPs is appropriate.

The random effects estimator is efficient for the first error components DGP, in which the explanators and disturbances are uncorrelated, but it is inconsistent in the second. On the other hand, the fixed effects estimator is consistent, but not efficient, if applied to the first error components DGP, and it remains consistent if applied to the second. We next explore how to test the claim that the explanators and disturbances are uncorrelated in the error components DGP. This test enables us to choose between the fixed effects and random coefficients estimators.

## Testing for Correlation Between Individual Error Components and Explanators

In an error components environment, how do we tell whether the explanators are correlated with the disturbances? The key lies in two features of error components DGPs. First, if the individual error components are correlated with the explanators, the fixed effects estimator is a consistent estimator of the parameters of the second error components DGP, and the random effects estimator is inconsistent. Second, if the individual error components are uncorrelated with the explanators, both estimators are consistent. Econometrician Jerry Hausman of MIT has exploited these facts to devise a test for the null hypothesis that the explanators and disturbances are correlated in an error components model.[6]

What is Hausman's reasoning in his search for a test to distinguish the two error components DGPs? He notes that if the individual error components are uncorrelated with the explanators, the fixed effects and random effects estimators will be the same in large samples, subject to sampling errors, because both are consistent. However, if the individual error components are correlated with the explanators, the fixed and random effects estimates will differ in large samples, subject to sampling errors, because only the fixed effects estimator is consistent. **Hausman's specification test for error component DGPs** asks whether the fixed and random effects estimators of the slopes differ significantly in the second error components DGP.

Hausman's test statistic for the test is

$$W = \frac{s_\mu^2 (\hat{\beta}_1^{LSDV} - \tilde{\beta}_1^{RE})^2}{\sum\sum(X_{it} - \overline{X}_i)^2},$$

where $s_\mu^2$ is the residual variance from the fixed effects estimator, as defined in Equation 16.9, and $\tilde{\beta}_1^{RE}$ is the random effects estimator. $W$ is asymptotically distributed chi-square with $k = 1$ degree of freedom. In a multiple regression, the test statistic is a weighted sum of the differences in the various coefficients, with the weights determined by the estimators' variances and covariances. The degrees of freedom is the number of slope coefficients in the error components model.

In Chapter 13, we encountered the Hausman–Wu specification test for detecting omitted, mismeasured, or endogenous variables when we are concerned that some explanators may or may not be correlated with the disturbances in what is otherwise the Gauss–Markov setting. That test relied on a regression and an associated $F$-statistic, the form of the test devised by Wu.[7] Hausman's contribution was to unify a host of specification tests, including that studied by Wu, the choice between OLS and IV estimators, and that studied here, the choice between fixed and random effects estimators in an error components DGP. The Hausman formulation of the test for detecting omitted, mismeasured, or endogenous variables (often called a Wald test) asks whether the OLS estimates equal the IV estimates of the model, just as here the Hausman test compares the random effects and fixed effects estimates. Hausman's Wald test and the Hausman–Wu $F$-test are asymptotically equivalent, but some econometricians argue that the $F$-test performs better in small to moderately sized samples.

Similarly, there is a regression formulation of Hausman's Wald test for choosing between random effects and fixed effects estimators. It, too, uses an $F$-statistic and is asymptotically equivalent to Hausman's Wald test. The regression used for this $F$-test involves the dependent and independent variables from the error components model, each transformed as required for conducting FGLS by performing OLS on suitably transformed variables. Let's call these variables $y^*$ and $x^*$, respectively. The regression adds as an explanator the deviations of the $X$-variables from their group means, which we earlier in this chapter denoted by $x$. For a single explanator, the regression estimated for the regression version of the Hausman test is

$$y_{it}^* = \beta_0 x_{oit}^* + \beta_1 x_{1it}^* + \beta_2 x_{1it}. \qquad \textbf{16.10}$$

According to the DGP, the true model does not include $x$, so $\beta_2$ is, in fact, zero. If the disturbances in the error components model are, in fact, uncorrelated with the explanators, OLS applied to Equation 16.10 is consistent, so we would rarely reject the null hypothesis that $\beta_2 = 0$. Consequently, to test the null hypothesis that the disturbances in the error components model are uncorrelated with the explanators, we test the hypothesis that $\beta_2 = 0$. With one explanator, this is a $t$-test. With multiple explanators, we test the null hypothesis that all the $x$-variables have zero coefficients in the analogous multiple regression. The associated $F$-statistic has $k$ and $(nT - 2k - 1)$ degrees of freedom.[8] This $F$-test performs better than Hausman's Wald test in small to moderately sized samples. When we reject the null hypothesis, we should use the fixed effects estimator. When we fail to reject the null, we should use the random effects estimator.

Most econometric software packages that handle panel data compute Hausman's test statistic. Some use the Wald statistic, others use the $F$-statistic, and still others offer both. Applied econometricians tend to use the form of the test that they find in their favorite software package. In a multiple regression model, the Wald statistic is asymptotically distributed chi-square with $k$ degrees of freedom, where $k$ is the number of slope coefficients in the error components model. Large values of Hausman's Wald statistic and large values of the regression-based $F$-statistic both lead us to reject the null of no correlation between the individual error components and the explanators.

## Two Examples: Manufacturing Firms and Russian Households

When examining panel data with error components, should we use the fixed effects estimator or the random effects estimator? *Hausman's Wald statistic can guide our choice between the random effects and fixed effects estimators.* To illustrate the choice and the role of Hausman's test, we return to the samples of French firms and Russian children analyzed earlier. In the sample of manufacturing firms, we reject the null hypothesis of no correlation between the individual error components and the explanators, as the test results in Table 16.4 indicate. The elasticities of output with respect to capital and labor do not differ appreciably between the two estimators, but the preferred fixed effects estimator rejects the null of constant returns to scale, whereas the random effects estimator does not.

In the sample of Russian children, we fail to reject the null hypothesis of no correlation between family error components and the explanators, as the test results in Table 16.5 indicate. (For purposes of comparison, these test results are

**TABLE 16.4** Hausman Specification Test of French Firms' Error Components' Correlation with Explanators

Correlated Random Effects—Hausman Test
Test cross-section random effects

| Test Summary | Chi-Sq. Statistic | Chi-Sq. d.f. | Prob. |
|---|---|---|---|
| Cross-section random | 33.851727 | 2 | 0.0000 |

Cross-section random effects test comparisons:

| Variable | Fixed | Random | Var(Diff.) | Prob. |
|---|---|---|---|---|
| LOGKAP | 0.312343 | 0.298934 | 0.000076 | 0.1235 |
| LOGLABOR | 0.658524 | 0.693189 | 0.000037 | 0.0000 |

**TABLE 16.5** Hausman Specification Test of Russian Kids' Error Components' Correlation with Explanators

| | —Coefficients— | | |
| z_haz_6 | Fixed Effects | Random Effects | Difference |
| --- | --- | --- | --- |
| totcal6 | .0011625 | .0004738 | .0006887 |
| totexpn6 | $-5.82e - 07$ | $1.95e - 08$ | $-6.02e - 07$ |
| meduc6 | .2857359 | .0626431 | .2230928 |

Test: Ho: difference in coefficients not systematic

chi2(3) = (b − B)′[S^(−1)](b − B),S = (S_fe − S_ re ) = 5.56

Prob > chi2 = 0.1350

presented in the format used by Stata 8.0.) In this case, therefore, we prefer the more efficient random effects estimator.

## What We Do and Don't Learn from Hausman's Test

If the correct model is either our first or second error components DGP, Hausman's test handily distinguished between the two. There is another alternative, however. A third error components DGP could allow for measurement error in the explanatory variables. Such measurement errors would make both the fixed effects and the random effects estimators inconsistent, but the consequent biases might differ between the two estimators.

If the explanators suffer from measurement error, such error might be practically unimportant in random effects estimation, but practically important in fixed effects estimation. The fixed effects estimator relies on the deviations of the explanators from their individual means. Measurement error might be large relative to the variation of the $X$'s within individuals, which would make measurement error bias large for the fixed effects estimator. The random effects estimator relies additionally on the variation in mean $X$'s across individuals. If in that variation measurement error is relatively unimportant, measurement error bias in the random effects estimator might be markedly smaller than in the fixed effects estimator.

In an earlier sample of French firms than the one we use, Jacques Mairesse's fixed effects estimates of the elasticity of output with respect to capital were much smaller than his random effects estimates. Mairesse attributed much of the difference to measurement error bias.[9] In our later sample of French firms, the fixed and random effects estimators yield very similar output elasticities, suggesting that measurement error is a less serious problem in our data.

In cases in which the measurement error bias of fixed effects estimation is seriously worse than that of the random effects estimator, the Hausman test should not lead us to use the fixed effects estimator. An IV estimator is the best choice in such cases. Absent a good instrument, we prefer the random effects estimator to the fixed effects estimator. Thus, when using Hausman's test with panel data, we should consider carefully the possibility that fixed effects estimators suffer from considerable measurement error bias.

## Testing for Unobserved Heterogeneity

Hausman's test lets us choose between competing unobserved heterogeneity DGPs. How might we test for the absence of unobserved heterogeneity altogether? Testing the null hypothesis of no individual effects differs between the distinct intercepts and error components DGPs. In the distinct intercepts DGP, the test asks if the individual intercept terms are all equal. In the error components DGP, the test asks if the variance of the individual components of the disturbance term, the $\nu_i$, is zero. The former test uses a standard $F$-statistic. The latter uses a test statistic devised by the same econometricians, Trevor Breusch and Adrian Pagan, of the Australian National University, who also devised the Breusch–Pagan test for heteroskedasticity described in Chapter 10.

In the distinct intercepts DGP, if there are no individual distinct intercepts, then there is a common intercept term for all observations, that is, $\beta_{01} = \beta_{02} = \cdots = \beta_{0n} = \beta_0$. We can test this hypothesis with a standard $F$-test, asking whether the coefficients on all dummy variables estimated by LSDV are equal. The test would involve $(n - 1)$ restrictions on the coefficients of the model. The distinct intercepts model has $(k + n)$ coefficients, including $k$ slopes and $n$ intercept terms. The degrees of freedom for the $F$-test of the null hypothesis of no distinct intercepts is therefore $(n - 1)$ and $(nT - k - n)$, where $nT$ is the number of observations in the panel. For computing the $F$-statistic, the unconstrained model uses the LSDV or fixed effects estimator, and the constrained model applies OLS to the model with only one intercept term for all individuals.

In the error components DGP, if there are no individual effects, the individual component of the disturbance term is always zero, that is, $\nu_i$ is always equal to its mean, zero, and therefore has zero variance. Breusch and Pagan offer a test statistic for the null hypothesis that $\sigma_\nu^2 = 0$ in the first error components DGP. They based their test on the residuals from OLS applied to the error components DGP. The **Breusch–Pagan variance test** statistic is

$$L = \frac{nT}{2(T - 1)} \left[ \frac{\sum_{i=1}^{n} (T\bar{e}_i)^2}{\sum_{i=1}^{n} \sum_{t=1}^{T} e_{it}^2} - 1 \right]^2,$$

in which the $e_{it}$ are the OLS residuals and the $\bar{e}_i = \sum_{t=1}^{T} e_{it}$, the average residual for the $i$-th individual. $L$ is distributed chi-square with one degree of freedom.

If there are error components correlated with the explanators, those error components cannot have a zero variance. Thus, the test for no individual error components appropriately takes place only within the first error components DGP. In an error components environment, we first conduct Hausman's test and then, if in doubt about the existence of individual error components, we conduct the Breusch–Pagan test.

## Summary

This chapter discusses data that have both time series and cross-sectional dimensions. We call these panel data. Panel data provide an opportunity to protect ourselves from a particular sort of omitted variables bias. If an omitted variable remains the same for an individual over time, the temporal dimension of a panel data set allows us to control appropriately for such unobserved heterogeneity across individuals. We distinguish between two kinds of unobserved heterogeneity: (i) distinct intercepts that do not vary from one sample to the next; and (ii) error components that do vary from one sample to the next. Error components DGPs come in two flavors, those in which the individual error components are uncorrelated with the explanators, and those in which the individual error components are correlated with the explanators.

The efficient estimator for distinct intercepts DGPs is called the fixed effects estimator. In essence, the fixed effects estimator introduces a dummy variable for each individual in the sample, although the estimator itself only estimates the slope coefficients in the model. If we want to estimate the individual intercept terms, we use OLS applied to the model with the full set of individual dummy variables. This estimator is called the least squares dummy variable (LSDV) estimator.

The efficient estimator for the error components DGP that has individual error components uncorrelated with the explanators is a FGLS estimator called the random effects estimator. The random effects estimator takes optimal account of the correlation among disturbances for an individual when assigning weights to observations. If the individual error components are correlated with the disturbances, the random effects estimator is not consistent. In this latter case, the fixed effects estimator is once again the efficient estimator.

Whether to specify a distinct intercepts DGP or an error components DGP depends on the sampling context. Will we repeatedly sample the same individuals, whose individual effect will be persistent across samples? If so, a distinct inter-

## An Organizational Structure for the Study of Econometrics

### 1. What Is the DGP?

Unobserved heterogeneity: distinct intercepts

Unobserved heterogeneity: error components with and without individual effects correlated with explanators

### 2. What Makes a Good Estimator?

――――

### 3. How Do We Create an Estimator?

Fixed effects estimator

Random effects estimator

### 4. What Are an Estimator's Properties?

――――

### 5. How Do We Test Hypotheses?

Hausman's test for error components correlated with explanators

Breusch–Pagan variance test for individual error components

cepts DGP is appropriate. Will we sample different individuals in each sample, so that individual effects will vary from one sample to the next? If so, an error components DGP is appropriate.

If the DGP is an error components DGP, we can test for correlation between the individual error components and the explanators using Hausman's test. To ascertain whether there are individual effects at all, we can, in the distinct intercepts DGP, conduct an $F$-test of the hypothesis that all the individual intercepts are equal, or, in the error components DGP, we can use Breusch and Pagan's test of the hypothesis that the variance of the individual error components is zero.

Observations may be clustered in data sets other than those that provide a cross section of time series. For example, a sample of several divisions of several auto manufacturers would require the same tools as panel data if there is a shared firm effect for all the divisions of a given company. The firm and the division would be the two dimensions of the data. The individual effect would be common to all divisions in a given firm.

## Concepts for Review

## Questions for Discussion

1. The distinct intercepts model implicitly includes a dummy variable for each individual. If the number of individuals is large, there can be many such dummies; for example, there are about 3,000 counties in the United States. If the number of such dummies is large, might OLS have a lower mean squared error than the fixed effects estimator? Why?

2. Can you envision panels in which it is a mistake to specify individual effects as constant over the sample period? How do the error components and distinct intercepts models impose unchanging individual effects?

3. If you work as an economist for a brokerage house and track 10 companies for your firm, what sort of DGP do you think you should rely on if you have panel series data about your companies?

4. If you work for the U.S. government's Securities and Exchange Commission and are studying industry-wide effects using the same data as in Problem 3, on what sort of DGP do you think you should rely?

## Problems for Analysis

> For the data sets that you will need to solve the problems in this section, go to **www.aw-bc.com/murray**.

1. Economic theory says that the demand for beer should vary with the level of taxes on beer. Philip Cook has investigated this relationship; the file beertax1.*** contains a panel of his state data for the years 1975–2000.[10] The variables are the state's tax rate on beer (*beer_tax*), per capita beer sales in the state (*beer_sales*), income (*income*), the federal numerical code for the state (*fips_state*), and the year of the observation (*year*).
   a. Which kind of DGP is more appropriate for these data, a distinct intercepts DGP or an error components DGP? Briefly explain.
   b. Using OLS, regress the log of beer sales on the log of the tax rate, the log of income, and an intercept term. What are the estimated income and price (tax rate) elasticities of the demand for beer?

   c. Re-estimate the relationship in (b) using a fixed effects estimator that accounts for fixed effects for each state and each year. How do these estimated elasticities compare with those in (b)?

   d. In the regression in (c), separately test the hypotheses that the state fixed effects are unnecessary and that the yearly fixed effects are unnecessary.

   e. Re-estimate the relationship in (b) using an estimator that accounts for random effects for each state and fixed effects for each year. Conduct a Hausman test to assess the appropriateness of the random effects estimator. What do you conclude?

   f. Based on the evidence in these data, do higher beer tax rates decrease beer consumption?

   g. Based on the evidence in these data, do higher beer tax rates increase consumers' total expenditures on beer, inclusive of taxes?

2. Do a firm's existing plant and equipment (*capitalvalue*) and its stock value (*stockvalue*) affect the firm's investment decisions (*invest*)? Yehuda Grunfeld addressed this question in an early econometrics study. The file grunfeld.*** contains the panel data for 10 firms over 20 years that Grunfeld used in his study.[11]

   a. Which kind of DGP is more appropriate for these data, a distinct intercepts DGP, or an error components DGP? Briefly explain.

   b. Regress investment on the firm's capital value and stock value. Use both OLS and random effects estimation. Compare the estimated coefficients and standard errors.

   c. Conduct a Hausman test to check whether random effects estimation is warranted in these data.

   d. Re-estimate the model in (b) incorporating fixed effects for each year. Test whether these annual fixed effects are necessary.

3. David Mustard has investigated the effects of arrests and convictions on murder rates.[12] The data set mustard.*** contains a subset of Mustard's data; mustard.*** contains panel data for each county (*county*) in four U.S. states, for each year from 1985 to 1992 (*year*). The dependent variable is the log of the murder rate in a county in a given year (*lratmur*). The explanatory variables are arrest rates (arrests per reported crime in percent, *arrmurd*) and conviction rates (convictions per murder in percent, *convmurd*) for murder. Data are not available for all counties in all years, so this is called an "unbalanced panel."

   a. Which kind of DGP is more appropriate for these data, a distinct intercepts DGP or an error components DGP? Briefly explain.

   b. Estimate the log of the murder rate as a function of the arrest and conviction rates for murder. Use the random effects estimator to account for the unobserved heterogeneity of the counties. Conduct a Hausman test. What do you conclude about the appropriateness of the random effects estimator?

   c. Re-estimate the log of the murder rate as a function of the arrest and conviction rates for murder. Use the fixed effects estimator to account for the unobserved heterogeneity of the counties and also use the fixed effects estimator to account for time period–specific effects. Test the null hypothesis that the time series dummies are unnecessary. What do you conclude?

d. Mustard used his data to study how omitting arrest rates from a crime regression biases the estimated effect of conviction rates on the crime rate. What do you conclude about the extent of omitted variable bias that would arise from omitting the arrest rate? Speculate why the bias is in this particular direction.

 4. Medicaid is the U.S. health insurance program that serves poor children. Kristine Lykens and Paul Jargowsky have studied the effect that Medicaid has on poor children's health.[13] The file medelig.*** contains a panel of 125 groups of Hispanic children in low-income families observed by Lykens and Jargowsky in 1988 and 1991. The variables in the file are as follows:

AGE         Mean age of kids in group
EDUC1       % of group without high school diploma
EDUC2       % of group with high school diploma
EDUC3       % of group with some college
EDUC4       % of group with bachelors degree
EDUC5       % of group with bachelors degree plus
FAMINC      Mean family income in group
MALE        % boys in group
MEDELIG     % of group Medicaid eligible
MEDPINS     Interaction of pinsur and medelig
NACUTE      Mean number of acute medical conditions in group
PINSUR      % of group covered by private health insurance
PSU         Primary sampling unit number (randomly recoded)
SPF         % of group who are single parents
YEAR91      = 1 if year is 1991;  = 0 if year is 1988

The acute medical conditions (*nacute*) were those reported for the two weeks preceding the interview. Because these were quite variable, Lykens and Jargowsky aggregated the observations by 125 geographic area (aggregating the observations by census primary sampling units).

a. Which kind of DGP is more appropriate for these data, a distinct intercepts DGP or an error components DGP? Briefly explain.

b. Regress the number of acute medical conditions on all demographic variables (*educ2, educ3, educ4, educ5, spf, male, age, faminc*—but excluding *educ1* to avoid perfect collinearity), *medelig, medpins, pinsur,* and *year91.* Use a random effects estimator to account for unobserved heterogeneity in the psu groups. (The interaction variable *medpins* allows for Medicaid eligibility to not matter for kids covered by private insurance. By focusing on Medicaid-eligible children rather than on Medicaid-recipient children, the analysis circumvents the endogeneity that stems from families with sick children receiving Medicaid.) Conduct a Hausman test to determine whether the random effects estimator is appropriate for analyzing these data.

c. Re-estimate the relationship between Medicaid eligibility and health outcomes for children in (b) using a fixed effects estimator. Do you conclude that increased Medicaid eligibility improves health outcomes for Hispanic children?

d. Test the null hypothesis that Medicaid eligibility has no effect on the health outcomes of children already covered by private insurance.

5. Earnings functions are seldom estimated with data on individuals' native abilities. This omission could bias estimates of the return to education if schooling and ability are correlated. Orley Ashenfelter and Alan Cecelia Rouse of Princeton University gathered earnings data from a sample of 680 identical twins to overcome the unobserved ability heterogeneity that might bias OLS estimates of the return to education.[14] Their data are in the file bothtwins2.***.[15] The variables in that file are

PAIR          The id number for the twin pair
IDIV          The id number of the twin within the pair( = 1 or = 2)
AGE           Age
AGE2          Age squared
EDUC          This twin's education as reported by self
EDUCT_T       Other twin's report of this twin's education
FEMALE        Female
LWAGE         Natureal log of hourly wage

This problem calls for examining the twins data using fixed and random effects estimation. In this data set, each twin appears as a separate observation. There are 680 observations.

a. Is the appropriate DGP a distinct intercepts DGP or an error components DGP? Briefly explain.

b. Use the random effects estimator to estimate a multiple regression model for the log wage (*lwage*) in which the explanators are education (*educ*, self-reported education), age (*age*), age-squared (*age2*), dummy for being white, and a dummy for being female (*female*). What is the estimated effect of education on the log of wage? Compare this estimate with the OLS estimate for one twin from each pair and with OLS across all of the twins. (The variable *indiv* is one for the first twin in each pair and two otherwise.) Why are the estimated standard errors different in these three regressions?

c. Focus on the random effects estimation in (b). What is the result of a Hausman test in which the null hypothesis is that the individual effects are contemporaneously uncorrelated with the explanators?

d. Use the fixed effects estimator to re-estimate the model in (b).The fixed effects estimator drops any variables that are fixed within groups.

e. What is the likely effect of measurement error in the education variable on the fixed effects estimator? Use sibling's report of the individuals education (*educt_t*) as an instrument for education to ascertain whether measurement error in self-reported education seriously biases the fixed effects estimator of the return to education. Do this by comparing the IV fixed effects estimator with the random effects estimator.

f. Conduct IV estimation coupled with the random effects estimation strategy (which we call "random effects IV estimation"). Does a Hausman test indicate any correlation between the explanators and unobserved ability?

g. Based on evidence from these data, should economists worry about omitted ability variable bias in conventional wage regressions?

6. The data set Japan1.*** contains measures of the natural logs of output, the capital, and labor for a panel of Japanese manufacturing firms.[16] With these data we can estimate a Cobb–Douglas production function.

   a. Is a distinct intercepts DGP or an error components DGP appropriate for this problem? Briefly explain.

   b. Estimate a Cobb–Douglas production function for Japanese manufacturing firms from these data. Use OLS, but include a dummy variable for each year (by assuming period-specific fixed effects). Test the null hypothesis that the time dummies are unnecessary. Also test the null hypothesis that the coefficients on labor and capital sum to one, that is, that returns to scale are constant.

   c. Re-estimate the Cobb–Douglas production function in (b). Use a random effects estimator to account for the unobserved heterogeneity of firms, but continue to include the fixed period effects. Conduct a Hausman test. Is the random effects estimator appropriate for analyzing these data?

   d. Re-estimate the Cobb–Douglas production function in (b). Use a fixed effects estimator that accounts for the unobserved heterogeneity of firms and time period effects. Test the null hypothesis that the returns to scale are constant in Japanese manufacturing. Compare your estimates from this estimation with those from (b) and (c). Do the differences make you skeptical about using fixed effects estimation with these data? Briefly explain your concern.

7. Consider a distinct intercepts DGP with just two observations per group and $n$ groups. Assume there is only one explanatory variable plus the distinct intercepts. Prove that the fixed effects estimator yields the same estimate for the slope coefficient as regressing the difference in the dependent variable for each group against the difference in the explanator for the group. This latter regression has $n$ observations, one for each group.

8. Public infrastructure is critical for a country or region's productivity. The Greatest Hit in Chapter 11, p. 458, reports David Aschauer's seminal work on how public infrastructure has affected productivity in the United States. Following on Aschauer's work, Alicia Munnell gathered state-level data on infrastructure and productivity.[17] The file productivity.*** contains Munnell's data for 1970–1986 for the 48 contiguous U.S. states. The variables in the file are

   | | |
   |---|---|
   | *state* | Numerical code for the state |
   | *year* | Year |
   | *privcap* | State's private capital stock |
   | *hwy* | State's highways and streets |
   | *water* | State's water and sewer facilities |
   | *pubcap* | State's public capital stock |
   | *gsp* | Gross state products |
   | *emp* | State's labor input measured (non-agricultural payrolls) |
   | *unemp* | State's unemployment rate |

   a. Regress the log of state product on an intercept, year, the unemployment rate, and the logs of employment, private capital, and public capital, using OLS. Are the signs and patterns of statistical significance as you would expect? What do these results indicate about the importance of the public capital stock for a state's gross output?

b. Repeat the regression in (a) using state-specific random effects. Do these find the same magnitude of effect for public capital as with OLS? Are the signs and statistical significance of the other variables as you would expect?

c. Does the regression in (b) cast doubt on the estimated standard errors reported in (a)?

d. Briefly explain why we can conclude that the OLS and random effects estimators are probably biased in this DGP.

e. Estimate the regression in (a) using state-specific fixed effects. Do you find the same magnitude of effect for public capital as with OLS and random effects estimation? Are the signs and statistical significance of the other variables as you would expect?

f. How would you summarize the findings about the productivity of public capital from these data?

9. In 1975, U.S. airlines were deregulated, allowing them to charge whatever prices they wished and to choose routes for their flights more freely than previously. One anticipated gain from deregulation was cost reduction, to be derived in part by allowing airlines to reduce excess capacity. Badi Baltagi, James M. Griffin, and Sharada R.Vadali estimate that airlines did, indeed, reduce excess capacity following deregulation.[18] Their analysis combined data on variable costs and factor shares to efficiently estimate excess capacity for 23 airlines in the years 1971–1986. Here, we use their data to estimate a cost function for airlines and to ask whether costs were higher prior to deregulation than they were after. The file deregulate.\*\*\* contains the following variables:

*airline*  A number indicating the airline in the observation

*pf*    The price of fuel

*pl*    The price of labor

*pm*   The price of materials

*reg*   = 1 if the observation is from the regulated period; = 0 otherwise

*stage*  Average length of the airline's flights that year

*vc*    Variable costs (fuel plus labor, plus materials)

*y*    An index of annual passenger miles flown by the airline

*year*   The year of the observation

Not every airline is observed every year. Costs per passenger mile might differ between airlines that make short flights and airlines that make long flights. The variable *stage* can account for this effect.

a. Regress the log of costs on an intercept term, the regulation dummy, year, and the natural logs of the three price variables and of *stage*, using OLS, firm-specific random effects, and firm-specific fixed effects.

b. What is the interpretation of the regulation dummy's coefficient in these regressions?

   c. What is the interpretation of the year's coefficient in these regressions?

   d. Briefly explain why we can conclude that the estimated standard errors reported for OLS are probably incorrect.

   e. Briefly explain why we can conclude that OLS and the random effects estimators are probably biased.

   f. What does the fixed effects regression imply about the effect of deregulation on airlines' variable costs?

   g. How do you counter the objection that technical change would have reduced airline costs even without deregulation?

   h. Add the squares of the logged explanators to the fixed effects regression in (a). What does this regression suggest about the conclusions in (f)?

   i. Are the added terms in the regression in (h), taken together, statistically significant? Show the needed test result.

   j. Some have argued that deregulation enables airlines to better plan their flights. This could mean that more efficient flight lengths were chosen after deregulation. How does this affect the interpretations in (f) and (h), and how would you take this consideration into account?

## Endnotes

1. Mark Twain, *Life on the Mississippi* (Boston: J. R. Osgood, 1883).

2. An actual study of military recruiting would need to allow for *both* state distinct intercepts and recruiting district error components. Moreover, the DGP might also need to account for serial correlation in the temporal dimension of the disturbances. Such a DGP requires more complex estimators than those developed here, but the spirit of those more complex estimators is captured here.

3. Yair Mundlak, "Empirical Production Functions Free of Management Bias," *Journal of Farm Economics* 43, no. 1 (1962): 44–56.

4. Pietro Balestra and Marc Nerlove, "Pooling Cross Section and Time Series Data in the Estimation of a Dynamic Model: The Demand for Natural Gas," *Econometrica* 34, no. 3 (1969): 585–612.

5. For example, Zvi Griliches and Jacques Mairesse, "Productivity and Research—Development at the Firm Level," in *Research and Development, Patents and Productivity*, ed. Zvi Griliches (Chicago: Chicago University Press, 1984): 271–297.

6. Jerry A. Hausman, "Specification Tests in Econometrics," *Econometrica* 46 (1978): 1251–1272.

7. D. M. Wu, "Alternative Tests of Independence Between Stochastic Regressors and Disturbances," *Econometrica* 41 (1973): 733–750.

8. If there are variables among the explanators that do not vary with time, those are excluded from the x-variables in the model (but not from the x*-variables), and the number of degrees of freedom in the numerator and denominator is altered accordingly.

9. Jacques Mairesse, "Time-series and Cross-sectional Estimates on Panel Data: Why Are They Different and Why Should They Be Equal?" *The Econometrics of Panel Data* 2., ed. G. S. Maddala, Elgar Reference Collection series. *International Library*

*of Critical Writings in Econometrics*, Vol. 1. (Cheltenham: Aldershot, 1993): 424–438.

10. Philip Cook, *Alcohol Control in Moderation: A Sober Assessment of Costs and Benefits*, forthcoming.

11. Yehuda Grunfeld, *The Determinants of Corporate Investment*, unpublished PhD thesis, University of Chicago, 958.

12. David B. Mustard, "Reexamining Criminal Behavior: The Importance of Omitted Variable Bias," *Review of Economics and Statistics* 85, no. 1 (February 2003): 205–211.

13. Kristine Lykens and Paul A. Jargowsky, "Medicaid Matters: Children's Health and Medicaid Eligibility Expansions," *Journal of Policy Analysis and Management* 21, no. 2 (2002): 219–238.

14. Orley Ashenfelter and Cecelia Rouse, "Income, Schooling, and Ability: Evidence from a New Sample of Identical Twins," *Quarterly Journal of Economics* 113, no. 1 (February 1998): 253–284.

15. For simplicity, responses of identical twin pairs who disagree about age, race, or sex have been altered slightly to ensure agreement.

16. Jacques Mairesse kindly provided these data.

17. Alicia Munnell, with the assistance of Leah M. Cook, "How Does Public Infrastructure Affect Regional Economic Performance?" *New England Economic Review*, Federal Reserve Bank of Boston, September/October (1990): 11–32.

18. Badi H. Baltagi, James M. Griffin, and Sharada R. Vadali, "Excess Capacity: A Permanent Characteristic of U.S. Airlines," *Journal of Applied Econometrics* 13, no. 5 (1998): 645–657.

# Chapter 17

# Forecasting

*It's a poor sort of memory that only works backward.*

—THE RED QUEEN[1]

Laius, king of ancient Thebes, worried about the future, so he consulted the leading forecaster of his day, the oracle at Delphi. The oracle offered two forecasts. First, Laius would have no children. Second, if Laius happened to have a child, it would be a son who would kill Laius and marry his own mother. (Such conflicting counsel about the future remains a staple of forecasters' work.) Alas, it was the second forecast that proved accurate, as all who have heard of Oedipus and his complex recall. Another literary lord of note, Macbeth, was seduced to murder by an alluring forecast that he would be king—Lady Macbeth thought it only wise to help fate along by slipping poison to a houseguest. Modern-day leaders worried about the future are no less inclined than Laius or Macbeth to ask for forecasts. What will GDP growth be next year? How many voters will cast their vote for the incumbent in the next election?

The oracle at Delphi sniffed gasses rising from a crack in the earth to divine the future; the witches in Shakespeare's *Macbeth* sipped their inspiration from "grease that's sweated from the murderer's gibbet" and other tasty tidbits.[2] Today's oracles stir measurements of past events, filtered through statistical machinery, to formulate their forecasts of the future. This chapter introduces the concepts and tools with which today's economic and political oracles foretell the fates of nations, presidents, and corporate profits. Students looking for an introductory textbook on forecasting can turn to Francis Diebold's *Elements of Forecasting* that inspired the organization of this chapter.[3]

## 17.1 Conditional Forecasting

**HOW DO WE MAKE FORECASTS?**

The second forecast by the Delphic oracle has the flavor of our regression analyses. *Given* that Laius would have a child, the oracle forecast the child would murder Laius. Our regression models also offer such **conditional forecasts**. When interpreting regressions, we say that *given* the explanators taking on specific values, we predict $Y$ to be the ordinary least squares (OLS) fitted value obtained using those explanatory variable values. This section examines the conditional forecasts economists make using the regression models we learned in previous chapters.

716

## Conditional Forecasts and Prediction Intervals

In the context of Chapters 1 through 16, it is inviting to predict that the value a variable $Y$ will take on next, in period $T + 1$, will be

$$\hat{Y}_{T+1} = \hat{\beta}_0 + \hat{\beta}_1 X_{T+1}. \tag{17.1}$$

Economists most frequently use predictions like $\hat{Y}_{T+1}$ when they are examining several possible values for $X_{T+1}$. "What if $X_{T+1}$ is 100? What would we predict $Y$ to be? What if $X_{T+1}$ is 150? What would we predict $Y$ to be?" and so on. Economists working as policy analysts engage in many such "what if" exercises, because they help government officials anticipate and plan for alternative futures. Because the predictions in such analyses are conditional on what $X$-values we consider, we call such predictions conditional forecasts.

We have encountered conditional forecasts before, in Chapter 5. There, we learned about prediction intervals, which are designed to give a range of conditional forecasts for $Y$, given $X$. A 95% prediction interval is constructed such that in 95% of samples (including in the sample the future observation $T + 1$), the prediction interval includes the actual $Y_{T+1}$. We also learned that prediction intervals can err in two ways. First, the estimates of $\beta_0$ and $\beta_1$ can be wrong. Second, the disturbance term, $\varepsilon_{T+1}$, can make the conditional forecast wrong. If the DGP satisfies the Gauss–Markov Assumptions and the disturbances are normally distributed, the variance of the conditional forecast's errors is

$$\sigma_{F0}^2 = \sigma^2[1 + (1/n) + (X_{T+1} - \overline{X})^2/\textstyle\sum(x_i^2)], \tag{17.2}$$

and the 95% prediction interval is

$$\hat{\beta}_0 + \hat{\beta}_1 X_{T+1} \pm 1.96\sigma_{F0}. \tag{17.3}$$

Conditional forecasts presume that we know $X_{T+1}$. The policy analysts' examination of several "what if" scenarios is one way to deal with uncertainty about $X_{T+1}$. But what if we want to pin down one specific forecast, or one specific forecast interval? If we don't know $X_{T+1}$, and usually we do not, we have to replace $X_{T+1}$ in Equation 17.1 with its own predicted value. Using a predicted value for $X_{T+1}$ adds one more source of potential error to forecasts, an error in predicting $X_{T+1}$. Little is known in general about forecasting with predicted $X$-values, other than that the appropriate prediction interval would be wider than that in Equation 17.3. Policy analysts' "what if" scenarios can provide valuable insights into the effects of uncertainty about $X_{T+1}$ in specific cases.

Using a predicted value for $X_{T+1}$ generally pushes back the forecasting problem one more step—how are we to estimate $X_{T+1}$? Because the statistical properties of forecasts of $Y$ based on forecasts of $X$ are not well understood, this chapter focuses mainly on forecasting methods that do not require predictions of one variable to forecast another. However, two frequently encountered cases of conditional forecasting do not require predicting $X_{T+1}$: (i) when $X$ is a time trend and (ii) when $X$ is replaced with several dummy variables indicating quarters, months, weeks, or any other specific periods of the year. If we know which period we are forecasting for, we know the values of any time trend or seasonal dummy appearing in Equation 17.1. The next two sections discuss the use of time trends and seasonal dummies in forecasting.

## Linear Time Trends

In Chapter 4 we examined a DGP in which the data are a time series and the explanatory variable is time itself, $t$. That time trend, the variable $t$, and an intercept were the only explanators in that model:

$$Y_t = \beta_0 + \beta_1 t + \varepsilon_t$$

$$t = 1, \ldots, T \qquad \textbf{17.4}$$

$$E(Y_t|t) = \beta_0 + \beta_1 t$$

and assume that the Gauss–Markov Assumptions are satisfied in this DGP. In this DGP,

$$E(Y_t) - E(Y_{t-1}) = \beta_0 + \beta_1 t - \beta_0 - \beta_1(t - 1) = \beta_1$$

because the index of time changes by one from one period to the next. When the mean of $Y$ grows over time in this constant fashion, we say there is a **deterministic trend** in the data. Because the $E(Y_t|t)$ is a linear function of time, we also refer to this as a **linear time trend.**

OLS is consistent when there is a deterministic time trend in the model and the Gauss–Markov Assumptions otherwise apply. (Chapter 12 noted that the OLS estimator even converges on the true value at a faster than root $n$ rate when the explanator is time.) A deterministic trend also preserves the asymptotic normality of the OLS estimator in this DGP. Consequently, if there is a deterministic time trend in the DGP, we can consistently estimate the parameters of the model with OLS and construct valid prediction intervals in which the conditioning on $X$, the time trend, is valid.

To illustrate a time trend, Figure 17.1 shows the fitted regression line for 19 years of footwear production for the United States regressed against time, as in Equation 17.4.[4] (These data are in the datafile footwear.*** on this book's companion Web site, **www.aw-bc.com/murray.**) Production declines steadily and approximately linearly across the years. However, note that the negative linear time trend cannot continue indefinitely—footwear production cannot become nega-

**Figure 17.1**

Annual Footwear
Production in the
United States

*Source:* 1999 M3 Fore-
casting Competition

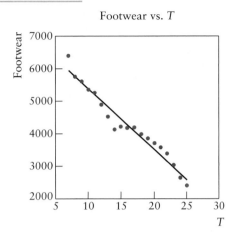

tive. This example highlights the fact that deterministic trends, downward or upward, cannot be counted on to continue forever. Forecasting trends invariably
takes us out of the range of observations on the explanatory variable, time. Using
the fitted values of regressions outside the observed range of the explanators is always particularly risky, because we have no confirmation that the functional form
is actually as we assume it to be.

## Exponential Growth Trends

Growth in a variable need not be linear. Section 4.5 described how a regression
can capture exponential growth by making the natural log of Y the dependent
variable in a model with a linear time trend:

$$\log(Y_t) = \beta_0 + \beta_1 t + \varepsilon_t. \qquad \textbf{17.5}$$

In this specification,

$$\frac{d(\log(Y_t))}{dt} = \frac{1}{Y_t}\frac{dY_t}{dt} = \beta_1,$$

so the regression coefficient, $\beta_1$, is the rate of growth of Y per time period.

To illustrate exponential growth, Figure 17.2 plots the number of U.S. citizens who traveled abroad in each of 26 years. (These data are in the datafile
tourists.*** on this book's companion Web site, **www.aw-bc.com/murray.**) Panel
(a) of the figure shows the regression line fit from Equation 17.4 with the number
of tourists as the dependent variable. Panel (b) shows the regression line fit from
Equation 17.5, with the log of the number of tourists as the dependent variable.

**Figure 17.2**

U.S. Citizens Touring Abroad

*Source:* 1999 M3 Forecasting Competition

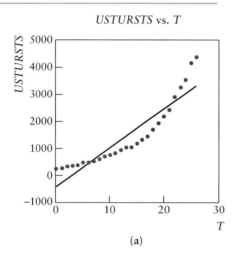

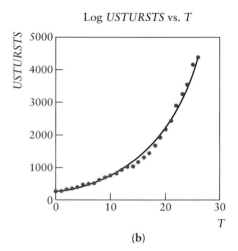

(a)

(b)

## Polynomial Trends

A time trend need not be linear, nor need it be exponential. Time can appear in a regression in any polynomial form; for example, it could appear in quadratic or cubic form, as in

$$Y_t = \beta_0 + \beta_1 t + \beta_2 t^2 + \varepsilon_t$$

or

$$Y_t = \beta_0 + \beta_1 t + \beta_2 t^2 + \beta_3 t^3 + \varepsilon_t.$$

**17.6**

Figure 17.3 reports 41 years of total revenues of Class I (large) railroads in the United States, excluding AMTRAK, plotted against time. Panels (a) and (b) show the fitted line from estimating the linear and exponential relationships of Equations 17.4 and 17.5 for rail revenues. (These data are in the datafile rail-rev.*** on this book's companion Web site, **www.aw-bc.com/murray.**) Neither model fits the data well. Panels (c) and (d) show the fitted line from estimating the quadratic and cubic relationships given in Equation 17.6.

The quadratic and cubic models in Panels (c) and (d) of Figure 17.3 fit the observed railroad revenue data markedly better than do the linear or exponential growth models. Which model should we rely on; the quadratic or the cubic? How should we choose the order of the polynomial when modeling the railroad revenue data in Figure 17.3? More generally, how should we to choose the powers of $t$ to include in a forecasting model?

**Figure 17.3**

Annual Rail Revenues for Class I Railroads (Excluding Amtrak)

*Source:* U.S. Department of Transportation

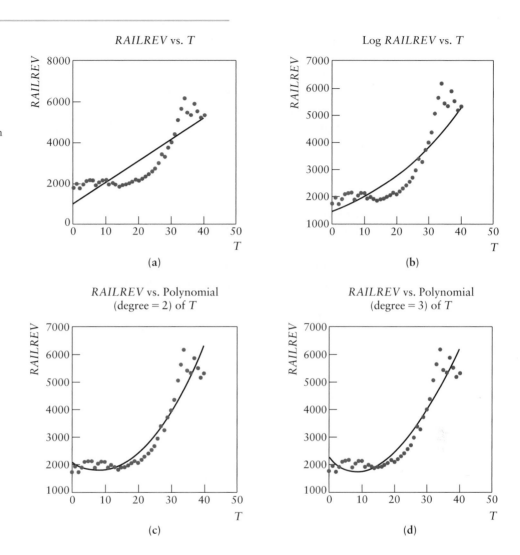

## Information Criteria for Choosing Among Models

Almost all of the regression models discussed in earlier chapters have been used to get at the behavioral and institutional relationships that causally determine the dependent variables of interest. For example, we put price in a demand curve because we think price influences consumers' choices. When we include the square of price, it is because we think (and perhaps the data indicate) that consumers' response to price is not linear, but quadratic. Forecasters bring a different perspective to specifying their models. Forecasters are largely uninterested in the causal connections among variables. Instead, they want models that can fit future data well. Any explanators that improve the prospects of fitting the data well are good explanators in the eyes of forecasters. This section discusses several measures of a model's goodness of fit.

An intuitively appealing measure of how well a model will fit the data in periods beyond the sample is how well the model fits data within the sample. We have already encountered two measures of the within-sample fit of a model, the coefficient of determination, $R^2$, and the adjusted $R^2$, $\overline{R}^2$. The coefficient of determination, $R^2$, is

$$R^2 = 1 - \frac{\Sigma e_i^2}{\Sigma y_i^2}.$$

This is not a good measure for choosing which powers of $t$ to include in the model because it always grows larger as more powers of $t$ are added to the model. If we rely on the $R^2$ to decide which variables to include, we will tend to make our models too complex, seduced by the better fit more variables provide. Forecasters have found that although adding explanators to a model always increases $R^2$, adding too many explanators damages post-sample fit. For forecasters, there is a trade-off between good fit and the number of explanators included in the model.

The adjusted $R^2$ penalizes models for added explanators, balancing a smaller sum of squared residuals against adding explanators that do not really belong in the model. The adjusted $R^2$ is

$$\overline{R}^2 = 1 - \left[\left(\frac{\Sigma e_i^2}{\Sigma y_i^2}\right)\left(\frac{(T-1)}{(T-k-1)}\right)\right] = 1 - \left[\left(\frac{\Sigma e_i^2}{(T-k-1)}\right)\left(\frac{(T-1)}{\Sigma y_i^2}\right)\right],$$

**17.7**

where $k$ is the number of explanators. But the adjusted $R^2$ is not the only measure that penalizes models for additional explanators. Forecasters rely on three alternative statistics for choosing between models with more or fewer explanators, such as more or fewer powers of time:

1. The adjusted $R^2$
2. The Akaike information criterion (AIC)
3. The Schwarz information criterion (SIC)

What varies in Equation 17.7 as the number of explanators changes and the number of observations and the values of $y$ do not is

$$s^2 = \frac{\Sigma e_i^2}{(T-k-1)}.$$

Thus, forecasters who rely on the adjusted $R^2$ to choose a model seek the model with the smallest estimated variance for the disturbances, $s^2$. However, most forecasters penalize models more for additional explanators than does the adjusted $R^2$. These forecasters use alternative criteria, usually either the Akaike information criterion or the Schwarz information criterion for selecting a preferred model.

The **Akaike information criterion (AIC)** for selecting a preferred model is to choose the model for which

$$AIC = \Sigma e_i^2 \left( \frac{\exp\left( \frac{2k+2}{T} \right)}{T} \right)$$

is smallest. Econometricians like the AIC because in large samples it tends to pick from a given set of models the model for which the variance of the prediction for period $(T + 1)$ is closest to that prediction's variance in the true (but unknown) model.

The **Schwarz information criterion (SIC)** is to choose the model for which

$$SIC = \Sigma e_i^2 \left( T^{\frac{k+1}{T} - 1} \right)$$

is smallest. The SIC penalizes models more harshly for additional explanators than does the Aikaike criterion. Econometricians like the SIC because in large samples it will tend to pick the model that is the best approximation to the true underlying model. For every model, $s^2 <$ AIC $<$ SIC. The adjusted $s^2$ grows slowest and the SIC fastest as $k$ rises. Consequently, when the criteria lead to different model choices, the SIC leads to the smallest model and the adjusted $R^2$ to the largest. The adjusted $R^2$ is the oldest of the three measures, but it has become the least preferred among econometricians. Econometricians differ about whether the AIC or SIC is the better measure in practice.

Note that the adjusted $R^2$, AIC, and SIC all share the trait of being based on observations that are in the sample that we use to estimate the various models. When lots of data are available for estimating a forecasting model, it is often wise to refrain from using all of the data for estimation, and instead choose and estimate the forecasting model using part of the data. Then, we can validate the model by examining its performance in the portion of the sample not used in estimating the model. Such validation exercises are especially effective in revealing when a model has been "over fit" with, for example, a polynomial of too high an order.

## An Example of Model Choice: Forecasting Railroad Revenues

Table 17.1 reports the adjusted $R^2$, AIC, and SIC for four models of railroad revenues, all of which express expected revenues as polynomials in time. (These data are in railrev.*** on this book's companion Web site, **www.aw-bc.com/murray.** They are the same data used for Figure 17.2.) The polynomials range in order from one (linear) to four (quartic). Better models have higher adjusted $R^2$ and

**TABLE 17.1** Criteria for Choosing Powers of Time in Forecasting Railroad Revenues

| Model | $\overline{R}^2$ | AIC | SIC |
|---|---|---|---|
| Linear | .750 | 16.08 | 16.16 |
| Quadratic | .906 | 15.12 | 15.25 |
| Cubic | .914 | 11.81 | 12.00 |
| Quartic | .911 | 11.87 | 12.11 |

lower AIC and SIC statistics. On all three criteria, the cubic polynomial in time best fits these data.

Figure 17.4, Panel (a), shows the fitted values (1947–1987) and 20 years of forecasts (1988–2007) for the four polynomial models and for the exponential growth model of Panel (b) in Figure 17.3. The quartic polynomial leads to unacceptable forecasts, as it predicts negative revenues very soon into the forecast period. The other models are much more alike to one another than to the fourth-order polynomial. Panel (b) shows just the polynomial models of order one to three and the exponential growth model. Viewed without the terribly performing quartic model, we can see that the other models do offer dramatically different forecasts from one another. By the end of the sample period, 1987, the models are already yielding sharply different fitted values. By the end of the forecast period,

**Figure 17.4**

Fitted Values of Railroad Revenues for 1947–1987 and Forecast Values for 1988–2007

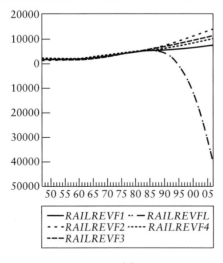

(a)

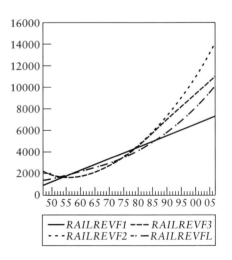

(b)

2007, the quadratic model forecasts revenues more than double those forecast by the linear model. The cubic and exponential growth models are in closer agreement to one another.

These railroad data illustrate the risks of forecasting deterministic trends to continue over long periods of time. With relatively little evidence to choose among the several functional forms, modest differences in choice of functional form can lead to dramatically different forecasts.

## Seasonal Dummies

Time trends capture persistent changes in data that accumulate over time. *Seasonal dummy variables* capture recurrent changes in data. There are numerous examples of such recurrent seasonal changes in variables. Retail sales surge in the fourth quarter of the year because of holiday purchases. Durable goods purchases slump during that same quarter. Unemployment rises in June and July as recent graduates flood the job market. Stock market activity on Mondays differs from that on Fridays, each affected in its own way by the stock markets closing down over the weekend.

**Seasonal dummy variables** indicate the day, week, month, or quarter of an observation. They are a natural way to incorporate seasonal effects into regression models and into conditional forecasts. Figure 17.5 graphs one real, but unnamed, company's quarterly sales for 36 quarters. Sales trend upward over the sample period. Do they also display seasonality? (The data are in the file sales.*** on this book's companion Web site, **www.aw-bc.com/murray.**) Table 17.2 reports a regression of sales on time, a constant, and seasonal dummies for quarters 2, 3, and 4. The coefficients on the quarterly dummies report differences between the intercept for that quarter and quarter 1. Quarter 4 is statistically significantly different from quarter 1.

Dummy variables are not the only way to capture systematically recurrent influences on $Y$. For example, from year to year, specific months differ in how many stock market trading days they have. If we want to forecast a month's stock market trading volume, the number of trading days is an explanator we would like to include in our model. Because the number of trading days depends only on the number of weekdays (less holidays) in a given month, we can calculate this explanator exactly for use in a conditional forecasting model. For convenience, we call all systematically recurrent influences **seasonal effects**. The coefficients on seasonal dummies measure such seasonal effects. Because seasonal variables are known in advance, we can use them as explanators in regression models and can then include their effects in building useful prediction intervals, such as that in Equation 17.3.

Seasonal effects complicate forecasting in that they require that we estimate their magnitude for use in our forecasts. Seasonal effects can also complicate policy analyses of time series data. Unemployment illustrates the problem. Unemployment

**TABLE 17.2** A Regression Model for Sales with Time Trend and Quarterly Effects

Dependent Variable: SALES
Method: Least Squares
Sample: 1984:1 1992:4
Included observations: 36

| Variable | Coefficient | Std. Error | t-Statistic | Prob. |
|---|---|---|---|---|
| C | 3306.944 | 246.4285 | 13.41949 | 0.0000 |
| Q2 | 414.1146 | 275.6768 | 1.502174 | 0.1432 |
| Q3 | −432.881 | 276.1604 | −1.567502 | 0.1271 |
| Q4 | −915.434 | 276.9645 | −3.305240 | 0.0024 |
| T | 50.88542 | 9.431624 | 5.395191 | 0.0000 |

| | | | | |
|---|---|---|---|---|
| R-squared | 0.619250 | Mean dependent var | | 3963.889 |
| Adjusted R-squared | 0.570121 | S.D. dependent var | | 891.4131 |
| S.E. of regression | 584.4564 | Akaike info criterion | | 15.70749 |
| Sum squared resid | 10589267 | Schwarz criterion | | 15.92742 |
| Log likelihood | −277.734 | F-statistic | | 12.60457 |
| Durbin–Watson stat | 1.369605 | Prob(F-statistic) | | 0.000003 |

rose in June 2003. Is this a sign of a weakening economy? Not necessarily. Unemployment rises every June, as new graduates enter the job market, seeking work. Did unemployment rise more than usual this June? If so, the increase is a sign of a weakening economy. To assess the health of the macroeconomy, the United States Department of Labor adjusts unemployment figures and reports them with their seasonal effects removed. We call such statistics **seasonally adjusted data.**

**Figure 17.5**

One Company's Quarterly Sales

*Source:* 1999 M3 Forecasting Competition

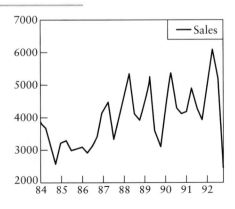

# An Econometric Top 40—Two Golden Oldies

## The Early Macroeconometric Modelers—Tinbergen and Klein

The macroeconomists of the 1930s, '40s, and '50s created the tools for estimating simultaneous equations models. Today, the models they inspired are used frequently by industry to forecast future economic outcomes. Although the models are relied on primarily for their forecasting capabilities, their creators initially answered the need for macroeconomic models that could describe the workings of the economy in aggregate form. The ambition of the macroeconomic model builders was immense: to write down a system of equations that aptly describes the workings of an entire economy and then estimate the parameters of that system.

In the 19th century, Leon Walras and Vilfredo Pareto of the Academy of Lausanne both developed general equilibrium models of national economies. These models, with a market for every good, were too vast for empirical implementation, however. In the 1930s, several macroeconomists made the key abstraction that would inspire the macroeconometricians. Instead of studying the markets for specific commodities, the early macroeconomists (most particularly, Dutch Nobel laureate Ragnar Frisch, Michael Kalecki of the Institute of Business Cycles and Prices in Warsaw, and, the giant among giants, Cambridge University's John Maynard Keynes) focused on broad aggregates of goods, lumping together all consumption, all investment, and all government spending into three key analytical categories. The simplicity of the broadly aggregated categories made the new macro models empirically manageable.

This Hit introduces two of the earliest multi-equation macroeconometric models, one the 1939 brainchild of Dutch Nobel laureate Jan Tinbergen, the other the 1950 creation of University of Pennsylvania Nobel laureate Lawrence Klein.[5] These two models were prototypes for many macroeconometric models that followed later. The aggregative strategy of macroeconomics did free Tinbergen, Klein, and other macro model builders from accounting for each and every good in the economy, but the empiricists among the macroeconomists nonetheless believed from early on that successful implementation of macro models would still require more detail than pure theorists would grapple with. Tinbergen's 1939 model, for example, contains 31 equations for estimation, plus another 17 "identities" (equations that link some variables by known institutional or accounting relationships) that require no estimation.

Tinbergen's model typifies macroeconometric models in breaking the economy into "sectors," or subsets of equations. Tinbergen's model has four sectors: (i) a final demands sector—three consumption functions and three investment demand functions, each treating a different aggregate of goods; (ii) a price-wage sector—five behavioral equations to determine the prices of goods and the wage rate for workers; (iii) a financial sector containing 10 behavioral equations; and (iv) an income distribution sector, also containing 10 behavioral equations.

Tinbergen's pioneering model appeared before most advances in simultaneous equations estimation. He estimates his model by OLS. He pays little heed to which variables in his model are exogenous and which are endogenous. And he falls into almost every other error that subsequent simultaneous equations research exposed. Indeed, much of the econometric research on simultaneous equations following

Tinbergen's work was an effort to learn how to do correctly what Tinbergen had ambitiously attempted before anyone else.

In his book, Tinbergen puts his estimated equations to three chief uses: first, he describes the U.S. economy; second, he asks whether the economy is stable; and third, he assesses competing theories of the business cycle. He does not use his macroeconometric model for either of the two purposes for which modern macroeconometricians most often use their models—he does not forecast the future of the economy and he does not simulate alternative public policies.

By the time econometricians had solved many of the statistical problems posed by Tinbergen's effort, macro modeling had advanced beyond Tinbergen's formulation of the economy. Klein's work went beyond Tinbergen's in both its economics and its statistics. Klein's model is a leaner machine than Tinbergen's, or, rather, three leaner machines, because Klein's book provides three alternative models. The largest of Klein's three models (which he called "Model III") contains only 12 behavioral equations to be estimated and four identities. Nonetheless, Klein's Model III was, in its very Keynesian flavor, the precursor of later, much larger Keynesian macro models. Klein's model I, with only three behavioral equations and three identities, has remained a teaching tool for macroeconometric courses for several generations.

Klein's Model I contains (i) a consumption function in which consumption ($C$) depends on wages and salaries in the public and private sectors ($W_g$ and $W_p$)and on property income ($P$):

$$C_t = \alpha_0 + \alpha_1(W_{gt} + W_{pt}) + \alpha_2 P_t + \varepsilon_t^C;$$

(ii) an investment equation in which investment ($I$) depends on current and lagged property income and on the initial stock of capital ($K$):

$$I_t = \beta_0 + \beta_1 P_t + \beta_2 P_{t-1} + \beta_3 K_t + \varepsilon_t^I;$$

and (iii) a wage equation in which wages depend on current and lagged national product ($Y$) and a time trend ($T$):

$$W_t = \gamma_0 + \gamma_1 Y_t + \gamma_2 Y_{t-1} + \gamma_3 T_t + \varepsilon_t^W.$$

The three identities in Model I are (i) national private product equals consumption plus investment plus government spending ($G$) minus government wages ($W_g$):

$$Y_t = C_t + I_t + G_t - W_{gt};$$

(ii) national income ($N$), which equals national product minus net exports and taxes ($X$), equals wages plus property income:

$$N_t = Y_t - X_t = W_{pt} + P_t;$$

and (iii) the change in the capital stock equals investment:

$$K_t = K_{t-1} + I_{t-1}.$$

All the variables in Klein's model are real, not nominal; the model offers no account of the general price level. The success (and limitations) of Klein's model in prediction and as a policy evaluation tool inspired a new generation of economists to build larger macro models that could better capture the complexities of a modern economy.

In 1969, Tinbergen received the Nobel prize in economics. His Nobel citation read "for having developed and applied dynamic models for the analysis of economic processes." In 1980, Klein received the Nobel prize in economics. His Nobel citation read "for the creation of econometric models and the application to the analysis of economic fluctuations and economic policies."

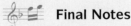 **Final Notes**

The simultaneous equations framework, and the estimation procedures associated with it, are a rich legacy of the macroeconometricians who preceded Robert Lucas, of rational expectations fame. Their history illustrates the changing methods and changing fashions of the economics community. The models were initially intended as descriptors of the actual economy, and the simultaneous equations methods of the modelers were meant to pin down the actual parameters that reflect the workings of the macro economy. But when Lucas cast doubt on the usefulness of such models as descriptions of the economy's actual workings (as described in a Greatest Hit at the end of Chapter 8; see p. 333), economists continued to use the models as devices for forecasting. Today, macro models are more apt to be estimated with OLS than with simultaneous equations methods, because the OLS methods tend to work relatively well when making forecasts.

■

Government statistical agencies often report data in both seasonally adjusted and seasonally unadjusted form. Graphs of seasonally adjusted data highlight more persistent features of the data, without the distraction of seasonal effects adding to the fluctuations in the data.

Figure 17.6 illustrates the contrasting roles of seasonally unadjusted and seasonally adjusted data. The figure shows quarterly data on GDP from 1991, quarter 1, to 2001, quarter 4, provided by the U.S. Bureau of Economic Analysis. Panel (a) contains the seasonally unadjusted data; Panel (b) shows the seasonally adjusted data. GDP typically falls in the first quarter of every year. The seasonally unadjusted data reveal this seasonal pattern in GDP. The seasonally adjusted data highlight the steady upward growth in GDP across the decade of the 90s. (Both the seasonal pattern and the general upward trend in GDP are apparent in longer time series on GDP. Such data are in the file gdp001.*** on this book's companion Web site, www.aw-bc.com/murray.) Most econometricians prefer to use seasonally unadjusted data in econometric models because statistical agencies

**Figure 17.6**

U.S. GDP by Quarter 1991:1–2001:4

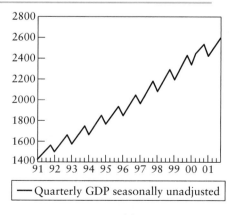

— Quarterly GDP seasonally unadjusted

(a)

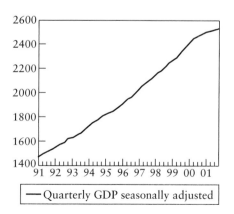

— Quarterly GDP seasonally adjusted

(b)

frequently adjust one series differently than they do another, which is appropriate for studying individual series, but which can induce misleading estimates of dynamic effects in regression models.

## 17.2     Univariate Forecasting

Conditional forecasts flow naturally from the regression models of Chapters 1–16, but conditional forecasting frequently stumbles on our ignorance of the future values of the explanators, $X_{T+1}$, $X_{T+2}$, and so on. Consequently, economic forecasters often abandon explanators and instead forecast a variable's future values based only on its own past values. The intuition for this strategy is that many economic variables change quite smoothly, so that values in the near future often look much like the values in the recent past. This section examines three statistical models that forecasters use in univariate forecasting. Because we have already studied first-order autoregressions (Chapter 11), which are a special case of one of these three models, the section begins with first-order autoregressive forecasting models.

### Forecasting with First-Order Autoregressions

The autoregressive model of Chapter 11 is an example of a model in which future values tend to look much like the values observed in the recent past. We can sometimes forecast autoregressive variables accurately from their own past values. In Chapter 11, it was the disturbances that were autoregressive. For forecasters, it is $Y$ that sometimes follows a first-order autoregressive (AR(1)) process:

$$Y_t = \alpha_0 + \alpha_1 Y_{t-1} + \varepsilon_t, \qquad \textbf{17.8}$$

in which $|\alpha_1| < 1$. We saw in Chapter 11 that autoregressive models can be expressed in terms of the current and lagged disturbances:

$$
\begin{aligned}
Y_t &= \alpha_0 + \alpha_1 Y_{t-1} + \varepsilon_t = \alpha_0 + \alpha_1(\alpha_0 + \alpha_1 Y_{t-2} + \varepsilon_{t-1}) + \varepsilon_t \\
&= \alpha_0 + \alpha_1(\alpha_0 + \alpha_1\alpha_1(\alpha_0 + \alpha_1 Y_{t-3} + \varepsilon_{t-2}) + \varepsilon_{t-1}) + \varepsilon_t \\
&= \alpha_0 + \alpha_1\alpha_0 + \alpha_1^2\alpha_0 + \alpha_1^3 Y_{t-3} + \varepsilon_t + \alpha_1\varepsilon_{t-1} + \alpha_1^2\varepsilon_{t-2} \\
&= \cdots = \frac{\alpha_0}{1 - \alpha_1} + \sum_{j=0}^{\infty} \alpha_1^j \varepsilon_{t-j}. \qquad \textbf{17.9}
\end{aligned}
$$

Equation 17.9 reveals why we restrict $|\alpha_1|$ to less than one. We need $|\alpha_1| < 1$ so that the $\alpha_1^j$ terms in Equation 17.9 shrink with $j$; otherwise, that sum would be infinite.

In Chapter 11, the disturbances in the autoregressions were independent, mean zero, identically distributed random variables. We call such disturbances

**white noise innovations**. The disturbances in time series models are called "innovations" because they capture what happens afresh in a specific time period. "White noise" innovations draw their name from statistical studies of radio signals. Those studies call static, signals that convey no information, "white noise." In time series models, if the disturbances are white noise innovations, each disturbance is a genuine surprise, completely unrelated to what has happened in the past. The Gauss–Markov Assumptions declare that disturbances are white noise innovations. In Chapter 11 we learned that if the disturbances in Equation 17.9 are white noise and distributed $N(0, \sigma^2)$, then $Y \sim N\left(\frac{\alpha_0}{1 - \alpha_1}, \frac{\sigma^2}{1 - \alpha_1^2}\right)$ and $\text{cov}(Y_t, Y_{t-r}) = \frac{\alpha_1^r}{1 - \alpha_1^2}\sigma^2$.

Equation 17.9 provides a formula with which we can forecast future values of $Y$. Our best guess of disturbances after time $T$ is zero, their expected value. We forecast forward from time $T$ by using $Y_T$ and the estimated values of $\alpha_0$ and $\alpha_1$, $\hat{\alpha}_0$ and $\hat{\alpha}_1$. With these replacements and a suitable change of indices, Equation 17.9 allows us to construct a forecast, $Y_{T+r}^F$, for any period, $(T + r)$:

$$Y_{T+r}^F = \hat{\alpha}_0 \sum_{j=0}^{r-1} \alpha_1^j + \hat{\alpha}_1^r Y_T. \qquad \textbf{17.10}$$

## Forecasting with Higher Order Autoregressions

The AR(I) model is often too simple to portray observed data accurately. We frequently need more complex time series models if we are to do a good job forecasting. Higher order autoregressions are a natural extension of the AR(I) model. In the AR(I) model, today's value of $Y$, $Y_t$, inherits a fraction of yesterday's $Y$, $Y_{t-1}$. In an **autoregression of order $p$**, today's $Y$ inherits fractions of each of $p$ preceding $Y$'s, $Y_{t-1}, \ldots, Y_{t-p}$. We denote autoregressions of order $p$ by **AR($p$)**. Thus, $Y_t$ follows a $p$-th order autoregressive process if

$$Y_t = \alpha_0 + \varepsilon_t + \sum_{j=1}^{p} \alpha_j Y_{t-j},$$

in which $\varepsilon_t$ is white noise.

As in AR(1) processes, in AR($p$) processes, past innovations never entirely stop affecting current outcomes. The correlation between $Y_t$ and $Y_{t-j}$ tends to shrink as $j$ grows, but it does not disappear altogether. Statisticians call

$$\rho_j = \text{cov}(Y_t, Y_{t-j})/\sigma^2$$

the $j$-th order autocorrelation coefficient. They call coefficients $\alpha_1, \alpha_2, \ldots, \alpha_p$ in an AR($p$) process **partial autocorrelation coefficients** of order 1 through $p$. Just as

$|\alpha_1|$ needs to be less than one in the AR(I) model so that the sum in Equation 17.9 is not infinite, the coefficients $\alpha_1, \ldots, \alpha_p$ are also restricted; a necessary condition for the partial autocorrelation coefficients is that $\sum_{i=1}^p \alpha_i < 1$. (Chapter 18 discusses DGPs in which this condition is violated.) *An identifying characteristic of AR(p) processes is that their autocorrelation coefficients of higher order shrink, but do not disappear altogether, and their partial autocorrelation coefficients of order (p + 1) and higher are zero.*

We can test hypotheses about partial autocorrelation coefficients using the standard $t$- and $F$-tests of regression analysis. Econometricians have also devised a test statistic for assessing the hypothesis that the first $r$ autocorrelations, $\rho_1, \ldots \rho_r$, are zero. The test statistic is

$$Q = T\sum_{i=1}^r \rho_i^2,$$

which, in large samples, is distributed approximately chi-square with $r$ degrees of freedom under the null hypothesis that first $r$ autocorrelations are zero.

## Estimating Autoregressive Models

Table 17.3 reports the estimated autocorrelation coefficients and partial autocorrelation coefficients for two samples of 635 observations generated from autoregressive processes. The estimates in Panel A are based upon data chosen at random from an AR(1) process in which $\alpha_1$ equals 0.9. The estimates in Panel B are based on data chosen at random from an AR(2) process in which $\alpha_1$ equals 1.20 and $\alpha_2$ equals $-0.64$. (Notice that in some higher order autoregressions, $\alpha_1$ may be greater than one, as in the second here. Notice, too, that partial autoregression coefficients are sometimes negative, as in the second here.) The figure presents both the numerical estimates and a graphical depiction of the estimates. The asterisks and periods in the first two columns of each panel reflect the magnitude of the estimated coefficients. The column headed $r$ indicates the order of the estimated autocorrelation and partial autocorrelation shown in a given row of the table.

The slow shrinking of the estimated autocorrelation coefficients and the quick drop to near zero of the estimated partial autocorrelations that we see in Table 17.3 are typical of autoregressions. In the AR(1) process in Panel A, the estimated partial autocorrelation coefficients become close to zero at order two; in the AR(2) process, in Panel B, the drop in estimated partial autocorrelation coefficients occurs at order three. Econometricians often use such printouts to decide what order of autocorrelation to allow for when they first specify a model for a given set of data. The Q-statistics reported in Table 17.3 are for testing the null hypothesis that the first $r$ autocorrelations are all zero.

The AR(1) processes in Chapter 11 and in this chapter assume $|\alpha_1| < 1$. This assumption precludes infinite and ever-growing variances. When modeling

**TABLE 17.3** Estimated Autocorrelations and Estimated Partial Autocorrelations for Samples from Two Autoregressive Processes

*Panel A*
Sample: 1947:02 1999:12
Included observations: 635

| Autocorrelation | Partial Correlation | r | AC | PAC | Q-Stat | Prob |
|---|---|---|---|---|---|---|
| .\|*******\| | .\|*******\| | 1 | 0.905 | 0.905 | 522.10 | 0.000 |
| .\|****** \| | .\|. \| | 2 | 0.810 | −0.044 | 941.75 | 0.000 |
| .\|****** \| | .\|. \| | 3 | 0.719 | −0.037 | 1272.5 | 0.000 |
| .\|***** \| | .\|. \| | 4 | 0.629 | −0.046 | 1526.0 | 0.000 |
| .\|**** \| | .\|. \| | 5 | 0.548 | −0.002 | 1719.1 | 0.000 |
| .\|**** \| | .\|. \| | 6 | 0.477 | −0.003 | 1865.2 | 0.000 |
| .\|*** \| | .\|. \| | 7 | 0.407 | −0.037 | 1971.9 | 0.000 |
| .\|*** \| | .\|. \| | 8 | 0.345 | −0.006 | 2048.7 | 0.000 |
| .\|** \| | .\|. \| | 9 | 0.289 | −0.011 | 2102.8 | 0.000 |
| .\|** \| | .\|. \| | 10 | 0.248 | 0.042 | 2142.7 | 0.000 |
| .\|** \| | .\|. \| | 11 | 0.225 | 0.064 | 2175.6 | 0.000 |
| .\|** \| | .\|. \| | 12 | 0.199 | −0.037 | 2201.3 | 0.000 |
| .\|* \| | .\|. \| | 13 | 0.181 | 0.020 | 2222.6 | 0.000 |
| .\|* \| | .\|. \| | 14 | 0.168 | 0.017 | 2240.9 | 0.000 |
| .\|* \| | .\|. \| | 15 | 0.151 | −0.025 | 2255.8 | 0.000 |
| .\|* \| | .\|. \| | 16 | 0.136 | −0.002 | 2268.0 | 0.000 |
| .\|* \| | .\|. \| | 17 | 0.120 | −0.018 | 2277.5 | 0.000 |
| .\|* \| | .\|. \| | 18 | 0.108 | 0.012 | 2285.0 | 0.000 |
| .\|* \| | .\|. \| | 19 | 0.093 | −0.019 | 2290.7 | 0.000 |
| .\|* \| | .\|. \| | 20 | 0.083 | 0.027 | 2295.2 | 0.000 |
| .\|* \| | .\|. \| | 21 | 0.071 | −0.017 | 2298.5 | 0.000 |
| .\|* \| | .\|. \| | 22 | 0.069 | 0.042 | 2301.6 | 0.000 |
| .\|. \| | .\|. \| | 23 | 0.058 | −0.042 | 2303.8 | 0.000 |
| .\|. \| | .\|. \| | 24 | 0.048 | −0.002 | 2305.4 | 0.000 |

*(continues)*

**TABLE 17.3** *(continued)*

*Panel B*
Sample: 1947:02 1999:12
Included observations: 635

| Autocorrelation | Partial Correlation | r | AC | PAC | Q-Stat | Prob |
|---|---|---|---|---|---|---|
| .\|\*\*\*\*\*\* \| | .\|\*\*\*\*\*\* \| | 1 | 0.745 | 0.745 | 354.14 | 0.000 |
| .\|\*\* \| | \*\*\*\*\*\|. \| | 2 | 0.272 | −0.635 | 401.57 | 0.000 |
| \*\|. \| | .\|. \| | 3 | −0.136 | 0.020 | 413.42 | 0.000 |
| \*\*\*\|. \| | .\|. \| | 4 | −0.328 | 0.017 | 482.29 | 0.000 |
| \*\*\|. \| | .\|. \| | 5 | −0.296 | 0.026 | 538.48 | 0.000 |
| \*\|. \| | .\|. \| | 6 | −0.143 | −0.018 | 551.67 | 0.000 |
| .\|. \| | \*\|. \| | 7 | −0.002 | −0.059 | 551.68 | 0.000 |
| .\|. \| | .\|. \| | 8 | 0.055 | −0.032 | 553.63 | 0.000 |
| .\|. \| | .\|. \| | 9 | 0.029 | −0.031 | 554.18 | 0.000 |
| .\|. \| | .\|. \| | 10 | −0.023 | 0.012 | 554.51 | 0.000 |
| .\|. \| | .\|. \| | 11 | −0.053 | −0.014 | 556.36 | 0.000 |
| .\|. \| | .\|. \| | 12 | −0.057 | −0.046 | 558.44 | 0.000 |
| .\|. \| | .\|. \| | 13 | −0.029 | 0.039 | 558.98 | 0.000 |
| .\|. \| | .\|. \| | 14 | 0.013 | 0.004 | 559.09 | 0.000 |
| .\|. \| | .\|. \| | 15 | 0.040 | −0.017 | 560.11 | 0.000 |
| .\|. \| | .\|. \| | 16 | 0.044 | 0.012 | 561.37 | 0.000 |
| .\|. \| | .\|. \| | 17 | 0.026 | −0.018 | 561.82 | 0.000 |
| .\|. \| | .\|. \| | 18 | −0.001 | 0.000 | 561.82 | 0.000 |
| .\|. \| | .\|. \| | 19 | −0.025 | −0.018 | 562.25 | 0.000 |
| .\|. \| | .\|. \| | 20 | −0.031 | 0.024 | 562.87 | 0.000 |
| .\|. \| | .\|. \| | 21 | −0.021 | −0.020 | 563.16 | 0.000 |
| .\|. \| | .\|. \| | 22 | 0.001 | 0.022 | 563.16 | 0.000 |
| .\|. \| | .\|. \| | 23 | 0.012 | −0.033 | 563.25 | 0.000 |
| .\|. \| | .\|. \| | 24 | 0.018 | 0.043 | 563.46 | 0.000 |

higher order autoregressions, we make an analogous assumption. An implication of this assumption is that the sum of the partial autocorrelation coefficients must be less than one. We restrict attention to variables for which (i) the variance of the time series variable does not depend on time and (ii) the covariance between one observation on a time series variable and a subsequent observation on that time series variable depends *only* on the distance in time between the two observations, *not* on the specific time period in which either observation occurs. In the language of Chapter 12, we restrict attention to variables that are covariance stationary. Chapter 18 analyzes models in which some or all variables are not covariance stationary.

The assumption that the covariances depend only on $|t - t'|$ requires that the shocks to a variable persist similarly in different parts of the time period under study—shocks happening in 1988 influenced 1990 in the same way that shocks in 2001 influenced 2003. In essence, we assume that the DGP that applies to one span of years is not different from the DGP that applies to another span of years.

## Forecasting with Moving Averages

Autoregressive processes imply that disturbances in the distant past continue to affect outcomes today, even if only in a small way. Not all real-world processes have this trait. In some processes, past shocks stop having an effect after a while. For example, if a company hires a surprisingly large number of workers this period, it may take several periods for the company to return to its established employment goals, but it is unlikely that employment in the firm is permanently affected by accidental surges or shortfalls in employment in one period. To model processes in which shocks to the system have effects for a limited time only, statisticians devised **moving average models**, denoted by **MA(q)**, where $q$ indicates how long a shock continues to influence $Y$.

In a moving average, today's observation, $Y_t$, is a weighted sum of today's innovation and some specified number of recent past innovations. The innovation in the sum that longest pre-dates the current period defines the order of the moving average. In a $q$-th order moving average process, today's realized value will be independent of all realized values that occurred more than $q$ periods ago, but it will be correlated with some realized values as far back as $q$ periods. Thus, if $\varepsilon_t$ is the innovation in period $t$, so it is distributed with zero mean and variance equal to $\sigma_\varepsilon^2$, and independently of the innovations in any other period, then $Y_t$ is a $q$-th order moving average if

$$Y_t = \beta_0 + \varepsilon_t + \sum_{j=1}^{q} \beta_j \varepsilon_{t-j}.$$

Thus, in a moving average process, the realized value today includes an inheritance from $q$ periods' innovations, an inheritance that contains some multiples — often but not necessarily fractions — of the past periods' innovations.

*An important difference between moving averages and autoregressions, is that in moving averages, past shocks eventually have no further influence, but in autoregressions, the past never entirely dies away.*

Notice that $\text{cov}(Y_t, Y_{t-r})$, the covariance of $Y_t$ and $Y_{t-r}$, is zero for $r > q$. The $\varepsilon$'s are white noise, and hence uncorrelated. When $r > q$, $Y_t$ and $Y_{t-r}$ share no common $\varepsilon$, so the two variables are uncorrelated. The $r$-th order **autocorrelation coefficient**, $\rho_r$, is

$$\rho_r = \frac{\text{cov}(Y_t Y_{t-r})}{\text{var}(Y_t)};$$

it measures the degree of correlation between observations on a variable observed at two different moments in time $r$ periods apart. *An identifying characteristic of MA(q) processes is that the autocorrelation coefficients of order $(q + 1)$ and higher are zero.*

## Estimating Moving Average Models

Table 17.4 reports the estimated autocorrelation coefficients and partial autocorrelation coefficients for two samples of 635 observations generated from moving average processes. The estimates in Panel A are based on data drawn at random from a first-order moving average process in which $\beta_1$ equals $-0.9$. (With $\beta_1$ equal to $-0.9$, a shock today is largely offset by an almost equal opposite effect the next period.) The estimates in Panel B are based on data drawn at random from a second-order moving average process in which $\beta_1$ equals 0.4 and $\beta_2$ equals to 0.8. The slow shrinking of the estimated partial autocorrelation coefficients and the quick drop to near zero of the estimated autocorrelations are typical of moving averages. In the first-order moving average in Panel A, the estimated autocorrelation coefficient goes to zero at order two; in the second-order autoregression, in Panel B, the drop in estimated autocorrelation coefficients occurs at order three. Notice that the distinctive pattern of the moving average processes is the opposite of the autoregressive processes. Econometricians often use such printouts to decide for what order of moving average or autocorrelation to allow when they first specify a model for a given set of data.

## Forecasting with ARMA models

We can imagine situations in which a process has elements of both moving averages and autoregressions. Some events have effects that end after several periods, and other events have effects that never die out entirely. To model such mixed processes, statisticians use a **mixed autoregressive–moving average (ARMA)** process. An ARMA process is the sum of an autoregressive component and a moving average component:

$$Y_t = \sum_{j=1}^{p} \alpha_j Y_{t-j} + \varepsilon_t + \sum_{j=1}^{q} \beta_j \varepsilon_{t-j}. \qquad \textbf{17.11}$$

Because of the autoregressive element in an ARMA process, each observation $Y_t$ is correlated with *every* previous innovation, and hence every previous observation $Y_{t-j}$, as with autoregressions. Some parts of new shocks die away, though, as with

**TABLE 17.4** Estimated Autocorrelations and Estimated Partial Autocorrelations for Samples from Two Moving Average Processes

*Panel A*
Sample: 1947:02 1999:12
Included observations: 635

| Autocorrelation | | Partial Correlation | | | AC | PAC | Q-Stat | Prob |
|---|---|---|---|---|---|---|---|---|
| ****\|. | \| | ****\|. | \| | 1 | −0.490 | −0.490 | 153.28 | 0.000 |
| .\|. | \| | ***\|. | \| | 2 | −0.008 | −0.326 | 153.32 | 0.000 |
| .\|. | \| | **\|. | \| | 3 | 0.029 | −0.200 | 153.86 | 0.000 |
| .\|. | \| | *\|. | \| | 4 | −0.028 | −0.167 | 154.36 | 0.000 |
| .\|. | \| | *\|. | \| | 5 | −0.016 | −0.166 | 154.52 | 0.000 |
| .\|. | \| | *\|. | \| | 6 | 0.034 | −0.107 | 155.28 | 0.000 |
| .\|. | \| | *\|. | \| | 7 | −0.020 | −0.096 | 155.54 | 0.000 |
| .\|. | \| | .\|. | \| | 8 | 0.026 | −0.044 | 155.97 | 0.000 |
| .\|. | \| | .\|. | \| | 9 | −0.014 | −0.035 | 156.10 | 0.000 |
| *\|. | \| | *\|. | \| | 10 | −0.066 | −0.134 | 158.93 | 0.000 |
| .\|* | \| | *\|. | \| | 11 | 0.083 | −0.060 | 163.36 | 0.000 |
| .\|. | \| | *\|. | \| | 12 | −0.032 | −0.062 | 164.04 | 0.000 |
| .\|. | \| | *\|. | \| | 13 | −0.020 | −0.091 | 164.29 | 0.000 |
| .\|. | \| | .\|. | \| | 14 | 0.039 | −0.055 | 165.29 | 0.000 |
| .\|. | \| | *\|. | \| | 15 | −0.023 | −0.062 | 165.63 | 0.000 |
| .\|. | \| | .\|. | \| | 16 | 0.020 | −0.023 | 165.88 | 0.000 |
| .\|. | \| | .\|. | \| | 17 | −0.023 | −0.047 | 166.22 | 0.000 |
| .\|. | \| | .\|. | \| | 18 | 0.030 | −0.004 | 166.79 | 0.000 |
| .\|. | \| | .\|. | \| | 19 | −0.040 | −0.050 | 167.84 | 0.000 |
| .\|. | \| | .\|. | \| | 20 | 0.054 | 0.011 | 169.77 | 0.000 |
| *\|. | \| | *\|. | \| | 21 | −0.077 | −0.068 | 173.71 | 0.000 |
| .\|* | \| | .\|. | \| | 22 | 0.068 | −0.017 | 176.77 | 0.000 |
| .\|. | \| | .\|. | \| | 23 | −0.019 | −0.012 | 177.01 | 0.000 |
| .\|. | \| | .\|. | \| | 24 | −0.014 | −0.022 | 177.14 | 0.000 |

*(continues)*

moving averages. If the order of the moving average component of the ARMA process is $q$, as here, and the order of the autoregressive component is $p$, as here, we say the variable follows an ARMA($p, q$) process. We can, and frequently do, estimate ARMA processes with an intercept term added to Equation 17.11.

**TABLE 17.4** *(continued)*

*Panel B*
Sample: 1947:02 1999:12
Included observations: 635

| Autocorrelation | Partial Correlation | | AC | PAC | Q-Stat | Prob |
|---|---|---|---|---|---|---|
| .\|**** \| | .\|**** \| | 1 | 0.460 | 0.460 | 135.29 | 0.000 |
| .\|**** \| | .\|** \| | 2 | 0.470 | 0.328 | 276.59 | 0.000 |
| .\|. \| | ***\|. \| | 3 | 0.051 | −0.349 | 278.24 | 0.000 |
| .\|. \| | *\|. \| | 4 | 0.016 | −0.080 | 278.42 | 0.000 |
| .\|. \| | .\|** \| | 5 | −0.003 | 0.247 | 278.42 | 0.000 |
| .\|. \| | .\|. \| | 6 | −0.005 | −0.037 | 278.44 | 0.000 |
| .\|. \| | **\|. \| | 7 | −0.041 | −0.223 | 279.50 | 0.000 |
| *\|. \| | .\|. \| | 8 | −0.061 | 0.032 | 281.91 | 0.000 |
| *\|. \| | .\|* \| | 9 | −0.081 | 0.098 | 286.19 | 0.000 |
| *\|. \| | *\|. \| | 10 | −0.099 | −0.137 | 292.50 | 0.000 |
| .\|. \| | .\|. \| | 11 | −0.045 | −0.003 | 293.84 | 0.000 |
| .\|. \| | .\|* \| | 12 | −0.042 | 0.101 | 294.96 | 0.000 |
| .\|. \| | .\|. \| | 13 | −0.006 | −0.044 | 294.98 | 0.000 |
| .\|. \| | .\|. \| | 14 | 0.012 | −0.028 | 295.08 | 0.000 |
| .\|. \| | .\|. \| | 15 | 0.002 | 0.038 | 295.09 | 0.000 |
| .\|. \| | .\|. \| | 16 | 0.027 | 0.027 | 295.54 | 0.000 |
| .\|. \| | *\|. \| | 17 | −0.005 | −0.073 | 295.56 | 0.000 |
| .\|. \| | .\|. \| | 18 | 0.016 | 0.019 | 295.72 | 0.000 |
| .\|. \| | .\|. \| | 19 | −0.030 | −0.010 | 296.33 | 0.000 |
| .\|. \| | .\|. \| | 20 | 0.016 | 0.024 | 296.50 | 0.000 |
| .\|. \| | .\|. \| | 21 | −0.025 | −0.023 | 296.93 | 0.000 |
| .\|. \| | .\|. \| | 22 | 0.035 | 0.037 | 297.72 | 0.000 |
| .\|. \| | .\|. \| | 23 | 0.003 | 0.006 | 297.73 | 0.000 |
| .\|. \| | .\|. \| | 24 | 0.012 | −0.046 | 297.82 | 0.000 |

Table 17.5 reports the estimated autocorrelation coefficients and partial auto-correlation coefficients for a sample of 635 observations generated from an ARMA process $\alpha_1$ equal to 0.7 and $\beta_1$ equal to 0.6. The slow shrinking of the estimated partial autocorrelation coefficients and the quick drop to near zero of the estimated autocorrelations are typical of moving averages. The pattern of auto-

**TABLE 17.5** Estimated Autocorrelations and Estimated Partial Autocorrelations for a Sample from an ARMA(1, 1) Process

Sample: 1947:02 1999:12
Included observations: 635

| Autocorrelation | Partial Correlation | | AC | PAC | Q-Stat | Prob |
|---|---|---|---|---|---|---|
| .\|****** \| | .\|****** \| | 1 | 0.802 | 0.802 | 410.16 | 0.000 |
| .\|**** \| | ***\|. \| | 2 | 0.493 | −0.420 | 565.38 | 0.000 |
| .\|** \| | .\|* \| | 3 | 0.279 | 0.186 | 615.26 | 0.000 |
| .\|* \| | *\|. \| | 4 | 0.136 | −0.145 | 627.18 | 0.000 |
| .\|. \| | .\|. \| | 5 | 0.036 | 0.020 | 627.99 | 0.000 |
| .\|. \| | .\|. \| | 6 | −0.031 | −0.049 | 628.62 | 0.000 |
| *\|. \| | .\|. \| | 7 | −0.059 | 0.032 | 630.87 | 0.000 |
| *\|. \| | .\|. \| | 8 | −0.066 | −0.039 | 633.66 | 0.000 |
| .\|. \| | .\|. \| | 9 | −0.054 | 0.046 | 635.54 | 0.000 |
| .\|. \| | .\|* \| | 10 | −0.010 | 0.066 | 635.60 | 0.000 |
| .\|. \| | .\|. \| | 11 | 0.033 | −0.028 | 636.30 | 0.000 |
| .\|. \| | .\|. \| | 12 | 0.050 | 0.010 | 637.89 | 0.000 |
| .\|. \| | .\|. \| | 13 | 0.039 | −0.046 | 638.86 | 0.000 |
| .\|. \| | .\|. \| | 14 | 0.009 | −0.019 | 638.92 | 0.000 |
| .\|. \| | .\|. \| | 15 | −0.009 | 0.027 | 638.97 | 0.000 |
| .\|. \| | .\|. \| | 16 | −0.013 | −0.004 | 639.08 | 0.000 |
| .\|. \| | .\|. \| | 17 | 0.001 | 0.052 | 639.08 | 0.000 |
| .\|. \| | .\|. \| | 18 | 0.018 | −0.014 | 639.29 | 0.000 |
| .\|. \| | .\|. \| | 19 | 0.037 | 0.054 | 640.19 | 0.000 |
| .\|. \| | .\|. \| | 20 | 0.060 | 0.009 | 642.53 | 0.000 |
| .\|* \| | .\|. \| | 21 | 0.071 | −0.003 | 645.86 | 0.000 |
| .\|* \| | .\|. \| | 22 | 0.070 | 0.005 | 649.10 | 0.000 |
| .\|. \| | *\|. \| | 23 | 0.043 | −0.071 | 650.31 | 0.000 |
| .\|. \| | .\|. \| | 24 | 0.008 | 0.030 | 650.35 | 0.000 |

correlations is not what we would expect from a pure MA process or from a pure AR process. In such cases, we turn to the ARMA specification.

Efficiently estimating regression models that have moving average disturbances was for a long time a difficult problem, even if the model contained only a constant term. However, models with autoregressive disturbances have always been quite manageable, using generalizations of Chapter 11's Cochrane–Orcutt estimator, for example. Advances in computer technology and in nonlinear estimation techniques have overcome the difficulties in estimating moving average processes. Today's computers and software have little difficulty in estimating Equation 17.11 by maximum likelihood. Table 17.6 reports maximum likelihood estimates of the process underlying the data used to build Table 17.5. (The EViews program that generated the random AR, MA, and ARMA samples for Tables 17.3–17.5 is in the file armamodels.prg on this book's companion Web site, **www.aw-bc.com/murray**. In the program, you can change the coefficients of the AR, MA, and ARMA models to create different AR, MA, and ARMA processes and to examine samples from those processes.)

In *Time Series Analysis: Forecasting and Control*, now in its third edition, statisticians George Box, of the University of Wisconsin, and Gwilym Jenkins, of the research firm Gwilym Jenkins and Partners, argued that forecasting with ARMA($p$, $q$) models is generally superior to forecasting with multiple regression models that contain numerous explanatory variables.[6] Many forecasters still rely on the Box–Jenkins approach today.

---

**TABLE 17.6** Maximum Likelihood Estimates of an ARMA(1, 1) Process

Dependent Variable: ARMA11A
Sample: 1947:02 1999:12
Included observations: 635
Convergence achieved after 6 iterations
Backcast: 1947:01

| Variable | Coefficient | Std. Error | t-Statistic | Prob. |
|---|---|---|---|---|
| C | 0.246497 | 0.175333 | 1.405880 | 0.1603 |
| AR(1) | 0.637621 | 0.034049 | 18.72682 | 0.0000 |
| MA(1) | 0.610691 | 0.034740 | 17.57907 | 0.0000 |
| R-squared | 0.724325 | Mean dependent var | | 0.251920 |
| Adjusted R-squared | 0.723452 | S.D. dependent var | | 1.890807 |
| S.E. of regression | 0.994334 | Akaike info criterion | | 2.831226 |
| Sum squared resid | 624.8585 | Schwarz criterion | | 2.852267 |
| Log likelihood | 895.9143 | F-statistic | | 830.2756 |
| Durbin–Watson stat | 1.972550 | Prob(F-statistic) | | 0.000000 |

Box and Jenkins offered numerous examples in which their methods outperformed multiple regression models. Subsequently, economists have confirmed that univariate forecasts of economic variables based on ARMA equations such as Equation 17.11 perform remarkably well in comparison to forecasts made from more complex multiple regression models, though the ARMA models do not always dominate the structural models. The secret to the success of the relatively simple ARMA models is their reliance on a small number of parameters that can, nonetheless, approximate well the time series pattern of most covariance stationary series. We call models that rely on a small number of parameters **parsimonius**. In practice, few ARMA models have more than three or four parameters—an ARMA(2, 2) model is considered unusually complex.

In specifying forecasting models, parsimony is often a good trait. With a small number of parameters, the ARMA model parameter estimates are rather efficient, and therefore estimation introduces relatively small errors into ARMA forecasts. In contrast, multiple regression models and simultaneous equations models with a large number of parameters almost surely misestimate some parameter or another by a substantial margin. These estimation errors often translate into substantial forecasting errors. ARMA models do not always forecast better than multiple regression models, but they often do, and when they do not, the differences in performance are frequently modest.

Given their generally comparable forecasting performance, a telling advantage of ARMA models is that building an ARMA model does not require as much knowledge about the variable being forecast as does building a good multiple regression model. For example, building an ARMA model does not require decisions about which explanatory variables belong in the model and which do not.

The relatively small number of parameters that work to an ARMA model's benefit in forecasting works to the model's disadvantage in any other uses—ARMA models tell us nothing about the relationship between a variable and its determinants. In exposing that relationship, multiple regression always dominates ARMA models.

Box and Jenkins proposed a three-step strategy for making forecasts with ARMA models. This **Box–Jenkins forecasting strategy** for forecasting a single variable, $Y$, from its own past history has three steps:

1. Determine $p$ and $q$ for $Y_t$.
2. Estimate the parameters of the ARMA$(p, q)$ process that defines $Y_t$.
3. Forecast the future values of $Y_t$ based on the model estimated in (2).

Step 1 requires some artistry because there is no standard methodology for choosing among alternative values for $p$ and $q$. Box and Jenkins recommend that we examine plots of the autocorrelation and partial autocorrelation coefficients, such as those in Tables 17.3–17.5, to determine candidate models.

Step 2 requires estimating the $(p + q)$ parameters $\alpha_1, \alpha_2, \ldots, \alpha_p$ and $\beta_1, \beta_2, \ldots, \beta_q$. Standard algorithms are available for maximum likelihood estimation of these parameters.

Many econometric software packages provide commands for creating the Box–Jenkins forecasts of Step 3. Just as we can forecast AR(1) processes with Equation 17.10, we can forecast ARMA($p$, $q$) variables using estimates of the coefficients of the ARMA process. For example, the forecast for $Y_{T+1}$ is

$$Y_{T+1}^f = \sum_{j=1}^{p} \tilde{\alpha}_j Y_{T+1-j} + 0 + \sum_{j=1}^{q} \tilde{\beta}_j e_{T+1-j}, \qquad \textbf{17.12}$$

where zero is our best guess of next period's white noise innovation, the $e_i$ are residuals from the estimation of Equation 17.11, and tilde ( ~ ) indicates an estimated parameter. Subsequent periods' forecasts use previous periods' forecasts for values of $Y$ not yet observed and use zero to predict white noise innovations after period $T$.

## 17.3     Multivariate Forecasting with Vector Autoregression (VAR)

Autoregressive models are easier to estimate than are moving average models. The ease of estimating models with autoregressive disturbances makes economists eager to rely on an important theorem that states that almost all moving average and ARMA processes can be arbitrarily well approximated by an autoregression of sufficiently high order. We call **noninvertible** the exceptional moving average and ARMA processes that autoregressions cannot approximate well. Usually, economists restrict their attention to autoregressive processes in their econometric models, capitalizing on the ease with which they can be estimated and their usefulness as good approximations to other time-series processes. In a particularly powerful formulation, economists forecast several variables at once by combining several autoregressions into a set of equations that we call a *vector autoregression (VAR)*.

### Vector Autoregressions

Vector autoregressions are generalizations of the simpler univariate autoregression. A univariate autoregression expresses the current realized value of a variable as depending on its own lagged values and a current white noise innovation, as in:

$$Y_t = \varepsilon_t + \alpha_0 + \sum_{j=1}^{q} \alpha_j Y_{t-j}.$$

A natural extension of the autoregressive formulation is to add lagged values of another variable to the right-hand side of Equation 17.13, as in:

$$Y_t = \varepsilon_t + \sum_{j=1}^{q} \alpha_j Y_{t-j} + \alpha_0 + \sum_{j=1}^{q} \beta_j X_{(t-j)} \qquad \textbf{17.13}$$

The final step to create what is called a vector autoregression is to also express $X$ in a form similar to Equation 17.13:

$$X_t = \varepsilon_{Xt} + \sum_{j=1}^{q} \tau_j X_{(t-j)} + \gamma_0 + \sum_{j=1}^{q} \gamma_j Y_{(t-j)}, \qquad \textbf{17.14}$$

in which $Y$ is the dependent variable in Equation 17.13. We call Equations 17.13 and 17.14, taken together, a vector autoregression. In general, a **vector autoregression (VAR)** contains several regressions. In each regression of a VAR, the variable on the left-hand side is the value of one variable at time $t$ and the variables on the right-hand side are the lagged values of all the variables that appear on the left-hand side of any one of the VAR equations. Naming the two variables $X$ and $Y$ in Equations 17.13 and 17.14 is convenient because it is familiar. However, in a vector autoregression, the distinction between independent and dependent variables, as we know it from ordinary regression models, and the distinction between endogenous and exogenous variables, as we know it from simultaneous equations models, may no longer apply. VAR models like those in Equations 17.13 and 17.14 describe how two or more random variables, here $X$ and $Y$, unfold over time, based on their joint past histories.

We can include more variables (and their lagged values) into VAR equations, in which case we would also have additional VAR equations, one for each variable. OLS estimates of VAR equations are used frequently to make economic forecasts. Computer packages can compute forecasts based on estimates of Equations 17.13 and 17.14, much as the Box–Jenkins procedures bases forecasts on estimates of ARMA equations such as 17.12.

Some economists use estimates of Equations 17.13 and 17.14 for more than just forecasting. They use them to ask how a shock to one variable, in the form of a one-unit increase in the disturbance for that variable, causes the variables in the system to vary in subsequent periods, if no other shocks disturb the system at the same time. In effect, these economists assume that Equations 17.13 and 17.14 capture the combined effects of all the structural relationships among the variables.

## Granger Causality

Although forecasters are less interested in the causal relationships among variables than are other users of econometrics, one favorite tool of forecasters, vector

# An Econometric Top 40—A Classical Favorite

## Money, Income, and Causality

The quantity theory of money's most recent champion was Nobel laureate Milton Friedman of the University of Chicago, who resurrected the age-old quantity theory to battle the Keynesian economists of the 1960s and 1970s about the role of money in the macroeconomy. One claim of Friedman and his followers was that changes in the money supply cause changes in real GDP.

In 1972, economist Christopher Sims of Princeton University adapted the then-new notion of Granger causality to ask whether money causes real GDP, or real GDP causes money.[7] Sims's causality test differs slightly from what has become the standard Granger test. Sims pointed out that an implication of Granger's reasoning is that if causality runs *only* from X to Y, then in a regression of Y on current, past, and future values of X, the future values will have zero coefficients. In essence, if X causes Y, past and current values of X will forecast Y's value, without any help from future values of X. Thus, if future values of X appear significantly in the relationship, it is because Y influences X, argues Sims. Sims carefully explained several special cases in which his claims would not hold and then argued that those cases were not a concern in his study.

Sims first regressed the log of real GDP on the current log of the money supply, eight lags of the log of the money supply, and four future values of the log of the money supply. The regression accounted for possible serial correlation in the disturbances. He then reversed the roles of real GDP and the money supply in the regression. Sims found that he could not reject the null of one-way causality from money to income, but that he could reject the null of one-way causality from income to money. These findings buttressed the quantity theory views of Friedman and his followers.

### Final Notes

There were many skirmishes in the macroeconomic debate between the Keynesians and the quantity theory advocates. Sims fired one artillery barrage among many. However, Sims's paper had much wider impact, because it alerted the economics community to the potential of Granger's theoretical work for studying applied questions about which variables cause which. Furthermore, Sims eloquently described the connection between causality, as viewed by Granger, and exogeneity, as worried about by econometricians: Testing for Granger causality amounts to testing for exogeneity. As a consequence, Granger causality testing emerged as a standard step taken by applied econometricians to check whether their time series data warrant assuming that an explanator is exogenous.

∎

autoregressions, is used by other economists to study the causal relationships among variables. Differentiating correlation from causality is always a challenge for economists. Regression equations don't, by themselves, resolve the matter. Economic theory and common sense must inform our interpretations of regression equations when we try to answer the correlation versus causality question. Nonetheless, vector autoregressions can shed some light on the causality question.

In 1969, econometrician and Nobel laureate Clive Granger of the University of California, San Diego, introduced a technical definition of causality for use in econometric models. Granger said that if $X$ causes $Y$, knowing past values of $X$ would allow us to forecast $Y$ better than just knowing past values of $Y$. That is, if the expected value of today's $Y$ given $Y$'s history depends on the past values of $X$, there is evidence that $X$ affects $Y$. Granger noted that $Y$ may cause $X$ as well. If the expected value of today's $X$, given $X$'s history, depends on the past values of $Y$, there is evidence that $Y$ affects $X$. When $X$ and $Y$ both cause one another, we say there is "feedback" between them. Technically, we say that $X$ **Granger causes**

### An Organizational Structure for the Study of Econometrics

**1. What Is the DGP?**

The Gauss–Markov Assumptions plus a deterministic linear time trend

Models with seasonal effects

Seasonally adjusted data

White noise innovations

Autoregressions of order $p$

Moving average processes of order $q$

Mixed autoregressive moving average processes

Vector autoregressions

**2. How Do We Create an Estimator?**
————

**3. What Are an Estimator's Properties?**
————

**4. How Do We Test Hypotheses?**
————

**5. How Do We Make Forecasts?**

Conditional forecasts

Adjusted $R^2$

Akaike information criterion (AIC)

Schwarz information criterion (SIC)

Box–Jenkins forecasting strategy

$Y$ if the coefficients on lagged values of $X$ in Equation 17.13, the autoregression equation for $Y$, are not all zero. Similarly, we say that $Y$ is said to Granger cause $X$ if the coefficients on lagged values of $Y$ in Equation 17.14, the autoregression equation for $X$, are not all zero. When Granger causality runs one way and not the other, the burden is on the analyst to explain why a causal link, if there is one, doesn't run from the Granger-causing variable to the Granger-caused variable.

Conducting a Granger causality test of the hypothesis that $X$ Granger causes $Y$ has two steps: (i) regress $Y$ on lagged values of $Y$ and lagged values of $X$; (ii) perform an $F$-test of the hypothesis that the coefficients on the lagged $X$-variables are all zero. If we reject the null in (ii), we conclude that $X$ Granger causes $Y$. Granger causality tests err easily when relevant variables are omitted from the VAR.

## Summary

This chapter introduced forecasting methods commonly used by economists. The chapter began with conditional forecasts, which are forecasts made from standard regression equations. Most conditional forecasting relationships face the difficulty of providing future values for the explanatory variables of the model. The usual approach is to try several different values for the explanators and to offer different forecasts for each scenario. Economists can, however, exactly specify future values for two kinds of explanators, time trends and seasonal dummies. Because forecasting models are not concerned with specific coefficients and their estimates, but rather with the ability of the model to predict future outcomes, forecasters often choose which variables to include in a forecasting model on the basis of the fit of the model. We introduced three commonly used statistics for choosing these variables: the adjusted $R^2$, the Schwarz information criterion, and the Akaike information criterion. Each of these measures trades goodness of fit against the benefits of a smaller number of estimated coefficients in a model.

Many economists forgo standard regression models when forecasting. They instead turn to forecasting variables from their own pasts, using models that specify a variable to be a mix of autoregressive and moving average components. The chapter describes the Box–Jenkins methodology for forecasting with ARMA models. Economists who saw that autoregressions could fit many individual time series next turned to multivariate models with an autoregressive structure. The chapter introduced these vector autoregression models and concluded by describing how vector autoregressions are used to explore the causal linkages among variables.

# Concepts for Review

# Questions for Discussion

1. "As long as a model predicts well, it doesn't matter whether it makes economic sense." Critically discuss this claim.

2. The manager of TechEnergy knows that the demand for energy is influenced by the time of year, in particular, the four (quarterly) seasons of spring, summer, fall, and winter. However, she is not sure how to explain this to the company's shareholders. She would like you to prepare a short statement as to how the season of the year can be incorporated into their traditional energy demand forecasts. Their existing model of energy demand currently considers only autoregressive and moving average terms. In preparing the statement, you will need to explain what is meant by "seasonality" and how this information can be taken into account in the econometric model. In addition, describe, and briefly defend, the criteria you would use to determine whether the existing model or your proposed "seasonality" model performs better.

3. A debate has arisen between Professor Ray L. Wurld, an applied econometrician, and Professor Abby Stract, an economic theorist, over the meaning of causation as it is often used within the context of a vector autoregression and econometrics, in general. Stract argues forcefully that "we learned long ago that correlation does not imply causation; Granger acts as if this were not true." Wurld replies, "Granger doesn't look at simple correlation. Conditioning on past values of both variables makes the test more plausibly a test of causation." Take one side in this debate and discuss your position with someone who opts for the opposite side. The discussion should provide a thorough critique and defense of Professor Granger's concept of causality.

# Problems for Analysis

> For the data that you will need to solve the problems in this section,
> go to **www.aw-bc.com/murray**.

 1. MacroPolicy, Inc., provides forecasts of the money supply to various durable goods manufacturing firms. The money supply information helps managers determine their operational strategies in light of the policymaking actions of the Federal Reserve. For example, when the money supply is predicted to rise, these manufacturers will likely experience lower inventory costs as interest rates fall. These manufacturers are typically not interested in the statistical properties of MacroPolicy's forecasts and only want to know where the money supply will be at some point. Your job is to provide them that information and, as such, you need to determine the best performing model from a number of competing alternatives. In addition, you will need to interpret your forecasts in a manner that the managers of these firms can use. Open the data set money1.\*\*\*. The narrow measure of money (*M1*) is denoted *fm*1.

a. Estimate the following four models using OLS. The variable $T$ is a deterministic time trend.

$$fm1_t = c + \beta T_t + \varepsilon_t$$
$$fm1_t = c + \beta_1 T_t + \beta_2 T_t^2 + \varepsilon_t$$
$$\log(fm1_t) = c + \beta T_t + \varepsilon_t$$
$$\log(fm1_t) = c + \beta_1 T_t + \beta_2 T_t^2 + \varepsilon_t$$

b. Compare the Akaike information criterion (AIC) value and Schwarz information criterion (SIC) value for the two fm1 models and also for the two log(fm1) models to determine which model in each pair performs best. Note that the AIC and SIC are useful for assessing performance between models that use the same dependent variable only.

c. Plot the fitted values against the actual values for the money supply for each model. Describe the differences in model results that you see.

 2. The U.S. housing industry constitutes a major sector in the economy. First, the number of new houses being built adds directly to the gross domestic product once the houses are completed. Second, building of more houses is typically followed by more purchases of durable goods like washers and dryers, as well as many home furnishings. Thus, it is not surprising that construction firms, as well as macroeconomists, would find accurate forecasts of housing starts informative. Builders would use this information to plan accordingly for their supplies, equipment, and labor. Macroeconomists might use forecasts of housing starts as an indicator of where the economy is headed in the months ahead. Open housing1.\*\*\*. The file contains monthly data on the number of housing starts (1-unit structure), and this variable is denoted *startnsa*.

a. Plot the number of housing starts (*startnsa*) and observe the repetitive pattern in the data.

b. Estimate a model of *startnsa* in which the variable of interest is regressed on a constant and a dummy variable that takes on the value 1 in December and 0 for all other months. Is the coefficient on the December dummy variable statistically significant? What does it indicate about the possibility of seasonal patterns in the data? Plot the residuals from this regression along with the fitted and actual values for housing starts. Is there any remaining seasonal pattern?

c. Estimate a model of housing starts using the explanators from part (b), but now also allowing for monthly seasonal effects in each month. You should include 11 seasonal dummy variables for the months February through December as well as a constant term. Re-examine the residuals from this regression, along with the fitted and actual values for housing starts. Is there any remaining seasonal pattern?

3. New housing starts likely depend on a number of conditions in the economy, in addition to exhibiting seasonal patterns. For example, demand for housing may exhibit persistence as potential buyers wait to see if new houses that better suit their needs become available. In additional, there may be relevant macroeconomic factors not captured by the season of the year. Open housing1.\*\*\*. The file contains monthly data on the number of housing starts (1-unit structure), and this variable is denoted *startnsa*.

a. Estimate an ARMA(1, 1) model of housing starts controlling for monthly seasonal patterns. You should include 11 seasonal dummy variables for the months February through December and a constant term. Re-examine the residuals from this regression, along with the fitted and actual values for housing starts. Is there any remaining seasonal pattern?

b. Compare the forecasting performance of the model estimated in part (c) of Problem 2 with that estimated in part (a) of this problem. Which model performs better? Explain why you expect some difference in model performance between these two competing models.

4. Many states are now allowing administrators at public colleges and universities to have more say in setting their own tuition rates. Advocates of this policy believe that deregulating tuition will more accurately reflect the market pressures that schools face. To make sound judgments regarding such legislation, state lawmakers require a thorough understanding of many education-related factors. In particular, forecasts of future enrollment and the detection of any trends are needed. Open educ172.\*\*\*. The data are from the National Center for Education Statistics, U.S. Department of Education. The variable *toten* represents the total number of students enrolled in colleges and universities.

a. Consider the following four models. Describe the type of trend and growth rate behavior that each model implies. The variable $T$ is a deterministic time trend.

$$toten_t = c + \beta T_t + \varepsilon_t$$
$$toten_t = c + \beta_1 T_t + \beta_2 T_t^2 + \varepsilon_t$$
$$\log(toten_t) = c + \beta T_t + \varepsilon_t$$
$$\log(toten_t) = c + \beta_1 T_t + \beta_2 T_t^2 + \varepsilon_t$$

b. Use the Box–Jenkins technique to determine the ARMA specification of each of the models in part (a), taking the trend variables as given.

c. Based on the AIC and SIC values, determine which model performs the best for *toten*? For log(*toten*)? Note that the AIC and SIC are useful for assessing performance between models that use the same dependent variable only.

d. Plot the fitted values against the actual values of *toten* for each of the models estimated in part (b). Describe the differences in results that you see. What is happening to total college student enrollment?

5. The time series behavior of the consumer price index (CPI) has been a topic of interest for economists in both the United States and the United Kingdom (UK). Forecasting future prices is important for both businesses and policymakers. For central bank policymakers, these forecasts may help determine whether or not interest rates should be made higher or lower. Firms need these forecasts to inform them about price pressures in the economy. Typically, higher prices (i.e., inflation) mean that wages will also rise, and thus labor costs may put a squeeze on profits. Moreover, the direction of prices will help firms plan their purchases of materials and supplies and also manage the demand of their products better. Open the data set peelsact.***. This data set contains annual UK data from 1700 to 1998.

a. Plot both *cpi* (the consumer price index for the United Kingdom) and the log(*cpi*). Describe what has happened to the general level of prices over this long sample period.

b. Clearly, many factors may have contributed to the rise in prices over this sample period including changes in money supply, technology, tastes and preferences, and political environments. In fact, it may be argued that it would be nearly impossible to identify all the economic factors that may have contributed to this rise in prices over such a long period. When faced with this type of situation, it is often appropriate to specify a univariate forecasting model. Use the Box–Jenkins technique to select the best univariate model for log(*cpi*).

c. Examine the residuals from the model you chose in part (b). Do they appear consistent with the assumptions of the Box–Jenkins approach? Would you consider this a good forecasting model? Why or why not?

6. TechEnergy is considering building a small wind energy plant in either Albuquerque, New Mexico, or Tucson, Arizona. The plant would involve the erection of wind turbines that would have the capacity to produce enough electricity to power 10,000 homes for 1 year. A critical factor in the location decision is to determine in which area more accurate wind speed forecasts can be obtained. Open weather1.***. The variables *tuswnd* and *albwnd* are the historical average daily wind speed series for Tucson and Albuquerque, respectively, measured in miles per hour.

a. Examine the autocorrelation functions for both *albwnd* and *tuswnd*. Based on this information, describe any differences and/or similarities you observe between the two wind speed series.

b. Use the linear trend model to decide whether there is a deterministic time trend in these two data series.

c. Based on your findings about the trend in part (b), use the Box–Jenkins technique to specify a univariate forecasting model for each wind speed model. Can you recommend one location over the other based on TechEnergy's location criterion of forecasting?

7. TechEnergy is considering building a small wind energy plant in either Albuquerque, New Mexico, or Tucson, Arizona. The management team foresees that spot markets for wind energy will develop in the future, and thus they will have the ability to sell their output on the open market. Currently, they enter into contracts with major utilities that specify the price at which they can sell all the output they can produce. They also know that if they enter the open market, they will be subject to the variability in energy demand that traditional suppliers experience. Namely, the demand for electricity depends critically on the weather, with the demand on hot days and cold days being especially high. One way to manage this variability in demand is to use financial derivatives based on temperature. These derivatives are available through the Chicago Mercantile Exchange, or CME. Open weather1.***. The variables *tustmp* and *albtmp* are the historical average daily temperature series for Tucson and Albuquerque, respectively. TechEnergy may be able to hedge unusual temperature variations in Albuquerque, provided they can determine the statistical relationship between the temperatures in the two cities. If a predictable statistical relationship exists, successful hedging may be attainable.

a. Construct a two-equation vector autoregression for *tustmp* and *albtmp*. Use the AIC to select the appropriate number of lags.

b. Use the test for causality that has been attributed to Professor Granger. Can TechEnergy feel comfortable operating in both areas (i.e., is it possible to exploit a statistical relationship between the two temperature series)?

8. Changes in the money supply are thought to be related to changes in the short-term interest rate. Open the data set money1.***. The broad measure of money is denoted *fm1* and the short term interest rate is denoted *ir*.

a. Estimate a vector autoregression (VAR) of the following form:

$$\Delta \ln(fm1)_t = \alpha_0 + \sum_{i=1}^{3} \alpha_i \Delta \ln(fm1)_{t-i} + \sum_{i=1}^{3} \beta_i \Delta ir_{t-i} + \varepsilon_t$$

$$\Delta ir_t = \delta_0 + \sum_{i=1}^{3} \delta_i \Delta ir_{t-i} + \sum_{i=1}^{3} \lambda_i \Delta \ln(fm1)_{t-i} + \varepsilon_t$$

b. Interpret the individual estimated coefficients. Does it appear that changes in the money supply and changes in the interest rate are related? How so?

c. Perform Granger's test of causality to determine if changes in the money that cause changes in interest rates, or changes in interest rates cause changes in the money supply.

d. In light of your answer to part (c), how would you describe the relationship between changes in the money supply and changes in the interest rate?

# Endnotes

1. Lewis Carroll, *Alice's Adventures In Wonderland* (London: Macmillan, 1865).
2. William Shakespeare, *Macbeth*.
3. Francis X. Diebold, *Elements of Forecasting* (Cincinnati: South-Western College Publishing, 2004).
4. The data used in Figures 17.1, 17.2, and 17.5 are from the 1999 M3 Forecasting Competition. The competition is discussed at length in M. Hibon Ord and S. Makridakis, eds., *International Journal of Forecasting* 16, no. 4K, 2000.
5. Jan Tinbergen, *Business Cycles in the United States of America 1919–1932* (League of Nations: 1939). Lawrence R. Klein, *Economic Fluctuations in the United States, 1921–1941* (New York: John Wiley, 1950).
6. George E. Box and Gwilym M. Jenkins, *Time Series Analysis: Forecasting and Control* (San Francisco: Holden-Day, 1970).
7. Christopher A. Sims, "Money, Income, and Causality," *American Economic Review* 62 (1972): 540–552.

# Chapter 18

# Stochastically Trending Variables

*But the long run is a misleading guide to current*
*affairs. In the long run we are all dead. Economists*
*set themselves too easy, too useless a task if in*
*tempestuous seasons they can only tell us that when*
*the storm is long past the ocean is flat again.*[1]

—JOHN MAYNARD KEYNES, 1923

Disentangling the trends that rule the economy in the long run from the fluctuations that churn the economic seas in the short run requires both theoretical and empirical sophistication. Keynes transformed theoretical macroeconomics with his famous book *The General Theory of Employment, Interest and Money* (1936). Since Keynes, empirical studies of time series data on gross domestic product (GDP), consumption, investment, unemployment, inflation, and interest rates have become a mainstay of macroeconomics. Macroeconomic variables often grow persistently over time, albeit with the ups and downs that Keynes highlights.

Short-run macroeconomic shocks that affect the economy in one period often have consequences that spill into subsequent periods. The short-run and long-run changes in the economy can have intimate connections, as we shall see in this chapter. Chapter 11 discussed at length the special form of short-run fluctuations called first-order autoregressions. That discussion restricted the autocorrelation coefficient to less than one in magnitude. This chapter reveals a connection between autocorrelation coefficients equal to one and variables that grow or shrink persistently over time. It then delves more deeply into the consequences of these trending variables for econometric analysis, revealing that our standard estimators and test statistics can be wildly misleading when our models contain such variables.

## 18.1 Time Trends

**Trends,** which are persistent upward or downward movements of variables over time, are well captured by graphs. This section uses graphs to depict trends and to motivate a richer analytical investigation of different kinds of trends. The exposition in this section and the next owes much to James Stock and Mark Watson's "Variable Trends in Economic Time Series."[2]

Figure 18.1 plots real per capita GDP, real per capita consumption, real per capita investment, and the Consumer Price Index (CPI) against time for the period 1948–1998. All four macroeconomic variables trend upward over time. Trending variables appear frequently in economic models, both as dependent variables and as explanators. For example, consumption functions have the trending consumption variable as dependent variable and the trending income variable as explanator. Unfortunately, trending variables can upset the consistency and asymptotic normality of least squares estimators, so we need to understand the connections between these variables and our usual estimation procedures.

Economists call the steady long-term changes in variables trends. This section begins by examining two kinds of trends. The macroeconomic variables in Figure 18.1 seem better described by one sort of trend than by the other. This section also investigates how ordinary least squares (OLS) remains consistent and asymptotically normally distributed when the model contains one kind of trend as an explanator, but may lose its attractive properties when the other kind of trend is present.

## Deterministic Trends

Some variables, such as age, increase a constant amount from one period to the next. This is one sort of trend. For another example, in Chapter 4 we examined a data-generating process (DGP) in which the data are a time series and the explanatory variable is time itself, $t$. Here, we also include an unknown intercept in the relationship:

$$Y_t = \beta_0 + \beta_1 t + \varepsilon_t \qquad t = 1, \ldots, T,$$
$$E(Y_t) = \beta_0 + \beta_1 t$$

and assume that the other Gauss–Markov Assumptions are satisfied in this DGP. In this DGP,

$$E(Y_t) - E(Y_{t-1}) = \beta_0 + \beta_1(t) - \beta_0 - \beta_1(t - 1) = \beta_1, \qquad \textbf{18.1}$$

because the index of time changes by one from one period to the next. When the mean of $Y$ grows over time in this constant fashion, we say there is a **deterministic trend** in the data. Because the $E(Y_t)$ is a linear function of time, we also refer to this as a **linear time trend**. When the dependent variable is measured in logs, $\beta_1$ is the growth rate of the variable per period.

The proof of the consistency of OLS in Chapter 12 does not preclude deterministic time trends. OLS is consistent if the disturbances and explanators are contemporaneously uncorrelated and the disturbances are homoskedastic and the covariances among the disturbances depend only on how far apart in time the observations are from one another.

We call disturbances **covariance stationary** if (i) the covariance between disturbances at any times $t$ and $t'$, $\sigma_{tt'}$ depends only on $|t - t'|$, the distance between the

**Figure 18.1**

GDP, Consumption, Investment, and the CPI, 1948–1998

*Source:* U.S. Department of Commerce

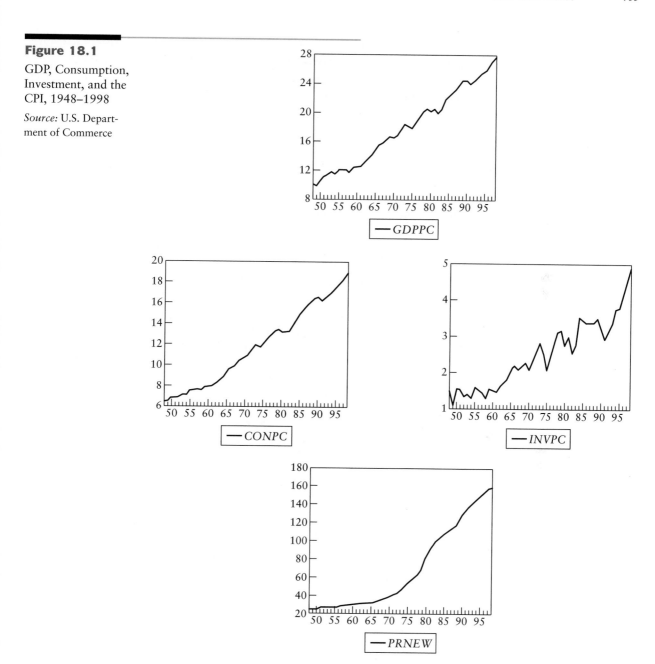

observations in time and (ii) the disturbances are homoskedastic. If any aspect of the joint distribution of observations (not just the variances or covariances) depends not only on how far apart the observations are from one another, but also on when in time the observations take place, we say the time series is **nonstationary.**

Although using time as an explanator does not alter the consistency of OLS, it does alter its asymptotic variance. In the absence of a time trend, the variance of $\hat{\beta}_1$ in a sample of $n$ observations, which is also the variance of $(\hat{\beta}_1 - \beta_1)$, the errors made in estimating $\beta_1$, is

$$\frac{\sigma^2}{\Sigma x_i^2} = \frac{\sigma^2}{n\left(\frac{1}{n}\Sigma x_i^2\right)} = \frac{\sigma^2}{nQ},$$

in which we define $Q = \frac{1}{n}\Sigma X_i^2$ to be a finite nonzero constant. In the no-trend case, the variance of $\hat{\beta}_1$ converges to zero as $n$ goes to infinity because of the $n$ in the denominator and despite the fact that $Q$ is a finite, nonzero number. In this case, the distribution of estimation errors collapses around zero as $n$ increases. In Chapter 12, we saw that we could compare the variances of consistent estimators if we first magnified their errors, so that the errors distributions would not collapse as $n$ grows. If we magnify $\hat{\beta}_1$'s estimation errors by multiplying each error by the square root of $n$, the magnified errors' variance is $\sigma^2/Q$, which converges to neither zero nor infinity as $n$ grows. Thus, magnification by the square root of $n$ is the appropriate magnification for studying the asymptotic distribution of $\hat{\beta}_1$. We concluded in Chapter 12 that $\hat{\beta}_1$ converges at a "root $n$ rate."

In contrast, when the explanator is a time trend,

$$\hat{\beta}_1 = \frac{\sum_{t=1}^{T}(t - \bar{t})y_t}{\sum_{t=1}^{T}(t - \bar{t})^2},$$

where

$$\bar{t} = \frac{1}{T}\sum_{t=1}^{T}t = \frac{1}{2}(T + 1)$$

and

$$\sum_{t=1}^{T}(t - \bar{t})^2 = (T - 1)(T + 1).$$

The OLS estimator of the slope is still normally distributed in large samples when the explanator is a deterministic trend. In this case, the variance of $\hat{\beta}_1$ in a sample of $T$ observations,

$$\frac{\sigma^2}{T\left(\frac{1}{T}\sum_{t=1}^{T}(t - \bar{t})^2\right)},$$

converges to zero because *both* $T$ and $\frac{1}{T}\Sigma(t - \bar{t})^2$ are growing toward infinity. Thus, when $Y$ contains a time trend, the distribution of $\hat{\beta}_1$ collapses at a faster than root $n$ rate. When a consistent estimator converges at a faster rate than root $n$, we say the estimator is **super consistent**. On the other hand, the OLS estimator of the intercept term remains just consistent, with its usual normal distribution.

The OLS estimator remains consistent, even super consistent, when there is a deterministic trend in the model. It also remains asymptotically normally distributed. Consequently, when a deterministic time trend is present in our DGP, we can conduct asymptotically valid inferences about the parameters, using our standard test procedures. The same results apply to multiple regression models that include a deterministic trend.

## Macroeconomic Variables and Deterministic Trends

Trending macroeconomic variables pose no special problems for econometrics if their trends are deterministic. Do the variables in Figure 18.1 reflect the influence of a deterministic trend? If they do, OLS based on one sub-period of the data should provide reasonably good forecasts of future values of the macroeconomic variables. We need only project future values as lying along the trend line. However, Figure 18.2 shows that, in practice, forecasts of the macroeconomic variables in Table 18.1 based on one period do poorly in forecasting subsequent periods. (The problems we see here in the levels of the variables would also appear if we measured the variables in logs. Macroeconomists usually work with the logarithms of these variables.)

Figure 18.2 repeats the graphs of Figure 18.1, but adds for each variable a forecasting line based on OLS estimates using the observations from 1948 to 1960. The graphs show that the forecasts and observed values do not mesh well. Indeed, the actual values are generally outside the 95% prediction bands for the forecasts, which are not shown. Although the macroeconomic variables do continue to trend after 1960, the trend seems to have changed. If you eyeball the data and try to forecast the variables in Figure 18.1 based on a different subperiod, you see that the forecasting performance of a deterministic trend model will generally be poor for these variables. The trends in the data seem to change more than once.

Figure 18.3 shows what a variable containing a deterministic trend is likely to look like. It shows a randomly drawn sample from a DGP in which $Y$ contains a deterministic trend and the disturbances satisfy the Gauss–Markov Assumptions. This graph is quite unlike those in Figure 18.2, but it typifies sample observations for a deterministically trending variable.

## Stochastic Trends

To accommodate variable trends such as we see in Figure 18.2, statisticians devised **stochastic trends**. A stochastic trend is similar to a deterministic one, but in-

**Figure 18.2**

Forecast and Actual Values of GDP, Consumption, Investment, and Inflation 1948–1998

*Source:* U.S. Department of Commerce

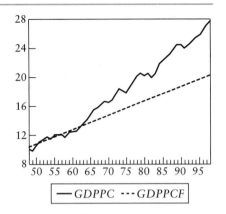

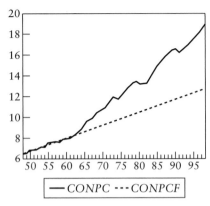

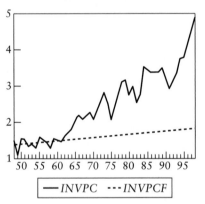

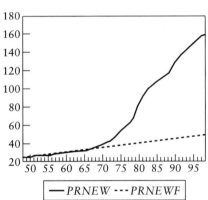

stead of the trending variable changing by constant increments each period, it changes by a random amount. We define a stochastic trend, $Z$, as a variable for which

$$Z_t = Z_{t-1} + \alpha + v_t \qquad \text{18.2}$$

or

$$Z_t - Z_{t-1} = \alpha + v_t \qquad \text{18.3}$$

where $\alpha$ is a constant and $v_t$ is a random variable with $E(v_t) = 0$.

For a deterministic trend, the contribution of the time trend to $Y$ grows by $\beta_1$ each period, from $\beta_1 t$ to $\beta_1(t + 1)$. In contrast, suppose

$$Y_t = Z_t + \varepsilon_t.$$

**Figure 18.3**

A Deterministically
Trending Variable
(1,000 Observations)

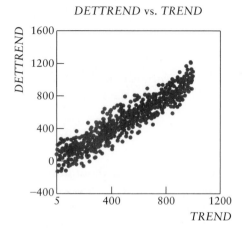

*DETTREND* vs. *TREND*

The stochastic time trend's contribution to $Y$ grows by $\alpha$, on average, each period, but the growth,

$$Z_t - Z_{t-1} = \alpha + \nu_t,$$

is random, not constant.

An alternative expression for a stochastic trend arises because

$$Z_{t-1} = Z_{t-2} + \alpha + \nu_{t-1}.$$

It is possible to express $Z_t$ in terms of $\alpha$, $t$, and the $\nu$'s alone. To do this, first substitute for $Z_{t-1}$ in the definition of a stochastic trend, to write

$$Z_t = Z_{t-2} + \alpha + \nu_{t-1} + \alpha + \nu_t.$$

Repeating this procedure of substitution over and over, we obtain

$$Z_t = \alpha t + \nu_0 + \sum_{j=1}^{t} \nu_j = \alpha t + \sum_{j=0}^{t} \nu_j,$$

if we assume the process began at $\nu_0$ in period zero. Like $\beta_1 t$, $Z_t$ contains all past increments to $Z$ ($\nu_0$, $\alpha + \nu_1, \ldots, \alpha + \nu_{t-1}$), plus a new increment ($\alpha + \nu_t$). For a deterministic trend, the increments are exactly the same in every period. For a stochastic trend, the increments are random variables. Notice that if $\alpha \neq 0$, a stochastic trend contains a deterministic trend component, $\alpha t$.

Like other random variables, each stochastic trend has a mean and a variance. The mean and variance of a stochastic trend are, respectively,

$$E(Z_t) = E\left(\alpha t + \sum_{j=0}^{t} \nu_j\right) = \alpha t + \sum_{j=0}^{t} E(\nu_j) = \alpha t + 0 = \alpha t.$$

and

$$\text{var}(Z_t) = \text{var}\left(\alpha t + \sum_{j=0}^{t} \nu_j\right) = \sum_{j=0}^{t}\text{var}(\nu_j) + 2\sum_{j=0}^{t}\sum_{k>j}\text{cov}(\nu_j, \nu_k).$$

The variance of $Z_t$ generally grows without bound as the sample size grows. For example, if the $\nu_t$ are homoskedastic,

$$\text{var}(Z_t) = t\sigma_\nu^2 + 2\sum_{j=0}^{t}\sum_{k>j}\text{cov}(\nu_j, \nu_k),$$

which will grow without bound as long as $\text{cov}(\nu_j, \nu_k)$ is bounded below $\sigma_\nu^2$ for $j$ not equal to $k$. For another example, if the variances of the $\nu_t$ themselves grow without bound (for example, if $\nu$ itself contains a stochastic trend) and negative covariances are not too strong, then the variance of $Z_t$ is also unbounded as the sample size grows. Because the variance of stochastically trending variables grows over time, stochastically trending variables are not covariance stationary.

## Random Walks

Stochastic trends are intimately related to the autoregressions introduced in Chapter 11. The relationship is most evident when we examine a **random walk**, a special type of stochastic trend in which the value of $\alpha$ is zero, so that

$$Z_t = Z_{t-1} + \nu_t, \qquad\qquad \textbf{18.4}$$

and in which the $\nu_t$ are homoskedastic and serially uncorrelated. In this special case,

$$E(Z_t) = E\left(\sum_{j=0}^{t}\nu_j\right) = \sum_{j=0}^{t}E(\nu_j) = 0,$$

and

$$\text{var}(Z_t) = \text{var}\left(\sum_{j=0}^{t}\nu_j\right) = \sum_{j=0}^{t}\text{var}(\nu_j) = t\sigma_\nu^2.$$

A stochastic trend in which $\alpha$ does not equal zero, but in which the $\nu_t$ are homoskedastic and serially uncorrelated, econometricians call a **random walk with drift**. The formula for a random walk with drift is the same as that for a stochastically trending variable, given in Equation 18.2:

$$Z_t = Z_{t-1} + \alpha + \nu_t,$$

but here the disturbances must be homoskedastic and serially uncorrelated.

**Figure 18.4**

Eight Random Walks of 1,000 Observations

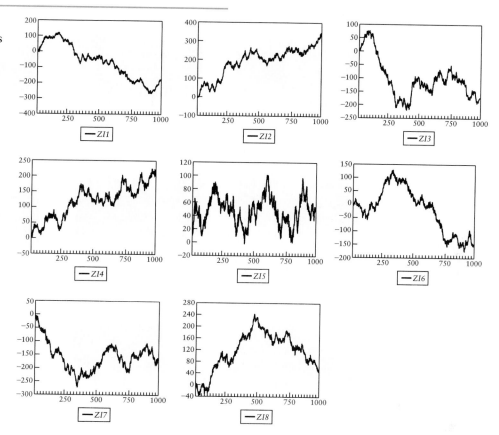

Picturing random walks, and contrasting those pictures with images of variables that do not contain a stochastic trend, reveals the striking character of stochastic trends. Figure 18.4 displays eight realizations of 1,000 observations for a random walk, $Z$, where

$$Z_t = Z_{t-1} + \nu_t,$$

in which $\nu$ satisfies the Gauss–Markov Assumptions. Notice the meandering pattern of a random walk. Observe that the variables in Figure 18.4 are sometimes more than zero, sometimes less — $Z$ has a mean of zero. Notice, too, that the persistence of observations more and less than zero in any one sequence of observations makes the eight pictures quite different from one another.

Figure 18.5 displays eight realizations of 1,000 observations on a variable $Y$,

$$Y_t = \varepsilon_t,$$

**Figure 18.5**

Eight Line Graphs of
1,000 Independent
Observations

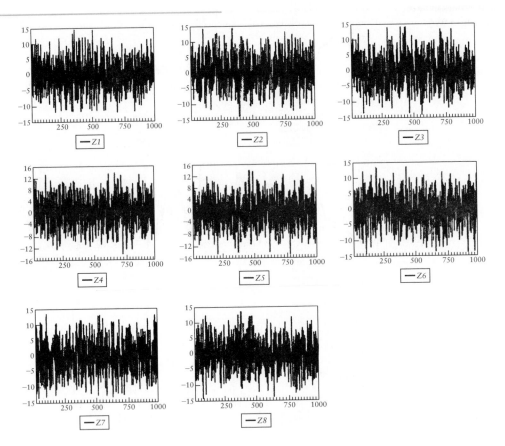

in which the observations do not follow a random walk, but instead satisfy the Gauss–Markov Assumptions. $Y$'s mean of zero is fairly observable in the figure. These graphs are closely related to those in Figure 18.3, but here there is no deterministic trend.

Figure 18.6 displays eight realizations of 1,000 observations on a variable $Y$,

$$Y_t = \varepsilon_t,$$

this time with the $\varepsilon_t$ following a first-order autoregressive pattern, with an autocorrelation coefficient $\rho = 0.9$, so that

$$\varepsilon_t = 0.9\varepsilon_{t-1} + \nu_t.$$

The observations do not cross zero as often as in Figure 18.5, but the contrast with the random walk series in Figure 18.4 is still sharp.

**Figure 18.6**

Eight Line Graphs of 1,000 Serially Correlated Observations, $\rho = 0.9$

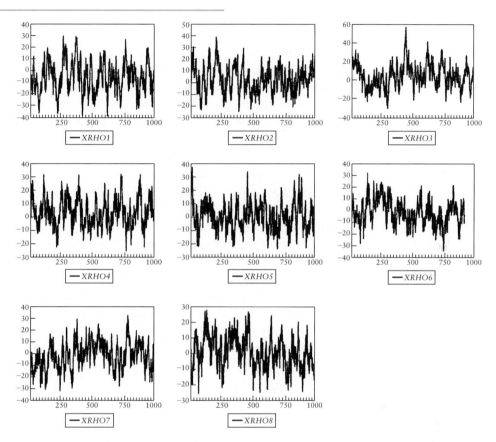

Because the $\nu$'s are uncorrelated with one another, the $\nu$'s in a random walk are often called **innovations**—they are the new, uninherited part of today's disturbance that is unrelated to what has happened in the past. The random walk is sometimes called "the drunkard's walk," because a drunk's next step is not systematically related to the drunk's previous step. If a drunk takes steps north, east, south, or west, with each step chosen at random, a random walk describes the distance the drunk travels along the north–south axis or along the east–west axis. Innovations with a mean of zero are sometimes called **white noise innovations**.

We can see the link between random walks—and hence stochastic trends—and first-order autoregressions when we compare the random walk expression

$$Z_t = Z_{t-1} + \nu_t$$

with the general form for a first order autoregression introduced in Chapter 11:

$$Z_t = \rho Z_{t-1} + v_t.$$

The random walk is a first-order autoregression in which $\rho = 1$. When we examined first-order autoregressive disturbances in Chapter 11, we restricted attention to the case in which $|\rho| < 1$ (for which $var(Z_t) = \sigma_v^2/(1 - \rho^2)$) to avoid the unbounded variances that accompany $\rho = 1$. In Chapter 11, and again here, we ignore the case in which $|\rho| > 1$ because the explosive behavior of such cases does not seem relevant to many economic settings. If $|\rho| > 1$, past shocks have ever-increasing impacts on the dependent variable.

The random walks in Figure 18.4 epitomize traits that are common among stochastically trending data, which are relatively smooth. They wander widely over time, and once they depart from their expected value, they may stray from it forever. Tilting the graphs in Figure 18.4 would show these same data with a nonzero drift.

The data in Figures 18.5 and 18.6 epitomize traits common among series that do not trend stochastically. Such data seldom remain long on one side of their expected value, and realizations far apart from one another in time are little correlated. Tilting the graphs in Figures 18.5 and 18.6 would show these same data with a deterministic trend.

## 18.2    Stochastic Trends in Regression Models

**WHAT ARE THE PROPERTIES OF AN ESTIMATOR?**

When a deterministic trend appears in a regression model, it does not change the attractive properties of our usual estimators or invalidate our usual test procedures, because the OLS estimators are still unbiased and normally distributed. What happens, then, when a stochastic trend appears in a regression equation? For example, if

$$Y_t = \beta_0 + \beta_1 Z_t + \varepsilon_t,$$

where $Z_t$ contains a stochastic trend, would $\hat{\beta}_1$ consistently estimate $\beta_1$? Would $\hat{\beta}_1$ be asymptotically normally distributed?

Because

$$\hat{\beta}_1 = \beta_1 + \frac{\sum z_t \varepsilon_t}{\sum z_t^2},$$

$\hat{\beta}_1$ is consistent if

$$\text{plim}(\hat{\beta}_1) = \beta_1 + \text{plim}\left(\frac{\sum z_t \varepsilon_t}{\sum z_t^2}\right) = \beta_1,$$

that is, if

$$\text{plim}\left(\frac{\sum z_t \varepsilon_t}{\sum z_t^2}\right) = 0.$$

We know that when neither $Z$ nor $\varepsilon$ is stochastically trending, $\hat{\beta}_1$ is consistent and asymptotically normally distributed. But what if *either* $Z$ or $\varepsilon$ is stochastically trending? Does $\hat{\beta}_1$ remain consistent? Is $\hat{\beta}_1$ still asymptotically normally distributed? The answers are not obvious because the unbounded variances of stochastically trending variables can make the Law of Large Numbers and the Central Limit Theorem inapplicable. Estimators that are usually consistent and asymptotically normally distributed may lose these attributes in models that include stochastically trending variables. The Central Limit Theorem proves more fragile than the Law of Large Numbers in this regard. There are some cases in which the Law of Large Numbers prevails but the Central Limit Theorem fails.

This section addresses in more detail the consistency and normality of OLS when explanators or disturbances contain stochastic trends, beginning by highlighting a difference between the role of random disturbances in equations containing deterministically trending variables and their role in equations containing stochastically trending variables. This difference in the role of disturbances sheds light on the performance of our usual estimators in one class of models with stochastic trends. We move on to explore other classes of models that contain stochastic trends, asking how our usual estimators perform in each class.

## Stochastic Trends and Reversion to Trend

Stochastic disturbances play fundamentally different roles for variables that contain deterministic trends than for those with stochastic trends. Consider first a variable $Y$ that contains a deterministic trend. The change in $Y$ from one period to the next for such a variable is

$$Y_t - Y_{t-1} = \beta_0 + \beta_1(t) + \varepsilon_t - \beta_0 - \beta_1(t-1) - \varepsilon_{t-1} = \beta_1 + \varepsilon_t - \varepsilon_{t-1}.$$

Here, $\varepsilon_{t-1}$, the deviation of $Y_{t-1}$ from the trend line $\beta_0 + \beta_1 t$, is "removed" as a new deviation, $\varepsilon_t$, is added in. Stated intuitively, $Y$ reverts to its trend line each period, before experiencing some new shock. It is this **reversion to trend** (also called **mean reversion**, a name that embraces the possibility that $\beta_1 = 0$) that accounts for the propensity of observations in Figures 18.3 and 18.5 to bounce randomly back and forth around the trend lines in those graphs. Serially correlated disturbances with an autocorrelation coefficient $|\rho| < 1$ also display mean reversion, but with some stickiness of successive observations above and below the trend line, as is evident from Figure 18.6, in which the autocorrelation coefficient of the disturbances is $\rho = 0.9$.

In contrast to a Y that contains a deterministic trend, a Y that contains a stochastic trend does not revert to its mean. Consider a variable W that contains a stochastic trend:

$$W_t = Z_t + \varepsilon_t,$$

where $Z_t = Z_{t-1} + \alpha + \nu_t$. Two random disturbances are at work here, $\varepsilon$ and $\nu$. The two disturbances enter the changes in W from one period to the next differently from one another:

$$W_t - W_{t-1} = Z_t + \varepsilon_t - Z_{t-1} - \varepsilon_{t-1} = \alpha + \nu_t + \varepsilon_t - \varepsilon_{t-1}.$$

As with Y, $\varepsilon_{t-1}$ gets removed from W as $\varepsilon_t$ gets added in. But as $\nu_t$ gets added in to $W_t$, the corresponding $\nu_{t-1}$ does not get "removed"—W does not revert to its trend (or mean) from one period to the next. The absence of mean reversion in stochastically trending variables accounts for the poor forecasts made when we modeled our macroeconomic variables with deterministic trends in Figure 18.2.

Stochastically trending variables do not revert to their mean. Once on one side of their mean, they have a persistent tendency to stay there. Nontrending variables, in contrast, bounce back and forth across their means in random fashion (albeit somewhat sluggishly, if the disturbances are serially correlated). The result of these differing behaviors is that in very large samples, stochastically trending variables and nontrending variables become uncorrelated. In particular, if an explanatory variable in a multiple regression is stochastically trending and the disturbance term satisfies the Gauss–Markov Assumptions (and is therefore not a trending variable), the explanator and the disturbances are asymptotically uncorrelated. This particular case sheds light on the performance of OLS when an explanator is stochastically trending and the disturbances are not.

## When an Explanator Trends Stochastically and Disturbances Don't

If an explanator is stochastically trending, but the disturbances are not, OLS consistently estimates the explanator's coefficient. To understand why this is so, consider the case of a single explanator.

Recall that the correlation coefficient for Z and $\varepsilon$ in a sample is

$$\frac{sample \ \text{cov}(Z, \varepsilon)}{\sqrt{sample \ \text{var}(Z)} \sqrt{sample \ \text{var}(\varepsilon)}} = \frac{\frac{1}{n}\Sigma z_t \varepsilon_t}{\sqrt{\frac{1}{n}\Sigma z_t^2}\sqrt{\frac{1}{n}\Sigma \varepsilon_t^2}}.$$

Because $Z$ and $\varepsilon$ are asymptotically uncorrelated when $Z$ contains a stochastic trend and $\varepsilon$ does not, their sample correlation coefficient converges in probability to zero:

$$\text{plim}\left(\frac{sample\ \text{cov}(Z,\varepsilon)}{\sqrt{sample\ \text{var}(Z)}\sqrt{sample\ \text{var}(\varepsilon)}}\right) = \text{plim}\left(\frac{\frac{1}{T}\Sigma z_t\varepsilon_t}{\sqrt{\frac{1}{T}\Sigma z_t^2}\sqrt{\frac{1}{T}\Sigma\varepsilon_t^2}}\right) = 0.$$

The formula for the sample correlation coefficient is quite close to the formula for the errors OLS makes in estimating the slope coefficient. We need only replace $\frac{1}{T}\Sigma\varepsilon_t^2$ with $\frac{1}{T}\Sigma z_t^2$ in the denominator to obtain the formula for $(\hat{\beta}_1 - \beta_1)$. Consequently, we can infer the plim of $(\hat{\beta}_1 - \beta_1)$ from that of the sample correlation coefficient for $Z$ and $\varepsilon$.

If we replace $\frac{1}{T}\Sigma\varepsilon_t^2$ with $\frac{1}{T}\Sigma z_t^2$ in the correlation coefficient expression, the new expression will converge to zero even faster than the correlation coefficient because while $\frac{1}{T}\Sigma\varepsilon_t^2$ converges to $\sigma^2$, a nonzero constant, $\frac{1}{T}\Sigma z_t^2$ grows without bound. Thus,

$$\text{plim}\left(\frac{\frac{1}{T}\Sigma z_t\varepsilon_t}{\sqrt{\frac{1}{T}\Sigma z_t^2}\sqrt{\frac{1}{T}\Sigma z_t^2}}\right) = \text{plim}\left(\frac{\Sigma z_t\varepsilon_t}{\Sigma z_t^2}\right) = 0.$$

Because the probability limit of $(\hat{\beta}_1 - \beta)$ is zero, $\hat{\beta}_1$ is a consistent estimator of $\beta_1$. The convergence of $(\hat{\beta}_1 - \beta_1)$ to zero stems from a key difference between the denominator and the numerator of the formula for $(\hat{\beta}_1 - \beta_1)$. In the denominator, both the $z$'s that make up $z^2$ have unbounded variances, whereas, in the numerator, only $z$ has an unbounded variance; the disturbance, $\varepsilon$, does not. We therefore expect the denominator to grow relative to the numerator, as the sample size grows.

The increased rate of convergence that results from replacing $\frac{1}{T}\Sigma\varepsilon_t^2$ with $\frac{1}{T}\Sigma z_t^2$ in the correlation coefficient expression suggests an especially rapid convergence of $\hat{\beta}_1$ to $\beta_1$; $\hat{\beta}_1$ is, in fact, super consistent when the explanator is stochastically trending and the disturbances are not. Unfortunately, while the Law of Large Numbers survives the unbounded variance of $Z$ in this case, the Central Limit Theorem does not. When the explanator is stochastically trending and the disturbance is not, $\hat{\beta}_1$, though super consistent, is not asymptotically normally distributed. *In general, in multiple regression models in which the disturbances are not trending, OLS super-consistently estimates the coefficients of stochasti-*

*cally trending explanators, but that OLS estimator is not asymptotically normally distributed.* Unfortunately, OLS is not consistent when the disturbances and explanators both contain stochastic trends.

## 18.3    The Consequences of Stochastic Trends for Regression

**WHAT ARE AN ESTI-MATOR'S PROPERTIES?**

Dependent variables, explanatory variables, and disturbances can all contain stochastic trends. Such stochastic trends can undermine the consistency and the asymptotic normality of all the estimators we have studied. When our usual estimators and test procedures are undermined, we need alternative methods of estimation and inference. To know when to use such alternative methods, we need formal tests to expose stochastic trends.

This section identifies the various cases in which stochastic trends make the Law of Large Numbers or the Central Limit Theorem inapplicable and thereby undermine our usual procedures. For simplicity, we focus on a DGP with one explanator and an unknown intercept,

$$Y_t = \beta_0 + \beta_1 X_t + \varepsilon_t,$$

in which the disturbances are contemporaneously uncorrelated with the explanators. The explanator $X$ may or may not contain a stochastic trend, and the disturbances may or may not contain a stochastic trend. Notice that if the disturbances contain a stochastic trend and $X$ does not, $Y$ must contain a stochastic trend. Notice, too, that if $Y$ contains a stochastic trend and $X$ does not capture that trend, then the disturbance term must contain a stochastic trend. And finally, if $Y$ contains a stochastic trend that is fully accounted for by $\beta_1 X$, then the disturbances do not contain a stochastic trend. We also assume in this chapter that all nontrending variables that appear in regressions are measured as deviations from their means, and therefore have a mean of zero. The results generalize to the multiple regression case.

We have already examined one case in which the Central Limit Theorem fails, that in which $X$ is stochastically trending, but the disturbances are not. In all, four cases must be considered:

1. When neither $X$ nor $\varepsilon$ contains a stochastic trend (the case we have studied in previous chapters), $\hat{\beta}_1$ is consistent. This is the standard result, proved in Chapter 12. In this case, $t$-tests based on the $t$-distribution and, in the multiple regression case, $F$-tests based on the $F$-distribution, are asymptotically valid. Perhaps the most surprising result in this arena is that adding stochasti-

cally trending explanators does not alter these traits of the OLS estimator of the coefficient on an explanator with mean zero that contains no stochastic trend, as long as the disturbances have no trend.

2. When $X$ contains a stochastic trend, but $\varepsilon$ does not contain a stochastic trend (the case we examined in the subsection on mean reversion), $\hat{\beta}_1$ converges in probability to $\beta_1$. Unfortunately, the asymptotic distribution of $\hat{\beta}_1$ is not generally the normal distribution, so our usual $t$- and $F$-tests are generally not valid. (If we can rewrite the equation so that the parameters of interest are on explanators that do not contain a stochastic trend, as we sometimes can, and as in case (1), though, then the usual $t$- and $F$-tests are valid in this case, too.[3]) Then $\hat{\beta}_1$ is super consistent, converging at a faster than root $n$ rate.

3. When $X$ contains no stochastic trend, but $\varepsilon$ does contain a stochastic trend (an unlikely case to encounter in practice), the numerator of

$$\frac{\frac{1}{T}\Sigma x_t \varepsilon_t}{\frac{1}{T}\Sigma x_t^2}$$

has a term with an unbounded variance, $\varepsilon$, and the denominator converges to a nonzero constant (under our usual large-sample assumptions). The Law of Large Numbers and the Central Limit Theorem both fail in this case. Instead of converging to $\beta_1$, $\hat{\beta}_1$ converges to a random variable. OLS is not consistent. Our usual tests are invalid.

4. When both $X$ and $\varepsilon$ contain stochastic trends, there are two terms with unbounded variances in both the numerator and the denominator of

$$\frac{\frac{1}{T}\Sigma x_t \varepsilon_t}{\frac{1}{T}\Sigma x_t^2}.$$

The Law of Large Numbers and the Central Limit Theorem both fail in this case. Instead of converging to $\beta_1$, $\hat{\beta}_1$ converges to a random variable. OLS is not consistent. Our usual tests are invalid. We call the regression of a stochastically trending variable on another, unrelated, stochastically trending variable a **spurious regression** because in this case, if $\beta_1 = 0$, ordinary $t$-tests will far too often reject a true null of $\beta_1 = 0$.

In multiple regression models, if our interest is in several parameters, the validity of tests deteriorates to the worst case among those parameters. If all the

**TABLE 18.1** The Consistency of OLS and the Validity of Conventional Tests in the Face of Stochastic Trends*

|  | Nontrending Disturbances | Stochastically Trending Disturbances |
|---|---|---|
| Nontrending Explanators | LLN holds <br> CLT holds | LLN fails <br> CLT fails |
| Stochastically Trending Explanators | LLN holds <br> CLT fails** | LLN fails <br> CLT fails |

*When the Law of Large Numbers (LLN) holds, OLS is consistent. When the Central Limit Theorem (CLT) holds, our usual $t$- and $F$-statistics follow the $t$- and $F$-distributions asymptotically.
**Except for a useful special case.

parameters involved in a test fall into case 1, the usual $t$- and $F$-tests apply. If one or more parameters of interest are on a variable that does not fall into case 1, $t$- and $F$-tests involving those parameters are not valid—the $t$- and $F$-distributions provide incorrect critical values. If one or more of the parameters of interest is on a variable that falls into cases 3 or 4, conventional tests involving those parameters are inconsistent. Econometricians have used Monte Carlo methods to obtain valid critical values for the $t$- and $F$- statistics in case b.

Table 18.1 summarizes these four cases, noting when the Law of Large Numbers fails and when the Central Limit Theorem fails. Because the consistency of OLS and the validity of our usual tests vary with whether the explanators or the disturbances contain stochastic trends, tests for the presence of stochastic trends are essential. We call such tests **unit root tests**.

## Spurious Regressions: An Example

When both explanators and disturbances are stochastically trending, both the Central Limit Theorem and the Law of Large Numbers fail, and OLS is inconsistent. This section illustrates the pitfalls of spurious regressions. Economic theorists hypothesize that households, being rational, do not suffer from "money illusion"; that is, the general price level, and changes in the general price level, do not influence households' decisions about real economic outcomes, such as real consumption. Rather, theorists say, only real income and relative prices determine real consumption choices. A seemingly straightforward test of the money illusion hypothesis proves misleading because the regression used is spurious.

**Figure 18.7**

Real Per Capita Consumption and the Rate of inflation, 1948–1998

*Source:* U.S. Department of Commerce

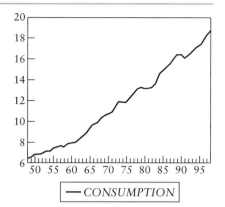

— CONSUMPTION

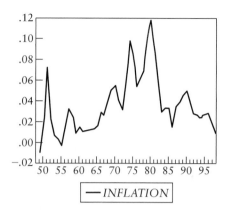

— INFLATION

To test the money illusion proposition, we might regress the log of real per capita consumption on the rate of inflation to see if inflation affects consumption. The data for this example are contained in the file illusion.*** on this book's companion Web site (**www.aw-bc/murray.com**). Figure 18.7 plots both real per capita consumption and the rate of inflation for the years 1948–1998. We can see that consumption trends upward, but inflation displays no obvious upward trend.

Without a trend of its own, inflation cannot account for the upward trend in consumption, so we include a time trend in the regression between the log of real per capita consumption and the inflation rate to capture that aspect of consumption's behavior. (We opt for the log of consumption, so that our coefficients can be interpreted as "a one percentage point increase in the inflation rate alters consumption by $\beta_1$ percent.") In essence, the regression asks whether changes in inflation account for deviations of the log of consumption from its trend. Table 18.2 contains the regression results.

Because the Durbin–Watson statistic is low, we report Newey–West serial correlation–consistent standard errors. According to our standard *t*-distribution critical values, the *t*-statistic of 3.07 on inflation would lead us to reject the null hypothesis that the log of real per capita consumption is unaffected by inflation. The conclusion seems to be that consumers suffer money illusion. Such a conclusion is, in fact, unwarranted.

On further examination, we will see that inflation appears to contain a stochastic trend. So, too, do the disturbances in the regression. This is case 4, described earlier. The OLS estimator of the coefficient on inflation is not consistent, nor are our *t*-statistics asymptotically normally distributed. A standard *t*-test based on this regression is likely to be misleading. The Newey–West standard errors, consistent if the disturbances are serially correlated but untrending, are

**TABLE 18.2** The Log of Consumption Regressed on the Log of Inflation and a Time Trend

Dependent Variable: LOGCONSUME
Method: Least Squares
Sample(adjusted): 1949 1998
Included observations: 50 after adjusting endpoints
Newey–West HAC Standard Errors & Covariance (lag truncation = 3)

| Variable | Coefficient | Std. Error | t-Statistic | Prob. |
|---|---|---|---|---|
| C | 1.834504 | 0.014162 | 129.5402 | 0.0000 |
| TREND | 0.022140 | 0.000444 | 49.86247 | 0.0000 |
| LOGINFLATION | 6.50E-05 | 2.12E-05 | 3.067837 | 0.0036 |

| | | | | |
|---|---|---|---|---|
| R-squared | 0.991297 | Mean dependent var | | 2.422840 |
| Adjusted R-squared | 0.990927 | S.D. dependent var | | 0.329768 |
| S.E. of regression | 0.031411 | Akaike info criterion | | −4.025176 |
| Sum squared resid | 0.046373 | Schwarz criterion | | −3.910455 |
| Log likelihood | 103.6294 | F-statistic | | 2676.795 |
| Durbin–Watson stat | 0.576557 | Prob(F-statistic) | | 0.000000 |

inconsistent if the disturbances contain a stochastic trend. *An informal indicator of a spurious regression is a very low Durbin–Watson statistic.* Our money illusion regression suffers a low Durbin–Watson.

If consumption and inflation both contain stochastic trends, this model with consumption as the dependent variable and with inflation and a time trend as explanators is, indeed, an instance of case 4:

$$\ln(consumption_t) = \beta_0 + \beta_1 t + \beta_2 \, inflation_t + \varepsilon_t.$$

Under the null hypothesis of no money illusion, $\beta_2 = 0$ and

$$\ln(consumption_t) = \beta_0 + \beta_1 t + \varepsilon_t.$$

If the log of consumption contains a stochastic trend, then in this last equation $\varepsilon_t = \sum_{j=0}^{t} \nu_j$, which itself trends stochastically (though with a mean of zero, as in a random walk). Both the Law of Large Numbers and the Central Limit Theorem fail; OLS is inconsistent, and the usual tests based on OLS are invalid.

Regressing the log of real per capita consumption on inflation is a classic spurious regression: Two unrelated stochastically trending variables (here the logs of consumption and inflation) are regressed on one another. Standard *t*-tests far too often reject the true null of no relationship between the variables in such regressions.

How are we to know whether a regression is spurious? What should we do if it is? To answer these questions, we first need a test for the hypothesis that a variable or disturbance is stochastically trending. We then need a strategy for estimating models that contain stochastically trending variables. Section 18.4 covers tests for unit roots, that is, those for the presence of stochastic trends. The remaining sections of the chapter then discuss estimation strategies for models that contain stochastically trending variables.

## 18.4    Testing for Unit Roots

How Do We Test Hypotheses?

Spurious regressions, like that in the preceding section, highlight our need to determine whether variables contain stochastic trends. A variable may have no trend, only a deterministic trend, only a stochastic trend, or both deterministic and stochastic trends. This section poses a testing framework consistent with all these possibilities. In particular, the tests we learn will let us determine whether the money illusion regression in the previous section is, indeed, spurious.

### Allowing for Both Deterministic and Stochastic Trends

Consider the various patterns of trend and no trend we wish to allow for. First, if there is a deterministic trend in an explanator or disturbance $Z$, and no stochastic trend, we could write

$$Z_t = \beta_0 + \beta_1 t + \nu_t.$$

If there is a stochastic trend in $Z$,

$$Z_t = Z_{t-1} + \alpha + \nu_t.$$

A more general specification that includes both deterministic trends and stochastic trends is

$$Z_t = \rho Z_{t-1} + \beta_0 + \beta_1 t + \nu_t.$$

In the deterministic trend case, $\rho = 0$. In the stochastic trend case, $\rho = 1$, $\beta_1 = 0$, and the drift parameter is $\beta_0$. Cases in which $0 < \rho < 1$ are without a stochastic trend, but have some serial correlation in $Z$. A curious feature of $\beta_0$ in this specification is that it captures the drift in the stochastic trend case, but the intercept in the deterministic trend case. (In the special case in which $\rho$ equals one and $\beta_1$ does not equal zero, the model would indicate that the drift in the random walk itself contains a deterministic trend—the drift would be $\beta_0 + \beta_1 t$. We almost never observe this case in economic data.)

Sometimes we know enough about the variable in question to exclude from the outset the possibility of a deterministic trend. For example, inflation rates in the United States do not display a steady upward or downward movement (see Figure 18.7), so we think they contain neither a deterministic trend nor a stochastic drift. Nonetheless, inflation rates may contain a stochastic trend—just one without drift. Because omitting an irrelevant variable increases the efficiency of OLS, we should omit $\beta_1 t$ when we know to do so.

When there is no steady upward or downward movement in $Z$, the troublesome possibility is that $Z$ might still follow a random walk. The alternative is that $Z$ contains no trend at all, but just has some mean, $\beta_0$. Absent steady upward or downward movement in $Z$, we could simplify the specification for hypothesis testing to be

$$Z_t = \rho Z_{t-1} + \beta_0 + \nu_t.$$

In this case, we juxtapose the case in which $Z$ follows a random walk, for which $\rho = 1$ and $\beta_0 = 0$ ($\beta_0 = 0$ because there is no drift in the data, by supposition), as in

$$Z_t = Z_{t-1} + \nu_t,$$

the case in which $Z$ contains no trend ($\rho = 0$), but has mean $\beta_0$, as in

$$Z_t = \beta_0 + \nu_t.$$

Once again, cases in which $0 < \rho < 1$ are cases without a stochastic trend, but with some serial correlation in $Z$.

Because OLS loses its convenient traits and no longer yields valid standard tests when there are stochastic trends, our chief interest is in testing the hypothesis that $\rho = 1$ against the alternative that $\rho < 1$. If we reject the null hypothesis that $\rho = 1$, we can conclude that the variable $Z$ is not stochastically trending. Unfortunately, under the null hypothesis that $\rho = 1$, the regression

$$Z_t = \rho Z_{t-1} + \beta_0 + \beta_1 t + \nu_t$$

falls into case 2 in our earlier typology, because the explanator, $Z_{t-1}$, is stochastically trending and the disturbance is not. In this case, OLS is consistent, but the standard $t$-tests do not apply, so we cannot use the usual critical values of the $t$-distribution to test the null hypothesis that $\rho = 1$. The OLS estimator of $\rho$, $\hat{\rho}$, is consistent, but not asymptotically normally distributed because the unbounded variance of the explanator, $Z_{t-1}$, undermines the Central Limit Theorem.

To illustrate the deviation of the asymptotic distribution of $\hat{\rho}$ from the normal distribution, Figure 18.8 shows Monte Carlo results for the distribution of

**Figure 18.8**

The Distribution of
$T(\hat{\rho} - 1) + 1$ When
$Z$ Follows a Random
Walk

*Source:* John Elder

$T = 50; \mathrm{E}(\beta_{\mathrm{ols}}) = .90$

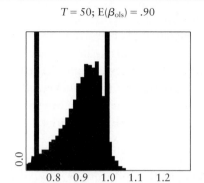

$T = 100; \mathrm{E}(\beta_{\mathrm{ols}}) = .95$

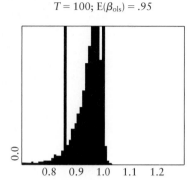

$T = 500; \mathrm{E}(\beta_{\mathrm{ols}}) = .99$

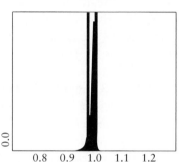

$T(\hat{\rho} - 1) + 1$, which, under the null hypothesis that $\rho = 1$, is one plus our estimation error magnified by $T$.[4] (Recall, we magnify our errors to observe the shape of their distribution as the errors concentrate around zero in large samples.) We magnify the errors by $T$, rather than by the square root of $T$, because of the super consistency of $\hat{\rho}$; $\hat{\rho}$ converges at the rate $T$. Adding one to the magnified errors centers the distribution around $\rho$, when $\rho = 1$. We see in Figure 18.8 that even in large samples, the distribution of errors is skewed to the left asymptotically. In fact, two thirds of the estimation errors are negative when $T = 500$ and $\rho = 1$. The OLS estimator of $\rho$ is not asymptotically normally distributed. When $\rho = 1$, we observe $\hat{\rho}$-values far below one much more often than the normal distribution would lead us to expect. Negative values of $(\hat{\rho} - 1)$ are less surprising when $\rho = 1$ than the normal distribution would lead us to believe.

## The Dickey–Fuller Test for a Unit Root

Because $\hat{\rho}$ is skewed toward values less than 1 when $\rho = 1$, a traditional $t$-test of the hypothesis that $\rho = 1$ against the alternative that $\rho < 1$ too often rejects the null hypothesis. Failure to account for the true nature of the distribution would lead us to think too often that $\rho < 1$, when in fact $\rho = 1$. In 1979, statisticians David Dickey of North Carolina State University and Wayne Fuller of Iowa State University used Monte Carlo methods to salvage the usual $t$-test statistic.[5] They computed approximately correct critical values for the $t$-statistic that we can use instead of the misleading critical values we might otherwise take from $t$-tables.

To simplify the applied economists' task, Dickey and Fuller slightly modified the straightforward estimation of $\rho$. They chose to estimate the model in the following form:

$$Z_t - Z_{t-1} = (\rho - 1)Z_{t-1} + \beta_0 + \beta_1 t + v_t.$$

The convenience of this form is that the null hypothesis of a unit root ($\rho = 1$) becomes a test that the coefficient on $Z_{t-1}$, ($\rho - 1$), is zero. It is the $t$-statistic for this test that regression packages always report, so we can obtain the needed $t$-statistic directly from the standard regression output. Because we rule out $|\rho| > 1$ as implausible, the **Dickey–Fuller test** is a one-sided test in which the alternative is that ($\rho - 1$) $< 0$. Thus, if our $t$-statistic is sufficiently negative, we reject the null of a stochastic trend.

Table 18.3 contains the critical values for the Dickey–Fuller test for several significance levels, assuming that the $v_i$ in the general trend specification just given are homoskedastic and serially uncorrelated. Dickey and Fuller have shown that the asymptotic distribution of the OLS estimator of ($\rho - 1$) will depend on whether the equation is specified with or without drift, so critical values are provided for both cases. Notice that the critical values are much larger than the corresponding asymptotic critical values for the $t$-distribution: 2.33, 1.96, and 1.64.

**TABLE 18.3** Dickey–Fuller $t$-test Asymptotic Critical Values

$H_0$: unit root

| Significance level | .01 | .025 | .05 |
|---|---|---|---|
| Critical value without $\beta_0$ and $\beta_1 t$ (No drift) | −2.58 | −2.23 | −1.95 |
| Critical value without $\beta_1 t$ (With drift) | −3.43 | −3.12 | −2.86 |
| Critical value with $\beta_0$ and $\beta_1 t$ | −3.96 | −3.66 | −3.41 |

*Source:* A. Banerjee, J. Dolado, J. W. Galbraith, and D. F. Hendry, *Cointegration, Error Correction, and the Econometric Analysis of Non-Stationary Data,* (Oxford: Oxford University Press, 1993, pp.102–103).

Thus far, we have followed Dickey and Fuller in assuming that the $v_i$ were serially uncorrelated. The test statistics in Table 18.3 are incorrect if, in fact, the $v_i$ are serially correlated. We can allow for serial correlation in the disturbances in the testing specification by adding lagged changes of $Z$ as explanators, as in:

$$\Delta Z_t \equiv Z_t - Z_{t-1} = (\rho - 1)Z_{t-1} + \beta_0 + \beta_1 t + \beta_2 \Delta Z_{t-1} + \beta_3 \Delta Z_{t-2} + v_t.$$

We refer to the variable $\Delta Z_t$ as the change in $Z$, or the first difference of $Z$. Common practice adds one or two lags in annual data and four in quarterly data. **Augmented Dickey–Fuller (ADF) tests** are tests of $\rho = 1$ based on such equations with lagged $\Delta Z$ values among the explanators. The critical values for these tests differ from those in Table 18.3. Econometric software packages that conduct ADF tests using residuals report either the needed critical values or the P-values for the observed test statistics.

The critical values in Table 18.3 would apply to tests for stochastic trends in either explanators or disturbances (or in dependent variables). We do not observe the disturbances associated with our observations, however. Instead, we examine residuals from a regression as if they were disturbances. The Dickey–Fuller and ADF critical values for the null hypothesis that $\rho = 1$ are different when the variable examined is a series of residuals. The new critical values depend on the number of stochastically trending regressors in the equation from which we obtain the residuals. Econometric software packages that conduct ADF tests report either the needed critical values or the P-values for the observed test statistics.

## The Spurious Regression Example Continued

The Dickey–Fuller tests allows us to determine whether the earlier analysis of money illusion did, indeed, involve a spurious regression. We first ask whether inflation contains a stochastic trend, disallowing a deterministic trend from the outset. In a preliminary step, we regress inflation on lagged inflation and a constant. Table 18.4 reports this regression. The $t$-statistic for the null hypothesis that $\rho = 1$ is

$$t = (\hat{\rho} - 1)/0.093 = (0.745 - 1)/0.093 = -2.74,$$

which is smaller in magnitude than the 5% critical value for the Dickey–Fuller test, $-2.86$, so we fail to reject the hypothesis that inflation contains a unit root.

Notice that the $t$-statistic of interest, $-2.74$, does not appear in Table 18.4. The Dickey–Fuller formulation that regresses the change in inflation on lagged inflation and an intercept term spares us computing the $t$-statistic—it appears in the output, as in Table 18.5.

The ADF test for a unit root in the disturbances requires taking the residuals from the regression of the log of real per capita consumption on inflation and a

**TABLE 18.4 Inflation Regressed on Lagged Inflation**

Dependent Variable: INFLATION
Method: Least Squares
Sample(adjusted): 1950 1998
Included observations: 49 after adjusting endpoints

| Variable | Coefficient | Std. Error | t-Statistic | Prob. |
|---|---|---|---|---|
| C | 0.009878 | 0.004322 | 2.285528 | 0.0268 |
| INFLATION(−1) | 0.744708 | 0.093047 | 8.003606 | 0.0000 |
| R-squared | 0.576797 | Mean dependent var | | 0.037520 |
| Adjusted R-squared | 0.567792 | S.D. dependent var | | 0.027664 |
| S.E. of regression | 0.018187 | Akaike info criterion | | −5.136268 |
| Sum squared resid | 0.015546 | Schwarz criterion | | −5.059051 |
| Log likelihood | 127.8386 | F-statistic | | 64.05771 |
| Durbin–Watson stat | 1.592026 | Prob(F-statistic) | | 0.000000 |

**TABLE 18.5 The Dickey–Fuller Regression for a Stochastic Trend in Inflation**

Dependent Variable: D(INFLATION)
Method: Least Squares
Sample(adjusted): 1950 1998
Included observations: 49 after adjusting endpoints

| Variable | Coefficient | Std. Error | t-Statistic | Prob. |
|---|---|---|---|---|
| C | 0.009878 | 0.004322 | 2.285528 | 0.0268 |
| INFLATION(−1) | −0.255292 | 0.093047 | −2.743704 | 0.0086 |
| R-squared | 0.138056 | Mean dependent var | | 0.000402 |
| Adjusted R-squared | 0.119717 | S.D. dependent var | | 0.019384 |
| S.E. of regression | 0.018187 | Akaike info criterion | | −5.136268 |
| Sum squared resid | 0.015546 | Schwarz criterion | | −5.059051 |
| Log likelihood | 127.8386 | F-statistic | | 7.527909 |
| Durbin–Watson stat | 1.592026 | Prob(F-statistic) | | 0.008573 |

**TABLE 18.6** Dickey–Fuller Test for a Stochastic Trend in Disturbances

Dependent Variable: D(RESID01)
Method: Least Squares
Sample(adjusted): 1951 1998
Included observations: 48 after adjusting endpoints

| Variable | Coefficient | Std. Error | t-Statistic | Prob. |
|---|---|---|---|---|
| RESID01(−1) | −0.373080 | 0.109515 | −3.406672 | 0.0014 |
| D(RESID01(−1)) | 0.241801 | 0.143911 | 1.680215 | 0.0998 |
| C | −0.000763 | 0.003127 | −0.244101 | 0.8083 |
| R-squared | 0.207414 | Mean dependent var | | −0.000894 |
| Adjusted R-squared | 0.172188 | S.D. dependent var | | 0.023793 |
| S.E. of regression | 0.021648 | Akaike info criterion | | −4.767375 |
| Sum squared resid | 0.021088 | Schwarz criterion | | −4.650425 |
| Log likelihood | 117.4170 | F-statistic | | 5.888095 |
| Durbin–Watson stat | 1.752872 | Prob(F-statistic) | | 0.005352 |

time trend and regressing the change in those residuals on the lagged residual and one lagged change of those residuals. Table 18.6 reports this regression. As noted earlier, the critical values in Table 18.3 pertain to Dickey–Fuller tests applied to a stochastically trending explanator or disturbance. We do not observe the actual disturbances, which is the variable of interest to us here, so we instead conduct a Dickey–Fuller test on the residuals. The critical values are different than those in Table 18.3 when we're examining residuals; the critical values depend on the number of explanators in the regression underlying the residuals. When the number of explanators is one, the 10% significance level critical value is −3.64. Consequently, the $t$-statistic on the lagged residual in Table 18.6, −3.41, is too small in magnitude to reject the null hypothesis of a stochastic trend in the disturbances.

The stochastic trend in the disturbances does seem to arise from a stochastic trend in real per capita consumption, as suggested. The ADF test for a stochastic trend in real per capita consumption, allowing for an alternative of a deterministic trend, requires regressing the change in consumption on lagged consumption, a time trend, an intercept, and two lagged changes of consumption, as Table 18.7 reports. The $t$-statistic on lagged consumption, −2.05, is too small in magnitude to reject the null hypothesis of a stochastic trend in real consumption per capita. The ADF distribution indicates that such extreme values of the $t$-statistic would occur in 56% of samples if consumption contains a stochastic trend. The $t$-distribution,

**TABLE 18.7  Augmented Dickey–Fuller Test**

Null Hypothesis: LOGCONSUMPTION has a unit root
Exogenous: Constant, Linear Trend
Lag Length: 1 (Automatic based on SIC, MAXLAG = 10)

|  |  | t-Statistic | Prob.* |
|---|---|---|---|
| Augmented Dickey-Fuller test statistic |  | −2.046418 | 0.5618 |
| Test critical values: | 1% level | −4.156734 |  |
| 5% level |  | −3.504330 |  |
| 10% level |  | −3.181826 |  |

*MacKinnon (1996) one-sided p-values.

Augmented Dickey–Fuller Test Equation
Dependent Variable: D(LOGCNSUME)
Method: Least Squares
Sample(adjusted): 1950 1998
Included observations: 49 after adjusting endpoints

| Variable | Coefficient | Std. Error | t-Statistic | Prob. |
|---|---|---|---|---|
| LOGCNSUME(−1) | −0.153723 | 0.075118 | −2.046418 | 0.0466 |
| D(LOGCNSUME(−1)) | 0.236333 | 0.146687 | 1.611139 | 0.1141 |
| C | 0.299004 | 0.136269 | 2.194223 | 0.0334 |
| @TREND(1948) | 0.003404 | 0.001709 | 1.992120 | 0.0524 |
| R-squared | 0.109924 | Mean dependent var |  | 0.021721 |
| Adjusted R-squared | 0.050586 | S.D. dependent var |  | 0.018116 |
| S.E. of regression | 0.017652 | Akaike info criterion |  | −5.157835 |
| Sum squared resid | 0.014022 | Schwarz criterion |  | −5.003401 |
| Log likelihood | 130.3670 | F-statistic |  | 1.852498 |
| Durbin–Watson stat | 1.939214 | Prob(F-statistic) |  | 0.151277 |

in contrast, would give rise to $t$-statistics as extreme as −2.05 in less than 4.7% of samples.

Because we are unable to reject stochastic trends in either inflation or the disturbance term in the money illusion equation, we cannot reject the claim that the money illusion regression is spurious. Therefore, the seeming conclusion that consumers suffer money illusion, based on the usual $t$-distribution of the $t$-statistic, is unwarranted.

## 18.5    How to Overcome the Spuriousness of Spurious Regressions

How Do We Make
an Estimator?

Nobel laureate and econometrician Clive Granger of the University of California, San Diego, and econometrician Paul Newbold of the University of Nottingham were the first to identify spurious regressions in economics.[6] They showed that in regressions of one randomly walking variable on another, unrelated, randomly walking variable, standard $t$-tests far too often reject the (true) null hypothesis of no relationship. Granger and Newbold suggested an alternative estimator for such models that yields consistent normally distributed estimators, for which our standard test procedures are valid. The Granger and Newbold strategy extends to spurious regressions that involve stochastically trending variables that are not random walks.

### Granger and Newbold's Strategy

Granger and Newbold focus on a spurious regression in which both the dependent and independent variables follow a random walk. Following them, consider a dependent variable, $Y$, and a purported explanator, $Z$, that both follow random walks. Then

$$Y_t = Y_{t-1} + \nu_t = \sum_{j=0}^{t} \nu_j$$

and

$$Z_t = Z_{t-1} + \mu_t = \sum_{j=0}^{t} \mu_j.$$

If $Y$ and $Z$ are, in fact, unrelated, then in a regression equation

$$Y_t = \beta_0 + \beta_1 Z_t + \varepsilon_t,$$

$\beta_1$ equals zero and $\varepsilon_i = \sum_{j=0}^{i} \nu_j$. This regression would then fall into case 4 and would be a spurious regression. OLS estimation of this equation is inconsistent.

Granger and Newbold draw our attention to the *changes* in $Y$ and $Z$ and find there a viable basis for estimating $\beta_1$. They note that

$$\Delta Y_t = \nu_t \text{ and } \Delta X_t = \mu_t.$$

Neither $\nu$ nor $\mu$ contains a stochastic trend. Granger and Newbold point out that if we difference both sides of the original regression equation, we obtain

$$\Delta Y_t = Y_t - Y_{t-1} = \beta_0 + \beta_1 Z_t + \varepsilon_t - \beta_0 - \beta_1 Z_{t-1} - \varepsilon_{t-1}$$
$$= \beta_1(Z_t - Z_{t-1}) + \nu_t = \beta_1 \Delta Z_t + \nu_t.$$

In this regression equation, neither the explanator, $\Delta Z_t$, nor the disturbances, the $\nu_t$, contain stochastic trends. The disturbances in this first differenced regression equation satisfy the Gauss–Markov Assumptions. OLS consistently estimates $\beta_1$, and our usual $t$-test is valid.

Granger and Newbold's strategy doesn't require that $Y$ and $Z$ follow random walks; the $\nu_t$ and the $\mu_t$ may be heteroskedastic or serially correlated. As long as both $\nu$ and $\mu$ are covariance stationary, OLS consistently estimates $\beta_1$ and our usual tests for *DGPs* with serially correlated or heteroskedastic disturbances validly apply to the estimation of the regression in changes.

Granger and Newbold's strategy is useful when faced with a spurious regression. If there are no stochastic trends in either $Y$ or $Z$, though, we should avoid analyzing our data in first differences. Differencing the data has two potential drawbacks when $Y$ and $Z$ contain no stochastic trends. First, differenced explanators often vary less than undifferenced explanators. The efficiency of OLS decreases when the explanators have less variation. Second, analyzing the data in first differences when $Y$ and $Z$ contain no stochastic trends can induce serial correlation where there otherwise is none. For example, assume $Y$ and $Z$ contain no stochastic trends, and the disturbances, the $\varepsilon_t$, satisfy the Gauss–Markov Assumptions. In this case, the differences in the $\varepsilon_t$, the $\nu_t$, become

$$\nu_t = \varepsilon_t - \varepsilon_{t-1}$$

and

$$\nu_{t-1} = \varepsilon_{t-1} - \varepsilon_{t-2}.$$

The appearance of $\varepsilon_{t-1}$ in both disturbances makes the $\nu_t$ correlated, even though the $\varepsilon_i$ are uncorrelated with one another. The efficiency of OLS decreases when used with serially correlated disturbances, and the computation of estimated standard errors becomes more difficult.

## Integrated Variables

The spurious regression problem plagues many regressions involving nonstationary explanators and nonstationary disturbances. We can apply Granger and Newbold's strategy for avoiding spurious regressions when the troublesome nonstationary variables have the further trait of being **integrated**. The defining trait of integrated random variables is that taking differences enough times reduces them to covariance stationary variables. We call stochastic trends whose innovations are covariance stationary **integrated of order one**, written **I(1)**. We call covariance stationary innovations **integrated of order zero**, written **I(0)**. "Integrated" as used here is analogous to its use in calculus, where it denotes a summing up of many small rectangles to compute the area under a curve. A random walk, for example, is the sum of all its past innovations, but the first difference of a random walk is just a white noise innovation. Because a white noise innovation is I(0), a random walk is I(1).

We call stochastically trending variables whose first differences are I(1) **integrated of order two,** written **I(2).** Higher orders of integration arise by similar extensions. Except for I(0) variables, variables that are integrated have growing variances and are therefore nonstationary. Granger and Newbold's solution to the spurious regression problem applies directly to nonstationary variables that are I(1). The strategy extends for application to higher order spurious regressions— we need only difference the data enough times to yield a regression with I(0) dependent and independent variables.

Generally, variables that are accumulating sums of other variables usually contain stochastic trends. For example, wealth is the accumulation of all past savings, so we can expect wealth to be an integrated variable. But what is the order of integration of wealth? That depends on the order of integration of savings. If savings are I(0), wealth is I(1). If savings are (I)1, wealth is I(2).

Table 18.8 reports a Dickey–Fuller test of the hypothesis that savings contains a stochastic trend. We do not reject that null hypothesis. Table 18.8 also reports a

**TABLE 18.8** Dickey–Fuller Tests for Stochastic Trends in Savings and in the Change of Savings

Null Hypothesis: SAVINGS has a unit root
Exogenous: Constant, Linear Trend
Lag Length: 0

|  | | t-Statistic | Prob.* |
| --- | --- | --- | --- |
| Augmented Dickey-Fuller test statistic | | $-0.744842$ | 0.9622 |
| Test critical values: | 1% level | $-4.211868$ | |
| 5% level | $-3.529758$ | | |
| 10% level | $-3.196411$ | | |

Null Hypothesis: D(SAVINGS) has a unit root

Exogenous: Constant

Lag Length: 0

|  | | t-Statistic | Prob.* |
| --- | --- | --- | --- |
| Augmented Dickey-Fuller test statistic | | $-6.842962$ | 0.0000 |
| Test critical values: | 1% level | $-3.615588$ | |
| 5% level | $-2.941145$ | | |
| 10% level | $-2.609066$ | | |

Dickey–Fuller test of the hypothesis that changes in savings contain a stochastic trend. We reject that null hypothesis. Consequently, we conclude that savings appear to be I(1). Wealth (the accumulation of all past savings) is, therefore, I(2).

## Money Illusion Revisited

We saw earlier that a regression of real per capita consumption on inflation is a spurious regression because both the explanatory variable and the disturbances are nonstationary. Can we overcome this spurious regression problem using the Granger and Newbold approach? Are first differences of real per capita consumption and inflation I(0)? Or would a regression of changes in consumption on changes in inflation be another spurious regression? Table 18.9 reports Dickey–Fuller tests applied to changes in per capita consumption and in inflation. We reject the presence of stochastic trends in either variable. (The critical values reported in the table differ between the two tests because of computer rounding errors in making the two sets of computations.)

Because changes in consumption and in inflation contain no stochastic trends, we can apply Granger and Newbold's strategy to the money illusion

**TABLE 18.9** Dickey–Fuller Tests Applied to Changes in Consumption and Changes in Inflation

Null Hypothesis: D(INFLATION) has a unit root
Exogenous: Constant
Lag Length: 1 (Fixed)

|  |  | t-Statistic | Prob |
|---|---|---|---|
| Augmented Dickey-Fuller test statistic |  | −7.530328 | 0.0000 |
| Test critical values: | 1% level | −3.577723 |  |
|  | 5% level | −2.925169 |  |
|  | 10% level | −2.600658 |  |

Null Hypothesis: D(LOGCONSUME) has a unit root
Exogenous: Constant
Lag Length: 1 (Fixed)

|  |  | t-statistic | Prob. |
|---|---|---|---|
| Augmented Dickey-Fuller test statistic |  | −4.613124 | 0.0005 |
| Test critical values: | 1% level | −3.574446 |  |
|  | 5% level | −2.923780 |  |
|  | 10% level | −2.599925 |  |

**TABLE 18.10** OLS Estimates of Changes in Consumption Regressed on Changes in Inflation

Dependent Variable: D(LOGCONSUMPTION)
Method: Least Squares
Sample(adjusted): 1950 1998
Included observations: 49 after adjusting endpoints

| Variable | Coefficient | Std. Error | t-Statistic | Prob. |
|----------|-------------|------------|-------------|-------|
| C | 0.021778 | 0.002585 | 8.423839 | 0.0000 |
| D(INFLATION) | −1.43E-05 | 1.35E-05 | −1.059364 | 0.2948 |
| R-squared | 0.023321 | Mean dependent var | | 0.021721 |
| Adjusted R-squared | 0.002540 | S.D. dependent var | | 0.018116 |
| S.E. of regression | 0.018093 | Akaike info criterion | | −5.146616 |
| Sum squared resid | 0.015386 | Schwarz criterion | | −5.069399 |
| Log likelihood | 128.0921 | F-statistic | | 1.122252 |
| Durbin–Watson stat | 1.537751 | Prob(F-statistic) | | 0.294848 |

model by examining first differences of consumption and inflation. Table 18.10 reports the regression of changes in real per capita consumption on changes in the rate of inflation that Granger and Newbold recommend. The Durbin–Watson statistic is on the lower edge of the uncertain region, indicating that there might be serial correlation in the disturbances. Table 18.11 reports feasible generalized least squares estimation of the same relationship. The $t$-statistic on the change in inflation variable's estimated coefficient in Table 18.11 is −1.31. We fail to reject the null hypothesis of no money illusion, contrary to the conclusion we drew earlier based on the faulty application of the $t$-distribution to the parameter estimates from a spurious regression. These data support economists' expectation that consumers do not suffer from money illusion.

Granger and Newbold recommend that when we analyze integrated economic data, we should work with first differences so as to avoid estimating spurious relationships among the variables. But Granger and Newbold limited their attention to regressions involving stochastically trending variables that will almost surely stray far from one another. They did not say anything about estimating relationships among integrated variables that might persistently remain closely related to one another. Are there such variables among those with stochastic trends? And if there are, should we treat regressions involving them differently?

**TABLE 18.11 FGLS Estimates of Changes in Consumption Regressed on Changes in Inflation**

Dependent Variable: D(LOGCONSUME)
Method: Least Squares
Sample(adjusted): 1951 1998
Included observations: 48 after adjusting endpoints
Convergence achieved after 17 iterations

| Variable | Coefficient | Std. Error | t-Statistic | Prob. |
|---|---|---|---|---|
| C | 0.021093 | 0.003283 | 6.425021 | 0.0000 |
| D(INFLATION) | −2.20E-05 | 1.67E-05 | −1.312290 | 0.1961 |
| AR(1) | 0.225651 | 0.179073 | 1.260101 | 0.2141 |

| | | | | |
|---|---|---|---|---|
| R-squared | 0.084000 | Mean dependent var | | 0.021236 |
| Adjusted R-squared | 0.043289 | S.D. dependent var | | 0.017984 |
| S.E. of regression | 0.017590 | Akaike info criterion | | −5.182513 |
| Sum squared resid | 0.013923 | Schwarz criterion | | −5.065563 |
| Log likelihood | 127.3803 | F-statistic | | 2.063324 |
| Durbin–Watson stat | 1.882416 | Prob(F-statistic) | | 0.138882 |
| Inverted AR Roots | .23 | | | |

Our usual estimation procedures fail us when estimating a spurious regression because the dependent variable, the explanator, and the disturbance term all contain stochastic trends. If the relationship is

$$Y_t = \beta_0 + \beta_1 Z_t + \varepsilon_t,$$

the unbounded variances of $Y$, $Z$, and $\varepsilon$ ensure that $Y$ and $Z$ will tend to differ wildly from one another over time, even if the coefficient $\beta_1$ isn't the zero that characterizes the classic spurious regression case. To estimate $\beta_1$ in such cases, one must follow the Granger–Newbold strategy of analyzing differenced data. OLS applied to the levels of the data is inconsistent.

If we add nontrending explanators to the spurious regression specification, estimating their coefficient falls into case 3—OLS estimates of the coefficients of such nontrending variables and standard tests about them are inconsistent. However, when we follow Granger and Newbold and analyze the model in differences, we estimate these variables' coefficients consistently, and our standard tests apply.

If both $Y$ and $Z$ contain stochastic trends, is it possible that $\varepsilon$ does not contain a trend? In such a case, $Y$ and $Z$ would tend to vary wildly, but $Y$ and $\beta_1 Z$

would not tend to differ greatly from one another—the difference between $Y$ and $\beta_1 Z$ would be $\beta_0 + \varepsilon_t$, which would contain no stochastic trend to make the difference fluctuate greatly. In such a DGP, estimating $\beta_1$ would fall into case 2; OLS would consistently estimate $\beta_1$, but our standard test procedures would not apply. For $Y$ to contain a stochastic trend when $\varepsilon$ does not requires that the trend in $\beta_1 Z$ accounts for the trend in $Y$. The two stochastically trending variables, $Y$ and $\beta_1 Z$, must contain the same trend. In such cases, econometricians say that $Y$ and $Z$ are *cointegrated*.

The finding that consumption, inflation, and savings are integrated variables is commonplace for macroeconomic variables—many do appear to be I(1) or higher. However, a caveat is in order. In a Dickey–Fuller test, the null hypothesis is that the variable is integrated. If the test has low power, we will fail to reject the null frequently when it is false. The Dickey–Fuller test, and other tests of the null hypothesis that a variable is integrated, often have low power. Consequently, although many macroeconomic variables look like integrated variables, they also look like variables with a serial correlation coefficient close to, but not equal to, one. The estimation methods described in this chapter as alternatives to OLS are attractive when the variables in question are truly integrated. *However, we seldom know with great confidence whether variables are integrated. When variables might be integrated, we should remain skeptical of econometric results unless our results are robust to treating the variables as either integrated or not.*

## Integration and Forecasting

Econometricians are often interested in estimating specific parameters in a regression model. But another frequent activity of econometricians is forecasting the future values of economic variables. What are the consequences of integrated variables for economic forecasting?

The mixed autoregressive–moving average (ARMA) forecasting methods of Box and Jenkins, described in Chapter 17, extend naturally to forecasting integrated variables. The ARMA estimation procedures that underlie ARMA forecasts are not consistent when applied directly to nonstationary variables, but if a nonstationary variable is integrated of order $d$, we can take first differences $d$ times to arrive at an I(0) variable. ARMA forecasting methods are consistent when applied to I(0) variables, so we can validly forecast the innovations that underlie an integrated variable using ARMA methods. We can then construct forecasts of the integrated variable by accumulating the forecast innovations. For example, assume that $Y$ is I(1). Its first differences, $\Delta Y$, are then I(0). Suppose the first $k$ ARMA forecasts of $Y$'s innovations are $\Delta Y^f_{T+1}, \Delta Y^f_{T+2}, \ldots, \Delta Y^f_{T+k}$. The first $k$ forecasts of $Y$ are then

$$Y^f_{T+r} = Y_T + \sum_{j=1}^{r} \Delta Y^f_{T+j} \qquad r = 1, \ldots, k.$$

This adaptation of the ARMA forecasting method is called **integrated mixed autoregressive–moving average (ARIMA)** forecasting. If the variable to be forecast is of order $d$, its autoregressive component is of order $p$, and its moving average component is of order $q$, we say that the variable follows an **ARIMA($p$, $d$, $q$)** process.

## 18.6    Common or Shared Trends

WHAT IS THE DGP?

Spurious regressions arise when we analyze stochastically trending variables that are unrelated. In this section, we examine stochastically trending variables that are related. Economists frequently conclude that some macroeconomic variable or another contains a stochastic trend. What do they mean by one variable "containing" a stochastic trend? An example makes the point. Real per capita GDP in the United States has many determinants, each influencing its observed value. If one of those determinants—for example, real per capita consumption—is stochastically trending, we say real per capita GDP contains a stochastic trend. Figure 18.9 shows both real per capita GDP and real per capita consumption for the United States from 1948 to 1998. We have already observed that both variables appear to trend stochastically. Visual inspection suggests some trend is common to the two variables, as they seem to trend closely together. This shows that stochastically trending variables genuinely related to one another may share the same stochastic trend; we call this a **common trend**. In this section, we explore the econometrics of variables with common trends.

The GDP example offers further insights into shared trends. If several determinants of GDP are stochastically trending—for example, consumption and investment—real per capita GDP might contain several stochastic trends. For example, if technology were improving in a stochastically trending fashion and

**Figure 18.9**

Real per Capita GDP and Real per Capita Consumption, 1948–1998

*Source:* U.S. Department of Commerce

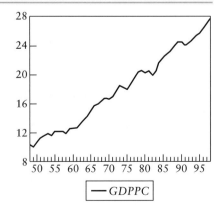

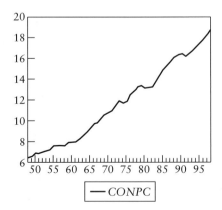

**Figure 18.10**

Real per Capita Consumption and Real per Capita Investment, 1948–1998

*Source:* U.S. Department of Commerce

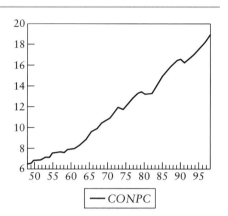

— CONPC

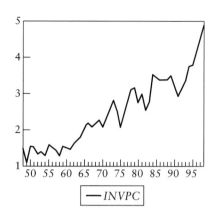

— INVPC

influencing investment, while cultural norms about materialism were stochastically trending and influencing consumption, then real per capita GDP would contain two distinct stochastic trends, technology and culture, one shared with real per capita investment and the other with real per capita consumption.

Alternatively, the supposedly several stochastically trending determinants of GDP may themselves share a single common stochastic trend. Figure 18.10 shows real per capita consumption and real per capita investment for the United States. Although visual inspection provides a less clearcut conclusion than it did for Figure 18.9, these two determinants of GDP do seem to trend similarly. GDP, consumption, and investment might all share one single stochastic trend. Caution is in order in interpreting Figures 18.9 and 18.10. Such graphs can be misleading. For example, notice that in Figure 18.10, consumption rises by about 12 over the time span shown, whereas investment grows by less than 5. By cleverly choosing the scale of the graphs, the two variables appear to have very similar slopes. "Optical econometrics" is a poor substitute for regression analysis! The evidence for common trends given by Figures 18.9 and 18.10 is quite weak. We need more sophisticated tools to determine *whether* two variables share a common trend. But first, we need to better understand how two variables *can* share a common trend.

## Cointegration and Error Correction

How can stochastically trending variables, those that wander with increasing variance over time, "stick together" in obedience to some underlying long-term relationship between them? Such variables, dubbed **cointegrated variables**, move together by periodically adjusting to one another's locations; we call this adjustment process **error correction**. The mathematics of cointegrated variables and error correction are sophisticated, but the concepts themselves are not. The tale of a drunk and her dog clarifies the link between error correction and cointegrated variables.[7]

A drunk is not the only creature whose behavior follows a random walk. Dogs, too, wander aimlessly when unleashed. Each new scent that crosses the dog's nose dictates a direction for its next step, with the last scent forgotten as soon as the new one arrives. Thus, we can model the meanderings of both drunks and dogs along a line by the random walk. In this example, a drunk woman proceeds according to

$$Y_t - Y_{t-1} = \varepsilon_t,$$

and the dog proceeds according to

$$Z_t - Z_{t-1} = w_t,$$

where $\varepsilon_t$ and $w_t$ are stationary white noise steps that the woman and dog take each period. Both the drunk and the dog follow increasingly variable paths, and for each, the best forecast of future location is current location.

But what if the dog belongs to the drunk? The drunk sets out from the bar, about to wander aimlessly in random-walk fashion. But periodically, she intones "Oliver, where are you?" and Oliver interrupts his own aimless wanderings to bark. He hears her; she hears him. He thinks, "Oh, I can't let her get too far off; she'll lock me out." She thinks, "Oh, I can't let him get too far off; he'll wake me up in the middle of the night with his barking." Each assesses how far away the other is and moves to partially close that gap.

Now neither drunk nor dog follows a random walk; each has added what we formally call error correction to her or his steps. But if we were to follow either the drunk or her dog, we would still find them wandering seemingly aimlessly in the night; as time goes on, the chance that either will have wandered far from the bar grows. The paths of the drunk and the dog still contain stochastic trends. *However, the error correction adjustments ensures that the paths share a common stochastic trend.* Figure 18.11 shows four sample paths of 1,000 steps for both the drunk and her dog. The vertical axis measures how far from the bar they are. The horizontal axis tracks their steps, from 1 to 1,000. In the four graphs, we see both the increasingly varying meandering of the drunk and dog from the bar, and their propensity to stay roughly together.

Significantly, despite the stochastic trends in the paths, we can still say, "If you find the drunk, the dog is unlikely to be very far away." Because our claim is right, the distance between the two paths contains no stochastic trend, and the walks of the woman and her dog are said to be cointegrated of order zero. For a set of series to be cointegrated of order $r$, each member of the set must be integrated of the same order, $r + 1$; thus the term *co*integrated. A set of series, all integrated of order $r$, is said to be cointegrated if and only if some linear combination of the series—with nonzero weights only—is integrated of order less than $r$. Such a relationship is called a **cointegrating relationship**. Because random walks

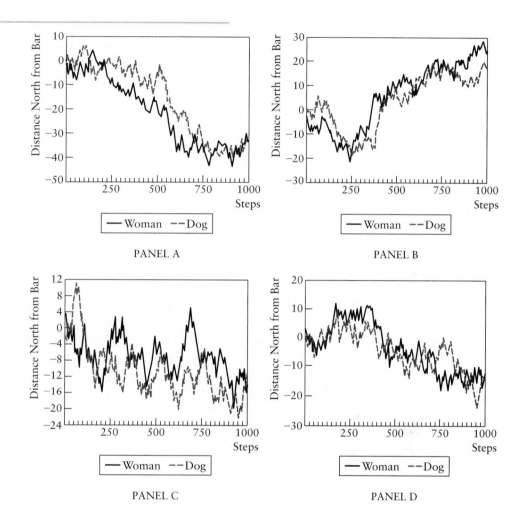

**Figure 18.11**

Four Paths for the Drunk and Her Dog

PANEL A

PANEL B

PANEL C

PANEL D

are I(1), cointegrated variables built from random walks, as with the drunk and dog who supplement their random walking with an error correction term, are cointegrated of order one.

More mundanely, we can model the drunk's and dog's cointegrated meanderings as

$$Y_t - Y_{t-1} = \varepsilon_t + \alpha_1(Y_{t-1} - Z_{t-1}) \qquad \textbf{18.5}$$

and

$$Z_t - Z_{t-1} = w_t + \alpha_2(Y_{t-1} - Z_{t-1}), \qquad \textbf{18.6}$$

where $\varepsilon_t$ and $w_t$ are again white noise steps of the woman and her dog. The coefficients $\alpha_1$ and $\alpha_2$ indicate how quickly the woman and dog close the distance between them. We call such coefficients **speeds of adjustment**.

The second terms on the right-hand side of each equation are error correction mechanisms by which the two wanderers probably stay close together; $(Y_{t-1} - Z_{t-1})$ is a cointegrating relationship between $Z$ and $Y$. In economic contexts, the cointegrating relationship is a long-run equilibrium relationship among the variables in the relationship. The error correction terms in the equations reflect how the variables adjust to that long-run equilibrium when they stray from it.

Notice that if the distance between dog and woman contained a stochastic trend, then the woman and the dog would probably grow far apart over time, despite their efforts to stay together. If this were the case, contrary to our expectations, the paths of the woman and the dog would not be cointegrated of order zero. Nobel laureates and econometricians Robert Engle of New York University and Clive Granger of the University of California at San Diego proved in 1987 that if the drunk and dog follow paths that are both I(1) and consistent with the error correction behavior in Equations 18.5 and 18.6, the paths must be cointegrated.[8] Furthermore, the converse holds. If (i) a set of stochastically trending variables are linked by error correction mechanisms such as those in Equations 18.5 and 18.6 and (ii) all the variables in those error correction equations are nontrending, then the stochastically trending variables are cointegrated.

In the case of the drunk and her dog, the difference in their locations contains no stochastic trend. In general, cointegration does not require *the difference* between the variables to contain no stochastic trend. There need only be *some* linear combination of the variables that contains no stochastic trend. It is this cointegrating relationship that belongs in the error correction term when modeling changes in $Y$ or $X$. *The key to cointegration is that the cointegrated variables contain multiples of a common stochastic trend.* If nonstationarity stems from a common stochastic trend, we can find a linear combination of the variables that cancels out that trend, resulting in a new, nontrending variable. A more general specification of an error correction model for the changes in cointegrated variables $Y$ and $X$ is

$$\Delta Y_t = \alpha_0 + \gamma_y(Y_{t-1} - \beta_1 X_{t-1}) + \eta_t$$

and

$$\Delta X_t = \phi_0 + \gamma_x(Y_{t-1} - \beta_1 X_{t-1}) + \nu_t.$$

In this more general specification, the cointegrating relationship is

$$Y_t = \beta_1 X_t + \mu_t,$$

which appears in both error correction terms. The rate at which $Y$ adjusts toward this long-run relationship is given by $\gamma_y$. The rate for $X$ is given by $\gamma_x$.

Just as the Dickey–Fuller regression sometimes needs augmenting with lagged changes of the dependent variable to account for serial correlation, error correction equations often need similar augmenting to account for serial correlation. Consequently, the dynamics of the short-run changes in a cointegrated variable $Y$ are sometimes better modeled by including lagged change variables in the error correction model:

$$\Delta Y_t = \alpha_0 + \alpha_1 \Delta Y_{t-1} + \alpha_2 \Delta X_{t-1} + \gamma_y(Y_{t-1} - \beta_{1t-1}) + \eta_t.$$

More than two stochastically trending variables might be cointegrated. If $m$ stochastically trending variables are cointegrated, they may contain up to $m - 1$ common stochastic trends, each corresponding to a different cointegrating relationship. In the tale of a drunk and her dog, imagine a husband who is also inebriated. If the husband heeds both his wife and her dog, the second cointegrating relationship involves all three variables. If the husband heeds his wife, but ignores the dog, the second cointegrating relationship is between his position and hers.

## Testing for Cointegration

Granger and Engle proposed that we test for cointegration by using the Dickey–Fuller test to determine whether the disturbances in a regression contain a stochastic trend. This is the same procedure used in the money illusion example to determine whether the regression of consumption on inflation was spurious. The critical values in Table 18.3 only apply to Dickey–Fuller tests for stochastic trends in explanators, disturbances, or dependent variables. Because we do not observe the disturbances associated with our observations, Granger and Engle propose we examine the residuals from a possible cointegrated regression as if they were disturbances. As noted earlier, the Dickey–Fuller and ADF critical values for the null hypothesis of the disturbances that contain a unit root are different when the variable examined is a series of residuals. The new critical values depend on the number of stochastically trending regressors in the equation from which we obtain the residuals. Econometric software packages that conduct ADF tests report either the needed critical values or the P-values for the observed test statistics.

## 18.7    Estimating Cointegrated Relationships

How Do We Make an Estimator?

How are we to estimate the parameters of models that involve cointegrated variables? We don't need to worry about spurious regression results, because the disturbances now contain no stochastic trend. OLS is consistent, even super consistent, when explanators contain stochastic trends and the disturbances do not. But what are we to do about the continuing invalidity of our usual test statistics?

More formally, if Y, $Z_1$, and $Z_2$ are cointegrated variables, estimating the slopes in

$$Y_t = \beta_0 + \beta_1 Z_{1t} + \beta_2 Z_{2t} + \varepsilon_t$$

is an instance of case 2. The explanators are stochastically trending, but the disturbance is not. OLS is consistent, but our usual test statistics are no longer valid, except for one special case. How are we to conduct inference when variables in our model are cointegrated?

If we add a mean zero I(0) X to this model, as in

$$Y_t = \beta_0 + \beta_1 Z_{1t} + \beta_2 Z_{2t} + \beta_3 X_t + \varepsilon_t,$$

estimating the slope coefficient for X is an instance of case 1; OLS is consistent and the associated $t$-statistic is asymptotically normally distributed. Our standard procedures are valid for estimating and testing the coefficients on variables such as X, but the question, addressed in this section, remains, "How are we to draw inferences about the coefficients on variables such as the Z's?"

## Stock and Watson's Dynamic OLS Estimator

To draw inferences about the coefficients on variables such as the Zs, econometricians James Stock of Harvard University and Mark Watson of Princeton University propose that we add seemingly superfluous nontrending variables to the cointegrated regression of interest to obtain a specification that falls into the exception to case 2—the respecified model could be rewritten in a way that makes $\beta_1$ and $\beta_2$ coefficients on a nontrending variable.[9] If the innovations of Y, $Z_1$, and $Z_2$ are serially uncorrelated, it suffices to add to the cointegrated regression the changes in the randomly walking explanators. The OLS estimators of $\beta_1$ and $\beta_2$ then asymptotically support our usual $t$- and $F$-tests based on the $t$- and $F$-distributions. This strategy for estimating $\beta_1$ and $\beta_2$ is called **dynamic OLS (DOLS)**.

Serial correlation in the innovations of $Z_1$ and $Z_2$ complicate dynamic OLS somewhat, requiring that we add not only the contemporaneous changes of $Z_1$ and $Z_2$, but also both past and future values (lags and leads) of those changes. The resulting equation again is an exception to case 2, and our usual estimators and test procedures apply to the estimation of $\beta_1$ and $\beta_2$. For example, if we add the contemporaneous changes in $Z_1$ and $Z_2$, plus two lags and leads of those changes, and estimate the parameters of

$$
\begin{aligned}
Y_t = {} & \beta_0 + \beta_1 Z_{1t} + \beta_2 Z_{2t} + \beta_3 X_t + \mu_t \\
& + \gamma_1 \Delta Z_{1,\,t+2} + \gamma_2 \Delta Z_{1,\,t+1} + \gamma_3 \Delta Z_{1,\,t} + \gamma_4 \Delta Z_{1,\,t-1} + \gamma_5 \Delta Z_{1,\,t-2} \\
& + \tau_1 \Delta Z_{2,\,t+2} + \tau_2 \Delta Z_{2,\,t+1} + \tau_3 \Delta Z_{2,\,t} + \tau_4 \Delta Z_{2,\,t-1} + \tau_5 \Delta Z_{2,\,t-2},
\end{aligned}
$$

where

$$\Delta Z_{j,\,(t+k)} = Z_{j,\,(t+k)} - Z_{j,\,(t+k-1)},$$

the OLS estimators of $\beta_1$ and $\beta_2$ are consistent and efficient. If there is also serial correlation in $\mu_t$, we should use the Newey–West serial correlation–consistent estimated standard errors for those OLS estimators. Little is known about how many leads and lags of the changes in $Z_1$ and $Z_2$ we ought to include. In practice, adding two leads and lags is standard. It is necessary to add equal numbers of leads and lags for the respecified model to be an exception to case 2.

Dynamic OLS is a simple and efficient approach to estimating the coefficients of a cointegrating relationship. Its chief advantage is that we can apply our standard $t$- and $F$-tests to the coefficient estimates we obtain from dynamic OLS.

## An Example of Dynamic OLS: Interest Rates and Deficits

Dynamic OLS allows us to draw inferences about relationships among stochastically trending variables. For example, when large, persistent budget deficits constrained U.S. economic policy for much of the 1980s and 1990s, many economists argued that these deficits discouraged private investment by driving up the long-term interest rates. But do deficits drive up interest rates? We address that question with DOLS in this example.

First, we model the long-term interest rate, measured by the 10-year treasury bond rate, as a function of the short-term interest rate, measured by the 1-year treasury bond rate, inflation, the U.S. government's real deficit per capita, and the change in real per capita income (to capture increased demand for investment). The data for this example are contained in the file deficit1.*** on this book's companion Web site (**www.aw-bc.com/murray**).[10]

Augmented Dickey–Fuller tests that we do not report do not reject the hypotheses that the interest rates, inflation, the per capita deficit, and the level of income per capita contain stochastic trends. ADF tests do reject the hypotheses that the changes in these variables contain stochastic trends. We conclude that the levels of these variables are I(1) and that their changes are I(0).

Table 18.12 reports the OLS regression of the long-term interest rate on the short-term rate, inflation, the deficit, the change in income, and a constant. If the variables in this model are cointegrated, the OLS coefficient estimates are consistent, but the reported $t$-statistics do not follow the $t$-distribution. In particular, we should remain skeptical of a claim that the $t$-statistic on *USDEF*, the deficit variable, supports the claim that deficits matter for long-term interest rates.

Table 18.13 reports an augmented Dickey–Fuller test for a stochastic trend in the disturbances of the regression reported in Table 18.12. We perform a Dickey–Fuller test, not an ADF test, because the Durbin–Watson statistic in the

**TABLE 18.12** OLS Estimates of a Model of Long-term Interest Rates

Dependent Variable: FYGT10
Method: Least Squares
Sample(adjusted): 1953 1998
Included observations: 46 after adjusting endpoints
Newey–West HAC Standard Errors & Covariance (lag truncation = 3)

| Variable | Coefficient | Std. Error | t-Statistic | Prob. |
|---|---|---|---|---|
| C | 1.264513 | 0.119566 | 10.57584 | 0.0000 |
| FYGT1 | 0.826709 | 0.035165 | 23.50950 | 0.0000 |
| INFL | −0.055646 | 0.032913 | −1.690684 | 0.0985 |
| USDEF | 0.006687 | 0.000389 | 17.18137 | 0.0000 |
| DY | 8.754592 | 135.1886 | 0.064758 | 0.9487 |
| R-squared | 0.984579 | Mean dependent var | | 6.750272 |
| Adjusted R-squared | 0.983074 | S.D. dependent var | | 2.822053 |
| S.E. of regression | 0.367148 | Akaike info criterion | | 0.936220 |
| Sum squared resid | 5.526714 | Schwarz criterion | | 1.134986 |
| Log likelihood | −16.53307 | F-statistic | | 654.4105 |
| Durbin–Watson stat | 1.707091 | Prob(F-statistic) | | 0.000000 |

**TABLE 18.13** Augmented Dickey–Fuller Test for a Stochastic Trend in Disturbances

Augmented Dickey–Fuller Test Equation
Dependent Variable: D(RESID01)
Method: Least Squares
Sample(adjusted): 1954 1998
Included observations: 45 after adjusting endpoints

| Variable | Coefficient | Std. Error | t-Statistic | Prob. |
|---|---|---|---|---|
| RESID01(−1) | −0.859757 | 0.150067 | −5.729148 | 0.0000 |
| C | 0.005599 | 0.052582 | 0.106474 | 0.9157 |
| R-squared | 0.432891 | Mean dependent var | | 0.004738 |
| Adjusted R-squared | 0.419702 | S.D. dependent var | | 0.463033 |
| S.E. of regression | 0.352726 | Akaike info criterion | | 0.797177 |
| Sum squared resid | 5.349879 | Schwarz criterion | | 0.877474 |
| Log likelihood | −15.93649 | F-statistic | | 32.82314 |
| Durbin–Watson stat | 1.900856 | Prob(F-statistic) | | 0.000001 |

original regression suggests the disturbances are not serially correlated. The 5% significance level asymptotic critical value for the Dickey–Fuller test with three stochastically trending explanators in the original regression is −4.11. Our Dickey–Fuller test statistic is −5.73. We reject the null of a stochastic trend in the disturbances. The interest rates, inflation, and the U.S. deficit are cointegrated.

Because the stochastically trending variables in this model are cointegrated, according to the ADF test, the OLS estimates of their slopes are consistent, but the associated $t$- and $F$-statistics are not distributed according to the $t$- or $F$-distributions. In particular, the $t$-statistic on the U.S. deficit variable may be misleading. To obtain $t$-statistics that do follow the $t$-distribution, we re-estimate the model, augmenting it with simultaneous changes of the stochastically trending explanators and two leads and two lags of those changes. Table 18.14 reports the DOLS results.

The $t$-statistic for $USDEF$ is asymptotically normal in a DOLS regression. Because that $t$-statistic is 5.59 here, we can confidently reject the claim that deficits do not matter for long-term interest rates. According to these data and this test, the large deficits of the 1980s and 1990s did make financing private investment, which relies on long-term borrowing, more expensive.

## Estimating an Error Correction Model

One lesson from story of the drunk and her dog is that cointegrated variables are always linked by an error correction mechanism. Because the long-term interest rate is cointegrated with the other four variables of the model reported in Table 18.12, we can specify the changes in the long-term interest rate in the error correction form:

$$\Delta FYGT10_t = \alpha_0 + \gamma(fygt10_{t-1} - \beta_1 fygt1_{t-1} - \beta_2 infl_{t-1} - \beta_3 USDEF_{t-1}) + \eta_t.$$

$$\textbf{18.7}$$

Alternatively, to account for serial correlation, the dynamics of the short-run changes in the long-term interest rate might be better modeled by adding lagged change variables to Equation 18.7:

$$\Delta FYGT10_t = \alpha_0 + \alpha_1 \Delta fygt1_{t-1} + \alpha_2 \Delta infl_{t-1} + \alpha_3 \Delta USDEF_{t-1} \qquad \textbf{18.8}$$

$$+ \alpha_4 \Delta dyt_{t-1} + \gamma(fygt10_{t-1} - \hat{\beta}_1 fygt1_{t-1} - \hat{\beta}_2 infl_{t-1} - \hat{\beta}_3 USDEF_{t-1}) + \eta_t$$

If our interest is in the short-run behavior of the dependent variable, the error correction specifications provide information that is inaccessible in the dynamic OLS specification. In particular, the coefficient $\gamma$ tells us about the dynamic adjustment of the long-term interest rate to divergences from its long-run equilibrium relationship with the other variables.

**TABLE 18.14** Dynamic OLS Estimates of a Model of Long-term Interest Rates

Dependent Variable: FYGT10
Method: Least Squares
Sample(adjusted): 1956 1996
Included observations: 41 after adjusting endpoints
Newey–West HAC Standard Errors & Covariance (lag truncation = 3)

| Variable | Coefficient | Std. Error | t-Statistic | Prob. |
|---|---|---|---|---|
| C | 1.202463 | 0.119648 | 10.05002 | 0.0000 |
| FYGT1 | 0.813292 | 0.035775 | 22.73359 | 0.0000 |
| INFL | 0.092467 | 0.038396 | 2.408234 | 0.0249 |
| USDEF | 0.003175 | 0.000568 | 5.588180 | 0.0000 |
| DY | 107.5782 | 182.8579 | 0.588316 | 0.5623 |
| DFYGT1 | −0.152899 | 0.049003 | −3.120187 | 0.0050 |
| DINFL | −0.193304 | 0.048039 | −4.023887 | 0.0006 |
| DFYGT1(1) | 0.011808 | 0.047289 | 0.249708 | 0.8051 |
| DFYGT1(−1) | −0.177982 | 0.063800 | −2.789681 | 0.0107 |
| DFYGT1(2) | 0.001897 | 0.039765 | 0.047715 | 0.9624 |
| DFYGT1(−2) | −0.238609 | 0.056676 | −4.210044 | 0.0004 |
| DINFL(1) | −0.150721 | 0.049082 | −3.070790 | 0.0056 |
| DINFL(−1) | −0.057203 | 0.036712 | −1.558122 | 0.1335 |
| DINFL(2) | −0.008720 | 0.046960 | −0.185684 | 0.8544 |
| DINFL(−2) | −0.059687 | 0.039356 | −1.516577 | 0.1436 |
| DUSDEF(1) | 7.73E-05 | 0.001207 | 0.064025 | 0.9495 |
| DUSDEF(−1) | −0.001182 | 0.001430 | −0.826582 | 0.4173 |
| DUSDEF(2) | 9.39E-05 | 0.000837 | 0.112190 | 0.9117 |
| DUSDEF(−2) | −0.001035 | 0.000667 | −1.552038 | 0.1349 |

| | | | | |
|---|---|---|---|---|
| R-squared | 0.995385 | Mean dependent var | | 7.110691 |
| Adjusted R-squared | 0.991609 | S.D. dependent var | | 2.715883 |
| S.E. of regression | 0.248775 | Akaike info criterion | | 0.359766 |
| Sum squared resid | 1.361561 | Schwarz criterion | | 1.153861 |
| Log likelihood | 11.62479 | F-statistic | | 263.6248 |
| Durbin–Watson stat | 2.335789 | Prob(F-statistic) | | 0.000000 |

Because all the variables in the error correction specification are I(0), OLS consistently estimates the error correction model, and our usual tests apply. However, the error correction variable is unobserved because $\beta_1$, $\beta_2$, and $\beta_3$ are unknown. To estimate the error correction specification, we need consistent estimates

# An Econometric Top 40—A Classical Favorite

## Rational Expectations, Permanent Income, and the Consumption Function

The modern understanding of stochastically trending variables can require us to transfer old wines to new bottles, Here, we examine a classic study of Friedman's permanent income hypothesis and show how to modify that study to account for its stochastically trending variables.

Early tests of Friedman's permanent income hypothesis focused on its implication that the average and marginal propensities to consume are equal. For example, in Chapter 7, we tested the equality of average and marginal propensities to consume indirectly, by testing the hypothesis that the consumption is a straight line that passes through the origin. In 1978, Robert Hall of MIT offered a deeper investigation into Friedman's permanent income hypothesis.

Hall built on the then-new insight that if we form our expectations rationally, we will efficiently employ all currently available information. The rational expectations assumption bears directly on Friedman's theory because Friedman's concept of permanent income is grounded in consumers' expectations about what their lifetime worth will be. In Friedman's view, permanent income is the yield we obtain from the implicit current interest on our expected lifetime worth. Hall's insight is that if, as Friedman contends, we consume a fixed fraction of our permanent income, and if we form our expectations of our permanent income rationally, then yesterday's consumption, which was based on yesterday's efficiently formed expectations, embodies all of yesterday's relevant information. In particular, Hall noted that if Friedman is right and expectations are rational, conditional on knowing yesterday's consumption, yesterday's income pro-

vides no additional information pertinent to today's consumption level. In equation form, Hall argued that in

$$\ln(consumption_t) = \beta_0$$
$$+ \beta_1 \ln(consumption_{t-1})$$
$$+ \beta_2 \ln(disposable\ income_{t-1}) + \varepsilon_t.$$

the coefficient on lagged income would be zero.

Hall extended his argument to all other past variables that would have been known to the consumer in period $(t - 1)$. If Friedman's theory is correct and expectations are formed rationally, no variable's lagged value provides us information pertinent to today's expected consumption that is not already embedded in lagged consumption. Hall tested Friedman's theory using data from 1948 to 1977. Hall's OLS estimation provides similar results when we use data from 1948 to 1998. We conduct the analysis in terms of the natural logs of real per capita disposable income and real per capita consumption. Hit Table 18.1 reports the OLS regression. In 1978, cointegration was an unknown concept. Hall interpreted the very small $t$-statistic on lagged income as evidence consistent with Friedman's permanent income hypothesis, unaware that his $t$-statistic did not follow the $t$-distribution.

We now know that the presence of stochastically trending variables in Hall's regression invalidates conventional $t$-tests. However, a more sophisticated analysis continues to support Hall's finding. The data for this exercise are contained in Hall.\*\*\* on this book's companion Web site (**www.aw-bc.com/murray**). Hit Table 18.2 contains dynamic OLS estimates of Hall's regression model, with changes in log

**HIT TABLE 18.1** An OLS Regression of Consumption on Lagged Consumption and Lagged Income

Dependent Variable: LOG(CNSMPTN)
Method: Least Squares
Sample(adjusted): 1949 1998

Included observations: 50 after adjusting endpoints

| Variable | Coefficient | Std. Error | t-Statistic | Prob. |
|---|---|---|---|---|
| C | 0.026932 | 0.026101 | 1.031838 | 0.3074 |
| LOG(CNSMPTN(−1)) | 0.969680 | 0.142612 | 6.799445 | 0.0000 |
| LOG(DISPINC(−1)) | 0.026953 | 0.143889 | 0.187318 | 0.8522 |

| | | | |
|---|---|---|---|
| R-squared | 0.997033 | Mean dependent var | 2.422840 |
| Adjusted R-squared | 0.996907 | S.D. dependent var | 0.329768 |
| S.E. of regression | 0.018341 | Akaike info criterion | −5.101259 |
| Sum squared resid | 0.015810 | Schwarz criterion | −4.986538 |
| Log likelihood | 130.5315 | F-statistic | 7896.917 |
| Durbin–Watson stat | 1.690193 | Prob(F-statistic) | 0.000000 |

**HIT TABLE 18.2** A Dynamic OLS Regression of Consumption on Lagged Consumption and Lagged Income

Dependent Variable: LOG(CNSMPTN)
Method: Least Squares
Sample(adjusted): 1950 1998

Included observations: 49 after adjusting endpoints

| Variable | Coefficient | Std. Error | t-Statistic | Prob. |
|---|---|---|---|---|
| LOG(CNSMPTN(-1)) | 0.839111 | 0.146759 | 5.717629 | 0.0000 |
| LOG(DISPINC(-1)) | 0.153479 | 0.147868 | 1.037951 | 0.3050 |
| DLC(-1) | 0.744198 | 0.262678 | 2.833117 | 0.0069 |
| DLY(-1) | −0.66223 | 0.250210 | −2.646734 | 0.0112 |
| C | 0.022421 | 0.026344 | 0.851094 | 0.3993 |

| | | | |
|---|---|---|---|
| R-squared | 0.997379 | Mean dependent var | 2.434039 |
| Adjusted R-squared | 0.997141 | S.D. dependent var | 0.323434 |
| S.E. of regression | 0.017294 | Akaike info criterion | −5.18048 |
| Sum squared resid | 0.013159 | Schwarz criterion | −4.98744 |

consumption and log income added to the model, as called for by dynamic OLS. The $t$-statistic on lagged income, 1.04, is valid in the dynamic OLS regression, so we conclude that Hall was, indeed, correct that the data support Friedman's permanent income hypothesis.

Hall went on to test whether the value of all common stock, lagged one period, predicts consumption conditional on lagged consumption. In this case, Hall found evidence against the permanent income hypothesis. He suggested a modification of the permanent income theory to account for this conflict between the data and the theory in its original form.

 **Final Notes**

Hall's insight provided a deeper basis for testing the permanent income hypothesis, a basis

that focused on the notion of expected wealth that is central to Friedman's view. Hall's recognition that rational expectations have strong implications for the microeconomic theory of household behavior spurred many other economic investigations far afield from the permanent income hypothesis, as researchers took Hall's insight and applied it in other realms.

Hall's conclusions about Friedman's models are not contradicted by a more modern analysis that accounts for the complications that stochastically trending variables pose for econometrics. We cannot count on being so fortunate in all studies involving such variables. The methods of this chapter provide tools to better test innovative ideas that rely on time series data.

■

of $\beta_1$, $\beta_2$, and $\beta_3$, so we can include as a variable an estimate of the divergence of the variables from their long-run equilibrium. Both OLS and dynamic OLS provide such consistent estimates, but the dynamic OLS estimates are preferable because (i) they are more efficient, (ii) they tend to suffer smaller biases in small samples, and (iii) their distributions allow us to use our standard test procedures.

## Lessons About Time Trends

What lessons have we learned about time trends? First, we now know that many macroeconomic variables appear to contain stochastic trends, not deterministic trends. As a consequence, we know to be on guard against spurious regressions and misleading test statistics. In practice, we should do the following:

1. Use Dickey–Fuller or ADF tests at the outset of any time series study to ascertain which of our variables contain stochastic trends and which do not
2. Ascertain whether the disturbances contain a stochastic trend after any regression involving stochastically trending variables
3. Re-estimate the model in differenced form if the regression is spurious, as suggested by Granger and Newbold

*An Organizational Structure for the Study of Econometrics*

### 1. What Is the DGP?

Deterministic trends

Stochastic trends

Stationary variables

Integrated variables

Spurious regressions

Cointegrated regression

Error correction model

### 2. What Makes a Good Estimator?

_____

### 3. How Do We Create an Estimator?

Regress first differences to avoid spurious regressions

Dynamic OLS for cointegrated relationships

### 4. What Are an Estimator's Properties?

Beware of the nonconverging spurious coefficient estimator.

Beware of nonstandardly distributed $t$'s and $F$'s.

Dynamic OLS test statistics follow standard distributions.

### 5. How Do We Test Hypotheses?

Dickey–Fuller tests

Trace and maximum eigen-value tests

Augmented Dickey–Fuller tests

### 6. How Do We Make Forecasts?

Integrated mixed autoregressive–moving average (ARIMA(p,d,q)) forecasts

4. Use dynamic OLS and an error correction regression to examine the long-run and short-run behavior of the data, if the variables in a bivariate regression are cointegrated (uncovered by analyzing the OLS residuals for a stochastic trend in a model with stochastically trending dependent and independent variables)

5. Because Dickey–Fuller and ADF tests often have low power, we seldom know with great confidence whether variables are integrated. When they might be,

we should remain skeptical of econometric results unless our results are robust to treating the variables as either integrated or not.

## Summary

This chapter reviewed the distinction between deterministic and stochastic trends. Deterministic trends do not alter the convenient traits of the least squares estimators and their kin or of the hypothesis tests based on those estimators. Stochastic trends, in contrast, often alter the convenient traits of the usual estimators and tests derived from them. When both the explanator and the disturbances contain stochastic trends, least squares regressions become spurious, far too often rejecting a true null of no relationship between the explanator and the dependent variable. When the disturbances contain no stochastic trend, but the explanators do, OLS remains consistent, even super consistent, but, except for a special case, $t$-statistics and $F$-statistics for such explanators do not have their usual asymptotic properties. The chapter introduced Dickey–Fuller and augmented Dickey–Fuller (ADF) tests to determine whether explanators or disturbances contain stochastic trends.

We noted that the solution to spurious regressions is differencing the data before performing OLS. Estimating models in which the disturbances are not stochastically trending and some explanators are stochastically trending is more complicated. When there exists a linear combination of stochastically trending variables that contains no stochastic trend, we say those variables are cointegrated. Among $k$ stochastically trending variables can be anywhere from zero to $(k - 1)$ cointegrating relationships. For cointegrated variables, there is always an error correction mechanism by which the cointegrated variables cling (probabilistically) to their shared long-run equilibrium relationship. We can estimate a cointegrating relationship among a set of variables with dynamic ordinary least squares (DOLS). $F$-tests and $t$-tests based on DOLS have the standard distributions asymptotically.

## Concepts for Review

## Questions for Discussion

1. Why are there time trends in an economy? Why might those trends be stochastic?

2. Is the notion of a stochastic trend a literal description of an economic phenomenon, or a useful approximation?

3. Why might there be long-run equilibrium relationships in the economy that would give rise to cointegrating relationships?

## Problems for Analysis

For the data sets that you will need to solve the problems in this section, go to **www.aw-bc.com/murray.**

1. A time series that has a unit root may be made stationary by first-differencing the series. Succinctly explain why distinguishing between a variable with a unit root and a variable without a unit root is important in time series econometrics.

2. Suppose that the long-term interest rate ($r_L$) and the short-term interest rate ($r_S$) are both integrated of order one.
   a. Explain what is meant by integrated of order one, I(1), and the implication of these interest rate variables being I(1).
   b. The theory of the interest rates suggests that $r_L$ and $r_S$ should be cointegrated. Explain what is meant by cointegration.

3. Whether or not a variable contains a unit root is important information for an econometrician when specifying a model to estimate.
   a. Thoroughly describe the Dickey–Fuller and augmented Dickey–Fuller (ADF) methods of testing for a unit root in economic time series.
   b. Compare the DF and ADF statistics. Under what conditions would you choose to use the ADF test? Under what conditions would you choose to use the DF test?

4. Nelson and Plosser examined 14 macroeconomic time series, including stock prices and real GNP, to determine whether or not these series are better characterized as

"stationary fluctuations around a deterministic trend, or as non-stationary processes that have no tendency to return to a deterministic path."[11]

   a. Explain what is meant by "stationary fluctuations around a deterministic trend."

   b. Explain what is meant by "non-stationary processes that have no tendency to return to a deterministic path."

5. Suppose that the long-term interest rate $(r_L)$ and the short-term interest rate $(r_S)$ are both I(1).

   a. Specify a two-equation error correction model of long- and short-run interest rates.

   b. Thoroughly explain how you would go about examining the short-run dynamics and long-run relationships implied by the model.

6. The theory of the term structure of interest rates suggests that a long-run equilibrium relationship exists between the short-term interest rate and the long-term interest rate. In fact, it has been observed that when the Federal Reserve changes the short-term rate, the long-term interest rate eventually moves in the same direction. Open the data set month1.\*\*\*. The short-term interest government Treasury bill rate is denoted by *tbillyr1*, and the long-term government bond rate is *tbond30*.

   a. Plot *tbillyr1* and *tbond30*. Do they appear to move together over time? Is one rate usually higher than the other? Which one?

   b. Test for unit roots in each interest rate.

   c. Test for the existence of cointegration between these two interest rates, using the method of Engle and Granger. What do you find?

   d. Another way to test for the existence of a long-run stable relationship between the long- and short-term interest rates is to examine the spread (i.e., arithmetic difference) between them. Define a new variable called *spread* = *tbond30* − *tbillyr1*. Plot the spread. Does it look like the spread is about the same magnitude over the sample period (on average)? Conduct a unit root test of your choosing on the spread. Compare your conclusion with that in part (b).

7. The notion that overall stock market returns are fairly stable over the long run suggests that investors might do well by constructing a portfolio that mirrors a major stock market index such as the S&P 500. Of course, all investors know that stock returns may be up in one year and down in another, and thus by stable returns over the long run we really mean that an investor can expect to earn some "average" level of returns provided she holds the stocks long enough. This average level of returns is often put in terms of the long-run historical average. For investment planning purposes, it would be helpful to know two pieces of information. First, what is the long-run average of stock returns? Second, is this long-run average a decent predictor of future returns? In other words, are stock returns mean-reverting? Open the data set month1.\*\*\*. The variable denoted *return* is the monthly return on the S&P 500 stock market index.

   a. Plot *return* over the entire sample period. Is it easy or difficult to determine whether or not market returns are stable over time, in the sense that the historical average is remaining about the same over long periods of time? Briefly explain why or why not.

     b. Use the Dickey–Fuller and augmented Dickey–Fuller statistics to determine whether or not *return* has a unit root. What can you say about the mean-reverting properties of stock returns?

     c. Suppose that you found return to have a unit root. What would this imply about using the historical average return as an indicator of future returns?

 8. In 1982, Charles Nelson and Charles Plosser alerted macroeconomics to the potential importance of understanding stochastically trending variables. They conducted augmented Dickey–Fuller tests to determine whether any of 14 macroeconomic time series were I(0).[12] The file nelplo.\*\*\* contains the time series Nelson and Plosser used.

     a. Plot each series against time to familiarize yourself with the shape of the data.

     b. Conduct augmented Dickey–Fuller tests to determine whether the individual series in the file are I(0), I(1), or I(2).

9. A variant of "Fisher's hypothesis" suggests that a long-run relationship exists between the price level in the economy and the nominal interest rate—namely, that prices and/or the interest rate adjusts to maintain a balance between the two, thus implying a stable real interest rate over time. Open the peelsact.\*\*\* data set. The data are annual observations of the short-term interest rate ($r$) and the consumer price index (*cpi*) for the United Kingdom from 1700 to 1998.

     a. Estimate the cointegrating regression $r_t = c + \beta_1 \ln(cpi)_t + \varepsilon_t$. Test to see if the interest rate and log price level are cointegrated.

     b. Write out the error correction model implied from your results in part (a). Estimate the model using just one lagged value of the changes in interest rates and prices. Interpret the results, including the speed of adjustment terms. Does Fisher's hypothesis hold?

 10. The data set money.\*\*\* contains observations on the U.S. per capita money supply (measured by M1) and per capita gross national product from 1948 to 1998.

     a. Are these variables I(0), I(1), or I(2)?

     b. Are the variables cointegrated?

     c. Explain how you would estimate the rate of change of per capita GNP with respect to the money supply.

     d. What is the economic interpretation of the slope in part (a)?

 11. The file illusuk.\*\*\* contains data on United Kingdom real consumption and inflation from 1949 to 2003. Analyze those data for money illusion following the same steps used in this chapter to analyze U.S. money illusion. Do the U.K. data lead us to conclude that there is no evidence of money illusion in the United Kingdom?

12. Economists working for the construction industry must understand the long-run relationship that may exist between mortgage rates and the number of new houses being built. One way in which to model this relationship is by using an error correction model. Open the data set housing1.\*\*\*. The file contains monthly data on the number of housing starts (1-unit structure), and this variable is denoted *startnsa*. The 30-year fixed mortgage rate is denoted *fixed30*.

     a. You are going to estimate an error correction model of housing starts (*startnsa*) and the 30-year fixed rate (*fixed30*) used for obtaining a mortgage. However, before going any further, consider the possibility that housing starts have a seasonal pattern. Regress *startnsa* on a constant and 11 monthly seasonal dummy variables. Create a new variable called *startsa* that is equal to the residuals from the regression of housing starts on the seasonal factors. This new variable represents seasonally adjusted housing starts. Plot both *startnsa* and *startsa* and describe their differences and similarities.

b. Using *startsa* and *fixed30*, estimate an error correction model of the following form:

$$\Delta startsa_t = \alpha_1 + \alpha_2 \Delta startsa_{t-1} + \alpha_3 \Delta fixed30_{t-1} + \gamma_1(startsa_{t-1} + \lambda_i fixed30_{t-1}) + \varepsilon_t$$

$$\Delta fixed30_t = \beta_1 + \beta_2 \Delta startsa_{t-1} + \beta_3 \Delta fixed30_{t-1} + \gamma_2(startsa_{t-1} + \lambda_2 fixed30_{t-1}) + \nu_t$$

c. Interpret the results in part (b), including the speed of adjustment coefficients.

13. Professors Campbell, Lo, and MacKinlay (1997) note that if the stock market is "weak form" efficient then a trader will not be able to earn superior returns using an information set that contains only the past history of the stock prices or returns themselves. In other words, all the information contained in the history of price movements has already been incorporated into current prices or returns. Financial market researchers have often used the augmented Dickey–Fuller (ADF) statistic to test whether or not a particular stock market is efficient.

a. Explain why and how the ADF test may be used to test for "weak form" stock market efficiency.

b. Open the data set month1.***. The variable *logsp500* is the log of the monthly closing price of the S&P 500 stock market index. Perform the ADF test on *logsp500*. Based on your results, is this market efficient or not?

14. Financial market participants examine the relationships between the prices of many assets to determine if there is any information that may help them predict future price movements. One popular model that is generally attributed to Clive Granger and Robert Engle is the error correction model. The model is particularly informative, as it can provide information about short-run dynamics and long-run trends. The short-run dynamics are typically inferred from the estimated coefficients on the lagged changes of variables in the system, and the long-run or common trend represents the presence of cointegration. If cointegration exists, then the two prices will not drift arbitrarily far apart from each other, and thus the investor has insight as to future price movements following a disturbance in the market. Open the dj1.*** data set. The log of the Dow Jones futures price is denoted *f*, and the log of the spot price is denoted *s*.

a. Conduct the augmented Dickey–Fuller test on both *s* and *f* to confirm they are I(1). By itself this result suggests that the two series are each "weak form" efficient in that no additional information contained in their own past history can be exploited to make superior returns.

b. A stronger form of market efficiency, known as the semi-strong form, suggests that no superior returns can be obtained even with publicly available information on other relevant price histories. An error correction model is a test of the semi-strong form of market efficiency. Estimate the following:

$$\Delta f_t = \alpha_1 + \alpha_2 \Delta f_{t-1} + \alpha_3 \Delta s_{t-1} + \gamma_1(f_{t-1} + \lambda s_{t-1}) + \varepsilon_t$$

$$\Delta s_t = \beta_1 + \beta_2 \Delta f_{t-1} + \beta_3 \Delta s_{t-1} + \gamma_2(f_{t-1} + \lambda s_{t-1}) + \nu_t$$

Examine the estimated coefficients on the lagged changes in $f$ and $s$. What do they tell you about market efficiency? Forecasting? Are the two series cointegrated? If so, which series adjusts to eliminate a disequilibrium, or do they both? How do you know? Explain.

15. During the early- to mid 1990s, there was a rapid increase in U.S. stock market prices. In the late 1990s, and shortly thereafter, stock prices fell sharply. These stock market changes brought sharp increases and declines in personal wealth. One way such changes in the stock market can affect GDP is through wealth's effects on consumption behavior. But how large is the effect of a change in wealth on consumption? Carol Bertaut addresses this question using data from several countries.[13] The file wealth.*** contains Bertaut's quarterly U.S. data from 1960 to 2001. The variables in the file are

DLCONS        Change in the log of real consumption
DLINCOME      Change in the log of real personal disposable income
LCONS         Log of real consumption
LINCOME       Log of real personal disposable income
LWEALTH       Log of real net worth

a. Graph the logs of consumption, income, and wealth against time. If the variables do not contain stochastic trends, do they contain deterministic time trends?

b. Conduct augmented Dickey–Fuller tests for unit roots in each of the variables in part (a). What do you conclude?

c. Conduct augmented Dickey–Fuller tests for unit roots in the first differences of each of the variables in part (a). What do you conclude?

d. Use Stock and Watson's dynamic OLS estimator to estimate a consumption function in which the dependent variable is the log of consumption and the explanators are the logs of income and wealth. Use two leads and lags of the changes in the logs of income and wealth.

e. Use the residuals from the DOLS regression in part (d) to test the null hypothesis that the logs of consumption, income, and wealth are not cointegrated. What do you conclude?

f. What are the estimated long-run elasticities of consumption with respect to income and wealth, respectively? Do you reject the null hypothesis that wealth does not affect consumption? The ratio of wealth to consumption is about 5:3. The marginal propensity to consume out of wealth is the elasticity of consumption with respect to wealth divided by the wealth–consumption ratio. What is the estimated long-run marginal propensity to consume out of wealth?

g. Using the residuals from part (d) estimate the error correction model corresponding to the model in (d). Does consumption adapt fully to discrepancies in the previous period between consumption and its long-run expected value? If not, how much of the discrepancy is closed each period?

16. TechEnergy is considering building two small wind energy plants, one in Albuquerque, New Mexico, and the other in Tucson, Arizona. Each plant would involve the erection of wind turbines that would have the capacity to produce enough electricity to power 10,000 homes for 1 year. A critical factor in the operations strategy of TechEnergy is to determine the time series properties of wind speed in these two areas. In particular, the time series properties will help determine the type of turbine blades as well as exact placement of the turbines to provide maximum efficiency. TechEnergy can economize on design and process costs if the wind speed in the two locations follows the same DGP. Open the weather1.*** file. The variables *tuswnd* and *albwnd* are the historical average daily wind speed series for Tucson and Albuquerque, respectively, measured in miles per hour.

a. Conduct a series of tests to determine whether or not these wind speed series follow a random walk process, follow a random walk with drift process, and/or whether they can be considered I(1) or I(0). (*Hint:* Begin with the most general unit root test and work your way through the various models.)

b. Based on your results in part (a), construct an ARMA or ARIMA model for both *tuswnd* and *albwnd*. Use the Box–Jenkins method or the AIC method to determine the best fitting specifications. Do the two wind speeds appear to behave similarly or not?

 17. Economists model the behavior of potential home buyers as if they are solving a portfolio choice problem. One aspect of this analysis is that home buyers will consider the house as an investment, or asset, which will reap a better return when the interest rate they use to finance the purchase is lower, all else being equal. The portfolio approach also suggests that home buyers will shy away from buying if they can receive a better (risk-adjusted) return elsewhere. Efficient markets will thus ensure that an equilibrium occurs in which there is a long-run stable relationship between the number of new houses and the interest rate used to finance home purchases. Open the data set housing1.***. The file contains monthly data on the number of housing starts (1-unit structure) and this variable is denoted *startnsa*. The 30-year fixed mortgage rate is denoted *fixed30*.

a. Plot *startnsa* and *fixed30*, being sure to place their values on opposite axes. Does there appear to be a relationship between financing costs and housing starts? Describe this relationship.

b. Estimate a vector autogression with *startnsa* and *fixed30* and perform a Granger causality test. What is your conclusion about the relationship between these two variables?

c. Examine each variable using the augmented Dickey–Fuller test and determine whether they are I(1) or I(0).

d. Test for the cointegration of *startnsa* and *fixed30*. Is your conclusion about a relationship between these two variables altered at all (compared with your answer in part b)? If so, how?

## Endnotes

1. John Maynard Keynes, *A Tract on Monetary Reform.* (London: Macmillan, 1923).

2. James Stock and Mark Watson, "Variable Trends in Economics," *Journal of Economic Perspectives* (Fall 1988). Figures 18.1 and 18.2, which appear in that paper (using the logs of variables), were the foundation for that paper's introduction, as they are here.

3. James H. Stock and Mark W. Watson, "Variable Trends in Economic Time Series," *Journal of Economic Perspectives* 2, 3 (Summer 1988): 147–174.

4. John Elder kindly shared with me PowerPoint slides from which Figure 18.8 is drawn. His paper with Peter Kennedy, "Testing for Unit Roots: What Students Should Be Taught," *Journal of Economic Education* 32, no. 2 (Spring 2001): 137–146, shares much in common with the approach of this chapter.

5. D. A. Dickey and W. A. Fuller, "Distributions of the Estimators for Autoregressive Time Series with a Unit Root," *Journal of the American Statistical Association* 74 (1979): 427–431.

6. Clive Granger and Paul Newbold, "Spurious Regressions in Econometrics," *Journal of Econometrics* 2 (1974): 111–120.

7. This section draws heavily from Michael P. Murray, "A Drunk and Her Dog: An Illustration of Cointegration and Error Correction," *The American Statistician* 48, no. 1 (February 1994): 37–39. John Elder and Peter Kennedy, "Testing for Unit Roots: What Should Be Taught?" *Journal of Economic Education* (Spring 2001): 137–146, also influenced this chapter's treatment of cointegration.

8. Clive W. Granger and Robert F. Engle, "Co-integration and Error Correction: Representation, Estimation and Testing," *Econometrica* 55 (1987): 251–276.

9. James H. Stock and Mark W. Watson, "A Simple Estimator of Cointegrating Vectors in Higher–Order Integrated Systems," *Econometrica* 61, no. 4 (1993): 783–820.

10. The model used here is adapted from Gregory Hoelscher, "New Evidence on Deficits and Interest Rates," *Journal of Money, Credit, and Banking* 18, no. 1 (February 1986): 1–17. He estimated the model by OLS and FGLS.

11. Charles Nelson and Charles Plosser, "Trends and Random Walks in Macroeconomic Time Series: Some Evidence and Implications," *Journal of Monetary Economics* 10 (1982): 139–162.

12. Ibid.

13. Carol C. Bertaut, "Equity Prices, Household Wealth, and Consumption Growth in Foreign Countries: Wealth Effects in the 1990s," Board of Governors of the Federal Reserve System, International Finance Discussion Papers, no. 724 (April 2002).

# Chapter 19

# Logit and Probit Models: Truncated and Censored Samples

*Heads I win. Tails you lose.*

—A PLAYGROUND SCAM

Your brother joined the U.S. Army this morning. He will fly helicopters. You worry, and wonder about the probability that a helicopter pilot in the Army will be killed while serving. Later today, you have an appointment with a university career counselor. You hope they know the probability that a college graduate with a 3.3 GPA and a score of 580 on the Graduate Management Aptitude Test (GMAT) will be accepted to a good masters of business administration (MBA) program. We often wonder about the probabilities that bear on our everyday lives. Economists wonder about probabilities, too. Does attending the Head Start program increase the probability that a poor child will complete high school? Do higher cigarette taxes reduce the probability that young people will begin smoking?

Many variables, such as test scores, GPA, age, and gender, influence probabilities. Economists frequently study the determinants of probabilities using regression techniques. Unlike dependent variables such as consumption or earnings, though, probabilities are restricted to the narrow range of values between zero and one. Our measures of the outcomes associated with probabilities are even more narrowly circumscribed. For example we might learn that a Head Start child does or does not eventually graduate from high school. The variables that describe the outcomes associated with probabilities take on only two values, zero or one—they are binary, or dummy, variables.

Earlier chapters dealt with dummy variables as explanators. This chapter discusses probabilities and dummy variables as dependent variables. When dummy variables appear as explanators, they imply only that different groups of observations have different intercept terms. We find here that when dummy variables appear as dependent variables, the consequences are more wide-reaching than that. We will learn that sometimes least squares regression techniques usefully estimate a model that has a dummy variable or a probability as its dependent variable, but the bounded nature of dummy variables and probabilities often calls for alternative estimation procedures.

## 19.1    The Linear Probability Model

The probability that a college graduate will be admitted to a good MBA program depends on the student's grades, GMAT scores, and other considerations. To model a probabilistic outcome such as admission, we need a specification that links the binary outcome, admitted or not, to its explanators. For example, we can specify the relationship between a dummy variable and its explanators as a linear regression model:

$$D_i = \beta_0 + \beta_1 X_i + \varepsilon_i, \qquad 19.1$$

in which $\varepsilon_i$ is the deviation of the $i$-th individual from the expected value for an individual with $X = X_i$. (Instead of denoting all dependent variables of interest by $Y$, this chapter uses $D$ to indicate dependent variables that are dummy variables.)

Statistical theory tells us that the expected value of a binary, zero-one, random variable equals the probability, $\pi$, that the random variable takes on the value one. According to Equation 19.1, if $X_i$ is fixed across samples, the probability, $\pi_i$, that the binary variable $D_i$ takes on the value one, often called "the probability of success," is

$$E(D_i) = (1)\pi_i + (0)(1 - \pi_i)$$
$$= \pi_i = \beta_0 + \beta_1 X_i. \qquad 19.2$$

Thus, Equation 19.1 is a model of both binary outcomes and their probabilities. The flip side of Equation 19.2 is the probability that $X$ takes on the value zero:

$$(1 - \pi_i) = 1 - \beta_0 - \beta_1 X_i. \qquad 19.3$$

If the explanator $X$ is a random variable, we could alternatively consider the probability that $D_i = 1$, conditional on $X_i$, written $\pi(D_i|X_i)$. In terms of Equation 19.1, this conditional probability is

$$E(D_i|X_i) = \pi(D_i|X_i) = \beta_0 + \beta_1 X_i.$$

*Because D takes on only two values (zero and one), each disturbance for a given observation, $\varepsilon_i$, also takes on only two values.* The values $\varepsilon_i$ takes on are

$$(1 - \beta_0 - \beta_1 X_i),$$

which occurs with probability $\pi_i$ (equal to $\beta_0 + \beta_1 X_i$), and

$$(0 - \beta_0 - \beta_1 X_i),$$

which occurs with probability $(1 - \pi_i)$, which is equal to $(1 - \beta_0 - \beta_1 X_i)$.

Because it expresses the probability of success, $E(D_i)$, as a linear function of $X_i$, we call this binary dependent variable version of the linear regression model a linear probability model. Notice that for some $X$-values between minus and plus infinity, the $E(D_i)$ is negative, and for some others it is greater than one. For the model to make sense, we must restrict $X$ to the range within which $E(D_i)$ lies between zero and one. In many data sets, the observed $X$-values fall in the required range, but in many others they do not.

## OLS Estimation of the Linear Probability Model

How are we to estimate the linear probability model? We can often consistently estimate $\beta_0$ and $\beta_1$ in the linear probability model using ordinary least squares (OLS), but feasible generalized least squares (FGLS) provides more efficient estimates. To see that FGLS is more efficient than OLS, first notice that the expected value of $\varepsilon_i$, $E(\varepsilon_i)$, equals zero:

$$E(\varepsilon_i) = (1 - \beta_0 - \beta_1 X_i)(\beta_0 + \beta_1 X_i) + (0 - \beta_0 - \beta_1 X_i)(1 - \beta_0 - \beta_1 X_i) = 0;$$

consequently, if the explanators are contemporaneously uncorrelated with the disturbance terms, OLS is an unbiased estimator of the linear probability model. OLS is not, however, an efficient estimator of the linear probability model because the disturbances are not homoskedastic. The variance of a binary random variable, $W$, with probability of success $\pi$, is

$$\begin{aligned} \text{var}(W) = E([W - E(W)]^2) &= (0 - \pi)^2(1 - \pi) + (1 - \pi)^2\pi \\ &= \pi^2(1 - \pi) + (1 - \pi)^2\pi \\ &= \pi(1 - \pi)[\pi + (1 - \pi)] = \pi(1 - \pi). \end{aligned}$$

In particular, the variance of $\varepsilon_i$ is

$$\pi_i(1 - \pi_i) = (\beta_0 + \beta_1 X_i)(1 - \beta_0 - \beta_1 X_i),$$

which varies with $X_i$. Because the variance of the disturbances depends on $X_i$, the linear probability model's disturbances are heteroskedastic. Consequently, generalized least squares (GLS) is a more efficient estimation procedure than OLS for the linear probability model. Unfortunately, knowing the variances of the disturbances requires knowing $\beta_0$ and $\beta_1$, which are unknown, so GLS is not a feasible estimator. Instead, we can use FGLS to estimate the linear probability model. It has two steps in this case:

1. Estimate Equation 19.1 by OLS and compute the fitted values, the $\hat{D}_i$.
2. Divide both sides of Equation 19.1 by $\sqrt{\hat{D}_i(1 - \hat{D}_i)}$, the estimated standard deviation of $\varepsilon_i$, and use the transformed variables to do OLS again.

An alternative to FGLS is to estimate the model by OLS, but to use White's heteroskedasticity-consistent standard errors to make inferences or build confidence intervals.

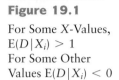

**Figure 19.1**

For Some $X$-Values,
$E(D|X_i) > 1$
For Some Other
Values $E(D|X_i) < 0$

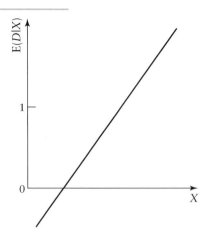

*For some range of values of X, the linear probability model may prove a good approximation to the distribution of D, but the model is badly flawed for some values of X.* Figure 19.1 illustrates the point. For some values of $X$, the probability that $D = 1$, given $X$, $E(D)$ is negative, and for other values of $X$, $E(D)$ exceeds one—both of which are meaningless as probabilities. To side-step this problem, we can restrict the range of allowed $X$-values to those for which all the $E(D_i)$ lie between zero and one. However, even when the $X$-values are restricted in this way to limit the values of the actual $E(D_i)$, fitted values of $E(D_i)$ may prove negative or greater than one.

## An Example of Linear Probability Models: National Football League Victory

"Let me root, root, root for the home team. If they don't win, it's a shame . . ." is the refrain of a popular baseball song.[1] However, home team pride isn't the only reason people care about the outcome of ball games. Many fans have a financial stake in games' outcomes as well. Sports betting is a popular—and sometimes an abused—activity around the world.

This example examines the relationship between the outcomes of professional football games in the United States and a pregame indicator of who will win a particular game. The indicator, popular among gamblers, is the "point spread." The point spread is an estimate of how much the team will lose by; if the point spread is negative, the spread's magnitude is the team's predicted margin of victory. A point spread of 20 for a team predicts that the team will lose by 20 points; a point spread of −20 predicts the team will win by 20 points. Sports fans often wonder, "If the point spread against the home team is 20 points, how likely is it

**TABLE 19.1  What Point Spreads Say About the Probability of Winning in the NFL: I**

Dependent Variable: WIN
Method: Least Squares
Sample: 1 644
Included observations: 644
White Heteroskedasticity-Consistent Standard Errors & Covariance

| Variable | Coefficient | Std. Error | t-Statistic | Prob. |
|----------|-------------|------------|-------------|-------|
| C | 0.500000 | 0.018849 | 26.52593 | 0.0000 |
| SPREAD | −0.025180 | 0.003068 | −8.26065 | 0.0000 |
| R-squared | 0.087582 | Mean dependent var | | 0.500000 |
| Adjusted R-squared | 0.086161 | S.D. dependent var | | 0.500389 |
| S.E. of regression | 0.478346 | Akaike info criterion | | 1.366137 |
| Sum squared resid | 146.8993 | Schwarz criterion | | 1.380012 |
| Log likelihood | −437.8960 | F-statistic | | 61.62496 |
| Durbin–Watson stat | 2.034242 | Prob(F-statistic) | | 0.000000 |

that the home team will win?" A linear probability model can answer this question and others like it.

Our data is all the game outcomes for home teams in the NFL in the 2001–2002 regular season. Table 19.1 contains the linear probability model estimates of $\beta_0$ and $\beta_1$ in a model of the probability of winning, given the spread. The data for the analysis are contained in the file football.*** on this book's companion Web site (www.aw-bc.com/murray). The variable win is a dummy that indicates that the home team won. The variable spread is a continuous variable that reflects the quoted spread for the home team in the game. The point-spread data are from one particular gambling house.

Table 19.1 reports the OLS estimates of the linear probability model, accompanied by White's heteroskedasticity-consistent standard errors. The estimated intercept is 0.50, so we estimate that the home team wins half the games in which its point spread is zero. We estimate that each one-point increase in the spread alters the team's probability of winning by $\hat{\beta}_1$, or −2.52 percentage points. The negative sign on the spread variable's coefficient reflects the fact that positive spreads indicate a disfavored team.

At the average spread for the home team, 5.88, the predicted probability of the home team winning is 35.2% ($0.5 - 0.0252 \cdot 5.88$). A spread of 20 points or more would lead us to predict a probability of winning less than zero—a senseless result. In this data set, the largest point spread is 17.5 points, so there are no senseless fitted values within this data set, although there could be. The next sections examine alternative models for limited dependent variables that restrict predicted probabilities to the range zero to one for all possible $X$ values.

## Maximum Likelihood Estimation of the Linear Probability Model

When the disturbances are heteroskedastic, the GLS estimator of the intercept and slopes of a straight line is the BLUE estimator. Unfortunately, linear estimators do not apply to many of the models that economists use to represent probabilities. To set the stage for estimating those alternative models of probabilities, it is instructive to examine an alternative to GLS estimation of the linear probability model. The maximum likelihood estimators (MLE) of the slope and intercepts are the estimates that make the observed data least surprising.

In the linear probability model, in which a dummy variable is the dependent variable, the dependent variable, $Y$, takes on only two values, zero and one. The maximum likelihood estimation (MLE) estimators for $\beta_0$ and $\beta_1$ are the values of $\beta_0$ and $\beta_1$ for which the observed pattern of zeros and ones would be least surprising. To construct the MLE estimators for $\beta_0$ and $\beta_1$ in the linear probability model, notice that Equations 19.2 and 19.3 give the probabilities for each dependent variable's two possible outcomes, one and zero. If we arrange the data so that the first $n_1$ observations in a simple random sample of $n$ observations are ones and the rest zero, the probability that we would observe this pattern of zeros and ones is

$$L = \prod_{i=1}^{n_1} (\beta_0 + \beta_1 X_i) \prod_{i=n_1+1}^{n} (1 - \beta_0 - \beta_1 X_i).$$

($\prod$ is like $\Sigma$, except that the terms are multiplied together, instead of added.) Maximizing this function $L$ with respect to $\beta_0$ and $\beta_1$ yields the maximum likelihood estimates of those population parameters. These are the estimates of $\beta_0$ and $\beta_1$ for which the observed data are most likely to arise. MLE estimates are generally consistent and asymptotically efficient. (See the Maximum Likelihood Estimation Web Extension on this book's companion Web site, **www.aw-bc.com/murray,** for a more detailed treatment of maximum likelihood estimation.)

Estimating the linear probability model by either OLS or by MLE is easy to do with existing econometric software packages. However, the fact that the linear probability model allows fitted and predicted probabilities outside the range zero and one pressed econometricians to develop alternative models that preclude such outcomes. *All the models of binary outcomes that econometricians use provide formulae, akin to Equations 19.2 and 19.3, that give the probabilities that each observation takes on the value zero or the value one, even when the models do not provide a linear-in-the-parameters form like Equation 19.1—which often they do not. Econometricians frequently use these probabilities to rely on maximum likelihood estimation for estimating limited dependent variable models.*

Before the advent of high-speed personal computers and powerful econometric software packages, economists frequently settled for linear probability models because they were easy to implement and frequently informed us correctly about what variables influence a particular probability. Today, estimating models that rule out negative fitted probabilities and those in excess of one is little more difficult than performing OLS. Few economists currently rely on linear probability models. We study them here because applying OLS to a linear probability model is the natural first approach to estimating probabilities in econometrics. Exposing the limits of linear probability models justifies the more complex specifications that follow. The next sections introduce alternatives to the linear probability model that avoid negative fitted probabilities and those in excess of one.

## 19.2    Probit and Logit Models

WHAT IS THE DGP?

The linear probability model misspecifies the relationship between a probability of success and its explanators. As Figure 19.1 makes clear, the linear probability model implies that for some $X$-values, probabilities exceed one, and that for some other $X$-values, probabilities turn negative. This cannot be right. Figure 19.2 offers an alternative view of the relationship between a probability and an explanator. In the figure, as $X$ approaches negative infinity, the probability approaches zero, and as $X$ approaches positive infinity, the probability approaches one. The rate at which the probability changes slows as $X$ grows in magnitude; in the middle range of $X$-values, the probability rises rather sharply with $X$, but the rate of increase declines as $X$ becomes very large or very small. Figure 19.2 depicts an inherently nonlinear relationship between $X$ and the probability of success. This section introduces two nonlinear models, the *probit* and *logit* models, that economists commonly use to estimate the relationship between probabilities and explanators.

### Latent Variables That Determine Binary Outcomes

Some football teams are a little stronger than their opponents; others are much stronger. The speed of a team's runners, the agility and strength of its linemen, and the passing accuracy of its quarterback all contribute to a team's strength. Similarly, some individuals are a little more employable than others and others

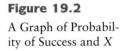

**Figure 19.2**

A Graph of Probability of Success and $X$

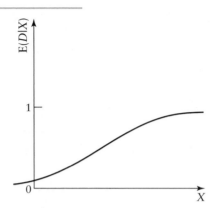

are much more employable than most. Education, experience, and other characteristics contribute to an individual's employability. But chance also contributes to an individual's employability in a given job search and to a team's relative strength on a given day. For example, an employer's need for someone to start work right away can make a person ordinarily passed over employable.

A team's strength relative to its opponent and an individual's employability are summary measures that are not directly observed. Instead we observe traits that contribute to the overall measures. More starkly, we also observe the clearest indicator of a team's relative strength, the outcome of the game, and the clearest indicator of an individual's employability—having a job. In general, we expect the team with better traits to be stronger on any given day, and the individual with better traits more likely to be employed at any given moment. A good combination of traits makes for a better summary measure of strength or employability, on average, and a better summary measure on average makes success more likely. The probit and logit models of binary outcomes rely on this notion of an unobserved underlying aptitude for success to underpin a nonlinear model of binary outcomes.

Suppose there is an unobserved continuous variable, $Z_i$, a team's relative strength or an individual's employability, that differentiates individuals with $D_i = 1$ from individuals with $D_i = 0$. For convenience, suppose $D_i = 1$ if $Z_i > 0$, and $D_i = 0$ otherwise. The stronger team wins ("they were the better team today, the score shows that," laments the Yankee manager after losing to a last-place team). The employable individual (an individual with $Z_i > 0$) gets a job. However, the realized value of $Z$ need not be the same as its expected value. The $E(Z)$ measures an individual's propensity to have $D = 1$; the actual value of $Z$ (if you could observe it) determines what actually happens to the individual. For example, the New England Patriots have a very high $E(Z)$, but they do lose sometimes; people with college educations are usually employed, but sometimes they are unable to find work.

We call an unobserved summary variable, $Z$, that determines a binary outcome a **latent variable**.

## Probit and Logit Models

The probit and logit formulations of limited dependent variable models are grounded in the assumption that some latent variable determines the binary outcome of interest to us. These models express the expected value of $Z_i$, not the expected value of the binary outcome, $D_i$, in terms of parameters, such as $\beta_0$ and $\beta_1$, and explanators, such as $X$. Thus we have:

$$Z_i = \beta_0 + \beta_1 X_i + \varepsilon_i.$$

The binary outcome $D_i$ equals 1 if $Z_i$ exceeds 0, and equals 0 otherwise. An alternative way to describe when $D_i$ equals 1 or equals 0 is to say that $D_i$ equals 1 if $\varepsilon_i > -(\beta_0 + \beta_1 X_i) = (-\beta_0 - \beta_1 X_i)$, and equals 0 otherwise. For example, someone with an expected value of $Z$ equal to, say, 5 will be employed as long as $\varepsilon_i$ isn't less than $-5$.

The cumulative distribution function for $\varepsilon_i$, $F(w)$, tells the probability that $\varepsilon_i$ takes on a value less than $w$. Figure 19.3 (see p. 826) displays the cumulative distribution function for the standard normal. The probability that a standard normal, $Z \sim N(0,1)$, takes on a value less than $-1.96$ is 0.025. The probability that a standard normal takes on a value less than zero is one half, and so on. In the figure, the distance from the horizontal zero axis to the cumulative distribution function is $\Pr(Z < w)$. Viewed the other way around, in the figure, the distance from the probability function to the horizontal line for 1.0, $[1 - F(w)]$, is $\Pr(Z > w)$.

The disturbances need not be distributed like the standard normal, but they must have some distribution function. Let's call that function $F(w)$. Recall that $D_i$ equals 1 if $Z_i$ exceeds 0, that is, if $\varepsilon_i > (-\beta_0 - \beta_1 X_i)$. Consequently, if the cumulative distribution function for $\varepsilon_i$ is $F(w)$, the probability that $D_i = 1$ is

$$\Pr(D_i = 1) = [1 - F(-\beta_0 - \beta_1 X_i)]. \qquad \textbf{19.4}$$

Similarly, the probability that $D_i = 0$ is

$$\Pr(D_i = 0) = F(-\beta_0 - \beta_1 X_i), \qquad \textbf{19.5}$$

because $D_i$ equals 0 if $Z_i$ is less than or equal to 0, that is, if $\varepsilon_i \leq (-\beta_0 - \beta_1 X_i)$.

How likely is it that we would see a particular pattern of some $D$'s being equal to one and others being equal to zero in a random sample? That is, what is the likelihood, $L$, for a set of $n$ observations, distinguished by whether $D_i$ equals one or zero? If the observations are independent of one another, the probability expressions for $\Pr(D_i = 1 | X_i)$ and for $\Pr(D_i = 0 | X_i)$ suffice to determine $L$. If the first $n_e$ individuals in a sample are employed and the remaining $(n - n_e)$ are not employed, then the likelihood of seeing such a sample, $L$, is

$$L = \prod_{i=1}^{n_e} [1 - F(-\beta_0 - \beta_1 X_i)] \prod_{i=n_e+1}^{n} F(-\beta_0 - \beta_1 X_i), \qquad \textbf{19.6}$$

if the observations are statistically independent.

To fully specify the likelihood in Equation 19.6, we must choose a specific form for the cumulative distribution function, $F(w)$. Once we have a specific likelihood function, $L$, we can use maximum likelihood estimation to estimate $\beta_0$ and $\beta_1$ by maximizing the function $L$ with respect to $\beta_0$ and $\beta_1$. These values of $\beta_0$ and $\beta_1$ make the observed sample less surprising than would any other values for $\beta_0$ and $\beta_1$. MLE estimation is generally consistent and asymptotically efficient.

## The Probit Model

There are two commonly used functional forms for $F(w)$ in Equation 19.6. The first is the cumulative distribution function from the normal distribution. The normal distribution arises in so many other statistical contexts that it is a natural choice for use in modeling binary outcomes, and many econometricians choose the cumulative standard normal distribution function for $F(w)$ when analyzing limited dependent variables. The resultant model is called the **binomial probit model**, or, more commonly, the **probit model**. Economists estimate the probit model by maximum likelihood.

When we estimate the probit specification, we obtain estimates of the coefficients of

$$E(Z_i) = \beta_0 + \beta_1 X_i.$$

Recall that in the binary outcome models for individual data, we assume that the binary random variable of interest takes on the value one if

$$Z_i = \beta_0 + \beta_1 X_i + \varepsilon_i > 0;$$

that is, $D_i = 1$ if $\varepsilon_i > (-\beta_0 - \beta_1 X_i)$. Because the standard normal distribution is symmetric around zero,

$$\Pr(\varepsilon_i > (-\beta_0 - \beta_1 X_i)) = \Pr(\varepsilon_i < (\beta_0 + \beta_1 X_i)).$$

Consequently, the estimated probability, $\tilde{\pi}$, that the binary dependent variable $D_i$ takes on the value one is

$$\tilde{\pi}_i = \widetilde{\Pr}(D_i = 1) = F(\tilde{Z}_i) = \Pr(\varepsilon_i < \tilde{Z}_i),$$

where $\tilde{Z}_i = \tilde{\beta}_0 + \tilde{\beta}_1 X_i$, F is the cumulative standard normal distribution function, and $\varepsilon_i \sim N(0, 1)$. The estimated probability, $1 - \tilde{\pi}$, that the binary dependent variable $D_i$ takes on the value zero is

$$1 - \tilde{\pi}_i = \widetilde{\Pr}(D_i = 0) = 1 - F(\tilde{Z}_i) = 1 - \Pr(\varepsilon_i < \tilde{Z}_i).$$

Maximum likelihood estimation of $\beta_0$ and $\beta_1$ in the probit model chooses the estimates of $\beta_0$ and $\beta_1$ for which the likelihood function in 19.6 is maximized, that is, the estimates for which the observed data are least surprising.

Because the normal cumulative distribution function is nonlinear, a nonlinear relationship exists between the probability of success and X, and between the probability of success and $\beta_1$. In the probit model, the derivative of the probability with respect to $X_i$ is not equal to $\beta_1$, as it would be in the linear probability model, but instead the derivative varies with both $\beta_1$ and $X_i$. In the probit model,

$$\frac{d(prob[D_i = 1])}{d(X)} = \frac{d(F[\beta_0 + \beta_1 X_i])}{d(X)} = \beta_1 f(\beta_0 + \beta_1 X_i),$$

where $f(\cdot)$ is the standard normal probability density function.

## An Example of the Probit Model: The Decision to Hold Interest-Bearing Assets

A study in 2000 by economists Casey Mulligan of the University of Chicago and Xavier Sala-i-Martin of Columbia University illustrates the probit model at work. Mulligan and Sala-i-Martin report that in the Survey of Consumer Finances, 59% of U.S. households report holding no interest-bearing financial assets, apart from employer-held pensions and IRAs.[2] Why, ask the two economists, don't more people hold financial assets? They argue that getting into the market for interest-bearing assets requires some fixed transactions costs—learning about the market and keeping track of the investment—that deter people with smaller assets from making the move out of cash or checking accounts. The foregone interest income is less than the transaction costs for these individuals. On balance, individuals hold interest-bearing assets if the net benefits from holding the assets is positive. The latent variable, Z, in this example, then, is the net benefit to the household from holding interest-bearing assets.

The foregone interest from not holding assets is the product of the interest rate and the level of assets. Thus, the probability that a household owns interest-bearing assets should depend on the level of the household's assets and on the interest rate. Mulligan and Sala-i-Martin suggest further that the learning costs may be lower for people with retirement fund assets, such as IRAs and pensions held with their employers, because exposure to such retirement investments might bring added general understanding of interest-bearing assets.

The data set financials.\*\*\* on this book's companion Web site (**www .aw-bc.com/murray**) contains the Survey of Consumer Finances data analyzed by Mulligan and Sala-i-Martin; this file is too large to be used with the student version of EViews. The data are from a single year, so we have no variation in interest rates with which to estimate the effect of interest rates on whether individuals hold interest-bearing financial assets. The variable *havrasst* is one if the individual has non-retirement-fund interest-bearing assets and is zero otherwise. The variable *lnfinast* is the natural log of the individual's total financial assets, cash, checking accounts, and interest-bearing financial assets. The variables *pension* and *iras* are dummy variables indicating the individual has a pension or an IRA. The variable *dist* is the distance from the individual's home to the nearest financial institution. Table 19.2 reports the probit results. People with larger asset holdings are, indeed, more likely to hold interest-bearing assets, and people with retirement assets such as IRAs and pensions are also more likely to hold non-retirement-fund interest-bearing assets.

The reported LR statistic in the output corresponds to the overall *F*-statistic reported in linear regressions; its corresponding P-value is the probability that we would see data like that in the sample if the included explanators do not matter at all. We reject that null hypothesis here.

How likely is an individual with $1,000 in assets to hold interest-bearing assets if he or she has no retirement accounts? The probit estimates allow us to compute an answer to this question. The natural log of 1000 is 6.91. Combining this 6.91 value for *lnfinast* with the estimated coefficients for *lnfinast* and the intercept, we obtain

$$\hat{Z} = -5.569 + 0.638 * 6.91 = -1.16,$$

where $\hat{Z}$ is the estimated expected net benefit from holding interest-bearing assets for a household with assets of $1,000 and no retirement programs.

The probability that a standard normal distribution takes on a value of $-1.16$ or less is 0.12. The model predicts that individuals with assets of $1,000 and no retirement programs have a 12% probability of holding interest-bearing assets. If the individual does have a pension plan, the probability of holding other interest-bearing assets rises:

$$\tilde{Z} = -5.569 + 0.638 \cdot 6.91 + 0.243(1) = -0.92.$$

Because $\Pr(Z < -0.92)$ equals 0.18, an individual with $1,000 and a pension plan has an estimated 18% chance of holding other interest-bearing assets—markedly higher than the 12% chance we estimate for an individual with no pension plan.

**TABLE 19.2 Probit Estimates of The Probability of Holding Interest-Bearing Assets**

Dependent Variable: HAVRASST
Method: ML - Binary Probit (Quadratic hill climbing)
Sample (adjusted): 3 3143
Included observations: 2842 after adjustments
Convergence achieved after 5 iterations
Covariance matrix computed using second derivatives

| Variable | Coefficient | Std. Error | z-Statistic | Prob. |
|---|---|---|---|---|
| C | −5.569306 | 0.205488 | −27.10289 | 0.0000 |
| LNFINAST | 0.638343 | 0.023260 | 27.44422 | 0.0000 |
| PENSION | 0.243126 | 0.069047 | 3.521156 | 0.0004 |
| IRAS | 0.208079 | 0.075085 | 2.771245 | 0.0056 |
| Mean dependent var | 0.620690 | S.D. dependent var | | 0.485301 |
| S.E. of regression | 0.312913 | Akaike info criterion | | 0.623138 |
| Sum squared resid | 277.8818 | Schwarz criterion | | 0.631516 |
| Log likelihood | −881.4797 | Hannan-Quinn criter. | | 0.626160 |
| Restr. log likelihood | −1886.308 | Avg. log likelihood | | −0.310162 |
| LR statistic (3 df) | 2009.656 | McFadden R-squared | | 0.532696 |
| Probability(LR stat) | 0.000000 | | | |
| Obs with Dep = 0 | 1078 | Total obs | | 2842 |
| Obs with Dep = 1 | 1764 | | | |

## The Logit Model

As noted earlier, the second commonly used cumulative distribution function, $F(w)$, for the disturbances in a latent variable model is the **logistic distribution,** for which

$$F(w) = \frac{\exp(w)}{[1 + \exp(w)]},$$

and for which, therefore,

$$1 - F(w) = \frac{1}{[1 + \exp(w)]}.$$

The latent variable model that uses the logistic distribution is called the **binary logit model** or, more commonly, the **logit model**. Economists usually estimate the logit model by MLE.

For the logit model, the probability that $D = 1$ is

$$\pi_i = \frac{\exp(\beta_0 + \beta_1 X_i)}{1 + \exp(\beta_0 + \beta_1 X_i)} = \frac{1}{1 + \exp(-\beta_0 - \beta_1 X_i)}, \qquad \textbf{19.7}$$

and the probability that $D = 0$ is

$$\pi_0 = 1 - \pi_i = \frac{\exp(-\beta_0 - \beta_1 X_i)}{1 + \exp(-\beta_0 - \beta_1 X_i)}. \qquad \textbf{19.8}$$

Equations 19.7 and 19.8 highlight the nonlinear relationship between the probabilities of succeeding and failing and $X$, and between the probabilities of succeeding or failing and $\beta_1$. In the logit model, the derivative of the probability of success with respect to $X_i$ is not equal to $\beta_1$, as it would be in the linear probability model, but instead the derivative varies with both $\beta_1$ and $X_i$. In the logit model,

$$\frac{d(prob[D_i = 1])}{d(X)} = \frac{d(F[\beta_0 + \beta_1 X_i])}{d(X)} = \frac{\beta_1 \exp(\beta_0 + \beta_1 X_i)}{[1 + \exp(\beta_0 + \beta_1 X_i)]^2}.$$

We can apply MLE using the logit's likelihood function by maximizing

$$L = \prod_{i=1}^{n_e} \left[ \frac{1}{1 + \exp(-\tilde{\beta}_0 - \tilde{\beta}_1 X_i)} \right] \prod_{i=n_e+1}^{n} \left( \frac{\exp(-\tilde{\beta}_0 - \tilde{\beta}_1 X_i)}{1 + \exp(-\tilde{\beta}_0 - \tilde{\beta}_1 X_i)} \right),$$

with respect to $\tilde{\beta}_0$ and $\tilde{\beta}_1$, given the observed $X$-values. The values of $\tilde{\beta}_0$ and $\tilde{\beta}_1$ that maximize the likelihood function are the MLE estimates—consistent and asymptotically efficient estimates of the logit model's coefficients.

Maximum likelihood is the most common estimation procedure used to estimate probit and logit models. In the past, when econometricians did not have powerful computers and sophisticated econometric software packages, MLE was frequently too computationally burdensome for easy application. Today, with powerful computers on their desks, most econometricians use it whenever individual data are available.

## An Example: The NFL and Point Spreads Once More

Let's return to the data of football.*** on this book's companion Web site (**www.aw-bc.com/murray**) to estimate a logit model of the relationship between the home team's probability of winning and its spread. In this example, the latent variable, $Z$, is the strength of the home team relative to its opponent for the day.

**TABLE 19.3** **What Point Spreads Say About the Probability of Winning in the NFL: III**

Dependent Variable: WIN
Method: ML - Binary Logit (Quadratic hill climbing)
Time: 17:21
Sample: 1 644
Included observations: 644
Convergence achieved after 3 iterations
Covariance matrix computed using second derivatives

| Variable | Coefficient | Std. Error | z-Statistic | Prob. |
|----------|-------------|------------|-------------|-------|
| C | 6.55E-17 | 0.082525 | 7.94E-16 | 1.0000 |
| SPREAD | −0.109814 | 0.015211 | −7.219175 | 0.0000 |
| Mean dependent var | 0.500000 | S.D. dependent var | | 0.500389 |
| S.E. of regression | 0.477754 | Akaike info criterion | | 1.301076 |
| Sum squared resid | 146.5357 | Schwarz criterion | | 1.314951 |
| Log likelihood | −416.9466 | Hannan-Quinn criter. | | 1.306460 |
| Restr. log likelihood | −446.3868 | Avg. log likelihood | | −0.647433 |
| LR statistic (1 df) | 58.88031 | McFadden R-squared | | 0.065952 |
| Probability(LR stat) | 1.68E-14 | | | |
| Obs with Dep = 0 | 322 | Total obs | | 644 |
| Obs with Dep = 1 | 322 | | | |

Table 19.3 reports the individual logit model estimates.

In the logit model, an intercept of zero corresponds to a probability of success of 50% when the explanator is zero. In Table 19.3, the intercept term is statistically insignificant and very nearly zero in magnitude. In this logit model we do not reject the null hypothesis that the home team has a 50% chance of winning games in which the spread is zero. In the linear probability model, we also did not reject the null hypothesis that the home team has a 50% chance of winning games in which the spread is zero. The mean spread in our sample is, in fact zero, with a standard deviation of 5.88 points. Applying Equation 19.7, using the estimated coefficients from Table 19.3, we estimate that at a spread of 5.88 (one standard deviation above the mean), the home team has a 34.4% chance of winning. This is not far from the 35.2% chance we estimated with the linear probability model.

Applying Equation 19.7 for point spreads of 5.88 and 6.88, we find that the estimated effect of a one-point change in the spread from 5.88 to 6.88 is

$$\frac{\exp(0.0 + 0.1098 \cdot 6.88)}{1 + \exp(0.0 + 0.1098 \cdot 6.88)} - \frac{\exp(0.0 + 0.1098 \cdot 5.88)}{1 + \exp(0.0 + 0.1098 \cdot 5.88)}$$

$$= .320 - .344 = -.024.$$

The linear probability model estimate of the effect of the same change in the spread was $-0.025$, the estimated slope coefficient of the model in Table 19.1. Linear probability models often give results similar to those from the logit model near the observed mean of the explanators.

The reported Prob > chi-square statistic in the output corresponds in function to the overall $F$-test reported in linear regressions; it is the probability that we would see data like those in our sample if none of the included explanators affect the dependent variable. We reject that null hypothesis because this reported P-value is so small.

This example highlights how we can easily use maximum likelihood to estimate models that are nonlinear in their parameters but how obtaining useful quantitative assessments from such models is more complicated than from models that are linear in their parameters.

## Comparing the Probit and Logit Models

With two common cumulative distribution functions to choose between when specifying F($w$) in Equation 19.6, it is natural to ask how the two specifications compare. The logistic and normal cumulative distribution functions have very similar shapes. The chief difference is that the logistic model has proportionately more "outliers"; that is, more realized values lie far from the mean. Figure 19.3 shows both the logistic and the standard normal cumulative distribution functions. The variable along the horizontal axis is $z$ . In the probit and logit models, $z = (\beta_1 X)$. The height of these functions at a given $z = (\beta_1 X)$ is the probability of success at that $X$. The fatter tails of the logistic distribution bring an initially faster accumu-

**Figure 19.3**

The Probit and Logit Cumulative Distribution Functions

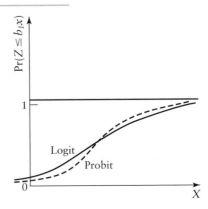

# An Econometric Top 40—A Classical Favorite

## The National Health Insurance Experiment

A Chapter 15 Greatest Hit described the chief findings of the National Health Insurance Experiment (NHIE) conducted by the RAND Corporation in the 1970s and early 1980s (see p. 649).[3] The RAND team included economists, statisticians, and physicians. The most important finding from the experiment was that modest cost sharing by patients (with a cap on maximum out-of-pocket expenditure) reduces medical expenditures but does not measurably change health outcomes for the average person. The cost-sharing lesson changed insurance practices in the United States. The fraction of major companies with cost-sharing insurance plans rose from 30% to 63% in the years immediately following the publication of the experimental results. The consequent savings from avoided medical expenses was about $7 billion by 2000, and they continue to accumulate. The cost of this lesson, the cost of the experiment, was less than $100 million (current). Here, our focus is on the modeling strategy the RAND economists used to study medical expenditures.

The National Health Insurance Experiment randomly selected families at six sites. It then randomly assigned the chosen households to one of 14 treatment plans or to a control group. It placed some households in a health maintenance organization (HMO); it gave the rest of the treated households a variety of fee-for-service plans. The chief differences among fee-for-service plans were the level of co-payment and the maximum out-of-pocket expenditure households might have to pay. Because the NHIE was a truly randomized experiment, very simple tools sufficed to provide consistent estimates of the differences in the effects of the

plans. For example, differences in means between the plans would consistently estimate the differences in the effects of the plans on the individuals in the treated households, which we call the "treatment effects" of the plans.

In their regression analysis of the plans, RAND's economists included a dummy variable for each plan, plus explanators such as age, sex, and income. The regressions also included important interactions, such as those between the effects of plans and income or between the effects of plans and a dummy variable indicating whether the individual is a child. Because the households were assigned randomly to the plans, there is no worry about omitted relevant variables—randomization ensures there is no correlation between such explanators and the treatment dummies. Including relevant measured traits does decrease the residual's variance, though, and therefore provides more efficient estimates of the treatment effects. Including interactions between the plans' effects and income or between the plans' effects and a dummy variable indicating whether the individual is a child is particularly important; policy makers need to know whether a particular plan is especially effective for low-income families or families with children.

The simple differences in means between plans would not efficiently use the information in the experimental sample—nor, in fact, would the straightforward regression of expenditures on the explanators just described. When the Gauss–Markov Assumptions apply, OLS is the best (most efficient) linear unbiased estimator. When the disturbances are also normally distributed, OLS is the best unbiased estimator.

But when the disturbances are not normally distributed, OLS may be inferior to some nonlinear estimation strategies. This is the case in the NHIE.

The RAND analysts noted three features of the experimental data on medical expenditures that suggest the need for a more sophisticated empirical strategy. First, many individuals made no use of their insurance—their expenditure was zero. Having many observations with the same value for the dependent variable, in this case a common value of zero, sharply departs from the assumption of normally distributed disturbances. Second, among those individuals with some expenditures, expenditures were highly skewed. The normal distribution is symmetric, not skewed. Third, the distribution of medical expenses was very different for individuals who used only outpatient services (patients not admitted for a hospital stay) than it was for those who used some inpatient services (patients admitted for a hospital stay). A mixture of distributions, with some observations following one distribution and others following another distribution, is apt to undermine the finite sample normality of linear estimators.

To account for the three major traits of the medical expenditure data, the RAND analysts used a four-equation model. The first equation is a probit model of the individual's choice to use medical care or not. This equation captures the reality that many individuals given insurance used no medical services during the year. Maximum likelihood estimation of such a model is efficient. The second equation is another probit model, this time estimating the conditional probability of having at least some inpatient expenditures, given that the individual has nonzero medical expenditures. This equation allows separate analyses of the expenditures of those who only use outpatient services and the expenditures of those who use some inpatient services. Again, maximum likelihood is efficient for this probit. The third and fourth equations explain the log of medical expenditures for those who use only outpatient services and the log of medical expenditures for those who have some inpatient expenditures. The use of logs accounts for the skewed distributions of these expenditures. The log of expenditures for each group indicates much more nearly normal disturbances than for both sets of expenditures taken together or for either measured in level rather than log. (Furthermore, by first estimating the probits, the analysts free themselves to take logs of medical expenditures because the regressions apply only to the individuals with nonzero expenditures.) The four-equation model provides consistent estimates of the treatment effects of the various plans, but with much smaller mean square errors than would a single expenditure equation estimated by OLS.

The NHIE provides panel data on household members' expenditures over several years. Random individual effects make the observations over time for each individual correlated with one another. Individuals in the same family are also likely to share a common random family effect that is fixed across family members and over time. The RAND analysts calculated robust standard error estimates that account for these clusterings of observations.

It is the estimates from this four-equation model that lead to the conclusion that modest cost sharing, with caps on maximum out-of-pocket expenditures, would appreciably reduce medical expenditures. It is a companion study of medical outcomes for experimental households[4] that further concludes that the reductions in expenditure are not accompanied by inferior health outcomes.

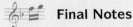 **Final Notes**

The RAND analysis illustrates how limited dependent variable models are frequently blended with ordinary regressions in important policy analyses. Economic decisions frequently have the character that households or firms first choose whether to spend money on an item at all and then decide how much to spend if they are going to spend anything. Most people do not buy a house, a car, or major appliances every year. Data on household expenditures on these goods include many zeros. Models that first estimate a probability of expenditure and then estimate an expected level of expenditure, given nonzero expenditure, estimate the structure of demand for such goods more efficiently than do linear regression models.

Relative to social science research, randomized social experiments are very costly undertakings (although relative to many biological or physical science research projects such as the human genome project, they are not). Using the data collected in such experiments as efficiently as possible is important, and more efficient estimators give policy makers more information from these costly experiments. In the case of the RAND study, the four-part model led to estimates that were markedly more reliable than least squares estimates would have been, especially for the smaller samples of data that were available as the experiment was in progress. The added reliability meant insurance companies, their customers, and government were more apt to reap the benefits of lowered health care costs without worsened health outcomes from those policies that the experiment uncovered.

∎

lation of observations as we come from the far left than is the case for the standard normal distribution, and then a slower convergence toward one as we move toward the far right. *Empirically, it is usually difficult to distinguish between the probit and logit models.* In practice, one specification or the other sometimes fits better into a given theoretical framework, and economists then choose between the probit and logit on that basis. At other times, the choice of a probit or a logit specification is arbitrary and usually unimportant.

In particular, the probit and logit models usually provide similar estimates of how a one-unit change in an explanator would affect the probability of interest. The derivatives from the linear probability model also usually differ only a little from these probit and logit estimates when we evaluate the probit and logit estimates near the mean X-values.

## 19.3    Truncated and Censored Samples

WHAT IS THE DGP?

Groucho Marx often quipped, "I refuse to join any club that would have me as a member." Unfortunately, econometricians sometimes encounter this attitude among the data they seek—some observations just won't appear in our data, even though they do so in a population of interest. For example, suppose we wish to study the determinants of income in the United States, but have available to us only a simple random sample of U.S. welfare recipients. U.S. welfare rules limit participation to families with incomes below legally mandated levels. All samples of welfare-eligible families exclude families with incomes above these levels. People with incomes above the mandated level never appear in samples of welfare recipients. How are we to estimate the expected value of the dependent variable in the population when our samples systematically exclude particularly large or small observations on the dependent variable, as in the case of samples of welfare recipients' incomes? This section addresses this question.

The 19th-century English anthologist Francis Turner reported that "love to his soul gave eyes; he knew things are not as they seem."[5] Econometricians sometimes encounter this attitude, too, among the data they seek—some observations look different than they really are. In particular, observations sometimes refuse to say just how big or small they are. For example, suppose we wish to study the demand for tickets to New York Yankees baseball games, where the number of tickets sold is a function of price. For most games, the stadium is not full, and the number of tickets sold truly tells us how many people wanted to buy tickets. But some games are sold out, and we know only that at least 57,478 (the stadium's capacity) people wanted tickets—the number of tickets people actually wanted is masked. How are we to estimate the expected value of the dependent variable in the population when observations on the dependent variable larger (or smaller) than some particular number appear only as that number, as in the case of samples of Yankees baseball game ticket sales?

Some data-generating processes (DGPs) exclude all observations for which the observed value of the dependent variable is larger than some specific value $a$, or smaller than some other specific value $b$ (or both). We call such samples **truncated samples.** Samples of welfare recipients are truncated when the dependent variable is income; no individuals with incomes above the mandated welfare-eligibility level $b$ are sampled.

Other DGPs include all the observations that would appear in the data if we were drawing a simple random sample but exclude the actual value of the dependent variable if that value is above a specific value $a$ (or below a specific value $b$), replacing the actual dependent variable value with $a$ or $b$, as the case may be. We call such samples **censored samples.** Samples of Yankees baseball games are a censored sample when the dependent variable is tickets demanded; we would have observations in which the number of tickets demanded is greater than $b$, 57,478. Truncated and censored samples both make OLS an inconsistent estimator of a regression equation's slopes and intercept.

Truncated samples differ from censored samples in that truncated ones omit observations altogether if the dependent variable lies outside the allowed range, whereas censored ones include such observations. In a censored sample, if the dependent variable lies outside the allowed range for a given observation, that censored observation contains the boundary value for the dependent variable instead of the actual value, but it contains complete information about the independent variables. This section introduces estimators of the slope and intercepts of a straight line that are consistent estimators when samples are truncated or censored.

## Estimation with a Truncated Sample

A strategy for estimating a regression equation with a truncated sample comes into view when we look at an example of what the DGP *can't* be. Consider the example of estimating the determinants of income from a sample of welfare-eligible households. For simplicity, consider households who all face the same income cut-off for welfare eligibility, $Y^c$. The DGP can't be

$$Y_i = \beta_0 + \beta_1 X_i + \varepsilon_i,$$

with

$$\varepsilon_i \sim N(0, \sigma^2).$$

For each X-value, some realized values from the normal distribution make a family's income exceed the limits mandated by law. For example, families with the X-values illustrated in Figure 19.4 who have shocks to their incomes (that is, disturbances) that leave them at or below the welfare cutoff are eligible for welfare; other families with the same X-values, but more fortunate random shocks to their income, are not. The right-hand tail of the distributions in the figure are not

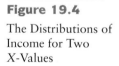

**Figure 19.4**

The Distributions of Income for Two X-Values

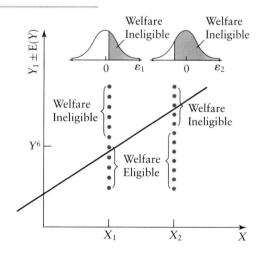

descriptive of the truncated sample DGP—the families in the right-hand tail do not appear in any sample of welfare-eligible households. Only when

$$\varepsilon_i < Y^c - \beta_0 - \beta_1 X_i$$

does a household appear in the sample. Because the truncated sample excludes observations with disturbances larger than or equal to $Y^c - \beta_0 - \beta_1 X_i$, the expected value of the disturbances is not zero across samples. This makes OLS an inconsistent estimator of $\beta_0$ and $\beta_1$.

Figure 19.4 also suggests an alternative specification for regression models observed in truncated samples. The alternative specification assumes the underlying disturbances, the $\varepsilon_i$, are normally distributed. If the shocks to income in the population of all families who face income eligibility cutoff $Y^c$ are normally distributed, then the shaded areas in the figure show the shapes of shocks to income for welfare-eligible families for the two illustrative values of X. These distributions are normal ones, with some portion of their right-hand tail cut off. We call these **truncated normal distributions**.

The shaded areas in the Figure 19.4 have areas less than one because some households are not welfare eligible. To use the shapes in Figure 19.4 to represent probability densities for the welfare-eligible subpopulation, that is, for our truncated sample, the area under the probability density curve must equal one. Consequently, to arrive at the truncated normal probability density function, we must divide the densities for incomes up to $Y^c$ in Figure 19.4 by the shaded area for the corresponding X-value. That shaded area is the $\Pr(\varepsilon_i < Y^c - \beta_0 - \beta_1 X_i)$, which, for a standard normal, equals

$$\Pr\left(\frac{\varepsilon_i}{\sigma} < \frac{Y^c - \beta_0 - \beta_1 X_i}{\sigma}\right) = F\left(\frac{Y^c - \beta_0 - \beta_1 X_i}{\sigma}\right),$$

where F(.) is the cumulative distribution function for the standard normal.

The density for a random variable $Y_i$ that is distributed $N(\beta_0 + \beta_1 X_i, \sigma^2)$ is

$$\frac{1}{\sqrt{2\pi\sigma^2}} e^{-\frac{1}{2}\left(\frac{Y_i - \beta_0 - \beta_1 X_i}{\sigma}\right)^2} = \frac{1}{\sqrt{2\pi\sigma^2}} e^{-\frac{1}{2}(Z_i)^2},$$

where $Z$ has a mean of zero and variance of 1. This density is related to the density for the standard normal, which is

$$f(Z_i) = \frac{1}{\sqrt{2\pi}} e^{-\frac{1}{2}Z_i^2}.$$

We can therefore rewrite the density for $Y_i$ as

$$\frac{1}{\sigma}f(Z_i) = \frac{1}{\sigma}f\left(\frac{Y_i - \beta_0 - \beta_1}{\sigma}\right).$$

In this case, the probability density function for income in our truncated sample, $g(Y)$, is

$$g(Y_i \mid Y_i < Y^c) = \frac{\dfrac{1}{\sigma}f\left(\dfrac{Y_i - \beta_0 - \beta_1 X_i}{\sigma}\right)}{F\left(\dfrac{Y^c - \beta_0 - \beta_1 X_i}{\sigma}\right)}, \qquad 19.9$$

in which $f(.)$ and $F(.)$ are the standard normal density and distribution functions, respectively.

Because their right-hand tails are missing, these truncated distributions have means less than $\beta_0 + \beta_1 X_i$, the means conditional on $X_i$ for the entire population. The truncated distributions also have a smaller variance than the normal distribution from which they are cut. The shape of distribution, and the corresponding means and variances, depends on $X$ because $X$ affects what shocks to income make a family income-ineligible for welfare. Statisticians have determined that the mean of the truncated income is

$$E(Y_i \mid Y_i < Y^c) = \beta_0 + \beta_1 X_i - \sigma\frac{f\left(\dfrac{Y^c - \beta_0 - \beta_1 X_i}{\sigma}\right)}{F\left(\dfrac{Y^c - \beta_0 - \beta_1 X_i}{\sigma}\right)}$$

$$= \beta_0 + \beta_1 X_i + \sigma\lambda_i, \qquad 19.10$$

in which

$$\lambda_i = -\frac{f\left(\dfrac{Y^c - \beta_0 - \beta_1 X_i}{\sigma}\right)}{F\left(\dfrac{Y^c - \beta_0 - \beta_1 X_i}{\sigma}\right)}.$$

Recall that in the truncated sample, $Y_i$ is always less than $Y^c$.

When the sample omits observations for which $Y_i < Y^c$, so that the left-hand tail is omitted, it is the density function over the unshaded area that tells us the shape of the truncated observations' density functions. For example, a study of the determinants of education based on a sample of U.S. soldiers would have no education levels below 12 years, because only high school graduates can enlist in the U.S. Army. In this case, the probability density function for education in our truncated sample is

$$f(Y_i | Y_i < Y^c) = \frac{\frac{1}{\sigma} f\left(\frac{Y_i - \beta_0 - \beta_1 X_i}{\sigma}\right)}{\left[1 - F\left(\frac{Y^c - \beta_0 - \beta_1 X_i}{\sigma}\right)\right]}, \qquad 19.11$$

in which now $Y^c = 12$. In this same case, the formula for the mean of the distribution of Equation 19.11 is

$$E(Y_i | Y_i > Y^c) = \beta_0 + \beta_1 X_i + \sigma \lambda_i, \qquad 19.12$$

in which now

$$\lambda_i = \frac{f\left(\frac{Y^c - \beta_0 - \beta_1 X_i}{\sigma}\right)}{\left[1 - F\left(\frac{Y^c - \beta_0 - \beta_1 X_i}{\sigma}\right)\right]}.$$

Equations 19.10 and 19.12 reveal that OLS applied to

$$Y_i = \beta_0 + \beta_1 X_i + \varepsilon_i \qquad 19.13$$

suffers from omitted variable bias if we use a truncated sample—it omits $\sigma \lambda_i$. How, then, can we consistently estimate $\beta_0$ and $\beta_1$?

Because $\lambda_i$ depends on the unknown slope and intercept parameters and $\sigma$ is unknown, we cannot simply add either as an additional explanator in a linear regression and use OLS to estimate $\beta_0$ and $\beta_1$. We can use the density functions in Equations 19.9 and 19.11 to form the likelihood function for the truncated sample, though, and consistently estimate $\beta_0$ and $\beta_1$ with MLE.

Notice that the coefficient on $X$ in Equation 19.13 is the marginal effect of $X$ on income or education in the population of all families who face the income-eligibility cutoff $Y^c$, whether or not they are welfare-eligible. In contrast, the marginal effect on the mean income of those who are welfare-eligible is the slope on $X$ plus the effect of a change in $X$ as it operates through $\lambda$ in Equation 19.10 or Equation 19.12, that is, plus the effect of a change in $X$ as it affects the probability that an individual is welfare-eligible or in the military.

As always, MLE requires that we know the distribution of the disturbance terms in our DGP. That the truncated normal distribution accurately reflects the true DGP is a common, but strong assumption.

## Estimation with a Censored Sample

How are we to estimate the expected value of a dependent variable when faced with a censored sample? OLS inconsistently estimates $\beta_0$ and $\beta_1$ when the samples are censored, just as when samples are truncated, but censored samples contain more information than truncated ones, and efficient estimation requires that we incorporate the additional information into our estimation procedure.

What is the character of the added information in a censored sample? In the example of the demand for Yankees tickets, we observe the price of tickets ($X$) and the number of tickets demanded ($Y$) for games in which the stadium is not full, as in a truncated sample. The distribution of tickets demanded at various prices for demands below capacity are truncated distributions, just as in Figure 19.4. The cutoff, $Y^c$, is now 57,478, the seating capacity of Yankee Stadium. However, unlike the case of the truncated sample of welfare-eligible families, in a censored sample we observe the explanator values for cases in which $Y_i > Y^c$ and we know the stadium is full on those days. What we don't know is how many more tickets than 57,478 people want to buy for sold-out games.

Because we do not have complete information on ticket demand, we cannot estimate the demand for Yankees tickets by applying OLS to

$$Y_i = \beta_0 + \beta_1 X_i + \varepsilon_i.$$

As in the case of truncated samples, the mean value of the disturbances is not zero when the sample is censored.

In 1958, economist James Tobin of Yale University proposed a consistent estimator for censored sample regressions. He assumed that the underlying distribution for the disturbances is the normal, in which case,

$$\varepsilon_i \sim N(0, \ \sigma^2),$$

which implies that a probit model describes the probability that any one observation is censored.[6] Given normal disturbances, the probability that the stadium is sold out is

$$\Pr(sold\ out) = \Pr(\varepsilon_i \geq 57{,}478 - \beta_0 - \beta_1 X_i)$$

$$= 1 - F\left(\frac{1}{\sigma}(57{,}478 - \beta_0 - \beta_1 X_i)\right)$$

$$= 1 - F(Z_i),$$

in which $Z_i = \frac{1}{\sigma}(57{,}478 - \beta_0 - \beta_1 X_i)$. If the first $n_1$ of $n$ observations is sold-out games, and the rest are games not sold out, then the likelihood function for Tobin's model is

$$L = \prod_{i=1}^{n_1}(1 - F(Z_i)) \prod_{i=n_1+1}^{n} f(\tfrac{1}{\sigma}(Y_i - \beta_0 - \beta_1 X_i)).$$

# An Econometric Top 40—A Classical Favorite

## Women's Wages and Women's Choice to Work

What wage offers await women in the labor market? We have seen so many applications of wage equations in previous chapters that we are perhaps conditioned to look to wage equation estimates to answer this question. But women's wages pose a particular puzzle. Many women do not work in the marketplace. What wage opportunities do they forgo to remain outside the paid workforce? Are the wages of women who do work in the marketplace indicative of the wages forgone by women who do not? Differences between the wage opportunities of women who work for pay and women who don't could markedly affect the observed wage because many women are not in the paid workforce.

In 1974, Nobel laureate James Heckman of the University of Chicago tackled the question of women's wages in a classic paper.[7] Heckman showed that even if the women who work differ systematically from women who don't, we can consistently estimate the average wage faced by all women based only on the wages of working women. The key, Heckman showed, is to model and estimate women's decision to work or not work, and to exploit that information when estimating women's wage equation. Heckman's approach applies, sometimes with sophisticated adaptation, to a broad class of instances in which samples are tainted by self-selection.

### Heckman's Model

Heckman's model begins with two equations. The first equation indicates a woman's reservation wage, $W_i^R$,

$$W_i^R = \alpha_0 + \alpha_1 H_i + \alpha_2 M_i + \varepsilon_i^s.$$

A woman's reservation wage is the minimum wage she would accept to work $H$ hours for pay, given the woman's exogenous traits, $M_i$, such as marital status. The second equation indicates the market wage for women with exogenous productive characteristics $X$, such as education or work experience:

$$W_i^M = \beta_0 + \beta_1 X_i + \varepsilon_i^d.$$

Together, these supply and demand equations determine the market wage and the number of hours worked for each woman. Heckman assumed that hours of work always adjust in the marketplace to produce an equilibrium wage, so $W_i^R = W_i^M = W$. The exogenous factors, $M$ and $X$, need not be different; for example, education might influence both a woman's reservation wage and her worth to a firm.

Heckman assumed that $\varepsilon_i^s$ and $\varepsilon_i^d$ individually satisfy the Gauss–Markov conditions, are jointly normally distributed, have variances $\sigma_s^2$ and $\sigma_d^2$, and have only a contemporaneous correlation with one another, reflected in $\text{cov}(\varepsilon_i^s, \varepsilon_i^d) = \sigma_{sd}$. To simplify the analysis, Heckman assumed that the demand for women's work is perfectly elastic; the wage offered does not depend on hours worked.

The central difficulty for analyzing the supply and demand for labor is that we do not observe wages for the women who are not in the labor market. The reduced form equation for hours worked for pay is

$$H = \frac{(\beta_0 + \beta_1 X_i - \alpha_0 - \alpha_2 M_i)}{\alpha_1} + \frac{(\varepsilon_i^d - \varepsilon_i^s)}{\alpha_1}.$$

Women with $H > 0$ will be in the labor force; all other women will be out of the labor force. We only observe the wages of those women who work. One group of women who will tend not to work are those who receive well below their expected wage offers, that is, women for whom $\varepsilon_i^d$ is much less than zero. Average observed wages will tend to be above-average offered wages, as the worst wage offers are not accepted.

Were it not for the self-selection of women into the labor force, we could estimate the demand for labor by OLS, since there are no endogenous variables on its right-hand side. If women were omitted from the labor market purely randomly, OLS would still be appropriate. Women in the market and women out of the market would have the same distribution of $\varepsilon_i^d$ and $\varepsilon_i^s$. But women's participation in the labor market is systematic, not purely random, and consequently, OLS will yield biased estimates of the demand equation.

Women like receiving better wage offers, so they prefer positive values for $\varepsilon_i^d$. Indeed, $\varepsilon_i^d$ has to make a woman's wage opportunity bigger than her reservation wage, or she will not work. Consequently, the distribution of $\varepsilon_i^d$ among working women will differ from that of women not working: Women not in the labor force will tend to be those who get unfavorable $\varepsilon_i^d$ values, and women in the workforce will tend to be those who get favorable $\varepsilon_i^d$ values. For women with a given education ($X$-value), those who work will have above-average values of $\varepsilon_i^d$ and those not in the workforce will have below average values of $\varepsilon_i^d$. Consequently, $\mathrm{E}(\varepsilon_i^d | a \, women \, works) > 0$, upending unbiased estimation of $\beta_0$ by OLS.

Moreover, how much $\mathrm{E}(\varepsilon_i^d | a \, women \, works)$ exceeds zero will vary with $X$, upending unbiased estimation of $\beta_1$ by OLS. Consider two women with the same reservation wage, but very different skill levels, one being highly skilled, the other having low skills. Further suppose both women would work if paid the expected wage for an average-skilled worker.

The woman with high skill levels would leave the labor force only in rare cases in which she receives a wage offer far from the expectation for her skill level ($\varepsilon_i^d \ll 0$). The woman with low skill is also driven from the market if she receives so very low an $\varepsilon_i^d$, but since her expected wage is below that of an average-skilled worker, it takes a *positive* shock ($\varepsilon_i^d > 0$) to draw her into the labor force. Thus, for high-skill (high-$X$) women, fewer of the lower $\varepsilon_i^d$ values are swept from the analysts' view than is the case among low-skill (low-$X$) women. Thus, $\mathrm{E}(\varepsilon_i^d | a \, women \, works)$ is not only less than zero, but it varies systematically with $X$.

## Heckman's Two-Step Estimator

Heckman's article shows precisely how $\mathrm{E}(\varepsilon_i^d | a \, women \, works)$ varies with $X$ if the disturbances in the model are normally distributed. This knowledge permits us to correct the selection bias in OLS. Key to determining $\mathrm{E}(\varepsilon_i^d | a \, women \, works) = \mathrm{E}(\varepsilon_i^d | H_i > 0)$ is the probability that a woman is out of the labor market, given her values of $M$ and $X$. Thus, central to Heckman's solution is observing $M$ and $X$ for the nonworking women. Many data sets contain data for both working and nonworking women, so Heckman's approach is quite feasible.

Because Heckman assumes the disturbances in his model are normal, a probit model yields the probability that a woman does not work. If $H_i \le 0$,

$$\left[ \frac{(\varepsilon_i^d - \varepsilon_i^s)}{\alpha_1} \right] \le$$
$$-\left[ \frac{(\beta_0 + \beta_1 X_i - \alpha_0 - \alpha_2 M_i)}{\alpha_1} \right],$$

or, since $\alpha_1$ will be positive in a supply equation,

$$(\varepsilon_i^d - \varepsilon_i^s) \le -(\beta_0 + \beta_1 X_i - \alpha_0 - \alpha_2 M_i).$$

Next, let's define the variance of $(\varepsilon_i^d - \varepsilon_i^s)$, which equals $(\sigma_s^2 + \sigma_d^2 - 2\sigma_{sd})$, to be $\sigma^2$. Because $(\varepsilon_i^d - \varepsilon_i^s) \sim N(0, \sigma^2)$,

$$(\varepsilon_i^d - \varepsilon_i^s)/\sigma \sim N(0,1).$$

Thus, we can use the standard normal cumulative distribution function, $F(.)$, to express the probability that a woman is out of the labor market as

$$\text{Prob}(H \leq 0) =$$
$$F\left(\frac{-(\beta_0 + \beta_1 X_i - \alpha_0 - \alpha_2 M_i)}{\sigma}\right).$$

For expositional convenience, we define $z_i = \dfrac{[-(\beta_0 + \beta_1 X_i - \alpha_0 - \alpha_2 M_i)]}{\sigma}$. Notice this relationship amounts to a probit model in which not working is the binary variable of interest. Estimating this probit model is the first step in Heckman's two-step procedure for estimating a wage equation for women.

Heckman showed that the variable $z$ that is critical to determining the probability that a woman does not work is also closely related to $E(\varepsilon_i^d | H_i > 0)$. We do not observe the $z_i$, but we can estimate them, using the fitted values from a probit model of women not working. Heckman showed that for women who work, we can write

$$W_i^M = \beta_0 + \beta_1 X_i + \gamma \frac{f(z_i)}{[1 - F(z)_i]} + \mu_i^d$$

H19.1

where $f(.)$ is the normal probability density function and $F(.)$ is the normal cumulative distribution function. In Equation H19.1, $E(\mu_i^d | H_i > 0) = 0$. The term involving $f(z_i)$ and $F(z_i)$ in Equation 19.1 accounts for how restricting the sample to women working for pay changes the expected value of the disturbance. The OLS estimator would be a consistent estimator of Equation H19.1 if we observe

the $z_i$. Unfortunately, we do not usually observe the $z_i$. However, Heckman showed that OLS is also a consistent estimator of Equation H19.1 if we replace the unobserved $z_i$ values with the fitted $z_i$ values from a probit model of women not working; this is the second step in Heckman's procedure. With today's better computers, Heckman's model is now usually estimated using maximum likelihood estimation (MLE).

## An Example of Heckman's Method

Heckman applied his model to a sample of 2,100 women who appeared in the 1967 National Longitudinal Survey. Hit Table 19.1 contains the maximum likelihood estimates of a wage function for women using Heckman's procedure. The table reports standard wage equation estimates for the same sample of women estimated by full information maximum likelihood applied to the supply of labor and demand for labor equations simultaneously, but with no accounting for selection bias.

### HIT TABLE 19.1 A Model of Women's Wages with Selection Correction

Dependent Variable: Log of offered wage

| Explanator | Coeff. | Std. Err. |
|---|---|---|
| Education | 0.0761 | 0.0075 |
| Experience | 0.0480 | 0.004 |
| Constant | −9.82 | 0.11 |

**With No Selection Correction**
Dependent Variable: Log of offered wage

| Explanator | Coeff. | Std. Err. |
|---|---|---|
| Education | 0.0681 | 0.007 |
| Experience | 0.0195 | 0.0025 |
| Constant | −0.36 | 0.086 |

Correcting for selection bias obtains a higher estimate of the effect of education on the wages offered women, just as Heckman's analysis leads us to expect, but the magnitude of the difference is not great in absolute size or relative to the estimated standard errors.

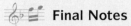

## Final Notes

Econometricians must frequently cope with samples that are not random. Heckman's work showed that careful attention to the behavior of individuals could sometimes allow econome-tricians to overcome the limits of nonrandom samples. Since Heckman wrote, models with endogenous limited dependent variables have grown in variety and complexity. In 2000, Heckman received the Nobel prize in econom-ics "for his development of theory and methods for analyzing selective samples."

∎

We can consistently estimate Tobin's model with MLE. Econometricians call censored sample DGPs with normal disturbances the **Tobit model**.

Notice that the coefficient on $X$, $\beta_1$, is the marginal effect of $X$ on $E(Y|X)$ in the population. For example, if $X$ is the price of a ticket, the coefficient tells us what happens to the number of tickets demanded if the price is lowered by one dollar. This may or may not be what we want to know. Tickets demanded, $Y_i$, are not always tickets sold, $Y_i^*$—the excess demand for sold-out games does not translate into ticket sales. Equation 19.10 gives the expected number of tickets sold across days when the game is not sold out, conditional on $X$. The expected number of tickets sold, $Y_i^*$, includes the effect of tickets sold on days when the game is sold out:

$$E(Y_i^* | X_i) = F(Z_i)(\beta_0 + \beta_1 X_i + \sigma\lambda) + (1 - F(Z_i))57{,}478.$$

The derivative of the expected number of tickets sold with respect to $X$ is

$$\frac{d E(Y_i^* | X_i)}{dX} = \beta_1 F(Z_i), \qquad\qquad \textbf{19.14}$$

a result that is not easy to prove.

Each time we estimate a censored regression model, we must carefully con-sider what the model's coefficients mean in the context of our problem and what derivatives are of interest to us. The Yankee Stadium example illustrates these concerns. For short-term planning, when the stadium's capacity is fixed, the effect of ticket price on tickets sold from Equation 19.14 may be more relevant than the effect on tickets demanded. For long-term planning, when the stadium might be altered to increase capacity, the effect of prices on tickets demanded becomes more relevant than Equation 19.14.

As always, MLE requires that we know the distribution of the disturbances terms in our DGP. Assuming that the normal distribution accurately reflects the true DGP for a censored sample is a common but strong assumption.

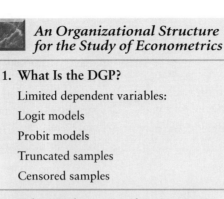

## Summary

This chapter treats the estimation of models in which the dependent variable takes a limited range of values. When the dependent variable takes on only the values zero and one, the expected value of the dependent variable can be interpreted as a probability.

The chapter begins with the linear probability model, in which the dependent variable of an ordinary linear regression is a variable restricted to the range zero to one. Because the linear probability model can yield nonsense results, the chapter next introduces two models that successfully restrict predicted probabilities to the zero–one range, the probit and logit models of binary outcomes.

Probit and logit models prove useful when estimating models in which some observations are excluded or altered when the dependent variable exceeds a specific value or falls short of another specific value. We call samples in which observations are excluded in this way truncated or those that are altered in this way censored. The chapter shows that OLS inconsistently estimates ordinary regression models when the data are from truncated or censored samples. The chapter then explains how we can use MLE to consistently estimate ordinary regression models with data from truncated and censored samples.

## Concepts for Review

| | |
|---|---|
| Binary logit model 824 | Logit model 824 |
| Binary probit model 820 | Probit model 820 |
| Censored samples 830 | Tobit model 839 |
| Latent variable 819 | Truncated normal distributions 832 |
| Linear probability model 813 | Truncated samples 830 |
| Logistic distribution 823 | |

## Questions for Discussion

1. "Saying the expected value of an employment dummy variable equals, say, 0.75 makes no sense. A worker is employed, or not. A patient dies, or doesn't. Saying 'on average the patient is 75% dead' makes no sense at all." Discuss.

2. Some sporting events can end in a tie. Suppose wins are recorded as ones, losses as zeros, and ties as one-half. Would a linear model that expressed this variable as a linear function of variables like the point spread be a linear probability model? How would you treat observations of one-half if you were looking to estimate the probability of winning? The probability of losing?

3. Can you think of simultaneous equations systems in which a limited dependent variable appears as an explanator in some equations and also as a dependent variable in its own equation?

## Problems for Analysis

For the data sets that you will need to solve the problems in this section, go to **www.aw-bc.com/murray.**

1. Use a probit model and the data in football.*** to estimate the probability of an NFL team winning at home when the spread is at its mean of 5.88 against them. How much does the probit model predict that the probability would change, were the spread to change from 5.88 to 6.88? What is the estimated probability of winning when the spread is 20, based on the probit model? How do these results compare with the logit results in the chapter?

2. How likely is an individual with $1,000 in assets to hold interest-bearing assets, if he or she has no retirement accounts? Use a logit model and the data in financials.*** to form your estimate of the probability. How much does the probability change if the individual has a pension? How do these results compare with the probit results in the chapter?

3. Sports betting has been going on as long as there have been sports. The file pntsprd.*** contains data, compiled by Hal Stern, for the 1989, 1990, and 1991 National Football League seasons. The variables in the file are the following:

| | |
|---|---|
| *favrite* | points scored by favored team |
| *fbeatspr* | = 1 if favored team beat the spread (underdog + spread < favrite); = 0 otherwise |
| *fwins* | = 1 if favored team wins; = 0 otherwise |
| *home* | = 1 if the favored team is the home team; = 0 otherwise |
| *spread* | The bookies' spread for the game |
| *underdog* | Points scored by the underdog team |
| *ubeatspr* | = 1 if underdog beat the spread (underdog + spread > favrite); = 0 otherwise |
| *wash* | = 1 if neither team beats the spread (underdog + spread = favrite); = 0 otherwise |
| *year* | Year of season |
| *yr89* | = 1 if season year is 1989; = 0 otherwise |
| *yr90* | = 1 if season year is 1990; = 0 otherwise |

a. Use a linear probability model to estimate the probability of a favored team winning if at home when the spread is at its mean of 5.31. Include *home* and dummies for the year of the season in the model, as well as *spread*.

b. How much does the linear probability model in (a) predict the probability of a favored team winning if at home in 1991 would change were the spread to change from 5.31 to 6.31?

c. Re-estimate the relationship in (a) using a logit model. What is the estimated probability of a favored team winning if at home in 1991 when the spread is at its mean of 5.31?

d. How much does the logit model in (c) predict the probability of a favored team winning if at home in 1991 would change were the spread to change from 5.31 to 6.31?

e. Re-estimate the relationship in (a) using a probit model. What is the estimated probability of a favored team winning if at home in 1991 when the spread is at its mean of 5.31?

f. How much does the probit model in (e) predict the probability of a favored team winning if at home in 1991 would change were the spread to change from 5.31 to 6.31?

g. What is the estimated probability of a favored home team winning in 1990 when the spread is 10, based on the linear probability, logit, and probit models in (a), (c), and (e)?

h. Do *spread*, *home*, or the year dummies, individually or collectively, enable one to predict successfully whether the favored team or the underdog will beat the spread in a game? Try all three models.

4. Most people in China do not belong to the ruling Communist Party. A sample of citizens in six Chinese cities gathered by Fang Cai, Margaret Maurer-Fazio, Xin Meng, and Hansheng Wang with funding from the Ford Foundation affords us a glimpse of

who the party members are.[8] The file partymember.*** contains data for a random sample of 1,021 working-age adults from the cities of Beijing, Chungchang, Nanjing, Tianjing, Wuhan, and Xian. The variables in the file are the following:

Beijing        = 1 if the individual lives in Beijing; = 0 otherwise
Chungchang   = 1 if the individual lives in Chungchang; = 0 otherwise
Nanjing       = 1 if the individual lives in Nanjing; = 0 otherwise
Tianjing      = 1 if the individual lives in Tianjing; = 0 otherwise
Wuhan         = 1 if the individual lives in Wuhan; = 0 otherwise
Xian          = 1 if the individual lives in Xian; = 0 otherwise
pmember       = 1 if the individual is a communist party member; = 0 otherwise
Female        = 1 if the individual is female; = 0 otherwise
yrs_edu       Individual's years of education
edu_mother    Years of education of individual's mother
edu_father    Years of education of individual's father

a. Estimate linear probability, probit, and logit models of the probability that an individual is a party member. Include all of the available variables, but omit Tianjing to avoid perfect multicollinearity.

b. How should we interpret the coefficients on the city dummy variables in the linear probability model in (a)?

c. Speculate why mothers' educations are more important than fathers' educations for whether individuals are party members. Is this what we observe in the data?

d. Are the relative magnitudes of the estimated coefficients on mother's education and own occupation sensible? Briefly explain.

e. For a male in Tianjing with the mean number of years of education and whose father and mother both have 5 years of education, what would be the estimated effect of 4 more years of education for the individual on the probability that the individual is a party member? Report estimates from each of the three models.

f. What would be the estimates in (e) if the city were Beijing instead of Tianjing?

 5. Who chooses to attend college? The data in college2.*** are a sample of 1,341 high school graduates from the High School and Beyond Survey, which reported on college attendance in October 1980 following high school graduation the June before. The variables in the file are the following:

college     Attends college from high school
female      Dummy for female
test        Test score
urban       Dummy for urban HS
suburban    Dummy for suburban HS
income      Family income in 2005 dollars
gpa         High school GPA

a. Estimate linear probability, probit, and logit models of the probability that a high school graduate attends college. Include all of the available variables; attendance at a rural high school is the omitted category that avoids perfect multicollinearity.

b. For males graduating from an urban high school with a GPA of 3.0 and a test score of 65, what is the difference in estimated college attendance rate between individuals with a family income of $25,000 and individuals with a family income of $35,000? Provide estimates for the three models in (a).

c. Are the college attendance rates for graduates of urban and suburban high schools with other traits in common statistically significantly different from one another in the logit model estimated in (a)?

 6. States vary widely in the benefits that their temporary assistance for needy families (TANF) programs offer low-income single parents. Does a state's generosity influence women's decisions to migrate from one state to another? One way to ask whether the probability that a low-income woman would move out of state depends on the generosity of her state's welfare program. The file dropouts.*** contains a random sample of white high school dropouts with incomes below the median income for their state. These are women who are economically vulnerable and who might need the benefits of the welfare system in the future. In the 2000 census, these women were asked where they lived in 1995. The variables in the file are the following:

| | |
|---|---|
| *age* | The woman's age |
| *age2* | The square of woman's age |
| *childunder5* | Woman has a child under 5 in household |
| *generosity* | Log of the state's maximum TANF benefit to the state's 20th percentile income |
| *married* | = 1 if the woman is married and spouse is present; = 0 otherwise |
| *move* | = 1 if the woman changed states between 1995 and 2000 |
| *neighbunemp* | Average unemployment rate of neighboring states |
| *nchild* | Number of children woman has in household |
| *reallocalinc* | Log of real local median income |
| *northeast* | = 1 if woman lives in Northeast |
| *south* | = 1 if woman lives in South |
| *midwest* | = 1 if woman lives in Midwest |

a. Estimate linear probability, probit, and logit models of the probability that a female low-income high school dropout changed state of residence between 1995 and 2000. Include all of the available variables; living in the West is the omitted category that avoids perfect multicollinearity. What can you infer about mobility from these estimated models?

b. Compare your probit results in (a) with those in the following table that are based on a larger random sample of census respondents than is in dropouts.***:

*Dependent Variable: MOVE*
*Method: ML - Binary Probit (Quadratic hill climbing)*
*Included observations: 42741*
*Convergence achieved after 7 iterations*
*Covariance matrix computed using second derivatives*

| Variable | Coefficient | Std. Error | z-Statistic | Prob. |
|---|---|---|---|---|
| C | 0.271807 | 0.417140 | 0.651596 | 0.5147 |
| AGE | 0.021958 | 0.010843 | 2.024972 | 0.0429 |
| AGE2 | −0.000309 | 0.000156 | −1.979219 | 0.0478 |
| MARRIED | 0.056344 | 0.016114 | 3.496480 | 0.0005 |

| | | | |
|---|---|---|---|
| NCHILD | −0.008964 | 0.006936 | −1.292397 | 0.1962 |
| CHILDUNDER5 | 0.053259 | 0.019208 | 2.772791 | 0.0056 |
| REALLOCALINC | −0.327604 | 0.080860 | −4.051475 | 0.0001 |
| NEIGHBUNEMP | −0.094626 | 0.019177 | −4.934233 | 0.0000 |
| GENEROSITY | −0.040677 | 0.003911 | −10.401111 | 0.0000 |
| NORTHEAST | −0.131205 | 0.027329 | −4.800908 | 0.0000 |
| MIDWEST | −0.103761 | 0.038886 | −2.668324 | 0.0076 |
| SOUTH | −0.038938 | 0.026920 | −1.446431 | 0.1481 |

| | | | |
|---|---|---|---|
| Mean dependent var | 0.130601 | S.D. dependent var | 0.336967 |
| S.E. of regression | 0.335918 | Akaike info criterion | 0.768906 |
| Sum squared resid | 4821.593 | Schwarz criterion | 0.771338 |
| Log likelihood | −16419.91 | Hannan-Quinn criter. | 0.769674 |
| Restr. log likelihood | −16563.28 | Avg. log likelihood | −0.384172 |
| LR statistic (11 df) | 286.7468 | McFadden R-squared | 0.008656 |
| Probability(LR stat) | 0.000000 | | |

Are you able to draw richer inferences from the results in the table? Why? The difference between the results in (a) and those in the table reflects a common truth about limited dependent variable model estimation. What do you think that lesson is? Why do you think it might be so?

c. Offer a brief explanation for the estimated sign of each variable's coefficient in the table, apart from the region dummies and the intercept term.

d. According to the results in the table, at what age does the probability of moving reach its maximum?

7. Does alcohol dependency interfere with people's ability to work? John Mullahy and Jody Sindelar addressed this question using data from the 1988 National Health Interview Survey.[9] Their study examined the employment of U.S. men and women between the ages of 25 and 59, and used several measures of alcohol dependency. This problem examines their employment status (the alternative is to either unemployed or out-of-the-labor-force.) The file alchemploy.*** contains a sub-sample of Mullahy and Sindelar's data: African-American males 30 to 59 years of age. This file is too large for the student version of Eviews. The variables in the file are:

*stalccon*   Per capita alcohol consumption in the person's state.
*stunempl*   Unemployment rate in the individual's state
*momalc*     = 1 if individual's birth mother was an alcoholic;  = 0 otherwise
*dadalc*     = 1 if individual's birth father was an alcoholic; = 0 otherwise
*educ*       Individual's years of education
*beertax*    Tax rate on beer in the individual's state
*married*    = 1 if the individual is married;  = 0 otherwise
*poorhlth*   = 1 if the individual is in poor health;  = 0 otherwise
*employed*   = 1 if the individual is employed; = 0 otherwise
*alcdep*     A measure of alcohol dependency/abuse; = 1 if dependent; = 0 otherwise.

    a. Estimate a linear probability model, a probit model and a logit model in which the dependent variable is the employment indicator and the explanators are the state's unemployment rate, the individual's education, marital status, health status, and the alcohol dependency measure.

    b. Determine for each model the estimated effect of alcohol dependency on the probability of being employed for an individual with average values for the other traits.

8. Who smokes? The data set smoker.*** contains a random sample of 1,196 U.S. males.[10] This file is too large for the student version of EViews. The variables in the file are:

*educ*     education
*age*      age
*income*   family income
*pcigs*79  price of cigarettes in individual's state in 1979
*ageeduc*  the product of age and education
*smoker*   = 1 for smokers; = 0 for non-smokers

    a. Estimate a linear probability model, a probit model and a logit model in which the dependent variable is *smoker* and the explanators are education, age, the price of cigarettes and income.

    b. Determine for each model the estimated effect of one additional year of education on the probability of smoking for an individual with average values for the other traits.

    c. Add to the models the product of age and education. Interpret the estimated coefficient.

    d. Determine for each model the estimated effect of one additional year of education on the probability of smoking for an individual with average values for the other traits.

    e. Repeat (d), but for an individual whose age is 20 years less than the average. How much of the difference between the effect calculated in (d) and the effect calculated here is due to the direct effect of a different age and how much is due to the altered effect of education for a different age?

9. Thomas Mroz of the University of North Carolina applied Heckman's sample selection estimation procedure to a sample of women from the 1975 Panel Survey of Income Dynamics.[11] Mroz's data are in the file mroz.***. The data set contains 753 observations on married white women, aged 30–60. Observations 1–428 are on women with hours of work greater than zero, whereas the final 325 observations are for women who did not work in 1975. There are a total of 22 variables in the data set. Mroz's variables and their names are

*lfp*    = 1 if woman worked in market; = 0 otherwise
*whrs*   Woman's hours of work in 1975
*kl6*    Number of children less than six years old
*k618*   Number of children aged between 6 and 18 years old
*wa*     Wife's age (years)
*we*     Wife's educational attainment (years)
*ww*     Wife's average hourly earnings in 1975 (1975 dollars)

*rpwg*   Wife's wages at time of interview in 1976 (1976 dollars)

*hhrs*   Husband's hours worked in 1975

*ha*     Husband's age (years)

*he*     Husband's educational attainment (years)

*hw*     Husband's wages in 1975 (1975 dollars)

*faminc* Total family income (1975 dollars)

*mtr*    (1 − wife's marginal tax rate) evaluated at zero hours work (percent)

*wmed*   Wife's mother's educational attainment (years)

*wfed*   Wife's father's educational attainment (years)

*un*     Unemployment rate (percent) in county of residence

*cit*    = 1 if family lives in large city; = 0 otherwise

*ax*     Wife's previous labor market experience (years)

*hmed*   Husband's mother's educational attainment (years)

*hfed*   Husband's father's educational attainment (years)

You will also need the property income of the family plus the husband's income, which together theory says a woman will consider in her work decision. This variable is

$$prin = faminc - (whrs0*ww).$$

a. Following Mroz, create the following transformations of variables to use as explanatory variables in the labor force participation equation:

$$ax2 = ax^2$$
$$wa2 = wa^2$$
$$wa3 = wa^3$$
$$We2 = we^2$$
$$we3 = we^3$$
$$wawe = wa \cdot we$$
$$wa2we = wa2 \cdot we$$
$$Wawe2 = wa \cdot we2$$
$$whrs = whrs0.$$

b. Estimate an hours worked equation using Mroz's data and Heckman's technique. Use *lfp* as the probit dependent variable, and a constant, *kl6*, *k618*, *wa*, *we*, *wa2*, *we2*, *wawe*, *wa3*, *we3*, *wa2we*, *wawe2*, *wfed*, *wmed*, *un*, *cit*, and *prin* as the explanatory variables. Use *whrs* as the dependent variable in the hours worked (labor supply) equation with a constant term, *kl6*, *k618*, *wa*, *we*, *wa2*, *we2*, *wawe*, *wa3*, *we3*, *wa2we*, *wawe2*, *wfed*, *wmed*, *un*, *cit*, and *prin* as the dependent variables.

c. Estimate the labor supply equation for the 428 working women *without* correcting for sample selection. Discuss how the results differ from the corrected estimates.

## Endnotes

1. Jack Norworth and Albert Von Tilzer, "Take Me Out to the Ballgame," 1908.
2. Casey B. Mulligan and Xavier Sala-i-Martin, "Extensive Margins and the Demand for Money at Low Interest Rates," *Journal of Political Economy* 108, no. 5 (2000): 961–991.

3. Joseph P. Newhouse and the Insurance Experiment Group, *Free for All? Lessons from the RAND Health Insurance Experiment* (Cambridge: Harvard University Press, 1993); Willard G. Manning, Joseph P. Newhouse, Naihua Duan, Emmet B. Keeler, Arleen Leibowitz, and M. Susan Marquis, "Health Insurance and the Demand for Medical Care: Evidence from a Randomized Experiment," *American Economic Review* 77, no. 3 (June 1987): 251–277.

4. Newhouse and the Insurance Experiment Group, *Free for All? Lessons from the RAND Health Insurance Experiment* (Cambridge: Harvard University Press, 1993); Robert Brook et al., "Does Free Care Improve Adults' Health?" *New England Journal of Medicine* 309 (December 8, 1983): 1426–1434.

5. From "The Dream of Maxim Wledig," either by Francis Turner Palgrave, English poet and critic, 1824–1897, or quoted by him in one of his anthologies of English poetry.

6. James Tobin, "Estimation of Relationships for Limited Dependent Variables," *Econometrica* 26 (1958): 24–36.

7. J. Heckman, "Shadow Prices, Market Wages, and Labor Supply," *Econometrica* 42: 679–694.

8. The Urban Labor Market Integration Project was funded by the Ford Foundation's Beijing Office.

9. John Mullahy and Jody Sindelar, "Employment, Unemployment, and Problem Drinking," *Journal of Health Economics,* 15 (1996): 409–434.

10. These data were used in John Mullahy's "Instrumental-Variables Estimation of Count Data Models: An Application to Models of Cigarette Smoking Behavior," that appeared in *The Review of Economics and Statistics* in 1997.

11. Thomas Mroz, "The Sensitivity of an Empirical Model of Married Women's Hours of Work to Economic and Statistical Assumptions," *Econometrica* (July 1987). These data were used later in Ernst Berndt, *The Practice of Econometrics* (Reading, MA: Addison-Wesley, 1991). Thanks to Ernst Berndt for pointing me to Thomas Mroz to obtain these data for use here.

# Statistical Appendix

# A Review of Probability and Statistics

*There is no more common error than to assume that, because prolonged and accurate mathematical calculations have been made, the application of the result to some fact is absolutely certain.*[1]

—Alfred North Whitehead

This appendix reviews the fundamental notions of probability and statistics that we rely on in econometrics.

## SA.1 Probability

The probability that the steel ball on a roulette wheel will stop at double zero is 1 in 37. The probability of a false-positive result on the most common tuberculosis test is 0.05. The probability of precipitation tomorrow is 25%. The probability that Hillary Clinton will be elected president is less than 1 in 10. Statements about probability are commonplace in everyday life, in science, and in politics. This section distinguishes among simple, joint, and conditional probabilities, and explores the connections among these three concepts. It then discusses both discrete and continuous random variables and their associated probability functions.

### Simple and Joint Probabilities

The next spin of the roulette wheel will put the ball in double zero. It will rain tomorrow. Hillary Clinton will be president. These are all simple propositions, in the sense that they claim a single thing will occur. When we state the probability that such a proposition is correct, we call the probability a **simple probability**.

The next spin of the roulette wheel will bring double zero, and the spin after that will also bring double zero. It will rain tomorrow and the high temperature will be greater than sixty degrees. Hillary Clinton will become president and Bill Clinton will serve in the U.S. Senate. Each of these propositions asserts two things. When we state the probability that such a complex proposition is correct, we call the probability a **joint probability**.

An **event** is something that might happen. In abstract form, consider the events A and B. A could stand for "it rains tomorrow" and B could stand for "the

**Figure SA.1**

Simple and Joint
Probabilities

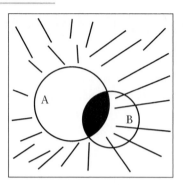

high temperature tomorrow is greater than 60°F." We denote the probability that event A occurs Pr(A) and the probability that event B occurs Pr(B). Pr(A) and Pr(B) are simple probabilities. We denote the probability that *both* A *and* B occur Pr(A and B). Pr(A and B) is a joint probability.

Figure SA.1 illustrates these probabilities graphically. The box in the figure contains all the weather outcomes that are possible tomorrow. The circle marked A represents all the weather outcomes in which there is rain tomorrow. The circle marked B represents all the weather outcomes in which the high temperature tomorrow is greater than 60°F. The box in the figure has an area equal to 1. The area of A is drawn equal to the probability that it rains tomorrow; that is, the area of the circle A is Pr(A). Similarly, the area of the circle B is the probability that the high temperature tomorrow will exceed 60°F, Pr(B).

Figure SA.1 is drawn so that the intersection of the circles A and B, the shaded area in the figure, equals Pr(A and B). The intersection represents all the weather outcomes for tomorrow in which there is rain and the high temperature is greater than 60°F. We call the area covered by both circles together the **intersection** of the events. We call the area covered by one circle or the other, or by both, the **union** of the events "it rains tomorrow" and "the high temperature tomorrow exceeds 60°F," and it represents all the weather outcomes in which it rains tomorrow or the high temperature exceeds 60°F, or in which both occur. We say that the probability of the union is Pr(A or B), with the "or" interpreted to include cases in which both A and B occur. Figures such as SA.1 are called **Venn diagrams**. (Often Venn diagrams are drawn without making the areas exactly match the pertinent probabilities.)

The probability of A or B, Pr(A or B), is linked to the simple and joint probabilities:

$$\text{Pr(A or B)} = \text{Pr(A)} + \text{Pr(B)} - \text{Pr(A and B)}.$$

**Figure SA.2**

More Simple and
Joint Probabilities

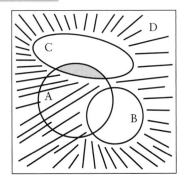

We subtract out Pr(A and B), so that we do not double count the shaded area in Figure SA.1 when calculating the total area covered by the events A and B together.

The cross-hatched area in Figure SA.1 is all the weather outcomes in which there is no rain. We call this collection of weather outcomes the **complement** of the event that it rains. The joint probability of an event and its complement is always 1 (either it rains or it doesn't).

Consider a third event, C, in which the high temperature tomorrow is less than 40°F. Figure SA.2 adds this event to the Venn diagram of Figure SA.1. Notice that there is no overlap of the circles B and C—the high temperature being above 60°F and below 40°F are *mutually exclusive*. With a third event, we have a larger collection of joint probabilities that we could ask about. What is the probability that A, B, and C will all occur? That is, what is Pr(A and B and C)? Note that the term "joint probability" also refers to the probability of the conjunction of three events. To check your understanding of joint probability, look at Figure SA.2 and ask yourself: What is Pr(A and C)? What is Pr(A and B)? What is Pr(B and C)?

Notice that Pr(A and C) is the shaded area in the figure covering the events in which it both rains and the high temperature is below 40°. Notice, too, that Pr(B and C) = 0; there is no overlap between the circles B and C. We say that B and C are **mutually exclusive**. Mutually exclusive events have a joint probability of zero. Because Pr(B and C) = 0, Pr(A and B and C) = 0, too.

The cross-hatched area in Figure SA.2 covers all the weather outcomes in which the high temperature is 40–60°F. Call this event D. The events B, C, and D share no overlap. They are mutually exclusive. They also include all the weather outcomes. We therefore call them **exhaustive**. Events that are both mutually exclusive and exhaustive have probabilities that sum to one:

$$Pr(B) + Pr(C) + Pr(D) = 1,$$

because B, C, and D are mutually exclusive and exhaustive.

**Figure SA.3**

The Joint Probability
of Three Events

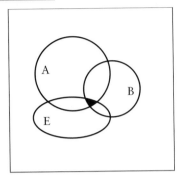

Pr(A and B and C) = 0, so their intersection in Figure SA.2 is empty and we cannot see it. Figure SA.3 adds a different event, E, to Figure SA.1, an event for which we can see the intersection of A, B, and E. Suppose the event E is that the barometer is falling throughout the day tomorrow. The circle E identifies all the weather outcomes tomorrow in which the barometer is falling all day. The joint probability that it rains tomorrow, with a high temperature above 60°F, and the barometer is falling all day, Pr(A and B and E), is the intersection of the three circles, A, B, and E, which is shaded in the figure.

## Conditional Probability

If it is raining tomorrow (A), what is the probability that the high temperature is above 60°F(B)? Notice that we are not seeking a simple probability here, because we are restricting our attention to a subset of tomorrow's weather outcomes, those in which the high temperature is above 60°F; we are asking how likely it is that it is raining when the high temperature is above 60. When we make probability statements that restrict attention to a subset of all possible outcomes, we call the probability a **conditional probability**. We denote the conditional probability of B given A, Pr(B|A). In Figure SA.1, Pr(B|A) is denoted by the fraction of A that is also in B.

Whether a probability is simple or conditional depends on our point of view. For example, Figures SA.1–SA.3 restrict attention to tomorrow's weather, which is a subset of all days. If we begin with a perspective of all days, the probability that it will rain, given that we are attending to tomorrow, would be a conditional probability, not a simple probability. At the outset of each analysis, we must define our **universe**, the collection of all events of interest to us. Conditional probabilities are those that attend to a subset of that universe, rather than to the whole universe. In Figure SA.1, for example, the probability of B, given A, is the fraction of A that is also B; in this conditional probability, it is as if A were our universe of discourse.

Notice that $\Pr(B|A)$ is generally not the same as $\Pr(A|B)$. In Figure SA.1, $\Pr(A|B)$ is the fraction of the area B (all the weather outcomes in which the high temperature is above 60°F) that overlaps with area A (the weather outcomes in which there is rain). This is different from $\Pr(B|A)$. $\Pr(A|B)$ is the probability of it raining tomorrow, given that the high temperature tomorrow is above 60°F. This conditional probability is related to a joint probability and a simple probability. The conditional probability of it raining tomorrow, given that the high temperature tomorrow is above 60°F, is

$$\Pr(A|B) = \Pr(A \text{ and } B)/\Pr(B).$$

This mathematical relationship provides us with a formal definition of a conditional probability in terms of joint and simple probabilities. We can also ask what is the probability that the temperature tomorrow will be above 60°F, given that tomorrow it rains:

$$\Pr(B|A) = \Pr(A \text{ and } B)/\Pr(A).$$

We read the formal expression $\Pr(A|B)$ as "the probability of A, given B." Unfortunately, the English language has many ways of expressing such conditionality. "Among rainy days, what is the probability that the high temperature will be above 60°F?" "If it rains tomorrow, what are the chances that the high temperature tomorrow will be above 60°F?" "Suppose it rains tomorrow. What, then, is the probability that the high temperature tomorrow will be above 60°F?" "What is the probability that we will find the temperature is above 60°F tomorrow, given that it rains tomorrow?" Because there are many ways to express conditionality, we must think carefully to determine whether we are seeking a simple probability or a conditional probability. Similarly, if we are seeking a conditional probability, we must think carefully to determine what it is conditioned on.

In applications, we sometimes know both the simple and the conditional probability, but we need to ascertain a joint probability. In such cases, we can manipulate the definition of conditional probability to compute joint probabilities:

$$\Pr(A)\Pr(B|A) = \Pr(A \text{ and } B) = \Pr(B)\Pr(A|B).$$

For example, suppose we know a particular family has three children, two girls and a boy, but we know nothing more about the children. What is the probability that both the first child and the second child from this family to attend school will be girls? The probability that the first child to attend school will be a girl is 2/3, because we have no reason to think one child or another is more likely to go to school first. The probability that the second child to attend school will be a girl, given the first was a girl, is 1/2 (because two children are left, a boy and a girl). Thus the probability that both the first and the second child to attend school are girls is $(2/3) \cdot (1/2) = 1/3$.

This calculation also leads us to the answer to a more complex question: What is the probability that one of the first two children to attend school is a boy? This complex event (either the first or the second child to attend school is a boy) is the complement of the event that the first two children to attend school are girls. Thus the probability that one of the first two children to attend school is a boy is $(1 - 1/3)$, or 2/3.

## Statistical Independence

The conditional probability of an event can be the same as the simple probability; that is, sometimes $Pr(A|B) = Pr(A)$. For example, we could argue that if we toss a coin twice, getting heads the first time has no effect on what we will get on a second toss. When $Pr(A|B) = Pr(A)$, we say A and B are **statistically independent events**. In the example from the previous section, the event "the second child to attend school is a boy" is not statistically independent of the event "the first child to attend is a girl"; the simple probability of a boy being the second to go to school is 1/3, whereas the probability of a boy being the second to attend, given a girl is the first to attend is 1/2.

When event A is statistically independent from event B, the joint probability of the two is the product of their simple probabilities. To see this, note that if A and B are statistically independent, $Pr(A|B) = Pr(A)$, in which case, $Pr(A \text{ and } B) = Pr(A)Pr(B)$. Moreover, if A is statistically independent from B, then B is also statistically independent from A, so $Pr(A|B) = Pr(A)$ implies $Pr(B|A) = Pr(B)$. For example, if the probability of getting a 500 on the verbal SAT is statistically independent of the student being white, then Pr(getting 500 on the verbal SAT| the student is white) = Pr(getting 500 on the verbal SAT).

## Bayes's Rule

The Reverend Thomas Bayes was the first to formulate a fundamental probability rule. **Bayes's rule** is that

$$Pr(B|A) = Pr(B)Pr(A|B)/Pr(A).$$

Bayes's Rule follows from manipulating the earlier relationship

$$Pr(A)Pr(B|A) = Pr(A \text{ and } B) = Pr(B)Pr(A|B).$$

Bayes's Rule is profound. *If one takes a subjectivist view of probability, in which probabilities express degrees of belief, Bayes's Rule tells us how new information (A) alters our beliefs (about B) if we adapt logically to new information.*

The left side of Bayes's Rule is the probability we assign to a proposition B, *after* receiving the information, A (that is, $Pr(B|A)$, which is sometimes called the **posterior probability** of B). On the right-hand side of Bayes's Rule, we find the probability we assign to B *prior* to learning that A is true (that is, $\Pr(B)$, which is sometimes called the **prior probability** of B), together with the ratio of $\Pr(A|B)$ to $\Pr(A)$. The ratio of $\Pr(A|B)$ to $\Pr(A)$ tells us whether the new information, A, is relatively surprising or relatively unsurprising if B is true. If A is relatively surprising if B is true (so $\Pr(A|B) < \Pr(A)$), then we revise downward the credibility we ascribe to B; if A is relatively unsurprising if B is true (so $\Pr(A|B) > \Pr(A)$), we ascribe more credibility to B.

In some applications of Bayes's Rule, we do not know $\Pr(A)$ directly, but we do know the probability of B and the probability of B's complement, $B^c$, as well as knowing both $\Pr(A|B)$ and $\Pr(A|B^c)$. Because A can occur either when B occurs, or when $B^c$ occurs, we can rewrite $\Pr(A)$:

$$\Pr(A) = \Pr(B)\Pr(A|B) + \Pr(B^c)\Pr(A|B^c).$$

We can, therefore, rewrite Bayes's rule as

$$\Pr(B|A) = \frac{\Pr(B)\Pr(A|B)}{\Pr(A)} = \frac{\Pr(B)\Pr(A|B)}{\Pr(B)\Pr(A|B) + \Pr(B^c)\Pr(A|B^c)}.$$

## The Probability Rules

In sum, there are five key probability rules:

1. $\Pr(A) + \Pr(B) + \Pr(C) = 1$ if A, B, and C exhaust all possibilities.
2. $\Pr(A \text{ or } B) = \Pr(A) + \Pr(B) - \Pr(A \text{ and } B)$.
3. $\Pr(A)\Pr(B|A) = \Pr(A \text{ and } B) = \Pr(B)\Pr(A|B)$.
4. $\Pr(B|A) = \dfrac{\Pr(B)\,\Pr(A|B)}{\Pr(A)} = \dfrac{\Pr(B)\Pr(A|B)}{\Pr(B)\,\Pr(A|B) + \Pr(B^c)\,\Pr(A|B^c)}.$
   and
5. If A and B are statistically independent, $\Pr(A|B) = \Pr(A)$ and $\Pr(B|A) = \Pr(B)$.

## Random Variables and Their Probability Functions

To illustrate the concepts of random variables and probability functions, consider the example of verbal Scholastic Aptitude Test (SAT) scores. Like many phenomena of interest to economists, verbal SAT scores take on many numerical values; scores range from 200 to 800, increasing by tens. Each of these values marks a possible event: (A) a student receives a score of 500 on the verbal SAT, (B) a student receives a score of 510 on the verbal SAT, (C) a student receives a score of 520 on the verbal SAT, and so on. Associated with each score is a corresponding probability for that event. A **random variable** takes on various numerical values, and associated with each value is a probability. A **probability function** assigns to each value that a random variable takes on its corresponding probability. Thus, there is a probability function associated with each random variable. For a random variable $S$ (for verbal SAT score), the probability function $p(s)$ provides the probability that $S = s$. These probabilities are simple probabilities. The link between this notation and the probability notation that we used earlier is that we can say that $p(s) = \Pr(S = s)$, with $p(s)$ defined for every value that $S$ takes on.

If we have two random variables, say $S$ and $A$, where $S$ is verbal SAT score and $A$ is Age, the age at which a student first takes the SAT, we can define a **joint probability function**, $p(s, a)$, which provides the joint probability that $S = s$ and $A = a$. When there are multiple random variables, the notation can be ambiguous. For example, with the two random variables $S$ and $A$, $p(6)$ might refer to either $\Pr(A = 6)$ or the probability that $(S = 6)$. To avoid such ambiguity, when a probability function does not have *all* the random variables as arguments, we subscript $P(\cdot)$ to indicate which variable's probability function we mean, as in

$$p_S(6) = \Pr(S = 6)$$

and

$$p_A(6) = \Pr(A = 6).$$

Simple probability functions and the joint probability functions are closely related. Notice that the values of $A$ are mutually exclusive on a given administration of the exam—if a student takes the SAT for the first time at age 17, that student can't be (simultaneously) taking the SAT for the first time at age 18, or at any other age. Similarly, the scores are mutually exclusive. On a given administration of the exam, a student who gets a score of 510 cannot get any other score.

Suppose, for illustrative purposes, that the age of exam takers is restricted to 16, 17, and 18. Test takers who get a score of 510 are one of these three mutually exclusive ages. The fraction of students who get a 510 is the sum of the fraction who both get a 510 and are 16, the fraction who both get a 510 and are 17, and the fraction who both get a 510 and are 18. That is,

$$p_S(510) = \Pr(S = 510) = p(s = 510, a = 16)$$
$$+ p(s = 510, a = 17) + p(s = 510, a = 18)$$
$$= \sum_A p(510, a)$$

where $p_S(s)$ is the simple probability function for $S$, and the notation $\sum_A$ indicates a summation over all the values that the random variable $A$ (age) takes on—more elaborately, $\sum_A$ means "evaluate the expression that follows at each value that $A$ takes on and sum those terms." This summation process is how simple probability functions are generally obtained from joint probability functions. Thus, the simple probability function for age among test takers is

$$p_A(a) = \sum_S p(s, a),$$

where the summation is over all possible test scores. In early statistical work, before the advent of calculators or computers, the sums that yielded simple probability functions were written in the margins of tables that displayed the random variables and their joint probabilities. Because of this, the simple probabilities became known as **marginal probabilities**.

The notion of random variables and joint probability functions generalizes to multiple random variables. If $G$ is a binary variable taking on the value 1 for females and the value zero for males, then the joint probability function for score, age, and gender is $p(s, a, g)$. We obtain the simple, or marginal, probability function for $S$ by summing the joint probability over all age and gender combinations:

$$p_S(s) = \sum_A \sum_G p(s, a, g).$$

Similar constructions connect the marginal probabilities for age and gender to the joint probability.

The "marginal" probability notion applies equally well to linking the joint probability function for score and age to the joint probability function for score, age, and gender:

$$p_{S, A}(s, a) = \sum_G p(s, a, g).$$

## Conditional Probability Functions

Conditional probability functions assign an appropriate conditional probability to random variables of interest. We define

$$p_{X|Y}(x|y) \equiv \frac{p(x, y)}{p_Y(y)},$$

where $X$ and $Y$ are random variables. Thus, the conditional probability function for $X$ given $Y$ is the joint probability function for $X$ and $Y$ divided by the marginal probability function for $Y$.

**Figure SA.4**

The Marginal Probability Function For Age Among Students Taking the SAT

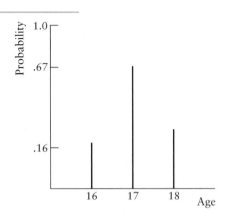

## Graphically Depicting Probability Functions

SAT verbal scores, years of age, and gender are variables that take on a finite number of discrete values: Verbal SAT scores begin at 200 and rise to 800 in increments of 10; we have decided to measure age as 16, 17, or 18; we denote gender by 1 or 0 (female or male). We commonly graph the probability functions for such variables by placing the values of a random variable along the horizontal axis and measuring the accompanying probability on the vertical axis.

Figure SA.4 shows a graph of the marginal probability function for the age at which a student first takes the SAT. The picture assumes that 2/3 of students take the exam at 17, 1/6 take the exam at 16, and 1/6 take the exam at 18. Figure SA.5 uses a three-dimensional graph to plot the probabilities for combinations of age and gender; the figure assumes that the probabilities do not differ by gender, given age.

## The Binomial Probability Function

A frequently encountered example of a probability function for a discrete random variable is the binomial distribution. Suppose a salesperson makes $n$ statistically independent sales pitches per day with each having the same probability of success, $p$.

Any one sales pitch will either succeed ($x = 1$) or fail ($x = 0$). The probability function for any single sales effort is

$$p(x) = p^x(1 - p)^{1-x}.$$

For $x = 1$, the probability is $p$; for $x = 0$, the probability is $(1 - p)$.

Because the sales pitches are statistically independent, if we denote the outcomes of the pitches, in order, $X_1, X_2, \ldots, X_n$, then

$$p(x_1, x_2, \ldots, x_n) = p_{X_1}(x_1) \, p_{X_2}(x_2) \ldots p_{X_n}(x_n)$$

**Figure SA.5**

The Joint Probability Function for Age and Gender Among Students Taking the SAT

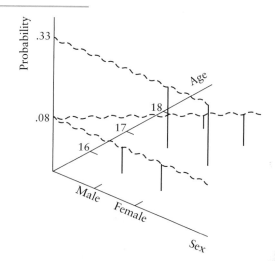

with each element in the product equal to $p$ or to $(1 - p)$ depending on whether that sales pitch was a success or a failure.

Any particular sequence of $s$ successful and unsuccessful sales pitches includes $s$ successes and $(n - s)$ failures. The probability of any one such sequence is thus

$$p^s(1 - p)^{n-s}. \qquad \text{SA.1}$$

Numerous sequences of success and failure can result in exactly $s$ successes. Each such sequence has the probability given by Equation SA.1. The probability that some such sequence, with exactly $s$ successful pitches, occurs is $p^s(1 - p)^{n-s}$ times the number of sequences with exactly $s$ successes. How many sequences of $n$ sales pitches have exactly $s$ successes? The answer is

$$\frac{n!}{s!(n - s)!}. \qquad \text{SA.2}$$

Why is this the formula for the number of sequences with exactly $s$ successes and $(n - s)$ failures? We can arrange $n$ distinct items $n!$ different ways. The numerator in Equation SA.2 would be a count of the number of sequences if each $x$-value were distinct. But we don't have $n$ distinct items, $s$ of the items are indistinguishable 1's; if we treat all the items as distinct (as the numerator in Equation SA.2 implicitly does), we use these $s$ 1's $s!$ times in any arrangement of the remaining items, so we overcount by a factor of $s!$. Similarly, the $(n - s)$ 0's are not distinct items, but the numerator treats them as if they are distinct. Treating them as distinct, we would overcount by a factor of $(n - s)!$. The denominator in Equation SA.2 just compensates for the overcounting in the numerator.

Consequently, the probability function for the number of successful sales in $n$ independent trials is

$$p(s) = \frac{n!}{s!(n-s)!} p^s(1-p)^{n-s},$$

which is called the **binomial probability function.**

## Statistically Independent Random Variables

Just as events can be statistically independent, random variables can also be statistically independent. The two statistical independence notions are linked, but the statistical independence of random variables is a stricter notion than that of events. For two random variables to be statistically independent, each and every event one random variable represents must be statistically independent of each and every event the other random variable represents.

Some random variables take on only a finite number of different values. We call these **discrete random variables.** We say two discrete random variables, $X$ and $Y$, are **statistically independent random variables** if and only if

$$p_{X|Y}(x|y) = p_X(x),$$

for every value $X$ and $Y$ can take on. This condition implies and is implied by

$$p_{Y|X}(y|x) = p_Y(y),$$

holding for every value that $X$ and $Y$ can take on. These conditions imply that

$$p(x, y) = p_X(x)p_Y(y).$$

We say that a set of discrete random variables $X_1, X_2, \ldots, X_m$ are **jointly statistically independent random variables** if and only if

$$p(x_1, x_2, \ldots, x_m) = p_{X_1}(x_1)p_{X_2}(x_2)\ldots p_{X_m}(x_m)$$

for every combination of values $X_1, X_2, \ldots, X_m$ can take on.

To illustrate the stringency of the statistical independence of random variables, we pose a hypothetical case. Suppose that the event being 17 is statistically independent of being female (so the probability of taking the test for the first time at 17 is the same for males and females) and that this independence of gender holds for 16- and 18-year-olds as well. We can therefore say that in this universe, age and gender are statistically independent random variables. Further, suppose that the probability of any particular verbal SAT score is the same for 17-year-olds as for the population as a whole. That is, the event being 17 is statistically independent of each of the many events depicted by particular test scores. With all

**Figure SA.6**

The Probability Function for a Continuous Random Variable

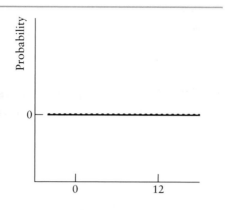

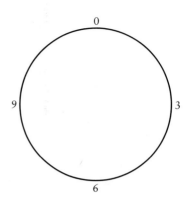

these events statistically independent, we can still find that the variables score, age, and gender are not jointly statistically independent. Suppose that the probability of any scores except 200 and 210 are the same for 16-, 17-, and 18-year-olds, but that the probability of a 200 is slightly higher for 16-year-olds than for 18-year-olds and the probability of a 210 is slightly lower for 16-year-olds than for 18-year-olds. The events "a score of 200" and " a score of 210" are not statistically independent of being 16 or of being 18. The random variables score and age are not statistically independent. In such a case, score, age, and gender are also not jointly statistically independent.

Data drawn in a manner that yields jointly statistically independent observations are much easier to analyze than are other statistical data. We often analyze such independent cases before analyzing more realistic complex cases.

## Continuous Random Variables and Their Zero Probabilities

We have thus far focused on random variables that take on discrete values. Many variables are continuous, though, such as height and weight. **Continuous random variables** take on an infinitude of different values. Continuous random variables are often not sensibly analyzed with probability functions. The difficulty continuous random variables often pose is that any specific height or weight has a zero probability of occurring, even though many heights and weights are neither impossible nor equally likely to occur. Figure SA.6 depicts the probability function for such a case—with the probability function zero everywhere, we do not learn much from the figure. Also in Figure SA.6 is a wheel with properties we now describe. The wheel exposes the problem and illustrates a solution.

Our hypothetical wheel has a circumference of 12 inches. The wheel is marked 0 at one point, and is then marked 3 one quarter of the way around the wheel, 6 halfway around, and 9 three quarters of the way around. We can measure the distance around the wheel from zero to any point as precisely as we'd like. This wheel we can spin, much like the wheel on TV's *Wheel of Fortune* game. When the wheel stops spinning, some point is under a pointer, and we can identify how far from zero the pointer points. There are an infinite number of points at which the wheel can stop.

The wheel is designed so that not all points are equally likely to come under the pointer. Points from zero to six are twice as likely to occur as points beyond six and before zero. In particular, points from zero to six are equally likely to occur, and one of those points occurs with probability 2/3. Points beyond six and before zero are also equally likely to occur, and one or another of them occurs with probability 1/3.

What is the probability that a point from zero to six occurs? If we assume that this probability is $k > 0$ (so the probability of all other points from zero to six is also $k$, and the probability of all points beyond six and before zero is $1/2k$), we arrive at a contradiction. Consequently, the probability of points between zero and six must be zero, as must be the probability of points beyond six and before zero. What is the contradiction that leads us to this odd conclusion?

The points between zero and six are mutually exclusive and equally likely. The probability that one point occurs from any subset of these points is the sum of the probabilities of the points in the subset. If one point has probability $k$, two points have probability $2k$, three points have probability $3k$, and so on. By assumption, no matter how small $k$ is, it is bigger than zero. Consequently, I can select enough points, say $m$, so that $mk > 1$. But that would imply that the probability of this subset of $m$ points has a probability of occurring bigger than one, which is impossible. Thus, $k$ cannot be greater than zero; $k$ must equal zero. Figure SA.6 does, indeed, show the probability function for the random variable "distance of the pointer from zero." This probability function is quite uninformative, masking entirely the fact that points from zero to six are twice as likely as points beyond six.

## Continuous Random Variables and Probability Densities

A more useful depiction of the wheel and its probabilities appears in Figure SA.7. The heights in the figure measure what we call **probability density**. A **probability density function** assigns to each value of the random variable its corresponding probability density. Equally likely points on the wheel will have the same probability density. In the figure, probabilities are measured by areas under the probability density function. For example, the area under the function from zero to 12 is 1—some point must arise. The area from 0 to 6 is two thirds, whereas that from 6 to 12 is one third. Numbers below 0 and above 12 cannot occur and receive a probability density of zero. Numbers from 0 to 6 get twice as high a prob-

**Figure SA.7**

The Probability Density Function for an Unbalanced Wheel and the Probability that 6 < X < 12

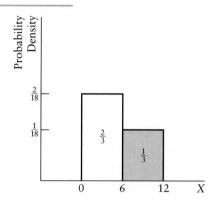

ability density as numbers above 6 and below 12. In Figure SA.7, the shaded area is the probability that the uniformly distributed random variable $X$ takes on a value between 6 and 12.

Just as we distinguish among marginal, joint, and conditional probability functions, we distinguish among marginal, joint, and conditional probability density functions. The connections among the probability functions that are made by summations are accomplished by a related mathematical procedure called integration (summing areas, in essence) among the probability density functions.

Readers familiar with calculus will recognize the integration operation, so for their benefit, the marginal probability density function, $f_X(x)$, for a random variable $X$, when there are other random variables $Y$ and $Z$, is tied to their joint probability density function, $f(x, y, z)$, by

$$f_X(x) = \int_Y \int_Z f(x, y, z)\, dy\, dz.$$

Similarly, the marginal probability density function for $X$ and $Y$, $f_{XY}(x, y)$, is

$$f_{XY}(x, y) = \int_z f(x, y, z)\, dz.$$

And the conditional probability density function for $X$ given $Y$ is

$$f_{X|Y}(x|y) = \frac{f_{XY}(x, y)}{f_Y(y)}.$$

Continuous random variables $X$ and $Y$ are statistically independent if and only if

$$f(x, y) = f_X(x)\, f_Y(y)$$

**Figure SA.8**

A Normal Probability Density Function and the Probability that $2 < X < 3$

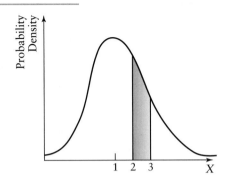

for all values of $X$, $Y$, and $Z$. More generally, a set of $m$ continuous random variables, $X_1, X_2, \ldots, X_m$ are statistically independent if and only if

$$f(x_1, x_2, \ldots, x_m) = f_{X_1}(x_1)f_{X_2}(x_2)\ldots f_{X_m}(x_m),$$

for all values the random variables take on.

## The Normal Probability Density Function

The most commonly encountered probability density function is the **normal distribution**:

$$f(x) = \frac{1}{\sqrt{2\pi}\sigma} e^{-\frac{1}{2}\left(\frac{x-\mu}{\sigma}\right)^2},$$

which is graphed with a bell-shaped curve, as in Figure SA.8. The curve in Figure SA.8 has $\mu = 1$ and $\sigma = 2$. The shaded area in the figure is the probability that this normally distributed random variable $X$ takes on a value between 2 and 3.

Three properties of normally distributed random variables make the normal distribution particularly easy to use:

1. A sum of a normally distributed random variable and a constant is normally distributed.
2. A product of a normally distributed random variable and a constant is normally distributed.
3. A sum of normally distributed random variables is normally distributed.

## The Standard Normal Distribution

Figure SA.8 shows the probability that a normally distributed random variable $X$ with $\mu = 1$ and $\sigma = 2$ takes on a value between 2 and 3. If $\mu$ or $\sigma$ were different, we would need a different bell-shaped curve to show the probability that $X$ falls between 2 and 3. Needing different curves for each combination of values for $\mu$

**Figure SA.9**

A Standard Normal
Probability Density
Function and the
Probability that
$0.5 < Z < 1.0$

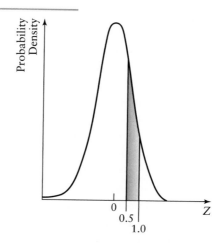

and $\sigma$ would be very cumbersome, especially in the past, when we didn't have computers to perform fast calculations for us. Fortunately, we can transform probability statements about any normally distributed variable into equivalent statements about a variable following the standard normal distribution, and from that one standard distribution we can obtain any probability assessments we need about normally distributed variables.

For any normally distributed random variable, $X$,

$$Z = \frac{(X - \mu)}{\sigma}$$

is distributed normally with $\mu = 0$ and $\sigma = 1$. This distribution, denoted N(0, 1), is called the **standard normal distribution.**

Figure SA.9 show this standard normal distribution. The shaded area in the figure is the probability that $Z$ lies between 0.5 and 1.0, which corresponds to $X$ lying between 2 and 3. When $X$ equals 2,

$$Z = (2 - 1)/2 = 0.5.$$

When $X$ equals 3,

$$Z = (3 - 1)/2 = 1.0$$

Thus, the probability that $Z$ lies between 0.5 and 1.0 corresponds to the probability that $X$ lies between 2 and 3. Other probability statements about other normally distributed random variables can be similarly transformed into equivalent probability statements about $Z$. We can therefore compute normal probabilities using $Z$ and the standard normal distribution, as long as we know $\mu$ and $\sigma$.

# SA.2 Statistics

Empirical knowledge is generally uncertain. An economist may examine individual incomes for a sample of American households observed by the government in 1974 and 2004. The economist wants to ascertain whether incomes in the United States were more or less unequally distributed in 2004 than in 1974. Not having seen every household, however, the economist's knowledge about the population is uncertain. An econometrician observes government spending and income in 50 states across the past 50 years. What the econometrician hopes to learn from such data is what would have happened to states' spending had incomes been different, or what will happen to states' spending in the future. Not having observed all states in all possible circumstances, our knowledge about the population is uncertain. Our uncertainty makes all these *statistical matters*.

**Statistics** is a field of inquiry; it inquires into how best to learn about the whole from data about only a part of the whole. Statistics are manipulations of the numbers in a data set. One early statistical inquiry was how to use statistics to describe a set of numbers succinctly. For example, how can we succinctly describe how unequally income was distributed among thousands of households observed in 2004? Later statistical efforts sought to model the probabilistic processes that give rise to data. For example, if polled households are selected using a chance mechanism, how can we mathematically describe the resulting sampling process? Still later, statisticians focused on how to best draw from sample statistics inferences about the processes that give rise to data. Some such inferences involved making estimates of the properties of the processes that give rise to data. For example, if 40% of households in our sample say they favor candidate A, what should we guess is the proportion in the population who favor A? Other such inferences involved testing hypotheses about the processes that give rise to data. For example, if 40% in the sample say they favor candidate A, can we reasonably reject the hypothesis that 20% in the population favor A?

## Descriptive Statistics for a Single Variable

A large collection of numbers can be unwieldy. We use descriptive statistics to summarize collections of numbers. The most common descriptive statistics for a single set of numbers are the mean, the median, the mode, and the variance (and the closely related standard deviation).

The **mean** of an observed set of numbers is the arithmetic average of those numbers. If the numbers are $Y_1, Y_2, \ldots, Y_n$, then the mean is

$$\overline{Y} = \frac{1}{n}\sum_{i=1}^{n} Y_i.$$

The mean of a normally distributed random variable equals the distribution's parameter, $\mu$.

The **median** is the number above which lie half the observed numbers $Y_1, Y_2, \ldots, Y_n$ and below which lie the other half of the numbers $Y_1, Y_2, \ldots, Y_n$. The median is unaffected by increasing the size of elements of $Y_1, Y_2, \ldots, Y_n$ that are above the median or decreasing the size of elements of $Y_1, Y_2, \ldots, Y_n$ that are below the median. It is therefore relatively insensitive to outlying observations. In contrast, the mean can be heavily influenced by outlying observations. Because the normal distribution is symmetric about its mean, the median of the normal distribution equals the mean of the distribution, $\mu$.

The **mode** is the most frequently occurring value among an observed set of numbers $Y_1, Y_2, \ldots, Y_n$. The mode of the normal distribution is also $\mu$.

The **variance** of an observed set of numbers is defined as

$$\text{var}(Y_1, Y_2, \ldots, Y_n) = \frac{1}{n}\sum_{i=1}^{n}(Y_i - \overline{Y})^2.$$

(Some textbooks, and some software packages, divide by $(n-1)$, instead of $n$, to define the variance of an observed set of numbers. This book, and some other textbooks and software packages, divide by $n$ because that makes the variance *the mean* squared deviation of a variable from its own mean.)

The **standard deviation** is the square root of the variance. The variance and the standard deviation provide a measure of how spread out the numbers are about their mean. The variance of a normally distributed random variable equals the distribution's parameter $\sigma^2$.

## Descriptive Statistics for Two Variables

Several other descriptive statistics summarize the relationship between two series of numbers. The **covariance** of two sets of numbers, $Y_1, Y_2, \ldots, Y_n$ and $X_1, X_2, \ldots, X_n$ is defined as

$$\text{cov}(X, Y) = \text{cov}(Y, X) = \frac{1}{n}\sum_{i=1}^{n}(X_i - \overline{X})(Y_i - \overline{Y}).$$

(Again, some textbooks divide by $(n-1)$ instead of $n$ to define the covariance. This book divides by $n$ so that the concept is a mean.) The covariance measures how strongly $X$ and $Y$ vary together on the same or opposite sides of their means.

The **correlation coefficient** is defined as

$$\text{corr}(X, Y) = \rho_{XY} = \frac{\text{cov}(X, Y)}{(\sigma_Y)(\sigma_X)},$$

where $\sigma$ stands for "standard deviation." Unlike the covariance, which can take on any value, the correlation coefficient is bounded such that $-1 \le \rho_{XY} \le 1$ no matter what values $X$ and $Y$ take on, so long as neither standard deviation is zero.

An advantage of the correlation coefficient over the covariance measure is that, unlike the covariance measure, the correlation coefficient does not change when the units of measure for $X$ or $Y$ change.

When examining two sets of numbers, $X$ and $Y$, subscripts frequently distinguish their means and variances, as in $\mu_X$ vs. $\mu_Y$ and $\sigma_X^2$ vs. $\sigma_Y^2$.

## Populations and Samples

We can describe a set of numbers with no knowledge of where the numbers came from. But often, we wish to link the data in hand to a larger frame of reference. For example, we might wish to make inferences about all voters based on a sample of voters. To make such inferences sensibly, we need to know something about the relationship between all voters and the voters in our sample.

We would be delighted if we knew that our sample of voters mirrored the collection of all voters. Then, we could confidently describe all voters based on our sample. Such close representation of the whole by a part is seldom achieved—and when it is achieved, we seldom know that it is. In lieu of an infeasible insistence on such "representative samples," statisticians suggest we rely instead on probability-based sampling procedures. One commonly encountered probability sampling procedure is *random sampling*.

A **sample** is a set of random variables, $Y_1, Y_2, \ldots, Y_n$, drawn from a population of interest. The $Y_i$ are the $n$ observations of the sample. The variable of interest to us, $Y$, has some distribution in the population. For example, $Y$ might be income and the population might be all elderly persons in the United States. In a sample from this population, $Y_1$ would be the income of the first person observed in the sample and $Y_2$ would be the income of the second person observed in the sample, and so on. Formally, the distribution of $Y$ in the population is described by a probability function, $p(y)$, or a by probability density function, $f(y)$.

A sample is said to be a **random sample** if the marginal probability function for the $i$-th observation, $p_i(y_i)$, equals the population probability function $p(y)$ for every $i, i = 1, \ldots, n$ (or the probability density function for the $i$-th observation, $f_i(y_i)$, equals $f(y)$ for every $i, i = 1, \ldots, n$). *In a random sample, the distribution across samples of each observation mirrors the distribution of the variable of interest in the population.* A random sample is a **simple random sample** when the observations in a random sample are mutually statistically independent.

Researchers do work with other probability samples besides random samples—for example, stratified probability samples. We do not discuss such samples in this appendix, however.

## Descriptive Statistics and Populations

The descriptive statistics that interest us when we summarize sets of data are the same traits of data that often interest us when we think about a population. What is the mean income in the population? What is the variance of income in the population? What is the covariance between two variables in a population?

In a sample, we obtain the mean and variance of the observed values of $X$ or $Y$, and the covariance between the observed values of $X$ and $Y$, by computing these statistics with the appropriate formulae. When these statistics are computed from sample data, we call them sample statistics—the sample means of $X$ and $Y$, the sample variances of $X$ and $Y$, and the sample covariance of $X$ and $Y$. We can, in principle, compute corresponding statistics in populations to obtain population means, variances, and covariances. When computing populations statistics, the appropriate relative frequencies for the different values $X$ or $Y$ takes on are the probabilities of those values occurring. Notice that the variance and covariance statistics are themselves means. The former is the mean squared deviation of a variable from its own mean. The latter is the mean of the products of the deviations of two random variables, each from its own mean. Means in populations are also called **expected values** and are indicated by E( ). Thus, the population mean of $Y$ is $E(Y)$; the population variance of $Y$ is $E([Y - E(Y)]^2)$, and the population covariance of $X$ and $Y$ is $E([X - E(X)][Y - E(Y)])$.

Formally, the mean of a discrete random variable $Y$ in a population is

$$E(Y) = \sum_Y y_j\, p(y_j),$$

where the summation is over all the values $Y$ can take on. The mean of a continuous random variable in a population is

$$E(Y) = \int_Y yf(y)\, dy,$$

where the integration is over the range of $Y$.

The variance of a discrete random variable in a population is

$$\text{var}(Y) = E[(Y - E(Y))^2] = \sum_Y \left(y_j - E(Y)\right)^2 p(y_j),$$

where the summation is over all values $Y$ can take on. The variance of a continuous random variable in a population is

$$\text{var}(Y) = E[(Y - E(Y))^2] = \int_Y \left(y - E(Y)\right)^2 f(y)dy,$$

where the integration is over the range of $Y$. The standard deviation of $Y$ in a population is the square root of the variance.

The covariance between two discrete random variables, $X$ and $Y$, in a population is

$$\text{cov}(X, Y) = E[(X - E[X])(Y - E[Y])] = \sum_X \sum_Y (x_j - E[X])(y_k - E[Y])p(x_j, y_k),$$

where the summations are over all the values $X$ can take on and all the values $Y$ can take on, respectively. The covariance between two continuous random variables in a population is

$$\text{cov}(X, Y) = E[(X - E[X])(Y - E[Y])]$$

$$= \int_Y \int_X (x - E[x])(y - E[Y])f(x, y)\, dx\, dy,$$

where the limits of integration are the ranges of $Y$ and $X$, respectively.

In general, the expected value of a function, $g(Y)$, is

$$E[g(Y)] = \sum_Y g(y)p(y),$$

(where the sum is over all the values $Y$ can take on) if $Y$ is a discretely distributed random variable and

$$E[g(Y)] = \int_Y g(y)f(y)dy,$$

(where the integral is over the range of $Y$) if $Y$ is a continuously distributed random variable.

Similarly, $E[g(Y_1, Y_2, \ldots, Y_m)]$ is

$$E[g(Y_1, Y_2, \ldots, Y_m)] = \sum_{Y_1} \sum_{Y_2} \cdots \sum_{Y_m} g(y_{1j_1}, y_{2j_2}, \ldots, y_{mj_m})\, p(y_{1j_1}, y_{2j_2}, \ldots, y_{mj_m})$$

(where the sums are over all the values the random variables can take on) if the random variables are discretely distributed, and

$$E[g(Y_1, Y_2, \ldots, Y_m)] = \int_{Y_1} \int_{Y_2} \cdots \int_{Y_m} g(y_1, y_2, \ldots, y_m)$$

$$f(y_1, y_2, \ldots, y_m)dy_1\, dy_2 \ldots dy_m,$$

(where the integrals are over the ranges of the random variables) if $Y$ is a continuously distributed random variable.

## The Algebra of Expectations

In econometrics, we frequently investigate the expected values of random variables. The following list summarizes the basic rules for manipulating expected values.

We call these rules the **algebra of expectations**. The proofs of these rules follow:

1. The expected value of a constant times a random variable is the constant times the expected value of the random variable:

$$E(kY) = kE(Y),$$

where $k$ is a constant and $Y$ is a random variable.

2. The expected value of a constant plus a random variable is the constant plus the expected value of the random variable:

$$E(k + Y) = k + E(Y),$$

where $k$ is a constant and $Y$ is a random variable.

3. The expected value of a sum is the sum of the expected values:

$$E\left(\sum_{i=1}^{n} Y_i\right) = \sum_{i=1}^{n}[E(Y_i)],$$

where each $Y_i$ is a random variable.

**Proof of 1**   The expected value of a constant times a random variable is the constant times the expected value of the random variable:

$$E(kY) = \sum_Y ky_j\, p(y_j) = k\sum_Y y_j\, p(y_j) = kE(Y),$$

where the sums are over all values $Y$ can take on.

**Proof of 2**   The expected value of a constant plus a random variable is the constant plus the expected value of the random variable:

$$E(k + Y) = \sum_Y (k + y_j)p(y_j) = \sum_Y (kp(y_j) + y_jp(y_j))$$

$$= \sum_Y kp(y_j) + \sum_Y y_jp(y_j) = k\sum_Y p(y_j) + E(Y),$$

but $\sum p(y_j) = 1$, so

$$E(k + Y) = k + E(Y).$$

**Proof of 3**   The expected value of a sum is the sum of the expected values:

$$E(Y_1 + Y_2 + \cdots + Y_m) = \sum_{Y_1} \sum_{Y_2} \cdots \sum_{Y_m} (y_{1j_1} + y_{2j_2} + \cdots + y_{mj_m})$$

$$p(y_{1j_1}, y_{2j_2}, \ldots, y_{mj_m})$$

$$= \sum_{Y_1} \sum_{Y_2} \cdots \sum_{Y_m} y_{1j_1}\, p(y_{1j_1}, y_{2j_2}, \ldots, y_{mj_m})$$

$$+ \sum_{Y_1} \sum_{Y_2} \cdots \sum_{Y_m} y_{2j_1}\, p(y_{1j_1}, y_{2j_2}, \ldots, y_{mj_m})$$

$$+ \cdots + \sum_{Y_1} \sum_{Y_2} \cdots \sum_{Y_m} y_{mj_1}\, p(y_{1j_1}, y_{2j_2}, \ldots, y_{mj_m})$$

$$= E(Y_1) + E(Y_2) + \cdots + E(Y_m).$$

Just as there are both probabilities and conditional probabilities, there are expectations and conditional expectations. The expected value of $Y$, conditional on $X$ being equal to a specific value, $x$, is the mean of $Y$ across all observations in which $X = x$. We denote the conditional mean of $Y$, given $X$, by $E(Y|X)$. Similarly, the conditional variance of $Y$, given $X$, is $\mathrm{var}(Y|X) = E\left([Y - E(Y|X)]^2 | X\right)$. If $Y$ and $X$ are statistically independent, then $E(Y|X) = E(Y)$ and $\mathrm{var}(Y|X) = \mathrm{var}(Y)$.

The **Law of Iterated Expectations** states that $E(E(Y|X)) = E(Y)$. A consequence of the law is that $E(\mathrm{var}(Y|X)) = \mathrm{var}(Y)$. Intuitively, the law says that if we average the means of subpopulations of $Y$ across a group of mutually exclusive and exhaustive set of subpopulations, with each subpopulation mean weighted by the probability of that subpopulation occurring, we obtain the population mean. For example, the average of boys' average test score and girls' average test score in a class gives the average test score for the whole class, as long as we weight the two averages by the relative frequency of boys and the relative frequency of girls in the class, respectively.

## The Algebra of Variances

In econometrics we also frequently investigate variances of random variables. The following list summarizes the basic rules for manipulating variances. We call these rules the **algebra of variances**. The demonstration of those rules follows; the demonstrations rely on the rules of the algebra of expectations (on p. 871).

1. The variance of a constant times a random variable is the constant squared times the variance of the random variable:

$$\mathrm{var}(kY) = k^2 \mathrm{var}(Y),$$

where $k$ is a constant and $Y$ is a random variable.

2. The variance of a constant plus a random variable is the variance of the random variable:

$$\text{var}(k + Y) = \text{var}(Y),$$

where $k$ is a constant and $Y$ is a random variable.

3. The variance of a sum is the sum of the variances, plus two times the sum of all the covariances among the variables in the original sum:

$$\text{var}(\Sigma Y_i) = \Sigma \text{var}(Y_i) + 2 \text{Sum of all the covariances among the } Y_i$$

$$= \Sigma \text{ var}(Y_i) + \sum_{i=1}^{n} \sum_{\substack{j=1 \\ j \neq i}}^{n} \text{cov}(Y_i, Y_j),$$

where $Y_i$ and $Y_j$ are random variables. (Because

$$\text{cov}(Y_i, Y_j) = \text{cov}(Y_j, Y_i),$$

each covariance appears twice in the summation.)

**Proof of 1**    The variance of a constant times a random variable is the constant squared times the variance of the random variable:

$$\text{var}(kY) = \text{E}[(kY - \text{E}[kY])^2] = \text{E}[(kY - k\text{E}[Y])^2]$$
$$= \text{E}[k^2(Y - \text{E}[Y])^2] = k^2\text{E}[((Y - \text{E})Y])^2]$$
$$= k^2\text{var}(Y).$$

**Proof of 2**    The variance of a constant plus a random variable is the variance of the random variable:

$$\text{var}(k + Y) = \text{E}[([k + Y] - \text{E}[k + Y])^2] = \text{E}[([k + Y] - k - \text{E}[Y])^2]$$
$$= \text{E}[ (Y - \text{E}[Y])^2] = \text{var}(Y).$$

**Proof of 3**    The variance of a sum is the sum of the variances, plus two times the sum of all the covariances among the variables in the original sum:

$$\text{var}\left(\sum_{i=1}^{m} Y_i\right) = \text{E}\left[\left(\sum_{i=1}^{m} Y_i - \text{E}\left[\sum_{i=1}^{m} Y_i\right]\right)^2\right] = \text{E}\left[\left(\sum_{i=1}^{m} Y_i - \sum_{i=1}^{m} \text{E}(Y_i)\right)^2\right]$$
$$= \text{E}\left[\left(\sum_{i=1}^{m} [Y_i - \text{E}(Y_i)]\right)^2\right].$$

Let $y_i = [Y_i - E(Y_i)]$. Then,

$$\operatorname{var}\left(\sum_{i=1}^{m} Y_i\right) = E\left[\left(\sum_{i=1}^{m} y_i\right)^2\right] = E\left[\sum_{i=1}^{m}\sum_{j=1}^{m} y_i\, y_j\right]$$

$$= E\left[\sum_{i=1}^{m} y_i^2 + \sum_{\substack{i=1 \\ }}^{m}\sum_{\substack{j=1 \\ j\neq i}}^{m} y_i\, y_j\right]$$

$$= E\left[\sum_{i=1}^{m} y_i^2\right] + E\left[\sum_{i=1}^{m}\sum_{\substack{j=1 \\ j\neq i}}^{m} y_i\, y_j\right]$$

$$= \sum_{i=1}^{m} E(y_i^2) + \sum_{i=1}^{m}\sum_{\substack{j=1 \\ j\neq i}}^{m} E(y_i\, y_j)$$

$$= \sum \operatorname{var}(Y_i) + 2\sum_{i=1}^{m}\sum_{j>i}^{m} \operatorname{cov}(y_i\, y_j).$$

## Estimation of the Population Mean by the Sample Mean

Statisticians' interest in population means leads them to ask how they might estimate population means from a sample of data. For example, veterans are a population of considerable interest to both politicians and citizens. What is the mean income of veterans 10 years after they leave military service? Gathering data on all veterans is very costly, so statisticians would answer this question by collecting a sample of veterans and recording their incomes. A natural candidate estimator of the population mean, $\mu$, is the sample mean,

$$\overline{Y} = \frac{1}{n}\sum_{i=1}^{n} Y_i.$$

The overbar on a random variable is often used to indicate the sample mean for that random variable. The sample mean is an intuitively appealing candidate for estimating the population mean, but does a deeper analysis of $\overline{Y}$'s traits confirm that it is a good estimator of the population mean?

Statisticians developed probability sampling procedures, such as simple random sampling, to allow analysis of the probabilistic properties of estimation procedures, such as estimating the population mean with the sample mean. In simple random samples, every individual in a population is given the same chance of being chosen for each and every observation, and observations are drawn independently of one another. Giving each individual the same chance of being chosen means the mean and variance of each observation will be the same as the population mean, $\mu$, and the population variance, $\sigma^2$, respectively.

The independence of observations from one another in a simple random sample ensures that the covariances between observations will be zero. For example,

$$E[(Y_1 - E[Y_1])(Y_2 - E[Y_2])] = \sum_{Y_1} \sum_{Y_2} [(y_{1j_1} - E[Y_1])(y_{2j_2} - E[Y_2])] p(y_{1j_1}, y_{2j_2}),$$

where the sums are over all the values that $Y_1$ and $Y_2$ can take on. Because the observations are statistically independent,

$$p(y_1, y_2) = p_1(y_1) p_2(y_2),$$

so

$$E[(Y_1 - E[Y_1])(Y_2 - E[Y_2])] = \sum_{Y_1} \sum_{Y_2} [(y_{1j_1} - E[Y_1])(y_{2j_2} - E[Y_2])] p_1(y_{1j_1}) p_2(y_{2j_2})$$

$$= \sum_{Y_1} (Y_{1j_1} - E[Y_1]) p_1(y_{1j_1}) \sum_{Y_2} (Y_{2j_2} - E[Y_2]) p_2(y_{2j_2})$$

(because when we change the value of $Y_2$, the value of $Y_1$ remains constant)

$$= 0,$$

because

$$\sum (y_{2j_2} - E[Y_2]) p_2(y_{2j_2}) = \sum_{Y_2} (y_{2j_2}) p_2(y_{2j_2}) - \sum E[Y_2] p_2(y_{2j_2})$$

$$= E(Y_2) - E(Y_2) \sum_{Y_2} p(y_{2j_2}) = E(Y_2) - E(Y_2) = 0.$$

Thus, if ours is a simple random sample with $n$ observations, we know that

$$\text{cov}(Y_i, Y_j) = 0 \qquad i \neq j,$$

as well as

$$E(Y_i) = \mu \qquad i = 1, \ldots, n,$$

and

$$\text{var}(Y_i) = \sigma^2 \qquad i = 1, \ldots, n.$$

From these conditions, it follows that $E(\overline{Y}) = \mu$ and $var(\overline{Y}) = \sigma^2/n$:

$$E(\overline{Y}) = E\left(\frac{1}{n}\sum_{i=1}^{n} Y_i\right) = \frac{1}{n} E\left(\sum_{i=1}^{n} Y_i\right) = \frac{1}{n}\sum_{i=1}^{n} E(Y_i) = \frac{1}{n}\sum_{i=1}^{n} \mu = \frac{1}{n}\, n\mu = \mu.$$

$$var(\overline{Y}) = var\left(\frac{1}{n}\sum_{i=1}^{n} Y_i\right) = \left(\frac{1}{n}\right)^2 var\left(\sum_{i=1}^{n} Y_i\right)$$

$$= \left(\frac{1}{n}\right)^2 \left[\sum_{i=1}^{n} var(Y_i) + 2 \sum_{i=1}^{n}\sum_{j>i}^{n} cov(Y_i, Y_j)\right]$$

$$= \left(\frac{1}{n}\right)^2 \left[\sum_{i=1}^{n} \sigma^2 + 2(0)\right] = \left(\frac{1}{n}\right)^2 n\sigma^2 = \sigma^2/n.$$

When the expected value of an estimator equals the population parameter it estimates, we say the estimator is an **unbiased estimator**. (A **population parameter** is a trait of a population that can be described with a single number.) *The sample mean from a simple random sample (indeed, from any random sample) is an unbiased estimator of the population mean.* Because $\overline{Y}$ is an unbiased estimator of $\mu$, the errors we make estimating $\mu$ with $\overline{Y}$,

$$e = \overline{Y} - \mu,$$

have a mean of zero: $E(e) = 0$. The variance of the estimation error, $var(e)$, equals $\sigma^2/n$, because $e$ differs from $\overline{Y}$ only by a constant. In addition to being an unbiased estimator of the population mean, $\overline{Y}$'s distribution collapses around the population mean as the sample size, $n$, grows large, because the variance of $\overline{Y}$, $\sigma^2/n$, goes to zero as $n$ grows large. When an estimator's distribution collapses around the true value as $n$ grows large, we say the estimator is **consistent**.

## Distribution of the Sample Mean

The expected value of the sample mean from a simple random sample equals $\mu$. The variance of the sample mean from a simple random sample equals $\sigma^2/n$. If the population is normally distributed, so is the sample mean: The sample mean is a sum of normals times the constant $1/n$, and is, therefore, normally distributed. We write these results in the compact form $\overline{Y} \sim N(\mu, \sigma^2/n)$.

*If the population is not normally distributed, the sample mean is usually not exactly normally distributed, but in large samples it is usually approximately normally distributed.* This result follows from the famous **Central Limit Theorem**. One simple version of the Central Limit Theorem is the following: *Under frequently encountered conditions, a sum of mean zero independent random variables becomes approximately normally distributed as the number of elements in* *the sum grows large. The most often violated condition for this Central Limit Theorem is that the variance of the variables in the sum be bounded.*

To apply the Central Limit Theorem to the sample mean, note that

$$E(Y_i - \mu) = 0 \quad \text{and} \quad E\left[\frac{1}{n}(Y_i - \mu)\right] = 0.$$

Consequently, by the Central Limit Theorem,

$$\sum \frac{1}{n}(Y_i - \mu) = \overline{Y} - \mu$$

is approximately normally distributed (with finite variance $\sigma^2/n$, so the variance of the sum is, indeed, bounded). The sample mean differs from $(\overline{Y} - \mu)$ by only the constant, $\mu$, so the sample mean is also approximately normally distributed.

## Estimation of the Population Variance

When we do not know the mean of the population, we usually don't know the variance either. A second task for statisticians is to estimate the population variance, $\sigma^2$, from sample data.

The sample mean proves to be an attractive estimator of the population mean—the sample mean is an unbiased estimator and as the sample size grows, the variance of the sample mean collapses toward zero, converging statistically on the true mean. Perhaps surprisingly, the sample variance is not a comparably attractive estimator of the population variance. The sample variance from a simple random sample,

$$\hat{\sigma}^2 = \frac{1}{n}\sum_{i=1}^{n}(Y_i - \overline{Y})^2,$$

is a biased estimator of the population variance.

## Deriving the Bias of $\hat{\sigma}^2$ as an Estimator of $\sigma^2$

To uncover the bias in $\hat{\sigma}^2$ as an estimator of $\sigma^2$, first rewrite $\hat{\sigma}^2$ as

$$\hat{\sigma}^2 = \frac{1}{n}\sum_{i=1}^{n}([Y_i - \mu] - [\overline{Y} - \mu])^2,$$

which adds and subtracts $\mu$, leaving $\hat{\sigma}^2$ unchanged. Next, examine the expected value of $\hat{\sigma}^2$:

$$E(\hat{\sigma}^2) = E\left[\frac{1}{n}\sum_{i=1}^{n}([Y_i - \mu] - [\overline{Y} - \mu])^2\right]$$

rewritten as

$$= \frac{1}{n}\sum_{i=1}^{n}\mathrm{E}\Big[([Y_i - \mu] - [\overline{Y} - \mu])^2\Big]$$

$$= \frac{1}{n}\sum\mathrm{E}[(Y_i - \mu)^2 + (\overline{Y} - \mu)^2 - 2(Y_i - \mu)(\overline{Y} - \mu)],$$

which, upon breaking the one sum into three:

$$= \frac{1}{n}\sum\mathrm{E}\Big[([Y_i - \mu)^2\Big] + \frac{1}{n}\sum\mathrm{E}\Big[(\overline{Y} - \mu)^2\Big] - \frac{2}{n}\sum\mathrm{E}[(Y_i - \mu)(\overline{Y} - \mu)]$$

$$= \frac{1}{n}\sum\sigma^2 + \frac{1}{n}\sum(\sigma^2/n) - \frac{2}{n}\sum\mathrm{E}[(Y_i - \mu)(\overline{Y} - \mu)]$$

$$= \frac{1}{n}(n\sigma^2) + \frac{1}{n}(n[\sigma^2/n]) - \frac{2}{n}\sum\mathrm{E}[(Y_i - \mu)(\overline{Y} - \mu)].$$

But

$$\mathrm{E}[(Y_i - \mu)(\overline{Y} - \mu)] = \mathrm{E}\left[(Y_i - \mu)\left(\Big[\frac{1}{n}\sum(Y_j - \mu)\Big]\right)\right]$$

$$= \mathrm{E}\left(\frac{1}{n}\sum_{j=1}^{n}[(Y_i - \mu)(Y_j - \mu)]\right)$$

$$= \frac{1}{n}\sum_{j=1}^{n}\mathrm{E}[(Y_i - \mu)(Y_j - \mu)].$$

The preceding expression is equal to

$$\frac{1}{n}(n\sigma^2),$$

because the $Y$'s being mutually independent implies that

$$\mathrm{E}[(Y_i - \mu)(Y_j - \mu)] = 0 \qquad \text{for } i \ne j$$

and

$$\mathrm{E}[(Y_i - \mu)(Y_j - \mu)] = \sigma^2 \qquad \text{for } i = j.$$

Consequently, $\mathrm{E}(\hat{\sigma}^2)$ further simplifies from

$$\frac{1}{n}(n\sigma^2) + \frac{1}{n}(n[\sigma^2/n]) - \frac{2}{n}\sum\mathrm{E}[(Y_i - \mu)(\overline{Y} - \mu)]$$

to

$$\frac{1}{n}(n\sigma^2) + \frac{1}{n}(\sigma^2) - \frac{2}{n}(\sigma^2)$$

or

$$\frac{1}{n}(n\sigma^2 - \sigma^2) = \frac{(n-1)}{n}\sigma^2.$$

Thus, we conclude that

$$E(\hat{\sigma}^2) = \frac{(n-1)}{n}\sigma^2 < \sigma^2.$$

The sample variance is biased toward zero, systematically underestimating $\sigma^2$.

## Whence the Bias of $\hat{\sigma}^2$ in Estimating $\sigma^2$?

The source of the bias of $\hat{\sigma}^2$ in estimating $\sigma^2$ is the reliance of $\hat{\sigma}^2$ on the sample mean, $\overline{Y}$. Because this bias reappears in slightly altered guise in econometric estimation, the source of the bias is worth some detailed exploration. To understand that source, we examine one potential unbiased estimator of the population variance.

We just showed that sample means unbiasedly estimate their exact population counterparts. Consequently, one unbiased estimator of the population variance is the mean squared deviation of the sample observations from the population mean:

$$\tilde{\sigma}^2 = \frac{1}{n} \sum_{i=1}^{n} (Y_i - \mu)^2.$$

$\tilde{\sigma}^2$, itself a sample mean, is the sample analogue of the population variance (which is, itself, a population mean), and as such is an unbiased estimator of the population variance. The estimator $\tilde{\sigma}^2$ is infeasible because we do not know $\mu$; we won't be able to use $\tilde{\sigma}^2$ in practice. But $\tilde{\sigma}^2$ helps us understand the bias of $\hat{\sigma}^2$.

The downward bias in $\hat{\sigma}^2$ stems from the tendency of observations to lie closer to their own mean, $\overline{Y}$, than to the population mean, $\mu$. It is a mathematical fact that the sum of observations' squared deviations from their own mean, $\overline{Y}$, is smaller than the sum of those observations' squared deviations from any other number. Consequently, unless our sample mean is, by chance, exactly equal to the population mean, $\hat{\sigma}^2 < \tilde{\sigma}^2$ and, because $\tilde{\sigma}^2$ is on average equal to $\sigma^2$, $\hat{\sigma}^2$ is on average less than $\sigma^2$. The sample variance from a simple random sample is a (downward) biased estimator of the population variance because $\hat{\sigma}^2$ relies on its own mean instead of on the unknown population mean, $\mu$.

## An Unbiased Estimator of $\sigma^2$

Fortunately, there is a simple fix for the bias in $\hat{\sigma}^2$. Because

$$E(\hat{\sigma}^2) = \frac{(n-1)}{n}\sigma^2,$$

$$E\left(\frac{n}{n-1}\hat{\sigma}^2\right) = \frac{n}{n-1}\frac{n-1}{n}\sigma^2 = \sigma^2.$$

Thus,

$$s^2 = \frac{n}{n-1}\hat{\sigma}^2 = \frac{\sum_{i=1}^{n}(Y_i - \overline{Y})^2}{n-1}$$

is an unbiased estimator of $\sigma^2$. In large samples, the difference between $s^2$ and $\hat{\sigma}^2$ is trivial. In small samples, the difference can be substantial.

One lesson to remember from the estimation of the population variance is that estimators that seem natural do not always have the most desirable statistical properties. In this example, the sample variance is inferior to $s^2$ as an estimator of the population variance.

## Confidence Intervals

The sample mean is almost surely an incorrect guess of the population mean, even when the sample mean is the best estimator to use. To provide a guess in which we have more confidence, we must rely on a range of guesses: "the population mean equals $\overline{Y}$, give or take something." **Confidence intervals** are estimators that provide a range of guessed values for the population parameter of interest.

To build a 95% confidence interval, we need a rule that offers an interval, such as "$\overline{Y} \pm c$," with which to guess the population mean. We would like the interval to be as narrow as possible, so that our guess is as precise as possible, but we also require that the interval be wide enough to ensure that in 95% of samples, our chosen interval covers the true value (from which follows the interval's name). A 90% confidence interval is constructed so that the true parameter falls within the chosen confidence interval in 90% of all samples. Other percentages can be selected, too. How are we to build such intervals?

Figure SA.10 shows the distribution of $\overline{Y}$ when the population mean is $\mu$ and the population is normally distributed with variance $\sigma^2$. The standard deviation of $\overline{Y}$ is $\sigma/\sqrt{n}$. Ninety-five percent of all sample means lie between

**Figure SA.10**

The Distribution of $\overline{Y}$

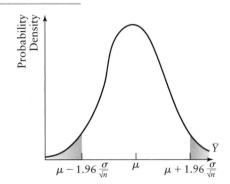

$\mu - 1.96\, \sigma/\sqrt{n}$ and $\mu + 1.96\, \sigma/\sqrt{n}$. (We could construct asymmetric intervals that also contain 95% of all sample means, but those intervals would be wider than this one, and we seek as narrow an interval as possible.) Consequently, in 95% of samples, $\overline{Y}$ lies within $1.96\, \sigma/\sqrt{n}$ of $\mu$. If we make our confidence interval $\overline{Y} \pm 1.96\, \sigma/\sqrt{n}$, the interval will include $\mu$ in 95% of samples.

A 95% confidence interval for the population mean is thus

$$\overline{Y} \pm 1.96\, \sigma/\sqrt{n},$$

when $\overline{Y}$ is the sample mean from a simple random sample.

## Confidence Intervals Using $s^2$ to Estimate $\sigma^2$: Step 1

$\overline{Y} \pm 1.96\, \sigma/\sqrt{n}$ is a 95% confidence interval when the population is distributed $N(\mu, \sigma^2)$, because across all samples

$$\Pr\!\left(\frac{\overline{Y} - \mu}{\sigma/\sqrt{n}} < -1.96\right) = \Pr\!\left(\frac{\overline{Y} - \mu}{\sigma/\sqrt{n}} > 1.96\right) = 0.025.$$

that is, only 5% of all sample means lie more than 1.96 standard deviations (of the sample mean) from the true mean.

Usually, we do not know $\sigma^2$ when we are guessing $\mu$. Instead of using $\sigma^2$ to build a confidence interval, we use $s^2$. The first step in building such a confidence interval is to substitute $s$ for $\sigma$ in the 95% confidence interval formula:

$$\overline{Y} \pm 1.96\, s/\sqrt{n}.$$

But this one step alone is not enough, because it is not true that

$$\Pr\!\left(\frac{\overline{Y} - \mu}{s/\sqrt{n}} < -1.96\right) = \Pr\!\left(\frac{\overline{Y} - \mu}{s/\sqrt{n}} > 1.96\right) = 0.025$$

when the population is distributed $N(\mu, \sigma^2)$. The 1.96 in this expression is taken from the standard normal distribution. The expression

$$\frac{\overline{Y} - \mu}{\sigma/\sqrt{n}}$$

follows the standard normal distribution, because the only random variable in the expression is $\overline{Y} \sim N(0, \sigma^2/n)$. But the estimated standard deviation of $\overline{Y}$, $s/\sqrt{n}$, is itself a random variable. Thus,

$$\frac{\overline{Y} - \mu}{s/\sqrt{n}}$$

has a normally distributed variable, $\overline{Y}$, in the numerator, and the random variable $s$, which follows some other distribution, in the denominator. We call

$$\frac{\overline{Y} - \mu}{s/\sqrt{n}} = t_{n-1} \qquad\qquad \text{SA.3}$$

a *t*-statistic with $(n - 1)$ degrees of freedom; the $(n - 1)$ reflects the denominator in the random variable $s^2$:

$$s^2 = \frac{\sum(Y_i - \overline{Y})^2}{(n - 1)}.$$

To construct a valid confidence interval for $\mu$, we need to know the distribution of the *t*-statistic, which we will now consider.

## The *t*- and Chi-square Distributions

The Guinness Brewery's quality-control official, William Gosset, writing under the pseudonym Student, explored the distribution of the *t*-statistic defined by Equation SA.3, and determined in 1908 how that statistic is distributed. Gosset wanted to assess the quality of batches of beer without opening the number of bottles needed to invoke the Central Limit Theorem for assessing the distribution of the *t*-statistic, in order to avoid excessive costs to the brewery. To describe Gosset's new distribution, we first turn briefly to the distribution of *squared* standard normals.

A squared standard normal follows what is called **the chi-square distribution with one degree of freedom**. This is a skewed distribution with mean 1 and variance 2. A sum of *n* independent squared normals follows what is called **the chi-**

**square distribution with $n$ degrees of freedom**—with mean equal to $n$ and variance equal to $2n$. For example, if I knew the mean of $Y$, $E(Y)$, I could examine

$$\sum \left[ \frac{Y_i - E(Y)}{\sigma} \right]^2 \quad i = 1, \ldots, n,$$

which would be distributed as chi-square with $n$ degrees of freedom. Statisticians have shown that when we replace $E(Y)$ by the sample mean of $Y_i$, as in

$$\sum \left[ \frac{Y_i - \overline{Y}}{\sigma} \right]^2,$$

we obtain another chi-square variable, this one with $(n - 1)$ degrees of freedom. (The one degree of freedom is "lost" when we replace $E(Y)$ with $\overline{Y}$ because the dependence of $\overline{Y}$ on each $Y_i$ "costs" us one independent squared normal in the sum.) Because $\left( \sum (Y_i - \overline{Y})^2 \right)/\sigma^2$ is distributed chi-square with $(n - 1)$ degrees of freedom,

$$\frac{(n - 1)s^2}{\sigma^2} = \frac{\sum [Y_i - \overline{Y}]^2}{\sigma^2}$$

is distributed chi-square with $(n - 1)$ degrees of freedom as well.

Now we are ready to describe the distribution of the standardized $t$-variable we just defined. Notice that

$$t = \frac{[Y - E(Y)]}{s},$$

but, if we define a standard normal variable $Z$,

$$Z = [Y - E(Y)]/\sigma,$$

where $Z$ would be distributed $N(0, 1)$, then

$$[Y - E(Y)] = Z\sigma,$$

so that

$$t = \frac{Y - E(Y)}{s} = \frac{Z\sigma}{s} = \frac{Z}{s/\sigma}.$$

The statistic $t$ is the ratio of a standard normal, $Z$, to the square root of a chi-square random variable that has been divided by its degrees of freedom:

$$\frac{s}{\sigma} = \sqrt{\frac{\left\{\dfrac{(n-1)s^2}{\sigma^2}\right\}}{(n-1)}}.$$

Such a ratio follows the **$t$-distribution with $(n-1)$ degrees of freedom** when the numerator and denominator are statistically independent. It is nontrivial to prove, but the numerator and denominator are independent in the $t$-statistic when we have a simple random sample.

Like the standard normal distribution, the $t$-distribution is symmetrical, with a mean of zero, but it has "fatter tails," that is, large values are more apt to occur with the $t$-distribution than with the normal distribution. There are convenient tables for calculating probabilities associated with statements about $t$-distributed variables, but we need tables (or at least parts of them) for each value of the degrees of freedom. As the number of degrees of freedom grows large, the $t$-distribution converges to the standard normal distribution.

We adopt a standard convention and say that $t_{n-1}^{0.025}$ is the number such that

$$\Pr\left(\frac{\overline{Y} - \mu}{s/\sqrt{n}} < -t_{n-1}^{0.025}\right) = \Pr\left(\frac{\overline{Y} - \mu}{s/\sqrt{n}} > t_{n-1}^{0.025}\right) = 0.025.$$

We can obtain $t_{n-1}^{0.025}$ from published $t$-tables.

## Confidence Intervals Using $s^2$ to Estimate $\sigma^2$: Step 2

We can now complete the construction of a 95% confidence interval for $\mu$ based on $\overline{Y}$ and $s^2$: $\overline{Y} \pm t_{n-1}^{0.025}\, s/\sqrt{n}$ is a 95% confidence interval for $\mu$ when $Y$ is normally distributed.

The interpretation of a 95% confidence interval requires some care. Strictly speaking, the 95% probability underlying the confidence interval refers to the fraction of all samples (weighed by their probability of occurring) that yield sample means such that the confidence interval includes the population's mean. It is, in general, incorrect to say about a realized value of the confidence interval based on a specific sample (for example $17 \pm 5$), "the probability that the population mean falls within this interval is 0.95." For some statisticians, called classical statisticians, the error is ascribing a probability to a population parameter. Parameters are what they are, say the classicists. A specific interval either covers the true parameter or it doesn't. There is no probability involved. For other statisticians, called Bayesian statisticians, the error is in not accounting for the prior probability that the true parameter lies in this particular interval. For example, estimates of a price elasticity of demand will sometimes be positive, by chance, even though demand curves virtually always slope downward. A 95% confidence interval for a demand elasticity that includes no negative values is almost surely wrong—the probability that a demand elasticity is positive is very small, almost no matter what your sample of data says.

## Across-Sample Properties of Estimators

We have already studied one across-sample property of estimators: unbiasedness. When the expected value of an estimator is equal to the population parameter of interest, the estimator is an unbiased estimator of that parameter. We call unbiasedness an **across-sample property** because the expectation is taken across the population of all possible samples. Formally, an estimator $\theta$ is an unbiased estimator of a population parameter $\tau$ if and only if $E(\theta) = \tau$. There are other across-sample properties of estimators. We note some of the most important here.

*Efficiency:* An estimator is an **efficient estimator** if it is an unbiased estimator and no other unbiased estimator has a smaller variance. When comparing two unbiased estimators, the estimator with the smaller variance is the "more efficient" of the two.

*Mean Absolute Error:* In addition to knowing whether an estimator makes errors on average, we often want to describe the magnitude of errors made by the estimator. The mean absolute error is one such descriptor. Formally, the **mean absolute error** of an estimator $\theta$ used to estimate a population parameter $\tau$ is $E(|\theta - \tau|)$.

*Mean Square Error:* Larger mistakes in estimation are sometimes disproportionately costly, relative to smaller errors. A measure of the magnitude of estimation errors that assigns a disproportionate importance to larger errors is the mean square error. Formally, the **mean square error** of an estimator $\theta$ used to estimate a population parameter $\tau$ is $E((\theta - \tau)^2)$. The mean square error is studied more often than the mean absolute error because squares are mathematically more tractable than absolute values. If an estimator has the smallest mean square error among all estimators of $\theta$, we call the estimator the **minimum mean square error estimator.**

## The Relationship Among Variance, Bias, and Mean Square Error

For any estimator $\theta$, there is a relationship among mean square error, variance, and bias:

$$MSE(\theta) = var(\theta) + [bias(\theta)]^2.$$

To prove this, begin with the mean square error of the estimator $\theta$ used to estimate a population parameter $\tau$: $E((\theta - \tau)^2)$.

$$E[(\theta - \tau)^2] = E[(\theta - E(\theta) + E(\theta) - \tau)^2] = E[([\theta - E(\theta)] - [\tau - E(\theta)])^2]$$

$$= E([\theta - E(\theta)]^2 + [\tau - E(\theta)]^2 - 2[\theta - E(\theta)][\tau - E(\theta)])$$

$$= E[(\theta - E(\theta))^2] + E[(\tau - E(\theta))^2] - 2E[(\theta - E(\theta))(\tau - E(\theta))].$$

The first term in this last expression is the variance of $\theta$. The second term is the expected value of a constant (because both $\tau$ and $E(\theta)$ are constants). The final term is the expected value of a random variable, $(\theta - E(\theta))$, times a constant, $(\tau - E(\theta))$. Thus we can rewrite the last expression as

$$var(\theta) + (\tau - E(\theta))^2 + (\tau - E(\theta)) E[(\theta - E(\theta))].$$

The second term in this expression is the square of the bias (if any) in $\theta$ when $\theta$ is used to estimate $\tau$. The final term equals zero because the mean of deviations of a variable, $E[\theta - E(\theta)]$, from its own mean is always zero. Thus we arrive at the conclusion we anticipated:

$$E[(\theta - \tau)^2] = MSE(\theta) = var(\theta) + [bias(\theta)]^2.$$

For unbiased estimators, the mean square error equals the estimator's variance. More generally, researchers may face a trade-off between bias and variance when choosing among estimators.

Academic researchers tend to prefer unbiased estimators, even at the cost of increased mean square error. One reason for this is that academic researchers envision their studies as one among many. Across many researchers' work, variance will be ameliorated—in effect, replications of a study increase the effective sample size and reduce variance. In contrast, if all researchers use the same biased estimator, the bias is not ameliorated when studies are pooled. For this reason, academic researchers are often particularly interested in finding efficient estimators—the unbiased estimators with the smallest variance.

In many practical applications, in which there are no replications, but just the one statistical inquiry, it doesn't matter whether errors stem from bias or variance—mistakes are mistakes. In such cases, researchers are more willing to suffer bias for reductions in variance, if the gains are large enough. Forecasters, for example, are generally interested less in unbiasedness than in making their mean square errors small. Finding minimum mean square error estimators is sometimes harder and sometimes easier than finding efficient estimators. (In settings in which biased estimators are acceptable in principle, the phrase "more efficient" is sometimes applied to smaller mean squared error, rather than smaller variance.)

## Testing Hypotheses About the Population Mean

Estimation is not the only task for statisticians. Often statisticians assess the validity of claims such as "Most Americans like hot dogs," or "Veterans' mean earnings are less than the mean for other Americans," or "the short-run demand for cocaine is price inelastic." Each of these claims puts forward a hypothesis about the world. Statisticians study how we can assess such claims when we have only a sample of data about the tastes of Americans for hot dogs, or the incomes of veterans, or purchases of cocaine. Examining how statisticians test hypotheses about population means, in particular, provides an opportunity for laying out their framework for testing hypotheses more generally.

Classical statisticians provide a procedure for testing hypotheses about the population mean, $\mu$, based on the sample mean, $\overline{Y}$, and the estimated standard deviation of the sample mean, $\sqrt{\sigma^2/n}$. Classical statistical tests of hypotheses have six steps:

1. State the hypothesis to be tested (called the **null hypothesis**) and the alternative to it (called the **alternative hypothesis**).
2. Choose a statistic (called the **test statistic**) with which to summarize the sample data.
3. Choose a probability of rejecting the hypothesis tested when it is true (called the test's **significance level**).
4. Determine what values of the test statistic (called the **critical region**) will lead us to reject the hypothesis being tested.
5. Compute the test statistic for the sample in hand.
6. Reject the hypothesis being tested, or don't, depending on whether the realized value of the test statistic falls in the critical region.

In the background of every hypothesis test are the statistical assumptions we rely on in the test and don't question when conducting the test. We call these assumptions the test's **maintained hypothesis**. For example, if we assume that veterans' earnings follow the normal distribution, and use that assumption in the course of testing a hypothesis about the mean of veteran's earnings, then that assumption is a part of our maintained hypothesis. If the maintained hypothesis is incorrect, the hypothesis tests' validity becomes vulnerable to challenge.

Suppose we wish to test the null hypothesis that the mean of a normally distributed population $\mu = \mu^0$, against the alternative claim that $\mu \neq \mu^0$. For example, we might hypothesize that the mean income in a population of families is $65,000, against the alternative claim that the mean income is not $65,000.

## The $t$-Statistic

If we are testing a hypothesis about the population mean, a natural statistic to examine to test hypotheses about the population mean is the sample mean, $\overline{Y}$. We do know the probability distribution for $\overline{Y}$: $\overline{Y} \sim N(\mu, \sigma^2/n)$, so we could make probability statements about $\overline{Y}$, as we need to if we are to settle upon a significance level for the test, but the distribution is different for every value of $\mu$ and for every value of $\sigma^2/n$. We find it more convenient to summarize the data by

$$t = \frac{\overline{Y} - \mu^0}{s/\sqrt{n}},$$

which is distributed $t_{n-1}$ if the null hypothesis is true. This statistic is called the $t$-statistic. There are $t$-distribution tables that show probability values for the $t$-distributions associated with different numbers of degrees of freedom, $(n - 1)$.

## The Significance Level of a Test

If we are to ever reject the null hypothesis when it is false, we will almost always also risk rejecting the null hypothesis when it is true. Statisticians begin a test by settling on the risk they are willing to take of rejecting the null hypothesis when it is true. They generally make this risk low, say 1%, or 5%, or 10%. Statisticians call this probability of rejecting the null when it is true the **probability of Type I error.** This probability is also called the significance level of the test.

## Critical Regions and the Power of a Test

Once a statistician has chosen a significance level, the goal is to minimize the probability of failing to reject the null hypothesis when it is false. This probability of rejecting the null hypothesis when it is false is called the **probability of Type II error.** Type I and Type II errors, rejecting the null when it is true and failing to reject the null when it is false, are the only types of errors one can make when testing a hypothesis. Statisticians ensure that the probability of Type I error is small. They cannot simultaneously always ensure that the probability of Type II error is small. Sometimes, statistical tests with low significance levels (a good thing) have a low probability of rejecting the null when it is false (a bad thing). The probability of rejecting the null hypothesis when it is false is called a test's **power.** The power is equal to (1 − probability of Type II error). The goal of minimizing the probability of Type II error once a significance level is chosen can also be called the goal of maximizing the power of a test, given the significance level. Unfortunately, we cannot always design powerful tests for low significance levels.

The alternative hypothesis $\mu \neq \mu^0$ includes instances in which the population mean is greater than $\mu^0$ and instances in which the population mean is less than $\mu^0$. In the former cases, the $t$-statistic will tend to be positive; in the latter cases, the $t$-statistic will tend to be negative. Consequently, values of the $t$-statistic far above zero and values far below zero both suggest that the null hypothesis is false.

**Figure SA.11**

The Distribution of the *t*-Statistic Given the Null Hypothesis is True

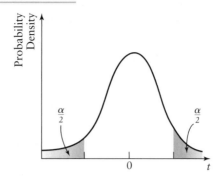

In such a case, we divide the critical region into two parts, values larger than some **critical value,** and values smaller than some other critical value. Because the *t*-distribution is symmetrical and has a mean of zero, the critical values are equal in magnitude, but opposite in sign. Figure SA.11 shows the distribution of the *t*-statistic if the null hypothesis is true. The shaded area in the figure is the critical region for the test if the significance level of the test is $\alpha$. One half of the probability mass for Type I error (the significance level) is placed in each tail of the distribution. This is called a **two-tailed test**. The critical values are $t_{n-1}^{\alpha/2}$ and $-t_{n-1}^{\alpha/2}$.

We can always construct a test procedure with a power of one—we need only always reject the null hypothesis. However, such a test would have a significance level of 100%—we would always reject the null when it is true (as well as when it is false). Similarly, we could reduce the probability of Type I error, the significance level, to zero by never rejecting the null hypothesis. Never rejecting the null would imply a power of zero—we would never reject the null when it is false (or when it is true). These extremes are not helpful. We must balance significance level and power, trading risk of one type of mistake for risk of another type of mistake.

Figure SA.12 shows the distribution of the *t*-statistic if instead of equaling $\mu^0$, the population mean actually equals ($\mu^0 + 5$). The critical values for the test statistic are shown as in Figure SA.11. The shaded area on the left plus the lightly shaded area on the right equal the significance level of the test. The darkly shaded regions in this picture are the probability that the observed *t*-statistic will fall into the critical region if the population mean equals ($\mu^0 + 5$). This area is the power of the test against the alternative that the population mean equals ($\mu^0 + 5$).

*More efficient estimators make more powerful tests.* Figure SA.13 shows again, with dotted lines, the distribution of the *t*-statistic given the null hypothesis were true, as in Figure SA.11, and with a solid line, the distribution of the *t*-statistic if the null hypothesis were false, as in Figure SA.12. If the sample size had been larger, so that the variance of $\overline{Y}$ were smaller, the critical region of the test would have been smaller, as indicated in Figure SA.13 by the placement of the critical re-

**Figure SA.12**

The Distribution of
the $t$-Statistic Given
the Null Hypothesis
is False and
$\mu = \mu^0 + 5$

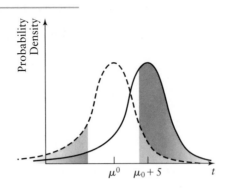

**Figure SA.13**

The $t$-Statistic's
Power When the
Sample Size Grows

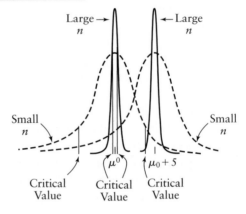

gion based on the distribution of the $t$-statistic given the larger sample size if the null hypothesis were true. Moreover, the distribution of the $t$-statistic given the null were false would also have a smaller variance if $n$ were larger. Thus, the power of the test becomes larger for two reasons: The critical region shrinks and the distribution of the $t$-statistic when the null is false becomes more concentrated within the critical region.

Had the original alternative hypothesis been that the population mean is greater than $\mu^0$, that is, if we believed the population mean could not be negative, $t$-statistics much less than zero would be less surprising under the null hypothesis than under the alternative hypothesis, so such negative $t$-statistics would not incline us to reject the null hypothesis. In such cases, we would place the entire critical region on one side of zero. Such tests are called **one-tailed tests**.

## Rejecting and Failing to Reject Hypotheses

When the observed $t$-statistic falls into the appropriate one- or two-tailed critical region, we "reject the null hypothesis." Otherwise we "fail to reject the null hypothesis." Because tests may lack power against some alternatives, we generally hesitate to "accept the null hypothesis," when we fail to reject it—there are too often other hypotheses, quite different from the null in practical terms, that we would fail to reject were they the null hypothesis.

When we reject the null that $\mu = \mu^0$, we say that the sample mean is "statistically significantly different from $\mu^0$." When we fail to reject the null that $\mu = \mu^0$, we say that the sample mean is "not statistically significantly different from $\mu^0$." The word "statistically" is very important here. For example, the sample mean may be statistically significantly different from zero and still be practically little different from zero. Or, the sample mean may be not statistically significantly different from zero and yet be a very large number—we just measure the mean so imprecisely that this large number does not lead us to reject zero as a possible value for the population mean. Practical, or economic, significance has a different meaning than statistical significance.

## Hypothesis Tests About a Population Variance

We do not test a hypothesis that the variance of a population, $\sigma^2$, has a specific value often, but such a test is possible if the underlying population is normally distributed. Under the null hypothesis $H_0: \sigma^2 = \sigma_0^2$, the test statistic

$$C = \frac{(n-1)\,s^2}{\sigma_0^2}$$

is distributed as a chi-square random variable with $(n-1)$ degrees of freedom. (See the description of the chi-square distribution given earlier.) Critical values for this test statistic can be obtained from a standard chi-square table. The test is two-tailed if the alternative is that the variance of the population differs from $\sigma_0^2$.

More often, one asks whether two populations have the same variance, $\sigma^2$. For example, one might ask if food expenditures in Zambia vary more about their mean than is the case in Kenya. This test is straightforward if one assumes that our DGP applies in both countries, but with possibly differing values for $\mu$ and $\sigma^2$ between the two countries. To test the null hypothesis that $\sigma^2$ is the same in both countries, one would first estimate $\mu$ in each country using the estimator $\overline{Y}$. One would then compute

$$estimated\ variance = \sum \frac{(Y_i - \overline{Y})^2}{(n-1)}$$

in each country, $s_z^2$ and $s_k^2$, for Zambia and Kenya, respectively. The numbers of observations may also differ across countries; let them be $n_z$ and $n_k$.

## The *F*-Test

Under the null hypothesis that the variances are equal in the two countries, we use the test statistic called an **F-statistic**,

$$F = \frac{s_z^2}{s_k^2}.$$

What is the distribution of this test statistic? If the populations are normally distributed and the samples in the two countries are independently drawn, the F-statistic follows what we call the F-distribution.

If we have two independent chi-square variables, $v_1$ and $v_2$, with degrees of freedom $n_1$ and $n_2$ respectively, then

$$F = \frac{(v_1/n_1)}{(v_2/n_2)}$$

follows the **F-distribution with $n_1$ and $n_2$ degrees of freedom**. There are tables for this distribution that apply when we put the larger sample variance in the numerator. Under the null hypothesis that the variances in Zambia and Kenya are equal, we can rewrite our F-statistic as

$$F = \frac{(n_Z - 1)s_Z^2/[\sigma^2(n_Z - 1)]}{(n_K - 1)s_K^2/[\sigma^2(n_K - 1)]},$$

which is the ratio of two independent chi-square variables, each divided by its standard deviation. Thus, our F-statistic has an F-distribution with $n_z - 1$ and $n_k - 1$ degrees of freedom. Critical values for this test statistic can be drawn from an F-table. The test is two-tailed.

## Asymptotic Unbiasedness and the Consistency of Estimators

The algebras of expectation and variance sometimes prove intractable when we try to use them to find efficient estimators (those with minimum variance among unbiased estimators). At other times, we cannot design unbiased estimators—we must accept some degree of bias in any feasible estimator. In such contexts, statisticians turn to an alternative perspective on what constitutes good estimators—they ask how the estimators perform as the sample size grows toward infinity.

If we cannot avoid bias altogether, there would be some comfort in knowing that as our sample size grows large, the bias in our estimator will grow small. An estimator is said to be **asymptotically unbiased** if the limit of its bias is zero as the sample size grows large. To define such an asymptotic property requires some care in thinking about our estimators.

$$1/2 \ (Y_1 + Y_2)$$

is a different estimator than

$$1/3 \ (Y_1 + Y_2 + Y_3),$$

which is a different estimator than

$$1/4 \ (Y_1 + Y_2 + Y_3 + Y_4),$$

and so on. However, each of these estimators is a sample mean for a sample with some number of observations. We describe *a sequence* of sample means, $\overline{Y}_n$, as the collection of all of these estimators, from one observation to $n$ observations. The asymptotic properties of the sample mean refers to what happens, in the limit, to the last sample mean in the sequence as $n$ grows large. Asymptotic unbiasedness requires that the asymptotic value of the expected value of $\overline{Y}_n$, called the **asymptotic expectation of $\overline{Y}_n$,** be equal to the population mean, $\mu$:

$$\lim_{n \to \infty} \left( E \left[ \frac{1}{n} \sum_{i=1}^{n} Y_i \right] \right) = \lim_{n \to \infty} (E[\overline{Y}_n]) = \mu.$$

Every unbiased estimator is asymptotically unbiased, but some biased estimators are asymptotically unbiased. For example, the sample variance is a biased estimator of the population variance, but because its expectation is

$$\frac{(n-1)}{n} \ \sigma^2,$$

and

$$\lim_{n \to \infty} \left( \frac{n-1}{n} \right) = 1,$$

the sample variance is an asymptotically unbiased estimator of the population variance.

An even more appealing asymptotic characteristic of an estimator than asymptotic unbiasedness is consistency. An estimator is consistent if as $n$ grows large, the distribution of the estimator collapses on the true value. Formally, an estimator $\overline{Y}_n$ is a consistent estimator of $\mu$ if

$$\lim_{n \to \infty} [\Pr(|\overline{Y}_n - \mu| > c)] = 0$$

for any $c > 0$. We say that the estimator $\overline{Y}_n$ **converges in probability** to $\mu$. In words, we can find a sample size, $n$, large enough that the probability that the estimator is further than $c$ from the population mean is smaller than any chosen nonzero number. Sufficient conditions for an estimator to be consistent are that it be both asymptotically unbiased and have a variance that converges to zero as the sample size grows without bound.

The variance of the sample mean from a simple random sample is $\sigma^2/n$, which converges to zero as $n$ grows. Thus, as we learned earlier, the sample mean is a consistent estimator of the population mean.

## The Law of Large Numbers

The **Law of Large Numbers** states that a sequence of sample means converges in probability to its asymptotic expectation as the sample size grows without bound. The Law applies quite broadly. In particular, it applies to sample means whose variance converges to zero as the sample size grows without bound. If the variance of the estimator grows without bound as the sample size grows, the Law of Large Numbers may fail. The consistency of the sample mean from a simple random sample as an estimator of the population mean is just one example of the Law of Large Numbers. We encounter many applications of the Law of Large Numbers in econometrics.

## The Central Limit Theorem

We know that if the population is normally distributed, the sample mean is also normally distributed. The Central Limit Theorem claims that the sample mean is asymptotically normally distributed under broad conditions, even if the population is not normally distributed. The most often violated Central Limit Theorem assumption is that the population has a finite variance.

The notion of an asymptotic distribution is subtle. Estimators that converge in probability collapse to a degenerate distribution concentrated at one point. Comparing these degenerate distributions tells us little about the performance of the estimators in large finite samples. Statisticians choose to describe the asymptotic distributions of estimators from another perspective. In effect, the statisticians look at the distributions under a microscope as the distributions are collapsing.

The first shift in focus is from the estimators themselves to the errors they make. For consistent estimators, these errors shrink to zero. Consequently, when we magnify the errors, they still shrink to zero! The second shift is to look not at the errors themselves, but to "magnify" the estimation errors by multiplying the errors by a number that grows with the sample size, such as the square root of $n$, or $n$ itself.

For example, the error, $e$, made by estimating the population mean with the sample mean can be expressed as

$$e = \overline{Y} - \mu = \left(\frac{1}{n}\sum_{i=1}^{n}Y_i\right) - \mu = \left(\frac{1}{n}\sum_{i=1}^{n}Y_i\right) - \frac{1}{n}n\mu = \left(\frac{1}{n}\sum_{i=1}^{n}Y_i\right) - \frac{1}{n}\sum_{i=1}^{n}\mu$$

$$= \frac{1}{n}\Sigma(Y_i - \mu).$$

The variance of these errors is $\sigma^2/n$, which shrinks to zero as $n$ grows. But if we magnify the errors by multiplying them by the square root of $n$, the variance of the magnified errors is

$$\text{var}(e\sqrt{n}) = n\,\text{var}(e) = n\sigma^2/n = \sigma^2.$$

The variance of the errors shrinks to zero, but the variance of the magnified errors converges to a nonzero constant. The distribution of the magnified errors does not shrink to zero. Consequently, we can study the nondegenerate distribution of the magnified errors. We call this distribution of the magnified errors the **asymptotic distribution** of the estimation errors, and we call the variance of the asymptotic distribution the **asymptotic variance** of the estimation errors. (Notice that had we multiplied the errors by $n$, the variance of the magnified errors would have grown without bound, and we would again have been unable to see the shape of the limiting distribution. We call the power of $n$ that makes the distribution neither collapse nor explode the **convergence rate** of the estimator.)

The Central Limit Theorem asserts that the sum of mean zero random variables is asymptotically normally distributed under suitable conditions. The two most frequent violations of the conditions are (i) that the random variables are too strongly correlated to support the theorem and (ii) that the asymptotic variance of the sequence is unbounded.

A simple random sample from a population with a finite mean satisfies the Central Limit Theorem's assumptions, so the sample mean's errors are asymptotically normally distributed. Because the sample mean differs from its estimation errors by a constant, the sample mean is also asymptotically normally distributed. The asymptotically normal distribution of the sample mean makes $t$-tests applicable in large samples even when the underlying population is not normally distributed. In large samples, the $t$-distribution converges to the normal distribution, so in large samples we use the critical values from the normal distribution.

## Summary

This appendix reviewed the basic concepts of probability and statistics that are useful in econometrics.

## Concepts for Review

## Endnote

1. Alfred North Whitehead, *Introduction to Mathematics* (Oxford: Oxford University Press, 1948): 27.

# Glossary

**Across-sample properties** The traits of estimators seen when looking at the estimators across the population of all samples.

**Adjusted $R^2$** A measure of goodness of fit that imposes a penalty for additional explanatory variables.

**Akaike information criterion (AIC)** A measure of goodness of fit that imposes a penalty for additional explanatory variables.

**Algebra of expectations** The rules for manipulating the expectations operator.

**Algebra of variances** The rules for manipulating the variance operator.

**Alternative hypothesis ($H_1$)** The hypothesis with which we are left if we reject the null hypothesis.

**AR($p$)** Autoregression of order $p$.

**ARMA process** A stochastic process that is a mixture of autoregressions and moving averages.

**Asymptotic bias** The difference in arbitrarily large samples between the expected value of an estimator and the population parameter the estimator is estimating.

**Asymptotic distribution** The shape an estimator's probability density function tends toward as the sample size grows large; more formally, the distribution obtained by multiplying an estimator's errors by the appropriate function of $n$ such that the resulting distribution does not become degenerate (with zero variance or infinite variance) as $n$ grows arbitrarily large. The chief use of asymptotic distributions is for statistical inference when the finite sample distribution of an estimator is unknown.

**Asymptotic normality** A property of some asymptotic distributions; such asymptotic distributions follow the normal distribution.

**Asymptotic properties** The traits of estimators in arbitrarily large samples.

**Asymptotic standard error** A standard error that is valid in arbitrarily large samples.

**Asymptotic unbiasedness** A property of some estimators; the bias of such estimators has a limit of zero as the number of observations grows without bound.

**Asymptotic variance** The variance of an asymptotic distribution.

**Asymptotically efficient** A property of some consistent estimators; such consistent estimators have the smallest asymptotic variance among consistent estimators with the same convergence rate.

**Attenuation bias** The bias in OLS estimates that arises from mismeasuring the explanatory variable in a bivariate regression.

**Attrition bias** The bias that arises in OLS estimators when some individuals who began as subjects in a study have subsequently dropped out.

**Autocorrelation coefficient** The fraction of last period's disturbance that is repeated in today's disturbance.

**Autoregression of order $p$** The linear relationship between a disturbance at time $t$ and its first $p$ lagged values, plus an innovation.

**Autoregressive** A property of some random variables (most notably, some disturbances); for such random variables, each period's value can be expressed as a linear function of one or more past periods' disturbances, plus an innovation.

**Autoregressive conditional heteroskedasticity (ARCH)** A specification of heteroskedastic disturbances in which a disturbance's variance in one period can be expressed as a linear function of past periods' squared disturbances, plus an innovation.

**Auxiliary equation** A regression equation not of direct interest itself, but estimated as one step in the process of estimating a regression equation of direct interest.

**Average effect of the treatment on the treated** In program evaluation, the average causal effect of a program or treatment for those individuals who actually participate in the program.

**Average effect of the treatment on those we intend to treat** In program evaluation, the causal effect of a program or treatment on those individuals who actually participate in the program, averaged across everyone the experimenters made eligible to participate, whether or not they actually participated.

**Bayes's rule** A formal probability relationship that declares how new information should alter one's prior probability assessments.

**Best linear unbiased estimator (BLUE)** Among all linear, unbiased estimators, the estimator with the smallest variance. OLS is BLUE under the Gauss–Markov Assumptions.

**Bias** The difference between the expected value of an estimator and the population parameter the estimator is estimating.

**Biased estimator** An estimator whose expected value differs from the population parameter the estimator estimates.

**Biased test** A test in which the power is less than the significance level for one or more specific alternatives.

**Binary variable** A variable that takes on the value 1 for observations that fall into a particular category, and a value of 0 for observations that do not fall into that category. Also called a *dummy variable*.

**Binomial logit model** A nonlinear regression model for a binary dependent variable and a single explanatory variable; the model relies on a logistic distribution.

**Binomial probit model** A nonlinear regression model for a binary dependent variable and a single explanatory variable; the model relies on a normal distribution.

**Bivariate regression** A regression with an intercept and a single explanatory variable.

**Box–Jenkins forecasting strategy** A strategy for univariate forecasting based on a mixture of autoregressive and moving average relationships.

**Breusch–Godfrey test** A test for serial correlation.

**Breusch–Pagan test** A test for heteroskedasticity.

**Breusch–Pagan variance test** A test for there being no individual error component in an error component's DGP.

**Censored sample** A sample in which values of the dependent variable above or below predetermined bounds are altered to equal the boundary values when recorded.

**Central (or Key) Limit Theorem (CLT)** The proven claim that in large samples sample means are generally approximately normally distributed, even if the population is not or, more formally, that the sum of independent random variables, or of even weakly dependent random variables, divided by the sum's standard deviation, has an asymptotically normal distribution.

**Ceteris paribus** "All other things being the same."

**Chi-square distribution** The probability distribution resulting from adding the squares of independent standard normal random variables. The number of squared standard normals in the sum is called the degrees of freedom of the chi-square distributed variable.

**Chow prediction test** An $F$-test that allows one to test for model stability when one subperiod is too short to allow separate estimation of the model in the two subperiods of interest.

**Chow test** An $F$-test of the null hypothesis that a model's coefficients are the same across subsets of observations.

**Classical favorite** Regression results that have been cited in excess of 300 times.

**Clustered** A trait of some sample observations; such observations have a shared component to their disturbances that makes the disturbances correlated across observations.

**Cobb–Douglas production function** The specification that says the log of output depends linearly on the logs of labor and capital.

**Cochrane–Orcutt estimator** An estimator for a linear regression model with first-order autoregressive disturbances.

**Coefficient of determination** The fraction of the variation in the $Y_i$ attributable to variation in the $X_i$; denoted by $R^2$. This is the most commonly used measure of the goodness of fit of a line. In a model with an intercept and a single slope coefficient, the formula for $R^2$ is

$$R^2 = \frac{\hat{\beta}_1^2 \sum x_i^2}{\sum y_i^2};$$

more generally,

$$R^2 = 1 - \frac{\sum e_i^2}{\sum y_i^2}.$$

**Cointegrated variables** A set of variables containing stochastic trends that can be placed into a linear combination that is stationary and that, therefore, does not contain a stochastic trend.

**Cointegrating relationship** A stationary linear combination of variables containing stochastic trends.

**Collinear** Property of a group of variables; regressing one variable in such a group against the others yields a high $R^2$. When variables are collinear, estimating their individual effects precisely might be difficult.

**Column rank** The number of linearly independent columns in a matrix.

**Column vector** A one-dimensional array of numbers in which the numbers are arrayed in a single column.

**Conditional forecast** A forecast of one variable made assuming we know the values of that variable's explanators.

**Conditional logit model** A model in which there are several possible outcomes, only one of which actually occurs, and in which the independent variables are the traits of the outcomes.

**Confidence interval** A guessing mechanism that produces intervals that cover the true parameter value in a known percentage of all samples. Thus, if a mechanism produces correct intervals in 95% of all samples, we call it a 95% confidence interval.

**Confidence level** The proportion of samples in which a confidence interval will contain the population parameter that is being estimated.

**Conform** A property of some pairs of matrices; such pairs satisfy the rules for being multiplied together.

**Consistent estimator** An estimator with a distribution that collapses around the estimated population parameter as the sample size grows.

**Contemporaneously uncorrelated** A property of some groups of random variables (which may include disturbances); the random variables in such a group are not correlated with one another in any one observation.

**Contemporaneously uncorrelated asymptotically** A property of some groups of random variables (which may include disturbances); in the limit, as the sample size grows without bound, the random variables in such a group are not correlated with one another in any one observation.

**Control group** In program evaluation, the group in an experiment that the experimenters make ineligible for the program; the group with which the "experimental group" is compared to determine the program's effect.

**Controlled experiment** An experiment in which the experimenter can keep two groups, one called the experimental group and the other the control group, identical, but for the treatment (such as a vaccine or a training program) under study in the experiment.

**Converges at the rate root $n$** A property of some estimators; such estimators' squared errors shrink as fast as $n$ grows; more formally, an estimator's squared errors divided by $n$ have a finite, nonzero variance in the limit as $n$ grows.

**Converges in probability** A property of some estimators; for such estimators, the probability limit of the estimator equals a constant.

**Covariance** A measure of linear association between two variables.

**Covariance restriction** In simultaneous equations models, information about the covariance between contemporaneous disturbances in two equations, about the contemporaneous correlation of a variable with an equation's disturbances, or about the correlation between two variables.

**Covariance stationary** A property of some time series variables; the variances and intertemporal correlations of such variables' observations do not depend on the specific time period of an observation (the first, third, twenty-fifth, etc.), though the covariances between observations may depend on how far apart in time the observations are from one another.

**Critical region** The set of values for a test statistic that will lead us to reject the null hypothesis.

**Critical values** The values of the statistic that separate the critical region from the rest of the distribution.

**Cross-sectional data** Data gathered from a population at a moment in time.

**Data-generating process (DGP)** What we know about where our data come from, combining what we assume about the underlying population of interest with what we assume about how data are chosen from that population.

**Data mining** Estimating a wide variety of specifications of a regression relationship and choosing the one that most appeals to the analyst.

**Degrees of freedom** A numerical trait of some statistical distributions that distinguishes among members of a family of distributions.

**Dependent variable** The variable to be explained in a regression equation; the left-hand-side variable.

**Deterministic time trend** An explanator in a regression model that adds a fixed amount to the expected value of the dependent variable each time period. Also a "time trend."

**Dickey–Fuller test** A test for a unit root; that is, the test determines whether a variable contains a stochastic trend.

**Difference in differences (diff-in-diffs) estimator** An estimator often used in program evaluation that, in essence, uses each of two groups as a control group for itself when estimating the effect of a program that was applied to one group, but not the other.

**Dimensions** The number of rows and columns in a matrix.

**Distinct intercepts DGP** In panel data, a DGP with separate intercept terms for each cross-sectional group.

**Disturbance or disturbance term** See *Error term.*

**Double logarithmic specification** A regression model in which both the dependent and independent variable are the natural logarithms of variables. Also called a *logarithmic specification.*

**Dummy variable** A variable that takes on the value 1 for observations that fall into a particular category, and a value of 0 for observations that do not fall into that category.

**Dummy variable trap** Including as explanators in a regression a set of dummy variables that are perfectly collinear with one another or with the intercept term.

**Durbin–Watson statistic** A test statistic for first-order autoregressive disturbances.

**Dynamic OLS (DOLS)** An estimator for regression models with cointegrated variables.

**Econometrics** The blending of economic theory, mathematics, and statistics.

**Efficiency** An unbiased estimator's variance. An unbiased estimator with a smaller variance than another is "more efficient."

**Efficient** A property of some unbiased estimators; such an unbiased estimator has a smaller variance than any other unbiased estimator. An unbiased estimator with a smaller variance than another is "more efficient."

**Endogenous variable** A variable whose value is determined within the system of equations under consideration and which therefore might be correlated with the disturbances of equations in which it appears as an explanator.

**Error components DGP** In panel data, a DGP in which disturbances are correlated within cross-sectional groups.

**Error correction** An out-of-equilibrium variable closes a fraction of its distance from its equilibrium value.

**Error term or error** The variable in a regression equation that reflects everything that makes a particular observation differ from the mean of the dependent variable conditional on the explanatory variables; also called *stochastic term, stochastic disturbance,* and sometimes just *disturbance.*

**Estimate** The numerical value taken on by an estimator in a specific sample.

**Estimated standard error of the regression** The square root of $s^2$, $s$, where

$$s^2 = \frac{\Sigma(residuals^2)}{(n - k - 1)},$$

where $n$ is the number of observations and $k$ is the number of slope coefficients in the regression.

**Estimator** A rule for guessing a population parameter from sample data.

**Exactly identified** A trait of some parameters; for such parameters, the restrictions in the DGP are just barely sufficient to allow the parameter to be consistently estimated.

**Exclusion restriction** In simultaneous equations models, information that an exogenous variable is not an explanator in a particular equation.

**Exogenous variable** A variable whose value is determined separately from the equations under consideration and is, therefore, uncorrelated with the disturbances of the equations being estimated.

**Explanator or explanatory variable** In regression analysis, a variable that accounts for variation in a dependent variable. Also called *independent variable*.

**F-distribution** The distribution resulting from forming the ratio of two independent chi-square random variables, each divided by its degrees of freedom.

**Feasible generalized least squares (FGLS)** Generalized least squares estimation, but using estimated variances and covariances for the disturbances.

**First-order autoregressive disturbances** Disturbances such that each period's disturbance equals some fraction of the previous period's disturbance, plus an innovation.

**First-order autoregressive process** A time series variable that can be expressed as a fraction of its own immediately preceding value, plus an innovation.

**First-order serial correlation** A property of some random variables (most notably, some disturbances); for such random variables, the value of the variable in one period is correlated with the variable's immediately preceding value.

**Fitted values** The estimated values of the dependent variable formed by inserting the observed explanatory variable values into an equation in which the estimated parameters are substituted for the actual values.

**Fixed across samples** Unchanging from one sample to the next.

**Fixed-effects estimator** The OLS estimator of slopes applied to panel data while allowing for a separate intercept for each cross-sectional group.

**Forecast error** The difference between a guess of the future value of a time series variable and the variable's actual future value.

**Forecast interval** In forecasting, a range of guesses for the future value of a time series variable.

*F*-statistic A statistic used to test multiple hypotheses about the parameters of a regression model.

**Full information estimators** A particularly efficient class of estimators for systems of equations.

**Full information maximum likelihood (FIML)** A particularly efficient estimator for systems of equations.

**Functional form** The specific mathematical form used to express the relationship among variables of interest.

**Gauss–Markov Assumptions** Uncorrelated, homoskedastic, zero-mean disturbances, with *X*'s fixed in repeated samples.

**Gauss–Markov Theorem** "OLS is BLUE under the Gauss-Markov Assumptions, and any linear combination of OLS coefficients has a smaller variance than the same combination of any other unbiased linear estimators of a regression model's coefficients."

**Generalized least squares (GLS)** Ordinary least squares applied to observations transformed to account for the variances and covariances of their disturbances.

**Generalized method of moments (GMM) estimation** An estimation strategy that relies on knowing moments of the population of interest and exploiting the Law of Large Numbers' assurance that sample moments are consistent estimators of population moments. GMM estimators are generally consistent but often are inefficient.

**Golden Oldies** Regression results so well known or so long known that the original papers are often not cited when the results are used.

**Goldfeld–Quandt test** A test for heteroskedasticity.

**Granger causes** *X* "Granger causes" *Y* if lagged values of *X* are statistically significant in a regression of *Y* on its own lagged values and lagged values of *X* (that is, if past values of *X* help predict *Y* even when we know the past values of *Y*).

**Grouped data** Observations averaged over a number of individuals (persons, firms, etc.). In grouped data, binary variables become proportions.

**Hausman's specification error test for error component DGPs** A test for correlation between the explanators and disturbances in an error-components DGP.

**Hausman–Wu specification test** A test for troublesome explanators.

**Heteroskedastic** Having differing variances.

**Heteroskedasticity** Some or all of the disturbances in a regression model have differing variances.

**Homoskedastic** Having equal variances.

**Homoskedasticity** All of the disturbances in a regression model have identical variances.

**Identified** A trait of some parameters; for such parameters, the restrictions in the DGP suffice to consistently estimate the parameter.

**Identity matrix** A square matrix with ones on the diagonal and zeros off the diagonal.

**Inconsistent estimator** An estimator that does not converge in probability to the population parameter that the estimator estimates.

**Inconsistent test** A statistical test whose power does not approach one against every alternative as the sample size grows.

**Independence of irrelevant alternatives** An assumption implicitly underlying multinomial and conditional logit models.

**Independent variable** In regression analysis, a variable that accounts for variation in a dependent variable. Also called *explanator* or *explanatory variable*.

**Indirect least squares** An estimation procedure that consistently estimates exactly identified equations that contain troublesome explanators.

**Innovation** A mean-zero component of a disturbance that is uncorrelated with past disturbances.

**Instrumental variable or instrument** A variable correlated with a troublesome variable, but uncorrelated with the disturbances.

**Instrumental variables (IV) estimation** An estimator that can consistently estimate linear regression models that contain troublesome explanators.

**Integrated** A trait of some nonstationary variables; such nonstationary variables can be transformed into stationary variables by differencing them some number of times.

**Integrated mixed autoregressive–moving average process** An integrated variable that, once differenced enough times to create a stationary variable, can be expressed by an ARMA process.

**Integrated of order $r$, or I($r$)** The trait of a variable that can be transformed into a stationary variable by differencing it $r$ times; $r$ can be zero, in which case the variable is stationary.

**Interaction term** An explanatory variable in a regression model that is the product of two other explanatory variables.

**Intercept term** The coefficient on an explanatory variable that has a constant value of one.

**Inverse of a matrix** For a square matrix, the square matrix that results in an identity matrix when the two matrices are multiplied together.

**Joint hypothesis** A hypothesis that entails several restrictions on the parameters of a model.

**Just identified** See *Exactly identified*.

**Lagrange multiplier tests** A class of tests that require only estimates of the constrained model.

**Large sample properties** See *Asymptotic properties*.

**Latent variable** A variable we do not observe.

**Law of Iterated Expectations** The rule that $E(E[X \mid Y]) = E(X)$.

**Law of Large Numbers (LLN)** A theorem that says that, under very general conditions, a mean from a random sample converges in probability to the corresponding population mean.

**Least squares dummy variable (LSDV) estimator** The OLS estimator applied to panel data while including a separate intercept for each cross-sectional group. The slope estimates of the LSDV estimator are identical to those of the fixed-effects estimator.

**Likelihood ratio statistic** Twice the difference between (i) the logarithm of the likelihood function evaluated at the unconstrained maximum likelihood estimates of the population parameters and (ii) the logarithm of the likelihood function evaluated at the maximum likelihood estimates of the population parameters given the null hypothesis is true.

**Likelihood ratio test** A test that compares the log of the likelihood of the observed data under the null hypothesis, $L^0$, with the log of the likelihood of the observed data if the maximum likelihood estimator were correct, $L^{mle}$. Asymptotically, the statistic follows the chi-square distribution.

**Limited dependent variable** A dependent variable whose range is not plus to minus infinity—for example, a binary dependent variable, an integer dependent variable, and a dependent variable that takes on just three values.

**Limited information estimators** A class of estimators for systems of equations.

**Limited information maximum likelihood (LIML)** An estimator for systems of equations.

**Linear constraints** Constraints among the coefficients that can be written as a linear combination of the coefficients.

**Linear estimator** An estimator that can be expressed as a weighted sum of the observations on the dependent variable.

**Linear in the independent and explanatory variables** The dependent variable can be expressed as a weighted sum of the explanatory variables plus a random disturbance.

**Linear probability model** A linear regression in which the dependent variable is a proportion or a binary outcome.

**Linear regression models or linear regression** A relationship that expresses a dependent variable as a weighted sum of the population parameters of interest, plus a random disturbance, and in which the weights are observed variables.

**Linear time trend** An explanatory variable that increases by one from one time period to the next. In a regression with a time trend, the expected value of the dependent variable tends to grow steadily over time.

**Local average treatment effect** The average treatment effect for a nonrandom subset of individuals in the population (most notably, the subset of individuals who are induced by an experiment to undertake treatment, who otherwise would not have).

**Logarithmic specification** A regression model in which the both the dependent and the independent variables are the natural logarithms of variables. Also called a *double logarithmic specification*.

**Logistic distribution** A probability density function that underlies the logit model.

**Logit model** A nonlinear regression model with a binary dependent variable; the model relies on the logistic distribution.

**Log-likelihood function** The logarithm of the probability (or probability density) of the observed values of the dependent variable occurring, expressed as a function of the model's parameters.

**Log-odds** The natural logarithm of the probability (or, in a sample, the proportion) of success minus the natural logarithm of the probability (or, in a sample, the proportion) of failure.

**Log-odds model** A linear regression model with the dependent variable equal to the log-odds for some event.

**Maintained hypothesis** The assumptions we make about the DGP and do not test. If our maintained hypothesis is wrong, our hypothesis tests may be faulty.

**MA($q$)** A moving average of order $q$.

**Matrix multiplication** The operation by which matrices are multiplied.

**Maximum eigenvalue statistic** A test statistic used in testing hypotheses about cointegration.

**Maximum likelihood estimation (MLE)** An estimation procedure that guesses that the population parameters have the values that make the realized observations as likely to occur as possible.

**Mean absolute error** The arithmetic average, across the population of samples, of the absolute difference between an estimator and the population parameter the estimator estimates.

**Mean reversion** A property of stationary time series variables; the expected value of such a variable at $(t + r)$, conditional on the variable's values prior to $t$, always approaches the variable's unconditional expected value as $r$ grows large.

**Mean square error** The arithmetic average, across the population of samples, of the squares of the errors made with the estimator in guessing a parameter of interest.

**Measurement error bias** The bias in OLS estimates that arises from mismeasuring an explanatory variable.

**Method of moments estimation** See *Generalized method of moments (GMM) estimation.*

**Mixed autoregressive–moving average (ARMA)** A property of some time series variables; such a variable can be expressed as a linear combination of one or more of its lagged values and its lagged innovations, plus a new innovation.

**MLE** Maximum likelihood estimation.

**Monte Carlo comparisons** Comparisons of estimators that use computers to draw samples of data, over and over again, and use those samples to implement one estimator or another many, many times.

**Monte Carlo exercise** Using a computer to apply an estimator many, many times, each time for a newly drawn sample of observations.

**Moving average of order $q$** A property of some time series variables; such a variable can be expressed as a linear combination of its preceding $q$ innovations, plus a disturbance term.

**Multicollinear** A property of some groups of variables; regressing one variable in such a group against the others yields a high $R^2$. When variables are multicollinear, estimating their individual effects precisely might be difficult.

**Multicollinearity** The state of high correlation among some explanators in a regression model. Multicollinearity can make precise estimation of individual variables' effects difficult.

**Multinomial models** Models in which there are several possible outcomes, only one of which actually occurs, and in which the independent variables are the traits of the individuals who are choosing the outcome.

**Multinomial logit model** A model in which there are several possible outcomes, only one of which actually occurs, and in which the independent variables are the traits of the individuals who are choosing the outcome. The model relies on the logistic distribution.

**Multinomial probit model** A model in which there are several possible outcomes, only one of which actually occurs, and in which the independent variables are the traits of the individuals who are choosing the outcome. The model relies on the multivariate normal distribution.

**Multiple regression model or multiple regression** A regression model with several explanatory variables.

**Natural experiment** An experiment that relies on chance circumstances mimicking the conditions of a randomized experiment.

**Newey–West heteroskedasticity and serial correlation consistent variance estimator** An estimator of the variance of OLS estimators that is consistent for regression models with homoskedastic or heteroskedastic disturbances and serially correlated or serially uncorrelated disturbances.

**Noninvertible** A trait of some moving averages; such moving averages cannot be arbitrarily well approximated by any autoregression of finite order.

**Nonlinear regression** Regressions that are not linear in the parameters which we need to estimate.

**Nonresponse bias** In randomized experiments, the bias that can arise in OLS estimators when some individuals selected to participate in the experiment decline to participate.

**Nonstationary** The trait of a sequence of random variables that their distributions depend on specifically which observation (the first or the twenty-third or the hundredth, etc.) we are considering.

**Null hypothesis ($H_0$)** The hypothesis that we are subjecting to refutation; also the hypothesis that we will take as true for purposes of determining relevant distributions for our test statistics.

**Observationally equivalent** Not empirically distinguishable from one another, no matter how many data one has.

**Omitted variable bias** The bias stemming from not including in a regression model a variable that influences the expected value of the dependent variable. If an omitted influential variable is uncorrelated with the included explanators, no bias results.

**One-tailed test** A test in which the critical region is at one extreme.

**Order condition for identification** The requirement that for an equation's parameters to be identified the equation must exclude at least one nontroublesome explanator for each troublesome explanator it includes.

**Ordinary least squares (OLS) estimators** The estimators of an intercept and slopes that minimize the sum of squared residuals in a specific sample. Under the Gauss–Markov Assumptions, the OLS estimator is both BLUE and the MLE.

**Overidentified** A trait of some parameters; for such parameters, the restrictions in the DGP yield a surfeit of riches for estimating the parameters consistently.

**Panel data** Data that has two dimensions, such as data with observations for several time periods for each of several individuals.

**Parameter** An unknown numerical trait of a population.

**Partial autocorrelation coefficients** The coefficients on the lagged values of a variable in that variable's autoregression.

**Perfectly collinear** A trait of some groups of variables; one variable in such a set of variables can be expressed exactly as a linear combination of the others.

**Perfect multicollinearity** When one variable in a set of variables can be expressed exactly as a linear combination of the other variables.

**Perform the regression of $Y$ on its explanators** Estimate the relationship between a dependent variable $Y$ and its explanatory variables. Also "regress $Y$ on its explanators."

**Plim** See *Probability limit*.

**Pop tunes** Regression results that appear among the book's greatest hits because they are particularly interesting.

**Population** A well-defined group that is the focus of statistical inquiry.

**Population parameter** See *Parameter*.

**Positive definite** A trait of some symmetric matrices; for such a symmetric matrix $Q$, $AQA' > 0$ if $A$ is not all zeros. If $Q$ is positive definite, $Q^{-1}$ exists and is also positive definite.

**Power of a test** The probability that a test will reject a null hypothesis, given that it is false. The power will vary across specific alternative hypotheses.

**Prais–Winsten estimator** An estimator for regression models with first-order autoregressive disturbances.

**Predetermined variables** Variables whose values at each time $t$ are determined before $t$, and that might, consequently, be uncorrelated with period $t$'s disturbance.

**Prediction error** See *Forecast error*, but applied to a non–time series variable.

**Prediction interval** See *Forecast interval*, but applied to a non–time series variable.

**Probability limit** The value to which a sequence of random variables converges if the random variables' distribution collapses as $n$ grows large. Also denoted *plim*.

**Probability of type I error** The probability of rejecting the null hypothesis given that it is true. Also called the *significance level* or *size* of the test.

**Probability of type II error** The probability of not rejecting the null hypothesis given that it is false. This probability is one minus the power of the test.

**Probit model** A nonlinear regression model for a binary dependent variable.

**P-value** The probability of seeing a value of the test statistic as extreme as, or more extreme than, we do, given that the null hypothesis is true.

**Quasi-maximum likelihood estimation (QMLE )** An estimation procedure that uses maximum likelihood estimation based on an incorrect distribution for the errors. QMLE estimates parameters consistently in a surprisingly large number of cases.

**$R^2$** The proportion of the variance in the dependent variable that is accounted for by variation in the explanatory variables. Also called the *coefficient of determination*.

**Random coefficients** Coefficients in a linear regression model that are themselves random variables.

**Random effects estimator** A feasible generalized least squares estimator for error component DGPs.

**Randomized experiment** An experiment in which individuals from the population of interest are randomly assigned to the experimental and control groups.

**Random number generator**  A computer program component that can create a series of numbers drawn from a specific probability distribution.

**Random variable**  A variable whose value is determined probabilistically. A random variable is defined by the values that it takes on and their associated probabilities or probability densities.

**Random walk**  A random variable constructed by accumulating random increments from one time period to the next. The mean of the amounts added each period may be zero or nonzero.

**Random walk with drift**  A random walk in which the expected value of each period's increment is nonzero.

**Rank condition for identification**  A sufficient condition for identifying the parameters of an equation.

**Reduced form or reduced form equations**  In systems of equations, the equations that express the endogenous variables of the system as functions of only the predetermined variables and the disturbances of the system.

**Recursive**  A property of one or more equations in a system of equations; such an equation's dependent variable depends on one or more endogenous variables, but those endogenous variables do not depend, directly or indirectly, on the dependent variable.

**Regime shift**  When the coefficients of a regression relationship change over time.

**Regression**  The relationship between the expected value of one variable and the value of one or more other variables.

**Regression specification error test, or RESET test**  A test for omitted variables.

**Regressor**  See *Explanatory variable*. Also called an *independent variable* or *explanatory variable*.

**Regression of Y on its explanators**  The estimated relationship between a dependent variable Y and its explanatory variables.

**Regress Y on its explanators**  Estimate the relationship between a dependent variable Y and its explanatory variables. Also *perform the regression of Y on its explanators*.

**Residuals of the regression or residuals**  The differences between the actual and fitted values of observations on the dependent variable.

**Reversion to trend**  Mean reversion in a model with a deterministic time trend.

**Right-hand rule**  A heuristic device for knowing how to multiply matrices.

**Robustness**  A property of some estimators; such an estimator retains its sampling process despite some nontrivial changes to the DGP.

**Root $n$ consistent**  A property of some consistent estimators; multiplying such a consistent estimator's errors by $\sqrt{n}$ leads to an asymptotic distribution with a finite, nonzero variance.

**Row rank** The number of linearly independent rows in a matrix.

**Row vector** A one-dimensional array of numbers in which the numbers are arrayed in a single row.

**Sample selection bias** The bias that can arise in OLS estimates when observations are not a random sample of the population of interest.

**Sample statistics** Mathematical rules for manipulating the numerical observations in a sample.

**Sampling distribution** The distribution of an estimator across the population of samples.

**Sampling properties** The statistical traits of an estimator across the population of all samples.

**Scalar** A single number not in an array of numbers, usually in the context of matrix algebra.

**Schwarz information criterion (SIC)** A measure of goodness of fit that imposes a penalty for additional explanatory variables.

**Seasonal dummy variables** Dummy variables indicating the season or month of an observation.

**Seasonal effects** In time series, the dependence of a regression equation on the season of the observation.

**Seasonally adjusted data** Data corrected for its seasonal effects.

**Seemingly unrelated regressions (SUR)** An estimator for several equations with contemporaneously correlated disturbances.

**Self-selection bias** The bias that can arise in OLS estimators when an individual's choices influence whether the individual appears in our samples.

**Semilogarithmic or semilog** Using the logarithm of a variable as the dependent variable in a model, while measuring the regressors in levels of the variables.

**Serial correlation** In time series data, correlation between the values of a variable or of the disturbance.

**Serially correlated** A property of some time series variables (most notably, disturbances); two or more observations on such a time series variable are correlated with one another.

**Serially uncorrelated** A property of some time series variables (most notably, disturbances); no two observations on such a time series variable are correlated with one another.

**Significance level** The probability of Type I error in a classical hypothesis test; that is, the probability of rejecting the null hypothesis, given that it is true. Also called the *size* of the test.

**Simultaneity bias** The bias in the OLS estimator that arises when an explanator is correlated with an equation's disturbance because the explanator is itself directly or indirectly determined by the equation's dependent variable. Also called *simultaneous equations bias*.

**Simultaneous equations** A set of equations that jointly determine variables of interest.

**Simultaneous equations bias** The bias in the OLS estimator that arises when an explanator is correlated with an equation's disturbance because the explanator is itself directly or indirectly determined by the equation's dependent variable. Also called *simultaneity bias*.

**Size** The significance level of a test.

**Size distortion** The trait of a test in which the actual significance level of the test is not the significance level that is presumed for the test.

**Specification** The formal characterization of the process generating one's data.

**Specifying the functional form of a model** Picking a specific mathematical form for an economic relationship.

**Specifying the stochastic structure of the model** Making assumptions about the distributions of the random components of a model, such as the disturbances.

**Speed of adjustment** In an error-correction model, the fraction of the gap between a current and an equilibrium value that is closed in one period.

**Spurious regression** A regression run between two unrelated variables that both contain stochastic trends.

**Square matrix** A matrix with the same number of rows as columns.

**Standard error of an estimator or standard error** The standard deviation of an unbiased estimator.

**Standard error of the expected value of $Y$ given $X^*$** The standard error of the predicted value of a dependent variable.

**Statistically significant** A trait of an estimate; in particular, the trait that in this sample one rejects the null hypothesis that the parameter estimated or the difference between parameters that is estimated is not zero.

**Statistically significantly different from** One rejects the null hypothesis that two entities are equal.

**Stochastic disturbance** See *Error term or error*.

**Stochastic specifications** Specifications that include a probabilistic, or random, component.

**Stochastic structure of a model** The formal characterization of the probabilistic aspects of the process generating one's data.

**Stochastic term** See *Disturbance or disturbance term*.

**Stochastic time trend** An explanator in a regression model that adds a randomly incremented, cumulative amount to the expected value of the dependent variable each time period.

**Stochastic trend** A random walk, with or without drift, that is an additive component of a variable. When a variable is the sum of a stochastic trend and other determinants, the variable "contains" the stochastic trend.

**Structural equations or structural form** Equations that describe the behavioral and institutional relationships of a system.

**Super consistent** A trait of some consistent estimators; such consistent estimators converge at a rate faster than root $n$.

**Symmetric matrix** A matrix in which the $ij$-th element equals the $ji$-th element for all $i$ and $j$.

***t*-distribution** The distribution of the ratio of a standard normal to the square root of an independent chi-square random variable that has been divided by its degrees of freedom.

**Test statistic** The mathematical manipulation of sample observations that one examines when conducting a hypothesis test.

**Three-stage least squares (3SLS)** A particularly efficient estimator for systems of equations.

**Time series data, or time series** Data gathered over time.

**Time trend** An explanator in a time series regression model that makes the expected value of the dependent variable a function of the observation's specific time period.

**Tobit model** A model that incorporates some kinds of censored data.

**Trace** The sum of a matrix's diagonal elements.

**Trace statistic** A test statistic used in testing hypotheses about cointegration.

**Transpose** The transformation of a matrix in which the rows are turned into columns and vice versa.

**Treatment effect** The causal effect of a program or other treatment on the expected value of a variable.

**Treatment group** In an experiment, the group who are placed in the program or are subjected to the treatment being studied; also, the group being contrasted with a control group.

**Trends** Influences that make a variable's expected value change steadily over time.

**Troublesome variable** An explanator that is correlated with the disturbance term.

**Truncated normal distribution** The distribution of a normal random variable from which all values above or below some predetermined bound have been excluded.

**Truncated sample** A sample in which observations with values of the dependent variable above or below predetermined bounds have been deleted from the sample.

***t*-statistic** The statistic used to test a single hypothesis about one or more regression parameters.

**Two-stage least squares (2SLS)** An estimator that consistently estimates regression models with troublesome explanators by first constructing a proxy for the troublesome variable and then replacing the troublesome variable with its proxy in OLS.

**Two-tailed test** A test in which the critical region is divided between the two extremes of the test statistic.

**Type I error** The probability that one will reject the null hypothesis, given that it is true.

**Type II error** The probability that one will fail to reject the null hypothesis, given that it is false. The probability of Type II error depends on what specific alternative hypothesis is true.

**Unbiased** A trait of some estimators; such estimators are right on average across the population of all samples.

**Unbiased estimator** An estimator whose expected value equals the population parameter being estimated.

**Underidentified** A trait of some parameters; such parameters cannot be estimated consistently because the DGP offers too few restrictions.

**Unit root tests** Tests to determine whether a variable contains a stochastic trend.

**Unobserved heterogeneity** Omitted variables whose values are constant for an observed individual over at least the time span of one panel data sample.

**Variance of the conditional forecast error** The variance of the errors made by a conditional forecast in predicting the future values of a dependent variable.

**Vector** A one-dimensional array of numbers in which the numbers are arrayed in either a single column or a single row.

**Vector autoregression** A system of equations made up of autoregressions, each autoregression including lagged values of *all* of the dependent variables in the system.

**Wald statistics** Test statistics based on how much the hypothesized parameter values differ from the unconstrained estimates.

**Wald tests** Test based on how much the hypothesized parameter values differ from the unconstrained estimates. Wald tests sidestep computing the constrained model.

**Weak instrument** An instrumental variable that is so weakly correlated with the troublesome variable that IV estimation using it overcomes little of the bias of OLS and suffers considerable size distortion.

**Weak test** A test with low power.

**White noise innovations** Mean-zero components of a disturbance that are homoskedastic and statistically independent over time.

**White test** A test for heteroskedasticity.

**White's heteroskedasticity consistent standard errors** An estimator of the standard errors of OLS estimators that is consistent with both homoskedastic and heteroskedastic disturbances. Also called *White's robust standard errors*.

**White's heteroskedasticity consistent variance estimator** An estimator of the variances of OLS estimators that is consistent with both homoskedastic and heteroskedastic disturbances.

**White's robust standard errors** See *White's heteroskedasticity consistent standard errors*.

**Within-sample-properties** Traits of an estimator in a single sample of data.

# Index